UNCLOUDY DAYS

The Gospel Music Encyclopedia

by Bil Carpenter

Backbeat Books
San Francisco

Published by Backbeat Books
600 Harrison Street, San Francisco, CA 94107
www.backbeatbooks.com
email: books@musicplayer.com

An imprint of the Music Player Network
Publishers of *Guitar Player, Bass Player, Keyboard, EQ*, and other magazines

United Entertainment Media, Inc.
A CMP Information Company

CMP
United Business Media

Distributed to the book trade in the US and Canada by
Publishers Group West, 1700 Fourth Street, Berkeley, CA 94710

Distributed to the music trade in the US and Canada by
Hal Leonard Publishing, P.O. Box 13819, Milwaukee, WI 53213

Interior design & composition by Leigh McLellan Design
Cover design by Richard Leeds–BigWigDesign.com
Front cover photos: The Gay Sisters: courtesy of the Gay Family Estate;
    Candi Staton: Robert Shanklin; The Staple Singers: courtesy of
    Stax/Fantasy Records; Ricky Dillard: courtesy of Crystal Rose Records;
    Mahalia Jackson: Michael Ochs Archives.com
Back cover photos: Tramaine Hawkins: A&M Records; Kenoly Brothers: Dave
    Lepori for NGMR Records; Patti LaBelle: Robert Shanklin; John P. Kee:
    Robert Shanklin; Angelic Gospel Singers: courtesy of Margaret Allison;
    Richard Smallwood: courtesy of Richard Smallwood; Ron Kenoly:
    Integrity Records

Library of Congress Cataloging-in-Publication Data

Carpenter, Bill, 1965-
    Uncloudy days : the encyclopedia of black gospel music / by Bil Carpenter.
        p. cm.
    Includes bibliographical references.
    ISBN-13: 978-0-87930-841-4
    ISBN-10: 0-87930-841-9 (alk. paper)
    1. Gospel musicians—Bio-bibliography. 2. African American
musicians—Bio-bibliography. I. Title.
    ML102.G6C37 2005
    782.25'4'0922—dc22   2005013792

Printed in the United States of America

05 06 07 08 09   5 4 3 2 1

Contents

Foreword

HOW WELL I REMEMBER as a child hearing the music of many of the great artists mentioned in this book. The songs written and sung by these artists are the backbone of gospel music as we know it.

My mother, Mamie, had such an appreciation for and was such a fan of recording artists like the Angelic Gospel Singers and Mahalia Jackson that she was always buying new music and bringing it home. The Hawkins family children would listen and learn much of this great music. Practically every Sunday afternoon at 3:00 p.m. we were on a program to sing somewhere in the San Francisco Bay Area. Those old records gave us a wealth of material to perform, and we loved every minute of it.

It is important to preserve our great gospel music heritage. So many of the songs tell us where we once were, where we are now, and where we will be on that uncloudy day. The history of those singers who have contributed so much to us as a people is vital so that we do not forget the place from which God has brought us. It is also of great significance that this generation and generations to come finally have a written encyclopedia through which they can relive this history.

I am grateful to Bil Carpenter for having the vision to write this book, so cleverly titled *Uncloudy Days.* The concise profiles of these legendary artists will tell their stories, from humble beginnings to great successes.

Thank God that we can all succeed and overcome. Oh, happy day!

Edwin Hawkins
Grammy award–winning
composer of "Oh Happy Day"

Introduction

My mother, Oceola, used to work evenings at the Morrison Hotel in Chicago. At night, my father—everybody called him Pops—had to think of a way to keep his four kids quiet until it was bedtime. So he started us to singing. He had sung in groups all of his life, and he decided to teach us to sing around 1948. He sat us on the floor in a circle and began to give us parts to sing. He gave us parts that his brothers and sisters used to sing down in Mississippi. There were 14 of them, seven girls, seven boys. They had so many children that they ran out of names. My uncle and Pops were the last two kids, so they named my uncle Sears and they named Pops Roebuck. Sears and Roebuck.

At some point my Aunt Katie lived with us, and she heard us singing. She said that we sang good enough to sing at her church, so she arranged for us to sing there. We caught the streetcar, and Pops had his guitar with no case. We sang "Will the Circle Be Unbroken." It was the only song Pops had taught us all the way through. The people at her church liked us so much that they clapped us back three times, so we had to sing that song over and over again. They took up an offering of $7. It was some money that could help with the family bills, so Pops said, "We gon' learn some more songs." That's when our career was born.

Our first big hit was a song we recorded for Vee-Jay Records called "Uncloudy Day." Josiah K. Alwood, a traveling preacher, wrote that song in 1879. It had become a church classic and had been sung by many artists long before we knew anything about it. But when Pops came up with the bluesy, guitar-driven arrangement that he gave the Staple Singers' rendition in 1957, it was as if the song was brand new. We had no idea that people would react to the song and love it like they did. That was our first million-seller, and it laid the foundation for all the other things we would do later in our career. Suddenly, churches all over America were booking the Staple Singers, and Pops was able to quit the various manual labor jobs he held to keep food on our table.

Gospel music has been good to our family and has inspired us to keep the faith in those times when we felt down. We've had our share of ups and downs. When we crossed over from straight gospel songs to message songs, a lot of people wanted to throw us out of the church. But time has brought about a change, and now all kinds of gospel artists have recorded Staple Singers songs, so that's some vindication that we were doing the right thing all along—we were just ahead of our time.

This book, *Uncloudy Days*, is a celebration of every form of gospel music. Almost everyone you can ever think of is in here, from the legends to the folks you might have forgotten about, but it's all good because it's all to God's glory. I hope you enjoy reading this book about a lot of my old friends that was written by another old and special friend, Bil Carpenter.

Mavis Staples
Rock and Roll Hall of Fame inductee and Grammy Lifetime
Achievement award winner with the Staple Singers;
recipient of three 2005 W.C. Handy awards

Acknowledgments

THANKS TO EVERYONE AT Backbeat for all of their diligent work on making this book happen. Thank you Matt Kelsey (publisher) for passing the book idea on to Richard Johnston (senior editor) who gave it the green light. Without the enthusiasm of you both, this encyclopedia would just be an idea instead of a reality. Thanks to Nancy Tabor (managing editor), for giving me extra time beyond my deadline to whip the book into shape. Many kudos to my editor, Gail Saari, and my copyeditor, Lunaea Weatherstone. I often told Lunaea that I'd go crazy (or perhaps, crazier) if I had to do the tedious work she does to make sure all of the facts are factual and that all of the spelling is on point. Also, much thanks to Kevin Becketti and Steve Moore for all the marketing strategies and Nina Lesowitz for the great publicity on the book. Kate Henderson was the first person I dealt with on a regular basis at Backbeat and she set the tone for the great working relationship I've enjoyed with everyone since then. Richard Leeds conjured up a terrific cover design for the book, Leigh McLellan has done a great layout design for the entire book and Amy Miller (production editor) has brought all the pieces together. My friend, Denise Stinson of Walk Worthy Press in Detroit, has given me invaluable advice on this book, my contract, and so many things. Thank you all so much.

I have many public friends who have been supportive throughout my career. Special thanks to Mavis Staples, Yvonne Staples, Edwin Hawkins, Candi Staton, Vickie Winans, Ann McCrary, CeCe Winans, Cedric and Angie Winans Caldwell, Debbie Winans-Lowe, and Bryan Wilson. Bryan is a COGIC robot who spewed all sorts of great facts about COGIC singers at me. Gordon "Gordo" Ely was an invaluable outlet. In between his fits (tantrums?) of telling me off and laying me out, he led me to several artists I never would have thought of including in the book. Gregory Gay schooled me on a lot of the more obscure gospel artists. Dan Ewald loaded me with all the CCM trivia I could slide into the book. Music professionals such as Lee Hildebrand; Opal Nations; Seamus McGarvey; Percy Williams (Siirius Satellite); Keith Solis (ABC Radio); Jacquie Gales-Webb (WHUR Radio); Stacy Merida at Sony Music, Pastor Jerome Bell (a pastor who doesn't act like a pastor – and you know that's a compliment from me) of the Maryland Family Christian Center in Forestville, MD; Pastor Shane Wall of the Feast of the Lord Church in Orangeburg SC; Rev. Andre Gates (a Rev. with no church to pastor? What's up with that? I love it!) and my instant-message buddy Sonja Norwood (Willie's wife, Brandy and Ray J's mom, and Sy'rai's grandma), have all contributed in some way to this book. Thank you all.

I'm grateful for my best friend ever in the public relations field, Erma Byrd, who was already looking for ways to hook me up with some media before the book was even finished. Sheila Frazier, the still-gorgeous starlet, turned me on to entertainment PR in the first place when she allowed me to be her assistant during Bill Clinton's 1992 presidential campaign. I probably seemed more like a lap dog than an assistant, but I digress. Other PR pals such as Phyllis Caddell, JoJo Pada, Edna Bruce, Andrea Williams, Veda Brown, and Gwendolyn Quinn have also been looking out for me and I love you all for it. Also, I must thank Yvonne Shinholster Lamb for being a mentor and getting me my writing gig at the *Washington Post* back in the day, and Garry Clifford for getting me my writing job at *People* magazine – also back in the day. With all of this back-in-the-day stuff, it sounds like I'm 105 years old, doesn't it?

As could be expected, I was highly stressed as my book deadline approached, but several friends kept me smiling through it all: Veryl Howard, who always finds something crazy to call about at midnight; Roderick Jemison and his wife Shannon, who sent work, money, and advice my way; Paulette Desuzia for her uncensored tongue (the FCC needs to ban your mouth); and Donte Alexander, who was always talking off the wall when he wasn't doing serious leg work for me related to the Houston-based gospel artists in the book. Thanks to my late business partner Vincent Young for the push to do this book. Thanks to the late Donald McIntyre for the push to tell the truth but not to hurt anybody's feelings (exactly, how do you do that?). Special thanks to my other business partner Robert Shanklin for being extremely helpful with all sorts of things – like lending me his assistant, a monumental sacrifice. I thank Winona Coles, our early silent partner, for being there to do anything to launch Capital Entertainment. I also thank Ric Dunn, Marcel Williams, and George Valentine for incredible Web site designs in our early years. Marvin Williams has been a great asset in recent years with my Web site and Darren Jones has gone beyond the call of an intern (an intern who draws the line at photocopying) to do many things to help not only me, but Capital Entertainment clients as well. My assistant, Tierra Elsey, has been a right hand and a right foot in keeping me organized and pushing me to take what I do a little more seriously.

My late aunt, Pauline Carpenter, was my first introduction to gospel music. When I was a teenager, I always enjoyed visiting her and my other relatives in Indiana during summer vacation. Great memories, good times. I learned my way around and loved to take long walks up and down North Meridian Street. I'd sing to myself the whole way. But, my real musical memories of those summers were at the storefront church Pauline attended. I don't recall what denomination it was. All the women in the choir dressed in white nurse uniforms (white stockings, white pantyhose, and even little white nurse caps). I never understood that part of it. The church seated no more than 75 people. Even when hardly anyone was there, it felt cramped and sweaty. Still, every Sunday, I looked forward to Pauline singing something and I was never happier than when she sang, "I Really Love the Lord." It was simply beautiful the way her voice rose and wailed the words. After we finished service at Pauline's church, we would often go to two or three other churches before the day was over. She would sing at all of those churches and it was sort of like a no-frills version of the gospel concert tours I would eventually go on as a publicist for various recording artists. That was my first time hearing true gospel music and I've been in love with the genre ever since. Without her planting that seed, I may have never gravitated towards this type of music at all. So, I thank you, Pauline, for introducing me to gospel music.

The foundation of everything in life is based on our family roots. I thank my parents, William (Jay) and Via Carpenter, for always encouraging my musical thirst for knowledge. It's my father's doo wop records and my mother's Gladys Knight & the Pips 45s that were the basis for my musical evolution. My brother Derek, my cousins Kia Gaskins, Mercedes Maynard, and Tony Massie have always kept me musically enriched.

All of my aunts have also pushed music at me from the crib: Sande Randall, Cathy Randall, the late Marian Randall, and Margie Carpenter. My Uncle, Willie Randall (They call him "Fatman" but he's not fat; I never understood that either) gave me three LPs (Gladys Knight & the Pips' *2nd Anniversary*, the Jacksons' first album on Epic, and the *Car Wash* soundtrack) when I was nine years old and I've been collecting these memories and music from that day to this one.

Anthony Heilbut wrote the original primer on Gospel music, *The Gospel Sound: The Good News and Bad Times*, in 1971. Tony is a gem of a man who just wants the whole world to know about this gospel music. He kindly offered me advice and information for this book. Thank you, Anthony, for your unselfish gesture. Last but not least, Eric Le Blanc came out of retirement to help me get many of these birth and death dates correct. He's such an authority in the field of old-school music, and I apprciate all of the time he devoted to helping me get it right the first time.

It's only when I began to sit down and write this public *thank you* note that I realized just how many people I actually know and need to thank. However, I don't think Backbeat would thrill to the idea of me thanking another 500 of my closest friends (smile), so to the rest of you who have touched my life, I'll just say thank you—you know who you are.

Bil Carpenter

Overview

A S I JOT DOWN THESE THOUGHTS, it's a good time to be in gospel music. A very good time indeed. In the early days of the 20th-century gospel music industry, people chose careers in gospel music either because they felt a divine calling to do it, or because they were afraid lightning would strike them dead if they dared to sing anything but gospel music. Surely no one went into a gospel music career expecting to make a decent living out of it. Even the top gospel artists of that day often worked day jobs to keep food on their tables. For instance, Lee Williams of the Spiritual QCs spent 30 years as a truck driver before he quit his job and depended solely on singing for his livelihood. Only a select few artists such as Sallie Martin, Rev. James Cleveland, and Gertrude Ward, who all had business acumen as well as performing talent, were able to maximize their money-making potential as artists. In addition, they all had side businesses to enhance their personal wealth.

It's a different day now. Music ministers at large churches can command a six-figure annual salary for coming in each Sunday morning and simply leading the church in worship and praise for half an hour before the pastor preaches. In an *Atlanta Journal-Constitution* interview about the money choir conductors make, producer Kevin Bond said, "I know people who make as little as $15,000 and I know people who make as much as $200,000." When the reporter asked Byron Cage if he had heard of conductors making six figures, he didn't hesitate. "I do," Cage said of himself. Then there are those who complain that choir conductors are the new slave masters. They benefit from having a choir, but the choir members who do the actual singing don't personally benefit. Ricky Dillard defended this long-standing choir rule. "Patti LaBelle doesn't get paid what the LaBelles get paid," he said in the same article. "It's Patti's show. It's Ricky Dillard and the Chorale. It's Ricky's show. I started this, and this is my thing."

It's a new day for gospel artists financially, but the roots of the music are based in faith and hope for a better world. The word "gospel" is an elision of two Old English words meaning God and story. So the gospel is a God-story, or as we've come to know it, the good news about God. The word is believed to have first appeared in print in 1874 with the publication of Philip Bass's book *Gospel Songs*. Of course, this translates as "songs that tell God's story." The black gospel music idiom grew out of the North American plantations and cotton fields where Negro slaves toiled from dawn to dusk from 1620 through the late 1800s. The harsh plight of the slave has been well-documented, so there's no need to revisit that story here. However, it was that harsh reality that quickened the slaves' faith in an afterlife that would reward them for this miserable life they lived on earth. The passion associated with black gospel was born under the glaring eye of the overseer. As the French philosopher Voltaire once said, "If there were no God, man would have to invent him." A belief in God and a heavenly reward were perhaps the only hope that kept many slaves going. In a sense, without hope, all hope dies.

A song that sums up this hope is "Uncloudy Day." The lyrics were written by Josiah Kelly Alwood, a circuit preacher who rode on horseback through muddy swamps to remote hamlets throughout Ohio spreading the gospel message in the 1800s. The music was written by his old friend J.F. Kinsey circa 1882. It wasn't written from the perspective of the slaves' trials and tribulations, but the lyrics resound as if it had been:

Oh, they tell me of a home far beyond the sky
Oh, they tell me of a home far away
Oh, they tell me of a home where no storm clouds rise
Oh, they tell me of an uncloudy day

Oh, they tell me of a home where my friends have gone
Oh, they tell me of that land far away
Where the tree of life in eternal bloom
Sheds its fragrance through the uncloudy day

Oh, they tell me of a king in his beauty there
And they tell me that my eyes shall behold
Where he sits on the throne that is whiter than snow
In the city that is made of gold

Oh, they tell me that he smiles on his children there
And his smile drives their sorrows all away
And they tell me that no tears ever come again
In that lovely land of the uncloudy day

It is against this backdrop that the Negro spirituals such as the morbid "Nobody Knows the Trouble I've Seen" and "Swing Low, Sweet Chariot" (a code message for the Underground Railroad that allowed Southern slaves to escape to freedom in the North) were born out of that pain and despair of being enslaved and disenfranchised.

As the 20th century opened, de jure slavery was a relic of the past. However, racism, segregation, Jim Crow, and all manner of humiliation were heaped upon black Americans. Again, gospel music served as the outlet for these frustrations and brought some peace to believers. As the grand dame of gospel, Sallie Martin, once said, "Maybe sometimes people sing it [gospel] if they're burdened, they express their feelings through the song. Then again, even if they're not, they feel happy, they can give it out like that, but it's a thing of the soul."

This book is a collection of soul stories, stories that briefly explain the journeys of some of the greatest gospel singers the world has ever heard. It's unfortunate that gospel music has often been ignored by the public at large and abandoned by its African-American heirs who view it as a vestige of a past they would rather forget. Of people distancing themselves from gospel, Patti LaBelle told *Billboard* magazine in February 1991: "I think sometimes people think it's just too black. That it is something that's going to make you greasy, and old, and wake up craving grits and greens or something. It's not a color thing, either. It's with a whole lot of people. It's like that stuff might get on me or something. And when people sing gospel, like, you break up your face."

Libraries and bookstores are filled with scores of reference books on various aspects of pop music. There are plenty of books on jazz, classical, and blues music. The dearth of books on gospel music would cause one to think that there was no interest in gospel music. Yet, according to a 2003 Recording Industry Association of America (RIAA) study, Christian music accounted for 5.8 percent of all US consumer music sales. By contrast, classical sales were 3 percent, jazz was 2.9 percent, and soundtracks were 1.4 percent. Blues, children's, and new age music didn't even account for 1 percent of the sales market. In spite of these statistics, one would be hard-pressed to find any books on gospel music. If one found such a book, it would probably be Anthony Heilbut's 1971 classic *The Gospel Sound* or perhaps Bernice Johnson Reagon's 1992 tome *We'll Understand It Better By and By*. However, those books focus on a few select gospel artists in scholarly detail. By contrast, this book, like any encyclopedia, covers every major artist who has contributed to gospel music history, and scores of others who have had much less of an influence yet still merit inclusion. Here are more than 600 gospel music personalities dating back to the Dinwiddie Colored Quartet, who made the first gospel recording for RCA Victor Records in 1902.

Every day someone dies and with them dies some unrecorded history. Shamefully, Edna Gallmon Cooke and Ruth Davis of the Davis Sisters are examples of two major gospel pioneers who have left this world without leaving one decent interview from which posterity can glean. Fortunately, this book is capturing the voices and history of some of the artists who were not deemed worthy of press coverage during their lifetimes. I interviewed Rev. Willie Morganfield (who wrote "What Is This?") just three weeks before his unexpected death. His death propelled me to reach as many artists as I could to get their stories down. Some were happy to talk and the stories poured like fine wine. Others didn't remember much or, perhaps, chose to forget. Still others, like Betty Ransom Nelson, didn't want the attention and politely passed on my interview request altogether.

Willing or unwilling, their abbreviated stories are finally here in one place for the world to know. Although the Bible is the book on which they based how they lived their lives, I hope this book will become sort of a bible on how successful they were with living "The Life I Sing About in My Song," as the Thomas Dorsey tune suggests. All of the first wave of gospel legends such as Willie Mae Ford Smith, Thomas Dorsey, and Mahalia Jackson have passed on to their final reward. The second wave, those who came to prominence in the 1950s, are quickly dying out. Fortunately, I've been able to interview a few of those legends such as the late Marion Williams and Roscoe Robinson from the Five Blind Boys of Mississippi. The book discusses the ups and downs, the good times and the bad.

Within these mini-histories, we see the whole range of human behavior. There are gospel artists who'd rather die before they'd allow a secular song to flow from their lips. There are those who won't sing them publicly, but will sing them privately for friends. There are others who will sing gospel or pop with no qualms depending on the occasion. In spite of the Bible's admonitions about fornication, there are artists here who sired children out of wedlock. There are artists who have committed adultery. There are artists who have openly lived a gay lifestyle. There are others who once were gay but left the lifestyle behind. Some have struggled with alcohol and drugs. Others are known to have been rude, stingy, or petty at times. But these facts are not told for sensationalism. They are told to show that we are all human and that we are all striving toward some sense of destiny in our lives. Along the way, we encounter trials and tribulations, which either break us or make us.

The strife in a gospel singer's life often comes from within his or her own community. Sallie Martin knew Aretha Franklin when she was a child gospel prodigy and, like so many of her generation, was disappointed when Aretha began to sing pop music. Martin once quipped of Franklin, "You can't be on both sides of the fence at one time. You're here tonight and to-morrow night you're something else." Many hardliners still feel that way about artists who sing both sacred and secular music.

Even some gospel songs have been labeled as secular once they start receiving secular radio airplay. Such was the case when Donnie McClurkin's "We Fall Down" reached the Top 40 on the R&B singles chart in 2001. "When it first came out, all the Christian radio stations played it," McClurkin told *Rolling Out* magazine. "Then, when secular stations started play-ing it, some people in the Christian community began to declare it unscriptural. I think that is indicative of what some of us believe… that [gospel] music is exclusive to us. But gospel music is not made for those who know God; it's made for those who don't…. We kept God in one direction for so long, and then we have new people bringing it to the next level. We have Kirk Franklin, who was just about killed because of what he built. I'm telling you, don't look at gospel in a traditional setting because it never has been. Mahalia [Jackson] wasn't tra-ditional in her time. They wouldn't let Mahalia play in church because she twisted her hips, had a band with drums and a bass guitar. They said she wasn't saved." Blues great B.B. King, who began his career with the Famous St. John's Gospel Singers in the 1940s, once said, "If they found out we had a guitar, some churches would cancel our show. To some, the guitars made us look like a rebel group."

This is just a taste of the history you will uncover in the pages of *Uncloudy Days*. I hope that you'll be as fascinated by these personalities as I am.

Bil Carpenter

A-7

A CONTEMPORARY GOSPEL band hailing from Manchester, Georgia, these siblings were raised in the House of the Living God church and all graduated from the Christian Way Academy. The group began as the A-Boyz and Girls. The girls were Miriam Harris (born February 13, 1978), Naomi Harris (born April 3, 1975), and Elain Childs-Parks (born February 22, 1965). The boys were drummer Arcelious Harris (born August 27, 1986), organist Alonzo Harris (born July 31, 1982), lead singer Alexander Harris (born September 9, 1980), guitarist Adronicus Harris (born May 14, 1977), keyboardist Antipas Harris (born March 10, 1976), and second lead singer Antonio Owens (born March 24, 1968), who is their godbrother. After the girls left the group, the guys performed as the A-Boyz. They wrote and produced their debut CD *The A-Boyz Project* for their own independent MNM Records label in 2000. The project lacked national distribution, so it never charted. However, it received enough radio airplay on the single "I'm Here 4 U" to win them television appearances on Candi Staton's *Say Yes* and BET's *Bobby Jones Gospel.* Currently, several members of the group are attending or have graduated from colleges such as Yale University and Boston University. Their fields of study include law, social work, and theology. Now that they are young men and not boys, the group has changed its name to A-7. "The A stands for the uniqueness of all of them having A for their first names," says group manager Alexander Harris. "The 7 stands for perfection in the Bible." They made a comeback in 2005 with a self-titled CD on Triple A Entertainment Records.

Lee Roy Abernathy

A SOUTHERN GOSPEL SONGWRITER born August 13, 1913, in Canton, Georgia, Abernathy distinguished himself early on as a piano player. He was a member of the Homeland Harmony Quartet in the late 1940s when they recorded for White Church Records. Later, Abernathy and Carroll "Shorty" Bradford billed themselves as the world's only two-man quartet. The duo performed four-part harmony in their live act of the period. Abernathy and his wife, Louise, began the first mail-order piano courses back in 1945 and also were instrumental in creating a market for Southern gospel sheet music. He performed with a number of groups thereafter and wrote gospel hits such as "Moving Up to Gloryland" and the boogie-woogie–styled "A Wonderful Time Up There," which Pat Boone crossed over to the pop charts where it peaked at No. 4 in 1958. Abernathy ran unsuccessfully for the Georgia governorship in 1958. He died May 25, 1993.

Shirley Ables

ONE OF WASHINGTON, DC's local gospel queens during much of the 1980s, Shirley Ables was born February 1939 in the nation's capital. Ables formed the Joy Gospel Singers in the 1970s and quickly built a solid and influential local representation for their spirited take on traditional gospel music. For a handful of years, they were in great demand to open for national acts passing through Washington, such as Shirley Caesar. Although they recorded some local albums, their only national recording was 1985's *Shirley Caesar Presents Shirley Ables—My Jesus* LP, issued on Exodus Records. Produced by Sanchez Harley and Loris Holland, it was an overall mediocre contemporary gospel recording that opened with a pseudo disco track called "Praises." The best song was written by Caesar and Ables, the catchy and clever mid-tempo takeoff on a Rolaids antacid commercial campaign called "How Do You Spell Relief?" It received decent gospel airplay nationally but would have benefited from the promotional push a more aggressive, larger recording label would have brought the project. In 1992, Ables's group won the Wammie (Washington, DC's version of the Grammy awards) for best gospel group, and in 1993 they won for best gospel song for "Keep on Praying." In 2003, the group was inducted into the International Gospel Music Hall of Fame. Ables is now the First Lady of the Westbrook Baptist Church in Washington, DC, where her husband, Rev. Homer Starks, is the pastor.

Abyssinian Baptist Church
Adam Clayton Powell, Jr.

ONE OF BLACK AMERICA's most fabled churches, the Abyssinian Baptist Church in Harlem was founded by the gifted orator Adam Clayton Powell, Sr. His son, Adam Clayton Powell, Jr., was born November 29, 1908, in New Haven, Connecticut. After studying at Columbia and Colgate Universities, Powell became a civil rights activist. He later earned a doctorate in divinity at Shaw University and was installed as pastor of his father's church in 1937. He discarded most of the Biblical teachings and only stressed the actual words attributed to Jesus Christ in the Bible. After winning a New York City council seat in 1941, Powell, a Democrat, made history in 1945 when he became the state's first black congressman. He would eventually spend more than 25 years in the position.

From the start, Powell went to Capitol Hill to press, not to impress. He was unbothered by the Congressional status quo and etiquette. He went there to open doors for blacks and did so with a militant arrogance that often riled and irritated his white congressional counterparts on both sides of the aisle. One of his first accomplishments was demanding a haircut at the segregated congressional barbershop. He then commanded his mostly black staff to integrate all of the segregated areas of the Capitol, including the cafeteria and the gymnasium. Powell strong-armed the Congress into allowing black journalists access to the Capitol press gallery. Possessing a big ego, Powell ignored those he felt ignored his concerns. When Adlai Stevenson ran on the Democratic presidential ticket in 1956, Powell campaigned for Republican Dwight Eisenhower instead. During his chairmanship of the education committee, Powell deliberately mispronounced the names of members, showed up late to the hearings, and was known to filibuster until he received concessions for his own favored legislation. In 1966, he held a "Black Power" conference in his congressional office to the consternation of many white congressmen.

For all his good intentions, personality issues sometimes sidetracked Powell's effectiveness. He was not a team player. Not only did he take no flak from his congressional colleagues, he also dismissed his own staff members who disagreed with his plans. Others quit in frustration. Regardless, Powell manipulated the media and used closed-door negotiating to push through minimum wage, anti-lynching, and educational legislation that benefited not only blacks but other working class people as well.

When he wasn't fighting for the working class, Powell was earning a reputation as a flamboyant playboy. His movie star handsomeness and gregarious charm made Powell irresistible to women. He had three tumultuous marriages (the union with jazz pianist Hazel Scott provided much tabloid fodder throughout the early 1950s) and numerous love affairs. In addition, he was a chain smoker and a heavy drinker. He was the celebrity preacher of the day. He officiated the 1948 wedding between Nat King Cole and Maria Ellington (the marriage that produced Natalie Cole) at Abyssinian. Long before prosperity preachers hit the scene, Powell pushed the gospel of capitalism. He even defended thievery among the working class: "A man's respect for law and order exists in precise relationship to the size of his paycheck."

Powell himself had a vague sense of the law. While appearing on a TV show in the early 1960s, Powell called Esther James "a bagwoman" for Italian numbers runners in Harlem, where Powell felt that blacks, not Italians, should run numbers. James filed a libel suit against Powell. Although James had a long police record that supported Powell's contention, the media turned on him. Powell was painted as beating up on a widowed grandmother. Meanwhile, most reports downplayed James's criminal record and highlighted Powell's verbal assault. The New York Supreme Court awarded James a $246,000 judgment, which Powell refused to pay. His congressional enemies used it as an opportunity to expel him from Congress. After winning re-election, Powell was denied a seat when the new Congress convened on January 10, 1967. He was charged with misuse of House funds, contempt of a court order, and conduct unbecoming a member of the House. On top of everything else, Congress fined Powell $25,000 and stripped him of his seniority.

While Powell's legal team appealed his case to the U.S. Supreme Court, Powell went to Bimini in the Bahamas with a group of friends he referred to as his 12 disciples. He spent his days fishing, boating, and visiting the local watering holes. In June 1969, the U.S. Supreme Court ruled Powell's exclusion from the House unconstitutional and cited racism as the cause. He was finally reseated. However, the mainstream press had painted Powell as a villain and he never recovered from the blight on his character. He was defeated by Charles Rangel for re-election in 1970 and retired. A year later, he resigned as pastor of Abyssinian Baptist Church and relocated to Miami, where he died on April 4, 1972. He was cremated and his ashes were scattered over South Bimini. In 2003, Showtime produced a film on Powell's life entitled *Keep the Faith, Baby*.

RECOMMENDED RECORDING: Right after he was denied his congressional seat, Powell flew a studio staff down to Bimini and recorded a set of sermonettes entitled *Keep the Faith, Baby* (Jubilee, 1967), a phrase Powell often invoked from his pulpit. The LP was recorded in a studio with a small but enthusiastic audience of Powell's nomadic fraternity. On "My Dear Colleagues," Powell compared his congressional tormentors to the Roman senators who stabbed Julius Caesar. Other tracks espoused Powell's views on the Vietnam War (against it) and black economic empowerment (for it). On the latter, Powell said, "Learn, baby, learn… so that you can earn, baby, earn!" He also said, "The only thing the white man respects is your vote and your dollar." The album was a moderate success, resonating mostly with Powell's supporters in Harlem. The LP inspired Esther James to rebuke him with her own LP *No Man is Above the Law – I Kept the Faith* (Faith Records, 1967). Side one of the album was James telling her life story and refuting Powell's claims. Side two was performed by a male Calypso group calling itself Lord Faith and the James Men. Among the songs in tribute or defamation to Powell were "Hold the Dough" and "Bimini Boat Song."

Alfred Ackley

BEST KNOWN FOR COMPOSING the hymn "He Lives," Ackley was born January 21, 1887, in Spring Hill, Pennsylvania. He studied music at the Royal Academy of Music in London where he excelled in playing the cello. In 1914, he was ordained into the Presbyterian Church and began to lead evangelistic meetings. At one such meeting, a Jewish student asked why he should worship a dead Jew (Jesus), at which Ackley proclaimed, "He lives!" From that experience, Ackley wrote the hymn that was first published in 1933 by the Rodeheaver Company, which was responsible for publishing many gospel songs in the 1950s. Ackley died July 3, 1960.

Oleta Adams

OLETA ADAMS (born May 4, 1962, in Seattle) first appeared on the national music scene in 1990 with the same sort of critical acclaim that greeted jazz vocalist Angela Bofill's debut a decade before. She was esteemed by hard-nosed jazz enthusiasts for her rich alto (just as Bofill once was) and superb skills at the piano, yet pop audiences appreciated her as well. Her defining moment was when her rendition of Brenda Russell's "Get Here" served as an unofficial American patriotic anthem during the 1991 Gulf War. In the years since, Adams has not enjoyed another hit of that magnitude and her recording output has been intermittent, but she remains a regular performer on the smooth jazz and club circuit.

Adams's family moved to Yakima, Washington, when she was 11 years old. Early on, Adams gravitated to the piano and excelled quickly. She was soon recruited to play and sing in the choir at the Pilgrim Rest Baptist Church where her father pastored (her dad, Pastor Ed, is a frequent guest on TBN's *Praise the Lord* program). In fact, at one point, Oleta was either directing or singing in four different choirs at the same time. In junior high school, she took classical voice lessons from her Julliard-trained teacher Lee Farrell who groomed Adams for an operatic career. Although she won a scholarship to Pacific Lutheran University in Tacoma to study opera, Adams decided not to enroll. Instead, Adams headed for Los Angeles in the early 1970s on a mission to make her voice heard. She raised $5,000 to produce her own exquisite demo tape, but she quickly found that her soothing music was out of step with the current disco and punk music trends. With guidance from Farrell, Adams left LaLa Land for Kansas City. She quickly began making a name for herself as a lounge chanteuse with her own band and a show that attracted celebrity spectators such as Billy Joel and Eartha Kitt. She paid her dues there. "You work through anything," she once told the *Sacramento Bee*. "The blender, the waitresses, groups from conventions coming through, even people falling over you drunk."

Many of the national artists Adams encountered when they performed on local bills with her tried to help her get a recording contract. The British band Yes arranged an audition for Adams with Atlantic Records head Ahmet Ertegun. Jazz guitarist George Benson even tried to land her a record deal, but none was forthcoming. But fortune finally struck in 1985. Roland Orzabal and Curt Smith of the duo Tears for Fears (best known for the No. 1 pop song "Everybody Wants to Rule the World") saw her perform at Kansas City's Hyatt Regency Hotel. They were moved by her show, but did not make it known to her that they were there or that they enjoyed her music.

A while later, Adams's band broke up, she and her drummer boyfriend John Cushon were on shaky ground, and after years of seemingly fruitless toil, she began to believe that she'd never become a recording star. At an emotional low point, "I gave my life to Christ, and it was like a big weight coming off my shoulders," she told Lynn Norment in an *Ebony* magazine interview. Later, while Orzabal and Smith were back in Britain working on the Tears for Fears album *The Seeds of Love*, they placed a surprise call to Adams and invited her to sing background on the album. She toured Europe with the band and became very close with them. They helped secure her a recording deal with the British Fontana Records label. With Orzabal as producer, her debut album *Circle of One* was recorded in London. The project was immediately successful as "Rhythm of Life" reached No. 9 on the R&B singles chart and No. 21 on the adult contemporary chart in 1990.

Adams's second single, a remake of the Brenda Russell hit "Get Here," received a promotional push that no money could ever buy. The song was released amid the 1991 Gulf War to free Kuwait from occupation by Iraq. The plaintive love song was transformed into a war anthem for families of soldiers, who could empathize with the line of the song that reads: "I don't care how you get here, just get here when you can." Many radio stations played the song in memory of those who died in combat, and many listeners called in dedications for loved ones who were on the battlefield. The increased airplay and media exposure propelled the song all the way to No. 5 on the pop charts, No. 3 on the adult contemporary chart, and No. 8 on the R&B chart. On the strength of "Get Here," the title song "Circle of One" was issued as a third single, which reached the Top 30 on the R&B, dance, and AC (adult contemporary) charts. The album sold a million copies and won Adams a Grammy nomination that year.

Her next albums, *Evolution* in 1993 and *Moving On* in 1995, sold respectably but did not begin to approach the success of *Circle of One*. In 1997, Adams fulfilled a personal dream to record a gospel album when Sony's gospel imprint, Harmony Records, released *Come Walk with Me*. Many R&B artists have done gospel projects that received a lukewarm response from the church world. Black gospel radio programmers did not embrace Adams's music, but it found a surprising home with white Christian radio programmers. The single "Holy Is the Lamb" not only received airplay on black gospel stations, but also received airplay on those tough-to-crack (for black artists) inspirational and AC Christian radio formats. The album climbed up to No. 4 on the gospel chart and an equally impressive No. 10 on the CCM (contemporary Christian music) chart.

The gospel project was a sacrifice in more ways than one as Adams's secular label was none too pleased about the recording. "At the time I had a secular deal with Mercury Records along with a Christian deal at Harmony Records," she told *Venice* magazine. "Mercury didn't find out about my Christian deal until I got into the studio to record my second record, then they debated about stopping the recording of it. But I wouldn't allow it to be stopped. I knew this was something I needed to say and needed to do as a part of my Christian faith. Then the business end of things happened and I found out the same problems exist in secular music that are also in Christian music. There are still racial prejudices even in the Christian world. At one convention I was told, 'We won't need you to do a liner [a radio drop] because we don't play your music.' And I'm like, 'The album's not even out yet. How do you know?' They [black gospel radio programmers] have an idea about gospel music that if it's really gospel, I should be singing with a big choir really yelling and screaming. But my music is more contemporary Christian. There's so much polarization, and I can't figure out why I thought we were serving the same God and that it didn't matter. But it did, it caused some sadness in me. Then I was let go by Mercury before I could even start a new record with them."

In late winter 2001, Pioneer Entertainment released Adams's *All the Love* CD, a mix of smooth love songs and pop-styled gospel songs. Adams covered Avalon's megahit "I Can't Live a Day Without You" and included other spiritual songs such as "Just Before I Go to Sleep," "The Power of Sacrifice," "When You Walked into My Life," and "In the Beginning." One of the most poignant selections was "Learning to Love You More," which Adams dedicated to her sister, Debbie. "Right at the height of success… I went home for the holidays and found out my sister had been in a coma for two months because she was hit by a car," Adams told *Venice* magazine. "They put her in a nursing home [where] nobody touched her because they said she had AIDS, which she did not. So they didn't brush her teeth or wash her hair. They didn't care because she was a drug addict, a woman, and a black person. The red flag went up for me and my battle cry began. I got her help and that meant I had to become her legal guardian and deal with her day to day. It was challenging because I lived in a different city and I was touring. I kept praying to God, saying, 'If you're going to remake her, please give her a different heart.' I think he said, 'Okay, I'm going to give you a different heart too.' I found that love means loving the unlovable. Now, we can say 'I love you' to each other. That's something we hadn't said to each other since we were kids."

RECOMMENDED RECORDING: *Come Walk with Me* (Harmony Records, 1997).

Yolanda Adams

ONE OF THE FEW GENUINELY distinctive vocal stylists in modern day gospel, Yolanda Adams has become the most heralded female gospel artist of the new mil-

lennium. Her rendering of V. Michael McKay compositions such as "Through the Storm" and "The Battle Is the Lord's" as well as other signature tunes such as "What About the Children" put her name on the gospel map in the 1990s and made her one of the most sought after women in gospel. However, it was her signing with Elektra Records in 1999 and the subsequent million-selling album *Mountain High, Valley Low* which transformed her into a superstar throughout the urban pantheon and brought her a new legion of faithful followers in the same manner that *Stomp* catapulted Kirk Franklin into superstar status.

Born August 27, 1961, in Houston, Texas, the eldest of six children, Adams grew up listening to everything from jazz and classical to gospel music. Her schoolteacher mom, Carolyn, and high school coach dad, Major, were both great singers and encouraged a wide range of music to be played in their household. Among

Yolanda Adams

Adams's favorite performers were James Cleveland, the Edwin Hawkins Singers, Nancy Wilson, and Stevie Wonder. Adams was particularly close to her father. When she was 13, he died of injuries suffered in a car accident. Her religious faith equipped her to cope with her father's death. "At 13, I'm picking out flowers, a casket, and making all the arrangements because my mom is like, 'I don't want to see it; my husband is gone,'" Adams told *Essence* magazine. "She was 33, and the love of her life was gone. She was like, 'What am I going to do?'"

Adams knew what *she* was going to do. She attended her father's alma mater, Texas Southern University, and continued to live at home and assist her mom with raising her siblings. At one point, she had dreamed of being a fashion model and then decided to become a news anchor. When an internship at a Houston TV station didn't translate into a permanent job, she became a schoolteacher like her parents. She taught elementary school on weekdays and sang with the Southeast Inspirational Choir on the weekends. It was while performing with the choir that she was spotted by producer Thomas Whitfield. Originally, Whitfield had composed the *Just as I Am* LP for a singer named Lydia Wright. However, he had Adams record the same album instead. In 1988, he placed the record with Sound of Gospel Records. The album eventually climbed to No. 8 on the gospel chart. Veteran vocalist Candi Staton gave Adams a big boost when she had Adams perform several times on her weekly TBN television musical series *New Direction*. The appearances helped fans put a face with the voice they'd been hearing on the radio.

Around the same period, Adams married Troy Mason, but she divorced him two years later and told *Gospel Today* that it was an abusive relationship. Meanwhile, her career continued to escalate as she moved to Benson/Tribute Records. There her LPs *Through the Storm* and *Save the World* produced the gospel megahits "Through the Storm," and "The Battle Is the Lord's," respectively. At last, Adams was able to leave the security of a teaching salary and sing gospel full time. With Adams's beautiful features and volcanic voice, Benson saw the potential for her to cross over to R&B radio. They crafted an urban radio campaign around the relatively weak song "Gotta Have Love," which reached No. 97 on the *Billboard* R&B chart in 1994.

As the decade wore on, Adams continued to create top-selling gospel projects such as the albums *More than a Melody*, *Live in Washington*, and 1998's *Songs from the Heart*. At that point in her career, Adams and her long-time manager, Shiba Freeman Haley, had been longing for a record label to take Adams's ministry to the next level of fame and recognition. They knew that Benson/Tribute was ill equipped to do so, so when Adams's contract was fulfilled, they began scouting for a new record deal. They met with virtually every major gospel label executive, even John Sussewell at the independent CGI Records, which was having spectacular success with Vickie Winans. They were still undecided as to what direction to take when fate stepped into the picture.

After seeing Adams perform live at New York's Beacon Theater, Elektra Records' chairwoman Sylvia Rhone sought the singer out and offered her just the kind of recording deal she was hoping for: a label that dreamed big but would allow Adams to remain gospel. "I didn't think signing with Elektra was as much of a leap as some might think because of the faith [Rhone] had in me," Adams said. "Her vision was the same as mine." Rhone paired Adams with Janet Jackson's producers, Jimmy Jam and Terry Lewis. They crafted a slick, urban album subtly expressing Adams's faith on most tracks, but coming out boldly on the Richard Smallwood–produced tune "That Name." The album *Mountain High, Valley Low* was issued in fall 1999.

Elektra's seasoned PR team of Lisa Jefferson and others used their mainstream media contacts to net Adams set-up media coverage she'd never had before. She received placement articles in high-end magazines such as *Interview* and *Jet*. There were television appearances on *Donny & Marie* and other programs. With such a media rollout and ace radio promoters working the album's first urban single, "Yeah Yeah Yeah," the CD debuted at No. 1 on the gospel chart. With jazz legend Nancy Wilson at her side, Adams went on BET's *Bobby Jones Gospel* TV show to explain for those who may have been confused as to whether her signing to Elektra meant she was leaving gospel—she wasn't leaving gospel, she was just taking it to a larger audience.

Initially, it looked like the much-hyped venture wasn't working out. A few weeks after its release, Adams's album fell out of the No. 1 slot on the gospel album sales chart and the "Yeah" single never took off on urban radio. In January 2000, Elektra pushed out "Fragile Heart" as the follow-up single, but it too failed to ignite urban radio programmers. Finally, by the spring Elektra picked a song Adams co-wrote, "Open My Heart," as the third single. With a similarity to Major Harris's quiet storm R&B classic "Love Won't Let Me Wait," the ballad "Open My Heart" saved the project.

Eventually, the song reached No. 10 on the *Billboard* R&B singles chart and shot all the way to No. 1 on the *Radio & Records* urban AC chart. As the album took off, Adams was invited to perform on coveted TV programs such as *The Rosie O'Donnell Show*. The album regained its No. 1 slot on the gospel chart, claimed the same space on the CCM chart, climbed to No. 5 on the R&B album chart, and rose to No. 24 on the pop album chart. The album eventually went double platinum. After years of being nominated and never winning a Grammy, Adams finally won her first Grammy for best contemporary soul gospel album in 2000.

"Elektra saw an opportunity to take my music where I wanted to take it, which is to the masses," Adams told GospelCity.com in 2001. "And to take it in such a fashion that it didn't compromise my faith or any of my beliefs in God. As a matter of fact, what they did was pour more money into the production and promotion of my album, which is what you have to do in order to sell records…. But what Elektra has done is made all the gospel labels step up. Because, let's just tell the truth, [the other labels] figured, 'Oh, let's just put an album out, we'll see what it does, we'll buy a couple of ads and if it sells, well, that's good. If it doesn't sell, well…you know, whatever.'"

Elektra immediately cashed in on Adams's success by rushing out a mediocre live album featuring versions of almost the entire *Mountain High, Valley Low* album plus a duet of "I Believe I Can Fly" with Gerald Levert. Then Adams's first Christmas album was hurriedly put together and rushed into the marketplace. As if there was not enough of Adams suddenly on retail shelves, Adams's former labels rushed out various compilation CDs of her prior material to exploit her new fame.

By the time Adams's December 2001 CD *Believe* was released with the inspirational urban single "Never Give Up," Adams had become a household name in black homes. However, many gospel radio announcers began grumbling on air about Adams hosting the Soul Train Awards and singing pop songs such as "Imagine" on a John Lennon television tribute. They also suggested that her lyrics were being watered down and that she was selling her soul for secular fame. "I would really do God a disservice if I say I want to be like him, but I don't want to share with anybody in the secular market and just go to churches and do church music, period," she told GospelCity.com. "That would do him a disservice because he said go into the highways and the hedges and compel men. No, it's not duplicity. What I'm doing is I'm standing up and being the person that I always am. The same person who hosted the Stellars was the same person who hosted the Soul Train Awards. You didn't see me get out of line, you didn't see me cuss. It would be different if there was some nakedness or some stuff I didn't do on the Stellars. And that's what I have to get people to understand. I'm not going to over-explain myself, or try to say that this is what I'm doing, please accept it. They have a choice. You either watch it or you don't. You accept it or you don't accept it. But I know what God told me. He told me that I would be able to go into any genre of music or any platform and represent him." She even told *Ebony* that "In Mahalia's day, folks told her the same thing. In Andrae Crouch's day, folks told him the same thing. In Thomas Dorsey's day, they told him the same thing. So I guess I'm on the right track."

RECOMMENDED RECORDING: *The Essential Yolanda Adams* (Sony Legacy) combines Adams's early traditional hits like "The Battle Is the Lord's" with contemporary new songs such as "Open My Heart."

African Methodist Episcopal Church

ONE DAY IN 1787, the black members of the segregated St. George's Methodist Episcopal Church in Philadelphia were praying in their designated area of the church when a white man told them to get up and go to another part of the church. Insulted by their rough treatment that day and the church's segregation in general, a black church member named Richard Allen (1760–1831) and others dropped their church membership and formed the Free African Society. They formed the organization with the idea of creating an environment of freedom to worship without segregation. Allen then brought together blacks from other Methodist and Episcopal churches and formed the African Methodist Episcopal (AME) church in Philadelphia at a special convocation April 9–11, 1816. They strictly followed the tenets of the Methodist church, all but the rule of segregation. Today, the church has more than 2.5 million members.

Doris Akers

ONE OF THE MOST UNDERRATED gospel composers of the 20th century, Doris Mae Akers wrote more than 500 songs, including "Lord, Don't Move That Mountain," "You Can't Beat God Giving," "God Is So Good to Me," "Sweet, Sweet Spirit," and "Lead Me, Guide Me." Born May 21, 1923, in Brookfield, Missouri, Akers studied piano as a child, wrote her first song at the age of ten, and formed a five-piece jazz band, Dot Akers and Her Swingsters, as a teenager. She moved to Los Angeles in 1945. "I picked her up in California," Sallie Martin told oral historian James Standifer. "She doesn't read a single note, but she can hear every tone that's supposed to be there."

Akers joined the Sallie Martin Singers as a singer and pianist, and toured with them for a handful of years. In 1947, she wrote her first professional song "I Want a Double Portion of God's Love," which Brother Joe May turned into a hit for Specialty Records in 1950. Soon other artists were requesting the songs from Akers's prolific pen. Her songs featured elegant lyrics and were not overly black in tone. Instead, they bridged black and white gospel music, often with a choral pop sound. In the late 1940s, Akers co-founded the Simmons-Akers Singers with Dorothy Simmons (born September 10, 1919, in Powhatan, Louisiana), also a member of the Sallie Martin troupe. They shared lead vocals with Simmons's lyric soprano contrasting nicely with Akers's mezzo-soprano voice. Never big sellers, they recorded albums such as 1957's "Sing Praise unto the Lord" on RCA Records before disbanding in the '60s. Later, Akers was the soloist and

director of the Sky Pilot Choir, a multiracial Los Angeles gospel choir. In 1972, Inez Andrews turned Akers's "Lord, Don't Move that Mountain" into an R&B hit and a gold record. As the golden age of gospel faded by the '70s, so did Akers's profile. She was largely forgotten by then and, in the last years of her life, she was minister of music at Grace Temple Deliverance Center in Minneapolis where she enjoyed teaching music to choirs and coaching young singers. Visiting the doctor about a broken ankle in August 1994, Akers learned that she had inoperable spinal cancer. After months of excruciating pain—and few complaints—she died at the Heritage of Edina Nursing Home on July 26, 1995. A testament to the popularity of her songs is the diverse group of singers who recorded them over the years, including Elvis Presley, Mahalia Jackson, Conway Twitty, Tennessee Ernie Ford, and the Dixie Hummingbirds.

Allen & Allen

KEYBOARDIST BRUCE ALLEN and saxophonist Allen T.D. Wiggins met on the campus of Bethune-Cookman College in the early 1990s. Allen was graduating and Wiggins was just starting his studies. In 1994, they formed an inspirational jazz duo and produced their first CD, *Allen & Allen*, for CGI Records later that year. They recorded other smooth jazz instrumental albums for the label, including *A-Blazing Grace* (1995), *A Christmas Like Never Before* (1995), *Come Sunday*, (1996), and *New Beginning* (Platinum, 1998). Although they had not had a chart hit on either the gospel nor smooth jazz charts, the group was sufficiently in demand for concerts to launch their own recording label in 2001. The Allen & Allen Music Group has released four albums by the duo. The latest CD, *Unconditional Love* (AAMG, 2004) features songs from their previous albums, including the beautiful love song "Answer to My Prayer."

Earline Allen

BACK IN THE 1950s, she was known as the Songbird of Texas in the Church of God in Christ (COGIC) de-

Left to right: COGIC *missionary Inez Hornes, her husband, Rev. Bennie Allen and his wife, Earline Allen, February 1974 in Houston.*

nomination. One of ten children, Allen was born June 9, 1923, in Houston. All of her family was musically inclined toward blues music styles. "I had this special call on my life," she says, "and none of them had this desire to be saved. They all followed after secular music. Every dance you can name, they could do it. I never learned dancing until I was saved and that was a holy dance. I used to hear my mother talk about the old time church services and how people came with this hunger to be saved and it always intrigued me." When she was 15 years old, Allen was saved. "Now, I could sing," she says, "but when I got saved, I was anointed."

In 1938, she met Bishop Bennie Earle Allen Sr., an 18-year-old preacher from Galveston who came through Houston for a revival. They courted for three years and married on June 26, 1941. Allen was very active in the COGIC denomination and devoted herself to music ministry. "There wasn't a church here in the city of Houston that had an organ," she says. "Then in the early 1940s the Buckstreet COGIC where I got saved got an organ. We only had one person who could play it and she played by music. She couldn't pick up 'I'm a Soldier in the Army of the Lord' by ear, and she couldn't play the old testimony types of songs that we used to sing when we'd testify. This is the way our services were structured. We had prayer, then a reading of the scriptures, and when we got up from our prayer service, we testified about what the Lord had done for us and that would go on for 30 to 45 minutes or so. But we don't do that much anymore in our churches. We

do praise and worship now. Everybody is following the praise and worship trend."

"But I got saved when you testified about the goodness of the Lord," she continues, her dramatic voice rising and falling for emphasis. "It caused other people to come to the Lord because they listened to your testimony, and some people had been saved out of all kinds of lifestyles. They would give their testimony about how God would deliver them and brought them out. They would come in to the service and we had what they called slaying in the spirit. The power of God would get on those folks and they would hit the floor and roll. So that's where we got the term Holy Rollers from.... But when they came up off the floor, they'd be speaking in tongues and it was an amazing thing to see. We also tarried for the Baptism of the Holy Ghost. They'd bring you to the church and set you on the altar. We would pray for each other until the people's language changed and they began to speak in tongues. They got that from where the 120 tarried in Jerusalem waiting for the power of the Holy Ghost, and when the Holy Ghost came it was like a sound from heaven rushing like a mighty wind that filled them all right where they sat."

With her church background and vibrant soprano, Allen was a perfect candidate for a long recording career. "We did not have the money to invest, which is the only reason I did not record," she says. Her only recording was a song she wrote called "I'm Gonna Rest One Day on the Other Side." She recorded the song for a KCOH radio promotion to advertise her musical, *The*

Story of My Life in Song. As the narrator told the story, she sang the songs. It was presented at the Anderson Memorial Church (Cage Street COGIC) in Houston and was the last project Allen dedicated to her own career. She then spent the next two decades coaching choirs around Houston. "I sang so hard from the time I was 16 until I was 40 that I developed singer's nodules," Allen says. "The doctors said I would lose my singing voice without surgery. They went in and performed the surgery and when I came out, I could not sing a word and could not speak. I cried, I went into trauma because here I am doing something to get better. I thought about the time when I turned down an opportunity to sing secular music but gave that up to serve the Lord."

Although she regained her speaking voice, Allen says that her singing voice was never the same. She eventually quit her music positions and began to focus on educational studies. "The more I studied, the more I liked it," she says. She pursued religious studies at a number of colleges, including the Southern Bible Seminary and Mount Hope Bible College.

In 1985, Allen founded the Greater Emmanuel Bible Institute in Houston. But she didn't stop there. At the age of 77, she enrolled in a doctoral program at the Houston Graduate School of Divinity, where she maintained an A average. Allen fell ill with an esophageal problem in the middle of her curriculum. She could not eat or drink regular meals for two years, and her doctors did not believe that she would survive. "Nobody thought I'd make it, but I made it and graduated with my class in 2002," she says. "The only thing I hate is that I received some Cs on my transcript. They fed me antibiotics for so many months that I lost some of my hearing, so when I returned to my program, I did not always hear everything." However, Allen was successful with her primary goal: "I wanted to know scripture for myself so that I could understand it and interpret it and share it with others."

Rance Allen

LONG BEFORE THERE WAS A BeBe and CeCe Winans or a Kirk Franklin, the Rance Allen Group was making decidedly urban-flavored gospel music, strategically designed to appeal to an unchurched black audience back in the early 1970s. Their songs, such as "Just My Salvation," "Ain't No Need of Crying," "I Belong to You," and "I Got to Be Myself," were all classically fine examples of the foundation Allen's group laid for the urban gospel artists who would follow two decades later.

One of a dozen children, Allen was born November 19, 1948, in Detroit and has been performing since he was five years old. He preached and sang early on and was called Little Rance Allen, the boy preacher. "We were raised in a family where you went to church every single night," Allen once told GospelFlava.com. "To keep our interest, my grandmother went to a pawn shop and brought instruments, drums, guitars, and amplifiers." In addition to the singing and preaching, Allen was a player—a piano player, that is. Using James Cleveland records and occasionally a Ray Charles tune as his guides, Allen began to play the piano at the age of seven and picked up the guitar two years later. His grandparents booked him and drove him to his engagements, but he once told liner notes writer Lee Hildebrand, "I didn't have a life like most kids had. I wasn't allowed to go out and play baseball with the guys and do the things a kid does. After I found out that this preaching was all work and almost no play, I started to slow down a little bit. I didn't get back into things again until the age of 17. That was when I decided all over again for myself that I wanted to be a preacher."

Eventually Allen decided to start a gospel singing group. With older brother Tom on drums, younger brother Steve on bass, and Rance on guitar, the brothers recorded their first song for the Reflect label in Monroe, Michigan. In 1971, they won a Detroit talent contest where Stax Records promotion man Dave Clark was a judge. Clark liked what he heard and got them signed to Stax Records, an R&B label in Memphis that gave birth to Otis Redding and Carla Thomas.

At the time, Allen was taking everything he was hearing on R&B radio and transforming the song lyrics into gospel songs so that he could play them in church. He took the Temptations' "Just My Imagination" and Archie Bell and the Drells' "There's Gonna Be a Showdown" and made them church songs. "People were not used to what I was doing," he told Lee Hildebrand. "I used to get some flak or bad things said about me, but every time something bad was said, someone would come along and say something good. I just happened to remember all the good things and not the bad."

Back at Stax, company president Al Bell loved the group so much that he created a subsidiary specifically to promote the Rance Allen Group, the Gospel Truth label. The group's first single on Gospel Truth was "Just My Salvation," which didn't chart, but it got a nice buzz going about the group and particularly Allen's earth-quaking falsetto. Gospel Truth began placing the trio on secular bills to expose their new style of gospel. "I had reservations about it," Allen told Hildebrand. "I prayed about it and found that my answer was 'Yes, you should play anything you get, Isaac Hayes or whoever, you should play it.' The first thing they put us on was a great big coliseum thing with Isaac Hayes. It was the first time we had played before an audience that big—something like 12,000 people. We lit up ourselves and lit the audience up too. It was a new experience for us." In spite of their girth, the Rance Allen Group's performance was electrifying. Allen employed some of Chuck Berry's guitar tricks such as shuffling across the stage as he ferociously played his guitar behind his back. With such theatrics and the group's powerful voices, the audience was always happily exhausted after a Rance Allen Group performance.

The fellows' single "I Got to Be Myself" became their first bona fide hit when it reached No. 31 on the R&B chart in 1971. They followed in 1972 with the LP *Truth Is Where It's At*, which featured their awesome take on James Cleveland's "That Will Be Good Enough for Me." The *A Soulful Experience* LP peaked at No. 35 on the R&B chart in 1975 as the single "Ain't No Need of Crying" climbed to No. 61 on the R&B survey. However, by 1975, financial misappropriations among label executives, pending lawsuits, and other problems shut Stax Records down. Burned but not baked, the Allen group snagged a deal with Capitol Records where they released the LP *Say My Friend*. They didn't feel embraced and produced no hits there. Fortunately, by that time, Fantasy Records had bought the Stax catalog and lured the Rance Allen Group back to the company to release the *Truth Is Marching On* LP, which

barely made the R&B Hot 100 in 1977. However, before departing Fantasy/Stax circa 1980, the group produced two more decent-sized R&B hits, "Smile" and the Top 25 R&B ballad "I Belong to You" in 1979.

The Rance Allen Group was without a deal for a while before Myrrh Records picked them up circa 1983 for the first of three LPs. The only one that hit was *I Give Myself to You*, which hit No. 5 on the gospel chart in 1985. There was another recording dry spell before Allen's old friend from his Stax days, Al Bell, started Bellmark Records and led the Allen group there. In 1991, the group rolled out with a tight, R&B-friendly album called *Phenomenon*. The lead single "Miracle Worker" received massive gospel airplay and even reached No. 32 on the R&B single chart. The album became the Allen group's first No. 1 gospel album ever and it also reached No. 33 on the R&B album chart. It would be five years before the next album, *You Make Me Wanna Dance* hit No. 7 on the gospel chart in 1996 and another six years before the group's Deitrick Haddon–produced *All the Way* CD hit the gospel chart in 2002 on the strength of the "Do Your Will" radio smash. While Allen still enjoys recording, preaching is clearly his first calling, which is

Rance Allen/ Bellmark Records photo

why he records sporadically these days. He pastors at New Bethel Church of God in Christ in Toledo. "I have a purpose in mind when I record," Allen told Lee Hildebrand. "I'm trying to attract someone's ears without scaring them to death or sounding fanatical, but what I'm actually trying to do is win them over to Christ."

RECOMMENDED RECORDINGS: *The Best of the Rance Allen Group* (Stax) features the group's most solid, timeless hits such as "That Will Be Good Enough for Me."

Ametria

SHE WAS BILLED AS THE First Lady of Hip-Hop Gospel when MCA released her eponymous debut CD in 2000, but Ametria never found an audience to justify the title. It's odd that someone with no track record and no signature hits would be tagged the First Lady of anything, but that's what MCA tried to make the gospel audience believe. If her album had taken off, there's no doubt that Ametria might have garnered that title since her debut featured hip-hop all-stars such as Mary J. Blige, Montell Jordan, JoJo Hailey from Jodeci, and Wanya Morris of Boyz II Men.

Born Ametria Doss in Wisconsin circa 1981, Ametria explained her career launch to GospelFlava.com in 2000. "When I was 16, a friend in church was looking for talent," she said. "He liked what he heard and then I auditioned for Joseph Carn. At that point, we did a demo of some gospel songs and he said that I've got to record. From there, I met Bilal Allah [A&R representative for MCA] and showcased for him. We vibed, I met the president of MCA and the rest is history." At the time, Ametria explained that what separated her music from R&B singers such as Monica and Brandy was her faith. "The difference between me and the others is that I'm singing for the Lord," she said. "I know my mission and my purpose. I'm here to let young people know that the Lord is there for them. There are so many negative things in the world. If young people would just trust and believe in the Lord, he'll lead and guide us into great things."

But great things were not to be. Frankly, for all the resources available to MCA, they have not had recent success with gospel music. They botched Vickie

Winans's *The Lady* album circa 1990 and a decade later they failed to find success with CD releases of Pam & Dodi, Youth Edition, and Ametria. All the artists produced fine, commercial CDs that sold less than new artists sell at independent gospel record labels that don't have MCA's muscle behind them. The press on the stars contributing to Ametria's CD *It's Not About Me* alone should have generated enough buzz to move more copies. Mary J. Blige wrote and produced "No Weapon" and "God Is So Good." Montell Jordan wrote and arranged "Prayer Changes Things" and "I Find Shelter." JoJo from Jodeci wrote and produced "What the World Needs" as a duet. Wanya from Boyz II Men joined her for the album's second duet. If the slick, urban music and Ametria's dry, Mary J. style of singing were too progressive for gospel radio, the album should have at least been pushed at urban radio. It wasn't, and it only sold a little over 10,000 units according to SoundScan—a major disappointment for a label of MCA's magnitude.

Carl Anderson

ONE OF THE BEST SONG STYLISTS of the baby boom generation, Carl Anderson is best known for playing Judas in the original Broadway production of *Jesus Christ Superstar* than for the many sophisticated urban pop recordings he made later in his career. Born Carlton Earl Anderson on February 27, 1945, in Lynchburg, Virginia, his twin brother Charles Edward died of bronchitis 11 months later. It was a family of 12 children, and they worshipped at the Rivermont Baptist Church. Anderson sang with a high school chorus and then entered the air force. After his discharge, he finished high school and enrolled at Howard University in Washington, DC, where he formed the rock band Second Eagle, which performed songs from the concept LP for *Jesus Christ Superstar*. At the same time, producers were mounting a Broadway production of the rock opera, which tells of the last seven days of Jesus Christ's life from the viewpoint of Judas. Agents for the show sought to stop Second Eagle from performing the songs in their concerts. However, a William Morris Agency representative showed up at a Palm Sunday concert in 1971 to confront the group and instead was moved by Anderson's voice.

Anderson was cast as Ben Vereen's understudy in the Broadway production. He eventually inherited the role, and it made him a star.

Anderson reprised his role in Norman Jewison's film adaptation of *Jesus Christ Superstar* and went on to launch a moderately successful recording and night-club career. In 1980, he signed to Columbia Records where his smooth jazzy albums were peppered with in-spirational songs such as "Somebody Up There Likes Me." Aside from collaborations with Nancy Wilson and others, Anderson's only major hit was the 1986 duet "Friends and Lovers" with soap opera star Gloria Loring. It reached No. 1 on the adult contemporary charts and No. 2 on the Hot 100. Anderson's 1994 CD *Heavy Weather Sunlight Again* featured the inspira-tional "God's Gift to the World" and he played Rev. Samuel in the Steven Spielberg/Quincy Jones motion picture *The Color Purple*. Anderson quietly battled leukemia for years before succumbing to the disease on February 23, 2004, in Los Angeles.

RECOMMENDED RECORDING: *Jesus Christ Superstar* (MCA Records, 1986) features Anderson at his vocal peak, singing psychedelic gospel songs.

Marian Anderson

AMERICA'S FIRST BLACK OPERA superstar, contralto Marian Anderson was born February 27, 1897, in Philadelphia. She joined the Union Baptist Church Choir when she was six years old. When she was 12, her father died and left the family penniless. Anderson went to work as a singer to help support the family. After winning a number of singing contests, Anderson tired of hearing people say, "A wonderful voice—it's too bad that she's a Negro." In 1925, she decided she might have a better chance of launching a singing career in Europe. On the continent, Anderson sang for King Gustav of Sweden and King Christian of Denmark among other royals. She became the toast of the classical world. Finnish composer Jean Sibelius asked her to have coffee with him and after she sang a bit for him at the table, he called to a waiter, "Not coffee, champagne!" After win-ning over the hearts of Europe, Anderson returned to the States in 1935, where she made a name for herself in a recital at New York's Town Hall. Sol Hurok became her manager and soon made her the third-largest opera draw in the US. Hurok and Howard University officials tried to arrange for Anderson to sing at the D.A.R. Con-stitution Hall in 1939, but Anderson was flatly refused because of her race. The conservative, elitist Daughters of the Revolution's refusal to allow Anderson to perform set off a firestorm of media attention. First Lady Eleanor Roosevelt intervened, and the Department of the Inte-rior arranged for Anderson to perform a free Easter concert on the steps of the Lincoln Memorial on April 9, 1939. The media attention reached a fever pitch and drew more than 75,000 people to the concert and mil-lions more through the radio broadcast.

In spite of her advanced age and declining vocal prowess, the Metropolitan Opera made Anderson the first black woman to sing on their stage on January 7, 1955, when she was 57 years old. She starred in Verdi's *Un Ballo in Maschera (A Masked Ball)*. Because of her name recognition and the other racial barriers she had broken, the Met picked her for the honor of being their first black artist over younger artists such as Robert McFerrin. Anderson later sang for Queen Elizabeth, President Eisenhower, and President Kennedy. She also served as the US Goodwill Ambassador in 1957 when she toured the globe for the State Department. During the 1964–1965 season, Anderson embarked on a fare-well tour that ended on Easter Sunday, April 18, 1965, to a standing-room-only crowd at Carnegie Hall. She then retreated to her Connecticut farmhouse with her hus-band, Orpheus Fisher. A deeply religious woman, An-derson recorded a number of religious-themed albums for RCA Records even after she stopped giving concerts. Her biggest recording was *Ave Maria*, which sold over 750,000 copies. However, it was typical for her other recordings to sell 250,000 copies each. The 1999 BMG Records reissue of the 1956 LP *Spirituals* is comprised of the original album and several other spiritual perfor-mances. In 1992, Anderson moved to Portland, Oregon, to live with her nephew, conductor Oscar De Priest. Fol-lowing a stroke, she died of congestive heart failure on April 8, 1993.

RECOMMENDED RECORDING: The 30-song collection

Spirituals features Anderson's operatic approach to Negro spirituals such as "Deep River," and to pop gospel such as "He's Got the Whole World in His Hands." (RCA/BMG, 1999).

Robert Anderson

AN INTERESTING EARLY GOSPEL influence on Albertina Walker and others during gospel's golden age, Robert Anderson had a crooner's (think of Bing Crosby or perhaps even a slightly livelier Perry Como) way of opening a hymn with his full, controlled baritone. His trick was that just when the listener thought he'd end the song soft and pretty, Anderson would conclude it with a thunderous, bluesy shout style that moved the congregation to its feet every time he sang in church. "They crowned him the king of gospel singers because he could really sing," Bertha Melson sighs. "He started a lot of singers singing." Born March 21, 1919, in Anguila, Mississippi, Anderson's family moved to Chicago when he was a child. He picked up the piano by ear and as a teenager assisted Roberta Martin in coaching the Sunday school choir at the Metropolitan Community Church. In 1933, he joined her Martin-Frye Quartet, which also included Eugene Smith, Willie Webb, Norsalus McKissick, and James Lawrence. In 1936, the name was changed to the Roberta Martin Singers. Once Martin's group took off, they performed several times a week. Since he didn't care much for the hectic travel schedule, Anderson left the group in 1939 and began to sing solo. His electrifying performance of "Something Within" at the National Baptist Convention in 1943 established him nationally.

Although Anderson was a great singer, he also seemed to be somewhat of a lazy singer. He didn't care to carry a whole concert program on his own, so he began to search for other singers to back him and to share lead vocal duties. In 1947, he formed the Gospel Caravan, an all-female troupe that included 17-year-old Albertina Walker. That was also the year that he wrote his most noted gospel song, "Prayer Changes Things." Back in 1942, he had formed an Indiana-based publishing company, Good Shepherd Music House, which published his songs such as "Why Should I Worry" and

"Oh Lord, Is It I?" The Gospel Caravan's first singles (listed as Robert Anderson with Vocal Chorus Accompaniment on the label) were "In My Home Over There" and "King Jesus (Will Roll My Burdens Away)," both of which were released in September 1949 on Chicago's Miracle Records. The recordings generated no heat and by November the label had taken out an ad in the black *Chicago Defender* newspaper inviting its readers to suggest gospel songs for Anderson to record since they obviously were not supporting the ones he chose to record. After the label lost its only draw, Sonny Thompson (who had sold 200,000 copies of the instrumental blues "Long Gone" in 1947) to King Records, the label eventually folded.

In 1951, Lewis Simpkins, Miracle's former A&R representative, opened United Records in Chicago. It was an R&B/blues label with artists such as Roosevelt "Honey Dripper" Sykes and Nature Boy Brown. Simpkins added his friend Anderson to the roster too. Anderson's first recording for the label was "My Expectation." After Simpkins died in 1953 of leukemia at the age of 35, his business partner Leonard Allen took over the label. He didn't have an ear for gospel and let Anderson go. Allen brought on more blues artists but could not maintain a strong enough presence in the R&B market to keep the company from closing in 1957. After Albertina Walker left to form her own group, Anderson gradually retired from regular performing. Over the years, he sang at special occasions but wasn't interested in the grind of regular performing and recording—perhaps one reason why he is not as celebrated as some of his gospel peers. However, he did direct the choir at the Hertzell United Methodist Church until his death on June 15, 1995, in Hazel Crest, Illinois.

RECOMMENDED RECORDING: There's nothing currently in print, but an original 78-rpm of "Prayer Changes Things" is worth tracking down.

Inez Andrews

INEZ ANDREWS ONCE CRACKED, "They don't pay me to sing; they like to hear me holler." Since the launch of her national career with the Caravans back in 1957, Andrews has created a reputation for herself as a distinctive squalling contralto who can hit high C at the drop of a piano key. After many successful years as a star member of that group, Andrews launched an equally successful career as a soloist. Gospel DJs nicknamed Andrews the Songbird for her passionate chirping, and ABC Records supposedly named its gospel imprint after her. Born Inez McConico on October 19, 1935, in Birmingham, Alabama, Andrews's father was Baptist and her mother was Holiness. Her mother died when she was two and her father and other relatives raised her, but she always had her feet in both churches. After a brief marriage at the age of 18, Andrews found herself working as a domestic to support her two young daughters. She was making $18 a week and would occasionally get extra money performing on the weekends as a fill-in for Dorothy Love Coates in the Gospel Harmonettes. For brief spells, she also performed with Carter's Chorale Ensemble and the Raymond Raspberry Singers. However, it was on a Nashville concert date subbing for Coates that Andrews met James Cleveland. He was playing piano for one of the groups that night and was impressed by Andrews's voice. He told Albertina Walker who then recruited Andrews for the Caravans in 1957.

Andrews's first song with the group was "Soldiers in the Army." The addition of Andrews and later Shirley Caesar took the Caravans to another level of stage presence and fame. While the group was always good, the buzz was around seeing Andrews and Caesar trade vocal licks that sent their audiences into hysterics. By 1960, Andrews was a household name in gospel circles. Her high notes coupled with her preaching style of singing earned her the title of the High Priestess. She once told historian Anthony Heilbut, "I know I sang hard. Sam Cooke did a program with us in Los Angeles and screamed so much to keep up, he got sick. He said, 'Girl…you the only singer ever put me to bed.'"

While with the Caravans, Andrews became best known for her rendition of "Mary, Don't You Weep." The song was an old church standard that had already fallen into the public domain, so Andrews took the core of the song and reworked her own version of it as a sermonette. The six-minute opus became one of the songs most identified with the Caravans and reportedly sold a half million copies. "I was one of the first females to come out with sermonettes," she told *Black Stars* in February 1979. "Nobody would do that except a male, they thought. So I got a sermonette together, we recorded it, and it went good. I can always count on 'Mary' to eat."

In the early 1960s, she formed the Andrewettes and toured Europe to great success. She briefly returned to the Caravans before going solo in 1966. She eventually found her way to Peacock Records, which launched its Songbird gospel subsidiary around Andrews. Eventually, Peacock sold its catalog to ABC Records (an offshoot of the television network), which was able to push gospel beyond the walls of the church. As Andrews was recording one of her first albums under ABC, she was in the studio with her producer, Gene Barge, who said that she needed another song to complete the album. "I don't have time to learn anything new, so we'll sing what I know," she recalled in *Black Stars*. "After we went over, I don't think he particularly liked it, but I did, and I was the artist so I took advantage of it." The song that she came up with was Doris Akers's "Lord, Don't Move That Mountain." After its release as a single, the song topped gospel play lists everywhere and crossed over to the R&B singles charts where it peaked at No. 48 in 1973. Reportedly the song eventually sold a million copies and temporarily made Andrews the hottest gospel singer in the country. Throughout the 1970s, Andrews turned out well-received gospel albums with radio singles such as "Headline News" and "More Church in the Home." However, after ABC was sold to MCA Records circa 1977, the gospel roster was dropped.

For several years Andrews continued to perform off of her name until the mid '80s when she began to record for Jewel Records. The label was a shell of its former self, and the records were poorly produced and hardly promoted. She also recorded for Savoy Records without much success. The LP *If Jesus Came to Your Town Today* on Miracle Records finally put Andrews back in the groove when it reached No. 31 on the gospel chart in 1988. A one-off CD with Word Records in 1992 resulted in the fine *Raise Up a Nation* (backed by the Thompson Community Choir) album, which reached No. 30 on the gospel chart. She then recorded a stunning grassroots album for Shanachie Records, *Two Sides of Inez Andrews*, which reunited her with Eddie Williams, her pianist from the Caravans. The album was critically acclaimed but not heavily promoted on gospel radio in 1996. Aside from occasional Caravans reunions, which never seem to be adequately promoted, Andrews rarely performs anymore. She assisted her third husband, Wendell Edingburg (a mortician), with running their flower shop until his death in the summer of 2004.

RECOMMENDED RECORDING: The measly ten-song 1999 CD *Headline News* is the only compilation in circulation. It includes "Lord, Don't Move That Mountain" but not "This Is Not the First Time I've Been Last."

Angelic Gospel Singers

THE ANGELIC GOSPEL SINGERS were always right under the radar in the 1950s but definitely on the screen. They never displayed the flamboyant showmanship of the Clara Ward Singers, nor the dramatic vocalizing and histrionics of the Caravans, but they were consistent audience pleasers. During the 1950s and 1960s,

Angelic Gospel Singers / Courtesy of Margaret Allison

they created a body of authentic, piano-based quartet songs such as their signature song "Touch Me, Lord Jesus." Considering that they were formed and based in Philadelphia, it's interesting that their music carried a distinctly Southern tone.

Perhaps the Angelics' Southern groove has to do with their founder and leader, Margaret "Babe" Allison, being born in McCormick, South Carolina (September 20, 1921). The family moved to Philadelphia in 1925 because her father had better job prospects there. "I was never actually a singer in church," Allison told *Rejoice* magazine in 1992. "I started playing the piano at the age of 12 and the church didn't have a permanent piano player, so I had a chance to play for the church." In her late teens, Allison joined a female chorus named the Spiritual Echoes. Inspired by the events of a dream, she formed the Angelics in 1944 with her sister Josephine McDowell and former Echoes members Ella Mae Norris and Lucille Shird. Sometimes they performed at up to four churches a day and sang the hits of the days, which were usually by male groups like the Fairfield Four.

In 1947, they signed to Gotham Records. "They weren't into gospel really," she says. "There was a promoter here named Otis Jackson. He suggested that we go to this company and let them hear us. So we went and the man who owned the company said, 'I want you to do something no one else has recorded, with your own arrangement, because I want you to establish your own sound.' So I did 'Touch Me, Lord Jesus.'" The soon-to-be-classic 78-rpm (backed with "When My Savior Calls Me Home") hit *Billboard* magazine's R&B Top 20 and sold more than 100,000 copies.

Suddenly the Angelics were a hot property and, other than the Ward Singers, one of the few visible female gospel groups of the time. Gotham ran into problems with the Internal Revenue Service for tax evasion and eventually closed. A bidding war ensued for who would pick up the Angelics. They decided on Chess Records in Chicago and cut an album there. Before the album was released, Jewel Records in Shreveport bought the masters from Chess. Finally, before Jewel released the album, Nashboro Records in Nashville bought the masters from Jewel and signed the group to a contract that lasted 27 years. Over the years, they scored with hits such as "My Sweet Home," "He Never Left Me Alone," "Standing on the Highway," and "Sometimes I Feel My Time Ain't Long." Most of their songs were written by Allison and played in her simple, Southern gospel piano arrangements. In 1982, Allison decided not to renew the contract with Nashboro. "They wanted us, but I refused to sign," she said. "They weren't doing me right by my royalties. By then they had lost all their gospel artists. The company had been sold three times. The last owner wasn't pushing the material, wasn't paying me right [as an artist], and wasn't even paying me my writer's royalties. So, I figured, why should I continue?"

From the 1950s straight through the end of the contract, the Angelics could be counted on to sell 10,000 to 20,000 copies of each LP they released. Those were more than respectable sales for the gospel market of the period, but they never enjoyed another smash hit like "Touch Me, Lord Jesus." Still, others saw great potential in the group. In the 1960s, talent scouts Michael Stewart and Ben Zuccor approached Allison about them managing the group. "They had Mahalia Jackson and they wanted the Angelics," Allison said. "They wanted to change our name to the Sweethearts of America. They weren't going to stop us from singing gospel, but they were going to change our arrangements to be more in tune with the music of the time. They told us our name would be up in bright lights and we'd be in movies. That's how the whole thing was presented to us, but none of us in the group were really interested."

By the 1970s, things had significantly slowed down as Allison battled chronic back problems and the original members of the group bounced in and out of the ensemble. Allison signed to Malaco Records in 1983 and often used singers her grandchildren's age to round out her group (Theresa Burton and Daryl Richmond have served the longest). It took a while for Malaco's radio team to reconnect the group with radio, but they hit pay dirt in 1987 when "I've Got Victory" reached No. 26 on the *Billboard* gospel charts. The following year's "Out of the Depths" solidified their comeback. It peaked at No. 28 on the gospel chart and spawned smash traditional gospel hits with Allison's self-written songs "Somebody's Praying for Me,"

"Thank You Lord for One More Day," and the radio-killer "It Could Have Been the Other Way." When Malaco began selling six figures with choirs such as Georgia Mass and Mississippi Mass, they seemed to lose interest in the Angelics. All their albums since (including the excellent *He's My Ever Present Help*, featuring "I'll Go") have not moved respectable units. Allison still sings when she's asked and says, "Everywhere I go, people say 'Sing "Touch Me, Lord Jesus" if you don't sing nothing else,' and I do."

RECOMMENDED RECORDINGS: Any CD or vinyl on the group's Nashboro years is bound to be good. However, since all of that is out of print, *Out of the Depths* (Savoy/Malaco) is a very good substitute.

Angelo & Veronica

THIS LATIN, GOSPEL-SOUL DUO held so much promise when they first appeared on the music scene in the early 1990s. In spite of a fire-baptized performance style that connected well with black gospel audiences, they never caught on commercially with either black gospel radio or CCM radio. This was partly due to the fact that their recording label, Benson Records, could never figure out exactly how to market and promote them to a white audience, and the label completely failed to capitalize on the black church's embrace of the couple.

Angelo Petrucci (born in 1959) and Veronica Petrucci (born Veronica Beth Torres in 1969) both came from Catholic families, but didn't have a strong sense of faith until their college years. Boston-native Angelo's dad was a professional guitarist and his mother worked at a radio station and played piano. Angelo began playing bass at the age of six. His dad fell sick when Angelo was 13 and had him take over his gigs. The young teenager was soon gigging four to five nights a week while attending school during the day. After his parents became born-again Christians, they tried to reach Angelo with the gospel message to no avail. It wasn't until his mother gave him a tape of Commissioned's "Running Back to You" that his heart slowly began to melt. "As a musician I was impressed with their music," Angelo said in 1994. "My mother suggested I record their music. I didn't know what she was doing, but she knew that if I learned the lyrics and recorded the songs that they would get into my heart and eventually they did."

Meanwhile, Veronica was raised in the Bronx until the age of five. The family then moved briefly to New Jersey before relocating to Puerto Rico. It wasn't until she was in high school that the family moved to Manhattan. After graduating from a Catholic high school, she enrolled at the Berklee College of Music in Boston at the age of 17. There she joined the gospel choir and was introduced to gospel music. "I think the first gospel I heard was by Tramaine Hawkins," Veronica said in 1994. "I was blown away not just by the music but by what she was saying. God was talking to me through that music and that really helped turn my life around." She rededicated her life to God and continued on her quest to become a professional pop singer. Angelo, also a Berklee student, had seen her perform in the choir, but they didn't meet until she came by the nightclub where his Top 40 band was playing one night. They connected instantly and began to sing as a duo in nightclubs for a year. They sang the R&B hits of the day by artists such as Johnny Gill, Luther Vandross, Whitney Houston, and occasionally, even a BeBe and CeCe Winans tune.

As their faith strengthened and they listened to more and more gospel music, they felt God calling them to sing gospel music. "I didn't know you could sing for the Lord and actually make some sort of living at it," Veronica said. As the duo wrote and recorded their demo, the songs took on the urban flavor of their favorite gospel artists. Angelo sent the four-song demo to a well-connected friend in Los Angeles for some feedback. A couple of weeks passed with no word, so Angelo called him and asked what he thought of the tape. He recalled his friend saying, "The music is slamming, but what's with these lyrics? They're talking about God, they're talking about Jesus." The friend said that with a lyric adjustment he could guarantee that some major recording artists would record the songs. The duo refused to change a single word. When Angelo hung up the phone, they both felt rejected as they walked into his mother's dining room. His mother asked why they looked so sad. When they told her what happened, she suggested they pray on the spot.

The very next day someone from Benson Records called Angelo's mother at WEZE Radio to track a song. She talked to the person about the duo's demo and the person suggested that she send the tape to Tara Griggs, an executive at Benson. "[Before this] we looked at the back of record covers and sent the tape to the addresses," Angelo recalled. "It's not like we were at the GMA [Gospel Music Association] and gave it to someone. We didn't know that there was a GMA. We didn't even know the names of people at the labels to send the tape to, we just sent them. We sent to Sparrow, Star Song, and every one we could find."

Three days later, Tara Griggs called to say she was interested. A week later, an executive from Star Song Records flew up to Boston to spend a weekend with the duo, who were married by this time. "Tara created all the excitement there at Benson," Veronica remembers. "She was a very big supporter of us." After meeting with both labels, the duo decided to go with Benson because they appeared more proactive and were ready to get the duo in the studio right away.

Angelo & Veronica's debut album, *Higher Place*, was released in 1992 and peaked at No. 35 on the CCM chart. "That was done in 14 days and you can tell by the singing," Angelo recalls. "Those are all first and second takes." The duo received a Dove award nomination as best new artist, and there was considerable buzz about the soulful couple's gospel-styled delivery of R&B-styled church music. Their next album, *Angelo & Veronica* appeared in 1993 and clearly showed the duo's love for urban music. Reminiscent of Chaka Khan's "I'm Every Woman," the dance track "Real Thing" showed off Veronica's powerful vocals, which could hold their own against gospel's most noted belters such as Vanessa Bell Armstrong and Tramaine. Angelo's smoldering old-school vocals shone on Quiet Storm numbers such as "Alone." The album was supported with a 60-city tour where they shared a bill with Michael English, First Call, and Mark Lowry.

At the time, CCM radio rarely played a record that did not sound completely pop in style. Nothing on the duo's album—including their cover of the Carole King pop standard "You've Got a Friend"—sounded pop, and they received very little CCM radio play. In addition, their music was not actively promoted to urban or gospel radio. The issue of race not only affected their radio play, but also where they sang. "It really hurts me when white people won't bring us to their church because they think we're black and vice versa," Angelo told this writer during an interview for *CCM* magazine. Veronica then added, "There are churches that won't have us because they find out we're white, so it goes both ways. It's been very eye-opening and that's definitely one of our platforms, to speak out against racism…. We do mostly black churches and the ones who are inviting us are making the statement against racism and we just praise God for that."

As they continued to speak, Angelo spoke candidly about the racial double standard in Christian music and how shocked he was to find it affecting his recording budgets. "We're up against financial battles too," he said. "When I produced my songs I didn't get what every other guy got because mine were the black cuts. Bryan Lennox [one of the producers] got more money because his songs were going to the money [white CCM] area. This is what bothers me. I tell these guys [at Benson Records], you ever open up *Billboard* magazine, guys? It's important to know that black music, in today's culture, is getting attention. That's what our kids are listening to…. It's frustrating to see that it's not getting as much attention [from within the industry]. This is my point. If it's black, it should get 50 percent as much attention as the white guy, as the white music does. It doesn't have to have more attention, but make it equal…. How would God want it? God would want it fair. It's not a statement about anyone personally. It's just about being fair…. In order to give everything I have in my music, if it's considered R&B, I want it to be [well produced]…. When someone listens to the white cuts on the record they say, 'Man, this sounds great! But Angelo's cuts? They sound kind of weak.' Well, why does his sound weak? People don't know money goes behind records. I'm still not given the best of what is allowed to me…. It's like Fred Hammond—his hands are tied. If he comes out with a weak record, a lot of times it's because he doesn't have the money [to produce] because of the culture [at these record labels who don't invest in gospel music like they do in CCM music]."

The story that was first written for the January 1994 issue of *CCM* was drastically edited by *CCM*'s editor at the time, who complained that Angelo & Veronica's comments were only one side of the story. She went on to say that since Benson was a major sponsor of *CCM* magazine, and, therefore, paid everyone's salary involved, it would be foolish to provoke them to anger with a negative story. The story was reduced to a puff piece as most of their stories were at the time. It was the last story this writer wrote for the magazine.

The message the duo wanted to trumpet was never heard and business continued as usual. They continued to make solid, irresistibly commercial CDs that failed to sell, such as 1995's *Give Your Life*, which peaked at No. 39 on the CCM chart, 1996's *Not Enough*, and finally, 1999's *Change*. As Veronica said at the time, "It's so wonderful that we have a group like Four Him and a group like Commissioned. Because it serves the same purpose, but what ministers to one doesn't minister to the other and that's just the way it is."

RECOMMENDED RECORDING: *Angelo & Veronica* (Benson) is their best album, a fine line between urban gospel and pop music. They shine on the funky disco number "The Real Thing."

Maya Angelou

PERHAPS AMERICA'S MOST visible and best-known living poet of the last 20 years, Maya Angelou's distinguished pedigree jumped a few levels when she read a poem at President Bill Clinton's 1992 inaugural ceremony. She had already been a household name for three decades in most black homes, but reading "On the Pulse of Morning" on the steps of the Capitol brought her international fame and recognition. Suddenly, inquiring minds the world over wanted to read Angelou's poems and personal narratives that celebrated the perseverance of the human spirit and the divine spirituality that motivates us all to higher callings.

Born April 4, 1928, in St. Louis, Missouri, Angelou has certainly led an eventful life. At the age of three, her parents separated and her grandmother in Arkansas raised her. When she was seven years old, she was raped by her mother's boyfriend and blamed herself for years. She had to testify against him in court and was so shaken that she hardly spoke to anyone until she was 13.

She had a baby out of wedlock and to support herself, she became a madam at a brothel. Later, she became San Francisco's first black cable car operator. After a brief marriage to a Greek sailor, she began to sing calypso music at the Purple Onion Club in Hollywood. From 1954 to 1955 she performed in the European road company of *Porgy and Bess*. In 1957, she recorded a world music LP entitled *Miss Calypso*. She performed in theater productions for years before becoming a journalist in Africa, where she fell in love with an anti-apartheid activist named Vuzumzi Make. For a couple of years, she doubled as an administrator at the University of Ghana while editing the *African Review*.

In 1966, author James Baldwin introduced her to an executive at Random House Publishing who encouraged her writing, and in 1970 they published the first volume of Angelou's autobiography, *I Know Why the Caged Bird Sings*, which covered her life through her teen years. The riveting memoir became a bestseller, as did subsequent volumes on her life and poetry, including *Oh, Pray My Wings Are Gonna Fit Me Well*, *Gather Together in My Name*, and *The Heart of a Woman*. Angelou continued to act from time to time, and in 1972 Perception Records released *The Poetry of Maya Angelou*, a classic LP. She won an Emmy nomination for portraying Alex Haley's grandmother in the ABC miniseries *Roots*. She brought her old friend Bobby Jones to sing gospel in the telefilm of her screenplay *Sister, Sisters*, which aired on NBC in 1981.

While Angelou's work is not evangelical, it is spiritually based and emphasizes the resiliency of the human spirit when it connects with God. As James Baldwin once wrote of her, "Her portrait is a Biblical study of life in the midst of death." In 1993, she won a spoken word Grammy for "On the Pulse of Morning," and in 1995, she won in the same category for "Phenomenal Woman." The latter inspired Angie & Debbie's 1997 single "Never Gonna," which addressed the characteristics of a virtuous woman according to Biblical standards. Angelou was the centerpiece of Ashford & Simpson's inspirational album *Been Found*, which featured her reciting narratives amid their singing. The title song and "What If" both hit the R&B Hot 100. Then Bobby Jones invited her to appear on his Gospo Centric CD *Just*

Churchin'. Angelou also sang and recited a spiritual on the UTV Records compilation *Church: Songs of Soul and Inspiration* in 2003.

Since 1981, Angelou has been a professor at Wake Forest University in Winston-Salem, North Carolina. Sprinkled throughout her works are nuggets of Biblical wisdom, such as this musing from *I Know Why the Caged Bird Sings*: "I find it interesting that the meanest life, the poorest existence, is attributed to God's will, but as human beings become more affluent, as their living standard and style begin to ascend the material scale, God descends the scale of responsibility at a commensurate speed."

Anointed

FOR A HALF DOZEN YEARS in the 1990s, the hottest dark-skinned act in contemporary Christian music was the quartet (then trio, and finally duet) known as Anointed. With their soul-inflected vocals and slick pop rhythms they soared to the upper echelon of the CCM music world, which has never been kind to most black recording artists. Songs such as "Under the Influence" and "It's in God's Hands Now" firmly established their reputation and young adult fan base.

The four original members of Anointed were all born in Columbus, Ohio, and grew up singing in church. Steve Crawford (born in 1973) and his sister Da'dra Crawford-Greathouse (born in 1969) teamed with Mary Tiller (born in 1970) and Denise "Nee-C" Walls (born in 1970) to form a group circa 1992. They soon won a production deal with Brainstorm Records, an independent label distributed by Word Records. The group produced and wrote the entire project, which was recorded within two weeks. With its classic soul elements, the CD *Spiritual Love Affair* reached No. 32 on the gospel chart. The success of the project led to the group signing directly to Word Records where producers Mark Heimermann and Chris Harris molded the group's soon-to-be popular pop style. The sophomore project *The Call* took off in the white Christian market with a bullet, and what little black audience the trio had cultivated largely deserted them as their audience became overwhelmingly white. An album that sold nearly 300,000 units, *The Call* garnered a Grammy nomination and three Dove awards. The single "It's in God's Hands Now" reached No. 40 on the R&B singles chart and No. 37 on the club chart. The idea that they abandoned black gospel for CCM radio bothered them, though. "That's a misconception," Walls told *Gospel Industry Today* magazine. "A lot of people think that we were signed to a gospel label and then we crossed over to CCM. From our first album, we were entering as contemporary Christian artists. We weren't offered a gospel label contract."

At the height of their success circa 1995, Mary Tiller was either squeezed out of the group or quit, depending on whom one consults. She filed a $2.5 million lawsuit against the group and its management. She alleged that their manager sexually harassed her. "The lawsuit was something that I never intended to do," Tiller told *CCM* magazine. "It was definitely a last resort." She went on to say that she asked the group to drop their management because of her allegations, "They felt like there were reasons they couldn't leave and didn't want to get involved in something they felt was a personal issue between him and me." Denise Walls later succinctly told *CCM*, "There wasn't anything we could do about it."

As a trio, the group continued to do well in the Christian pop market, but by 1999 Walls also opted to leave the group. Reduced to a duo, the Crawford siblings took on a more urban-flavored sound, resulting in the 2002 release *If We Pray*. It was a good album, but their weakest seller. Word Records was sold to the Warner Music Group during that period. The black music division was closed and Anointed was dropped from the roster. Down, but not out, Sony Music's gospel division quickly signed them. Meanwhile, Tiller and her husband Larry run her Mary Tiller Ministry in which she sings and speaks at church conferences. She's also released one CD entitled *The Journey* for her own Eve of Destiny recording label.

RECOMMENDED RECORDING: *The Best of Anointed* (Word Records, 2003) includes their best-known songs.

Anointed Pace Sisters

FOR A GOOD FOUR YEARS in the early 1990s, the Pace Sisters (a brood of nine) were the most talked about sister group in gospel. They could shout, howl, and mesmerize an audience with the acrobatic vocals they loved to wrap around traditional gospel-styled songs. It even seemed as though Latrice, Melonda, LaShun, Duranice, Phyllis, Dejauii, Leslie, and Lydia might be poised to take the Clark Sisters' claim as the most talented and acclaimed sister act to emerge from the Church of God in Christ (COGIC). However, that buzz didn't last.

The Atlanta-based Pace Sisters hailed from a long line of church singers and preachers. They sang in church all their lives but didn't sing together until high school when they began to do talent shows. They also performed in COGIC convocation concerts before they became part of Rev. Gene Martin's Action Revival Team. Following that professional learning experience, the Paces recorded two albums for the Atlanta-based Faith Records label. In 1992, they achieved instant national stardom when their debut album on Savoy Records, entitled *U-Know* reached No. 2 on the *Billboard* gospel chart and stayed there over a year. They rode on that success until they delivered their second CD, *My Purpose*, in 1995. It only reached No. 17 on the gospel chart and by that time they had been away from their fans for too long and the project was not embraced as enthusiastically as their debut. A series of family problems kept the group sidelined until they re-emerged in 2003 with their third CD, *It's Already Done*, on their own label, Gospel Pace Music.

RECOMMENDED RECORDING: *U-Know* (Savoy) made the group's name, and it's the best bet for someone wanting to explore their sound.

Arc Gospel Choir

THIS MANHATTAN CHOIR was formed from the members of the Addicts Rehabilitation Center, a treatment facility for those dealing with substance abuse. The choir was formed to raise funds to keep the center (founded by James Allen) open. Merging gospel lyrics with doo wop harmonies, the choir recorded "He's My Light" featuring doo wopper Harold Wright, best known for singing "Little Darlin'" with the Diamonds in the 1950s.

India.Arie

ONE OF THE MOST POPULAR neo-soul artists of the new millennium, India.Arie's music touches on love, faith, and self-esteem from an inspirational standpoint. India.Arie's father is former pro basketball player Ralph Simpson. Born October 3, 1975, in Denver, she lived in Memphis and Detroit before relocating to Atlanta at the age of 13. While in high school Arie began playing guitar at the encouragement of her mother. In Chocolate City she joined an artist's collective called Groovement, and she released an independent CD of her songs through the EarthShare label. A pivotal slot on the 1998 Lilith Fair tour garnered major-label interest in Arie, but since Motown was the only label offering her creative control, she signed with them and rejected all other offers. Her debut CD *Acoustic Soul* was released in 2001 to a very slow start. Motown bought television commercials since radio didn't play the music. The single "Video" was ignored by urban radio. The self-love ditty didn't take off until after Arie made a television appearance on *Oprah*. With that attention, the song rose to No. 14 on the R&B chart and No. 47 on the Hot 100. The album eventually went platinum and also featured inspired songs such as "Strength, Courage and Wisdom" and "I See God in You." Arie's second CD, *Voyage to India*, featured even more faith-inspired tracks such as "God Is Real" and minute-long spiritual interludes such as "Healing" and "Gratitude."

Vanessa Bell Armstrong

WHEN VANESSA BELL ARMSTRONG hit the music scene with "Peace Be Still" (with its sweeping notes and jazzy phrasings) in the 1980s, the black gospel world greeted her with awestruck wonder, and *Totally Gospel* magazine asked whether she was the new Queen of Gospel. Born October 2, 1953, in Detroit, she says her mother had a dream that Armstrong would sing for the Lord when she was still in the womb. So, early in life, Armstrong sang at church and became known in local church circles. Starmaker Mattie Moss Clark recruited her at the age of 13 and had Armstrong singing with her various choirs. "She fussed a lot and I guess that made me feel loved," Armstrong told *Gospel Industry Today* in April 1998. "A lot of people couldn't handle it. Sure, I got upset, I got mad, I got embarrassed—but I knew she wanted the best out of me. She always taught me that whenever I sang, to sing like it's my last performance." Around the age of 18, she recorded "Put a Little Love in Your Heart" with a local choir. Her first husband, Samuel Armstrong, suggested that she stop singing around the house and sing for the public like God intended. He packed her off to the GMWA (Gospel Music Workshop of America) convention in Los Angeles and arranged for her to sing "He Looked Beyond My Faults" before pivotal gospel industry executives and radio announcers. The bit won her a recording contract with Muscle Shoals Records.

Eventually, Samuel Armstrong left his job at an auto plant and began managing his wife's career. Her first LP, *Peace Be Still*, was a traditional gospel album heavy on vocal dynamics and simple musical arrangements. The album shot to No. 3 on the *Billboard* gospel chart in 1984 and a star was born. Her next project, *Chosen*, went to No. 1 and the last Muscle Shoals project, *Following Jesus*, also sold well. During this period, Andrae Crouch chose Armstrong to sing the theme song for the NBC sitcom *Amen* and she co-starred with the Winans in the touring stage play *Don't Get God Started*. The buzz led R&B label Jive Records to sign Armstrong to a long-term contract. From the beginning, they intended to cross Armstrong over to the urban charts while maintaining her gospel following.

Jive gave Armstrong a beauty makeover and paired her with top R&B producers such as Loris Holland. *Peace Be Still* took her from her churchy roots to slick urban-styled ballads and dance songs with inspirational messages. The album featured the pleasant minor R&B radio hits "Pressing On" and "You Bring Out the Best in Me," which stalled at No. 80 on the R&B singles chart in 1987. In the ensuing years, Armstrong would face many obstacles. She divorced, experienced financial reverses, her album sales at Verity Records plummeted, and she had a fierce reputation for being difficult. On top of all of this, she experienced a health setback with a stroke-like palsy that crippled her singing ability for a spell. However, she eventually bounced back, although she has yet to enjoy another major gospel radio hit.

RECOMMENDED RECORDING: Armstrong's Jive/Verity recordings have never been particularly popular, so skip the Verity hits compilation and get the *Greatest Hits* (Muscle Shoals, 1991) compilation, which features "I'm Going Through," "Peace Be Still," and "He Looked Beyond My Faults," among others.

Ashford & Simpson

THIS POP-SOUL MUSICAL DUO is known for hit records such as "Solid," "I'll Be There for You," and "Is It Still Good to Ya?" in the late 1970s and '80s. After a brief matriculation at Eastern Michigan College with no declared major, Nickolas Ashford (born May 4, 1942, in Fairfield, South Carolina, but raised in Willow Run, Michigan) moved to New York City. He found work as a busboy, where the pay was so low he couldn't afford an apartment, so he slept on park benches instead. While visiting the White Rock Church in Harlem in 1964, Ashford spotted pianist Valerie Simpson (born August 26, 1946, in New York City) belting out a spiritual from the choir loft at the church her grandmother pastored and was instantly smitten. When they officially met, they decided to sing together. Ashford wrote gospel songs and Simpson could play them, so they began to compose songs. They recorded for Glover Records, as Valerie & Nick, but it was so hard building a following that they decided to stick to songwriting.

They sold a batch of songs to a music publisher for $75 and scored their first hit when Ray Charles recorded their tune "Let's Go Get Stoned" in 1966. They were then signed to Motown Records as staff songwriters. During their tenure there, the couple wrote such pop classics as "Ain't Nothing Like the Real Thing," "Ain't No Mountain High Enough," "Heaven Must Have Sent You," and "Reach Out and Touch Somebody's Hand." The duo wrote prolifically, and

when they had extra material in the can with no one to record it, Motown executives sent Simpson into the studio to record a solo LP. In 1971, the LP *Exposed* was released, which included two rousing gospel songs, "Sinner Man (Don't Let Him Catch You)" and "There Is a God." The latter was nominated for a Grammy award for Best Soul Gospel Performance.

By 1975, Ashford and Simpson were married and had left Motown and joined Warner Brothers as a recording duo. They recorded several stellar soul hits during their tenure. The couple continued to write and produce for other artists. Gladys Knight and the Pips recorded their "God Is" on their 1981 LP *Touch*, and Nickolas did a gospelized version of "Heaven Must Have Sent You (Precious Lord)" on their *Marriage Enrichment* CD. Apart from singing, the duo has various business ventures. They opened the posh New York restaurant 20/20 in 1986, but closed it after the employees were stealing the food and gobbling the profits. They now run a New York eatery called the Sugar Bar, which features a wide variety of live music performances, including gospel music.

Darwin Atwater

ONE OF THE FEW ARTISTS making noise in gospel music with classical flourishes, composer Darin Atwater was born July 11, 1970, in Washington, DC. He began to play piano by the age of four, conducted an ensemble by 12, and yet, majored in accounting at Howard University because his father was an IBM executive. It was when his cousin introduced him to Nathan Carter, the late director of the Morgan State University Choir in Baltimore, that he refocused on studying music. After majoring in piano at Morgan State and the Peabody Conservatory, Atwater turned professional. In 1995, he premiered his own piano concerto with the National Symphony Orchestra. That success carried over to other symphonies and he soon found himself collaborating with gospel artists such as Richard Smallwood and Shirley Caesar. Atwater then launched the Soulful Symphony, an ambitious orchestra fusing gospel and classical music with a full string section. "I was bankrolling it myself," he told the *Baltimore Sun* newspaper in 2004. "It has been a lot of blood, sweat, and tears for me personally." The ensemble struggled at first since black gospel audiences are not typically open to classical music. However, the Baltimore Symphony Orchestra (BSO) named Atwater a composer-in-residence in May 2004, and with a $300,000 grant from the Eddie and C. Sylvia Brown Foundation, the Soulful Symphony found a home with the BSO for at least three years. "The Soulful Symphony is about establishing a repertoire that speaks to the African-American vernacular in ways that have not been done before," Atwater told the *Sun*.

RECOMMENDED RECORDINGS: Atwater hasn't yet recorded projects under his own name. However, his string arrangements have appeared on Shirley Caesar's *Christmas with Shirley Caesar* (Myrrh, 2000), Karen Clark-Sheard's *Second Chance* (Elektra, 2002), and Donald Lawrence's *I Speak Life* (Zomba, 2004). He's also done production work on projects by Richard Smallwood, Yolanda Adams, and others.

Aunt Jemima

SOME MAY WONDER WHY Aunt Jemima would merit inclusion in this book, but it's not the head-scratcher that some might expect. Many a gospel singer was raised on a breakfast of Aunt Jemima pancakes and just as many gospel singers have resembled her. For years, the assumed image of a female gospel singer was that of a gaily robust, obese, dark-skinned black woman. Even today, this image still fits many people's image of a gospel singer.

Aunt Jemima was not a real person; the concept was created in 1889. Newspaperman and entrepreneur Chris L. Rutt was attending a minstrel show at a theater in Missouri when the idea came to him. The white minstrels were performing a popular song of the day called "Aunt Jemimah," which poked fun at the black cooks who cooked for the white plantation owners. The minstrels had red bandannas in their hair, aprons around their waists, and their faces were painted black. Rutt and his business partner, Charles G. Underwood, had just bought the Pearl Milling Company, invented an instant pancake recipe, and were searching for a creative way to market the product. They quickly got a trademark on the Jemima image and began marketing their product. However, they were soon broke and sold their interest in the company to the R.T. Davis Milling Company in 1890. The Davis Company decided to go a step beyond the image of Aunt Jemima and actually find someone to portray the character. They found a 59-year-old former slave from Kentucky named Nancy Green (1834–1923) who worked as a maid for a judge in Chicago.

The Davis Company introduced the living Aunt Jemima at the World's Columbian Exposition in Chicago in 1893. It was a big promotion where they constructed the world's largest flour barrel and had Aunt Jemima on hand to cook flapjacks, sing songs, and regale the spectators with humorous stories of the Old South. Maintaining a warm smile, Green spoke to the crowds who flocked to see her as she cooked and served up thousands of pancakes during the event. She attracted so much attention that police had to keep the crowds moving so that the next group of people could file by Aunt Jemima's stove and say hello. The gamble paid off sweetly in the coming weeks as the Davis Company received more than 50,000 orders from around the world for Aunt Jemima's pancake mix. Officials at the fair awarded Green a medal for her showmanship and proclaimed her the "Pancake Queen." The Davis executives were so thrilled with her success that they gave her a lifetime contract. Green traveled the country on promotional tours and her face was plastered on giant billboards coast to coast. Although the company made big money off of the product, they eventually ran into financial problems and had to sell to the Quaker Oats Company in 1926. Nancy Green maintained her lifetime contract until she was killed by a car on the south side of Chicago on September 24, 1923.

Green's image was used for years after her death until Anna Robinson was hired in 1933 as the second Aunt Jemima. She was a featured attraction at the Chicago Century of Progress Exposition. A portrait was painted of Robinson (who died in 1951) that was used in later promotional pictures of the character. The first Aunt Jemima of the television age was Edith Wilson (born September 2, 1896). Wilson was a second-rate blues singer, not especially gifted, but good enough to make a living and to cut some records for Columbia Records in 1921. Her biggest moment was the trio record she recorded with Louis Armstrong and Fats Waller called "My Man Is Good for Nothing but Love." They were billed as the Thousand Pounds of Harmony. Wilson was in the cast of the *Amos 'n' Andy* radio show and acted in the Humphrey Bogart movie *To Have and Have Not*. She began her role as Aunt Jemima in 1948 and her tenure lasted until 1966. She portrayed the role on radio, television, and in personal appearances. Wilson died after a fall on March 30, 1981. At various times over the years, other women portrayed Aunt Jemima on a regional basis. She was portrayed by a real-life cook, Ann Short Harrington (1900–1955), who worked for the Kappa Sigma fraternity in Syracuse before going to work for former New York governor Thomas E. Dewey. Harrington appeared on local New York television programs and commercials during the early 1950s. Ethel Ernestine Harper was a schoolteacher before she began her period of pancake making in the 1950s.

As the early civil rights movement took shape in the post–World War II years, many black organizations, including the NAACP, began to boycott the sponsors of network television programs such as *Beulah* and *Amos 'n' Andy* for what they charged were negative characterizations of black people. Aunt Jemima was not immune to this criticism. Her critics said that a black mammy with a do-rag on her head was a throwback to slavery and therefore unacceptable. Eventually, Quaker Oats modernized Aunt Jemima's appearance to look like just an amiable cook.

Debbie Austin

A CLEVELAND NATIVE, AUSTIN sang with the city's United Voices of Faith Choir when she was 13 years old. In 1970, she began an eight-year association as a member of Shirley Caesar's Caesar Singers backup group. She formed her own group, Unity, in 1979 and they released their *For the Prize* LP for Savoy Records the following year. That album and their sophomore set *Never Defeated* were both produced by Rev. James Cleveland. Austin recorded erratically over the next few years without achieving any lasting radio hits. Among her standout

recordings were "Everyday Is Thanksgiving" and "God Is Our Fortress." She appeared in the 1992 Pauly Shore/Brendan Fraser comedy film *Encino Man*. Aside from hosting an Akron, Ohio–based radio show on WTOF in the 1990s, Austin was a choir director and youth counselor with the city's St. James COGIC until she died of heart failure on May 13, 2002, at the age of 50.

Jean Austin

A GUTSY ALTO WITH A PENCHANT for thick, traditional choir arrangements, Birmingham-bred Jean Austin first sang professionally in vocal ensembles by Brother Joe May and the Dorothy Norwood Singers. In 1973, ABC Records released her debut LP *The Soul of Jean Austin*. A thrilling collection of songs produced by legendary R&B radio promoter Dave Clark, the standout tracks included Austin's powerful vocals wrapping around the ballads "Lord, I Ain't a Stranger Now" and "The Storm Is Passing Over." There were a handful of other recordings, but Austin eventually disappeared from the national musical landscape and was last known to live in Cleveland, Ohio.

Ayiesha

ONE OF TOBY MAC'S MANY PROTÉGÉS, the R&B-flavored vocalist Ayiesha was born on July 2, 1979, in Hempstead, New York. Born to Caribbean parents, Ayiesha was raised in a Christian household that encouraged her singing. Her family financed her debut CD *What You Do to Me*, which exuded a fresh, urban-centered vibe. Toby Mac met Ayiesha on a vacation stop. He was enamored with her voice and signed her to his Goatee Records label with her debut project scheduled for a 2006 release.

Percy Bady

ONE OF GOSPEL'S MOST CONSISTENT and prolific producers of recent years, Percy Bady was born in July, 1961. He was raised in a church-going Chicago family where his father preached the gospel and his mother taught Sunday school. By the age of three, Bady was playing piano by ear. He began to play keyboards at church and fell in love with the production expertise of producers such as Quincy Jones. He studied music formally at Chicago's Roosevelt University and continued to perfect his gifts by playing in churches. At one such church, Rev. Milton Brunson of the Thompson Community Singers heard Bady. Thus began a 15-year association where Bady was the primary keyboardist and songwriter for a number of the choir's albums. In the ensuing years, Bady has played on sessions for some of gospel's biggest hits, such as Marvin Sapp's "Not the Time, Not the Place," BeBe and CeCe Winans's "Lost Without You," and R. Kelly's "I Believe I Can Fly," which has been adopted by many gospel singers. In the late 1990s, Bady signed a production deal with Gospocentric Records that allowed him to put his golden touch on virtually every hit project the label churned out during the period. He was also able to bring his younger brother, drummer Ray Bady, to the label to record his solo debut. After years of producing others, Bady finally stepped into the limelight in 2003 with *The Percy Bady Experience* CD. It was a solid piece of urban radio-friendly message music with cameos by Dorinda Clark-Cole, Marvin Sapp, and BeBe Winans. In spite of the big production and all-star lineup, the CD only managed to peak at No. 18 on the *Billboard* gospel album sales chart, a huge disappointment to the label, which expected a much bigger seller.

Bob Bailey

BEST KNOWN IN NASHVILLE circles as a background singer for Reba McEntire, Vince Gill, and a score of country artists, Bob Bailey was born on February 19, 1956, in Middletown, Ohio, where he sang at New Era Baptist Church as a child. His family often sang together at public events even after they relocated to Portland, Oregon, in 1961. Bailey enrolled at the University of Oregon on a classical voice scholarship in 1974. He dropped out after three years to tour the world with the Christian band New Hope. When he returned to the

US, he was asked to join Jim and Tammy Bakker's *PTL Club* in Charlotte, North Carolina. He sang regularly on the program for three years and recorded an LP, *Looking Forward*, for Goodlife Records in Phoenix, Arizona.

Bailey left *PTL* in 1981 and moved to Nashville where he began to write songs in earnest for Lorenz Creative Services. The company bought his LP back from Goodlife and reissued it on Benson Records. His second LP was his most successful. The album, *I'm Walkin'*, appeared on Airborne Records and was nominated for a Grammy award in 1984. One more LP, *Bob Bailey*, featured not just church songs but also inspirational message songs such as "Inner City Blues" "Project Girl," and "Heaven Help Us All."

In between his own gigs, Bailey was in demand as a session singer. However, Bailey eventually fell from grace. He became a drug addict amid conflicting emotions that arose over his feelings of rejection and racism in the music industry. A friend, Michael McKinney, delivered Bailey to a drug treatment facility over the Thanksgiving holiday in 1989. After his complete recovery in 1992, country star Wynonna Judd embraced Bailey by taking him on the road with her for over a decade as one of her background vocalists. In addition to his work with Judd, Bailey travels to Europe to give gospel concerts. He's a marquee attraction in Denmark.

Pearl Bailey

A QUADRUPLE-THREAT PERFORMER (singer, dancer, actress, and comedienne), Pearl Bailey was one of Hollywood's first black superstars in the 1950s. A preacher's kid, Bailey was born March 19, 1918, in Newport News, Virginia. She began as a dancer and got her big break by replacing Sister Rosetta Tharpe in the Cab Calloway Orchestra. From there, she made her Broadway debut in a 1946 production of *St. Louis Woman*. An elegant but sassy woman, Bailey earned a quick reputation as a party girl. She drank, cursed like a sailor, and had a string of paramours that brought her as much attention as her talent. She recorded for Columbia, Coral, and Mercury Records. Her suggestive *For Adults Only* albums in the early 1960s were bestsellers. She later took an all-black cast of *Hello, Dolly!* on a successful world tour in 1967–69 and starred in her own ABC TV series in 1971. In the late 1970s, Bailey enrolled at Georgetown University and majored in theology. She eventually earned her Bachelors degree and often spoke out on religious matters on her frequent talk show appearances on programs such as *The Merv Griffin Show*. She enjoyed a 40-year marriage to drummer Louie Bellson. Bailey wrote an armful of bestselling books, served as a special ambassador to the United Nations, and was awarded the Presidential Medal of Freedom in 1988. She suffered from heart ailments over the last 20 years of her life and died of coronary disease on August 17, 1990, in Philadelphia. An inspirational, grandmotherly figure to the world in later life, one of Bailey's best-known quotes was, "People see God every day, they just don't recognize him."

RECOMMENDED RECORDING: Although she could sing in a rich alto, Bailey's music is distinctive for her dry, slurred vocal renderings amid her humorous asides. She sprinkled songs of faith throughout her vast catalog, but she released one very valuable (currently out of print) LP, *Searching the Gospel*, on Roulette Records in 1966. It featured her bluesy but highbrow renditions of "Ave Maria," "Every Time I Feel the Spirit," and "His Eye Is on the Sparrow."

Philip Bailey

SEVENTIES SUPERGROUP Earth, Wind & Fire's amazing falsetto and percussionist, Philip Bailey enjoyed a brief moment as a Christian music star in the 1980s. He was born on May 8, 1951, in Denver, Colorado. Raised a Catholic, Bailey went to a Baptist church as a teenager for the social aspect and to hear the music. A friend from Colorado, Harry Jones, snagged a job with Warner Bros. Records in Los Angeles. When he heard that a gospel group from the roster, the Stovall Sisters, was looking for a new percussionist, he told Bailey about the job. Bailey won the position and moved to Los Angeles circa 1970. Soon he was promoted as the group's musical director. He even had a solo in their concerts. It was dur-

ing this period that he reconnected with Verdine White of Earth, Wind & Fire, which was also on the Warner label. He had met him some time before when the band was passing through Colorado. After Warner dropped the Stovall Sisters, Bailey received a fateful call. Verdine and his brother Maurice White reformed Earth, Wind & Fire after the original band members left. They asked Bailey to join them. The new group signed to Columbia Records and over the next decade they were one of the Top Ten bestselling groups of the music business. They scored numerous pop and soul hits such as "Get Away," "That's the Way of the World," "Shining Star," and "Boogie Wonderland," among others.

During the period, Bailey says his life was a mess. "There was a year or so like in 1976 where I don't even know what happened," he recalls. He began to think about God and the meaning of his life more intently because of his circumstances and also because of a frantic fan. "We did this song called 'Jupiter.' One lady caught me and got through all of our security. She came running, wide-eyed, breathlessly and said, 'What is the answer to Jupiter?' and she was dead serious! It was just a stupid song we wrote. I said, 'Baby, it's just a song.' But after that I went to my room, and I was taken aback. I thought, 'People really believe we have answers, and my life is a mess!' So I prayed for God to reveal himself to me." Over the next few years, Bailey says that God put people in his path to minister to him. On a plane ride, a woman sat next to him and asked him if he was a Christian. He told her that he attended church. "No, do you have a relationship?" he recalls her saying. "You mean like you talk to him and he talks back to you?"

He had never heard it phrased quite that way and set out on a spiritual quest. The pastor who preached at his mother's funeral gave him a Dake's Bible. When Earth, Wind & Fire was on a European concert tour with Santana, Santana's lead vocalist Leon Patillo, a born-again Christian, spotted Bailey reading the Bible and they struck up a conversation about faith. They soon became very close encouragers of each other's spiritual growth. After Patillo led Bailey through a study of the Book of John, Bailey says, "That's when I fell in love with God."

Bailey then started an organization, Living Epistles Fellowship, sort of a social club for secular artists who were Christians. They socialized with former singer and Motown producer Frank Wilson's Christian Entertainers Fellowship in Los Angeles. Soon a band of vocal Christian celebrities in Hollywood such as Deniece Williams, producer/songwriter Jerry Peters, songwriter Skip Scarborough, Marilyn McCoo and Billy Davis, Jr., and Ray Parker, Jr., among others, began to speak out about their faith. One of the first events was the 1980 "Living Proof" rally at R.F.K. stadium in Washington, DC, where secular artists convened to sing and testify about their faith. In 1981, Bailey and songwriter Terry McFadden had a vision to stage a high-end program, "Jesus at the Roxy," which took place at the infamous Los Angeles nightclub. "We had strings, horns, narrators into the music, and it all culminated in the song 'Make Us One,'" Bailey recalls. "Most of us artists had parts in it. It was such an unthought-of event, we sent out invitations. We did two shows a night for two nights. We didn't have PR people. All the hot entertainers of that time were on the street trying to get tickets into the show. *Entertainment Tonight* and all those people came to us…. There were many people who to this day were impacted in their life by that show."

That point in Bailey's life grounded him in his faith. "I didn't do anything musically the first few years that I was saved because I didn't want it to be a fad or to distract from my walk," Bailey says. In 1985, Bailey's solo career was red-hot as his "Easy Lover" duet with Phil Collins had become a massive hit on the pop, dance, adult contemporary, and R&B charts. Prior to the record's release, he had decided that it was time to make a gospel album. Leon Patillo introduced him to executives at his record label, Myrrh Records, and Bailey signed on the dotted line.

Bailey's debut LP, *The Wonders of His Love*, was released in spring 1985. Myrrh Records put him on a three-month tour with Christian pop star Amy Grant who had a nontraditional audience for a gospel artist. Grant's then-husband, Gary Chapman, sang "Easy Lover" with Bailey during the tour. Bailey's gospel songs such as "Come Before His Presence" and "I Will No Wise Cast You Out" received diverse radio play on both black and white gospel radio formats. Bailey turned to more stellar gospel projects such as 1987's *Triumph* and 1989's *Family Affair*. But he was disappointed in the Christian music industry's business practices and the rumor mill that looks for secret sins. He made his exit when his contractual obligations were completed. "I went into the Christian music thing very naïve," he confesses. "I was just thinking things were going to be done a different way and for a different reason on that side. I was asked to do the same things I was asked to do in the secular world. They wanted to capitalize off of 'Easy Lover.' I think if I didn't have 'Easy Lover,' I probably wouldn't have been able to even get a gospel label to sign me. That was sobering…. Plus, there wasn't any more loyalty in Christendom than in the secular thing. It was all about making money. So, my thing was I might as well stay over in the secular thing where it's more money…. There are a lot of dead bodies from dealing with Christian record companies. For me, it just made me dig in deeper to my personal relationship with God."

Jim and Tammy Faye Bakker

JUST LIKE SONNY NEEDED Cher, Jim Bakker needed Tammy to make him look good. But, just like Cher, Tammy needed Jim to run the show and build the infrastructure. During the 1970s and early '80s, Jim and Tammy Bakker were the hottest couple in Christian television. Every gospel artist wanted to be a guest on their daily talk show, which was modeled after the hit talk shows of the day such as *The Tonight Show with Johnny Carson*. Life for the bubbly couple began in Minnesota. They both were born into poor, devout Assemblies of God families. Jim was born January 2, 1939, in Muskegon, Michigan, and Tamara Faye LaValley was born March 7, 1942, in International Falls, Minnesota. After the Bakkers married in 1961, they became traveling evangelists. In the mid-'60s, they met Pat Robertson, who was launching the Christian Broadcasting Network (CBN). The Bakkers became the first hosts of the network's debut program, *The 700 Club*, in 1966. The Bakkers eventually had a falling out with Robertson and left CBN. They later hooked up with Jan and Paul Crouch and, in 1973, formed the embryonic foundation of what is now the Trinity Broadcasting Network. However, Paul Crouch and Jim Bakker had differing visions for the network. According to Crouch's book, *I Had No Father but God*, Bakker left the ministry without saying good-bye. In Bakker's autobiography, he says that he and Tammy were forced out of TBN. They eventually formed Heritage USA and launched *The PTL Club* television program, which eclipsed the success of other Christian networks at the time.

The PTL Club was a tremendous media outlet for gospel artists who were not able to perform their latest singles on network, primetime talk or variety programs. Along with featuring regular singers such as Howard and Vestal Goodman, Rosey Grier, Candi Staton, and Willa Dorsey, the show was America's introduction to BeBe and CeCe Winans. Tammy Bakker had heard Joe Cocker and Jennifer Warnes's version of "Up Where We Belong" on the house system in a department store and thought it would be a great song for BeBe and CeCe. They rearranged the song as a gospel tune and BeBe and CeCe's PTL Records LP *Lord, Lift Us Up* was sent to more than a million PTL supporters for a cash donation, giving the Winans their first million-seller (technically). The network was also an outlet for Tammy Bakker's Southern gospel songs, which she sang with black Pentecostal fervor. She recorded a dozen LPs during that period. Two of her biggest were 1985's *Don't Give Up (You're on the Brink of a Miracle)* and 1986's *Enough Is Enough*. Tammy's signature song was the catchy Mike Murdock tune, "You Can Make It," which became a Sunday morning staple in churches coast to coast.

The Bakkers' extravagant lifestyle and million dollar homes caused some to question the financial practices at the ministry. In 1984, they began to sell lifetime memberships for $1,000 that allowed supporters a three-night annual stay at PTL's luxury hotel and resort center. The ministry sold more memberships than they could accommodate and only one 500-room hotel was ever built. Everything unraveled in March 1987 when news came to light of Jim Bakker's tryst with PTL secretary Jessica Hahn and the $265,000 hush money he was paid. Rev. Jerry Falwell convinced Bakker to step

down for a month so that the scandal would pass, at which point Falwell would reinstate Jim Bakker as CEO. However, Falwell barred the Bakkers from coming back once he learned of all of the governance troubles at the ministry. The Bakkers stayed at their Beverly Hills home during the period. Tammy wrote their side of the story in the song "The Ballad of Jim & Tammy." Set to the music of Tom T. Hall's "Harper Valley P.T.A.," the 12-inch single was released via Sutra Records, a dance label, in 1987. It's now considered a collector's item.

Jim Bakker was eventually sentenced to 45 years in prison for fraud and conspiracy to commit fraud. He was a model prisoner and served almost 5 years of his sentence. While he was in prison, he and Tammy divorced. They both married others and set up new ministries. After Jim's 1996 book *I Was Wrong* was published, he moved to Branson and set up a new television ministry. Tammy (now Tammy Faye Messner) has kept a significantly higher profile. She has appeared in a variety of network sitcoms, such as *The Drew Carey Show*, and starred in the television show *Tammy Faye's House Party* and a talk show with Jim J. Bullock. Tammy's heart-in-hands emotions, extreme makeup, and "we're all family" personality have endeared her to gay audiences, who relate to her survivor instincts. *The Eyes of Tammy Faye* was a campy movie based on Tammy's life story, and she was also a star of the 2003 MTV reality series *The Surreal Life*, which saw her rooming with pornographer Ron Jeremy, rapper Vanilla Ice, model Traci Bingham, and actor Erik Estrada. It was a ratings blockbuster. In spring 2004, Tammy was diagnosed with inoperable lung cancer, but pledged to fight and triumph over it. After all, her autobiography is titled *I Will Survive…and You Will Too*.

Trace Balin

ONE OF THE HARDEST SINGING women to ever rise from the CCM (contemporary Christian music) industry, Trace Balin's gritty vocals (think of a female Rod Stewart) distinguished her Christian pop music from her early '90s competitors such as Kim Boyce and Cindy Morgan. The sheer roughness of her earthy vocals lent an edgy quality to songs that otherwise might have been considered bland and formulaic.

Born in 1946 with a crystal-clear voice, Balin started her career singing in Ohio coffeehouses before her big first break, singing behind country singer Freddy Fender. After years as support singer, Balin was poised to sign with a major record label in 1986 that had every intention of making her a pop star. Unfortunately, she caught pneumonia and the virus lasted eight months. At the end of the illness, there were nodules on her vocal cords that left her with an audible rasp. When they heard what had happened to Balin's voice, the label executives dropped her from the roster, so she decided to try Christian music, and the rasp became her trademark. She signed to Word Records imprint Day Spring, where her debut LP *Champions* was released in 1987. She's never had a staggeringly big hit record, but she received decent radio play for songs such as "Eye of the Hurricane," "Never Let It Be Said," "Only for You," and "We Need Each Other." If any one song could be considered her trademark performance it would be the rock-edged "If I Don't Have Love," which features a performance even Tina Turner might covet. Her only chart LPs were *Here and Now*, which peaked at No. 34 on the CCM album chart in 1990, and *Out of the Blue*, which hit No. 29 in 1991. In the intervening years, Balin has recorded the independent CDs *Glory Road* and *Tracy Balin, Past and Present*.

Although she has not been visibly in the musical forefront of late, Balin has contributed background vocals to such popular albums as Steven Curtis Chapman's *The Great Adventure* and assorted projects by Babbie Mason, Pam Thum, and Mark Lowry.

Rev. Robert Ballinger

A CHICAGO-BASED SINGER/PIANIST born June 9, 1930, Ballinger recorded for Peacock, Chess, and United Records in the 1950s. He was a hard singer and enhanced his songs with a bluesy keyboard style. Among his standout recordings was "John Saw the Number" for Peacock in 1964. With blues great Willie Dixon on bass and Odie Payne on drums, Ballinger fiercely tackled the keys on that jump tune. He died in December 1965 at the age of 34.

Bishop Jeff Banks

BORN JUNE 7, 1927, in Pittsburgh, Banks was raised in the COGIC denomination where his parents were both choir singers, so it's no surprise that he followed in their footsteps. Banks, a piano player, and his younger brother, Charles, joined the Mary Johnson Davis Singers in 1947 as soloists. They were with her until 1953 when they formed the Famous Banks Brothers duo. Their first record "Can I Get A Witness?" put them on the gospel map. Sibling duos were rare in gospel at the time, so the Banks Brothers set the stage for those who would follow, such as the O'Neal Twins. Their style incorporated elements of call and response, double leads, and harmonic modulations that distinguished their sound. Eventually, they both felt called to pastor in Newark, New Jersey. Banks founded the Revival Temple Holiness (COGIC), and Charles started the Greater Harvest Baptist Church. Charles was the first to record a choir. He formed the 60-voice Back Home Choir from the church and landed a recording deal with Vee-Jay Records where they recorded the LP *Wonderful*, which featured solos by his brother and a gutsy Georgia-born singer named Carrie Smith. They performed at prestigious venues such as Madison Square Garden, Carnegie Hall, and the Newport Jazz Festival through the 1960s.

Meanwhile, Banks's Revival Temple Mass Choir released several successful albums for Savoy Records beginning in the 1980s. One of the most memorable was *Caught Up in the Rapture*, which peaked at No. 12 on the gospel chart in 1988 and spotlighted the smash ballad radio single "You Can Make It if You Try," featuring solo turns by Rev. Milton Biggham, Nancey Jackson, and Donald Malloy. Unfortunately, Bishop Banks died suddenly on January 31, 1997, in Newark.

Willie Banks and the Messengers

BORN MAY 11, 1929, in Raymond, Mississippi, Willie Banks first sang gospel with his mother when he was five years old. In 1968, Banks formed his own group, Willie Banks and the Southernaires. They eventually signed with Peacock Records where they made their debut with the LP *Heaven Must Be a Beautiful Place*, a then-contemporary quartet album. In 1972, Banks disbanded that group and formed the Messengers, who immediately recorded for the Nashville-based HSE Record label. They recorded a handful of quartet LPs there such as *Mother Why?* and *For the Wrong I've Done.* In 1979, the latter received a Grammy nomination for Best Soul Gospel Performance. On July 6, 1981, the group was dealt a terrible hand when its touring van went over an embankment near Atlanta and fell 50 feet. One member of the group was killed on the spot, and Banks lay near death praying for help. He made a pact with God that if his life was spared, he would always sing God's praises. His life *was* spared and his group went on to record for Malaco Records, where they kept traditional, toe-tapping gospel music alive over the course of several low-selling LPs. Willie Banks died on February 1, 1993, and posthumous albums such as *The Legend Lives On* and *The Best of Willie Banks* were his first albums to hit *Billboard*'s gospel chart in years.

RECOMMENDED RECORDING: *The Best of Willie Banks* (Malaco) is only ten tracks, but they are ten of the best.

F.C. Barnes

IN AN INDUSTRY THAT SUGGESTS that one must be less than 30 years old to garner your first gold record, Rev. F.C. Barnes enjoyed the surprise gospel gold record of the 1980s when he and Janice Brown's folksy "Rough Side of the Mountain" blanketed the gospel airwaves and became the megahit of the decade on gospel radio. Born Fair Cloth Barnes on June 22, 1929, in Rocky Mount, North Carolina, Barnes grew up in church. He played and sang with the Marks Chapel Baptist Church until he was called to preach in 1955. He then attended United Christian College in Goldsboro, North Carolina, and earned a doctorate degree. In 1959, he founded the Red Budd Holy Church. He was content to simply pastor for years until he felt the desire to sing again. He teamed with Rev. Janice Brown and they began to sing at church events around the state. They were unlikely stars. Brown sported a Jheri curl, prescription glasses, and simple housedresses; Barnes was an older, fatherly man. But when they hit the pulpit, their natural charisma came to the surface and engaged their captive congregations.

In 1983, Barnes wrote a simple, backwoods track about triumph over tribulation, "Rough Side of the Mountain." Barnes and Brown's laidback, but sincere reading of the song became a quick gospel standard and remained in the *Billboard* gospel Top Ten for over a year. In a genre of music where 20,000 was considered good sales and 50,000 was a blockbuster, "Rough Side of the Mountain" sold half a million copies within two years— an astounding success. The hit streak continued until Brown got married and left the duo. Barnes recorded with varying success with other aggregations, but his most lasting recent hits have been his own solo recordings such as "Come On in the Room" and "God Will Heal the Land." Today, Barnes pastors the St. Paul Holy Church in Maple Hill, North Carolina.

RECOMMENDED RECORDING: *The Classic Collection* (AIR) is a simple ten-song CD with the thrilling "For Your Tears I Died," "You Ought to Have Been There," and, of course, "Rough Side of the Mountain."

F.C. *Barnes & Sister Janice Brown /*
photo courtesy of AIR *Records*

Luther Barnes

ONE OF THE MUSICIANS MOST responsible for keeping the quartet sound alive amid the contemporary vibes of the Winans and Commissioned, Luther Barnes and his various groups gave young adults of the 1980s that old-time religion. Born Luther Lee Barnes on March 10, 1954, in Rocky Mount, North Carolina, Barnes first sang onstage at the age of nine. His father, F.C. Barnes, formed a group called the Barnes Juniors, comprised of little Luther's four uncles. He sang with them until he joined another family group, the Sunset Jubilaires. By all accounts, Barnes was a model son. "We didn't have the street life some men had growing up in the city and that kind of thing," he says. "And that helped me stay grounded and honor God. I've traveled a lot and seen a lot. I definitely can appreciate the choir and home field of North Carolina. It's been very good for me, growing up in a Biblical home. There were times I felt they shielded me from things I wanted to be involved in. But now when I look back I am grateful that I wasn't involved in drugs, heavy smoking, partying, and all those kinds of things. It's just been a blessing."

After graduating from high school in 1973, Luther Barnes became the lead singer for the Sunset Jubilaires. He was nothing like the usual quartet lead singers. Whereas most quartet soloists were extremely animated or outright clowns when they sang, Barnes was poised and cool even as a teenager. While maintaining his place in the Jubilaires, Barnes earned a degree in music education from St. Augustine College and put it to use as a high school music teacher and private piano tutor. However, the desire to perform was so strong that Barnes and the Jubilaires cut their first LP, *I'll Take Jesus for Mine*, in 1981 for AIR Records. He finally broke through with his LP *See What the Lord Has Done* with the Red Budd Gospel Choir in 1985. The catchy, uptempo quartet track was sung in Sunday morning services coast to coast during that period. Over the years, Barnes has continued to churn out steady old-school hits such as "So Satisfied" and "I Can't Make It Without You."

Possessing a smooth tenor, Barnes has branched out in recent years with some pop-gospel songs such as the beautiful ballad "Half a Man" from his *Come Fly Away with Me* album in 2002. Although his music has mostly upheld the older gospel traditions, Barnes sees himself as an innovator. "At an early age, I would always listen to the difference between the sound of gospel music and the sound of popular music," he says. "The Temptations and all those artists sounded so much better. And then I'd turn on the gospel stations and the bass was just weak. You could hardly hear the beat. The words weren't correct and the whole musical pattern wasn't either. I said, 'Goodness, why can't gospel come up and be just as right musically as the other forms of music?' I thank God for people such as Kirk Franklin and James Cleveland who have helped us get our act together to upgrade our music."

RECOMMENDED RECORDING: *The Best of the Early Years* (AIR) covers all of Barnes's beloved '80s hits.

Barrett Sisters

WITH THEIR MELODIOUS vocal blend, the Barrett Sisters started singing in Chicago's Morning Star Baptist Church in the 1940s. Under the direction of their aunt Mattie, a chorus director at Central Baptist Church on the South Side, they started to sing professionally as the Barrett and Hudson Singers. However, Delois Barrett (born December 3, 1926) was called to join the Roberta Martin Singers while she was still a student at Englewood High School. Norsalus McKissick asked her to sing "He Will Remember Me" at a church musical that Roberta Martin was headlining. Martin loved Delois's rich soprano and took her on the road. Delois was a year late graduating because of her touring with the Martin Singers. When Martin recruited Bessie Folk and Delois circa 1944, she turned over the vocal solos to them. Delois shined on Roberta Martin Singers classics such as "The Storm Is Passing Over." She remained with the group for 18 years. During those years, Delois's middle sister Rodessa (born August 26, 1932) was a choral director at the Galileo Baptist Church, and her baby sister Billie studied at the American Music Conservatory and sang as a soloist for a while. Although the Roberta Martin Singers were still active, Delois left the group in 1962. She wanted to stay nearer her home and her husband, a minister. She didn't make much money on the road; few gospel singers did in that day. A friend since her teens, gospel-turned-blues star Dinah Washington, often suggested that Delois switch to blues singing. Though she was tempted, Delois never did. She and her sisters formed the Barrett Sisters and released their first LP on Savoy Records in 1963. They never had many hits, but they are best known for "What Shall I Render?" and "I'll Fly Away."

Delois Barrett has known tragedy. Her parents died relatively young. One of her daughters died of hepatitis at the age of 14. Delois was reduced to singing at funeral parlors to make ends meet in the 1970s (she sang at evangelist Katherine Kuhlman's funeral). The sisters received a necessary career boost in 1982 when the critically acclaimed documentary film *Say Amen, Somebody* chronicled the sisters' journey. They have recorded a couple of albums, such as *What a Wonderful World* for I Am Records in 1990. However, they are no longer considered recording artists. They are now in demand as performing artists on college campuses and at traditional churches that appreciate the warm harmonies that earned them the title the Sweet Sisters of Zion.

Fantasia Barrino

THE THIRD SEASON WINNER of Fox Television's *American Idol* talent competition is straight out of the church. Fantasia Barrino was born June 30, 1984 in High Point, North Carolina. She was singing by the age of five and much of that singing was in the church. Barrino's grandmother and mother pastor at Mercy Outreach Church of Deliverance in Archdale, North Carolina. Barrino enjoyed church so much that she'd break into a holy dance that her family called the BoBo. She always dreamed of a singing career and her personal American idol is Aretha Franklin, whose fire she brought to her own singing. Barrino's first recording was with her relatives. They recorded a gospel CD called *Miracles* as the Barrino Family for First Lite Records.

During her high school years, Barrino became pregnant and had to drop out to deliver her baby daughter, Zion. Her family gathered around her and supported her during that period. In August 2003,

Barrino's older brother encouraged her to try out for the *American Idol* auditions in Atlanta. They drove to Atlanta and found 10,000 aspiring stars in line. They waited for hours but grew hungry and weary. Barrino convinced a security guard to save her space while she and her brother went to get some nourishment. When they returned, the line had been moved to another location and they were not accepting any more applicants. She and other singers who were turned away stood outside and sang to each other. A passing security guard heard Barrino and promised to get her in for an audition some way. After three preliminary auditions, Barrino passed the test to go to Hollywood for the actual show.

Throughout the competition, Barrino's rock-edged crackle of a voice pleased the judges and viewers alike. However, as news of her having a child out of wedlock appeared in the press, many viewers withdrew their support of Barrino by saying that she wasn't a good role model for young girls. Barrino responded on *MTV News*: "Don't look down on me, pray for me." As the competition drew to a close, it was obvious that Barrino was one of the best singers in the program. On May 26, 2004, she won the competition and a million-dollar J Records contract. Her first single, the inspirational anthem "I Believe," written by Tamyra Gray, reached No. 1 on the *Billboard* pop singles chart and sold over 100,000 copies its first week. With all the good fortune that's come Barrino's way, she still credits her faith as her source of inspiration. "I've been in church all my life," she told *MTV News*. "I always thank the people, but if it hadn't been for God, I wouldn't be here. He's the one that puts the breath in my body. He gave me the gift. So every time I sing I offer it back up."

Fontella Bass

ALTHOUGH FONTELLA BASS has been labeled a one-hit wonder by rock music scribes for her 1965 smash "Rescue Me," she has used that one song to maintain an active and vital career over the years. Bass was born July 3, 1940, in St. Louis, Missouri, to gospel singer Martha Bass of the legendary Clara Ward Singers. Her kid brother, David Peaston, would make noise as an

R&B balladeer in the 1980s. Bass grew up in church singing and playing the piano. She launched her career playing keyboards in Little Milton's band in the early 1960s. On the side, she began to make records for Ike Turner's Prann Records label. Eventually, Milton's bandleader, Oliver Sain, left to form his own group. He took Bass and singer Bobby McClure with him as featured singers with his band. Bass and McClure were soon signed to Checker Records where they enjoyed two instant R&B smashes with "Don't Mess Up a Good Thing" and "You'll Miss Me When I'm Gone" in 1965. Bass's first solo single, the rousing "Rescue Me," soared to No. 1 on the R&B chart and No. 4 on the pop chart that same year.

Over the next couple of years, Bass would place equally fine songs such as "Recovery," "I Surrender," "I Can't Rest," and "You'll Never Ever Know" into the upper reaches of the R&B charts, but she never made the transformation into a major artist. After her solo career waned, Bass moved to Paris with her then-husband, trumpeter Lester Bowie, and was a featured vocalist with his avant-garde jazz group, the Art Ensemble of Chicago. She sang "Theme de Yo Yo" on their 1970 LP *Les Stances à Sophie*, considered a classic turning-point album in the fusion of funk and avant-garde jazz. They eventually moved back to the States where Bass recorded without fanfare for Jewel Records in Shreveport. In 1980, Bass teamed up with her mother and brother for the traditional gospel album *From the Root to the Source* on the Soul Note label. As a trio, they recorded such church evergreens as "God Has Smiled on Me" and "He Touched Me." In 1995, Bass recorded a critically acclaimed CD *No Ways Tired* for Elektra Records' Nonesuch imprint. In spite of terrific reviews from rock critics, both gospel radio and Christian media ignored the album. Her 2001 CD *Travelin'* on the Justin Time Records label featured gospel tracks such as "Walk with Me" and "In the Garden." The Voices of St. Louis Choir backed her. Although Bass clearly prefers to perform gospel music of late, she occasionally will do a concert or special television appearance where she'll reprise "Rescue Me" and other soul songs. And on most Sunday mornings, Bass can be found singing at Mount Beulah Missionary Baptist Church in her hometown.

Martha Bass

MARTHA BASS WAS BORN March 7, 1921, in St. Louis. Her mother, Navada Carter, was a well-known gospel singer in the area. In 1929, Bass joined the choir at the Pleasant Green Baptist Church. She later attended and graduated from the National School of Nursing while continuing to sing in church. Bass came up through the National Baptist Convention meetings in the 1940s where gospel grand dame Willie Mae Ford Smith mentored and trained Bass's deep, dark contralto to excite congregations all over the country. In her heyday, Bass sang in programs with Rev. James Cleveland, the Davis Sisters, and Joe Mayes of East St. Louis. She was later a featured soloist with the Clara Ward Singers from 1955 to 1960. Thereafter, Willa Ward hired Bass as the sales manager at the Ward Singers' record shop in Philadelphia. Later, Bass recorded five solo LPs for Checker Records including the hit album *I'm So Grateful*. Her last recording was in 1980 when she joined her offspring, Fontella Bass and David Peaston, to perform the bare bones, traditional gospel LP *From the Root to the Source* for the Soul Note Records label. Bass taught Sunday school up to two years before her death. She died of a heart aliment at the Barnes-Jewish Hospital on September 24, 1998.

Freda Battle

A FORMER GOSPEL RADIO announcer, Freda Battle was born April 1957 in Boston. She worked as an announcer at WLVG, WEZE, and WILD, an R&B radio station, where her Sunday morning gospel show was No. 1 in the ratings for years. In 2004, Battle and her backing choir, the Temple Worshippers, released their debut CD *Serious Praise* on Axiom Records.

Kathleen Battle

A PURE SOPRANO, Kathleen Battle rose to fame in the 1980s with her indomitable operatic roles such as Zerbinetta and Rosina, which showed off her excellent acting skills. She was born August 18, 1948, in Portsmouth, Ohio. After working her way to the top rung of the opera world, Battle was unceremoniously booted from the prestigious Metropolitan Opera for allegedly unprofessional conduct in 1994. The singer was said to be rigidly demanding, and many of her former colleagues wore T-shirts that read: "I Survived the Battle." In Battle's defense, many of her critics were known to be as demanding. Although she was no longer welcome at the Met, Battle continued to thrill with her recitals and fill auditoriums worldwide. Over the years, she's recorded a handful of faith-inspired albums. Among them are 1997's CD *Grace*, which featured sacred songs such as Mozart's "Laudate Dominum" and Handel's "Rejoice Greatly." It reached No. 2 on *Billboard*'s classical crossover chart. Other albums such as *So Many Stars* (Sony Classical, 1995), *Kathleen Battle at Carnegie Hall* (Deutsche Grammophon, 1992), and the illustrious Jessye Norman collaboration *Spirituals in Concert* (Deutsche Grammophon, 1991) showcase many of Battle's glorious readings of sacred operatic works.

Helen Baylor

IN THE EARLY 1990s, IT APPEARED that Helen Baylor (born Helen LaRue Lowe) was poised to become to Christian music what Gladys Knight was to pop music in the 1970s: a gregarious personality with a soulfulness that could keep a black audience while also attracting a white one. The pop-styled instrumentation of songs such as "Can You Reach My Friend," "Stand My Child," and "Sea of Forgetfulness" firmly established Baylor in the Christian pop world, while her soulful alto gave her an equally firm black gospel foothold.

Born January 8, 1953, in Tulsa, Oklahoma, Baylor's family later relocated to the Los Angeles ghetto of Compton, California. As Little Helen, she recorded her first song, "More and More," for the Soultown label when she was just 13 years old. Over the course of her teenage years, Baylor opened for Aretha Franklin, Stevie Wonder, Redd Foxx, Moms Mabley, and B.B. King. By the age of 17, she'd left L.A. to join a touring production of the Broadway musical *Hair*. During this period, Bay-

lor began to use drugs. "I was the youngest person in the show," she says, "and I wanted to belong so badly."

After *Hair*, Baylor became the lead singer for the band Side Effect, which fused a 1940s bebop jazz sound with a somewhat funky disco rhythm and called the result vaudevillian soul. Their sound and style was similar to that of the zoot suit–clad Dr. Buzzard's Original Savannah Band, which was known at the time for "Cherchez La Femme." They were far more edgy than the Pointer Sisters, who dressed in World War II women's garb and sang jazz tracks like "Salted Peanuts" at the time. Baylor recorded with Side Effect during their most successful period in 1976–77 when she gave them their first chart hit with "Always There" (a No. 2 disco single). The song appeared on the LP most critics considered their best, *What You Need*. It was released by Fantasy Records in 1977 and rose to No. 26 on the R&B album chart. Their previous and subsequent albums were uneven, but this set (produced by the group's trombonist, Wayne Henderson) is remembered as a funk classic. It produced four Top 100 R&B singles, due in large part to Baylor's strident gospel-styled vocals, including "S.O.S.," "Finally Found Someone," and "Keep that Same Old Feeling," which peaked at No. 22 on the R&B chart.

After exiting the group, Baylor became an in-demand background vocalist for the Captain and Tennille and Rufus featuring Chaka Khan. She sang behind Khan on their 1978 gold-certified LP *Street Player*, which featured the R&B smash "Stay." While touring with Rufus, she met James Baylor, who would eventually become her husband, but her life was spiraling downward. "I was associating with drug dealers, shacking up with James Baylor, and pawning nice things just to buy a $25 bag of weed," she says. "I wasn't working much anymore because my reputation as a musician was going downhill."

Strung out, Baylor was at the end of her rope and could go no further when she showed up at Fred Price's Crenshaw Center Church in 1981. "I'd never completely let go of the God I knew as a child, but when I was a teenager I just didn't find Jesus very interesting," she recalled. "By 1981, when I went to church with my grandmother, I knew what I'd been missing. I cried at the altar and bought a Bible. But I still dabbled in drugs and it took me a year to finally turn my life over to the Lord completely." After straightening out her life and marrying James Baylor, she decided to sing gospel music. "I wanted to sing for God's glory, so I thought that God was going to open the doors for me to sing for and save the world," she told Today's Christian Music .com. "But it didn't happen. So, for the next six years, I struggled and got angry with God. Finally, I started working in my church, getting it together, and six years after I first felt the desire to sing again for his glory, God told me to go prepare to do just that."

Through her church connections, Baylor began to sing at church conferences and she even appeared on Richard Roberts's (Oral's son) nationally televised religious program, where she candidly discussed her exodus from the secular music business and overcoming drug demons. The appearance opened up innumerable ministry opportunities for the singer. Finally, in 1990 at the age of 35, Baylor recorded her first gospel album, *Highly Recommended,* for Word Records. The buzz about Baylor was so strong and positive that the album reached No. 24 on the CCM chart and No. 9 on the gospel charts. The breakout single was Baylor's rerecording of Debby Boone's 1985 CCM smash "Can You Reach My Friend."

The success of *Highly Recommended* drove the sales of the comparatively weaker albums *Look a Little Closer* and *Start All Over.* However, the combined sales of those two albums still did not equal the sales of her debut CD. Baylor's spoken monolog "Helen's Testimony," in which she talked of her drug addiction and her praying grandmother, fueled the success of her biggest selling album yet, *The Live Experience,* which crested to No. 1 on the gospel chart and No. 6 on the CCM chart in 1994. Featuring live versions of her hits up to that time, such as "Sea of Forgetfulness" and "Can You Reach My Friend," the project eventually sold over 200,000 units.

The next album, *Love Brought Me Back,* had a more classic soul feel with Baylor's reworking of soul man D.J. Rogers's title track. In addition, Baylor teamed up with her former Rufus acquaintance Tony Maiden to write tracks such as "The Lord Is My Shepherd," "Nobody Better," and "The Best Is Yet to Come." The album was

a strong seller, but she parted ways with Word Records and signed with Verity Records in 1999. The album *Live* featured a re-creation of "Helen's Testimony," but the plug-singles were gospelized reworkings of Christian pop artist Rich Mullins's "Awesome God" and the church standard "If It Had Not Been for the Lord." The album's more gospel-infected atmosphere made it a bigger gospel than CCM album. Signing with Diadem Records in 2002, Baylor released the urban inspirational CD *My Everything,* which was her first solo CD to miss the CCM charts, although it did rise to No. 11 for gospel and sold just under 50,000 copies. Baylor continues to make music and sing at conferences. In terms of her future, she's sure that she'll never return to secular music. "There's nothing wrong with other people doing secular music," Baylor has said, "but I'm sold out to preach the gospel message." In 2004, Baylor signed a new recording agreement with James Bullard's MCG Records label.

RECOMMENDED RECORDING: *Greatest Hits* (Word Records, 2002) features Baylor's hallmark moments such as "Helen's Testimony" and "Can You Reach My Friend?"

B.C.M. Choir

THE NASHVILLE-BASED BAPTIST, CATHOLIC, and Methodist Mass Choir was a very popular studio choir in the early 1970s, comprised of mostly black voices. They backed several country artists, such as pianist Floyd Cramer and Johnny Cash, and performed with Ray Stevens on his million-seller "Everything Is Beautiful." Elvis Presley also used the choir as accompaniment in his concerts. One of their first recordings was the *Hello Sunshine* LP on Salvation Records in 1972. Their cover of "My Sweet Lord" received a Grammy nomination that year. One of the standout cuts was their rendition of Mattie Moss Clark's "Salvation Is Free," which was led by gospel dynamo Ann McCrary. The choir later recorded for Nashboro Records and also Savoy Records before disbanding in the 1980s. In 2003, Universal Special Products released ten of the choir's '70s tracks on the *Oh Happy Day* compilation CD.

Beautiful Zion Missionary Baptist Church Choir

THE FIRST GOSPEL CHOIR TO HIT the R&B charts was not Kirk Franklin and God's Property's "Stomp." It was the Chicago-based Beautiful Zion Missionary Choir that placed the rocking hit "I'll Make It Alright" at No. 33 on the R&B singles chart in 1973. The song was led by Emma Richards, daughter of Beautiful Zion's pastor. Her expressive alto shone on the track, which was involved in some litigation at the time. The choir had heard the song on the radio and decided to record it when they made their debut LP on Myrrh Records. Inexperienced with copyrights, they didn't realize the song they based it on was Bobby Womack's "Lookin' for a Love." The case was settled and it was one of gospel's early R&B success stories. Former Myrrh Records executive Billy Ray Hearn (who later formed Sparrow Records) and signed the choir, always felt they were unique. "That harmony the black choirs used where all the guys are singing that tenor line, the sopranos and the altos," he sighs. "Oh, it had so much energy. It's so contagious when you're listening to it. It just draws you into it. And when they start singing I got so excited because they had such a unique sound from what had been heard. Now, if you had been attending a lot of black churches you would have heard this before, but it was never out to the white community." The choir's last R&B hit was the tune "Ride to the Mountain Top" from their last LP *In the Spirit* in 1973. Emma Richards now lives in Garland, Texas.

Margaret Becker

BACK IN THE 1980s, Margaret Becker enjoyed a launch as a hard-rocking, axe-playing (à la Bonnie Raitt) Christian vocalist with a penchant for introspective songs about the faith and trying to hold on to that faith amid a world of circumstance and doubt. Over the years, Becker's musical style has evolved from a fusion of rock sounds into a soulful pop blend. In the course of that career, she's enjoyed 14 No. 1 Christian radio hits, three Dove awards, and four Grammy nominations. Born July 17, 1959, in Bay Shore, New York to German/Irish Catholic parents,

Becker was raised on Long Island. Her household encouraged the arts and creative expression. She attended James Madison University and sang in coffeehouses on the weekends. While trying to find herself, Becker studied journalism and worked as a department store bill collector to keep food on her table. In spite of her Catholic upbringing, she didn't really develop a strong relationship with God until a friend ministered to her.

She told *CCM* magazine that "When I found God, and when I found out who he was and what he wanted with me, there was no choice. I had to live in such a way that people would know more about him. When I became a Christian, I knew that I would not be satisfied unless I was broadcasting to other people about Jesus in some manner, whether it was through digging a ditch in Guatemala, or whether it was through singing. I had to tell others about God's ability to love us. His desire to love us and the Man behind the Name that he chose to come to us with, by, in, and through. I applied to a whole bunch of Christian missionary organizations and never got accepted to any of them, so it became apparent to me that there was another way to go. I tried to deny it; I tried to work in a regular job for three and a half years, and it didn't work out. The Lord didn't give me a regular job; I always had piecemeal jobs and I could never get into a settled position that you could grow in or even have health benefits or anything like that. So I began to re-examine the music."

Taking another look at her musical skills and deciding she wanted to be a performing songwriter, Becker moved to Nashville in 1985. In a matter of weeks, she had acquired a songwriting contract with Sparrow Records. After a few months, the songwriting contract had expanded into a recording deal. Her first work was some guest vocals on label mate Steve Camp's 1986 *One on One* LP. The following year, Becker's debut LP *Never for Nothing* was released. Possessing a fiery delivery worthy of pop-rocker Pat Benatar (but smokier, less piercing), Becker quickly made a name for herself as a tough rocker with Christian hits such as "Fight for God" and the title tune. The following year, her project *The Reckoning* delivered further smashes with "Light in the Darkness" and "Find Me."

Perhaps the best album of her career and certainly one of the Top Ten best albums of 1990, *Immigrant's*

Daughter was a masterpiece. The title song told the story of Becker's maternal grandmother, whom she never met personally. Still, the song celebrates her grandmother's faith and sacrifice to come to America for a better life. The album was less hard-rocking as her two previous efforts, with Becker taking a more pop-rock approach. Her clever songwriting and easy-to-recall hooks made songs such as "Solomon's Shoes," "The Hunger Stays," and "This Is My Passion" stand out. Showing further good taste, Becker closed the album with an electrifying unplugged take on Curtis Mayfield's "People Get Ready." The album reached No. 18 on the *Billboard* CCM chart.

Over the next decade, Becker continued to maintain her artistic standard while delivering radio-friendly tracks such as "Deep Calling Deep," "Say the Name," and "Simple House." In 1994, Becker joined fellow CCM starlets Christine Dente and Susan Ashton for a stellar acoustic, pop-country CD entitled *Along the Road* (a mimic of the successful Emmylou Harris, Dolly Parton, and Linda Ronstadt *Trio* collaboration). It was critically praised but did not draw a large consumer audience. In spite of her popularity in live concert settings and consistent radio hits, Becker has never been a huge record seller either. When the 1999 CD *What Kind of Love* did not break any new commercial ground for the singer, Becker and Sparrow Records parted ways after 15 years of critically acclaimed music. In 2001, Becker recorded another trio record, joining singers Maire Brennan and Joanne Hogg (with Phil Keaggy) on guitar to create a Celtic CD of hymn-styled original songs entitled *In Christ Alone* for the Worship Together label.

RECOMMENDED RECORDING: *Steps of Faith: 1985–1992* (Sparrow Records, 1993) is a dozen of Becker's early Christian radio hits, which also happen to be her best work, with songs such as "Never for Nothing" and "Solomon's Shoes."

William Becton

THE 1995 OKLAHOMA CITY terrorist bombing was the catalyst for the crossover success of William Becton's R&B–styled inspirational number "Be Encouraged." By coincidence, the Washington, DC, native's custom (self produced) album was released around the same time of the bombing that killed hundreds of workers in a government building in Oklahoma City. A Washington area R&B radio station, WPGC, began to play "Be Encouraged" in memory of those who died. Soon most of the black radio stations in the market were playing the song. Other R&B stations along the Atlantic coast joined them until it was a national hit. During that period, Intersound Records offered Becton a distribution deal. They rushed the *Broken* CD to stores nationwide to capitalize on the single's success. Eventually, the song reached No. 32 on the R&B singles chart. The album spent 11 weeks at No. 1 on the *Billboard* gospel album chart and peaked at No. 25 on the R&B album chart.

It was a surprise hit for William Becton, Jr., who was born on December 31, 1968. At the age of four, he began to sing in the youth choir at his family's church. At the age of eight, he began formal musical training at the Sewell Music Conservatory where he studied piano. He graduated from the Duke Ellington School for the Arts in Washington, DC, and later studied at the University of the District of Columbia, where his professors Pearl Williams Jones and William Moore mentored him.

In 1991, Timothy Wright and Myrna Summers recorded one of his songs, which transformed him from amateur to professional instantly. His *Broken* project was the next step in his transformation. Following the success of that album, which easily sold over 300,000 copies, Becton released *Heart of a Love Song* in 1997. The hip-hop single "Workin' Out" reached No. 54 on the R&B chart. Although it reached No. 5 on the gospel album chart early after its release, the CD was a commercial failure. Becton's 2000 release *B2K: Prophetic Songs of Promise* was making serious noise on R&B and gospel play lists when the CGI/Platinum Records label (which had bought Intersound) was in the midst of a financial reorganization. The record was lost in the process and Becton shifted his attention toward other musical activities. He acted in some gospel plays and hosted a Sunday morning gospel show on WPGC before landing a national radio show with ABC Radio's nationally syndicated gospel network, Rejoice. In 1998,

Becton was ordained a minister and currently serves as an associate pastor at the Tabernacle Church in Laurel, Maryland. He made a moderate comeback in 2003 with the traditional-styled "Joy in the Morning," a clear departure from his prior contemporary styling.

Daniel Bedingfield

DANIEL BEDINGFIELD, one of England's current pop heartthrobs, was born December 3, 1979, in New Zealand, to Christian missionary parents. He grew up in seedy, working-class southeast London where he and his two sisters formed a vocal trio called the DNA Algorhythm. His musical influences were R&B artists, so R&B sensibilities are the foundation for his brand of pop, which has been described by some critics as Prince re-creating Michael Jackson tracks. Following a breakup with a girlfriend, Bedingfield wrote and recorded the pop-gospel house beat "Gotta Get Through This" in his bedroom with a microphone he hooked up to his computer. Released on Relentless in winter 2001, the song soared to the top position of the UK singles chart. Eventually, Universal Records issued the song in the US where it hit No. 10 on the Hot 100 pop chart. Other American hits have included the clean pop songs "James Dean (I Wanna Know)" and "If You're Not the One." Bedingfield has been known to include a reading of Psalm 23 in his live concerts.

Margaret Bell

YOUNGER SISTER OF GOSPEL BELTER Vanessa Bell Armstrong, Margaret Bell was less a belter than a sophisticated Christian pop singer, along the lines of a Whitney Houston. The Detroit-bred Bell grew up singing with her sisters, Charlene and Vanessa. While an Oral Roberts University student, Bell sang on the university's daily telecast and later became an understudy for the gospel musical *Don't Get God Started*. She spent time as a background vocalist on tours (even substituting for CeCe Winans on a BeBe and CeCe Winans tour when CeCe was pregnant) and recording sessions.

Her friend Mervyn Warren (a founder of Take 6) passed Bell's demo tape to Jim Ed Norman at the Warner Bros. Nashville office in 1989.

Norman signed Bell to the gospel imprint, Warner Alliance Records, with hopes of making her a multi-format, inspirational pop star. "I don't feel as if I'm straddling [two genres]; that's a strategy my company chose to do," she told *Billboard* magazine in 1991 upon the release of her debut CD. "But I am firm about who I am. I make it plain that even though 'Over and Over' is being worked R&B, it is still a gospel love song. I think because of the success of [other gospel acts], it takes the chains and shackles off. With the potential of gospel, [record companies] are seeing that it can reach all audiences. I think the Winans and Vanessa [Bell Armstrong] have really worked to break the mold."

Warner Bros. Records' national black music department was behind the project and helped coordinate lavish listening parties in various cities. However, in spite of some sporadic urban adult contemporary airplay and a lot of promotional dollars, the project never made a significant impact at urban radio and it only mustered a ranking of No. 23 on the *Billboard* gospel album sales chart. A second CD never surfaced, and Bell retired to a life of domesticity as the wife of former Philadelphia Eagles running back, Keith Byars. One of BeBe Winans's closest friends, she has continued to record on his various projects over the years.

Bells of Joy

THIS QUARTET ENJOYED one of the biggest gospel hits of 1951 when their "Let's Talk About Jesus" became a runaway hit. The song was recorded in January 1951 by an Austin, Texas, group and released on the Peacock Records label. After the song took off, the song's vocalist and co-writer A.C. Littlefield was the only member of the group willing to tour to support the record. Then Peacock president Don Robey (1903–1975) had the idea to get the Southern Tones to tour with Littlefield as the Bells of Joy. The group continued to perform thereafter but never enjoyed another hit of that magnitude.

Rev. Delores P. Berry

ONE OF THE LEADERS in a new wave of openly gay gospel singers, Rev. Delores Berry puts a sweet face on a lifestyle that is often cited as an abomination by traditional church leadership. She's recorded a half dozen full-throttle, traditional-styled albums of church standards rearranged to reflect acceptance of gays, lesbians, and transgendered people.

Born February 15, 1951, in Baltimore, Maryland, Berry was an only child. Her salesperson mother belonged to the Methodist church and her handyman father was with Holiness denomination. As a child, Berry attended both churches and any other house of worship she was invited to, even a synagogue. "I think that background helped me learn how to deal with different people of different faiths," she says. Regardless, it was an excellent training ground for her current position. "I knew that one day I would be a preacher; I felt it in my bones," she says. When Berry was 13 years old, her father died, after being chronically ill with asthma. His death brought Berry and her mother closer together. At the age of 16, she joined the Renaissance Choir and began to do the first real singing of her life. After graduating from high school, she attended college and prepared to enter the ministry within the Christian Methodist Episcopal denomination circa 1976.

At the same time, Berry was beginning to come to terms with her sexuality. "All of my life I knew that I was gay," she confides. "Even from the age of five. I didn't know what it was called, but I knew." The only person she had "come out" to was her best friend, Charlene, even though her extended family had at least 36 openly gay members. "I was ordained in the CME church, but a few months later I just couldn't be satisfied," she remembers of the day she finally told her church leadership. "I talked to my bishop and he informed me that there were a lot of us and that I just needed to be quiet. But I had been quiet since I was 5 and now I was 25."

Berry had seen the controversial Rev. Troy Perry (who founded the Universal Fellowship of Metropolitan Community Churches [UFMCC], a gay Christian denomination, in Los Angeles in 1968) on the *Mike Douglas* TV show and was familiar with the organization but never thought of joining it. After her bishop advised her to ignore her sexuality, Berry called a gay hotline in Baltimore. "A man named Louis Hughes answered the phone and I said, 'I'm a Methodist minister and I think I'm coming out. Where do I go?'" He sent her to a women's support group that met every Thursday evening. Someone there invited Berry to an MCC service. "That week I went and I felt like I could breathe," she recalls. "I had felt in the CME church—even after I was ordained and hands were laid on me for ordination—there was a part of me that had stayed in the pew."

In 1983, Berry was ordained within the UFMCC denomination and pastored for a time. "I always felt the call to evangelism as opposed to pastoring," she says. Although she prefers evangelism to pastoring, Berry has no faults with female pastors. She also counters those who cite St. Paul's writings as justification for women to be silent in the church. "What was happening was the men weren't taking their responsibility, so the women were taking over because the men wouldn't help," she says. "So he told the women to stop dealing with the issue and make the men do their part?… From that, we get that women shouldn't be preachers? Jesus had several women who did ministry with him [as did St. Paul, e.g., Phoebe and Priscilla]. They traveled with him and they had him in their homes. Helped him found churches. The way a lot of people embrace faith is out of fear. They don't read for themselves or do research for themselves. I feel responsible to help people understand who we are and how God uses us."

Berry is equally astounded that the Bible is used, in her opinion, to denigrate homosexuality. "One of my favorite things to point out is that there are only a few scriptures that speak in judgment of gay-lesbian people but there are so many more there that speak in judgment of heterosexuals," she says. "The other part is that people worked diligently to write down everything that Jesus said or did. But they missed, evidently, him saying anything about gay-lesbian people? There's not one thing there. So, since I'm a Christian and I follow Jesus Christ, I lean on the fact that he didn't single me out."

That philosophy carries over into Berry's music. She began financing her own CDs in the 1990s. "I change words when I sing songs," she explains. For instance, in the spiritual, "Swing Down, Sweet Chariot," she weaves in tolerance for gays. "I sing, 'I looked over Jordan and what did I see? Loving heterosexuals coming to welcome me. Lipstick lesbians coming to welcome me! Gay men in leather coming to welcome me!' I even say, 'People who haven't a clue, coming to welcome me. Millions of gay bishops coming to welcome me!'"

In recent years, Berry's weight has been a threat to her ministry. At her heaviest, she weighed 420 pounds. "Food was a comfort," she confides. "And I was also just plain greedy, I have to tell you the truth." After recording her *God Put a Rainbow in the Sky* CD in 2002, she had a heart attack. "They tell me that only 25 percent of my heart was working. That's a miracle. I feel like I kissed God's face and came back," she says. "I had gotten so big, I had the stomach reduction surgery. I lost 200 pounds. I lost 30 dress sizes. I was wearing a tight 54 and now I'm wearing a 24. I had a tummy tuck some months afterwards and had an infection from mesh that they used." She then had ten surgeries within seven months. "I had to heal from the inside out," she says. "That's what we all do regardless of the issue."

Berry's sexuality is not an issue anymore. She and her mate, Judy Kiser, had what they term a holy union in 1986. In the future, Berry would like to expand her ministry beyond the gay church circuit into the mainstream church world and beyond. "I want to be more responsible for this call that I have been blessed to live," she says. "I want to go out to churches that are not gay-friendly. I want to go wherever I can get in. I don't play guess who's coming to dinner. My primary focus is the power of Jesus Christ in our lives. The strength that God gives us. The blessings and comfort that the Holy Spirit gives us. I don't preach 'gay gay,' but I preach 'include everybody.' But I don't go where they don't know who I am—including my podiatrist."

What saddens her most is the guilt and anxiety gay Christians feel over their sexuality and that they have somehow fallen short of God's will. She says, "Somebody will say, 'Rev. Berry, will you pray for me? I know God doesn't love me' and I'll pray with them. Then I'll look out the church window when they leave and they're driving away in a brand new Mercedes, yet they feel unloved. I say there's something wrong with this picture."

RECOMMENDED RECORDING: *This Is Why I Sing* (1995) features hymns such as "Blessed Assurance," "His Eye Is on the Sparrow," and a rousing "Can't Nobody Do Me Like Jesus." www.RevDeloresBerry.com

Big Maybelle

A 1950S BIG-VOICED JAZZ/BLUES vocalist who never achieved the success her talent merited, Big Maybelle was born Mable Louise Smith on May 1, 1924, in Jackson, Tennessee. She grew up singing in the Sanctified Church but made her name as a bluesy pop artist in the 1950s. A handsome woman with a warm smile and more than ample weight, her voice could coo into one ear and blast out of the other ear as a howl. She was renamed Big Maybelle by producer Fred Mendelssohn who signed her to OKeh records in 1952. She recorded the original version of Jerry Lee Lewis's "Whole Lotta Shakin' Goin' On" and in 1956 cut her signature single "Candy" that was repopularized on *The Cosby Show* TV series in the 1980s. The song is also the best representation of her trademark vocal teardrop where she whimpers over the lyric at a climatic moment. Throughout those early years, Maybelle battled weight problems and an enduring heroin addiction. Unfortunately, she died after suffering a diabetic coma in a Cleveland hospital on January 23, 1972.

RECOMMENDED RECORDING: In 1968 she recorded her only gospel LP, *The Gospel Soul of Big Maybelle* on Brunswick Records. It featured eleven spirituals such as "Sweet Chariot," "He's Got the Whole World in His Hands," and "Dry Bones."

James Bignon

ONE OF THE FIRST PERFORMERS since James Cleveland to match a deep, dark baritone with a fantastic choir, James Bignon was born August 1954 in Savannah, Georgia. An only child, his parents were church musicians. He first sang as a boy soprano at St. John's Baptist Church in the city. Bignon began writing songs at the age of 11 and after graduating from high school in New York he played piano for Mildred Clark and the Melodaires. Later he toured with Dorothy Norwood and developed a reputation as a gifted pianist. Because of his Georgia roots and industry buzz, Rev. Milton Biggham asked Bignon to lead the Macon-based Georgia Mass Choir that Biggham formed in 1983. There were 873 people at the first rehearsal and it was soon narrowed to 150 voices. The choir quickly made a name for itself as it patterned its style on the traditional gospel format of the 1950s and emphasized rousing lead vocalists over ensemble harmonies. Some of their bigger hits under Bignon's direction were "Come On in the Room," "We've Got the Victory," "Hold On, Help Is on the Way," and "He's All Over Me." In 1995, Bignon selected ten members of the choir to be featured in Michael Flatley's *Riverdance* musical, which toured the country to sold-out performances that year. Not long after, Bignon left the choir to concentrate on a solo career and his own group ensembles, such as James Bignon and Deliverance, and James Bignon and God's Children. Although he and these R&B-flavored aggregations have achieved a modicum of success, albums such as *How Excellent Is Thy Name* and *Heaven Belongs to You* have been tepid sellers in comparison to his work with the Georgia Mass Choir.

BL&S Singers

THIS IS THE WASHINGTON, DC–BASED traditional black gospel trio of Barbara Best, Lois Tillery, and Sylvia Wayman. They recorded LPs such as *Just to Behold His Face* for Savoy Records in the early 1980s. However, their biggest success was the 1987 *Daybreak* album on Sound of Gospel Records. The project's radio popularity was

BL&S *Singers*

driven primarily by the catchy ballad "Romans 8:18" and secondarily by the uptempo track "The Anointing."

Scott Blackwell

A SECULAR REMIX MASTER who jumped ship and became a Christian remix master in the 1990s, Texas-born Scott Blackwell has enjoyed a position at the top rung in both music genres. Blackwell rose to prominence in New York in 1986 as a DJ and remixer for the likes of Debbie Gibson and ZZ Top before slipping into drug abuse. He eventually sobered up and became a Christian. He brought his mixing skills to the church house on his CD *Walk on the Wild Side* for Frontline's Myx Records in 1992. With his use of house rhythms and funk samples, Blackwell brought a new vibe to Christian music—even if very few were listening. "I can't get hung up in worrying about criticism, because I know I am doing what the Lord wants me to," Blackwell told *Billboard* in July 1995. "I know there are a lot of people who don't understand what I'm doing, but that's fine. I can only respond to that by sharing my heart on why I'm doing this. I know how damaging it is for kids to suck up secular music six or seven hours a day. And I know that a lot of these kids really enjoy dance music in all its different types of forms—house, rock, swing, hip-hop, rave, and all that. What the church needs to understand is that when there is a particular type of lifestyle adhered to a type of music in the world, it does not mean that the two are totally fused. Because I like hip-hop or Christian gangsta rap doesn't mean I have to follow the lifestyle associated with the secular variety." At last notice, Blackwell was still running his California-based N-Soul Records label, which has failed to gain a strong consumer base in spite of the quality of its work.

Robert Blair and the Fantastic Violinaires

THEY HAVE NEVER ENJOYED the mainstream appeal the Mighty Clouds of Joy experienced outside of the church community, but in their heyday the Fantastic Violinaires' quartet music was just as good. The group was organized by Wilson DeShields, Leo Coney, and Isaiah "Lil Shot" Jones as a trio in Detroit in 1952. Before they took their name, the group sang first and second tenor parts against the backdrop of a baritone. Some of their early fans said this sound reminded them of harmonizing violins so the group named themselves the Fantastic Violinaires. Eventually, the group chose newcomer Willie Banks as their lead vocalist. He was with them only briefly before starting his own group. In 1955, they received a new lead singer named Wilson Pickett, who went on to a far more successful R&B career with songs such as "Mustang Sally" and "In the Midnight Hour." During Pickett's tenure, he recorded only two sides with them, "Sign of the Judgment" and "My Work Will Be Done" on Gotham Records.

However, the lead vocalist most associated with the group was the late Robert Blair (born August 6, 1930, in Macon County, Mississippi), who joined the group in the early 1960s. Blair possessed a fiery tenor

that electrified audiences in his prime. After their initial LP, *Stand by Me* for Checker Records in 1965, a strategic placement at the Westbury Jazz Festival sent the group's career to new heights. In a short period, the quartet amassed an armful of gospel radio hits such as "Children, Are You Ready?" "Three Pictures," "Mother Used to Hold Me," and "I Don't Know What this World Is Coming To," which made a little noise on the secular market. According to the Violinaires, Rolling Stones superstars Keith Richards and Mick Jagger were fans of the group during this period and suggested that the Violinaires sing the Stones' song "Salt of the Earth," which was included on their 1969 LP *God's Creation*. The bluesy song was initially released on the Stones' 1968 LP *Beggars Banquet*.

In 1972, the Violinaires moved to Jewel Records in Shreveport where they recorded the hit "Dr. Jesus." By 1983, they had been signed by Malaco Records where they recorded more hits such as "Thank God for Mama" and "So Much to Shout About." After joining Atlanta International Records in 1988, the group enjoyed their first chart LP in years when the delicious *The Pink Tornado* reached No. 34 on the gospel album chart that year. The radio-friendly hits were a remake of Curtis Mayfield's "People Get Ready" and the R&B-flavored "Stop, Look and Listen." In the 1990s, the group recorded for both Paula and Prominence Records without any significant sales or radio impact. Still, they continued to tour the Southern quartet market. After a series of health setbacks, Blair died in March 2001. In tribute to him, the surviving members decided to keep performing in Blair's memory. They have since released one CD, entitled *Another Level*. Blair dubbed Titus Stallworth, who sang with the group when Blair was too ill to perform, "Baby Blair" because their voices were similar. Blair handpicked him as his successor and looked on him as a son. However, instead of taking over the Fantastic Violinaires as their lead singer when Blair died, Stallworth formed Lil Blair and the Violinaires, a group of young men singing that old-time religion.

RECOMMENDED RECORDINGS: Unfortunately, the group's best work for Checker Records has never been consciously and respectfully reissued on CD. Instead, a bunch of cheap, budget CDs have been issued over the years by archivists obviously so unfamiliar with the group's music that they don't even include some of their biggest hits. Their best CD for AIR Records in the 1980s was *The Pink Tornado*. However, to get a feel for the group in its prime, it's best to reach for vinyl such as *Mama Used to Hold Me* and *Salt of the Earth*.

Mary J. Blige

LIKE JAZZ ICON BILLIE HOLIDAY, Mary J. Blige does not have a great singing voice. However, just like Holiday, what she lacks in vocal beauty, she more than makes up for in raw emotion. That nakedness combined with the studio wizardry of Sean "Puff Daddy" Combs and Jodeici's DeVante Swing had music critics hyping Blige as the next Aretha Franklin in 1992. Her career has continued to flourish as she's embraced Christianity and brought more gospel-tinged verve to her secular recordings, such as her Grammy-winning *No More Drama*. Born January 11, 1971, in the Bronx, New York, Blige's life was tough from the start. Her father was absent from the home. She lived with her mother and sister in the Schobam housing projects in Yonkers where she developed a street-tough attitude in order to survive her environment. Her trials have been many: emotional and physical abuse, drug usage, and self-esteem issues. She dropped out of high school during her senior year. However, music was an outlet for Blige, who enjoyed soul music by Chaka Khan, Candi Staton, Marvin Gaye, Mavis Staples, and, of course, Aretha, among others. She was at a mall one day where she made a karaoke recording of Anita Baker's "Caught Up in the Rapture of Love." Her stepfather gave it to Uptown Records chief Andre Harrell, who recruited Blige to back up artists such as Father MC. Through the association with Harrell, Blige came to work with Sean Combs, who produced her 1992 debut CD *What's the 411?* which meshed rap and soul in a unique fashion that few women had tackled previously. It was an immediate hit and led to singles such as "All that I Can Say," "Not Gon' Cry," "Ooh Boy," and "You Remind Me," among many others.

Over the years, as she has come to grips with her past, Blige has found peace with God. In a candid interview with *Sister 2 Sister* magazine in 2001, she spoke of her admiration for televangelists such as Joyce Meyers and Dr. Fred Price. Price officiated at the marriage of Blige to Kendu Isaacs in December 2004. They helped bring each other back to God. "I'm sick of being sad," Blige told *Sister 2 Sister*. "And if real happiness is in Christ, then that's where I want to be. I don't care what people say, 'Well, she still got on tight shorts.' It ain't about your clothes. It's about what comes out of your mouth, how you act around people, how you treat your people, not how tight your jeans are. And it says 'Come as you are' in the Bible to the church, but there is an appropriate way that you should dress for the church. You let somebody walk in there who doesn't have a loose dress to wear to church, the whole church will talk about it. So, no. I don't go to church. I just listen to the word from the TV church and take what I need to take from them without going there and being a fraud and a hypocrite and acting like I'm catching the Holy Ghost."

In 2000, Blige collaborated on the CD debut of gospel newcomer Ametria. Blige wrote and produced the tracks "God Is So Good" and "No Weapon" for the *It's Not About Me* project. Ametria has the same raspy, dry vocal style as Blige, but did not find the same kind of commercial success. Blige has also sprinkled her own albums with homages to God. Her live CD *The Tour* featured a brief interlude called "Thank You Lord" written by Rodney Jerkins. Her album *Love & Life* featured the Donald Lawrence–penned "Ultimate Relationship." However, her own composition "Testimony" from the *No More Drama* project was her strongest statement of faith and actually received gospel radio airplay in 2001.

Professor Harold Boggs

THE COLUMBUS, OHIO–BASED ENSEMBLE's single "Will I Be Remembered?" was described in this manner in a 1957 *Billboard* magazine review: "Choir and rollicking instrumental backing shouts out an urgent question with strong emotional feeling and good beat. Merits plenty of spins and sales." The small troupe of singers (with a big, full choir sound) first recorded for the secular King Records label in 1952. However, beginning in 1955, the bulk of their recordings appeared on Nashboro Records through the 1960s. Their greatest claim to fame was the 1964 hit "I've Fixed It with Jesus." Boggs (born Harold Garfield Boggs in 1928) performs the song in concert with his other male singers, known as the Specials. Midway through, his husky tenor wailed the verse and chorus. Backed by swirling organ vamps, the song climaxed with Boggs cracking his voice on the final lines of the song—a delicious example of '60s traditional gospel. His last recordings were for the Sound of Gospel label in the early 1990s.

Tim Bowman

FOR YEARS, MANY FOUND the mixing of jazz and gospel to be sacrilegious. However, after keyboardist Ben Tankard opened the door to such a marriage in the early 1990s, the stage was set for the entrance of guitarist Tim Bowman. In a relatively short period, Bowman has become the face of smooth jazz gospel. Standout tracks such as "I'll Be There," "Smile," and "The Only One" have garnered mainstream smooth jazz radio play and placed Bowman's gospel-inspired music right alongside the grooves of George Benson, Dave Koz, and Boney James, among others.

Born April 22, 1959, in Detroit, Bowman was steeped in church activities and developed his love of music at the International Gospel Center Church in Ecorse, Michigan. "There was a guitarist at church who just blew me away," Bowman says of the day in 1970 when his 11-year-old hands were first inspired to pick a guitar. "When I saw him, I said I want to do this," Bowman remembers. "I used to watch a lot of *Hee Haw* [a syndicated country variety television show in the 1970s] and I used to see Roy Clark play the guitar on there. He was the man! His precision and ability to do it all was incredible. He'd do classical and then jazz and then country. He was flawless. Then, later on, George Ben-

son had a huge influence on me. I heard this guy on the guitar wailing and I said that's how I want to play. He was playing fast, but he played with this great emotion and great phrasing. The way he played over the chords, he could almost make the guitar talk. It was amazing. You just didn't hear that kind of music in church at the time." Bowman played in church for eight years and won a two-year scholarship to the Detroit Music School. One of Bowman's mentors was Joe LeDuca, who became known in later years as the music producer for the *Xena: Warrior Princess* TV series.

After graduating from high school, Bowman devoted his time to playing in a gospel group called International Sound of Deliverance, which also featured his sister, Vickie, who would soon marry aspiring gospel

Tim Bowman

artist Marvin Winans. Around this time, Winans's group, the Winans, was having its annual anniversary concert at Mercy College. They needed a guitarist and gave Bowman a call. Gospel legend Andrae Crouch soon landed them a record deal and the Winans' career soared as they became the bestselling gospel group of the 1980s with their smash hits "Tomorrow" and "The Question Is." Bowman stayed on as guitarist and eventually music director for six years. There was lots of media and constant touring for the Winans. Although it was a whirlwind of opportunity, Bowman wanted to get off the merry-go-round. "I was getting burned out from the traveling and I missed spending time with my wife and kids," he recalls.

Bowman amicably left the group in 1987 and took a variety of well-paying 9-to-5 jobs. He seemed content to play music as a hobby until he and his wife, Wanda, had a revelatory midnight chat. "We were up late," Bowman recalls, "and my wife said, 'You ought to do a CD.'" Although it had not occurred to him previously, Bowman thought it was a good idea and started laying down tracks. He played them for veteran producer Jerry Peters, who in turn played them for other people, who agreed that Bowman should pursue a record deal. All the label executives Bowman spoke to tried to change the songs and the album's smooth jazz concept, so he decided to manufacture the album himself.

In May 1996, Bowman printed up 2,000 copies of his CD *Love Joy Peace* and started promoting the album around Detroit. The city's primary smooth jazz radio station WJZZ started playing four tracks concurrently ("Give Me You," "Love, Joy, Peace," "I'll Be There," and "Speak to Me") in heavy rotation. In five weeks, 1,000 CDs on consignment at various Detroit record shacks were sold. By October 1996, the Salem, Oregon–based Insync Music label had repackaged the album and released it nationally. The album peaked at No. 19 on the *Gavin* smooth jazz charts and No. 20 on *Radio & Records* magazine's album chart in spring 1997. The single "I'll Be There" rose to No. 18 on *Gavin*'s Top Twenty singles chart. His follow-up CDs *Paradise* and *Smile* have received similar press attention and radio play. Unfortunately, Insync had only Christian distribution when the CD had little gospel radio airplay. "It was crazy,"

Bowman adds. "People were going store to store looking for the CD and they would have to go to a little Christian store on the outskirts of town, where they'd only have one copy and wouldn't order any more." Bowman has continued to make other hit albums such as 2004's *This Is What I Hear*. It was his first for Liquid 8 Records and his best seller yet.

RECOMMENDED RECORDING: All of Bowman's smooth jazz CDs are good, but the best is *Paradise*, which features tasty covers of Angie and Debbie Winans's "Light of Love," Vickie Winans's wailer "Lord, Don't Move the Mountain," and the ultra-cool funk of "The Only One."

Kim Boyce

IN THE EARLY 1990s, Kim Boyce was Amy Grant's contemporary and Christian music's answer to Madonna. Boyce sang high-energy dance music and pop-inflected CCM songs such as "Here" and "You Can Be Mine" that made her instantly radio-friendly and brought her a hip, young church audience. However, her music did not begin to tap into the latent seriousness of Madonna's music, although her hooks were competitive. Her music and her voice were light and optimistic. Moreover, Boyce was drop-dead beautiful, so male journalists loved to write about her as they fussed over her glamour girl photos. However, Boyce was never comfortable with the emphasis on her beauty over her ministry gifts, and she eventually bowed out of the industry at the top of her game and at the peak of her career. Still, her musical verve broke ground that even Grant had not yet broken (Grant didn't do a club song until 1991's remix of "Baby Baby") as she helped pave the way for Cindy Morgan, Stacie Orrico, and other church gals who like a bass line with their hosannas.

The eldest of three girls, Kimberly Anne Boyce was born in 1961 in Winter Haven, Florida. Raised in a God-fearing home, she accepted Christ at the age of seven and sang with her family's group, the Melody Three Singers, around the state for a number of years. She enrolled at the University of South Florida as a journalism major and entered the Miss America pageant. She became Miss Florida in 1983—the same year Vanessa Williams won her crown. Later, Boyce moved to Nashville where she did background vocal sessions for a number of artists, including Kenny Marks and Carman. She eventually snagged a recording deal with Myrrh Records and issued her debut LP *Time and Again*, which featured five Top Ten Christian hits, including "Darkened Hearts" and "Helpless."

The bigger she became, the more Boyce fought Christian media's questioning whether her pop-styled music was aimed at general market acceptance. "I don't need this to be a career," Boyce emphatically told *CCM* magazine during that period. "I have other talents. I was studying broadcasting in school, and I was pretty good at it. I had some major offers to work as a newscaster or correspondent. But that was number two to me. Christian music was the first love. Also, if I wanted to do music for the sake of doing music, I wouldn't do Christian music. For the amount of work you have to put into it and for the level of hardship, I doubt that anyone in pop music has to work any harder. If I was going to do it just to make money and be famous, I'd do pop music, because of those reasons. At the same time, I wouldn't have to be accountable to people scrutinizing your lyrics and what you really mean and how your life is.... I don't know if anyone knows this, but I've had offers to do secular things. There have been enough tempting things that have come along that, if I wanted to do them, I could. I'm not saying that I would make a pop record and put Madonna out of business; I'd never be that presumptuous. But at the same time, the offers have been there. I have chosen Christian music because I believe in it and because I know this is where God has called me to be."

On top of that, Boyce's manager at the time did a great job of marketing her but also caused financial problems. "He created a major debt for me," she told *CCM*. "The stress of me being responsible for that almost wiped me out." Moreover, the manager ignored Boyce's career as he pursued a pop career for another client. Finally, Boyce bought her way out of the remaining time on their contract. "I had to give up a large amount of money that he owed me to get out of the management deal," she confessed to *CCM*. "I had to decide whether or not I was going to sue him. I didn't feel good about going into that because of the emotional stress that it would put on me, as well as the area in scripture of suing a brother. So I had to forget it and say, 'That money is my settlement, and I'm paying you that money to get out of my contract.' We finally signed the papers and were done with it, and I was free to pursue new management." By the late 1990s, Boyce had changed her style to adult contemporary Christian music and devoted herself to domesticity. She married and had two children. She and her husband, singer Gary Koreiba, now run the Pierce Arrow Theater in Branson, Missouri.

RECOMMENDED RECORDING: Sadly, Boyce's chosen low profile has caused a new generation of CCM fans to grow up ignorant of her music. Therefore, Word Records hasn't issued a hits compilation, fearing there's no commercial interest. Until there is such interest, Boyce's first two LPs on vinyl are a good primer for anyone interested in Christian dance music.

Leomia Boyd

REDEEMED RECORDS ONCE TAGGED Leomia Boyd the Queen of Soul Gospel. Her sheer talent and career endurance merit such a title, but her sales success doesn't. Although she's recorded a variety of fulfilling and thrilling traditional-styled albums over the years, she's never enjoyed a national hit. Born August 3, 1952, in Aberdeen, Mississippi, Boyd grew up on a farm. "It was a normal life for a country person," Boyd said in 1988. "There wasn't nothing to do but go to church. Go out in the fields and pick cotton, then go back to church and sing a little." After graduating from Aberdeen High School, Boyd went to work. She married James Boyd and had four daughters. Although she enjoyed her work and her life, she felt a calling to sing professionally. "One day my husband told me that if that's what I felt I should do, then I should go for it," she recalls.

In 1981, Boyd left her job as a high school teacher's aide and began singing wherever they'd hand her a microphone. With her fiery vocal style, Boyd soon landed a contract with Jewel Records where she recorded the LPs *Changed* and *I'm Depending on You*. When Jewel folded, AIR Records was waiting in the wings to sign her. Her first AIR LP, *I'm Ready*, wasn't ready for gospel radio. For her second AIR album, Leonard Williams of the Williams Brothers produced the eight-song collection entitled *That's the Way the Lord Works*. Boyd wrote half the cuts, such as "Holy Ghost Fire," which showed off her ferocious vocal style, similar to that of Inez Andrews without the piercing high notes. However, gospel radio still didn't pick up on the album. Unfortunately, subsequent recordings on smaller labels such as *Sweeter in the Light* on Redeemed Records have done nothing to improve Boyd's lot. It's a sad commentary that more gospel fans don't enjoy her stellar music. When asked in 1988 where she'd like to see her career in ten years, Boyd replied, "Ten years from now I really can see myself being the next Mahalia Jackson, that's my goal. I want to be just as big a household word as Mahalia, Shirley [Caesar], Vanessa [Bell Armstrong] because I believe the Lord has plenty out here for all of us. All we gotta do is strive for it and he'll give it to us. If we do it and humble ourselves in his name, he'll granteth our wish and if that's my wish, then, I don't have no other reason not to believe that if he done it for them, he can also do it for me."

RECOMMENDED RECORDING: Hands down, Boyd's best project was *That's the Way the Lord Works*, only available on vinyl at secondhand record shops.

Boys Choir of Harlem

ARGUABLY, THE MOST PRESTIGIOUS and renowned youth choir in recent history, the Boys Choir of Harlem have gone where few choirs have gone. They've sung for presidents, made major television specials, and toured the world. Over the course of their career, they have backed Luciano Pavarotti and Kathleen Battle at one end of the spectrum and Kanye West and Eddie Murphy on the other. They've even performed on an Alvin and the Chipmunks project. Walter Turnbull founded the choir in 1968. The Mississippi native moved to New York to launch his career as an operatic tenor. After per-

forming with the New York Philharmonic for a while, Turnbull wanted to do something to inspire inner-city kids in Harlem. At that point, Turnbull founded the Boys Choir of Harlem, which was not merely a choir. Through membership in the choir, Turnbull and his associates strictly taught the youth good manners and social etiquette and stressed the importance of academic achievement and community service. In those lean early years, Turnbull drove a taxi to raise more money for the Boys Choir of Harlem. The choir began with a dozen or so kids but eventually grew to several dozen. A great human interest story, the choir attracted national attention via major press coverage such as CBS's *60 Minutes* and NBC's *Today Show*. Although the choir has recorded several albums and appeared on several recording projects, their only album to chart is 1992's *Christmas Carols & Sacred Songs* (Blue Note Records) CD, which reached No. 11 on the *Billboard* gospel chart in 1997—five years after its initial release. In 2002, a 25-year employee with the choir was accused of sexual abuse with a minor. Two years later, the board of directors demanded that Turnbull resign his post as president of the organization because he did not act fast enough to dismiss the accused pedophile. "We are absolutely devastated by this news," Steven Butler, an opera singer and artist-in-residence at the choir's academy, told the *New York Amsterdam News* in January 2004. "I have nothing but the most profound respect for Dr. Turnbull, and I have no idea why he is being asked to resign. He is a no-nonsense disciplinarian and no one can do what he has done for these children for over 35 years." In a neighborhood where 70 percent of kids drop out of high school, 98 percent of the 1,000 kids who have passed through the choir have graduated from high school and gone on to college or launched successful enterprises. "My kids come from the same kinds of families [as other kids in Harlem]," Turnbull told *60 Minutes* correspondent Morley Safer. "The difference is that there is somebody willing to do something for them, and they are willing to do something. There is an opportunity…. We instill in these kids the belief that they can be the best at anything they choose. Music lifts every voice, not just children who can sing and dance well, but also those who are not blessed with natural talent yet still have a dream of becoming somebody."

Boyz II Men

THIS PHILADELPHIA-BASED R&B vocal quartet is known for their smooth, clean love songs such as "On Bended Knee," "One Sweet Day" (with Mariah Carey), and "End of the Road." Formed in 1988, Boyz II Men consists of Shawn Stockman (born September 26, 1972), Nathan Morris (born June 18, 1971), Michael McCary (born June 7, 1958), and Wanya Morris (July 29, 1973). They were the bestselling group on the Motown Records label in the 1990s, recording inspirational songs such as "The Color of Love" and "Song for Mama." They have also recorded outright gospel songs such as "Dear God" from their *Evolution* CD and "Humanity" with Shirley Caesar from the *Prince of Egypt* soundtrack.

Professor Alex Bradford

IF LITTLE RICHARD HAD BEEN a gospel singer, his name would have been Professor Alex Bradford—and had Bradford become a rocker, his name would have to be Little Richard. Bradford is to gospel what Richard was to rock 'n' roll: an innovative though flamboyant piano-playing singer with a husky voice and acrobatic stage presence. Just as Richard laid the foundation of rock for Elvis Presley and others to stand on, Bradford laid the cornerstone for gospel's male vocalists to build upon. His dynamically delivered 1950s hits such as "Too Close to Heaven," "I Won't Sell Out," "Lord, Lord, Lord," and "He'll Wash You Whiter than Snow" earned him the title of the "Singing Rage of the Gospel Age."

Born January 23, 1927, in Bessemer, Alabama, Bradford had a unique childhood for a Depression-era child. His father worked in the coal mines, and his mother was a cook and sometime beautician. She noticed something theatrical about her son and gave him piano and dancing lessons, a luxury during those rough economic times. By the age of four, he was performing in black vaudeville shows and received additional tutoring from jazz pianist Mildred Belle Hall. Bradford gravitated toward the applause of the crowds and the whole theater scene. He was soon bored with the simple Baptist services his family attended and, over his father's

objections, joined the more exciting Sanctified Church at the age of six, although his mother reminded him who was in charge and forced him back to the Baptist services. He continued to perform when he could and at the age of 13 he joined a children's choir, the Protective Harmoneers. In short order, he also had his own local radio show where he'd sing and play the piano live. After a tangle with a racist cop, Bradford's parents sent him to New York where he formed a quartet called the Bronx Gospelaires. He didn't last long there and returned to Bessemer to finish high school at a prestigious Negro private school, the Snow Hill Institute. It was during this period that he developed a deeper appreciation of gospel music (he had been a blues fan) by artists such as Arizona Dranes, the Swan Silvertones, and others.

Bradford excelled in his studies and was eventually appointed as a teacher's assistant. He had such an authoritative personality that his classmates nicknamed him "Professor" and he kept the name throughout his

Alex Bradford/ Courtesy of Specialty/Fantasy Records

career. During World War II he served in the army and entertained at camp shows. When he was discharged in 1947, he took a preaching gig at the Universal Spiritual Church in Birmingham, but soon fled to Chicago with a dream of joining the Roberta Martin Singers. Martin befriended him from a distance but never let him join her group. His other hero, Mahalia Jackson, offered him a job as her traveling companion and personal secretary. Then he heard of an opening in the Willie Webb Singers. Bradford got the spot and sang lead on Webb's version of the hymn "Every Day and Every Hour." Roberta Martin was always looking for hit songs, so she took a second look at Bradford and began to record his songs, such as "Since I Met Jesus" and "Let God Abide." At the same time, he made some recordings for Apollo Records in 1951, but they didn't go over well. Still, he was in rabid demand in person for his over-the-top, choreographed concerts that were guaranteed to "wreck the house" nightly.

Circa 1953, Bradford founded the Bradford Specials, a gospel quintet, and began recording for Specialty Records. His rough and energetic vocal style was rare in gospel at the time, so his aerobicized workout of his composition "Too Close to Heaven" became an easy million-seller. Their other records would combine the fervor of gospel with the pizzazz of Broadway. Bradford continued to churn out decent-selling hits, but none as big as "Too Close." He and Sallie Martin teamed up for the huge hit "He'll Wash You Whiter than Snow." At his height, Bradford kept church gossips loaded with ammunition. He was known to drink, party hard, waste money on extravagant gifts, and his flamboyant manner caused some to believe he was a homosexual—all church taboos.

Soon there was more talk about Bradford's offstage life than his recordings and he began to slide in popularity. Then Broadway producers approached him about starring in Langston Hughes's *Black Nativity* musical on the Great White Way. The show was a tremendous success and had an equally successful London run. During the 1960s, Bradford prodigiously recorded music for the Columbia, Savoy, Gospel, Checker, and Nashboro labels. In spite of the recorded output and some fine moments, none of these recordings made much gospel noise.

In the 1970s, Bradford recorded a series of good but poorly promoted LPs for Cotillion Records, such as 1972's *Black Man's Lament*. Though still a relatively young man with a boyish handsomeness, Bradford was then seen as a has-been. He took a job directing the choir at the Greater Abyssinian Baptist Choir in Newark. He did occasional concerts with his wife, Alberta, before a two-year stint with the play *Don't Bother Me, I Can't Cope*. Historian Tony Heilbut has suggested that Bradford had aspirations to become a pop star on the order of Tom Jones. However, those opportunities were not available to Bradford. His last project was Vignette Carroll's *Your Arms Too Short to Box with God*. The musical, which introduced Jennifer Holiday to the theater world, was an instant Broadway smash. However, Bradford had ongoing creative differences with Carroll. During that tense period, Bradford suffered a massive stroke and lingered for a few days before passing away on February 15, 1978.

RECOMMENDED RECORDING: Fortunately for fans of Bradford, a good deal of his music is in print. The Fantasy Records compilation *Too Close* is the first place to start as it features 29 solid songs from the Bradford Specials' 1950s work at Specialty Records, including "Too Close."

Calvin Bridges

IN THE 1980s, CALVIN BRIDGES's recorded approach to gospel was considered contemporary, although his approach to songwriting was decidedly traditional. Therefore, most of his recordings were ignored while his compositions were hits when sung by others. Born January 1952, Bridges grew up singing and playing keyboards in church and became an in-demand studio musician in the late 1970s. He began his career as a keyboardist/organist at Curtis Mayfield's Curtom Records studio in Chicago where he played on Leroy Hutson's forgettable disco LP *Unforgettable* and Linda Clifford's masterpiece LP *If My Friends Could See Me Now*, which featured the smash "Runaway Love." He also backed Tyrone Davis on some sides for Columbia Records before going into gospel exclusively. In the gospel arena,

Bridges became a top session player for Savoy Records where he played behind heavyweights such as Rev. Clay Evans, Luvonia Whitley, and Albertina Walker. In 1981, Bridges recorded the Myrrh Records LP *So Much to Be Grateful For*, which set the foundation for his career as a gospel artist/choir leader. His music was often synthesized with a subtle British punk sound (perhaps the Eurhythmics doing gospel?), which may be what attracted European audiences to his music in subsequent years. However, Bridges's greatest impact has been in the traditional gospel fold where Rev. Clay Evans enjoyed a hit with "Going to Be with the Lord" and Albertina Walker found three hits with "Spread the Word," "Wait on the Lord," and "I Can Go to God in Prayer." In spite of his prior experience as a performer, Bridges oddly won a Stellar award as best new artist in 1986 and founded the Chicago Praise Ensemble in the late 1980s. The group experienced two respectably successful hit LPs, *Renew My Spirit*, which rose to No. 12 on the gospel chart in 1987, and *Awesome*, which peaked at No. 26 in 1988. Although Bridges's group was never a major player in the gospel field, they are best known for their songs "Chosen" and "Rose of Sharon." In spite of his credentials, Bridges has never enjoyed as much fame at home as he has abroad, where he and his ensemble have performed extensively throughout Europe.

Brooklyn All-Stars

THEY WERE BIRTHED at the tail end of the Golden Age of Gospel in 1958, but the Brooklyn All-Stars still made a significant impact on gospel music for a solid two decades. They were formed in New York's Brooklyn borough back in 1950 but never cut a record until they signed to Peacock Records in 1958 and recorded "Rest Awhile" and "Meet Me in Galilee" in those initial sessions. At the time, the group was comprised of founder Thomas J. Spann (basso), Herbert Robinson, Hardie Clifton (falsetto tenor), and Sam Thomas. Like most gospel groups starting out, they were cheated by plenty of concert promoters and were often poorly compensated even when they were paid. After a while, Robinson left to join the more established Sensational Nightin-

gales and was replaced for a while by Paul Owens, who eventually left as well. In 1967, the All-Stars joined Nashboro Records and saw their songs released on the subsidiary Silver Cross and Gospel recording labels. One of their most popular was "No Cross, No Crown." The 1970s were their most lucrative period when they recorded the alleged million-sellers "When I Stood on the Banks of the Jordan" and "He Touched Me and Made Me Whole" for Jewel Records. Since the 1980s, the group has recorded sparingly, although they continue to perform with a rotating membership at various blues and gospel festivals. They may not have gained the fame and fortune of their peers such as the Blind Boys, but they have influenced singers such as pop superstar Aaron Neville. "The voices that intrigued me," Neville said in the liner notes to one of his greatest hits CDs, "were not only the Moonglows, Flamingos, and Orioles, but those cowboys yodeling in the movies. I loved that sound. I also loved the gospel groups, especially Sam Cooke with the Soul Stirrers, the Blind Boys, the Pilgrim Travelers, and the Brooklyn All-Stars. I studied the way their harmonies were woven, and I learned to sing each part, from bottom bass to top tenor."

RECOMMENDED RECORDING: Any Jewel Records vinyl on the group is the best bet since everything on the group is out of print.

Brooklyn Tabernacle Choir

THIS FIVE-TIME grammy-winning choir was founded by Carol Cymbala in 1972, a year after she and her husband, Jim, took over the then-struggling, now-affluent Brooklyn Tabernacle Church in Brooklyn, New York, which Carol's parents founded some years prior. White choir director Cymbala began the choir with nine voices and has seen it grow to 275 mostly black voices, comprised of people from all walks of life, from physicians and lawyers to former street people. Their sound is not the rowdy, traditional black gospel sound. Instead, it is a polished but passionate pop-gospel style that has earned the group five Top Ten bestselling gospel CDs and helped bring praise and worship music into the black gospel fold. In the early 1980s when Cymbala had a hard time finding good material for the choir to perform, she began to write their music. "I just want to see people drawn to Jesus Christ," Cymbala has said. "I want the music to be the arrow that points them to him."

RECOMMENDED RECORDING: *Hallelujah: The Very Best of the Brooklyn Tabernacle Choir* (Atlantic Records, 2000) features 15 of their most spirited performances from the 1990s.

Bishop Ronald Brown

A GIFTED SPEAKER, Bishop Ronald Brown (born March 14, 1947, in Savannah, Georgia) was raised from birth by his aunt, Ida Cooper, and called to preach as a teenager. Brown and singer Vickie Winans (then Vickie Bowman) were married in the mid-'70s and had one son, Mario. Nicknamed "Skeeter," Mario eventually took the last name of Vickie's second husband (Marvin). Mario Marvin has gone on to become a millionaire music producer and has collaborated extensively with P. Diddy. For more than two decades, Bishop Brown has pastored at Faith Tabernacle Deliverance Temple in Orangeburg, South Carolina. There he recorded an album of traditional church songs called *Having Good Old Fashioned Church* for his own custom label. With the help of church member Shane Wall, who single-handedly worked a national marketing and distribution campaign to promote the CD, the album became one of the biggest gospel hits of 1996 with 50,000 in sales. The songs that made the most radio impact were "Down by the River," "There's a Storm Out on the Ocean," and "Something on the Inside."

Ruth Brown

DURING THE 1950s Ruth Brown was *the* best-known female R&B singer in the country. Her string of million-selling smashes such as "Teardrops in My Eyes," "5-10-15 Hours," and her signature tune "(Mama) He Treats Your Daughter Mean" established the genre that Etta James and Aretha Franklin would take to new levels of acclaim. It's been said that Atlantic Records was about to close its doors when Brown's hits made the company a boatload of money in a short period of time and saved it from bankruptcy. Afterwards, Atlantic was nicknamed The House That Ruth Built.

Born Ruth Weston on January 12, 1928, in Portsmouth, Virginia, Brown first sang in church and was inspired by jazz artists such as Dinah Washington and Billie Holiday. In 1945, she ran away from home with trumpeter Jimmy Brown, whom she eventually married. She sang briefly with Lucky Millender's band before Cab Calloway's sister, Blanche, got her a singing gig at the Crystal Caverns nightclub in Washington, DC. A local DJ, Willis Conover, liked her show and recommended her to Ahmet Ertegun and Herb Abramson, who owned the struggling Atlantic Records. They liked what they heard, and her first record "So Long" was an immediate hit in 1949. Before Brown, most black female singers sang jazz, blues, or standards. She was the first real R&B singer and she developed her own distinctive style. "They started calling me the girl with the tear in her voice because of that little squeak I had," she told *Goldmine* magazine. "It was an accident, it just happened. It was a crack that happened and I said, 'Oh, that's terrible!' But Herb said, 'Oh no, it isn't! Leave it in.' In fact, they got to the point where, if I was getting ready to go and record, and I had a bad throat, they'd say, 'Good!'"

Over the next decade, Brown delivered classics such as "I'll Wait for You," "I Know," "Sure Nuff," "Oh What a Dream," and "Mambo Baby." In the 1960s, Brown's hits dried up and consequently she was dropped from Atlantic. She took various jobs as a school bus driver and a maid to support her two sons. Her old friend Redd Foxx brought her back into the business in the 1970s when he was riding high on *Sanford and Son*. She began to get club dates through his help. Brown starred in the short-lived NBC sitcom *Hello, Larry* circa 1979 and as Motormouth Mable in the 1985 John Waters film *Hairspray*. In 1989, she really came into her own in the Broadway musical *Black and Blue*. In her Tony award acceptance speech, Brown received a standing ovation when she remarked, "It's taken me 40 years to walk up those five steps." The new fame led to recording contracts with Fantasy Records and then with Rounder Records.

In the 1980s, Brown and her attorney Howard Beagle fought a nine-year legal battle with Atlantic Records for back royalties for Brown's 1950s recordings, which had been reissued many times over though she didn't receive a penny for them. The label claimed they had not recouped Brown's recording budget yet, but a judge felt otherwise. Brown settled on an undisclosed sum and her efforts led Atlantic to establish the Rhythm & Blues Foundation (and its Pioneer Awards), which aids aging artists with hospitalization and other benefits.

RECOMMENDED RECORDING: Brown's newfound fame over the last two decades led Polygram Records to reissue her 1962 *Gospel Time* LP in the late 1980s. The album featured her traditional versions of "Milky White Way," "Just a Closer Walk with Thee," and "Satisfied." The album was produced by Shelby Singleton (who would eventually produce Tammy Wynette and the Staple Singers). It was recorded in Nashville with the city's best musicians, including organist Ray Stevens (who went on to record "Everything Is Beautiful"), guitarists Jerry Kennedy and Harold Bradley, and pianist Harold "Pig" Robbins. The Milestone Singers were the background vocalists. Brown, who has always kept her faith intact, even preached her way through a rocking version of "Morning Train." It's a fine set and a welcome addition to the collection of anyone who enjoys traditional gospel with polish.

Shirley Brown

IN THE 1970s BLACK WOMEN started talking on their records—they called it rapping. They rapped about the unfaithful men they were in love with, and sometimes they confronted the other woman. Laura Lee, Candi Staton, Denise LaSalle, and Millie Jackson were a few of the popular female rappers of the time. However, no one had a bigger rap record than Shirley Brown did when "Woman to Woman" hit the scene in 1974. With a gospel-charged upper vocal range similar to Aretha Franklin's early in her career, Brown delivered the song as passionately as anyone could. The influence of the song was so massive that it led to answer songs such as Barbara Mason's "From His Woman to You" and Lonnie Youngblood's "Man to Woman."

Born January 6, 1947, in West Memphis, Tennessee, Brown grew up in St. Louis, Missouri. She began singing in church as a child and soon developed a reputation outside of her church for her dynamic solos. "I grew up under the supervision of powerhouse, soul-stirring preachers, singing in the choir at the tender age of nine years old," she told the *Memphis Commercial Appeal* in 1997. "That's something you'll never forget. It goes with you a long, long way." After bandleader Oliver Sain produced her first recordings for A-Bet Records, Albert King secured a deal for her at Stax Records. When singer Inez Foxx turned down the chance to record "Woman to Woman" because she couldn't see herself singing the story line, it was offered to Brown, who had no qualms. The song about a love triangle spent two weeks at No. 1 on the R&B charts and peaked at No. 22 on the pop chart.

Thus far, Brown has never had another hit of that magnitude, although she's made further R&B chart noise with "It Ain't No Fun," "It's Worth a Whippin'," and "Blessed Is the Woman (with a Man Like Mine)," and "You Ain't Woman Enough to Take My Man" picked up where "Woman to Woman" left off. Over the years, Brown has recorded for Arista Records, 20th Century Fox Records, Soundtown Records, Chelsea Avenue, and Black Diamond Records, but she's had her most recent success at Malaco Records. On some of her most recent albums, Brown has fulfilled a lifelong dream of recording gospel and message songs. On her 1997 CD *The Soul of a Woman* she dedicated Dottie Rambo's "He Looked Beyond My Faults" to her son, Prentiss Brown, who died in 1997 at the age of 29. Backed by the Mississippi Mass Choir, Brown turned in a *tour de force* performance. "In [my son's] last days, he'd sing the first verse, I'd sing the second," Brown told the *Appeal* that year. "When he was a young boy coming up in the Baptist church, that was his only favorite song, really.... I was trying to write a song in tribute to my son, and I just got writer's block. I think, spiritually, that's what the Lord was trying to say to me. This is the song—you've had it here all the time."

Maurette Brown-Clark

A GIFTED SINGER, composer, and arranger, Maurette Brown-Clark was born May 5, 1966, in Long Island, New York. She's been singing since the age of four and performed extensively with her family's gospel group as a teenager. She graduated from the University of Maryland and had a professional job when she had an epiphany in 1990. On a plane ride, she read an inspirational magazine article about a former classmate who had found his niche in life. "I came face-to-face with my own mortality," she says. "I didn't want to have lived and died without touching anyone." She began asking God what she should do and she says that he instructed her to start a music ministry. For a while, Brown-Clark was a background singer for CeCe Winans and Hezekiah Walker. She eventually found her way into Richard Smallwood's group Vision as a featured vocalist on the song "Angel" on Smallwood's 1996 CD *Adoration: Live in Atlanta.*

The buzz about her dynamic, yet finely controlled performance on "Angel" won her the attention of Verity Records, who signed her to a deal in 1998. Her debut CD *How I Feel* was poorly promoted and had sluggish sales, but it won Brown-Clark a Stellar award for Best

Milton Brunson / Mike Borum for Rejoice Records

New Artist in 1999. Receiving the Stellar put an end to a running joke between the singer and her mother. "We used to watch the Stellars and she'd say, 'We'll be down there one day.' And I'd say, 'Yeah, when we buy some tickets and sit in the nosebleeds.'" When the CD failed to generate sales, Verity dropped Brown-Clark from their roster. Eventually, she resurfaced on AIR Records, which specializes in traditional gospel music. They failed to adequately market Brown-Clark's contemporary sound on the mild-selling CD *By His Grace* in 2002.

Milton Brunson and the Thompson Community Singers

PERHAPS THE MOST celebrated gospel choir of the 1980s, the Thompson Community Singers (aka the Tommies) were formed by Milton Brunson (born June 28, 1929) in 1948 while he was still a student at Chicago's McKinley High School. "We wanted to get together and sing spirituals and everything else," Brunson told *Totally Gospel* magazine in 1988. "We just wanted to sing." They set up shop at St. Stephen's Church in the Windy City where pastor Rev. Eugene Thompson guided and encouraged their ministry. Thompson introduced the choir to several of his influential colleagues in the ministry who booked them for concerts and allowed their reputation to flourish. They eventually named the choir after him.

Over the years, the choir became a significant training corps for aspiring neighborhood singers. They made their first recordings in 1963 for Vee-Jay Records where they recorded the radio hits "Old Ship of Zion" and "Motherless Child." Before the label closed in 1966, the choir recorded two excellent full-length LPs, *The Soul of the Thompson Singers* and *Yes, Jesus Loves Me.* After his ordination in 1962, Brunson founded the Christ Tabernacle Missionary Baptist Church, where he once preached, "Instead of putting a needle in your vein, put some education in your brain. If you want to get high, get high on Jesus." Brunson continued to preach as the choir's name continued to grow. Later they recorded for Hob Records where they cut such LPs as *Moods, Images and Reflections* (1974) and enjoyed hits with "I'll Trade a Lifetime," "I Thank God," and "I Love to Praise His

Name." Then it was off to Nashboro's Creed label imprint where they recorded the outstanding call and response song "Rise and Walk," featuring Jessy Dixon on organ, and the LP *To All Generations* (1979).

In spite of their longevity and prior success, the choir rose to another level when they joined Word Records in the 1980s. The *Miracle Live* LP reached No. 6 on the *Billboard* gospel chart in 1984. They followed up with five No. 1 albums in a row: *There Is Hope* (1986), *If I Be Lifted* (1987), *Available to You* (1989), *Open Our Eyes* (1990), and *My Mind Is Made Up* (1992). However, they won their only Grammy award thus far in 1995 for the CD *Through God's Eyes*. As the choir's fame spread, so did the notoriety of Brunson's tight ship. "Well, I'm strict," he once said. "If that's what you want to call it. I don't play when it's time to do things." Gospel personality Bobby Jones took it a step further by writing in his memoirs that Brunson "was an arrogant man, difficult to get to know."

Throughout the choir's history and his role as a pastor, Brunson was also a celebrated radio announcer. He hosted Chicago gospel radio programs on WXFM, WVON, WCFL, and finally WGCI. Following Brunson's death on April 1, 1997, his wife JoAnn (who joined the choir when she was 14 years old) became the director of the choir. She eventually dropped the Thompson Community Choir name and adopted their nickname the Tommies as their official name. Their 50th anniversary was marked by a hits CD, *50 Blessed Years*, in 1998 and a U.S. Post Office building at 324 Laramie Avenue in Chicago was posthumously named in Brunson's honor. In 2002, the Tommies returned to the music scene with a contemporary, urban-flavored studio CD, *Real*, produced by Percy Bady. In spite of the delicious funk of the title song, perhaps the style of the song and absence of Brunson were too much of a departure for their fan base. The album never caught on and sold poorly in comparison to their prior Word Records projects. When Word Records closed their black music division, the Tommies were unceremoniously dropped from the label as was the rest of the black roster, with the exception of Shirley Caesar.

RECOMMENDED RECORDING: Clearly, the 1980s were the most successful period of the choir's long career.

Great Moments (Word Records) features their biggest hits from that period.

James Bullard

POP MUSIC HAS CLIVE DAVIS, and gospel has James Bullard. Arguably, he has guided more successful gospel recordings than any single person in the history of gospel music. Born April 6, 1942 in Atmore, Alabama, Bullard moved to Cleveland in his twenties where he formed a vocal trio called BOS—Bullard, Oliver, and Ship—which toured and recorded together with considerable success from 1958 to 1970. After the group disbanded, Bullard became an executive with Cleveland-based Way-Out Records, where he supervised the debut of "I'm Glad He Knows My Heart," which became a huge hit by the Sensational Saints. Bullard began to hone his skills as a marketer, personally visiting record shops around the country and selling thousands of units in the process. "I just saw what I was doing as common sense, and it was working," he recalls. "I started to focus on that more and more. That's when I first starting seeing a vision for taking this music to the people in ways that hadn't been done before."

Bullard later formed his own label, BOS, named after his former recording trio. To keep the rent paid, Bullard began doing promotion work for Birthright Records, which had a roster of artists that included Edwin Hawkins. Impressed with Bullard's work for them, Birthright merged its label with BOS and allowed Bullard to retain ownership of BOS. Bullard's sales expertise pushed Hawkins's album sales into six figures. A good man can't be held down, so in 1978 Roadshow Records (which had artists such as Tina Turner and the soul group Enchantment) brought Bullard on staff specifically to make Shirley Caesar a household name. Bullard accepted the charge, which resulted in her 1978 bestseller LP *From the Heart*.

However, Bullard didn't really make good on his promise to make Caesar a household name until he moved on to head up Word Records' black music division in 1980 and brought Caesar along for the ride. Her debut LP for Word Records, *Rejoice*, had tremendous smash hits with "Gotta Serve Somebody" and "Satan,

You're a Liar." The album also won Caesar her first Grammy award in years. Over the next decade, Caesar easily became the most recognizable woman in gospel due to Bullard's marketing skills and a wave of hits such as "Martin," "Jesus, I Love Calling Your Name," and "Go." During the 1980s, Bullard also was responsible for Word's successful associations with Edwin Hawkins, Al Green, the Clark Sisters, and the Mighty Clouds of Joy, among others.

In the 1990s, Bullard's help was needed at the classically based Intersound Records, which had plans to open a black gospel division. Bullard brought to the label hit projects for Vickie Winans, the Mighty Clouds of Joy, and Candi Staton, whom he had wanted to sign at Word back in 1982. By 1997, Bullard had left Intersound and formed MCG Records with legendary session player Jerry Peters. The label has enjoyed incredible success with classic traditional gospel music, particularly with the various CDs by Lee Williams and the Spiritual QCs.

Solomon Burke

FOR A BRIEF PERIOD IN THE 1960s, Solomon Burke's majestic costumes and soulful crooning earned him the title of King of Soul—that was just before James Brown and Otis Redding came along and redefined exactly what soul music is and was. His gospel vocals, country arrangements, and romantic story lines coalesced for a unique musical adventure that came to life on classic cuts such as "Cry to Me" and "Everybody Needs Somebody to Love."

Born March 21, 1936, in Philadelphia, Burke was named for the biblical King Solomon and has carried that mantle of royal lineage all of his life. He was weaned on church music and preachers. His grandmother got him a guitar, so he began singing and playing at church. Influenced by Superman, he put on a cape and won over the congregation. He was preaching at his family's church and hosting his own gospel radio show before he was a teenager. In 1955, Burke recorded a mix of gospel and blues songs for Apollo Records such as "To Thee," "You Can Run but You Can't Hide," and "I Need You Tonight." He recorded briefly for Singular Records before signing to Atlantic Records in 1961. Under the di-

rection of legendary producer Jerry Wexler, Burke turned out a string of R&B radio hits such as "Just Out of Reach," "Cry to Me," "If You Need Me," "Got to Get You Off My Mind," "Tonight's the Night," and "Goodbye Baby (Baby Goodbye)." At the height of his fame, Burke's show rivaled James Brown's for excitement. He'd step onstage wearing a royal robe, a scepter in his hand and a crown on his head. That was to get the attention of the audience, but he held the audience with his dramatic performances, which seemed like the wildest of church services rather than a soul concert.

From the 1970s to the present, Burke has vacillated between gospel and secular musical projects. He recorded the 1979 LP *Lord We Need a Miracle* (Savoy Records), 1998's *We Need a Miracle* (Malaco), and the 1999 CD *Not by Water but Fire this Time*. Although he was no longer a chart-topper, Burke's intimate, thrilling club performances have transformed him from a has-been into a favored soul gentleman among the most prestigious rock music critics. Records he recorded for a variety of small labels through the 1990s sell respectably with virtually no radio play on the strength of Burke's print press. His 2002 CD *Don't Give Up on Me* earned him his first Grammy award. A former mortician who used to sell popcorn during intermission at his own shows, Burke worked a number of jobs at once to support his 21 children. In spite of all of that, he's never forsaken his highest calling. He is bishop of the House of God for All People Church in Los Angeles.

RECOMMENDED RECORDINGS: Virtually anything Burke has ever recorded is sweet ear candy. All of his gospel performances pack the passion that his love songs do. However, the collection to own is *You Can Run but You Can't Hide* (Mr. R&B Records), a Swedish import CD that features many of Burke's great teenage gospel songs he recorded for the Apollo label in the 1950s.

Mosie Burks

ALTHOUGH SHE DOESN'T HAVE SOLO billing with the Mississippi Mass Choir, almost everyone who has come to see the choir in concert over the last decade has come specifically to see the sassy, silver-haired vocal dynamo who has made the old Dorothy Love Coates tune "They Got the Word" one of the most popular black gospel songs in recent memory. The third-oldest of 13 children, Burks was born June 17, 1933, in Forest, Mississippi, where her family worked the delta cotton fields. Burks's mother died young, and Mosie became mother to her siblings. She graduated from Money Vocational High School but was unsure as to whether her future path would be music or teaching. "I really believed there was more than one Mahalia Jackson because I was going to be the other one," she laughs. "I grew up singing. I always loved to sing. We had an old Gramophone and we had one big ole album. I used to play that thing. It was nothing but blues and stuff on it, but I used to play it all the time just so I could hear music. I believed I would be a singer, but my desire was to teach school. The only song on [that LP] I remember is 'Ain't You Sorry Mama?' Now, who in the world wrote that I'll never know! It wasn't Muddy Waters. My parents used to put us in the wagon, and go into Forest, Mississippi, and that's when I would hear Muddy Waters. It was actually him in person, but we never got a chance to go to it. We stayed in the wagon. My parents wouldn't allow us to go into the juke joint. But I could hear them [from the wagon]: Muddy Waters, John Lee Hooker, all kinds of blues singers like that."

Burks was the only one in the household who attended church. "My parents did not attend church," she recalls. "But my grandparents did. So I ended up in their church for a while. We moved a lot. Whichever farm was paying the most, that's where you moved to, so I would join whatever church I was near. My mother would get me up for Sunday school because she knew I wanted to go. It was 13 of us in the house, but I was the one she'd wake up. She'd say, 'Mosie, it's time, do you want to go to Sunday school?' and I'd say, 'Yes, ma'am.'" When she came of age, Burks matriculated at Jackson State University and decided to work the first semester before enrolling because she didn't have money to buy new clothes and school books. Her plans changed when her mother died in 1955. "She was only 40," Burks recalls with sadness. "She had a lot of children and worked so hard in the fields. That's why I hated the cotton fields. I hated the work that was put

on them. Then come home and fix dinner, washing and ironing and with that many children. I literally hated that place and I declared that if I ever grew up, I'd never stay there."

Burks's father moved his other children to Jackson where Mosie was cleaning houses for a living. He abandoned them there. "My dad left me with the children, that's a sad story," she continues. "I moved back in with them. It was the winter, December, a $10 a week house. I was working for $20 a week and I had seven children, and he left us there and that's when I really learned how to trust God. I always trusted him, but I really learned how to depend on him. To catch a bus at night and come in and stop at the store with the dollar that I had and pick up food and come home and cook the last meal for the children and go to bed. They were happy, but they didn't know what I knew: I didn't have nothing for the next day. I would get on my knees and pray and the next day—this kind of chokes me up a little— somebody would knock on my door and say, 'Mosie, here's some eggs and here's a piece of bacon.' I didn't know they knew we were in the condition we were in, and I'd just shout and praise the Lord. But the Lord granted me to feed them young 'uns and keep them clothed. And I put them through school and all…."

"One day I was working for somebody and the man was out of town. He called and I answered his telephone for his wife. He asked me who I was, and I told him I was the maid. We talked a little longer and then I put his wife on. When he got home, he said to his wife, 'Mosie is not a maid. I don't know why she's here.' I thought he meant I didn't know how to clean up. But that's not what he meant. He told me I was not a maid and to go back to school. I thank God for those two people. They were my employers, but they insisted that I go to school. So I started going back to the library, studying and reading. I would see him at a distance, and he'd always wave and ask me how I was doing."

Eventually, she made her way to Tougaloo College as a voice major. She also married in 1957 and had three children. "I had a great husband," she confesses. "I was his queen. He was one of those people who didn't believe in you working. He worked for a produce company so he'd bring home things they'd throw away, like peas, and we'd shell 'em all up and can them. So we were able to make it by really well…. Then my husband became deathly sick [a hit-and-run accident victim, all of his vital organs were damaged] so I dropped out again and I never went back." When her husband became ill, Burks went to work for Bell South. "I had practiced and learned how to pass a test," she says. "Out of those 40 people who took the test that day, two people passed and I was one of them…. I worked split shifts so I could go home and give him his medicine and then go back to work." Her husband was never able to work again and lived another 13 years before passing away in 1984. Burks remarried in 1992. "The Lord blessed me with another husband and now I'm his baby," she laughs. "The other one, I was his queen. This one I'm his baby."

Burks and her husband were both retired from their respective jobs in 1994 when a friend called Burks and told her about an audition for the Mississippi Mass Choir. "I said no, I'll let that be for young people," she says as she looks back on that day. Though she refused the invitation, someone called to tell her that she had been selected to audition at Anderson Methodist Church. Burks said they made a mistake and that she'd never put her name down. The person said that it was down. "Rather than argue I decided to go for the heck of it," she says. She sang "What Do You Know About Jesus," and three months later, she received a letter affirming that she'd been selected as a new member of the choir. Although Burks had no ambition or interest in soloing, she was chosen for a solo. She was thinking of dropping out of the choir because the choir's rehearsals took up a lot of her time, and her new husband wasn't pleased with her schedule taking her away from him. The problem was solved when he was hired to handle the choir's merchandise table on the road. Burks then led a ragtime-styled bouncy number, "When I Rose this Morning," which propelled the *I'll See You in the Rapture* CD to No. 1 on the *Billboard* gospel sales chart in 1996.

The song was such a rousing hit that Malaco Records executives wanted to pair Burks with another great song on the follow-up CD *Emmanuel: God with Us*. Burks recalls, "There was a song called 'They Got the Word' that was written by Dorothy Love Coates. I knew of her music and always loved it. Jerry Smith [from Malaco] said I needed to do another song and that song

had come in my spirit before he asked me what I wanted to do. I knew it was going to be that one, so I discussed it with him and he said this is it." To say the album was a hit would be an understatement. The album remained on the gospel chart for 55 weeks, sold more than 200,000 copies, and made Burks the face of the choir for the gospel public. While the fast-paced song ran laps around radio station play lists, the song's writer—Dorothy Love Coates—was raising her blood pressure. She was angry that the album's producer Jerry Smith listed himself as the songwriter for her song. Originally entitled "The Great Coronation," the song was listed as "They Got the Word" in the album's credits. "She was a great lady to me," Burks says. "I'm sorry to hear she allowed bitterness to enter her life and remain. That's one thing I will not do. I will not allow something that is not good for me to remain with me. I don't do that. I refuse to eat it, so therefore I don't have to digest it." Oddly, Malaco executives said that they thought the song was in the public domain and they didn't realize that Coates had written it, although Malaco holds the publishing rights on the song.

When the slight was recognized, Malaco began to pay Coates author royalties on the song. In addition, they paid tribute to Coates on their follow-up CD *Amazing Love* by recording a medley of her hits. Coates died on April 9, 2002, before the album was released in June of that year. "When she passed away we were touring," Burks recalls. "I really wanted to go to the funeral. I just really wanted to be there for her and sing that song ['They Got the Word']."

Burks also got the word about keeping fit at any age. Not your typical grandma, Burks works out in the gym three days a week, making use of free weights and the track course. Burks's popularity has led Malaco to take her in the studio to record her first solo CD, which will be released in the near future. Burks was profiled in Disney's 2004 nostalgic, feel-good motion picture *America's Heart & Soul*, which found director Louis Schwartzberg touring the country in search of inspirational stories on a number of everyday people, ranging from a Colorado cowboy to the founders of Ben & Jerry's Ice Cream.

In spite of a lot of adversity early in her life, Burks is quite happy with the way her life has unfolded. "In the back of my mind, I always wanted to sing, but I never saw any way possible that it could come about," she gushes. "I loved Mahalia Jackson and I would sing 'How I Got Over' and a great deal of her songs. We were poor people, but I found out we weren't poor. We just didn't have what someone else had. Rosetta Tharpe was one of the persons I liked to listen to. These were women who really played a part in my life. They don't know what they did for me then and what they do for me now."

Kim Burrell

A MUSICIAN'S SINGER, Kim Burrell is cited as a vocal influence by contemporary urban teenyboppers such as B2K's Omarion and Kelly Rowland of Destiny's Child. Her style is comparable to jazz stylists on the order of the late Betty Carter. She never sings the same note twice. Her phrasing and mood creates a new, uniquely personal rendition every time she sings a song. The dynamic manner in which Burrell utilizes her vocal instrument has helped fuel the admiration of her fellow musicians.

Born August 26, 1973, in Houston, Texas, Burrell grew up on the music of D.J. Rogers, Thomas Whitfield, and the Clark Sisters. However, she mostly credits her own family as being her biggest musical influences. "We were all musically inclined," she told *Gospel Industry Today* magazine. "We gathered around the piano more than we gathered around the radio. My biggest influences were my mom, who sings like a songbird, and my dad, who plays like a musical genius. They caused me to do what I do."

She first drew attention as a songwriter and soloist on the Trinity Temple Full Gospel Mass Choir's *Holy One* album, which also featured Kirk Franklin's earliest work. She later funded her own custom CD, *Try Me Again*, on Pearl Records in 1997. She literally sold the CD out of the trunk of her car and racked up 50,000 sales as she crossed the country singing at church events. Frank Cooper and Max Siegel recruited her as the debut artist on Tommy Boy Records' gospel imprint in 1998.

Her CD *Everlasting Life* reached No. 10 on the gospel sales chart. "*Everlasting Life* brought me numerous relationships outside the gospel industry and strengthened my relationships with those inside the gospel industry," Burrell told *Gospel Industry Today*. "Stevie Wonder, Chaka Khan, Robert Townsend, Puff Daddy, Lil' Kim, Mary J. Blige, and R. Kelly are all people that are in constant contact with me as a result of *Everlasting Life*."

On the strength of the first album, the second Tommy Boy Gospel CD, *Live in Concert*, was highly anticipated. Recorded at G.E. Patterson's Temple of Deliverance Church of God in Christ in Memphis, it featured live performances of songs from Burrell's two previous projects and three new tracks. Buoyed by mainstream magazine reviews and an appearance on *CNN Headline News*, the album peaked at No. 4 on the gospel album chart in 2001. "Usually my albums are not what people consider consumer-friendly," Burrell told *Gospel Industry Today*. "Musicians usually enjoy them more than the average music buyer… This time around, we've recorded a project that is both consumer-friendly and a musician's delight."

In accessing her place in gospel, Burrell is focused. "I recently saw a documentary on Mahalia Jackson," she told *Gospel Industry Today* in 2000. "I want to compare myself to her. She was not a well-learned person from what I can tell. But she knew what she sang about, and she knew what she believed. I want to be as confident as she was. I want to always keep that level of confidence, because I think that's what has gotten me this far. The artists of Mahalia's day might not have always known every trick of the trade, but they became successful in business."

RECOMMENDED RECORDING: Burrell's *Live in Concert* is the best representation of her work and unique gifts.

Ruth Busbee

A PROTÉGÉ OF THOMAS WHITFIELD, Busbee began singing at the age of five in the COGIC denomination. She was trained at the Frisbee School of Music in Detroit and made her professional debut with the Howard Lemon Singers in the 1970s. She later worked with the Thomas Whitfield Company Choir before Savoy released her debut LP *He Loves Me* in 1978. Although it featured Whitfield and his players on the production, Busbee's high-pitched voice seemed an ill fit for this bluesy, traditional style of gospel music.

Juanita Bynum

OVER THE YEARS, BLACK AMERICA has enjoyed the spectacle of many superstar preachers such as Bishop T.D. Jakes, Rev. Ike, Fred Price, Creflo Dollar, and even the deified Martin Luther King, Jr. However, black America has never had a preaching woman even begin to approach the stature and name recognition of Juanita Bynum. She burst on the scene in a big way when her videotape *No More Sheets* sold a million copies in the late 1990s and opened up worldwide ministry opportunities that have brought her thousands of faithful followers, who treat her more like a rock star than a prophetess of God.

Born in January 16, 1959, in Chicago, Bynum and her four siblings were raised in a strong Christian home. Along with church attendance, she performed in school plays. One school production of *My Fair Lady* was so good that a Hollywood talent scout wanted Bynum to audition for sitcoms such as Diahann Carroll's *Julia* show. However, Bynum's mother, Katherine, turned down such offers because she wanted her daughter to be grounded in the Bible, not show business.

Although Bynum sensed that her life's work would be involved with church work, she wasn't sure how it would be manifested. In the meantime, she married at the age of 21 and moved to Port Huron, Michigan, where she devoted herself to the marriage. Then her husband left her less than two years into the marriage. "I married for sex and for what the man looked like," she told *Essence* in 2001. "Everybody told me he wasn't right, but I was screaming, 'I'm in love. I can change him.'" Her mental collapse following the 1983 breakup put her in the hospital for three weeks. After her divorce was finalized, she fell in and out of many men's beds. They promised her expensive gifts and good times, but she wasn't genuinely happy. "I got tired of men with their hands in my underwear," she confessed later on the *No More Sheets* video. "It was too expensive."

Over the years, Bynum worked a number of menial jobs to keep her head above water before she was forced onto welfare. She returned to Chicago and enrolled in beauty school to become a hairdresser. After two years of styling, she was off of public assistance. She then got a job as a flight attendant for Pan-American Airlines, which allowed her to travel around the country and make a very good living. However, in 1991 Pan-American went out of business and Bynum began to fulfill that ministerial calling she first sensed as a child. "My friends said that God shut Pan-Am down because I wouldn't go and preach," she's said. "I knew God was saying that this was my destiny, but I didn't want to hear it."

Through her church, Bynum began speaking at small gatherings. In 1996, she met Bishop T.D. Jakes, who was just beginning to build a name outside of the church world at that time. He invited her to his church's singles' conference in Dallas that year. Jakes knew little of Bynum's past but said that he felt God had something momentous for her to say. Her message at a small women's breakfast went over so well that he asked her to speak at his main event that night. She had nothing prepared to say, but "When I got on that platform," she told *Essence*, "that message had a voice of its own. It wasn't from me—it was from God."

It is the core of that message that served as the foundation for her *No More Sheets* book, which was published by Jakes's then-publisher, Pneuma Life. The book detailed Bynum's sexual escapades and what she felt was behind them. The way out, she reasoned, was through knowing God and who he designated you to be. "Once you get past material things, you can go directly into a relationship saying, 'I need a friend,'" she told *Essence*. "We marry for a couch and we call sex love, but when the sex gets low and the couch gets old, we don't have a friend. That's why I don't have the same criteria for a mate that I once had. I used to think a man had to throw a big rock on my finger." With her past emotional issues settled, Bynum married Thomas Weeks in 2003.

While Bynum was packing church auditoriums with her dynamic speaking, she also decided to start recording praise and worship albums. Showing off her rich, low alto, Bynum's first CD, *Morning Glory, Vol. 1:*

Peace, reached No. 12 on the gospel chart in 1999. In 2002, she reached the gospel Top Ten with *Morning Glory, Vol. 2: Behind the Veil*. She was also a featured vocalist on a gospelized remake of "Because You Loved Me" on *The Williams Brothers: The Concert* CD. Music aside, Bynum has experienced controversy in the church market. She was criticized by some for spending a million dollars on her wedding, while others reject her Holiness theology and believe she uses the gospel to enrich herself. In spite of those concerns, Bynum's music is authentic praise and worship, which stirs the hearts and emotions of those who flock to her meetings.

Shirley Caesar

SINCE THE DEATH IN 1972 of the original Queen of Gospel, Mahalia Jackson, many music critics have crowned Shirley Caesar the heir apparent to Jackson's throne. There are others who arguably feel that Albertina Walker, who gave Shirley her big break and opened the door for a dozen other gospel stars, is more deserving and should be crowned the queen. Regardless of that debate, in terms of sheer sales alone, Caesar is by far the most successful and prolific woman in gospel since Jackson. She began her career with Walker's Caravans, one of the Top Five gospel acts of the 1950s. Caesar then branched out on her own as a solo artist in 1966 with her own unique style of delivering songs and sermonettes that made her an immediate crowd pleaser and a consistent record seller. Over the years, she has made songs such as "Don't Drive Your Mama Away," "No Charge," "Faded Rose," "Jesus," and "Hold My Mule" into absolute gospel classics. If gospel aficionados argue over whether Caesar is the queen or not, one thing everyone agrees on is that she is the First Lady of Gospel.

Born October 13, 1938, in Durham, North Carolina, her early life was filled with church socials, revival meetings, and the like. Caesar's mother, Hallie, devoted her life to the church, and her father, Big Jim Caesar, was a tobacco worker who sang with the Just Come Four, an a cappella quartet in the 1930s. She loved to go watch her father sing and by the age of ten, she had begun singing in church. In 1950, tragedy struck when Caesar's father died of a seizure. For years, she thought her father

had died because he had whipped her that day for breaking a streetlight. The day he died was the day Caesar became a woman. The take-charge youngster began to take her singing seriously, especially since her mother, who was a semi-invalid by this point, was left with 13 children to rear alone. Caesar started touring as a gospel soloist with evangelist Leroy Johnson, whom people used to call "One Leg Leroy" because he only had one leg. Known as Baby Shirley, Caesar made frequent appearances on Johnson's television show in Portsmouth, Virginia. Through his contacts, she cut her first record, "I'd Rather Have Jesus," for Federal Records. "I missed growing up because I took care of my mother from the time I was 12 years old," Caesar has said. "When I graduated from high school, I walked across the stage crying because I knew I hadn't really applied myself. I knew I was an adult now and couldn't go back to being a little girl." She immediately enrolled in North Carolina State College, not knowing exactly what her future would hold. During some leisure time circa 1958, Caesar went to see a Caravans concert when they came through town. The tale goes that one of the members was absent and Caesar went up to Albertina Walker and told her that she knew all the song parts and could sing it. Although Walker smiled, she said no, and Caesar persisted until Walker gave in and allowed Caesar to sing. Legend has it that Caesar sang the Caravans' songs better than they did and Walker asked her to join the group. She dropped out of college and went on the road with America's premier female group.

Two of the primary soloists with the Caravans at the time were Cassietta George and Inez Andrews. Andrews was known for her high-C squalls and for virtually hollering a song to get an audience on its feet. When Caesar joined the group, the pairing of Caesar and Andrews became a show-stopping spectacle. Fans wanted to see them outsing each other. They both had a preacher's approach to a song, half singing and testifying amid moments of preaching to the choir. Caesar's alto was light with a Mexican vibrato (very fast), and Andrews had a piercing alto that she'd build into volcanic explosions of high notes. Caesar would wow the crowd with her "Sweeping Through the City," and Andrews would then pulverize them with "I'm Not Tired Yet." Caesar would come back with "Hallelujah, It's

Done" only for Andrews to turn the place upside down with "Mary, Don't You Weep." It was exhausting for the singers, but the audiences got their money's worth. By the 1960s the Caravans had eclipsed the Ward Singers and become the biggest female draw in gospel music.

Around 1961, Caesar was receiving offers to perform apart from the group. She began taking the dates, but her commitment to the group often got in the way of her scheduling. "I've always been a go-getter," Caesar once said. "I believe in progress and I don't believe in stagnation. I'd already gone as far as I could with the Caravans. Secondly, I had a call to ministry and you're not as free when you're in somebody else's group. What would happen is that Albertina [Walker, the group founder] would say, 'We're off to such and such a time.' And I'd say, 'Can I have these dates?' because people were calling for a revival and she'd say yes. So I'd make those dates and I'd book them. Then somebody would call the group for a concert and Tina would say, 'I'm sorry, you can't go.' And there I was disappointing an audience of people."

Shirley Caesar

In 1966, Caesar solved the problem by leaving the Caravans altogether. Andrews had long been gone by this time, and Caesar was the last remaining star, so the group quickly declined following her exit. Caesar lost no time establishing herself as a solo artist with the Caesar Singers as her backing group. However, she experienced new trials as the boss. Before, Walker and her handlers dealt with the promoters and the business transactions. Caesar learned quickly that just because a man was promoting a gospel concert didn't mean he was a Christian. "They capitalized on me having a soft heart," she once said. "They didn't cheat me, though lying and cheating go hand-in-hand. If I look out there and see the concert hall is running over and you say to me, 'I didn't make enough money to pay you,' well, I've learned to go on stage anyway because the audience is not to be blamed for that. Plus, if I don't go out there, it's not going to reflect on the promoter in the public's eyes. It's going to reflect on me, so that's what I've got to do. I've never taken anyone to court—not that I shouldn't have, but I've never done it. We had a Shirley Caesar Cruise a few years ago. A lot of people in Baltimore went on that and the promoter paid me half of what we were supposed to get and then he wrote me a check for the rest. So I came home and put the check in the bank and paid the group from his check and the check bounced…. I had to make his check good because once I made the checks to the group, they went and cashed their checks…. You can cheat me, but you can't get around justice being done as far as the Lord is concerned, because what you sow is what you reap. Good will come back to you. But if you sow the wind you're going to reap the whirlwind."

By 1969, Caesar had signed to Scepter Record's Hob gospel imprint. Scepter was the company that produced hits for pop acts such as Dionne Warwick, the Shirelles, and Chuck Jackson. Caesar became the biggest act on Hob and in 1969 hit pay dirt with the sermonette "Don't Drive Your Mama Away." In the song, the mother raises two sons. The good son grows up to become a wealthy doctor. The bad son runs off and gets caught up in street life. When the mother grows old, she moves in with her wealthy son, but he and his wife turn against her because she doesn't speak good English and doesn't fit in with their middle-class friends. They put her out, and the bad son shows up to say that she can come live with him even though he eats beans out of the can and doesn't make much money. Caesar preaches the story over a roaring crowd for a good five minutes before she actually begins singing. It's a song in the great tradition of Caesar's vocal hero, Edna Gallmon Cooke, who was the first gospel singer to popularize sermonettes in the 1950s. The song went on to become her first million-seller.

In 1971, Caesar won her first Grammy award for "Put Your Hand in the Hand of the Man from Galilee." As Caesar's name began to grow beyond the gospel field via profiles in *Ebony* magazine and the like, along came offers to sing pop music, to which she'd always quip, "I would sing rock and roll if you let me rock for Jesus and roll for God."

Considering her hard line, it's interesting that some fans accused her of backsliding and singing the devil's music when she recorded an old country song. Caesar had heard Melba Montgomery's version of "No Charge" and decided to record it. "I laid on the floor, wrote out all the words, and tried to tell the story the way she was doing it, and Mom said, 'That's the ugliest song!' I was trying to sing it like her and I couldn't do it," Caesar says. "But when I finished putting it together, boy, Mom loved it. After the song started getting play, my mother started getting phone calls from people accusing me of singing rock and roll. I said all I'm doing is singing about this disobedient boy. Then I did a version where I'm talking about the way Jesus went to the cross and it's no charge. The record company released the religious version of it that went like 'When Jesus went to the cross, he hung, bled, and died, he did it at no charge, and when you add in the cost of real love, there's no charge.' The record company saw how well it was selling and they cut the religious part on the end of it off. But it sold more copies than any other record I've ever done. Second to that was probably 'Don't Drive Your Mama Away' and 'Hold My Mule.'"

The million-selling single reached No. 40 on the R&B chart and No. 91 on the pop charts in 1975. Most gospel music in the 1970s wasn't selling gold, so fans and radio announcers started calling Caesar the First Lady of Gospel. After her contract with Hob Records was finished, Caesar signed to Roadshow Records,

which had artists such as Tina Turner at the time. It was there that she first met executive James Bullard who helped steer her records beyond the gospel world. On the heels of "No Charge," Roadshow released the LP *First Lady* in 1978 and watched it climb to No. 36 on the *Billboard* R&B album charts—Caesar's first LP to do so.

By 1980, Roadshow was out of business and Bullard had become the black gospel A&R chief at Word Records in Waco, Texas, and taken Caesar with him. Her first project was *Rejoice*, which featured her spine-tingling version of Bob Dylan's 1979 smash "Gotta Serve Somebody." Dylan has since said that Caesar's version is his favorite rendition of the song. In the early '80s, one of Caesar's signature songs came to her in the most unique way. A stranger approached her with a song he had written called "Jesus." It was a rainy night and she was due to catch a plane and didn't feel like being bothered at the moment. He was persistent that she listen to it. "I wish I had time, but I don't," she recalls saying. He asked to go with her to the airport and he would sing it on the way. When she arrived at the airport she found that her plane was canceled, so she went back home and looked at the song again. "I didn't like the verses, but I liked the tune. Right there on the spot, I wrote two new verses. I got no credit for that. I wrote two verses on 'Never.' On 'Lord, Let Your Spirit Fall on Me,' I wrote both of those verses. I kind of thought they'd be nice enough to give me the credit, but I was naïve. Even on 'Jesus' I didn't get co-publishing. At any rate, it's such a powerful song that it didn't even matter because it blessed so many people."

It was just the beginning of Caesar's second breath of a career. Every album she has recorded since then has placed on the gospel chart and produced radio hits such as "Yes, Lord, Yes," "He's Working It Out for You," and "Hold My Mule." During the 1980s she found time to finish the Bachelors degree she began when she was with the Caravans in the 1950s. She earned a Master's degree from Duke University and was an elected politician on the Durham city council for a while.

As the years have passed, Caesar's tough stance against secular singers has mellowed. Back in the 1970s, she told *Jet* magazine that secular singers should not sing gospel and vice versa. However, she sang a duet, "Steal Away," with Destiny's Child member Michelle Williams in 2001. More eyebrows rose when she recorded the *Shirley Caesar and Friends* CD, which featured collaborations with gospel and R&B artists. Among the secular singers on the set were Patti LaBelle, Faith Evans, and Gladys Knight. The duet with Evans, entitled "Hurting Woman," received some R&B radio airplay in 2004. Caesar had come a long way from 1991 when she told *Rejoice* magazine, "A song like 'Baby Baby' [Amy Grant], I don't think that's a gospel song. I see contemporary gospel as being gospel with only the music changing, not the words. Anytime you've got a song and the Lord is not mentioned to the extent that it's going to help somebody, you're not listening to a gospel song." Today, Caesar is married to Bishop Harold Williams and pastors the Mount Calvary Word of Faith Holy Church in Raleigh, North Carolina. After nearly a quarter century with Word Records, Caesar established her own Shu-Bel Recording label in 2005.

RECOMMENDED RECORDINGS: Caesar's finest moment was her 1978 LP *First Lady* (Roadshow), which featured her sadly delicious country ballad "Faded Rose," the funky "Message to the People," and her disco-styled take on Stevie Wonder's "Jesus Children of America." The 2003 CD *Greatest Gospel Hits* (Word) features 15 of Caesar's biggest hits from her long tenure with Word Records.

lished artists looking out for him. He did some vocal work on Commissioned's LP *Will You Be Ready?* Daryl Coley turned him on to a recording session that Coley could not do because he was signed to another label. The Wilmington-Chester Mass Choir's Christopher Squire introduced him to AIR Records where he started a nine-member vocal group called Purpose. Their debut produced hits such as "Transparent in Your Presence" and "Dwell Among Us." While in Atlanta, Cage began a ten-year stint as a music director for the 20,000-member New Birth Missionary Baptist Church. Since 1998, Cage has been minister of music at Ebenezer AME Church in Ft. Washington, Maryland.

For a while, it seemed that Cage's greatest contribution to gospel music would be as a songwriter, having written songs such as Jonathan Creer's "Count It All Joy" (1993), Wilmington-Chester Mass Choir's "Anytime, Anywhere" (1994), Full Gospel Baptist Fellowship Mass Choir's "Yet Praise Him" (1998), and the Greater St. Stephen Mass Choir's "You Are My Potion" (1999). Still, Cage is actively seeking to carve out a niche for himself in the secular marketplace with an urban style of gospel in the mode of Kirk Franklin. "My greatest desire," Cage has said, "is that the Lord takes this music to the masses. I look at myself as just a vessel that I pray God is going to use to get his music to many, many of his people and draw them closer to him."

Byron Cage

ONE OF THE MANY MARQUEE choir conductors to rise since the advent of Kirk Franklin in the early 1990s, Byron Cage was originally best known for introducing the choir Purpose back in 1995. His 2003 CD *The Prince of Praise* catapulted him into gospel stardom on the radio strength of "There Is a Name" and "The Presence of the Lord Is Here."

Born on December 15, 1962, Cage was raised in Detroit. Both of his parents sang and he attended the same church that the DeBarge singing family attended. The late choir conductor Donald Vails was a mentor to Cage at the time, as was Thomas Whitfield. Cage began singing in earnest as a teenager. He had lots of estab-

Cedric and Victor Caldwell

PERHAPS THE MOST SOPHISTICATED producers in modern gospel music, Victor and Cedric Caldwell's jazzy hands have produced slick gospel tracks on music by Whitney Houston, Take 6, Andrae Crouch, Chantée Moore, Bobby Brown, Donnie McClurkin, and CeCe Winans, among others. The Grammy-winning duo takes the traditional gospel idiom and enhances it with flourishes of smooth jazz and the polish of classical music.

The Caldwell brothers consider their parents, Dr. and Mrs. Virgil Caldwell, significant factors in the creation of Caldwell Plus (their early duo name and later the name of their production company). Dr. Caldwell was a band director when the two brothers were growing up.

Consequently, they were exposed to music and to piano lessons at a very early age. "Our parents used various means of parental persuasion to see to it that we practiced regularly," recalls Cedric, who began studying classical piano at the age of seven. Victor, five years younger than Cedric, says that a daily practice session was a requirement, and their mother made sure of that, with belt in hand. Of course, he adds, "There were times when I would slip by and go outside without practicing." At the church their father pastors, Victor was the Sunday school guitarist for several years and Cedric was the church pianist until he went away to attend college.

The two continued their musical studies through high school, and both attended Middle Tennessee State University. Cedric graduated with a Bachelor of Arts degree in music and continued on to receive his Masters degree in education. When Victor entered MTSU toward the end of Cedric's stay, the Caldwell brothers decided to write as a team. Upon leaving MTSU, Cedric moved to Chattanooga, Tennessee, where he was a junior high school band and choir teacher for seven years. In 1983, Victor left for Nashville after receiving his Bachelor of Science degree in audio engineering. He worked at LSI studio as a staff engineer. Easy access to recording facilities enabled Victor and Cedric to put their compositions on tape. Later, Victor began playing on sessions as a studio musician and as bass guitarist for the contemporary Christian group the Imperials.

One day, Victor gave a demo of Caldwell Plus songs to Chris Smith, general manager of Morgan Music Group. Smith was so overwhelmed by the tape that, according to Cedric, "He started calling people and carrying the tape around with him." He also signed the brothers as exclusive writers. Shortly after that, they became staff producers for the group's production company. Soon they were co-producing the Spinners, Jane Powell, and contemporary Christian artist Andrea Marcee. Smith communicated his enthusiasm for the Caldwells' music to some key executives at MCA Record's Master Series label. After they landed a contract with the label, Victor and Cedric began planning for their debut album, *As We Bop.*

Even though Victor and Cedric are brothers, they approach music from different, though complementary, angles. "I came from the jazz side," says Cedric. "Victor was into recording and the technical aspect." Victor says he will often come up with the form and changes for a tune, then will give it to Cedric, who writes the melody and sometimes alters some chord changes. The mix of contemporary jazz and smooth urban grooves on their debut project was well-received in the jazz community, but the duo opted not to do another album for the label because they decided to go into gospel music instead.

After traveling as pianist for R&B gospel duo BeBe and CeCe Winans for several years, Cedric decided to devote himself to only gospel music. In late 1994, he and Victor formed Caldwell Plus Productions. Traditionally, a record company must work through several different organizations in order to produce an album; they rent a studio and hire a producer, an engineer, and musicians. Cedric and Victor realized that their talents and abilities enabled them to consolidate the entire production process by producing the songs, engineering the sessions, playing the instruments, and renting the studio. Since the inception of their production firm, they have produced a number of stellar tracks. They produced the B-side to Whitney Houston's mega

Caldwell Brothers / photographer Erick Anderson *for* Father's Image

million-seller "I'll Always Love You," CeCe Winans's platinum Grammy-winning album *Alone in His Presence*, and Donnie McClurkin's breakthrough singles "Stand" and "Speak to My Heart."

In early 1997, the Caldwells teamed up with Cedric's wife Angie and her sister Debbie to found Against the Flow Records. The first release by Angie & Debbie, entitled *Bold*, peaked at No. 3 on *Billboard*'s gospel charts and remained a top-seller for over a year. Since then, they have produced acclaimed albums by Ann McCrary and Mom & Pop Winans, as well as Angie Winans's Grammy-nominated smooth jazz CD *Melodies of My Heart*. The Caldwells put the label on hold when their distributor went out of business in 2002. They have continued to produce hit recordings for Patti LaBelle, T.D. Jakes, Smokie Norful, and Brandy, among others.

Bridgette Campbell

THE YOUNGEST OF FOUR PKS (pastor's kids), Campbell was born in July 1974 in Mayfield, Illinois, and first sang in church at the age of three. She sang throughout grade school and won her big break singing on Ricky Dillard and the New Generation Chorale's *A Holy Ghost Take-Over* CD in 1993. She led the songs "He Will Forgive," "If My People," and "Lord, You Are All." In 1994, Campbell began touring with her brother, Jesse Campbell. The Hughes Brothers, who produced the films *Menace II Society* and *House Party*, launched a Capitol Records–distributed label, Underground Records, with Jesse as their flagship artist. The handsome young singer enjoyed a brief spell as a sex symbol. His R&B croonings such as "The Comfort of Your Man," "Baby Baby Baby," and "When You Cry I Cry" were minor radio successes. They were also expressive and seductive without emphasizing the act of sex. After Jesse's promotional tour was over, he and Bridgette returned to gospel work. Jesse did background vocals on Evelyn Turrentine Agee's "God Did It" and other songs. Bridgette backed Calvin Rhone, Heaven Sent, and B. Chase Williams and the Shabach Choir. She kept performing cameos on a series of projects, including a very high-profile vocal on Fred

Hammond's "Don't Pass Me By" on the 2000 *Purpose by Design* video. After touring with Jesse Dixon in Europe, Campbell starred as CoCo in the Judge Greg Mathis and Phyllis Stickney play *Been There, Done That*. With such a full résumé, the full-voiced singer didn't wait to be discovered. She produced and released her own CD, *Bridgette*, on From the Heart Records in 2003 before Light Records released her national debut, *Been Good*, in 2004.

RECOMMENDED RECORDING: *Been Good* (Light Records, 2004) has jazzy moments but is largely a contemporary throwback to traditional gospel music with plenty of foot-stomping beats and hooks. Campbell possesses a firm, striking voice that reaches right through the earphones and captures the listener.

Lamar Campbell

"I'M A RADICAL PRAISER," Lamar Campbell once said, and he has gone to great lengths to prove the point with his urban contemporary choir, Spirit of Praise. Born February 13, 1964, in Indianapolis, Indiana, Campbell comes from a tight family where he enjoyed the company of three siblings. He was raised in the Haughville Seventh Day Adventist church and taught himself to play several instruments. After graduating from Broad Ripple High School, Campbell attended Butler University. He soon became a music minister and formed a group in 1987. Campbell admits to developing an arrogance about the group's success. In order to humble himself, he disbanded the group and refocused his life on God's work. He became music minister at Light of the World Christian Church and formed Spirit of Praise in 1995. They signed with EMI Gospel on his birthday and their eponymous first CD debuted at No. 21 on *Billboard*'s gospel charts in spring 1998. Since the choir's debut, they have toured with CeCe Winans and appeared with Aaron Neville on NBC's *Today Show* and CBS's *Late Show with David Letterman*. Among their successful radio singles are "Stand Up on Your Feet" and "When I Think About You."

Canton Spirituals

FOUNDED IN CANTON, MISSISSIPPI, in 1946, the original group was led by singer and songwriter Harvey Watkins, Sr. The current lead singer, Harvey Watkins, Jr., performed with the group intermittently since he was a child. The original members were Eddie Jackson, Theo Thompson, and Roscoe Lucious. They recorded for small local labels and performed regularly throughout the Southeastern United States. It wasn't until they signed with J&B Records in 1985 that they developed a national following. That's the year their LP *Mississippi Po Boy* was released. They released several other respectable hits over the next decade. Their 1995 *Live in Memphis* CD for Blackberry Records spent 169 weeks on the gospel chart and sold just under 500,000 copies. When they recorded for Verity Records in the late 1990s, they enjoyed the biggest hits of their career with songs such as "Been Good" and "Clean Up." The group is keeping that down-South quartet tradition alive with just a touch of modern instrumentation to attract younger listeners.

Caravans

IN THE 1950s, THE CARAVANS lacked the Clara Ward Singers' flashy costumes and stage clowning, but they more than made up for it with the quality of their many classic hits such as "Mary, Don't You Weep," "I Won't Be Back," and "Sweeping Through the City." Even more so, the group was esteemed for the number of gospel legends it birthed, including Shirley Caesar, Inez Andrews, Bessie Griffin, James Cleveland, and its founder, Albertina Walker.

Walker formed the Caravans in Chicago in 1952 with the original roster of Ora Lee Hopkins, Elyse Yancey, and Nellie Grace Daniels. The personnel changed regularly. Walker, a shrewd leader, recognized that her voice wasn't always the best fit for every song and she routinely showcased the talents of others. At various times over the next five years, the group included Bessie Griffin, Dorothy Norwood, and their pianist, James Cleveland. However, the 1958 aggrega-

tion of Inez Andrews, Shirley Caesar, Walker, and Delores Washington was the most successful grouping. The combination of Caesar's youthful energy and squalling soprano, Andrews's shrieking high-Cs, Washington's sweet high notes, and Walker's crusty rasp made for a delicious listening experience.

By the early 1960s, the Ward Singers had tailored their performances to the supper-club crowd in Las Vegas. Instead of proclaiming the gospel, they served up a pop-styled message of love and brotherhood. The Caravans stole the Wards' previous position as the No. 1 female gospel group with their music, which remained church-based and thoroughly gospel. Personnel such as Josephine Howard, Delores Washington, and pianist James Herndon had replaced those who left for solo careers, as Andrews did in 1962. Aside from the aforementioned hits, they continued to enjoy hits into the sixties with cuts such as "Make It In" (1961), "I Won't Be Back" (1962), "No Coward Soldier" (1963), and "Walk Around Heaven" (1964) for the Vee-Jay Records label.

In 1966, Caesar, who had become the star attraction, left the group, and within months only Walker remained. She recruited a new set of Caravans that included teenager Loleatta Holloway, who would have disco hits such as "Run Away" and "Love Sensation" a decade later. After a few good but uneventful LPs for Savoy Records through 1971, Walker finally retired the group. In the years since, there have been numerous Caravans reunions with Caesar, Andrews, Walker, Washington, Norwood, and the late Cassietta George.

RECOMMENDED RECORDINGS: *The Best of the Caravans* (Savoy Records, 1977) features classics such as "Mary, Don't You Weep." Another good buy is the CD *Seek Ye the Lord/The Soul of the Caravans* (Collectables Records, 2001) which features two of their best albums for Vee-Jay Records.

Bob Carlisle

BOB CARLISLE POSSESSES ONE of the best voices in Christian music—full, rich, and handsome. He also owns one of the bestselling songs in Christian music history, "Butterfly Kisses." Carlisle was born September 9, 1956, in Santa Ana, California. His career started in the late 1970s with numerous recording sessions for artists such as Bryan Duncan and Sandi Patti. Over the years, he sang and played guitar for Christian bands such as Good News and Psalm 150. However, his longest association was with the Allies, who formed in 1984. They had a bluesy, Southern rock sound that mixed well with Carlisle's soulful vocals. Their albums *Allies*, *Shoulder to Shoulder*, *Long Way to Paradise*, and *Man with a Mission* were all Top 25 CCM best sellers. In 1992, Carlisle went solo, moved to Nashville, and wrote Dolly Parton's No. 1 comeback hit "Why'd You Come in Here Lookin' Like That?" After striking up a deal with Sparrow Records, he enjoyed radio hits such as "Giving You the Rest of My Life" and "Getting Stronger."

By 1996, Carlisle had moved on to Diadem Records where he enjoyed a moderate hit from his *Shades of Grace* CD, entitled "Mighty Love." He wrote another tune for his daughter, Brooke. "I was alone in my office one night, and I came to the realization that I don't have this child under my roof for too much longer," Carlisle told *Billboard* magazine in 1997. "I pulled out some photos of me walking her on a horse and different things that are depicted in the song, and I just came unglued. The song poured out of me. It was just a gift for her." The song was called "Butterfly Kisses" and became a decent Christian radio hit. It received new life when Clive Calder took over Diadem's parent company, Zomba Music. Calder was reviewing all of the music on the label and came across the song. He felt it had mainstream potential and had his ample radio team push the song on pop radio. The song eventually shot up to No. 1 on the adult contemporary pop singles chart and the repackaged CD *Butterfly Kisses* sold over 2 million copies in 1997. Carlisle has yet to match that success with his subsequent recordings. He did create the first rendition of "We Fall Down," which turned out to be the biggest recording of Donnie McClurkin's career thus far.

RECOMMENDED RECORDING: *Collection* (EMI, 2002) doesn't include "Butterfly Kisses," but it does have Carlisle's other great Christian radio singles.

Carman

SUPERSTAR OR SUPER WHACK, Carman has been called both. He was one of the bestselling CCM recording artists of the 1990s with an amazing string of 20 gold records and big-budget music videos. He was born Dominic Licciardello on January 19, 1956, in Trenton, New Jersey. His father was a meat cutter and his mother was a musician. He always enjoyed music and played both the drums (in his mother's band) and the guitar as a teenager. When he came of age, he went to Las Vegas to launch a career as a pop artist in 1976. He sang in clubs for a couple of years until he was invited to an Andrae Crouch concert. "I gave my life to the Lord at one of his concerts," he told *Totally Gospel* magazine in April 1987. "I saw the spiritual intensity. The anointing was in his songs, it changed my life." Carman then devoted himself to launching a Christian music ministry. He moved to Tulsa, Oklahoma, and began attending Bishop Carlton Pearson's church. Carman released his first LP, *Some-O-Dat*, in 1982 and sold it out of the trunk of his 1973 Vega.

Carman kept hustling until his CCM singles such as "Sunday's on the Way" began to receive airplay. Eventually, Myrrh Records saw the potential and signed Carman to a recording deal. With his swarthy, handsome looks, Carman became an instant Christian sex symbol and women bought his music in droves. He began to tailor his music toward the youth market and developed an equally strong following among both male and female youth. Songs such as "Lazarus, Come Forth" and "Champion" made him an instant favorite. Furthermore, Carman's dramatic music videos illuminated the messages behind his songs to a greater degree than his lightweight vocal performances. The critics often viewed his music, particularly his urban raps like the ridiculous "Who's in the House" from *The Standard* CD, as laughable. "We have touched a lot of people with what the critics have rejected," Carman told *CCM* magazine. "I am used to being criticized, but one thing no one has ever asked me was, 'Why do you do it?' And there is a specific reason. It is because, before I actually went into ministry full time, the Lord impressed upon my heart to do two things: unite the generations and unite the denominations."

Regardless of what critics thought, the public could not get enough of Carman. His donation-only concerts (complete with elaborate sets, laser lights, and choreography) filled football stadiums nationwide during the 1990s. His 1994 concert at Texas Stadium in Dallas had an attendance of 71,132—the largest Christian gathering in America up to that time. In recent years, Carman has cut back on his live concert performances and toned down the funk element in his music for a softer, more adult contemporary style as opposed to the young sound he espoused earlier.

RECOMMENDED RECORDING: *Heart of a Champion* (2000) is a deluxe two-CD set of Carman's biggest hits such as the novelty tunes "Satan, Bite the Dust!" and "Who's in the House."

Kurt Carr

ONE OF THE MOST POPULAR choir leaders of the new millennium, Kurt Carr toiled in the vineyard a good decade or more before he realized true fame and glory. His breakout and breakthrough CD *Awesome Wonder* established him as a major force in gospel music in 2000. The diminutive, highly energetic conductor with the little boy's voice has made good for himself. Born October 11, 1964, in Hartford, Connecticut, to a nonchurchgoing home, Carr began to attend services on his own at the age of 13. He grew up on the standard church fare for kids in the 1970s: Walter Hawkins, James Cleveland, and Andrae Crouch. "I had a natural ear for music, and my mother saw my interest in gospel, so she bought me a Walter Hawkins album around that time," Carr says. "It literally changed my life. I listened to it every single day for at least a year or two, and I taught myself how to play piano from those songs."

Carr graduated from the University of Connecticut with a degree in fine arts. He was later mentored by the classically trained Richard Smallwood who taught him to incorporate a variety of musical influences into black gospel. Carr's most significant training ground was the years he spent under the tutelage of Rev. James Cleveland. "Rev. Cleveland taught me hymns and other standard gospel songs," Carr told *Gospel Industry Today*

magazine in 2000. "While working with Rev. Cleveland I was exposed to many great pioneers of gospel music, including the Caravans, Shirley Caesar, and the Mighty Clouds of Joy. What I didn't realize is this exposure would be the foundation to support my ministry of music today." He began working with Cleveland in 1986 as his pianist. He eventually became the singer's musical director and remained so until Cleveland's death in 1991—the same year he made his first CD, *Together*, for Light Records. The album by the Kurt Carr Singers featured the gospel version of Mikki Howard's "Love Under New Management" and rose to No. 11 on the gospel album chart.

After Light Records closed, Carr was signed by Gospo Centric Records, which made noise with his *Serious About It!* CD in 1994. Because of the mega-success of lablemate Kirk Franklin around the same time, Carr and other artists on the label's roster were somewhat ignored as the label's resources were poured into capitalizing on the Franklin phenomenon. Therefore, it was 1997 before Carr's next CD, *No One Else*, was released. That album was his biggest yet, selling well over 100,000 copies. Carr's 2000 CD *Awesome Wonder* surprised the gospel music industry by catapulting the singer to instant celebrity status within black church circles. Churches across America were suddenly singing songs from the CD, which eventually sold a half million copies. Carr also serves as creative director/music minister for the West Angeles Church of God in Christ in Los Angeles.

Wynona Carr

IN SPITE OF HER LOW PROFILE, Wynona Carr was one of gospel's best modern gospel composers and performers of the 1950s. The narrow-minded church world of the period wasn't ready for this beautiful woman who was way ahead of her time. Her sensual voice, thought-provoking lyrics, and secular music style was never appreciated by the gospel world at large. She later switched to pop music but never got lucky and died in obscurity. Many of the songs she wrote for herself were eventually covered by other better-known artists such as vocal group Manhattan Transfer, who used her song "Operator" as the closing song each week on their 1975 CBS television variety show.

Born on August 23, 1924, in Cleveland, Ohio, Carr learned piano by the age of eight and enrolled at the age of 13 in the Cleveland Music College. As a teenager, she sang in Baptist churches around the city and in 1944, she relocated to Detroit where she was soon directing a local choir and eventually formed her own group, the Carr Singers. She also toured with the Wilson Jubilee Singers, who were formed from the Wings Over Jordan Choir. While sharing a show bill with the Pilgrim Travelers, Carr caught the attention of the group's manager, J.W. Alexander. He paid for her initial demo and sent it to the group's recording label, Specialty Records. Label owner Art Rupe, a white man with a flair for picking black talent, signed Carr on. In 1949, she showed up in Los Angeles for her first recording session. Carr brought to the sessions her education as an arranger, musician, songwriter, and vocalist. Rupe respected what Decca Records had accomplished with Sister Rosetta Tharpe and he added "Sister" to Carr's name hoping to capitalize indirectly off of Tharpe's vast fame at the time. A proud woman, Carr was initially angered by the comparison and the strategy, but put her feelings aside. Backed by the Austin McCoy combo, her debut 78-rpm was the jump tune "Each Day" backed by the ballad "Lord Jesus."

Some of Carr's next singles were a revamp of "St. James Infirmary" as "I'm a Pilgrim Traveler" and a re-working of Roy Brown and Wynonie Harris's "Good Rockin' Tonight" as "I Heard the News (Jesus Is Coming Again)." By transforming familiar secular songs into gospel ones, Carr was doing what Rance Allen would be hailed as a genius for 20 years later. However, in her time it was considered sacrilegious. Churches still believed in just a simple piano for gospel music and found anything else to be worldly. Consequently, Carr received very little radio airplay and lukewarm acceptance when she appeared on church programs. Oddly enough, she wrote prolifically and was able to make more money through sheet music sales than through record sales. She also took a regular position as organist and choir director at C.L. Franklin's Bethlehem Baptist Church. It was there that she met Joe Von Battle, who would record Aretha

Franklin's first tracks a couple of years later. He produced Carr's first and only decent-size gospel hit, 1953's "Ball Game," a vivid tale of a showdown between Jesus and Satan using baseball terminology.

In hindsight it's easy to see why Carr was not successful as a gospel artist. Most gospel artists didn't emphasize their beauty and she was a beautiful woman who dressed the part. Most gospel artists wrecked churches by holding elongated notes and impassioned squalling. Carr's sensual alto with its subtle rasp was more akin to Pearl Bailey than to the average gospel singer. She sang with much passion, but it was the earthy, swinging passion of the juke joint rather than the humble, backwoods swagger of most church folks. They could not relate to her vocal delivery and they scratched their collective heads over the lyrical content of her well thought-out songs.

Gospel thrived on clichés and simple lyrics about the Christian faith. "Ball Game" aside, the church world rejected the romping "Dragnet for Jesus" and even the clever "15 Rounds with Jesus." The song "15 Rounds with Jesus" showed Carr boxing Satan to defend God's honor. "I'm gonna win this fight for Jesus and I'm going 15 rounds," she sang. "I only have one worry, I know that he won't fight fair, but with my God to guide me, I can whip him anywhere." The problem for most gospel fans is that they didn't fight God's battles. They let God fight their battles for them. Ambitious, Carr was constantly pleading with Art Rupe to do more for her career. He seemed to have a soft spot for her, advancing her money when she needed it and giving her what was in his power to give. He wanted her to have a hit record as much as she did and teamed her with his top draw, Brother Joe May. They recorded several songs, but the closest to a hit was "What Do You Know About Jesus?"

Rupe was able to get Carr added to a mainstream tour with Sister Rosetta Tharpe and Madame Marie Knight in 1954. That tour took Carr to a mostly white audience that had never experienced her brilliant music before. Those two factors, along with the between-show girl talk between the headliners who had dabbled in secular music and been criticized by the church, caused Carr to leave gospel music altogether. The tour concluded in December, and in January 1955 Carr sent

Rupe a letter asking him to allow her to sing pop music instead of gospel. "Look what Epic did for Roy Hamilton's 'You'll Never Walk Alone,'" she wrote in one epistle. "I could play all the clubs and not be limited to my own people."

Rupe agreed to give it a try but as a backup. He suggested she drop "Sister" from her name to distinguish her new musical direction from her old one. Besides, he reasoned, if the pop sortie failed, she might want to return to gospel. She dropped both "Sister" and "Carr" and just became Wynona. While she began working on songs for her secular debut as a pop artist, Carr pushed Rupe to get other artists to record her compositions. She spoke to Tharpe directly about recording some of her tunes and suggested that Rupe get Kay Starr to record "Operator." Meanwhile, Carr's first pop tryouts "Please Mr. Jailer" (which would show up more than 30 years later in the movie *Cry-Baby*) and "Hurt Me" were only regional hits—not the national hits she was looking for. Rupe kept massaging Carr's ego, though she was given to severe mood swings. One day she was optimistic and the next fatally depressed about her career. Her next songs, "What Do You Know About Love?" and "Give Me Your Hand to Hold," were very good, but just didn't catch on. In 1957 "Should I Ever Love Again" reached No. 15 on the black singles chart and Carr's career was finally on its way. In the midst of her greatest success, Carr was diagnosed with tuberculosis and retired to her parents' home in Cleveland for what would be a two-year recovery. Clubs wanted her to perform, but she couldn't and her career suffered irreparable damage.

By the time Carr bounced back to health in 1959, she was basically a new artist who had to start all over again. Sonny Bono (of Sonny and Cher fame), who was Little Richard's chauffeur at the time, produced the rousing "I'm Mad at You" in 1959, but it failed to find an audience. Carr began to receive some concert dates, but her career was stalled. She left Specialty Records, which was on the verge of folding anyway, and signed with Frank Sinatra's Reprise label in 1961. The label sported sophisticated acts such as Sammy Davis, Jr., so Carr had high hopes that Sinatra's influence and prestige would open doors for her career. In spite of slick

Neal Hefti arrangements, her mix of faith-inspired ("Down by the Riverside") and pop songs ("I Gotta Stand Tall") still could not find a regular audience. She performed at venues around Cleveland throughout the 1960s, but as she moved into her forties she realized all her chances had been spent. At that time, if a female singer didn't make her mark before the age of 40, it was unlikely that she ever would because the industry (especially in the pop field) would write you off. Carr had no intentions of going back to gospel, so she quit the business and spent her remaining years in a depressive state of mind, passing away on May 12, 1976. Aside from Manhattan Transfer, other artists who have covered Carr's gospel songs include the Edwin Hawkins Singers and Joe Liggins ("Don't Miss that Train"), the Five Blind Boys of Mississippi ("Our Father"), the Persuasions ("Ball Game"), and the Sallie Martin Singers, who recorded several of her songs.

Mel Carter

BEST KNOWN FOR A STRONG two-year run on the pop charts in 1965–1966, Carter's smooth tenor shined best on the No. 1 adult contemporary chart hits "Hold Me, Thrill Me, Kiss Me" and "Band of Gold." During that stretch, his other hits included "(All of a Sudden) My Heart Sings," "Love Is All We Need," and "Take Good Care of You." He was never a soul singer. Instead, he was a black man with a mainstream pop style similar to that of Johnny Mathis or Nat King Cole.

Born April 22, 1939, in Cincinnati, Ohio, Carter first sang at a penny arcade when he was four years old and later had a brief gig with jazz great Lionel Hampton. As a teenager, Carter sang with the Raspberry Singers gospel group before forming his own gospel ensemble, the Cavetts. He sang briefly with the Gospel Pearls before Quincy Jones discovered him and signed him to Mercury Records in 1959. He later signed with Sam Cooke's SAR/ABKCO Records where he recorded the syrupy "When a Boy Falls in Love" in 1963. A switch to Imperial Records led to his aforementioned hits such as "Hold Me, Thrill Me, Kiss Me." Known as an all-around entertainer, Carter maintained a Hollywood presence as a television actor on such shows as *Sanford and Son, The Rifleman,* and *Magnum, P.I.* while continuing his recording and stage work. In 1984, Carter recorded a gospel LP for Inyx Records called *Willing.* It included songs such as "Lift Him Up" and "When I'm Weak." The album won Carter his only Grammy and NAACP Image award nominations thus far.

CBS Trumpeteers

VERY POPULAR IN THE LATE 1940s through the mid-'50s, this Baltimore-based quartet started as simply the Trumpeters in 1946 when Joseph Johnson founded the organization. They began a radio show on WCAO in Baltimore where they sang live on the air. The buzz from the show led to a national radio show on CBS Radio and a record deal with Score Records. Their biggest hit was the bluesy "Milky White Way" in 1947. More than a decade later, Elvis Presley recorded a version of the song. The Trumpeters changed their name in the 1950s to mirror their CBS Radio show, but eventually faded from the musical landscape as musical styles changed.

CBS *Trumpeteers / uncredited publicity photo, courtesy of Capital Entertainment archives*

Eric Champion

HE WAS NEVER A MAMMOTH STAR like his contemporaries such as Steven Curtis Chapman, but Eric Champion more than held his own and created some of contemporary Christian music's most eclectic and rhythmically appealing music of the early 1990s. Born May 12, 1970, in Daytona Beach, Florida, Champion traveled and performed with his parents' music ministry as a child. He had a gift for instruments and learned to play a variety of them, from keyboards to accordions. After high school, Champion attended Oral Roberts University where he studied acting. Meanwhile, he was writing music and recording demo tapes. His mother sent one of those tapes to producer and Myrrh Records executive Chris Christian, who circulated them among his industry colleagues. Eventually, Christian artists such as Mike Eldred, Truth, and Area Code were recording his ditties. He wrote "Imagine Love" for Kim Boyce and co-penned "Here I Am" with Rebecca St. James for her debut CD in 1994.

By 1990, Champion's self-titled debut CD was in stores and had yielded dance-styled fan favorites such as "We Are the Young," "Everyday People," and "Forever Love." Over the balance of his albums, Champion leaped from electronica to pop and back to dance vibes, totally confounding the music critics and defying categorization. In 1992, he created one of the best Christmas CDs that almost no one has heard, featuring a shimmering dance version of "Little Drummer Boy," downright funky versions of "Angels We Have Heard on High" and "God Rest Ye Merry Gentlemen," a doo-wopish "Away in a Manger/Silent Night" medley, and a futuristic take on "It Came Upon a Midnight Clear." Instead of taking the easy listening stance many take with holiday music, Champion also crafted four strong original songs, including a Beach Boys-styled "Hot Christmas" (a humorous tune where he celebrates Christmas with a Florida tan) and the jazzed-up "Somebody's Santa."

In spring 1993, Champion's *The Answer* spent three weeks at No. 1 on the CCM charts, and two years later he visited that position again with *Touch.* His last project, *Transformation,* was for Essential Records and resulted in two Top Ten CCM singles, "Dress Me Up" and "Life Form," in 1996. By the age of 27, Champion had tired of industry politics and the pressure to produce megahits. He moved to the Orlando, Florida, suburb of Deland where he's now married with kids.

In 2003 he told CCM magazine that he planned to make another album in the future. "It's neat to make music," he said. "I still love pop music, and I'm sure people that hear the new stuff will hear some of the old stuff as well because that's just who I am." Since that time, Champion has recorded some independent music that is available on his Web site at www .ericchampion.com.

Gary Chapman

UNFORTUNATELY, HE'S BEST KNOWN as Amy Grant's ex-husband; but Gary Chapman is a fine, soulful singer in his own right. Born August 19, 1957, in Texas, he came to know Grant when he wrote her 1979 hit "My Father's Eyes." The two eventually married, but they had numerous ups and downs over Chapman's well-documented battles with the bottle. They divorced in 1999. Before the breakup, they collaborated on songs and toured together. Chapman has written songs for artists ranging from Kenny Rogers to T.J. Shepherd. At the same time, he carried on a successful solo career with hit songs such as "Where Do I Go?" and "Where Are the Broken Hearts?" He also hosted *Prime Time Country*, a nightly talk show on The Nashville Network (TNN) for four years before it was cancelled in 1999.

Charles Fold Singers

ONE OF REV. JAMES CLEVELAND's favorite ensembles for collaborations, the Charles Fold Singers backed him on the gospelized cover of Gladys Knight and the Pips' "The Best Thing that Ever Happened to Me" from the late 1970s. Fold was born June 4, 1934, in Cincinnati, Ohio. His ensemble gained fame for the nine traditional gospel LPs they recorded with Cleveland. From this union came bestselling albums such as *This Too Will Pass*, *Thank You, Lord, for One More Day*, and *Lord, Let Me Be an Instrument*, which won a Grammy for Best Soul Gospel Traditional Album in 1981. The Fold Singers have also recorded 25 years' worth of music of their own for Savoy Records, with "Never Will I Turn Back" being one of their larger hits. Today, Fold is the music director at the Lincoln Heights Missionary Baptist Church in Cincinnati. "Music rouses something in you that probably nothing else can bring out," he once told the *Cincinnati Enquirer*. "Music can make you cry. It can make you laugh."

Ray Charles

AN AMERICAN MUSICAL INSTITUTION, Ray Charles was perhaps the most influential black singer of the 20th century. His influence was broad and reached deep into the country market, the rock field, the soul arena, and even into the gospel world. He was born September 23, 1930, in Albany, Georgia. Glaucoma stole his eyesight when he was seven years old, and Charles subsequently studied music at the Augustine School for the Deaf and Blind.

His parents died before he became an adult, but his mother instilled in him a faith and self-reliance he carried the rest of his life. "She made me do everything other kids did," he told *Parade* magazine in August 1988. "I had to make my bed. I had to scrub the floor and wash the dishes. My mom taught me how to cook…. She knew I was going to lose my sight, she knew she had to teach me how to do normal things, to learn so I could take care of myself when she was gone."

By the time he was 15, Charles's mother was gone. He dropped out of school and moved to Florida where he made his first recordings. "Ray loved blues singers like Joe Turner, but most of all he loved gospel singers," Renald Richard told Charles's biographer Michael Lydon. "He used to talk all the time about Archie Brownlee, the lead singer with the Five Blind Boys of Mississippi, how much he liked him. Then he started to sound like him, turning his notes, playing with them to work the audience into a frenzy." Charles put those skills to good use when he became a star in the '50s and '60s. He turned out a long line of hit records that could have easily been gospel with a change of lyrics. Among his standards during the period were "I Can't Stop Loving You," "Hallelujah, I Love Her So," and "What'd I'd Say?"

During the '60s, Charles was a heroin addict and a womanizer. He eventually overcame his addictions and continued to perform until shortly before his death. In spite of his ups and downs, he still felt fortunate. "There's nothing written in the Bible, in the Old or New Testament, where it says: If you believe in me, you ain't going to have no trouble…" Charles told *Parade* magazine. "Although I've had bad things happen to me—let's face it, let's be honest about it—would you say I'm better off, more well off, than most sighted people?… I'm blessed that I'm able to say that to you." Charles passed away from liver disease on June 10, 2004.

RECOMMENDED RECORDINGS: Sprinkled throughout the Charles catalog are gospel songs that most gospel audiences have never heard. There are a couple of gospel numbers, "My God and I" and "Heaven Help Us All," on Charles's inspirational compilation Ray Charles Sings for America (Rhino Records, 2002).

Julius Cheeks

IF EVER A SINGER SANG for their supper, it was truly Rev. Julius Cheeks. He was perhaps the hardest-singing singer of his generation in the 1950s, and his gritty, baritone vocal style was adopted by R&B stars such as James Brown and Wilson Pickett. Cheeks was born on August 7, 1929, in Spartanburg, South Carolina. His widowed mother, Big Chick, raised 13 children on her own. Cheeks quit elementary school when he was in the second grade, so that he could earn money by picking cotton. He was illiterate and could barely write his own name. Music took Cheeks's mind off his circumstances. His next-door neighbors had a radio and he spent many a Sunday at their house listening to quartets singing across the airwaves. In 1946, he joined a gospel quartet calling itself the Baronets. They shared a bill with the Five Blind Boys of Mississippi one night when the Blind Boys' manager, Barney Parks, took a hard listen to Cheeks's voice. The next day, Parks showed up at Cheeks's regular gig at a gas station. Parks handed him $10 and told him to be in Charleston that night. Parks put Cheeks in a group known as the Sensational Nightingales. Cheeks immediately fell into place as a

stage clown who would get the audience revved up over his jokes and his out-of-nowhere shrieks and wails. He quickly became known as the hardest singer in gospel. In spite of his success with the group, Cheeks made nothing but meal money. He left the group and joined the Soul Stirrers for a better paycheck. The Nightingales lured him back with better pay, and they soon enjoyed a string of hits on Peacock Records, such as "Last Mile of the Way."

By 1960, Cheeks had retired from the group and was preaching full time. He eventually formed a group called the Sensational Knights (aka the Four Knights), but they failed to gain much attention. He later disbanded the group and joined the Mighty Clouds of Joy briefly in the late 1960s before going solo in the 1970s. He also recorded a handful of solos during the period such as the chilling "There's a Man Going Around Taking Names" and "If Serving God Is Wrong (I Don't Want to Be Right)," a play on a Luther Ingram R&B song about romantic infidelity. Cheeks preached at churches in Baltimore, Newark, and finally in Miami where he died on January 27, 1981. Cheeks sang so hard and pushed his voice to its limits so often that he eventually lost much of the texture that distinguished it early on. However, the diminishing voice did not curb his stage dynamics. Though ragged and uneven at the end of his life, he still pushed it to the sheer delight of his dwindling audience. Candi Staton, whose group the Jewel Gospel Trio used to open for the Nightingales, says, "Julius sang so hard that he just sang himself to death." Cheeks's daughter, Judy, experienced brief fame in England when her 1994 single "Reach" spent four weeks at No. 1 on the UK club charts.

RECOMMENDED RECORDINGS: Unfortunately, there's nothing comprehensive on the Nightingales in print. As for Cheeks's solo recordings, "Somebody Left on That Morning Train" (Savoy Records) is out of print but in circulation.

Chicago Mass Choir

A CHOIR BASED ON THE LARGE GMWA gospel format, they've enjoyed gospel hits such as "I Go to the Rock,"

"Nobody Like Jesus," and "He That Believeth" in the 1990s. The genesis of the group was with James Chambers, who founded the Ecclesiastes Community Choir (ECC) in 1971. Various members of the choir formed the Chicago Mass Choir in 1988. When Chambers fell ill, he left the choir in the hands of Abe Cook, the choir's vice president. Both Cook and Chambers died in the early 1990s. Dennis Cole took over leadership for a while, before Chambers's cousin Feranda Williamson assumed the role. "Education and encouragement to approach learning as a lifelong endeavor are our highest purpose," she once said. "We can be quick to point out where young people are falling short, but we have to ask ourselves what are we doing to educate them and show them a different and better way of life? This organization is driven by a passion to give something of value back to the community by helping and empowering others."

Aquannette Chinnery

A ST. THOMAS NATIVE, Chinnery excelled in school. She skipped high school and enrolled in the College of the Virgin Islands when she was 14 years old. At the age of 18, she became the school's youngest graduate when she earned a B.A. in chemistry. She continued her studies in the US where she earned an M.S. from MIT and a J.D. from Rutgers University. At the same time, Chinnery loved music. She taught herself to play music as a child and sang in college choruses. She was lead vocalist for the Tidalwave Gospel Band for a spell. In her varied career, she has continued to sing while practicing law, working as a biochemist and a fashion model, and earning a reputation as a gifted painter. In 2003, the title song of her CD *Who Is Like Unto You?* became a No. 1 smash in St. Thomas. The project mixed traditional gospel with traditional Caribbean rhythms such as soca, reggae, and calypso.

Choir Boyz

IN THE 1990s, R&B MUSIC had Boyz II Men and the black church world had the Choir Boyz. The quintet resembled the vocal style of Boyz II Men with a churchy twist.

Darrell Holmes, Derek Owens, Richard Yerby, Martin Wilson, and Randy Roberts were all raised in Christian households. At some point in their teenage years, various members fell prey to the temptations of blunts, babes, and boom boxes. One member even served prison time. The Baltimore natives formed a group in 1991 and released their debut CD *Ordered Steps* in 1999 on Platinum Hill Entertainment. Their style is traditional gospel harmonies with 21st century, mid-tempo R&B rhythms.

Christianaires

BEST KNOWN FOR THE 1993 HIT "Two Wings" with its driving blues rhythm, this Sontag, Mississippi–based quartet was formed in the 1970s by siblings Paul and Tyrone Porter with their cousins Arnold and Ronald Brown. In 1981, they made their debut with the album *A Message in His Song*. They have since recorded for an assortment of independent record labels, including Malaco, AIR, Platinum, and Marxan Records. Their 1993 album *The Vision Becomes Clearer* featured their first big hit, "Two Wings," a cover of the James Cleveland tune. They have an energetic, soul-drenching live performance style. However, another big radio hit has eluded them in spite of a regular release schedule of new music and frequent concerts with the leading quartet stars.

Angélla Christie

GOSPEL'S LEADING FEMALE SAX PLAYER, Angélla Christie was born February 19, 1963, in Los Angeles but grew up "everywhere," as she's put it. Her parents were Christian missionaries, but in spite of their watchful eye, disciplinary problems led Christie to spend a year in a Texas girls' home. Still, she had musical aspirations to become a rock guitarist. Her mother had other ideas, though. She picked up a saxophone from a pawnshop for $300 when Christie was 14 years old and stood her before the church to perform a solo. "I was so terrified that Sunday that I cried and hid my horn in my closet hoping to avoid the inevitable," she recalled. "But after playing and experiencing the overwhelming response of worship and praise offered to God, I was encouraged and motivated to do more of what I did…"

Eventually, Christie attended the High School of Performing and Visual Arts in Houston and later graduated from Houston Baptist University with a degree in music. Upon graduation, she decided to go professional. However, a woman performing jazzy instrumental gospel songs (where you could not hear the message of "Amazing Grace" even if you knew the melody) was not instantly embraced by the church community or gospel recording labels. "What do you do when God calls you and the record companies don't? I really didn't know anything about establishing a ministry, recording an album, or booking dates, but I knew I couldn't negate the calling or wait for a record company to confirm it. Like Nike, I just did it!" She recorded an independent album entitled *Because He Lives* and traveled the church circuit where she opened for BeBe and CeCe Winans, John P. Kee, and Shirley Caesar. After playing sax on Yolanda Adams's 1991 *Through the Storm* CD, Christie issued her first nationally distributed LP, *Walk with Me*, on Artifex Records. She recorded two more instrumental albums there before AIR Records signed her in 1996. Her *Hymn & I* CD reached the Top 30 gospel album chart in 1999, and the following year she toured with Adams, Caesar, and Mary Mary on the blockbuster "Sisters in the Spirit" concert tour. Her most recent project is *Draw the Line* on her own recording label, ACSM.

Church of God in Christ (COGIC)

ELDER CHARLES HARRISON MASON (1866–1961) was raised in Memphis, where his family worshipped in the Missionary Baptist Church denomination. Mason was an itinerant evangelist until a warehouse owner allowed him to hold revival meetings at a gin house near Jackson, Mississippi. In 1897, Mason said that God revealed to him what to name his church: the Church of God in Christ (COGIC). While attending a Los Angeles revival in 1907, Mason heard W.J. Seymour preach from the biblical book of Luke 24:49. The passage spoke of the city of Jerusalem tarrying until the Holy Spirit came upon them. The revival became a fanatical outpouring of emotion as the congregation sought to bring the Holy

Spirit into their presence through ferocious praying. Over the years, the COGIC denomination's musical convocations have produced some of gospel's most fervently unique and popular artists such as Andrae Crouch, the Clark Sisters, and the Hawkins Family. The church now boasts a membership of more than 8 million.

Clark Brothers

THE CLARK SISTER THAT MOST FANS have forgotten about is Denise Clark. She left the Clark Sisters over issues with her sisters and has never gained a footing as a national artist. Therefore, it's no surprise that her sons' debut CD received none of the fanfare given to the debut of her sister Karen's daughter, Kierra. Originally formed in 1985, the Clark Brothers (Lorenzo, Larry, and Derrick) disbanded for a time and then regrouped in 1996. Their style is nothing like that of their aunts; their sound is jazzy and mellower. Lead singer Larry writes and leads most of their work. They released the CD *We Need Your Love* on their own Grace & Mercy Music group label in 2000.

Clark Sisters

THROUGH THE 1980s, the Clark Sisters had the most exciting and talked about stage show in the entire gospel field. There were no laser lights and no big rig props, it was just the girls and their band, and they never ceased to turn whatever church they entered inside out and upside down. As astounding as their biggest hit records such as "My Redeemer Liveth," "Is My Living in Vain?" and their R&B breakthrough "You Brought the Sunshine" were on wax, they paled in comparison to the colors the sisters rinsed them with in concert. Therefore, it's no surprise that the Clark Sisters' music and intricate vocalizing have influenced the vocal styles of Mariah Carey, Faith Evans, Exscape, Kelly Price, Mary Mary, Kenny Lattimore, and Smokie Norful, among others.

"The Clark Sisters set the trend for female vocalists in the contemporary gospel music arena," says Tim A. Smith, a longtime Detroit radio announcer for WDTR in Detroit. "Their preacher-like vocal squalls and jazz-

Clark Sisters / photo by Arnold Turner. Courtesy of BET Celebration of Gospel, January 2005.

influenced scatting acrobatics have been imitated by thousands of singers of all musical genres. They've both inspired and paved the way for such talents as Witness, Virtue, Trin-i-tee 5:7, Kim Burrell, and Faith Evans."

The Clark Sisters' mother, the legendary Mattie Moss Clark, was the president of the music department for the Church of God in Christ (COGIC) and coached and recorded choirs around the country for years. She dragged her children with her and pushed her daughters to sing just as her own mother had pushed her to play the piano years before. The five Clark sisters (Jacky, Twinkie, Denise, Dorinda, and Karen) were reared in Detroit and professionally assembled as a group in 1973. "Our mother taught us about the music business," Karen Clark-Sheard told *GMMC* magazine. "Growing up we had to miss a lot of the things that kids normally do because Mama might have some songs for us to sing. Although many days we had to miss playtime, in the long run it's working for the good. Everything Mama taught us, we've used. Looking where we are now, it was worth the sacrifice." Jacky laughs, "Yeah! We didn't play long. If Mama got a song, we had to come in from whatever we were doing and go over the song and learn it."

Perfectionist extraordinaire Mattie would even awaken the girls in the middle of the night if she felt the Lord had given her a song. While this was hard on the girls' playtime, it was also hard on the singers in Mattie's choirs, who often complained—behind her back—that Mattie favored her daughters over other singers. If she was teaching a choir and they couldn't get the song right, Mattie would call her daughters out and have them flawlessly sing a song they had probably learned, sleepy-eyed, in the middle of the night. "I trained my girls to get the sound I wanted," she told her biographer Eugene McCoy. "If I could not get it from others or knew that they did not have what I was after, I used the girls to get the sound." If the girls' singing didn't help the choir learn the song, Mattie would throw shoes, purses, or even hymnbooks at the slackers until they got the song right. Good thing there were no bricks around.

No bricks were needed for the Clarks. They incorporated all of Mattie's vocal ideas along with their own nuances and fused it with the R&B styles being pioneered by Stevie Wonder and other secular singers of the 1970s. When they were barely teenagers, their Uncle Bill Moss produced their debut LP *Jesus Has a Lot to Give* in 1973 for his Bilmo Records. The next year, they followed up with *Mattie Moss Clark Presents the Clark Sisters* and hit the road to promote the projects. "We actually started out with Shirley Caesar," Dorinda told *GMMC* magazine in 1994. "She would take us around on the road with her, giving us an opportunity to sing. That's something not too many people know about."

After creating a considerable buzz in the gospel world with their nonconformist style, the Clark Sisters signed with the Detroit-based Sound of Gospel Records label in 1976 and produced a string of gospel smashes such as "Nothing to Lose" and "A Praying Spirit." As they honed their performance skills, the piano-playing Elbertina "Twinkie" Clark composed the bulk of their recording material. The Clarks continued fusing blues, jazz, classical, swing, and disco into their brand of gospel that clearly separated it from the rest of the pack.

The 1980s saw the Clark Sisters leap outside the church walls as their music gained acceptance in secular venues. Their first live recording, *Is My Living in Vain?*, remained at No. 1 on the *Billboard* gospel chart for over a year. *Record World* magazine voted them Best Female Gospel Group of the year. Things continued to roll in their favor. In 1981, the Clarks starred in the motion picture *Gospel* along with James Cleveland and Shirley Caesar and recorded what would become their biggest success to date, "You Brought the Sunshine." It wasn't until two years later that the track achieved crossover status on R&B radio (peaking at No. 16 on *Billboard*'s R&B chart via an Elektra Records issue of the single) and dance clubs across the country. Like its groundbreaking predecessor, Edwin Hawkins's "Oh, Happy Day," "You Brought the Sunshine" was criticized for going into avenues that gospel music traditionally wouldn't venture into, according to the church. The sisters' answer was, "Our job is to reach those who wouldn't normally listen to gospel." The song even found its way into a Sunny Delight orange juice commercial in 1983—the ultimate crossover.

Ironically, the success of "You Brought the Sunshine" overshadowed the Clarks' critically acclaimed 1982 LP, *Sincerely*, which won an NAACP Image award and a Grammy nomination. The album included the staples "I'm Encouraged" and "Name It and Claim It," and was recorded on the now-defunct New Birth Records. Unfortunately, legal disparities with Sound of Gospel Records put their recording career on hiatus for the next couple of years. The sisters claim they never received royalties for their big hits during their time with Sound of Gospel. Also, to their despair, "Sincerely" was the last recording to feature Denise's vocals. She decided to leave the group to raise a family and begin her own ministry, although she continued to tour with them intermittently and joined them for their show-stopping performance on the 1985 Grammy awards.

In 1986, the Clarks joined Word Records' Rejoice imprint, which focused on black gospel music. They quickly issued *Heart and Soul*, which featured the radio hits "Jesus Is a Love Song," "Balm in Gilead," and "Pray for the USA." Their next album, *Conqueror*, was nominated for a Grammy in 1987, and 1989's *Bringing It Back Home* was their last album for the label and the last one with Twinkie. She left the group to launch a solo ministry in 1991. "It was devastating," Jacky told *SCORE* magazine in 1994. "I had always said that the Clark Sisters were like a car: Twinkie was the engine, Dorinda was the battery, Karen was like the spark plug, and I was the steering wheel…. It was like the engine had dropped out of the car."

On top of this loss, Mattie had fallen ill. In 1992, one of her legs was amputated and in 1993 she had a stroke. She died on September 22, 1994. With their chief songwriter and musical guide on her own and their mentor now watching from heaven, for the first time the Clarks were forced to look outside of their close-knit unit for musical direction.

Their childhood friend BeBe Winans had become a huge hit as half of the BeBe and CeCe Winans contemporary gospel duo. Teaming with Winans's and Anita Baker's then-producer Michael Powell, they produced a delicious slice of urban soul/gospel entitled *Miracle*. They were signed to Winans's Benjammin Production company, and he was planning to release the project through Capitol Records as he had done with Angie & Debbie a year before, but Capitol decided to shut down their black music division and only retain the gold-selling BeBe and CeCe on the label. Winans then sold Sparrow Records (which distributed BeBe and CeCe's Capitol CDs in the Christian market) on the idea of releasing the project. The Top Ten gospel CD earned the sisters an appearance on *The Arsenio Hall Show*, an in-studio concert on *The Tom Joyner Morning Show*, and a rave review from *USA Today* in 1994.

The Clarks felt that Sparrow didn't promote them as hard as the label pushed their white acts. They asked for a music video and an urban radio campaign, but label executives argued—in spite of the Clarks' history on the urban charts—that black gospel didn't sell enough to merit such an extravagant expenditure. More than pleased with the sales of *Miracle*, Sparrow asked for another album, but the Clarks decided that no deal was preferable to a halfhearted one. With the exception of BeBe and CeCe, Sparrow lost all of their black acts, including such artists as Richard Smallwood and Daryl Coley, within a couple of years. Sparrow didn't drop them; they left. Although the Clark Sisters have continued to perform intermittently since that time, they have not recorded an entire project since *Miracle*. They have all recorded solo projects and occasionally come together for a special track on each other's CDs.

Dave Clark

THERE'S NO TELLING HOW DIFFERENT the music business might be had there been no Dave Clark, the first African-American record promoter. Born March 6, 1909, in Jackson, Tennessee, Clark grew up in Chicago. While attending the Juilliard School of Music in New York, Clark juggled jobs as a newspaper columnist and song-plugger. In 1938, he began to promote records, the first of which was Jimmy Lunceford's "Walking Through Heaven with You." He became great at his job in a hurry and was soon promoting for Decca, Chess, Apollo, and United Records. In 1954, he became promotion director at Duke-Peacock Records where he worked with blues singers like Bobby Blue Bland and gospel artists such as the Dixie Hummingbirds and the Sensational Nightingales. In 1971, Stax Records' boss Al Bell brought Clark's experience to his label to promote the Staple Singers and Isaac Hayes among others. Clark was instrumental in helping Bell launch Stax's gospel imprint, Gospel Truth Records, and helped run the division. Clark brought unique R&B-styled gospel artists such as the Rance Allen Group and the Howard Lemon Singers to the label.

After Stax filed bankruptcy circa 1975, Clark worked with TK Distribution for a while before Malaco Records founder Tommy Couch hired him. "Dave was responsible for changing Malaco from a production company to a real record company, where we manufactured and distributed all our product ourselves," Couch

told *Billboard* magazine after Clark's death. "He was a real record man, and many—if not all—of the big artists that we signed came to Malaco only because of Dave." At Malaco, Clark continued to fight for gospel just as strongly as he did for blues music. He worked well into his eighties and still held the title of vice president of promotion at Malaco when he died in a nursing home of natural causes on July 22, 1995.

Mattie Moss Clark

PERHAPS NO OTHER PERSON has had more influence on music in the Church of God in Christ (COGIC) denomination. It's been said that Mattie Moss Clark was the first conductor to teach three-part harmony when she taught it to the Southwest Michigan State Choir of the Church of God in Christ. In addition, she was a songwriter, vocalist, pianist, and arranger who recorded 35 LPs during her lifetime. Clark was also president of COGIC's National Music Department for 25 years, and founded the Clark Conservatory School of Music in Detroit. Over the years, Clark recorded with such COGIC legends as James Moore, Vanessa Bell Armstrong, Elder James Lennox, Rev. Richard "Mr. Clean" White, and Betty Ransom Nelson. She also helped launch the careers of Walter Hawkins, Hezekiah Walker, Commissioned, Richard Smallwood, and, of course, the Clark Sisters, among scores of others.

Born March 26, 1925, in Selma, Alabama, Mattie Juliet Moss was the second of eight children born to Fred and Mattie Moss. The family was poor, but full of Christian faith. Mother Moss was a guitarist and pianist herself and insisted that little Mattie take piano lessons at the age of four. By the age of five, she was playing at her mother's church services. Mattie's brother Edwin helped hone her keyboarding skills. Mother Moss told Mattie of seeing visions of her daughter leading a great choir. After high school, Mattie sought to go to Fisk University and study classical music, but when her father died, Mattie decided to stay near her mother by attending Selma University. Instead of pursuing a classical career, she continued to accompany her mother during her religious services. In 1947, Mattie joined her sister in Detroit where she eventually met and married a COGIC pastor, Elder Elbert Clark. They had five daughters, Jacky, Denise, Twinkie, Dorinda, and Karen, and one son, Leo. While tending to motherhood, Clark continued to direct choirs. By then, she knew music would be her life's work and didn't allow motherhood to interfere with her career. She dragged her children with her and pushed her daughters to sing just as her own mother had pushed her to play the piano.

Clark hit gospel with a revolutionary approach in the 1950s and 1960s. Gospel was still largely a pipe organ genre when she started. Clark's songs could not be played with just the traditional instrumentation. Her rhythmic music demanded a Hammond B3 organ, drums, and tambourines. Churches that wanted their choirs to sing Clark's compositions were forced to buy the extra instruments to make the songs work. Once the churches had the instruments and personnel, music ministers began to play with different sounds and became more innovative in the church worship service. Over the years, Clark recorded more than two dozen LPs with her various choirs and musical ensembles. Among her radio hits were "Lord, Do Something for Me," "Salvation Is Free," and "Climbing Up the Mountain."

Mattie Clark was known to be an austere taskmaster when it came to her coaching and directing skills. A woman who didn't mind waking up her own children in the middle of the night to teach them a new song didn't have any problems telling strangers how she wanted them to sing. Dr. Earline Allen, who directed COGIC's Houston jurisdiction state choir, invited Clark down to work with the choir when Clark's *Salvation Is Free* LP was a radio smash circa 1970. "She knew what she wanted from singers," Allen recalls. "Everybody says she was so stern. She was tough. You had to get it or get out [when you were] working with Mattie Moss! She would tell us to sing a certain song and she would sing the part for the sopranos. She would sing the part for the altos and then she'd do the tenors' part. She would tell the sopranos—and it seemed to me to be so extremely high—she would sing it and then she'd say, 'I'm an alto and you're a soprano, so you better sing it right.' That was the way she talked." Clark worked until health problems prevented her from doing so. In the end, she suffered with diabetes and high blood pressure. One of her legs was am-

putated and her health declined further. She passed away at the age of 69 on September 22, 1994.

Mildred Clark and the Melodyaires

A TRADITIONAL QUARTET WITH just a touch of contemporary soul, the Melodyaires formed in Kansas City, Missouri, in the 1960s. Mildred Clark and her sisters grew up in the COGIC denomination and formed a gospel group, the Seaberry and Cofield Singers. Later, they morphed into the Kansas City Melodyaires and began to perform nationally. Eventually, the group landed a recording deal with the secular ABC Records' Songbird gospel division where they recorded an armful of stellar albums. The label experienced its biggest hits with Inez Andrews, the Mighty Clouds of Joy, and Tessie Hill. Groups such as the Patterson Singers and the Melodyaires suffered from a lack of personal attention from the short-staffed label and never gained the major hits their talents merited. Their best album during the period was perhaps *Lord, I've Really Been Trying*, which earned them a positive review in *Billboard* magazine. In 1979, the group moved on to Savoy Records where they unveiled the LP *God's Got Everything You Need*, which featured a nice gospel reading of Sam & Dave's "Hold On, I'm Coming." In 1986, they recorded *Help Me Jesus* for Heat Records in Akron, Ohio. The simple, two-step title song showed off Clark's breathy, subtly expressive alto to fine effect. It was as fine as anything they ever recorded and should have become their signature song. Their last recording was the *You Got to Be Right* LP for Wajji Records (a Washington, DC–based label) in 1990.

Twinkie Clark

SHE WAS ALWAYS VIEWED as the brain behind the Clark Sisters because her songs comprised the bulk of their repertoire, so when she left the group in the early 1990s many feared the Clark Sisters' glory days were over. Born Elbertina Clark on November 15, 1954, she was nicknamed "Twinkie" because her sister Jacky said that she had twinkling eyes as a child. Twinkie has played the organ and piano since her youth and became a star at COGIC conventions because of her dazzling pianissimo. After attending Howard University, she returned to the Clark Sisters and began to write powerful songs such as "You Brought the Sunshine," "There Is a Balm in Gilead," and "Is My Living in Vain?" By the 1990s, Clark felt led to branch out on her own and do more personal ministry in churches. Her debut solo CD *Comin' Home* appeared on Tyscot Records in 1992. Clark has recorded a half dozen projects, but they have only been purchased by her die-hard fans and she has yet to enjoy a sizeable hit as a solo artist. However, her 2004 CD *Home Once Again: Live in Detroit* is her highest charting project. It debuted at No. 9 on the gospel album sales chart and became her first solo album to reach the R&B album sales chart.

Jacky Clark-Chisholm

ONE SAD FACET TO THE Clark Sisters' legacy is the poor treatment that eldest sister Jacky Clark (born December 29, 1951) has received from gospel radio announcers and critics who fail to mention her when they are waxing poetic about Twinkie, Karen, or Dorinda Long considered the least vocally talented member of the family, she has constantly had to fight for her own recognition. When the Clarks performed at a benefit Patti LaBelle sponsored circa 2002, a *Gospel Today* magazine article on the event mentioned every sister except Jacky. She has a light, attractive voice that has led Clark Sisters gems such as "Wonderful Counselor" and "No Doubt About It." Clark-Chisholm recorded a praise and worship project, entitled *Expectancy*, that was released on the small Detroit-based Entheos Records in spring 2005.

Dorinda Clark-Cole

THE PREACHER IN THE Clark Sisters family, Dorinda Clark-Cole (born October 19, 1957) is also known for her jazzy runs and vocal hiccups. As with her sister Karen, fans marvel over her precise vocal jibs and jabs that slap listeners like bolts out of the blue. While scouting around for a solo recording contract, Clark-Cole recorded some tracks with the Alaska Mass Choir. JDI

Records released that project in the spring of 2002 to the dismay of Gospo Centric, which thought the initial radio acceptance of the record might hurt their solo project for the artist. With J. Moss handling some of the production, Clark-Cole's self-titled CD hit the stores on July 11th and was a fine mix of contemporary and traditional COGIC-style running numbers. Gospel radio embraced the songs "I'm Coming Out" and "I'm Still Here," which took the album to No. 5 on the gospel chart. The project's success gave Clark-Cole a platform to talk about a depressing point in her life when she considered suicide. "I had an experience that made me feel very disillusioned, very betrayed, because it involved a conflict between Christians," she says. "I was raised in church, and somehow I didn't think this kind of conflict would take place in my life, because I knew God. It was a terrible challenge, and it helped me to see that anyone can have challenges that can cause you to say, 'I don't understand this. Where is God?' I felt like God had left me, and I came very close to attempting suicide. My pain was that severe…. I share this story because I want people to understand that we all go through situations we can't handle—only God can help us, only he can be the source of our light, our joy, our inner peace. There on that highway, I sensed him saying to me, 'Are you going to let everything I've invested in you go down the drain?' He stopped me before death took me. His grace pulled me back, and I want people to know that you don't have to let your problems take you out. God is greater than those problems. A lot of my songs come from that ministerial standpoint."

Karen Clark-Sheard

THE BABY OF THE CLARK SISTERS, Karen Clark-Sheard possesses a vocal range and style closest to that of the young Aretha Franklin than any other artist in modern gospel. Perhaps, Franklin saw some of herself in the singer when she picked Clark-Sheard to sing on a CBS tribute in the early 1990s. Clark-Sheard's vocal gymnastics have influenced a generation of gospel artists and even R&B stars such as Faith Evans and Mariah Carey.

Born November 15, 1960 in Detroit, Clark-Sheard sang with her sisters all of her life before she stepped out as a solo artist in 1997 with her CD *Finally Karen*. Produced by Donald Lawrence, Stanley Brown, and J. Moss, the studio half of the music was urban contemporary, such as Clark-Sheard's duet with Faith Evans, "I'm Nothing Without You," which received some play on urban AC radio. The second half of the CD was recorded live at Bailey Cathedral Church of God in Detroit for a Clark Sisters reunion on "Jesus Is a Love Song" and the showstopper "The Will of God," featuring a riff battle between Sheard and her daughter Kierra "KiKi" Sheard. The album peaked at No. 2 on *Billboard*'s gospel chart and sold well over 400,000 units—by far the biggest seller of any Clark Sisters–related projects. In the midst of Clark-Sheard's success, Island Records decided to close their urban division, leaving Clark-Sheard in recording limbo for a few years.

Then Clark-Sheard resurfaced on Elektra Records with the CD *2nd Chance* in 2002. The album was aimed at crossing over to the R&B chart like Yolanda Adams's "Open My Heart" single the previous year. Although it peaked at No. 2 on the gospel album sales chart, it was not the huge seller Elektra anticipated. Gospel radio announcers took a cool hand to spinning the mechanical rhythms that didn't remind them of church at all. The 2003 follow-up CD, *The Heavens Are Telling*, was a little more church-oriented, with the hit gospel radio single, "You Are Welcome." However, Elektra Records went through reorganization during Clark-Sheard's tenure and the project sold even less than *2nd Chance*. Clark-Sheard then signed to Word Records and geared up for a return to her church roots on a project slated for release in late 2005. On June 16, 1984, Clark-Sheard married J. Drew Sheard (born January 1, 1959 in Detroit) who is now pastor of the Greater Emmanuel Institutional Church of God in Christ in Detroit. They have two children: J. Drew Sheard II, a music producer, and Kierra Valencia Sheard, a gospel vocalist with EMI Gospel Records.

Otis Clay

ONE OF THE BEST AND MOST underrated deep soul singers of the 1960s and 1970s, Clay was cut from the same gritty mold that gave the world R&B stars such as Otis Redding and Wilson Pickett. He never made it to the upper echelon of the soul music pedestal, but his talent, professionalism, and persistence have kept him working steadily over the years.

Born February 11, 1942, in Waxhaw, Mississippi, Clay was raised in Chicago. At the age of 12, Clay joined his first gospel quartet, the Pilgrim Harmonizers. Years later, while still a member of the group, Clay sneaked off and cut some smooth R&B sides for Columbia Records in 1962. The records were never released, so in 1963 he joined the Gospel Songbirds briefly before moving across town to sing with the Sensational Nightingales. He only stayed a year—the money was terrible and bad promoters canceled too many dates. Clay left the gospel field and began recording for One-derful Records. His first single, "I'm Satisfied/I Testify," showed off his hard-driving gospelized vocal style and put him on the *Cash Box* R&B charts. In 1968, One-derful went out of business and sold his contract to Cotillion Records for $5,000. The first order of business was a frantic cover of the Sir Douglas Quintet's "She's About a Mover," produced by Rick Hall in Muscle Shoals. By 1972, Clay had moved over to Hi Records in Memphis where he laid down "Trying to Live My Life Without You" in 1972.

Although Clay's fallen off the charts and off of most people's lips in America, he is virtually a superstar among soul fans in Japan where he's recorded two stunning live albums boasting funky horn lines, pulsating grooves, and the most gritty vocals ever put to wax.

RECOMMENDED RECORDING: Clay recorded the kind of bluesy, retro soul gospel album that most of today's gospel artists would be afraid of recording lest they be labeled as old-fashioned. Whatever they call it, Clay's *The Gospel Truth* (Blind Pig Records, 1993) is a brilliant album with real musicians and honest, heart-to-heart songs about the faith, including "Have Mercy Jesus" and "Sending Up My Timber."

Clefs of Calvary

THIS CHICAGO-BASED GROUP leaped into doo wop gospel action in the 1960s. Its founder, James Phelps, was born April 2, 1932, in Shreveport, Louisiana. He moved to Chicago in the 1950s where he performed with gospel groups such as the Gospel Songbirds and the Holy Wonders. He formed the Clefs of Calvary in 1961. Phelps's leads defined the group's output for New York's Tru-Sound label where they recorded the LPs *Baptised* (1962) and *God's Light* (1963). His voice resembled Sam Cooke but with a harder edge. In 1964, the Soul Stirrers needed an extra voice for a television appearance. They asked Phelps to join them. After the show aired, members of the Clefs of Calvary felt betrayed that Phelps had sung with another group and asked him to leave the group he founded. Phelps joined the Stirrers full time and the Clefs disbanded. When the Stirrers began to record for Chess/Checker Records, producer Gene Barge singled out Phelps as a secular soloist. Phelps enjoyed a Top 20 R&B hit with "Love Is a Five Letter Word" in 1966. He left the Stirrers during that period so the gospel audience would not criticize the Stirrers as they had been criticized when they allowed Sam Cooke to return and sing with them after launching his secular music career. Phelps recorded other R&B material through the 1970s, but never experienced another big hit.

Ashley Cleveland

IF BONNIE RAITT SANG GOSPEL, she might sound something like Ashley Cleveland. Born February 2, 1957, in Knoxville, Tennessee, the whiskey-voiced guitarist attended high school in the San Francisco Bay Area, racked up more than 200 recording sessions with artists such as Reba McEntire and Etta James in the 1980s, and toured with John Hiatt before she cut her own demo in 1988. That tape led to a contract with Atlantic Records where she created a critically acclaimed, roots-styled rock album that walked a tightrope between the Christian market and the pop world with lyrics of faith and romance. The album fell through the marketing cracks and was cited by *Billboard* magazine as one of the Ten Most Overlooked Albums of the Year. Cleveland then wound up at Reunion Records, a large, independent Christian label enjoying crossover pop success with Kathy Troccoli at the time, where she cut the stunning bluesy Christian rock CD *Bus Called Desire*. Again, it fell

through the cracks on the CCM side. Her next CD, *Lesson of Love*, didn't move much product, but Cleveland made history as the first woman to be nominated for a Grammy in the Christian rock category, which she won in 1995 and again in 1998 for the CD *You Are There*. Eventually, Cleveland withdrew from the major labels since they never knew how to market her music. "I did make an effort to cater to the Christian market," she told *CCM* magazine in 2003. "But I think I was also beginning to realize that I was not a good fit as a contemporary Christian artist. Simultaneously, I realized I was too Christian for mainstream, so I have gone back to my initial artistic mission statement and am comfortable and happy with where I am now—even though it is something of an island." Cleveland now records what she wants for 204 Records and caters it to a small but loyal group of admirers.

Rev. James Cleveland

SINCE THOMAS DORSEY WAS DEEMED the Father of Gospel, James Cleveland's success earned him the next best title: the Crown Prince of Gospel. From the 1950s on, Cleveland laid the foundation for the elevation of choir music into a sophisticated art form. Implementing diverse elements of jazz and pop, blues and Sanctified church rhythms, he created a new sound for gospel choirs. It is therefore no surprise that he's hailed as the paradigm by which all other choirmasters are judged. In spite of his prodigious talent as a composer, arranger, choral director, and ambassador for gospel music, Cleveland left this world in a cloud of scandal that has sullied his reputation for some. Still, his musical accomplishments remain uncompromised.

Born in Chicago on December 5, 1932, in the heart of the Great Depression, Cleveland was the only son among three children. His father, Ben, worked on WPA projects to keep food on the table and, as a kid, Cleveland took a newspaper job to help make ends meet. "I was Mahalia Jackson's paperboy," he once said. "I'd go over to her apartment on Indiana Avenue and leave her paper and then put my ear to the door to try to hear her singing. If she wasn't at home, I'd go over to her beauty shop—she used to be a hairdresser, you know—

and just sit around there and listen to her hum songs while she was straightening hair."

Cleveland began pretend-playing piano at the age of five. "We couldn't afford a piano," he told Anthony Heilbut in *The Gospel Sound.* "So I used to practice each night right there on the windowsill. I took those wedges and crevices and made me some black and white keys. And, baby, I played just like Roberta [Martin]. By the time I was in high school, I was some jazz pianist." His grandmother took him to church with her every Sunday and he loved the services. When Cleveland was eight years old, Thomas Dorsey, the minister of music at Pilgrim Baptist Church, sat him on top of a box at church and had him sing "All I Need Is Jesus." That was the beginning of his music career. He was said to have a beautiful boy soprano at that age and he soon joined the youth choir where he was also coached by Little Lucy Smith and Dorsey as to how to play the piano. At the age of 15, Cleveland joined the gospel group the Thorne Crusaders. As he grew older, it was harder for him to reach his high notes, so he sang louder and strained to reach them, and eventually his once beautiful soprano grew into a gruff rasp. "My beautiful boy soprano just went haywire on me when my voice changed," he says. "Later on I sang so hard that I strained my voice. That's why it sounds like a foghorn now."

When he started performing, Cleveland literally begged and hustled his way onto programs. In 1950, he joined Norsalus McKissick and Bessie Folk to form the trio called the Gospelaires. They weren't together long, but his work with the group caught the ear of gospel star Roberta Martin. Cleveland had already begun to compose songs, so she recruited him to write for her group. "I sold all of those tunes to Miss Martin for little or nothing," he says. "Of course, she made fabulous sums of money off of them, but that wasn't my interest at the time. My mother was still doing day work for eight hours a day and sometimes she would come home and I'd have the money there in my hand—more money than she was making as a grown woman—and it was a big deal." Some of the best-known songs Cleveland wrote for Martin were "Grace Is Sufficient," "Stand by Me," and "I've Got a Newborn Soul (Since the Holy Ghost Took Control)."

Soon Albertina Walker recruited Cleveland to play piano with her group, the Caravans. He was more than a piano player, though. He wrote songs for them and in their concerts he often narrated hymns while the group sang under him and the music played. Such instant success led to a large ego and a reputation for being temperamental. When he felt ignored or treated less than fairly, Cleveland would abruptly quit the group and join other groups until he cooled down and Walker asked him to return. During those years, he spent time with the Gospel Chimes, the Gospel All-Stars of Brooklyn, and the Meditation Singers. While with the Chimes, he recorded some pop-styled ballads, as well as some rousing shout songs. In 1959, he cut a gospelization of Ray Charles's "Hallelujah, I Love Him So" with the All-Stars that would hint at his future desire to make an impact in secular music. As the decade closed, Cleveland had begun to fuse pop instrumental styles with full choir voices to create a unique, somewhat polished, but still rock-solid gospel sound in church music. Within weeks of the record's success at radio, choirs across the country began to mimic what Cleveland was pioneering.

A rising star, Cleveland was being courted by two record labels. Vee-Jay Records wanted him and he wanted to sign with them, but Harold Lubinsky at Savoy Records had a keen ear for music and convinced him to sign there instead. Savoy's A&R man, Fred Mendelssohn, decided the first LP should be a choir recording. They recorded the Angelic Choir in the cellar of an old church in New Jersey under terrible recording circumstances. They recorded in mono but once the choir became filled with the Holy Spirit, their vocal passion more than compensated for any technical limitations of the recording. That first LP, *Christ Is the Answer,* surprised everyone and sold 100,000 copies right away. In 1962, Cleveland recorded his first masterpiece with Rev. Lawrence Roberts's First Baptist Church Choir in Nutley, New Jersey. The LP *Peace Be Still* sold 800,000 units within the year and transformed Cleveland virtually overnight into a gospel superstar at a time when it was rare for any black music (gospel or otherwise) to sell many LPs. At the time, gospel album sales of 10,000 copies were considered smash hits, so Cleveland's sales afforded him the luxury of commanding $2,000 a night for concerts. Even at the then-staggering rate, he was booked a year in advance. His success continued in Europe where he performed a sold-out, two-week engagement at the Olympia Theater in Paris and a command performance for Prince Rainier and Princess Grace in Monaco. In 1966, his single "Without a Song" peaked at No. 18 on the *Cash Box* magazine R&B singles chart. Cleveland's rapidly growing income afforded him the opportunity to finance his pet projects such as the creation of the Gospel Music Workshop of America (GMWA).

In 1968, legendary COGIC choir conductress Mattie Moss Clark and Elma Hendricks convened a Sing-A-Rama in Detroit at C.L. Franklin's New Bethel Baptist Church. They formed a 1,000-voice choir and had Cleveland come in as a special guest. Cleveland so enjoyed the music and teaching classes that he told Clark he would like to create a similar convocation and maybe call it the Music Workshop of America. Clark suggested that he add "Gospel" to the title to let prospective attendees know it was gospel music only. Cleveland wasted no time in putting the word out. The first GMWA convention took place in August 1968 at the King Solomon Baptist Church in Detroit. The idea was to perpetuate the legacy and appreciation of gospel music through classes and provide an opportunity to expose new talent. More than 3,000 people came from around the country for the first meeting. This soon became gospel music's annual summer celebration where record labels premiered their new music and radio announcers had the opportunity to acquire new music and socialize with the movers and shakers in the gospel field.

In 1963, Cleveland relocated from Chicago to Los Angeles and began to pastor at the New Greater Harvest Baptist Church. He was fired in 1970 for emphasizing music over preaching. The choir quit in protest and followed Cleveland as he founded the Cornerstone Institutional Baptist Church in November of that year. Over the years, Cornerstone's membership swelled way beyond the 2,000 seating capacity and Cleveland had to add a second service to accommodate the overflow. A hallmark of the church was the creation of a permanent choir, the Southern California Community Choir, which would remain one of the leading choirs of the decade. They backed Cleveland on the 1974 LP *In the Ghetto*, which won him the first of his four Grammy awards. By the mid-'70s, Cleveland had recorded such gospel smashes as the ballad "God Is," "I Had a Talk with God," "Christ Is the Answer," "Please Be Patient with Me," and his gospel reworking of Gladys Knight and the Pips' "The Best Thing That Ever Happened to Me." His 1977 LP *Live at Carnegie Hall* produced another *Cash Box* magazine black radio hit with "Say You Love Me," which made the Hot 100. His marquee name also led to other appearances. Cleveland was one of the many celebrities recruited for Elton John's 1976 opus *Blue Moves*, a bombastic two-LP set that was widely panned by music critics for its excess. As *Rolling Stone*'s Stephen Holden wrote, "*Blue Moves* is no different than most double albums in that it contains nowhere near enough good songs to justify the extended length, but songs are no longer the focus. Instead, *Blue Moves* is preoccupied

Rev. James Cleveland

with sound, with instrumental interludes and tidy segues, to the exclusion of sense. It attempts to satisfy the ears while leaving the emotions completely unaroused. In fact, *Blue Moves* is the musical equivalent of a dumb but gorgeous one-night stand. Unfortunately, it is also intended as a sort of farewell album and is clearly meant to have a more lasting effect. Instead it sounds like it's time for John to take a rest."

The album was meant to express many of John's personal views and shades toward his thinking on controversial matters such as suicide and poverty. The album contained four gospel-inspired numbers, "If There's a God in Heaven (What's He Waiting For?)," "Boogie Pilgrim," "Where's the Shoorah?" and "Bite Your Lip," which closed the album. Of course, many gospel purists criticized Cleveland for allowing himself and his choir to back a secular singer, especially one with an androgynous stage presence who sometimes displayed homoerotic elements to his concerts and his songs. Cleveland shrugged it off as spreading light in the darkness.

Cleveland was a millionaire at this point in his life, with a lavish lifestyle. He lived in a mansion, owned luxury cars, and expensive rings adorned his chubby fingers. When asked whether his opulence might cause some of his church members to feel he was misusing their tithes and offerings, Cleveland said, "Most of them know I acquired all of this before I started pastoring. My church gives me no salary. I work completely free. All of my time is donated to the church along with most of my money. So I never get any static from anybody. I get my money from my music, personal appearances, music writing, and record royalties. If I want to go to a nightclub, I go. I don't feel religion was meant to make pleasure less enjoyable. I go to see movies—I get sermons from movies. I even get inspiration from movies. Religion, like gospel, should involve itself with all phases of life."

For someone with such a seemingly open mind, his mind was closed to the '70s phenomenon of gospel rock. Cleveland had written secular songs in the '60s for Laura Lee and other R&B artists and loved the sensual sounds of Donna Summer's music. However, when the Staple Singers and the Mighty Clouds of Joy had crossover hits, he was firmly against what they were doing. "Rock gospel is just not the same," he said at the time.

"Gospel music expresses love for Christ and it cannot be sung as rock gospel or rock music. In true gospel music, the message is paramount, not the music. In rock gospel, the music is more important than the message." The Mighty Clouds' Johnny Martin, in an interview with *Jet* magazine, retorted, "It's easy for him to say that rock isn't gospel. He's making plenty of money and his records, since they are choir oriented, are always being played on the radio. In our case, being a quartet, we need hit records to survive. The average station that plays gospel doesn't play quartets. They play choirs."

By the 1980s, Cleveland's music continued to sell, although he scaled back his participation and allowed others to sing and write much of the music. As a result, the quality wasn't as good, but his name still made sales. In 1981, the GMWA was held in Los Angeles and during the festivities Cleveland became the first gospel artist to receive a star on the Hollywood Walk of Fame. That same year Elton John had Cleveland and his choir back him on "Fascist Faces" from his LP *The Fox*. But for the most part, Cleveland let the music produce itself with the set of young imitators he surrounded himself with who were dying to produce. Cleveland and his manager, Annette Thomas, spent much of their time creating enterprises that did not depend on record sales. He owned the Southern Kitchen Restaurant in Los Angeles, and he was a backer in the Subrena Booking Agency, which was the largest gospel-booking firm at the time.

After years of keeping Savoy Records afloat, Cleveland formed King James Records in 1985 with distribution through Sound of Gospel Records. In addition to his own records, the company produced projects on Billy Preston and the Harmonizing Four. All of the projects were dismal sellers. Cleveland closed the company in 1990 and returned to Savoy Records where he enjoyed one more No. 1 gospel LP when *Having Church* hit the record bins. That year, the GMWA convention was held in Washington, DC, at the downtown convention center. Cleveland was there, and he didn't look good. A heavy man, shaped like a halfback during his prime, Cleveland had lost considerable weight and collapsed at one point during the convention. He went back to Los Angeles where he recuperated at home. Cleveland was known to occasionally smoke and drink, and his representatives said that he had respiratory problems. On February 9, 1991, Cleveland passed away. Thomas told the press that he died of congestive heart failure, but a drama loomed on the horizon.

More than 4,000 people and a who's who of recording artists packed the Shrine Auditorium in Los Angeles for Cleveland's four-hour funeral service. "Rev. Cleveland had an open casket," Gospel TV personality Bobby Jones wrote in his memoirs of Cleveland's wake. "And twice they dressed him in different outfits.... I was also a little embarrassed by the situation because I noticed the bottom of his shoes were scuffed. I thought if they were going to go through all the trouble of changing his costume, they could have put some new shoes on him."

The funeral fashion show was nothing compared to the show that would soon break out between Cleveland's heirs and his church. Jones also noted in his book that, "Not only was [Cleveland's] convention business in disarray, but also his church and his personal affairs. I thought that a man with that kind of intelligence, and having been sick as long as he was, would have considered the possibility of his passing and made provisions for people to handle his estate…. Only one other person had worked with him trying to manage all his business, and that person's business practices were very questionable."

The person Jones alluded to was Annette Thomas. Just months after Cleveland's death, *Jet* magazine reported that members of his Cornerstone Church (located at the corner of Slauson and Western) were up in arms over Thomas's plans to sell the church for $4.5 million. According to Cleveland's estate attorneys, the singer had been subsidizing the church out of his own pocket. According to them, he speculated that the income flow would cease with his death and that the church would have to be sold and a new more economical location would have to be found to hold services. The interim pastor, Eugene Bryant, was in the middle between Thomas and a group of church members who sued Cleveland's estate to prevent the church from being sold. In April 1992, L.A. Superior Court judge Stephen O'Neil ruled that the church could not be sold before a hearing later that month. The church was eventually allowed to be sold and for a time was turned into a Pick 'n Save discount store.

The biggest scandal erupted when a court suit was filed by a man named Christopher Harris against the Cleveland estate charging that Cleveland was a practicing homosexual who had sodomized him when he lived in the singer's Los Angeles home between 1985 and 1988. Furthermore, the suit claimed that Cleveland did not die of heart disease, but that he died of complications from AIDS and had exposed Harris to the virus. In a *Jet* magazine story, Harris was revealed to be 15 years old when Cleveland took him in, and according to his attorney, "It was not consensual sex. There were three years of unprotected intercourse."

The next sting came from 34-year-old Andre McIsaac (who claimed to have changed his name to Cleveland as a teenager), who claimed to have been raised as Cleveland's adopted son. He staged a news conference in October 1991 arguing that he was due half of Cleveland's estate (estimated at the time to be worth $4–6 million). McIsaac's attorney alleged that Annette Thomas authorized the creation of a trust and appointed herself trustee on Thursday, February 8, 1991—the same date Cleveland was admitted to the Brotman Medical Center in Culver City, reportedly suffering from respiratory problems. Thomas's attorney, Donald Garner, countered that she had consulted with Cleveland about the trust prior to his lapsing into a coma and that the singer gave her his power of attorney. He died two days later. After the press conference concluded, Jean Ervin, the mother of Cleveland's only biological child, LaShone, turned to the press and disputed McIsaac's claims. While she showed the press private trust documents willing $100,000 to LaShone and $10,000 to McIsaac, Ervin said that McIsaac was just one of many homeless, fatherless children Cleveland took in over the years and that he was never formally adopted. Years later, people close to the cases are mum as to the final outcome. No more news hit the press, so it's likely that all cases were settled out of court with gag orders. It was a sad postscript for a man who forever changed the way we view and hear choirs.

RECOMMENDED RECORDING: *James Cleveland with the World's Greatest Choirs* (Savoy Records, 1995) features 14 of Cleveland's best-known hits, such as "Peace Be Still," "I Don't Feel No Ways Tired," and "Jesus Is the Best Thing That Ever Happened to Me."

Dorothy Love Coates

ONE OF THE PIONEERS OF GOSPEL who honestly never reaped the benefits of her work, Dorothy Love Coates wrote songs that read and sang like hymns. Her compositions were so perfect that for decades musicians routinely rerecorded her songs and credited themselves as the writers because they thought they were public domain songs. Coates's group, the Original Gospel Harmonettes, churned out hit after hit in the 1950s, such as "Ninety-Nine and a Half Won't Do," "Get Away Jordan," "You Can't Hurry God (He's Right on Time)," "I'm Sealed," and "You Must Be Born Again." Perhaps they are not remembered as well as the Clara Ward Singers and the Caravans because they lacked the show business flash of the Wards and the variety of skilled vocalists the Caravans had. What they did have were great songs, tight harmonies, and a lead singer with a husky, ragged voice that popped, snapped, and crackled as she relived every song as if it were her personal testimony.

Coates was born Dorothy McGriff on January 30, 1928, in Birmingham, Alabama. Her preaching father abandoned the family early on, and Coates went to work scrubbing floors to help support her mother and five siblings. A pianist from an early age, Coates played for several groups before forming the Royal Gospel Singers in the 1940s. She'd also married Willie Love, who sang with the Fairfield Four quartet. In 1947, Coates was recruited to join the Original Gospel Harmonettes. The group had been formed in 1940 by Evelyn Starks Hardy (pianist) as the Harmoneers with Odessa Glasgow Edwards (contralto), Vera Kolb (soprano), Mildred Miller Howard (mezzo-soprano), and Willie Mae Brooks Newberry (alto). Hardy's Sanctified approach to the piano gave the group a distinct sound, and Howard was their lead singer. By the 1950s, the group's name had evolved into the Gospel Harmonettes. There were other groups performing under the name, so they changed the name once again to the Original Gospel Harmonettes to distinguish themselves from the upstart groups. An appearance on Arthur Godfrey's *Talent Scouts* television show won them a recording contract with RCA Records. Eventually, Coates, who was then working as a well-known

regional soloist, was brought in to share vocal chores with Howard.

As time wore on, more creative control was surrendered to Coates, but she temporarily left the group when her daughter was born with epilepsy. Just over 21 years old, Coates was already divorced, broke, and physically weakened from a rough bout with pneumonia. In fact, some fans thought that she had lost one of her lungs from all of her rough singing. In 1951, Coates rejoined the group in time for them to sign with Specialty Records. Their first recordings were a cover of Roberta Martin's "I'm Sealed" and "Get Away Jordan." Coates added a whole verse to "Get Away Jordan" but received no writing credit for it. After the song took off and made money for the label, the songwriter, and everyone involved with it but her, Coates decided to write her own songs.

In 1953, Hardy stopped touring, although she continued to record with the group. She was replaced with pianist Herbert "Pee Wee" Pickard on the road. Over the next few years, the Harmonettes churned out classic after classic, including "No Hiding Place," "You Must Be Born Again," "Ninety-Nine and a Half Won't Do," and "That's Enough." Everything they sang was rough and passionate and loved by gospel radio. More exciting than hearing the group on the radio was seeing them in person. Coates, more so than her dignified co-laborers, made concert audiences listen to her. A tall woman sweeping across stage or charging down church aisles in long choir robes, she was a sight to behold. She sang hard as Ruth Davis of the Davis Sisters and she preached throughout and in between songs. Art Rupe, who owned Specialty Records, used to fear that Coates sang so hard that she'd have a heart attack. Words cannot adequately express the dramatic arm gestures, facial contortions, and physicality Coates brought to her live performances.

In addition, Coates's direct manner made her a hilarious presence on stage as the audience couldn't help but laugh at her candor. In his book *The Gospel Sound*, Anthony Heilbut writes of how a concert promoter once told Coates that his packed concert bill was running late and he had to cut her performance time, but that 15 minutes was enough time to get her message through. She angrily went on stage and told the audience what the promoter had to say: "He says I can get my message through in 15 minutes?…" Heilbut quotes her as saying. "'Well, Jesus Christ came down through 42 generations, hung on a rugged cross, suffered, bled, and died for your sins and mine. That was 2,000 years ago and some folks still ain't got the message.' As the saints say, the church went up and folks were ready to throw their purses at the stage to show solidarity with Coates."

Around 1958, the Harmonettes retired at the top of their game. They were third only to the Caravans and the Ward Singers in popularity. Meanwhile, Dorothy married Carl Coates, the bass and guitarist for the Sensational Nightingales. During that period, she became a housewife and also began to become involved in civil rights protests in Birmingham, often working closely with Martin Luther King, Jr. Many of Coates's songs carry a political theme, however, the answer can always be found in her faith.

In 1961, Coates re-formed the Harmonettes with her sister Lillian McGriff, Willie Mae Garth, and Cleo Kennedy. They made new hits with "Come On in the House," "I Won't Let Go of My Faith," and "Lord, You've Been Good to Me." After recording for Savoy when they reunited, the group switched to Vee-Jay Records in 1964. They briefly recorded for Columbia's black subsidiary, OKeh, in 1968. There they recorded the classic "Strange Man." By the late '60s, many artists were recording Coates's material or using it as the backdrop for their own. The Supremes' "You Can't Hurry Love" is said to be based on "You Can't Hurry God," and Wilson Pickett transformed "Ninety-Nine and a Half Won't Do" into a secular song. At least Pickett changed the lyrics, but Coates's own gospel peers such as Sister Rosetta Tharpe and James Cleveland did word-for-word renditions where they credited themselves as the writers. Edna Gallmon Cooke and Mattie Moss Clark credited their versions of "You Must Be Born Again" to themselves. Calvin Rhone, Dorothy Norwood, Donnie McClurkin, and Patrick Henderson have claimed "He's Right on Time" as their own, just as Ray Charles claimed "That's Enough" for himself. Even Pop Winans's producers appropriated "God Rose

in a Windstorm" as their own. All this proves is that Coates's writing was so good that people knew that no one in their lifetime had written such classics.

Of course, a good attorney could have helped Coates with these copyright infringements, but she probably didn't trust them either. "I feel like I'm feeding the entire gospel field," she told Heilbut. "They all take my songs or my sayings. And then these promoters bitch about paying me 1960 prices…" She mentioned a specific promoter, "That Negro wanted me to come up from Birmingham, carrying six people, and [was going to] pay me two hundred and fifty dollars." This writer spoke to Coates a number of times on the phone about an interview. She always said she'd be glad to do it, but she was either too busy or wasn't in the mood. However, whenever the call was placed, she was sitting by the phone, always pleasant though somewhat suspicious of what the real intentions were. She'd been ripped off so much that she was pessimistic and untrusting.

Coates's first husband, Willie Love (1925–1991) had passed away, and life was still a struggle after all of her contributions to gospel music. She lived modestly and sang at local churches, although she was paid in small change or warm embraces from the congregation. In the last decade of her life, Coates appeared in films such as *The Long Walk Home*, with Whoopi Goldberg, and Oprah Winfrey's *Beloved*. She died of heart failure on April 9, 2002, in Birmingham.

RECOMMENDED RECORDING: *The Best of Dorothy Love Coates & the Original Gospel Harmonettes* (Specialty/ Fantasy Records, 1991) includes 24 classic tracks, such as "No Hiding Place."

Natalie Cole

SOME GENERATION X MUSIC FANS may have the wrong idea about Natalie Cole based on her recent career evolution into a smooth jazz and standards chanteuse, with adult contemporary hits such as "Unforgettable" and "Take a Look" comprising her current repertoire. However, for a while back in 1976 Cole was heralded by the media as the new Queen of Soul. *Rolling Stone* magazine suggested that Cole was about to take Aretha Franklin's throne in an inglorious revolution. Back then, Cole was burning up the R&B and pop charts with her church-styled wailing on smash hits such as "This Will Be," "I've Got Love on My Mind," and "I'm Catching Hell." During that period, Cole had married her producer, who was also a Baptist preacher, so many of her R&B LPs were sprinkled with inspirational, if not outright gospel numbers. Over the years, as Cole has triumphed over drug addiction and recommitted her life to Christ, she has done a handful of gospel songs that are worth seeking out.

Natalie Cole was born February 6, 1950, in Los Angeles to legendary pop crooner Nat King Cole and his wife, Maria, a former jazz singer herself. She was raised in the prestigious Hancock Park area of Los Angeles, which was all white before the Coles moved into the neighborhood. Cole grew up around a who's who of celebrities her parents knew and performed with. She made her stage debut at the age of 11 when she appeared in a black version of *Gigi* called *I'm with You* with her father and Barbara McNair at the Greek Theater in Los Angeles. Cole had a very nurturing relationship with her father and a more strained relationship with her mother. Maria was light-skinned and pedigreed. Nat was dark and became socially acceptable to the family of Cole's mother only hesitantly because he was a popular musician. Many blacks of the era were raised with the concept that the lighter the skin, the better the person. This conflict caused self-esteem issues for young Natalie. "When my mother was angry with me, she used to say I was just like my father," she told *Parade* magazine in 1993. "That put me in an uneasy position as a kid: What does that mean?"

She went on to say, "I was very popular in school, but even then, I knew that I was liked for who my father was, not for myself. I was smart enough to know there was a reason why I was able to infiltrate all these different areas, where I ended up the only black there—or the only black in that position, because the other blacks were servants…. It makes you very insecure and you go out of your way to get people's attention." After her father's death from lung cancer in 1965, Cole's mother moved the family to Massachusetts where she was briefly married to a white man. Maria was appalled at Cole's friendliness with their household servants and stressed the importance of becoming a member of upper-class society and gaining an education, so Cole graduated from the University of Massachusetts at Amherst as a psychology major. While on campus, she became fast friends with future blues star Taj Mahal. He introduced her to the rock and blues scene. Cole interacted with poor people from the inner city for the first time and it was eye-opening for her. She became a bar waitress and played in a band, Black Magic, on weekends. This period was also her introduction to LSD, heroin, and membership in the Black Panther party. "I became a rebel overnight," she told *Parade*. "I had this big afro, and I marched on the administration to get a black studies program. Black history was very important to me, and I was surprised with what I learned. When I came home, I said to my mother, 'How come you didn't tell us about all this other stuff?' She was like, 'Well, you didn't need to know.'"

Eventually, Cole concealed who her father was and began performing solo club dates. Her performing repertoire included songs such as "Honky Tonk Women" and Sly Stone's version of "Que Sera Sera." Around 1974, Cole's manager hooked her up with two young producers in Chicago, Chuck Jackson and Marvin Yancey. They felt an instant bond, and the trio created a whole album of music, which they shopped at every major label. Everyone turned it down except her dad's old label, Capitol Records, which was once nicknamed The House That Nat Built. Her gold-selling debut LP *Inseparable* reached No. 18 on the pop charts and featured the smash hits "This Will Be" and the title tune. In 1976, she won Grammy awards as Best New Artist and Best Female R&B Vocalist. Cole's sophomore LP *Natalie* showcased even more of Yancey's gospel influence in the production. Even love or lack-of-love ballads such as "No Plans for the Future" and "Touch Me" have a gospel feeling. One of the album highlights was "Keep Smiling," a hip-shaking, no-holds-barred inspirational church romp. That album went gold just as Cole and Yancey married on July 31, 1976.

Cole's third album, *Unpredictable*, began to showcase that she was more than just a soul shouter. Released in spring 1977 and driven by the single "I've Got Love on My Mind" and the dance track "Party Lights," it was Cole's first platinum seller. The album's diversity was displayed on the jazzy "Peaceful Living" and the bluesy "Be Mine Tonight." The highlight was the six-minute sermonette "I'm Catching Hell." Set to the lilting rhythm of a Sunday morning revival waltz, Cole testifies about the ups and downs of relationships. On the tail end of the track she even uses the church language of "This is my story, this is my song…."

On her fall 1977 LP *Thankful*, the Cole-Yancey-Jackson trio continued to keep their gospel piano style as the foundation for love songs such as the album's No. 1 single "Our Love." The funky track "Be Thankful" was another pleasingly outright church number with organ wailing as Cole and the background singers riffed back and forth. The beautiful ballad "Nothing Stronger than Love" was a less obvious, but clearly faith-inspired song.

Cole's 1978 album, *Natalie…Live* is reminiscent of Al Green's concerts, which are fusions of church and juke joint. Recorded at L.A.'s Universal Amphitheater and New Jersey's Latin Casino, the two-LP set gets a thorough church treatment. Forceful background singers, serious testifying on Cole's part, and elongated versions of Cole's three-minute hits, make this a platter perfect for a Sunday morning revival service. The live versions of "I've Got Love on My Mind," "Be Thankful," "I'm Catching Hell," "Lucy in the Sky with Diamonds," "Our Love," and "I Can't Say No" are all in the seven-minute running time range. For her part, Cole sings as if she's in a choir loft. Fans who only know of Cole from her pop standards may be surprised to hear how hard and bluesy she wails on songs such as "Cry Baby" before an entirely enthusiastic audience. Of particular note to gospel fans will be the spiritual reading she gives Doris Day's "Que Sera Sera." The audience almost loses its mind as Cole does a low-down call and response with her background singers and holds ferociously gritty notes during a preaching introduction to her gospelized version of Etta James's "Something's Got a Hold on Me," which segues into an athletic workout on her own gospel song "Be Thankful."

By the 1980s, hits were less steady for Cole and her marriage had ended. In addition, she was hooked on cocaine. At one point, her multi-million dollar fortune had dwindled to $300,000 and her mother had to take over her financial affairs. Soon there was yet another crisis to deal with—just as Yancey and Cole were about to reconcile their marriage, he suffered a massive stroke and died. She was suddenly a single mother with a drug problem. Aside from recording a few LPs that never really hit the high notes the labels were hoping for, Cole spent most of the 1980s detoxifying. At one point, Cole went into a drug rehabilitation center, but got hooked again after her exit from the center. After she underwent the detox program at the Hazelton Clinic in Minnesota in 1983, Cole was finally able to triumph over her addiction. She told *Parade*, "I felt it was my last chance to deal with some real problems, perhaps my last chance to save my life. I discovered that I was still grieving about my dad, in a lot of pain about my mother and a lot of shame about how I had done all these things. I learned about forgiveness. I learned about love and about my relationship with my dad. I'm still working through it—this feeling that I would never measure up, not ever be worthy to be called his daughter."

After her rehabilitation, Cole renewed her faith in God, and in 1989 she joined friend Deniece Williams on the duet "We Sing Praises" for Williams's gospel CD *Special Love*. After joining Elektra Records in 1991, Cole enjoyed a spectacular career renaissance when her CD *Unforgettable*, an album of standards made famous by her father, was released and topped the pop charts. The album sold eight million units, won three Grammy awards, and set Cole into a new career direction as a lady of song instead of an R&B belter. Before the record's release, some thought an album of standards would be career suicide. "I consider myself a singer," Cole once said of such speculation, "but not any particular kind of singer. I like to sing everything from Joni Mitchell to Count Basie."

Since then, Cole has, for the most part, left her R&B repertoire behind her and now performs standards with big bands and orchestras. She often says that one day she'd like to record a gospel album. Two of the highlights of Cole's 1999 CD *Snowfall on the Sahara* are her renditions of Roberta Flack's "Reverend Lee" and Bob Dylan's gospel tune "Gotta Serve Somebody." On October 12, 2001, Cole married Nashville preacher Kenneth Dupree; they divorced in 2004. Although the marriage ended, she still maintained her faith. She's made appearances on TBN's *Praise the Lord* and shared her testimony. "I was raised Episcopalian," she told *LA Focus* in February 2003. "We went to church every Sunday, but it's very doctrinal. It's lovely, but not personal. So I was saved in the doctrinal sense, but Jesus didn't really become real to me until I was an adult…. It's just as damaging to sit up and say I'm a Christian and then turn around and do something stupid. So sometimes I have to let my actions speak for themselves and hope that they glorify God. That even though I'm in the secular business, that even though I do make money, we're all given different gifts and I believe my gift is a ministry as well."

Daryl Coley

A SINGER'S SINGER, Daryl Coley is beloved by gospel and jazz musicians everywhere for his precise, improvisational vocal technique and his wide vocal range. In spite of several bona fide gospel hits such as "'Till

Daryl Coley / photo courtesy of Sparrow Records, 1996

Sunday Comes" with the Tri-City Singers and others, he's never been able to translate his critical acclaim into popular commercial appeal. If Coley had a CD sale for every compliment his performances receive, he'd be the biggest-selling gospel artist of all time, but his fans don't seem consistently inclined to support him at the cash register.

Born October 30, 1955, in Berkeley, California, Coley grew up on jazz music and learned to play keyboards and clarinet. At Castlemont High School, Coley and his classmates Rodney Franklin and bassist Freddie Washington studied under the late Philip Grida, their music mentor, and performed with the school group, Castleleers. Coley later formed the New Generation Singers. In 1977, he began to play keyboards for the Hawkins family. He wrote "I Am Determined," which became a hit for Tramaine Hawkins. He also sang on Hawkins family tracks "Do Your Best" and "He'll Understand." In 1983, Coley performed with Rev. James Cleveland for a while before venturing off into secular music briefly in 1984. Danniebelle Hall encouraged him to stay with gospel when they ran into each other at a GMWA convocation.

That year, Coley did background vocals on albums by Sylvester and on a Nancy Wilson and Ramsey Lewis project. "When Rodney started doing his albums [on Columbia] he would bring me in to do vocal arrangements and to sing and stuff," Coley says. "On one album Rodney did, Stanley Clark was his producer and so through that process, Stanley knew me when it came time for him to produce Nancy Wilson and Ramsey Lewis. They were looking for a vocalist…. They had picked somebody to sing the song and [Nancy] listened to it and said, 'Uh uh, baby, that ain't the one.' So Stanley called me late one night and said, 'Daryl, I got to do this album for Ramsey Lewis and Nancy Wilson. The thing is set up for tomorrow, can you come do it?'… Nancy came in and we did this duet. Well, I had grown up listening to her and I was sitting there just in awe. She's a sweetheart, a sweet lady, she's not grand. None of that. She was just talking with me and we were just singing stuff. I was throwing her old songs at her and she was like, 'What you know about those songs?' and that's how we built a relationship. And after that, she took my number. You know how you think people are just being nice or so forth? After a year, I had done my first album, *Just Daryl*. She went to a record store because she listened to gospel and they had this big poster. She said to herself, Daryl's got an album? She bought my album, spent a week with it—she did a photo shoot with nothing but that album playing. She called me on the phone crying, telling me how she was blessed by the music."

That album was the 1986 LP *Just Daryl* for Plumeline Records. The album reached the gospel Top Ten and earned him a Grammy nomination for Best Male Gospel Soul Vocalist. After an LP for Light Records, it was Coley's association with Sparrow Records that would make him a star. His 1990 debut LP *He's Right on Time* zoomed to No. 3 on the gospel album chart and made Coley the man of the hour. His 1992 album *When the Music Stops* reached No. 1 on the gospel chart and remains his best seller. Subsequent albums for Sparrow and later Verity Records have been good. They have charted high initially but quickly fell off the charts and radio play lists. Although Coley's radio appeal appears to have waned, he remains a fan of other singers.

"I'm a supporter of gospel," he says. "I go to the record store and purchase CDs and tapes. At home, I guess it's because a lot of gospel music just doesn't minister to me. I have those picks and chooses that do and I enjoy good gospel music, but some of it that's out there I just don't care to have in my collection. I listen to classical music. A lot of Beethoven and a lot of jazz. Also, I listen to a lot of female vocalists. I don't listen to a lot of males. Oleta Adams, Natalie Cole, Nancy Wilson, Sarah Vaughan, Ella Fitzgerald, some early Aretha, Chaka Khan, and I love Patti Austin. Then I listen to the Yellow Jackets, Joe Sample, Kenny G, but usually band stuff. I love Harry Connick, Jr., and for gospel, I'd love to do a big band album. A 35-piece brass band! That's what I'm talking about doing. Something different!"

Mitty Collier

NEVER A BIG NAME OUTSIDE of the deep soul coterie that worshiped artists such as Big Maybelle and Theola Kilgore, Collier is best known for her aching, piercing contralto on bluesy, church-inspired 1960s songs such as "I Had a Talk with My Man Last Night" and "No Faith, No Love." Born June 21, 1941, in Birmingham, Alabama, Collier sang in church as a teenager and was a member of the Hayes Ensemble, a gospel outfit that toured throughout the Southeastern states in the late 1950s. She attended Miles College for a while before going to Chicago to visit her brother in the summer of 1959. She ran into her former French teacher there and he began suggesting that she participate in talent shows. She won WGES DJ Al Benson's talent show at the Regal Theater for six weeks straight. Ralph Bass from Chess Records was in the audience one of those nights, liked what he heard, and signed Collier to a recording contract.

Collier recorded a number of admirable but lukewarm sellers such as "Part Time Love" and an answer song "I'm Your Part Time Love." Her breakthrough came with "I Had a Talk with My Man Last Night," a secularization of a gospel song. "We got it from a gospel song that James Cleveland had done," she told *Goldmine* magazine. "We had a musician at the studio who played for church. His name was Leonard Caston. So he had this album and he came down to the studio and played it, because he was going to teach some songs from it to his church. Billy Davis, who was my manager and producer, heard the song and kept telling Leonard to play it over and over. And so they took it and changed the words, and we cut it in the next couple of weeks or so." After a 13-week run on the charts, the song peaked at No. 3 on *Cash Box* magazine's R&B chart in fall 1964. The producers figured that if the formula worked, why not try it again? They then took Cleveland's "No Cross, No Crown" and transformed it into Collier's smoldering ballad "No Faith, No Love," also a Top 40 R&B hit. Her final hit was the *Billboard* Top Ten R&B single "Sharing You" in 1965. She was then sent to producer Rick Hall in Muscle Shoals hoping to create another hit, but those recordings failed to reignite Collier's career. In 1969, she joined soul singer William Bell's Peachtree Records in Atlanta where the hits dried up altogether. After a brief time with Entrance Records, Collier made her exit from secular music in 1972 and devoted her life to church work. Her debut gospel LP *The Warning* featured "I Had a Talk with God Last Night" in its original form. Over the years, she made sporadic recordings such as *Hold the Light* in 1977 and *I Am Love* in 1987. In spite of a handful of fine, soul-drenched church recordings, Collier has never been embraced by the gospel music industry outside of Chicago, where she writes a church column for the *Chicago Defender* newspaper and ministers at a church.

Freddie Colloca

A DYNAMIC CHRISTIAN POP ARTIST with the same looks and stage manner that catapulted Enrique Iglesias and Ricky Martin to the top of the pop charts in the late 1990s, Freddie Colloca is ready for his close-up. He was born February 14, 1975, in Buenos Aires, Argentina. His father, Rev. Roberto Colloca, pastors the Iglesia Vida Abundante in Miami where young Freddie first led worship and played piano when he was ten years old. His father, also an accomplished musician, has been a major influence on Colloca's life and music. Since his teen years, Colloca has been performing at youth camps and for church groups. In the late 1990s, he formed a band called Mainstream. In 2001, Colloca's debut CD *Dance El Ritmo* on One Voice Music was released to positive press attention. His albums are basically pop dance affairs. Although he has yet to become a chart success story, he has developed a good following with further albums such as *Unconditional* and *Cancion de Mi Corazon*.

Commissioned

DURING THE 1980S, Commissioned was second only to the Winans in popularity among gospel vocal groups. Whereas the Winans brought a mellow adult contemporary vibe to gospel music, Commissioned brought a funk band feel to gospel. During the decade, they filled gospel airwaves with a dozen fan-friendly hooks such as "I'm Going On," "Running Back to You," "Ordinary Just Won't Do," and "Will You Be Ready?"

After bassist Fred Hammond returned from a concert tour with the Winans circa 1982, he was hyped on starting his own group to express his own musical ideas. He and Michael Brooks, who had auditioned for the same Winans tour, founded Commissioned with Mitchell Jones, Michael Brooks, Mike Williams, Keith Staten, and Karl Reid. Because their music was very R&B with an occasional rock edge, a lot of churches were hesitant to book them. However, Mattie Moss Clark was not afraid. She booked the group to perform at the COGIC annual convention and it gave them a needed boost. They all held day jobs while they worked on their debut LP *I'm Going On*, released on Light Records in 1985. Aside from the edge in their music, the group mixed the group vocals high instead of burying them below the instrumentation as most groups did at the time. This was revolutionary and gave a fuller sound to the music. The album was a big hit and dates were rolling in, so they were all able to quit their jobs within a matter of months.

Over the next few years, Commissioned ruled the airwaves with songs such as "I'm Going On," "'Tis So Sweet," "Unworthy," and "Go Tell Somebody." As the group progressed, they each were called to their own ministries. By 1991, Keith Staten had left for a solo career as a praise and worship artist with Integrity Music. Michael Brooks had gone into the ministry and managed Witness, a female version of Commissioned that he founded. For Commissioned's 1991 CD *7*, Marvin Sapp, Eddie Howard, Jr., and Maxx Frank joined the group. Their hit cycle continued and the project featured the hits "I Love Thinking of You" and "Victory."

In 1994, Fred Hammond and Michael Williams made their last contributions to the group on the Top Ten album *Matters of the Heart*. The album featured cameos by Run D.M.C., Chucki Booker, and Dawkins & Dawkins. The group covered rock star Phil Collins's "Another Day in Paradise," and "We Shall Behold Him" became a radio smash.

There were still more personnel changes in store. Montrel Darrett joined the group for the hit album *Irreplaceable Love* in 1996, but Marvin Sapp exited the group by the time Commissioned went into the studio to record the 2000 CD *Time*, which featured two new members, Chris Poole and Marcus Cole. With virtually all of the group's original members off on their own, many felt that Commissioned's glory days were past. But there was one last hurrah left in the band. All of the original members came together in

2002 for a sold-out national concert tour, and the CD *Commissioned Reunion* sold more than 100,000 copies and was one of the bestselling projects of that year. Alas, it seems to have been the end of the road for the '80s supergroup. They have now retired the name, but the sound lives on.

Benjamin Cone, Jr.

ONE OF A DOZEN or so preachers who gained notoriety in the 1990s for their story songs, Benjamin Cone, Jr., was raised in Waycross, Georgia. After becoming an ordained minister, he relocated in Jackson, Mississippi, where he is director of Good Samaritan Ministries of Mississippi, a community philanthropic organization. Cone's thunderous baritone and precise articulation can be heard on an assortment of Malaco Records story songs and sermonettes (such as "It's Hammer Time" or "The Trial of Jesus") that hark back to the glory days of C.L. Franklin's greatest spoken word gospel projects.

Consolers

ONE OF THE FAVORED gospel acts of the 1950s, the Consolers created a legacy of common folk, traditional-styled church music. With just an acoustic guitar and two roughshod vocals, this married duo provided the public with an array of plaintive sermonettes, praise tunes, and guilt-laden songs about wayward children.

Sullivan Pugh was born on October 1, 1925, in the city of Morehaven, Florida, where his father was a farmer. Pugh's wife, Iola Lewis, was born July 22, 1926. They were both raised in church and shared a love for singing and revival meetings. "We met at a church," Pugh says of his late wife. "It was a tent service that was going on. I went there and I used to play the piano a little, so the pastor let me play the piano for the services. So I kept going back nightly to play and one night she came to the service and that's when we met." Although he says it wasn't love at first sight, it eventually evolved into love. "It was a good thing for both of us," he smiles.

Since they both had sung in local Miami groups, they decided to sing together circa 1951 and began to tour the Eastern US seaboard. From the beginning, their singing style possessed more commonality with a revival tent meeting than with technical singing. Sullivan's rough, ragged baritone was loud and upfront in equal competition with Iola's field-holler alto. On many of their songs, it's as if they are literally yelling the lyrics more than singing them. However, that style works well with the rootsy, acoustic music of the Consolers. "We were calling ourselves the Consolators when we first started out," Pugh recalls. "We were told by a DJ up in New York—this is before we made any records, we went up there and were singing—he said the proper word to use [grammatically] would be the Consolers. So we took his advice and changed it."

Back home in Miami, Henry Stone, a white entrepreneur who had a love for bluesy black music, was beginning to make a name for himself in the music business. When he was in the army during World War II, Stone befriended several Negro soldiers and played trumpet in an integrated army band. After his discharge, he worked for Jewel Records and Modern Records as a promoter. By 1947, he moved to Miami and launched his Seminole Distribution Company. Using an Apex reel-to-reel tape machine, Stone made a bunch of low-cost recordings of artists ranging from Ray Charles and John Lee Hooker to the Consolers. "He was trying to record a lot of the local gospel singers," Pugh explains. "We heard about it and got in touch with him. We did a couple of songs on that label." The first recording was a song Pugh wrote called "How Long Has It Been (Since You've Been Home)?" Pugh says of his inspiration for the song, "That was my very first song I ever wrote. It was a part of my life. I was very close to my family and they were close to me. That was the story." They recorded alternately as the Miami Soul Stirrers and the Spiritual Consolers for Stone's labels, Deluxe and Glory, in the 1952–53 period. Twenty years later, Stone would experience million-sellers such as Betty Wright's "Clean Up Woman," Gwen McCrae's "Rockin' Chair," and K.C. and the Sunshine Band's "Shake Your Booty." In 1952, however, he wasn't having a lot of success with the Consolers.

"We had signed a contract with him," Pugh says. "When that fell through, he told me, 'Well,. I'm not going to try to hold you to the contract. Why don't you try and get with a record label that's already established? I wish you much luck.' We had heard about Nashboro Records and they were very good. They were one of the companies we wrote to and it wasn't very hard at all. We sent a letter and Nashboro asked us to send a demo and that's what we did."

Although Pugh was from Florida, he had the spare Delta blues style of guitar that Mississippi-reared Pops Staples would popularize in the late 1950s with the Staple Singers. The Consolers' first single on Nashboro was the mid-tempo tune "Give Me My Flowers" in October 1955. The song was based on a story Pugh heard as a youngster. "I was told a story many years ago about a lady that was trying to…" he thinks a moment. "Well, she was going to a funeral and she took some food. And everybody was laughing at her because she took food to the funeral and everybody else was taking cards and flowers. She got a little upset with them and said, 'If our deceased friend can see those flowers you got there, then she can eat my soup.' So that's where I got the idea to write that song."

It went on to become one of the bestselling gospel songs of the period and the song most associated with the Consolers. When soul singer Candi Staton was a child, she sang in a group called the Jewel Gospel Trio. They were often on the same bill as the Consolers. "I remember that the house went up every time they sang that song," she recalls. "They didn't really say much to anybody else when we were backstage. They'd come in, pass by everybody, speak to whoever they had to speak to in order to be paid, do their part of the service, then turn around and leave. As a child, I often watched them leave and wondered why they didn't speak to anybody. Even though they were very dynamic on stage, I think they were a little shy face-to-face with people. It was funny to see them ride off because their car had bad springs or something, so whenever they drove off, their car would be jumping up and down because they were inside that buggy praising God like there was no tomorrow."

Over the next 20 years, the Pughs were one of the top-selling acts in gospel with hit songs such as "Waiting for My Child" and a re-recording of "How Long Has It Been." By the 1970s, with the contemporary gospel revolution, the Consolers had lost their radio appeal with their old-school traditional style, but continued to perform regularly in the South. "We went with Savoy Records out of New York for a couple of recordings," Pugh says. "It didn't work out too good because when Nashboro sold out, we went with Savoy Records. Then Savoy sold out to Malaco Records. Then we went on and signed with Atlanta International Records. We stayed there for a short while, but none of those records was as successful for us as Nashboro was."

The 1990s were especially quiet for the group, as Iola's health declined. "She suffered like most black people with sugar diabetes and high blood pressure," Pugh says. "I guess it got the best of her." She died October 11, 1994. There was not a lot of family left for Pugh to lean on. They never had children of their own, although they raised Iola's nephew as their own child. Pugh had two minor strokes in early 2004 and is working to get back to his full strength. "When I'm feeling pretty good, I get in there and rehearse on my guitar," he says. "But I've been very sick. They say I had a light stroke. Matter of fact, the doctor said I had two strokes. But I play anywhere that I can. If I feel up to it, I go. The doctors say to keep doing what I enjoy doing and it will work in my favor."

Money often works in people's favor too, so Pugh is asked whether he received royalties on all the songs he's written. "I have no complaints whatsoever," he replied. "I did nicely with Nashboro and a lot of the records that we put out went on to be considered as big sellers in gospel. Oh, yes, I get royalties. I mean it's nothing to brag about. But it's nice to be remembered down through the years." Shirley Caesar and Pops Staples remembered him. Staples covered "Waiting for My Child" on his 1994 Grammy-winning *Father Father* CD, and Caesar cut a very passionate, bluesy rendition of "How Long Has It Been" on her 2001 *Hymns* CD.

RECOMMENDED RECORDING: *Lord Bring Me Down* (MCA Special Products, 1998) is a mere ten songs, including "Give Me My Flowers" and "Waiting for My Child," but those are the Consolers' biggest hits.

Edna Gallmon Cooke

ONE OF THE SMOOTHEST, JAZZIEST of church singers
from the Golden Age of Gospel in the 1950s, Cooke
was never a huge star in terms of sales and radio play.
She was a consistent performer with a loyal following.
Her phrasing was similar to that of early Billie Holiday.
They were both sopranos with light vocal styles, yet
they punched a lot of emotion into their music in spite
of their vocal limitations. Cooke was better known for
her recorded sermonettes than for her singing, and no
one could deliver a fire-and-brimstone message as sincerely and innocently as Madame Cooke.

"She was a good friend of ours," the Consolers' Sullivan Pugh says. "A very lovely lady, a sincere gospel
singer." According to Eric LeBlanc's research, Cooke was
born August 26, 1899, in Columbia, South Carolina (not
1917 as has been cited elsewhere). Her father, Rev.
Eddie J. Gallmon, was a shouting preacher at Springfield
Baptist Church in Washington, DC. Cooke hailed from
a family that was well educated musically and academi-
cally. She attended Temple University in Philadelphia
and taught primary school for a period of time in Washington, DC.. She once considered a career in classical
music, but her real desire was to become a pop star. "She
wanted to be a show girl," J. Lowe, one of her featured
singers, says. "She was very classy and wanted to become
a Billie Holiday type of pop singer. But she met Willie
Mae Ford Smith and that changed everything." Cooke
joined the Holiness Church denomination, which
stressed dignity and sacred living. Cooke's natural elegance and subtle Barbara Stanwyck–like beauty earned
her the title Madame Cooke. Throughout the 1940s,
Cooke toured as "the Sweetheart of the Potomac."

After her first husband died, Cooke met her second
husband, Barney Parks (a shrewd businessman who had
founded the Dixie Hummingbirds) at a Philadelphia
concert in 1951. "It didn't take long," he laughs, for a romance to blossom. He soon became her husband and
her manager. "He guided her toward the stardom she
achieved," Lowe says. In November 1953, Cooke released
"Evening Sun" on the Nashville-based Republic Records
label (a subsidiary of Bill Beasley's Tennessee Records, which had R&B acts such as the Clips and the

Rovers). The lilting country ballad featured Cooke's sermonizing, backed by the Radio Four. At Nashboro she
recorded tracks such as "Nobody but You Lord," "The
Mule Talked," "Heavy Load," and "Seven Steps to Hell."

After her initial vocal recordings didn't take off,
Cooke began to employ the sermonette style of preaching her father used so effectively during her youth. Instead of wailing like many of her peers, she used her
voice in other ways to steal the audience's affection.
She'd moan and bend a note beyond recognition until
the audience gave her a standing ovation and was ready
to throw their shoes at the stage in approval. In those
successful days, Cooke cut quite a picture. She'd arrive
at the concert venue in a long, shiny Fleetwood Cadillac and step out of the car wearing a mink stole, her
hair perfectly coiffed. "She'd walk straight through the
back door and to her dressing room," Lowe says. "She
never went in through the front door. She never hung
out in the lobby. She wasn't common and didn't socialize, therefore, people kept her on a higher level than
the artists who would be out front socializing and in-
teracting. She didn't care if you were Sam Cooke or
anybody else. She stayed in her dressing room until
they called her to stage. She'd be in there reading her
Bible. She was real, she didn't play church."

Cooke toured with a pianist, Marge Cheeks, and
male backup group, the Sons of Faith. She would appear on bills with the hardest gospel singers around
but always held the audience captive. "It didn't matter
how many male groups came before her," Lowe says.
"When the emcees said, 'Now, we're going to Washington,' that meant Madame Cooke was about to come
on, and the people were ready for her. People were on
the edge of their seats just anticipating what she was
going to do. It was amazing to see such a stylish
woman do that. She'd come on stage almost dragging,
very slow and build from there. By the time she came
to the end of her program—she always closed with
'Heavy Load'—she'd start prancing across the stage
and she never lost that million-dollar smile. She'd say,
'On a Monday, I got rid of my heavy load.' Then she'd
go through the days of the week and at the end of each
day, she'd say, 'I got rid of my heavy load.' The music
would run so fast that it was almost like there was no

beat, but the tension she created between the music and what she was saying had the whole audience jumping. If I can say this, she was an anointed pro. She knew her audience."

All of the artists on the road had respect for Cooke. "She was my idol," Candi Staton says. "She was beautiful like a movie star and I wanted to be just like her. She was just such a step above everybody else." Roscoe Robinson, who replaced Archie Brownlee in the Five Blind Boys of Mississippi, says, "Madame Cooke was something else. She didn't mix with anybody. She'd get on me for slipping into the hotel with a woman. She'd be sitting outside her room in a chair reading the Bible. She tried to keep us all straight. She'd [speak up] to anyone she felt wasn't going the right way."

In 1961, Cooke recorded her biggest hit, the spoken "Stop, Gambler." She wrote the track in which she discussed how, before Jesus was hung on the cross, he was disrobed and gamblers gambled for who would get his robe. Using card deck terminology, she preached: "Look at that next gambler, he's throwing down the ace spot now, representing the highest card in the deck: God the Father, the one who made you. If I were you, I'd stop, gambler. I wouldn't use that card anymore." Cooke was no gambler. She and Parks didn't have the hard luck stories that many gospel artists faced. "I don't remember a time that she wasn't paid," Lowe says. "She wouldn't go on stage if she wasn't paid because that was how Barney Parks taught her. Even if she was paid, she wouldn't pay us, her singers, until she got on the phone and Barney said it was all right. She was a total professional." In addition, Cooke and Parks owned two hotels, one in Augusta, Georgia, and one in Hendersonville, North Carolina. The one in Hendersonville was connected to Edna's Diner on Pettigrew Street.

But all was not well. "She wasn't well when I met her," Parks says. "She was just a strong person and she loved what she was doing. She had a bad kidney, so the doctors took that one. Then the other one went bad. She wasn't the type to complain. We were down in Louisiana one time and she had to go to the hospital for three to four days." But Cooke would not leave the road. "It was rough seeing her that way," Lowe says. "Sometimes she'd lean on me so hard, but when she hit that stage, she was like another person. She'd do her program

and then almost stagger back to the dressing room." Lowe and Augustus Hawkins, her other background singer, were on the road with Cooke a week or so before the end. They drove her back to Henderson. "The look on her face, I didn't think she was going to make it that time," Lowe says. "The way she gripped my hand when we were leaving her said a lot. She said, 'I know you're going to stay with this business, so remember this: put the records out before the singer. Make the records hits before you introduce the singer.' That's just what I did. I went back and forth between gospel and R&B, but I always remembered what she said."

"The night before she went into the hospital [for the last time], Edna was over in Oxford [a North Carolina city]," Parks recalls. "She decided to go to her primary doctor in Philadelphia. She was with this guy named Gerald Alston who went on and joined the Manhattans [a soul group known for the song "Kiss and Say Goodbye"]. He rode as far as Philadelphia with her. At the time, we had a business here and I had to stay with the business. Gerald looked after her. She sang that night, but she just wasn't well. Once she was in Philadelphia at the hospital, Edna called me three days before she passed. I was supposed to go up to Philadelphia to see her over the weekend. She called me and said, 'Baby, don't come up on the weekend. I'll be home soon.' I don't know how she got to the phone or how she was talking like she did because she was really not well. I believe she knew she was dying. Two to three days later, her aunt called me and told me I better hurry if I wanted to see Edna alive. Before I could get there on the train, she passed." It was September 4, 1967. Cooke's body was taken to Washington for the funeral and then transported to her native South Carolina for burial. "Madame was the biggest female soloist of that time for black people," Lowe says. "Just as Mahalia was the biggest female soloist for the white audience. Madame was the biggest star for the black world."

Sam Cooke

ONE OF GOSPEL AND SOUL music's most important ambassadors, Sam Cooke composed gospel classics that are still sung today. He also made gospel music palatable to youth during a period when the demographics skewed old. He went on to become one of America's first black sex symbols and created a string of smooth, pop soul hits such as "Send Me" and "Cupid" that still have music critics hailing him as one of the best soul singers who ever lived.

One of eight children born to a Baptist minister and his wife, Cooke was born on January 22, 1931, in Clarksdale, Mississippi. He sang in his father's church and when the family moved to Chicago toward the end of the decade, he became immersed in the immense Chicago gospel scene. He and three of his brothers formed a gospel group called the Singing Children before Cooke abandoned them to join the Highway QCs. It was through the QCs that Cooke met the Soul Stirrers' baritone R.B. Robinson, who groomed Cooke to eventually take over for the Soul Stirrers' lead vocalist, R.H. Harris. Initially, when Cooke joined the group in 1950, he imitated Harris with disastrous results. He eventually developed his own style and his signature yodel that put him over the top. Add to that his youth and pretty boy looks, and the Soul Stirrers had the most successful run of their career. Cooke sang lead on smash hits such as "Wonderful," "Nearer to Thee," and his own compositions "Touch the Hem of His Garment" and "That's Heaven to Me." "Sam Cooke never sang too hard," Aretha Franklin wrote in her memoirs. "He sang hard occasionally, though, and when he did you were in for the best time of your life…. I was so influenced by him that Daddy told me to stop emulating Sam and instead express my own heart and soul."

A fan of pop groups such as the Ink Spots, Cooke had always longed to try his hand at secular music. In 1956, he recorded the love song "Lovable" under the name Dale Cook so as to not offend his gospel audience in case the record failed and he needed to go back to church singing for his bread and butter. It tested well enough for Cooke to leave the Soul Stirrers altogether and go solo. His 1957 debut under his own name, "You Send Me," sold two million copies and established him as an overnight sensation. Over the next few years, clean pop hits such as "Bring It on Home to Me," "Cupid," and "Twisting the Night Away" gave Cooke leverage to create his own enterprises. He and his manager, S.R. Crain (born June 7, 1911), formed a publishing com-

pany and SAR Records where they began to record a plethora of gospel and R&B acts. Cooke was still on great terms with the Soul Stirrers. They provided background vocals on some of his recordings, and he showed up on their concert bills whenever he could. Contrary to what has been reported in the past, associates of Cooke say that the fans never booed Cooke when he showed up, unannounced, on programs with the Soul Stirrers. "No, there was none of that," Roscoe Robinson laughs. "They were happy to see that Sam still remembered us little gospel folks."

Unlike most black artists of the period, Cooke enjoyed a diverse, integrated audience of young and middle-aged fans. He performed at sock hops, on *American Bandstand* on TV, as well as in sophisticated hotel lounges. Life was good and Cooke was a millionaire within a few short years. Although he was married with a child, Cooke was known to have a wandering eye. It caught up with him on December 11, 1964. The details are sketchy and shrouded in mystery. Cooke is believed to have had a rendezvous with an Asian hooker at the

Sam Cooke / Courtesy of Specialty/Fantasy Records

Hacienda Hotel in the Watts section of Los Angeles. Depending on who is to be believed, she either took his clothes or his money and left the scene. Cooke, in a rage to get to her, bolted out of the hotel room half-naked and shouting to the black hotel manager, Bertha Franklin, about the woman who had just robbed him. Not knowing who Cooke was, Franklin panicked and shot him dead. There was a media frenzy when the news hit the wire services. Black fans claimed a conspiracy, many in the mainstream press suggested that Cooke had raped a woman, and his old friends thought he had been framed by business interests who felt Cooke was too independent. Because Cooke was black, the LAPD didn't seriously investigate the homicide, and more than 40 years later, there are still more questions than answers as to what really happened to Cooke on that ill-fated evening. Regardless of how he died, Cooke's music lives on and continues to inspire new generations of listeners.

RECOMMENDED RECORDING: *Portrait of a Legend* (ABKO, 2003) is a 30-track CD that includes two of Cooke's best-known gospel numbers, "Touch the Hem of His Garment" and "Jesus Gave Me Water." It also includes virtually every pop song that Cooke is identified with, such as "You Send Me" and "Everybody Loves to Cha Cha Cha."

Denny Correll

IF DENNY CORRELL HAD STUCK with rock music in the 1970s, he could have eventually become a Rod Stewart or Joe Cocker. With his raspy, blues-infused voice he would have been a serious contender; but he felt his calling was to the Christian music industry, which to this date does not support Correll's hard-edged, blues-based style of music. There are no Christian blues artists on the order of Correll, Larry Howard, or Trace Balin recording for the major labels today.

Born Dennis Correll on February 19, 1946, Correll's entrée to the rock world would be through Blues Image. The band was formed in Tampa, Florida, in 1966 by guitarist/lead vocalist Michael Pinera, percussionist Manuel Bertematti, and drummer Joe Lala. They were joined later by Welsh bassist Malcolm Jones and keyboard player Frank Konte. In 1968, the band moved to New York City where they managed a club called the Image. They regularly played their bluesy rock at the club and ended up snatching a recording contract with Atlantic Records' Atco subsidiary. Their eponymous debut LP didn't make any noise, but their 1970 follow-up LP *Open* featured the No. 4 pop smash "Ride Captain Ride." Not long after, Pinera left the group and Correll became their primary vocalist. The band's subsequent material such as the *Red, White & Blues* LP didn't make the score, and they eventually broke up. In 1975, Correll recorded a single, "Good Old Rock and Roll," on A&M Records. Correll and some other members then formed Manna. After that stint was over, Correll recorded what most music critics consider his shining achievement as a musician, the *Standing in the Light* LP that appeared on Marantha Records in 1979. Over the next few years, he released an array of poorly received LPs for Myrrh, including *How Will They Know*, *Something I Believe In*, and *Living Water*. He died of heart failure on November 30, 2002, in Newport Beach, California.

Guy Costley

AN EXTREMELY WELL-ROUNDED ATHLETE (from football to archery and stilt walking), dancer (studied under *The Wiz*'s choreographer George Faison), singer (attended the Brooklyn Academy of Music), and actor (honed his skills at the Papermill Playhouse), the New Jersey–based performer Guy David Costley has appeared in McDonald's commercials, network television films, and played the minister of music in Vy Higgensen's off-Broadway musical, *Mama, I Want to Sing*. He briefly made some noise in the dance market with his percolating gospel track "Somebody Here" on the New Jersey–based garage music label Movin' Records in 1992.

Craig Brothers

THIS TEENAGE SIBLING DUO was introduced by Rev. James Cleveland. They made a handful of quasi-contemporary gospel LPs for Savoy Records in the 1980s. Their LPs include *James Cleveland Presents the Craig Brothers* (1980) and *He Wants a Place* (1982).

Beverly Crawford

ONE OF THE BRIGHTEST ARTISTS to arrive on the gospel scene in the last dozen years, Beverly Crawford's raw talent is a pleasant throwback to the gospel queens of the Golden Age of Gospel. She can moan like Mahalia Jackson, squall like Inez Andrews, testify like Shirley Caesar, and sing like nobody's business. Still very youthful and exuberant in her performances, she has not yet established a signature song, but it's certain to come in time. In the meantime, she's best known for songs such as "Run to the Water" and "Ride on King Jesus."

One of seven children, Crawford was born in August 1964 in Gainesville, Florida. Her father was pastor of the Holy Temple of God Church, and she served as his worship leader when she came of age. After singing throughout her adolescence, Crawford sang Candi Staton's disco song "Honest I Do" at a high school talent show where an impressed secular record label executive then offered her a record deal. Her mother turned it down saying, "No, that's not the kind of music we want to sing." Crawford went on to sing with her sisters as the Camp Sisters. In 1989, Crawford's husband taped a concert they did at a church and sent it to various record labels. The only person who responded, a year later, was Bobby Jones. She was booked to do his BET television show and soon became a regular.

Crawford told *Gospel Today* magazine, "After I had been with Bobby Jones about three years, [my husband] Todd said, 'I'm going to put the word out that you're ready to go solo.' I told him, 'Nobody wants to sign me.' But then I talked with Demetrus Alexander about it." Alexander signed Crawford to Warner Alliance Records in 1994, and her debut CD *Jesus, Precious King* appeared the following year. After another album, Warner closed its gospel division and Crawford eventually ended up on T.D. Jakes's Dexterity label where songs such as "Run to the Water" became respectable radio hits. "If I step on a stage and there's one person in the audience, I'm going to give the same thing I'd

Left to right: Beverly Crawford, Candi Staton, Vickie Winans, Shirley Caesar, and BAM Crawford / *photo by Bil Carpenter*

give a million," Crawford says, "because that life matters to God, and that may be the one life that he's going to use me to change. In Christ, we're all family and friends, and my greatest job is simply to be available for him to use me as he chooses."

Clay Crosse

ONE OF THE MOST SOULFUL Christian artists on the scene, Clay Crosse came out with a bang and seems to have vanished with a whimper. From 1993 to 1997, Crosse held his own with Steven Curtis Chapman and Michael W. Smith with a half dozen No. 1 Christian singles such as "His Love Is Comin' Over Me." Born February 11, 1967, Crosse's mother was pianist at Leawood Baptist Church in Memphis. He sang at their church and then got a singing job at an amusement park. At the same time, he took a courier job at Federal Express and worked on a demo during his time off. Singer Gary McSpadden was in town performing, so Crosse took the demo to him. Listening to it on his way home, McSpadden pulled his car to the side of the road and flagged down his son, Shawn, who was following him in another car. "You've got to hear this," he yelled. Shawn liked it too and signed Crosse to McSpadden/Smith management, which he ran with his business partner, Ron Smith.

They got Crosse signed to Reunion Records in 1993. Using producers Peter Bunetta and Rick Chudacoff (who'd worked with Kenny G, Smokey Robinson, and Kathy Troccoli), he produced a soulful CCM debut CD, *My Place Is with You*. The album has sold 70,000. "The last thing I ever want to be is plastic or fake or cheery. At the same time, I don't want to be a stick in the mud and gloomy," Crosse said then. "I want to sing songs that relate to what I'm feeling. A lot of people are content and have joy at all times, but most are not overly happy all of the time. …. Ultimately, this album is about joy… the joy of finding Jesus Christ, but I think it paints a realistic picture of the struggle of trying to walk through life serving him."

Crosse followed in 1995 with *Time to Believe*, which doubled the sales of his debut CD and earned him a Dove award for New Artist of the Year. The third album, 1997's *Stained Glass*, sold even better and gained him a Dove nomination for Best Male Vocalist of the Year. In 1999, he released *I Surrender All: The Clay Crosse Collection Vol. 1*. His 2000 release *Different Man* didn't really catch on with radio and only sold 40,000.

"As Christians, we should have some sort of filter system in our lives, and I had just shut mine off altogether," Crosse said in an interview on his Web site. "I got to a point where these influences and the lasting images I had from my past began to manifest themselves in real ways in my life. The past is sad to think about, but I do have a real joy now. I have a peace that I didn't have before. I am really at a broken place, and that's a good thing. My focus has certainly changed. I used to deal with real issues of pride, and the whole industry thing was very important to me. But that has all changed. I feel like God has made me a little more lowly, but I feel his power in my life like I never have before. I want his will in my life—in my career and in my marriage. I feel such a freedom now. Do I want to sell more records? Yeah. But is that why I'm excited? No. I'm excited because I really have something to say and I want you to hear it. The title of this album even challenges me to continue to ask myself, 'Am I really a different man?' I want to be able to say, 'Yeah, that's me!' A different man means someone who is seeking God wholeheartedly. God's word to me has been to just let go of all of these other distractions and to follow him completely. We have to take an aggressive stance and commit our lives wholeheartedly to Christ…. My career is still important, but it's not all-consuming. Everything is different. I'm not just touring anymore, I'm crusading. I'm so excited—not because I have a new album, but because I have a lot to say. The book of Romans says, 'In all things God works for the good of those who love him.' I want to tell my story because I hope it will give others the courage to change."

Cross Movement

THIS PHILADELPHIA-BASED RAP ensemble is perhaps the most respected hip-hop group to rise from the Christian music industry. John "The Tonic" Wells, William "Ambassador" Branch, Brady "Phanatik" Goodwin, and Virgil "T.R.U.-L.I.F.E." Byrd all belonged to other Christian rap groups in the past but came together as a group in 1994. Their street-hard, real-issue approach to Christian rap won them applause beyond the four walls of the church. Suddenly record labels were offering contracts, but the group decided to remain independent. Their first project was 1997's *Heaven's Mentality*, which sold well at their packed concerts. Although the group has produced music videos such as "Know Me (Huh, What?)" and "House of Representatives," they have failed to connect to the Christian mainstream. Their 2003 CD *Holy Culture* debuted at No. 134 on the *Billboard* pop album chart and No. 10 on the CCM chart, but fell off the charts the following week and never returned. Still, it sold 90,000 units. The group has suffered from poor distribution and a lack of marketing dollars. However, they continue to hang in the game and keep making music that leaves their fans wondering why they aren't superstars yet. It all rolls back to the idea that the Christian music industry still isn't ready for hip-hop. "I'd like to do a hip-hop/R&B-based tour in the spring, but I'm too concerned that our industry won't respond," DC Talk's TobyMac told *Billboard* magazine in 2001. "I live in a city [Nashville] where our Christian hit radio station barely plays hip-hop/R&B, while our mainstream hit radio station plays 75 percent hip-hop/R&B. Our industry has a problem that needs to be resolved. Our industry makes hip-hop/R&B music a bubble within a bubble, whereas in the mainstream it's included in a wider pop offering."

In 2004, John Wells was diagnosed with an anxiety disorder that hit him as he was performing onstage in Orlando. "Before I knew it, I was being carted away in an ambulance, and they weren't sure what was going on with me," he told *CCM* magazine in February 2005. "I was having an irregular heartbeat, high blood pressure, irregular breathing. I basically thought it was over, and I was checking out." With his health on the mend, Wells insisted to *CCM* that the Cross Movement isn't finished. "I think we're continuing to put our hands to the plow in terms of trying to be elders to, specifically, the Christian holy hip-hop culture…. We're really gearing ourselves up to make disciples."

Andrae Crouch

PERHAPS NO ONE PERSON has had as much influence on contemporary gospel music as Andrae Crouch. From the example he has set as a composer of songs such as "My Tribute: To God Be the Glory," "Through It All," and "Soon and Very Soon" to his use of backing groups and nontraditional instrumentation, Crouch has truly earned his title as the Godfather of Gospel Music.

Crouch and his twin sister, Sandra, were born July 1, 1947, in San Francisco, California. Crouch's father owned a dry cleaning business and was pastor at Christ Memorial COGIC, where Crouch's musical foundation was laid. He was singing and playing the piano before he was ten years old. At the age of 16, he formed Andrae Crouch and the Disciples with Sandra on drums/percussion, Fletch Wiley, Perry Morgan, and Billy Thedford. The group often sang on Audrey Meier's famed Monday Night Sing concerts in Southern California. One day, Meier introduced Crouch to Tim Spencer at Manna Music Publishing, who went on to publish Crouch's first song, "The Blood Will Never Lose Its Power." Crouch had written the song when he was 15 and was so disenchanted with his work that he threw it in the trash. Sandra saw its beauty and retrieved it, and

40 years later, it's one of the most recorded songs in gospel music history.

Next, Spencer introduced Crouch's music to Light Records founder Ralph Carmichael. The group's 1970 debut LP *Take the Message Everywhere* featured "The Blood Will Never Lose Its Power," "What Makes a Man Turn His Back on God," and "Without a Song." Crouch's unique vocal arrangements and pop music styling helped usher in what would become known as the Jesus Movement—a cultural revolution among young Christians to make their faith simple and their music hip during the age of the hippies. As a testament to his broad appeal, Crouch and his group performed on the *Tonight Show with Johnny Carson* in 1972. The debut and subsequent albums were great successes with the white Christian market in part due to the aggressiveness of Light's distributor, Word/Myrrh Records.

Billy Ray Hearn is the founder of Sparrow Records, and he was the vice president of Word Records when the label distributed Crouch's music via Light Records. "I was a renegade with Myrrh," Hearn jokingly recalls. "There are a lot of things I did that they had never done before." As a favor to his pal Ralph Carmichael, Hearn helped Crouch cross over to the black audience and begin the praise and worship movement in the black church. "I started promoting Andrae Crouch to the white stations and to the black gospel stations," Hearn says. "The black stations like WQBH in Detroit with Martha Jean the Queen. She had never played Andrae Crouch because he was mainly being sold to the white crowd. So I got her to play that. And then I was really instrumental in getting Andrae accepted by the black community because he wasn't. He was basically a white artist and I got him to cross over into the black stations."

Since Crouch was at the center of the contemporary Christian music field's praise and worship revolution with songs such as "Jesus Is the Answer," it's no surprise that once he crossed over to the black church, there was a ripple affect. Soon other black gospel artists began to introduce worship songs into the black church. Former soul singer Candi Staton contributed "I Will Praise" (adopted by churches from coast to coast) and "Glorify Your Name." By the 1990s artists such as Fred

Hammond, Judy McAllister, and Ron Kenoly had taken worship music to a new level of prestige.

Crouch was at the center of it all. By the end of the 1970s, he had become a top concert draw and his 1978 *Live in London* project captured the excitement of his concerts. Crouch even became popular in Hollywood, where he appeared as himself on the CBS sitcom *The Jeffersons*, *Soul Train*, a Barbara Mandrell special, and even on NBC's *Saturday Night Live*. After scoring a huge hit with the ballad "I'll Be Thinking of You," which graced both the Hot 100 R&B singles and the R&B album charts with its presence in 1979, Crouch signed to Warner Bros. Records. Crouch's records became even more ambitious. The 1981 *Don't Give Up* LP marked the beginning of "he" replacing "Jesus" in gospel songs. Among the songs were "I'll Be Good to You, Baby." It was a title that had Crouch fans asking whether Crouch had left gospel to become a love song singer. In fact, the song was an anti-abortion ballad. The album still proved successful and reached No. 51 on the R&B album sales chart. After one more LP, *No Time to Lose*, Crouch took a self-imposed sabbatical from recording. He had been arrested for cocaine possession in 1983, but the charges were eventually dropped for lack of evidence. Although he denied any wrongdoing, the story hit the press and somewhat sullied Crouch's stellar reputation. It was time for a break.

During his break, Crouch served in his parents' church and also devoted time to film scores. He collaborated with Quincy Jones on the soundtrack for *The Color Purple*. That work led to other score work for the films *The Lion King* and *Free Willy*. In addition, his Andrae Crouch Singers choir was in A-list demand for secular recording sessions in Hollywood for artists such as Diana Ross, D-Knowledge, Michael Jackson, Elton John, Julio Iglesias, and others. They received a bit of criticism from the church community when they backed pop star Madonna on her 1989 hit "Like a Prayer." In the video for the controversial song, Catholic-reared Madonna portrayed herself as being crucified. Church groups found the images sacrilegious. Pepsi-Cola yanked their Madonna commercials from the air because of public outrage.

During the early 1990s, Crouch was dealt an emotional blow when his mother died of cancer. "For many months I was bitter," he told *CCM* magazine in May 1994. "I was wondering why God didn't heal her. Why did he take her? I knew it wasn't right for me to feel that way, but I said, 'What happened to my prayers that he would heal anything if I asked it in his name?' What happened to that?" A year later, his father also died of cancer. "I had matured by then," Crouch said. "I didn't ask those questions anymore." Out of those tragedies, Crouch birthed *Mercy*, his first studio album in almost a decade. Fueled by the radio success of the R&B-styled ballad "The Lord Is My Life," featuring El DeBarge, and "Nobody Else but You," the project won Crouch his seventh Grammy award and put him firmly back in the public eye. "Andrae Crouch was definitely missed," says Percy Williams, a gospel announcer with WBLS radio in New York City. "And people were eager to hear his new offerings. The response was phenomenal. Though he had been absent for some time, listeners were well aware of and graciously welcomed the return of his ministry and artistry." In the time since, Crouch has created other fine CDs such as the Top Ten *Pray* and the all-star holiday masterpiece *The Gift of Christmas*. He and Sandra are planning to launch their own recording label, Slave Records, in 2005.

Sandra Crouch

THE TWIN SISTER OF GOSPEL pioneer Andrae Crouch, Sandra Crouch is an accomplished musician in her own right. She's been by her brother's side at every step in his career. In 1964, when they were 16, they founded Andrae Crouch and the Disciples. A drummer and percussionist, Crouch played tambourine on numerous West Coast recording sessions by Janis Joplin and Mongo Santamaria. She even played percussion for jazz great Gabor Szabo and numerous Motown sessions with Diana Ross. Over the years, she's written several songs, such as "Jesus Is the Answer," which she co-wrote with Andrae.

In 1983, Crouch recorded her first solo LP, *We Sing Praises*. It won a Grammy award and produced the radio hits "He's Worthy" (led by soprano Jean Johnson), "Holy Spirit" (led by Howard Smith), and "We Sing Praises," which Crouch sang the lead on. Her next CD,

We're Waiting, in 1985 included the massive hit "Completely Yes," sung by church choirs nationwide. Her last CD, *With All of My Heart,* was released on Sparrow Records in the autumn of 1992. To promote the project, Crouch went on a concert tour, *Gospel: Good for the Soul,* with Daryl Coley and the Richard Smallwood Singers. In 1998, Andrae defied the COGIC denomination's policy against female preachers and ordained Sandra as a co-pastor of their late father's church, Christ Memorial COGIC.

Benny Cummings

"I HAVE HIS CD IN MY CD PLAYER NOW," gospel-soul singer Richard Hartley says of Benny Cummings. "He was the epitome of the modern choir master, skilled at writing, directing, producing, and playing the piano. He was at the forefront of the contemporary choir movement." Cummings and his twin brother were born in 1951, but his music sounds as if it were born around 1991. Although the COGIC denomination is known for its great musicians, it isn't known for contemporary music, but rather, for innovative traditional gospel music. In the late 1970s, when Cummings began to record the New York–based King's Temple Choir for Nashboro Records, he was creating innovative contemporary music for the time. The music had the backdrop of traditional gospel, but the intense vocal harmonies, liberal use of synthesizers (a rarity at the time), and thick chord progressions made the Benny Cummings experience something out of the ordinary. Gospel star Donnie McClurkin even sang with the choir for a spell during his youth. The group was mostly an East Coast phenomenon with radio successes such as "Every Step of the Way," "Sign of the Judgment," Jesus Is Knocking," and "Hold Out" (1981). In the 1980s, Cummings developed a close working relationship with John Lennon and Yoko Ono. He sang background vocals on Lennon's final LP, *Double Fantasy,* in 1980. He also recorded vocals on several Ono solo projects. After his LP *By His Stripes* on Gospearl Records in 1987, Cummings recorded a couple of independent albums for Sound Solutions Records. Although Cummings passed away in the 1990s, it's a reminder of his influence that his

music has been covered by such current innovators as DeAndre Patterson, the Shekinah Choir, and Ricky Dillard and the New Generation Chorale.

Daddy Grace

IN THE EARLY-TO-MIDDLE 20th century, Sweet Daddy Grace was one of the most beloved and controversial evangelists in black America. Operating from his United House of Prayer for All People in New Bedford, Massachusetts, Bishop Charles Manuel "Sweet Daddy" Grace was a dynamic preacher. He was an even more impressive showman. Whether one believed his theology or not, Grace always gave a great show. He wore expensive tailored clothes, sported gaudy jewelry, and was even known to paint his fingernails. At his height of fame, the self-proclaimed "boyfriend of the world" presided over hundreds of churches, had a multi-million dollar manufacturing operation, and boasted three million followers.

Born Mercelino Graca on January 15, 1881, in Brava (Cape Verde Islands), his family moved to New Bedford in 1903, and Grace worked on a railroad line as a short order cook. Much of his early life is a mystery, as he did not want the public to know of his humble beginnings. After an early marriage ended in divorce, Grace changed his name to hide his prior identity and founded the United House of Prayer for All People in 1921. He set up House of Prayer affiliate churches all over the US and even in Egypt. Grace catered his sermons to the black poor and preached a theology of prosperity and upward mobility. For some people, he inspired them to reach for higher aspirations in life. Others paid his church tithes and offerings expecting a financial blessing in return for their sacrifice. Although he preached to the poor, Grace had no program to aid the indigent. His sermons were meant to enrich himself. He did not depend on church contributions alone, though. He also manufactured a "healing" soap that cleansed the body and allegedly reduced body fat. He sold his own brand of hair pomade, toothpaste, coffee, cookies, and cosmetics. Grace also owned an insurance company and burial plots. During his lifetime, he was clandestinely one of the richest men in America. He even bought one of John Rockefeller's homes.

In his heyday, Grace required his congregations to attend services seven days a week. They began with 20 minutes on their knees in prayer, followed by an hour of boisterous praise and worship accompanied by the gifts of the spirit such as speaking in tongues, tarrying before the Holy Ghost, and being slain in the spirit. The loud commotion often flooded the surrounding neighborhood and the police were called in by angry neighbors to keep the peace. Much like Muhammad Ali in his prime, Grace was his own best advertisement. He exuded a cocky arrogance, which both distracted and attracted followers. He once said, "If you sin against God, grace can save you, but if you sin against Grace, God cannot save you." Another time, Grace said that "If Moses came back now, he'd have to follow this man," pointing to himself.

Over the years, Grace spent time in prison and was in and out of trouble with the IRS for tax evasion. He was also frequently hauled off to court to defend himself against charges of being a charlatan and ripping off the poor. Grace finally died in his 85-room Los Angeles mansion in 1960. More than 5,000 spectators came out for his funeral, which was preached by himself—he had recorded his own eulogy on tape some years before.

Damita

TO MANY IN THE GOSPEL FOLD, she's merely the spouse of Deitrick Haddon, but Damita is a rising star in her own right. Runway-model looks, electrifying stage energy, and a diverse contemporary sound that stretches from rock to the blackest of grooves, Damita has all that it takes to become a major star on the gospel scene. She and her twin sister Marguerita were born September 4, 1971, in Detroit, Michigan. Their father, Walter Bass, was assistant pastor at the Southwestern Church of God through the 1970s, then he pastored a church in Meadville, Pennsylvania, for four years before he moved his family back to Michigan and pastored a church near Sumter. "My parents were very strict," Damita says. "We were not allowed to listen to

any music other than gospel. As children, we would have to sneak and listen to secular music. We would listen to Aretha Franklin, the Sugar Hill Gang. We tried to hear all that we couldn't hear at home. Sometimes we'd get caught listening to something and my father would say, 'What's that I hear? That don't sound like gospel!' And we'd have to turn it off. We weren't allowed to wear make-up. We couldn't wear shoes that showed our toes. It was very restricting at times."

However, there were no restrictions to her singing gospel. She would wake in the morning to the sounds of James Cleveland on the record player as her mother, Ruby, cleaned the house. Damita used to harmonize with her sister and her cousin Sheila Smith, and soon they were performing at church and other public places. At one point, they decided to form a group called Adoration and Praise. The legendary gospel conductor Mattie Moss Clark often dispensed advice to the young group. "She would talk to us about staying together and working [on our] technique. We sang in her Michigan State Choir. Her advice was to open our mouths and sing. She knew when you weren't singing too. She knew when you were lip-synching. I was at a rehearsal and I was so tired of singing, so I just started moving my mouth. She said, 'You ain't singing!' and called me out in front of everybody. She was extremely tough, but I appreciated the attention she gave us."

After graduating from McKenzie High School, Damita won a lead role in the touring gospel musical *Mama Don't*, which went on the road for a year. The play's producer funded Adoration and Praise's demo album. After performing at a surprise birthday party for the president of TM Records, the group was offered a contract by the president. They added Pamela Taylor to the group, became a quartet, and released their a cappella LP *Time Is Running Out* in 1991. It was a strong seller and reached No. 17 on the gospel chart, leading to some touring opportunities, but they eventually broke up due to personality conflicts.

Afterwards, Damita said, "I just worked in the church, sang in the choir. Our choir did an album and I traveled with that. I had little solo songs that became known. I traveled with Deitrick Haddon and Voices of Unity. There were plenty of times I could have stepped out there and said I want to do a solo thing, but I wanted to wait on God." After Damita had sung with Haddon's Voices of Unity a while, they developed a strong friendship that evolved into a romance. They eventually married circa 1996 and Damita continued singing leads with Voices of Unity. At one point there was a buzz about Haddon as an upcoming star in the music business, and executives from Atlantic Records began to watch him with possible interest in signing him to the label.

The appealing element to the Voices of Unity was Damita as much as it was Haddon himself, so the executives passed on signing Haddon. "Some of the executives had heard me sing with Deitrick's group and when they found out I wasn't signed to a label, they offered me a contract," she said in 2000. Haddon was assigned to produce Damita's debut album. Among the first batch of songs they submitted to the label were four awesome duets, including "Visions" and "You've Been Good." However, it was rumored that executives felt the project was becoming too much of a Haddon album instead of a Damita album, so the duo was sent back into the studio to come up with more songs. Atlantic only kept five of the original fifteen songs Haddon submitted for consideration. They dropped all the duets except for "Wedding Song," which was recut by legendary producer Arif Mardin. One of the other saved songs, "Hold on 2 Your Faith," was originally a mellower pop-styled track, which they transformed into a rocking number. They also added a remake of Mother's Finest's "Truth" with a rap by Toby McKeehan of DC Talk and a beautiful urban AC song called "Won't Be Afraid" by an outside producer.

After the eponymous album hit the streets in autumn 2000, Damita went on a promotional tour for *Bride* magazine and made the rounds of gospel media. In spite of a slick, non-gospel CD cover and a decent marketing budget, the gospel radio response was lukewarm and Atlantic's hopes of making Damita an across-the-board star died. The targeted single "Hold On to Your Faith" was not even added to some of the primary gospel radio stations' play lists. There was more success on Christian rock radio where "Truth" made the Top 20 and on urban AC radio where "Won't Be Afraid" hit the Top 30—no small accomplishment. Perhaps the fact that the album made some noise on three distinctly dif-ferent radio formats may answer why it wasn't a bigger hit. After Warner Bros. Records bought Word Records (which had already merged with Atlantic's Christian division) in 2002, most of the black artist roster was allowed to end their contracts with Atlantic, including Damita. She is currently on the praise team at Paula White's Church Without Walls in Tampa, Florida.

Alvin Darling

ALVIN DARLING WROTE songs such as "He's All Over Me" for Bishop Jeff Banks and the Revival Mass Choir and "A Mother Cries" for Dorothy Norwood. He and Norwood wrote the megahit "Somebody Prayed for Me" in 1994. The Alvin Darling Ensemble recorded albums for Inspirational Sounds and Savoy Records in the late '70s and early '80s.

Montrel Darrett

A SINGER WITH A RETRO '70s soul vibe, Darrett's music touches on a variety of contemporary issues from a Christian perspective. But he has always stressed that he is not a church singer. "I'm not a gospel singer," he once said. "I'm an artist who loves God." Perhaps his failure to distinctly classify himself as such (in spite of recording for EMI Gospel Records) is why he has yet to be embraced fully by the gospel community.

Born in 1965 in Evansville, Indiana, Darrett lost both of his parents to cancer early in life. At the age of 11, his family relocated to Nashville where they lived in the notorious John Henry Hill projects, where crime and drugs ran hand in hand. In spite of his mother's rearing him in church, Darrett served jail time for drug offenses. He eventually straightened out and earned a football scholarship to Nebraska State University before he joined the navy. It was after a tour of duty during the 1991 Gulf War that Darrett recommitted himself to Christianity. He had recorded his first song, "Walk Around Heaven," as a child and decided to come back to music on his return. After singing stints with John P. Kee and Commissioned, Darrett snagged a solo recording deal with EMI Records where he recorded the stellar

Chronicles of the Soul CD. The album had a mellow Isley Brothers–Marvin Gaye groove. The songs subtly reflected Darrett's faith and the album touched on a number of everyday issues. The album received high praise in a few mainstream publications such as *Rap Pages* and *Billboard* but scarce attention in the gospel world. EMI serviced "Free" as a single to urban radio. However, it only received scattered radio play, mostly in the deep South. Not long after the CD's release, Darrett's daughter was killed in a car accident. After producing a few tracks on other EMI Gospel artists, Darrett and the label parted company.

Davis Sisters

LONG BEFORE FEMALE gospel aggregations were in vogue, the Davis Sisters surfaced on the landscape with such a powerful presence that most gospel audiences were initially taken aback. They were gospel's hardest singers, and they often dressed in uniforms or gender-neutral clothing. Other singers hated to share stages with them because—whether they were male or female groups—the Davis Sisters were likely to steal the show based on their dynamic vocal theatrics.

The Davis Sisters were raised in the Fire Baptized Pentecostal/Holiness denomination, known for its fire-and-brimstone messages and athletic worship services where the congregation tarried until the Holy Ghost came. At their home church in Philadelphia, Mount Zion, the pastor often called the Davis Sisters to sing before the congregation as children. Even during their teens, the Davis Sisters' stage presence was so assured and their vocals so mature and powerful that they developed a reputation throughout the city as "house rockers." In 1945, they formally began to perform as a group. They accepted invitations to perform in nearby states where their fame grew to the point where they were nicknamed the Famous Davis Sisters because their name and reputation preceded them.

Ruth "Baby Sis" Davis (April 19, 1927–January 2, 1970), Thelma Davis (1930–January 2, 1955), Audrey Davis (born January 24, 1932; died January 1982), Alfreda Davis (born 1935; died 1989) and their piano-playing cousin Curtis Dublin (1928–December 29,

1964) first recorded for Gotham Records in 1947, but their first major hit was "Jesus Steps Right In" in 1952. By that time, they had added Imogene Green (1930–1986) to the lineup. Ruth and Greene cut loose on the August 1952 follow-up hit "By and By." The sisters were on a roll and kept churning out uptempo, scream and shout, pew-jumping hits such as a cover of Alex Bradford's "Too Close to Heaven," "Twelve Gates to the City," and "He Understands, He'll Say Well Done."

Thelma died in 1955. It's been written that she died in a house fire, but family friend Willa Ward (of the Clara Ward Singers) says, "There wasn't any fire. She got sick and died." A while later, Jackie Verdell joined the group and specialized in performing dramatic ballads that showcased her rich, controlled contralto. In her memoirs, Aretha Franklin wrote: "I also considered Jackie Verdell of the Davis Sisters one of the best and most underrated female soul singers of all time. It was through Jackie that I learned the expression 'Girl, you peed tonight,' meaning you were dynamite. Several nights Jackie sang so hard she literally had a spot or two on her robe from peeing. Singing far too hard, I also peed here and there in the early days; I quickly realized no one should sing that hard." Verdell later recorded for Peacock Records from 1961 to 1964.

After Gotham went out of business, the Davis Sisters recorded for Savoy Records until 1962. By the 1960s the group had begun to lose steam as radio programmers focused on younger groups, and they were sidelined by several personnel changes and personal traumas. Ruth's health problems (diabetes and liver and kidney disease) ended her life just after New Year's in 1970, and the group was finally finished as their mascot was laid to rest. "I loved them, all of them," Dorothy Norwood says. "Jackie Verdell was one of my best friends. I was living up in New Jersey and I would go down to the Davis Sisters' house all the time. We occasionally would sing together on programs." She saw Ruth Davis just before her death. "I saw her in Atlanta. She was sick but she made the concert. She had a problem, I think it was in her stomach. I remember the man got up at the funeral and made a statement. He said about a month or two ago, the Davis sisters had a program. It wasn't at that church but somewhere else in [Philadelphia]. He said they probably had 50 people and now you can't get in here [the place is so packed with mourners]." The remaining sisters all died virtually anonymously over the next 20 years.

RECOMMENDED RECORDING: Though a quintet, the Davis Sisters sounded like a small choir with their full, rich sound. Sadly, all of their fine music remains out of print. Anything one can find on the Savoy Records label is a listening epiphany.

Billy Davis, Jr.

A SOULFUL TENOR WITH a gorgeous upper range, Davis was born June 26, 1940, in St. Louis, Missouri. He sang with the St. Louis Gospel Singers as a teenager and recorded one single for the Hudson label called "Lord I'm Satisfied" in the late 1950s. Davis won fame and fortune as a featured vocalist with the Fifth Dimension pop vocal group in the 1960s. They recorded such classic pop singles as "Wedding Bell Blues," "Last Night I Didn't Get to Sleep at All," and "Aquarius/Let the Sunshine In," which spent six weeks at No. 1 on the Hot 100 pop singles chart in 1969. That same year, Davis married group member Marilyn McCoo, and they eventually enjoyed a career as a duo with the smash, Grammy-winning single "You Don't Have to Be a Star (to Be in My Show)" in 1976. Although they remained happily married, the duo performed separately after 1981. They recorded the praise tune "Praise Ye the Lord" on Davis's 1982 traditional-styled black gospel LP *Let Me Have a Dream*, backed by a James Cleveland Choir. They later did a beautiful love duet of "I Believe in You and Me" (it shows off his delicious upper range and was popularized later by Whitney Houston) for McCoo's 1983 RCA LP *Solid Gold*. Davis is an avid entrepreneur. He's invested in several businesses over the years in between occasional stage work in musicals such as *Dream Girls*. In the 1990s, Davis triumphed over prostate cancer. In 2001, McCoo and Davis had recurring roles on the UPN TV series *The Jamie Foxx Show*.

RECOMMENDED RECORDING: *Let Me Have a Dream* (Savoy Records, 1982) features Davis's energetically soulful renditions of black church classics such as

"Steal Away" and his beautiful rendition of Danniebelle's "Let Me Have a Dream."

Clifton Davis

BEST KNOWN AS Rev. Reuben Gregory on the 1980s sitcom *Amen*, Clifton Davis has had a long career in and out of church. Born October 4, 1945, in Chicago to an evangelist, Davis and two of his thirteen siblings formed a gospel trio during their teens. Davis became a minister while attending a Seventh Day Adventist high school, the Pine Forge Institute. From there, he enrolled at Oakwood College where he formed the Chapel Four, a gospel quartet. After college, he worked in a mental hospital until he saw a play called *The Apple Tree*, starring Alan Alda. Seeing the actors bring those characters to life inspired Davis to act professionally. After a bit part in Barbra Streisand's film *Funny Girl*, he began to get more roles. He appeared in an all-black production of *Hello, Dolly!* starring Pearl Bailey and Cab Calloway and was nominated for a Tony award for his role in *Two Gentlemen of Verona*. Strikingly handsome in his youth, Davis made a fluid transition to television acting with roles on *Love, American Style*. In 1972, he and his then-girlfriend, Melba Moore, had their own variety show on ABC. Davis was using drugs and was abusive to Moore, who soon escaped the relationship. Davis became known as a notorious playboy who had affairs with Nancy Wilson and Victoria Principal, among others. But all women were not moved by his charm. According to an early 1970s *Sepia* magazine article, when he propositioned Cher (who was married to Sonny Bono at the time), she turned him down flat.

Davis had a second wind on the hit sitcom *That's My Mama* in 1974. During this period, Davis was briefly a Motown songwriter. His most famous composition was "Never Can Say Goodbye," which has sold millions of copies and been recorded by such artists as the Jackson 5, Gloria Gaynor, the Supremes, Johnny Mathis, and Isaac Hayes. After falling out of the limelight and surviving a cocaine overdose in 1979, Davis re-emerged in 1986 as the co-star of the comedy church sitcom *Amen*, which ran for four years on NBC. During that period, Davis became an associate pastor at a Seventh

Day Adventist church in California. In 1991, he recorded a lackluster LP, *Say Amen*, for Benson Records. Davis's suave but unsoulful vocal skills did not ignite gospel audiences and the album floundered. He did become popular in the Christian community based on his *Amen* role. He's hosted several gospel or Christian awards television programs and is a recurring host on the Trinity Broadcasting Network's *Praise the Lord* program.

Louise "Candy" Davis

LOUISE "CANDY" DAVIS (born Anna Louise Davis) has been relegated to one-hit-wonder status. She enjoyed one of the most memorable gospel hits of the 1980s with the rocking chair ballad, "Better than Blessed." In 1986, the LP of the same name peaked at No. 5 on the *Billboard* gospel sales chart and spent 65 weeks on the chart.

Mary Johnson Davis

ALTHOUGH SHE DOESN T have a long discography and is virtually unknown today, Mary Johnson Davis is credited with bringing bluesy curlicues and elaborate vocal runs to the black gospel idiom. It has been written that Mahalia Jackson and Clara Ward both borrowed heavily from Davis's unique vocal style. Born November 26, 1899, in Pittsburgh, Pennsylvania, she first sang as a soloist with piano accompaniment by her first husband, Eddie Clifford Davis. She then formed a female vocal group that included Frances Steadman, Berniece Johnson, and Thelma Jackson. A soprano with formal, precise enunciation and an operatic tone, she could easily slide into soaring, robust vocal gymnastics that captivated audiences in the 1940s. Mahalia Jackson was so overcome by Davis's vocal technique that she allegedly fainted when she first heard her sing at a church service. In spite of the hushed respect of her musical peers, Davis's talent did not translate into a lucrative career. She worked in a department store in her later years and died—virtually unnoticed—in August 1982.

DC Talk

THE GOSPEL HIP-HOP trio DC Talk was arguably the biggest group in the CCM world for much of the 1990s. Kevin Max (born August 17, 1967, in Grand Rapids, Michigan), Toby McKeehan (born October 22, 1964, in Washington, DC), and Michael Tait (born May 18, 1966, in Washington, DC) formed their group on the campus of Jerry Falwell's Liberty University in Lynchburg, Virginia, where they were all students in 1987. They produced a rap song called "Heavenbound," which became a campus hit. At that point they felt they could really go professional and started performing at birthday parties. Forefront Records discovered them and signed them to a recording deal in 1989. Although Tait and McKeehan were from Washington, DC, the "DC" in their name isn't geographic. It stands for "Decent Christian." Their first album, *DC Talk*, a fusion of pop-styled hip-hop music with blatant gospel lyrics, sold 100,000 units. From the beginning, McKeehan was the primary songwriter and mastermind behind the group. Although kids instantly gravitated toward DC Talk, some Christian parents didn't know how to take two white guys and a black guy rapping in the name of Jesus. Some felt it was sacrilegious. Others didn't like bringing urban culture into the CCM fold. "They say use the church music for the church and keep the street music out in the street, and I can understand their viewpoint. But as long as the word is being spoken explicitly and you're not blaspheming Christ in any way, I think it can be used as an effective tool to minister the gospel," McKeehan told the *Washington Post*. Regardless of the skeptics, the trio continued to build on their success with each new CD.

Free at Last in 1993 scored them their first gold CD, and they followed it with *Jesus Freak*, their first platinum CD (eventually double platinum). The latter CD's single "Just Between You and Me" reached No. 29 on the *Billboard* Hot 100 singles chart and the video received MTV airplay. The accompanying album is considered by many critics to be the trio's most ambitious. They skipped the hip-hop that made them famous and developed a more pop-rock sound while maintaining their passionate but unpreachy gospel lyrics. The follow-up album, *Supernatural*, took a more mainstream approach. It was less gospel and more message-oriented than their prior projects. At the time of its release in 1998, the album held the distinction of being the highest charting Christian CD ever on the *Billboard* Hot 100 album chart when it reached No. 4, thanks in large part to a pact with Virgin Records to promote DC Talk in the pop world. It too went platinum.

McKeehan, ever the entrepreneur, founded Gotee Records (he has a goatee) in 1994 and the label has flourished with Christian acts such as Out of Eden, the Katinas, and gold-selling Jennifer Knapp. Circa 2001 DC Talk decided to take a break from performing together and release solo projects. Kevin Max, often viewed as the eccentric member of the group, released the alternative rock CD *Stereotype B* and has written a couple of poetry books. Tait formed the rock band Tait, which scored with its Top Ten CCM CD *Empty*. Under the name of TobyMac, McKeehan released the Top Ten CD *Momentum*, which had a distinct R&B vibe. In spite of the group's many twists and turns, McKeehan once said, "Our mission is the same as any Christian's is: to go and tell the world about Jesus Christ."

Archie Dennis

ONE OF THE LEADING black gospel psalmists of the 1970s, Dennis's warm, dignified baritone endeared him to many white congregations during the period. Born December 20, 1935 in Pittsburgh, Pennsylvania, he came from a musical family. His mother sang in an a cappella quintet and his father sang with the family group the Dennis Four. As a youth, Dennis and his sister, Patricia, sang regularly at the Northside Church of God before branching out to sing with the Valetta Smiley Singers. After finishing high school, Dennis sang gospel with the Metropolitan Singers and Brooklyn's Arthur Miller and the Milleraires. Dennis kept moving up in ministry as he sang on recording sessions for Maceo Woods and the Roberta Martin Singers in the 1960s. From 1971 to 1977, he was a featured singer with Billy Graham's organization, performing on television and at crusades. In 1986, he became pastor of the Lord's Church in Monroeville, Pennsylvania. He died on October 26, 2001. Dennis never recorded for a major label as a soloist and most of his recorded output for labels such as Nor-Vel was beyond the range of commercial gospel music. His best-known song was the self-written tune "I've Never Seen the Righteous," recorded in 1978.

Clevant Derricks

ONE OF THE GREAT GOSPEL songwriters during the Golden Age of Gospel, Clevant Derricks was born May 13, 1910, in Chattanooga, TN. He later relocated to Dallas where he began to preach and write songs to inspire and uplift his congregation during the Great Depression. The Stamps-Baxter publishing firm heard his songs and purchased the publishing rights to "Just a Little Talk with Jesus," "When God Dips His Love in My Heart," and "We'll Soon be Done with Troubles and Trials." The publishing company placed these songs with several major artists such as Tennessee Ernie Ford and others. Jerry Lee Lewis and Elvis Presley did a duet of "Just a Little Talk with Jesus" in 1956 at Sun Records. Years later, Derricks was peddling some new songs to Aaron Brown of Word Records. Derricks mentioned that he had written other songs but had never received any royalties. Brown became Derricks's personal champion. He contacted BMI vice president Frances Preston, who helped Derricks establish his copyrights, and his estate received royalties for the first time. Brown enjoyed Derricks's demos so much that he gave him a contract with Word's country music division, Canaan Records. He rerecorded some of his early tunes along with his new compositions. The LPs such as 1976's *Satisfaction Guaranteed* were not big sellers, but brought Derricks much joy in the months before he passed away in April 1977.

Teri DeSario

A ONE-HIT WONDER in the pop world thanks to her 1980 smash single "Yes, I'm Ready" with K.C. and the Sunshine Band, Teri DeSario experienced the same fate in the CCM field in the 1980s. Born in 1950, DeSario played the recorder and the harp during her high school years. After marrying horn player Bill Purse, they both joined the jazz group Abacus. The Bee Gees' Barry Gibb heard their demo and was so impressed with DeSario's voice that he wrote her a song ("Ain't Nothing Gonna Keep Me from You") and snagged her a record deal. The first project was a commercial failure, but fate intervened after DeSario bumped into an old high school friend, Harry Wayne Casey, who had made a name for himself by that time as the leader of K.C. and the Sunshine Band. The bump led to a hit as K.C. produced her next project, *Moonlight Madness*. As a duo they did a beautiful cover of Barbara Mason's '60s classic "Yes, I'm Ready." The soulful ballad reached No. 1 on the *Billboard* adult contemporary chart, No. 2 on the pop chart, and No. 20 on the black music singles chart. After her follow-up LP bombed as strongly as her album debut, DeSario left pop music for the CCM field. She released two LPs, *Voices in the Wind* and *A Call to Us All*, which both made the *Billboard* CCM album chart, but did not create a strong or loyal fan base for the singer in the genre. Eventually, DeSario merged into the musical background where she did background vocals on Rockwell's pop hit "Somebody's Watching Me" and on Carmen's *Live... Radically Saved* album. She also co-wrote and sang on Philip Bailey's *Wonders of His Love* gospel album. In the ensuing years, DeSario has also done session work on *Truth & Light: Music from the X-Files*, *Maranatha Christmas Classics*, and *WOW Worship Blue*.

Destiny's Child

THE 1990S ANSWER TO Diana Ross and the Supremes, Destiny's Child is the bestselling female pop group of the last decade. The group was founded in 1990 with Beyoncé Knowles (born September 4, 1981), Kelly Rowland (born February 11, 1981), Letoya Luckett (born March 11, 1981), and Latavia Roberson (born November 1, 1981). Knowles's father, Matthew, became the group's manager and began grooming the preteens for superstardom. All church girls, their name comes from the biblical book of Isaiah. The girls went on Ed McMahon's *Star Search* talent competition but did not win. They continued working in Houston and opened for youthful acts such as SWV. In 1997, they landed a recording deal with Columbia Records where they eventually cut such pop smashes as "No No No" and "Bills Bills Bills." After Roberson and Luckett split from the group because of a management dispute, Michelle Williams (born December 1, 1980) stepped in. As a trio, the group excelled with further pop successes such as "Survivor" and "Independent Women." In spite of their sensual, sexy stage attire, they all profess to be Christians and have sung gospel on programs such as the Stellar awards and BET's *Celebration of Gospel*. Their 2001 CD *Survivor* features a stunning gospel medley that includes a bit of Richard Smallwood's "Total Praise." Aside from managing the group and Beyoncé's career, Matthew Knowles has gone into gospel management with artists such as Shirley Caesar and Ted & Sheri. In 2005, the group announced they were disbanding after the promotion of their *Destiny Fulfilled* CD

William DeVaughn

"BE THANKFUL" WAS a quasi-religious R&B hit that gave William DeVaughn a few moments of fame in 1974. Born in 1948 in Washington, DC, DeVaughn was an ardent Jehovah's Witness and a government worker when he sought to realize his dream of becoming a recording artist. He spent $900 to produce a custom album in Philadelphia at the hallowed Omega Studios where many great '70s soul records were created. The company's vice president, Frank Fioravanti, so liked the track "Be Thankful" that he decided to peddle it to various recording labels. Roxbury Records released it and it went on to sell more than two million copies. Backed by a cool, laid-back groove, DeVaughn sang of retaining a sense of gratitude regardless of one's station in life. The song told the story from the perspective of someone who lived and survived the black ghetto: "Diamond in the back/sunroof top/digging the scene with a gangster lean." He once told the *Washington Post*, "I was trying to create some lyrics that would help them [young black men in the ghetto] keep their self-esteem. That's what a lot of guys were doing back then. They would have their big hats on—those Sly & the Family Stone hats—profiling, rolling through the neighborhood." With DeVaughn's soft falsetto and mellow sound, many thought the song was a new Curtis Mayfield record at the time, which probably helped propel the record when fans called radio request lines asking to hear it. Even gospel radio stations played the song. The single shot to No. 1 on the R&B chart and No. 4 on the pop chart.

The remainder of the album carried a heavier spiritual message on such songs as "Give the Little Man a Great Big Hand," "We Are His Children," and "Blood Is Thicker than Water." Those songs received some radio play, but DeVaughn was almost doomed from the beginning. Most fans didn't catch the subtle spiritual message in his music, so when they showed up for his concerts, they were ill prepared for his hard-nosed sermonettes and many were turned off. He never regained another big hit and eventually went back to his government work. After the rap boom, many rap artists began to sample "Be Thankful." Since DeVaughn wrote the track and owned it, its popularity has given him a handsome supplemental income. "All that I have accomplished, I feel it is a spiritual blessing from the Creator," he told the *Post*. "Without His blessing, none of this would have come about…. I feel things are turning exactly the way they should."

Dez (Desiree Coleman)

SHE'S BETTER KNOWN for piercing high notes than for a specific song, but Desiree Coleman had all the right tools to make it big in music. With exotic good looks and a five-octave vocal range, Coleman was cast as the child star of Vy Higgensen's *Mama, I Want to Sing* off-Broadway musical in the 1980s. Coleman stayed with the show for four lucrative years. Through the fame the show brought her, she met Patti LaBelle, who managed her for a while and also featured her in her "Stir It Up" music video. When her run with the play was over, Coleman recorded a pop album for Motown Records that was much hyped but failed to connect with an audience in the 1988–89 period. Motown eventually dropped her and she fell out of sight. During that downtime, Coleman married basketball star Mark Jackson of the L.A. Clippers. In 2001, she resurfaced simply as Dez with a gospel CD *Sing for Me* on the Destiny Music recording label. She had a number of producers

for the project, including Wyclef Jean. Through marketing muscle and promotional teams, the album managed to reach No. 7 on the gospel album chart and even No. 54 on the R&B album chart, but the project still failed to establish her as a gospel star.

Ricky Dillard

GOSPEL SHOWMAN Ricky Dillard's New Generation Chorale is one of gospel's most thrilling ensembles of the last 20 years. What the group lacks in stage finesse and vocal technique is more than made up for in vocal passion and stage histrionics. It's quite a sight to see the slim, fastidious singer spastically conduct a choir of full-figured singers to dip, shake, and grind to the tune of his invisible conductor's baton. There's no choir exactly like them in gospel today. Born February 25, 1964, in Chicago, Dillard was raised on the east side in the Mason Court projects by a single mother with four children and a tenacious faith in God. At the age of three, he was watching and pretending to conduct choirs. At five years old he began directing the junior choir at St. Bethel Baptist Church. In 1981, he formed the first gospel choir at Bloom High School. "There were so many church kids

Ricky Dillard/ photo courtesy of Crystal Rose Records

there and they liked to sing," he said. "So I started a group called Ricky Dillard and Company and we sang at school. One of my teachers, Don Bondurant, said, 'You should start a gospel choir' and I did." In spite of his love of performing, Dillard thought his future lay in radio announcing. He attended Columbia College for a couple of years, but dropped out because "the curriculum bored me and I was really tired of school anyway." He took a job as a front desk clerk at a Holiday Inn and later worked as a file clerk while performing in a professional backup group called Love, Salvation & Devotion (LSD) on the weekends. In 1984, Dillard joined Milton Brunson's Thompson Community Singers. At the same time, he started hanging out with renowned club DJ Frankie Knuckles and began recording dance and hip-hop records. Aside from a half dozen guest appearances on various dance tracks, Dillard recorded his own dance album *Let the Music Use You*, which was released in Europe. In spite of his growing success in the club market, Dillard says, "My heart was in the gospel. I always wanted to do gospel. The other stuff was just an opportunity to record. I wanted to bring a more contemporary style into gospel for choirs."

Dillard founded the New Generation Chorale in 1988 and the next year they won the McDonald's Chicagoland Choir competition. One day he met producer Butch McGee in a parking lot. McGee had heard of him and signed Dillard's group to Malaco Records on their reputation alone. New G's first album, *The Promise*, was released in 1990 and won them a Grammy nomination and a GMWA Excellence award in 1991. The next year the choir was featured in Steve Martin's movie *Leap of Faith*. By the time their second live album *A Holy Ghost Take-Over*, debuted in 1993, hitting No. 3 on the gospel chart, Dillard was a consultant on Whoopie Goldberg's *Sister Act II* movie and the choir had appeared on a PBS television special, *Going Home to Gospel*, featuring Patti LaBelle and Albertina Walker. In 1994, New G won their first Stellar award for contemporary choir of the year and recorded all the background vocals for gospel queen Albertina Walker's CD *He Keeps on Blessing Me*. In 1995, New G's third album, *Hallelujah*, was a Top Ten gospel hit and the choir had its first club hit. They collaborated with Frankie Knuckles and Adeva on "Walkin'" from their *Welcome to the Real World* album. The Virgin Rec-

ords single became a Top 20 hit on *Billboard* magazine's club chart.

By 1996, New G had moved to Detroit-based Crystal Rose Records, which had put Donald Lawrence and the Tri-City Singers on the map. Their debut "Worked It Out" reached No. 8 on the gospel chart. The group's follow-up CD *No Limit* reached No. 10 on the gospel album chart and became their biggest seller to date, racking up sales of over 100,000 units. The group then backed Ann Nesby on her 2002 dance hit "Let Your Will Be Done," which reached No. 3 on the *Billboard* club chart. Dillard's 2004 CD *Unplugged…. The Way Church Used to Be* was a major comeback project. It earned both Grammy and Dove award nominations in 2005.

Dion DiMucci

A '60S DOO WOP ICON known for pop classics "The Wanderer" and "Runaround Sue," Dion was born July 18, 1939, in the Bronx, New York. With his New York street-tough image and his affinity for blue-eyed soul music, Dion and the Belmonts were an instant hit in the late 1950s with songs such as "A Teenager in Love." In 1960, Dion went solo and created a decade of Top Ten pop hits. By the 1970s, Dion had triumphed over a heroin addiction and become a born-again Christian. In 1978, he cut his first Christian LP, *Only Jesus*, for Word Records. His biggest Christian radio hits include "I Put Away My Idols," "Sweet Surrender," and "Still in the Spirit." His 1985 track "Crazy to Fall in Love" was done in the doo wop style that made him famous. Although he has maintained his faith, Dion stopped recording Christian music in the late 1980s.

Dinwiddie Colored Quartet

IN 1902, THE SAME YEAR that the Pepsi-Cola Company was founded and the teddy bear (in homage to President Teddy Roosevelt) was created, the Dinwiddie Colored Quartet recorded the first gospel recording. The group hailed from Pennsylvania and was formed initially to raise money for the John A. Dix Industrial School in Dinwiddie, Virginia. Their members included first tenor Sterling Rex, second tenor Clarence Meredith, first bass Harry Cruder, and second bass J. Mantell Thomas. The group recorded a half dozen sides in October 1902 for Monarch Records, including "Down on the Old Camp Ground" and "We'll Anchor Bye and Bye." The songs were released on three singles in a matter of weeks. They were reissued in 1906 under the RCA Victor logo.

Dana Divine

THE 2001 DANCE RECORDING "The Gospel Slide: The Jesus Apostles March" was one of the biggest songs of the year on gospel radio play lists. With her takeoff on the rap duo Grandmaster Slice & Izzy Ill's 1990 "Shall We Dance (Electric Slide)" track that spawned the Electric Slide urban dance craze, Dana Divine sought to ignite a similar reaction in the church world. She was born Dana Lynn Stovall on September 28, 1972, in Chicago. Her grandfather, Bill Foster, was one of the early black filmmakers. He created silent films such as *The Railroad Porter* (1912) and *The Birth of a Race* (1918). The latter was an answer film to D.W. Griffith's controversial and racially polarizing 1915 epic *The Birth of a Nation*.

As a child, Divine played the clarinet and the piano. She grew up watching her mother play piano at churches throughout the Chicago area. She spent her teen years in Los Angeles where she began to compose songs in earnest during her leisure. Later, she made a living doing singing telegrams. There was still time for school as well. Divine earned a B.A. in marketing from the University of Illinois, and a M.A. in media communications from Governor's State University. Additionally she studied in London at the Sussex University as an exchange student for a year.

In the early '90s, Divine sang background vocals on Will Smith's "Ring My Bell" and R. Kelly's "Hey Love." She also wrote "Thinking About Your Love" for British soul siren Ruby Turner's hit 1991 CD *The Other Side*. Divine has also collaborated with Chicago's best dance producers Hula, Mark Pichiotti, Frank Orrall, and Maurice Joshua. For five years, Divine produced and hosted *S.T.A.G.E! (Stand Tall And Get Excited!)*, a children's television program in Chicago.

One of Divine's songs, "Runnin'," is used on Sony PlayStation II and is also used as a ringtone for cell phones. Her dance track "Brighter Days" became a dance hit via Cajmere's rendition. Divine's CD *A Nu Language*, another contemporary collection, was released to positive radio response in 2004. "God continues to speak to all people today," Divine says. "He is speaking to them in contemporary terms. The methods that he uses may be holy hip-hop, spoken word, miming, interpreted dance, gospel-house music, etc. These are his 'Nu Languages.' The message is the same, but the language is different. Through the calling of the Holy Spirit, he will continue to draw men and women unto him, no matter what style of music is used."

Jessy Dixon

IN THE 1970s, Jessy Dixon and his various choir ensembles were the go-to singers for pop artists who needed a nice full gospel choir sound on a specific track. Dixon later made a few notable gospel albums but has never gained a reputation within the gospel industry as an essential artist. Born March 12, 1938, in San Antonio, Texas, Dixon moved to Chicago as a teenager. His first gig was playing piano for the Clara Ward Singers. He later joined James Cleveland's group, Gospel. He wrote songs for Cleveland (such as "God Can Do Anything but Fail") who recorded and popularized them enough that other gospel singers began to request Dixon's songs. Eventually, Dixon formed his own group, the Jessy Dixon Singers, who were booked by the organizers of the Newport Jazz Festival to perform their song "The Wicked Shall Cease Their Troubling" at Radio City Music Hall in 1971. There Paul Simon spotted them and added the singers to his touring entourage for a couple of years and used them as backup on his smash hit "Still Crazy After All These Years." The exposure led to session work with Natalie Cole, Cher, and Diana Ross.

In the late 1970s, Dixon focused more on re-establishing his gospel roots. Signed to Light Records, he released *It's All Right Now* in 1979, which was a huge success. He followed up with the LPs *Songs of Pentecost*, *I Know What Prayer Can Do*, and *He's Able*, which were all moderate sellers. In 1993, Dixon enjoyed his biggest radio hit with "I Am Redeemed." Aside from regular concert tours to Europe, Dixon was not very visible on the American gospel landscape for a long time before he joined Bill and Gloria Gaither's successful *Home-coming* concerts in the early 1990s.

"He was tremendous at what he did," says Cinque Cullar, who once sang with Dixon. "He commanded his audience. You never saw him out of place one time. From the time he came out of his hotel room to the time he went back, you never knew what he did. He stayed away from the group and when we saw him, it was time to go. Him being the leader, it was a respect thing. I learned to separate myself from my own choir members when I started a choir, so they maintain that respect. Don't let them know where you live, don't hang out with them, don't go bowling with them. Don't socialize with them, but love them—that way you maintain that respect. Be open and let them trust you."

Marcia Dixon

PERHAPS ENGLAND's foremost black gospel journalist, Dixon is known largely for her writings on faith and gospel personalities in London's *Voice* newspaper. Her knowledge and expertise on faith matters has led to feature interviews on BBC television and Choice FM, two of the country's most recognized media outlets. "Over the years numerous people have told me how my religious writings have touched them," Dixon says. "I've received a letter from individuals stating that after they read an article I had written they decided not to kill themselves. Ministers have told me that some of the articles have challenged them to become more active in the community and reach out to disadvantaged groups, whilst gospel artists have said that my page is the one they turn to when they need to find out what's happening within the gospel music community. All this proves to me is the power of God-inspired writing."

Dixon was born in London, where she later earned a social science diploma. In September 1988, Dixon became a religious editor and began editing the "Soul Stirrings" column in the *Voice*, Britain's leading black newspaper. The newspaper gave Dixon a tremendous platform which she used to further the careers of a number of able gospel artists. In the middle 1990s, Dixon founded the MJR gospel talent agency. Among her clients were Luciano Pavarotti and Sting. The company also organized the Winans' farewell UK press tour circa 1997. She later closed the enterprise and formed the MD public relations firm in 2002. Her business was nominated for a Young Entrepreneurs award at the European Federation of Black Women Business Owners Awards in 2004. Capitalizing on England's *Pop Idol* TV competition, Dixon was hired to coordinate the GMTV/Voice Gospel Challenge 2001–2003. In spite of her varied endeavors, Dixon remains in position at the *Voice* where her articles continue to touch thousands upon thousands. "My purpose as a writer is to inform, challenge, and inspire people into action," Dixon says. "When people tell me as a result of reading my words it's inspired them to fulfill their purpose in life, it makes me know I've fulfilled my part."

DJ Disciple

THIS BRAGGADOCIO American disc-spinner has been adopted by Europe as one of their favorite DJs because of his blend of traditional Big Apple house music with worldbeat rhythms. He was born David Banks on September 2, 1965, in Brooklyn, New York. His father played piano with jazz trumpeter Miles Davis and his brother played bass with singer/guitarist George Benson. He got his start in the group Brooklyn Soul Boys and the Street Preacherz, a gospel outfit. From there, he began to DJ at the Wild Pitch club in Manhattan. That led to a ten-year run as a host on 91.5 Radio FM in New York. His *My True Colors* album launched him on the global dance scene. He later mixed popular inspirational songs such as "Put Your Hands Up" by the Black & White Brothers. He's played at most of the leading dance clubs in the world, such as London's Ministry of Sound, Torres de Avillas in Barcelona, Club Lemon in Tel Aviv, Jazid in Oslo, and Pacha in Ibiza. He also owns his own recording label, Catch 22, which has produced a number of fine club songs.

DJ Maj

A CHRISTIAN RAPPER and mixer (born Ric Robbins on October 9, 1970, in Lafayette, Louisiana), DJ Maj first gained attention as a party DJ. In 1992, Robbins ventured to Nashville where he found instant work as a mixer with DC Talk and performed on their CD *Free at Last*. The work continued to snowball into sessions with Out of Eden, T-Bone, Audio Adrenaline, and GRITS. His hip-hop songs showed up on projects by Hip Hope, GRITS, Lil iROCC Williams, Reality Check, and Silage. Robbins also found time to host a radio show on Nashville's WAY-FM for five years before launching the syndicated radio program "Virtual Frequency" in 2000. In 1997, Robbins released an independent CD entitled *Sabbatical Transit*. He has since recorded three hit CDs for Gotee Records including 2001's bestselling *Full Plates: Mix 2*, which featured the No. 1 Christian rhythmic chart hit "Deception."

Creflo Dollar

ONE OF THE MOST SUCCESSFUL televangelists of the last decade, Creflo Dollar preaches a gospel of prosperity to his audiences. Born January 1962 in College Park, Georgia, Dollar graduated from Lakeshore High School and earned a B.A. in history from West Georgia College. He began his career as a high school teacher and later became an educational therapist for the Brawner Psychiatric Institute of Atlanta. In 1986, Dollar founded World Changers Christian Center, a nondenominational church in College Park, Georgia. His first services were held at an elementary school with eight followers, and he has watched that enterprise grow to a 20,000-member megachurch. According to an *Atlanta Journal-Constitution* article in 2000, Dollar or his ministry owns a $5 million private plane, a million-dollar mansion that Dollar lives in, and a Rolls Royce that he drives.

Dollar is not without his detractors. Some have labeled the pastor "Cash Flow" Dollar because of his emphasis on money. Others have criticized him for being aloof and not even allowing members of his congregation to shake his hand. During boxer Evander Holyfield's 2001 divorce from his wife Janice, Dollar's name surfaced in court papers because Janice's attorneys wanted an accounting of $4 million Holyfield gave to Dollar's ministry and over $150,000 he gave directly to Dollar prior to filing for divorce. Janice also wanted to know the nature of the counseling sessions Holyfield had with Dollar. The marriage reportedly crumbled in part because Holyfield impregnated two other women in the last couple of years of his marriage to Janice. As his pastor, Dollar counseled him on spiritual matters. When the court asked Dollar for a deposition in the case he refused and was cited for contempt of court. Dollar said he would go to jail first but before it came to that, the Holyfields settled their divorce out of court. Dollar also drew some minor criticism from church folks for appearing in a music video by the notorious rapper Ludacris called "Welcome to Atlanta," which also featured Jermaine Dupree. Long wishing to get into the music industry, Dollar and his wife, Taffi (born October 1964) founded Arrow Records in 2000. The first project was the CD *From the Heart*, which reached No. 8 on the gospel chart in great part to Dollar's frequent hyping of the CD on his daily television broadcast. The CD showed Dollar to have a weak singing voice and little charisma as a vocalist. Wisely, Arrow signed other artists such as Generation J.

Thomas Dorsey

HE WAS NAMED THE Father of Gospel Music and with good reason. Not only did Thomas Dorsey coin the term "gospel music," but he wrote some of gospel's foundational standards such as "Take My Hand, Precious Lord" and "Peace in the Valley." Thomas Andrew Dorsey was born on July 1, 1899, in Villa Rica, Georgia, to an organ-playing mother and a Baptist preacher father. In spite of his church heritage, Dorsey became a blues pianist called Barrelhouse Tommy and later Georgia Tom. He wrote saucy double entendres such as "Tight Like That" and he played with blues queen Ma Rainey and Tampa Red. In 1918, he moved to Chicago where he played in a number of jazz and blues bands before forming his own group, the Wildcats Jazz Band.

In 1928 Dorsey suffered a nervous breakdown and retired from music. During his convalescence a minister convinced Dorsey not to give up music. He suggested that he give up blues and return to church music. Initially, he was rejected by many in the church because of his secular background. He took a hard stance and rejected all blues offers, although there were no forthcoming church opportunities.

In 1932, Dorsey organized a choir at Chicago's Pilgrim Baptist Church and also founded the first black Christian music publishing house. Soon tragedy struck. Dorsey's wife died in childbirth, as did the son she was carrying. On the verge of another breakdown, Dorsey locked himself in his room for three days and out of his grief, wrote what would become "Take My Hand, Precious Lord." In the years to come, the song would rival "Amazing Grace" as America's favorite gospel song.

After Sallie Martin joined his traveling singing troupe at Ebenezer Baptist Church and began popularizing Dorsey's songs across the country, Dorsey allowed her to manage his sheet music store, which had been disorganized and unprofitable. Martin cleaned it up and made it lucrative. In 1933, Dorsey, Martin, and their associates Thomas Frye, Magnolia Lewis Butts, and Beatrice Brown founded the National Convention of Gospel Choirs and Choruses, an annual convention that would serve as the harbinger for the Gospel Music Workshop of America. The main purpose of the convention was to introduce and teach Dorsey's songs to choir conductors who could take them back to their churches and popularize them with those local congregations. Hence, the idea was that amateur church musicians would then buy the sheet music in order to learn to play the songs. Dorsey further cemented his name by touring the country with his "Evenings with Dorsey" where a variety of singers performed his songs and kept them popular. In 1939, Dorsey composed "Peace in the Valley" for Mahalia Jackson who often recorded his demos for him. The song would go on to become a million-seller for country star Red Foley and later for Elvis Presley.

As other singer-songwriters such as Rev. James Cleveland took center stage in the 1960s, Dorsey gradually began to withdraw from active performing and even songwriting. He became semi-reclusive, only emerging every summer to appear at his convention, which dwindled in popularity as Cleveland's Gospel Workshop of America became more contemporary and popular. He died January 23, 1999.

Willa Dorsey

"BOY, WHAT A SINGER!" Billy Ray Hearn says of Willa Dorsey, whom he produced in the early 1970s for Word Records. "The things she'd do with her voice were simply fantastic." Though largely forgotten now, Willa Dorsey was quite a trailblazer in the 1960s. She was perhaps the first black woman to integrate many mainline white churches with her operatic gospel songs. Born on July 2, 1933, in Atlanta, her parents died when she was a teenager and she was shuffled between relatives until she came of age. Gospel composer Thomas Dorsey was her cousin, so he taught her some things about hymn singing. She began singing weekly on WERD, America's first black-owned and operated radio station, in the early 1950s. Then she sang with the Atlantanaires, a local group that opened for all the big gospel concerts traveling through the city. When Dorsey appeared on a bill with the Sallie Martin Singers, Martin approached her and offered Dorsey a job with her group when she finished high school. Dorsey spent a year with the group and then attended Clark College before deciding that she wanted to sing opera instead of gospel music. She then lived between Los Angeles and Portland, Oregon, where she studied opera with Robert McFerrin (father of performance artist Bobby McFerrin), who was a Hollywood vocal coach on films such as *Porgy and Bess*.

By the 1960s, Dorsey felt that she belonged in the church market and recorded with the Mighty Faith Increasers Choir for King Records in 1962. She then recorded an LP for Christian Faith Records before getting the break of her life. Her agent at the time introduced Dorsey to the Hollywood Christian Group, a Christian social club for Christians in show business. There she met cowgirl legend Dale Evans, who got Dorsey booked into the New York World's Fair where she introduced Dorsey with as much warmth as if she had been her own daughter. That opportunity led to many engagements such as the invitation for Dorsey to sing at the People's Church in Toronto where Billy Graham preached on many occasions. After her appearance there, white congregations in the United States started to invite Dorsey to sing for them. "I broke the barrier for black singers in the white churches," she says humbly. "They consider me the mother. I was the first to sing at the Christian Booksellers Convention (CBA). Andrae Crouch sang there the year after me and he said, 'Willa, what do I do? How should I act?' I appreciated him asking me. I sang at a lot of white churches where they would come up to my face and tell me, 'You are the first black to stand at our pulpit.' I was accustomed to it, I wasn't offended because I had seen that all of my life growing up in Atlanta. One time, I was at a church and we were on an elevator going to the rehearsal room when a lady got on with us. She just caught my eye and rolled her eyes at me! Man, if looks could kill you, I'd be dead."

However, for as many of those stories, Dorsey has just as many stories of kindness from whites. Her agent, Richard Yancy, arranged for her to sing "God Bless America" at a Jewish organization's God and Country Awards banquet at the London Palladium in the late 1960s on a billing with opera great Marilyn Horne. "Lawrence Welk was a recipient that year," she recalls, "and a month later, he called me himself on the telephone and asked me to sing on his television program." Dorsey proved to be an audience favorite and a ratings winner. She sang virtually every religious or inspirational song that Welk and his musical director, George Cates, ever liked. "They wanted me to sing 'Can't Help Lovin' that Man of Mine,'" she recalls. "But I told them I couldn't sing that song. At that time, I had a drug rehabilitation center and I had to pray over those young people and pray them out of drunken stupors. I told them, 'I don't want to lose my anointing with God. So I have to stay on the straight and narrow.' So George Cates said, 'We're trying to make a star out of you and you're trying to reach souls.'"

Although Dorsey continued to appear on the show, she didn't appear as often because of her decision to only sing religious or patriotic songs. The Welk program on ABC did help win her a recording contract. In 1968, she released what she considers her first real LP, *The World's Most Exciting Gospel Singer*, which earned a Grammy nomination. In the usually black category of Best Soul

Willa Dorsey

Gospel Performance, where Dorsey was nominated with the Davis Sisters, the Swan Silvertones, and Rev. James Cleveland, for the first time the honor went to a white artist, Dottie Rambo. Dorsey is most recalled for her 1970 LP *Stand Tall*. The patriotic title song was her signature tune. A *Billboard* magazine review at the time stated that "Willa Dorsey is undoubtedly one of the most original singers to ever emerge on the gospel scene. With a voice that has not only classical tones but an almost unbelievable range, she can do things to a song that few other gospel artists have been able to achieve. Listening to Miss Dorsey is an unforgettable experience." After her time with Word, Dorsey recorded *Spirituals for All Seasons* on the First Baptist label and *Willa Dorsey in Holland* on Megadureco Records. In the 1980s, Dorsey was a regular and featured psalmist on Jim and Tammy Bakker's *PTL Club* television program, where she would sing hymns and assorted gospel numbers on a regular basis. In the 1990s, she survived a rough bout with ovarian cancer that left her comatose for a time, but she's recovered and now testifies about her struggle. "Oh, baby, I've seen heaven," she says. "I've been to the other side." In 2002, Dorsey received an honorary doctorate from the Anointed Waters School of Urban Ministries in Los Angeles. Dorsey is affiliated with the Maranatha Church in Northeast Portland, Oregon.

Rev. Isaac Douglas

BORN IN 1940 IN Philadelphia, Pennsylvania, Douglas first sang with the Gospel Troubadours. He then joined the Edwin Newberry Singers where he was spotted by Raymond Raspberry, who recruited him to lead the Raspberry Singers. He also moonlighted as the second lead for the Ruth Davis Singers in the early 1960s. Eventually, Douglas moved to New York where he formed the Isaac Douglas Singers, who made their name on the song "Lord Have Mercy." From there, he co-founded the New York Community Choir, which backed poet Nikki Giovanni on her quasi-gospel LP *Truth Is on Its Way*. That album reached No. 15 on the R&B chart in 1971. Douglas's *Harvest Is Plentiful* LP on Creed Records reached No. 2 on the *Jet* magazine Soul Brothers Top Ten Gospel Album chart in May 1975. The choir later recorded for RCA Records and enjoyed a moderate R&B hit with "Express Yourself" in 1977. Douglas went on to work with a dozen other choirs including the Birmingham Community Choir. While he was working with various choirs, Douglas also recorded as a soloist for Nashboro Records' Creed imprint. His gruff vocals complimented the traditional style of the gospel music he cultivated. He died in 1988.

Margaret Douroux

DAUGHTER OF ESTEEMED PASTOR Earl A. Pleasant, Douroux was born March 21, 1941, in Los Angeles. She is a noted gospel historian, performer, and songwriter. She's composed songs for Albertina Walker, Rev. James Cleveland, Dorothy Norwood, and the Mighty Clouds of Joy, among others. In 1997, she recorded the CD *Already Done* with the Heritage Mass Choir for JDI Records. Douroux is minister of music at the Greater New Bethel Baptist Church in Inglewood, California.

Oma Drake

A LEADING BACKGROUND vocalist in the 1970s, Drake appeared on albums by Barbra Streisand, Billy Preston, and Neil Diamond, among others. She was dropped from Motown Records in the 1960s for being too fat, though she cut a nice duet with Marvin Gaye while she was there. Among the gospel-related projects her powerful voice can be heard on are Billy Preston's 1972 LP *Music Is My Life*, which featured the standout gospel cuts "God Loves You" and "Make the Devil Mad (Turn On to Jesus)." She also had featured vocals on John Hurley's 1972 LP *Delivers One More Hallelujah*. A 1983 *Billboard* review was a love fest for the album *Will You Be Ready?*: "Backed by a choir that manages to capture the church sound in a studio, Drake cuts loose on 'Pray to the Father', 'One More Day', 'Will You Be Ready', and the bouncy 'I Believe in You.' Drake is a great talent, and it is high time she was showcased like this." Drake is also known alternatively as Oma Heard and Oma Page.

Dr. Alban

THIS SWEDISH CLUB DJ enjoyed fleeting fame and several dance/club chart hits between 1993–1995. He dynamically fused spirituality and rhythm on the transcontinental smash 12-inch single "Sing Hallelujah!" which peaked at No. 15 on the *Billboard* dance chart in late summer 1993.

Dramatics

BEST KNOWN AS THE GRUFF lead vocalist for the Dramatics soul quintet, L.J. Reynolds was born January 27, 1953, in Saginaw, Michigan. He began his career as Larry "Chubby" Reynolds for Tri-Spin Records in the 1960s. He was then lead singer for the Relations on Mainstream Records in 1969. After a number of small label records, Reynolds finally scored in 1971 with "Let One Hurt Do" on Law-ton Records. Finally, in 1973 Reynolds replaced William Howard in the Dramatics. In 1980, he left the group and signed a solo deal with Capitol Records. After he failed to blow up as a solo artist, Reynolds rejoined the Dramatics in 1986. In 1991, Reynolds recorded his first gospel album for Bellmark Records, a self-titled set that featured songs such as "Amazing Grace" and "Jesus Is My Kind of People."

Arizona Dranes

BILLED AS "The Blind Gospel Singer" in the 1920s, Arizona Juanita Dranes is remembered as the first black female pianist to record a song. She was born May 4, 1889, in Greenville Town, Texas. She came up in the COGIC denomination and served as worship leader and pianist for COGIC bishops such as Emmett Morey Page, Riley Felman Williams, and Samuel M. Crouch, Jr. It was during her tenure with Crouch that OKeh Records talent scout Richard Jones spotted her performing during one of Crouch's services and decided to sign her to a recording deal. In 1926, she went to a Chicago recording studio, sat down to the piano and sang, "My Soul Is a Witness for My Lord." It was the first recording by a black female pianist. Her somewhat barrelhouse blues approach to keyboarding with her nasal alto proved to be a succulent elixir for gospel music fans of the time. She recorded more than 30 songs during her time at OKeh. She died circa 1960.

O'Landa Draper

A CONTEMPORARY choir director who was clearly on the rise when he died suddenly in 1998, O'Landa Draper was born September 29, 1963, in Memphis, Tennessee. His mother was a successful concert promoter and Draper grew up around the business. After entering Memphis State University in 1981, Draper majored in music. He was directing the school's gospel choir when producer Thomas Whitefield took an interest in mentoring him. Eventually, Draper formed the Associates Mass Choir. The group began to build their reputation and landed a recording deal with Word Records in 1990. Their biggest exposure came when the choir backed pop star Billy Joel on his "River of Dreams" video and single in 1993. The song hit No. 1 on the adult contemporary chart, and the album did equally well on the album chart. The choir was never a big seller at Word, but their performances were always energetic and appealing. The choir is perhaps best known for "My Soul Doth," an old a cappella tune. "The excitement around that song was in O'Landa directing," says fellow choir conductor Ricky Dillard, who is equally known for his stage clowning with his own New Generation Chorale. "It was an a cappella, but a fresh a cappella. It was like a soulful spiritual and it centered around the vocal abilities of the Associates. When they'd sing it in a concert, they brought it to life. It was like a scripture reading set to music. You know how in the storefront churches, the saints would stand up and testify." Sadly, Draper died of kidney failure at the age of 34 on July 21, 1998. Following his death, Draper's mother assumed control of the choir and she has kept them on the road, although their popularity has dwindled considerably without their founder.

Drinkard Singers

ANNE L. DRINKARD MOSS was born April 16, 1927, in Newark, New Jersey. As teenagers, she and her sisters Lee Warrick and Emily "Cissy" Houston formed a gospel group called the Drinkard Singers (their maiden name). They eventually added family friend Judy Guions Clay. The group recorded for Chess, Choice, Savor, Verve, and RCA Victor Records. Moss sang lead on "I'm in His Care" from their much-acclaimed 1957 Newport Jazz Festival LP. Following the appearance, they became the first gospel group signed to RCA Records where they recorded their signature tune, "Rise, Shine." Houston later formed her own group, the Sweet Inspirations, in the late 1960s. Moss died January 1, 2003.

Phil Driscoll

PERHAPS THE BEST-KNOWN gospel trumpeter in America, Phil Driscoll was born November 9, 1947, in Seattle. His first instruments were a plastic trombone and a toy guitar when he was three years old. But he also played real instruments throughout his childhood and eventually formed Baylor University's first jazz band when he was a student there. During that period, he recorded his first LP, *A Touch of Trumpet*, in 1969 backed by the Stockholm Symphony Orchestra. Driscoll's big break came when he was a contestant in a CBS television talent-search series *The All American College Bowl* where he beat out then aspiring pop duo Karen and Richard

Carpenter. After the competition, Driscoll wrote songs for pop artists such as Joe Cocker, Stephen Stills, and Leon Russell. By 1981, he had become a Christian and began recording for Benson Records. With a raspy voice similar to that of Ray Charles, Driscoll began to sing and play trumpet on his albums. The 1983 project *I Exalt Thee* earned him a Dove award and a Grammy nomination. His fully orchestrated but soulful albums of mostly instrumental praise and worship music were instantly embraced by both black and white church audiences. His 1984 LP *Keep the Flame Burning* finally earned him a Grammy. In the late 1990s, Driscoll formed his own label, Mighty Horn and has recorded several CDs through that company.

Roby Duke

WHEN HIS FATHER'S BAND, the Delta Rhythm Boys, fired their bass player, 12-year-old Roby Duke took the job and launched his career. Born December 9, 1956, in Greenwood, Mississippi, he had been playing since he was eight years old. His first album *Not the Same* appeared on MCA's Songbird gospel imprint in 1980. From there, he recorded three LPs for Word Records that featured the Top Ten CCM radio hits "Down to Business" and "Our Love." Duke moved to Seattle in the 1990s. There he became a consultant for Roland Instruments. He now works with Masali Music Publishing.

Bryan Duncan

CCM'S BLUE-EYED SOUL-MAN, Bryan Duncan was born March 16, 1953, in Ogden, Utah. The son of a preacher, Duncan spent his teen years in North Carolina where he learned to play guitar and piano. While in college, he founded the Sweet Comfort Band in 1972 with drummer Rick Thomson and bassist Kevin Thomson. Randy Thomas was their guitarist and Duncan played keyboards. They recorded a half dozen albums for Light Records without much commercial success. "We were under the mistaken impression that if our music was absolutely incredible, it would propel us into a successful career and ministry," Duncan once told *CCM* magazine.

"So while we were focusing on our musical presentation, a number of bands passed right by us because they were focusing on communicating to the audience. It was disillusioning to us that someone could put out a substandard record, create an image and get the right marketing, and actually do better than if you were a good artist. That was probably the most demoralizing thing for SCB. Once we realized that excellence was not what was being looked for by the majority, it was like the end of the vision. We didn't know what else to do."

While his band was hoping for a hit, Duncan was pouring concrete on construction sites during the week to pay his bills and support his family. "For the last two years of SCB, I was beginning to want out," he told *CCM* in 1986. "I was feeling really stale musically and spiritually and feeling a lot of frustration on the business end of things. I began to feel a real pessimism and bitterness settling into my life. I wasn't offering any hope in my lyrics because I wasn't seeing any hope. I had forgotten that God had a plan for my life, that God loved me, and not just the people I was singing for."

The group split in 1984 and Duncan went solo immediately. He continued to record for Light Records where he released *Have Yourself Committed* in 1985 and watched it rise to No. 26 on the *CCM* chart. The next two albums hit the *CCM* Top Ten and his superb *Strong Medicine* project went all the way to No. 5 in 1989. The title track was a bluesy, old-school soul ballad that Duncan sang with reckless abandon. His future albums would fuse his rough-hewn vocals with the soulful approach to Christian pop he preferred to sing. By this point, Duncan's self-penned compositions were creating hit after hit for his new recording label, Word Records. The songs such as "Love Takes Time," "I'll Not Forget You," "You Don't Leave Me Lonely," and "When It Comes to Love" made him one of CCM's most popular artists of the 1990s.

By the end of the decade, Duncan and Word had parted company. He joined Diadem Records, which lacked the promotional and marketing muscle Word provided Duncan. His debut CD *Joyride* in 2001 featured Donnie McClurkin and Darwin Hobbs. Although it had the classic soul grooves Duncan loved, the songs were not as strong as his prior work and the record failed to find a home at CCM radio. In spite of the ups and downs of his career, Duncan remains philosophical. "We get sidetracked into thinking that when we get into something like a music ministry that we could have a big career. I don't think the Lord sees it that way," he's said. "I don't think the Lord necessarily wants us to be huge. I think he wants obedience. He wants us to be holy. We fall into this thing where we measure our success spiritually by our success in the music business or our field, and I think that's missing the point."

Leontine Dupree

THIS GARY, INDIANA–BASED songwriter and playwright recorded the singles "I'm Guilty" and "Color Me Foolish" and the LP *Standing on His Word* for Nation Time Records. She recorded the LPs *Leontine Dupree Featuring the Voices of Chicago* and *One More Sunny Day Featuring Christ Temple Community Choir* for Savoy in 1982. She has continued to perform regionally and cut a CD entitled *Chicago Headline News* in 2004.

Bob Dylan

CONSIDERED BY MANY to be the greatest thinking-songwriter of the 20th century, Bob Dylan has created a body of thought-provoking songs about the politics of love, hate, and war. Songs such as "The Times They Are A-Changing," "Just Like a Woman," "Like a Rolling Stone," and "Blowin' in the Wind" were as indicative of the 1960s as were civil rights demonstrations and antiwar protests. Born Robert Allen Zimmerman on May 24, 1941, in Duluth, Minnesota, Dylan was raised in Hibbing. He played guitar from the age of six and eventually picked up the harmonica as well. While studying art at the University of Minnesota, Dylan began performing folk and blues songs in local coffeehouses under the name of Bob Dylan (in tribute to the poet Dylan Thomas). Eventually, Dylan found his way to Manhattan in 1961 where he immersed himself in the Greenwich Village folk community. While there, he began regular visits to his folk idol, Woody Guthrie (composer of "This Land Is Your Land"), who was gradually dying of Huntington's Chorea. Once settled, he began playing

New York clubs and quickly built a following. A performance at Gerde's Folk City, a coffeehouse venue, won Dylan an enthusiastic review in the *New York Times* by its no-nonsense music critic Robert Shelton. Based on the review, Columbia Records A&R executive John Hammond (who had recently discovered and signed Aretha Franklin) sought him out and signed him to a contract that continues to this day more than 40 years later. Although his eponymous debut LP was issued to encouraging acclaim, it was his sophomore LP *The Freewheelin' Bob Dylan* that set Dylan's career into high gear. Composed entirely by Dylan, the album featured classics such as "Blowin' in the Wind," "Masters of War," "Hard Rain's A-Gonna Fall," and "Don't Think Twice, It's All Right." Dylan was then romantically involved with Joan Baez who was already a folk superstar. She began recording his songs and popularizing them to even greater degrees. Soon Peter, Paul and Mary and the Byrds were recording his songs, as were scores of other performers.

Over the years, Dylan developed a mystique as an eccentric hermit of a musician who was rarely seen on popular television shows. He and his songs were often discussed, but he was rarely seen. This "something" just added to the excitement and appeal of Dylan to his loyal fans. To many, Dylan was the representation of the anti-establishment musician. In fact, a closer examination of Dylan's music reveals someone who is not anti-establishment as much as he's dismayed by the establishment. Therefore, when the Jewish Dylan revealed in 1978 that he had become a born-again Christian, many fans felt betrayed. He took a conservative fire-and-brimstone approach to his newfound faith. Working with renowned producer Jerry Wexler (an avowed atheist), who had produced Aretha Franklin's greatest R&B sides at Atlantic Records, Dylan's 1979 LP *Slow Train Coming* fused blues-rock instrumentation with a solid evangelistic message that was best demonstrated on the album's first single, "Gotta Serve Somebody," which reached No. 24 on the pop charts. The album peaked at No. 3 on the *Billboard* album chart and sold a million copies. The album also earned the singer his first Grammy award for one of his own projects.

Dylan followed that success with two more gospel LPs, 1980's *Saved* and 1981's *Shot of Love*. Both albums reached the pop Top 40 and received airplay in the Christian music market. However, the pop music press panned these albums as much for their musical value as for Dylan's faith, which seemed to especially bother many of them. Following these releases, Dylan returned to secular music, fueling speculation that his born-again experience was a bust. He's never publicly commented either way, although he has continued to perform some of the songs in his concerts. Dylan did fully participate in the 2003 compilation *Gotta Serve Somebody: The Gospel Songs of Bob Dylan*. The album places 11 of Dylan's gospel songs in the hands of bona fide black gospel singers such as Helen Baylor, Shirley Caesar, and the Mighty Clouds of Joy. He closed the superb album by re-recording his "Change My Way of Thinking" with the legendary Mavis Staples, one of the few people who has known Dylan long enough to have the privilege of calling him Bobby.

Sheila E.

ONE OF PRINCE'S MANY female protégées in the 1980s, Sheila E. (born Sheila Escovedo on December 12, 1959, in Oakland, California) proved to be a superb musician in her own right with a series of high-profile projects. Her mother is Creole and her father, Pete Escovedo, is a Mexican percussionist who once played with the Santana band. As a kid, Sheila was a tomboy. She ditched five years of violin lessons to play soccer and to run track because she dreamed of competing in the Olympics. By the age of 13, she fell in love with the skins (drums). She played so hard that she once said, "Sometimes my hands go numb. I look down at the drums and see blood over everything." Her first gig was playing in her father's Latin jazz-fusion band. She then started backing her father on a couple of his LPs before she toured with the likes of Herbie Hancock, George Duke, and Diana Ross. In 1983, she toured with Marvin Gaye and Lionel Richie. Then Prince reached out to have her play drums on his song "Erotic City," the flip side of his "Let's Go Crazy" hit. From there, he signed her to his Paisley Park label. The title song from her first LP *The Glamorous Life* hit the Top Ten on the pop charts. What the soft-voiced singer lacked in vocal power, she made up for with instrumental expertise. The song was one of the most memorable and classic hooks of the '80s. She recorded other pop hits such as "A Love Bizarre" and "Koo Koo." Sheila played drums in Prince's live shows (he loved to shock the audience with female musicians who could play as hard as men) and later was a musical director on both Magic Johnson's and Wayne Brady's ill-fated syndicated talk shows. In recent years, she's been more vocal about her Christian faith, including appearing on religious television programs. Sheila was raised a Catholic, but only attended church under duress. When she was 18, she became a born-again Christian. "I was doing session work in Los Angeles, and there were a lot of Christians, very famous people in the secular mind," she told Crosswalk.com in 2002. "I saw how they acted and I said, 'I don't want to be a Christian because the things that they are doing are so wrong.' I felt I was better off not being a Christian. I was very discouraged because of how Christians were acting and because, back then, the thing to be or become was born again. It was like a fad, you know? So I just got turned off."

Sheila E. left faith behind until the 1990s when she suffered a physical breakdown after ten nonstop years of exhaustive world tours. After a low where she dropped to 85 pounds and thought she would die, Sheila E. recommitted herself to God and began attending Beverly "BAM" Crawford's Bible Enrichment Fellowship International Church in Los Angeles. "I found a good church and my pastor is just wonderful and anointed, and our musical ministry is just incredible," she told Crosswalk.com. "I'm getting the best of both worlds—good Word and good praise and worship. Church is about praise and worship, the foundation. It's totally changed my life. I can't even imagine, when I think about the things that I had done not being a believer, his grace is so amazing." Her 2001 CD *Heaven* on Concord Records is an enjoyable smooth jazz, retro soul project that features subtle but direct references to God and other matters of faith. In 2005, Sheila E. served as music director for the "Sisters in the Spirit" arena gospel tour featuring Yolanda Adams and Prophetess Juanita Bynum.

Eartha

WHEN THE NEWS BROKE that Eartha was up for a Grammy in the Best R&B Female category in 2003, a lot of people were surprised, but they figured that she's an entertainment legend and deserves to be so acknowledged. Then, when they learned that she was also nominated in the gospel category, all the gospel industry folks were wondering, 'When did Catwoman from the original *Batman* TV series record a gospel album?' Everyone eventually realized that these Grammy nominations did not belong to the legendary star of stage, screen, and television, Eartha Kitt. Instead, they belonged to a lesser-known, 5'11" black woman with blonde hair and a fashion model's face.

Virtually everyone was scratching their head and asking who she was. The Eartha in question is Eartha Moore, born in Los Angeles circa 1975. Her mother, Zinna Smith, was an organist and guitarist. Moore often followed her mother to rehearsals and learned to play drums at the age of six. Little is known of her history, but Eartha attended Marvin Winans's Perfecting Church for a while and was mentored by Dr. Iona Locke, the noted evangelist. In 2000, Eartha released the independent CD *This I Know*. From there, she offered the 2002 CD *Sidebars*. In spite of smoky vocals and musicianship (she plays drums, keyboard, guitar, trumpet, and saxophone), Eartha is still looked upon with some derision in the gospel community. At the time of the 2002 Grammy announcements, the CD had produced no radio hits and had only sold 52 copies nationwide, according to SoundScan.

"Eartha had an okay record, but for something to get picked that people were so unaware of is mind-boggling," *Billboard* R&B editor Gail Mitchell said in a *USA Today* article on the controversy in 2003. Although Eartha's label AFRT said that the CD sold 10,000 copies in non-traditional places and that 50,000 copies had been given away, the artists she was up against in the R&B category were all million-sellers such as Aaliyah, Ashanti, Mary J. Blige, and Jill Scott. Gospel radio announcers were not amused either. "Her neo-soul style is closer to D'Angelo or Angie Stone than to Dorothy Norwood or Shirley Caesar," says Barbara Johnston, an announcer at WYBC in Connecticut at the time. "I was giving away product, and usually people call in to get anything. After I played Eartha's song, the phone didn't ring once." Although Eartha lost in the Grammy R&B category, she won in the gospel category, beating out such established gospel artists as Fred Hammond, BeBe Hammond, Deitrick Haddon, and Commissioned. Whereas most artists use a Grammy win as a stepping-stone to other career opportunities, Eartha has vanished—for the time being—in spite of her obvious musical gifts.

East St. Louis Gospelettes

THIS IS AN ELECTRIFYING, R&B-styled female sextet who made their largest impact during the late 1970s. Founded circa 1964 in East St. Louis, the group initially recorded for Checker Records. They released three LPs there in the 1960s, including the hit *You Can't Hurry God*. In spite of some moderate gospel success, it wasn't until they met Benny Ashburn during a California vacation that their career went into overdrive. Ashburn managed the pop-soul band the Commodores, who were known for songs such as "Three Times a Lady" and "Brick House." The group was introduced to Ashburn by their mutual friend Henry Nash, who booked both groups at some point in his career for Subrena Artists in New York. The Gospelettes were soon booked to open for the Commodores on a 96-city tour in 1980. In addition to their own 20-minute set, the Gospelettes closed each concert by backing the Commodores on their classic song "Jesus Is Love." From there, it was onward and upward for a time. The group performed at venues such as the Sahara in Las Vegas and hired a publicist. Most gospel artists during that period never enjoyed the fruits of a personal publicist. After their success with the Commodores and a move to New Birth Records in New York, the group changed their name in 1983 to Frances Moore-Lee and Burning Bush in order to appeal to a crossover R&B audience. In spite of a fine final LP, *I Love You, Jesus*, which included their own version of "Jesus Is Love," it was their last outing.

Duke Ellington

GENERALLY CONSIDERED the most important composer in the 20th century jazz world, Duke Ellington gave us such jazz standards as "Sophisticated Lady," "It Don't Mean a Thing (If It Ain't Got that Swing)," "Take the 'A' Train," and "I Got It Bad (and That Ain't Good)" among scores of others. He also created some beautiful sacred pieces that have withstood the test of time. Born Edward Kennedy Ellington on April 29, 1899, in Washington, DC, he was the son of a White House butler. Although his family was working class, they had dignity. Ellington was raised with an air of superiority that allowed him to look beyond the racial climate of his times and achieve great success as a composer. He began to play the piano around the age of seven and knew with certainty that it would be his lifetime vocation. He dropped out of high school at the age of 17 and pursued music full-time. His group, the Washingtonians, relocated to New York in 1923 and began to record for a number of recording companies, including Vocalion and Columbia. By 1927, Ellington's band had set up residency at the famed Cotton Club in Harlem where their concerts were broadcast live over the radio. These regular broadcasts made Ellington's band nationally known within a matter of months. After the gig earned them some movie cameos and touring opportunities, the Ellington Orchestra left the Cotton Club in 1931 and scored their first hit with "Mood Indigo." From that point on, Ellington helped define the idiom of jazz and swing music as he composed and recorded hit after hit after hit.

With a café au lait complexion, wavy hair, a good build, and a sense of refinement, Ellington quickly became a sex symbol and one of the best-dressed men in music. It is impossible to overstate the magnitude of the respect and public admiration for Ellington from the 1940s to his death. His allure might be comparable to that of a rock star or a boy band in today's world. Therefore, every work Ellington released received a great deal of attention and scrutiny. In 1945, he wrote the suite "Black, Brown and Beige" for a Carnegie Hall concert that was dismissed and disdained by the jazz press who had not yet come to appreciate his work on its artistic merits. He was still seen as a commercial artist by many

(such as today's boy bands are). The suite was a high-art set of instrumental interludes, whose highlight was the introduction of the classic song "Come Sunday." In spite of critical dismissal of the work, Ellington did not set it aside. He revisited the work many times over the years and finally recorded it in 1958.

The most controversial project of Ellington's career was the 1965 religious concerts he staged at New York's Fifth Avenue Presbyterian Church and at San Francisco's Grace Cathedral. Somehow, the prevailing thought was that religion had no place in jazz or that it was sacrilegious to apply religious music to a jazz setting. Ellington was not phased. "Every man prays in his own language, and there is no language that God does not understand," he told *Ebony* magazine in 1966. That same year he won the Grammy for Best Jazz Composition for the track "In the Beginning God" from the LP releases of those sacred concerts.

In his last years, Ellington continued to perform until his death from lung cancer on May 24, 1974, in New York City. His son, Mercer, kept his father's orchestra alive until his own death in 1996 and Mercer's son has held the reins ever since. In 1999, there was a media love fest celebrating the centennial of Ellington's birth, with news stories on the importance of Ellington, television specials, and a deluge of reissues of the Duke's long out-of-print recordings.

RECOMMENDED RECORDINGS: *Concert of Sacred Music* (BMG, 1998) is a thrilling live album of jazz music with sacred lyrics. The album opens with the booming baritone of Brock Peters on the track "In the Beginning God." Ellington's group then takes the listener through such tunes as "Come Sunday," "David Danced Before the Lord with All His Might," and "The Lord's Prayer." One of the vocalists was Queen Esther Marrow. Ellington's usual all-star players included Johnny Hodges, Louie Bellson, Paul Gonsalves, and Cootie Williams. It was a project that the Duke called "the most important thing I've ever done." If one has the interest, virtually all of Ellington's religious work can be found on a variety of import CDs.

Ruth Ellington-Boatwright

JAZZ GREAT DUKE ELLINGTON's only sibling, Boatwright was born July 2, 1915, in Washington, DC. She was educated at Columbia University and Ellington named her president of his music publishing company, Tempo, in 1941. Along with handling her brother's legal matters, she hosted a talk show on New York's WLIB radio station in the 1950s. She continued to run Ellington's music interests after his death in 1974. She sold a good deal of Ellington's works to the Smithsonian Institution in 1991 and half of his publishing company in 1995. Boatwright was a churchgoer and was instrumental in founding the jazz music ministry at St. Peter's Lutheran Church in Manhattan where Rev. John Garcia Gensel was the designated jazz pastor. She died on March 13, 2004.

Lorraine Ellison

ALTHOUGH LORRAINE ELLISON is scarcely remembered by any but the most fanatical of 1960s soul music aficionados for her earth-quaking ballad "Stay with Me," her approach to that classic and whatever else she sang was pure gospel. Born in 1943 in Philadelphia, Pennsylvania, she first recorded with the gospel group the Ellison Singers, who cut the LP *This Is Another Day* for the Sharp/Savoy label in 1962. They changed their name to the Golden Chords and briefly recorded for Columbia Records in 1963. The failure of all of these records led Ellison to move into R&B music in 1964 when she joined Mercury Records' roster. Her smooth Top 25 R&B cover of Jerry Butler's "I Dig You Baby" was deceptive. Possessing a piercing soprano with raw emotional power, her soul-drenched ballad "Stay with Me" finally gave her the hit she always coveted. The track has to be heard to be believed because it simply defies description. Issued by Warner Bros.' black recording division, Loma, the song climbed to No. 11 on the *Billboard* R&B charts in 1966. Ellison met the one-hit wonder jinx, though, because in spite of the flawless recordings that followed, she never had another sizeable hit. No matter what she sang, Ellison's love for gospel was always the foundation. Even love songs such as "Heart Be Still," "A Good Love,"

"I Want to Be Loved," and "You Don't Know Nothing About Love" only needed the name of Jesus to be inserted to be considered some of the hardest, most passionate gospel songs ever recorded. When it became apparent to her after almost ten years with Warner Bros. Records that they were unable to create any hits for her, Ellison opted to record songs she felt like recording. Her last recording sessions included gospel songs such as Cassietta George's "Walk Around Heaven," "I'll Fly Away," "Many Rivers to Cross," and "No Relief." Warner never released them during her lifetime. By all accounts, Ellison was a warm, amiable person whose mean-spirited husband brought her much grief. She died on August 17, 1985, with barely a notice.

Tommy Ellison and the Five Singing Stars

BORN IN 1932 in South Carolina, Tommy Ellison started his career singing with Edna Gallmon Cooke, the Chosen Gospel Singers, and the Harmonizing Four. In the 1960s, he formed the Five Singing Stars as a contemporary group with a traditional gospel flavor. At the same time, his brother James "Budd" Ellison was playing R&B piano and composing songs for R&B/funk trio LaBelle. In the 1970s, the Singing Stars recorded hits such as "Father, Please Stand by Me," "Newborn Soul," "God Loves You," "Guilty," and "Hard to Get Along." Over the years, they recorded for HSE Records, Nashboro, and AIR Records. One of their recent CDs, *Going to See My Friend*, featured fine gospel versions of two classic R&B tunes, the Manhattans' "Shining Star" and the Chi-Lites' "Oh Girl," which they renamed "Don't Leave Me Jesus."

Gordon Ely

BILLBOARD MAGAZINE's black gospel music critic since 1994, Ely's reviews on the subject can either make or break recordings in the gospel music market. He was born on May 21, 1964, in Richmond, Virginia. From 1989 to 1999, Ely was a music writer and columnist for the *Richmond Times-Dispatch* where he interviewed such pop music legends as Rosemary Clooney, Ray

Charles, and Bon Jovi. Although *Billboard* magazine had reviewed black gospel product during the course of its 100-plus year history, it was not until Ely was hired in 1994 that they had a full-time black gospel album critic. In addition to *Billboard*, Ely is a regular contributor to other music publications, wrote the liner notes for Time/Life's triple-platinum *Songs 4 Worship* CD, and is recognized as a seminal figure in bringing widespread, mainstream attention to the gospel music genre.

"The roots of almost all truly indigenous American music can literally be traced to the African-American church, from the often improvisational, a cappella spirituals of pre-emancipation blacks, to 20th-century blues, jazz, R&B, soul, and rock 'n' roll—and even modern hip-hop and urban contemporary sounds," says Ely. "Unbridled lyrical expression, as well as a dizzying display of musical forms and artistry, running a gamut from despair and confusion, to hope and determination, are the very essence and definition of black gospel music. Indeed, it is 'American music' at its deepest point of connection with both the heart and soul of all who walk the pathways of this good and gracious, yet still deeply troubled land."

Emotions

EASILY THE MOST POPULAR female R&B trio of the latter 1970s, the Emotions came to be known and exalted for their smooth, aching classic soul ballads such as "Don't Ask My Neighbors," "Flowers," "Walking the Line," and "A Feeling Is" Their uptempo smashes such as "Best of My Love," "Don't Wanna Lose Your Love," and "Boogie Wonderland" (with Earth, Wind & Fire) are exceptions. Soul fans wanted to hear the group sing about finding love and losing love as only they could. Throughout their career, the group has continued to sprinkle their repertoire with the gospel music and message of their youth. Jeanette (born February 1950), Wanda (born December 17, 1951) and Sheila (born January 17, 1953) Hutchinson were all born in Chicago. Their father, Joe Hutchinson, once sang with the Wings of Heaven gospel group. He began grooming his daughters for a singing career in 1957. They began as the Heavenly Sunbeams and later sang as Three Ribbons

and a Bow (three girls in ribbons and their guitar-playing dad sporting a bow). They developed a repertoire of 150 mostly sacred songs, a few secular tunes, and a couple of classical pieces. They performed around the Chicago area, singing live on radio, doing several radio commercials for Al Abrams Pontiac, opening for Mahalia Jackson and Staple Singers concerts, and appearing on the local *Jerry Van Dyke Show*. In 1962, the girls (under the name the Hutch Stereos), recorded their first song, "Santa Got Stuck in the Chimney," for Local Records. They then recorded for the Vee-Jay Records subsidiary Tollie Records and also for One-derful Records as the Sunbeams. In 1967, they changed their name to the Emotions "because we knew how to arouse emotions," Sheila once told writer Robert Bowman. They began recording for the local Brainstorm Records and its Twin Stacks subsidiary, where they recorded songs such as "I Can't Stand No More Heartaches" and "I Can't Control these Emotions."

Around this period, the Staple Singers had joined Memphis-based Stax Records and began to make greater headway in the R&B field. Pervis Staples had stopped performing with his family's group and was managing other artists. He took the Emotions on and booked them on a talent show at the Regal Theater where first prize was a chance to record one song for Stax Records. They won, and once they were in the studio recording, executives realized that the group needed a long-term contract instead of a one-time record. They were teamed up with producers Isaac Hayes and David Porter. Their first hit was a song Sheila wrote called "So I Can Love You," which reached No. 3 on the R&B chart. After that, most of their R&B songs such as "Show Me How," "I Could Never Be Happy," and "Put a Little Love Away" were only moderate hits. Their producers struggled with keeping their songs current yet clean. Porter once told Bowman that "being as young as they were and with their dad with them, we had to juggle our thoughts as to how to be clean yet suggestive.... We went through great pains to be sure that we didn't turn mummy and daddy off with the songs." During their time at Stax, Jeannette left the group to start a family. Their cousin Theresa Davis (born August 22, 1950 in Chicago) took her place for a while. The group was booked to be part of the documentary film *Wattstax*, which was shot live at the Los Angeles Memorial Coliseum on August 20, 1972. It featured Stax's most popular artists such as the Staple Singers, Carla and Rufus Thomas, Isaac Hayes, and others. There was a lot of media buzz about the concert, which celebrated the triumphant spirit of the L.A. black community in Watts in the wake of racial unrest. The show was a likely career springboard for all artists involved. Just as the Emotions were about to take the stage, their segment was cancelled because the show was running long. They were heartbroken to not be able to sing even one song when the popular artists sang up to four songs.

Days before the concert, the Emotions had sung a particularly rousing rendition of the gospel standard "Peace Be Still" at a local church in the city with Wanda on lead. They sang harder than most of their fans would come to know them for and it's a delicious piece of sanctified soul. It was an arrangement their father came up with when they were children that built into a vocal climax and was always a sure-fire hit with crowds. Stax had filmed that performance and some secular performances they had done that week. The filmmakers liked "Peace Be Still" best of all, so they spliced that performance into the film instead of one of their secular songs. Unfortunately, R&B radio wasn't playing overtly gospel songs at the time and because they were secular artists, gospel radio refused to touch the Emotions' 45-rpm single. What could have been a wonderful showcase for the Hutchinson sisters through the movie and the single ended up having no effect on their career at all. They floundered for the rest of their time with Stax, and when the company finally closed in 1975 it didn't mean much to the group because their records weren't selling anyway. Not long after, family friend Ron Ellison told Hutchinson that he had played some of the group's new demos for Charles Stepney, who worked with Earth, Wind & Fire's Maurice White. Stepney loved what he heard, so Ellison wanted to bring him and the Emotions together. The meeting led to Stepney signing them to Kalimba Productions. White's group was the biggest, funkiest R&B group in the country and they secured Columbia Records to release the Emotions' new music. Jeannette had returned from maternity leave and Randle retired from the group.

The debut 1976 LP *Flowers* featured the smash R&B hits "Flowers," "I Don't Wanna Lose Your Love," and "You've Got the Right to Know." The title song had gospel overtones and a brotherhood message, but the album also featured a cappella renditions of the gospel standard "God Will Take Care of You" and their own gospel tune "We Go through Changes." The Emotions toured with Earth, Wind & Fire to promote the project, which reintroduced the group almost as if they were a brand new trio. It was as if "So I Can Love You" was a fluke and the group was being taken seriously for the very first time. The Emotions' smooth love songs were not as much sensual as they were playful and kittenish. The young women always came across as somewhat bashful and innocent about their love songs and maintained a clean image among singers with racier images such as Chaka Khan and Donna Summer. Jeanette took another maternity break and was replaced by their baby sister, Pamela (born September 19, 1958), for the recording and promotion of their next LP, *Rejoice*. The title track was a funky gospel song set to the tone of R&B-styled message music similar to what the Staple Singers and Rance Allen had been recording at the

The Emotions / photo courtesy of Stax/Fantasy Records

time. However, the breakout single was the uptempo "Best of My Love," which gave the ladies the first and only No. 1 R&B and pop hit of their career to date. They followed up with the Quiet Storm staple "Don't Ask My Neighbors," one of the most beautiful love songs ever recorded. Black radio also played their version of the Edwin Hawkins Singers' song "A Long Way to Go," "A Feeling Is" and the quasi-gospel "Blessed" during the summer of 1977. After going gold with *Flowers*, this LP was their first to go platinum, and they won the Grammy award for Best R&B Group for the track "The Best of My Love."

After a tour with the Commodores was completed, Jeanette returned to the group to stay and Pamela returned to college. At that point, they began working on their last gold LP to date, 1978's *Sunbeam*. The album featured the Top Ten R&B smash "Smile" and another soon-to-be Quiet Storm staple, "Walking the Line." They toured with the Brothers Johnson and had their own elaborate flowered stage set design (a nod to their big hit "Flowers") where they sat in chair-size flowers and sang their songs to an ecstatic audience. Following their tour, they were back in the studio with Earth, Wind & Fire recording "Boogie Wonderland" which became a massive worldwide hit. In the late fall of 1979, the Emotions released the critically disappointing LP *Come into Our World*, which nonetheless featured a beautiful cover photo and one minor dance hit with "What's the Name of Your Love?" Their last Columbia LP *New Affair* was poorly promoted and was the worst seller of their career, although they had slightly better radio airplay than with the previous album on the songs "Turn It Out" and "Now that I Know." During this period, the sisters began to work behind the scenes. They had long written many of their own hits such as "So I Can Love You," "Me for You," and "Don't Wanna Lose Your Love." They now began to write for other artists. Wanda and Jeanette worked on the Jennifer Holiday project *Feel My Soul*, and Sheila began singing in commercials back in Chicago. Wanda and her husband Wayne collaborated with Maurice White on Earth, Wind & Fire tunes such as "Let's Groove," "Fall in Love with Me," "Side by Side," and "Thinking of You."

In 1984, the Emotions returned to the record store shelves with their album *Sincerely* on Red Label Records.

The album produced three admirable singles, "You're the One," the dance track "You're the Best," and the wrenching ballad "Are You Through with My Heart?" In spite of some good music, it did not become a big comeback recording and they moved on to Motown Records where they released the 1985 LP *If I Only Knew*, which also did not improve their fortunes. Adding to their sadness was their father's death from cancer that year. He was strong-willed and strict, but he loved his girls and his death shattered them. After his passing, they dropped out of the national limelight for a time.

By 1990, they were itching to become active again. Pamela and Jeanette did background vocals on gospel singer Helen Baylor's "There's No Greater Love" track. Wanda and Jeannette sang on Earth, Wind & Fire's *Heritage* CD that year. In 1992, the group recorded "I Want to Thank You for Your Love" for the motion picture soundtrack for *Bebe's Kids*. Soon they were doing dusties (oldies but goodies) concerts and performing on a consistent basis. While attending an acting class, Jeanette came up with an idea to create a theater piece around the sisters' career. The musical *Bigger Than Bubblegum* debuted in 1995 and received strong reviews. It then began to tour across the country. They also produced their first CD, *The Emotions Live*, in 1996 on their own Sunbeam Records label. Along with their R&B hits, the album featured several original gospel songs. The sisters now include a gospel segment in their concert dates and have seen nostalgia develop around their old music, which has been featured in movies such as *Summer of Sam* and *Boogie Nights*. After their heyday was over, the Emotions have continued to make excellent background vocals for a number of artists, including LL Cool J, Patrice Rushen, Lionel Richie, Nancy Wilson, and Smokey Robinson. In 2001, they received the Rhythm and Blues Foundation's Pioneer Award.

RECOMMENDED RECORDING: There is no single compilation featuring the gospel tunes of the Emotions. They have sprinkled their offerings throughout their discography. However, the progressive Christian thinker will appreciate their 1977 LP *Rejoice* (Columbia Records). Along with the squeaky-clean love songs such as "Don't Ask My Neighbors" and "Best of My Love," there are the spiritually drenched tunes "A Long Way to Go," "Blessed," and "Rejoice."

Escoffreys

THIS BRITISH SISTER ACT was named the Best Female Group by the Black Gospel Association from 1985 to 1987. The Escoffreys were very visible during the 1990s. They were signed to Atlantic Records' East-West imprint in 1990 and enjoyed crossover hits such as "Look Who's Loving Me." They won the DMI at the London Gospel Music Awards in 1994. Marcia Escoffrey has taught at seminars since then and backed artists such as Elton John, Eric Clapton, and Sting in recording sessions. Her sister Sandra died in the summer of 1999.

E.T.W.

A CHRISTIAN RAP TRIO formed on the campus of Oral Roberts University in 1985, they made their greatest impact in 1991 with the Top Ten CCM single "Destined to Win." The group was comprised of Mike "MCL King" Hill (born 1965), Elroy "MC Free" Forbes (born 1967), and Johnnie "Johnnie Jam" Williams (born 1962). They recorded for Forefront Records until 1997 when they released their final project, *Ain't Nobody Dyin' but Us*. Their sound was harder and more street-edged than DC Talk's pop rap.

Anthony Evans

THE SON OF TELEVANGELIST Tony Evans, who pastors the Oak Cliff Bible Fellowship in Dallas, Anthony Evans (born 1979) grew up with a diverse spectrum of Christian music influences, from Commissioned to Steven Curtis Chapman. He graduated from Jerry Falwell's Liberty University where he sang with the school's Sounds of Liberty singing group. Following college, Evans sang with the inspirational Christian group TRUTH for two years. He then toured with Kirk Franklin as a background singer before nailing a recording contract with INO Records. His 2004 CD *Even More* debuted at No. 17 on the gospel album chart.

Clay Evans

CLAY EVANS WAS ONCE best known as Jesse Jackson's personal pastor through a popular television commercial promoting his music in the 1970s, but gospel fans have long known him as a great traditional gospel artist who has created gospel gems such as "Room at the Cross." Born on June 23, 1925, in Brownsville, Tennessee, Evans was three years old before he began to talk. When he finally uttered his first words, his grateful mother, Estanualy, prayed that his voice would be used for God's service. As a child, Evans often sang with the family gospel group that his mother sang and played keyboards for. After graduating from Carver High School in Brownsville, Evans's family moved to Chicago. There he briefly sang with the Lux Singers before he joined an a cappella group, the Soul Revivers, who often shared local bills with the Highway QCs during gospel's Golden Age. In 1950, at the age of 25, Evans founded the Fellowship Missionary Baptist Church with three siblings and two friends as his first members. Over the years, the church's name would change to Mount Carmel before Evans rechristened it Fellowship Baptist Church. His sister, LeDella Reid, formed the 200-voice choir that has backed Evans on most of his albums.

Evans's local fame grew quickly through his "What a Fellowship" radio broadcast, and his church's growing congregation brought it political clout. Sometimes that clout worked against him. For instance, in 1965 when Evans was building a new church and invited Dr. Martin Luther King, Jr., to speak, he felt the sting. The bank loaning the church money for construction withdrew the loan because the white bank executive viewed King as a racial troublemaker. As a consequence, the building would not be completed until eight years later, when it was affectionately nicknamed "The Ship."

Evans began recording his choir back in the 1960s but really didn't hit his commercial stride until the 1980s when his Savoy Records LPs such as *I'm Blessed*, *I'm Going Through*, and *What He's Done for Me* all hit the Top Ten on the gospel chart. As contemporary gospel artists such as Andrae Crouch were embraced by youth, the traditional choir settings and impassioned vocals of Evans's choir connected with the elders of the black church, who often felt that gospel music was getting away from God with its contemporary beats and loosely bible-based messages. Many of them wanted to get back to the basics of the early Reagan administration, when the country, at least temporarily, took on a neo-conservative atmosphere that the president set in motion. Evans's music reminded church mothers (women comprised the bulk of black church membership) of the good old days when children had manners and it seemed that the world was a much kinder place—in spite of segregation.

Evans's popularity has continued, although much of his initial audience of senior citizens has died off. In 1996, his *I've Got a Testimony* LP reached No. 1 on the gospel album chart on the strength of the radio hits "It's Me Again," "Lead Me On," "God Rose in a Windstorm," and "Lost Sheep." Evans performed on the Stellar awards and *Bobby Jones Gospel* television broadcasts that year. Nearing the age of 80, Evans is still mentally sharp, in his pulpit preaching every week, and recording hit albums such as *Constantly*, which hit the gospel Top Ten in 2002.

Linda Evans

LINDA EVANS SANG R&B for Ariola in 1979. She then recorded a self-titled LP for Good News Records in 1984, which was distributed by A&M Records. The label was founded by Freddie Piro, who was partially responsible for the emergence of the Jesus Music Movement in the early 1970s through his recording of the group Love Song. The label would later produce fine recordings for Roby Duke, Becky Fender, and Howard McCrary. By the 1990s, the label had closed.

Madame Hurd Fairfax

THE FIRST BLACK FEMALE gospel singer to ever record was Madame Hurd Fairfax. The Baptist stalwart recorded for Paramount Records in 1923. Out of those springtime sessions came tunes such as "They Needed a Songbird in Heaven," "Somebody's Knocking at Your Door," "The Swallows," and "Troubles Don't Last Always."

Fairfield Four

DURING THE World War II era, the Fairfield Four were one of gospel music's most popular and hardest singing quartets. They were originally formed as a gospel duet in the 1920s by the pastor of Nashville's Fairfield Baptist Church to soak up the idle time of his sons, Harry and Rufus Carrethers. Soon, John Battle joined and they became a trio. In the 1930s, they became a quartet and recorded for RCA Victor and Columbia Records where their renditions of hymns featured the vocal contrasts of a booming baritone and a sweet tenor. In spite of their record deals, they did not really draw widespread national attention until the Sunway Vitamin Company sponsored a daily 15-minute national radio broadcast that emanated from WLAC in Nashville. They never made much money and by 1950 the group had broken up. One former member, Rev. Sam McCrary (born October 27, 1913), briefly resurrected the group at various times over the years, but spent most of his life as a Nashville pastor. In 1980, promoter Doug Seroff reunited the surviving members of the group for a concert in Birmingham, Alabama, that led to a renewed interest in the group among high-art culture fans. In 1989, after they won a National Endowment for the Arts award, Warner Bros. Records signed them up. At the time, the group was comprised of Walter Settles, W.L. Richardson, Isaac Freeman, and McCrary. Their 1992 label debut CD *Standing in the Safety Zone* reached No. 22 on the gospel chart—the highest of their erratic recording career. It was not a commercial success but a critical one. The follow-up CD, 1997's *I Couldn't Hear Nobody Pray*, featured appearances by Elvis Costello, Pam Tillis, and Garrison Keillor. It too was more a critical than cash register success, but it did win a Grammy award. They have released a couple more albums on small labels but remain in good demand on the college and blues concert festival circuit. They also had a cameo appearance in the George Clooney film *O Brother, Where Art Thou?*.

In 2002, at the age of 73, Isaac "Dickie" Freeman, the group's baritone, was coaxed into recording a barebones, grassroots-style traditional gospel album entitled *Beautiful Stars*, produced by Jerry Zolten for Lost Highway Records. When Zolten initially came to him, Freeman said, "I'd never thought about doing a solo album. Not after all those years of singing as part of a quartet. But he said, 'I'm behind you. I think it would be a good idea.'" Indeed it was a good idea. The CD garnered rave reviews in dozens of publications including *USA Today* and the *New York Times*. Freeman still performs with the Fairfield Four, which is completely comprised of non-original members.

Lola Falana

IN THE 1970S AND '80S, Lola Falana reigned as the undisputed Queen of Las Vegas—the first woman (of any color) to pull down $100,000 a week entertaining at any of the top hotel casinos there. Her protégée relationship with Sammy Davis, Jr., brought her clout and entertainment industry respect. Along the way the leggy dancer made many firsts. She was the first black woman to become spokesperson for a major perfume line when she became Faberge's Tigress woman in 1975 and the first black celebrity spokesperson for Hanes pantyhose. She was also the first black woman to sign a contract with ABC for four television specials in 1976. Her exotic attributes put her in league with the great beauties of the day such as Raquel Welch and Ann-Margret.

Falana was born on September 11, 1943, in Philadelphia, Pennsylvania. Her father was a Cuban immigrant and her mother was African-American. She grew up taking dance lessons and always had a relationship with God. After high school, she moved to New York to become a star. The early years were rough, but she eventually earned a job with blues queen Dinah Washington as a dancer. She was later discovered by Sammy Davis, Jr., who cast her in *Golden Boy* on Broadway. With her star on the rise, she recorded modest hits for Mercury Records and Reprise Records such as the gorgeous summer song "Coconut Grove." Falana later moved to Italy where she became a superstar model and spaghetti-western film star. When she returned to the States, she appeared on several network television programs, such as *Laugh-In* and *The Mod Squad*.

Along the way, she began to perform in Las Vegas where she paid many dues and worked her way up to the top rung of the entertainment industry there. Her energetic show featured dancing, lavish costume changes, and a lot of inspiration. In addition, she was a perennial fixture on television during the period. In 1987, that all came to a halt when Falana was stricken with multiple sclerosis. Over some months she had noticed that it had become more difficult to do the high-energy dance routines she had become known for. One night, in the middle of performing, her voice slurred and she couldn't get her rhythm. For the first time in her career, people walked out on her show. Weeks later she was diagnosed with MS and her doctors said there was nothing they could do for her. She sought solace in her lifelong faith. "God was trying to get my attention, but I wasn't listening," she says. "It took him allowing me to have MS to get my attention."

Even as her arms fell out of their sockets, she lost her sight, and she was paralyzed on one side, Falana's faith strengthened. There were days she literally crawled on her belly just to get to the bathroom. After almost two vexing years, she says God restored her health. In 1990, she made a triumphant return to the Vegas stage. "I wanted to say farewell," she says. "I wanted to show the world that God had healed me and that if I chose to continue performing that I could continue. However, I chose to go from [being] a star to a servant of Jesus Christ." Still in her prime, Falana began evangelizing. Her ministry trips have taken her throughout the US and to places as far as Bosnia. She's currently raising

Lola Falana, July 1994 / photo by Robert Shanklin

money for African children who have been orphaned by the AIDS epidemic sweeping that continent. A life-long Episcopalian, she was led to join the Catholic faith. She sees herself as being a part of a revolution in the Catholic Church that emphasizes the ministry of Jesus Christ and everyday miracles like herself. However, Lola Falana takes the gospel everywhere. She speaks to Baptist church groups, Pentecostal groups, Charismatic groups, and any other group that welcomes the Good News. When the MS first struck her, Falana says she lost much of her singing ability. She has seen it gradually come back to her and once it does, she hopes to make an inspirational music CD.

Father Divine

SHAM ARTIST OR SHEPHERD? Father Divine was much loved by his loyalists and much despised by his detractors during his lifetime. Father Divine was a controversial figure who did much to aid the poor during the Great Depression but also raised eyebrows when he allowed his followers to proclaim him Almighty God. It is believed that he was born George Baker circa 1879 in Rockville, Maryland. As a teenager, Baker was mentored by a traveling evangelist named Samuel Morris, who called himself Father Jehovah. After a decade of collaboration, Baker went his own way in 1912 and began to set up his own ministry. He ended up in the affluent white neighborhood of Sayville, New York, where he and his first wife, Mother Divine, lived communally with other members of their congregation. Neighbors were always uncomfortable with the black couple integrating their neighborhood, but they were especially bothered by the transient blacks who often came to visit. Divine was thrust into the national spotlight in November 1931 when neighbors called the police because one of his prayer meetings became too loud. White policemen arrived on the scene and arrested Divine for disturbing the peace. He saw himself as the victim of racism, so he refused bail and pleaded his innocence. He was tried and convicted. Judge Lewis J. Smith sentenced him to a year in jail and a $500 fine. Divine went to jail, and two days later the judge suddenly died. Divine openly hinted to a newspaper reporter that the magis-

trate's death was no accident, saying, "I hated to do it!" When the news broke, many blacks across the country believed Divine possessed supernatural powers.

In 1932 when he was released from prison, Divine moved his church to Harlem, where he was welcomed as a hero. The Depression was in full swing, so Divine set up Peace Missions—charity depots funded by his church to feed, clothe, house, and instruct the poor in the tenets of his faith. Divine preached a faith of racial equality, universal brotherhood, and prosperity. Those who joined the faith were told to pay off their debts and set their financial houses in order. In addition, there was a strict code of teetotalism, no smoking, and celibacy for those who were not married. However, Father Divine biographer Sara Harris, in her book *Holy Husband*, wrote that Divine amassed millions off the backs of the poor and engaged in unchaste relationships with the group of young women he surrounded himself with. After the first Mother Divine died, Divine married a white Canadian woman named Edna Rose Ritchings. She took over the ministry when Father Divine died in 1965. His body was enshrined at the couple's Philadelphia estate.

Fernando

IN THE EARLY 1990s, there was a temporary boom of Hispanic gospel artists. It appeared as a hot new trend, but just as quickly as it came, it left. None of the artists made a big commercial impact on the industry, and it's surprising that considering the emergence of Hispanics as the largest minority group in the US, there have not been more Hispanic gospel artists. Nonetheless, one of the first was a smooth-singing, potential pinup boy named Fernando. He was born in 1960 to Ecuadorian Catholic parents, Jorge and Ines Quinde. His mother began to attend a Protestant church when Fernando was in the seventh grade, and Fernando made the leap of faith with her. He began recording for the Movin' Up label. His first album *True Love* appeared in 1990. In 1992, he came back with *Latin Perspective* and followed with his best album, *Fernando*, in 1996. His fourth album, *En la Interseccion*, was issued on Caiman Records in 1997. Fernando possesses a firm tenor that just floats over his R&B-style rhythms with just a touch of Latin flavor that makes for a very fine listening experience. Recently, he's worked as a voice-over actor in Hollywood

Fireside Gospel Singers

COMPRISED OF Houston Whitney, Edward Hall, Albert Phillips, and Thomas Gilbert, this group recorded for Nashboro Records in the early 1950s. One of their standout tunes is "Get Your Soul Right," a riveting, hard-singing workout between Whitney and Phillips.

Fisk Jubilee Singers

THE FISK FREE COLORED SCHOOL for newly freed slaves was founded in 1866 by Union Army General Clinton B. Fisk. In 1871, Geoff L. White, a treasurer and music instructor at Fisk University in Nashville, decided to raise some money for the school, which was facing bankruptcy, by launching a concert tour. Against the better judgment of school officials, White found nine Fisk students (all former slaves or the children of former slaves) who could sing and set out on a tour that traced the path of the Underground Railroad. White borrowed money to finance their classical music tour, which he expected would bring in big funds. However, the classical repertoire didn't go over well. White then decided to change the song selections to Negro spirituals and slave tunes his secretary, Ella Shepherd, had learned as a child. To emphasize the point, he also named the group the Jubilee Singers, a reference to the recent emancipation of the slaves in 1865. With the group's polished sound and determination to save their school, they began to develop an audience in Ohio. From there, they trekked to Brooklyn, New York, where abolitionist minister Henry Ward Beecher was so overcome by their performance at his church that he lobbied his wealthy parishioners to donate generously to the school's cause. The tour eventually took them all over the US and to Europe. They raised $150,000, enough money to buy the school's present-day campus, which sits on what was once Union Fort Gillem.

RECOMMENDED RECORDING: The CD *In Bright Mansions* (Curb, 2003) is a modern recording by the current choir. It was recorded in a 19th century church with century-old arrangements to create the ambiance of the original Fisk Jubilee Singers.

Five Blind Boys of Mississippi

ONE OF THE MOST influential groups in all of early gospel music history, the Five Blind Boys of Mississippi were formed in the 1930s by Archie Brownlee (born October 19, 1925, in Turrell, Mississippi; died 1960), Joseph Ford, Lawrence Abrams, and Lloyd Woodard— all students at the Piney Woods School for the Blind near Jackson, Mississippi. They began performing as the Cotton Blossom Singers circa 1936 to help raise money for the school. They also began recording field recordings for the Library of Congress folklorist Alan Lomax the next year. After the men graduated from school, they performed secular music for white audiences as the Cotton Blossom Singers and sang spirituals for black congregations as the Jackson Harmoneers. They expanded to a quintet with the addition of Melvin Henderson, who was later replaced by Percell Perkins (who was not blind) in the 1940s. During that period, Perkins became their manager and they changed their name to the Five Blind Boys. They made their first commercial recording for Excelsior Records in 1946, but did not hit it big until they joined Don Robey's Peacock label in 1950. Their single "Our Father (Which Art in Heaven)" reached No. 10 on the R&B chart in January 1951. They recorded a dozen radio hits over the next decade, and the centerpiece was always Brownlee's spine-tingling howls, screams, and yodels. His vocal theatrics had a profound effect on the development of Ray Charles's vocal style. Unfortunately, Brownlee died after a sudden bout of pneumonia on February 8, 1960, in New Orleans. After Brownlee's death, Roscoe Robinson and Wilmer Broadnax shared lead vocal chores. Various incarnations of the group survived into the 1990s, although all of the original members had either died or retired by 1982.

Roberta Flack

ONE OF ADULT FM RADIO'S most cherished artists, Roberta Flack began her recording career eclectically. On her first albums, she often mixed in her favorite gospels alongside her sophisticated love songs. Born February 10, 1940, in Black Mountain, North Carolina, the velvet-voiced chanteuse began to play classical piano at the age of nine. At 13, she performed Handel's *Messiah* in its entirety before her church congregation. After earning a scholarship, Flack enrolled at Howard University in Washington, DC, where she graduated with a degree in music education. While in the city, Flack began to sing pop songs at Mr. Henry's Club while also teaching music at a public school. Jazz great Les McCann spotted her at Mr. Henry's and arranged an audition for her at Atlantic Records. After being signed to the label, Flack's breakthrough hit was "The First Time Ever I Saw Your Face," which was a No. 1 pop single in 1972. Flack's early LPs featured songs such as "Reverend Lee" about a wayward minister and the awesome six-minute opus "I Told Jesus" in which Flack took the classic hymn and transformed it into a dramatic jazzy vocal workout. Her third LP, *Quiet Fire*, featured three spiritual tunes: "Go Up Moses," "Bridge over Troubled Water," and "Sunday and Sister Jones." Her 1972 duet LP with former Howard University alumnus Donny Hathaway featured their stirring version of "Come Ye Disconsolate." Through the end of the 1970s Flack recorded other spiritually inspired music, such as "Some Gospel According to Matthew" and "God Don't Like Ugly," which she recorded first with Hathaway and later reprised with Peabo Bryson. The singer, who is best known for such smooth pop songs as "Tonight, I Celebrate My Love" and "Killing Me Softly," was also a Ph.D. Candidate at the University of Massachusetts while continuing to record her own unique brand of music in her own incomparable way. "I am a person who has managed to last because I have chosen to stay true to my own identity and principles, and true to my own experience," Flack told the *Washington Post*'s Richard Harrington. "I am a black person who sings the way I do. I am not a black person who sounds anything like Aretha Franklin or anything like Chaka Khan. I know what I am and I don't want to—and I shouldn't have to—change in order to be who I am."

RECOMMENDED RECORDING: *First Take* (Atlantic) only has one gospel song, "I Told Jesus," but it's well worth buying for that track alone.

Tony Fontaine

A MID-LEVEL CROONER (in the Frank Sinatra mold) with a soulfulness in his style was primarily known for the songs "Cold, Cold Heart," "Visions of Bernadette," and "Syncopated Clock" for Mercury Records in the 1950s. After a 1957 car accident, he dedicated himself to church life and gospel music and often appeared at Pentecostal religious crusades. He briefly recorded gospel music for Word Records circa 1961 and collaborated with one of their popular artists of the period, Gloria Roe. The Assemblies of God church denomination sponsored the 1963 motion picture *The Tony Fontaine Story* with Fontaine tackling the lead role. Some of his recordings are listed as Tony Fontane as well as by Tony Fontaine. He died of cancer at the age of 47 on July 1, 1974 at the West Hills Hospital in the Los Angeles area.

Cedric Ford

SINGER-SONGWRITER Cedric Ford was born September 28, 1968, in Chicago. A protégé of Dorothy Norwood, he and Faith Howard used to sing in a group called Visions: A Choral Ministry. The choir backed Howard's godmother, Albertina Walker, on a number of her projects. Walker and Dorothy Norwood produced an album for Howard on Salvation Records that featured a duet with Ford. Norwood was impressed by Ford and took him under her wing. She produced his 2000 CD *Cedric Ford Featuring Visions: A Choral Ministry*. He and Norwood co-wrote "Grandma's Song" for the project. The album won him a GMWA Excellence award nomination as Male Vocalist of the Year. Norwood recut the song on her 2002 CD *Live at Home*. In recent years, Ford has worked as a church music minister and co-starred in the David E. Talbert stage play *The Fabric of a Man* with Shemar Moore and Cheryl "Pepsi" Riley in 2001. He won an NAACP Theater nomination as best supporting actor for his role.

Blind Mamie Forehand

THIS RURAL EARLY-20TH century gospel singer is best known for her mournful, bluesy, shrill vibrato on the 1927 recording of "Honey in the Rock," which featured her husband on guitar and her sink-drip ringing of a triangle. That track is featured on the CD *Sacred Roots of the Blues* (BMG Records, 2004).

Fortitude

AN URBAN CONTEMPORARY gospel quartet, Fortitude's music was born in their childhood experiences. The childhood stories behind the group are poignant. Cinque's (born Cinque Cullar on May 14, 1974) father struggled with an addiction; Teddy's (born Hugh Jackson on June 11, 1974) and Jamie's (born Jamie Simon on December 21, 1975) fathers faced other personal challenges; and Roc's (born Leon Guyton on September 19, 1975) father died when Roc was only 11 years old. Worst of all, when Roc came of age, he lived on the edge. He was in a street gang until he had an epiphany one dark night. Roc and three of his buddies were sitting in a parked car, shooting the breeze. "Gunshots came from out of nowhere," he recalls. "I'm a big guy and so were my friends, so there was nowhere that we could duck down. We were in a little car, a Buick Century. I looked to the left of me and this guy was literally on the other side of the street shooting from behind a bush. He had a nine-millimeter and emptied a whole clip. None of us got hit from that short distance! I was thinking to myself, "Man, none of us got hit!' And what made me turn my life around isn't that I was afraid, it's that I wasn't afraid. It sounds kind of funny, but I thought to myself, 'I've gotten myself in too deep with this stuff [if] I'm not afraid

about someone shooting at me.' So I said, 'Lord, I'm done.'" Roc turned in his guns to the gang member he reported to and told him he was out.

Free from the street life, Roc immersed himself in music with his best friend, Teddy. Initially, they met through Roc's cousin. "He was always telling Teddy that I could out-sing him," Roc laughs. "So we finally met and we hit it off. My father was dead and his wasn't in the home, so we had that in common. That brought us closer together. We were inseparable in a minute." They started singing together at Concord Baptist Church. Their pastor had a dream of forming a record label and he wanted Roc and Teddy to be his first recording artists. "We didn't feel like we were really ready yet," Roc says. "We suggested to him that he record another local community youth choir first since we had helped to develop the choir and write some of their songs." By the time the choir's CD was released, Teddy and Roc were ready. One of the songs they had written for the choir's CD had Jamie's name written all over it, so they brought him in to record it. "We had grown up listening to Jamie in Walt Whitman and the Soul Children, so he was like a mentor to us," Roc says. "When we heard what Jamie did with the song, we asked him to join us and he agreed to do it."

After Jamie joined the group in 1998, he asked if his buddy from the Soul Children days, Cinque, could also join. "We didn't really know Cinque, but knew of him," says Roc. "We'd see him at local church functions. We had never even thought of having four people in the group. But it was amazing—we all came together just like that."

Once the group was solidified as Nu Wave, they released their debut CD *So Grateful to You* (Imani Faith). The album generated enough attention to win the group a Stellar award nomination for Best New Artist. In the subsequent years, the group remained active with spot concert dates while holding down positions at their respective churches. They also contributed to other projects, including the song "With this Ring," a Verity Records wedding CD.

Fast-forward to Nashville in the spring of 2003. Word's A&R man, Desmond Pringle, saw Fortitude perform in a showcase and signed them to Word Records.

After they signed with Word, label executives felt the name of Nu Wave was too familiar. "We had to change our name," Cinque says. "We wanted something that talked about the four of us, so we came up with Fortitude and the label liked that." The group went in the studio and cut songs with an array of solid producers such as Derek "DOA" Allen, Roger Ryan, Asaph, Berris Bolton, and Desmond Pringle. "All four of us have different musical approaches," says Cinque. "I love great heartfelt gospel ballads. Roc is the big sensitive guy who writes and sings from the soul. Teddy gives strong vocals, with an exciting presence that really connects to the audience. Jamie is a wonderfully talented singer-songwriter and inspired brother. We can have one song and each one of us will interpret it differently. All four of us have unique contributions. That's the beauty of Fortitude."

Clarence Fountain and the Five Blind Boys of Alabama

ONE OF THE LEADING hard-singing quartets of the Golden Age of Gospel in the 1950s, the Blind Boys made a spectacular career renaissance after 2000. The group's leader, Clarence Fountain, was born November 28,

Blind Boys of Alabama /
photo courtesy of Specialty/Fantasy Records

The original Five Blind Boys of Alabama.

1929, in Tyler, Alabama. The guys met in 1939 when they were students at the Talladega Institute for the Blind in Alabama. Fountain had joined the school's male chorus. "The chorus was like a glee club," Fountain said in an EMI Records biography. "Most of our teachers were white, and we were taught a lot of material by white songwriters, like 'Tenting Tonight on the Old Camp Ground.' But we used to listen to black gospel music on the radio, on WSGN in Birmingham. That station played records by groups like the Golden Gate Quartet and the Soul Stirrers, and we loved it. My buddies and I decided to form our own group and sing like they did, with four-part harmony. For a while we called ourselves the Happy Land Jubilee Singers and we toured all around the country. Then a promoter put us on a show with another blind group, the Jackson Harmonies from Mississippi. He billed it as a contest between the blind boys of Alabama and the blind boys of Mississippi. The name worked so we stuck with it."

The guys would often sneak off the school grounds and sing at a nearby military installation where the troops loved them. Buoyed by the soldiers' enthusiasm for their music, the Happy Land Jubilee Singers dropped out of school in 1945 and sought to make a name as recording artists. In 1947, their lead singer, Velma Bozman Traylor, accidentally shot himself to death. He was replaced by Rev. Paul Exkano, who shared lead vocals with Fountain. The Happy Land Jubilee Singers made their recorded debut with "See Everybody's Mother but Mine" for Coleman Records in 1948. By the time the group began to record for Specialty Records, they had officially changed their name to the Five Blind Boys of Alabama. Gospel promoters capitalized on the name by pairing the group on concert bills with the Five Blind Boys of Mississippi. The competing hard-singing quartet showdowns were some of the most remarkable concerts of the period. It would come down to Fountain's fiery lead versus his counterpart, Archie Brownlee. "Every night I had to battle it out with him," Fountain told Seamus McGarvey of *The Gospel Truth* magazine. "Who would the people like the best—and may the best man win! At the end of the show, we would come down the aisle, shake hands, and collaborate together. That was really exciting. Archie, he could sing you to death."

They drew large crowds and ambulances to transport saints overcome by the boisterous singing.

The group left Specialty in 1957 and recorded for Vee-Jay, Savoy, and an assortment of labels over the next decade. In 1969, Fountain left the group to pursue an undistinguished solo career. His lack of success as a soloist brought him back to the group a decade later. On the other hand, the group didn't do much without Fountain either. Their fortunes began to change in 1983 when the group was cast in a gospel adaptation of Sophocles' *Oedipus at Colonus*. Retitled as *The Gospel at Colonus*, the musical toured the country to rave reviews. By the time it hit Broadway in 1988, the show had won an Obie award and given the Blind Boys a new, mostly white audience. One of their new fans was rock legend Peter Gabriel, who signed them to his Real World label. Their debut *Spirit of the Century* found them applying their rough, bluesy vocals to songs by Mick Jagger, Tom Waits, and Ben Harper, among others. The album climbed the gospel charts, but the audience was not black gospel. Thanks to Gabriel's muscle, the Blind Boys were booked on high-profile programs that don't usually book gospel artists, such as *The Late Show with David Letterman*. These appearances coupled with blues festival concerts gave them a rock music audience in addition to their theater audience. The CD won the group their first Grammy in 2001. In 2004, founding member, George Scott, retired from touring with the Blind Boys. However, he continued performing on their records until his death on March 9, 2005. He suffered from diabetes and heart ailments.

4 HIM

A SUBTLY SOULFUL CCM pop quartet, 4 Him was formed in 1990 when its members Andy Chrisman (born May 17, 1965), Mark Harris (born August 1, 1962), Marty Magehee (born June 27, 1962), and Kirk Sullivan (April 2, 1959) left the Christian choral group TRUTH. With Sullivan handling most lead vocals, the group has racked up an amazing number of No. 1 Christian radio hits such as "Measure of a Man," "For Future Generations," and "The Basics of Life."

Aretha Franklin

NO R&B SINGER save for Sam Cooke has had more influence on gospel artists than the Queen of Soul, Aretha Franklin. Although she has only recorded a handful of gospel projects over the course of her career, she personifies gospel for secularists who don't know the field, and the gospel world still looks on her as one of their own. She's one of the very few soul singers who would be welcomed into virtually any black church on a Sunday morning. She's been forgiven for singing secular music, whereas many of her secular peers such as Candi Staton and Al Green inspire more ambivalent feelings among church audiences because of their secular pasts. Perhaps it is because when Franklin did venture into R&B music, she did not leave the church behind as Staton and Green once did. She never stopped singing gospel in her secular concerts and always credited the church and church mothers such as Clara Ward and Mahalia Jackson for grooming her voice.

Franklin was born March 25, 1942, in Memphis, Tennessee. Her mother was a gospel singer and her father, C.L. Franklin, was a preacher. Franklin regularly sang with her sisters, Carolyn and Erma, at her father's New Bethel Baptist Church in Detroit, but soon it was apparent that Franklin was especially gifted. Her father began to feature her at his speaking engagements and she made her first recording as a gospel artist at the age of 14. It was recorded live at her father's church and featured songs such as "Never Grow Old" and "Precious Lord." There were only 1,000 copies of the LP pressed by the local Battle Records label in 1956. Chess Records' gospel division, Checker, bought the masters and reissued the album as "Never Grow Old." The album merely fueled the already substantial buzz about the child prodigy with the big, dramatic voice. She even filled in for Shirley Caesar on a Caravans date in Florida once. "Naturally I knew all the parts from lying on the floor by the record player in the study listening to them for hours," Franklin recalled in her memoirs.

While many recording artists influenced Franklin's vocals, Franklin pointed to Clara Ward as a strong influence on her keyboard technique. "I wasn't really that conscious of the gospel sound," Franklin told *Ebony* in

1966, "but I liked all Miss Ward's records. I learned to play them because I thought one day she might decide she didn't want to play and I'd be ready." Aside from Ward and Art Tatum, Franklin's hands-on piano skills came from James Cleveland, who lived with her family for a while. "Most of what I learned vocally came from him. He gave me a sense of timing in music, and timing is important in everything." She fused his proclivity for big chords and dramatic flourishes with Erroll Garner's tremolos and easy swing in such a way to highlight the cadence of her vocal hues and thereby create her own uniquely dramatic performance style.

It was her friend Major Holly, a bassist for Teddy Wilson's band, who convinced her to seek a secular career. Taking the lead from her friend Sam Cooke, who left gospel for the broader fame and lucre of pop music, Franklin signed to Columbia Records in 1960. The label sought to make her an all-around entertainer in the mode of Judy Garland. She sang standards, show tunes, blues, and even cover tunes. While many of her recordings at the label were excellent, they were not commercial. Consequently, Franklin enjoyed several turntable hits (radio play but poor sales) such as "Operation Heartbreak" and "Runnin' Out of Fools." This went on until 1967 when famed R&B producer Jerry Wexler signed Franklin to Atlantic Records with the goal of molding her into the gospel-infused R&B star he knew she was born to become. Franklin was an immediate success at Atlantic and finally had the commercial appeal to match her radio success. She scored with such gritty, Southern soul ditties as "I Never Loved a Man (The Way I Love You)," "Respect," "Chain of Fools," "Dr. Feelgood," "Don't Play That Song," and "Call Me" among many others. The string of hits prompted DJ Pervis Spann to crown Franklin the Queen of Soul and the title has stuck ever since.

At Atlantic, Franklin freely expressed her gospel roots and often included outright gospel or spiritual songs on her R&B albums. Her 1968s LP *Aretha Arrives* featured the gospel "I Ain't Gonna Let Nobody Turn Me Around," and the LP *Lady Soul* from the same year featured a stunning rendition of Curtis Mayfield's "People Get Ready." The 1970 LP *Spirit in the Dark* featured spiritual-overtoned songs such as the title cut and "When the Battle Is Over." The 1971 LP *Live at*

Fillmore West featured gospel-drenched renditions of "Bridge over Troubled Water," "Reach Out and Touch Somebody's Hand," and "Spirit in the Dark" as an impromptu duet with Ray Charles.

However, fans of Franklin's gospel music point to her quintessential recording from 1972: the much hallowed *Amazing Grace* LP. On the two-record set recorded at New Bethel, Franklin was backed by her former piano teacher Rev. James Cleveland and the Southern California Community Choir. She chose to record some of the traditional gospel songs she grew up loving. With Franklin and Cleveland trading turns at the piano, the audience was treated to an emotional, spirit-charged evening that included such numbers as "Mary, Don't You Weep" and "How I Got Over." The LP reached the Top Ten on both the R&B and the pop charts and yielded a moderate R&B single with Marvin Gaye's "Wholly Holy." The album won a Grammy as Best Gospel Album and in the years since has sold more than two million copies. The influence the album has had on gospel musicians cannot be overstated as Franklin's mainstream success prompted more record labels to take gospel music more seriously. Meanwhile, the high standard of Franklin's production caused many gospel artists to raise their own standards in order to compete.

At the close of the 1970s, Franklin's record sales had slumped and her career need rejuvenation. She found it in Clive Davis, who wooed Franklin to Arista Records and crafted a comeback that resulted in smash hits such as "Jump to It," "Freeway of Love," and "A Rose Is Still a Rose." After the untimely death of her father in 1984 and a variety of other personal problems, Franklin had the itch to record another gospel album. "It's long overdue," she told *Totally Gospel* in 1988. "My fans have all but demanded it. Everywhere I'd go, people would ask me, 'When are you going to do another gospel album?' This has been going on for the past four years. There was always another taping, always another photo shoot, always another this, another that. You just have to put your foot down and say this is it!" She called in friends like Joe Ligon of the Mighty Clouds of Joy, Rev. Jasper Williams, Mavis Staples, Rev. Jesse Jackson, and conductor Thomas Whitfield to make her new album sparkle with the authentic gospel flourishes Franklin relished. Again, she picked traditional gospel songs she loved as a child such as the Ward Singers' "Packin' Up and Getting' Ready to Go" and "Beams of Heaven."

The ensuing double LP *One Lord, One Faith, One Baptism* won another gospel Grammy for the singer and reached No. 1 on the gospel album chart. It sold over 300,000 copies at the time and was reissued on CD with new bonus tracks in 2003 based on fan demand. Rhino Records reissued the *Amazing Grace* album on CD in 1999 with all of the recordings, 29 songs in all, to the delight of fans of Franklin's gospel music. Whereas music critics often try to separate Franklin's R&B material from her gospel material and suggest that she left the church, she always sets them straight. "I never left the church," she emphatically told *Totally Gospel*. "I did then and do now carry the gospel along with me."

RECOMMENDED RECORDING: *Amazing Grace* (Atlantic/Rhino) is Franklin's best gospel effort and features several riveting gospel performances. Start with this album and then enjoy the others.

C.L. Franklin

TO MANY, HE WAS just Aretha's daddy, but to a generation of churchgoers in the 1950s, C.L. Franklin was the most famous and exciting preacher on the gospel circuit. For those who did not have the opportunity to witness his soulful sermonizing in person, he made more than 76 LPs of his sermonettes and songs such as "The Eagle Stirreth Her Nest," "The 23rd Psalm," "A Bigot Meets Jesus," and "I Heard It Through the Grapevine." He was known as the Man with the Million Dollar Voice because that voice had sold well over a million records. A handsome man, smooth talker, fashionable dresser, and ladies' man, Franklin was one of the most esteemed and sought-after preachers of the period.

Born Clarence LeVaughn Franklin on January 22, 1915, in Sunflower County, Mississippi, he was called to preach at the age of 14. After high school, Franklin attended Greenville Industrial Seminary and LeMoyne College before pastoring several churches including Memphis's New Salem Baptist Church and Buffalo's Friendship Baptist Church. He made his final move in 1946 when he founded the New Bethel Baptist Church in Detroit. Franklin began to record his soul-stirring sermons for Checker Records in the 1950s. He toured with all the great gospel stars of the era. A reputed womanizer, Franklin may have had a romantic relationship with the great Clara Ward according to her sister Willa's book. Through the 1970s, Franklin continued to preach, although he did not do the whirlwind preaching tours he did in the '50s and '60s. He seemed content to watch his children prosper as daughters Erma, Aretha, and Carolyn all became successful entertainers. His son Cecil managed Aretha, and his other son Vaughn was a military man. Then tragedy struck on June 10, 1979. Franklin was at his Detroit home on LaSalle Boulevard watching television in his bedroom when a group of thugs broke into the house hoping to steal some antique windows. They didn't realize Franklin was in the house. He caught them off guard and shot them with his own handgun. They returned fire, catching the pastor in his right knee and groin. Aretha was performing in Las Vegas when she heard the news and rushed home to be by her father's side. He had already lapsed into a coma. In her autobiography, Aretha wrote that the criminals were caught and convicted for their crimes.

The Franklin children hoped their father would come out of the coma, so they had 24-hour nursing care for him rather than putting him in a nursing home. His medical bills were well over $2,500 a week, and Aretha worked constantly to raise money to pay the mounting debts. Eventually, they admitted Rev. Franklin into the New Light Nursing Home on Grand River where he died four days later of heart failure on July 27, 1984. Rev. Franklin's open casket wake was held at the Swanson Funeral Home, where he was dressed in a cream-colored suit with a white Bible at his side. The funeral took place at the New Bethel Baptist Church with a who's who of black celebrities in attendance. Three thousand were crammed inside the church and another six thousand stood outside to listen to Rev. Jesse Jackson eulogize Franklin over the loudspeakers. Franklin was buried at Detroit's Woodlawn Cemetery. Aside from his immense influence on other ministers, Franklin also influenced singers. Blues legend Bobby "Blue" Bland told the *Chicago Sun-Times*' Dave Hoekstra in December 2003, "One of my favorite sermons of his was 'The Eagle

Stirreth Her Nest.' I'm from the church, which is an-other reason my lyrics have to tell stories. Rev. Franklin would do the squall when he got real wound up. The reason I paid attention to that is that I used to sing real high. I had my tonsils removed and lost that falsetto. So I had to come up with a gimmick. I started closing my throat and worked on it until I got a flavor for it and it would blend to whatever key I was in."

RECOMMENDED RECORDING: *The Eagle Stirreth Her Nest* (Checker/MCA) is probably the best known of Franklin's sermons and a great place to become ac-quainted with his style.

Kirk Franklin

KIRK FRANKLIN INTRODUCED gospel to a new generation of churched and unchurched kids in 1994 with his breakthrough hit "The Reason Why We Sing." Born Jan-uary 26, 1970, in Dallas, Texas, Franklin's life was rough from the outset. He was abandoned by his parents and raised by his Aunt Gertrude who kept him grounded in church. At the age of 11, he was leading the adult choir at Mt. Rose Baptist Church. During puberty, he began to rebel and hang with a rough crowd. When one of his friends was fatally shot, Franklin realized that he was on a path to destruction and returned to church where he began to compose songs. Any time a major gospel artist would come through town, such as BeBe Winans or Daryl Coley, Franklin sought their advice on the music business. In 1991, he formed a choir called the Family. They recorded a local project and eventually passed a demo of it to Coley. At the time, Coley, his wife Jenell, and Vicki Mack-Lataillade were planning to go into business together. Vicki was going to launch Gospo Centric Records. She would run the label, Coley would be the A&R chief, and Jenell would manage the artists. The first few artists the label released, such as Betty Griffin-Keller and A-1 Swift, didn't fare too well. "Jenell kept asking Vicki to listen to the Kirk Franklin demo," says Neily Dickerson, who was the vice president of artist development for the label. "That tape was in Daryl's car for months because he kept forgetting to give

it to Vicki. Meanwhile, Kirk was calling Daryl all the time to see if he played the tape for anybody. Daryl is that kind of person, he'll help any artist he thinks has talent in whatever way he can. He just forgot to bring in the tape. Finally, Jenell and I went and got the tape. We went in the office and played it all day for two days. After [hearing] it all through the day, Vicki said, 'Is that the same guy? I think I kind of like that. I might be able to sell 30,000 copies of that.' I said, 'No, I think you can sell 100,000 copies.' Vicki laughed and told me I was crazy."

After Mack-Lataillade cleaned up the crudely pro-duced recording and had it mixed enough times to get the flaws out of it, she released it. The Family's self-titled CD debuted at No. 32 on the gospel album sales chart in July 1993. After a moderately successful run of the sin-gle "The Reason Why We Sing" for a few months, the song seemed to have run its course. What happened next would change the course of modern gospel. "It was a team effort," Dickerson says. "It wasn't a brainstorm. It wasn't planned. Ike Owens—our East Coast radio promoter—had the idea to send it to WOWI, an R&B radio station in Virginia. He gave it to the program di-rector, Steve Crumbley, and he loved it. He played it every day and all through the day for weeks. The listener response was incredible. The refreshing thing about it is that Steve personally started calling his program direc-tor friends like Elroy Smith in Chicago and they began to play it without us having to give away a free trip or pay for some radio announcer's daughter's college tui-tion—those things you sometimes had to do in the past to get records played."

After Elroy Smith began to play the song on WGCI in Chicago, the same listener response developed there. At the time, syndicated radio host Tom Joyner was still connected to WGCI. He was a top announcer there be-fore he launched his national radio show. When Joyner, whose show was based in Dallas (where Kirk Franklin and the Family lived) began to play the song, it really took flight. "Kirk had already recorded his second album and we were ready to put it out," Dickerson con-tinues. "It was called *Whatcha Lookin' 4*. Artwork and everything was done and we saw this song taking off at R&B radio and we said, 'Hold up. Let's see how much more we can sell.' It had sold 100,000 at that point and everybody was happy because we had put all of these other albums out and nothing had hit yet." It eventually reached No. 28 on the R&B singles chart a year later.

Franklin was pushing for the CD in the can to be released before the music was considered dated. However, everyone at the label kept the second album on hold and rushed out a Christmas CD instead. "I'll never forget the date because it was July 3rd, which is my mother's birthday," says Dickerson. "We all went down to Dallas and rented a studio. We had a Christmas tree; we had someone bring in turkey and dressing. We were wearing green and red. We had the Christmas spirit going, and that whole album was recorded in one day." Franklin had a nice Christmas gift that year. His first CD was certified platinum, and he had a second R&B hit with the Christmas song "Jesus Is the Reason for the Season."

Franklin's hard urban sound on his crossover songs, the slick video choreography, and R&B samples on his music gave some gospel artists pause. "There were times when I would look at him and I would frown on it, because I was not used to that kind of gospel," Shirley Caesar once told *Gospel Industry Today* magazine. "But when the Clark Sisters and the Hawkins Family came out, they called that contemporary. Twenty years later it's traditional, compared to what we're listening to now. So give it another 15 years and what he's doing will be traditional."

Franklin rejuvenated gospel in the 1990s and other labels began to invest more money in the budgets of their gospel artists. Meanwhile, Franklin continued to enjoy massive radio hits such as "Melodies from Heaven" (1996) and God's Property's "Stomp," which featured a Funkadelic sample and guest vocals by Cheryl "Salt" James of Salt-N-Pepa. The album for the latter sold more than two million copies and spent two weeks at No. 1 on the R&B singles chart. But with the success came lawsuits from members of the choir who saw records selling without them receiving royalties on them. "I will never forget one of the first things that a member of the Family told me back in 1994," Franklin told *Gospel Industry Today* magazine. "He said he didn't understand how he could sing a song and not get publishing from that song…. He just didn't understand why publishing goes to the songwriter…. It was ignorance about how business works. I wrote 90 percent of that album and produced it. Being songwriter and publisher means what I do is not recoupable. I automatically get paid from record one…. From the first royalty check, they had issues with me. The God's Property lawsuit brought other lawsuits, like Men of Standard [suing their record label]."

After the cases were settled, Franklin continued to pour energy into his career. He spent a lot of time developing an ABC sitcom (that he was to star in), which was shelved before it was ever produced. His 1999 all-star anthem "Lean on Me" (which featured Bono, R. Kelly, Mary J. Blige, and Crystal Lewis) only reached No. 26 on the R&B singles chart and No. 79 on the pop singles chart—a far more modest success than what the label expected with such a lineup of mainstream superstars. In fact, it was the presence of those pop stars that caused many Christian stations to ban the song from their play lists. Only when the label remixed a new version of the song with only Crystal Lewis and Franklin did gospel and CCM radio stations begin to play the song. For his next project, Franklin returned to a more traditional church sound. The CD *The Rebirth of Kirk Franklin* sold more than 90,000 units the week of its release in 2002 and featured cameos by legendary artists such as Willie Neal Johnson, Shirley Caesar, and Richard Smallwood. In recent years, Franklin has confessed to *Charisma* magazine to overcoming a pornography addiction and has begun preaching. While the world waits to see what's next for the most influential gospel artist of his generation, he is humbled. "I'm just afraid that if I go for popularity, riches, No. 1 charts, limos, and private jets, God will say, 'You're no good for me.' And then he'll cut me off," he told *Gospel Today*. "I'm nothing but dirt that God's blessed."

RECOMMENDED RECORDING: From a production standpoint, *The Nu Nation Project* (Gospo Centric Records, 1998) is perhaps Franklin's crowning achievement. It's an album that easily competes with anything in the urban mainstream. In addition, it features the hit singles "Lean on Me," "Revolution," and his very funky rendition of Bill Withers's "Gonna Be a Lovely Day."

Alfonso Freeman

THE SPITTING IMAGE OF his Academy Award–winning father, actor Morgan Freeman, Alfonso Freeman is a very smooth, polished gospel singer. Born September 13, 1959, in Los Angeles, he didn't know his father the first decade of his life. His mother, Loletha, raised eight children in impoverished Compton, an area notorious for its mean streets. Alfonso was her only child with Freeman. One day while Loletha was watching television, the PBS series *The Electric Company* came on, and there was Morgan Freeman. She screamed for Alfonso to come out and see his father for the first time. When Alfonso was 19 and working for a telemarketing company, he found his father's phone number in a directory and called him. "I was really nervous because he could have hung up the phone and been like, 'I ain't got no kid.' But when I mentioned my name and said it's me, he said, 'Hey, how are you!'" They spoke periodically over the next five years. When Alfonso was 24, Morgan showed up at his front door and they finally met face-to-face. They confronted their mutual feelings about each other and have remained connected ever since.

However, Alfonso repeated the same mistakes his absentee father made: he abandoned his wife and kids. He had affairs and eventually divorced his wife. "I think that was the deepest depression I had ever experienced in my life. At the time, I had two jobs," he told *LA Focus* magazine. "I just had this deep crushing feeling of depression going through divorce and looking at my life and all the mess I was in. I'll never forget—I left [work], got in my car, and I just started crying, stomping the floor of my car and wailing. I seriously wanted to drive into a wall. I don't know what it was that kept me from going that far." Eventually, he returned to the faith of his youth. Over the years, Alfonso has performed in stage plays such as *Jesus Christ Superstar* and movies such as *The Shawshank Redemption*. In autumn 2003 Alfonso released his first solo gospel CD *I Want to Believe*.

RECOMMENDED RECORDING: *I Want to Believe* (FMedias Entertainment, 2003) is a revelation. It's simply amazing that Freeman had not been recording all of his adult life. This project is a sophisticated, smooth jazzy-soulful project of mid-tempo and ballad songs such as

"New Mercies" and the title song. His warm tenor fits nicely in between those of Al Jarreau and George Benson.

Rodney Friend

RODNEY FRIEND is a smooth gospel vocalist in the vein of '80s pop-soul singer Ray Parker, Jr., of *Ghostbusters* fame. Friend's light but soulful vocals graced a trio of moderately successful LPs for Brenda and Phillip Nicholas's Command Records gospel label in the late 1980s. From the beginning, Friend's sound was a soft mix of urban adult rhythms with strong gospel lyrics. The first album, *Worthy*, reached No. 19 on the gospel chart in 1986. His best album was *Don't Lose Sight*, which reached No. 30 on the gospel chart in 1988. The title song was an upbeat, urban-friendly track which could have easily crossed over to R&B radio had the small Command label had the means to facilitate such a strategy. Friend's last chart entry was the uneven *So Much to Celebrate* LP, which peaked at No. 39 on the gospel chart in 1991. When his recording contract with Command was over, Friend continued to play keyboards/synthesizers on Nicholas's recording sessions. A prolific songwriter, Friend wrote or co-wrote songs such as Nicholas's "Tell Somebody," Crystal Lewis's "There's Always Time for You," and Daryl Coley's "Worthy Is the Lamb."

RECOMMENDED RECORDING: *Don't Lose Sight* (Command, 1988) is out of print, but it's his best project to date.

Futrel

A GOSPEL GIRL GROUP, Futrel made a brief impact on the gospel chart with their *Worth the Wait* CD in 1990. The project reached the Top 20 on the gospel album sales chart. Although they were dressed in 1940s period clothing on the cover (like the Andrews Sisters or early Pointer Sisters), the music was a nice blend of uptempo Christian pop ("I Died for You") and smooth R&B-styled ballads such as "I've Got the Victory." The group's lead vocalist and primary songwriter was Darlene Denette

Futrel. The group was rounded out by Janice Davis, Theresa Day, and Evie Young-Nelson. Their final project, *Declarations*, appeared on Tribute in 1993.

Billy and Sarah Gaines

PERHAPS THE MOST popular Christian pop duo of the 1980s, the husband-and-wife team of Billy and Sarah Gaines proved that many white Christian radio programmers were not biased against black recording artists as many black gospel artists (who did not receive radio play on white Christian stations) had charged. The programmers would play the music as long as it perfectly fit the format. As a consequence, the Gaines duo enjoyed little support from black gospel radio audiences since their music was very pop in tone. Songs such as "No One Loves Me Like You Do," "He Says," and "While You Wait" were huge CCM hits.

Billy Gaines was hit by a car when he was 12 years old, and music was part of his healing process. He learned to play the drums and then the piano. Sarah first sang with her family's group, the Thomas Singers. After meeting in Richmond, Virginia, Billy and Sarah married in 1977 and joined Living Sacrifice, a Christian pop group that toured with Danniebelle Hall. After Living Sacrifice disbanded in 1980, the couple moved to Nashville to cut an LP, but the label closed before it was released. Billy began to write songs and worked as a janitor and Pinkerton security guard while waiting for his big break. In 1986, the couple recorded their first project for Benson Records. Their 1990 single "While You Wait" spent four weeks at No. 1 on the CCM chart. They continued to record through the 1990s with their last project appearing on Warner Alliance Records in 1996. However, in the process of many career ups and downs, Sarah became disenchanted with the music business and retired from the duo. Billy continues to sing and minister at church conferences.

RECOMMENDED RECORDING: *Through the Years: Greatest Hits* (Benson Records, 1995) features ten of the duo's most popular songs such as "How Great His Heart Must Be."

Rev. J.M. Gates

LONG BEFORE BISHOP T.D. Jakes was filling sports arenas with his crusades, Rev. J.M. Gates was on the battlefield for the Lord and turning his sermonettes into bestselling records. During the 1920s, no preacher sold more records than Gates, who also is responsible for introducing the gospel music of former bluesman Thomas Dorsey and others into the black church market via his crusades. One such song was "There's Something About the Lord Mighty Sweet" that the Georgia Peach recorded in 1934. While some of his sermonettes were serious and a bit paternal, several of them were very funny. In "The Devil in a Flying Machine" he admonished his audience on the evils of riding in airplanes. He paid tribute to nappy locks on "Kinky Hair Is No Disgrace," and "Mannish Women" is both sexist and hilarious.

Gates was born July 14, 1884, in Hogansville, Georgia, and became a Baptist minister at Atlanta's Calvary Church in 1914. He recorded his first sermon, "Death's Black Train," in 1926 and saw it sell a staggering 35,000 copies by the end of the year. Gates's sermonettes were really skits more than straight homiletics. He would kick off the proceedings with a simple but direct message. His sidekicks, Sister Norman and Sister Bell, could be counted on to give a hearty "Yes, Lord!" at the appropriate point. Or they might ask an elementary but curious layman's question that Gates could then use to debate or to illustrate his overall object lesson, such as he does in the contentious "The Woman and the Snake" recording in which he and the women argue over who was the real root of evil in the Garden of Evil. Over the years, Gates recorded more than 200 sides for a variety of labels, including Victor, Bluebird, Columbia/OKeh, and Gennett. He was a prolific performer, although he didn't record for four years during the Great Depression. In 1934, he began recording again. His most popular sermons include "Death's Black Train Is Coming," "Oh Death Where Is Thy Sting?" and "Goin' to Die with the Staff in My Hands." Gates died of a cerebral hemorrhage on August 18, 1945, at his Atlanta home. It's been said that his funeral drew the largest crowd of any death in the city until the passing of Martin Luther King, Jr., in 1968.

Gay Sisters

UNFORTUNATELY, the one-hit wonder status many gospel historians accord the Gay Sisters gives younger generations the idea that they actually only had one hit. The truth of the matter is that the unique group had several hits, but their biggest hit, "God Will Take Care of You," was so massive and broad that many people forget that they did indeed have other notable hits, though the others didn't carry the impact of that one song.

In 1922, Fannie Lewis (1907–February 28, 1999) married Jerry Gay (January 1, 1897–September 30, 1978) in Atlanta. They later moved to Chicago where they raised their five children: Evelyn (1923–September 30, 1984), Robert (1924–1967), Mildred (1926–2002), Geraldine (born March 31, 1931), and Donald (born August 28, 1945). A solid Christian, Jerry ran two successful furniture shops and a scrap metal business during the Depression. He was able to feed and clothe not only his family, but also other families in his segregated, underprivileged neighborhood on Chicago's West Side. The family attended Elder Lucy Smith's All Nations Pentecostal Church, which was renowned in Negro church circles for the singers in its Sunday morning worship services. Fannie once asked professional musician Rosetta Nubin (who also attended the church) to pray that God would endow her daughters with the same musical skills. Nubin—who later gained fame as Sister Rosetta Tharpe—prayed the prayer and eventually the girls did develop musical gifts. They started by playing the piano. Evelyn developed a firm, traditional style of playing, while Geraldine cultivated a spontaneous style with dissonant chord progressions and creative passion. Evelyn was more ambitious. She accompanied Mahalia Jackson in live appearances in the 1940s and later played on recordings with the Soul Stirrers.

Inspired by Pastor Smith's stellar vocalizing, Mildred and Evelyn formed a duo in 1946. After Smith died, the family left her church and joined the COGIC denomination where they became heavily involved in the national musical department. They sang throughout the Midwest and developed a name for themselves. They went to New York to sing for T.S. Harden, who was once president of the National Baptist Convention.

He booked them at his church and churches throughout the East Coast. From time to time, Geraldine would join them but wasn't a permanent member at the time for a couple of reasons. First and foremost, she wasn't interested in gospel music. She longed to play jazz like her brother Robert (a trumpeter who played with Dizzy Gillespie and Sonny Rollins, who lived with them a while), but her strong-willed mother kept her from making the transition. Secondly, Jerry was extremely protective of his spoiled baby girl and didn't want her traveling on the road since she was newly married and expecting a child.

The sisters were in Los Angeles circa 1948 when Dolphin Records asked them to make a record. They recorded "Have a Little Talk with Jesus," but not much came of it. Then they met Herman Lubinsky on the East Coast and he invited them to join the Savoy Records roster in 1950. They initially recorded as the Famous Gay Sisters. Their first session was the old hymn "God Will Take Care of You." At the time, most traditional black church music wasn't considered sacred unless the tempo was slow and the words were drawn out. Evelyn rearranged the song by speeding the tempo a bit and not drawing the words out, a musical statement as revolutionary and controversial as Kirk Franklin's hip-hop flavored "Stomp" was to the black gospel world in the 1990s. In spite of those who found the song sacrilegious because of its bluesy rhythm, many embraced the new sound and it became a spectacularly successful hit upon its release. It sold an easy 100,000 units (an astounding amount of records for any genre to sell at the time), which in today's sales would be equal to the popularity of a platinum record. Although they were a duo on stage, there were songs led by Geraldine on the *God Will Take Care of You* LP.

"Geraldine had a great left hand on the piano," Donald Gay says of his sister. "And Evelyn had a great right hand. Geraldine was more jazz and Evelyn was more bluesy." Geraldine loved jazz musicians. She hung out with Miles Davis and followed her brother to his recording sessions. As the group forged on, it seemed like they were always running into roadblocks to further success. Evelyn wrote a song called "Is It Well with Your Soul?" which the sisters sang at All Nation's Church. "So who's sitting in the audience but [song-

Gay Sisters / all courtesy of
Gregory Gay, Gay Family Estate

writer] Kenneth Morris," Donald Gay recalls. "He took it and said he wrote it. Evelyn was young and didn't know about copyrights." Evelyn has been cheated out of songwriting royalties for other songs, such as "God Will Take Care of You."

"Evelyn wasn't a selfish person," Donald Gay says of his sister's naiveté. "If she found something good, she'd tell everybody. Next thing you know, the same ones Evelyn helped get on the label are then telling the label you don't need the Gay Sisters. For instance, when they were on Decca, which was owned by Bing Crosby and some other people, the Gay Sisters had a six-month contract with an option. Evelyn was known for her great piano intros, so she did this song 'Oh, Won't You Have Mercy,' with Peter Engle, the harpist, and William Petty on violin, which was unusual in gospel. Mahalia Jackson heard it and the song was doing very well, especially in the East. She was a funny person and she said, 'Nobody comes up over me.' The reason she became the queen of gospel singers was that she worked at keeping everybody else from being heard. In all honesty, she was very, very selfish. That's a fact. Mahalia got to the musicians' union in Chicago and she told Harry Gray, who was the local union president, to block the record because Petty wasn't a member of the union and Decca was a union label. Leonard Joy, the vice president of Decca, called Evelyn and told her there were too many issues with the record and that they would not be able to promote it any further." The recording then died a quick death.

Evelyn was a go-getter and determined to make the group appeal to as many diverse audiences as possible. Older audiences liked them because they sang hymns, and young audiences liked them because they were young and sang jazzy, modern gospel. They even reached out to the Apostolic church (The "Jesus Only" denomination that didn't believe in the Trinity) by recording "Walk Out in My Jesus Name," which reaffirmed the "Jesus Only" philosophy. As a result, many Apostolic church music ministers booked the Famous Gay Sisters for concerts based on that one song. They continued to make smooth-selling gospel radio hits such as "I'm a Soldier," "God Shall Wipe Away All Tears," and "The Little Old Church." By the time they

moved on to Checker Records circa 1960 Geraldine was back with the group, as was their younger brother Donald, but the hit streak had stopped. For a brief time, their father went on the road with them in much the same manner that Aretha Franklin used to open with a song before her father, C.L. Franklin, would minister. Jerry Gay copied the format. The Gay Sisters opened for him with a concert that was followed by his soul-stirring sermon.

Tragedy struck in 1964 when Geraldine confronted her womanizing husband about his fidelity. "He beat her up really bad," says Donald Gay. "He had already beat her and was coming at her again and Geraldine told him to back up. He didn't stop and she shot him." She spent several months in jail, where she gave birth to her youngest child, before a court inquest ruled the case as a justifiable homicide. Unshaken, the sisters looked to the future.

By the middle 1960s, the Gay Sisters had disbanded. The group never made decent money and rarely saw a royalty for their consistent record sales. Mildred joined the Clara Ward Singers for a time, Donald became a preacher, and Evelyn played piano on the *Jubilee Showcase* (a precursor to BET's *Bobby Jones Gospel* TV show) on Chicago's ABC television affiliate. By the 1970s, all of them were out of the music business and their only musical connection was at Sunday morning church services. They gave one last performance together for a bicentennial event in Washington, DC, in 1976. Rev. Gay continues to preach. He and Geraldine reunited for a gospel recording in autumn 2004 on the Sirens label, entitled *In the Right Hands*.

RECOMMENDED RECORDINGS: Mildred, Donald, and Geraldine regrouped in 1993 for a couple of sessions for Shanachie Records' *Soul of Chicago* gospel CD, which featured other stars from Chicago's Golden Age of Gospel. Because of Mildred's advancing age and poor health, Geraldine slowed down the tempo of their new recording of "God Will Take Care of You" because Mildred's breathing was labored and she couldn't keep pace with the song. It was a poor final recording for this group, who once shined so brilliantly. It's even sadder that none of the group's original recordings have been reissued on CD, and two generations of gospel fans have grown up with no clue as to the impact and beauty of their 1950s Savoy sides.

Gloria Gaynor

AMERICA'S FIRST DISCO QUEEN, Gloria Gaynor is best known for her 1979 No. 1 pop single "I Will Survive." She was born September 7, 1949, in Newark, New Jersey. The public came to know her with her 1976 disco million-seller "Never Can Say Goodbye." Other hits followed such as "Reach out, I'll Be There" and "How High the Moon." But the biggest was 1979's "I Will Survive," which spent three weeks at No. 1 on the pop singles charts. After the disco craze ebbed, Gaynor found it hard getting another hit. In addition, she had chronic back problems and issues in her marriage. She eventually became a born-again Christian and saw her marriage restored. She has recorded "I Will Survive" with religious lyrics in recent years and is a member of A.R. Bernard's Christian Life Center Church in Brooklyn, New York. The 2004 CD *The Answer* was a contemporary gospel collection.

Hulah and Carolyne Gene

THIS MOTHER AND DAUGHTER singing team was discovered by Rev. James Cleveland. They recorded briefly for Savoy Records circa 1972 with an uptempo take on the spiritual "Steal Away."

Generation J

A POP-STYLED CONTEMPORARY gospel quartet, Generation J was formed in 1998 when brothers Aaron Sanders (born 1984) and Pierre Sanders (born 1980) hooked up with their sibling cousins Leslie Hudson (born 1981) and Adrienne Hudson (born 1979) and began singing at Pastor Creflo Dollar's World Changers Church International in Atlanta. They grew up listening to the gospel vibes of the Archer Sisters, John P. Kee, and Shirley

Caesar. "We're Generation J—a generation for Jesus—and that's not just about a vocal group," says Pierre Sanders. "Generation J is about a movement. It's about a generation of people who have vision and meaning, and who want to encourage everyone that the life God has for us is a life of victory, filled with excitement and adventure in Christ."

Eventually, Pastor and Taffi Dollar discovered the group and signed them to their Arrow Records label. Their debut CD *Living Free* was released in 2002. Being associated with Dollar's high-profile ministry brought the group instant media attention. The startup label did not have major distribution, so the CD was hard to find, though it sold well at Generation J's concerts. They then performed on concert bills worldwide with a dozen of the industry's best gospel artists, including Mary Mary, Fred Hammond, CeCe Winans, Kim Burrell, and B.B. Jay. Perhaps the group's biggest break was opening for Jaci Velasquez on her 30-city "Unspoken" tour in fall 2003. Arrow then arranged a one-off deal with Word Records to release the group's CD *Secret Place* in summer 2004. Boosted by their energetic and contemporary rendition of the spiritual "Goin' Up Yonder," the project debuted at No. 2 on *Billboard*'s gospel chart. The group appeared on *Soul Train* and was featured in a spread in the urban youth magazine *Right On!*, but it was not enough to maintain Word Records' interest. When the group's sales declined, Word dropped Generation J from the roster and the Hudson sisters amicably exited the group for a life outside of show business. The Sanders brothers left Arrow Records in 2005 and have continued Generation J with just one new female vocalist.

Cassietta George

IN MANY WAYS, the great Cassietta George's career was similar to that of current gospel phenom Kim Burrell. Like Burrell today, George was beloved by her gospel peers for her sheer vocal techniques (a thin voice but dramatic performance style punctuated with warm pauses and pointed vocal leaps that never failed to garner rhapsodic ovations in concerts). But she never made a commercial impact with the public as a soloist.

George was born January 23, 1929, in Memphis, Tennessee, to a large family (four sisters and a brother). At the age of four, she began singing in her father's church. After finishing secondary school in Canton, Ohio, George returned to Memphis where she founded the female a cappella quartet Songbirds of the South in the early 1950s. She briefly sang with the W. Herbert Brewster Ensemble before joining the Caravans in 1954. She didn't lead a Caravans hit until 1962 when "Remember Me" was in radio rotation. Still, her biggest Caravans solo was on her co-penned (with Rev. James Cleveland) ballad "Walk Around Heaven," released in 1964 on Vee-Jay Records.

The tune "Walk Around Heaven" was not simply a gospel song. It had elements of a protest song and was written during a time of social revolution in America (civil rights agitation, college unrest, and a burgeoning women's rights movement). Bob Dylan had released "Blowin' in the Wind" in May 1963 and Sam Cooke had composed "A Change Is Gonna Come" in response to an October 1963 incident where he and his entourage were arrested for trying to register at a whites-only hotel in Shreveport, Louisiana. The overlooked line in "Walk Around Heaven" that supports the protest thesis is: "When I get to heaven, I'm gonna jump and shout—nobody will be able to put me out," a subtle reference to the many civil rights activists turned away from lunch counters and public lavatories in 1960s America. The song has since been elevated to classic status and recorded by artists such as Irma Thomas, Willie Neal Johnson, and the Mighty Clouds of Joy. Lorraine Ellison's 1974 Warner Bros. Records recording is arguably the best rendition of the song.

George left the Caravans in 1965 and recorded a dozen solo singles for Audio Arts Records in Los Angeles such as "Somebody Bigger than You and I." Her LP *Cassietta in Concert* was nominated for a Grammy in 1979. In the 1990s, Dorothy Norwood tried to resurrect George's career by producing the LP *Dorothy Norwood Presents Cassietta George*. However, the project failed in that regard and disappeared quietly. Cassietta George died of cancer on January 3, 1995.

Georgia Mass Choir

ONE OF THE MOST successful traditional choirs in the history of gospel, the 150-member choir has churned out a steady stream of toe-tapping hits such as the bluesy "Come on in the Room," "Joy," and "Sunday Morning Medley." The group was founded January 29, 1983, in Macon, Georgia, by Savoy Records director Milton Biggham. He held auditions and more than 600 people showed up for the 150 slots, from teenagers to senior citizens. Biggham is the group's lead singer and chief songwriter. The choir had some high-profile performances at the 1996 Olympic Games in Atlanta. Their biggest project to date was when film director Penny Marshall cast them to appear in the film *The Preacher's Wife*. Three of the choir's signature songs—"He's All Over Me," "Joy," and "Hold On, Help Is On the Way"—were featured on the movie's soundtrack, with Whitney Houston leading the songs. The choir also appeared behind Houston as she promoted the movie on television programs such as *Saturday Night Live*, *The Today Show*, and *Good Morning America*.

Georgia Peach

ONE OF THE GREAT soloists in the formative years of gospel music, Georgia Peach was born Clara Hudman Breese on October 10, 1899, in Atlanta, Georgia. Hudman didn't seriously begin to sing until her teens when she and her two brothers formed a trio that sang at the Mt. Moriah Baptist Church and other local assemblies. It appears that her father left the picture early on, leaving Hudman's mother to raise three children on her own. Hudman eventually dropped out of school and went to work as a caregiver for her pastor Rev. T.T. Gholston's terminally ill wife for two years. Six months after the woman died, Hudman married the pastor. His church split over the scandal. Half of the church was appalled, and the other half was envious that Hudman snagged the church's most eligible bachelor before they did. The fallout proved too much for Gholston who eventually became an alcoholic and was voted out of the church for preaching under the influence of unholy spirits. Hudman followed her husband to pastoral posts in Detroit and New York, but they eventually divorced. She left the denomination and joined a Pentecostal church, Refuge Church of Our Lord, where she began to sing again. A smooth, powerful contralto, her fans labeled her Georgia Peach because of her Atlanta roots and the warm, fuzzy feelings her music gave them. She died December 31, 1964, in New York City at age of the 64.

Jon Gibson

THIS BLUE-EYED SOUL singer enjoyed several CCM radio hits such as "God Loves a Broken Heart," "Jesus Loves Ya," and "Happy to Know Jesus" at the end of the Reagan-Bush administrations. Gibson was born January 3, 1968, in San Francisco and reared in San Jose. After his army discharge when he was 20, Gibson signed to Dick Griffey's Solar Record's Constellation imprint as an R&B artist. Solar had created R&B hits of the day such as Carrie Lucas's "Dance with You" and Shalimar's "Second Time Around." Griffey fooled many of his associates with Gibson's demo tape because the young singer sounded so much like Stevie Wonder. His debut LP *Standing on the One* followed. However, Gibson was conflicted about his pursuit of stardom and a desire to serve God via music. In 1986, he signed to the progressive Christian label Frontline, which specialized in gospel dance music and pop-gospel grooves. His first single, "God Loves a Broken Heart" from his *On the Run* LP, spent six weeks atop the CCM singles chart. His next LP, *Change of Heart*, featured CCM's first rap hit with "The Wall," featuring MC Hammer. Gibson's dream came true when Stevie Wonder played harmonica on his song "Body and Soul."

With his movie star good looks and soulful grooves, Gibson caused the CCM audience to begin to accept urban music, even if it was only through the voice of a white man. Still, it was a pivotal barrier that he broke down in Christian music. Had a black artist recorded the same songs and in the same manner, it's unlikely that they would have ever been played. Therefore, Gibson helped broaden the audience for urban music among white teenagers just as New Kids on the

Block was doing in mainstream America at the same time. Then the bottom fell out at Frontline Records. "When the company went down, the products stopped being made. It kind of sat in bankruptcy court and was transferred from one hand to the next," Gibson told *CCM* magazine. "It was way out of my control, and I didn't have a label to back me up. It had a real effect on me. I was really hurting. I struggled for about two years. I kind of sat up in the house on the hill and just felt sorry for myself."

In 1999, Gibson temporarily found a new label home when Gospo Centric Records signed him to record *The Man Inside* CD. It was a very good project with Gibson's trademark urban style complimented by production work by Tommy Sims, who has made a career of bringing R&B and gospel together in a pleasing crossover manner. However, the CD was a commercial failure, prompting Gibson to launch his own Imagery Records label in 2002. He released the praise and worship project *Soulful Hymns* that year. Since then, Gibson's duties as a husband and father have prevented him from having the time to run a label and his family. At last glance, he was seeking a new recording deal.

Leonard Givens

BEST KNOWN FOR his work with the '70s-era contemporary gospel group the Loving Sisters, Givens and his sister, Gladys, were the lead singers for the group, which recorded for ABC-Peacock Records. Givens, who possessed a smooth but emphatic tenor, later struck out on his own and produced the 1981 LP *A Song Is Born* on which he was backed by the Little Rock Mass Choir.

Joan Golden

IN MEMPHIS SHE'S known as "The Golden Girl of Gospel" of WLOK 1340 AM. For more than 40 years, five hours a day, Golden has brought gospel music to the denizens of Beale Street. A Memphis native, Joan Elizabeth Williams was born in 1937 and wanted to be a DJ even as a child. She was reared in church so there was no question in her mind that at some point, she'd become a gospel music announcer. After graduating from Booker T. Washington High School and AM&N State College in Arkansas, Golden began to sing and perform in church programs. In 1957, she joined WLOK. Among her popular show segments were "Something for the Girls and the Guys Too" and "The Golden Hour."

Golden Gate Quartet

IN 1925, FOUR STUDENTS at Booker T. Washington High School in Norfolk, Virginia, founded the Golden Gate Quartet. A.C. Eddie Griffin and Robert "Peg" Ford, a one-legged bass singer, recruited Henry Owens and Willie Johnson. By 1935, Griffin backed out of the group to devote time to his barbershop and was replaced by William Langford. Ford's failing health forced him out in 1936 and he was replaced by 16-year-old Orlandus Wilson. Their style was a hodgepodge of the Mills Brothers, the swing of the Three Keys, and the influence of preachers. The group's sound was a polished barbershop quartet style. In the late 1950s, they toured Europe extensively. Much of their success was outside of the church. They began recording for Bluebird/Victor producer Eli Oberstein in 1937 at a Charlotte hotel. They made several high-profile appearances on NBC Radio's "Magic Key" program. In 1938, John Hammond put them on a bill with Count Basie and Benny Goodman on a From Spirituals to Swing concert at Carnegie Hall. That led to their own CBS radio show and a regular gig at the posh Café Society in Manhattan. President Franklin Roosevelt loved the group and had them perform at his inaugural party at the D.A.R. Constitution Hall against the wishes of the organization, and they became the first black group to perform there. The quartet recorded sessions with Leadbelly, but soon after Langford left the group to found the Southern Sons. Clyde Riddick replaced him. They then recorded for Columbia Records and Mercury, and had cameos in films such as *Star Spangled Rhythm* and *Hollywood Canteen*. In 1948, Johnson left for the Jubilaires, and in 1959, Owens left to become an evangelist preacher. In 1955, the group toured Europe for the first time. They loved the easy racial atmosphere and in 1959, the group im-

migrated to France under the leadership of Wilson. They did not perform in the US again until 1994 when they returned to be inducted into the United in Group Harmony Hall of Fame. In October 1999, Wilson stepped down from performing with the group but continued to supervise them. He died December 30, 1999.

Gold West Singers

FORMED IN RICHMOND, California circa 1947, this group has had a variety of personnel over the years. They recorded for the Ajax and Music City labels in the middle 1950s. Never nationally known, one of their best recordings is the spirited "Jesus Is Everywhere," which features Rev. Robert Hartsfield on lead vocals. The group is also notable because two of its members went on to make names for themselves in secular music: Southern soulman Joe Simon and bluesman Johnny Fuller.

Gospel Clefs

THIS NEW JERSEY–BASED GROUP, founded by Leon Lumkins (some sources list him as Lumpkins), recorded for Savoy Records from 1957 to 1965. At the time, the group was unique for blending R&B sensibilities with their gospel sound. In the 1970s, they recorded crossover fare such as "Bridge over Troubled Water" for the SOA label. Sometimes Lumkins shared lead vocals with Rev. Huston. Their 1958 song "Open Our Eyes" (lead vocals by Charles Ferren) was later covered by R&B band Earth, Wind & Fire and folk singer Richie Havens.

Gospel Gangstaz

FORMER GANG MEMBER Mr. Solo became a Christian after he was almost shot to death. In 1989, he founded the rap group the Gospel Gangstaz. In addition to Mr. Solo, the group was comprised of former gangsters, such as Tik Tokk and Chille' Baby, to bring the church to the streets. They first recorded for Holy Terra Records where they released the albums *Do or Die* and *Gang Affiliated*, which sold 100,000 copies between them. In 1999, they signed with B-Rite Records where they cut the *I Can See Clearly Now* project. "The major-label debut for this South Central L.A. threesome packs a wallop, wrapping bone-rattling, bottom-heavy hip-hop grooves around masterfully constructed raps and infectious, melodic hooks," said a *Billboard* magazine review. "The trio… delivers its message of hope and encouragement without compromising the details of the harsh lifestyle from which its art arises or the stiletto-sharp edge of the music it engenders." The album rested on the gospel album sales charts for over a year and peaked at No. 3 on that chart.

In spite of the album's success, it was their last for B-Rite. In 2002, they debuted *Exodus* on the Native label, but it was not the success of their previous projects. After six weeks, it had dropped from both the gospel and the R&B album sales charts. "Gospel Gangstaz stand in a position to help, because we have seen how the gospel of Christ is real," Solo once said. "Our lives were changed from selling crack, drive-by shootings, car-jacking, and illicit sex, to a life of peace, joy, and happiness because of Christ. We want to go back to the hood and let our light shine."

Gospelaires

A VERY POPULAR NAME for gospel groups in the 1960s, the Gospelaires of Dayton, Ohio, were probably the most successful aggregation. Founded in 1954, they signed to Peacock in 1957 and released the LP *Just Faith*. Their lead singer was Rev. Charles McClain. They later recorded for Savoy Records where Bob Eli produced their hits "Joyful Joyful," "Remember Me," and "Jesus of Nazareth" in the 1970s.

David Gough

IF NAT KING COLE sang contemporary gospel music, he might sound something like David Gough, who is best known for his mid-tempo 2003 radio hit "Hold On." The eldest of three children, Gough was born August 14, 1949, in Detroit. His mother was a nurse's aide and his father worked in a Chrysler factory. They were not a particularly religious family, although they lived across the street from a COGIC church that Gough attended a handful of times. He absorbed all of the music he heard and when he was in high school, he discovered he could sing. "I was a teenager," he recalls. "My brother and I used to pantomime. We would do some Temptations dance routines and sing with hot sauce bottles to our mouths." After high school, Gough served in the navy for four years and was stationed in Southeast Asia. He and a buddy, Wilmore Hicks, formed a duo called Si & Dave. "We were singing some Top 40 and some older songs," he says. They were good enough to win an Australian talent contest. Later, when he was in Guam, Gough formed a multinational pop quintet called Five Way. They performed together for a couple of years before he returned to the US in 1972 and got married. Back in Detroit, he worked his way up the corporate ladder at Meade Paper Company. "I was still doing music on the side," he adds.

During that period, Gough says, "I gave my life to God. My wife Carol was instrumental in witnessing to me. She was already a Christian." With his newfound faith and some songs he'd written, Gough wanted to record an LP. He contacted all the major gospel labels, but they all ignored his demos, so he formed DoRohn Records in 1982. "I formed it to put my music out," he says candidly. "I was sending my music out but no one was picking up on it. I've always been an entrepreneur and had side businesses. I sold Shacklee products and other things and I'd take the money and put it back into the company." His first LP, *Good News*, was released that year, but he couldn't get distribution so the recording didn't sell well.

"I produced and manufactured it," Gough explains of the debut album. "I started calling distributors. I had never done this before, so I learned as I went along. The idea was to go through the Bible Belt areas and sell the albums. I noticed that there was a difference in black and white gospel music on the business side. At that time, Walter Hawkins had the *Love Alive* albums that were selling like crazy. Andrae Crouch was big at that time too. So I was talking to a distributor about my album and he told me he doesn't do anything with black music. I asked him if he handled Walter Hawkins's albums and he said no. So then I asked him about Andrae Crouch. Do you know what he said to me? He said, 'We don't consider him black.' I said, 'Well, have you looked at his picture lately?' and I hung up the telephone."

Gough continued to issue albums every two years or so and had moderate radio hits with "Highly Recommended" and "Heart Fixer." He received a great professional break when Dr. Bobby Jones heard his music and booked him to be on his BET program, *Bobby Jones Gospel*. By the early 1990s, Gough had branched out and began to sign other artists. "We didn't have big budgets," he says. "But we didn't stop doing what we were doing." The year 1989 was an ambitious one for Gough. He released saxophonist Bill Fridge's LP *He's the One We All Adore* and the Gospel Stock Chorale's LP *Excited*, which produced the radio hit "I'll Fly Away." He also signed Terrie Bledsoe, whose 12-inch single "Jesus Is a Friend of Mine" was arguably black gospel's first female rap song. "It was too soon for the black church," he says. "They weren't ready for her, but it caused some eyebrows to raise."

Over the years, Gough has recorded a total of nine albums, which all possess a pop soul groove more than a hard gospel styling. Surprisingly, his bestselling CD of all is his 2001 *This Christmas* project. Gough's recent labor of love is the Gospel Hall of Fame, which he founded in 1995 to honor gospel music pioneers. The Gospel Music Association (GMA) in Nashville, which ran a pre-existing Gospel Hall of Fame, subsequently sued him. After much legal wrangling and tough words from representatives on both sides, the matter was settled. The concession was that Gough's organization changed its name to the International Gospel Hall of Fame. "There are different factions that feel that some things shouldn't be done," he says. "But everything has been worked out. We are in the midst of working a deal to buy some land for the museum. This is a big part of our culture. We have to stay the course."

Grace Thrillers

FOUNDED IN JONESTOWN, Jamaica, in the early 1970s as a trio called the Heavenly Secrets, the group was initially comprised of Hilton Fay, Monica Holness, and Noel Willis. They operated out of the Full Truth Church of God Deliverance Centre under Bishop Shaw, who later renamed them the Grace Thrillers. The group expanded to include seven performers, and in 1978 they made their first tour outside of Jamaica. They did not record their first LP, *He's Alive*, until ten years later. Shirley Willis led many of their hits such as "Can't Even Walk," "I Wanna Hear the Story," and "I Must Tell Jesus." In 2003, Willis left the group and resurfaced in 2004 with her first solo offering, *Trust Him More*.

Amy Grant

CHRISTIAN MUSIC'S bestselling female artist ever, Amy Grant was born November 25, 1960, in Augusta, Georgia. Her father is a doctor who moved his wife and four children to Nashville while Grant was still a toddler. There she learned to play the guitar at summer camp and had an interest in a musical career. In 1975, she took a part-time job at producer Chris Christian's studio where she erased recording tapes. She eventually made a demo of her songs. Some spoke of faith, but they were not gospel songs as much as they were "thinking" songs that ruminated about life and faith. The demo made its way to Myrrh Records, which signed her to a deal when she was 16 years old. Grant's acoustic style ranged from John Denver's view of country music to Joni Mitchell's view of pop music. She scored several early hits, such as "Father's Eyes" and "Old Man's Rubble." However, it was Grant's 1982 Christian pop LP *Age to Age* that laid the foundation for her eventual mainstream superstardom. The first single, the bouncy "Sing Your Praise to the Lord," spent ten weeks at No. 1 on the CCM chart. She followed up with the divine anthem "El Shaddai" and the poppish ballad "In a Little While," which were both Top 5 Christian radio smashes that helped give Grant her first gold album. Myrrh, which struck a distribution deal with A&M Records during the period, then began to position Grant as a pop artist.

Grant's 1985 LP *Unguarded* featured the Top 40 hit "Love Will Find a Way" and "Wise Up," which featured some nice field-holler ad libs from Donna McElroy. Grant's albums continued to blend pop grooves with inspirational or conspicuous gospel lyrics. In 1991, she created her major pop breakthrough, *Heart in Motion*, which featured the No. 1 pop single "Baby Baby." The album sold four million copies in the US and spawned other hit singles in "Good for Me," "Every Heart Beat," "I Will Remember You," and "That's What Love Is For." Recent albums by Grant haven't fared as well on the Christian or the pop charts. In her personal life, Grant has found joy and peace. After a tense 17-year marriage to Gary Chapman, who struggled with alcohol abuse for years, Grant married country-pop star Vince Gill in 2000. It set off a mild controversy in the church community, where some people speculated that the Grant-Gill romance commenced before the Grant-Chapman divorce. Some Christian radio stations pulled Grant's music from their play lists, but the couple weathered the storm.

Natalie Grant

THE SOULFUL CHRISTIAN pop singer Natalie Grant got her start with the Christian touring group TRUTH. She was born December 21, 1971, in Seattle. After spending two years with TRUTH, Grant released a self-titled CD for Benson Records in 1999. When the project didn't take off, Benson didn't renew the contract. She later released *Stronger* on Pamplin Music in 2001 and *Deeper Life* on Curb Records in 2003. Her more recent project, *Worship with Natalie Grant and Friends*, on Integrity Music, is a praise and worship project that received airplay on both black gospel and CCM radio.

Denyce Graves

"I KNOW THAT I AM an inspiration to young black people just because I'm black and doing something that's not hip-hop or R&B or what they expected. I recognize the responsibility in that. I insist that they give tickets to inner city and underprivileged kids for all of my concerts and if they don't do it I buy the tickets myself." One of the most celebrated mezzo-sopranos in opera, Denyce Graves was born March 7, 1964, in Washington, DC. Her father (who is now a Baptist minister) left the family when she was two years old, leaving Graves's mother the task of struggling to raise three children on her own. In spite of the struggle, Graves's mother never took public assistance and taught her children the value of work and discipline. The whole family sang in a Pentecostal church, but Graves's voice stood out and her mother hoped she'd become a gospel singer. However, after a schoolteacher took Graves to an opera, she was hooked on arias. She studied voice at the Duke Ellington School for the Performing Arts and worked her way through Oberlin College Conservatory of Music and the New England Conservatory. After a two-year apprenticeship at the Houston Grand Opera ended in 1990, Graves's career went into overdrive. She wound up at the Metropolitan Opera in New York as the star of *Carmen*. The critics and audiences loved her, and it's become her signature role, though she's also in demand for recitals and other operas. Among the CDs Graves has recorded are *Angels Watching over Me* and *Cathedral Christmas*, both of which feature blatant gospel songs. She performed "America the Beautiful" and "The Lord's Prayer" on her *American Anthem* CD, which reached No. 8 on *Billboard*'s classical crossover chart. She recorded a brilliant version of "Ave Maria" for the all-star compilation CD *Church: Songs of Soul and Inspiration*. The project debuted at No. 1 on the gospel chart, and Graves considers it one of the greatest achievements of her career. "I grew up in church," she told *LA Focus* magazine. "I was raised on gospel music, and I've taken a very different life path. I feel that one of the most important projects that I've done is this one, and it's brought me full circle. I had to go along that path—through the conservatories and the studying in a very different area of music—only to arrive back at my roots. I believe that you hear God in this music, and I'd like people to feel the presence of God. In this crazy time and uncertain world, we couldn't have enough of that."

RECOMMENDED RECORDINGS: *Angels Watching over Me* (Camden/RCA) features 21 gospel classics such as "City Called Heaven" and "Every Time I Feel the Spirit."

James Grear

THE MINNEAPOLIS-BASED ensemble James Grear and Company have had a measure of success getting their urban gospel grooves played on urban radio. Their songs "Don't Give Up," "Beautiful Black People," and even their cover of Celine Dion's "Because You Loved Me" have become popular on urban AC radio, but they've yet to translate the radio play into significant sales and name recognition.

Born June 5, 1962, in Gary, Indiana, Grear was raised in the COGIC denomination where his parents were in church leadership. He made his church-singing debut at the age of five. While in high school, Grear formed James Grear and the True Holiness Singers. They performed locally for seven years. After a record deal fell through, Grear disbanded the group and moved to Minneapolis where he worked at a bank. He reconnected with the COGIC denomination there and formed a new group to raise money for the church. After their initial concert was a success, they were inundated with requests to perform. Grear named the group James Grear and Company circa 1987. Through friends in Sounds of Blackness (also based in Minneapolis), they did session work for Jimmy Jam and Terry Lewis's various productions. Finally, in 1997, they won their own record deal with Barnett Williams's Born Again Records in Los Angeles. By that time, Grear's group had spent a decade cultivating its slick, youthful urban approach to gospel music. The lead single, "Beautiful Black People" (written by group member Roosevelt George), was first played on the local R&B station KMOJ before it branched out across America and made it to No. 59 on the R&B Hot 100 in 1998—not an insignificant feat considering that the group was unknown and with a small independent label. The next single didn't have as strong a hook, but "Don't Give Up" managed to hit No. 89 on the R&B Hot 100. The CD of the same name rose to No. 8 on the gospel album and No. 34 on the R&B album charts. The album also included a nice rendition of "Because You Loved Me" that saw some urban AC radio play.

The group has followed up with albums such as *The Next Level* (which did not chart on any level), *What Will Your Life Say?* and *Gettin' It Together.* All of these projects were commercial failures, although they did feature some of their trademark crisp, clean retro soul vibes. The group's widest exposure has been backing Mariah Carey on a 2002 *Today Show* appearance and Sting on the soundtrack to *Hercules.* Perhaps Grear's most noble accomplishment is serving as a foster father to a group of young boys with special needs that he's taken into his home. "People know me for my gift for music," he once said in a Liquid 8 press release. "But I believe God's greatest gift to me is working with these children whose special challenges have taught me much over the years…. I have no doubt it was God's call on my life to become a foster parent."

RECOMMENDED RECORDINGS: Grear's best recording remains the *Don't Give Up* CD, which hosts their urban hits "Because You Loved Me," "Beautiful Black People," and the title song.

Greater Abyssinian Baptist Church Choir

NOT TO BE CONFUSED with Harlem's reserved Abyssinian Baptist Church Choir, this Newark, New Jersey–based choir was led by Professor Alex Bradford and they recorded for Jubilee Records in the 1960s.

Al Green

AS A SOUL SINGER, Al Green bridged the gap between the cornfields and the city street corners with his uptown-styled Southern soul music in the 1970s. With a soft gospel falsetto, Green became one of soul music's romantic leading men in the 1970s with hits such as "I'm Still in Love with You," "Let's Stay Together," and "How Do You Mend a Broken Heart." A series of tragic events led him back to the arms of Jesus and a gospel recording career by the end of the decade, only to re-emerge in the 1980s as both a soul-man and a soul-winner.

He was born Albert Greene (he dropped the "e" in later life) on April 13, 1946, in Forest City, Arkansas, into a religious family. "My father played bass in different R&B groups, but he only played Christian records at home," Green told *Pulse* magazine in 1989. "Eventually he formed a gospel group with me and my brothers called the Green brothers. I got bounced out when I was nine for listening to Jackie Wilson, 'cause at that time it was kind of taboo, you know." Before he was expelled, Green and the group toured throughout the South on the weekends until the family relocated to Grand Rapids, Michigan. At the age of 16, Green formed an R&B group, Al Greene and the Creations, with some high school buddies. Two members, Curtis Rogers and Palmer James, later founded the Soul Mates with Green. Their first single, "Back Up Train," hit the R&B charts in 1967 on the Hot Line Music Journal label. They released a couple more singles, but the group disbanded and Green went solo.

In 1969, Green opened for bandleader Willie Mitchell when he was touring in Midland, Texas. Mitchell liked Green's voice and snagged him a recording contract with Hi Records in Memphis. Mitchell had Green drop the hard, Otis-Redding style of singing he had been doing and adopt a smoother, more sensual style of vocalizing that showed off his falsetto. His first album for the label flopped, but his second one, *Al Green Gets Next to You* in 1970, spawned the smash R&B singles "Tired of Being Alone" and "I Can't Get Next to You."

1972 would be the banner year for Green's career. He released four smoldering ballads, which all zoomed to No. 1 or No. 2 on the R&B charts: "You Oughta Be with Me," "Let's Stay Together," "Look What You Done to Me," and "I'm Still in Love with You." Green's subsequent crossover to the pop charts solidified his status as a soul superstar. He filled 20,000-seat stadiums, had all the women he wanted, and kept churning out hits such as "Here I Am (Come and Take Me)," "Love and Happiness," "Call Me," "Sha-La-La (Make Me Happy)" and "Livin' for You."

Amid his fame, Green had a sobering experience at Disneyland in 1973. "We'd played with Smokey Robinson in San Francisco, then got a private jet to take us down to Anaheim for this special midnight show," Green told *Pulse.* "I went to bed collapsed and exhausted, and woke up in the middle of the night praising God. It was amazing; I'd never experienced anything like that before. I ran into the bathroom and tried to keep it from coming out, stuffed a towel in my mouth, but that's impossible to do—even if you have

a towel [laughs]." Green told Mitchell and the rest of his inner circle about his experience and how he felt God was calling him to some higher purpose. They downplayed it for fear that Green would stop his hit cycle. Green spent the next three years trying to please his record label with hit songs while simultaneously trying to do what he felt God was calling him to. "I spent a lot of that time doing songs where the lyrics were deliberately ambiguous about what their subject was, whether I was singing to a woman or someone else," he told *Pulse.* Songs such as "Belle," "I Tried to Tell Myself," and "Keep Me Cryin'" came during this period. They were all good songs, but not as memorable as his earlier tunes.

In 1974, Green felt God gave him the last hint that he needed to redirect his life. Green and his off-and-on girlfriend, R&B singer Laura Lee, were on the outs. He had taken up with Mary Woodson, who (unknown to Green) was married with three children. "I was in my apartment in a separate part of the house," he told *Pulse.* "She had just proposed to me, and I'd said I didn't know whether I wanted to marry her." Green was relaxing in his bathtub when the scorned Woodson

Al Green / Courtesy of A&M Records

came in with a boiling pot of grits and poured them down his back. She then went downstairs, put a gun to her head, and fatally shot herself. After almost eight months of skin graft operations and therapy, Green bought a rundown church called Full Gospel Tabernacle not far from Elvis Presley's Graceland mansion. He began to preach on Sundays while still singing his R&B during the week. Green and his producer Mitchell ceased collaborating together as Green drew closer to that Old Rugged Cross. Albums such as *The Belle Album* (1978) and *Truth 'N' Time* (1979) that subtly displayed his new faith were rejected by his traditional fan base. Finally, while performing in Cincinnati in 1979, Green fell off the stage and nearly injured himself seriously. Seeing the incident as yet another sign from God, Green gave up secular music completely and devoted himself to preaching and coordinating his first gospel album.

Still signed to Hi Records, Green and Hi struck a deal with Word Records' Myrrh imprint to issue his gospel material. The first album, *The Lord Will Make a Way*, appeared in 1980. The title cut was a duet with ex-girlfriend Laura Lee (known for "Women's Love Rights"), who had also become a born-again Christian and deserted her R&B career in the late 1970s. For this song, Green won his first of nine Grammy awards. He had never won previously, and all of the subsequent awards, with the exception of one, were in gospel categories.

In 1981, Green came up with his second gospel album, *Higher Plane*, which reached No. 62 on the R&B chart. In spite of his new career as a gospel artist, Green rarely made the rounds most gospel artists frequented to sell their products. He was still a big enough name in the secular field and still had enough fans willing to follow him into any kind of music that his gospel albums still sold far more than the average major gospel artist sold at the time. Besides, Green didn't need the money. He was still receiving royalties for his R&B records, so he never had to make a living as a gospel artist. In 1982, Green appeared in the gospel musical *Your Arms Too Short to Box with God* with Patti LaBelle. With his Hi contract at an end, Green reunited with producer Willie Mitchell for the album *He Is the Light*, his first for A&M Records in 1985. However, it was his album *Soul Sur-*

vivor that gave Green his first No. 1 gospel radio hit—the album hit No. 1 on the gospel album chart and No. 25 on the R&B album chart. The funky single "Everything's Gonna Be Alright" reached No. 22 on the R&B singles chart in 1987.

By the late 1980s, Green felt comfortable enough to develop a non-church concert repertoire featuring his R&B hits such as "Let's Stay Together" and "Love and Happiness." He would infuse those songs and others with drawn-out gospel emotion and also feature some of his religious material. A whole generation of new fans and their parents welcomed Green back into the pop world with sold-out concerts. Some in the church world fussed about Green performing his old R&B hits in secular venues while turning down most offers to perform in churches. For his part, Green often argued that his secular hits opened the door for him to share his faith with an audience that would not ordinarily attend a church service.

While his last gospel albums such as *One in a Million* and *Love Is Reality* failed to create strong radio hits, they still sold well—both sold over 50,000 units with very little promotion. Meanwhile, Green briefly returned to the pop world when he and Annie Lennox teamed up for their Top Ten pop rendition of "Put a Little Love in Your Heart" from the Bill Murray movie *Scrooged* in 1988. In 1995, Green created a new inspirational soul album entitled *Your Heart's in Good Hands*, which sold respectably and saw himself inducted into the Rock and Roll Hall of Fame. In recent years, Green's high-profile television appearances on *Ally McBeal* and a nostalgia for his classic soul sound have led to a plethora of reissues of Green's gospel and soul product. Since 2000, EMI issued *Greatest Gospel Hits* and Universal released *Testify: The Best of the A&M Years*. *Precious Lord*, *I'll Rise Again*, *The Lord Will Make a Way*, and *Higher Plane* are all back in print again. Then Green surprised everyone with his raucous duet with Ann Nesby, "Put It on Paper," which hit No. 1 on *Radio & Records* urban AC charts in 2002. Green says he'll eventually do more soul and gospel albums, but has complained that he feels creatively limited at times. "I am an artist," Green told *Pulse* in 1989. "And what I do is supposed to be enjoyed as a work of art. If the church world today were more open to that, I think I could cut more songs that would be more art-oriented instead of always religious-religious-religious oriented. But in the church, you know, we have our way of doing things and we're kind of set in the pattern, so therefore you're kind of in a bind about what you can do a little bit. Except me—I am the black sheep, liable to do anything. I mean, I still cut songs like 'The Mighty Clouds of Joy' that was done by B.J. Thomas some years ago. It's just art; that's what I think it is, anyway."

Green has found a way to mix the two in his live concerts, which receive raves from music critics. "The Rev. Al has more than a little Wayne Newton in him," *Washington Post* critic Sean Daly wrote on February 16, 2004, of Green's then-recent Constitution Hall concert. "And as he tossed roses to the ladies in exchange for long-lasting lipstick smears on his lapel and face, the night had the distinct feel of a rowdy church service on the Vegas Strip."

RECOMMENDED RECORDING: There are many Al Green gospel compilations on the market. For the more traditional material, EMI's *The Right Stuff* is the one to buy. It features his incomparable versions of "The Lord Will Make a Way Somehow," "Amazing Grace," and "People Get Ready" with Laura Lee. For more contemporary sounds, *Testify: The A&M Years* includes the funky "Everything's Gonna Be Alright" and "You Brought the Sunshine."

Linda Green-Tavani

IN THE LATE 1970S, Peaches & Herb was the hottest duo of the disco era. Their hip-shaker "Shake Your Groove Thing" reached the Top 5 on both the pop and R&B charts. It joined the *Saturday Night Fever* soundtrack and any number of Donna Summer tracks as a song that helped define that era. Peaches & Herb first formed in 1966 with Herb Feemster and his original Peaches, Francine Hurd. They scored a dozen major hits over the next four years, such as "Close Your Eyes" and "Let's Fall in Love." By 1970, the hits had dried up and Feemster became an officer with the Washington, DC, police department. By 1976, he had the itch to sing again. Through his original producer, Van McCoy, he met

model Linda Green (born June 27, 1949). She became his new duet partner and Peaches & Herb was reborn. After a single for MCA Records flopped, the duo hooked up with Feemster's childhood buddy Freddie Perren, who had become a great songwriter for the Jackson 5, among others. Perren placed their project with Polydor Records. The dance track "Shake Your Groove Thing" exploded immediately. But the best was yet to come. The ballad "Reunited" spent four weeks at No. 1 on both the R&B and pop singles chart. They continued to record radio hits such as "I Pledge My Love" and "Bluer than Blue" through 1983. The duo then parted ways. Green and her husband, Stephen, a songwriter, founded a ministry called WOW (Winning Our World) where they distribute Bibles and practical necessities worldwide. They have recorded three independent CDs, *Urban Missionaries* (1992), *Bought with the Blood* (1997), and *Perfect Love* (1999), which they've sold through their www.wowjam.com website.

Rosey Grier

OF COURSE, 6'5" (300 pounds at his peak in the 1950s) Rosey Grier is a household name as a football legend, sometime actor, and frequent television talk show guest in the 1970s. It's his foundational fame in those arenas that gave him the platform to become a respected leader in Christian church circles over the last 20 years.

Born July 14, 1932, in Cuthburt, Georgia, Roosevelt Grier (named after US President Franklin Roosevelt) and his ten siblings were raised on a small farm where his parents grew corn, peanuts, and watermelons. He and his father rode a horse-drawn wagon through the city every Saturday selling watermelons. In 1945, the entire family moved to Roselle, New Jersey, where they had relatives and better job prospects. At Roselle High School, Grier became an all-around athlete, excelling especially well in football. Upon graduation, he received 25 scholarship offers from postsecondary institutions. At his college choice, Penn State University, Grier sang with the Mysterious Cavaliers, a quartet. While maintaining at least a C average, Grier won All American honorable mention for tackling during his senior year.

In 1955, Grier received $7,000 to play for the New York Giants. Teaming Grier with Dick Modzelewski, Andy Robustelli, and Jim Katcavage, the four became one of the best defensive front-fours in the National Football League. The next year they creamed the Chicago Bears 47–7 and the Giants won their first NFL championship in 18 years. In 1957, Grier served in the army and returned to the Giants in late 1958. He went on to help the team win the Eastern Division title in 1959, 1961, and 1962. They did not win the NFL championship, but Grier was named All-Pro twice. One criticism of Grier's football days was that he was inconsistent. He once admitted, "My main fault as a football player was that if the opposite guy wasn't very good, I wasn't very good. But if he was good, I was great."

Teammate Kyle Rote got Grier into show business. Grier's guitar playing early in the morning used to bother Rote, who told Grier "If you really want to learn, I have a friend in New York." The friend was Michael Stewart, president of United Artists Records. Grier went to meet him. Stewart says, "This massive guy came in carrying his guitar like it was a toothpick, his amplifier like a woman's purse. And out of this hulk of a man came this plaintive high voice. It broke me up. He could sing." In 1963, Grier made his concert debut at Carnegie Hall to rave reviews. The same year he was traded to the Los Angeles Rams.

Once settled in Los Angeles, Grier began to make guest appearances on *Shindig, Hullabaloo, Mr. Novak,* and *The Man from U.N.C.L.E.* He was soon making more money as an actor than as a football player. (In 1964, the Rams paid him $26,000.) In addition to recording for Bell Records, Grier played the lead role in a musical version of *Othello* in 1966. The Rams players Deacon Jones, Lamar Lundy, Merlin Olsen, and Grier became known as "The Fearsome Foursome." Their defensive line was virtually impenetrable and God help the man who was tackled by one of them. After tearing an Achilles tendon in 1967, Grier retired from football in 1968.

Grier lent his support to Robert F. Kennedy's 1968 presidential campaign. In June 1968, at the Ambassador Hotel in Los Angeles, Grier and Ethel Kennedy were walking right behind Robert when Sirhan Sirhan fired several shots. Grier wrestled Sirhan to the ground until police took him away. At Kennedy's funeral Grier was a pallbearer, and he stood by Ethel during the services. Grier then became a delegate to the Democratic National Convention in Chicago and joined George McGovern's presidential campaign staff. The same year, KABC-TV in L.A. began *The Rosey Grier Show,* which was syndicated by ABC Films. The half-hour program was along the lines of a talk show format. Later in the year, he went with Bob Hope to entertain the troops in Vietnam.

In 1969, Grier portrayed a runaway slave named Gabe Cooper who found refuge on an Indian reservation on the *Daniel Boone* TV show. In 1975, he played Moose, a truck driver, on one of President Ford's favorite shows, *Movin' On.* In the late 1970s, Grier and his second wife divorced. On the suggestion of a friend, Grier began attending Fred Price's Crenshaw Christian Center Church. He soon became a born-again Christian. One week after Grier and his son attended church services, Little Rosey asked, "Can Mom come to church with us next week?" Although Grier was angry with his ex-wife, he invited her to placate his son. Soon she was saved, and Grier says, "God let me see Margie in a new light. It was as if she was a different woman altogether." They fell in love again and remarried in 1981. Today, Grier is in demand as a lecturer and conference speaker.

From the late 1960s to 1974, Grier recorded message songs such as "Bring Back the Time" for United Artists Records, "Beautiful People" and "Rat Race" for ABC Records, and "You're the Violin" for A&M Records. After recommitting his life to Christ, Grier recorded a fine gospel album entitled *Committed* for Word Records in 1986. The track "Be Bold, Be Strong" received some radio airplay, while "We Will Stand" featured background vocals by Little Anthony of the Imperials, Glenn Leonard (from a latter-day formation of the Temptations), and Grier's former football buddies Deacon Jones and Steve Archer.

Bessie Griffin

ALTHOUGH SHE IS virtually unknown today, Bessie Griffin briefly flirted with the sort of widespread mainstream fame that Mahalia Jackson enjoyed the last 20 years of her life. A chubby woman with sensual eyes, she had stage charisma, a rich contralto, and a moaning ability that slayed many a packed church. Born Arlette Broil on July 6, 1922, in New Orleans, her father was a sanitation worker with a thirst for hard liquor. Her mother was devout but died while Griffin was a child, leaving her to be raised by her grandmother, Louise Narcisse. Her grandmother worked in a pecan factory during the week and sang in church on Sunday mornings. Griffin followed in Miss Louise's footsteps and began to sing too. Her schoolmates ridiculed her name, so she changed it to Bessie. As a young woman, she spent a decade singing with the Southern Harps, a female quartet. During that time, she married and divorced Willie Griffin before jumping the broom a second time with Spencer Jackson.

Griffin made a few records in the late 1940s but didn't achieve national attention until Mahalia Jackson invited her to sing at one of her anniversary concerts at the Chicago Coliseum in the early 1950s. There was a terrific buzz about her Mahalia-styled contralto, and the shy singer ended up joining the Caravans before they hit it big. By 1954, she left them, since she wasn't making decent money, and toured with the preacher W. Herbert Brewster, Jr., for a year. Still broke, she left Chicago and moved back to New Orleans until 1959 when producer

Bessie Griffin / Savoy Records photo

Bumps Blackwell (who wrote Elvis's "Rip It Up" and Little Richard's "Good Golly Miss Molly") put her in the gospel musical *Portraits in Bronze.* While the show did not enrich Griffin, it did gain her Hollywood notoriety. Movie legends ranging from Bette Davis to Steve McQueen came to witness Griffin's stellar performances. She appeared on national television shows with Ed Sullivan, Dinah Shore, and Danny Kaye, among others. However, Griffin had no able managerial handlers to transform her Tinseltown buzz into consistent fame and fortune in the early 1960s. She recorded for several recording labels, but a hit record eluded her. She spent her final years performing for basically handouts, made a few recording sessions with Shanachie Records, and died of breast cancer on April 10, 1989, in Culver City, California.

RECOMMENDED RECORDING: One of her best projects is the out-of-print 1960s Savoy Records LP *The Gospel Soul of Bessie Griffin,* which features a spine-tingling rendition of "Come Ye Disconsolate" and her own riveting, self-written "Mother's Song." However, the only thing in circulation is the 2000 Shanachie CD reissue *Even Me,* which features 22 tunes from throughout Griffin's career, stretching from the church-wrecking 1954 "Too Close to Heaven" to her last work in the 1980s such as "I Can Put My Trust in Jesus." Also on the market is Griffin's 1963 concert *Live at the Bear in Chicago* (Sony Legacy, 1998) that demonstrates Griffin's middle-of-the-road approach to "When the Saints Go Marching In" and "Didn't It Rain."

Gloria Griffin

BORN DECEMBER 15, 1933, in Mississippi, Griffin was reared in St. Louis, Missouri, where she sang her first solo at an Easter pageant at the age of five. Her aunt Adie Mae Haynes formed the Haynes Singers, and Griffin sang with them during her high school years. At the age of 16, she moved to New York where she worked with singer Alvin A. Childs. Then she sang with the Clara Ward Singers for a spell before graduating to a short stint with the Caravans. Mahalia Jackson also served as a mentor to Griffin. Griffin joined the Roberta Martin

Singers in 1957 and became their shining star on the tuneful ballads "God Specializes," "God is Still on the Throne," and her own composition, "I'm So Grateful." In later years, she would testify, "The doctors said I could never sing another gospel song [after failing health]. But you know, God, He specializes." According to writer Tony Heilbut, Griffin would run up and down the church aisles as her audience was left hopping, hollering, and shouting themselves silly. She only recorded a handful of solo albums, most notably 1971's *Gospel's Queen* on Atlantic's Cotillion label. She died in the early 1990s.

LaShell Griffin

ONCE WOMEN IN THE MUSIC business reach 25 years old, they are told that they are too old to make it big. So imagine the country's surprise when a 36-year-old housewife and mother of five won Oprah Winfrey's Pop Star Challenge talent competition out of 15,000 people who sent in audition tapes in 2003. Born in Detroit, Michigan, Griffin was singing in church from the age of 13. After high school, she married Lee Griffin and they had five children. Over the years, Griffin's singing was confined to church on Sundays. During the week, she was the consummate homemaker, shopping for groceries, dropping the kids off at school, and doing volunteer work. Foot surgery slowed her down and laid her up in the fall of 2003. "While I was resting and recovering, I was watching a lot of television and found out about the Pop Star Challenge," she told *Christian Music Today*. "I had always enjoyed singing and I thought this very well could have been the chance for me to come forward."

Indeed it was. She and seven others were chosen out of the 15,000 audition tapes sent in for the Pop Star Challenge. They competed in front of celebrity judges and, in the end, the public voted for Griffin in the spring of 2004 largely because of her riveting performance of "The Greatest Love of All." Once she won the grand prize, a contract with Epic Records, she had ten days to record her CD, *Free*. "I fought hard to get those particular songs on the album because one thing I've always wanted to do was to bridge the gaps," she told *Christian Music Today*. "There's such segregation between Christ-

ian music and gospel music and inspirational music and pop music. I've always wanted to bring that all together, and this album is definitely going to do that. There's something on it for everybody. All the songs are so different. I have a little MercyMe flavor in there, also some Barbra Streisand, but then a bit of Jill Scott. There's just a big variety of different styles of songs. I tested out where I could and couldn't go, and it was beautiful."

RECOMMENDED RECORDING: Considering the secular music industry's disdain for overtly Christian music, when Griffin won the Pop Star Challenge, Epic Records executives were probably worried about the kind of record she would make. All along, Griffin's passionate faith and desire to sing gospel was apparent. This album seeks to blend inspirational pop with gospel, but it leans more toward the gospel end of the spectrum. The smooth, jazzy "Free," "He's Coming Back," and her cover of MercyMe's "I Can Only Imagine" stand out. However, the album as a whole should not have been rushed in ten days. In spite of Griffin's awesome vocal ability, which shines over every song (even the duds), that isn't enough to make this a memorable album. Aside from the gorgeous single "Free," it isn't memorable. But the singer certainly is!

GRITS

THE BLACK CHRISTIAN RAP duo of Teron "Bonafide" Carter and Stacey "Coffe" Jones is best known as GRITS. Their success, though limited, has been on the white side of gospel music rather than the black. "The black face scares them," Coffee told ChristianityToday.com in 2004. "Stacie Orrico, whom they've embraced, she's doing her version of urban music. Her beats are very urban-driven. That's why I don't think it's the music itself. They feel safer with a white face promoting that kind of music than with a black face."

The racial politics of Christian music has been an eye-opening experience for them. "There's a blatant division within our industry," Bonafide told *CCM* magazine in 2004. "We shy away from talking about race and about who's really running things. You see it in music, our churches, etc. In the Christian music industry, everything's predominantly white. Black music doesn't really exist in that genre. I always thought it ironic that Kirk Franklin never made the cover of *CCM* until he exploded on urban radio, but he had been doing it for all these years. Everybody was like, 'Oooh, let's embrace Kirk, because he's big!' Now Kirk sells magazines; that's why you want him on the cover…. We've been told our stuff is too urban, that it doesn't fit the format. Out of Eden has been told that. And that's basically telling us, 'You're too black.' That's where we come from! What do you expect? We get flak when we do music that's true to who we are, true to our people. That's why, for us, sometimes we'd rather be in a more mainstream environment. They're more diverse, and at times play more Christian songs than so-called Christian radio."

The duo met in 1991 when they were both part of DC Talk's dance troupe. In 1997, they were offered a deal by TobyMac's Gotee Records label to make an album. Their debut CD *Mental Releases* came in 1995 and they have recorded steadily. The Christian music critics love their music, but until their 2004 CD *Dichotomy A*, they had never enjoyed a major hit. That CD reached No. 12 on the CCM album sales chart and they were finally able to break the color barrier in the white Christian market.

"It hurts, especially when it's coming from your brothers and sisters: you're not accepted here," Bonafide said to *CCM*. "There are even moments where we feel as though we're the affirmative action of Christian music: 'Well, let's put GRITS up there just because we have to. We need somethin.'… I'd rather not be a part of it if we're going to get that treatment. We've turned down offers to tour and activities simply because they wanted us to be the token black group. We don't want to be tokens. If you want us there, it has to be because you really feel what we're doing."

Josh Groban

ALTHOUGH HIS MUSICAL tastes range from reggae star Bob Marley to opera star Luciano Pavarotti, Groban is neither in style. Instead, the young vocalist has combined an operatic approach to pop music with a naïve humbleness that has transformed him into a superstar

within three short years. Even more fascinating is the idea that Groban has popularized a classic pop style of music (think Bing Crosby with more vocal range and crescendo) among the Britney Spears and Justin Timberlake audience. Born Josh Winslow Groban on February 27, 1981, in Los Angeles, Groban was raised in an Episcopalian family. He sang all of his life and attended the prestigious Interlochen Arts Program. His vocal coach was a friend of mega-producer David Foster. When Foster needed a vocalist for a political function, the vocal coach recommended Groban.

After that event, Foster had Groban fill in for Andrea Bocelli at a Grammy rehearsal with Celine Dion. Backstage, Groban met Rosie O'Donnell, who booked him to sing on her show and the buzz began. At the same time, he enrolled as a musical theater major at Carnegie Mellon University. Then Groban was offered a Warner Bros. Records contract via Foster's 143 imprint. It was a good match for Foster, who had failed in his quest to transform the Christian pop group Plus One into major crossover stars. Groban's self-titled debut CD was released in November 2001 and featured two gospel songs, "Jesu, Joy of Man's Desiring" and a Charlotte Church duet, "The Prayer" (also covered by Yolanda Adams and Donnie McClurkin). The album shot to No. 1 on the *Billboard* classical album sales chart. A year later, his *Josh Groban in Concert* CD boasted another version of "The Prayer" with Angie Stone as his duet partner. The album's single was a stirring version of "O Holy Night," which began to receive play at inspirational Christian radio stations. In fall 2003, Groban's next CD, *Closer*, appeared and the anthemic single "You Raise Me Up" raised Groban up to even higher levels. Aside from peaking at No. 1 on the adult contemporary radio charts, the song received such broad play on Christian inspirational radio that the Christian trio Selah covered the song as well.

Rickey Grundy

BEST KNOWN FOR COMPOSING the choir favorite "Can't Stop Praising His Name" and for organizing a variety of choirs for recording artists, Rickey Grundy was born January 30, 1959 in Los Angeles. Something of a child prodigy, Grundy graduated from high school at the age of 15 and studied at the Southern California Conservatory of Music. In 1980, he made contributions to Keith Pringle's *True Victory* LP, which served as a launch to a very successful behind-the-scenes career in gospel music. In 1989, he recorded his first Sparrow Records CD *The Rickey Grundy Chorale*, which peaked at No. 10 on *Billboard*'s gospel survey and spent 29 weeks on the chart. In recent years, Grundy has toured throughout Europe extensively and done production work on several films, such as Tom Hanks's *The Ladykillers* and *Why Do Fools Fall in Love.*

Deitrick Haddon

SINCE HIS DEBUT PROJECT in 1995, the gospel music industry has been patiently waiting for Deitrick Haddon to dominate contemporary gospel music the way that Kirk Franklin did in the early 1990s. He was born in Detroit on May 17, 1973 to parents who are the pastors of High Praise Cathedral. Early on, Haddon listened to Stevie Wonder and Michael Jackson albums in between the gospel music he was weaned on. At the age of 13, he began directing the church choir. "When I was 16 or 17, I used to sing with a group called Perfect Peace and we wanted to be like Commissioned or the Winans," he told *Gospel Today* magazine. "We just thought we were going to blow up out of Detroit. We landed a record deal with Bellmark Records, but when we recorded our album they sat it on the shelf for two and a half years. That basically broke the group up. In the midst of that I knew I wasn't going to wait on a record label. I got busy and took my choir [Voices of Unity] and recorded an album." Tyscot Records released that album. It didn't chart, but the sales were encouraging. In 1998, Haddon's solo debut *This Is My Story* reached No. 31 on the gospel album sales chart. His other albums didn't chart high, but they sold very well over time. Even though Haddon earned hit radio singles such as "I'm Saved, I'm Saved" and "This Is the Day the Lord Has Made," he moved on from Tyscot to Verity Records with hopes that they could take his sales to a new level of success.

"It was very frustrating because any time you have people who are ahead of their time or see something that they want to do that's different from what everyone else is doing, it's hard," he told *Gospel Today*. "Eventually, you end up having to suppress what you really are and what God has given you and adapt to what people can handle. It's very frustrating when you have somebody that's very creative and wants to put their hand in everything and doesn't want to do the same old thing, but you have a label or radio announcers who say, 'That can't get played on our station or format,' or a label that doesn't know what to do with your material."

The deal Haddon struck allowed him to record as a solo artist for Verity Records while he produced his choir and other acts on Tyscot Records. Since he joined the Verity roster in 2002, his debut CD *Lost & Found* peaked at No. 5 on the gospel album sales chart and produced the hit "A Sinner's Prayer," which received a smattering of secular radio play. The 2004 CD *Crossroads* debuted at No. 1 on the gospel album sales chart and was poised to be Haddon's bestseller yet. "I want to be part of the group of young people that will take gospel music to the next level," he told *Gospel Today* at the time.

Jester Hairston

BY THE TIME HE HAD reached the age of 85, Jester Hairston had become a TV star thanks to his role as the wisecracking church deacon Rollie Forbes on the 1980s NBC sitcom *Amen*, starring Sherman Helmsley and Clifton Davis. However, long before that Hairston had a distinguished career as a conductor and songwriter. His songs such as "Amen" and "Mary's Boy Child" have been recorded by artists as diverse as Charlotte Church and Harry Belafonte. The grandson of slaves, Hairston was born July 9, 1901, in Belews Creek, North Carolina, and was raised in the Homestead section of Pittsburgh where his family worked in the steel mills. Always involved in church activities, Hairston won a scholarship from his Baptist church to study landscape architecture at the Massachusetts Agriculture College in 1920. There he played on the football team and sang in the glee club while also coaching local choirs. When his money ran out, Hairston dropped out until a woman impressed by his talent offered to finance his musical education. He eventually graduated from Tufts University in 1929.

Hairston made his way to New York where he met Hall Johnson, a Negro spirituals conductor who hired Hairston as his assistant. Johnson taught Hairston to respect spirituals and the history behind them. Soon Hairston had devoted himself to preserving the music of the slaves. When Johnson sold his screenplay *Green Pastures* to Warner Bros. in 1935, Hairston was allowed to conduct the music for the film. His biggest break came the following year when Russian composer Dmitri Tiomkin asked him to conduct the choir in the classic film *Lost Horizon*, which won an Oscar for best score. It was the start of Hairston and Tiomkin's 20-year collaboration on films. Through Hairston's efforts, big-budget films such as *Red River*, *She Wore a Yellow Ribbon*, and *Land of the Pharaohs* boasted the first integrated choirs on their soundtracks.

Hairston's work was not confined to the recording booth. He co-starred in both the radio and television versions of *Amos 'N' Andy* and also had bit parts in some Tarzan films. Years later, some blacks complained that the roles black actors of Hairston's generation played were demeaning. However, Hairston once said, "We had a hard time then fighting for dignity. We had no power. We had to take it, and because we took it the young people today have opportunities." He also appeared in feature films such as *The Alamo*, *To Kill a Mockingbird*, *In the Heat of the Night*, *Lady Sings the Blues*, *The Last Tycoon*, and *Lilies of the Field*, for which he composed the song "Amen." That gospel song is one of the most recorded songs in gospel history with the most versions by Elvis Presley, Johnny Cash, and Harry Belafonte. Over the years, Hairston wrote more than 300 spirituals. His best-known spiritual is the Christmas song "Mary's Boy Child," which has been covered by dozens of recording artists, including Neil Diamond, John Denver, Charlotte Church, and Mahalia Jackson.

Aside from various soundtracks for which he either arranged music or composed songs, Hairston never recorded an album. However, in 1989, Gasparo Records released an album of Hairston's spirituals recorded by the Belmont Chorale. After Hairston won the role of Rollie Forbes on *Amen* in 1986 and became a celebrity, he was in greater demand than ever to speak on college campuses about his choral work and the Golden Age of Hollywood. Even after the comedy show about the ups

Teresa Hairston / courtesy of Gospel Today *Magazine*

and downs of a Philadelphia black church went off the air, Hairston continued to speak candidly and with eloquence at college campuses well into his nineties. He also globe-trotted as a goodwill ambassador for the US State Department. Hairston died January 18, 2000, at the ripe old age of 98.

Teresa Hairston

WHAT KATHERINE GRAHAM AND Clare Booth Luce meant to mainstream journalism in the past is what Teresa Hairston means to gospel music journalism today. Through her magazines, *Gospel Today* and *Gospel Industry Today*, she has provided a platform for gospel artists and Christian personalities to share their testimonies and explain what motivates their ministries. Born Teresa Sanders on February 7th in Cleveland,

Gospel Today *magazine /*
courtesy of Gospel Today *magazine*

Ohio, Hairston is an accomplished pianist who began her career as a songwriter. "I started writing songs before I got into the industry," she told GospelFlava.com in May 2004. "It's been a lifelong thing for me. In fact, that was my first inspiration to get into the industry… I'd kind of let that gift lie dormant." Bowling Green State University Gospel Choir recorded one of her first gospel songs, "Just to Behold His Face," in 1980. She went on to write songs for artists as diverse as Albertina Walker and the Georgia Mass Choir. During that period, Hairston scored music for Savoy Records artists such as James Cleveland, Myrna Summers, and Milton Biggham. Later in the 1980s, Hairston took a position at Benson Records as the director of marketing and worked her way into an A&R executive position at the label, where she served as an executive producer on projects by Hezekiah Walker, Albertina Walker, and Thomas Whitfield.

In 1989, Hairston took $300 and launched a gospel magazine, *Score*. As the years marched on, Hairston changed the name to *Gospel Today*. While the magazine began strictly as a gospel music magazine, it has evolved into a Christian lifestyle and entertainment publication with a monthly circulation of 250,000. It is now the world's leading African-American religious magazine and has featured cutting-edge interviews with Natalie Cole about her past drug addiction, the other woman in Henry Lyons's sex scandal, and Fred Hammond about his divorce. Hairston has also produced the *Gospel Today Magazine Presents* series of praise and worship CDs on Verity Records, which has included such artists as Vickie Winans and Richard Smallwood.

Danniebelle Hall

DANNIEBELLE HALL WALKED into the spotlight during the infancy of contemporary Christian music. Although she was black, her work with Andrae Crouch and the Disciples and her subsequent solo career was largely supported by white Christians following the Jesus hippie movement of the late 1960s. While her earlier compositions such as the classic "Ordinary People" were embraced during the genre's birth, by the time the industry matured in the 1980s and Hall was middle-aged, she was viewed more as a black artist. Christian radio that played her before found that she no longer fit what they defined as the format, though her style of music had not changed. New recording labels promoted her to the black gospel world, but she had no professional roots there and could never get a foothold with her smooth vocals and pop orchestrations. She could easily have been compared to Roberta Flack, another pop-soul stylist who had a far more successful career in the white pop world than in the black R&B arena.

Born October 6, 1938, in Pittsburgh, Pennsylvania, Hall triumphed over a childhood of poverty and loneliness. She began playing an upright piano at the age of three and began playing at church at 12. At age 30, she formed a San Francisco Bay Area gospel quartet called the Danniebelles. They recorded an album and toured for four years. In 1972, Danniebelle joined her favorite gospel group, the already-legendary Andrae Crouch and the Disciples, who had fomented the

contemporary Christian music revolution in the late 1960s with their unique fusion of layered harmonies and soulful praise and worship music. Danniebelle's smooth alto was the lead on Disciples classics such as "Take Me Back" (1973), "Tell Them" (1975), "Soon and Very Soon" (1976), and "Quiet Times" (1977).

Danniebelle's lead vocals on so many Disciples hits led Light Records' (the label that recorded the Disciples) founder Ralph Carmichael (born May 27, 1927) to offer her a separate solo contract. Her albums while at Light included *Danniebelle* (1974), *Y* (1974), and *This Moment* (1975). In spite of their respectable sales and overall quality, they did not really connect with the masses. When Danniebelle joined the roster at Sparrow Records, her music finally found an audience.

Her 1977 label debut, *Let Me Have a Dream*, is the perfect balance between Christian pop and gospel soulfulness. The overall theme of the album was worship, as most contemporary Christian music was at the time. Produced by Bill Maxwell with background vocals by Jessy Dixon, piano by Joe Sample, and sax by Ernie Watts, the album was stuffed with songs that received widespread play on Christian radio at the time. From the opening plea of the beautiful "Let Me Have a Dream" (later covered by Billy Davis, Jr., on his Savoy Records gospel debut in 1980) to the closing Andrae Crouch–Keith Green composition "You're the Only One," it was a classic album from the start. Along with her signature tune "Ordinary People," it also featured another '70s Christian radio anthem, "We All Need Each Other."

Since Christian music's reach was successfully extending into Europe, Sparrow sent Hall to Sweden to record her next album, *Live in Sweden with Choralerna*. An awesome live album, it was recorded over several concert locations in Sweden and the crowds were ecstatic about Hall. The set opened with her rocking version of "I Go to the Rock." She performed a couple of delicious Jessy Dixon songs such as "That's What He's Looking For" and "He's the Best Thing That Ever Happened to Me." She also covered the Disciples' "My Tribute," but the true smash was "You Must Open the Door."

During the 1980s, Hall struggled to find another hit. She signed to Benson Record's black division, Onyx. They repackaged her 1973 Christmas album as *Songs of the Angels* in 1983. Her only original album for the label, *Unmistakably You* in 1984, did not sell and Benson didn't renew the option on her contract. She was caught between a white Christian music field that had grown up and no longer found her music relevant to their cause and a black gospel world that rejected her outright for not being one of them from the start.

Through the rest of the 1980s and early '90s, Hall had lean times where she performed when she could, but dates were few and far between. Finally, in 1994 she snagged a recording deal with CGI Records in Chicago where she released *Designer's Original*, an album that finally gave her a moderate gospel hit with the song "Ain't No Devil in Hell (Gonna Walk on the Jesus in Me)."

Just as she was getting her career back into high gear, Hall suffered a stroke in 1995, which led to a diabetic coma and renal failure. As she fought her way back to health, Hall was then diagnosed with breast cancer. She beat that, but ended up having her left leg amputated. During her ordeal, Hall's estranged husband of 26 years, Charles Hall, died in 1998. That same year, she resurfaced briefly for an Andrae Crouch and the Disciples reunion concert. The solo dates she did often turned out to do more harm than good. She had been on dialysis, which sapped her strength, and many of her church engagements were less than stellar. The word spread that Hall's shows were terrible and that sometimes she was brought on stage in a wheelchair. She forced herself to perform because she loved performing, but more so because she needed money for her staggering medical bills and daily dialysis treatments. Her only other income was small royalty checks for the songs she had written during her healthy years. Many artists have recorded her songs. "Hymn of Love" was recorded by Eartha Kitt, "Keep Holding On" by Pat Boone and Bobby Jones, "Like a Child" by the Mighty Clouds of Joy, and "Ordinary People" by the late James Cleveland and most recently by Delores "Mom" Winans.

For the last three years of her life, Hall lived in a Bay Area nursing home. Family and fans would send some money to help her with her living expenses. Her faith in God never wavered. She sent messages to her fans through her Web site, which her daughter maintained. Hall shared her health setbacks and plans for the future, but she mostly spoke of how her faith had never been stronger. Her last entry was in October 2000. She was moved to a San Jose–area hospital in November and her doctors were surprised that she was still alive. They scheduled her for angioplasty on her right leg to improve circulation and to have her gangrened toes amputated. In between surgeries, Hall began to choke. Fluid filled her lungs, she vomited, and her heart stopped beating. She was resuscitated but never regained consciousness. On Thursday, December 28th around 5:30 A.M. she slipped into eternity.

Andrae Crouch issued a statement on Danniebelle's passing: "When I think about Danniebelle, she was first and her music was second. She made many of the songs she recorded work because of her talent more than the song itself. She was the greatest. There is no other individual, no other talent quite like Danniebelle's. I was always in awe of her." Andrae and Sandra Crouch coordinated the funeral plans and called for donations to be sent care of the City of Refuge Church in San Francisco. "We all want Danniebelle to have a dignified service and nothing else," Sandra said at the time. "She gave and we want to pay tribute to a great psalmist." BeBe Winans and a contingency of other gospel stars packed themselves into Center of Hope Community Church in Oakland for the funeral.

RECOMMENDED RECORDING: *Remembering the Times* (EMI Gospel, 2001) is a 20-song collection recorded during Hall's tenure with Sparrow Records in the 1970s. Among the tunes are her signature track "Ordinary People." The bouncy "I Go to the Rock" and the mellow "That's What He's Looking For" also stand out.

James Hall & Worship and Praise

JAMES HALL'S WORSHIP and Praise Choir hit the music scene in 1995 with the smash hit *God Is in Control*. The youngest of eight children, Hall was born in Brooklyn, New York, in 1971. He began to sing at the age of five and once said, "My greatest joy was hearing the choir sing. I built a little cardboard church in my mother's bedroom and filled it with paper dolls that represented my choir. I would stand there and direct them." Hall got to direct real people when he was in high school and created the Worship and Praise Choir. He tried to secure a record deal for the choir but was rejected so often that he considered disbanding the group. "Every time I was at my lowest, someone would step into my life with a word of encouragement," he later said. "The pastor would preach on not becoming weary in God's service, or someone would tell me how this ministry had turned their life around. There was always a word to keep me going."

In 1992, the choir recorded the CD *God Is in Control* for a small label with cash flow problems. The record release was delayed several times while the owner tried to raise the money to adequately promote the project. After the choir booked themselves on the *Bobby Jones Gospel* TV show, the label was so inundated with retail requests for the CD that Intersound Records took over and promoted the album nationally.

Their subsequent CDs *King of Glory*, *Live from New York at Lincoln Center*, and *We Are at War* have all charted well and kept James Hall & Worship and Praise on the gospel radar. "Sometimes God blesses me with songs that are very traditional," Hall told *Gospel Music Exclusive* magazine in 1995. "But a lot of what I do is very contemporary. My father was a jazz nut, so I grew up hearing a lot of jazz, and there's definitely a flavor of that in there too. You'll hear different influences in different songs."

Vera Hall

AN INDIGENT BLACK singer discovered by folklorists John and Ruby Lomax in the 1930s, Vera Hall recorded spirituals such as "The Last Month of the Year" for the Library of Congress in the 1950s. She went to work for a white family at the age of 11 and married at 15. When she was 21, her husband was shot and she fell into a deeper state of destitution. Her life went from bad to worse. Her daughter distanced herself from Hall. A loose girl who wielded switchblades, the daughter gave birth to two children by two different men and died of hepatitis at the age of 20. Her daughter's death created such sadness in Hall that she rarely spoke her name.

She referred to her grandsons as her own sons, since she raised them after her daughter's death.

When the Great Depression set in, many wealthy white families lost their property and money. One such victim was socialite Ruby Pickens Tartt, whose husband lost his prestigious job as postmaster. She later worked with John Lomax on recording black singers in rural Georgia. They first recorded Vera Hall in July 1937, at which time she sang blues such as "I Been Drinking" and spirituals such as "God Knows I Am De One" and "God's Goin' Build Up De Zion Wall." Hall is credited with writing songs such as "The Last Month of the Year," "Trouble So Hard," "Death Have Mercy," "Another Man Done Gone," and "Boll Weevil Holler." Tartt helped secure royalties for Hall on those songs when others recorded them and popularized the songs. Over the years, "The Last Month of the Year" was recorded by Odetta, the Kingston Trio, the Staple Singers, and the Fairfield Four. In her last years, Hall was sickly and blind. She died on January 29, 1964, at the age of 58 and was buried in the Livingston Negro Cemetery. John Lomax wrote in a *Sing Out* magazine obituary, "Her performances were all graced with dignity and with love. Her sense of timing and beat were perfection itself. She has added to the flexibility of the African style, the mellowness and polish of the best of western European vocal art."

Fred Hammond

WHEN THE HISTORY of post-1980s gospel music is written, Fred Hammond will go down as a much greater influence than he's often given credit for. Kirk Franklin and Yolanda Adams may have enjoyed more crossover success, but Hammond is responsible for taking praise and worship music to an urban audience that once viewed the genre as the white man's diluted form of gospel. As a result, Hammond has fashioned numerous contemporary-styled worship songs such as "Glory to Glory" and "When the Spirit of the Lord," which have become standards among black choir repertoires every Sunday morning somewhere in America.

Hammond was born December 27, 1960, in Detroit. His father died when he was young, and his mother, Mildred, raised him and kept him in church. She also bought him his first bass guitar, a Norma. Once he mastered it, she bought him a Fender Precision. Hammond began to sing for his church's choir when he was 12 years old. His mother was a church musician and often brought him along to her choir rehearsals. During his leisure time, Hammond listened to music by the Edwin Hawkins Singers and Andrae Crouch, but he didn't stop there. He branched out beyond the church walls to enjoy the sounds of Sly & the Family Stone, the Ohio Players, and even blues guitarist Edgar Winter.

As a teenager, Hammond played with a group called Saved, along with Mitchell Jones and Michael Williams. They were offered a record deal by D.J. Rogers for his HopeSong label, but the label dissolved before the album materialized. Hammond then auditioned for the Winans band and earned a spot playing bass for them in 1980. After two years of touring with the Winans, Hammond came home to Detroit and formed Commissioned with his partners from Saved, Williams

Fred Hammond / *photo courtesy of* Verity *Records*

and Jones. He added Michael Brooks, who auditioned with him for the Winans (but wasn't accepted), Keith Staten, and Karl Reid. Their music encompassed the sacred and secular styles Hammond had been grooving to since his youth. Although many churches didn't support their progressive form of gospel, Dr. Mattie Moss Clark did believe in them. She featured them in key spots at her annual COGIC music convention in Memphis. Soon they were signed to Light Records, just like the Winans.

Once their debut LP *I'm Going On* hit the streets, they all quit their 9-to-5 jobs and were doing weekend concert dates to make a living. They deliberately mixed their vocals higher in the mix, which was revolutionary at the time, though it's commonplace now. "We tried to lock in spiritually and make sure that every part of our lives was cleaned up," Hammond says. "Personally, I felt that God was calling me to be married. I even felt that he had been telling me to find a wife before the record came out. I just knew that I couldn't be serious about my career and be dating while I was on the road. This was not a game. That feeling must have hit everybody because they all got married. We all did things for ourselves that settled us and kept us focused."

Commissioned enjoyed a steady string of contemporary gospel radio hits such as "Running Back to You," "Ordinary Just Won't Do," and "I'm Going On." In 1994, Hammond left the group and formed the Radicals for Christ Choir. Hammond eventually disbanded the choir and just recorded under his name. Since going solo, Hammond has earned three gold records for albums such as *Pages of Life: Chapters 1 & 2* and a string of funky praise and worship songs such as "Jesus Be a Fence All Around Me" and "No Weapon." On writing worship songs, Hammond told *U* magazine, "I didn't know worship. All I knew was going to church—sing some songs, listen to the choir, give an offering, listen to the preacher, have an altar call, and go home. That was Sunday morning worship. One day, I learned that worship is intimacy with God, a love affair with God…. It's not just raising your hands and getting emotional, worship is heartfelt, intimate relationship with God. Praise is something different."

"I really believe [Jesus] understood what we're really in, what the world is really in, and he was willing to go to any lengths to get it back," he continued. "He hung out with sinners, the crazy people, the sick people... real life, that's where it's at. I've always loved motorcycles, anything with wheels, and so now I've just learned that we can use these bikes to reach the community that I'm in—in Detroit—and I just really want these people to know the Lord. Last night, I was outside a bar sitting on my bike, and this woman came up and started talking to me. There's no telling how many people drove by and saw me hanging outside a bar talking to a woman. It's all about being approachable, being available for all those who would never come to a church. And I'm a church guy, so I know what that's about."

In looking at his success and the aftermath of his divorce, Hammond told *Gospel Today* magazine in 2004, "Some Christians seem to think that we're not supposed to have issues, but the truth is, we've all got issues—things that hold us back, things we pick up quickly, things we struggle with. They say, 'Well, all you've got to do is this or that' to take care of those issues or problems. But I've learned that one of the reasons I'm successful is because I've been through so much, and I relate to the common people who don't get it right off the bat."

RECOMMENDED RECORDING: *Hooked on the Hits* (Verity Records, 2003) features all of Hammond's best-known solo songs.

Happy Goodmans

"THE HAPPY GOODMAN FAMILY is a pioneer in gospel music," former Gospel Music Association President Frank Breeden once said. "They were one of the first groups to incorporate contemporary instruments in [Southern] gospel music, and that helped broaden its appeal to an audience who grew up on rock 'n' roll."

Alabama-born Willie Howard "Happy" Goodman (born November 7, 1921) began his and his family's career in Southern gospel music in 1940. He and his sister, Gussie Mae, created a group with their siblings Ruth, Sam (born March 19, 1931), Rusty (born September 2, 1933), and Bob (born February 4, 1938). In her auto-

biography, Howard's wife, Vestal Freeman Goodman (born 1930), recalled her mother-in-law naming the group. "You Goodman kids are always laughing and having fun," she wrote. "We may not have much of this world's goods, but we sure are happy. We're not just the Goodman family. We're the Happy Goodman family."

After the girls married and Rusty left to launch a career in country music, Goodman's wife Vestal joined the group and they became a quartet. They rode throughout the South in an old limousine to sing in camp meetings, revivals, and gospel singings for freewill offerings. A weekly, 30-minute show on WLTV Channel 13 in Bowling Green, Kentucky, helped their fame spread throughout the deep South. After being turned down by every gospel recording label, they financed their first two LPs, *I'm Too Near Home* and *It's a Wonderful Feeling*, in the 1962–1963 period.

Prior to that time, most Southern gospel music was recorded with just piano accompaniment. Using the same session musicians that played behind George Jones and other country stars, they brought Southern gospel to a new level of respect. By the 1960s, Bob had left the group and Rusty returned to become the group's principal songwriter. He wrote songs that have gone on to become Southern gospel classics, such as "I Wouldn't Take Nothin' for My Journey Now," "Had It Not Been," and "Leavin' on My Mind," which has become a standard at funerals throughout the South. Eventually, Word Records caught wind of the Happy Goodmans. They recorded for the label for 25 years and sold hundreds of thousands of records. Their album *The Happy Gospel of the Happy Goodman Family* won a Grammy in 1968 for Best Gospel Album.

Their fame continued to spread with their two popular gospel television programs, *The Gospel Singing Jubilee* and *The Happy Goodman Family Hour*, in the late 1960s and early 1970s. Their music has influenced country artists such as Dolly Parton and Ricky Skaggs. In 1980, the group disbanded. Rusty and Sam had seen the rise of contemporary Christian music artists Amy Grant and Sandi Patti selling like pop artists and wanted the group to get in on the new trend. "Howard and I had no desire to change," Vestal recalled in her memoirs. "...I didn't even know how to sing that kind of music. We finally came to an impasse... and we all decided it was time to go our separate ways. We had threatened to disband many times before, but this was the real thing. The breakup was amicable but not comfortable. We said things back and forth that we later regretted. Rusty, especially, was offended at Howard and me because of our refusal to change. Some of his comments seared our hearts."

Howard and Vestal reluctantly began performing as a duo at church conferences and the like. Ironically, the 1981 Grammy awards pitted the Goodmans against each other. Rusty's LP *Escape to the Light* was nominated for Best Traditional Gospel Album as was the Goodman Family's *Goin' Higher*. J.D. Sumner's various artists compilation won, but it was odd for the tight-knit Goodmans to be competing against each other. Soon, Howard and Vestal were invited to appear on Jim and Tammy Bakker's *PTL Club*, a sort of daily Christian *Tonight Show* format with celebrity interviews and music. The Goodmans were so full of life and downhome, offstage and on, that the Bakkers had them join the staff just to be near them on a regular basis. On the TV show they sang almost daily and shared their life experiences in a way that inspired the viewers. They soon developed an entirely new audience outside of the Southern gospel world. After three years on the show, the Goodmans left in 1988 when the Bakker's *PTL* scandal brought the Heritage USA ministry to its knees.

After the *PTL* debacle, the Goodmans were flat broke and singing every weekend to make ends meet, when Vestal was diagnosed with lymphoma. Her faith was strengthened through the ordeal and friends predicted she'd live to cause the Devil more trouble in the future. Miraculously, she was healed and Vestal hit the road again with Howard. In 1990, Rusty was diagnosed with cancer, and he summoned Howard and Vestal to make amends for their falling-out years before. The Happy Goodmans recorded once more for *The Reunion* LP that year. Amid his pain and medical treatments, Rusty wrote new songs for the project such as "Standing in the Presence of the King" and "Don't Give Up," which became even more poignant as his condition worsened. Sam's health was also deteriorating as he battled emphysema. Rusty's medical bills were insurmountable, and Bill Gaither organized a star-studded benefit concert at Christ Church in Nashville. Amy Grant, BeBe

and CeCe Winans, Michael W. Smith, and 27 others came out and sang. There had been tentative plans for a reunion concert tour, but Rusty died on November 11, 1990. Sam's death followed on August 5, 1991.

Afterwards, the Goodmans became a trio with Johnny Minick. Over the years, they recorded three CDs that remained true to their soulful, traditional style of Southern gospel: *Set Your Sails, Joy for the Journey*, and *The Final Stand*. In 1995, Vestal recorded her first solo LP, *Hallelujah*, for Word's Canaan subsidiary. Her CDs *Moments* and *Hymns for Life* were both released in 1997 and peaked at No. 4 and No. 9 on the Southern gospel charts. From these albums came her renditions of classics such as "Sweet Hour of Prayer" and Hank Williams's "I Saw the Light."

In 1998, the Happy Goodmans were inducted into the Gospel Music Hall of Fame. During that period, they began to enjoy a career resurgence with their appearances on Bill Gaither's successful *Gaither Homecoming* videos and television specials. In 2000, the Goodmans released the CD *Fifty Years*, which has sold over 100,000 units as a CD and been certified gold as a home video. Although plagued by bad knees that made it hard for him to walk, Howard performed almost until the end of his life. He died of complications from knee surgery and pneumonia on November 30, 2002, at Vanderbilt University Medical Center in Nashville after about seven months of convalescence. Just a year later, Vestal, who still grieved his loss, died of complications from a bad case of the flu on December 27, 2003 in Celebration, Florida.

Gabriel Hardeman

PHILADELPHIA'S OWN tunesmith Gabriel Hardeman and his wife and collaborator Annette were responsible for two of the most enduring Quiet Storm soul ballads of the 1980s: Stephanie Mills's No. 1 smash "I Feel Good All Over" and Miki Howard's No. 2 smash "Love Under New Management." In recent years, they have sought to make the same sort of impact in the gospel world with varied success.

Hardeman was born December 13, 1943, in Atlanta. Annette was born November 19, 1954, in Chester,

Pennsylvania. Hardeman's first writing success came in 1979 when James Cleveland and the Philadelphia Mass Choir recorded his song "I Know the Man." He later formed the Gabriel Hardeman Delegation, an amalgamation of musicians and vocalists, and released the 1981 *Talk* and 1983 *Feels Like Fire* LPs on Birthright/Word Records. The latter won them a Grammy nomination and received some airplay on R&B radio stations. In the late 1980s, Hardeman and Annette (who once sang with the disco trio First Choice, of "Dr. Love" fame), began to write clean love songs for artists such as Stephanie Mills ("I Feel Good All Over") and Miki Howard ("Love Under New Management"). Both songs were gold-selling works. In the 1990s, the Hardemans took a time-out. Gabriel graduated from Lutheran Theological Seminary and began a new career as a teacher and athletic coach. Meanwhile, he continued to write songs for Teddy Pendergrass, Edwin Hawkins, and Grover Washington, Jr. The Delegation also continued to provide background vocals for studio recordings on Patti LaBelle and Phil Perry, among others.

In 2001, the Delegation returned to the airwaves with the slick gospel-soul CD *To the Chief Musician* on Crystal Rose Records. The CD hit the *Billboard* gospel album sales Top 40 chart and enjoyed massive radio play for the funky single, "Hold Out, Deliverance Will Come." The album is a delicious fusion of old school and Bible school and a perfect paean to the Chief Musician—Jesus. In 2003, the Hardemans relocated to Atlanta and have set up a new ministry there.

Sanchez Harley

ONE OF THE MOST prolific of modern gospel producers, Sanchez Harley has collaborated with a who's who of the gospel world, from Kirk Franklin and Lamar Campbell to Albertina Walker and Shirley Caesar. The only child of two teachers who met on the campus of Tennessee State University, Harley was exposed to music at an early age. Though he was born in Jacksonville, Florida, he was raised in Baltimore, where the family was very active in the Waters AME Church. He studied piano for ten years, and while attending Douglas High School he played sax in the All City Concert Band. In 1973, he won a

scholarship and attended Tennessee State University in Nashville. He was one of the first blacks to play a horn in the school's marching band.

Later Harley co-founded the group Bottom & Company, which recorded hit songs such as "Spread the News" and "Do You Wanna Do a Thing Here for the Party" for Motown Records. In the 1980s, Harley and his arranger-partner, Lloyd Barry, began to get involved in arranging records. "The arranging work was all in either country or gospel and I didn't want to do country," Harley laughs. They began working for Word Records and their artists such as Shirley Caesar. Harley built on those experiences and became a much sought-after producer. Among his proudest achievements was producing the *March On!* soundtrack for Warner Bros. Records, which celebrated the 30th anniversary of the 1963 March on Washington. The album featured Will Downing, Cybil Shepherd, and Take 6, among others. Harley even conducted the San Francisco Symphony when they backed Patti Austin on the track "Oh Freedom."

Harley also produced the Gospel Music Workshop of America's successful 25th anniversary album and has continued to produce a battery of leading and legendary gospel artists such as Albertina Walker, Bishop Paul Morton, the Christianaires, Hezekiah Walker, and Kirk Franklin. In recent years, Harley formed the Chez Musique recording label, which has experienced great success with the traditional gospel group RiZen.

Larnelle Harris

ONE OF THE FIRST black vocalists to be accepted in the CCM field in the 1970s, Larnelle Harris's warm, operatic baritone has wrapped itself around Christian pop songs such as "I've Just Seen Jesus," "How Excellent Is Thy Name," and "More Than Wonderful." Born in 1947, Harris graduated from Western Kentucky University. An excellent operatic singer, saxophonist, and percussionist, Harris toured with the Spurrlows, a Christian vocal group, as their drummer between 1970–1972. The Spurrlows persuaded Harris to return to his Christian roots and dedicate himself to Christian music. "I used to play the clubs all the time," Harris told the *Los Angeles Times* in June 1987 of his past gigs singing Top 40 music

Larnelle Harris / photo courtesy of Benson Records

Richard Hartley and Soul Resurrection

REV. RICHARD HARTLEY is a combination of spiritual shepherd, standup comedian, fashion model, and new millennium singing songwriting choirmaster. His 2003 CD *Love Is All We Need* received great reviews but was ignored by traditional gospel radio announcers. Considering that he was raised in the Church of God in Christ (COGIC) denomination, which has produced gospel revolutionaries such as the Clark Sisters and Edwin Hawkins, it's no surprise that Hartley has a unique approach to the Good News. On top of that firm foundation, add the fact that Hartley grew up with R&B star Kelly Price back in their old Queens stomping grounds, earned his union card in Broadway musicals such as *Mama, I Want to Sing*, and has performed with music super-legends such as Mariah Carey, Diana Ross, and Aretha Franklin, and it is clear that Hartley brings a diverse set of revolutionary urban vibes to his musical table.

"I don't see what I do as being revolutionary," Hartley says. "This is just who I am and these are the sounds that have been swirling around in my head for years." The youngest of three children, Hartley was born November 27, 1961, in what was once an all-Jewish ghetto in the Queens borough. They lived in the Hammels Projects on 81st Street. It faced the Temple of Israel, a beautiful old synagogue. "I just fantasized that one day it would be my church as I passed on my way to the beach," Hartley reminisces. "It was so stately." But his family wasn't Jewish; they attended a COGIC assembly elsewhere in their neighborhood. By the age of six, Hartley knew he could sing and that he would sing one day. He started singing in the church choir with his older brother, Stuart, who encouraged Hartley's musical proclivities.

After graduating from the City University of New York and studying music engineering at the New York Center of Media Arts, Hartley took a job as a drug/health counselor for the Board of New York in 1985. One day, just for fun, Hartley accompanied a friend to an audition for Vy Higgensen's off-Broadway production *Mama, I Want to Sing*. He ended up auditioning too and won a role. Soon he was taking a sabbatical

and German lieder in nightclubs. "Then I decided I could not do that…. I was new to my commitment as a Christian, and club people were bad [influences]…. You make little concessions: you may be an abstainer in terms of drinking or smoking, and then you say, 'Well, this is not so bad.' It is difficult [to sing gospel] when I am not a true example of what it is like to be a Christian."

Harris was a member of the Christian group First Gear for a while before going solo in 1976. That year, he released his debut LP *Tell It* for Word Records. Harris was popular from the beginning but reached a new level when he and Sandi Patti teamed up to record "More than Wonderful" in 1983. That same year, Harris became the first black man to win the Dove award for male vocalist of the year. Meanwhile, Harris racked up CCM radio hits such as "How Excellent Is Thy Name," "I Miss My Time with You," and "I've Just Seen Jesus." In 1984, Harris began a moonlighting gig with Bill Gaither's Gaither Vocal Band quartet. Harris has never enjoyed a moment on the black gospel chart, but most of his albums have done well in the Christian market, proving that the right black artist with the right non-black material can make a successful jump between the genres.

from his counseling position and ended up holding several principal roles in the long-running musical. Through the musical, Hartley toured to more than two dozen countries. Over time, these opportunities manifested into separate concert tours for Hartley to Australia, Europe, and Japan where they are very popular and have released music albums.

Hartley grew up in the same neighborhood as R&B songstress Kelly Price. Aside from being friends, they were both members of the COGIC church and used to sing together as teenagers. When Price landed a job as one of Mariah Carey's backup singers in the early 1990s, she pulled Hartley into Carey's camp as a background singer too. Hartley appeared in Carey's "Anytime You Need a Friend" music video and on her NBC television special in 1993. Later, when Price became a star in her own right, she had Hartley go on tour with her as a background singer. Just when his musical dreams were becoming a reality, Hartley was dealt a serious blow. In the summer of 1992, his brother Stuart died suddenly. "That was my lowest point spiritually and emotionally," Hartley says. "I lost my music partner and blood brother. Stuart was the center of everything we did musically. I don't know that I have triumphed over that loss yet. I can say that I'm still here and that the Lord is blessing! The music is what keeps me going."

Hartley continued to perform because he knew Stuart would not have wanted the music to die, so he began to assemble small groups to back recording artists. During this period, he performed with Aretha Franklin, Mavis Staples, and many other music legends. In 1996, Hartley formed Soul Resurrection to resurrect the musical bond he shared with Stuart. "It was an attempt to keep the legacy that Stuart and I started," he says. Among the eight-member ensemble's troupe are Hartley's sister, Wanda, a percussionist, and his wife, Stacey. In the ensuing years, Soul Resurrection became an in-demand backup group for established artists when they appeared on television shows such as *Late Night with David Letterman*, *Showtime at the Apollo*, the Grammy awards, and the Soul Train Music awards. The group also was featured in the Madison Square Garden musical *This Is My Song*, which starred Tramaine Hawkins, Cissy Houston, and Shirley Caesar.

In spite of positive reviews, Hartley's 2003 Shanachie Entertainment debut CD *Love Is All We Need*, a mix of Caribbean and dance rhythms with quasi gospel messages, failed to connect with gospel radio. Still, he continues to push forward, expanding the borders of black gospel. "The basic message of the Bible is love," Hartley says. "Soul Resurrection's sound is different in that it is a sound unique to my life experiences and not just church sounds. It has the same spiritual substance of church music, but it reflects more personal artistry than community choirs usually do. We hope to blaze a path that unifies R&B and gospel as one."

Lorenzo Harrison

ONE OF THE MOST influential sacred steel guitarists in the embyonic stage of the genre, Lorenzo Harrison's music has greatly impacted young steel guitarists such as Robert Randolph. Born October 26, 1925, in Aurora, Colorado, Harrison was influenced by Willie Eason, who became known as Little Willie and His Talking Guitar. Eason and his brother, Troman, were responsible for introducing the steel guitar into black church worship services. Eventually, Harrison began playing with the Jewel Dominion Players within the Church of the Living God denomination. Harrison was known for slowing down the tempo, adding chords, and putting a boogie-woogie swing to it. Aside from recording his own songs for obscure record labels, Harrison also played behind the Jewel Gospel Singers (Candi Staton, Maggie Staton, and his daughter, Naomi Harrison) when they recorded for Nashboro Records in the 1950s. He managed the group and became vice president of the Church of the Living God in 1955. He was eventually elevated to bishop and died in 1986. "Lorenzo Harrison and all of them were the greatest musicians I've ever heard," Robert Randolph once said. "Had they come out 20 or 30 years ago, they'd have been in the position I'm in. The church was stricter with them than with me, because of the time. They're my main motivation, what they did for the whole tradition. They were playing in church to a small congregation—there are only 12,000–13,000 people in our whole church organization—and now we have over 200 steel players, and a bunch of kids who want to be steel players. They started that, and it never got out of the church so they could show their abilities."

Steve Harvey

ONE OF THE MOST popular comedians of the new millennium, Steve Harvey was born January 17, 1957, in Cleveland, Ohio. After working more than a dozen years as a standup comic, Harvey became host of *Showtime at the Apollo*, a syndicated talent show, in 1994. His obvious talent for the funny led to his own top-rated WB Network sitcom, *The Steve Harvey Show*, which ran from 1996 to 2002. He was recruited to host the Stellar awards, a gospel broadcast in 1999 with Lynn Whitfield and CeCe Winans. Seeing how good Harvey was with a gospel audience, BET Television then hired him to host their top-rated annual *Celebration of Gospel* specials. Harvey, who is also a Christian, has interviewed a variety of gospel artists on his popular morning radio show at KKBT, an R&B and hip-hop station in Los Angeles. The parents of four children, Harvey and his wife have given substantial contributions to the community via their Steve and Mary L. Harvey philanthropic organization.

Edwin Hawkins

HE'S CREDITED WITH being the bridge between old-school and contemporary gospel. If Edwin Hawkins never recorded anything other than 1969's "Oh Happy Day," he would still retain a lofty place in gospel music. However, this master composer has created a legacy that clearly makes him one of the cornerstones of modern gospel.

Hawkins was born August 18, 1943, in Oakland, California. One of six children, he grew up in the Campbell Village projects, where his parents, Mamie and Dan Lee Hawkins, encouraged his musical skills at an early age. Hawkins began to play the piano by age five and when he was seven took over the keyboards for his family's vocal group. They recorded a custom project years later in 1957. Hawkins's father was a tough taskmaster, so everything Hawkins and his siblings did was done

with excellence lest they incur their father's wrath. Hawkins excelled on many fronts. By the age of 16, he hosted a weekly Sunday night radio show and sang regularly at various churches in the Bay Area.

As active members of the Ephesians Church of God in Christ (COGIC), family friend Betty Watson and Hawkins formed the Northern California State Youth Choir in the early 1960s. "There was already a Southern California State Youth Choir," Hawkins recalls. "And in our church, the choir would go to these conventions every year. So Betty and I put together a choir for people in Northern California to be represented at the convention. After we came back from the convention, we all enjoyed working together, so we decided to stay together and make a record."

They recorded a custom LP, *Let Us Go into the House of the Lord*, in 1968. The tune "Oh Happy Day" was on that project. "My mother had an old hymnal and I had a knack for rearranging hymns," Hawkins says. "'Oh Happy Day' was an old hymn and I rearranged it. It was actually one of the least likely songs to become a hit. There were some much stronger songs on there. We were going to hand-sell the album in the Bay Area. We ordered 500 copies. Lamont Bench, a Mormon guy, recorded that album on a two-track system. Those 500

Edwin Hawkins / photo courtesy of Edwin Hawkins

copies sold, then a DJ at KSAN Radio in the Bay Area got a copy of it and started playing it." Soon "Oh Happy Day" was stealing radio play on an FM radio station in New York City and other major cities. In her book *We'll Understand It Better By and By*, gospel historian Bernice Johnson Reagon wrote, "A graduate student at the time, I remember hearing the remarks of an African-American DJ when he introduced the song on WVON, a soul music radio station in Chicago: 'Here's a new song climbing the charts. I don't know what to call it. It sounds like gospel and it sounds like soul. Whatever it is, the beat has a groove. I like it and I'm gonna play it.'"

The burgeoning success of the recording was a life-changing experience for Hawkins. "I wasn't planning to go into the music business and I wasn't looking for a record deal. The record's success decided my fate. I learned the business the hard way." Sixteen major recording labels were interested in either buying or licensing the underground hit, but Buddha Records made the best offer. "Some people thought the label had something to do with the religion because of Buddha, but that was just a name," Hawkins says. "A Jewish guy named Neil Bogart [who later founded Casablanca Records and launched the careers of KISS and Donna Summer] owned it. We signed the contract Easter Sunday night in 1969. He and his partners flew out to see me and brought me a check for $5,000. Coming from the projects, that was a lot of money to me."

It was then decided to change the ensemble's name to the Edwin Hawkins Singers. Dorothy Morrison was the featured vocalist on the track and developed a bit of fame as the singer of the surprise hit. A national single and album were rushed out, and with Buddha's muscle, "Oh Happy Day" reached No. 4 on the US pop singles chart and No. 2 on the UK pop singles survey. It spent two weeks at No. 2 on the American R&B singles chart as well. The group was suddenly the toast of Hollywood. They performed on network television programs such as Dick Clark's *American Bandstand, The Hollywood Palace, The Smothers Brothers Comedy Hour,* and *Happening '68,* among others. In 1970, the group won a Grammy award for Best Soul Gospel Performance for "Oh Happy Day" (to date, the best-selling black gospel single of all time with 7 million copies sold) and won the

same Grammy category the next year for their tune "Every Man Wants to Be Free." Although the song was embraced by some elements of the church world, it was largely a secular hit that had great appeal during the peace and love hippie movement of the time. With this in mind, the group was then featured behind labelmate Melanie's breakthrough single, a hymn entitled "Lay Down (Candles in the Rain)," which rose to No. 6 on the pop charts in 1970.

Of course, showing up on secular TV shows, appearing in rock music magazines, and singing music that seemed like blues to traditional gospel ears brought Hawkins much criticism from some in the gospel music community. "We preach, and the Bible teaches, to take the gospel into all the world, but when it all comes down, we don't want to do that with our music," Hawkins says.

Edwin Hawkins / June 1987 Totally Gospel magazine, courtesy of Capital Entertainment archives

"And the church world is quick to criticize that....I think sometimes that it is out of jealousy. Someone has succeeded, and people don't like it. A lot of that goes on."

Buddha pushed the choir's fame further than any other gospel choir had gone up to that time. They recorded prodigiously during the period to keep the momentum going. Other bestselling albums included *He's a Friend of Mine* and *Children Get Together*. The 1972 LP *I'd Like to Teach the World to Sing* received a rave review in *Billboard* magazine in April of that year: "The rich warm voices of the internationally famous Edwin Hawkins Singers are presented here in another album of inspirational songs. 'Give Me a Star,' 'Oooh Child,' and 'I Don't Know How to Love Him' are included along with an arrangement of 'Shine' that could prove to be the one to bring some of the 'Oh Happy Day' success." The title song was featured in a very successful Coca-Cola campaign that year and kept the choir in the forefront.

During the late 1970s, Hawkins continued to maintain his star appeal with hit albums such as *Wonderful*. In the early 1980s, he cut back on live performances and concentrated on event performances. In 1981, through a partnership with dentist Byron Spears's Birthright Records, Hawkins released *Live with the Oakland Symphony Orchestra*, which featured the gospel megahit "Worship the Lord." It was so successful that Birthright released *Live with the Oakland Symphony Volume II* the following year. In 1983, Hawkins founded the annual Music & Arts Seminar as a nonprofit organization to mentor and develop new gospel talent. Each year, the seminar records a live album of the songs new artists have developed. Some of the artists either discovered or participating in the concerts over the years have included Yolanda Adams, Daryl Coley, and LaShun Pace.

Following his association with Birthright Records, Hawkins recorded for Polygram's Fixit Records label, where he charted with the Hot 100 R&B hit "If at First You Don't Succeed (Try Again)" in 1990. From there, Hawkins joined Sony's Harmony imprint where he released several of the Music & Arts Seminar live recordings. In 1999, Hawkins celebrated the 30th anniversary of "Oh Happy Day" with the excellent album *Love Is the Way*. The album featured a newly recorded club version of "Oh Happy Day" and the contagiously soulful, mid-tempo track "Lord of All." The project received great reviews and reached No. 31 on the gospel album sales chart. In 2004, Hawkins formed his own label, TRI Recordings, and released the CD *All the Angels: Music & Arts Love Fellowship Mass Choir*.

Proving his stature as a great gospel composer, Hawkins has seen scores of artists record his songs, including Rev. Clay Evans ("Everything Will Be Alright"), Jennifer Holliday ("This Day"), Brooklyn Tabernacle Choir ("Mine All Mine"), and Ron Kenoly ("Worship the Lord"). Hawkins's original version of "Oh Happy Day" has sold more than 7 million copies since 1969. In addition, Hawkins's arrangement has been covered by more than four dozen artists ranging from the Oak Ridge Boys and Elvis Presley to Aretha Franklin and Joan Baez—once again proving that Hawkins is one of the most influential musicians of this era.

RECOMMENDED RECORDING: *Oh Happy Day: The Best of the Edwin Hawkins Singers* (Buddha Records, 2001) is the place to get Hawkins's breakthrough recordings from the early 1970s. His Birthright material has yet to be reissued on CD.

Tramaine Hawkins

IF THERE HAD BEEN no Shirley Caesar and no Mahalia Jackson, Tramaine Hawkins would have undoubtedly been crowned the Queen of Gospel in the 1970s. In addition to her dynamic church-wrecking soprano, Hawkins boasted a regal aura, stylish stage costumes, and runway model beauty. She looked and carried herself like the gospel royalty she's become. Born October 11, 1951, in San Francisco as Tramaine Aunzola Davis, she was raised in Berkeley. Her family had a long, deep church history. Her grandfather was Bishop E.E. Cleveland (a founder of the COGIC black Pentecostal denomination), and her aunt is Bishop E.C. Reems, an influential female evangelist. Hawkins grew up singing in COGIC church convocations. As a child she sang with the Sunshine Band and the Heavenly Tones. She also sang with the Northern California State Choir, which later morphed into the Edwin Hawkins Singers after their 1968 homemade recording of "Oh Happy Day"—the biggest-selling gospel single to date—became a surprise pop smash. After the group began performing in secular venues on bills with the Jackson 5 and the Supremes, Hawkins left the group because she didn't feel comfortable sharing stages with pop artists.

It wasn't the first time she was faced with the option of performing in secular venues. Earlier, Hawkins had been asked to become a founding member of the R&B trio the Honey Cones. She had initially pondered the idea, but eventually decided that she was called to strictly sing gospel and rejected the offer. The group went on to have R&B smashes such as "Stick Up," "Want Ads," and "The Day I Found Myself." After leaving the group, she spent 11 months touring with Andrae Crouch and the Disciples where she had a featured vocal on "I'm Coming Home, Dear Lord" with Billy Thedford on the group's 1971 *Keep on Singin'* album. Meanwhile, Hawkins had been dating Edwin Hawkins's younger brother, Walter, and married him in 1970.

Eventually, Walter Hawkins left his brother's group to found and pastor the Love Center Church in Berkeley. They also formed a church choir and recorded their first LP, *Love Alive*, in 1975. Although the album was credited as Walter Hawkins and the Love Center Choir, Tramaine Hawkins did the bulk of the singing. Her dramatic vocals on the eight-minute, gut-wrenching ballad "Changed" and the uptempo "Goin' Up Yonder" were instant gospel radio classics that quickly made the Hawkinses gospel's most celebrated couple. In a field where 20,000 units was considered a hit, the *Love Alive* album sold a staggering 300,000 copies. It even led to opportunities for the couple in the mainstream African-American press. In 1978, they followed up with the equally successful *Love Alive II*, which featured Hawkins on "Be Grateful." Soon Walter Hawkins had formed the Hawkins Family (which included Tramaine, his cousin Shirley Miller, and his sister Lynette among other revolving members) and theirs became the most exciting show in gospel music. They packed secular concert venues and put on an electrifying performance that mostly revolved around the vocal theatrics of Tramaine and Walter. Although Walter was a brilliant performer, the star was clearly Tramaine. With her mahogany skin, flowing hair, custom-made stage outfits, and commanding stage presence, her sophisti-

cated image and style were comparable to that of Diana Ross or Nancy Wilson.

Noting Hawkins's charisma, Light Records offered her a solo contract. After some initial hesitance, she recorded the albums *Tramaine* and *Determined*, which were both major gospel hits and featured her classics "Highway" and "I'm Determined." Then she decided to leave the label. "At that time I didn't feel that the people at Light Records were desirous of my career expanding outside of the church market," she told *Totally Gospel* magazine in 1988. "I've always felt that gospel music ought to be heard and available to everybody, not just the Christian market. Teenagers were buying R&B and pop, but they weren't going to stores buying gospel music…. I felt there was a whole market out there for the ministry's sake. I wanted to give them music with substance because of the fact that young people are so influenced by music." She found a producer and came up with a demo that they peddled to several major labels before A&M Records took a chance on it. "They decided that they might have something," she continued. "They went for it because they felt that they could make some money off of it, that it was marketable. Our main focus was on the ministry aspect of the whole situation."

Tramaine Hawkins / A&M Records publicity photo

A&M's gamble paid off nicely, although many church traditionalists labeled Hawkins a backslider for the secular-sounding music she began to create. The techno dance track "Fall Down" zoomed to No. 1 on the *Billboard* club chart and No. 7 on the R&B chart in 1985. Their second single was the funky "In the Morning Time," which hit No. 21 on the club chart and No. 26 on the R&B chart. In addition to those tracks, gospel radio also heavily played the ballad "With All My Heart." The album *The Search Is Over* peaked at No. 2 on the gospel charts and hustled all the way to No. 33 on the R&B album chart. The follow-up LP *Freedom* didn't fare as well. It was produced by the Jacksons, who were having trouble producing hits on themselves, let alone anyone else. The first single, "Rock," went to No. 22 on the club chart and No. 56 on the R&B chart. Gospel radio rejected "Rock" altogether, but they did play "Daniel."

After her 12-inch days at A&M were over, Hawkins signed with Sparrow Records in 1988 and recorded a more traditional gospel LP *The Joy That Floods My Soul*, which resulted in the gospel radio hits "We're All in the Same Boat Together" and "What Shall I Do?" The gospel industry embraced her again and said that she had returned to her church roots—implying that her repertoire at A&M was not gospel—but Hawkins had a problem with that assessment. "I'm not particularly crazy about the term that they're using now, because going back to something, to me, means that you've left something," she said at the time. "I don't feel spiritually or otherwise that I've left the church." She followed with a *Live* LP featuring guest appearances by guitarist Carlos Santana, saxophonist Stanley Turrentine, organist Jimmy McGriff, and the Edwin Hawkins Singers. Buoyed by the radio hits "The Potter's House" and "Lift Me Up," the album won Hawkins her first Grammy award in 1990.

After a four-year recording hiatus, Hawkins moved over to Columbia Records where Mahalia Jackson had been transformed into a household name 40 years before. Label executive Dr. George Butler hoped to do the same with Hawkins. However, the CD *To a Higher Place* failed to make that happen. In their efforts to make Hawkins appeal to non-churched adults, the album featured inspirational standards such as "Trees," a corny duet with Mahalia, and uneventful pop songs. The production was excellent, but the songs weren't, and the soul that made Hawkins such a church-wrecker was hidden behind strings and muted messages. Surprisingly, the best song on the project, a suave, R&B-styled ballad "That's Why I Love You Like I Do," was not even pushed as an R&B single. The sales were poor and Columbia did not exercise its option for a second CD. It would not be until 2001 that Hawkins would release another project, when she signed to Gospo Centric Records for a mediocre album called *Still Tramaine*. Produced by Walter Hawkins, who remained close to her even after their divorce, the album still sold upwards of 100,000 copies off of Tramaine Hawkins's legendary name in spite of no clear radio hit.

Walter Hawkins

HANDS-DOWN ONE OF gospel's best vocalists ever, Walter Hawkins enjoys an incredible vocal range and a jazz man's gift for vocal bends and turns. During the 1970s, he created gospel's most successful family act, the Hawkins Family, with a series of gospel radio smashes such as "What Is This?" "Goin' Up Yonder," and "Be Grateful." He was born May 18, 1949, in Oakland, California. His brother, Edwin, had already made a name for himself in 1969 when "Oh Happy Day" became an international hit. While studying for his Master of Divinity degree from the University of California at Berkeley, Hawkins recorded his first LP, which was released as *Selah* and *Do Your Best* at varying times by Fantasy Records in 1972. An October 1972 *Billboard* review made these comments: "Walter Hawkins is a pianist of enviable accomplishments while his vocal prowess is in no way disputable. He's gathered around him an exceptional crew of sidemen and vocalists and the total effect is completely invigorating. Tom Fogerty, Merl Saunders, and Brian Gardner produced; top cuts [include] 'Where Will You Run,' 'Searchin',' and 'It Pays.'"

The following year, with a commission from his pastor, E.E. Cleveland at Ephesians COGIC, Hawkins founded the Love Center Church on MacArthur Boulevard in East Oakland. The Love Center Choir recorded their first album as a church family. Hawkins used

$1,800 he borrowed from his mother-in-law to complete the project. It was called *Love Alive* and debuted on Light Records in 1975. Although the album was credited as Walter Hawkins and the Love Center Choir, it was really Hawkins's wife, Tramaine Hawkins, doing the bulk of the singing. Her dramatic vocals shone on the project. "Changed" and the uptempo "Goin' Up Yonder" were instant gospel radio classics that quickly made them gospel's most celebrated couple. A runaway smash, the *Love Alive* album sold a staggering 300,000 copies. It even led to opportunities for the couple in the mainstream African-American press.

In 1978, they followed up with the equally successful *Love Alive II*, which featured Hawkins and his sister Lynette on the smash single "Be Grateful." The songs "Never Alone," "Right On," "Until I Found the Lord," and "I'm Goin' Away" were also huge songs on gospel radio. During this time, Hawkins created the Hawkins Family (which included Tramaine, his cousins Shirley Miller and Lawrence Matthews, and his sister Lynette among other revolving members). They were soon staging a concert program that became gospel's hottest ticket. They packed secular concert venues and put on an electrifying performance that mostly revolved around the vocal theatrics of Tramaine, Walter, and Lynette.

The Hawkins Family's success continued to grow. Their self-titled 1980 LP featured their hit "What Is This?" By that point, Tramaine had recorded her first solo album and Walter Hawkins's first solo project appeared in 1982 when he released *I Feel Like Singing*, which included the hit "Do Your Best." Over the course of the decade, Hawkins focused on his church and on producing and writing songs for other artists. "Now I want to break out of the Hawkins chorale," he told *Billboard* in September 1992. "I want to do some other people and see what happens with that kind of collaboration."

In 1990, Hawkins invited Daryl Coley and Yvette Flunder in for the *Love Alive III* recording, which became the biggest seller of the *Love Alive* album series. The radio favorites were "There's a War Going On," "I Love You, Lord," and "He'll Bring You Out." The LP spent 34 weeks at No. 1 on the *Billboard* gospel album sales chart during the almost 100 weeks it spent on the

survey. The album went on to sell over a million copies. The public could not get enough love, and 1993's *Love Alive IV* also peaked at No. 1 on the album sales chart and spent a year on the survey. In between projects, Hawkins was ordained a bishop on October 18, 1992 by the COGIC denomination.

Hawkins was quiet for a few years because some of the labels he was associated with experienced distribution and financial problems. He and the family made a welcome return in 1993 when Gospo Centric Records released the double CD *Love Alive V*, which reunited all of the original members of the Hawkins Family group, including Tramaine, who was no longer married to Hawkins but remained a close friend. Buoyed by Hawkins's solo on the stirring ballad "Marvelous," the album peaked at No. 5 on the gospel Top 40 and led to a successful cross-country Hawkins Family reunion concert tour.

As an elder statesman in gospel, Hawkins has become a favorite for cameo appearances on others' albums lately. The Mississippi Mass Choir had a sizeable hit with him on "Hold On, Soldier" in 1993, and Donald Lawrence and the TriCity Singers watched him steal the show on "Seasons" from their *Go Get Your Life Back* CD in 2002. Whereas many gospel fans consider Daryl Coley to be gospel's best living singer, Chicago radio announcer Gregory Gay makes a case for Hawkins. "Daryl has skill," he suggests. "But Walter has passion. Passion makes the difference."

As he continued to build his church ministry, in 2000 Hawkins bought a 30,000-square-foot auto dealership at 105th Street and International Boulevard, just blocks from his boyhood home, and relocated the Love Center Church there. "Early on I thought my ministry and my music were apart from each other. But now I see they work hand-in-hand," he once said. "I can go a lot of places with my music that I can't go as a pastor and vice versa. The purpose of both is getting the message out to people. I've had some material blessings and it's okay to have them, but to be blessed with peace of mind and joy in your life, that's when you will be truly fulfilled."

RECOMMENDED RECORDING: *Love Alive* (Light Records, 1975) remains the must-have project by Walter Hawkins.

Lynette Hawkins-Stephens

THE BABY OF THE Hawkins Family, Lynette Hawkins was born on August 20, 1954, in Oakland. Toward the middle 1970s, when her brother Walter was having success with the Hawkins Family recordings, she became one of his great soloists with her dynamic alto vocals that rivaled any woman in the gospel field of the time. During those years, Hawkins-Stephens led such Hawkins Family classics as "Be Grateful," "Right on Time," "There's a War Going On," "Dear Jesus," "I'm Not the Same," and "God Is Standing By." In 1987, she released her debut LP *Baby Sis*, which engendered the radio hit "Time Is Winding Up" and reached the Top Ten gospel album sales chart. She later had a quick hit with the title track of her 1991 Tribute Records CD *Walking in the Light*. In recent years, she has appeared on new recording projects by Donnie McClurkin and Jonathan DuBose, Jr.

Rev. Charles G. Hayes

DR. CHARLES HAYES was born December 10, 1937, in Verbena, Alabama. After graduating from Prentice High School in Montevallo, he moved to Chicago where he was ordained in 1957. In April 1959, he founded the Cosmopolitan Church of Prayer in the basement of Morris Jackson's home at 634 Woodland Park in Chicago. In those days, Hayes placed the folding chairs weekly and served as church pianist before he gave his sermon. Eventually, the church moved to a storefront on Cottage Grove Avenue. Hayes then began a Sunday night radio program. Although he was still in his twenties, people started calling him Father Hayes because his advice and counsel seemed so fatherly. In 1961, the church converted an old post office on South Langley Avenue into their sanctuary. It was at that venue that Father Hayes and the Voices of Cosmopolitan began to make records. Nicknamed the Warriors because of their driving and energetic vocal presence, they produced gospel hits such as "The Bridegroom Cometh," "Step Back and Let God Do It," and their signature tune, "Jesus Can Work it Out."

RECOMMENDED RECORDING: *The Collection* (Savoy Records) consists of 12 of the choir's most beloved songs, such as the seven-minute "Jesus Can Work It Out," which features the original and much-borrowed church hook: "How you gonna pay your rent, all your money spent?"

Heather Headley

THE TONY AWARD–WINNING Broadway star who originated the role of Nala (a feisty lioness) in *The Lion King* was born October 5, 1974 in Trinidad. Her parents pastored the Barataria Church of God there. Headley began playing piano at the age of four and soon began to sing as well. When she was 15 years old, her family moved to Ft. Wayne, Indiana, where her father became pastor of a local church. In spite of initial culture shock, Headley immersed herself in American music and graduated with honors from high school before earning a musical theater degree from Northwestern University. In 1997, she was cast in *The Lion King*. Critics applauded her mesmerizing performance and the buzz began. Soon she was called on to take the title role in Elton John and Tim Rice's Broadway musical version of *Aida*. She told *LA Focus* magazine, "Disney gave me an opportunity to do something that nobody else in the world could have given to me at that time. I'm glad they listened to God. They could have picked anybody. I had no name and yet they were saying we have the faith in this girl that she can be Aida, when I didn't have that much faith in me."

In her new role, Headley floored the critics again and won a Tony award in 1998. Soon there was a pool of recording labels wanting to transform this Broadway star into a soul star. A number of labels courted Headley and even gospel star CeCe Winans considered Headley for her recording label, but Headley decided to go with RCA Records. From the beginning, Headley's Christian faith guided what she would and would not sing on the pop-soul CD. "Because of my spirituality and everything I stand for and want to stand for, image is very important to me," she told *LA Focus*. "I can't tell you how many fights I had with A&R and everybody just about the songs. People bringing songs in and me saying 'I can't sing that.' There was one time somebody brought me a song and I was standing in the studio in tears, because it was one of those songs. It had sexual innuendos that were terribly uncomfortable for me. I didn't want to come across as the diva because it was a new world to me." Eventually, she won out and her debut CD, *This Is Who I Am*, was sophisticated and intelligent. The first single, "He Is," was about both God and her fiancé, and she closed the project with the God-inspired ballad, "If It Wasn't for Your Love." The album was propelled to gold status by the No. 1 urban AC single "I Wish I Wasn't." While some see a secular music career as incompatible with a Christian lifestyle, Headley is grateful to God for her secular success. "Mercy is God not giving us what we deserve, and grace is him giving us what we don't deserve," she told *LA Focus*. "This whole journey is grace, miraculous grace. It's not anything I deserve. I have not been a saint. I have not praised or prayed to him enough and yet he's given me these amazing blessings. I should be happy just living. That's grace enough."

Helen Robinson Youth Chorus

BORN JANUARY 31, 1915, in New Orleans, Helen Robinson organized the Helen Robinson Youth Chorus in 1951 as a way to constructively occupy the leisure time of her seven children and other youths in their neighborhood on Chicago's South Side. They began rehearsing in the parlor of Robinson's home at 32nd Street and Wentworth Avenue as they honed their harmonies. As they began singing around the Windy City, Robinson began to meet vital contacts such as Lorenza Brown Porter, a member of the Argo Singers. Down the road, Porter introduced Robinson to Vee-Jay Records co-founder Calvin Carter, who recorded several Chicago-based groups on his label, such as the Staple Singers and Pookie Hudson & the Spaniels. In September 1956, the group stepped into Universal Studios to record their first sessions, which included the songs "Time Is Winding Up" and "Dwelling in Beulah Land." With Vee-Jay behind them, the group began appearing on bills with national artists and traveling for out-of-state concerts. Vee-Jay only released one single before the group was unceremoniously dropped from the roster.

The choir moved on to Church Records where they recorded the single "Be Still and Know." From there, they recorded several songs for Specialty Records, but none of them were released at the time. It would be 1962 before the group's music was in Mom & Pop shops again. That year they recorded *Reflections from Heaven* on Ollie Lafayette and Margaret Aikens's Mag-Oll label. Robinson's daughter, Jeanette, was the choir's lead vocalist at the time, and she put a distinctive stamp on "Thy Grace Is Sufficient for Me" and "The Only Hope We Have," which have become obscure gospel classics.

Ironically, Mag-Oll's success with the choir prompted Vee-Jay to lure them back into the studio to record the LP *The Heart of Gospel* in 1964. Jeanette's fantastic leads captured the heart of Rev. James Cleveland, who tried to get her to join his ensemble, and a talent scout even offered her $1,000 to go pop, but she stuck with her mother and kept singing with the group. By 1967, the group had signed on to R&B label Atlantic Records, the same year that Aretha Franklin did. Their LP *Joy* featured the single "I'm Happy with Jesus." The album was reissued on Atlantic's Cotillion imprint in 1972 during a time when the label boasted gospel artists such as Myrna Summers and Marion Williams who was being produced by Roberta Flack at the time). The group ceased recording at that point but continued to perform intermittently in the Chicago area through the 1970s. Helen Robinson died of breast cancer on June 17, 1993, and Jeanette continues to keep her mother's name alive through the group she conducts, the Helen Robinson Scholarship Chorus.

Hellen Hollins Singers

THEIR NAME ISN'T AS familiar as it once was, but their signature tune "I Don't Know What You Came to Do" lives on. Once known as the Roberts Family Singers, they gained fame as the Hellen Hollins Singers in the late 1960s. Hollins was born circa 1940 and was a child when she joined the family group in 1948. They performed regularly, but without fanfare until 1967 when they signed a contract with Peacock Records. Hollins's husband, Milton Hollins, Sr. (November 15, 1936–April 15, 1991), wrote their biggest hit, "I Came to Praise Him," which was an instant gospel smash. They were never able to capture a hit as big as that tune. In 1975, they joined Hob Records. That year, they released the *Following Jesus* LP and were nominated as best gospel group of the year by *Ebony* magazine. In 1982, they recorded *He Gave It to Me* for Savoy Records, and their last known project was 1988's *Still Able* on Messiah Records. In 1991, "I Came to Praise Him" was reborn. The R&B trio Tony! Toni! Tone! sampled the song in "House Party II (I Don't Know What You Came to Do)." The song was featured on the soundtrack of the Kid 'N Play film *House Party II*. It reached the R&B Top 20 and the pop Top 50.

R.J. Helton

HELTON'S CLAIM TO FAME was Fox Television's wildly successful *American Idol* series in 2002, but he used that platform to launch a gospel career. The Nicaraguan native was born on May 17, 1981. As a baby he was adopted by an American couple who named him Richard Jason Helton and raised him in Cummings, Georgia. "I began singing when I was three years old," he says. "I would hear songs and memorize them and keep singing them around the house. My mother would freak out about me singing. One time at church I was very young and I got up in front of everyone to sing 'Jesus Loves Me' and I started laughing. It was very funny." He sang in church all of his life and grew up enjoying Christian music artists such as Plus One and Jars of Clay.

His big break came when he heard of auditions for the Fox Television talent contest series *American Idol* in May 2002. He made it to Los Angeles, but was voted off the show early and came back as a wild card. His performance of Stevie Wonder's "Lately" won the judges over and he advanced to the top ten finalists. Though he has a pleasant, smooth vocal, he was criticized by the judges for having a somewhat stiff and wooden stage presence. A well-mannered, humble

Christian, these qualities were often ridiculed in the press. When he was voted off the show as the sixth person to be eliminated from the competition, an *Entertainment Weekly* scribe wrote, "I'm sure there are a few prayer-loving teens who are weeping their eyes out, but the rest of us know what Simon knew all along: This guy was barely good enough to be a boy-band understudy." Aside from the grand prize winner Kelly Clarkson, Justin Guarnini, and Tamyra Gray, Helton was the only other top ten finalist to earn a record deal within a year of the show. He signed to Gospo Centric Records and released the CD *Real Life* in 2004. Musically, it was an uneven album, devoid of the hooks and catchy tunes that make pop music popular. It peaked at No. 14 on the CCM Top 40 album chart and quickly fell from sight. However, there were real-life stories behind the songs.

"I was sexually abused when I was seven by a family friend," Helton told the *Baltimore Sun* in March 2004. "I kind of put it away and didn't deal with it until recently. It takes a lot of time to heal from this, and I wrote 'Delicate Child' as part of the healing process—it took a year and a half for me to write the song. I wanted to be able to confront him, but he died recently and I never was able to…. I've already had lots of letters from people saying the song changed their lives and [they] dealt with their own issues because of the song."

Barbara Hendricks

OPERA SOPRANO Barbara Hendricks was born November 20, 1948, in Stephens, Arkansas. She earned a Bachelors degree in mathematics and chemistry from the University of Nebraska, but eventually furthered her musical training at the Juilliard School of Music in New York. She made her American debut in the San Francisco Opera. In 1977, Hendricks moved to Europe and currently holds Swedish citizenship. In 2004, she was awarded an honorary doctorate by Liege University in Belgium. A decade before, she received the Legion of Honor from French President Francois Mitterand.

RECOMMENDED RECORDINGS: Hendricks has recorded two stellar gospel albums. *Barbara Hendricks Sings Spir-*

ituals with Dimitri Alexeev (Angel/EMI, 1984) includes songs such as "Talk About a Child That Do Love Jesus" and "Fix Me, Jesus." Although her readings are often stoic and lack a knowing passion, Hendricks does technically superior work on *Give Me Jesus* (EMI, 1999), which boasts 21 tracks such as "My Lord, What a Mornin'" and "My God Is So High."

Gerard Henry

BET'S HOTTEST YOUNG gospel ambassador is Gerard Henry (aka Brother Gerard), who has hosted the network's Sunday morning television series *Lift Every Voice* since 1999. He was born January 22, 1972, in Manhattan, New York, to a postal carrier and a nurse. "I always wanted to be an actor," Henry says. As a teenager, he acted in a local television after-school special entitled *Second Best.* After graduating from a Teaneck, New Jersey, high school, Henry majored in film at the University of Maryland. After earning his degree, Henry was selective about what film work he would take since he had become a Christian. "Back in 1988 I made a commitment to the Lord," he says. "The love I was searching for was in Christ. That led me to God." It also led him to an internship at Black Entertainment Television (BET). He worked his way up to a job in business affairs. While there, he submitted an idea for a weekly gospel video program to BET executive Jeff Lee. In spite of Henry's youth and lack of experience, Lee liked the idea and saw Henry's potential. He green-lighted the show. "It wasn't exactly how I envisioned it," Henry says now. "I wanted it to have both black and white artists so that we could build a bridge between those two cultures within the church." Alas, BET decided to focus solely on black gospel artists. The show launched in 1999 as a half-hour program where Henry interviewed artists in between playing their latest video. A 2003 episode of Vickie Winans's 50th birthday party celebration remains the top-rated program in the show's history with a viewing audience of over 800,000. In the future, Henry would like to branch out into radio and other avenues of Christian entertainment. "The whole acting thing is still in me," he says. Henry's *Voices of Inspiration* book of quotes from Christian celebrities was a bestseller in 2005.

Jake Hess

A FOUR-TIME GRAMMY winner who sang with a number of significant Southern gospel quartets and was Elvis Presley's favorite male vocalist, Hess was known for songs such as "Who Am I?" "Wouldn't Take Nothin' for My Journey Now," and "Brighten the Corner Where You Are." He also sang at the funerals of both Elvis Presley (1977) and Hank Williams (1953). Born December 24, 1927, in Limestone County, Alabama, Hess was the youngest of 12 children. He always sang in church, and at the age of five, he and his brother sang in a group. At 14, he joined the Haleyville Melody Boys and at 16, he left home to sing with the John Daniel Quartet. He later sang with the Sunny South Quartet and the Original Melody Masters before joining the Statesmen Quartet in 1948. The group was known for taking the traditional Southern gospel sound, multi-part harmonies, and embellishing it all with touches of ragtime and jazz to make gospel more appealing to youth. Elvis Presley often attended Statesmen concerts and cited Hess as a major vocal influence on his musical style. Elvis biographer Peter Guralnick told the *Washington Post* that Presley wanted to emulate the voices of Hess and Roy Hamilton. "They were such virtuosos," Guralnick said. "Each had a voice that Elvis never felt he could fully emulate. What he did seek to do was to emulate the feeling they had in their singing."

In 1963, Hess formed the Imperials quartet, which set the stage for the forthcoming contemporary Christian music scene with its liberal use of drums and electric guitars. Their ascent would coincide with the counterculture movement of the late 1960s. The group backed Presley on a number of his gospel sessions including his 1967 LP *How Great Thou Art*, which also featured the No. 1 hit "Crying in the Chapel." During this period, Hess recorded several solo projects and won three consecutive sacred music Grammys between 1968 and 1970.

Hess fluctuated between singing with groups and solo pursuits thereafter. He collaborated with country icons such as Tammy Wynette, Hank Snow, and Connie Smith. He also recorded a hymns CD with former pro football star Terry Bradshaw. In 1981, Hess and other Southern gospel stars formed the Masters V and won a Grammy for their LP *The Masters V*. In 1991, he reformed the Statesmen Quartet, but chronic health problems forced him to retire in 1993. Bill Gaither coaxed him out of retirement during that period to perform in his hugely successful homecoming concerts," which featured several gospel stars sitting around a piano and singing songs in campfire style. In the late 1980s, he received SESAC's Lifetime Achievement award and was inducted into the Gospel Music Hall of Fame. Hess suffered a heart attack in December 2003 and his health progressively worsened. He died on January 4, 2004, at a hospital in Opelika, Alabama.

Howard Hewett

FANS OF 1980S SOUL MUSIC will recall Howard Hewett as the matinee-idol handsome lead vocalist on the trio Shalamar's biggest hits such as "Second Time Around" and "A Night to Remember." Hewett then launched a moderately successful solo career that netted such Top Ten hits as "I'm for Real," "Show Me," and the forgettable "Strange Relationship." However, over the last decade, Hewett has become more outspoken about his Christian faith and begun to record gospel music.

He was born October 1, 1955, in Akron, Ohio. His mother was a gospel music promoter who'd bring the Pilgrim Jubilees, James Cleveland, and the Five Blind Boys into the city for concerts. At the age of 11, Hewett became lead singer of the Hewett Family gospel group. Around age 14, he went into R&B. He played the bass for several local groups, but now says, "I wanted to sing more than anything," so he dropped the bass. Eventually, Hewett made his way to Los Angeles and joined the R&B trio Shalamar with Jody Watley and Jeffrey Daniels circa 1980. For the next few years, the group turned out a string of bestselling pop-soul hits such as "Second Time Around," "This Is for the Lover in You," and "A Night to Remember." In 1985, Hewett went solo and developed an image as a romantic crooner with soul charters like "Strange Relationship," "I Can't Tell You Why," and "I'm for Real."

One of the songs Hewett is best known for is "Say Amen" from his LP *I Commit to Love*. A surprise hit, the stirring gospel ballad reached No. 54 on the R&B singles chart in 1987. "The tune was straight from the Lord," Hewett told *Totally Gospel* in 1987. "While on a plane going to my wife's folks in Florida, I was listening to a rough track of the tune. This is when the Lord gave me the lyrics. A lady that was sitting next to me must have thought that I was crazy. She just didn't know the Lord was dealing with me, as the tears streamed down my face."

Hewett always fought with his record label, Elektra, to include one or two gospel songs on his R&B albums. Hewett says, "They said it didn't fit the image of a sex symbol for me to sing gospel songs." Still, he managed to place tracks such as "I Will Always Lift Up Jesus," "He's Not Ashamed of Me," and "I'll Let Everybody Know " on the remaining albums of his contract. Hewett, who continues to sing both R&B and gospel, finally was able to produce an entire gospel CD, *The Journey*, in 2001. The project reached the Top 40 gospel chart in 2001.

Vy Higgensen

PRODUCER AND PLAYWRIGHT Violet Higgensen brought the gospel musical *Mama, I Want to Sing* to life off-Broadway in the 1980s. Born in the Bronx to a strict Barbadian preacher and his wife, Higgensen wasn't allowed to hear secular music in her household. Her older sister, Doris Troy, left home and became a pop star with songs such as "Just One Look" in 1963. Higgensen launched a career as a secular DJ at WBLS radio in New York. In the early 1980s, she wrote a play based on her sister's life. *Mama, I Want to Sing* opened in March 1983 at Harlem's Heckscher Theater and ran for 1,500 performances—one of the longest off-Broadway production runs in theater history. The show then made several worldwide tours. Troy played her own mother in the show from 1984 to 1998. The show made Higgensen and her husband and business partner, Ken Wydro, wealthy and led to other productions such as *Mama, I Want to Sing II*, *Let the Music Play Gospel*, and *Born to Sing*. Over the years, celebrities such as Chaka Khan, CeCe Winans, Shirley Caesar, Deniece Williams, and others have appeared in Higgensen's productions.

Fairest Hill

A MOTIVATIONAL SPEAKER who moonlights as a gospel vocalist, Fairest Hill is the son of '70s gospel star Tessie Hill. He and his twin sister, Ferrell, were born October 29, 1959, in Detroit. They grew up near the infamous Brewster Projects where many Motown artists were reared. "I lived in a neighborhood where the rats were so big they beat up the cats and dogs," he's said. His father, Lonnie Bozy Hill, was pastor of the Original Church of God in Christ (COGIC). When Hill was a teenager, his father was involved in a car accident that left him in a vegetative state. His mother put her career aside and nursed him until his death. Hill took a job at a hospital to help the family pay bills while he attended the Detroit College of Business. He planned on becoming a CPA, but music was still in his blood. Hill and nine other friends formed an a cappella group, the Followers of Christ. They all attended Rhema Bible Training Center in Tulsa, Oklahoma, and performed together for a good decade. Soul star D.J. Rogers produced their only national LP, *Taking Back What the Devil Stole*, for Hope Song/Benson Records in 1983. Their music was a precursor to the music Take 6 would create by the end of the decade.

The group split over creative differences in 1989, and Hill threw himself into Youth on the Move, a ministry he had launched in 1986. Using examples from his own childhood, Hill began to speak in the public school system about self-esteem and professional dreams. He now speaks to student groups 250 days a year with his motivational messages. However, he hasn't left music behind. He's recorded a half dozen albums over the years for a number of small independent labels. His best is arguably 2000's *Full Circle*, which appeared on Insync Records. With his smooth tenor, Hill delivered a polished, classic, soul-styled, easy-listening gospel CD. Gospel radio jumped on the mellow ballad "Remember What Your Mama Said," and "Step Away," a motivational rap, had the infectious lilt of the best coffeehouse poetry readings. "They lack motivation," Hill has said of his young audience. "There's only one Dairy Queen in some of these small cities I go to. There's nothing to do but smoke and drink. The kids kill each other because they're frustrated and there's nothing else to do. I

go to a lot of places where others won't go because there's no money there. It's good to go to the big concert halls, but everybody's not going to go there to hear what you have to say. I'm marketing myself to the places that John P. Kee won't go and to the places that can't afford to get Kirk Franklin."

Kim Hill

WHAT THE THINKING man's singer-songwriter-guitarist Joni Mitchell was to folk-rock music in the 1960s and early '70s, singer-songwriter-guitarist Kim Hill was to Christian music in the early '90s. Born December 30, 1963, in Starksville, Mississippi, and raised in Memphis, the Ole Miss alumnus recorded her self-titled CD debut in 1988 for Reunion Records. With her warm, mannish alto (reminiscent of Anne Murray's laid-back vocal style), Hill scored two instant No. 1 Christian radio singles with "Faithful" and "Psalm 1." *Cash Box* magazine hailed her as the Best New Artist of 1989. Hill continued to gain an audience with her subsequent CDs, and then she surprised her fans by recording a secular country-pop album of relationship songs entitled *So Far, So Good* for Reunion Records. The rocking single "Janie's Gone Fishin" was a minor country hit in 1994, but the next year, Hill was back in the church fold recording CCM music again. Her biggest struggle has been ending a turbulent ten-year marriage. "What I thought would be the end of me, my life as I know it, my ministry, everything," she once said. "God has turned my ashes into beauty and my mourning into dancing. I had to learn that God hates divorce, but he does not hate divorced people. What Satan meant to destroy me, God has used to minister to hurting people. He has turned my misery into my ministry."

Lauryn Hill

THE 1998 CD *The Miseducation of Lauryn Hill* was bought by more than 12 million people and catapulted Lauryn Hill into stratospheric worldwide fame. It was considered a landmark hip-hop concept album that fused issues of politics, old-school soul, spirituality, and Caribbean influences with everyday stories. It showed the promise of a major artist emerging, but eight years later, Hill still hasn't recorded the once-highly anticipated sophomore CD. Furthermore, her critics have seen her embrace of faith as a distraction rather than a blessing. Born May 25, 1975, in South Orange, New Jersey, she was always attracted to the entertainment world. She had a bit role in the soap opera *As the World Turns*, which led to a bigger role in the Whoopi Goldberg film *Sister Act II*. One of the highlights of the film was Hill's passionate duet of "His Eye Is on the Sparrow" with singer Tanya Blount. While a Columbia University student, she formed the Fugees with Wyclef Jean and Pras. Their greatest success came with 1996's socially conscious rap CD *The Score*, which sold over 17 million copies behind the smash single "Killing Me Softly with His Song."

After riding that wave of success, which heralded Wyclef Jean as the group's mastermind, Hill was intent to show that she was just as gifted as her former beau. She then offered up *The Miseducation*, which won five of the eleven Grammys it was nominated for at the 1999 ceremony. The album featured several subtle double-entendre spiritual messages, such as the song about her son, "To Zion," which received some gospel radio play. Other songs echo faith while focusing on earthy matters, such as "Lost Ones," "Forgive Them Father," and "Final Hour." Unfortunately, musicians who worked on the album sued Hill, claiming that she took full credit for the project in which they also made significant contributions. Hill and Columbia Records settled with the musicians and never admitted any wrongdoing. Meanwhile, Hill did prove to be a fine producer on her own as she produced Aretha Franklin's 1998 smash "A Rose Is Still a Rose" and CeCe Winans's island groove, "On That Day," a tune that creatively spoke of the Rapture. Bishop Paul Morton has since covered the song.

In 2001, Hill returned with *MTV Unplugged No. 2.0*. Most music critics don't even look at it as a regular Hill album since it is so different from her debut and not what they anticipated. The two-CD acoustic set reflected Hill's growing interest in religion (due to her relationship with sage Brother Anthony). She played a simple style of guitar, and many of the 22 tracks spoke to some real or abstract element of faith, from "Oh

Jerusalem" to "I Gotta Find Peace of Mind." *Billboard* magazine's Melinda Newman called it "a fascinating glimpse into the mind of an artist who is so clearly still inside her own drama that she can't see her way out yet." Some of the drama included reports of Hill distancing herself from the Hollywood aspect of her career and seeking a more enlightened approach to music creation. Because of her new attitude, Hill reportedly turned down roles in films such as *Charlie's Angels* (Lucy Liu got the role instead) and Matt Damon's *The Bourne Identity*. Hill also dropped out of Oprah Winfrey's *Beloved* film when she became pregnant with one of her four children. Furthermore, Hill (who was already distrustful of the media) allegedly demanded that media outlets pay her for interviews during that period. *One World* magazine was given an interview quote of $10,000. There were no takers.

All of these rumors fueled speculation that Hill was in emotional turmoil. In December 2003, while playing at a papal-sponsored concert in Rome, she launched into a blistering tirade against priests who abuse children. While many sympathized with her statements, they felt it wasn't the time or place to make them. She was promptly escorted from the stage and left the country. Meanwhile, she's still rumored to be working on the follow-up album to *The Miseducation*. She did contribute the track "The Passion" to the 2004 CD *The Passion of the Christ*, an album of original songs inspired by the Mel Gibson film of the same name. "The film was a visual representation of what life is supposed to be for the people of God—a sinless man willingly gave himself up so that others might be saved," she said at the time. "I was inspired by the film and proud to contribute a song to this collection."

Tessie Hill

SHE CREATED ONE of the most popular gospel songs of the 1970s with the catchy "Great Things," but just as quickly as it rose, her star faded and her great talent was never fully exploited. Born October 8, 1934, in Monroe, Georgia, Hill was eight when her family moved to Detroit where she sang in the Polk Street Church of God in Christ (COGIC). The minister of music sent a tape of the choir (with Hill handling lead vocals) to Savoy Records. They were signed and issued a number of moderately selling LPs. Eventually, Hill broke free and signed a solo deal with Peacock Records where she recorded a handful of fine albums that were contemporary for the time. With her powerful vocal punches, Hill was named Top Female Gospel Artist of the year by *Record World* magazine in 1978. "When my mother's career was about to take off, that's when daddy was in that car accident," says her son, Fairest Hill. Tessie Hill brought her husband home and nursed him for two years until he died. "She gave up everything. Her record *He Keeps Doing Great Things* was doing well and she was in demand. She never got back on top again."

Professor James Earle Hines

BORN CIRCA 1916, Hines has been labeled by gospel historian Tony Heilbut as the first bona fide gospel superstar. In the liner notes to his CD *The Great Gospel Men*, Heilbut wrote of Hines, "When he performed, audiences could not contain themselves. Men and women ran into each other, people fell out of balconies. Ambulances were summoned; overwrought ecstatics collapsed. Male quartets began scuffling, trying to get similar responses. After such frenetic showmen as Hines or Brother Joe May, it became clear that gospel involved more than singing. If you didn't move the people out of their seats, into the aisles, and—ideally—leave them flat on their backs, you had not scored." Hines's talent was first recognized during the National Baptist Convention musicales. Later, he moved to Los Angeles where he began conducting the St. Paul Baptist Church Choir. Although his group performed simple harmonies, his dynamic use of his baritone on lead vocals gave their group a distinctive sound. Sallie Martin sang lead with them for a while before she formed her own group. The choir briefly recorded for Capitol Records where their rendition of "God Be with You" was a huge hit in 1947. Hines also trained the preteen Etta James, who became a child gospel prodigy under his tutelage and regularly sang on L.A. radio before moving to San Francisco in 1950. Later Hines formed a group called Professor J. Earle Hines and His Good Will Singers. They recorded songs such

as "Dig a Little Deeper" for Mr. R&B Records. Hines stopped performing in the 1950s and died September 5, 1960, in Cleveland, Ohio.

Bishop Al Hobbs

AS THE CHAIRMAN of the GMWA's Gospel Announcer's Guild, Al "The Bishop" Hobbs is one of the most powerful and influential figures in gospel radio. Born June 4, 1943, in Decatur, Alabama, Hobbs grew up in church. In the 1960s, Hobbs sang with Lucille Jones & the Traveling Notes, a Louisville, Kentucky–based group. He later made his way to Indianapolis as an announcer where he graced WTLC, a gospel radio station, with his sonorous baritone. In the 1980s, Hobbs opened Circle City Records and began to write music in earnest. Among his first projects was producing former R&B singer Laura Lee's second solo gospel LP *All Power* in 1984. Among the fine songs he wrote for that project were "I've Got My Mind Made Up" and "A Brand New Me." He and the Indianapolis Mass Choir had been recording albums since their 1980 *Live* LP on Savoy Records. Other albums and songs followed, including the 1982 hit "You Touched My Life." In 1992, Hobbs founded Aleho Records, which has issued several dozen CD projects. Among the hit recordings have been Sister Cantaloupe's comedy albums, Angela Spivey's various projects, and Mimi Redd's 1994 smash, "Order My Steps."

Darwin Hobbs

THEY CALL HIM the Luther Vandross of gospel and perhaps that's the reason his talents are not more appreciated in the genre. Die-hard gospel fans don't like mixing the secular and sacred. They don't want to think of Luther Vandross or someone imitating him when they listen to gospel. In spite of that, Hobbs is an awesome talent with a strong voice well suited toward the ballads that are Vandross's trademark.

Born in Cincinnati, Ohio, Hobbs was not raised in a churchgoing family. He was ten years old when his parents divorced and that singular event changed his life in many ways. After his mother's remarriage,

Hobbs and his five siblings were required to attend their stepfather's church, El-Bethel Baptist. It was there that Hobbs joined the children's choir and discovered his musical gift. "I opened my mouth and I could sing," he once said. He sang so well that the choir leader yanked him from that group and put him in the young adult choir. He began to sing throughout the city and studied formal classical music. At the age of 14, he dedicated his life to Christ and then decided to strictly become a gospel singer. He caught CeCe Winans on her "Alone in His Presence" tour in fall 1995. It proved life-changing for the robust singer. "During that time in my life I was sort of in a holding pattern, waiting for the timing of God with regard to my music," he's said. "I knew I didn't want this ordinary shallow ministry. Prior to CeCe's concert I had never experienced the glory of God mixed with such creativity and skill."

After the concert, Hobbs struck up a conversation with Winans's music director, Roger Ryan. The two stayed in touch and Ryan encouraged Hobbs to move to Nashville and jump-start his career. Hobbs and his wife, Traci, made the move in October 1996. Within a week of his relocation, Hobbs was getting session work as a background singer with artists such as CeCe Winans, Shirley Murdock, Bishop T.D. Jakes, Michael W. Smith, and Kathy Troccoli. Since that time, Hobbs has recorded on several artists' projects. In addition, he has recorded three CDs of his own for EMI Gospel. The best of those projects thus far is 2000's *Vertical*, a smooth album of reverential praise music with a sweet R&B backdrop. Although it was only nine tracks, they were all sonic masterpieces. Hobbs turned in a beautiful gospel rendition of Vandross's Quiet Storm staple "So Amazing" with the female quartet Virtue backing him. Disco queen Donna Summer gave a soft, sophisticated touch to their duet, "When I Look Up." The hallmark of the album was the funky soul duet with Michael McDonald, entitled "Everyday." Had EMI Gospel had an urban radio team, the song could have easily crossed over to mainstream urban radio. Hobbs's music has never received the embrace from gospel radio that it deserves and thus, he's still lacking that defining hit song. Until it arrives, Hobbs serves as a worship leader at Eddie Long's New Birth Missionary Baptist Church in Atlanta, Georgia.

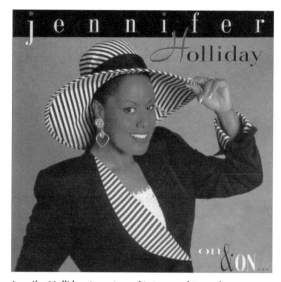

Jennifer Holliday / courtesy of Intersound Records

Jennifer Holliday

A BROADWAY LEGEND with a gospel wail to be reckoned with, Jennifer Holliday was born October 19, 1960, in Houston, Texas. The daughter of a preacher and his schoolteacher wife, Holliday grew up in church. After her father, Rev. A.L. Holliday, abandoned his wife and their three children, her mother, Jennie, took on another job to maintain a comfortable lifestyle for her family. Wanting to help her mother gave Holliday the tenaciousness to push her way through school and graduate. She made her way to Broadway in Vinette Carroll's smash stage production *Your Arms Too Short to Box with God*. In 1982, Holliday won the role of Effie in the original Broadway musical *Dream Girls*. The show was based on the trials and tribulations of the Motown trio the Supremes. Holliday brought the house down every night with her passionate performance of the song "And I Am Telling You I'm Not Going," for which she won a Grammy award.

Holliday became an overnight star and netted a recording deal with Geffen Records where she recorded a string of hit R&B albums that featured gospel songs such as Edwin Hawkins's "Give Us This Day," "Shine Your Light," and the 1985 Grammy-winner "Come Sunday." With such an earth-quaking vocal presence, fans often wondered when she'd finally record a gospel CD. That happened in 1994 when she released *On and On* on the Intersound Records label. "Because I do secular music," she told this writer at the time, "I thought a contemporary gospel album wouldn't make sense because the new way gospel is now, some of it, if you change the words, it could easily be secular. So, this is traditional. What prompted me to do it was the death of Thomas Whitfield…. I just got so sad [after he died]. Of course, I miss him as a person, but I used to always tell him we were going to get a chance to work on something together. I couldn't work on it before because when you say you want to do something gospel the secular record companies go, 'Please!' …Richard Smallwood had an album and he wanted me to sing, but my record company wouldn't let me. Edwin Hawkins, he's a friend of mine, the same thing…. I had to sing at Thomas's funeral and that was one of the hardest things I had ever done. All the time I was singing, I was wondering if the dead really can hear because of all those times he wanted me to sing one of his songs and I couldn't, and here he is dead and I have to sing in front of him. It did something to me and I wanted to do the project after that. I was very regretful that I didn't get to do that one thing with Thomas Whitfield. He asked me so many times." The *On and On* CD featured a song Whitfield wrote for Holliday, entitled "I Love You Just the Same." The album reached No. 10 on the *Billboard* gospel album sales chart in 1995 and has since become a collector's item.

Brenda Holloway

ONE OF MOTOWN'S most talented vocalists in the 1960s, Brenda Holloway provided the label with three solid classics that still receive daily airplay on oldies radio stations worldwide. In spite of that fact, Holloway was also one of Motown's best-kept secrets. Many people know her songs, but few recall her name. Born June 24, 1946, in Atascadero, California, she grew up in the notorious Watts neighborhood where she learned to play violin and sang in church with her sister Patrice. She made her recording debut at the age of 14 when she backed Patrice on her debut single "The Del Viking." Soon, the sisters were working as session singers. In 1964, Holloway sang

Mary Wells's "My Guy" at a Los Angeles radio convention that Berry Gordy was attending. He was struck by her smoldering vocals and signed her to a recording contract. Her first single was "Every Little Bit Hurts," which earned her an opening slot on the Beatles 1965 American tour. Other hits followed such as "Operator," "When I'm Gone," and "I'll Always Love You." In spite of her success, Holloway felt ignored by the label and didn't feel she was offered the prime songs. She then began to write her own songs. One of her first was "You've Made Me So Very Happy," which was a minor hit for her, but a huge hit for Blood, Sweat & Tears in 1968. It has since been recorded by dozens of other artists ranging from Rosemary Clooney to Gloria Estefan. That same year, Motown released Holloway's sophomore LP, but it went nowhere because she stopped promoting it upon her retirement from the music industry. She had retained her strong religious values and felt she needed to leave the industry in order to retain them. She married a minister and led a quiet life away from the spotlight until 1980 when she resurfaced with a brilliant gospel LP entitled *Brand New* on Fantasy Records. In recent years, Holloway has returned to the concert stage with sporadic but acclaimed performances. She also recorded a second Fantasy LP, *It's a Woman's World*, a pop collection, in 1999.

Holmes Brothers

VIRTUALLY UNKNOWN to the gospel world, the Holmes Brothers have made their living by completely spreading the Good News on the blues circuit. Sherman and Wendell Holmes were raised in Christchurch, Virginia, where they both sang in a church choir. Sherman studied clarinet and piano before taking up the bass, while Wendell learned trumpet, organ, and guitar. Sherman studied at Virginia State University briefly before quitting school in 1959 and heading to New York for a gig with singer Jimmy Jones. After Wendell finished high school, he joined his brother and they played in various bands before forming the Sevilles in 1963 (not to be confused with the Los Angeles–based group that had a Hot 100 pop hit with "Charlena" in 1961). The group lasted three years and backed John Lee Hooker among others. After the group disbanded, Sherman, Wendell, and their drummer, Popsy Dixon, continued to play in a variety of bands before they formally created the Holmes Brothers in 1979.

From the start, the group's sound was a mélange of deep blues and hard gospel. Matched with their three-part harmony and Americana music grooves, they created a sound unique to themselves. One of their favorite venues to play at was Dan Lynch's, a New York club where they met future pop star Joan Osborne when she was a struggling performer. It is also where they met producer Andy Breslau, who eventually brought the group to Rounder Records.

Since their debut CD on the label, *In the Spirit*, the group always includes one blatant gospel song on their projects. When rock star Peter Gabriel caught wind of their talents, he borrowed them from Rounder long enough to record their first entire gospel CD on his Real World Records, 1992's stunning *Jubilation*. It should be noted that it's Gabriel and his label that reintroduced Clarence Fountain and the Five Blind Boys to the music industry in 2001. That association has made them one of the biggest artists on the Americana concert circuit today. In 1997, the Holmes Brothers released their *Promised Land* CD, which features an awesome rendition of "I Surrender All." That same year, they hit the road with Joan Osborne, who was opening for Bob Dylan.

After signing with Alligator in 2001, the group's debut was *Speaking in Tongues*, a critically acclaimed CD of rootsy gospel that Osborne produced. Among the standout tracks are "Jesus Got His Hook in Me" and "King Jesus Will Roll All Burdens Away." The project led to appearances on *The Late Show with David Letterman* and rave reviews in *Rolling Stone*, *Newsweek*, and *USA Today*. In 2003, the brothers recorded Blind Willie Johnson's gospel classic "You're Gonna Need Somebody on Your Bond" for the *Crossing Jordan* TV soundtrack and on the Sister Rosetta Tharpe tribute CD *Shout Sister Shout*. Although the group's blues-rock approach to gospel doesn't fit modern-day gospel music formats, the saints don't know what they are missing. "Straight-out, raw and real soul shouts, Jimmy Reed–influenced country blues, and juke-joint salvation," a *Boston Globe* review stated. "The Holmes Brothers can get down or raise crowds to sweaty bliss with soul-power."

Frank Hooker

FOR A BRIEF MOMENT in the 1980s, Frank Hooker was the gospel world's answer to MC Hammer. His pop-gospel rap "Hear the Word" made some noise in 1987, but the world wasn't quite ready for a bespectacled 40 year old rapping about Jesus. Born Frank Ruppert Hooker in 1946, in the 1970s he formed Frank Hooker and the Positive People. They recorded for Panorama, a label distributed by RCA Records. Between 1979 and 1981, they placed four songs on the Hot 100 R&B singles chart. The biggest of these, "I Wanna Know Your Name," reached No. 40 on that survey in spring 1980. Hooker later moved into the Christian market and recorded *Hear the Word* for Command Records in 1987. The album coasted to No. 30 on the gospel album sales chart.

Israel Houghton

THIS SINGER-GUITARIST had a rough entrance into the world. At the time, his white mother was 17 years old and his absentee father was black. Living in the conservative town of Waterloo, Iowa, her parents gave her two options when they learned she'd be giving birth to a black child: either have an abortion or leave. With no man and no family by her side, she moved to San Diego to have her child. In her eighth month, she was walking down a street when a woman accosted her, witnessing to her about Christ. Israel's mother became a Christian and began to read the Bible daily. It seemed to her that the name Israel was on virtually every page, so she named her child Israel when he was born in 1971. Growing up in church, Houghton gravitated to music and in 1989 he became a full-time church musician. For a time, he was a member of Fred Hammond's Radicals for Christ Choir. In 1995, Houghton and his wife, Meleasa, founded New Breed Ministries. He released his first CD, *Whisper It Loud*, for Cadence Communications (distributed by Warner Bros. Records) in 1997, but it failed to connect with radio. After signing with Integrity Music, Houghton's praise and worship finally gave him a great radio success story. His 2002 CD *Real* and 2004's *Live from Another Planet* put him on the map with songs such as "There's a Lifting of

Israel Houghton/ photo by DRE Photography / Dr. D. 2004

Hands" and "Again I Say Rejoice." "I'm often asked by skeptics why I'm as passionate about worshipping God as I am," he says. "The answer is simple for me. In this age of disposable relationships, I could easily have become a statistic and, at best, a distant memory of a youthful mistake. Instead, a sovereign God rescued my mother and me and gave us hope, a future and a testimony of the providence of God. The very least I can do is enter into his gates with thanksgiving, his courts with a passionate praise, and eventually bow before his throne in intimate worship."

Cissy Houston

HER STELLAR HISTORY has been overshadowed by the fact that she is also superstar Whitney Houston's mother. But long before the world knew Whitney, they knew her mom's voice backing up Elvis Presley, Aretha Franklin, and countless other performers with her thunderous gospel ensembles. Along the way, she also recorded a good armful of LPs that never became great hits but were nonetheless significant pieces of soul and

gospel music. Born Emily Drinkard on September 30, 1932, in Newark, New Jersey, Houston came from a family of six other siblings. Her mother died when she was nine years old, and her father raised the kids on his own. Houston and her brothers and sisters were always singing in the house when other neighborhood kids were outside playing. Houston began singing at the New Hope Baptist Church when she was five years old and later directed the church's choir. In 1957, she formed the Drinkard Four, a group comprised of herself, her adopted cousin Judy Clay, and her older sisters Marie and Lee. They eventually evolved into the Drinkard Singers and performed at the Newport Jazz Festival in 1957. Backed by New Jersey's Back Home Choir, they made their debut with Verve Records that year on the LP *The Drinkard Singers and the Back Home Choir at Newport.* The following year they became one of the first gospel groups signed to RCA Records when their LP *A Joyful Noise* appeared.

By 1960, the Drinkards had disbanded and Houston has been cited in magazine articles as having formed a group called the Group (featuring her teenage nieces Dionne and Dee Dee Warwick) that was created specifically to do session work as background singers. However, all of the women involved give conflicting accounts on the evolution of their dynamic backing group. Warwick says that she and her sister Dee Dee formed the Gospelaires along with Houston, Clay, and Doris Troy. "We were a gospel group and we all came out of my church choir," Dionne says. "We weren't a recording group per se. We did the oohs, the ahs, and the occasional yea yeas." Troy told writer David Nathan that the group consisted of herself, Dee Dee, and Dionne, and that they only wanted to record gospel until she nudged them into secular music. Dionne says that their first secular backup gig came as an accident. "We were in the right place at the right time," she's said. "Someone asked us if we could do it, we did it, and one thing led to another." That first secular gig was backing Ronnie Hawkins on his tunes "Forty Days" and "Mary Lou."

The evolution of the group became further convoluted. Dionne left after Burt Bacharach discovered her when the group was doing a session for the Drifters. He secured a recording deal for her at Scepter Records. Dee Dee formed her own backup group called Dee Dee's

Girls, although she occasionally still performed with Houston, who formed the Sweet Inspirations. Troy and Clay went on to solo careers, only to get back with Dee Dee and Houston at various points in the 1960s. Houston's Sweet Inspirations became one of the top backing groups of the 1960s, wailing behind Barbra Streisand, Connie Francis, Neil Diamond, and literally hundreds of other recording sessions. The Sweet Inspirations were noted for their distinctive, full-bodied gospel approach to backing vocals. They weren't the innocuous Anita Kerr–type of backing group. Their vocals were as much a part of the recordings as the lead vocalist was. Listen to Aretha Franklin's "Chain of Fools" or "Ain't No Way" (that's Houston doing the high notes on the latter), and it's easy to hear how important their vocals were to the overall feel of the records.

Eventually, Houston's group recorded for Atlantic/ Stax records, scoring with a secular treatment of the Staple Singers' gospel "Why Am I Treated So Bad?" and toured with Aretha Franklin and Elvis Presley. By 1970, Houston had left the group and signed with Commonwealth Records. Her eponymous album of cover songs tanked. Moreover, the label went bankrupt and sold Houston's contract to Janus Records, which did an equally poor job of promoting her. In 1972, she recorded the first version of Gladys Knight and the Pips' "Midnight Train to Georgia," which was then entitled "Midnight Plane to Houston." It failed too, and then it was on to Private I Records. In 1978, Houston starred in Carmen Moore's opera *Gospel Muse*, conducted by the renowned Seiji Ozawa, and she recorded her biggest hit to date. In the thick of the disco era, she recorded "Think It Over," a scorching dance number that featured her bustling gospel vocals over a love-me-or-leave-me tracks. It reached No. 5 on the *Billboard* disco singles chart and No. 32 on the R&B single chart. However, the success wasn't duplicated. "You can become quite discouraged in this business," she once said. "But I took a lot when I first started and I will not let anything crush me. I've seen too many people crushed."

As the 1980s kicked in, Houston didn't appear on as many recordings and by the close of the decade, her daughter Whitney had become a superstar. People who had never bothered to look at LP credits were referencing Houston as Whitney's mom. Houston received

more press during that period than she ever had in her life. She appeared in Whitney's video "The Greatest Love of All" and recorded "I Know Him So Well" with her on Whitney's second LP. By the end of the 1990s, Houston had recorded two acclaimed traditional gospel CDs for House of Blues Records. Although her alto has become a little wobbly and her vibrato unpredictable, Houston still packed a lot of punch on tracks such as her gospelization of Marvin Gaye's "How Sweet It Is to Be Loved by You," which is nothing less than a masterpiece. Neither 1996's *Face to Face* or 1998's *He Leadeth Me* won gospel radio programmers over. She's received very little affection from that community, but both albums won Houston the first Grammy awards of her career for best Traditional Soul Gospel Album.

Whitney Houston

ONE OF THE LEADING pop superstars of the 1990s, Whitney Houston was born August 9, 1963, in Newark, New Jersey. Her mother, Cissy, was a founding member of the Drinkard Singers—a '50s-era gospel group that made some noise in the festival circuit and among integrated, middle-class audiences. Raised in church, Whitney was always singing gospel as a child. Because her mother was a background vocalist for many secular artists such as Elvis Presley, Houston also grew up enjoying pop music. As a teenager, she was briefly a background singer herself, backing her mother's big club hit "Think It Over," Chaka Khan's "Clouds," and Herbie Mann's *Mellow* album. In 1981, she convened a label auction to see who would offer her the best deal. Clive Davis of Arista Records made the most attractive offer and was most interested in grooming Houston. While Davis strategized, Houston worked as a Wilhelmina Agency model and had acting roles on TV sitcoms such as *Gimme a Break* and *Silver Spoons*. Her eponymous 1985 debut LP sold over ten million copies on the strength of hits like "How Will I Know" and "Saving All My Love for You."

From the beginning, Houston's style fused the fire of her gospel roots with a sophisticated pop polish that made her music universal. After meeting crossover gospel stars BeBe and CeCe Winans at an NAACP ceremony, they became fast friends with Houston. CeCe Winans once told *Jet* magazine that Houston knew BeBe and CeCe's songs better than they did. Houston recorded "Hold Up the Light" with them on their 1987 LP *Heaven*. When Houston recorded the music for the soundtrack to *The Bodyguard* in 1993, she allowed BeBe Winans and Cedric Caldwell to arrange the flip side to the "I'll Always Love You" single. That track was called "Jesus Loves Me." The single went on to become one of the biggest-selling singles in music history, holding the No. 1 spot on *Billboard*'s pop charts for 14 weeks as the album sold 15 million copies. Continuing to aid the Winans clan, Houston's Angel Way management company managed the careers of Angie and Debbie Winans. In 1995, Houston and CeCe teamed for "Count on Me" from the *Waiting to Exhale* soundtrack. They also did a gospelized rendition of "Bridge over Troubled Water" at that year's *VH1 Honors* telecast that became one of the most requested videos of the year. Houston has often spoken of her faith and desire to record gospel music. That opportunity finally came when she recorded the soundtrack to her 1996 film *The Preacher's Wife*. Backed by the Georgia Mass Choir, Houston turned in rousing, traditional church performances on gospel standards such as Dottie Rambo's "I Go to the Rock" and Richard Smallwood's "I Love the Lord."

Larry Howard

GOSPEL'S LEADING blues guitarist in the 1980s, Larry Donald Howard was born March 27, 1950. A classically trained musician, one of his first gigs was backing jazz legend Count Basie at a University of Miami music camp when Howard was 13 years old. When he returned home, he joined a neighborhood band and taught himself the guitar. He then formed the Southern rock band Grinderswitch, circa 1967. They earned a recording deal with Capricorn Records in 1972. Grinderswitch opened for top Southern rock and blues bands of the period such as the Marshall Tucker Band, B.B. King, the Charlie Daniels Band, Papa John Creach, Lynyrd Skynyrd, and the Allman Brothers.

Howard spent much of his time getting high on drugs. He tried to unhook himself from drugs by quit-

ting Grinderswitch in 1979 and moving back to Florida where he worked in his father's construction business. However, the drugs were just as prevalent there and Howard fell deeper into that abyss. On August 20, 1980—his wife Peggy's birthday—she had enough. They had a big fight, she left, and he overdosed. "The next thing I knew I was in the emergency room watching all those medical people working around my body," Howard says. "Suddenly, I saw them all stop and walk away. In that instant I remember crying out to God, 'If you'll put me back in that body, I'll do whatever you want me to do for the rest of my life.' The next instant I was on the examining table, completely sober and wide awake." When he was released, Howard found a church home and reconciled with his wife.

In 1984, Refuge Records owner Bob MacKenzie heard Howard's song "I Gave Jesus My Blues" and wanted to record an album on him. The debut LP *Shot* was released in 1986 and received a bit of Christian airplay, but was mostly embraced by secular blues radio stations looking for Sunday morning music that still fit their format. Over the years, Howard has recorded half a dozen other fine gospel blues projects, such as *Sanctified Blues*. In recent years, he's done a great deal of outreach to prisons and owns his own Omega Arts recording studio in Macon, Georgia.

Mark S. Hubbard and the United Voices for Christ

ONE OF THE MANY energetic young choir conductors who have taken a page from the Ricky Dillard-O'landa Draper school of conducting, Hubbard was born October 15, 1966, in Chicago. He accepted Christ as his savior when he was five years old and joined the Greater Holy Temple Missionary Baptist Church where his mother, Louarraine, was a bishop. He soon became a choir conductor there. Prompted by his zeal to spread the word, Hubbard organized the United Voices of Christ Choir in 1985. He started with three members and in time it grew to a membership of a hundred. In 1992, they recorded their first CD, *Trust in Jesus*, for Tyscot Records. It reached No. 28 on the *Billboard* gospel sales chart. Since 1998, Hubbard has served on the music staff of Bishop Larry Trotter's Sweet Holy Spirit Gospel Baptist Church in Chicago.

Lavine Hudson

SHE WAS POISED to become Christian music's answer to Whitney Houston in the late 1980s, but England's Lavine Hudson never made it that far. One of six children born to Pastor Austin and Elaine Hudson in the 1960s, she first sang in church at the age of seven. She perfected her gift singing in her father's COGIC congregation in Stockwell, England. Hudson grew up on the music of Aretha Franklin, the Clark Sisters, and Andrae Crouch. As a teenager, she sang with both the COGIC Mass Choir and the London Community Gospel Choir. After her studies at the College of Further Education, she worked at Lloyd's Bank.

She was rejected by the London School of Music for sounding too black. "[They said] 'You can sing, but we don't like the lyrics, you sound too black, you should think white if you want to succeed,'" she told *Totally Gospel* in 1988. "I just replied, 'I won't dilute the lyrics for nobody. I am black, and if I'm going to succeed, it will be because the Lord will have it be so and not because I had to think white.'" In 1983, Hudson moved to Boston where she worshipped at the COGIC Good Shepherd. She didn't have all of the funds for her tuition, so her church family raised money for her to enroll at Berklee College of Music.

After her education, Hudson returned to England where she became a featured vocalist on the London gospel television program, *People Get Ready*. Soon, she was courted by Virgin Records, who liked her just as she was and signed her to a recording deal. Her first LP *Intervention* was issued in 1988. The title song, a pop tune, reached the R&B Hot 100 singles chart, and the album managed to place at No. 19 on the Top 40 album sales chart. The album featured a duet with Derrick Brinkley and tracks produced by Twinkie Clark, Marvin Winans, and Nicholas Brown. In spite of the album's respectable sales, it was far from the platinum party Virgin Records was hoping to throw for Hudson. Her follow-up album, *Between Two Worlds*, was released in 1991. A stronger, more enjoyable album than the previous one,

the CD didn't chart at all and Hudson was eventually released from her contract. According to Marcia Dixon of Britain's *The Voice* newspaper, regrettably, Hudson has retired from the music business. "In the wake of Loose Ends' US success in the mid-'80s, UK record companies started scouting for young black talent," says Charles Waring, a music critic for Britain's *Mojo* magazine. "The two most significant young female singers to emerge were Mica Paris and Lavine Hudson. Mica had a rich, earthy tone... and was steeped in gospel music... as was Lavine, but Lavine had a purer tone and a greater gift for melismatic cadences ... In fact, for a time, she was regarded as the UK's answer to Aretha Franklin.... Her voice possessed a great elasticity and facility to communicate emotion."

George Huff

WITH HIS BIG SMILE and old-school vocal chops, George Huff wowed viewers of Fox TV's *American Idol* with his down-home renditions of Otis Redding's "Dock of the Bay" and the Temptations' "Ain't Too Proud to Beg" in 2004. Huff was born November 4, 1980, in New Orleans, where he was raised by his mother, Althea Washington. He began singing at the age of five and

George Huff / photo by Robert Shanklin, 2004

eventually sang in the choir at Greater St. Stephen's Full Gospel Baptist Church. After graduating from Sarah T. Reed High School, Huff enrolled as a music education major at the University of Oklahoma with the intent of becoming a teacher. While on campus, he sang in operas and the school gospel choir and worked as a cook in the university cafeteria. At the audition for *American Idol*, Huff was asked why he wanted to win the competition. He said, "I want to be an American Idol because I want to build homeless shelters all over the world, and I want people to be touched by my music, and I want to be rich!" He made it all the way to No. 5 on the show before he was voted off. However, his Christian testimony and raspy voice won him a recording deal with Word Records, the legendary gospel label. He is scheduled to release a mainstream inspirational CD in 2005.

Cathy Hughes

SHE'S ONE OF THE MOST powerful women in the history of radio, period, and she's certainly the biggest mogul black radio has ever known. Cathy Hughes's Radio One network owns 69 radio stations in 22 major urban markets throughout the United States. According to *Fortune Small Business* magazine, Radio One is the seventh largest US radio network. Hughes was born April 22, 1947, in Omaha, Nebraska. Her mother, Helen Jones Woods, was a trombonist for the International Sweethearts of Rhythm all-female jazz orchestra. Her father, Williams Woods, was Nebraska's first black CPA and an entrepreneur. In addition, Hughes's maternal grandfather, Laurence Jones, founded the Piney Woods Country Life School, a well-regarded black boarding school.

As a teenager, Hughes integrated the Duchesne Academy, an elite Catholic girls school in Omaha. She had a brief marriage at the age of 17 that produced her only child, Alfred Liggins, Jr. While in Omaha, she began her career in radio by volunteering with a black radio station and then working on a Ford Foundation project that encouraged minority ownership. In 1971, she migrated to Washington to be near a man she was dating. She then found work in Howard University's Communications Department where she was mentored by the dean, Tony Brown.

In 1973, Hughes moved over to the university's radio station, WHUR, where she served as general sales manager for five years. While there, Hughes developed the Quiet Storm radio format. "It was the forerunner of what is now called adult contemporary—mood music, romantic love songs, ballads—and it became the No. 1 urban format in the history of black radio," she told *Fortune Small Business* (FSB) magazine in September 2004. "I tried to get Howard University to license it, and they refused. So I decided to leave." In 1978, Hughes became general manager at WYCB, the nation's first contemporary black gospel radio station. "My career made a turn," she told *Out Front* magazine in 1998. "The management of the station and I had a conflict, and they suggested I buy my own station and that was the beginning of this path."

Hughes and her then-husband, Dewey Hughes, a Washington television pioneer, took advantage of the FCC's Distress Sale Policy, which allowed the agency to sell financially distressed radio stations to women and minorities for a third of the price. They bought the low wattage WOL radio station in Washington, DC, for $950,000 in 1980 with a $100,000 inheritance from her father and various business loans. There was no money to hire a drive-time radio announcer, so Hughes became the host of *The Cathy Hughes Morning Show* from 6:00 to 10:00 A.M. On that talk program, Hughes interviewed music personalities and community leaders like she was talking to her next-door neighbor. She used slang and spoke in a manner that her listeners understood. The show commanded tremendous respect, particularly in the working class black community it sat in at 4th and H Streets in Northeast Washington. Politicians sought an interview spot on the show during political campaigns and Hughes would welcome them. However, when politicians such as former DC mayors Marion Barry and Sharon Pratt Kelly didn't fulfill their campaign promises, Hughes blasted them on the air. She once accused Barry of pimping the city and called Kelly a party girl. "We're not going for the okey-doke," she'd snap and fire up her rowdy radio audience, which was distrustful of political leadership anyway. When her program finished for the day, the rest of the schedule was filled with oldies-but-goodies announcers such as a former cab driver named More Better Man, radio legend

Moon Man, and Joe Hartwell. On Sundays, there was paid religious programming in the morning, and the charismatically flamboyant Ray Edwards created an exciting Sunday afternoon gospel music play list.

However, AM radio was dying a quick death and the Hugheses could not attract enough advertising revenue to keep the station afloat. "I lost my marriage because of the company," Hughes told *FSB*. "My husband said, 'We'll never pay this back [the loans]. This is a tunnel with no light at the end, let's just walk.' I couldn't do that to my lenders. I had $1.5 million of other people's money; I would not have been able to live with myself." When Dewey Hughes demanded that Hughes move to Los Angeles with him or face divorce, she called what she thought was a bluff and stayed with the radio station. They later divorced, though they remained friends.

"I lost everything," Hughes told *FSB*. "I stood in my window one day as they repossessed my car. In 1982, I ended up living in the radio station, sleeping in a sleeping bag for 18 months…. I was literally washing up in the bathroom for the radio station. I cooked on a hot plate. It was crazy, because some days I might forget a personal item, and the staff would be embarrassed. The receptionist would say, 'You left your bra in the ladies' room.'"

Even when the bills were many and the receivables were few, Hughes didn't hide from collectors. "I made partial payments on every one of my bills each and every month," she told *FSB*. "It built up my credibility with lenders. I tell new entrepreneurs, don't hide from the phone calls and the letters. The minute I knew that one of my lenders or one of my creditors was on the phone, I immediately stopped what I was doing and went and had a discussion with that person." Black radio had a rough time attracting major radio sponsors, so Hughes saved the station by going to local businesses. "How does Cadillac know I sold 100 cars for them?" she asked *FSB*. "When the only black dealership in DC advertised with me, I would sponsor clinics for women, to show them how to change a flat tire or change oil. And sometimes 200 women would show up, and the dealer knew I sent them."

In 1985, Hughes's son, Alfred Liggins, Jr., a Wharton Business School graduate, joined the staff as an ad-

vertising salesman. He proved to be an encouragement to his mother. At one point when she was frustrated with the whole process, he pushed her to buy WMMJ, an FM station that would allow them to attract national advertising revenue that could keep both stations alive. Liggins worked hard at building his mother's business, and Hughes appointed him president and CEO in 1989. Since that time, the dynamic duo has formed Radio One and aggressively bought one low-ranking station after another and turned every one of them around and made them profitable. In 1999, Radio One went public on the American Stock Exchange and raised an instant $75 million to buy more stations. Along the way, it has been important for Hughes to have a gospel radio station in virtually every city. In fact, Radio One has created some of the first FM gospel frequencies in the country when they turned former secular stations such as WPZE 97.5 (Atlanta), WNNL 103.9 (Raleigh), and WJYD 106.3 (Columbus, Ohio), among others, into gospel stations that are killing their gospel competitors in ratings and advertising.

In 2003, Radio One launched the TV One television network, which features classic black television shows and new programming such as *B. Smith with Style*, Donna Richardson's gospel aerobics program, and *The Gospel of Music with Jeff Majors*. Hughes attributes her success to her faith in God. "Believe in God first and then believe in yourself," she says. "There will be nothing the two of you can't achieve."

June Hunt

TELEVISION HAS Dr. Phil and Christian radio has June Hunt. Her syndicated, late night radio program *Hope in the Night* provides therapeutic advice with Christian solutions to a national radio audience. In spite of her humble, folksy radio persona, Hunt comes from a wealthy family. Her father, H.L. Hunt, was a billionaire oil tycoon, one of America's richest men in the 1940s. Hunt had already sired ten children by two prior wives before having four more with his last wife (and June's mother), Ruth Ray Wright, who was once a secretary at Hunt Oil Company.

June Hunt was born December 31, 1944, in Dallas. Her father was a scrappy, hard-nosed character. A fifth grade dropout who won his fortune on shrewd speculations and wildcatting, Hunt lived frugally. He cut his own hair and drove his own car, which he parked several blocks from his own office building to avoid paying parking meter fees. His one major extravagance was his primary home in Dallas, a larger replica of George Washington's Mount Vernon estate. On the political front, Hunt was fiercely anti-communist and often lobbied politicians during the McCarthy era, though he didn't donate money to their war chests. June Hunt has often written and spoken of her father's abusive nature and the emotional scars it caused in her life.

June Hunt became a Christian as a young adult and began to sing Christian music. Over the years, she's toured on USO shows and sung at Billy Graham crusades. Upon her father's death in November 1974, June Hunt came into a significant inheritance. A year later, Al Bell signed Hunt to a recording contract at Stax Records' Gospel Truth subsidiary. With Hunt's pristine vocal range (similar in style to that of Julie Andrews) it seemed to be an odd choice, considering that Stax was the home of gutbucket blues artists such as Otis Redding and Rufus Thomas. After years of reckless spending, Stax was nearing bankruptcy. According to Stax historian Rob Bowman's book *Soulsville U.S.A.*, many familiar with the situation suggested that Bell only signed Hunt to get access to her money and save Stax Records with an infusion of cash. Bell denied the charges and said that he appreciated Hunt's songwriting skills. Whatever the case, Stax was out of business before any albums by June Hunt were released.

In the intervening years, Hunt was actively involved in youth ministries and public speaking. In 1986, she launched her first radio program, a daily devotional show called *Hope for the Heart*, which began on 23 stations and eventually spread to nearly 200 stations. In 1994, she began the counseling radio program *Hope in the Night*, also heard on more than 100 radio stations worldwide. Like June, her mother was also a strong Christian. She died of cancer in 2002. The following year, June Hunt was diagnosed with breast cancer but has survived and triumphed over the illness.

RECOMMENDED RECORDING: Hunt has recorded three CDs for her ministry: *Whisper of My Heart*, *Songs of Surrender*, and *Hymns of Hope*. Backed with a polished, symphonic tableau, Hunt's music tends to be covers of great church hymns such as "I Surrender All" and "Great Is Thy Faithfulness." Her pure, clean voice soars over these refined renditions.

Stephen Hurd

ONE OF THE MANY young leaders in the burgeoning praise and worship movement in black gospel music, Stephen Hurd was born in Washington, DC, in 1968. A church boy all of his life, Hurd graduated from the Duke Ellington School of the Arts and attended Howard University. He was consecrated as a minister in 1988 and began working in Washington area church vocal groups and choirs. In 1999, he formed Corporate Worship, a vocal group specializing in praise music. Over the next couple of years, they released the custom CDs *Corporate Worship* and *In the Overflow*. In 2004, Hurd enjoyed a national hit when the CD *A Call to Worship* reached the Top 40 gospel chart on the strength of the rumba-styled "Undignified Praise."

Norman Hutchins

IN A TIME WHEN most aspiring gospel artists are seeking to carbon copy the style and sounds of contemporary gospel performers such as Kirk Franklin and Mary Mary, Norman Hutchins is a throwback to the old style of traditional gospel music. A relatively young man (born in 1964), he specializes in bringing that old-time religion to a new generation of gospel fans. Hutchins became a youth minister at the age of 8 and earned enough money—up to $100 a night—to support his mother and 11 siblings. After getting married at the age of 19, he spent four years as pastor of the New Hope Church of God in Christ in Delaware, Pennsylvania. Then he felt led to move to Los Angeles where he held a series of menial jobs until he found a home for his vibrant voice in the West Angeles COGIC choir.

He sang on their Sparrow Records album, *Saints in Praise Vol. 2*, which ascended to No. 5 on the *Billboard* gospel chart in 1991. Soon after, the album's success led Sparrow Records to offer Hutchins a recording deal that was launched with the album.

When Hutchins joined the choir, his pastor named him director of social services for the 9,000-member church. His job was to serve the needy with food, clothing, and shelter. He routinely exceeded his $12,000 a month budget "Many times," he told *YSB* (Young Sisters and Brothers) magazine in 1994. "But you got a mother who walks in with seven children who've been sleeping under a bridge—you mean to tell me I'm supposed to go home to my wife and my three kids, feel good and go to sleep? I'm sorry. We've got to find a home for this family. Everybody wants to minister to people spiritually," Hutchins told the magazine. "They want to preach to you. They want to prophesy to you. But there's a time when people need natural ministry. 'My car needs fixing, my rent needs to be paid, food needs to be put on the table.' Things like that help people make it from point A to point B."

After Hutchins's second Sparrow album, *Don't Stop Praying*, failed to ignite, he was dropped from the label and went without a recording deal until he joined James Roberson's JDI records in 1999. His debut album *Battlefield* zoomed to No. 9 on *Billboard*'s gospel chart and sold well over 150,000 units. Ironically, the song that sold the album, "Battlefield," was recorded on his self-titled debut album for Sparrow but never went anywhere until he rerecorded it for JDI. He followed with a Christmas project entitled *Emmanuel*, which leaped to No. 6 on the gospel chart. Hutchins continued his run with a 2002 release, *Nobody but You*, which reached No. 7 on the gospel chart and sold over 50,000 units according to SoundScan.

Imperial Gospel Singers

FOUNDED BY Anna Smallwood in Philadelphia, the group recorded traditional gospel sides such as "Lazarus," "My Father's House," and "My Change Will Come" for Savoy Records in 1958–1959.

Maggie Ingram

BORN MAGGIE LEE DIXON on July 4, 1930, in Douglas, Georgia, she was the fourth of six children. Her parents were evangelists who instilled a deep faith and work ethic in their children. They didn't attend school regularly, but they regularly worked the cotton and tobacco fields to help their parents bring in revenue. Ingram always sang in church and her powerful voice suggested to her family that a career in music lay ahead. At the age of 16, she married a sharecropper named Thomas Ingram and they soon had five children. The family eventually moved to Miami, Florida, where Thomas became a pastor at Wells Temple COGIC. The wife and kids sang to enhance Thomas's sermons, and invitations to sing at other churches started to arrive. However, they didn't become a professional group until after Maggie and Thomas divorced. She took the five kids and moved to Richmond, Virginia, in 1961. They began to sing as a family group (the boys played instruments and the girls sang), Maggie Ingram and the Ingramettes, to bring in extra money. By 1964, the group was signed to Nashboro Records and they had released their first big hit "Time Is Winding Up." Possessing a big, dry wail of a voice, Ingram was always considered a vocal fire-starter. Just like kindling wood, she warms up slowly before blazing into a song and breaking out into a holy dance that usually sends her or her captive audiences prancing through the church aisles. In the 1980s, the group signed to Gospearl Records and recorded the *Miami Riot* LP, which reached No. 33 on the *Billboard* gospel album chart in 1988.

The Inspirational Choir of the Pentecostal First-Born Church of the Living God

AFTER THE LONDON Community Gospel Choir appeared on Trevor Philip's British TV show *Black on Black* in the 1980s, the response was so positive that the show solicited other gospel choirs to send in demos of their music. The Inspirational Choir was chosen to sing on an Easter episode of the program circa 1983. They were spotted by the British pop band Madness, who picked them to sing on the smash pop song "Wings of a Dove" from the 1984 LP *Keep Moving* on Stiff/Geffen Records. It was the first time that a British gospel choir reached No. 2 on the UK's *Music Weekly* pop singles chart. The Inspirational Choir later cut 12-inch singles on songs such as "Clean Heart" and "Pick Me Up."

RECOMMENDED RECORDING: *Gospel Songs* (Spectrum, 1994) features their takes on gospel classics such as "I've Got a Robe" and "Amazing Grace."

Jackson Family

A BLEND OF contemporary and traditional gospel, this young group of siblings sought to do in gospel what the Jackson 5 had done in pop music but never made it that far. Comprised of three girls (Marla, Monica, and Michele) and three boys (Monty, Matham, and Maury), the Jacksons were born to Luther Ray, a demolition man, and his wife, Joy. The kids always sang around their Lancaster, California, home. The eldest child, Monty, sang with the Heritage Singers from 1983 to 1987 before he lassoed his siblings together to form a gospel group. They landed a recording deal with Word Records where they recorded two smooth R&B-styled gospel albums, *Family* (1990) and *Make Us One* (1992), largely composed and produced by members of the group. Gospel radio programmers never embraced their sound or their tracks, and the Jackson Family vanished as quickly as they appeared.

Don Jackson

THE FOUNDER OF Central City Productions, which presents the annual Stellar awards gospel music ceremony, Don Jackson was born September 18, 1943, in Chicago. At Marshall High School, he played on the school's championship basketball team. He attended Northwestern University on a basketball scholarship and graduated in 1965 with a degree in communications. He then worked as an advertising executive at RR Donnelley and later for WVON radio. In 1970, Jackson founded Central City Marketing to promote and de-velop television programs geared toward the African-American audience. In 1985, Jackson launched the Stellar awards in partnership with WGN TV in Chicago to create a new avenue to expose black gospel music artists. In the first years of the show, it featured a diverse mix of presenters such as Oprah Winfrey and performers such as the Barrett Sisters. As the years progressed, the show was syndicated and began to feature more secular entertainment personalities in order to attract better national ratings. For instance, there was widespread grumbling from gospel artists that pop star Brandy received the Most Notable Achievement award from the Stellars for her work with her parents' philanthropic children's organization in 2001, when many gospel veterans had not been honored for their works. There had been complaints about other secular artists receiving performance, hosting, and presenter time on the program that is not afforded to gospel artists on the secular side. In recent years, the program has increased its ratings while also keeping flagship gospel artists the focus of the program.

Rev. Jesse Jackson

THROUGHOUT THE 1980S, Rev. Jesse Jackson was regarded by many to be America's unofficial spokesperson for black America. However, long before that period—when he ran two respectable campaigns for president of the United States in 1984 and 1988—Jackson had a substantial musical history. Born October 8, 1941, in Greenville, South Carolina, Jackson's parents, Noah Robinson and Helen Burns, never married. He took on the last name of his stepfather, Charles Jackson. Jackson's stepbrother, Chuck Jackson (not the '60s pop singer), went on to become a successful songwriter for Aretha Franklin and Natalie Cole in the 1970s. In 1959, Jesse Jackson went to the University of Illinois on an athletic scholarship but left because of campus racism. During this period, he became active in the civil rights struggle. He organized protest marches and sit-ins for the Council on Racial Equality (CORE). After graduating from the Chicago Theological Seminary, Jackson was ordained as a Baptist minister in 1968. In the late 1960s, Jackson launched Operation Breadbasket to strong-arm (via boycotts and negative publicity) government and private enterprise to hire blacks. To raise money awareness, Jackson had regular broadcasts on WVON radio in Chicago and he recruited artists such as the Staple Singers to sing on the programs. Chicago disc jockey E. Rodney Jones introduced Jackson to Stax Records President Al Bell, who became a close partner in Jackson's cause. Jackson recorded the *I Am Somebody* and *Pushing On* motivational sermonette LPs for Stax's Respect imprint. Jackson also was an emcee at the legendary Wattstax concert in 1972, often said to be black America's Woodstock.

Earlier, in 1971, Jackson founded People United to Save Humanity (PUSH) as an alternative to the policies of the Southern Christian Leadership Conference (SCLC) and other civil rights organizations. Jackson also had the celebrity endorsements of friends such as Roberta Flack, Nancy Wilson, and Aretha Franklin to bring credence to the good work he was doing through PUSH. He formed the PUSH Choir, which recorded albums such as 1979's *Push for Excellence* (Myrrh Records), featuring performances by the Hawkins Family and Andrae Crouch. In the 1980s, Jackson turned the leadership of PUSH over to Rev. Willie Barrow. In 1984, Jackson ran for president and drew blacks and white liberals to his campaign. After being chastised by Jewish groups for referring to New York as "hymietown" on the stump, Jackson gave a compelling unity speech at that year's Democratic convention. With his thick, garbled Southern accent, the preacher gave what most critics consider one of the best speeches of the 20th century. It was so popular that Constellation Records released it as the LP *Our Time Has Come* later that year. Jackson also spoke throughout Aretha Franklin's 1987 LP *One Lord, One Faith, One Baptism.*

In 1986, Jackson founded the Rainbow Coalition, a political organization, and geared up for one more presidential bid in 1998. Although he didn't win an office, he stayed in the news. Whether it was bringing a hostage home to the US or criticizing Hollywood for its treatment of black performers, Jackson always stirs the strongest of emotions even among blacks. Singer Millie Jackson dedicated her "Phuck U Symphony" to Jackson after he criticized black artists for performing in South Africa before the end of apartheid. In an-

other case, Jackson led a boycott of the Oscars and accused Hollywood of not hiring enough blacks in 1996. Actress Whoopi Goldberg, who hosted the ceremony that year, was outraged. "I thought it was bullshit," she told *Vibe* magazine in February 1997. "…There were more black people on that stage that night than had been there the whole entire time. [Jesse should] get in the fucking neighborhoods and say, 'Until the studios start putting out product we're involved with, we ain't gonna go see the movies,' but don't come out at the end of the line and say 'We're gonna beat you up!' Don't tell me there's a problem—I knowww! I got the scars. I got the scars right from you, putting down my work. And motherfucker, where are you now? Where's the follow-up? Fuck him!"

Mahalia Jackson

UNIVERSALLY RECOGNIZED as the mother of black gospel music, Mahalia Jackson remains gospel's best-known ambassador decades after her death. With her rousing contralto, Jackson's signature recordings of "I Will Move On Up a Little Higher," "Didn't It Rain," and "In the Upper Room," among a dozen others, are the definitive recordings that demonstrate how authentic gospel music should be sung.

She was born on October 26, 1911, in segregated New Orleans. Her father, Johnny, a preacher and a barber, already had a set of children other than the ones he shared with Jackson's mother, Charity. Jackson's parents were never married to each other, so she was sent to live with her mother's sister Duke after her mother died. Duke ran her levee shack like a dictatorship. She was tough and no-nonsense. Though Jackson's mother forbid her to listen to blues music, Duke wasn't as vigilant in that regard. Jackson listened to Bessie Smith and Ma Rainey tunes on the sly. Duke kept her busy with so many domestic chores that Jackson was not able to keep up in school. She dropped out of the eighth grade and took a job as a washerwoman in a laundry. Jackson wasn't even allowed much playtime. A tomboy, she loved softball, playing with snakes, and wading in the swamps to catch crawfish. Some of the vindictiveness and personality flaws Jackson would be accused of later in life could be traced to her youth. Once when she needed a new pair of shoes, she showed up at the barbershop and asked her father for some. He said that he couldn't afford any new shoes, but the biggest insult was that her step-siblings were there taunting her about asking their father for shoes. In addition, Johnny's pet name for Jackson was Chocolate because of her deep skin tone. In later life, Jackson was known to be jealous of light-skinned black women.

However, the church tempered much of Jackson's rough edges. "In our house we shifted everything down from Friday night through Sunday," she told the *Saturday Evening Post* in December 1959. "You either were a Christian and acted like it or you were put out of the church." Her aunt's shack was next door to a Sanctified Church. That rocking music had a profound effect on how Jackson would later approach her music. "They gave their songs a real powerful beat, a rhythm that came from way back in slavery times and probably before that from Africa," she told the *Saturday Evening Post*. "We Baptists sang real sweet and we did beautiful things with our hymns and anthems, but when those Sanctified people lit into 'I'm So Glad Jesus Lifted Me' they sang out with a real jubilant expression. I believe the blues and that rock 'n' roll stuff, all of them got their beat from the Sanctified Church people."

After Jackson's uncle went to Chicago to work as a bricklayer, he returned and regaled the family with fascinating stories of how blacks and whites shopped in the same stores and how everything was integrated in Chicago. He talked of how blacks up North were better paid than blacks down South. Chicago began to sound like the Promised Land to Jackson. "I began to have this longing desire to go up to Chicago and see for myself," she told *Life* magazine in November 1954. "The last thing at night before I went to sleep I would whisper to my pillow that someday the sun was going to shine down on me in Chicago." In December 1928, Jackson took her first train ride and was headed to Chicago with the notion of becoming a nurse. Once there, she stayed with her Aunt Alice. Everything her uncle told her appeared to be true and inspired Jackson to set some goals for herself. She loved blues music and picture shows but soon gave them up after her grandfather came to visit. She pestered him to go with her to

Mahalia Jackson sheet music / courtesy of Margaret Aikens

a show during a heat wave. He went, had a stroke, and died. Jackson's aunt blamed her for his death and Jackson felt such guilt that she vowed to God that she would never have anything to do with blues music again.

She soon joined the Greater Salem Baptist Church Choir. After she sang a superlative solo of "Hand Me Down My Silver Trumpet, Gabriel," the director appointed her the choir's regular soloist. She also sang in a group comprised of the pastor's sons, the Johnson Brothers. Before Jackson could start nursing school, her Aunt Hannah fell ill with heart trouble, and Jackson had to take a job to help the family make ends meet. "There wasn't any money for school, and I had to go back to the washtubs and ironing boards and to do maid's work in hotels. I earned $7.50 this way," she told *Harper's* magazine in August 1956. After the Johnson Brothers disbanded, Jackson began to sing as a soloist with Evelyn Gay as her piano accompanist. She had also attended beauty school and earned enough money to open her own beauty salon in 1939. Before that, she had married Isaac Hockenhull in 1935. A Fisk University graduate, he was a chemist by trade but could only find work in the US Post Office. A member of the black bourgeoisie, Hockenhull found gospel music plebian. "He didn't like my songs," Jackson told the *Post*. "He thought gospel singing wasn't educated. He wanted me to take voice training, to become a [classical] gospel singer. He'd say, 'Why do you want to waste your wonderful voice on that stuff! It's not art!… We finally came apart over it. A man who marries a woman doesn't want her running around all over the country either—even for the Lord. But sometimes you feel something deep down inside you that has to come out—that's the way my gospel singing was for me. I felt I had to express it or be torn apart by it, and finally this feeling ended my marriage."

Meanwhile, Jackson was building a name throughout the country from her frequent trips with composer Thomas Dorsey. To introduce his songs and build an audience for them, Dorsey toured the country in the 1930s and took either Sallie Martin or Jackson along to demonstrate the songs. Dorsey's relationship with Martin was one of convenience. He didn't much care for her singing or her romantic overtures, but she was instrumental in organizing his business and helping him make money. However, Dorsey was enamored of Jackson's voice and wrote songs such as "Peace in the Valley" with her in mind.

In 1937, Jackson recorded her first song, "God's Gonna Separate the Wheat from the Tares," for Decca Records. It was, at best, a modest success and she was dropped from the label. In 1946, she received her second chance at a recording career when she recorded "He Knows My Heart" for Apollo Records. It was such a poor seller that Apollo considered dropping her as well. Producer Art Freeman pleaded Jackson's case to the white owner, Bess Berman, who didn't care for Jackson's sometimes-sarcastic remarks and intrepidness. Freeman pushed Jackson to record W. Herbert Brewster's "I Will Move On Up a Little Higher" in 1948. It was an immediate hit and eventually sold 2 million copies. A great deal of its success was due to its appeal to jazz and blues enthusiasts.

"Its slow syncopated rhythms caught the fancy of jazz fans," according to poet Langston Hughes, who "bought it not for religious reasons, but as a fine example of a new kind of rhythmical Negro singing. The gospel song began to reach a public for whom it was not intended at all." The church community was not amused. For every churchgoer who appreciated Jackson's music, there was one who felt she was promoting Satan's kingdom simply because the song appealed to those outside of the church. In addition, the more conservative churches frowned upon Jackson's unrestrained performances and her propensity for swinging her ample hips to her bluesy backbeats. "They were cold to it," Jackson told the *Post* about several black ministers. "They didn't like the hand clapping and the stomping, and they said we were bringing jazz into the church and it wasn't dignified. Once, one of the preachers got up in the pulpit and spoke out against me. I got right up too. I told him I was born to sing gospel music. Nobody had to teach me, I was serving God. I told him I was serving God. I told him I had been reading the Bible every day most of my life, and there was a psalm that said, 'Oh, clap your hands, all ye people!'"

Jackson's next single, "Dig a Little Deeper" sold a half million copies off the coattails of "I Will Move On Up a Little Higher." Soon Jackson was being offered $10,000 a week to sing in nightclubs. "I never had it, so I don't miss it," she'd always say. Writer Studs Terkel invited Jackson onto his CBS radio show in Chicago and became fast friends with her for the rest of her life. His promotion of Jackson via his radio program further exposed her to the white audience. On October 4, 1950, Jackson headlined a concert at New York's Carnegie Hall that Joe Bostic arranged for her. As her car pulled up two hours before show time, she wondered out loud where "all those people" were going. The line was wrapped around the building to see Jackson. She once said, "I have hopes that my singing will break down some of the hate and fear that divides the black and white people in this country." Indeed it did, for whites and blacks who rarely attended the same program piled in together to see Jackson.

In the early 1950s, Columbia Records had signed Jackson and her career went into orbit. Although she retained her longtime pianist, Mildred Falls, most of Jackson's music for the label lost a bit of the musical earthiness that caused Columbia to sign her in the first

Mahalia Jackson and Duke Ellington / Columbia Records publicity photo

place. Producers such as Mitch Miller, Percy Faith, Jack Halloran, and arranger Marty Paich put Jackson in front of white background singers and string orchestras. They were certainly the most sophisticated gospel recordings of the time and they appealed to white audiences in unprecedented numbers. Jackson experienced unparalleled success for a black performer during the period. She was as well known as America's leading female pop singers such as Dinah Shore or Jo Stafford, something that only black women such as Ella Fitzgerald or Lena Horne could relate to during the period. Whereas most black artists were thought of as singles artists, Jackson was an album artist. Columbia didn't push singles as much as they pushed whole albums on Jackson. Along with rerecording "I Will Move On Up a Little Higher," Jackson recorded several new hits for the label such as "In the Upper Room," "Didn't It Rain" and "He's Got the Whole World in His Hands," which hit the Hot 100 pop singles chart in 1958. Most of Jackson's recordings were met by mainstream press with ecstatic acclaim. The television shows that booked her were the No. 1 rated ones such as *The Ed Sullivan Show* or *The Tonight Show*. The magazines that profiled Jackson were *Time* or *Newsweek*. She enjoyed fame and prestige foreign to even the biggest R&B stars.

As Jackson's star ascended, her audience became increasingly white, as black churches could no longer afford her concert fees. By the end of her life, Jackson's audience would be predominantly white and international. Suddenly, the black world was often critical of Jackson. Black periodicals rushed out stories on Jackson's failure to keep a husband. They noted that she chose her career over her first husband. During her second marriage to Sigmund Galloway, a suave but out-of-work musician, Jackson lost over 100 pounds due to the emotional strain of the relationship. Galloway was a womanizer who allegedly beat Jackson on occasion. They fought constantly and ended up having a bitter divorce that cost Jackson $20,000 in legal fees. The black media ate it up and the mainstream press barely mentioned it. In the 1960s, Jackson opened a chain of restaurants, Mahalia Jackson's Chicken Supper Restaurants. The Kentucky Fried Chicken chain's motto was "finger licking good," but Jackson's catchphrase was "tongue licking good." When the restaurants closed, the black press seized the moment to point to Jackson's declining fortunes.

Meanwhile, Jackson's gospel friends often felt they got short shrift. As wealthy as she had become (she easily made $100,000 a year in the 1950s and even more thereafter), Jackson was not generous with her money. Evelyn Gay, who was Jackson's first regular pianist, stopped playing for her in part because Jackson paid her very little and sometimes not at all. In her memoirs, Aretha Franklin recounted a story of how she once sang on a program that Jackson sponsored in Chicago. At the end of the program, Jackson thanked her for coming and Franklin shyly asked about her payment. Jackson waved it off and said that she would talk to Franklin's father about it but never did. "I left Chicago with my heart broken," Franklin wrote. There were other times when Jackson humiliated her black friends in front of white people. "Robert Anderson told this story many times," says Evelyn Gay's brother Donald. "They were driving through the South and her Cadillac was stopped by the police. In the car was Mahalia's cousin Alan Clark, who was her road manager, Robert Anderson, and Edward Robinson. The policeman was suspicious of why a black woman was in such an expensive car with three men. He thought they were up to no good. When he asked Mahalia who she was and what she was doing with these men, she said in her saddest voice, 'Officer, my name is Mahalia Jackson and I'm a gospel singer.' So then the policemen asked who the men were and she said, 'Officer, these ain't no men, these is sissies.'"

An ardent Democrat and civil rights proponent, Jackson knew firsthand about racism. Not only had she grown up with it, but when she became wealthy and bought a home in an upper-class white neighborhood in Chicago, it touched off a minor race riot among whites who didn't want any black—no matter how famous or talented she was—living in their neighborhood. Jackson sang at the 1956 Democratic National Convention that nominated Adlai Stevenson to challenge incumbent President Dwight Eisenhower. When Stevenson lost his bid, Jackson held no grudges. She sang at the Eisenhower White House. She later sang for President Kennedy's inaugural ball as well. She was Martin Luther King, Jr.'s favorite singer and he would often recruit her to sing at his Freedom rallies. She was there at the famous March on Washington on August 28, 1963, where King gave his hallowed "I Have a Dream" speech. He had given the speech many times before at local rallies, but it had never been witnessed

on national television. On that hot summer day where 250,000 gathered near the steps of the Lincoln Memorial to lobby for a civil rights bill, King was winding down his comments. Jackson, who was sitting on the podium, shouted out, "Tell 'em about the dream, Martin," according to King biographer Taylor Branch. King then went on to give the rousing speech that is now as well-known as Lincoln's Gettysburg Address.

As time wore on, Jackson was so popular that Columbia executives thought Jackson could be even bigger if she sang blues or pop music. "Anybody that sings the blues is in a deep pit yelling for help and I'm simply not in that position," she once told *Life* magazine. Her only concessions to secular music were inspirational songs such as "Danny Boy" or "A Satisfied Mind." The mere idea that she would be lumped in with entertainers was anathema to Jackson, who also scoffed at the idea of gospel nightclubs like New York's Sweet Chariot and who didn't believe in gospel-pop music. "The gospel is good news and good tidings and not entertainment," she once told *Down Beat* magazine in a passionate discourse. "They have watched me for 35 years, come December, slave to bring the gospel into places it had never been— Constitution Hall, Carnegie Hall, and places like that. I never brought it down…. The Flamingo Hotel in Las Vegas offered me $25,000 a week to appear there. I turned down the offer…. Gospel singing has become commercial and big business…. I'm very ashamed of the name 'pop.' Gospel isn't pop."

Still, the pop music establishment was so enthralled with Jackson's powerful vocal power and success that they felt she should be recognized for her musical accomplishments. The National Academy of Recording Arts and Sciences (NARAS) created a gospel music category in its annual Grammy awards presentation so that they could specifically honor Jackson. The Best Gospel or Other Religious Recording slot was inaugurated in 1961 and Jackson won the award for her LP *Every Time I Feel the Spirit*. She won it again the following year for the album *Great Songs of Love and Faith*. In the late 1960s, Jackson's Christmas music sold like pop music. Her *Silent Night* LP reached No. 11 on the pop album sales chart in 1966, and her *Christmas with Mahalia* LP hit No. 2 on the same chart in 1969. The world had opened to Jackson as well. She toured

Europe several times to standing-room-only crowds in every city.

In spite of her continued popularity, Jackson was failing fast. She had suffered from back and heart problems since the 1950s and it was catching up with her. In addition, her personal life was a mess again. Her second husband had maneuvered his way back into her life but refused to sign a prenuptial agreement when they reconciled, causing her further emotional grief. As she was touring Germany in 1971, she collapsed and was rushed to the US Army Hospital for treatment of circulatory problems. She made it home to the US and said that she was feeling better. Over the next year, her health deteriorated further. For two days before her death on January 27, 1972, Jackson wandered in and out of consciousness until an intestinal obstruction combined with heart failure claimed her life.

There were extravagant funerals in both Chicago and New Orleans. Eight thousand people crammed into the former's Arie Crown Theater, with another 5,000 outside. President Nixon sent condolences, Rev. C.L. Franklin preached, and Aretha sang. Professor Thomas Dorsey, Coretta Scott King, and Chicago mayor Richard Daley were all there singing Jackson's praises. In the Crescent City, more than 65,000 people filed past Jackson's coffin. Her funeral service featured an exhausting performance by Bessie Griffin and eulogies from Lou Rawls and Dick Gregory, among others. Upon Jackson's death, a *Washington Post* editorial read, "Long before soul became a vogue word, Mahalia Jackson embodied it." Jackson's legacy lives on. In 1976, she was posthumously awarded a Grammy award for "How I Got Over" and was later the first gospel artist to receive a star on the Hollywood Walk of Fame.

RECOMMENDED RECORDING: *The Essential Mahalia Jackson* (Sony Legacy, 2004) is the most sensible choice for bargain shoppers, with 37 tracks including live renditions of "He's Got the Whole World in His Hands," "Didn't It Rain?" "Elijah Rock," and "How I Got Over." It also features her studio renditions of Duke Ellington's "Come Sunday," "In the Upper Room," and "Move On Up a Little Higher."

Jackson Southernaires

THIS GOSPEL QUARTET was known for country-style story songs such as "Teddy Bear" and "Thank You, Mama, for Praying for Me." The Mississippi-based group was formed in 1940 by producer Frank Crisler and originally consisted of Huey Williams, Roger Bryant, Jr., Maurice Surrell, James Burks, and Luther Jennings. They improved upon the quartet tradition by adding guitar, bass, and drums to their music. Although they performed live for years, they didn't sign their first recording deal until 1963. Their debut project *Too Late* on Songbird was an instant success and kept them popular. Other hits followed such as "Don't Look Down on a Man" and "Get Right Church" with ABC/Dunhill Records. However, "Teddy Bear" was the biggest hit. "'Teddy Bear' was an old Red Sovine song," Frank Williams told *Totally Gospel* in April 1988. "We heard it and liked it, but it really didn't ring a bell with us until almost the same incident happened to us during the CB radio craze. Afterwards, we thought the song would be great and recorded it. Believe it or not, we rehearsed, did the rhythm, lead, and background vocal tracks all on one take." Not only was the song one of the most-played gospel tracks of the year, but it also won a Grammy nomination in 1979. They received another Grammy nomination for "Thank You, Mama, for Praying for Me" in 1991. Though Frank Williams, the backbone of the group, died on March 22, 1993, they continue to perform and record for Malaco Records.

RECOMMENDED RECORDING: *Greatest Hits* (Malaco, 1995) features a new version of "Too Late" and all their best-known songs.

Nancey Jackson

A NEWARK, NEW JERSEY, native with a soulful wail, Jackson has supplemented her solo gospel career over the years as a background vocalist on Celine Dion's "That's the Way It Is" and R. Kelly's "I Believe I Can Fly." Jackson first sang "I Feel Like Pressing My Way On" at her pastor father's church, St. John's Methodist Episcopal Reformed. Later she sang with Bishop Jeff Banks and the

Revival Temple Mass Choir, as well as with Rev. Milton Brunson. Her friend Loris Holland gave a demo of Jackson's music to Raina Bundy, who ran Sony Records' gospel division, Harmony, at the time. Jackson made a little noise with her rousing, club-flavored debut "I'm Free" in 1997. "The worst part of 1998 for me was when I began to release new artists like Nancey Jackson," Bundy told *Gospel Industry Today* in December 1998. "Just fighting to keep the integrity of who she is, while getting her positioned to become established in the industry was difficult. It was also difficult going through staff changes in the middle of this launch. Our problems were more internal, getting the organization set up and getting the right kind of help." Furthermore, Jackson told GospelFlava.com in 1999, "I'm not crazy about the hype that goes along with being an artist…. A lot of folks seem to think that we're in competition. We're all on the same team. There's also little encouragement from the veterans. I'm willing to admit that I don't know everything. If there's something that I'm not doing, extend some knowledge."

Judy Jacobs

ONE OF THE MOST dynamic, young praise and worship artists working the church circuit these days is Judy Jacobs. She's made a name for herself through numerous TBN *Praise the Lord* TV appearances and singing for evangelists such as Benny Hinn. Bishop T.D. Jakes has even called her dramatic singing "preaching wrapped in song." The youngest of 12 children, Jacobs was born September 27, 1957, in Lumbarton, North Carolina. She was raised in church and started singing around the age of five. When she was eight, she and her sisters began to sing in churches as the Jacobs Sisters. After attending Lee University in Tennessee, she began to sing with the pop gospel group Danny Murray and New Harvest. She appeared on their LPs on recording labels such as Harmony and Spirit Son. In 1989, she went solo and opened shop as His Song Ministries. Jacobs is a vibrant performer who virtually acts out her songs. Her warm alto is basically a pop voice but with a soulful edge that comes across due to her high-energy delivery.

Evangelists on television and in arenas often have Jacobs minister before they speak because she emotionally stirs the audience like very few artists. Since 1994, Jacobs has recorded several CDs for the His Song label she and her husband, Jamie Tuttle, own. Among her best-known songs are "No God Like Jehovah" and the riveting "My Deliverer."

RECOMMENDED RECORDING: Jacobs hasn't been around long enough to do a best-of collection, but until then *House of Healing* (2003) is a good representation of her high-octane ballads and her funky congregational sing-alongs.

Bishop T.D. Jakes

"T.D. JAKES IS A SMART MAN," Washington, DC, radio host Rev. Imogene B. Stewart blasted over the WOL radio waves early one Sunday morning in January 2003. "He knows that the black woman hates the black man and he has capitalized on your hatred for the black man." The feisty announcer voiced what many of Jakes's critics have murmured privately. They say Jakes has zeroed in on black women's weak spot—the black man—and has built his national audience on the back of black women's hurt and pain at the hands of their men. However Jakes has accomplished his fame and fortune, someone wants to hear it. He fills stadiums that no other black religious leader can fill. Millions have bought up his ego-boosting inspirational books and millions watch his daily TV programs. Shrewdly, Jakes has also transformed his female-friendly philosophy into a series of bestselling gospel CDs that have earned him the position as one of the Top Ten gospel artists of the last decade.

He was born June 9, 1957, the youngest of three, in Charleston, West Virginia. Jakes's mother, Odith, was a schoolteacher and his father, Ernest, owned a janitorial business. Jakes seemed born to preach the gospel. He memorized scripture early and stood in his family's living room and practiced preaching so loudly that one could hear his booming voice halfway down the block. Always an industrious and hard-working child, Jakes sold greens from his mother's garden and always gave each customer a receipt as if he was running a store. At the age of 12, he became a door-to-door Avon salesman. "He could convince the devil to buy," Bobbie Tolliver, an old acquaintance from his Vadalia neighborhood, once told the *Wall Street Journal.*

When Jakes wasn't selling or pretending to preach, he was often caring for his father. Ernest was a big man who developed hypertension and resulting kidney failure early in life. Jakes spent many late nights mopping blood up from the floor as his father was hooked to a dialysis machine. "I slept a lot in hospital waiting rooms," Jakes told the Religion News Service's Adelle Banks. "I was acquainted with grief all my life. In a sense I'm still reaching out to my father through other people. I see a little of myself in them, healing my own wounds, perhaps."

By the time Jakes turned 17 in 1974, he knew he was called to preach, but fought it. Instead, he became a psychology major at West Virginia State University. However, the conviction to preach became too strong. He eventually dropped out of college and became an associate minister at a local church. Driving his late model silver Trans Am, he'd occasionally preach at small churches within a couple of hours' driving distance. His church position didn't pay much so he took a full-time job at the Union Carbide plant and spent his weekends as an itinerant preacher, trading his sports car for a beat-up Plymouth Valiant and wearing suits with worn-out linings. At one of his meetings, a coal miner's daughter named Serita Jamison started sending him love notes. They eventually met, fell in love, and were married six months later.

The year 1982 turned out to be one of the worst in Jakes's life, as well as the beginning of his ministry. Union Carbide shut down and he lost his job. By this time, he and Serita had twins and needed to keep food on the table. Serita became a gospel radio DJ at night. Jakes dug ditches, laid gas lines with his brother, and redeemed used soda bottles. He went on welfare and lit his home with candles to keep from having a high electric bill. The death of Jakes's father that year pushed him more aggressively toward his ministerial calling. As he sought out whatever speaking engagements he could garner, Jakes began to earn a name for himself.

An hour away in Montgomery, Jakes began a weekend church, Greater Emmanuel Temple of Faith, in an old storefront. He laid the cinderblock himself to make the baptistery and filled the place with old movie house seats. During the initial services with a handful of people, Jakes played piano, led worship, and then preached the sermon. People started coming in off the streets. After a while, enough people were coming regularly that Jakes could stop doing manual labor and concentrate on the ministry full-time. In 1986, Jakes relocated the church to Charleston and called it Temple of Faith. There he drew a diverse crowd of blacks and Hispanics, and 35 percent of the church was white. It was there that the nucleus of his "Woman, Thou Art Loosed" seminars began.

In his new role as pastor, people started coming to Jakes for counseling, especially women who felt abused and abandoned by men. "The problems were very similar," Jakes later told the *Dallas Morning News.* "So I thought instead of counseling them one by one, maybe if I bring them together I could tell them all the same thing at one time." He began teaching a Sunday school class on the abuse women felt. "I just started teaching on it, and it ran over to the second class and the third and more people came every time…" Jakes mentioned the class to a pastor friend in Pittsburgh who suggested that he give the seminar for the women at his church. He did and, "It was obvious I had struck a nerve. I learned that pain is not prejudiced and that it recognizes no gender and that it reaches all ages and ethnicities. And though I was very different from them physically, I could relate to them on the basis of pain."

The big breakthrough came in Tulsa, Oklahoma. Jakes went to Bishop Carlton Pearson's annual Azusa pastors conference, which drew almost 5,000 church leaders every year. Jakes was sitting in the back and Pearson saw him sitting in the "cheap seats" as it were. "I wasn't talking to this man ten minutes before I knew he had a special anointing," Pearson says. "It wasn't just his voice, although I could tell by his voice that he could speak. It was the substance of what he was saying that told me he had a special gift." Pearson felt led to allow Jakes to speak, so he gave him a platform during his conference. At the time, Pearson had a weekly telecast on the Trinity Broadcasting Network. Various parts of his conference were aired on his program, including Jakes. "TBN was bombarded with calls from people wanting them to re-air that segment with Jakes," Pearson said.

That first national exposure for Jakes opened the floodgates. According to Pearson, his own ministry was running into some money problem, so he temporarily took his show off the air until he could raise more money to keep it on. In the meantime, TBN gave his old time slot to Jakes and from there Jakes became the *cause célèbre* of the Christian world. With the TBN exposure, ministers began booking Jakes for appearances at megachurches. At many of these gatherings, Jakes gave his "Woman, Thou Art Loosed" sermon. After awhile, someone suggested that Jakes turn the sermon into a book. Although Jakes was selling tapes of the sermon, he never thought of himself as a writer. As he started to write, the words flowed. By this time, he was doing well enough financially to invest $15,000 of his own money in publishing the book through Destiny Image Printers, a company that publishes books for preachers at a fee. In 1993, the first edition of *Woman, Thou Art Loosed* was published and within three weeks, all 5,000 copies had been sold. The publisher kept printing and the book eventually sold a million copies.

Without any media attention, Jakes soon began to draw significant crowds and then outstanding crowds. For instance, his first "Man Power" seminar, aimed at men who are hurt, drew 2,500 men in Detroit in 1993. The third such seminar drew 20,000 in Atlanta just two years later. With hefty profits coming in for his book sales and good love offerings from his speaking engagements, Jakes was able to move his family out of the poverty they struggled through for so long. He bought a mansion in Charleston with an indoor swimming pool and a bowling alley. He and his wife each bought an $80,000 Mercedes-Benz. While some were proud of Jakes's achievements, others began grumbling about his seemingly sudden wealth.

"I don't think I've tried to flaunt it, nor have I tried to hide it," he told the *Dallas Morning News* years later. "If it's not dishonest or illegal, it's irrelevant." Jakes was even more direct with the *Washington Post* when in reflection on that period, he said, "To say to me that because I'm a Christian or because I'm a min-

ister or because I'm black… that I'm excluded from everything everybody else has an opportunity to have insofar as the legal pursuit of health and wealth and life is discrimination."

In 1996 the *Charleston Gazette* ran a stinging story criticizing Jakes's nouveau riche status and his creature comforts. He held a press conference chiding the Charleston media for criticizing him when he was, in fact, bringing jobs to the depressed region and inspiring others to better their lot as he had done. Just that year alone, one of Jakes's conferences at his church had brought the city $3 million in revenue from out-of-state attendees staying in hotels, eating at restaurants, renting cars, and so on. Jakes felt betrayed by his hometown and began looking to relocate his ministry elsewhere. A couple of years later, Jakes told the *Washington Post*, "If you do anything, you're going to be controversial; if you do nothing, you're going to be ignored."

Soon after, Jakes learned that televangelist W.V. Grant's Eagle's Nest Family Church, a 28-acre complex in Dallas, was for sale. (Grant was found guilty of failing to report more than $375,000 in income to the IRS.) Jakes bought the Eagle's Nest for $3.2 million and moved his family and 50 staff members to Dallas. Several members of his Charleston congregation moved there as well. Jakes had the center totally renovated and renamed it the Potter's House, taking the name from a passage from the book of Jeremiah where God is compared to a potter who reshapes broken vessels. Jakes maintains that, through God, his ministry helps reshape broken lives. In addition to the spiritual nourishment at the Potter's House, the ministry also has programs that feed the hungry, educate the ignorant, shelter the homeless, and detoxify drug abusers

Once the move to Dallas was complete, Jakes bought an opulent mansion on White Rock Lake right next to the former H.L. Hunt (the oil magnate and father of gospel singer/motivational speaker June Hunt) compound. Moreover, according to the *Wall Street Journal*, the Potter's House brought in over $20 million in 1997 and more than half of that income was from Jakes's book and tape sales. By this time, Jakes was used to the criticism and didn't mince words when Religion News Service reporter Adelle Banks questioned him about his wealth. "Any time you say that if I was a Buddhist I could be wealthy, if I was the head of the Nation of Islam I could be wealthy, if I ran the Mafia I could be wealthy, but because I'm a Christian I'm forbidden from being wealthy, there's something real sick about that."

Something else that has fueled Jakes's fame and fortune is his recordings. Integrity Records wanted to branch off into black gospel, but their black gospel imprint, Glorious Records, had failed to create any hits and was abandoned. Label executives figured that if they launched a praise and worship CD with an artist with some degree of name recognition (as opposed to the unknown artists Glorious had produced) they might have an easier time establishing themselves in the gospel market. Bob Gurich, an Integrity executive, had spotted Jakes in West Virginia and thought that he might be a good candidate for the label's gospel aspirations. Integrity executives wisely sensed that with the crowds Jakes was drawing, at the very least Jakes could sell the product at his gatherings and the company would comfortably break even. Gurich was soon communicating with Jakes's product sales manager, Paul Jones. Mike Coleman and others from Integrity went to meet with Jakes and his music minister Marcus Dawson in West Virginia, but were unable to persuade him to sign a recording deal with the label. When it seemed the deal wasn't happening, Chris Long and Stacy Merida, from Integrity's A&R (Artists and Repertoire) department, stepped in and began courting Jakes more aggressively. Finally, the talks were in progress and Jakes's attorney was on his way down to Mobile to discuss the deal further. Flying back to Mobile from a business trip, Merida was reading one of Jakes's books. Unbeknownst to her, across the aisle sat Jakes's attorney, who asked her if she liked the book. She said that she did. "That's my client," she recalls him saying. "I then introduced myself and we had a laugh because I was one of the people he was scheduled to meet with the next day. So I ended up driving him to his hotel and we had some informal discussions about the deal."

After ironing out some rough spots of the deal, Merida was appointed A&R manager for the project. While all the terms had been agreed to, there was still no signed contract. Merida trekked to Dallas where Jakes had just moved his entire church. "He was busy talking to contractors and telling people to knock out this wall and to do this and to do that," Merida says. "I was frustrated because I was chasing this man all over the building while he attended to his business. I finally said, 'Can I please just have a few minutes to go over the song selections with you?' He calmed down and sat at the piano and began to go through what he would like to have on the project. Then I said, 'Are you going to sign the contract?' He said that he would and that he'd FedEx it. [When] I got back to Mobile and the FedEx came, I put on my red lipstick and kissed the contract and handed it in to my boss."

With Merida picking songs and singers, she, Jakes, and his musical team went about transforming the successful "Woman, Thou Art Loosed" concept into a musical CD. Recorded live at the Louisiana Superdome before 40,000 enthusiastic women, Jakes inspired high praise from the beginning of the service. "Put those hands together and give the Lord the biggest praise you've got," he commanded. "Don't save anything, don't hold anything back." With that invitation, Jakes's audience released their inhibitions and freely rejoiced and nodded in agreement as woman after woman, from Juanita Bynum to Vickie Winans, sang a personal song of inspiration that resonated with the women as a group. Jakes spoke in between songs and his baritone conveyed fatherly comfort as he spoke over a bed of music on the title song, a lush sermonette that brought the cheering women to their feet. When it was released, the album reached No. 3 on the gospel charts. Proving that the album's success was not a fluke, Integrity issued another CD the following year without any star attractions. *Live from the Potter's House* sold just as briskly as the first CD and also peaked at No. 3 on the gospel chart and reached No. 75 on the R&B album chart.

By 1998, Jakes was virtually a household name in black homes. His daily TV show was not only showing on TBN, but was airing on BET and later on the Word Network. When his contract with Integrity ended, he chose not to re-sign with the label. Jakes had a concept for an album of urban love songs that he didn't feel Integrity could adequately promote. Instead, he was aggressively courted by Island Records (an urban label with R&B artists such as the Isley Brothers and Dru Hill), in part due to the recommendation of producer

Donald Lawrence, who produced several artists on the label and had already befriended Jakes. Label chief Hiram Hicks nicknamed Jakes an "anointed Barry White." With Lawrence overseeing the album's production, *Sacred Love Songs* was born in 1999. Knowing that some in the church world would bristle at the idea of a Christian love song CD, Jakes clearly outlined the purpose of the album in the CD's liner notes by stating the need to "make Christ the center of our personal relationships" and that they are "meant to provide strength by understanding that marriage is a ministry." The songs, some of them sensual, celebrated sex within the institution of marriage and featured vocalists such as Tamar Braxton (Toni's sister), Marvin Sapp, and Shirley Murdock. While some traditionalists may have decried the CD, the project broadened Jakes's fan base among the youth market as the R&B single "The Lady, Her Lover and Her Lord" (sung by Murdock) reached No. 58 on the R&B singles. The album itself beat Jakes's prior CDs in sales and reached No. 2 on the gospel charts as it approached gold status.

Unfortunately, in spite of the sales of Jakes's project, Island Records was losing money on other projects and eventually closed their urban division. Jakes soon began negotiating with EMI Records to distribute his own recording label, Dexterity Records. In November 2001, he announced his partnership with EMI. "My call is more to ministry than to music," Jakes told *CCM Update* magazine that month. "It is exciting that I've come around full circle and am able to develop that interest in partnership with EMI."

Jakes went on to explain the meaning behind the name Dexterity Records. "Dexter is my middle name," he said, "and the term dexterity represents flexibility. I think there needs to be a greater flexibility in Christian music. I tried to express that in *Sacred Love Songs*, which was a modern day interpretation of the Song of Solomon. We don't want to be locked into one kind of Christian music, but we want to live up to the name Dexterity…. We're not trying to find as many artists as we can and do as many deals as we can. We want to be selective and only bring to the forefront those things I feel are really going to have benefit and not just duplicate what's already out there."

The label's first project was *The Storm Is Over* in 2001. The praise and worship CD featured the Potter's House Mass Choir with guest appearances by Donnie McClurkin, Deitrick Haddon, Beverly Crawford, and D'Atra Hicks. The album peaked at No. 5 on the gospel album chart and No. 56 on the Hot 100 pop album chart. In July of that year, Dexterity released Beverly Crawford's first CD for the label, entitled *Beverly and Friends*, and in early 2002 released R&B star Shirley Murdock's debut gospel CD, *Home*.

The albums by Crawford and Murdock sold respectably, but they were not massive hits. For the next massive hit, Dexterity had to look to another Jakes project. *Woman Thou Art Loosed Worship 2002: Run to the Water…the River Within* featured Judith McAllister, Darwin Hobbs, and Shirley Murdock. In addition to his usual sermonizing, Jakes actually sang an earthy rendition of "Amazing Grace" on the project, which rose to No. 2 on the gospel charts. Integrity capitalized on Jakes's continued popularity in 2002 by issuing *Get Ready: The Best of T.D. Jakes*, an album of songs compiled from his first two Integrity CDs. Although plenty of people bought the individual projects the first time around, the album still reached No. 11 on the gospel charts and was another steady seller.

In November 2002, Jakes debuted *God's Leading Ladies*, which became his first No. 1 album on the gospel charts. Aretha Franklin was listed as a participant in some of the advance advertisements for the CD, but wasn't on the final project. The CD did include gospel songs dealing with everyday issues by Patti LaBelle, Kelly Price, and Shirley Murdock. Three songs of particular interest to women were Ann Nesby's "You Always Cared," Karen Clark-Sheard's "Fatal Attraction," and "Praying Women" by the Winans women (Angie and Debbie, Vickie, and Mom).

Looking back on his awesome progress over the last decade, Jakes has produced a hit play (*Behind the Curtain*), authored 28 bestselling books (including a diet book), and been hailed as the best preacher in America by *Time* magazine. But in accessing his appeal, perhaps Imogene Cross, who saw him speak in Baltimore, said it best when Adelle Banks asked her what makes Jakes so appealing to her. "I felt like T.D. Jakes talked directly to my spirit, to my body, my soul. I know now what I have to do…. I've been crying on people's shoulders and getting nowhere, and now I'm going to be crying on Jesus' shoulder." As for those who continue to overlook Jakes's inspirational message to those who hurt, and the good works of his Potter's House, and prefer to dwell on how much money he earns, Jakes thinks success is the best inspiration to the poor and downtrodden in the inner city. "One of the reasons they do not go straight is they believe if they go straight they have to go to work at Wendy's or Burger King," he told the *Washington Post's* Bill Broadway. "Once they see a black man who is successful, who has written several books and been celebrated [across] the country and overseas, and he's not selling drugs, but he's driving the same kind of car the pimp or drug dealer is, and he's not illegal and he's not immoral, it encourages young men…. They say, 'Hey, if God can do it for him, he can do it for me, too.'"

RECOMMENDED RECORDING: The *Woman, Thou Art Loosed* (Integrity, 1996) project remains Jakes's best work. Many of his later projects have an assembly line feel of being manufactured to capitalize on his name recognition rather than being truly inspired gospel projects. Also good is *Sacred Love Songs*, a sensual R&B-flavored CD celebrating holy matrimony. It features vocal cameos by Shirley Murdock and Toni Braxton's sister, Tamar, among others.

Etta James

BEFORE ARETHA WAS crowned the Queen of Soul by DJ Pervis Spann in the late 1960s, many considered Etta James to be the queen. Best known for her vintage soul recordings of "All I Could Do Was Cry," "Tell Mama," "At Last," and "I'd Rather Go Blind," James began her career in the church and has recorded incredible gospel material at various points in her life. Born Jamesetta Hawkins on January 25, 1938, in Los Angeles to a black woman who had been raped by a white pool shark James believes was Rudolph "Minnesota Fats" Wanderone, James was raised by Lula and Jesse Rogers, a couple who ran the rooming house her mother stayed

at when she was born. James called them her grandparents, and they started her singing at St. Paul Baptist Church at the age of five. They wanted her to become a piano player, so they gave her lessons, but it was her loud, powerful voice that really caught the church's attention. The legendary Professor James Earle Hines coached James and took her under his wing. The church used the spectacle of this child prodigy to draw crowds and raise money for church projects. The rafter-raising services were broadcast live every Sunday on KOWL radio with Ray Charles's future manager, Joe Adams, as the emcee.

"My grandfather was a very egotistical man and he had an argument with the preacher, and he was like snatching his marbles and going home. He says, 'I'll take my kid out of your church,'" James recalled to *Living Blues* magazine. "And he thought the congregation would drop down, which at that time we were getting people from Hollywood. White people, they would come and look at shows, see the show at this Baptist church. We broadcast from 9:00 at night on Sunday to 11. My grandfather got mad and he took me away from the church. When he took me away from the church, I completely withdrew and he took me to another Baptist church and I would never sing anymore. I just got mad and said, "I ain't gonna sing!" because I knew he wanted me to sing at this other church. These two churches were runnin' in competition—so I wouldn't sing. I stopped singing altogether."

After her adopted grandparents died in 1950, James's mother reclaimed her child and took her to live in San Francisco. There James began to sing on street corners with a couple of other girls. They concocted an answer song to the Midnighters' suggestive "Work with Me, Annie." They came up with "Roll with Me, Henry." When the group came through town, they went to their hotel and sang it for them, but the Midnighters pretty much ignored them. A little later, they sang it for bandleader Johnny Otis, who took them down to Los Angeles (against the wishes of James's mother) to record it at Modern Records in November 1954. Otis felt James had the strongest vocal presence so he made her the lead. He changed her name from Jamesetta to Etta James. He took her nickname "Peaches" and assigned it to the other two girls, so they became Etta James and the Peaches. The salacious song title was changed to "The Wallflower" after some radio stations banned it, and the record became a No. 1 R&B hit in early 1955. Eventually the Peaches were dropped from the act and James was solo as she continued making hit records such as "Good Rockin' Daddy" and "W-O-M-A-N."

From the beginning, James had a high-voltage stage persona. She could belt the hardest notes and feel every nuance of a word. She took her incendiary vocals to Chess Records in 1960 where she continued to have hits such as the wrenching ballads "All I Could Do Was Cry," "At Last," "Trust in Me," "Stop the Wedding," "I'd Rather Go Blind," and the unearthly "Waiting for Charlie." She also tackled rough-riding tracks that brought the house down in live concerts, such as the gospel-flavored "Something's Got a Hold on Me," "Tell Mama," and "Security."

In the midst of her heyday, James was tortured by an addiction to heroin that nearly killed her. "I was trying to be hip," she told *Soul* magazine in 1974 following her recovery at a detox clinic. "I was 21 years old and on tour in Louisiana and at a party. They fooled me, they told me it's cocaine, but it was heroin. If I had known it was heroin, I wouldn't have taken it. And they told me it would take away my appetite, and I was always looking for something that would do that. I've always been fat. So I sniffed it. I got so sick from that, but after I got over the sickness, there was such a mysterious feeling." She was hooked for 15 years and, in the process, lost her money and career. Eventually, her probation officer recommended a psychiatric hospital in Tarzana where James stayed for several months and cleaned out her system. Once she was fully detoxed, she fought her way back into the music business.

James has since recorded a number of stellar blues, jazz, and even country albums for labels such as Island, Private Music, and Elektra Records. She was inducted into the Blues Hall of Fame in 2001. In 1986, her live LP *Live at Maria's Supper Club* on Fantasy Records featured a rousing rendition of "He's Got the Whole World in His Hands." In 1989, James realized a lifelong dream of recording a gospel LP when *The Gospel Soul of Etta James* was issued on K-Tel's Arrival gospel imprint. Her

2000 CD *Matriarch of the Blues* features a scorching revival of Bob Dylan's "Gotta Serve Somebody." In 2002, Curb Records reissued James's K-Tel recordings in two CD volumes called *Greatest Gospel Hits*, which feature her reverent and sometimes rocking versions of gospel standards such as "This Little Light of Mine" and "I Saw the Light." In her rare interviews, James has often alluded to the church's influence on her life and continues to carry her faith wherever she goes. She's a stronger person for enduring all of her trials and tribulations. That strength is heard in her music and is reflected in her crusty stage persona. "Life's been rough," she once told *Rolling Stone*. "But life's been good. If I had to go back and do it all over again, I would live it the exact same way. I've had people say to me, 'Can't you be more feminine?' And I would go, 'Feminine? Does that mean I have to put a bonnet on my head and a little apron on and bake some cookies or something?' People think that tough thing I do is an act. No, that's the way I am and the way I like to be."

Jason & deMarco

THEY CALL THEIR MUSIC spirit pop, a blend of pop music with spiritual messages. A spiritual pop duo with a twist, Jason & deMarco made the cover of *The Advocate*, a national gay newsweekly, in July 2004 with the scintillating headline, "Gay Christian Lovers." It was the first major national exposure for an act that had been making noise within the gay community for a couple of years, but had not yet made the leap to the pop mainstream.

Jason Warner (born 1975) is from Baltimore, Maryland, and deMarco DeCiccio (born 1976) was born in Canada. Warner comes from an Evangelical background. "I knew since I was a child that God had a plan for me, and when I realized I might be gay I thought it was a ploy from Satan to prevent me from [pursuing my ministry]," he told *The Advocate*. "I felt I needed to get past this thing and just fight it, and for years I lived that way. I finally realized that I couldn't fight it and accepted that this is who I am." Warner loved music and wanted to express his strong faith through it. After graduating from high school, he eventually joined the legendary CCM touring choir TRUTH in 1996. When he could no longer deny his sexuality, he informed the group that he was gay and was immediately kicked out. Warner attended the conservative Lee University in Cleveland, Tennessee, for a while and even sang with another CCM group called the Sound, but eventually went on a spiritual pursuit to get to know himself better. One day he found himself at the Sunrise Cathedral in Ft. Lauderdale, Florida, where he finally found a house of worship that supported him unconditionally.

In 2001, Warner made his way to Los Angeles where he met deMarco, who had been living there since 1999. deMarco was raised in an Italian-Canadian home and as a child was taught to sing by Catholic nuns. He took a more serious study of music and theater during high school and later as a student at York University. Once in Hollywood, deMarco pursued a career in entertainment and received a handful of on-camera roles in television commercials.

When Jason and deMarco met, they have said that they had an instant bond that was beyond sexual attraction. Since they were both men with strong faith and a desire to sing, they decided to perform as a duo and had their first concert tour in the summer of 2002. Their smooth tenors mix easily to create an adult contemporary sound similar in mood to the Australian duo Air Supply from the 1980s. However, unlike Air Supply, which was heavy on ballads, Jason & deMarco mix it up. Their repertoire features ballads, acoustic songs, and uptempo numbers. The type of songs they sing could easily be sung by another musical heartthrob, Josh Groban, who also has a predilection for big orchestral anthem songs such as the ones Jason & deMarco favor.

Jason & deMarco, who are also a couple, launched their "Songs for the Spirit" tour in 2003 to promote the CD *Songs for the Spirit*. They followed up in 2004 with the CD project *Spirit Pop*, which has an acoustic pop styling. Much of their sales are through their Web site, www.jasonanddemarco.com. Jason and deMarco have said that their goal is to redefine what people consider spiritual music. "It's not Christian music," they told *The Advocate*. "It's pop with a spiritual message. It has noth-ing to do with religion; it's about love, life, and the journey that we are all living." Jason continued, "If we can see ourselves as children of God, as whole and complete with all of our faults—and, through our music, if others can see that they are still loved by God—then our message has gotten through…. I wish the gay community could realize that it isn't God coming against them but humankind coming against them on the gay issue."

Chris Jasper

HE'S ACTUALLY NOT an Isley brother, but keyboardist Chris Jasper gained fame in the 1970s as a member of the soul band the Isley Brothers. It's Jasper's spooky, hypnotic Moog synthesizing that defined Isley Brothers hits such as "For the Love of You" and "Who's That Lady" as much as Ron Isley's sweet tenor. Born December 31, 1951, in Cincinnati, Ohio, Jasper studied piano as a child and attended the Juilliard School of Music in New York after high school. While visiting his sister on the east coast, Jasper met his cousin, Ernie (the youngest Isley brother) for the first time. The two began to have impromptu jam sessions that Marvin Isley soon joined in on. The trio formed a little group and would be playing their music when the older Isley brother (who had been singing professionally with songs such as the gospel-styled "Shout" and "This Ole Heart of Mine") would pass through.

In 1969, the elder Isley brothers (Ronald, Rudolph, and O'Kelly) signed a new production deal with Epic Records that allowed them more creative freedom. As they became less of a Motown pop act and more of a funk band, the Isleys decided to expand the group to include Ernie, Marvin, and Chris. For the next dozen years, the Isley Brothers were one of the bestselling groups in soul music. They turned out hits such as "Love the One You're With," "Summer Breeze," "Fight the Power," "Voyage to Atlantis," "Groove with You," "Don't Say Goodnight," "Harvest for the World," and "Between the Sheets." In 1984, Marvin, Ernie, and Chris split to form their own group, Isley Jasper Isley. They scored immediately with the smash brotherhood anthem, "Caravan of Love," which spent three weeks at

No. 1 on the *Billboard* R&B singles chart. In addition to some pop radio airplay, the song received massive radio play at progressive gospel radio stations.

Eventually, Isley Jasper Isley disbanded. Chris Jasper turned his mind toward producing himself and others for his own production company, Gold City. He enjoyed two big R&B hits with "Superbad" and "One Time Love" in 1988. Jasper also produced a wonderful soul singer named Liz Hogue who enjoyed a sultry Phyllis Hyman–tinged radio hit with "Dream Lover." Jasper soon had a religious metamorphosis and began to record smooth, Quiet Storm contemporary gospel music. His first gospel album, *Praise the Eternal*, appeared in 1992 and featured a more gospelish rendition of "Caravan of Love." Financially well-off, Jasper continues to produce gospel projects on himself. However, none of them have connected with gospel radio and the gospel world is largely unaware of his fine recordings.

Eva Jessye

SHE WAS BORN Eva Alberta Jessye on January 20, 1895, in Coffeyville, Kansas, and began writing poetry and songs as a child. When she was twelve years old, Jessye formed a female quartet. She attended college at Western University in Quindaro and Langston University in Oklahoma, then taught in segregated classrooms for a while but eventually moved to the East. She was a reporter for the *Baltimore Afro-American* newspaper in 1925 and moved to New York the following year. After meeting and becoming a protégé of composer Marion Cook, Jessye formed the Dixie Jubilee Singers, a chorale group, in 1926. Their repertoire ranged from ragtime to opera to gospel. One of their first gigs was singing radio jingles for Van Heusen shirts and performing on the popular radio shows of the day. In 1927, Jessye published her acclaimed book, *My Spirituals*, for Robbins-Engel Publishing in New York. The book collected unique and lesser-known spirituals into written form for the first time. Baritone Paul Robeson was just one of the performers who began to sing the spirituals from her book. In 1929, she coached the chorus for the first black Hollywood musical, *Hallelujah*. The chorus quickly became popular in radio studios and on movie

sets. When George Gershwin's *Porgy and Bess* opera opened on Broadway in 1935, Jessye was its choral director. The chorus was later transformed into her own Eva Jessye Choir, which toured throughout Europe and was also active in the civil rights movement. In 1978, Jessye became an artist-in-residence at Pittsburgh State University in Kansas where she donated four tons of memorabilia from throughout her career. She moved back to the University of Michigan at Ann Arbor (where she had established the Eva Jessye Afro-American Music Collection in 1974) and remained there until her death on February 21, 1992.

Claude Jeter

ONE OF THE GREAT falsetto voices of the Golden Age of Gospel in the 1950s, Rev. Claude Jeter was born December 26, 1914, in Montgomery, Alabama. After his attorney father died when Jeter was eight years old, his mother moved the family to Kentucky where Jeter finished high school. There he found work in the West Virginia coalmines and to pass the time, he formed the Four Harmony Kings (Jeter, his brother, and two fellow miners), an a cappella group, in 1938. He changed the group's name to the Swan Silvertones in 1942 when the group began to host a radio show on WDIR radio in Knoxville, Tennessee, that was sponsored by New York's Swan Bakery Company. They recorded for a number of record labels including King, Specialty, and Vee-Jay Records. Their decade with Vee-Jay was their most commercial period as producer Paul Owen refined their sound. They added instrumentation and stressed harmony and smoothness as opposed to the hard singing they did for Specialty Records. One of their acclaimed moments was 1959's "Mary Don't You Weep," in which Jeter sang "I'll be a bridge over deep water," reportedly inspiring Paul Simon to write "Bridge over Troubled Water" a decade later. In 1966, Jeter left the group to try his hand at a solo career. He was ordained in the Holiness church and moved to New York City where he began to evangelize. It's been said that Jeter's smooth falsetto was a vocal influence on soul stars Al Green and Eddie Kendrick.

Jewel Gospel Trio

THEY'VE BEEN forgotten by all but the most ardent gospel fans, but the Jewel Gospel Trio was an innovative female gospel trio in the 1950s. The group was formed by Bishop Mattie Lou Jewel circa 1953 with her granddaughter Naomi Harrison, Canzetta Staton, and Margaret Staton. The teenagers all attended Nashville's Jewel Academy boarding school. They first recorded for Aladdin Records in Los Angeles but cut their biggest hits for Nashboro Records beginning in 1955 with "Many Little Angels in the Band." They took turns leading songs, but Margaret led their biggest hit "I Looked Down the Line and I Wondered." Canzetta led their next biggest hits, "Jesus Is Listening" and "Too Late." The trio was the first group of the era to have their own regular band, which featured a steel guitarist and Hawaiian drums. They toured with the biggest groups of the day such as the Soul Stirrers and the Davis Sisters. Though they sang some ballads, the group was known for their jump songs. Gospel queen Albertina Walker chuckles, "Oh, yes. I remember them girls. They had so much energy and they *sang*! We almost hated for them to be on the show with us, but it was all good. Everybody was family back then."

By 1960, Margaret (Maggie) had left the group and enrolled in college. She later became an educator before resurrecting her singing career with a string of LPs for Winston-Derek Records in the late 1980s. Her sister, Canzetta (Candi), later launched a stellar secular music career in the 1970s before she returned to her gospel roots in 1982. Naomi (Bishop Naomi Aquila Manning) assumed leadership over the Church of the Living God ministry upon her grandmother's death in 1991 and died of colon cancer herself in 2002.

Mable John

THE OLDEST SISTER of famed crooner Little Willie John (best known for writing and recording "Fever," which was covered by Peggy Lee), John was raised in Detroit and was Berry Gordy's best buddy long before he founded Tamla/Motown Records in 1959. She used to spend the day helping Gordy peddle his songs to New York publishers. "He had no money and no way of getting around, but he had these people who wanted to hear his songs, so I drove him around," John says. One of those tunes, "Lonely Teardrops," eventually became a hit for Jackie Wilson and Gordy's career was on the way. He took John along for the ride.

When one of his songs, "Got a Job," didn't attract a buyer, Gordy decided to produce the record himself and then get a major label to distribute it. Recorded by Smokey Robinson & the Miracles, it was released via End Records, but bombed due to a lack of promotion. John and Robinson thought the record would do well if Gordy started his own label and marketed the records right. They worried him into founding Tamla/Motown in 1958 and the rest is history. John was the first female to record for the label, although many critics have erroneously stated that Mary Wells was the first. Wells was the first female on Motown proper, but Tamla preceded Motown. John, who had shared a bill with Billie Holiday two weeks before the singer's death, sang bluesy songs on which she was often backed up by the Primettes (later known as Diana Ross and the Supremes). In fact, backing John was their audition. John didn't recall their being especially talented, though they were determined to impress Gordy, particularly Diana Ross. Their ambition attracted Gordy and he signed them on.

Mable John / courtesy of Stax/Fantasy Records

Although none of John's singles for Tamla ever hit the national charts, she developed a strong following and repeatedly sold out shows at the Apollo in Harlem, the Howard Theater in Washington, and other venues. Sensing that Tamla/Motown was more geared toward popcorn soul than to the blues she was most comfortable singing, John left the label in 1964. As the Motown sound soared, John says, "I didn't feel that Motown was a place where I could survive." In conference with Gordy, John explained her dilemma, reassured him of their friendship, and asked for her contract release. They both cried. Gordy gave John some roses, a thousand dollars shopping money, and her release.

John finally came into her own when she joined Stax Records in late 1965 and put her bluesy style to good use. When she arrived in Memphis, Isaac Hayes and David Porter, who had been assigned to write for John, had nothing for her to record. Half the time, she had to track them down—they were usually chasing women—and drag them into the studio. She collaborated on almost every song they wrote for her, and the songs usually reflected some event in her life such as her 1966 million-seller, "Your Good Thing Is About to End." It was about her husband, who gambled, drank heavily, and spent too much time in the streets. The song has been so beloved that it's been covered by artists such as Lou Rawls, Bonnie Raitt, and the Captain & Tennille. "I've never considered myself a singer," John says, "I'm a storyteller."

The lusty "You're Taking Up Another Man's Place" hit No. 38 on *Cash Box*'s black music charts a few months later. Etta James covered the song on her *The Right Time* album and wrote in the liner notes that "Mable John is not only a beautiful writer, but a super-bad singer." Oddly enough, John might have had another soul classic attributed to her had Sam & Dave not recorded "When Something Is Wrong with My Baby." It was written for and first recorded by John, "But it was the first time that Stax found a ballad which really suited Sam & Dave, so they released their version rather than mine," she says.

Every song John did at Stax was a gem and no one at the company could understand why radio did not pick up on them. John feels that her lack of radio success may

have been because of a lack of promotion. "They had Sam & Dave, Isaac Hayes, Johnny Taylor, Otis Redding. That's a lot of people for a small company to promote... But I did well for myself and I can't complain."

Chicago DJ Lucky Cordell remembers John's emotional stage show vividly. "What Mable had was an ability to identify with or make the people identify with her. She had that ability to reach out into an audience and you really felt she was singing to you. She talked to the women 'Girls, you know what I'm talkin' about' and somebody'd say 'Yeah!' Then she had a little thing going where the women understood each other.... She didn't do drugs, I don't think she even drank, so her performances were always the best that she could give."

John became depressed following the sudden death of Little Willie in 1968. Berry Gordy and Diana Ross took care of all the funeral arrangements. "Willie and I had a bond between us that was closer than any I had with any other relative, and all of my family is very close. Diana [Ross] saved the day. I don't believe I could have gotten through that day without her help. She even had to dress me because I was so upset." John even contemplated leaving show business. Then Ray Charles (who had lost his mother and could relate to her personal loss) called to sympathize and share his personal grief with John. He coaxed her back into singing by appointing her the lead singer for the Raelettes in 1970.

Mable took the Raelettes to the Orient without Ray Charles and put together one of the most popular Raelettes groupings. They recorded on the Tangerine label and had several hit singles in the early 1970s such as "I Wanna Do Everything for You." Most singers leave groups to go solo, so when John did the reverse, Lucky Cordell says, "I was surprised, but I could see the logic. Her career was not happening anymore at Stax. She was still working because she's a good entertainer, dependable, and had a good following.... I think she felt to go with Ray Charles, who's an institution, that something might develop for her."

Mable left the Raelettes in 1976 to attend ministry school. In 1989, she became an associate pastor at the Sanctuary of Praise Church in Los Angeles. She's since founded her own Joy in Jesus Ministries and A Place to Pray, a non-profit charity center in L.A.'s Crenshaw neighborhood. Mable's first gospel album, *Where Can I Find Jesus,* was released on her brother's Meda Record label in 1992 and she's currently working on a sequel. For the last four years Mable has been hosting "Christmas All Over L.A." to feed and clothe L.A. homeless during the holidays. Mable recently received her doctorate of divinity degree and saw Stax Records release 25 of her rare 1960s recordings on the stellar compilation *Stay Out of the Kitchen.* She's also been honored with the Rhythm & Blues Foundation's Pioneer award for her vast career achievements.

Blind Willie Johnson

A GOSPEL-BLUES founding father, Blind Willie Johnson was a bottleneck slide guitarist and had a roughshod vocal style that added a deeper earthiness to his recordings. Johnson was born January 22, 1897, in Independence, Texas. His mother died when he was a child, and his father later remarried. When Johnson was nearly seven years old, the couple was arguing and the stepmother threw some lye. It missed Johnson's father but instantly blinded Willie. He later made money on street corners by playing the guitar and passing a hat, a practice he continued when he became a Baptist preacher. He and his wife, Angeline, performed bluesy hymns as a duet in various Dallas area churches in the late 1920s. In 1927, Johnson signed to Columbia Records and recorded some of his most enduring gospel-blues songs, "Mother's Children," "It's Nobody's Fault but Mine," and "Jesus Make Up My Dying Bed." They were all hits and more hits followed such as the Crucifixion story "Dark Was the Night — Cold Was the Ground," "God Don't Never Change," and "Let Your Light Shine on Me." Johnson didn't record after 1930, but continued to preach and sing on street corners. In 1947, the Johnsons' home burned down. In the course of healing from injuries sustained in the fire, Johnson developed pneumonia and died a week later. His wife turned to a nursing career and retired from public life. Johnson's music has been kept alive by cover versions by Bob Dylan, Pop Staples, Eric Clapton, and others.

RECOMMENDED RECORDING: *Dark Was the Night* (Columbia Records, 1998) consists of 16 of Johnson's aforementioned tunes and others such as "Church, I'm Saved Today" and "John the Revelator."

Isabel Joseph Johnson

A CHICAGO DJ AND gospel TV host on WCIU (the station that launched *Soul Train*), Johnson was born in 1919 in New Orleans. Her family moved to Chicago when she was ten years old. After graduating from DuSable High School in 1936, she married Wilbur Edward Johnson. She loved church and church singing, and in the 1940s, her pastor asked her to introduce singers on the church's afternoon radio program. Johnson opened a beauty shop and ran that for years before she began to broadcast a Sunday morning gospel radio program, *It's Time Truth Speaks* on WVON in the 1960s, sponsored by Leak & Sons Funeral Home. With her strong voice, Johnson's weekly catchphrase was an admonition to "pull the car over to the curb" so that one could listen to the music she was going to play without distraction. The radio show made Johnson so popular in the Chicago gospel community that WCIU didn't see it as a gamble to offer her her own local television program. Johnson hosted and produced *Rock of Ages*, a live gospel music showcase that aired from the 1970s through the 1980s. The program spotlighted both local and national gospel artists. Johnson retired from most of her ventures in the early 1990s, although her beauty shop is still open and running. She died May 4, 2000, of Alzheimer's disease.

James Weldon Johnson

THE GIFTED COMPOSER of the Negro National Anthem, "Lift Every Voice and Sing," James Weldon Johnson was born James William Johnson on June 17, 1871, in Jacksonville, Florida. His father was a headwaiter in a restaurant and his mother was Florida's first black female schoolteacher. It was a middle-class home that encouraged educational pursuits. After graduating from

Atlanta University, Johnson became principal at the school where his mother once taught. He then studied law and became the first black to pass the bar exam in Florida. Johnson and his brother, John Rosamond, a New England Conservatory of Music graduate, began collaborating on songs in 1897. Johnson wrote the lyrics and his brother wrote the music. In 1902, the brothers moved to New York to push their songwriting careers. However, Johnson became disgusted with the racial stereotypes common in black music at the time. He took further studies and wrote a novel called *The Autobiography of an Ex-Colored Man*. He also became active in the NAACP and the burgeoning civil rights movement. For the gospel community, he edited the superlative anthologies *The Book of American Negro Spirituals* (1925) and *The Second Book of American Negro Spirituals* (1926).

Johnson died on June 26, 1938, when the car he was riding in was struck by a train. Over 2,000 people attended his funeral in Harlem. Johnson's "Lift Every Voice and Sing" has been recorded by at least three dozen artists over the years, ranging from Ray Charles and the Boys Choir of Harlem to the Harmonizing Four and Art Blake & the Jazz Messengers. However, the most popular renditions are Kim Weston's torch song reading in 1970 that hit the Hot 100 R&B singles charts and Melba Moore's all-star version, which reached No. 9 on the R&B singles chart in 1990.

Keith "Wonderboy" Johnson

A NEW YORK NATIVE with a down-South vibe, Keith "Wonderboy" Johnson leaped on gospel's quartet scene in the late 1990s with energy and youth. Johnson was five years old when family members labeled him "wonderboy" for what they perceived as wondrous musical talents. He enjoyed going to Harlem's Apollo Theater to see great gospel acts such as John P. Kee and Rev. James Cleveland. Later, he became a member of the Boys Choir of Harlem before he founded his own quartet of young men with a passion for that old sound. Through a deal with World Wide Records in Houston, Johnson's first hit was 1998's "Hide Behind the Moun-

tain." Since then, he's enjoyed hits such as "Send a Revival," "I'll Fly Away," and "I've Got a Feeling."

In addition to the hit albums, Johnson has also acted in touring musicals such as *PMS: It's a Man Thang* and *What a Man Wants, What a Woman Needs*.

Mattie Johnson

A WASHINGTON, DC–based singer who launched the group Mattie Johnson and the Stars of Faith in the 1970s, Johnson was born circa 1946 in Aikens, South Carolina. Her mother, Martha Taylor, grew up working in cotton fields. She left Johnson and her siblings with their grandmother and moved to Washington, DC, in the 1950s to seek a better job with which to support her children. Taylor saved $10 a week from her job at Yale Laundry for three years so that her children could join her in the nation's capital. Johnson worked, at various times, as a cab dispatcher, cafeteria worker, and a nursing aide. She formed the Stars of Faith with her mother and her sister Frances Taylor in 1968. They added Debra Gambill, Linda Tyson, and Betty Clement to the group and recorded a number of fine, high-energy recordings for Savoy Records, the biggest of which was "He's a Friend of Mine" in 1980. "There was no one in the Washington area who could work a stage like Mattie," says singer Nadine Rae. "She was a very fun person to be around, always upbeat, and she brought that personality to the stage. Locally, she was the queen of gospel."

Part of the connection Johnson shared with her audience was her ability to touch her fans where they hurt. "When you look into the audience," Johnson told the *Washington Post* in March 1980, "you know that somebody is out there with marital problems, with children who are sick, some with money problems and can't pay the rent or put food on the table. There are those who are having problems on the job, some with children in trouble with the law. Things are so bad sometimes that all you can do is scream the name of Jesus. Sometimes that's the relief you need." Johnson was in the middle of another gut-wrenching concert in Washington, DC, when she suffered a massive heart attack and died on March 6, 1988.

Vernard Johnson

GOSPEL'S SAXOPHONE pioneer, Vernard Johnson was born September 6, 1948, in Kansas City, Missouri, where he began to play in area nightclubs at the age of 17. Johnson was born with asthma, a condition that would cripple the average saxophonist's ability to perform. He's said that he asked God to heal him and that prayer made the difference. "Many people don't believe it by listening to me play, but I was born with bronchial asthma," he told *Totally Gospel* magazine. "It was so bad that my folks couldn't even sleep at night for listening to me breathe. Even though I couldn't breathe correctly, I remember blowing a song on my horn for Jesus and then taking one deep breath and everything was gone. Gone out of my lungs! Jesus had touched me and now I play for him." A lifelong member of the COGIC church, Johnson has been recording gospel LPs for labels such as Savoy Records dating back to the early 1970s. After seeing Johnson perform at the New Orleans Jazz Festival, Elektra Records vice president of marketing David Bither signed Johnson to the label, where he recorded *I'm Alive* in 1991. In recent years, Johnson, who holds an earned doctorate from Southwestern Seminary, has been preaching, taking the gospel to prisons, and continuing to toot his horn.

Willie Neal Johnson

FAMED FRONTMAN for the Gospel Keynotes quartet, Willie Neal Johnson was born August 25, 1935, in Tyler, Texas. The eldest of six children, he and his siblings began to sing together as children. When he was a teenager, Johnson was chosen by Rev. C.W. Jackson to sing with his group, the Five Ways of Joy Gospel Singers. He later formed the Gospel Keynotes with longtime friends Ralph McGee, Rev. J.D. Talley, Charles Bailey, John Jackson, Lonzo Jackson, and Archie B. McGee. They signed with Nashboro Records where they enjoyed "Show Me the Way" as their first hit single. He soon was nicknamed "the country boy" because of his folksy, Southern manner. They made 20 more years of records such as "That's My Son" for Nashboro. Their 1981 LP *Ain't*

No Stopping Us Now garnered a Grammy nomination. In 1985, the group signed with Malaco Records where they have had a handful of moderate gospel hits. Johnson's last recorded vocal was a cameo on Kirk Franklin's *The Rebirth of Kirk Franklin* album in 2002. Johnson died of a stroke on January 10, 2001, at East Texas Medical Center. Since Johnson's death, the group now performs as the New Gospel Keynotes.

RECOMMENDED RECORDING: For their Nashboro sides such as "Clean Heart" and "Show Me the Way," check out *At Their Best* (Universal Records, 2001). Malaco has yet to release a compilation on the group's hits during their tenure there.

Bobby Jones

BOBBY JONES IS TO gospel music what Don Cornelius was to soul music and what Dick Clark was to rock 'n' roll in the 1950s and 1960s. His *Bobby Jones Gospel* television program was not only the most-watched program on the BET network for years, but it was also an imperative media outlet for gospel artists who didn't have the privilege of appearing on primetime television or news

Bobby Jones / photo courtesy of Word Records

programs to introduce their new musical projects. Jones was born September 19, 1938, in Henry, Tennessee. His parents were both alcoholics who, at times, made life miserable for Jones and his two siblings. His father was especially abusive, causing Jones to wrestle with lack of self-esteem and timidity. When he was 14, the family moved to Paris, Tennessee, where Jones began to assert himself and to chart his own destiny. He graduated from high school early, at the age of 15, and earned his degree in education from Tennessee State University when he was 19 years old. While pursuing his Masters degree, Jones taught elementary school in the Missouri and Tennessee school systems.

On the side, Jones indulged himself in music by performing with the Meister Singers. In 1967, he took a consultation position with McGraw-Hill. The job took Jones around the world until he tired of the travel demands and resigned in 1975. As if he didn't have enough to do, Jones also co-hosted a children's television show called *Fun City Five* for a season in 1973. But it was music that was winning his affection. He sang with the Royal Gospel Singers before founding the Love Train Choir circa 1974. The choir was comprised of those that society rejected: blacks, gays, and the physically challenged.

The year 1976 was a turning point for Jones. He had formed yet another choir, the New Life Singers, during that period and they released their debut LP *Sooner or Later* for Benson Records in 1976. In his autobiography, Jones wrote that he was so proud of the album that he invited members of the Hawkins Family to hear the project. "I invited them to my home for a reception and to hear what I recorded," he wrote. "Well, although I thought I was on the high end, I quickly got put in my place. I remember playing the album and they just laughed in my face. I was secretly so upset, but I didn't say anything." Regardless of whose assessment was more viable, the public spoke and the album was a commercial disaster.

However, Jones found success in television to offset the recording disappointment. He launched *The Nashville Gospel Show* with Theresa Hannah and Tommy Lewis that year. The weekly program aired on NBC's WSMV affiliate at 9:00 A.M. on Sundays. He also hosted a weekly talk show, *Bobby Jones World*, and a

news program called *Symposia*. The show ran for several years and made Jones a local star as he provided a platform for gospel artists to perform on television. But there was a plot hatching behind the scenes. According to Jones's memoirs, Hannah and Lewis felt that they were the stars of the program and that Jones was dispensable. Their attorney called Jones to arrange a meeting to discuss Hannah and Lewis having a larger role in the program. Jones refused to meet with him, so Hannah and Lewis persuaded NBC to drop Jones from the show he co-founded. Jones's attorney, Richard Manson, called NBC on his behalf and convinced them that Jones was indeed a star attraction. NBC relented and gave Jones his own show.

Jones didn't stop there. He constantly worked to improve his show and move it to the next level of excellence. Jones eventually took the show from NBC, which wasn't supporting it, and aired it elsewhere, including on the new cable network, Black Entertainment Television (BET). It was a decision that would make Jones a national personality as BET got off the ground in 1980. As the network grew into the conglomerate that it became, Jones's program grew with it and was its No. 1 rated program for over a decade. The program showcased secular artists singing gospel, gospel artists singing gospel, and amateur artists getting their first national exposure. Since gospel was not often welcomed into primetime television, the program was an incredible boost to the gospel music industry, which was in a slump for most of the 1970s but began to grow to unprecedented sales numbers by the 1990s.

On the recording side, things were often rough for Jones. He was not considered a good singer by most people's standards, and many of his other featured singers tended to over-sing their songs. However, there were times when Jones's vocals were more than enjoyable. On the title cut of the 1979 Nashboro LP *There Is Hope for this World*, Jones gave a surprisingly soulful and satisfying performance on the mid-tempo track. In general, though, most gospel connoisseurs dismissed Jones's musical contributions. One who did not was country star Barbara Mandrell, who was a regular watcher of Jones's program. They recorded the duet "I'm So Glad I'm Standing Here Today," which won a Grammy in

1984. Mandrell was proactive in pushing Jones's career. She had Jones and New Life open for her Las Vegas concerts and had them perform with her on various television shows

Over the years, Jones has recorded on virtually every major gospel label: Word, Nashboro, Creed, Benson, EMI/Sparrow, Malaco, and Gospo Centric. His 1994 Sparrow CD *Bring It to Jesus* reached No. 17 on the gospel album sales chart before Jones had the recording pulled. Although he felt it aimed to become his biggest-selling album, there was trouble in the ranks of the New Life Singers. Many of the singers had staged a revolt where, according to Jones, they demanded 80 percent of the album sales royalties and a percentage of ownership in his television show. Rather than fight with them, Jones killed the record before the group's actions did. He disbanded the New Life Singers and then created the Nashville Super Choir as his vocal backdrop. In 1998, Jones finally enjoyed a Top Ten gospel CD when *Just Churchin'* sold over 50,000 units according to SoundScan and gave him a steady radio hit with "Just a Closer Walk with Thee."

Just as things were looking up, Jones received an unexpected backlash when St. Martin's Press issued his autobiography, *Make a Joyful Noise*. Many in the gospel community were extremely offended at his candid remarks. For instance, he wrote about James Cleveland's body having costume changes during his funeral service. He accused various members of the Winans family of being jealous of him and made several other comments about gospel's leading figures that made the book the talk of the Gospel Music Workshop of America convention. Jones, who usually attends the annual gospel music mainstay, opted to stay away that year. Nevertheless, Jones still rides high with his *Bobby Jones Gospel* TV show, which remains a BET ratings winner after 24 years, the longest-running black gospel music television program in history.

Brent Jones & the T.P. Mobb

AN UP-AND-COMING gospel group that has been successful at merging a straight urban musical vibe with a Christian message, Brent Jones and his T.P. Mobb

are supplying Generation X with smooth grooves such as "Good Time" and "Midnight."

"If you print my age, I'll have to kill you," Brent Jones laughs. The singer was born May 7 in Los Angeles sometime in the latter half of the 20th century. An only child, Jones began taking piano lessons at the age of six. When he was 14, he became music minister of his home church. He was raised in the conservative Methodist denomination, but was influenced by artists who also had a gift for mixing R&B with gospel, such as John P. Kee and the Clark Sisters. "That's when I really became exposed to and inspired by gospel music," says Brent. "I thought it was such bomb music—so feel-good—but not enough people were hearing it. I decided right then that if there was any way I could, I wanted to get that music heard by the same masses that were listening to mainstream music.

"Early on, when New Edition came along, I had wanted to be the next New Edition," says Brent. "Then it was Jodeci, and on and on, until God touched my life and put it on my heart to be a gospel musician. He changed everything. When I was onstage, I didn't feel like being sexy. I felt like being anointed. I didn't want to just entertain people. I wanted to touch them with some of what the Lord had given me." In 1992, Jones formed the T.P. Mobb. When Sounds of Blackness cancelled a date at the House of Blues in Los Angeles, Gospel Brunch coordinator Sylvia St. James booked the Mobb. Their first recording gig was a guest spot on the *Motown Comes Home* project in 1994. They later produced their own debut project on their own Holy Roller Record label. The self-titled CD spawned the urban adult contemporary radio hit "Good Time," which helped the album reach No. 37 on the R&B chart in 1999. Their follow-up project, *Beautiful*, charted two steps higher in 2000 and included an astounding R&B-styled slow jam entitled "Midnight."

Jimmy Jones & the Sensationals

BASS SINGER Jimmy Jones has been all over the gospel music map. In the 1950s, he was a member of the Southern Sons Quartette and, later, the Harmonizing Four. In 1958, he recorded his first solo sides for Savoy

Records, including "Somebody Bigger than You and I" and "Before this Time Another Year." He sang with the Mighty Clouds of Joy briefly in the 1960s and then vanished from the landscape.

Rev. Paul Jones

RENOWNED PRIMARILY for his 1990 recording of "I Won't Complain," Rev. Paul Jones (born November 6, 1961) founded Houston's bustling Greater New Grove Baptist Church in 1981 when he was just 21 years old. In the ensuing years, the charismatic young pastor hosted a daily radio show on KWWJ and was a very active civic leader. Adamantly anti-drug, he mentored youth and sheltered the homeless. In addition, he developed a close friendship with singer Yolanda Adams and other rising singers on the Houston gospel scene. He enjoyed singing himself, although his voice was unrefined, and enjoyed a regional radio hit with his recording of Elder James Lennox's "I Won't Complain."

Ironically, Jones was in negotiations with Savoy Records when tragedy struck. On November 19, 1990, two friends found Jones's body at his home in an exclusive Houston neighborhood. Both his Jaguar and Jeep had been stolen from the garage. Initially, the *Houston Chronicle* carried reports that police were following up on unsubstantiated tips that Jones frequented adult bookstores where he picked up men for sexual encounters and that perhaps one of those men was his killer. However, police later traced the homicide to a 20-year-old convict and a 14-year-old accomplice who were caught speeding at 112 mph in a 55 mph zone. Police found that the duo knew that Jones was a prosperous minister. They waited until he was home alone and knocked on his door. When he opened the door, they forced their way in and robbed him of several personal possessions. Before they left with both of Jones's cars, they fired three bullets, fatally wounding Jones. In the wake of his death, Jones's rendition of "I Won't Complain" became a megahit and received a Stellar award nomination as Best Traditional Song.

RECOMMENDED RECORDING: The LP *I Won't Complain* only reached No. 32 on the *Billboard* gospel al-

bum sales chart, but that's not an accurate indicator of the title song's popularity. The independently distributed project spent half of 1992 on the sales chart and a couple of years in regular gospel radio rotation.

Jones Sisters

GAIL, PHYLLIS, AND CHERYL Jones had an interesting childhood. Their father, Rev. Howard Jones, was an evangelist with the Billy Graham Evangelistic Association in the 1950s and they grew up in Liberia where their father served the organization for many years. They sang early on in church and through their father's connections, they had their own weekly radio broadcast called *Singtime*, which was designed to encourage and inspire African youth. By the '60s, the family had moved back to their hometown of Oberlin, Ohio. Phyllis attended high school and Gail and Cheryl were college students when they cut their first LP for Word Records, entitled *Singing We Go*. In 1971, they released their final LP *People Get Ready*.

George Jordan

BORN IN 1944, the Chicago-based pianist and songwriter wrote "God Never Fails" for Mattie Moss Clark and the Southwest Michigan Choir. He has served as minister of music at Maceo Woods Christian Tabernacle Church in Chicago since the 1960s and has played the keys on most of Woods's albums, including the Top 30 R&B hit "Hello Sunshine" in 1969.

Kim Jordan

ONE OF THE BEST just-under-the-radar jazz pianists/vocalists to emerge in recent memory, Kim Jordan is a performer with a coveted résumé. Her work does not fit neatly within the confines of gospel music. However, it merits attention by the gospel community. "I am a funky keyboard artist," Jordan says. "I'm a combination of gospel, with a Latin feel, some blues, even classical—a conglomeration of many things."

She was born Kimberly Denise Jordan circa 1962 in Detroit. Her father, Rev. Dr. Joseph R. Jordan, is the pastor of the Corinthian Baptist Church in Hamtramck and her mother was a music teacher. Jordan began to play the piano in church when she was five years old and she later graduated from Howard University's School of Fine Arts.

Over the years, Jordan has played behind artists such as Roberta Flack, Vanessa Williams, and Stevie Wonder in concert. She played on recording sessions for bluesman Taj Mahal, Gil Scott-Heron, and R&B quartet Dru Hill. She toured with Scott-Heron for a dozen years. Jordan also wrote the tune "We Must Be in Love," which became a No. 11 R&B hit for the female soul group Pure Soul in 1995.

During that same year Jordan was moving to New York City to further her career when the eight-foot U-Haul truck carrying her possessions hit a six-foot overpass. Her face slammed into the steering wheel and she suffered a brain injury. When Jordan was well enough to return home, she sat at the piano and the information in her brain would not manifest in her fingers. She had to relearn how to play the piano. It took more than three years to remaster the keyboard. "That changed my focus on life," Jordan told the *Quad-City* newspaper in November 2003. "Before, I was just an arrogant kind of person. Now I have focus and meaning. I believe that's the purpose for my life. Everybody has a purpose and everybody has meaning in their life."

Instead of pursuing the secular music course she was on, Jordan changed her music focus to a gospel genre. In 2001, she issued her first solo CD *All for You* on her own ProSounity Music label. It's in limited distribution but available on her Web site: www.kimjordan.com. Known for her dramatic style of playing, Jordan turned in a thrilling project that fused mellow soul with jazz and capped it off with gospel lyrics.

"That is the whole main focus of why I do gospel jazz now," she told *Quad-City*. "I know that it's a miracle that I'm playing again, a complete miracle." As *Washington Post* writer Nina Killham once wrote, "Whatever she wants you to feel, you feel. She's captivating… she consumes you."

Tom Joyner

THE BEST-KNOWN black radio announcer in America today (ten million people—one third of the US African-American population—tune into his daily show each week), Tom Joyner was born in December 1949 in Tuskeegee, Alabama. According to a February 2002 cover story in *Savoy* magazine, Joyner was a shy but excellent student who matriculated at the Tuskegee Institute at the age of 16. He began to overcome his timidity by spinning records at the campus radio station. He and some friends then went to the town's only radio station, WBIL, and demanded that they play black music. "There was no Motown, no nothing, in a town that was 90 percent black," Joyner told *Savoy*. After earning his sociology degree, Joyner took a job as a news announcer on WRMA in Montgomery, Alabama. He then took an R&B DJ job at KKDA in Dallas. Soon after, John H. Johnson, publisher of *Ebony* and *Jet* magazines, hired him for his WJPC radio station in Chicago. Johnson became Joyner's mentor and began featuring him in *Jet* magazine to help build his national profile. When Joyner landed in Chicago, he became a star with shows that moved him from WJPC to WVON to WBMX to WGCI. In the early 1980s, Joyner became host of Johnson Publications' syndicated talk show, *The Ebony/Jet Showcase.* He made national headlines in 1985 when he held on to his morning-drive gig at WGCI and accepted an afternoon-drive gig at KKDA in Dallas. "This is mornings," he told *Savoy*. "This is afternoons. If I could get back and forth between the two, I've got job security, which is unheard of in this business. If one [station] fires me, I've got the other to fall back on." The daily commute earned him the titles of "the Fly Jock" and "the Hardest Working Man in Radio." Although neither station's management liked Joyner splitting his duties, their respective displeasure was moot. Because the stations were in different states, the competition clause in Joyner's contract was irrelevant. During the eight years that Joyner carried that load, his respective shows were routinely No. 1 in both their markets.

By the end of 1993, Joyner was planning to retire from the daily radio grind and just continue his syndicated CBS radio urban countdown show, *On the Move.* Then ABC Radio offered him a deal he could not refuse:

a daily, nationally syndicated program. In January 1994, *The Tom Joyner Morning Show* launched from ABC's Dallas studios on 29 stations. The program featured comedy skits, interviews with politicians, and plenty of classic soul music. It was an immediate hit and over the years, the show has featured gospel artists such as the Clark Sisters, Candi Staton, and BeBe and CeCe Winans. Joyner's show played a huge part in popularizing Kirk Franklin's breakthrough radio hit "Why We Sing" in 1995. Joyner has since frequently invited the leading gospel artists of the day to his show and introduced their music to a wide urban audience. Under the umbrella of Joyner's Reach Media, the morning show is now heard on more than 110 radio markets. In 2004, Joyner and his business partner David Kantor sold 51 percent of their ownership in Reach Media to Radio One for $55 million in cash and Radio One stock. Joyner is also a strong advocate for education and has raised millions of dollars for historically black colleges and other community causes via the Tom Joyner Foundation.

Jubilee Four

SOMETIME CIRCA 1960 a quartet of black singers was in a Hollywood recording studio waiting to back up a Reprise Records pop star on a recording session. While they were waiting for the singer's arrival, they began to sing to pass the time. The producer and engineer decided not to wait for the tardy singer any longer. They recorded the quartet and the Jubilee Four was born. The lead singer, Willie Johnson, had recorded with the Golden Gate Quartet for a while and also sang on some of folklorist Alan Lomax's Library of Congress recordings. The other singers included baritone Ted Brooks, tenor Jimmy Adams, and basso George McFadden. McFadden had sung with the Jubilaires on the popular *Amos & Andy* radio show.

Their debut Reprise LP *Lookin' Up* appeared in 1961 and featured a dozen religious standards and spirituals. Their style was clean, crisp, and pop-oriented. As a consequence, they were popular with predominantly white audiences. Several performances on Jimmy Dean's ABC television variety series in the early 1960s led to the top-selling Epic Records LP *Jubilee Four on TV*.

John P. Kee

KNOWN AS THE Prince of Gospel, Kee picked up where Rev. James Cleveland left off when he passed away in 1991. Although there are modern elements to his music, Kee has largely kept the traditional black choir style that Cleveland popularized alive and well with songs such as "Show Up," "New Life," and "Wash Me."

The next to last of 16 children, Kee was born June 4, 1962, in Durham, North Carolina. A handsome and gifted child, Kee excelled in school. He graduated from the North Carolina School of the Arts at the age of 14 and later attended the Yuba College Conservatory. Before he came of age, Kee was gigging with jazz legend Donald Byrd and funk band Cameo. When he was on the road with singer James Taylor, Kee began to sell drugs. "I was working mainly to support my drug habit," he told *Rejoice* magazine. "I didn't use crack, but I freebased, which is the same spirit," he told *Gospel Today* in 2000. When a cocaine exchange went awry, he saw a buddy murdered. "And that's been my testimony from day one," he continued. "To know that this brother died in my presence for forty dollars crushed me. But what it also did was allow me to go home and repent. That

John P. Kee / photo by Robert Shanklin

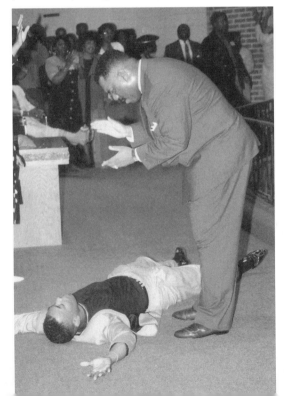

doesn't mean to go home and cry, but it means to re-evaluate your situation—to rethink who you are. That is what happened to me. I was hustling and selling drugs, but it stopped that day. God got my attention, and that was the day I surrendered my will to him. I didn't smoke any more coke or marijuana from that day on. I wasn't totally free because I was still running the girls [pimping], but God delivered and freed me, and I realized that salvation was a process."

Kee became a musician for Jim and Tammy Bakker's *PTL Club* in Charlotte. He started writing songs and sending them to artists. Some of the first to record them were Edwin Hawkins, who recorded "Jesus Lives in Me," and the New Jerusalem Baptist Choir, who recorded "Show Me the Way." In 1981, Kee founded the New Life Community Choir with 60 members. At the time, it was nicknamed the welfare choir because so many of the members came from the 'hood. In 1987, Kee made his debut with the *Yes Lord* LP on Tyscot Records. Then the choir recorded *Wait on Him* for Tyscot, which peaked at No. 4 on the gospel album sales chart and won three Stellar awards in 1989, including one for Song of the Year for "It Will Be Alright."

In spite of his past musical success stories, it was 1995's *Show Up* CD that put the gruff-voiced Kee in the exclusive club of singers with gold or platinum records. It was also proof that Kee was not just maintaining but increasing his fan base. In addition, the project won five Stellar awards, a Soul Train Music award, and a Grammy nomination. Not just an artist, Kee has also done arrangements or production work for Vanessa Bell Armstrong, Teddy Pendergrass, Bryan Wilson, Inner City Mass Choir, and Drea Randle, among others. In 1995, Kee founded the New Life Fellowship Center in Charlotte where he is the full-time pastor. He and his wife have eight children, another choir in the making.

Stanley Keeble

PRIMARILY KNOWN in the local Chicago gospel scene as one of Inez Andrews's longtime keyboardists and godfather to her son, Richard Gibb, Stanley Keeble was born March 8, 1937, in Chicago. He began taking piano les-

sons during his youth and after graduating from high school in 1955, he directed the choir at Rev. Clay Evans's Fellowship Baptist Church. In the 1960s, Keeble played keyboards for Jessy Dixon and Inez Andrews on recordings and in concerts. In 1968, Keeble formed the Voices of Triumph Choir which enjoyed a moderate, regional hit with "I Feel Good." Following the LP *Gospel Truth* for the local Torrid Records label in 1971, Keeble spent most of the next two decades continuing his college education, teaching in the Chicago Public schools, and serving as a chaplain at Presbyterian St. Luke Hospital for over a decade. Backed by the Voices of Truth Choir, Keeble returned to recording for the I AM Records LP *Can't You Love Him* in 1990. Keeble's deep, husky voice shined on the uptempo title song, which was a local hit. Later in the decade, Keeble hosted a weekly radio program, *The Joy Hour*, on the college radio station WKKC. His present passion and mission is the Chicago Gospel Music Heritage Museum that he founded in spring 2002. Keeble has struggled to raise money and find a permanent facility to house the museum. Still, he's optimistic. "The museum has not opened to the public as soon as I would like," Keeble says. "But I have collected many artifacts in preparation for the museum and continue to do so, and I trust that it will open in the near future."

Paul Kelly

AN UNDISTINGUISHED Southern soul singer who wrote the gospel classics "God Can" and "Stealin' in the Name of the Lord," Paul Kelly was born June 19, 1940, in Miami, Florida. In the mid-'60s, Kelly recorded for Selma Records, Buddy Killen's Dial Records, and Philips Records, but none of these deals produced any hit records. Disappointed with the poorly written songs his producers gave him to record, Kelly began writing songs as he strummed his guitar. Kelly's grandmother had raised him in church and he had seen a lot of church scandals as a child. Kelly says, "When I wrote 'Stealin' in the Name of the Lord' I really had nothing more in mind than the thought of preachers who played these games." He thought it might be a good song for his friend Sam Moore of Sam and Dave fame, but Moore rejected it. Kelly then recorded it himself and it was bought by the Happy Tiger label. At the time, the song was controversial and Kelly's live performances were met with boycotts and picket signs by churchgoers. "I believe in God," Kelly has said, "and I have faith in God, but not in religion. I feel that if Jesus came back today they'd kill him all over again."

After Happy Tiger fell on unhappy times in 1970, Buddy Killen arranged for Warner Bros. Records to buy the masters. In Warner's hands, the song rose to No. 14 on the R&B charts. At Warner, Kelly recorded a variety of message, gospel, and story songs. His next biggest hit was 1973's "Don't Burn Me" which peaked at No. 35 on the R&B chart. After fairly dismal sales on his succeeding LPs, Warner Bros. dropped Kelly from the roster. His final album, *Stand on the Positive Side*, featured the smoldering ballad "God Can." While Kelly's rendition sounded poorly produced and weakly sung, the song became a favorite of gospel singers and has been recorded beautifully by the Staple Singers and also notably by Dorothy Norwood. Kelly now lives in Ruby, South Carolina, and his most recent album was *Let's Celebrate Life*, issued on South Carolina's Ripete Records label featuring new versions of "Stealin' in the Name of the Lord," "My Journey's End," and "The Devil's Pipe." In spite of his spiritual songs, his tune "Personally" is his most successful and has been covered by Jackie Moore, Karla Bonoff, Ronnie McDowell, and Z.Z. Hill. Irma Thomas has recorded "New Rules," Meatloaf has done "Don't Burn Me," and Thelma Houston has recorded the definitive rendition of "Stealin' in the Name of the Lord."

R. Kelly

ONE OF R&B'S MOST popular male superstars of the last 20 years and an heir to the emotional baggage and musical genius of Donny Hathaway and Marvin Gaye, R. (Robert) Sylvester Kelly was born on January 8, 1969, in Chicago. He grew up in the projects and lost his mother to cancer when he was a teenager. Before she died, she instilled a sense of faith in Kelly. He popped on the R&B scene in the early 1990s with salacious R&B smashes such as "Sex Me," "Your Body's Callin'," and "Bump 'n' Grind," which spent an amazing 12 weeks at No. 1 on the R&B charts in 1994.

In spite of the raunchy tone of many of his songs, Kelly has always maintained one foot in the gospel world. In 1994, he produced the South Carolina–based retro soul quintet N-Phase's self-titled debut CD, which closed with a sparkling rendition of the Commodores' "Jesus Is Love." He produced tracks on gospel trio Trinitee 5:7's first two CDs and "That Extra Mile" from the Winans' 1993 *All Out* project. Perhaps the music of R. Kelly exemplifies the age-old struggle between good and evil that has vexed mankind since Adam and Eve.

Kelly has endured his share of trials and tribulations—literally. In recent years, he has been in and out of court defending himself from charges that he's molested a number of young girls. Kelly was also rumored to have married R&B crooner Aaliyah when she was 15 years old and he was 27. There's been an out-of-court settlement for a woman who claimed to have been sexually harassed by Kelly. Kelly has denied wrongdoing and expressed that his relationship with God has deepened. "There's a lot of people going through a lot of things right now that are deeper than me, you know," he told *Blender* magazine in 2003. "I see kids and people starving…. People think I'm going through something—but I know God is real. My own situation is not so heavy. We'll be all right."

Throughout the negative publicity that has swirled around Kelly over the last decade, he keeps doing what he does best: make music. Through his pain, he has written a number of songs of faith such as 1995's "Heaven Can You Hear Me?" and "Heaven I Need a Hug" in 2001. Although it's not a gospel song, Kelly's 1996 million-seller "I Believe I Can Fly" has been adopted as a gospel song by several gospel artists. It's been covered by Yolanda Adams, Jennifer Holiday (on the Essence awards), Dottie Peoples, Youth for Christ, Bishop William C. Abney, Jr., and gospel sax man Mel Holder. In 2004, Kelly, who has sought counsel from Bishop T.D. Jakes and attended Greater Salem Baptist Church in Chicago, actually recorded a gospel album. His 21-track "Happy People/U Saved Me" project is half church and half club. The blatant gospel single "U Saved Me" has been thoroughly embraced by the gospel world where it reached the Top Ten on *Radio & Records*' gospel singles chart in fall 2004.

"I'm a real person, and I love people," Kelly said in May 2002 of the public relations nightmare that had become his life. "That's my problem. I let people into my world, and they [mess] some things up. But I turn around and love them anyway, because that's what I want God to do for me. I forgive them because I want to be forgiven one day."

Roberta Kelly

SHE NEVER GAINED the fame she was due in America, but Roberta Kelly has certainly made her mark on pop music history. She was the voice of the 1975 global million-seller "Fly Robin Fly." Even more than that, Kelly created the first gospel-disco concept album with her 1978 *Gettin' the Spirit* LP. Kelly was born November 23 in New Mexico in the early 1950s and she and her sister grew up in a Los Angeles housing project in the Boyle Heights neighborhood. She always enjoyed music (jazz bassist Charles Mingus was her cousin), but her only church experience as a child was in the Catholic church. When she was 15 years old, Kelly started attending black churches. "And I saw what I missed. Even though I have the voice God gave me, if I had grown up in that [Pentecostal] environment, I could have done it. It makes me feel bad that I can't wail. I know I have the instrument, but I don't know how to do it."

Kelly and her sister then formed a soul group, the Uniques, with two men, and they performed throughout the Los Angeles area. "Hal Davis and Marc Gordon opened the California office of Motown and they knew of us singing with a group called the Uniques," she says. "They asked my mother if they could sign us to Motown. She said yes, but they didn't want the guys, only us. My sister was in love with one of them and eventually she married him. And I kind of liked the other guy. So we didn't sign, but we could have been one of the first groups at Motown [when they opened that new office circa 1972]."

Meanwhile, Kelly made a good living as an x-ray technician, though she continued to moonlight as a

Roberta Kelly / photo by Ron Slenzak, 1978. *Casablanca Records publicity photo*

singer. Eventually, she decided to move to Germany where her godparents were born and see what the future held there. Her first night in Munich, a friend took Kelly to the happening nightspot, the Domicile. It wasn't long before Kelly was meeting everyone on the German music scene—including another American expatriate, Donna Summer. "We were starving together in those days," Kelly says of the woman who instantly became one of her best friends and eventually, an international superstar. They both became protégées of German producers Giorgio Moroder and Pete Bellotte, who liked to match great black female voices with the then-nouveau European disco rhythms that became known as the Munich Machine.

Moroder and Bellotte struck a deal for Atlantic/Warner Bros. Records to release their European-made recordings on Oasis Records in America (They later switched distribution to Casablanca Records when they felt Warner Bros. wasn't enthusiastically promoting their releases.) One of the first Oasis releases was Kelly's 1974 single "Kung Fu's Back Again." During that period, Kelly recorded a song called "Fly Robin Fly" for producers Sylvester Levay and Michael Kunze. "I sang that with three other women, but we were only given 150 [German] marks," she says. "They formed another group named Silver Convention and sent them around the world miming to our music and getting rich. Years ago, I tried to sue, but the other girls would not do it." The 1975 disco track spent three weeks at No. 1 on the US pop singles chart and topped pop charts around the world.

Kelly didn't brood for long; she just concentrated on her solo career. She released a number of disco-oriented singles, but the first to score on the *Billboard* club charts was "Zodiacs," which reached No. 24 in 1977. The song was a big hit in Italy, and Kelly was in an Italian discothèque when the concept for her next album came to her. "[An interviewer] was talking about the hit and then he asks, 'What's the next thing for Roberta Kelly?'" she recalls. "And out of my mouth, without even thinking about it, I said, 'A gospel disco album.'" A week later, Kelly and Moroder met in Munich to discuss her next recording project. She continues, "Giorgio told me he had an idea for a gospel disco album. I fell on the floor when he said that."

Moroder produced this project with Bob Esty. Esty picked Edwin Hawkins's "To My Father's House" and George Harrison's "My Sweet Lord," and Kelly chose Hawkins's classic "Oh Happy Day." Esty wrote the title track and collaborated with Kelly on the remaining two tracks on the six-track LP. The song "Gettin' the Spirit" zoomed to No. 9 on the club play chart in 1978. "That album should have gotten all over the world," she exclaims. "Neil [Bogart, president of Casablanca Records] called me himself and apologized because I had to

take a backseat. They were working on Donna's movie *Thank God It's Friday*. They spent a million dollars on just promotion and it didn't do anything. What my album did, it did on its own without any promotion." Still, Kelly says, her dance floor rendition of "Oh Happy Day" did win her a Singer of the Year award in Brazil.

"I was not a born-again Christian then," she says. "If I died at that time, I would have gone right to hell." About a year later, Kelly became engaged to an Afro-German. At the wedding, the pastor invited the guests in attendance to "give their lives to Christ." Not only did Kelly become a born-again Christian that day, so did Donna Summer, her manager Susan Munao, and several other guests. "Nothing changed," Kelly says of her lifestyle. "I still cursed like a sailor and screamed and hollered at people. I just lived a very worldly life. But four years later, my husband left me for another woman. That was on a Tuesday and on Thursday, I was baptized in the Holy Spirit and I haven't looked back since. That's when my life changed."

Kelly walked away from recording for a while and spent three years working for Donna Summer while her daughter worked in Summer's fan club operation. In 1986, Kelly and her daughter moved to Spain for a year before taking up residence in Germany again. She continued to perform, but only sang gospel music. "I chose to only sing gospel," she says. "God didn't tell me to do that. It's just what I felt [I had] to do." In 1995, a German record label, Weltbild, sent Kelly to America to record a gospel album that was never officially released. The album, *Sound of Color*, included songs such as "He's Always There," "Down by the Riverside," "Go Down, Moses," and "Jesus Loves Me." "[The producer] was an alcoholic," Kelly says. "So they fired him and paid the rest of us off even though I had an option for another album."

The recent joy of Kelly's life is a choir she created comprised of third-generation Afro-German war babies. "They are some of the most beautiful children," she sighs. "On the one hand, they are put on a pedestal for that. However, in another way, they are not recognized as being German and are made to feel bad about it." She sees the choir as a vehicle to build their self-esteem. She's also excited that the original producers of "Fly Robin Fly" have granted Kelly permission to have the choir record "Fly Robin Fly" along with a rap written by Kelly for a new generation of listeners. Aside from that worthwhile cause, today Kelly works as a vocal coach for radio announcers on German Public Radio in Bavaria.

Ron Kenoly

RON KENOLY ROSE from an obscure Sunday morning congregational hymn leader into one of the most popular praise and worship leaders in the world. More than three million records later, Kenoly has distinguished himself as an unabashed cheerleader for Jesus Christ. His uplifting paeans such as "Lift Him Up," "Let Everything That Has Breath Praise the Lord," and "Use Me" (which he co-wrote) are regular fare at Charismatic churches around the globe. Moreover, Kenoly has carved out a niche for himself as a black man in a predominantly white field. His diverse audience continues to expand. He packs in upwards of 10,000 adults, toddlers, and grannies in civic arenas around the world 250 nights a year. Considering his great achievements, Kenoly's beginnings were humble.

The third of six sons, Kenoly was born December 6, 1944, in Coffeyville, Kansas, where he knew both joy and heartache. "My mother put happiness and love into our household," he says of Edith Kenoly, who worked as a housemaid. "We were poor, but she made us so happy that we didn't realize we were poor." His paternal influence was not as strong. "My father was in the military and gone all of the time," he says. After high school, Kenoly ventured to Hollywood. Faced with poor job prospects, he joined the air force in 1965. While in the military, he met and married his wife, Tavita. During this time he also joined the Mellow Fellows, a Top 40 cover band that toured military installations. "I can remember in our neighborhood there was one family that owned a TV," he recalls. "On Saturday nights they would turn it around and put it in the front window, facing the street, so everybody else could watch. I remember seeing Sammy Davis, Jr., and Nat King Cole for the first time, and I was profoundly impressed that here were two black men on a national stage—highly respected and highly talented. I knew right then that was what I wanted."

In 1968, Kenoly left the air force and resettled in Los Angeles where he planned to seek his fortune in the music business. Over the next few years, he made his money by singing demos of Jimmy Webb ("MacArthur Park") songs for the Audio Arts label. He also released his first single, "The Glory of Your Love (Mine Eyes Have Seen)," for the company. This opportunity led to recording deals with MCA, United Artists, and Warner Bros. However, it was at A&M Records that Kenoly had his greatest secular success. Label execs changed his name to Ron Keith because they "thought an Italian last name would confuse the R&B marketplace," Kenoly laughs. Simply entitled *Ron Keith & the Ladies*, the A&M album featured the R&B hit "I Betcha I'll Get Ya" and "Soul Vaccination," which was later covered by Tower of Power.

As his career took shape, Kenoly's family life suffered. He worshiped his career and neglected his wife

Ron Kenoly / Integrity Records promotional photo

and kids. His marriage became abusive—emotionally and physically. They separated and were nearing a divorce. "My wife rededicated her life to the Lord in 1975 and began praying for the healing of our family," he recalls. "I began to realize the goodness of God because I could see the changes he was making in her life, and I could see that while I never lost respect for God, I had never had a strong spiritual life. That's when the lights began to come on for me." Kenoly remained in R&B music another year to fulfill contractual commitments. When he left Los Angeles, he relocated to Oakland, California. There he took the humbling job of passing out towels at the Alameda College locker room while taking night courses. "I just surrendered my life to the Lord, allowing him to do some character building in me," says Kenoly. "I had to learn to be a husband and a father, and I had to learn how to relate to God as a father."

Kenoly taught music and physical education at Alameda College from 1978 to 1982. Still, the fire to sing burned within him. He tried to no avail to get a gospel record deal. "It was a real low point," Kenoly says. "But as much as I loved music, I loved God more. I couldn't go back to secular music even if it meant never singing again." One summer evening Ron sat alone in church for hours, playing, singing, praying, worshipping, and laying his burdens before the Lord. "From that night on, the record companies ceased to matter. The Lord had met me and shown me so much that I felt I had gone beyond what any company could offer me. Acceptance and rejection didn't matter anymore because all I knew was that I had been with God."

After he left the church that night, Kenoly produced a custom-made album entitled *You Ought to Listen to This* in 1983 and sold it wherever he sang. Word of his musical talents began to spread around the Oakland area, and he found himself invited to lead praise and worship at numerous churches. "I didn't even think of myself as a praise and worship leader," he explains. "All I knew was I would go and sing my songs and something special would happen."

Leading worship for high-profile pastors like Lester Sumerall and Jack Hayford brought Kenoly to the attention of evangelist Mario Murillo, who commissioned him to lead worship at his crusades. Through Murillo,

Kenoly met Pastor Dick Bernal, who founded the Jubilee Christian Center, a congregation in San Jose, California. Kenoly became the church's music minister in 1987 and was content to stay there without the thought of ever recording again. But in 1990 Don Moen, then the creative director for Integrity Music, heard about Kenoly's ministry and approached him about the possibility of recording one of his praise services.

Kenoly's album *Jesus Is Alive* was released in 1992 and became a surprise hit. What followed was *Lift Him Up*, which has since sold a half million copies and won an Angel award in 1993. The worship hits kept coming. *The God Is Able* set broke records for praise music, and *Billboard* magazine voted *Sing Out with One Voice* the No. 1 independent Christian music album of 1995. The next year's *Welcome Home* album earned Ron his first Dove award.

In between all of his record-breaking sales in the praise market and nightly touring schedule, Kenoly managed to find some time in 1998 to complete his doctorate in sacred music from the Friends International Christian University in Merced, California. "I'm still trying to figure out what all of this means," he muses. "I want to be a good steward of what God has given me, not just in terms of music, but in life experience and valuable lessons I can pass on to other people. He's holding me responsible for the visibility and the influence that he's allowed me to have. And, make no mistake; it has been him who has allowed it. I've never had a manager, a promoter, a booking agent. It's all just been the sovereign work of God. This is God's music and God's agenda. My main concern is just to always do with it what he wants me to do."

RECOMMENDED RECORDING: *High Places: The Best of Ron Kenoly* (Integrity Music, 1997) features Ron's best-known praise songs.

Kenoly Brothers

IF IT EVER BECAME acceptable for Christian music to encourage the idea of sex symbols, the Kenoly Brothers would be the number one candidates for the role. In a field that is not distinguished for handsome men, nor beautiful women for that matter, the Kenolys possess the physical attributes, vocal chops, and urban beats that would make them huge in the pop music realm. However, the lack of a major recording label to push their careers has prevented the duo from achieving all of their vast potential.

They are the sons of praise and worship leader Ron Kenoly. Bingo (Ronald) was born January 18, 1977, and Piqasso (Sam) was born March 14, 1979, both in Oakland, California. "I was 16 when I started singing," Bingo says. "I was watching a Jodeci concert on TV and K-Ci and JoJo were moving everybody in the audience and they moved me. I thought about how good they made me feel and I decided I wanted to make people feel like that too. I practiced every day. I listened to all the groups out there. My style came from listening to groups like Silk and Guy. I like all those ballads."

In spite of his father's successful recording career in Christian music, Bingo says, "I wasn't even trying to hear gospel for the first four years after I started singing. You couldn't get me to listen to gospel. The kind of gospel music I was hearing didn't move me. Then, in 1997, my brother and I decided to be a duo and God started giving me all these tight gospel grooves. We're taking back what the Devil stole. We're going to have the bomb music with respect for God. We're going to flip the script on that." For a brief time, Bingo did some modeling, which led to a role as a thug in Robert Redford's HBO movie *Grand Avenue*.

After graduating from Silver Creek High School in San Jose, Bingo performed secular music with a variety of aggregations. He and a buddy named Sidney formed a duo that didn't last long enough for them to name it. Then he rapped with his brother, Piqasso, for a year before he decided, "I don't want to rap. I want to sing. I knew these Pilipino cats who put in a word for me with this group called Ontilt and I was with them for two years. … I was still trying to find myself. We did heavy pop stuff like All-4-One. I respect what All-4-One does, but it's not what I wanted to do."

What Bingo wants to accomplish is more in line with R&B troubadours Mint Condition. "Stokley's vocal capabilities are unreal," he says. "Everybody in the band can play and sing well. They are excellent songwriters and have the tightest chord progressions. They've been blessed in songwriting and with Stokley as the lead singer. I want to be on that level. They've never come out with anything garbage. They are very picky… and I respect that so much. They are my musical role models."

Piqasso grew up around music, but didn't take an interest until 1995. "I was hanging with my brother and his friends," he says. "I didn't have anything to do; my friends weren't around, so I went with him. He and his friend needed a third part harmony and my brother forced me to sing…. The girls there liked it. The way they flipped out, I said, 'I think I kind of like this.'" He started practicing and training his voice on his own. The Kenoly Brothers began to participate in local talent shows. They won one at Piedmont High School, but Piqasso says, "We did Stevie Wonder's song 'Lately.' I didn't have the right motives then. I was doing it because I wanted the girls, and it didn't matter how I looked—they would swoon because I was singing."

On May 15, 1997, that all changed. "I had been traveling with my dad, but I just wasn't living my life right," Piqasso continues. "I was meeting all these people in churches and when I came home, I was living a different life. The Holy Spirit spoke to me and said I was throwing it all away. 'I gave you all this and this is how you treat me?' I was at a gathering in a room with people smoking, drinking, and doing other stuff that wasn't right. People asked what I do and I'd say, 'I travel with my dad, Ron Kenoly, a gospel singer.' I was a bad witness, so I stopped cold turkey. It was hard, but I was praying. Slowly but surely, I started to get rid of my bad influences and soon I didn't miss them. My brother saw the change in me and it inspired him to change too."

Following his spiritual reawakening, Piqasso served as the youth praise and worship leader at Jubilee Christian Center in San Jose for a little over a year. "That was the best education for me," he says. "I was singing at all the youth events and sometimes leading worship Sunday nights. I learned how to ad lib and to sing really well because I was constantly singing."

Since Ron Kenoly had experienced the music business from both the secular and gospel sides, he hammered home the point for his sons to own their own company because record labels rarely give artists their due monies. "We're taking everything on ourselves and doing it," Bingo says. "We didn't want to be a slave to anybody's contract. We want to build something our kids can inherit. The bottom line is, signing yourself to a label is like renting a house. You don't do it unless you have to, otherwise, you are just paying somebody else's bills." The duo's career together was born sometime in 1994. "I started traveling with my dad because he wanted me to explore what he did and to see what it was like on the road," Piqasso recalls. "He was gone a lot and it was a way for us to spend time together because we always had a cool relationship. He liked the way I dealt with people. So, at first, he had me selling product at his concerts. But my dad has always been our biggest fan, encouraging us to sing. My brother and I had won all these talent shows and we were like a main attraction around town. Dad saw how we were getting good and he asked if we wanted to sing on his *Welcome Home* album. We did a song called 'I Love to Love You Lord.'

"The album did really well and that song got such a good response that radio stations were playing it in different countries. It was No. 1 in Fiji and had A-1 rotation in New Zealand [it also won a Dove award]. So when I started traveling with my dad, he said, 'You need to start doing this song.' My brother was off doing his own thing at the time, so I went up there by myself and sang it. It was traumatic at first because I was just used to screaming girls, and the people at churches were a little more conservative so you didn't know right away if they liked it or not. They did like it. For the next two years I sang it and pretty much established my brother and me, even though he wasn't there. Finally, in mid-1997 we decided we wanted to record an album called *Who's There?* and our dad produced us. But I believe nothing happened with that because we were not ready yet. We still needed to grow spiritually."

They have grown and their songs reflect their spiritual maturity. "If I want to write a song about something, I'll say 'God give me the words to say.' He'll start giving me a melody and I'm like snap! I have to isolate myself and give my complete attention to that song," says Bingo. "'You Are My Joy' came about like that. I was driving in my car and I was telling the Lord how

much I loved him…. He said, 'If you love me so much, why don't you spend time with me?' I make time for TV and go hang out with my partners, so I said, 'I need to represent.' I was driving up the hill to my house and all of a sudden the words came right to me."

Although they had recorded a CD entitled *Who's There?…God's There* in 1997, the duo's first national release was 1999's *All the Way*. Issued on their NGMR Records label, it reached No. 30 on the gospel album sales chart. The ballad "You Are My Joy" received airplay on a dozen R&B radio stations such as Hot 105 in Miami. "We received virtually no gospel radio play," Piqasso says. "And we didn't have the money to push like it needed to go on the secular stations." In spite of that, the CD still sold over 40,000 copies—more than respectable figures that major labels grab for their mid-level artists.

The Kenolys' next album, *No Distance*, was just as thrilling a mix of Usher-R. Kelly–styled vibes with gospel lyrics as the first album. They saved up over $20,000 to promote an R&B single, which they had in "Too Close." It was a steamy, ultra-sensual single about an unmarried couple's decision to abstain from sex in order to please God. The song was most added on *Radio & Records'* urban AC chart in the fall of 2002. This time the duo's distributor let them down. "We finally had a hit," Bingo says, "and our distributor doesn't have the record in any stores anywhere that the song is getting played. It was No. 1 in some markets and it wasn't in the stores." In the urban market, radio and retail work together. When radio plays a song, if retail stores don't begin to show sales within a couple of weeks, radio programmers then drop the songs because they assume the consumer doesn't like it. In the Kenolys' case, Diamante/Butterfly had serious financial problems, which eventually led them to file for bankruptcy.

In spite of the blow to their careers, the Kenolys keep pushing. They plan to release a rough-edged solo rap CD on Bingo in 2005. Afterwards, the Kenoly Brothers will reunite for another smooth soul duo album. "We try to write universal music," Piqasso says. "We want [to appeal to] Chinese people, black people, white people, Indian people, all people. We think we've got the right balance to our style. We're not real soft and we're not real hard. We want to reach the girls, their boyfriends, and we're not opposed to reaching their parents either. We just want to reach everybody with this message about Christ."

B.B. King

UNIVERSALLY KNOWN as the King of the Blues for songs such as "The Thrill Is Gone" and "Cryin' Won't Help You," B.B. King's first ambition in life was to become a preacher. He was born Riley King on September 16, 1925, near Indianola, Mississippi. "Church was the highlight of the week," King wrote in his memoirs of his childhood. "Church was not only a warm spiritual experience, it was exciting entertainment, it was where I could sit next to a pretty girl, and mostly it was where the music got all over my body and made me wanna jump. Sunday was the day."

One of King's first musical influences was Rev. Archie Fair, who preached and played guitar at a little COGIC church in the Pinckney Grove neighborhood. When he was seven years old, King received his first guitar, a Silvertone out of the Sears & Roebuck catalog. Rev. Fair showed him how to hold it and showed him how to play his first chords. "I wanted to be a reverend," King wrote in his book. "Next year, I taught Sunday school to some of the younger kids. People looked at me like a church boy, and I was glad to be seen that way. Church had the singing, church had the guitar, church had folks feeling good and happy, church was all I needed. I'd be a guitar-playing preacher like Reverend, except for my stutter and the fact that I couldn't concentrate on my book learning."

Blues was the primary music heard in the area where King was raised. He listened to 78-rpms of Blind Lemon Jefferson, Lonnie Johnson, and Rev. J.M. Gates. He still was vacillating between becoming a preacher— or at least a gospel singer—and making something else his career avocation. King then formed the Elkhorn Jubilee Singers with some relatives. "Part of me still yearned to serve in the army of the Lord," King wrote. "But the truth is I never got that calling… I never heard that voice. If I had, I wouldn't have argued." King sang hymns on street corners, but no one would drop money into his hat until he started singing the blues. Almost 21 years old, King then moved to Memphis in 1946. Once there, he became a radio announcer on WDIA radio where he was dubbed "the Beale Street Blues Boy." When he started recording blues music for Bullet Records in 1949, the title was shortened to "Blues Boy" King. By the time King became a star on the blues circuit in the middle 1950s, everybody just called him B.B.

"I've heard that black folks are supposed to have this big conflict between singing for the world and singing for God," King wrote. "Some of them surely are divided. I am not. I liked Robert Johnson, the blues singer from Mississippi who they claim traded his soul to the devil for musical talent. But I consider that story bullshit. I would never trade my Godly feelings for anything. And in my mind, no blues artist ever has. That myth also makes it seem that blues talent is tainted talent. I don't believe that. I believe all musical talent comes from God as a way to express beauty and human emotion."

RECOMMENDED RECORDING: *B.B. King Sings Spirituals* (Diablo Music, 1998) is a ten-track reissue of King's 1959 Crown Records LP of the same name. It features King's bluesy guitar and wailing vocals on classic gospel tunes such as "Precious Lord" and "Save a Seat for Me."

Curtis King

ONE OF THE COUNTRY'S most underrated theatrical producers, Curtis King is the founder of the Black Academy of Arts & Letters in Dallas, Texas. Born December 20, 1952, in Coldwater, Mississippi, he majored in theater at Jackson State University. After acting in or directing several plays during college, King opened the Junior Black Academy of Arts & Letters (JBAAL) in 1977 from his dining room table and with $250 to his name. There was much struggle in the early years, but through his perseverance and a staff of people who would forgo paychecks to keep the center open, they made it through the hard times. His persuasive lobbying brought some of Hollywood's biggest black stars to Dallas to do King's productions for little or no pay. King treated the artists with dignity and respect. Limousines transported them, King's staff addressed them by their last name, and they

Curtis King / *photo courtesy of the Black Academy of Arts & Letters*

were treated with the smoothest of kid gloves. As a result, legendary actresses such as Esther Rolle and Beah Richards would come whenever King called.

One of King's favorite projects was the annual Martin Luther King, Jr., holiday concert featuring gospel and protest songs, backed by a rousing choir. The gospel artists featured in the program have included Vickie Winans, the Clark Sisters, and Mavis Staples. In 1993, King staged an elaborate 30th anniversary March on Washington concert at the Kennedy Center in Washington, DC It was hosted by *CBS News* anchor Dan Rather and featured a range of artists that included Richard Smallwood, Vickie Winans, Eartha Kitt, and Esther Rolle. The following year, King took a musical called *Black Music and the Civil Rights Movement* on a national tour. Again, the show featured gospel and protest songs. The artists on the bill included Myrna Summers and Jennifer Holliday.

King always jumps at the opportunity to bridge the gap between pop music and the gospel idiom. One of his biggest accomplishments has been the "Symphony with the Divas" concert, which is broken into pop, classical, and gospel segments. King recruited a mix of artists such as Dionne Warwick (pop), Florence Quivar (classical), and Beverly Crawford (gospel) for an astounding program that won several standing ovations when it premiered at Washington, DC's

Warner Theater in 1997. Over the years, the show has featured Oleta Adams, the Clark Sisters, and Melba Moore, among others. King has future ambitions to bring an all-gospel show to Broadway.

In 1997, the name of the JBAAL was formally changed to the Black Academy of Arts & Letters (BAAL). Nestled inside the Dallas Convention Center with over 250,000 square feet of space and a multi-million dollar annual budget, it's the largest African-American theater institution in the country. It's also the place in Dallas for touring productions and headline concerts to play. It's been said that if you haven't played the BAAL, you haven't played Dallas.

Gladys Knight

ONE OF THE MOST distinctive voices in soul music, Gladys Knight was born May 28, 1944, in Atlanta, Georgia. She captured America's heart in the 1960s when Gladys Knight & the Pips made their first recordings with songs such as "Giving Up" and "Letter Full of Tears." Knight, her brother Bubba, and two cousins, William and Edward, became household names with their 1970s pop-soul hits like "If I Were Your Woman," "Midnight Train to Georgia," and "Neither One of Us (Wants to Be the First to Say Goodbye)." With such a powerful vocal talent and having grown up in the Baptist church, it was only a matter of time before Knight finally delivered a gospel album. That time came in 1998 when she produced and released her first gospel project, *Many Different Roads*, on her own Many Roads recording label. The year before, some eyebrows arched when it was learned that Knight had forsaken her Baptist roots and joined the Church of Latter Day Saints (Mormons). The album managed to reach No. 21 on the gospel album sales chart. Her 2005 follow-up *One Voice* reached No. 2 on the gospel chart.

Marie Knight

A BIG STAR ON the gospel circuit in the 1950s, Marie Knight was Sister Rosetta Tharpe's partner in crime in creating the first gospel crossover songs such as "Up

Above My Head," "Precious Memories," and "Gospel Train." She was born June 1, 1918, in Sanford, Florida, but was raised in Newark, New Jersey. She sang throughout her years as a student at South Side High School and sang her first solo at the Oakland Avenue Baptist Church. Right after high school, Knight joined an itinerant singing group that led worship services for a Philadelphia-based missionary named Mrs. Robinson. However, it was after she hooked up with Sister Rosetta Tharpe in 1946 that Knight would lay the foundation for her career as a gospel maven.

Possessing a full-throttle contralto, Knight's thick voice was an even counterpoint to Tharpe's girlish wail. They first teamed up on the 1948 ballad "Precious Memories," which rose to No. 13 on the *Billboard* R&B singles chart. Early the next year, they teamed up with the Sam Price Trio and released the rousing "Up Above My Head, I Hear Music in the Air," which pulsated its way to No. 6 on the R&B singles chart and spent almost ten weeks on the survey—an astounding feat for a gospel recording. Knight wasn't finished, though. Just as that record waned, Knight rallied the Dependable Boys and the Sam Price Trio to back her on her Top Ten R&B smash, "Gospel Train." In 1950, they pulled 27,000 people to see them at Griffith Stadium in Washington, DC, and another 17,000 viewed their concert in Ponce de Leon Park in Atlanta.

In 1951, Knight recorded "Have Faith" with former heavyweight boxing champ Jersey Joe Walcott and then headlined a tour with Jersey Joe, the Nightingales, Dolly Lewis, and Vivian Cooper. When that tour was through, Knight became the first gospel artist to perform gospel music in upscale supper clubs such as the Blue Angel in New York and the Black Orchid in Chicago. After her record sales slumped, Decca executives reteamed Tharpe and Knight, hoping to create new recording magic and high sales. In 1955, they served up the tunes "Stand the Storm" and "Look Away in the Heavenly Land." The songs did little to change the record sales, so Knight joined an R&B concert tour called the "Lucky Seven Blues Tour" in 1956. On the bill with Knight were Earl King, Little Willie John, Otis Williams & the Charms, Jack Dupree, the Royal Jokers, and Hal Singer.

When news of Knight's participation in the R&B tour reached the black church community, her old fans were indignant. Knight was unbothered. She cut a 1956 pop LP with the male vocal group the Millionaires and joined B.B. King on the Rock 'N' Roll Jubilee tour. Soon Knight was recording love songs such as "Tell Me Why" and "As Long as I Love." The former became a moderate hit for Gale Storm in 1956. For the rest of the decade, Mercury executives vacillated between releasing pop and gospel records on Knight, who was rapidly losing her gospel fan base and not gaining a secular fan base. They'd release a pop tune and when that didn't hit, they'd release a gospel one and then start the whole process all over again. Even her fine 1961 recording of "Come Tomorrow" was only a hit when Manfred Mann did a cover of it. Knight, who also appeared in the film *Rockin' the Blues*, finally enjoyed a Top 40 R&B hit in 1965 with the torch ballad "Cry Me a River."

Knight then faded from the scene, only to resurface briefly in 1975 with the LP *Today* on the Labor label. It featured Louisiana Red on guitar and Floyd Waite on piano. She wrote "The Florida Storm" and filled the project out with Waite's "Pushing for Jesus" and standards such as "Step by Step" and "Where He Leads Me." In 1979, she recorded a Savoy Records set of traditional fare entitled *Lord, I've Tried*. In 2003, she recorded a new track for a Rosetta Tharpe tribute CD, *Shout Sister Shout* on M.C. Records. Since that time, Knight, who is still in fine voice, performed on the syndicated radio programs *Mountain Stage* and *WoodSongs Radio Hour*. She's also been interviewed on National Public Radio's *Weekend Edition* and performed in a Tharpe tribute concert with the Holmes Brothers and Odetta in 2004. She has since signed a booking contract with Concerted Efforts and is on the road again.

Patti LaBelle

ONE OF THE FEW artists black America never seems to tire of is the iron-lung powerhouse Patti LaBelle, who has thrilled audiences for more than 40 years with her gospelized vocal approach to her signature songs "Lady Marmalade," "If Only You Knew," and "Over the Rainbow." She was born Patricia Louise Holte on May 24, 1944, in Philadelphia. Her father worked at

Baldwin Locomotive and her mother was a food server at St. Agnes Hospital. Her first vocal influences were jazz singers such as Gloria Lynne, Dinah Washington, and Sarah Vaughn. "My bedroom became my nightclub, my concert stage, my sanctuary," she wrote in her autobiography, *Don't Block the Blessings*. "When I got home from school, I would grab a broom or a bottle or a brush—anything I could pretend was a mike—and stand in front of the bedroom mirror singing my heart out.... I wasn't homely little Patricia Louise with the big nose and the nappy hair and the broken family and the dirty little secret. I was beautiful. I was powerful. I was popular... I was Cinderella—Cinderella with a band and a beat and a tick and a tock that would never strike midnight again."

LaBelle met her fairy godmother in the Beulah Baptist Church Young Adult Choir. The choir director, Harriett Chapman, made LaBelle feel comfortable enough to do her first solo with the song "God Specializes," a Roberta Martin standard. "It touched me in a

Patti LaBelle / photo by Robert Shanklin

special way. Each time we sang it, it moved me deep down inside," LaBelle remembered in her autobiography. "When Mrs. Chapman said it needed a solo, for a reason I can't fully explain now, I raised my hand.... I was stirred by the music and moved by the spirit. Once I closed my eyes, it felt like a dream. It was as if I really wasn't out there in front of the young adults choir at all. I was back in my bedroom mirror, singing into my broomstick.... Halfway through the song, I was no longer just singing. I was chanting, I was incanting, I was crying, I was testifying, laying back on the notes until the song was no longer a song, but a sanctified call to God and I was no longer a teenage girl singing in a church choir but a messenger of the Lord singing on the front steps of heaven." When she finished, the room was dead silent. Some people were whimpering and brushing tears from their eyes. Mrs. Chapman was astonished at LaBelle's hidden talent and told her, "Patsy, from now on you will be our soloist."

LaBelle was the chosen soloist when she formed the BlueBelles with Cindy Birdsong, Nona Hendryx, and Sarah Dash in 1960. Although they recorded prolifically during the '60s, their only major hit was 1962's million-selling bubblegum tune, "I Sold My Heart to the Junkman." By 1970, they had taken British Vicki Wickham as their manager and she completely transformed them from a girl group into a space-age (based on their futuristic stage costumes) soul group. They turned in spectacular gospel-styled performances on Laura Nyro's 1971 old-school soul album *Gonna Take a Miracle*. Nowhere is the group's church background more evident than on the vocals on the title song. The trio (Birdsong had left to join the Supremes) named their publishing company Gospel Birds and, now named simply LaBelle, they became the most ferocious black female group of the 1970s, in or out of gospel. They could stand up against any singer in black music and sing the competition down to the ground. During the decade, they enjoyed several hits, including the chart-topper "Lady Marmalade," "Isn't It a Shame," and "Last Dance."

In 1977, the trio all launched solo singing careers. LaBelle's ability to hold extended notes, hit high C, and growl with the best of church singers shone throughout her repertoire. Her debut LP *Patti LaBelle* featured songs such as "I Think About You" and "You

Are My Friend," which could have easily been considered gospel with a slight change in lyrics. Reporters constantly asked LaBelle whether she'd ever record a gospel album. She always said that it was a dream of hers to record one, but was waiting for the right time. She made a concession in 1982, when she starred on Broadway in a successful revival of *Your Arms Too Short to Box with God.*

In the 1990s, LaBelle began to make gospel cameos. She recorded "The Sun Will Shine Again" with Whitley Phipps on his Coral Records LP of the same name in 1990. The following year, she starred in a PBS television special, *Going Home to Gospel.* It featured the Mighty Clouds of Joy, Edwin Hawkins, the Barrett Sisters, and Albertina Walker. Later in 1991, LaBelle's childhood church, Beulah, celebrated the 51st anniversary of Mrs. Chapman's service to the church choir. "I had to break another commitment to be there, but I needed to return to the church where it all began for me to pay tribute to the lady who encouraged me to step up," LaBelle said in her memoirs. "I needed Mrs. Chapman to know how much her faith in me would always mean…. That night, in November 1991, for the first time in three decades, I sang with the choir. I joined them to perform for Mrs. Chapman, to sing her favorite hymn: 'Jesus Keep Me Near the Cross.' That was the last time I sang with the choir and it was the last time I saw Mrs. Chapman." She died of cancer eight months later.

In 1992, LaBelle recorded "Ready for a Miracle" for Steve Martin's *Leap of Faith* movie soundtrack. She joined the 2003 Shirley Caesar & Friends duets project to record with Gladys Knight and Caesar on "I Know It Was the Blood," and sang "Always There" on T.D. Jakes's *God's Leading Ladies* CD in 2002. LaBelle also recorded the inspirational ballad "When You've Been Blessed (Feels Like Heaven)," which reached No. 4 on the R&B singles chart in 1992. It appeared on her CD *Burnin.'*

"I know what I do is blessed or God wouldn't have left me here to carry on," LaBelle wrote in her book. "He wouldn't have given me a voice that people want to hear…. People have told me they leave my concerts different than when they came…. I think it's why God put me here. I know it is. That's the only way I can explain why the older I get, the stronger my voice becomes. I can hold a note longer. I can take a song higher. I can carry a message farther. And I can't hold back. This is what I live for. To share my gift."

Ladies of Song

IN A WORLD OF Shirelles and Vandellas, the Ladies of Song were closer in style to the Andrews Sisters. This black female trio (and sometime quartet) was arguably the most sophisticated gospel group on the circuit in the 1960s. They didn't sing hard like the Davis Sisters, didn't have the varied voices of the Caravans, and didn't have the flamboyance of the Ward Singers. They were a thoroughly enjoyable group that sang traditional church songs with highbrow orchestrations to appeal to a white audience and just enough soul to keep the black bourgeoisie interested.

Sometime in 1961, Celeste Melton Scott and her sister Margaret Aikens Jenkins, who were raised in Chicago, joined Robbie Preston Williams in forming the group. Scott and Jenkins's mother, Marie C. Melton, was an evangelist who brought them up in church. Scott was a soloist with the National Baptist Convention and Jenkins was director of the West Adams Foursquare Church Chapel Choir. However, Jenkins's ambitions were not confined to the local assembly. A gifted songwriter, her songs were recorded by several artists. In addition, she and Ollie Lafayette formed Mag-Oll Records in Chicago and recorded groups such as the Helen Robinson Youth Chorus.

Meanwhile, the Houston-raised Williams, a preacher's kid, was a pianist and soloist with the Divine Guidance Church in Los Angeles. Her son, Billy Preston, was a child actor who became a professional organist in the 1960s before hitting it big as a pop artist in the 1970s. Williams's daughter, Rhodena, was also a pianist and became involved with the Gospel Music Workshop of America (GMWA) convention early on and conducted the choirs on several of their LPs over the years.

After the group came together, they began to perform on programs with Mahalia Jackson, who was one of their biggest supporters. With her push, they were soon appearing on television and were eventually noticed by Word Records and offered a contract in 1967.

Ladies of Song / photo courtesy of Margaret Aikens Jenkins

Their debut LP *Soul of Gospel* appeared in 1968 and the album *Everybody Will Be Happy* followed the next year. The track "Battlefield" from the latter held particular meaning for Jenkins, who recorded it as a tribute to her mother. "Mama was singing 'On the Battlefield,'" she recalls with tears in her throat. "She had a heart attack while she was singing in church." Ironically, Marie died suddenly in October 1971 when she too was onstage singing "Battlefield." After her death, the Ladies of Song sang no more.

Jenkins wrote most of the group's songs, such as "The Only Hope We Have." She also wrote a dozen songs that Mahalia Jackson recorded, including "A Spring in Galilee." Now in her eighth decade, she continues to perform on occasion and never misses a chance to witness about the goodness of the Lord in her girlish soprano. "Oh baby," she says. "Without him, we're nothing. He's the only hope we have."

LaRue

WITH THEIR EXOTIC Continental looks, they are probably the most attractive alternative rock artists Christian music has ever witnessed. However, beneath the sibling duo LaRue's Euro-styled music is a soulfulness that rises from Natalie's deep vocals and Phillip's passionate lyrics. They've already made a name for themselves with songs such as "Waiting Room," "Reason," "Fly," and "Picture Frame."

Natalie (born December 28, 1983) and Phillip (born October 9, 1981) LaRue came from a Christian household that moved around a lot. Their father's work took the family to Southern California, Oregon, and Arizona. While living in Phoenix, Phillip was a soccer and track buff and pondered a career in sports. However, at the age of 14, he came down with mononucleosis, which exacerbated into double pneumonia. He was on his back for months and during his recovery his parents gave him a guitar to occupy his time. He learned three chords and began writing songs. "My mom was the one who pushed us to write songs together," Natalie told *Release* magazine. "Phillip had started writing songs on his own, but they were a little too depressing. I wrote poetry, so my mom suggested that we try writing as a team."

After writing their first song, "Picture Frame," the duo began writing enough songs to stage concerts and performed around the Phoenix area at youth groups. Soon they were in the studio with local producer Ken Barry making a demo. He sent it off to a variety of Christian recording labels. A Reunion Records executive was interested in coming to the city to meet LaRue when their dad's business took them to Nashville to live. Once there, LaRue was signed to Reunion and began working on their debut CD with Newsboys producer Mike Linney and Christian rock legend Rick Elias.

The songs the duo wrote touched on a variety of issues that youth of any background could relate to, such as loneliness ("As She Cries") and finding a soul mate ("Someday"). "My so-called friends started putting me down and making fun of me, and it was a really hard time in my life," Phillip recalled to *Breakaway* magazine in 1999. "When I was at school I felt out of place and like an outcast. I felt like I had to do something to get noticed and known by others. I'd been ignoring God and decided to get back on track in my relationship with him. Shortly thereafter I became interested in… ministering to others through music." Phillip went on to say, "We want to encourage people to be real and to be honest. So many Christians go through life thinking they can't open up and let others know they have struggles. But that's one message we want to get across. We all go through things, and we've all made mistakes. We are not better than anybody else."

Their eponymous debut CD hit stores in August 1999. A *Billboard* magazine review said, "Their voices have a strength and sense of purpose that belies their young years, yet they still convey the infectious exuberance of youth…" The album's best cut was "As She Cries," a soulfully melancholy ballad that showed off Natalie's thick, richly textured lead vocals as Phillip harmonized behind her. A track that showed their lyrical playfulness was "Stars." On the song, which indicts the arrogant trappings of celebrity, they sing, "I am a movie star, I drive a big car. I'm on the silver screen, I am a citrus queen." With the video of "Reason" getting heavy rotation on the Disney Channel, the CD peaked at No. 30 on the CCM album sales chart and sold well over 100,000 units—a very impressive debut indeed.

LaRue has continued to build their audience with the successive albums *Transparent* (2001) and *Reaching* (2002). They have also shown up on several other projects. Natalie led a club song with DJ Maj on the *Soul Lift* soundtrack, which featured Johnny Cash and others. LaRue's song "Fly" was featured on the *Left Behind* soundtrack and "Reason" was on the *Whatever It Takes* compilation CD that benefited the Cassie Bernall Foundation (the young Christian teenager killed in the 1999 Columbine shooting). They co-wrote "I'm All Yours" with Rachel Lampa for her *Kaleidoscope* CD.

Coming from a tight-knit family, when LaRue travels, their parents and younger twin sisters, Brianna and Rachelle, often accompany them. Brianna was born with cerebral palsy and Natalie has said, "Brianna has had a huge impact on our lives and career.... She really knows who she is in the Lord and doesn't worry about what people think of her." They wrote a song in tribute to her inspiration and energetic spirit on "Transparent." LaRue say their goal is to touch people with God's message. "Years from now," Natalie says, "we want to look back and be able to say that whatever we did, wherever we went, and whatever

we've made plans to do, we were trying to share God's love and word with as many people as possible."

Denise LaSalle

ONE OF THE SASSIEST singers on the old-school soul circuit, LaSalle is also one of the best songwriters the genre has ever produced. Along with writing her No. 1 R&B hit, 1971's "Trapped by a Thing Called Love," LaSalle has written hit songs for Barbara Mandrell, Rita Coolidge, Ann Peebles, Lattimore, Little Milton, and the late Z.Z. Hill. She was born Denise Allen on July 16, 1939, in Belzoni, Mississippi. Her recordings for Westbound Records between 1970 and 1973 established her as an R&B artist with a gift for spinning a story that could make one laugh or cry. Among the hits from that period were the naughty "Man Sized Job," "Run and Tell That," and "Trapped by a Thing Called Love." After she moved on to ABC/MCA Records in 1976 and later Malaco Records in the 1980s and 1990s, LaSalle revealed a new side to her personality with a string of raunchy story songs about impotent men, whorish women, and unfaithful lovers, such as "Don't Mess with My Toot Toot," "Right Side of the Wrong Bed," and "Married but Not to Each Other."

LaSalle and her husband, James Wolfe, own the Jackson, Tennessee, radio stations WFKX, WZDQ, and WJAK. In 1996, Wolfe felt called into the ministry. In 1999, LaSalle recorded her first gospel CD, *God's Got My Back*, for her own Angels in the Mist Records label. It was one of the best gospel albums of the year with a warm soul feeling throughout. The funky title track was No. 1 on several gospel radio stations in the South. Among the standouts on the project was LaSalle's 11-minute rap on what's wrong with the world today on "Going through Changes." There was the beautiful R&B-styled ballad, "God Don't Make Mistakes," which provided comfort to those who have lost loved ones. Dipping into the shtick that made her secular raps so humorous, LaSalle used the format on "Still Talking About a Man," although the man in question here is Jesus Christ. Another smart turn was how LaSalle took the Spinners' secular hit "Mighty Love" and transformed it into a gospel tune, "His Mighty Love."

LaSalle performed at the GMWA convention and appeared on Candi Staton's TBN television show to promote the album. However, the album was poorly distributed by Southern Distributors in Atlanta, and many gospel radio announcers in the North refused to listen to the project because of LaSalle's secular music background. At the time, the album only sold 6,000 units according to SoundScan. Although she retained her faith to an even greater depth, LaSalle left the gospel field when she wasn't embraced. These days, she continues to give blues concerts where she will occasionally surprise the audience with one of her gospel numbers.

Lavender Light Gospel Choir

A NEW YORK CITY–BASED, 45-member chorus focused on providing spiritual and gospel music inspiration to the gay community, Lavender Light was founded in 1985. The original director was Gregg Payne, who stayed on for eight years. Their current director is the classically trained University of Wisconsin graduate Ray Gordon. Their repertoire consists of traditional black gospel, Negro spirituals, and anthemic tunes. Their first CD, *Lavender Light*, was issued in 1994 with such traditional fare as Janiece Thompson's strong lead on Sister Rosetta Tharpe's "Over My Head" and Dionne Freeney's urgent alto on "I Don't Know What You Came to Do." For their 2000 CD release, the chorus took on a slightly contemporary flavor. Entitled *Light in the House*, it featured the choir's take on Richard Smallwood's "I Will Sing Praises," Donnie McClurkin's "Speak to My Heart," and Shirley Caesar's "Sweeping through the City." The CD received a top rating in the gay magazine *The Advocate*.

Donald Lawrence & the Tri-City Singers

IN 1995, WHEN Donald Lawrence & the Tri-City Singers' sophomore CD *Bible Stories* was released, there was much excitement in the air. "This is going to be big," proclaimed Nashville's WFSK radio announcer Rev. Charles Howse. "This is one of the best albums we've

ever got in here. We're playing it heavy too. I was down in Atlanta and they were playing it heavy down there. This is going to be the hit of the summer." He didn't lie. That album remains the choir's best-selling project with a quarter million in sales. According to *USA Today*, "[They are] one of the most phenomenal choirs out now." Kirk Franklin has gotten media attention and accolades for bringing contemporary urban gospel into popularity in the 1990s, but much of the credit really goes to Lawrence, who mixed Franklin's breakthrough record "Why We Sing" and also produced many of the other songs that were responsible for taking contemporary gospel to the next level during that period.

The Tri-City Singers were initially formed in 1981 as a 34-voice ensemble comprised of members from the tri-city areas of Charlotte and Gastonia, North Carolina, and Spartanburg/Greenville, South Carolina. They sang at churches throughout the Carolinas. "When we first started going on the road, it was a long time before we started making enough money to cover our travel expenses," Lawrence said in 1995. "At the same time, we needed to be going out on the road to help promote our album and get our name out there. We had to put up with promoters who bring us to town and then don't have the money to pay us. We always did the shows anyway, so that meant we ended up paying our way to do these shows. We didn't have anyone giving us money, so I ended up incurring about $30,000 in debts."

Lawrence grew up with a love for music. Born May 4, 1961, he was raised by his godmother and taught himself to play the piano by the age of 15. Reared in the church, he mostly listened to gospel music by Twinkie Clark, Marvin Winans, and Thomas Whitfield. He earned a Bachelor of Fine Arts degree in musical theater from the prestigious Cincinnati Conservatory. In 1985, he formed the group Company with some of his friends. Their sound was akin to the a cappella that Take 6 would eventually become known for years later, a fusion of spiritual message music with an urban flavor. In 1987, he wrote a musical with his former college professor, Worth Gardner, called *Sing Alleluia*, which was staged at the Cincinnati Playhouse. A talent scout at the infamous Village Gate in New York then brought the show to that venue for an engagement. While in New York, Lawrence

Donald Lawrence / photo courtesy of Crystal Rose Records

met someone who secured him a role in the comedic play A Woman Like That, which starred R&B crooner Peabo Bryson. Promoter Bill Washington took the show on the road for eight weeks. Around this time, a friend of Lawrence's gave a tape of some of his music to R&B star Stephanie Mills. She liked it so much she asked him to produce some tracks for her. "I came straight from the church," Lawrence said in 1995. "So I turned her down for a year because I didn't know if I could do urban music or not." He eventually wrote two tracks for Mills's 1991 album, *Something Real*. He began traveling with her and writing her musical arrangements and, eventually, became her musical director. When members of the group En Vogue went to see Mills in concert, they came backstage and asked who did her arrangements. They hired Lawrence to be their vocal coach and arranger for their "Funky Divas" tour in 1993.

Lawrence's association with the Tri-City Singers began when a close friend, who had served as the group's musical director, resigned his position. He suggested that Lawrence take the position, which resulted in their 1993 *A Songwriter's Point of View* CD, which rose to No. 2 on the gospel chart and was pushed by the radio singles "Personal Friend of Mine," "Shut De Do," and "I Walk with the King." Nominated for several Stellar and NAACP Image awards, that debut was followed two years later with Tri-City's No. 1 breakthrough album, the Grammy-nominated *Bible Stories* in 1995. Lawrence then scored a Top 30 R&B hit, "Don't Give Up," from the *Don't Be a Menace* soundtrack. The song featured Karen Clark-Sheard, Hezekiah Walker, and Kirk Franklin with Lawrence. "We've always loved to entertain an audience, but that by itself is not nearly enough," group manager Vanessa Glenn-Durrah once said. "We want to be known as more than a group with cool stage moves and CDs full of great songs. We want to touch and change people's very lives through the power of God moving in what we do. All the success the last decade has brought us has been exciting, but Tri-City's greatest calling is—and will always be—first and foremost for ministry. We never could have lasted this long if it was for any reasons other than loving to sing and serve the Lord."

In the years since, Tri-City has enjoyed further hit albums such as *Hello Christmas* (which earned them a performance on NBC's *Today Show*), *Tri-City4.com*, and *Go Get Your Life Back*. In 2004, Lawrence decided to step down from his shepherd's post with the Tri-City Singers. He signed an imprint deal with Zomba/Verity Records for his recording label, Quiet Water. The first artists he signed were the Murrills and Dewayne Woods. His own solo album, *I Speak Life*, was released in September of that year.

RECOMMENDED RECORDING: *Restoring the Years* (EMI Gospel, 2003) features all of the group's radio successes, including "Never Seen the Righteous," "When Sunday Comes" with Daryl Coley, and "The Best Is Yet to Come."

Laura Lee

IN HER 1967–1975 SOUL music peak, Laura Lee was a tough-talking woman with a liberated stance on male-

Laura Lee / Hot Wax Records LP cover

female relationships that was unique for the time period, with brass-knuckle belters such as "Women's Love Rights," "Dirty Man," and "Rip Off." The wide-eyed Laura Lee was born on March 9, 1945, in Chicago and raised in Detroit. Her adoptive parents were Rev. Edward Rundless, an original member of the Soul Stirrers and pastor of the New Liberty Baptist Church, and his wife, Ernestine, who formed the Meditation Singers. Lee's vocal talents were apparent early on and by the age of nine she'd joined the Meditation Singers. The group recorded for Specialty Records at the time. Audiences love children and with her fire-rasp vocals, Lee often stole the show with her solos. Family friend James Cleveland formed a short-lived gospel trio of Lee with Jackie Burney and Aretha Franklin. They patterned themselves after the Caravans and sang their songs such

as "Lord, Keep Me Day by Day" and "Not Tired Yet." The group was just for fun because Lee had a real job already touring all over the country with the Meditation Singers. They performed in nightclubs such as New York's Sweet Chariot and the Paris Opera House. Frank Sinatra caught their act at the Flamingo Hotel in Las Vegas and offered Lee a recording contract. She told writer Lee Hildebrand, "He went up and asked my mother if he could pull me from the group and put me on his Reprise label. He said something like, 'This little bitty girl with the big voice—could we have her? We know we could go places with her.' But Mama was hesitant. I was still in my teens, and I was still dedicated to gospel."

Sinatra's offer got Lee thinking and when she was old enough, she decided to go pop in 1966 when she cut her first R&B record for the Ric-Tic label. From there she moved on to Chess Records where her first record was a secular song her friend James Cleveland wrote for her called "Stop Giving Your Man Away." It bombed, but she'd eventually record such gritty, Southern-soul styled records as "Need to Belong," "Dirty Man," and "As Long as I Got You" (said to be based on the Violinaires' gospel hit "I Don't Know"), which were all R&B hits. Lee's career was red-hot as she toured with Ike and Tina Turner and Wilson Pickett, among others. In 1969, Lee jumped over to Atlantic Records where she recorded "What a Man" (the chorus of which would be part of a million-seller for Salt-N-Pepa more than 20 years later). None of her singles there were big sellers, so she made another move, this time to Holland-Dozier-Holland's Hot Wax label. With the new label, Lee surpassed all of her prior success with sassy, feminist R&B smashes such as "Rip Off" (No. 3 R&B), "Women's Love Rights" (No. 11 R&B), and "Crumbs Off the Table" (No. 40 R&B).

Well before Millie Jackson and Denise LaSalle started trash-talking and recording somewhat X-rated material, Lee was putting out the same material without profanity. Her tough-as-nails attitude toward male-female relationships spoke to many. For instance, in "Rip Off" she seeks vengeance against an unfaithful man: "I'm tired of being neglected, I'm gonna slap him in the face with the unexpected. I'm setting him up for the rip off…" Then there was the what's-good-for-the-goose mentality on "Women's Love Rights" where she declares, "Stand up and fight for your love rights, love who you wanna, cuz a man is sure gonna." There's a demand for sexual satisfaction on "Crumbs off the Table" where she complains, "I'm hungry, but you ain't able! All you wanna give me is the crumbs off the table." On "Wanted, Lover: No Experience Necessary," she was even more direct as she spelled out her desire: "I want you to S-O-C-K-it-to-Me." Her 1972 album *Two Sides of Laura Lee* featured a funky, upbeat gospel track called "You've Got to Save Me," a nice nod to her gospel roots.

During a good period of the 1970s, Lee was in a romantic relationship with Al Green. After surviving a major operation and long recovery period, Lee ended her secular career. "I was tired and I just didn't want to be Laura Lee the entertainer anymore," she told her Chess liner notes writer David Nathan. Lee and Green recorded a stunning version of "People Get Ready" for his 1981 *Higher Plane* LP. That went so well that Green produced the stellar gospel LP *Jesus Is the Light of My Life* by Lee in 1983. It was distributed through Word Records. In 1984, she recorded one more superb traditional gospel album, *All Power*, for Tyscot Records. For years, Lee sang in Detroit churches and refused all offers to sing secular music. "For years, I did missionary work with other evangelists, bishops, and pastors," she wrote on her www.ladylauralee.com Web site in 2003. "I prayed as instructed... Thousands of people were healed, delivered, and set free from bondage. In doing his work, I seldom sang. In March 2003, God spoke to me and instructed me to go back and sing music of all kinds, whether it be gospel, soul, R&B, or pop, and sing only the truth. With the Lord in my heart and soul, I am on my way to do his will, with hopes I will be received with love, as I was on my last journey."

LeFevres

PERHAPS THE MOST influential family in the early days of Southern gospel music, the LeFevres' career lasted 50 years and their music has influenced a wide array of country artists. Brothers Urias (1910–1979) and Alphus (1912–1988) LeFevre were born and raised in Smithville, Tennessee. They attended Lee College in Cleveland, Tennessee. At the school, they joined the Bible

Training School Quartet No. 2 and began looking at music as a formal career. In 1934, Urias married Eva Mae Whittington (born 1917), a vocalist and piano player, who formed a trio with Urias and Alphus. In 1939, they moved to Atlanta where they performed as the LeFevre Trio and sang regularly on WGST radio. As their name grew, the group expanded to include other relatives and friends. At that point, they billed themselves as the LeFevres. In the 1940s, they began to record 78-rpms for Bibletone Records. They became known for songs such as "Scatter Sunshine," "I Walk with Jesus," and "Keep on the Firing Line." Their fame was further buttressed by regular appearances on WAGA TV in Atlanta. In 1959, their syndicated musical television series, *The Singing Caravan*, aired in 65 markets and featured the top Southern gospel acts of the day. As a testament to their success, the LeFevres did television commercials for SSS Tonic and Martha White Flour. The LeFevres were a successful music machine. They syndicated programs for Southern gospel and non-religious country acts. They published sheet music, operated a state-of-the-art recording studio, and owned a concert-booking agency. By 1976, the group's name and business had been sold to its longtime bass singer, Rex Nelon (1932–2000), who joined the group in 1957. After Eva retired in 1977, Nelon changed the group's name to the Rex Nelon Singers out of respect for the LeFevres since there were no longer any LeFevres singing in the group. In spite of bypass surgery and a nasty fall in recent years, Eva continues to perform intermittently, mostly with the wildly successful Bill Gaither Homecoming concerts.

Howard Lemon

ONE OF THE STRONG, contemporary, R&B-styled gospel groups to emerge in the 1970s, the Howard Lemon Singers recorded a couple of stellar albums that match the power of Stax labelmates the Rance Allen Group. Lemon began playing the piano at the age of five and later picked up the clarinet, trumpet, and trombone. At the age of 12, he progressed to studying classical piano and organ. A song he wrote, "No Greater Love," was recorded by the Voices of Tabernacle, under the direction of Rev. Charles A. Craig and Rev. James Cleveland. Marvin Gaye also recorded it later. Lemon founded the Howard Lemon Singers in the late 1960s. The group consisted of Joyce Moore, Esther Smith, William Garrett, and Orean Williams. They signed to Stax Records' Gospel Truth imprint in 1972. Their 1973 LP *I Am Determined* included a beautiful ballad "Stop, Look, Listen to Your Heart," which was a gospelization of the Stylistics' massive pop soul hit of the same name. Over the years, Lemon has collaborated with Mattie Moss Clark and Thomas Whitfield, among others. Today, Lemon serves as the music coordinator for the Pleasant Grove Baptist Church in Detroit.

Meadowlark Lemon

KNOWN AS THE Clown Prince of the Harlem Globetrotters basketball team for 24 years, Meadowlark Lemon was born April 25, 1935, in Wilmington, North Carolina. After the 6'6" Lemon graduated from high school, he briefly served in the army and played with the Kansas City Stars basketball team. In 1957 he joined the Harlem Globetrotters and became a household name with his near-perfect hook shot and zany on-court antics. He retired in 1979 and eventually devoted himself to the Christian ministry. Lemon recorded a quasi-disco LP, *My Kids*, for Casablanca Records that same year. Although the single was a hyped-up version of "Sweet Georgia Brown," the project included songs such as "God Put Love in Everybody." He's recorded other religious music in years since and his www.meadowlarklemon.com Web site features autographed basketballs and nutritional drinks. Lemon is now an ordained minister and lives in Scottsdale, Arizona. Lemon is one of only four former members of the Harlem Globetrotters to have his jersey (number 36) retired.

Lucylle Lemon & the Lemon Singers

A DETROIT-BASED, 60-member chorus that was popular in the 1950s, the group was founded by Lucylle Lemon (born July 14, 1916, in Detroit). A dynamic arranger,

composer, and directress, Lemon was a lifelong church singer, nicknamed "Girlie" because of her youthful vitality. Her group traveled around the country keeping traditional gospel music alive in the 1940s and '50s. They toured the Midwest with groups such as the Dixie Hummingbirds and Sam Cooke and the Soul Stirrers. Many of the church congregations they sang for in states such as Montana and North Dakota had never seen black people in person. "They were feeling our hair, trying to understand what it was like," David Winans, a group member, said in his autobiography.

"Everybody in the choir wasn't what you would call saved," Winans continued. "Some were just people who wanted to sing. I saw in the choir things being done that were against the teachings of the Bible." For example, Winans said the chorus wasn't invited back to a Nazarene church because some of the chorus members were caught smoking, which was frowned upon in that denomination. In spite of their national travel schedule, they were mostly known and revered in Detroit where Lemon was also called the "Doll of Gospel Music." In 1990, Sound of Gospel Records issued an LP of Lemon's regional singles entitled *Fill Me with Your Spirit* and in 2002 a tribute CD, *Detroit Remembers.*

Elder James Lenox

ERSTWHILE PASTOR OF Chicago's Greater Holy Temple Church of God in Christ (COGIC), Lenox was known for his deep, scratchy vocals on radio hits such as "I'm One of Them Today," "The King Is Coming," and "There Is No Failure in God." Born July 4, 1931, Lenox's father was a church bishop and Lenox began to sing at the age of five. He recorded traditional choir-oriented music for Savoy Records during most of the 1970s and 1980s. His wife, Aldrea, sang with both the Jessy Dixon Singers and the Dorothy Norwood Singers. It was circa 1982 that Lenox first introduced the song "I Won't Complain," popularized by Rev. Paul Jones a decade later. After his father passed away in 1986, Lenox assumed the pastorship of his father's church. Lenox died of prostate cancer in 2001. His son, Lamont Lenox (born May 24, 1956), records gospel music and hosts the syndicated TV series

Testify! Another son, Kelvin Lenox (born 1957), wrote songs for Edwin Hawkins, Angela Spivey, and others. He died of diabetes on January 18, 2004.

Crystal Lewis

ONE OF THE BLACKEST-sounding white singers that the CCM genre has ever produced, Crystal Lewis has enjoyed many hits such as "Beauty for Ashes" with Ron Kenoly, "Lean on Me" with Kirk Franklin, and "People Get Ready … Jesus Is Comin'" which received airplay on both black and white Christian music radio stations. She was born September 11, 1969, in Corona, California. Her father, Holland Lewis, was pastor of the Anaheim First Church of the Nazarene. Lewis grew up listening to LPs such as Michael Jackson's *Off the Wall* and Sting's *Nothing Like the Sun*, as well as music by the Stray Cats and Sade. Raised in a Christian home, Lewis and her sisters used to gather around the family piano and harmonize with their mother. Lewis first surfaced as a member of the cast of the youth musical Hi-Tops in 1985 and later fronted the rockabilly gospel band Wild Blue Yonder when she was 16. When the band was recording an album, Brian Ray (who was six years older than she) came in to photograph the cover. Lewis and Ray instantly fell in love against her parents' objections. Lewis was forbidden to see Ray, so she saw him in secret. "I got caught a few times," she told the *Los Angeles Times* in May 1998. "I knew I shouldn't be sneaking around, but I didn't know how else to do it. I had to have this relationship." When Ray proposed, her parents made Lewis return the ring. However, by the time Lewis was 19 and had gone through premarital counseling, her parents approved of the nuptials and the couple was finally married.

Lewis went solo in 1987 and snagged a recording deal with Frontline Records that produced moderate radio hits such as "God Is Somebody," "Rock Solid," and "You Didn't Have to Do It." She felt stifled about the lack of creative freedom and the label's insistence on making her a pop-dance artist. After Frontline went bankrupt, Lewis and Ray formed Metro One Records in 1992. Her first album, *Remember*, was a fusion of alternative rock with a soulful edge. Christian music critics loved her music from the start and their buzz helped Lewis develop something of an underground audience, although she was not yet a huge Christian radio star. That would change when in 1996 Myrrh Records, impressed with her independent record sales, began to distribute Lewis's music. The first album from the union, *Beauty for Ashes*, transformed Lewis into a Christian world superstar within a year's time. The gold-selling album reached No. 5 on the CCM chart and spawned the smash singles "People Get Ready… Jesus Is Comin'," "God's Been Good to Me," and the title song, a duet with Ron Kenoly.

In 1998, Lewis joined Interscope/B-Rite Records where Kirk Franklin's label handlers hoped to transform this pretty white girl with the big black voice into a megastar outside of the church world. They paired her with Franklin, U2's Bono, Mary J. Blige, and R. Kelly on Franklin's 1999 pop anthem "Lean on Me." Because of the caliber of artists on the session, the label was banking on an across-the-board smash single that would top the pop, R&B, and Christian music charts. In spite of a nice hook, impassioned vocals, and star personnel, the song was coolly welcomed on all fronts. It only reached No. 79 on the *Billboard* pop single chart, No. 26 on the R&B chart, and white Christian radio refused to play it for the most part, objecting to the appearance of secular artists on the song. The label then rushed out a version of the song with just Lewis and Franklin, which Christian radio did play. Lewis's most recent albums have been a little less radio friendly and more experimental in tone. Her proposed pop breakthrough project for Interscope fell through, and Lewis returned to the independent course that brought her to Myrrh Records' attention in the first place. Her next project, *Fearless*, was geared toward the pop world, but didn't cross over in 2000. A *Billboard* review said, "The R&B flavored pop songs on this… show an artist in peak form…. Lewis's voice is a rare jewel that shimmers and shines throughout this stunning album." Her most recent projects have included a Spanish album, a holiday project, and a new age hymns CD.

RECOMMENDED RECORDING: *More: Live* (Word, 2002) is the album to get as it shows Lewis in a live setting, performing all of her greatest hits.

Lexi

A FORMER ENGLISH TEACHER turned gospel singer, Lexi was born Alexis Nucklos in June 1966. She was raised in her grandfather's Ohio-based Pentecostal church where she sang since the age of five years old. In 1990, she signed with the Polygram-distributed Fixit Records label where she recorded her debut album, *Call Her Lexi.* Afterwards, she went on the road as a background singer for Gerald Levert for three years and later backed up Kim Rutherford, Anointed, Fred Hammond, and Dawkins & Dawkins. Lexi then worked as a schoolteacher until she was led back into the business. "I did not want to come back," she once said. "I had been tremendously hurt by certain business practices I had previously experienced in the music industry. I didn't want anything to do with gospel music or the music industry as a whole. But God had another plan for my life. The Lord told me to come back and do what I had to do for him." She resurfaced with the CD *That's the Way It Is* on boxer Evander Holyfield's Real Deal Records label in 2001. It was a smooth, R&B-flavored gospel project that reached No. 13 on the *Billboard* gospel album sales chart and No. 63 on the R&B album sales chart. At the time, Lexi said, "If this project opens the door for me to travel down the same roads traveled by Brandy, Monica, and Busta Rhymes, I'm available to be used." Unfortunately, her services were not utilized and she faded from the scene again until she resurfaced as a TV host on the Word Network in 2005.

Lil iROCC

AFTER THE SUCCESS of secular kiddy rappers such as Bow Wow and Lil Romeo in the late 1990s, Christian music executives wanted to jump on the bandwagon with a Christian alternative. They found that in Lil iROCC (which stands for "I rely on Christ completely"). Born March 3, 1990 in New Orleans, iROCC was raised in Atlanta. He began professional modeling at the age of three. When his mother, Treiva Williams, was undergoing treatment for cancer in 1997, she and her husband became Christians and joined Bishop Eddie Long's New Birth Missionary Baptist Church.

Lil iROCC / *courtesy of Authority Music*

iROCC began rapping when he was ten years old and signed up for a talent contest with V103 in Atlanta in December 2001. He was one of 15 finalists. "We just told him to get up there and have fun," his mother said. "And he just rocked it, and walked away with the grand prize." In 2000, his father met EMI Gospel executive Ken Pennell, who scored iROCC a deal with Forefront/EMI. Although there are not a lot of gospel radio stations that will play Christian rap music, iROCC's peppy radio single "All My People" received some airplay and his self-titled CD reached No. 26 on the *Billboard* gospel chart when it was released in summer 2003. There were immediate media comparisons to BowWow. "I know Bow-Wow," iROCC told HipHop2Go.net at the time. "He's cool so it doesn't bother me at all. The main thing that Bow Wow and I have in common [is] we are both hip-hop cats. Hip-hop tells your story—what's real to you. So that's what each of us is doing—rapping and 'reppin' about what's real to each one of us. Not a good or bad thing—just a real thing."

"I want to touch not just kids, but all people, and let them understand what this is all about," iROCC has said. "It's not about me. It's about God the Father. I want to lead people to Christ, and also let them know it's fun to be with God. When you have him, you don't have to be afraid of anything. The skits and the songs are really what I'm about. The songs are a lot of fun, but they also have something to say. I'm excited about God, and I live for Jesus Christ, but I make sure to never come across like I'm preaching at anybody. I just want other kids to see that it's okay for them to be excited about Christ, too."

Little Cedric & the Hailey Singers

HE MADE A BIGGER splash in the R&B world with the raunchy soul quartet Jodeci and later as a solo artist named K-Ci, but Cedric Hailey got his start as a gospel artist. A Charlotte, North Carolina, native, Hailey (born September 21, 1969) and his brother JoJo (born June 10, 1971) toured the Southeast with Donald "DeVante Swing" DeGrate and his brother Dalvin in various gospel groups. The DeGrates' father was a minister and both families were very active in the Pentecostal church. Hailey's debut LP *Jesus Saves* had appeared on Gospearl Records in 1986 and the DeGrates had recorded for a small label as well. The two sets of brothers were initially brought together by their girlfriends. Hailey was actually dating the same girl Dalvin was dating and they almost came to blows over her. In the end, they both dropped her and forged a mutual dream of R&B stardom. Their LP *I'm Alright Now* received a good review from *Billboard*: "Little Cedric sounds like a young Michael Jackson, and his songs have a very commercial black-pop sound. He's made a big splash in gospel and has the talent to be a legend tomorrow; this album is another step in the right direction."

Around the age of 16, DeVante ran away to Minneapolis hoping to land a job at Prince's Paisley Park outfit, but was rejected. He returned home and started writing songs, which he got JoJo to record. The duo trekked to New York to shop the demo to record labels. At the last minute, K-Ci and Dalvin decided to ride along. They walked into Uptown Entertainment with more than an hour's worth of songs and were about to be thrown out when rapper Heavy D overheard their music and talked Uptown President Andre Harrell into listening to the tape. Harrell liked what he heard and decided to sign them, not as a duo, but as a quartet named Jodeci (a fusion of their nicknames).

The brothers ventured far from their gospel roots with a somewhat wild, sensual repertoire of music. Their debut album *Forever My Lady* appeared in 1991 and went triple-platinum on the strength of the title song and "Come and Talk to Me." Displeased with their treatment at Uptown, the band flirted with taking their next CD, *Diary of a Mad Band*, to Dr. Dre's Death Row Records. Uptown retaliated by not promoting the CD, which still sold heavily because of the buzz about the group and was certified platinum.

Trouble knocked on their door in 1993 when a woman K-Ci met at a club and brought back to DeVante's apartment filed criminal charges against them both, saying that K-Ci threatened her and fondled her breasts while DeVante pointed a gun at her. Inspired by this incident, Jodeci released the CD *The Show, the After Party, the Hotel* in the summer of 1995. It too was a platinum seller. Around the same time, K-Ci released his first solo track. "If You Think You're Lonely Now" was a cover of a song by another gospel-turned-R&B star, Bobby Womack. The most surprising element to the song was how similar K-Ci's weathered vocals were to Womack's raspy voice. Since then, K-Ci and JoJo have recorded as a duo, emphasizing lush R&B ballads over the more raunchy fare Jodeci was known for.

Little Richard

THE OTHER KING OF rock 'n' roll (other than Elvis, that is), Little Richard is an American icon. When he burst on the music scene in the 1950s with his greased pompadour, heavy makeup and mascara, preacher's squall, and sensuous New Orleans boogie songs, Little Richard was not someone the public would soon forget. In fact, they never have. He's as infamous now as he was 50 years ago.

Born Richard Penniman on December 5, 1935, in Macon, Georgia, he was raised in church. It was through listening to gospel music by the Clara Ward Singers that he discovered group member Marion Williams's gospel yodel, which Little Richard would later incorporate into

Little Richard / courtesy of Specialty/Fantasy Records

his signature song, "Tutti Frutti." In 1955, he landed a recording deal with Specialty Records and recorded the salacious piano romp "Tutti Frutti" that features his catchphrase "Shut up!" and that Marion Williams yelp. Other smash hits followed such as "Long Tall Sally," "Rip It Up," "Good Golly Miss Molly," and "Lucille." Richard was one of the first black acts with a hard R&B style to cross over to the pop charts on his own terms.

When a plane he was on experienced trouble during an Australian concert tour in 1957, Richard retired from the music business and studied theology at the Oakwood Seventh Day Adventist College in Alabama, graduating four years later. By 1962, he had returned to rock 'n' roll. Future rock icons such as the Rolling Stones and the Beatles—both groups idolized Richard and borrowed heavily from his style—opened for him on his tours. He recorded several secular albums, but none approached the success of his earlier music. Richard also recorded several gospel LPs during the 1960s, including *Swingin' Shoutin', Really*

Movin' for Guest Star Records, *Clap Your Hands* for Spin-O-Rama, *Coming Home* for Coral Records, *King of the Gospel Singers* for Mercury Records, and *The Second Coming* for Reprise. Some of Richard's gospel music was far more reverential and subdued than one would expect from such an electrifying performer. However, he did flex his vocal muscle on the Coral Records LP on songs such as "Walk with Me, Lord."

In 1986, after his success in *Down and Out in Beverly Hills*, Warner Bros. had Richard do a new gospel album, *Lifetime Friend*. It was a commercial failure, not because a gospel album by Richard doesn't have an audience, but because it simply was not good. It was an extremely computerized, pop-rock production that often buried Richard's vocals too deep into the mix. Furthermore, the songs were not the solid songs an artist of Richard's stature deserved. Still, the rocking "Great Gosh Almighty" reached No. 42 on the *Billboard* pop singles chart that year.

London Adventist Chorale

FORMED IN 1981 under the direction of conductor Ken Burton, this choir created a unique repertoire of spirituals and classical pieces with just a touch of modern rhythm to keep the music fresh. In 1994, they won England's prestigious Sainsbury Choir of the Year award, which led to international bookings, great media exposure, and performances before the British royal family. In 2002, they performed at Queen Elisabeth's Golden Jubilee concert along with the BBC Symphony and Dame Kiri Te Kanawa at Buckingham Palace.

London Community Gospel Choir

THE UNITED KINGDOM'S first known black gospel choir was formed by Lawrence Johnson, Delroy Powell, and former electrical engineer Rev. Bazil Meade. Meade was born in Montserrat, but moved to London when he was nine years old. His mother commanded him to attend Sunday school in the New Testament church denomination. The music minister there taught him some guitar chords, which he learned sufficiently to play in church services. The female pastor then took him under her wing and he began playing organ on her speaking engagements. He studied Billy Preston's instrumental organ LPs for inspiration and skill development. When the pastor went to a new church, Meade was commissioned to assemble a church singing group. Later he formed a gospel funk band called Kainos.

In 1981, Johnson, Powell, and Meade formed the London Community Gospel Choir following the Brixton and Toxteth race riots. At the time, the three men met to stage a reconciliation concert that would show young blacks in a positive light and also spread the gospel through music. Following the success of their original concert, they made the choir a permanent group in August 1982. After their national debut in a Christmas performance on London's Channel 4 *Black on Black* television program that year, the station was bombarded with requests to see the choir again. That one appearance led to numerous television appearances, concert performances, and record albums.

Although they are a gospel choir, the ensemble (ranging from 50 to 150 members at any given time) boasts allure and showbiz slickness in their presentation (not to mention choreography and secular musical influences) that would probably be frowned upon in the traditional American church market. However, their inspirational music and creative verve have made them the choir of choice for many London recording sessions. They have backed such artists as Tina Turner, Stevie Wonder, Candi Staton, Elton John, George Michael, Sarah Brightman, Sting, Paul McCartney, and Boy George. Several former members, including Lavine Hudson, Nu Colors, and Ronny Jordan, have charted successful singing careers after exiting the choir. American audiences will probably best know them for performing on Disney's *The Lion King* soundtrack. They have also recorded a handful of custom albums in London. "Our music promotes a positive message which is relevant to everyone," Meade has said. "We are passionate about it because we believe what we sing. Whether we are singing at a prestigious event for royalty or on a street corner, we give one hundred percent every time."

RECOMMENDED RECORDING: *Hush and Listen* (Permanent Records, 1993) is a delicious gospel take on pop songs such as the Staple Singers' "I'll Take You There" (with British pop icon P.P. Arnold on lead vocals), Bob Dylan's "Knocking on Heaven's Door," and the Temptations' "Ball of Confusion" among others.

Greg Long

SOUTH DAKOTA–RAISED singer Greg Long (born December 12, 1966) dedicated his life to God at a Dallas Holm concert when he was 14 years old. He sang with his family's gospel group as a kid. In 1993, he signed with Myrrh Records and enjoyed a string of Christian pop radio hits such as "How Long," "Think About Jesus," "Jesus Saves," and "Love the Lord." In 2003, Long replaced Michael Passons in the Christian pop group Avalon. He and Avalon co-founder Janna Long are married with one child.

Janna Long

THE PRIMARY DISTAFF voice in the soulful CCM supergroup Avalon, Janna Long is a preacher's kid from Baltimore, Maryland. She grew up loving the vocal styles of Aretha Franklin and Patti LaBelle. Since 1995, Long has been proving that she can hang with her idols vocally. Her soaring voice graces Avalon's hits such as "Can't Live a Day Without You," "Testify to Love," and "Everything to Me." In 2002, Long released her debut solo CD on Sparrow Records, entitled *Janna*, which includes the funky, urban-styled hit "Greater Is He." "I don't think I break any new ground theologically, and I'm totally fine with that," she told *CCM* magazine in February 2003. "It's a record of songs that encourages the body of Christ. And stylistically, this record is a bit more gospel-geared and [has] more of an R&B flavor than anything I've done with Avalon."

Alvaro Lopez

A LEADING DRUMMER in the Latin Christian market, Alvaro Lopez was born in 1965. He played the drums as a kid in his native Mexico. At the age of 14, he became an accompanist for the well-known singer-songwriter, Emmanuel. That gig led to others with Mexican singing stars such as José José and Pedro Vargas. While on tour with Luis Miguel in 1987, Lopez experienced an emotional breakdown and attempted suicide. Some fellow musicians from Luis Miguel's band led him to a relationship with God. After he was back on his feet, those friends—Heriberto and Hector Hermosillo—formed the Christian group Torre Fuerte with Lopez. They toured throughout Latin America before Lopez left the group in 1997. He then formed Alvaro Lopez & the Res-Q-Band, which fuses Spanish lyrics and musical styles with hard funk and black gospel rhythms. "I felt the conviction of the Lord fall on me," he says. "I was beginning to lose my focus. Success and fame were starting to take over my thoughts as they had in earlier days. God showed me clearly that he had rescued me from all of that, and gave me the vision for the Res-Q-Band. My mission is now reflected in the name of my band—I want to rescue souls from death for the Kingdom of God."

Darlene Love

ONE OF THE '60s girl group vocal icons, Love was born Darlene Wright on July 26, 1938, in Los Angeles. This preacher's daughter came of age during the girl group boom of the early 1960s when the Shirelles and Chantels ruled the radio airwaves. Love joined the Blossoms in 1957 and they became the house singers on the *Shindig* teen television show. But Love's place in music history was secured when she became producer Phil Spector's favored singer. He used her strong alto as the lead voice on songs that were credited to other groups. That's Love wailing on the Crystals' "He's a Rebel" and Bob B. Soxx & the Bluejeans' "Zip-A-Dee-Doo-Dah." Eventually, Spector allowed Love to come center stage and record Hot 100 pop singles such as "Wait 'Till My Bobby Gets Back Home," "Today I Met the Boy I'm Going to Marry," and "A Fine Fine Boy" which all charted in 1963. Through the years, she has supported herself as a session singer with credits backing Elvis Presley, Luther Vandross, Dionne Warwick, and Aretha Franklin. She later concentrated on acting, starring as Danny Glover's wife in all four of the *Lethal Weapon*

films. In the late 1980s, an old friend from the Phil Spector days, Cher, took her on the road as a featured singer in her extravagant stage shows. In the 1990s, Love recorded a Columbia Records pop LP, *Paint Another Picture*, and acted on the CBS soap opera *Another World* before recording her first gospel CD, *Unconditional Love*, in 1998. The album was produced by gospel legend Edwin Hawkins but poorly received by the gospel community.

Patrick Love

BORN JULY 23, 1968, in Charlotte, North Carolina, his father was a dockworker and his mother a day care provider. Love enjoyed a middle-class upbringing and had a happy home life. He attended church most of his life but didn't get serious about his faith until he was 16. "I always had aspirations to be a football player," he says. "I dreamed of playing for the Dallas Cowboys. But I would also put on a gospel record and [pretend] I was performing. I wanted to do both." When he broke his arm in a football game, his doctors recommended that Love end his football fantasies in order to protect his hands so that he could continue to play the piano and the saxophone. After graduating from West Mecklenburg High School in 1986, Love attended Brookstone Accounting College. He met Donald Lawrence, who worshipped at the same church as Love, Salem Baptist Church. The pastor, Anthony L. Jinwright, thought they should know each other and introduced them. Love began to coach the A.L. Jinwright Choir and Lawrence got the choir a record deal with Crystal Rose Records (Lawrence was a co-owner). The choir's 1994 *Wait on the Lord* CD reached No. 18 on *Billboard*'s gospel chart. However, it was Love's next project, *The Vision*, in 1998 that put him on the map. Propelled by what he calls the "North Carolina Hump"—a catchy vamp that Charlotte artists such as John P. Kee and Donald Lawrence perfected in their mid-1990s work—the CD peaked at No. 16 on the *Billboard* gospel chart. The ballad "Write the Vision" was a major gospel radio hit and "I Can Depend on God" was a minor one. After that project, Love faded from the national stage but remains active on the Charlotte gospel scene.

Walt "Baby" Love

FOR YEARS, HE WAS the only national radio voice for urban mainstream radio, then Walt Love carved out a new niche as a syndicated gospel radio announcer. Born near Pittsburgh, Pennsylvania, in the 1940s, Love joined the army and became a paratrooper after high school. After his time abroad with the military, Love returned to Pennsylvania where he finished his service duty and became an announcer at Erie's WWGO. From there, he went to KYOK in Houston, Texas. When he moved across town to the then-powerhouse KILT, Love became the first African-American to host a show at a Top 40 radio station. For the next decade, Love was a hot property and moved all across the country to take key on-air positions in top markets. In 1970, he was with New York's WOR. In 1972, he was with Los Angeles' KHJ, and two years later he was back in the Big Apple at WXLO—all Top 40 stations.

By the 1980s, Love had moved into managerial positions at Chicago's R&B monument WVON before relocating back to Los Angeles for stints with KKBT, KGFJ, and KUTE. During the Reagan era, Love also became urban editor at *Radio & Records*, a music industry newspaper. It was during that period that the idea to launch his own gospel radio program began to germinate in Love's mind. "We became interested in wanting to do "Gospel Traxx" basically because I'm a born-again Christian and accepted Christ when I was a young boy," he told GospelCity.com. "Then, like most people, I went along just trying to serve the Lord but got distracted with the world, got distracted from the standpoint of meaning. Then when I became more of an adult in this business and began to look at things, I realized the only reason I was succeeding was because of my faith in God. When man stepped in my way, opportunities still came about and those opportunities came because of the Lord."

In 1995, Love launched "Gospel Traxx" and initially syndicated the show himself. However, before the year was through, Love had signed an agreement with SupeRadio to syndicate the show and market the program to advertisers. The show rapidly became a staple outlet for gospel music. After their initial agreement ended in December 1998, Love and SupeRadio embarked on a legal battle over advertising revenue. Love was eventually awarded $271,000 in damages, but when SupeRadio appealed, the case was vacated on a technicality.

Love is now syndicated through Excelsior Broadcasting through 2009 and featured on 125 stations. Love has become a major force in promoting gospel music. Since 1998, he's hosted national concert tours around the country that were promoted on his Sunday morning show. Love has also created three "Gospel Traxx" compilation CDs that have sold respectably. In addition to "Gospel Traxx," Love continues to produce his various urban radio shows such as "The Urban Countdown" (begun in 1984), which is the longest running African-American syndicated show in radio history. Love is an associate pastor at the First AME Church of Los Angeles. He and his wife Sonya (who also produces "Gospel Traxx"), head the 501C3 nonprofit organization, Walt & Sonya Love Foundation for Cancer and Lupus Research. In assessing Love's influence, Maurice DeVoe, a former KKBT programmer, told Billboard magazine, "He was a radio pioneer, someone who to this day still tries to find ways to reinvent the wheel and make black radio better."

Loving Sisters

THIS LITTLE ROCK, ARKANSAS–BASED sister act was founded in the 1950s by Gladys Givens McFadden (born September 10, 1934). Her father was a minister and she had six siblings (four sisters and two brothers). Two of her sisters sang in another gospel group, so she decided to start her own group with one of her other sisters, a friend, and that friend's sister. Since they were all sisters and getting along with each other, she named the group the Loving Sisters. The group consisted of Lorraine Leake, Ann James, Josephine Dumas, and McFadden. They had a regular gig singing on a local Sunday morning radio show. One Sunday, the quartet group the Pilgrim Jubilees were going through town and heard the Loving Sisters on the radio. The Jubilees contacted the group and suggested that they audition for the label they recorded for, Peacock Records. McFadden sent Peacock President Don Robey a demo tape and he signed them to his roster in 1962. He sent them to Universal Studios in Chicago where they recorded their first songs such as "Who Could Ask for More" and "Don't Let My Running Be in Vain."

Being in Little Rock at the height of the 1960s civil rights era, the Loving Sisters became very involved in the protest movement. Daisy Bates, a civil rights activist credited with helping push for the integration of Central High School in Little Rock, lived around the corner from McFadden. The Loving Sisters often accompanied Martin Luther King, Jr., at his speaking engagements. "We were doing things before he would speak during that Poor People's campaign," McFadden recalls. "We were in every state with him and Klansmen were trying to run us off the road and that's what we were singing about. You write from your own experiences. I wrote 'Trying Times' when we were marching in Tupelo, Mississippi. People were marching in front of the hotel and we were behind the barricade in the hotel and the hotel didn't want us to come out, so I was locked in there. I wrote that song because those were trying times." They also traveled extensively with C.L. Franklin. "He was the only preacher at that time who could command a large audience for a fee," she recalls. "We traveled with him all through Florida and the Southeast. We sang at his church in Detroit a number of times."

The Loving Sisters recorded several singles over the decade with Peacock. By the time Don Robey died in 1975, Peacock and the group's contract had been sold to ABC Records. During that period, they recorded gospel music that was ahead of its time. "I wrote almost everything that we ever sang," McFadden recalls. "A lot of what I wrote would fit into today's music. It had a rock flavor, but the words were gospel. We wrote according to our environment, but ABC didn't really know what to do with a gospel artist. By the time we were nominated for a Grammy for the *Amazing Grace* LP in 1978, ABC had been bought by MCA and they didn't know what to do with gospel either. People are still trying to find our music." Being with such a major mainstream recording label afforded them a very high production standard. The half dozen

or so albums they recorded during the period are some of the best, virtually forgotten, examples of contemporary gospel music. McFadden produced most of the music, which included real horns, real organs, and up-to-date rhythms. The music was meant to appeal to the fans of secular soul artists such as Natalie Cole and Marvin Gaye. Aside from a couple of straightahead gospel disco numbers, the music could easily fit in on any R&B play list. Central to the group's sound was McFadden's strong alto voice.

After their contract expired, the Loving Sisters began to fade from the national scene. "My mother was getting older and she would take care of our children when we were traveling," McFadden says. "Around the time that we did 'Lonesome Highway', we had a car accident and my mother said that if we were in an accident, all of us could be gone and then, she said, 'What would happen to me?' So we thought about her and how she was declining, and we decided not to travel so much and to stay home with her. She died in 1994 at the age of 94." In recent years, McFadden accepted Ernie Dodson's EMOBA (Museum of Black Arkansans) Excellence award and the GMWA's Pioneer of Praise award. The group continues to perform and, at the time of this writing, is rehearsing new music with the hopes of doing a new recording. "If we could get a major label involved, that would be great," McFadden laughs. "We're ready to come back."

RECOMMENDED RECORDING: It's long out of print, but *A New Day* (ABC-Peacock Records, 1975) is as fine an example of '70s contemporary gospel as one will find. From the biting funk and social commentary of "People Getting Married" to the country church steel guitar of "Old Home Town" to the laid-back, intoxicating horn lines of the ballad "We Are One," it is a warm, enjoyable listening experience.

Robert Lowe and the Queens Community Choir

ROBERT LOWE IS the pastor of New York City's Mount Moriah AME Church. His 30-member group is comprised of singers from his congregation and New York's

Queens borough. The group toured with pop star Kenny Loggins in the 1980s. Their 1990 debut project *Make Me Over* won them a GMWA Excellence award. Their most recent CD *Total Experience* appeared on their own record label, Moriah Music Group.

Herman Lubinsky

HERMAN LUBINSKY WAS responsible for fomenting the spread of black gospel music in the post–World War II era straight through the 1980s more than any other individual in the history of the genre. Through his Savoy Records label, Lubinsky produced and promoted gospel music to the black church community on a scale and with an intensity that remains unsurpassed. He was born August 30, 1896, in Bradford, Connecticut. A trailblazer, Lubinsky managed New Jersey's first radio station, WNEW, in 1924. He then opened a record shop at 58 Market Street in Newark. In 1939, Lubinsky had the idea that he could start making records as well as selling them. He formed Savoy Records from that same spot and named it after the New York ballroom. Beginning in 1942, Savoy produced some of the greatest jazz musicians, such as Charlie Parker, Erroll Garner, and Miles Davis. In 1948, Lubinsky opened a Los Angeles office that produced great R&B sides by Little Esther Philips and Johnny Otis. Lubinsky's son, Dick, says that his father often had to pay money under the table to get R&B records played. Being a frugal man, this didn't go over well and led him to concentrate on gospel, which didn't have the notorious pay-for-play practices that were prevalent in R&B radio.

"My old man's gotten a lot of bad rap as not being good to artists or for being tough," says Dick Lubinsky. "He was tough. He was tough on me, you know what I mean? My father was cheap! He loved making money, he just didn't like parting with it. If somebody tried to sell him something, he'd say, 'Oh, God, that's too much, I need it cheaper!' But if you went to buy something from him and start to chisel him, he'd say, 'Oh, you're killing me!' A lot of artists will say the old white independents screwed them. But my father never took a penny of royalties from those people, and the woman who worked for him for 45 years taking care of that, Helen Gottesman, she wouldn't take a nickel." With Lubinsky's good working relationships with gospel artists, Savoy Records severely scaled back its jazz and R&B sessions and primarily became known for its prodigious gospel recordings by the 1970s.

Lubinsky's gospel history dated back to 1943 when he created a Savoy Records gospel subsidiary called King Solomon Records. The New York–based quartet Kings of Harmony recorded the label's first gospel 78-rpm, "Fountain of Blood" with "Trees Are Bending" on the flip side. The imprint followed up with singles by the Johnson Jubilee Singers, Sister Dorothea Robinson & the Southern Belles, and the Heavenly Four of Alabama, among others. By 1949, Lubinsky had decided to issue gospel under the Savoy label, and the first release was the famous Ward Singers' "Just One Moment." Throughout the 1950s, Savoy enjoyed six-figure megasellers such as "God Will Take Care of You" (1951) by the Gay Sisters, "Twelve Gates to the City" (1955) by the Davis Sisters, "God Specializes" (1958) by the Roberta Martin Singers, and "Mary, Don't You Weep" (1958) by the Caravans, among many other bestsellers. In those early days, jazz producer Ozzie Cadena produced the label's first historic gospel sessions.

By the 1960s, Savoy was doing so well in the gospel field that they had gospel subsidiaries named Gospel and Sharp. "That's when we really got heavy into gospel," says Dick Lubinsky. "Everybody was leaving the other gospel companies to come to Savoy. At one point, my father had so many people wanting to record there that he started renting the studio out. He'd have a certain amount of records pressed up and give them to you so that you could go out there and try to get your own records on the radio. If you got a hit, you could come back to Savoy and he'd sign you. If you didn't, it was just a small loss. I used to see people come with a truck full of furniture and say, 'We want to be stars.' They brought everything they owned with them."

Much of Savoy's success is directly related to the production skills of a Jewish man named Fred Mendelsohn and a black pianist named Lawrence Roberts who came to Savoy as a producer when he was 15 years old in 1954. "He was the greatest black gospel producer there ever was," Dick Lubinsky says of Mendelsohn. "All the artists loved him. Rev. Lawrence Roberts, Professor Charles Taylor, Alex Bradford, and the Banks Brothers used to always make a fuss over him." The company knew they were on to something when they discovered Albertina Walker's protégé, James Cleveland. He had been rejected by Vee-Jay and Motown before Albertina Walker pushed Lubinsky to sign him in 1960. "When my father signed James Cleveland, we knew we had the biggest name in gospel," Dick Lubinsky recalls. "He put out an album for us called Peace Be Still that sold a million copies—not in one year, but over the years. If you consider the fact that African-Americans represent 12 percent of the American population and that maybe only one out of that 12 being a gospel fan, and take a guy like James Cleveland selling a million albums? With that limited clientele, that makes him on a per capita basis the biggest recording artist who ever lived. I tell that to everybody. He's No. 1, untouched, and he made some 60 albums for Savoy."

"Freddy Mendelsohn would discover a new choir like this Southwest Community Choir that was big at the time or Professor Charles Fold," Dick Lubinsky continues. "Freddy would start an album with Charles Fold and then he'd have James introduce the group and sing maybe one song on the album, which helped James, helped us, and helped the star, helped everybody. It was a tremendous innovation by Fred Mendelsohn... *Billboard* used to publish the top 35 gospel albums once a month, [and] 27 were by Savoy. Can you imagine?"

While Herman Lubinsky presided over the top gospel recoding label of the period, he was not necessarily a candidate for the church deacon board. Following the Cuban missile crisis, Cuban cigars were contraband and not legally available in the US. "My father called the Cuban consulate," Dick Lubinsky recalls. They realized that Lubinsky was an influential man with money and sent an emissary to his home with a box of $200 cigars. "The man handed my father the cigars and my father says, 'I'm not paying you for these. The man asks why and my father says, 'You remember when Castro confiscated the TWA planes? ... Well, I'm a TWA stockholder, so now I figure we're even.'"

Herman Lubinsky continued to run the label until 1973 when he was diagnosed with cancer. "They gave

him two weeks to live and he lasted another nine months," Dick Lubinsky remembers. "My father would be so bonged out on morphine and other drugs they give terminal cancer patients, he'd be making deals right out of his hospital bed that I had to countermand. His signature wouldn't even come out horizontal." By that time, Mendelsohn was effectively running the label, and Milton Biggham was eventually ushered in to help carry the load. Herman Lubinsky died on March 16, 1974. The National Estate Bank decided to sell the company. Motown Records executive Ewart Abner was one of several labels that bid for the label catalog. However, their $1 million offer was far below the value of the company, which was eventually sold to Columbia Pictures for their Arista label in 1975. The gospel catalog changed hands a couple of times and is now in the hands of Malaco Records. "They aren't doing much with it, are they?" Dick Lubinsky wonders. "That stuff could still sell today if it were repackaged and put out there, but I haven't seen anything." Malaco has done an uneven and questionable job of keeping the stellar Savoy catalog alive and in print. What reissues they have done have been budget-oriented with no significant liner notes, bonus tracks, or the slick artwork that usually accompanies CD reissues. However, in one sense, their frugal reissue approach is in step with Herman Lubinsky's original mission. In the book *The Gospel Sound*, Herman Lubinsky told gospel music historian Anthony Heilbut, "I always say I make records for the man with the dinner pail and the lady over the washtub."

Patrick Lundy

ONE OF MODERN gospel's most skillful composers and choirmasters, Patrick P. Lundy was born in 1967 in Thomasville, Georgia. In 1985, he moved to Washington, DC, to enroll at Howard University. During his time there, he served as an assistant director of the Howard University Gospel Choir under A. Paul Gatling's tutelage and also served Dr. Weldon Norris, who directed the Howard University Choir. He was in line to take over the Howard University Gospel Choir after

Gatling retired, but he formed the Ministers of Music Choir in 1994 instead. Their debut CD *We Sing the Power* appeared in 1995. They have since recorded the 2003 CD *Standin'*, a blend of contemporary gospel and a couple of spirituals, for the Allen & Allen Music Group. In the Washington, DC, area, Lundy works as a music director for the acclaimed Eastern High School Choir and also serves as senior associate minister of music at the Reid Temple AME Church.

Jeff Majors

IT CAN SAFELY BE stated that Jeff Majors is the leading harpist in gospel music because he's probably the only harpist in gospel music. That's not to diminish the impact of his repertoire, as much as to highlight the fact that the instrument most mentioned in the Bible is rarely played in modern gospel music. Majors hails from a long line of singing preachers, including the legendary Claude Jeter. An only child, he was born Jeff Majors Graham on November 3, 1955, in Washington, DC. When he was six, his trumpet player mother began taking him to her band rehearsals. She played with artists such as Pearl Bailey in the 1950s. Majors began playing the harp during his teenage years. "When I first picked up that harp," he recalls, "it almost seemed like it was laughing at me… as if it was saying, 'Okay, I've figured you out. Now you're going to have to spend some time with me if you want to figure me out.'" He studied for years under the watchful eye of Alice Coltrane, jazz great John Coltrane's widow. In the late 1980s, Majors began recording custom CDs displaying his skills on the harp, and by the 1990s, he had become a gospel announcer for Radio One's Baltimore gospel station. After the radio conglomerate began establishing gospel radio stations in other markets such as Detroit and Atlanta, the company syndicated his Sunday morning radio show to other FM stations within the network. When Radio One formed Music One Records they released Majors's CD *Sacred* with distribution through Universal Records. That stellar album featured Al Johnson and Genobia Jeter on vocals, Dexter Wansel conducting strings, and Kenny Gamble consulting on the project. It reached No.

32 on *Billboard*'s gospel chart. After that agreement ended, Music One had independent distribution for the albums *Sacred 2000* and *Sacred Holidays*. The former featured gospel legend Albertina Walker on the track "Just Another Day." After scouting a new deal, Sony picked up distribution for the label in 2002. The first release, *Sacred 4 You*, appeared, and the single "Somebody Bigger" featured R&B veteran Jean Carne on vocals and has made Majors's biggest impact on urban AC radio yet. Majors hosted a Sunday morning gospel television program on the ABC television affiliate WMAR in Baltimore for a while. He now hosts the national program *The Gospel of Music with Jeff Majors* on the TV One television network. Since Majors is the only harpist many people have ever seen or heard, kids are often intrigued by the large, majestic instrument. "The most fulfilling part of this ministry is seeing kids want to be a part of it," he says.

Jeff Majors / photo courtesy of Music One

Malcolm Dodds Singers

ONE OF THE MOST in-demand recording session backing groups during the 1960s, they backed artists as diverse as Neil Sedaka and Nina Simone. Dodds's pop group, the Tunedrops, enjoyed a hit with "It Took a Long Time" in the late 1950s, and he performed on Dick Clark's *American Bandstand* in 1957. However, the Harlem-reared composer-arranger is most closely identified with his collaborations with pop crooner Brook Benton, most notably on Benton's *If You Believe* (Mercury Records, circa 1961) religious collection that featured traditional, choral arrangements of "Shadrack" and "Just a Closer Walk with Thee" among others. Perhaps his greatest legacy is co-writing the "Look for the Union Label" slogan/theme song with advertising executive Paula Green for the International Ladies Garment Workers Union (ILGWU) in 1975.

Donald Malloy

FOR A BRIEF PERIOD in the late 1980s, Donald Malloy took the gospel world by storm as his ballad "Holy Spirit" became one of the most played gospel songs of the era. Born November 28, 1955 in Cheraw, South Carolina, Malloy sang in the Pleasant Grove AME Church youth choir from the age of six. Eventually, a chance meeting with Savoy Records executive Milton Biggham led to his association with that label. Biggham gave Malloy featured soloist spots on hit albums by Bishop Jeff Banks & the Revival Temple Mass Choir ("I'll Be Alright"). He also collaborated with other Savoy artists such as Rev. James Cleveland and Dorothy Norwood. However, it was his solos with the New Jersey Mass Choir (and their "I Want to Know What Love Is" with the pop group Foreigner) that launched his career. "Singing on 'I Want to Know What Love Is' really helped to open doors for me," he told *Totally Gospel* in 1988. "Television appearances, concert tours, just things that I never believed would happen to me." All of these experiences led to Malloy's debut solo LP *Holy Spirit* in 1987, which brought him fleeting fame as a soloist. He later recorded for CGI Records and AIR Records before cutting a new Savoy Records CD, *Jesus Reigns,* in 1999.

Rebecca Malope

CITED AS FORMER South African President Nelson Mandela's favorite singer, Rebecca Malope is considered the queen of South African gospel music. She was born in 1968 in Lekazi Township near the Kruger National Park. She did not receive a formal education, as she and her sisters spent their youth working on a tobacco farm. In 1986, Malope and her sister Cynthia left their township and headed to Johannesburg in search of a better life. Although she initially sang in various secular amateur contests, she eventually decided to sing only gospel because of her deep faith. She won the Shell Oil Company's "Road to Fame" competition, but was unable to secure a recording deal. She formed a partnership with songwriter Sizwe Zakho and music agent Peter Tladi to raise money to produce her debut album, *Rebecca*, which went gold. Subsequent albums also went gold, but it was her *Shwele Baba* CD that made her a superstar, selling 100,000 copies within three weeks of its release in 1995. Since then, her albums have all sold platinum and she's racked up sales of over ten million units in a country known for bootleg recordings. Her mellow voice is pleasant but undistinguished. Her popularity lies in her ability to merge traditional Zulu rhythms with Americanized gospel stylings. Since EMI began distributing her music circa 1997, her star has continued to shine with big budget music videos, concert tours with her Pure Magic Band, and international television appearances.

However, the road to fame has had many potholes. She lost her father, brother, and a sister in 1996, and she lost her mother to illness in 2003. In 2001, a gospel singer whom she mentored early in his career publicly accused Malope of having hired a hit man to kill him when she began to view him as a professional rival. However, she was never charged with that crime. In 2004, Malope adopted her sister Cynthia's daughters after Cynthia died of AIDS-related infection.

Mickey Mangun

THE MOLASSES-VOICED white gospel singer from Little Rock developed a national reputation during President

Bill Clinton's administration in the 1990s. Mangun first met Bill Clinton at a Christian camp in 1977. She and her husband became friends with the future president, and Clinton often visited their church, where Mangun's singing would bring him to tears. She is the worship and praise leader at the Pentecostals of Alexandria Church in Alexandria, Louisiana, where her husband, Anthony, is pastor. The church was founded by his parents, G.A. and Vesta Mangun, in 1950. Mangun has recorded independent projects over the years and some of her fan favorites include "Promise (Coming Down That Dusty Road)" and "Water Grave." In reflecting on the Manguns in his autobiography, Bill Clinton wrote, "Knowing the Pentecostals has enriched and changed my life. Whatever your religious views, or lack of them, seeing people live their faith in a spirit of love toward all people, not just their own, is beautiful to behold. If you ever get a chance to go to a Pentecostal service, don't miss it."

Madeline Manning-Jackson

FOUR-TIME OLYMPIAN Madeline Manning-Jackson was born January 11, 1948, in Cleveland, Ohio. While attending John Hay High School, she won her first national title in the 440-yard run at the girls' AAU championship. It won her a spot on the US Olympic team. At the 1968 Olympics in Mexico City, she was a surprise winner of the 800-meter race where she set an Olympic record as the first woman to break a time of two minutes. In 1972, she graduated from Tennessee State University where she also served on the school's track team, the Tigerbelles. In 1976, Manning-Jackson recorded a gospel LP, *Running for Jesus*, for the New-Pax Records label and released a biography, *Running on Faith*, written by Linda Jacobs Altman. In 1984, she was inducted into the National Track and Field Hall of Fame. The 1992 film *Going for God and the Gold* profiled Manning-Jackson and other Olympians about their religious faith. She was on-hand for the unveiling of the Wilma Rudolph postage stamp during the July 14, 2004, Olympic Golden Moments Salute Dinner. In recent years, Manning has been an evangelist/motivational speaker and continues to sing. She was

awarded an honorary doctorate of divinity degree from Oral Roberts University.

Queen Esther Marrow

A VETERAN SINGER who received a career resurgence in the 1990s with her various Broadway gospel revues, Marrow was born in Newport News, Virginia. She was raised by her grandmother and moved to New York as a teenager, where she found work in the city's garment district. When she sang an impromptu version of "Happy Birthday" at an office party, an impressed co-worker introduced her to a friend-of-a-friend-of-a-friend of jazz great Duke Ellington, who hired Marrow as a soloist for his 1965 *Sacred Concerts*. She toured with Ellington for the next couple of years. "I did a concert with Duke Ellington here in San Francisco… at Grace Cathedral Church," she told San Francisco's *Metropolitan Arts* newspaper in August 1999. "I thought I had died and gone to heaven! It was a Saturday evening, the sun was still up, and it was coming through the stained glass windows. It made this ray that came down! The church was packed and I stood there and I sang 'Come Sunday' with Mr. Ellington's orchestra. My God!… and Johnny Hodges playing that saxophone—Whew! It was unbelievable."

"I was singing with Harry Belafonte when Dr. King joined him, doing rallies that combined music with Dr. King's messages," Marrow said in a 2001 EMI Records press release. "I had been a part of the Movement prior to that, but meeting and getting to know Dr. King brought me deeply into it. He was every bit as magnetic and charismatic a man, one-on-one, as he was before thousands of people, and he was such a warm, gentle person. Aretha Franklin was traveling with us at the time, and one evening we were sitting in a back room with Aretha playing the piano, and both of us singing. Dr. King happened by and heard us, and just came up and joined right in. It was very much a family feeling."

In the 1970s, Marrow played Auntie Em in the Broadway hit *The Wizard of Oz* and had a recurring role as Oscar the Grouch's mother on the PBS children's television series *Sesame Street*. Throughout the years, Marrow also found herself collaborating with a varied coterie of artists on their recorded projects or in concerts, including Bob Dylan (she did background vocals on his 1985 *Empire Burlesque* and 1986 *Knocked Out Loaded* LPs), B.B. King, and Chick Corea. In 1990, Marrow wrote and starred in a musical, *Truly Blessed*, based on the life of Mahalia Jackson. The show received nominations for three Helen Hayes awards during hit runs in San Francisco and Washington, DC, before going on to a successful stint on Broadway.

Later in the decade, Marrow was approached by German producer Michael Brenner, who solicited her aid in putting together a gospel troupe to perform in Germany. She went back to New York to assemble the Harlem Gospel Singers, a seven-piece band and ten-voice chorus. After wowing Europe, the troupe returned to the United States. In 2000, Marrow and the Harlem Gospel Singers released two CD projects on Open Door Music. The first was *Live at the Cologne Philharmonic Hall*, and the last was simply entitled, *Queen Esther Marrow Featuring the Harlem Gospel Singers*. Both projects featured a number of rousing traditional black gospel and spiritual songs. In 2002, Marrow's sterling alto was found on her first solo CD, *God Cares*, for EMI Gospel, a fine set of more traditional gospel songs.

"Gospel music today, with the young people, I would say that it's going to sound very pop, sometimes even hip-hop," she told the *Metropolitan*. "And that's fine for the young people—as long as they keep sincerity there and alive. My goal is not going to be to hip-hop it so much that you don't know what it is. And I don't approve of dancing to gospel music. You will find gospel music in clubs and that is something I don't quite approve of. I think that we've got to have respect somewhere. And God is what we're singing about. The music is going to evolve, of course, but myself and the Harlem Gospel Singers are trying to keep it from going too far. I'm not knocking the young kids, but I want them to hear what I'm doing, too, so they know where their music comes from."

Roberta Martin

ONE OF THE LEADING gospel groups of the 1940s and '50s, the Roberta Martin Singers were a unique ensem-ble. Born February 12, 1907, in Helena, Arizona, Roberta Martin's family relocated to Cairo, Illinois, when she was ten. There she studied classical piano until she was asked to play for the young people's choir at Ebenezer Baptist Church. From that point on, she devoted herself to church music. In the gospel fold, she was inspired by the piano styles of blind pianist Arizona Dranes, who also influenced Clara Ward, and Bertha Wise, who helmed a vocal group from Augusta, Georgia.

Martin became a disciple of Thomas Dorsey when he assigned her to play for his Pilgrim church choir. In 1933, she co-founded the Martin-Frye Quartet with Thomas Frye. By 1935, the quartet had morphed into the Roberta Martin Singers. Possessing a thick contralto, Martin was the lone female surrounded by Norsalus McKissick, Willie Webb, Robert Anderson, James Lawrence, and Eugene Smith, who were all adolescents at the time. Martin's singers sang loudly and dramatically without a bass. Their sound was not harmonious. One could easily identify the backing voices. This lack of synchronicity made the group's urgent sound a distinctive and welcome change amid the repetitive quartets of the era. By the 1940s, Martin had added women to her group and further refined her sound with elements from her classical training. In 1939, she founded the Roberta Martin Studio of Music where she began to publish (and further popularize) her songs and the compositions of others. Among the gospel standards flowing from her firm were "Only a Look," "I'm Just Waiting on the Lord," and "He Knows How Much We Can Bear." In the 1960s, Martin began to wind down and take it easy as her health began to weaken. She died January 18, 1969, in Chicago, Illinois. More than 50,000 mourners attended her memorial service.

Sallie Martin

THOMAS DORSEY'S National Convention of Gospel Choirs and Choruses appropriately labeled Sallie Martin "the Mother of Gospel." Yes, she sang and her group, the Sallie Martin Singers, had a following, but that is not why she's Mama Gospel. She merits the title because the publishing firm she and Kenneth Morris launched in 1940, Martin & Morris Music, was responsible for popularizing gospel music during the idiom's infancy. Whereas Thomas Dorsey's publishing house only published his own compositions and Roberta Martin's firm only published songs she performed, Martin & Morris published and therefore popularized songs by all the important gospel composers of the day, such as William Brewster, Dorothy Love Coates, Alex Bradford, James Cleveland, Lucie Campbell, and Sam Cooke.

Born November 20, 1896, in Pittsfield, Georgia, Martin never knew anything about her father. She lived with her mother and her parents. Her mother was a traveling musician. After her mother's death circa 1912, the teenager decided to leave Pittsfield because she didn't want to be a cotton-picker like most people she knew. She quit school and moved to Atlanta where she took a succession of jobs such as babysitting, house cleaning, and laundry work. In 1916, the family of the children she babysat encouraged her to attend the Fire Baptized Holiness Church with them. She enjoyed the spontaneity of the service and decided then to become a Christian. Eventually she met and married Wallace Martin, two years her junior. A terrible fire in Atlanta in 1917 gutted most of their neighborhood, and the couple packed what they could and moved to Cleveland. A lot of the printed material on Martin states that she went to Chicago to live in 1927, but she told interviewer and archivist James Standifer otherwise. According to her interview, she first went to Chicago in 1919 and found work at a school, but her husband stayed back in Cleveland. He refused to come to Chicago because the job prospects were bleak, so she went back to Cleveland to be with him after a few months. She had grown to love Chicago and kept pushing her husband to go back with her. In 1922, they went to Chicago together. "He finally came on to Chicago and got a job," she said. "He had a job and then when he finally got out of the job, he just started where he'd have games and playing, men all in the house, drinking and would gamble all night.... So finally, it just came to a head. I said, 'Now we will just have to [separate because] I cannot take it....' We stayed separated until he passed away." The second time around in the Windy City, Martin got a hospital job while more actively pursuing a professional career in gospel music. Around 1929, she auditioned for the Pilgrim Baptist Church Chorus, conducted by Thomas Dorsey. Initially, Dorsey was leery of Martin's talents, but she was persistent about working with him because she knew that he was on the music fast track. He considered her singing style and her stage presence unrefined (she liked to move about the stage instead of singing flat-footed). Martin later said she'd permanently ruined her voice by singing too hard at a music convention. In addition, she didn't read music and had no interest in doing so. Dorsey simply was not impressed and rejected her without second thought. She auditioned for him again on two other occasions and was rejected both times. In later years, she'd scoff at people who complained that she couldn't sing and made the point that her voice took her out of the cotton fields. "'Aaw, she can't sing,'" she recalled them saying. "'All she does is talk her words and pat her feet...' You all know I'm still patting my feet and talking my words. I said, 'To tell you the truth I've been just about where I wanted to go.'"

Martin did not give up. As she saw it, Dorsey, a former blues star who was electrifying churches with his gospel songs, was her path to the next level in gospel music. Whenever she heard that he was appearing at a local church, she'd manage to get a solo near Dorsey's spot on the program. Every time, she'd sing a Sanctified song that lent itself to her whoops, groans, and perhaps a foot shuffle across the pulpit, stirring the church into a frenzy. Dorsey found it remarkable how Martin could bring the congregation to its feet, but she still was not for him. Finally, Martin sought the intervention of gospel composer Theodore R. Frye, whom she knew Dorsey respected. On Frye's recommendation, Dorsey reluctantly allowed Martin to join a traveling trio he formed to demonstrate his songs at church convocations. Aside from her ragged vocals, Dorsey so disliked Martin's voice cracking in the middle of a phrase and her unrepentant sharp tongue toward him, that it was a year before he allowed her to sing a solo. When she did sing a solo, people remembered the song and that, after all, was the purpose. "We went over it. I sang it that night," Martin said of that first solo, "I'm Claiming Jesus." "I didn't ever have to say any more. I could go anywhere that anybody would ask me to come... He [Dorsey] would send me like he was glad to do that because what songs he had, wherever I went, I carried the music. Then when I'd get through, I'd sell it."

It was obvious to Dorsey that Martin was a born saleswoman, and against his better judgment, he began to work with her. Dorsey founded the National Convention of Gospel Choirs and Choruses (NCGCC) and as the duo's fame spread, Martin became the first prominent gospel artist to tour the West Coast. As their relationship grew, Dorsey began to value Martin's business sense and he tolerated her tirades because he came to feel he needed her for his success as much as she felt she needed him. Dorsey was a creative mind and had little head for business, so he sagely delegated all such responsibilities to Martin, who organized his music store in short order. "I was running his business and everything and taking care of everything," Martin recalled to Standifer. "Because when I would go to the rehearsals I would notice his uncle's wife's sister, she would do maybe the cooking and going to the store, while Mr. Dorsey had an old bag that you keep money in placed in a drawer. He had an iron there, no rug on the floor, and an old desk. That was his room. We rehearsed right there in this room. I'd notice if she's going to the store she'd go there and she would get her some money out and not make any record or nothing. When he'd get there to carry us home, he had an old car and he'd carry us all home. When he'd get there he'd just go on and get the bag out of the sack, put it in his pocket and never look. So after quite a few rehearsals, that was when I said to him, 'You know, you have something here, but you don't know what to do with it.' He said, 'What do you mean?' I said, 'What I said.' He said, 'Can you do any better?' I said, 'I think I can.' He said, 'Well here it is.' I said, 'What are you going to pay me?' 'Four dollars a week.' I said, 'All right.'" She devised the best ways to market Dorsey's sheet music, charge singers for lessons, and save him money all around. In addition, Martin assembled small choruses throughout the South and the Midwest to sing his songs at church functions and make the songs popular so musicians would buy the sheet music to play the songs at their own churches. Within a few months, Martin had Dorsey's business in something it had never been in before: the black.

Martin continued to relentlessly nag Dorsey on what he was not doing to promote his business and they finally had a falling out in 1940 when Dorsey didn't defend her with some of his colleagues who suggested Martin, as a woman, was in over her head in running his business. "He was satisfied with the way I was running it," she recalled, "but the thing about it is he wanted to take what somebody else said and don't have enough grit to just say, 'Well, she's doing a mighty fine job with the business.'"

By this point, Martin was almost as well known as Dorsey was, so with financial backing from Rev. Clarence H. Cobb, she joined forces with gospel composer Kenneth Morris to open Martin & Morris Music. Just as she did to help Dorsey establish his publishing company, Martin went on the road to perform the songs from her publishing company. She took a young pianist named Julia Mae Whitfield as her accompanist. By all accounts, Martin picked up where she had left off with Dorsey and her company eventually became bigger than his. Now that her firm was stable, Martin formed the Sallie Martin Singers, the first professional female gospel group on record. The women rounding out her first grouping included Dorothy Simmons, Sarah Daniels, Julia Mae Smith, Melva Williams, and pianist/singer Ruth Jones, who would later be known as the jazz and blues vocalist Dinah Washington. At the time, Jones was only 16 years old and Martin said that she was "fast as you want." Martin told Standifer, "She could spot any man in that audience that she wanted to meet, and before they could say 'May the Lord be with us 'til we meet again,' Dinah would be out on that floor…. I know that her mother trusted her with me, so I just had to tell Mrs. Jones, 'Well, I just have to leave Dinah because I can't be responsible for her.'" It's been written that Roberta Martin was briefly a pianist for Martin's group, but Martin cleared that up in the 1981 interview with Standifer. Martin had encouraged Roberta to start her own publishing firm and suggested that they go on the road together to help build up Roberta's name. She took Roberta along for her previously scheduled Sunday School Congress appearances in South Carolina and Alabama, as well as an appearance in Texas. The Texas promoter was going to bill the show as Martin & Martin, but Roberta's associate had a problem with Sallie getting top billing. "She had a young man with her that was so jealous that if you… said Sallie and didn't say Roberta, he thought that you had committed a crime," Martin told Standifer.

In spite of her cranky reputation, Martin had a heart of gold and though she might have fussed constantly, she was always giving breaks to new singers and helping others in whatever way that she could as she traveled the country. In 1942, Martin's adopted daughter, Cora (born 1927) joined the group as its featured soloist. In 1946, Martin moved to Los Angeles where she set up a West Coast branch of her publishing company. While in L.A., Martin began adding male singers to her ensemble on a rotating cycle. During this period, Martin recorded her first 78-rpm records for Aladdin Records, including "He's a Friend of Mine," listed as Sallie Martin & Her Singers of Joy on the record label. They also recorded for Bronze and Exclusive Records without any particular success. In 1949, Martin gave Brother Joe May, who would soon become known as the Thunderbolt of the Middle West, his big national break when she allowed him to sing on the coveted pre-convention program of the NCGCC.

In 1950, Martin and Morris struck a great deal with Specialty Records owner Art Rupe. He designated them as the exclusive arranger, distributor, and publisher for all of his label's gospel music works. This partnership increased Martin & Morris's income significantly. Previously, much of the music they demonstrated was unrecorded and they depended on church musicians buying sheet music to play in services. Specialty's recordings were heard by the masses via radio, which expanded the buying market beyond church musicians. Suddenly, people who just wanted to learn to play their favorite gospel song were buying sheet music because they heard the song on the radio. Annual sales were well into six figures and the owners each made well over $100,000 a year—an incredible sum of money for the time.

Specialty eventually invited Martin's group to record there. In looking back, Martin's music is classic Golden Age gospel, but at the time, not much was thought of it. Martin's rough voice always got the attention of the congregation in her church circuit, but her group came up with very little that impressed radio announcers. Therefore, their first singles were songs that the sophisticated Cora led such as "Lord, I Need Thee Every Hour" and "Eyes Hath Not Seen." They were well received, but not major hits. Even Sallie Martin's gritty take on "Hold to God's Unchanging Hand," which had a great hook and passionate vocal, didn't resonate with radio. The Ward Singers, the Caravans, and the Davis Sisters had not come on the scene yet and gospel radio was still geared toward quartet singing and hymns. It was at Savoy that the group had their biggest hit with Martin's duet with Alex Bradford, "He'll Wash You Whiter than Snow," a tune where they matched each other note-for-note and wailed until the listener was exhausted. It's been written in many gospel histories that the Martin group disbanded in the late 1950s. It's possible, although records such as "Let Jesus Come into My Heart," "God Is Love," and "Precious Lord" did not appear until the early 1960s.

Although her group shut down, Martin didn't. By the 1960s, she was considered the wealthiest woman in gospel music, far richer than even the millionaire Mahalia Jackson. Like Dorothy Love Coates, the Staple Singers, and Jackson, Martin was an active participant in the civil rights movement and donated money to many worthwhile charitable causes. She continued to work at Martin & Morris through 1970 at which time she sold her interest to Morris. Much of her life story was chronicled in the acclaimed 1981 film *Say*

Top: Bonnie Bradford and Berda Young Patrick
Bottom: (*left to right*) Claudia Bradford, Sallie Martin, and Cora Martin

Amen, Somebody. Martin's appearance led to something of a career renaissance with NBC's *Today Show* profiling her and *Ebony* magazine doing a spread on her incredible life. Martin sang right up to the end of her life and continued to serve as vice president of the NCGCC.

When Standifer asked if her advanced age slowed Martin down onstage, she said that it didn't. "I must say, I was in Paris from the first of January to March 18th," she told him in 1981. "I sang every night except Monday night when I was off, Sunday we gave a matinee, and then Sunday nights. But, now, you see, I didn't try to ask just let me be the main spokesman or something and in that way, at night I sang two solo numbers and then with the group came on… I've tried to not just sing to be singing. I've tried not to just overwork myself for somebody maybe to say 'Amen.' Like when I was in Atlanta when these disc jockeys, they have a way of bringing groups in. They'd have two and three groups on one service. Well, now, they expect for you to try to out-sing the other ones so the people can shout or something. Well, you see, the last time I was there, there was this man, I told him, I said, 'Now, we're going to sing. But if you expect me to [do something extraordinary] for you to shout, you just might as well get up and go home now because I'm going to sing but I'm not going to overwork myself trying to make you shout."

Martin died in Chicago on June 18, 1988, at the age of ninety-two. In looking over her life, she once made this comment to a church gathering that adequately sums up her whole life: "If Mahalia is a Cadillac and Roberta is a Buick, I'm just a Model T Ford. But I make it over the hill without shifting gears, and that's what counts. Church, I make it over the hill."

Mary Mary

THE URBAN GOSPEL DUO Mary Mary picked up right where urban gospel duo Angie & Debbie left off when they semi-retired in 1999. This other sister act took their brand of contemporary gospel directly to the streets. The infectious urban single "Shackles (Praise You)" was serviced to gospel and mainstream black radio simultaneously with a big press rollout that made Mary Mary one

of the most talked about acts of that year. They have worked that smash single and lesser ones into a lucrative career as gospel's most popular duo of the moment. Erica Monique Atkins (born April 29, 1972) and "Tina" Trecina Evette Atkins (born May 1, 1974) were born into a large family with six other siblings in Inglewood, California. Their parents were gospel singers and the only music allowed in their home was gospel. All the kids sang in the evangelistic COGIC choir, but Erica and Tina often won solo spots. Eventually, a group of the siblings performed on *Bobby Jones Gospel* and the opportunity inspired them to make singing a career. In 1995, they were cast in Michael Matthews's successful Chitlin' Circuit gospel play, *Mama I'm Sorry* and his less-successful next play, *Sneaky*. When they came off the road, Erica became a courtesy clerk at Boys Market and Tina was a make-up artist at Nordstrom while they shared an apartment and tried to make it in the music business. Soon, Erica was on the road singing backgrounds for Brian McKnight and Brandy. Meanwhile, Tina went on the road backing Eric Benet and Kenny Lattimore. They were often uncomfortable with some of the songs they had to sing, so they both looked forward to the day that they could sing their own gospel-oriented songs they had been writing during their downtime.

A chance meeting with producer Warryn Campbell in 1996 proved to be the catalyst for Mary Mary. Raised in the church himself, he could relate to the sisters' quandary about singing secular music. He began to collaborate with them and took their songs, which they demoed, to his publisher, EMI Music. The sisters were signed to a publishing contract. Soon their songs were being recorded for the *Dr. Doolittle* and *The Prince of Egypt* soundtracks.

In 1999, Campbell met with a Columbia Records executive on another matter and happened to play some of Mary Mary's songs. The executive wanted them at the label and made it happen. Although the company issued a press release stating that the duo was the first gospel act signed to the label, it wasn't true. Tramaine Hawkins had just left the label circa 1997. In addition, Columbia had a long history with select gospel artists going back almost 50 years when they first signed Mahalia Jackson, the Queen of Gospel.

Campbell suggested they make their professional name Mary Mary instead of something like Erica & Tina. "We were thinking about the Marys in the Bible, and there are two specifically: Mary Magdalene, who was delivered from evil spirits, and of course Mary, mother of Jesus, both of whom were very instrumental in his ministries. It's all about Jesus and telling people who he is and of his love. That's the whole purpose behind Mary Mary," Erica says. With Campbell in the producer's chair, they crafted a slick urban CD that just happened to have gospel lyrics. The lead single, "Shackles," from the CD *Thankful* was an immediate success. It reached No. 9 on the R&B chart and No. 28 on the Hot 100. It was also a Top Ten pop hit in England, France, the Netherlands, and Australia. The project earned the duo a Grammy award for Best Contemporary Gospel Album, two Dove awards, three Stellar awards, and a Soul Train award. A second single, "I Sings," another tasty groove, never got off the ground at black radio because instead of requesting the new single, fans would just keep requesting "Shackles" again—making it a perennial recurrent on urban play lists. The best "I Sings" could do was No. 68 on the R&B chart.

In between projects, the duo joined ALW Entertainment's "Sisters in the Spirit" tour with Shirley Caesar, Yolanda Adams, and Angella Christie, which was sold out in more than 45 cities in 2000. The same tour was reprised the next year with Virtue replacing Christie, but it was cancelled for poor ticket sales. The promoter blamed the cancellation on the 9/11 tragedy, although the advance sales were sluggish prior to that, perhaps because it was virtually the same lineup as the year before, the tickets cost more, and none of the artists had any new material out at the time. During this time, Mary Mary were also featured on Kirk Franklin's single "Thank You," which was culled from the soundtrack for *Kingdom Come* (Gospo Centric, 2001).

Over the summer of 2002, Mary Mary finally released their sophomore CD, *Incredible*, after having its release date changed a couple of times. Rumors swirled that Columbia executives were not pleased with the results and had sent the duo back into the studio to come up with a better project. Usually, summer is the worst time to release a gospel project because consumers are on the beach or vacationing and not as inclined to shop for music. In spite of that, Columbia set the album up well and it sold over 45,000 copies in its first week of release, debuting at No. 1 on the gospel chart and eventually reaching No. 10 on the R&B album chart.

The first single, "In the Morning," was another smooth, classy dance number with an easy hook. In spite of the song's appeal and great message, it only reached No. 54 on the R&B chart. Although it did not cross over as strongly as the first project, the album was well embraced by the gospel community, which also strongly played "Trouble Ain't," "Ordinary People," and "Little Girl."

"When people see the covers of our albums, we sometimes hear them say, 'You don't look like gospel singers.' Well, we want to show that you can be a Christian in the music business and represent!" says Tina. "You can still be fashionable, wear your hair and clothes in a hip way, and deliver the message." Erica adds, "We want to show that with all the provocative, sexual images for young people in the music industry, everything doesn't have to be bootys and Bentleys! Young kids need to know that it's hard work to make it in the music business, but you don't have to be wild and weird to succeed."

The interesting thing about urban gospel artists such as Mary Mary is that many radio listeners are looking for the positive, alternative messages they sing. Moreover, they are drawing more people to listen to gospel radio since there is still little airtime for urban gospel on regular R&B stations. While many urban radio audiences are slowly shrinking, gospel radio is picking up listeners. Still, there are those critics who say that the only reason music such as Mary Mary's is accepted at urban radio is because of the music and that the message is being ignored. Of course, the duo disagrees. "I think for far too long, people have thought music couldn't sound good and have a message," Erica has said. "We just wrote from our hearts and put a hot record together. 'Shackles' should be played right after 'Back that Thing Up.'" Tina added, "As long as they keep listening to it, they'll get the music eventually. People will feel the music and feel good, and eventually they'll catch on. We want to sell millions of copies, all over the world, just like Santana."

Mase

IN THE LATE 1990S, Mase was all the rage in the rap world. With P. Diddy as his mentor, it's no surprise he became so big so fast. "Hands down the best rapper of all time," rap superstar Kanye West said of Mase in *Rolling Stone*. "He knew how to get his point across in the fewest lines. Most of his raps, people could just connect with them and understand and feel what he was saying off one listen. The best speakers know how to talk where everyone understands everything they're saying."

Born Mason Durrell Betha on August 27, 1977, in Jacksonville, Florida, Mase was raised in Harlem where he fell in with a rough crowd. He later began to rap to amuse his basketball buddies. His hoop skills earned him a scholarship to State University of New York, but rap won out. Under the name Mase Murder, he joined the group Children of the Corn. After one of the members died in a car accident, Mase went solo. In 1996, he traveled to Atlanta to a music conference to meet producer Jermaine DuPri, but met Sean "P. Diddy" Combs instead. Mase made his debut on Combs's remix of the 112 single "Only You." Soon he was doing cameo raps on several of Diddy's high-profile Bad Boy label rap songs, including his "Can't Nobody Hold Me Down," which spent six weeks at No. 1 on both the *Billboard* pop and R&B charts.

Mase was literally a rap superstar before he released his own album. Therefore, it's no surprise that his debut CD *Harlem World* reached No. 1 on the *Billboard* Hot 100 in 1997. It produced the hit songs "Feel So Good," "Lookin' at Me," and "What You Want." However with fame comes tabloids. Mase was arrested in 1998 for disorderly conduct and initially was thought to be soliciting a prostitute. He denied the allegations and the charges were eventually dropped. Shortly after his sophomore CD *Double Up* was released, Mase surprised the rap world by announcing his retirement from rapping because of his born-again Christian beliefs. He refused to even promote the CD by making a video or doing any concerts. After giving up his lifestyle of bling bling and loose women, Mase founded a church in Atlanta—S.A.N.E. (Saving a Nation Endangered), geared toward youth outreach—and began to do the Christian

talk show circuit. His laid-back manner and tediously slow speech pattern makes his preaching style different from the stereotypic, whooping type of black preachers. However, he has studied the Bible in depth and has a teaching style that has earned him preaching engagements on TBN's flagship *Praise the Lord* television program. In an October 2004 cover story in *Vibe* magazine, Mase talked of going broke after he left music. "One year, it seemed I was going to lose everything—my house, my mother's house," he said. "All the things I had pending, that if I would've kept doing music, I could've paid for. I think that was the hardest year of my life, 2001. That year, I began to miss monetary things, financial things. I'm over here doing right, and ain't nothing going right. And at that time, I was ready to come back [to music], but for monetary reasons. I remember that day, crying in my bathroom. What am I going to do? And then peace came on me. 'You're going to be all right.'"

In 2004, Mase made a comeback to the rap music scene with the CD *Welcome Back*, which opened at No. 4 on the Hot 100 pop album chart. It was not a gospel rap album, just a clean one. The initial singles "Breathe, Stretch, Shake" and "Welcome Back" were respectable radio hits, but not the blockbusters Mase was accustomed to in the past.

Babbie Mason

ONE OF THE MOST prolific songwriters in contemporary Christian music, Mason has written songs for more than two dozen leading Christian recording artists, including CeCe Winans, Helen Baylor, and even former Harlem Globetrotter Meadowlark Lemon. She was born in 1955 in Jackson, Michigan. Although she was a preacher's daughter and led the choir in her father's church (Lily Missionary Baptist Church), Mason aimed for a secular music career after high school. She sang in clubs at night and in church on Sunday mornings. Eventually, Mason had a life-changing moment. "One day while I was in college I was eating a bowl of lukewarm soup and the grease began rolling around and separating from the soup," she says. "And I remembered a scripture in Revelation, the third chapter. It was a letter and I felt like this letter was written for me. It said, 'I know your works and I know you're neither hot nor cold. I'm going to spew you out of my mouth.' The Lord was giving me a visual example of the way my walk had become and since that day I knew I had to be fully committed." After college at Michigan's Spring Arbor Christian College, Mason taught public school music and English classes while serving her church as pianist and choir conductor. After relocating to Atlanta, she recorded five independent Christian music LPs that received respectable radio play and earned her invitations to minister at churches across the country. By 1984, she set up her own ministry, left teaching for full-time evangelism, and by 1988 won a Word Records contract. The album *With All My Heart* featured the No. 1 CHR (Christian hits radio) single "Each One, Reach One." Her 1992 CD *A World of Difference* produced several radio hits including "God Has Another Plan" and "The Only Hope." In spite of her smoky, jazz-infected vocals, Mason has never found a home at black gospel radio. Her slick arrangements have been embraced by inspirational radio and contemporary Christian radio. Her 1996 CD *Heritage of Faith* featured the traditional toe-tapper "Stop by the Church," which was meant to introduce Mason to the black gospel market. Although the song received scattered gospel radio play, she still was not able to create a strong audience in the market. By 2000, Mason had left Word Records and joined Spring Hill Records where she delivered the delicious big band–styled Christian jazz album *Timeless*, which tanked in spite of its quality. Perhaps Christian radio just was not ready for an album that echoed the era of Ella Fitzgerald and Doris Day.

Milt Matthews

BORN MILTON RAY MATTHEWS in January 1947 in Wilson, North Carolina, his father was a blues singer with the Matthews Brothers and died when his son was only six. Matthews's mother worked as a domestic to support her four children. They all helped out around the house to take the burden off their mom and when they weren't home, they could be found at the local Baptist church where Matthews took up the guitar and keyboards. After graduating from high school, Matthews moved to Washington, DC, in 1965 to make enough money to move to New York. He did odd jobs there and was able to finally make that move in 1967. In the Big Apple he swept floors at the Greyhound bus station while trying to break into the music business. Patterning himself after Sam Cooke and Jackie Wilson, Matthews dreamed of becoming a singer, but his entry was as a session guitarist. He started writing songs and peddling them to performers. After a while, he gained a manager, Bo Fleming of Exuberant Productions. Fleming also managed boxer Joe Frazier, who recorded Matthews's song "I'll Always Love You" but never released it.

Things turned around in 1970 when Commonwealth United Records released Matthews's debut LP *Milt Matthews Inc.* A year later came the RCA-distributed Ember Records project *For the People.* Both albums were sales disasters, though British soul fans still seek them out. In spite of the dismal sales, Matthews began to open concerts for acts such as Smokey Robinson & the Miracles, Jon Lucien, and Millie Jackson. He then joined with Bryan Records where his single "All These Changes" hit No. 14 on the *Cash Box* disco chart in 1974. He made some non-charting singles for Abbott Records before switching to H&L Records (recording home to soul supergroup the Stylistics) where his single "Trust Me" hit No. 52 on the *Cash Box* R&B single chart in 1978. Later that year he toured Japan, but in 1980 he returned to Washington weary of being a "puppet" for the music industry. He could never pick his own songs or make input into his career and was tired of the game. He opened Flexible Studios to help record aspiring singers. "I remember how hard it was for me when I started," he told the Gospel Highlights newsletter in 1988. He also began singing with the gospel quartet the Kingsmen, who enjoyed a big regional hit with "It's Testifying Time" with him as the lead singer. Following that exercise, Matthews founded MM Records and released his first gospel LP, *Music Ministry*, in 1987. On it, he showed off his smooth baritone on a gospel remake of Frederick Knight's soul classic "Betcha Didn't Know That," and the album closed with a beautiful self-penned ballad, "Fishers of Men." Aside from local

Washington radio airplay on flagship gospel stations WYCB and WUST, the album never took off nationally due in part to the label's failure to secure a distribution deal. Since then, Matthews has faded from the gospel scene just as he had vanished from the soul scene.

Brother Joe May

WILLIE MAE FORD SMITH dubbed him the Thunderbolt of the Middle West and by most accounts he never failed to live up to that title. Brother Joe May was one of the greatest stylist and vocalists that gospel music has ever known. His anointed tenor possessed a powerful punch and an astounding range which he used to full effect to rouse congregations to their feet. Although he clearly took his position as a church leader seriously, May was also a great showman in the most positive sense of the word. Born on November 9, 1912, in Macon, Mississippi, his family worshipped in the Church of God denomination—where all men are called "Brother," hence his stage name. He began singing at the age of nine and performed at a number of church functions throughout the South where he quickly developed a stellar reputation as a gospel singer. All of his musical influences were gospel with the exception of blues belter Bessie Smith. After graduating from high school, May worked as a day laborer and in 1941 moved to East St. Louis where he found work at a chemical plant. It was in St. Louis that May first met gospel legend Willie Mae Ford Smith, who mentored him and basically transformed him into the male version of herself. His phrasing, stage presence, and vocal acrobatics all belonged to Smith. Smith introduced May at Thomas Dorsey's National Convention of Gospel Choirs and Choruses conventions all over the country. At a Los Angeles–based convention in 1949, May's talent was witnessed firsthand by Specialty Records executive J.W. Alexander, who worked with the Soul Stirrers, and who immediately signed May to a contract. May's debut single, "Search Me Lord," was such a rousing, million-selling success that he was able to quit his day job and sing full-time. He quickly followed up with the gold-selling "Do You Know Him?" As his national fame grew, May was often called the male Mahalia Jackson. In 1958, May left Specialty and signed with Nash-

boro Records where he began to record his own compositions. May obviously relished the stage and was a tireless performer. He worked himself strenuously. Aside from his private concert dates, he co-starred with Marion Williams in the Broadway production of *Black Nativity*, which eventually toured the US and Europe to ecstatic audiences. As the 1960s neared an end, May's health began to deteriorate, but he still pushed himself to meet every concert engagement. His grave condition was not even known to many members of his family. On the way to a concert in Thomasville, Georgia, May suffered a massive stroke and died on July 14, 1972. Soon after, both Specialty and Nashboro Records rushed out greatest hits LPs on May to exploit the nostalgia around his death.

Curtis Mayfield

CURTIS MAYFIELD was the conscience of soul music in the 1960s and 1970s, and his continuing influence on a new generation of composers and performers allows him to still be the small voice of right and wrong years after his death. Mayfield's compositions such as "People Get Ready" and "Amen" celebrated his quiet but insistent faith in God. His songs such as "Billy Jack" and "Freddie's Dead" were commentary on drugs and crime. There was the black pride of "Choice of Colors" and "We Who Are Blacker than Blue." Finally, there was the encouragement of "I'm So Proud," "Keep on Pushing," and "We're a Winner."

Born June 3, 1942, in Chicago, Mayfield was reared in church and loved performing early on. He first met a baritone named Jerry Butler when they both sang together in the Northern Jubilee Singers, a group that performed in Mayfield's grandmother's Traveling Soul Spiritualist Church denomination. Later they formed their own group called the Modern Jubilaires before Butler formed his own group and Mayfield joined another gospel group called the Alphatones. They fell out of touch until 1956 when Mayfield's family moved to Chicago's North Side where Butler lived. Butler persuaded Mayfield to leave the Alphatones and join a doo-wop group called the Roosters and a Chick (as the guitarist) that had just moved from Chattanooga, Tennessee, to Chicago. "The girl didn't come [with them] from Tennessee," Mayfield told *USA Today*, so they dropped Chick and just became known as the Roosters. "I went through hell for about a year singing with them as the Roosters because Chicago was just a little too sophisticated to take the name in. Finally, a fellow named Eddie Thomas told us, 'First thing y'all got to do is change that name. What you want to do is bring about some type of impression.' And that was it… we were able to get some respect."

Newly christened as the Impressions, the quintet was made up of Mayfield, Butler, Sam Gooden, and brothers Arthur and Richard Brooks. They landed a recording deal with Vee-Jay Records where they recorded "For Your Precious Love," which became a No. 3 R&B chart smash and sold a million copies. Because Butler led the song, Vee-Jay renamed the group Jerry Butler & the Impressions. This decision caused some tension within the group since Butler and Mayfield were not original members. Eventually, Butler struck out solo and the Impressions disbanded. The other guys went back to 9-to-5 jobs. Butler asked Mayfield to tour with him as his guitarist. Mayfield began to write hits for Butler such as "He Will Break Your Heart" in 1960. He soon formed his own publishing company and began to write songs for other artists as well. Eventually, Mayfield saved enough money to regroup the Impressions and assume leadership of the group. He brought Fred Cash in as Butler's replacement, began singing the leads in his soft tenor, and took the group to New York where they recorded "Gypsy Woman" for ABC-Paramount Records. It was a Top 20 smash and the beginning of a string of hits. Just as they were taking off, the Brooks brothers wanted to shift the group sound toward the jump style of rock 'n' roll that Little Richard and the Coasters were doing. When the other three members protested, the Brooks brothers quit the group and went on to record for End Records, where they produced no hits and watched their careers die.

Meanwhile, the Impressions were birthing a new revolution in music. Aside from Mayfield's distinctive falsetto and guitar playing, what made the Impressions a hit was Mayfield's songs. In the decade that would give birth to drugs, sex, and rock 'n' roll, Mayfield brought an entirely unique message to the music table.

"I used to write gospel [songs] and sing in a gospel group and actually, the only difference later was that instead of putting the word God in it, I would just leave it open for the individual to take in," he once explained. "As a matter of fact, 'Keep on Pushin'" was a gospel song and I changed some of the lyrics. Instead of saying, 'God gave me strength,' I'd say, 'I've got my strength and it don't make no sense not to keep on pushin'"

Using Biblical principles as his backdrop of inspiration, Mayfield created a canon of faith-inspired songs that touched on every aspect of life from romance on "I'm So Proud" to racial pride on "Choice of Colors." "My mother always read me lots of poems," he told *Newsweek* in 1996. "Paul Laurence Dunbar, I loved Dr. Seuss, limericks. These [became] the foundations for my hook lines and rhythmic patterns." Over the course of the '60s, the Mayfield technique resulted in the No. 1 R&B smashes "Choice of Colors," "It's Alright," and "We're a Winner," as well as Top 20 R&B charters such as ""Fool for You," "Woman's Got Soul," "Amen," and "Meeting Over Yonder."

If Mayfield had written and recorded nothing other than 1965's "People Get Ready," he would have a secure place in music history. One of the most covered songs in pop music, it's been recorded by Aretha Franklin, Rod Stewart, Margaret Becker, Ziggy Marley, and country legend Janie Fricke, to name a few. Tuning his guitar to the atypical key of F sharp, Mayfield shared the lead vocals with his two singing partners. The mellow-tempoed song is one of the most astounding fusions of a poetic gospel lyric with a pop sound. Artists with no religious affiliation love to sing the song for the pure beauty of its redeeming message and timeless groove.

> People get ready there's a train a comin'
> You don't need no baggage, you just get on board
> All you need is faith to hear the diesel's hummin'
> Don't need no ticket, you just thank the Lord
>
> So people get ready for the train to Jordan
> Picking up passengers cost to coast
> Faith is the key, open the doors and board 'em
> There's room for all among those loved the most
> There ain't no room for the hopeless sinner
> Who would hurt all mankind just to save his own

Have pity on those whose chances grow thinner
For there's no hiding place from the Kingdom's
      throne
So people get ready there's a train a comin'
You don't need no baggage, you just get on board
All you need is faith to hear the diesel's hummin'
Don't need no ticket, you just thank the Lord

In 1968, the Impressions' manager Eddie Thomas and Mayfield formed Curtom Records. The group continued to churn out hits for Curtom, but in 1970 Mayfield finally went solo. He adopted a harder, funkier sound and really began to detail the trials and tribulations of those growing up in inner city cesspools of drugs, crime, and indifference. Mayfield came out swinging with the track "(Don't Worry) If There's a Hell Below, We're All Gonna Go." This was only a hint at the graphic picture of ghetto life that Mayfield would paint on *Superfly*, the 1972 soundtrack to a blaxploitation film. It's universally praised by music critics as Mayfield's crowning achievement. As with Stevie Wonder's "Living for the City" and Marvin Gaye's "What's Going On?" the lead single "Freddie's Dead" was the story of a drug abuser's overdose.

The album was so successful that Mayfield was recruited to do more film soundtracks. The best of these was Gladys Knight & the Pips' *Claudine*, which described the ups and downs of a welfare mother bringing her children up in the ghetto. Aretha Franklin's *Sparkle* was the story of a singer who got caught up in the downside of the music industry. The Staple Singers did *Let's Do It Again* and Mavis Staples did its sequel *A Piece of the Action*. However, by the late '70s Mayfield's hits were just turntable hits, not big sellers. Through the 1980s he recorded infrequently and toured occasionally. By the 1990s, Mayfield's name was becoming popular again as a score of rappers began to sample his music in their songs. Then tragedy struck. On August 14, 1990, Mayfield was standing onstage at a free concert in Brooklyn tuning his guitar when a lighting rig fell on him. Mayfield was paralyzed from the neck down and in critical condition for weeks. He eventually was confined to a wheelchair and unable to move without assistance. Though a quadriplegic, he adjusted to his condition and

continued to live his life. Midway through the decade, Mayfield decided to record a new CD.

Initially, after his accident, Mayfield thought he'd never record again because he couldn't play guitar anymore. He couldn't even write songs because when he had a thought, he couldn't write it down until he called out for someone to write it down for him. It was frustrating, but he rarely complained. "You learn to live with it," he said in a 1996 interview. "It's as simple as that, or as hard as that, depending on one's mental ability…. You're always learning something about your body. One thing you learn quick is that paralyzed does not mean you don't hurt and ache and have chronic pain. I thought, 'I'll lie here and never hurt again.' That ain't the way it goes. Aches come and go. Some go dormant. You think it's over and it'll jump back at you. If you sit up a little too long, you can feel an ache in your butt. I think, 'Why should I ache? I'm paralyzed.'"

Recording for the project was a rough process. Mayfield could not sit up for long periods because his blood pressure would drop and cause him pain. He had no control of his diaphragm, his lungs were weak, and he had trouble catching his breath, so he lay on his back to record the songs with a microphone dangling over his mouth. But, for him, those inconveniences paled in comparison to not being able to play the guitar. "I still mourn to this day not being able to play my guitar," he told *USA Today* in 1996. "It's like having lost a brother. It helped me as a creative person."

The album *New World Order* was released in autumn 1996 and the title song reached No. 24 on the R&B chart. The project featured co-writers such as Narada Michael Walden and guest vocalists such as Mavis Staples and Aretha Franklin. Mayfield did a heavy round of press, mostly on his back and by phone to promote the CD. Many media types wondered if his paralysis had changed the status of his faith. "I'm not going to burden myself with 'Why me?'" he told *USA Today*. "Hell, it could happen to anybody. So how can I be mad? And mad at what?"

After the album's press cycle waned, Mayfield fell out of sight again, except for an occasional tribute such as the one he received when he was inducted into the Rock and Roll Hall of Fame. He died of complications from diabetes and his spinal injury on December 26, 1999, at the age of 57. Earlier that year, Rhino Records compiled a CD of some of Mayfield's best gospel recordings simply titled *Gospel*, which reached No. 40 on the gospel chart after he passed away.

MC Ge Gee

THE SISTER OF SLAIN Christian rapper D-Boy Rodriguez, MC Ge Gee was arguably the first female rapper in Christian music. Her mother, Cookie, was once a prostitute and heroin addict, who later found Christ and founded an anti-gang ministry with her husband, Demi. Of Puerto Rican heritage, Ge Gee was born Genie Rodriguez in the Bronx, New York, circa 1969. Her parents moved to Pennsylvania to create a women's ministry when she was a child. "I was four or five years old and seeing girls on heroin," she said in 1992. "I wasn't naïve as to what goes on in the streets. The only difference is I was used to seeing adults going through a lot of drugs and rehabilitation, but when we got here it was teenagers. It's basically ministry—once you're involved in it, nothing can shock you."

When she was 11 years old, the family moved to Dallas. "My mom wanted to move away from ministry, so we moved to Dallas and they ended up starting a gang ministry," she said in 1992. "It's funny how we ended up here. We never even knew about Dallas except for the TV show. We pictured it to be just one big ranch." Rodriguez went through growing pains. "I did go through a stage where I didn't want anything to do with it [ministry]," she said. "It turned me off for a while. One day I just had an awakening. I was forced to go to church and just had an attitude. I'd sit in the back of the church. And then one day, I couldn't blame God for people's actions. My brother was an example. He'd been through exactly what I had been and seen what I seen and he was strong as ever. So it was a cop-out to blame God for the freaky things people do."

Following in her brother's footsteps, Rodriguez released her first rap album, *I'm for Real*, for Frontline Records in 1989. From the beginning, it was not a marriage made in heaven. "They basically told me what kind of rapper I was going to be," she said. "They'd make the music and then tell me to write a rap to it. I feel like you need to write the rap, then you can start feeling what kind of beats you want and how you want to tie it together."

At the time, there were no major Christian female rappers, so Rodriguez felt that she'd be a good introduction for church folks. "Some people don't like hardcore, some don't like vague lyrics in rap, so maybe I can be a bridge because I don't consider myself hardcore," she said. "I'm not YoYo or somebody like that, but I'm certainly not a Vanilla Ice either. But I am reaching two audiences: the girls out there who want encouragement and the Hispanics who feel that Hispanics don't get anywhere in life."

Rodriguez had a big issue with many of the Hispanic rappers of the day such as Mellow Man Ace. "I'm turned off of a lot of the Hispanic rappers out there," she said then. "Because either they don't make a point to what they are saying or they leave Hispanics with a certain stigma, like t-shirts off and looking sweaty and trying to look sexy. They misrepresent us. I did consider that in my rapping that I'm not just a woman, not just a Christian, but I'm also Hispanic." Even though the rap world is all bravado and bling, Rodriguez was trying to broaden the scope of rap music. "I don't deal with it by trying to prove that I'm one of the guys. I just go on and I do what I do. They stereotype it as either being a male thing, a black thing, or not being a Christian thing. There are a lot of barriers we need to get over."

After D-Boy was killed in a drive-by in 1990, Rodriguez continued his legacy with *The Mission Continues*, her sophomore CD in 1991. "It's a spinoff of my brother's last album," she says. "The song [of his] I like the most is 'I Dropped the Mic.' In the rap, he was talking to rappers who make no sense in their raps. You know, they talk about gangstas, they talk about negative things, and my brother says drop the mic if you don't have anything positive to say. When he passed away, I was listening to his tape and starting to write for my second album, and I was thinking I have to pay tribute in some way to him and what he stood for. Then I thought of 'I Caught the Mic' to let him know

I'll carry it on." It was a little easier working on the second project. "I didn't have my brother to hide behind," she says. "I took a little stronger stand. If they have a song made up, they hate changing it. But that last time, I said, 'I'm sorry, but it's my money.' I know that it's my face and my name that goes on that tape. If you listen to my last one and want a good laugh, listen to 'Hawaiian Dream' because they forced me to do it."

There was no radio audience for Christian rap music at the time, so it was youth leaders at churches who kept Christian rappers working in the early 1990s. Rap was still new to the Christian world and Rodriguez received her share of angry letters from pastors who saw the genre as an unnecessary evil. "I got a letter of criticism from this pastor and he was letting me have it!" she says. "Several of my lines about being hung up on being Hispanic and hung up on being a woman got him. He said this isn't what Jesus died for and you're this and you're that. I [felt] this man doesn't even know what's in my heart, so I was getting ready to write him a letter. Then I thought, I'll shock him. I'll call him. We talked about an hour and a half and by the time we were done, he apologized and said that he misjudged me. Then he sent me two nice gifts in the mail to make up for it because he [had written] a letter that could really depress someone for a while." Frontline Records eventually closed and Rodriguez settled into a life outside of the limelight. She and her husband, Joe Lopez, a former DJ, still reside in Dallas.

MC Hammer

HIS CAREER DECLINE and bankruptcy provided fodder for late night television comics in the late 1990s, and he was never considered a rapper with street credentials by the rap intelligentsia. Nevertheless, MC Hammer still retains the best-selling rap CD of all time with *Please Hammer, Don't Hurt 'Em* which has sold over ten million copies in the US alone. Born Stanley Kirk Burrell on March 30, 1962, in Oakland, California, he was raised in a strict Christian home. As a teenager, he was a bat boy for an Oakland baseball team, where he danced and entertained the fans during breaks in the game. He was nicknamed "Hammer" because some of his friends felt

he resembled Hammerin' Hank Aaron—the Atlanta Braves' baseball star—and because he desired a career as a baseball player. When he wasn't picked up by a team, Hammer spent three years in the navy. Upon his discharge, he began to rap in local clubs. Some of his baseball contacts helped fund Hammer's own record label, which produced his first LP, *Feel My Power*, in 1987. He sold the LPs out of the trunk of his car and had a regional hit on his hands. Eventually, Capitol Records caught wind of his success and repackaged the LP as the CD *Let's Get it Started*. Then they watched it sell an easy two million copies off the strength of the smash single, "Turn this Mutha Out."

It was the next CD, *Please Hammer, Don't Hurt 'Em*, that made MC Hammer a household name. By taking the soundtrack to Rick James's "Superfreak" and putting a rap on top of it, he created one of the catchiest rap hooks ever with "U Can't Touch This." With his baggy parachute pants, bookworm glasses, and offbeat dance steps, Hammer took the street edge off rap and made it acceptable to suburban PTA mothers. As a result, Hammer took rap to places Public Enemy never

M.C. *Hammer / Capitol Records promotional photo*

could. He followed up with three more hit singles that year, including the gold-selling, gospel-themed "Pray."

In 1992, Hammer did another gospel tune, "Do Not Pass Me By," featuring Tramaine Hawkins. It reached No. 15 on the *Billboard* R&B singles chart and also hit the ILLBOARD Hot 100 singles chart. The rap community had so demonized Hammer that, in an effort to win their respect, he dropped the MC from his name and took on a hard-edged rap style and thug image that alienated him from his suburban following. Each new CD sold worse than the one before it. By 1996, Hammer had filed for bankruptcy. After a religious revival in his life, Hammer recorded the spiritually based albums *Family Affair* and *Active Duty* on his own label.

Thomas McClary

LIFE HAS BEEN interesting for Thomas McClary. Born in the segregated South, his folks were the most prominent black family in Eustis, Florida. He made headlines when he integrated his all-white high school there in 1963. He later co-founded the Commodores, a '70s pop band known for million-selling singles such as "Three Times a Lady," "Brick House," "Sail On," "Easy," "Still," and "Just to Be Close to You." In their heyday, music critics hailed them as the black Beatles because no black musical group had ever sold as many albums as the group did during the post-Nixon era. At the height of his fame, McClary says God called him away from his lucrative musical career to work with local churches in his hometown.

Born October 6, 1950, in Eustis, Florida, McClary was the youngest of eight children. His parents owned the 2,600-acre McClary Farm, which employed dozens of people. "They were one of the few families that didn't sharecrop," he recalls. "They owned their own land. They grew corn, sugar, and cotton. They did it all." Theirs was the first house in Eustis to have a color TV set and a private telephone. "People were always coming through just to use the phone or watch TV," he laughs.

In spite of the creature comforts, McClary was not spoiled. As a teenager, he rose at 3:00 A.M. daily to deliver newspapers with a one-armed friend who drove the car. He mowed lawns on Saturdays, was a brickmason on school break, and washed windows at a clothing shop. He played on his school's baseball and football teams and still made the dean's list every semester. Then he decided he wanted to attend the white high school near his home. "I was the first black to integrate the school system in the state," he says casually. "It was a real quagmire for me because I was the president of my class at the black school every year. I was quarterback, I was pitcher. My coaches didn't understand why I was doing it. They said, 'You're a star here, you have it made.' But there was this curiosity because I had always heard that the white schools are better."

It was a tough experience and media frenzy. McClary's family received death threats, and when McClary played football at school, the opposing team and its cheerleaders jeered, "Get that nigger." A female student accused him of making an inappropriate comment. The principal knew she was lying and told McClary so, but didn't discipline her. While singing in the school choir, three classmates took a cigarette lighter and ignited his clothes. "It was three guys standing behind me and they all put their hands behind their back so I didn't know which one did it. That was the only time I kind of lost it." What helped him through was his faith. "My parents were prayer warriors so it was through that faith and knowing that we're overcomers and that I made it through," he says.

In spite of the hostility, McClary never judged all whites by his classmates' behavior. A white classmate, Kent Reed, befriended him and endured nigger-lover slurs. "I couldn't use that as a criteria," he explains. "I had to really look at the character of each individual and chose my friends accordingly." Eventually, McClary had the last laugh. He won over the majority of the students and became the senior class valedictorian. Once high school was over, McClary was planning to matriculate at an Ivy League school until a friend teased him about getting back in touch with his black roots. On that advice, he enrolled at a historically black college, the Tuskegee Institute in Alabama. "I'm standing in the registration line and I hear this guy behind me whistling this saxophone solo by Eddie Harris called 'Listen Hear,'" he recalls. "He was going through all the riffs and I was thinking this guy's got to be a musician." McClary, who had been playing guitar since the tenth grade, turned around and asked the shy saxophonist to start a band with him. His name was Lionel Richie.

They formed the Mystics in 1967 and began to play around the Montgomery, Alabama, area. Another campus band, the Jays, needed to replace some members after they graduated. The Mystics and the Jays joined forces. To choose a new group name, they blindfolded a member and had him put his finger down on a word in the dictionary. His finger fell on the word commode. "They didn't think that would work," McClary chuckles, "so he did it a second time and he picked commodore." Renamed the Commodores, they aspired to be the black Beatles one day. They started off as a backing band for artists going through Montgomery, including Jerry Butler, Candi Staton, and the Ike & Tina Turner Revue.

The group studied music marketing and how Colonel Parker molded Elvis Presley into a star. "We made a decision to be different," McClary says. "We entertained people and put on a show. We examined how an artist could have several hit records and can't fill a room, and another group might have just one hit and could fill a coliseum." They jumped into an old Chevy attached to a U-Haul full of the group's instruments, and drove to Harlem in New York where they crashed with McClary's aunt. There they met Benny Washburn, who became their manager/mentor. He talked their way into an audition at basketball legend Wilt Chamberlain's club, Small's Paradise. The night of their gig, the group packed the venue with family and friends from Tuskegee who happened to be in the Big Apple. The club manager liked their show and the packed audience and booked them for the rest of the summer for $1,800 a week.

Eventually, the group auditioned and won a two-year opening slot on the Jackson 5's first major concert tour in 1971. "The big question was would a no-name group like the Commodores be able to maintain the crowd because everybody was there to see the Jackson 5. Not only did we maintain, but the write-ups became so incredible that Berry Gordy [founder of the Jackson 5's record company] said, 'Why aren't they signed? We're giving them all this exposure and someone else is going to come and take them.'"

Motown signed the group, but on the group's terms. They sought complete creative control and eventually they demanded the right to keep their song publishing rights—something Motown had never surrendered to any artist. "We were the first to get our publishing rights from Berry Gordy," McClary grins. "And the only way we were able to do that is because we were the first Motown act to sell LPs. All the other acts were known for selling singles. So when we came and started selling millions of albums and our contract was about to run out, Berry Gordy was not about to let us go. Our leverage was that we had to get our publishing rights. Stevie Wonder didn't have his publishing. His lawyer had a favored nations clause in his contract that [if] anyone got anything greater than Stevie, Stevie would automatically be promoted to get whatever that was. So he was grandfathered in by way of the Commodores."

Beginning in 1974, the band launched a string of Top Ten R&B and pop hits. They earned $500,000 a week in Las Vegas, and in the Philippines, they broke the Beatles' attendance record at the Areneta Coliseum. (The Beatles sold 207,000 tickets to the Commodores' 230,000 tickets.) The Commodores' pop-soul styling transcended race and touched emotions. "Some of the letters we'd get were amazing," McClary remembers. "One lady was dying of cancer. She said every time she put a certain song on, it would ease the pain. Lots of people got married off our songs. The emotions that it touched in people's lives are unbelievable."

"That was by design," McClary declares. "We had people write to us from around the world who didn't speak a lick of English but knew the spirit in which the songs were written. We earnestly sought for answers when we recorded those songs…. Even though music is subtle, it's very powerful. There are things musically that hide in our membranes. [People hear] a song and they remember what they were doing when the song came out. With that kind of power you have to be good stewards. We tried to be good stewards of that gift that God gave us even though we didn't give God the glory at that time. We feared God and knew that he was giving us those songs." One such song was undeniable. "Jesus Is Love" from the 1980 LP *Heroes* has become a gospel classic, and they used it to close their concerts.

In addition to major radio airplay on gospel stations, the song reached the R&B Top 40 in 1980.

1980 would be a turning point. Singer Kenny Rogers called out of the blue and asked Richie to write some songs for him. One of those songs, "Lady," spent nine weeks at No. 1 on the pop chart and took Richie's profile to a new plateau. Meanwhile, McClary and Richie wrote other songs together for Rogers and for Diana Ross. Soon the buzz was that Richie, who led most of the Commodores' singles, would eventually go solo. By 1982, Washburn had died, leaving them without the father figure who had kept them a solid unit. Without his presence, some members became jealous of Richie's increasing fame. Because of his tight relationship with Richie, other members often criticized McClary. In fact, McClary was a peacemaker. When a member left the group for a failed tennis career and then returned, the group didn't want him back, but McClary persuaded them to welcome him back into the family.

However, it was a broken family by the close of 1982. McClary and Richie both opted for solo careers. McClary cut a solo LP for Motown that produced the Hot 100 single "Thin Walls." He produced Klique's 1983 R&B hit "Stop Doggin' Me," which stayed at No. 2 on the R&B chart for four weeks. He had collaborations in the works with James Ingram, Melissa Manchester, the Four Tops, and a who's who of Hollywood. McClary's career was just on the verge of exploding when he received a call from God. "I heard an audible voice from God while I was in the shower," he recalls. "The voice said 'It's time for you to come home now.'" McClary jumped out of the shower, looked all round his house to see where the voice was coming from, and there was neither TV nor radio playing. The voice spoke again and McClary says, "I could not hold back the tears." McClary says that God was calling him to return to Eustis and work with local churches. He left his Hollywood home and stumbled onto a project of interviewing Apostolic preachers. He traversed the country, at his own expense, and documented the life of these religious leaders in a film, *The History of the Apostolic Faith*. After he finished packaging and marketing the project, McClary says God instructed him to donate all the proceeds to local churches. "I said, 'God, I just left all these big projects to do this project and now you want me to give the money back?'" McClary continued to obey and to work in the community. He won a zoning permit for a prime downtown youth center no one thought would ever be built. He gave motivational speeches at local groups and says, "It has been one faith walk after another." He met his wife, attorney Beryl Thompson, at one of those local groups. They married in 1992 and collectively have six children.

Today, McClary serves as minister of music at the New Destiny Christian Center in Orlando, a church that began with four members and blossomed into 4,500. Over the years, he has coached a number of local choirs but has now decided to transform New Destiny's mass choir into a professional choir and record their first CD. He's writing most of the songs but jokes that "I'll be getting others to sing them." He anticipates a release on his own Morning Star Records later this year.

McClary loves what he's doing, but says that a Commodores reunion tour may be in the making. In the meantime, all that slick soul music he and his bandmates recorded 30 years ago is funding the work he's doing for God. McClary keeps in touch with them and reminds them of the source of their good fortune. "I tell the guys all the time that God had to honor me and to honor his word," McClary explains. "I was a tither even back then. I tithed even though I wasn't saved because of my praying parents who feared God. My accountants used to laugh at me and wonder why I'd be giving six figures to the church. So it's not coincidental that the resurgence of that music has happened because God had to honor his word…. That's my testimony…. For the last 20-something years the royalties have not stopped. It's been incredible. I don't rub it in but try to tug at them and make sure they keep God first. I say to them 'You guys, just like Stevie Wonder was grandfathered in when we got our publishing rights, you were grandfathered in because I paid my tithes.'"

Bishop Clarence E. McClendon

IF THERE'S SUCH a thing as a sex symbol preacher, it's Clarence E. McClendon. He struts across pulpits like a rock star, and his relative youth and matinee idol looks have endeared him to a mostly female church audience. Born in 1965 in Decatur, Illinois, he began preaching at the age of 15. In 1991, he began pastoring the West Adams Foursquare Church in Los Angeles. He changed the name to Church of the Full Harvest International two years later. In 1997, McClendon took his message to television, which made him a superstar among charismatic Christian denominations.

In spring 2000, Integrity Music released the CD *Shout Hallelujah: Bishop Clarence E. McClendon Presents the Harvest Fire Mega Mass Choir*. The album reached No. 9 and spent 24 weeks on the *Billboard* gospel chart. The ultra-conservative Integrity Music label (which frowns upon divorce) stopped promoting the album during that period when it was learned that McClendon had divorced his wife of 16 years, Tammera, and later married Priscilla Delgado. *Charisma* magazine editor Lee Grady was incensed that an evangelist of McClendon's stature would consider divorce an option. "We are expected to forgive and forget—lest we be branded as judgmental," he wrote. "After all, if the offerings are flowing, and the preaching still gets the people to shout, then surely the anointing of God is on this man no matter what he did. Right? It sounds so merciful, but restoring a person into ministry after a moral failure is not that simple. We're supposed to give people time to heal. But the truth is that when it comes to marital breakdown or sexual sin, we Charismatics are way too eager to grant immediate pardons."

Although Integrity Music dropped McClendon from the roster, he denied any wrongdoing and weathered the storm. Under the umbrella of Clarence E. McClendon Ministries, McClendon's church boasts 12,000 members and his television program reaches 160 million people worldwide.

Debbie McClendon

THERE'S A STEREOTYPE that all gospel singers are big, fat, and greasy looking. When she first surfaced on the music scene in the 1980s, Debbie McClendon certainly wasn't that. She was a beautiful woman with a Polynesian look. She turned many heads, but she always turned

Debbie McClendon / Count It All Joy LP, 1987. *Photo by Harry Langdon, courtesy of* Star Song Records

them back toward Christ. With a high soprano, she delivered a small string of enjoyable CCM-styled albums of varying quality, although she never had a defining hit single in spite of major cheerleaders such as Andrae Crouch and Bill Gaither urging her on to the next level.

She was born Deborah Lynn McClendon on June 15, 1956, in Pasadena, California. Sandwiched between a younger brother, Paul, and an older sister, Rene, McClendon became a Christian at four years old. Her mother was very active in church and raised her children to be as well. "As a child, I always had a desire to sing," McClendon says. During her teens, she studied classical music for eight years. After graduating from John Muir High School, she attended Pasadena City College for a while.

Growing up, McClendon was musically influenced by the Bill Gaither Trio and Andrae Crouch. In 1982, she began to sing professionally by doing backup vocals for Crouch, Donn Thomas, and Barbara Mandrell. She then performed as a featured soloist for the Billy Graham Association, the Easter Seals Telethon, World Vision, the Full Gospel Businessmen's Association, and the Campus Crusade for Christ. Around this time, McClendon met Scott Smith, who was producing artists such as the Winans and Crouch at the time. He took an interest in her and introduced her to Christian songwriter Mike Murdock and asked him for money to finance a project on her. Murdock gave them $20,000 to create McClendon's first LP. Smith then presented the finished album to the A&R director at Light Records who rejected it outright. Smith didn't give up. He took the album to Light Records' President Ralph Carmichael, who listened to it and decided to release what became *I Can Hardly Wait* in 1985. Perhaps Carmichael should have listened to his A&R man. The album was a poor seller, though it had some good tracks, such as the Caribbean number "No, No Doubts" and the old-school, soul-flavored "I'm Free," as well as a slick cover shot by celebrity photographer Harry Langdon. The album did receive a Dove award nomination as best traditional gospel album of the year. The irony is that there were no traditional songs on the contemporary LP.

Light released McClendon from her contract and she soon found herself signed to Houston-based Star Song Records where she recorded the much better album, *Count It All Joy*, in 1987. One song in particular, "We Will Never Be Apart Again," features backing vocals by Walter and Lynette Hawkins, Alfie Silas, and Howard Smith. McClendon sang the song in tribute to her mother, Pearl, who had passed away in 1980. Other notable tracks include the bouncy urban rhythms of "He Won't Let Me Down" and the title track. Although it was not a major seller, it is McClendon's bestselling project to date. Around the same time, she recorded a country ballad with the Bill Gaither Trio called "Tell Me." Her voice was well suited to the song as she sang in a slightly lower register and her high notes were layered over a textured chorus on the fade that made a nice vocal blend.

Unfortunately, it's never been easy to fuse a classically styled singing voice with urban music. More times than not, McClendon's beautiful voice sounds too highbrow for the common man's music she is performing. Star Song was eventually sold to Sparrow Records and they dropped the artist roster. In 1989, McClendon signed to Frontline Records where she made her debut with her first CD *Morning Light*. This is perhaps McClendon's finest recording. She sang in a more earthy tone and the material was stronger. Early on in his career, Percy Bady armed McClendon

with three stellar tracks: the smooth soul of "Always," the praise and worship of "Worthy," and the ballad "My Song," a duet with Gene Miller. The set closed with a beautiful rendition of "I Surrender All" with simple piano accompaniment. The arrangement was the perfect backdrop to her classical vocal approach to the hymn. McClendon's final CD for Frontline, *Get a Grip*, was released amid the label's mounting financial problems, which eventually ended up in a bankruptcy filing and going out of business. The album wasn't spectacular, but it had some nice moments such as "Sweeter Than" and a remake of Larry Norman's "I Wish We'd All Been Ready." However, the album was not well promoted and it never found a radio footing as the music was deemed too black for white Christian radio and too white for black gospel radio. McClendon became a housewife and did occasional background vocals on CDs by Olivia Newton-John, Beverly Crawford, and Inspirational Charm. On her own legacy as a singer, McClendon told *Totally Gospel* magazine: "I always want to back up the songs I sing with the way I live."

Lisa McClendon

A CONTEMPORARY GOSPEL artist known for her retro-soul fusion into gospel, Lisa McClendon was born Edletha Lorraine McClendon on October 17, 1975, in Jacksonville, Florida. She became a born-again Christian at the age of 15 and became serious about her faith when she was 19 years old. Over the years, she enjoyed a wide range of vocal influences such as Harry Connick, Jr., Natalie Cole, and jazz legend Ella Fitzgerald. In 2002, she composed and recorded an independent retro-soul gospel CD entitled *My Diary, Your Life* for the independent Shabach recording label. Although it was poorly distributed, it created enough of a buzz that Integrity Music offered McClendon a recording contract. Her debut for the label, *Soul Music*, appeared in September 2003 and the spicy single "Hey Now" received respectable gospel radio airplay, bringing a Jill Scott vibe to sacred music. "My mission is to deal with life and issues," McClendon has said. "Things that are sugar-coated, such as immoral sex, lying, divorce, etc., I want to take the sugar off and just call it what it is, then offer hope. I want to go beyond the church walls… to go and teach all nations. Some people may never go to church. So I'll be a part of the church that goes to them."

Donnie McClurkin

GOSPEL'S FIRST MALE superstar since Andrae Crouch in the 1970s, Donnie McClurkin stumbled into fame in the late 1990s at epic proportions for a gospel artist who did not seek crossover success. Born November 9, 1961, in Amityville, New York, McClurkin's home was filled with domestic violence and drug abuse. He was saved by an aunt who sang background vocals with Andrae Crouch. "I had listened to Andrae's music nearly all of my life," McClurkin has said. "He had been a hero long before I ever met him. Entirely of his own initiative, he took me under his wing and became a teacher and role model to me. He was the influence in my life spiritually and musically."

During his youth, McClurkin played keyboards with his church's youth choir. He formed the McClurkin Singers with his relatives in 1979. Although he loved to sing, he felt called to preach. In between singing with his family and studying to preach, McClurkin formed the Restoration Mass Choir, which recorded the 1989 *I Feel Well* LP that first introduced McClurkin's classic song "Speak to My Heart." "We tried and tried, but no breaks came," McClurkin says. "So we entered the studio and recorded an album on Savoy Records and used the name New York Restoration Choir." Around that time, McClurkin was hired as an associate minister at Marvin Winans's Perfecting Church and also learned he had leukemia. After he battled the disease, McClurkin's friend Demetrus Alexander, a Warner Alliance Records executive, convinced him to record an album for the label. The 1996 eponymous album's various tracks were produced by Take 6's Mark Kibble, Andrae Crouch, and Cedric and Victor Caldwell. Angie and Debbie Winans supplied background vocals. It was a smooth, sophisticated album that still retained a churchy essence. McClurkin's almost operatic tenor soared over the radio hits "Stand" and "Speak to My Heart." Through BeBe Winans, Oprah Winfrey heard McClurkin's music and

invited him to perform on her television show. The opportunity catapulted his CD to No. 4 on the gospel charts and began to make McClurkin's name outside of the gospel fold as the album was certified gold.

Since he had by then developed a national platform, McClurkin used it as an opportunity to preach against the homosexuality he had often witnessed in church circles. He freely admitted that he had been molested as a child and later had homosexual relationships himself. "I don't believe that we should stand up and begin to cry out and denounce everybody, because some of them don't want to change," McClurkin says. "Our appeal should be to those who want to change. I don't need to stand on some soapbox and scream and holler with some kind of vengeance saying homosexuality is wrong. No, sin is wrong, and that includes lying and gossiping. There is no difference. Everybody is going to the same hell. The religious hypocrite will go to the same hell as the murderer and the homosexual. So my job is to say that sin is wrong and to kill the sin, not the sinner."

After Warner Bros. Records closed their Warner Alliance Christian division, McClurkin was signed to Verity Records. His first CD, *Live in London*, was more churchy than his debut. With an enthusiastic audience and fully aware of his preaching mantle, McClurkin fluctuated between testimonial style vamps and praise and worship music. His fans loved it and the album

Donnie McClurkin / photo courtesy of Verity Records

became an instant success without a clear single. In January 2001, Rev. Jesse Jackson made headlines when the media reported that the married minister had recently fathered a child with a woman young enough to be his daughter. In support of Jackson, sympathetic R&B DJs began to play a track from McClurkin's album called "We Fall Down," the chorus of which says, "We fall down, but we get up." The stronger the scandal became, the more airplay the song received. Verity Records rushed out a music video and the song reached No. 40 on the *Billboard* R&B chart.

Although the song became associated with Jackson's saga, McClurkin was moved to record the song after his own misstep. "I was in a place of really hurting, a place of disappointment," he told *Jet* magazine in 2003. "I had messed up so badly, and I know most Christians won't tell on themselves, but I don't have anything to hide because that's not the nature of God—he's forgiving. If you have a problem, you give it to him. I almost got to the point of giving up, not giving up my relationship with God, but my ministry. I had jacked up so badly, then the song came. I realized that I am no better than anyone else, but then, I am no worse either. My sin showed me that I was no better. No matter how much Jesus I spoke about, I was no better than anyone else. But then the mercy of God showed me that a sinner is just a saint who falls down." The CD *Live in London* reached No. 1 on the gospel chart, No. 22 on the R&B chart, and was certified platinum for sales of over a million copies. Even after his 2003 CD *Again* reached No. 1 on the gospel chart, McClurkin was still predicting that he would eventually stop recording altogether and concentrate on pastoring his church in New York.

Liz McComb

WHAT MAHALIA IS TO gospel music in America, Liz McComb is to France. There is no clear gospel community there, so McComb's earthy, traditional gospel music is just thought of as classic music, and she's often spoken of in the same light as Etta James, Nina Simone, Jessye Norman, and other such American song stylists. The improvisation, the syncopated chord patterns, the hushed moans, the cathartic wails, and the aggressively Pentecostal approach to the keyboard makes each one of her performances a truly unique, jazz-like exercise.

Born December 1, 1952, in Cleveland, Ohio, McComb is the sixth of a brood of seven children born to a factory worker and a housekeeper. Her father died when she was very young—McComb doesn't recall her age. "You remember what you want to remember," she says. The McComb home was Bible-centered and she began singing at age three. She and her sisters sang in a group called the Daughters of Zion. As a teenager, McComb imbibed jazz artists like Sarah Vaughn and Nat King Cole. After studying for a while at the Karamu House Theater, McComb moved to New York with hope of becoming a Broadway star. Her cousin Annie had lived and worked in Europe and knew a big concert promoter there. She got McComb to send an audition tape to the promoter. In the early 1980s, he put her to work in Europe as one of the Jean Austin Singers and then, as a member of the *Roots of Rock 'N' Roll* revue where she opened for the legendary gospel singer Bessie Griffin.

Over the next decade, McComb performed on bills with Ray Charles, James Brown, Taj Mahal, and other musical luminaries. One of her closest collaborators was Gregory Hunter, a graduate of *Dream Girls* on Broadway. They struck up an enriching friendship and musical partnership that lasted until his death. "After that I decided not to collaborate with anyone else," McComb says. "I loved him so much as a person. It was hard. I was taking care of him. His wife had died of AIDS. Then later he died of AIDS too." For a while, McComb was depressed and didn't want to perform. However, she had an experience that brought her up from her abyss. "[Gregory Hunter] came to visit me," McComb recalls. "Most people don't believe me when I say this. When I really knew it was him, I was laying on my bed watching TV and I had my hand over my head and my hand moved, but I didn't move it. Greg passed by to say goodbye."

During this trying period, McComb met Gerard Vacher, owner of the Cotton Club in Neuilly, France. Though theirs is a combative relationship, Vacher eventually became McComb's manager and guided her success through Europe. A relentless promoter, Vacher spent thousands out of his own pocket to promote McComb in America and throughout Europe, where she has recorded a dozen hit albums. Though she records classic music by Dorothy Love Coates and other gospel legends, McComb's best works are her own compositions, born out of her own experiences. "God has brought me to a level now to really be a vessel for him," she says. "No matter what has gone on in my life or the steps I have had to take to get there, and some have not been beautiful.... I fell in love with a European man. I loved that man and that man made me sing the blues and that's not what God wanted for me. I loved him and my mind was on him, so the Lord fixed it so that I had to get out of that. My mother said, 'God isn't pleased with what you're doing.' I had to hear her telling me about that. She was praying and speaking in tongues and said, 'You better wake up' and I did. I can truly say my steps have been ordered by the Lord. Sometimes we have to walk that walk in order to be assured in God. I think a lot of the young people want to do gospel... or they want to do a record just to do a record, but it doesn't have any substance. The word that I say now is real."

In 2001, Vacher negotiated a deal with the EMI-distributed, Detroit-based Yellow Rose Records to release McComb's first American CD. The eponymous album was comprised of a dozen songs from McComb's various European releases. The most outstanding were the original "What Happened to the Love?" and "Time Is Now," which both oozed a seductive after-hours feel as the lyrics probed into deeper elements of man's existence. The album reached No. 21 on the gospel chart, but did not build an American audience for this gifted singer with the voice that slides from smoothness to raspiness quicker than a blink. Vacher was frustrated that his six-figure marketing investment in McComb failed to make her an American star and gave up on America. He instead concentrated on maintaining her stature in Europe where she followed up with an EMI France Dixieland gospel CD entitled *Spirit of New Orleans* that received rave reviews from the French press and sold respectably through the Continent. "I lived a real story here," she says of her success. "I've made it thus far by the grace of God. I'm a flawed woman. I haven't lived everything that God said but I am now. I believe he took me through those things to bring me to where I am now."

Marilyn McCoo

THE BRONZE BEAUTY found fame as one-fifth of the 5th Dimension pop group in the 1960s with hits such as "One Less Bell to Answer" and "Aquarius/Let the Sunshine In." In the mid-'70s, McCoo and her husband, Billy Davis, Jr., became a duo with their smash hit "You Don't Have to Be a Star" and a hit CBS TV series. By the early 1980s, McCoo launched a solo career as she became co-host of the weekly musical TV series *Solid Gold* and performed her solo act regularly in Las Vegas and Atlantic City. She and Davis had become born-again Christians around 1979 and became active in Hollywood's Christian community thereafter.

The daughter of doctors, McCoo was born September 30, 1943, in Jersey City, New Jersey. She started singing early and as a teenager she appeared on Art Linkletter's *Talent Scouts*. After her family moved to Los Angeles, McCoo enrolled as a business major at UCLA while also pursuing a modeling career. She won the Miss Bronze California pageant in 1962 where she met photographer Lamonte McLemore, who was also a singer. Fast friends, McLemore and McCoo teamed up with Floyd Butler and Harry Elston to form the Hi-Fis, a vocal group. They performed in clubs until Ray Charles caught wind of them and had them tour with him in 1965.

Charles produced one single with them called "Lonesome Mood" before Bulter and Elston left the group to form the Friends of Distinction, which would go on to have a huge hit with "Going in Circles." While on tour with Charles, McCoo and McLemore met Marc Gordon who became their manager. Around that time, McLemore got in touch with two childhood friends from St. Louis who could both sing, Billy Davis, Jr. (born June 26, 1940) and Ron Townsend. There would be one more addition with schoolteacher Florence LaRue, who was Miss Bronze California in 1963. The new group was named the Versatiles. They signed to Bob Keene's Bronco Records where the A&R director, Barry White (who would make a name for himself as a soul singer/conductor some years later), had begun strategizing on the group's first record. When Gordon introduced them to famed guitarist Johnny Rivers, who had just founded Soul City Records, the group wanted to go with Rivers. Bronco released them from their contract. Rivers changed their name to the 5th Dimension and their first hit single "Go Where You Wanna Go" (a cover of a tune by the Mamas & the Papas) hit the Top 20 pop chart in 1966. Barely into their twenties, the black group appealed to youth—white youth—with their polished, pop sound and emphasis on tight, five-part vocal harmonies. In spite of the name of their record label, the 5th Dimension's sound was never cultivated for black radio, although they had consistently good success there. Over the next seven years, the group would churn out such classic AC radio staples as "(Last Night) I Didn't Get to Sleep at All," "Aquarius/Let the Sunshine In," "One Less Bell to Answer," "Never My Love," "Stoned Soul Picnic," "Workin' on a Groovy Thing," and "Up, Up and Away," which won four Grammy awards in 1968.

McCoo and Davis were married on June 26, 1969, at the height of the group's fame and rapidly became the focus of media attention as they led most of the group's bigger hits. Around 1975, McCoo and Davis departed the group and joined ABC Records as a duo. Their duo's material was still sophisticated, but had a more R&B feel than their music with the 5th Dimension. Their 1976 LP *I Hope We Get to Love in Time* featured the No. 1 pop and R&B smash "You Don't Have to Be a Star" and the Top Ten hit "Your Love." The former led to a Grammy as best R&B duo and a CBS summer replacement TV variety series, *The Marilyn McCoo & Billy Davis, Jr. Show.*

After a couple more LPs only created a tepid public response, McCoo went solo in 1981 with her marriage intact. She began co-hosting the hour-long weekly variety TV series *Solid Gold* with Andy Gibb after negotiations with the show's original host, Dionne Warwick, broke down. Meanwhile, McCoo & Davis reunited on wax for the song "Praise Ye the Lord" on Davis's gospel LP *Let Me Have a Dream.* In 1983, McCoo recorded an LP entitled *Solid Gold* for RCA Records that included the minor hit "Heart Stop Beating in Time" and a pre–Whitney Houston version of "I Believe in You and Me" (sung as a duet with Davis). McCoo left *Solid Gold* after the 1984 season, only to return as the sole host for 1986–88. While doing the show, McCoo also took an acting role on the soap opera *Days of Our Lives* for one season.

In 1991, McCoo recorded her first Christian/inspirational CD *The Me Nobody Knows* for Warner Bros.' Christian music division, Warner Alliance. Produced by Chris Christian, the album was a smooth pop affair that leaned toward the smooth jazz and Quiet Storm radio formats. The title song reached No. 24 on the CCM chart. Through the 1990s, McCoo starred in stage productions of *Show Boat, Dream Girls*, and *Man of La Mancha.* She also hosted the Easter Seals Telethon and the Lou Rawls Parade of Stars Telethon for the United Negro College Fund.

Louise McCord

A PROTÉGÉ OF Rev. James Cleveland, McCord grew up idolizing Delois Barrett Campbell of the Roberta Martin Singers. "Every run Delois made, I tried to make it," she said in Bernice Johnson Reagon's book *We'll Understand It Better By and By.* "You have to know what you're singing about in order to deliver a song. I tried to make those runs like Delois, but I couldn't make them until I really began to know the Lord." She recorded one fine LP for Stax Records' Gospel Truth imprint. The 1972 album *A Tribute to Mahalia Jackson* featured songs associated with Jackson, as well as message songs such as Bettye Crutcher's "Better Get a Move On." The album was produced by Stax's beloved promotion man, Dave Clark, in Detroit where Thomas Whitefield created the song arrangements and the Rance Allen Group provided the music (Rance Allen on lead guitar and organ, Steve Allen on bass guitar, and Tommy Allen on drums). She later recorded spectacular gospel music for Savoy Records such as "Trying to Find My Peace" but her career never took off.

Gwen McCrae

ONE OF SOUL MUSIC'S great treasures from the 1970s, Gwen McCrae's 1975 million-seller "Rockin' Chair" is one of the most identifiable songs of the era. Born Gwen Mosley on December 21, 1943, in Pensacola, Florida, as a child, she loved gospel music. "I was raised right up there in it," she told the *London Sunday Herald* in April

2004. "My mother played the piano in church, she had me there for prayer meetings, for Baptist Training Union meetings, all kinds of meetings—I was just a regular churchaholic! That's why I want to sing gospel, and why I always listened to gospel. James Cleveland, Shirley Caesar, the Mighty Clouds of Joy… those were my lookup people. It's what I wanted to do all my life."

After high school, she worked as a nurse for a while until she met a sailor named George McCrae in 1963. They married a week later and she joined his group, the Jivin' Jets. "I didn't want to do R&B," she told the *Herald*. "I was just helping out this little group in West Palm Beach in Florida. It started when I got married, and my ex-husband was in this little local group, and they said to him, 'Doesn't your wife sing? Will you ask her to sing with us?' and I turned right around and said, 'I can't do that!' You see, I had to go to church that day and do a song with my gospel group, and my voice went away from me. I couldn't get nothing out, so I said, 'Oh Jesus, please forgive me, I wasn't going to sing with that group,' and my voice came right back. Then it came to me that if you're married, you have to be obedient to your husband as well as to Jesus, so that's what I did. I helped out."

Eventually, they decided to sing as a duo and were discovered by singer Betty Wright who helped them get signed to her label, Alston Records. After a number of small hits, George temporarily retired from singing and became Gwen's manager. However, after a while, he itched to sing again. In 1975, they enjoyed massive solo hits. Gwen recorded "Rockin' Chair" and George recorded "Rock Your Baby," both of which reached No. 1 on the R&B singles chart and the Top Ten on the Hot 100 pop chart. Gwen enjoyed other hits such as "For Your Love," "Funky Sensation," and "Love Insurance" over the next few years. However, she and George eventually divorced. When this writer interviewed her in the late 1990s, she had nothing positive to say about him. In addition to accusing him of infidelities and spousal abuse, she charged that he moved to Europe to avoid having to pay child support in the United States. "If it wasn't for the grace of God," she said at the time. "I wouldn't be here now. I tell you, it's been hard for me." In 1995, McCrae became an evangelist. In 2004, she released her first gospel CD,

I'm Not Worried (Going Back to Church). It was traditional gospel with a retro-soul gloss. *Billboard* magazine scribe Gordon Ely wrote, "At the top of her form and in complete command of her material, McCrae proves herself to be no gospel dilettante. This album arrives like a postcard from a dear friend."

Now back in the gospel fold, the raspy-alto told the *Herald*, "When I was in the R&B scene, I gave my all, I gave my best. But it bothered me, because that wasn't where I wanted to be. I had children to raise, and I wanted to raise them. Some people just want to sing, they don't care about children, all they want to do is make it. I wanted to get my children grown first, and then worry about putting myself forward. And I've been a minister since I was 33. I thought to myself at that age, if Jesus could die for me on the cross at the age of 33, who am I that I can't give my life to him at the age of 33?"

Ann McCrary

BEST KNOWN AS one of the featured vocalists for BET's long-running *Bobby Jones Gospel* television series, Ann McCrary is a late bloomer with a long history in gospel music. Born August 24, 1950, at Nashville's General Hospital, McCrary's father, Rev. S.H. McCrary, was a founding member of the Fairfield Four quartet. She began singing at the age of two and was never far away when her father sang with the legendary groups of the 1950s. They all pitched in with watching over little Ann, and Bessie Griffin even taught her to sing "Since I Met Jesus." During one concert, Ann wandered onstage. "I pulled on my father's pants leg and asked if I could sing. He thought that was so cute, so he let me sing 'Since I Met Jesus.' The people began throwing money at the stage," she recalls. "Well, the promoter hadn't met his part of the contract, so there wasn't enough money for us to get home. After those people threw that money, it was enough and Daddy never left home without me after that."

As a teenager, McCrary joined the Baptist, Catholic & Methodist Mass Choir, while her older sister, Regina, began a long stint as a backing vocalist for Bob Dylan. They recorded for Nashboro Records and earned a

Grammy nomination for their album *Life*. McCrary was the lead vocalist on their hits such as a remake of Mattie Moss Clark's "Salvation Is Free." The group performed with or backed scores of country artists. They backed Ray Stevens on his million-seller "Everything Is Beautiful." They also sang with Johnny Cash and backed Elvis Presley on several occasions. McCrary's career came to an abrupt halt in 1968 when she married. "I was stupid," she says. "My husband wanted me to stay home because he was intimidated by my singing. For years, I was forced into silence, had three children, was a depressed mother and wife. I couldn't even go to church because he didn't want me to." McCrary's father was crushed that she could no longer attend church, but because he was a minister, he didn't feel it right for her to get a divorce. "I tried to make it work for the kids' sake," she says. But when she was confronted by her husband's mistress, "I began to re-evaluate my life. I had turned away from God and all his teachings because this man did not want that, but I hung in there because I thought that at least he loved me. That was a serious wake-up call." McCrary had a nervous breakdown in 1974 at an Italian hospital while her husband was in the air force. She was in the psychiatric ward for three months before being transferred to a hospital in Wichita Falls, Texas. When she was released, McCrary started going back to church. Her husband would point a gun at his head and threaten to kill himself if she went to church. "That kept me in check for years because I didn't want him to kill himself and for his children to know that he killed himself. But later on I said, if it's time for you to go, then I guess you gotta go." They finally divorced in 1988. Back in the church fold, McCrary formed the St. Mark Ensemble Choir and directed them for a dozen years. She also formed a gospel group called the CBS Singers (Cousins, Brothers, and Sisters) with her siblings and cousins. After her cousins dropped out, the group renamed itself the McCrarys. At the same time, McCrary began to get session work. On the secular side, she's done background work for Kenny Rogers, Wynonna, and Reba McEntire. On the gospel side, she's backed CeCe Winans, Michael Card, Yolanda Adams, Twinkie Clark, and Donnie McClurkin. She's sung lead on Hezekiah Walker and the Love Fellowship Crusade Choir's *Live in London at Wembley* CD, as well as the 1996 GMWA Women of Worship CD *The Crown Collection*, where she recorded "He Is Lord" with Nancey Jackson. She also sang lead on the Colorado Mass Choir's "I'm Going Away" and "Press."

All the session work caught the attention of Tara Griggs, who signed McCrary to a development deal with Benson Records. Before the album was released, Griggs left to take a position at Verity Records and no one else showed interest in McCrary's project, so it was shelved. Producer Cedric Caldwell approached her about recording for his upstart Against the Flow Records label, which had released the controversial but successful CD *Bold* by Angie & Debbie in 1997.

The album *What Is This?* showcased McCrary's robust vocal power on songs written by members of Take 6 ("Just Want to Give You the Praise"), Marvin Winans, and others. She shone best on hymns such as "How Great Thou Art" and the old Soul Stirrers' classic "No Room at the Inn." The title song was a trio recording with Donnie McClurkin and Steve Crawford of Anointed on the Brother Joe May classic which had been re-popularized by the Hawkins Family in the 1970s. It was an excellent album, but ATF's distributor, Diamante—drowning in financial trouble—didn't push the CD strongly. It was lost in the shuffle in spite of weekly promotions on Bobby Jones's highly rated TV show. The track "Just Want to Give You the Praise" was eventually lifted for Integrity Music's *Women of Faith: Gospel* CD, which also featured Oleta Adams and Dottie Peoples. McCrary currently records for New Day Christian Distributors in Nashville.

McCrarys

ONE OF THE BEST background groups in gospel, pop, or R&B music, the McCrarys have sung behind a who's who of the music industry. The sibling quintet of Alfred (born 1950), Charity (born 1952), Howard (born 1953), and twins Sam and Linda (born 1954) hail from a family of 12 in Ohio. Their first LP was a 1972 contemporary gospel album, *Sunshine Day*, for Light Records, which had not dabbled into much black music previously. Some of the members were still teenagers at the time, but the group wrote the majority of the music, which featured piano work from future jazz legend Joe Sample. The album was not a hit, but the group began to get steady work as background vocalists for artists such as Cat Stevens. In 1976, they provided backing vocals on Stevie Wonder's masterpiece LP, *Songs in the Key of Life.*

Wonder returned the favor on the McCrarys' (minus Howard) first positive-pop LP in 1978. They scored a Top Ten R&B hit with "You," which featured Stevie Wonder on harmonica. It was a funky, midtempo number with a positive message that could have easily been directed to God or a boyfriend/girlfriend. They followed with lesser chart hits such as "Don't Wear Yourself Out," "Lost in Loving You," and "Love on a Summer Night." Howard rejoined the group on their 1980 Capitol LP *All Night Music* after which they were dropped from the roster. They returned to gospel session work later in the 1980s, appearing on various albums by Andrae Crouch and Candi Staton among others.

Over the years, Howard has written songs for the Mighty Clouds of Joy, such as "The World Is Not Home," and he wrote the theme song for Jim and Tammy Bakker's PTL television show. Howard recorded a solo gospel album, *So Good*, for the Good News label in 1985. In addition, he has done voice work for the California Raisins and Hanna-Barbera's *Once Upon a Forest*. He has also toured as Rev. Winter in a sold-out London production of *Mama, I Want to Sing*, which starred his sister-in-law, Chaka Khan. (Her sister Tammy is his wife.) Today, the McCrarys often get together to sing on various TBN programs such as *Praise the Lord*. The McCrarys are related to the late Sam McCrary of the Fairfield Four. His daughters, Ann and Regina, are both featured singers on BET's *Bobby Jones Gospel* TV show.

Jackie McCullough

ONE OF THE MOST dynamic female preachers of the modern era, Jackie McCullough was born in Jamaica circa 1950. Her parents were both preachers who raised her in New York City. The late Bishop Leonora Smith prophesied that McCullough would someday become a preacher. She dreamed of a medical career and after finishing nursing school, McCullough worked at Harlem

Hospital as a registered nurse. After seven years of nursing, she felt the call to preach. She left nursing around the same time that she left a physically abusive marriage and her newborn infant had died. "The death of my baby and the death of my marriage propelled me into a deeper walk with the Lord," she told *Gospel International* magazine. "I wanted the proverbial traditional home: a husband, a child, a house, a career, and maybe something for God. I had my own agenda and all that was disrupted." She moved in with her parents and began to preach in prisons and on street corners. Eventually, she founded the Daughters of Rizpah in Pomona, New York, which serves as the headquarters for her traveling evangelistic meetings. That have taken her around the globe. Possessing a deep, boisterous rasp of a voice, McCullough recorded the CD *This Is for You, Lord* for Gospo Centric Records in 1999. Recorded live in Jamaica, the album had a festive feel with elements of R&B sprinkled through a congregational style of worship songs that were all co-written by McCullough. The album reached No. 11 on the gospel album chart but was not a strong enough seller to merit Gospo Centric recording another one.

Jimmie McDonald

ONE OF KATHRYN KUHLMAN'S featured psalmists during the last year of her life, Jimmie McDonald was also one of the first black singers to perform regularly at predominantly white evangelistic services in the 1970s. With his booming, operatic baritone, he set the pace for Kuhlman's healing services. He began recording albums such as *I Believe in Miracles* for Pilgrim Records in 1965. During his stint with Kuhlman, McDonald first met Benny Hinn, who has utilized McDonald's vocal talents at his crusades in the ensuing years.

V. Michael McKay

A GIFTED GOSPEL SONGWRITER on par with Thomas Dorsey in terms of the beauty and skillfulness of his work, he was born Varn Michael McKay in 1952. He wrote "The Potter's House" for Walter and Tramaine

Hawkins, "The Battle Is the Lord's" and "Through the Storm" for Yolanda Adams, and "I'm Still Here" for Albertina Walker. McKay is a two-time Dove award winner. He's published over 100 songs through his Schaff Music Publishing and lives in Houston, Texas.

Doc McKenzie & the Hi-Lites

IMAGINE A TRADITIONAL gospel quartet with a lot of funk and reverb and you've imagined the Hi-Lites. Doc McKenzie is noted for his smooth, laid-back vocal style that is highlighted by sudden roughshod squalls à la Joe Ligon of the Mighty Clouds of Joy. The Hi-Lites have never made a strong impact on gospel radio nationwide, but they have made a small impact in the Southeastern states radio community and managed to work steadily for three decades. They continue to be current and as in-demand as they've ever been—without a strong radio presence. "Since I was a small boy, I loved to sing and make music," McKenzie has said. "As I've grown in the Lord, I realize that this is not something I chose to do. Before I was placed in my mother's womb, I was anointed for this ministry, to bless God's people through song."

Milbert E.S. McKenzie was born on April 29, 1949, in Olanta, South Carolina, to a farming family. When McKenzie wasn't helping till the land, he could be heard singing at St. Mark's Holiness Church of Lake City. The church's Bishop R.C Eaddy nicknamed McKenzie "Doc" when he was three years old because of his ability to doctor anything. It's hard to believe, but he's said that he was music director for the church choir at the age of six and later learned to play the guitar. In 1965, McKenzie formed the Gospel Hi-Lites with his sister Beronzy McKenzie and his cousin Handy McFadden. After graduating from Carver High School in 1967, McKenzie joined his older brothers in Paterson, New Jersey, where they reconstructed the group as Doc McKenzie & the Gospel Hi-Lites. They performed on weekends while holding down 9-to-5 weekday jobs. In 1982, they released their first LP *What a Wonder the Lord Has Done* on Savoy Records. Soon after, McKenzie's brothers retired from the group, so he relocated to his native Lake City and recruited new members.

After the Savoy contract ended, they were without a label home until the 1990s when they recorded a number of poorly promoted LPs for Atlanta International Records, First Lite Records, Meltone Records, Shurfine Records, and MCG Records. In spite of warming the rosters of some of gospel's biggest independent labels, the Hi-Lites' greatest commercial success came with First Lite Records in the mid-'90s. Their 1995 CD *Man in the Middle* featured the 18-minute opus "Little Girl Fell," which was divided into three parts so that it could be played on the radio. Their other First Lite projects, *Ride with Jesus* and *Live*, both hit the Billboard Top 30 gospel album chart. Their 2001 MCG Records CD *Hold On* featured the great old-school R&B-styled title song, which reflects on maintaining marriages in a climate of divorce. The CD never charted, but the song gained enough buzz to earn them a slot to perform the song on the 2002 Valentine's Day episode of Candi Staton's TBN *Say Yes* television program. The group was dropped by MCG Records after that project and have since recorded for New Haven Records, still looking for a legitimate hit.

David Meece

ONE OF THE MOST popular contemporary Christian music artists of the 1980s, Meece was best known for the songs "Candle in the Rain" and "We Are the Reason." Born May 26, 1952, in Humble, Texas, Meece was a child prodigy. He began touring as a concert pianist by the age of ten. He toured Europe and was a featured soloist with the Houston Symphony (under the direction of conductor André Previn) by the age of 16. Music took Meece's mind away from trouble at home. "My father was a very abusive man," he once told *Teen Challenge* magazine. "He tried to kill my mother on numerous occasions. He tried to kill all of us. He was an alcoholic and a drug addict. Sharing this and explaining how God was able to take that nightmare of the beginnings of my life and turn it into the very place of ministry that I'm in today has been very liberating for me. It has become part of the healing process in my life."

Meece attended the Peabody Conservatory of Music in Baltimore on scholarship. During that time in his life, Meece, who was raised a Southern Baptist, became a born-again Christian and began to write songs about his faith. In 1976, he snagged a recording contract with Myrrh Records where he released his debut LP *David*. Over the years, the major complaint about Meece's music has been that he jumps from one category to another. One album is pop, the next is experimental, and then there's a blue-eyed soul project. In the CCM field, artists who are not easily categorized are not usually that successful. Thus, Meece's success has been erratic. His first big record was 1979's "I Can't Believe It's True," which reached No. 2 on the CCM singles chart. In spite of his disparate musical tastes, Meece has had the most success when he sings light pop songs—the type of soft tunes that were a harbinger for Michael W. Smith. When "We Are the Reason" was first issued in 1981 it only reached No. 14 on the chart, but has proven to be one of the most played songs on Christian radio. He's enjoyed No. 1 CCM singles with 1985's "You Can Go" and 1990's "The Man with the Nail Scars." Some collaborations with pop-soul singer Gino Vanelli yielded radio hits such as "Seventy Times Seven" in 1986. However, the following year's "Candle in the Rain" reached No. 2 on the CCM singles chart and has become the second-most popular song in Meece's catalog. Since the mid 1990s, Meece's career has taken on a subdued tone and he's recorded for independent labels.

RECOMMENDED RECORDING: *Odyssey* (Star Song, 1995) is a hits collection featuring Meece's best-known songs.

Bertha Melson

IN CHICAGO, she's known as the tiny woman with the big voice. Born March 4, 1933, in Chicago, Melson grew up with gospel legends Sam Cooke and James Cleveland. As a teenager, she was in an unnamed group with the latter. "I guess he called himself learning how to play," she cracks now, "because he couldn't play piano that good at first. Now, he could teach you a song and how to sing it, but he couldn't play worth two cents back then. We sang hymns, anthems, some songs that

he would write. He'd give them to us, we'd learn them, and then we sang them at Sunday afternoon church programs. Some other songs we sang, Maceo Woods wrote. Maceo and Sam Cooke and all of us came up together. We just sang for fun. We had a ball."

Melson continued singing after she married C. Hiram Melson, who was by all accounts one of the most dynamic preachers in Chicago during the 1950s. Melson says, "Sometimes you get too big for yourself. My husband was one of the best preachers in the city of Chicago.... Sometimes we let good things go to our head. If I went to church with him and they called on me to sing, he wouldn't let me. He said that only he was supposed to call on me to sing if he wanted me to sing." Melson says that her husband's church kicked him out for some impropriety, and she kicked him out later on.

Even as a single mother with two children, Melson didn't let anything stop her from ministering in song. "I'd have one child under one arm," she says. "I'd have the other under the other. When it was time to sing, one of the women there would hold my sons. I only had sons. I wouldn't want no daughters." Why not? "Girls is trouble." That remark leads into a discussion of women preachers. "God didn't tell me to preach," she says with indignation. "I notice all the lady singers nowadays call themselves ministers. God ain't told me nothing about all of that. Now, if I see a young person going down the wrong way and I think I can help them, I'll give them some advice."

In recent years, Melson has been slowed down a bit by arthritis. "I haven't stopped going," she insists about her concert appearances. "I just don't go as much." She's only recorded once, for Rev. Clay Evans's Fellowship Choir, but Savoy Records never released the song. Melson has a high-end alto, not unlike Marion Williams's warbling vocal style and has never made a living as a performer. She's worked at a local laundry for over 40 years to keep her bills paid; the singing is just to bless others. "Sometimes folks say, 'I don't go to that church because it's too small,'" she says. "But sometimes, that's where you get your greatest blessing. I just listen to them and smile and keep on stepping. The Lord puts you in places where he wants you to be."

Men of Standard

WHEN THEY APPEARED on the gospel horizon in 1996, the field was crowded with choirs and soloists. There were few hit male groups at the time. Men of Standard gave the gospel world the standard for what a smooth, urban crossover-styled gospel group should look and sound like. Formed by Isaac Caree, Michael Bacon, Bryan Pierce, and Lowell Pye, their harmonies were tight and, though spiritual, also sensual.

Caree is the son of noted gospel singer Nancy Wilson, who is well-known in Southeastern black church circles. He once toured with Phyllis Hyman and Billy Preston in the 1994 musical *Blues Bar*, but his and Pye's real training ground was in John P. Kee's New Life Community Choir. They eventually formed the Men of Standard with Pierce, who was a youth minister in New Orleans. They went through a few people before deciding on Bacon as the fourth member.

Their self-titled debut CD and the follow-up CD *Feels Like Rain* gave them a terrific industry buzz on the heels of the radio singles "Winter" and "Yet I Will Trust Him." In explaining their style, Lowell Pye said, "We wanted to be different. God is calling for more than just another group of singers. He's demanding that you live a holy lifestyle. I think we came up with the name Men of Standard because we wanted to let people know that you've got to have standards. We as a group want to set a standard. We don't want to compromise our beliefs for anyone. That's what the name stands for and we're sold on that belief."

After their initial success, the group sought to sever their ties with their publisher, Muscle Shoals. They sought a larger recording deal and more control over their career. After a protracted battle, they eventually stayed with the company. However, the three years away from the limelight hurt their career. Their subsequent CDs have performed badly, and the group has struggled to maintain their fan base as gospel music has now been flooded with equally young, urban contemporary gospel groups such as the Choir Boyz.

RECOMMENDED RECORDING: *The Men of Standard* (Muscle Shoals, 1996)

Joyce Meyer

A NO-NONSENSE Bible teacher, Joyce Meyer has become one of the most popular speakers in Charismatic church circles of the last 20 years. Born Pauline Joyce Hutchison on June 4, 1943, in St. Louis, Missouri, her life reads like a network television mini-series. Her father joined the military the day after she was born and returned three years later, a bitter alcoholic. He was abusive and molested Meyer from an early age. When she was nine, Meyer told her mother about the abuse, but she refused to believe it. When Meyer was 14, her mother returned from a shopping trip and saw her husband in a compromising position with her daughter. In her book *Beauty for Ashes*, Meyer wrote that her mother "looked, walked out and came back two hours later, acting as if she had never been there."

The lack of trust at home sharpened Meyer's resolve to become independent of her parents. She took a job at a dime store and began stealing things from work and from friends. In spite of her troubles, she was popular at O'Fallon Technical High School and her peers often sought her out for counsel. Not long after graduation in 1961, Meyer packed her bags into her black 1949 Chevrolet and left her parents' home. Later that year she married a fifth grade–dropout and car salesman. She was working as a payroll bookkeeper when her husband persuaded her to begin stealing money (years later, she returned the money). Once they pocketed the loot, the couple moved to California. The money was never enough for Meyer's husband, though. He once tried to slip her wedding ring off her finger while she was asleep so he could pawn it. She suffered a miscarriage and was depressed over his infidelities. She later became pregnant again, and after her son was born, she took him and left her husband.

Meyer has described that period as a living hell. She moved back home with her parents where her mother started having violent fits—one culminated in Meyer being beaten with a broom. One day, Meyer was outside her parents' home washing a car when she was approached by a young engineer named Dave Meyer. After five dates, they married on January 7, 1967, and he adopted her firstborn.

Although her new husband was attentive and warm, Meyer was still not happy. She became saved around the age of 13, but she had drifted in and out of church over the years. One day in 1976, after crying out to God for help that same morning, Meyer was leaving a beauty shop when she felt the presence of God come over her. A few weeks later, she began a Thursday morning 6:00 A.M. Bible study at Miss Hulling's Cafeteria at the corner of 8th and Olive Streets. Word soon spread about the bare-bones but dynamic teaching Meyer was doing, and she eventually had 500 women meeting in the pre-dawn hours to discuss the Bible. The class continued for five years until Meyer left the Lutheran church she had been attending and joined a small, storefront church called Life Christian Church as an assistant minister in 1982.

Meyer's Biblical insight was so sharp that her pastor, Rick Shelton, asked her to appear with him on his radio program, which gave her the idea to start her own radio show. Eventually, she bought her own 15-minute slot on WCEW in St. Louis, then bought radio time in six other cities, including Chicago. Meyer's bold speaking manner opened up opportunities to take on a deliverance ministry. "I had every person, I think, anywhere within 10 miles who had a demon come knocking at my door wanting deliverance," she told the *St. Louis Post-Dispatch*. "And I was staying up half the night, almost every night, Dave and I were casting out demons… our kids are back there sleeping and we're in the living room screaming at demons half the night."

In August 1985, Dave and Meyer founded Life in the Word ministry. In those days, they'd go speak for whatever small change churches threw at them. It often wasn't enough to even rent a hotel room, so the couple would sleep in their car in a McDonald's parking lot overnight. "We would believe in God literally for our socks and underwear," she's said. In 1993, Dave had a vision from God to take Meyer's ministry to television. He compiled a program based on her speaking appearances and bought time on WGN in Chicago and BET. Soon, speaking engagements poured in, and the TV and radio programs were heard on over 600 stations collectively.

Meyer finished the 1990s having triumphed over several obstacles. She recovered from breast cancer, and she healed strained relationships with her children. She also went to her father and forgave him for molesting her. On two occasions, he refused to acknowledge that he had done anything wrong. Still, Meyer bought her parents a home and showered them with the care she felt she lacked as a child. Finally, in November 2000, Meyer went to their home for Thanksgiving. Her father stood at the front door crying. "'I just need to tell you how sorry I am for what I did to you,'" she recalled him saying. She forgave him and ten days later, she baptized her father. In a 1998 *Charisma* magazine cover story, Meyer was cited as the most popular female minister in America.

Now that she's written more than 50 books (she currently has a lucrative contract with Warner Books) and fills basketball arenas for speaking engagements, Meyer's success has come under scrutiny. According to the *Post-Dispatch*, the ministry collects $95 million a year in revenue and employs 500 staff members. In late 2003, a Christian watchdog group, Wall Watchers, asked the Internal Revenue Service to investigate the legitimacy of Meyer's tax-exempt status. Wall Watchers' founder Rust Leonard questioned why the ministry bought Meyer a $2 million home, homes totaling $2 million for her four children, the luxury cars the family drives, and a $10 million corporate jet. "You can be a businessman here in St. Louis and people think the more you have, the more wonderful it is," Meyer told the *Post-Dispatch*. "But if you're a preacher, then all of a sudden it becomes a problem." She further commented to *Christianity Today* that "We do not spend irresponsibly and are prudent in the way we manage our ministry, returning 85 percent of all unrestricted donations back to help hurting people around the world."

Jun Mhoon

A MUSIC PRODUCER who tried to resurrect the Chicago gospel scene in the late 1980s, Jun Mhoon was born June 10, 1954, on Chicago's West Side. During elementary school, he joined the drum and bugle corps.

When he was 12 years old, he began to tour as the Staple Singers' drummer. He played behind other artists such as Jessy Dixon before he took an entry level position at the Warner Bros. Records warehouse in the Windy City. He soon rose to director of Midwest local marketing. He later joined RCA Records and participated in AEMMP (Arts, Entertainment, and Media Management Program) Records, Columbia College's student-run recording label. From there, Mhoon became a vice president at A&M Records. In 1987, Mhoon set up his own I AM Records where he churned out mostly gospel LPs on artists such as Dorothy Norwood, Pop Staples, and others. None of the albums sold very well and Mhoon closed the label. In recent years, Mhoon has reignited the label and begun to reissue his back catalog on CD for the first time.

Mighty Clouds of Joy

PROBABLY THE FIRST gospel quartet group to marry R&B instrumentation (electric guitars, congas, and so on) to traditional Southern gospel harmonies, the Mighty Clouds of Joy are arguably the most successful gospel quartet group in history.

From the beginning, the group's lead singer has been Willie Joe Ligon (born September 11, 1942, in Troy, Alabama). Ligon knew early on that he could sing, but was too shy to perform in public, preferring to sing at home. His mother suggested that he sing with his cousins to build his self-esteem. After going to Los Angeles at the age of 14 to spend some time with his uncle, Ligon ended up living there. While attending Jefferson High School in 1955, his singing in school functions attracted the attention of classmates Johnny Martin and Richard Wallace. Initially, the group also included the siblings Ermant and Elmer Franklin, but Ermant eventually left.

A neighbor took an interest in the group and tutored them on four-part harmonizing. They began to sing around the Los Angeles area where they were discovered by a local gospel disc jockey who offered to produce a demo tape on the group. At the time, Peacock Records was the label that made music that ap-

pealed to young gospel fans. The group sent a tape of the spiritual "Steal Away" to the label. Owner Don Robey signed them right away. "The president of Peacock liked 'Steal Away,'" Ligon said on the group's Web site. "But he wanted me to add something to make it longer. I'd been listening to Rev. C.L. Franklin on the radio for years, so I did this preaching kind of thing in his style to go along with our singing. That was different from what anybody else was doing, and it became our trademark." The record was issued in 1960 and their first LP *Family Circle* surfaced the following year.

By the close of the 1960s, the Clouds hit their stride and were selling consistently. R&B groups such as the Temptations, the Coasters, and the Contours were renowned for their slick choreography as much for their soulful singing. While some gospel groups of the 1950s had become known for their vocal dynamics and histrionics such as aisle-running during the climax of a song, it was unusual to have choreography implemented into what was considered at the time to be a worship service. Dancing was still considered satanic in many church circles, so the Clouds took a

Joe Ligon / photo by Aaron Rapoport, courtesy of Myrrh Records

chance when they developed choreography to accompany their youthful approach to traditional gospel music and started sporting flashy costumes like secular singers. However, there was little fallout as their mostly youthful audience loved the look and the dance steps. In addition, the group one-upped the standard quartet group sound (usually just guitar accompaniment) by adding bass, drums, and keyboards to develop their own distinct sound—to the horror of traditionalists and delight of the youth. They were soon labeled the Temptations of gospel.

In the 1970s, the group signed with ABC Records where they recorded music designed to cross over to the R&B charts. "They're taking gospel off the radio in most places," Johnny Martin told New York DJ Al Gee in 1975. "…to stay out here on the road [gospel groups need] a hit record like the rest of them, and if they don't have gospel on the radio anywhere, you have to cut something that they'll play on the radio."

The Mighty Clouds did give R&B radio something to play. From 1974 to 1984, they had a string of R&B hits with "Time," "Mighty Cloud of Joy," "There's a Love in the World," "Glow Love," "Midnight Hour Part 1," and their biggest hit, "Mighty High," which peaked at No. 2 on the *Billboard* disco chart in 1975. The record's success led to a group appearance on the *Soul Train* television show, the leading promotional outlet for black soul stars in the 1970s. Contrary to what the Clouds have said over the years, they were not the first gospel group to appear on the syndicated program. (The Staple Singers had done the show previously.) "We were very nervous that the public wouldn't understand our *Soul Train* performance," Ligon has said. "When our disco hit 'Mighty High' was played, we were shocked at the reaction of the kids dancing. We were ahead of our time. Now it's one of our most requested songs. The die-hard gospel fans gave us flak like you wouldn't believe. It wasn't churchy enough for them. They said we'd sold out and gone funky."

By the 1980s, the group returned to more traditional musical fare and re-established a relationship with gospel audiences with radio hits such as "I've Been in the Storm Too Long," "He's My Rooftop," and "Everybody Ought to Praise His Name." In 1993, they did a series of concerts with Paul Simon. Songs like "Loves Me Like a Rock" and other tracks with Simon reminded pop critics and baby boomers that the Clouds were still on the scene. The publicity led to college gigs before a new audience of young white students. "Before there was an Andrae Crouch, the Hawkins singers, or the Clark Sisters, there was the Mighty Clouds of Joy doing contemporary gospel. We were the forerunners of that, and when we were doing it we got a lot of complaints because at that time there wasn't much contemporary gospel…. We were the first to do contemporary gospel, then came groups like the Winans," Ligon told *Totally Gospel* in 1986. Today, the Mighty Clouds remain a hot commodity on the blues and gospel concert circuits.

RECOMMENDED RECORDING: The compilation *20th Century Masters—Millennium Collection: The Best of the Mighty Clouds of Joy* (Universal Music, 2002) features the Clouds' best early 1960s work for Peacock Records such as the sermonette "A Bright Side" and "Family Circle." Unfortunately, the group's stellar 1970s crossover recordings have yet to receive a decent CD reissue.

Mike-E

AN EARLY '90s Christian rapper, Mike-E was born Michael Ellis Wright circa 1959 in Detroit, where his father was a COGIC pastor. Influenced by the guitar skills of Carlos Santana and Prince, Mike-E released Christian rap CDs such as *Good News for the Bad Timez*, which reached No. 28 on the CCM chart in 1992, and *Pass It On* on former football star Reggie White's Big Doggie Records label. Mike-E's sister, Marvie, was once a member of Winans Part II and the female gospel group Witness. Along with playing guitar on a number of albums, Mike-E co-wrote songs with a number of artists, including Angie & Debbie Winans, with whom he wrote the CCM hit "Never Gonna." He's currently on the music staff at a Nashville church.

Douglas Miller

FOR SOME ODD REASON, gospel music has not produced many baritone singing stars. However, in the mid-'80s

Douglas Miller / photo courtesy of Joe Williams of Matador Management

Douglas Miller came as close as anyone to becoming a gospel megastar with his bottom-heavy baritone that shined brilliantly on tracks such as "Unspeakable Joy" and his signature tune "My Soul Has Been Anchored in the Lord." Born December 31, 1949, in Johnstown, Pennsylvania, he grew up singing in church. When he was a University of Akron student he was discovered by Mattie Moss Clark, who took him under her wing and guided his musical training. She introduced him at the COGIC's popular Midnight Musicals and generated a buzz about Miller's talent. Clark produced Miller's first two LPs for Gospearl Records. However, it was the title cut of 1984's *I Still Love the Name of Jesus* that established Miller nationally. The following year, the smoldering ballad "My Soul Has Been Anchored in the Lord" (which Miller wrote) pushed the LP *Unspeakable Joy* up to No. 6 on the gospel chart.

There is quite a story behind "My Soul Has Been Anchored in the Lord." It goes back to the days when Douglas's mentor, Mattie Moss Clark, negotiated a terrible recording contract for him with Gospearl Records. "My song 'When I See Jesus' was so hot that it had only been out three months and they wanted me to do another album," he recalls. "So I did 'Joy of the

Lord Is My Strength' and they released it the week of the COGIC convocation in Memphis. The owners sold so many records there that they went back to Baltimore and bought themselves a Mercedes-Benz. I got nothing." That wasn't the breaking point, though. The last straw was when the owners threw a party celebrating Miller's LP hitting No. 1 on the *Billboard* gospel chart. "They had a party celebrating the album going No. 1 and didn't invite me," he exclaims.

At that point, Miller started legal proceedings against Gospearl Records. "I was in Baltimore not knowing if I was going to have to go to court or not," he continues. "But when I came to Baltimore the owners sent me messages that if I didn't sing for them, I wasn't singing for anybody and they'd have me killed. That's how serious this got. One of them threatened my life. I was sitting up there in the hotel scared to come out of my room…. Sitting up in the hotel room, God gave me 'My Soul Is Anchored in the Lord' because I was going through a storm, brother."

Subsequent LPs failed to ignite audiences until Miller's 1990 LP *Live at the Top* on Word/Rejoice Records reached No. 15 on the gospel chart. It featured a Shirley Caesar duet and a live version of "My Soul Has Been Anchored in the Lord." In recent years, Miller has starred in touring gospel musical stage plays such as *God's Trying to Tell You Something*, *Secret Lover*, and *Lord, Save My Children from Destruction*.

Lucille Banks Robinson Miller

WASHINGTON, DC'S colorful first female gospel DJ was from another time and place. The eldest of Deacon Edward and Mary Lewis's six daughters, she was raised in the city's Metropolitan Baptist Church where the bourgeois blacks worshipped in the early half of the 20th century.

After a failed early marriage, she moved back in with her parents and they helped put her through Howard University where she majored in psychiatry and minored in music—she had taken piano lessons as a teenager. In 1937, Miller formed the Banks Seminary Choir, a youth ensemble. She then formed the Paramount School of Music and began to give private music lessons. Her entrance into radio was accidental. She was listening to Frances White's show on WOOK and thought the announcer used bad English. White's sister was Miller's beautician, so she volunteered to come in and correct the radio copy. White told Miller the station was looking for a daytime gospel host and that she should apply. Though Miller said she wasn't interested, White submitted Miller's name to WOOK President Richard Eaton anyway and he asked her to audition.

Miller arrived for her audition and nine white women were there. "If I was going to audition I wouldn't have a chance now. All those white people against me," she said in a 1992 interview with the *Washington New Observer*. In the end, she got the job because she was the only one with a general knowledge of music and because Eaton thought she was articulate. In 1953, she began a decade run at WUST, then two years at WOL, then back to WUST until she joined WYCB in 1979. At WYCB, Miller created the Love Club where she collected money over the air to send kids to college or to just buy them school clothes. "We have a lot of hate in this world, not enough love," she said. "If we did, we wouldn't have all the killings… parents killing children, children killing parents, children killing teachers, mothers throwing babies out of windows and putting them in trash cans. That's the result of no love. God is love and in order for the Lord to love us we have to love one another."

With her precise diction and raspy delivery, Miller became a leading emcee at gospel concerts over the years. Among the artists she befriended were Mahalia Jackson, Roberta Martin, and Rev. James Cleveland. Miller worked right into her eighties. "I tell them I don't have anything to retire," she said of the prospect of retirement. "Had I stayed in the school system I would've had a retirement, but I chose to teach in my home. I think I made the best choice because so far none of my boys have been in jail and they're doing pretty good." She died of leukemia in July 1998. Miller, who married four times and had three sons, was believed to be 87 years old.

Shirley Miller

SHIRLEY MILLER'S first time singing in front of a crowd was at a friend's funeral when she was five years old. She

enjoyed happier singing opportunities when she joined her cousin Edwin Hawkins's group in 1970. "Everyone associates me as being the lead singer of 'Oh Happy Day' on the original recording," the contralto told *Totally Gospel* in 1987. "Dorothy Morrison is the one who originally sang the song on the album. I didn't join the Singers until after the album was recorded. People tend to associate me with the song because I sing it in all of our personal appearances." In 1987, Miller released her debut LP *I Must Go On* on Light Records. On the strength of the title song, the album reached No. 9 on the gospel chart in 1987. "I was shy about stepping out on my own," she told *Totally Gospel* then. "It was about a year ago that I heard the voice of the Lord tell me to go out on my own. The doors were opening for me to do solo work. I became more secure each time I went out. I decided about a year and a half ago, with some finances the Lord blessed me with, to do a solo project. Walter [Hawkins] took the portion of the project that we had completed to Ralph Carmichael of Light Records. He liked it to the point that Light took the project and finished the remainder of the album."

Miller never followed up with another solo album. Aside from an occasional Hawkins family reunion and background session work with Donald Vails and Yvette Flunder in the 1990s, Miller has retired from the national stage.

Stephanie Mills

THE 4'9" VOCAL DYNAMO made her name as the star of the 1970s Broadway smash *The Wiz* and continued to expand her fame with a string of sophisticated, romantic love songs in the 1980s and 1990s. Born March 22, 1959, in Queens, New York, Mills first sang in the church choir. At the age of nine, she made her Broadway debut in *Maggie Flynn*. In 1974, she recorded her first LP, *Movin' in the Right Direction*, for Paramount Records. It was a flop, but a song from the album convinced producer Ken Harper that Mills might be perfect to play Dorothy in his black adaptation of *The Wizard of Oz. The Wiz* ran for four years and won seven Tony awards.

Mills recorded a slow-selling LP for Motown before signing to 20th Century Records in 1979 where she hit gold with the album *What Cha Gonna Do with My Lovin'*. She had a hit streak going with R&B smashes such as "Sweet Sensation," "I Never Knew Love Like This Before," and "I Feel Good All Over." By 1982, Mills had revealed to *Jet* magazine that she had become a born-again Christian, although she continued to record secular music. In 1994, Mills recorded her first gospel CD, *Personal Inspirations*, for Gospo Centric Records. Coming off of a string of gold records, Mills was unhappy with the label's promotional efforts on the album and the initial sales of 120,000 units. She opted not to record a second gospel album with them. However, her one set was a mix of contemporary and traditional styles. It was propelled to No. 8 on the gospel album chart by Mills's secular audience and moderate gospel radio airplay for "The Power of God," a gospel rendition of her R&B hit "I Have Learned to Respect the Power of Love." Mills's shimmering vibrato soared on John P. Kee's "He Cares," Mitty Collier's "I Had a Talk with God Last Night," and an electrifying version of the Caravans' "Sweeping Through the City." Her mechanical, computerized covers of Curtis Mayfield's "People Get Ready" and Tramaine Hawkins's "In the Morning Time" and "Everybody Ought to Know" were not as successful. At the time, Mills stopped performing secular music altogether and did some promotional dates with Donald Lawrence & the Tri-City Singers. Many promoters booked her for concerts without stipulating that she'd only be singing gospel. During that period, she was often booed when she left the stage without singing her R&B hits. Conversely, she was often shunned by the gospel world because of its long-standing distrust of secular singers who sing gospel after a born-again experience. Aside from some recordings with her pal, BeBe Winans, Mills has not recorded any further gospel projects.

Mississippi Mass Choir

PERHAPS THE MOST popular black gospel choir of the last dozen years, the Mississippi Mass Choir was formed in 1988 by the late Frank Williams (June 25, 1947–March 22, 1993), a member of the Jackson Southernaires and an executive with Malaco Records. He had long desired to start a mass choir, so when he convinced Jerry Mannery at Malaco of the idea, he began recruiting members. He recruited David R. Curry as the choir's first director. After open auditions and months of rehearsals, the choir recorded their first CD, *The Mississippi Mass Choir*, on October 29, 1988, at the Jackson Municipal Auditorium. That project reached all the way to No. 1 on the black gospel chart. Over the next few years, they enjoyed further hits like "God Don't Need No Matches," "It Wasn't the Nails," and "He Can Fix What Is Broke." However, no recording packed the wallop that the choir's 1999 CD *Emmanuel: God with Us* did when radio picked up on the rousing Dorothy Love Coates remake "They Got the Word." The song was led by Mosie Burks, a former telephone operator, who was prodded to join the choir by a friend. With her beautiful silver hair flowing and her trim, athletic figure swaying to the rhythm, the 70-plus singer's gritty alto shined on the rocking re-recording in 1999. The fame of that song and others that Burks has sung have led to a forthcoming solo project on Malaco Records and a role in the 2004 Disney film *America's Heart and Soul*.

Alda Denise Mitchell

BORN 1943, ALTO SINGER Alda Denise Mitchell co-produced her 1988 gospel LP *Oh Taste and See* with veteran R&B composer Skip Scarborough. It appeared on Chicago's I AM Records label, which was distributed by Word Records in the gospel market and by A&M Records in the mainstream market. In spite of the smooth production and heartfelt vocals, it failed to establish Mitchell nationally and she quickly disappeared from the national landscape.

Vernessa Mitchell

FOR A BRIEF MOMENT in 1978, Vernessa Mitchell's R&B quartet High Inergy was the hottest female group in R&B music when they saw their sensual soul ballad "You Can't Turn Me Off (In the Middle of Turning Me On)" bolt to No. 2 on the R&B charts and No. 12 on the pop charts. They followed up with the infectious Top 20 smash "Love Is All You Need." However, their appearances on *American Bandstand* and other major shows of the period were short-lived. After the group's fame faded, Mitchell initially found her way into the traditional gospel world, but eventually evolved into the biggest gospel diva in the dance/club world.

Born January 1, 1959, in Columbus, Georgia, Mitchell came from a family of eight kids and a minister father. She sang in the church choir, taught herself to play the piano, swooned to Sarah Vaughn records, and composed her first song in the sixth grade. After Mitchell and her sister, Barbara, were accepted into California's Bicentennial Arts Program in Pasadena, California, they met fellow singers Linda Howard and Michelle Martin there. The four formed a group and developed a one-hour show that they performed over the next eight months. Motown Records founder Berry Gordy's sister, Gwen, spotted them singing and brought them to the attention of Motown executives who signed them in 1977. They named themselves High Inergy because a lot of people said they had a lot of energy when they sang. They spelled Inergy with an "I" because Motown had an album out with the Supremes called *High Energy* and didn't want the two products confused.

Their debut LP *Turnin' On* featured the smash hits "You Can't Turn Me Off" and "Love Is All You Need," but their sophomore LP *Steppin' Out* floundered. "The Lord spoke to me and said, 'It's time to leave all this. I've given you your talent and I want you to use it for me,'" Mitchell once said. "With me being the daughter of a minister, I knew the voice of the Lord. When he called, I obeyed. I felt the message I was singing at Motown wasn't encouraging. That bothered me because I didn't want to be looked at as an artist who wasn't giving quality messages."

Mitchell then went to work for Dr. Wayne S. Davis at World Won for Christ Ministries in Inglewood, California. She was an administrative assistant there during the week and a minister of music on the weekends. "[My friends] would ask me how could I leave big money to work as a secretary," she recalled. "Some would even joke about my never recording again." Then her former Motown producer, Kent Washburn, contacted her. He had been born again and wanted to produce a gospel album on her at Command Records. "He sent me the same expertise, the same professional people I had at Motown," she recalled at the time, "only now we are all serving the Lord." Her debut album, *This Is My Story*, a mix of contemporary and traditional gospel, reached No. 19 on the gospel chart in 1985 and earned a Grammy nomination. Mitchell later switched to Word Records and Benson Records where she recorded LPs such as *Higher Ground, On a Mission*, and *Destiny*. A surprise hit with a dance remix on "Reap (What You Sow)," originally a track from the *Destiny* album, in 1996 led Mitchell to a new career as a gospel dance star. A David Morales mix on "This Joy" shot up to No. 5 on the club charts in 1998 with various 12-inch mixes being issued on the Groovilicious, Welcome Wax, and Strictly Rhythm labels. A Friburn & Urik mix on Mitchell's track "Issues" climbed to No. 12 on the club charts and was issued on the G2 label, while the British Expansion label issued "Be for Real." Mitchell has also worked with the remix master Junior Vasquez who mixed the vinyl of her "Trouble Don't Last Always." 2004's "Took My Life" was her best showing yet, reaching No. 2 on the Hot Dance Club play chart.

Ed Montgomery

THE FOUNDING PASTOR of Houston's 7,000-strong Abundant Life Cathedral Church has joined the ranks of fellow pastors T.D. Jakes and Carlton Pearson in launching a music career. His Ablife Records label has issued albums such as *I Still Believe*, which feature himself and others in leading urban, contemporary-styled gospel songs. Born circa 1952 in Cleveland, Ohio, Montgomery was raised by his grandmother, Iola Freeman. When he was 14, Montgomery began to play piano at Temple Baptist Church. "I was an organist who played with James Cleveland, Shirley Caesar, and the Caravans when they all came through Cleveland," he says. "I knew that I wanted to write and it first began with music, but the songs I wrote were so long that I realized that I must be wanting to do more. So from that point on I went into ministry and writing messages, and from messages into writing books."

Montgomery, who was influenced by esteemed preachers such as Dr. A.E. Campbell, Jr., and Caesar

Clark, attended Dallas's Bishop College (Paul Quinn College), the premier training ground for Baptist preachers of the time, in 1973. During that period, he formed a gospel group that included the daughter of one of the Barrett sisters. Through Montgomery's persistence, the group earned a summer job at the Six Flags Over Georgia amusement park. "We did an audition and we won out over 400 contestants," says Montgomery.

The sextet lasted for two and a half months. Montgomery then went into full-time ministry. He took a church in Bonham, Texas, 70 miles from Dallas and spent three and a half years there as its pastor. He then felt the Lord called him to start a church in Houston. "I took my wife, two children, and $500 in my pocket and got to the outskirts of Houston and asked the Lord which way to go," he says. "I remember driving west, found an apartment, and took a job selling pencils and paper clips. Six months later we started Abundant Life Cathedral Church [in 1981 with 31 members, including his family] and now we have 7,000 members."

In 1999, Montgomery formed Ablife Records to release music by his urban contemporary church choir, the Abundant Life Cathedral Choir. It was the fulfillment of a teenage dream. "When I was 17 years old I remember walking into a lawyer's office and asking him to set up a record label," he recalls. "Of course, he told me it would be $500 to incorporate and I had to walk out of the door because I didn't have $500. I just decided at this particular time to open up our own label in 1999 because we had a boatload of talent here at the church."

Montgomery showcased the choir at a time when preachers were developing an even greater profile as singers. Leading evangelists such as T.D. Jakes, Bishop Clarence McClendon, and Bishop Carlton Pearson were just a few of the hit-making recording artists who were also pastors. Montgomery's first national success was *I Still Believe*, which reached No. 11 on the gospel album chart in 2001. Their next CD, *The Live Experience*, was an even bigger hit, climbing all the way to No. 7 on the same chart in 2003. "I believe it is important within gospel music to keep a solid word base—in other words, not just a beat but substance," he says of the trend of singing preachers. "It is important for writers to have

that kind of substance in order to keep the message of the gospel pure in our generation, because most of the preaching of our generation is being preached over music. I believe your ministers are coming in because they are like Davids [the Biblical David, a musician]. Before they take positions as pastors, many of them were writers, many of them were musicians. I believe they are coming in right now to put the doctrine back in our message—the message of gospel music."

Dorothy Moore

BEST KNOWN FOR her 1975 quadruple million-seller "Misty Blue," Dorothy Moore cut some of the smoothest, yet down-home soul songs of the 1970s, such as "With Pen in Hand," "I Believe in You," and "Funny How Time Slips Away," all major R&B hits. Born October 13, 1946, in Jackson, Mississippi, Moore was raised on Monument Street by her great-grandmother. She sang in church and never dreamed of becoming anything but a singer. After graduating from Lanier High School, Moore attended Jackson State University where she formed a pop group called the Poppies. Their single, "Lullaby of Love," was released on Epic Records in 1966 and made the Billboard Hot 100, but the group fell apart over the other girls' lack of enthusiasm for traveling. Moore recorded for a number of small labels such as Avco, GSF, and Chimneyville as a soloist without producing any great hits. She also cut a few records for Malaco Records, including a ballad she didn't particularly like called "Misty Blue" circa late 1973. It was shelved. When Malaco was on the verge of going bankrupt, they started releasing anything good they could find in their vaults in hopes of getting a hit. They released "Misty Blue" around Thanksgiving 1975 and by the spring of 1976 it was the biggest hit in Malaco's history. The song eventually sold over four million copies and gave Moore at least two years of being a very hot commodity in the music business. Toward the end of the decade when disco was in full swing, Moore's ballads stopped attracting the attention of radio jocks. She recorded for a couple of labels in the early 1980s, but the results were not successful. In 1986, she fulfilled a lifelong dream to record a gospel album when she released *Giving It Straight to You* on Word Records' Rejoice subsidiary (the black division). It reached No. 23 on the gospel charts and featured Moore's earthy renditions of Lionel Richie's "Jesus Is Love" and Brother Joe May's "What Is This?" Another nice traditional that showed off Moore's approach to gospel was the moving "Captain of My Ship." In spite of the album's success, Rejoice didn't renew their option for Moore to do a second album. "I had went through so many things and I had to do that album," Moore told *Living Blues* in 1995. "It was time to get my feet back on the ground and go back home where it all started. I grew a lot, got closer to God, regrouped and just got stronger in that way. I've learned a whole lot of things. I learned that [gospel] wasn't something that you should look away from just because you're doing R&B. You don't get to go to church because you're singing on the weekends and what have you, but you don't give up on God just because you're not in church. I just gave everything to God and he leads me now in everything I do." Before the album was released, Moore had survived an emotionally draining divorce and gotten her life back in a happy state. In 1989, she did a new inspirational R&B CD entitled *Winner*, which featured a fine gospel song called "I Thank You." Later, she re-signed with Malaco Records where she did the fine soul albums *Feel the Love* and *Stay Close to Home* in the early 1990s. The latter's title song is a secularized gospel song. "Just a couple of lyric changes and that would be straight-up church," Moore says. Moore remains firm in her faith and has put both of her children through college. She never felt she needed to leave secular music and exclusively sing gospel like many former R&B singers. "I was never into drugs or anything," she says. "I don't have any horror stories like that." She hopes to record a gospel album again in the future, having released her first CD, *Please Come Home for Christmas*, on her own record label, Farish Street Records, in 2002.

Gatemouth Moore

ONE OF THE HALLOWED names in the blues music canon, Gatemouth Moore was born Arnold Dwight Moore on November 8, 1913, in Topeka, Kansas. He always sang as a youth and gained the nickname "Gatemouth" because of his loud singing voice. At the age of 16, he moved to Kansas City where he fronted a trio of jazz big bands led by Tommy Douglas, Walter Barnes, and most notably, Bennie Moten. Moore's life was spared in April 1940 when a fire broke out at the Rhythm Night Club in Natchez, Mississippi. The club, with one exit, was packed with fans to see Walter Barnes and his Royal Creolians. The windows were boarded up to prevent unpaid entry, and the walls were decorated with moss. The fire started near the door and ignited the moss. More than 200 patrons were trampled or trapped in the fire and perished—including the orchestra. Moore was outside on the tour bus when the fire started and was one of the few survivors who lived to tell the story.

After this tragedy, Moore went solo and began recording for the Chez Paree and Damon labels. In spite of his tag as a blues singer, his vocal style was more akin to 1940s crooners such as Billy Eckstein or Bing Crosby. Unlike most blues singers, Moore enunciated every syllable and sang his blues with a tongue-in-cheek sophistication. In 1945, he moved on to National Records where he wrote and recorded the blues classics "Did You Ever Love a Woman?" (covered by Louis Jordan and B.B. King), "Somebody's Got to Go" (covered by Rufus Thomas, Lonnie Johnson, and Victoria Spivey), "I Ain't Mad at You, Pretty Baby" (covered by Johnny Otis), and "Christmas Blues" (covered by Jimmy Witherspoon). In 1947, he re-recorded those tunes for King Records and brought pinup boy bluesman Wynonie Harris to the label as an artist.

In 1949, Moore was performing onstage when he had a vision of himself becoming a Christian. Instead of singing his scheduled blues number, he sang "Shine on Me," and when he left the stage, he left secular music to study theology. He was ordained at the First Church of Deliverance in Chicago by Rev. Clarence Cobb later that year. Moore then became the first gospel announcer at WDIA in Memphis while recording gospel music sides for Chess Records and later Coral Records.

Moore continued to record gospel and preach from then on. Johnny Otis was able to persuade him to re-record some of his great blues sides on his last LP

Great R&B Oldies on Otis's Blues Spectrum recording label in 1977. That set included the Moore composition "Beale Street Ain't Beale Street No More." In 2003, Moore reprised the tune in Richard Pearce's film *The Road to Memphis*, part of Martin Scorsese's acclaimed PBS film series *The Blues*. In recent years, Moore occasionally revamped his secular blues along with his gospel tunes at blues festivals. He died May 19, 2004, in Yazoo City, Mississippi, where he was the pastor of the Lithonia AME Church at the time of his death.

RECOMMENDED RECORDINGS: *Rev. Gatemouth Moore and His Gospel Singers* (Audio Fidelity, 1960)

Rev. James Moore

BORN EBRUARY 1, 1956, in Detroit, Moore was a student of the great choir conductor Mattie Moss Clark. His professional break came in 1974 when he was discovered at James Cleveland's Gospel Music Workshop of America (GMWA) convention in Chicago. Moore had a crusty voice and he loved to sing traditional-styled church songs. His debut album, *I Thank You Master*, appeared on Savoy Records a few months later. He recorded several more albums for a variety of labels such as Secret, Sound of Gospel, and Luminar, but it wasn't until his Malaco debut, *James Moore Live*, in 1988 that he made the *Billboard* gospel Top Ten and hit his stride. His guest vocals on the Mississippi Mass Choir's *Live at Jackson State University* propelled it to No. 1 on the gospel chart, and it won a gaggle of gospel awards. His star continued to shine on albums such as *Live in Detroit* and *I Will Trust in the Lord*. An ebullient, gregarious character, Moore loved to eat a lot and play a lot. Unfortunately, his somewhat reckless lifestyle led to a stroke and renal failure before the age of forty. He fought his way back to the stage, amid sudden blindness and regular dialysis. He continued to perform in gospel plays such as *Why Do Good Girls Like Bad Boys?* and concerts right up until his sudden death on June 7, 2000, at Methodist Central Hospital in Memphis, Tennessee.

RECOMMENDED RECORDING: The 1991 *Live in Detroit* CD is trademark James Moore. It features stand-

out performances such as his revival of Rev. James Cleveland's "I Stood on the Banks" and the 13-minute "He's All I Need."

Melba Moore

ONE OF BROADWAY's greatest stars of the 1970s, Melba Moore thrilled audiences in the hit musicals *Hair*, *Purlie*, and *Timbuktu*, among others. Born Beatrice Hill on October 29, 1945, in New York, Moore's early life was a bit bumpy. Born out of wedlock to a bandleader and a professional singer named Bonnie Smith, she was raised by her illiterate grandmother, a fierce Christian who beat Moore daily to get "Satan" out of her. Although her mother sent her gifts from the road, Moore felt trapped with relatives who did not demonstrate love, and her self-esteem suffered.

In the 1950s, Bonnie Smith married Clem Moorman and they took Moore to live with them in an integrated, middle-class neighborhood in Newark. Moore says that her stepfather made her feel loved so she changed her name to reflect his. Parental pressure forced her to attend Montclair College, and after graduating, she taught elementary school but hated it so much that she contemplated suicide. Hoping to break out of the rut she felt she was engulfed in, she married a man she didn't love. What really made her happy was performing. She beat out Donna Summer and others to replace Diane Keaton as Sheila in the Broadway production of *Hair*. After two years of fame in that role, Moore took the starring role of Luttibelle in Ossie Davis's musical *Purlie*. She won a Tony award for her performance.

The press from the musicals led to a recording contract with Mercury Records. None of those recordings were particularly successful, so she and boyfriend Clifton Davis starred in the CBS variety TV series *The Melba Moore-Clifton Davis Show* in 1972. At the time, Davis was physically abusive to Moore, and they ended their relationship as well as the program. After switching to Buddah Records and Epic Records, Moore began to experience big R&B hits with a soft disco groove in the late 1970s. Songs such as "This Is It," "Pick Me Up, I'll Dance," and "You Stepped into My Life" kept her on the charts. Many of her album tracks featured outright gospel songs such as the beautiful tune "Mighty Clouds of Joy" and the inspirational anthem "Lean on Me," which she currently sings with a more gospel flavoring.

Throughout the 1980s, Moore continued to churn out R&B hits such as "A Little Bit More," "Love's Comin' at Ya," and "Fallin.'" She starred in television films, another CBS TV series called *Melba*, and had a recurring role on the Falcon Crest primetime soap opera. In 1990, she enjoyed her last Top Ten R&B smash with the all-star recording of the Negro National Anthem, "Lift Every Voice and Sing." She and her second husband, Charles Huggins, formed Hush Productions, which managed stars such as Freddie Jackson. However, Huggins and Moore had a bitter divorce, Huggins took most of the marital property, and for a time, Moore was penniless. Since then, Moore has proved herself a survivor. She resurrected her career several times over and became closer to God. She's recorded a couple of fairly good but poorly distributed gospel CDs, *Solitary Journey* (Encore Music Group, 1999) and *I'm Still Here* (Shout! Glory Music, 2003), which she produced with Shirley Murdock. The live CD *A Night in St. Lucia* (Image Entertainment, 2002) closes with a rousing ten-minute version of "Lean on Me" reprised as "Lean on Jesus."

RECOMMENDED RECORDING: *Nobody But Jesus* (Believe Records/Lightyear, 2004) features Moore's urban contemporary takes on traditional fare such as "What a Friend We Have in Jesus" and "Precious Lord."

Frances Moore-Lee & Burning Bush

(see East St. Louis Gospelettes)

Cindy Morgan

CINDY MORGAN BEGAN her career as a Christian dance artist but has evolved into something of a meditative troubadour in the Bob Dylan vein. Born June 4, 1968, in Red Hill, Tennessee, she was one of six children and her father was a mechanic. She loved to play the piano and as a teenager found work playing gospel and country music at Dolly Parton's Dollywood amusement park

in nearby Pigeon Forge. Soon, Morgan migrated to Knoxville where she did session work until a Word Records executive noticed her talent and offered her a recording deal in 1990. "When I came into the industry, dance music was really hot, and I just wanted to sing," Morgan says. "When Word asked me what kind of music I wanted to do, I said I wanted to do something style-wise that was between Whitney Houston and Janet Jackson. I don't think I even had a deep understanding of ministry, or thought that much about it. I was driven. I was compelled to sing, to write. It's like I had this thing in me that said, 'You're never going to be you unless you do this.' I wasn't really thinking it through or planning out my future. I was just acting on an opportunity."

Although she didn't have a plan, her debut CD *Real Life* was a smash hit with a strong urban dance rhythm. The album enjoyed two No. 1 Christian radio singles, "Let It Be Love" and "It's Gonna Be Heaven." The album won six Dove award nominations and she walked away with the Best New Artist of the Year award in 1993. The next couple of CDs followed the same formula. Then Morgan changed producers and took on a more pop direction à la Amy Grant. Moreover, her music became even more lyrically driven by faith with worshipful songs such as "Praise the King." Morgan's latter pop songs such as "The Loving Kind" and her rendition of Todd Rundgren's "Love Is the Answer" maintained an urban edge.

RECOMMENDED RECORDING: The 1999 CD *The Best So Far* is a 14-song collection of Morgan's best hits ranging from the dance material like "Let It Be Love" to the worship song "Praise the King."

Willie Morganfield

HE HASN'T WRITTEN many gospel classics, but Rev. Willie Morganfield's "What Is This?" was enough to earn him a place in gospel history. Born July 11, 1927, in Stovall, Mississippi, Morganfield always sang gospel. He sang with the Old Kings of Harmony, the New Orleans Chosen Five, and he coached the Four Stars in Cleveland. "I didn't get professional until I moved to Memphis in 1959 because I wasn't doing good in Cleveland," he recalls. By that time, his parents lived in Memphis where his father pastored King Solomon's Church. He moved to Memphis to restart his life. "When I got there Joan Golden was at my daddy's church that Sunday morning. Daddy asked me to sing a song and Joan heard it and she asked me if I ever thought about recording and I told her no. She said she knew a guy named Harmon Brown that was looking for somebody to record. He said that I had to write my own songs and come up with the money to record them. I think it was $335 I had to pay and I didn't have that. One of my daddy's members let me have that money. I wrote two songs: 'Can't See Why Everybody Won't Serve the Lord' and 'Only the Lord Can Help Us in Times Like These.' He recorded them but they didn't do good. They just played them locally. And then when I wrote 'What Is This?' that caught on fire."

The song came to Morganfield while listening to the radio one day. "I heard a preacher preaching," he says. "He was on the radio. I had prayed for a song that would help somebody else, not so much helping me. He got to preaching and he said 'Who wouldn't serve a God like this?' and it kind of threw me off because I kind of felt him without seeing him. The Lord just told me to write and I wrote 'What Is This?' He gave me the words." The copyright lists Joan Golden as a co-writer. "Joan Golden didn't help me write that," he explains. "I just gave her credit because she's the one who helped get me on record.…. When she played it on the radio, the man had to come in and take the mike from her because she got happy on the air. So I gave her credit because I didn't have nothing to pay her." He recorded the song in November 1959 and by January 1960 Morganfield says it was No. 1 on gospel stations across the country.

Eventually, Brother Joe May caught wind of the song and made a version that surpassed the original in sales and recognition. Morganfield recalls, "Joe May [was likely to be] in trouble because his company was trying to record it as if he wrote it [because they got half of publishing on whatever he wrote]." The song has such a classic sound that many artists have assumed it was an old hymn and listed the song as public domain in album credits. Because the song was so strongly associated with May, many others continued to list him as the composer. These circumstances have hampered Morganfield from receiving his proper royalties over the years. "BMI sued May's record company and made them put it like it was supposed to be. I don't even worry about that. I know I wrote it, the Lord know I wrote it, and most folks I know, know I wrote it. If I don't get nothing out of it, it don't bother me because that's not my motivation. I'm a pastor and the Lord has blessed me." Among the other artists who have recorded the song are Morgan Babb, Walter Hawkins, Dorothy Moore, the Seven Sons of Soul, Ann McCrary, and Donnie McClurkin. In 1975, Morganfield began to pastor at the Bellgrove Church in Clarksdale, a post he held until his sudden death from cardiac arrest in November 2003.

Bishop Paul Morton

ONE OF THE MOST popular televangelists of recent years, Bishop Paul Morton was born on July 30, 1950, in Windsor, Ontario, Canada. When he was 22 years old, Morton moved to New Orleans. In 1975, he was installed as pastor of the Greater St. Stephen Missionary Baptist Church. At the time, the church had 647 members and over the years, through Morton's proactive missionary work and dynamic preaching, the congregation has grown to 20,000. In 1992, the church changed its name to Greater St. Stephen Full Gospel Baptist Church. The previous year, Morton had released his first LP, *Jesus, When Troubles Burden Me Down*, on Onyx Records. That and a 1995 sermon project "Dealing with Impossibilities" were not big sellers. However, the LP *We Offer Christ* was one of the Top 30 albums of 1994. In 1999, Morton released a solo CD, *Crescent City Fire*, on Gospo Centric Records. It leaned to the hip-hop side, but was a sales disaster. The breakthrough project was 2004's *Let It Rain* CD on Morton's own Tehillah Records. Backed by the FGBCF (Full Gospel Baptist Church Fellowship) Mass Choir, the album included the gospel hit singles of CeCe Winans/Lauryn Hill's "On that Day" and Bishop Morton on the soul-stirring, climactic title song.

Bill and Essie Moss

BORN MAY 1929 in Selma, Alabama, Bill Moss is the younger brother of the late Mattie Moss Clark. A keyboardist, in the 1960s Moss crafted a traditional style of bluesy, Southern gospel with just a touch of contemporary styling to keep it from sounding old-fashioned. He and his wife, Essie (affectionately called the Missionary for her evangelistic performance style), merged their names to create Bilesse Records. Their classic Bill and Essie Moss & the Celestials' 1969 LP *Already Been to the Water* is their masterpiece. Along with the title cut, "Everything Will Be Alright" was also a smash hit. Moss continued to build momentum when he issued the *Solid Rock* LP in 1971. In May of that year, a *Billboard* magazine review said, "Moss writes diversified gospel music with unusually persuasive lyrics, sets them to driving rhythms and soars into some rockin' soul… he shows that with the Celestials and Mt. Carmel Choir he's a strong bidder for stardom." Moss also wrote the black empowerment funk track "Sock It to 'Em Soul Brother" which he recorded for Bell Records. An instrumental version followed from Elijah and the Ebonies on Capsoul Records. He wrote another hit for Teegarden & Van Winkle. He started another label, Bilmo Records, in the early 1970s. In addition to his own records, he produced and released the first two LPs made by his nieces, the Clark Sisters, *Jesus Has a Lot to Give* (1973) and *Mattie Moss Clark Presents the Clark Sisters* (1974). Essie (born July 1933) has recorded the LPs *The Road Is Rough* (Jewel Records, 1982) and *I Am Truly Saved* with the Missionary Baptist Church Choir (AIR Records, 1987).

J Moss

THE SON OF GOSPEL pioneers Bill and "Missionary" Essie Moss and cousin to the Clark Sisters, James Moss was born in September 1971. His childhood was immersed in music. His parents pushed him to study the piano and his father further encouraged him to write songs. He often spent summer vacations from school on the road touring with his father's group, the Celestials. In 1984, Bill Moss paired his sons, James and Bill Jr., as a duo calling itself the Moss Brothers. They re-corded the contemporary gospel/rap LPs *Time to Seek the Lord* (1985) and *Cry It Out* (1988) for Gospearl Records. The duo disbanded when Bill Jr. went off to college. Eventually, James attended Michigan State University for two years, but quit because he was more concerned with music than school books.

Moss formed PAJAM Productions with Paul Allen and Walter Kearney and they produced some local Detroit artists. Money was scarce so Moss juggled several odd jobs to keep his rent paid, taking a computer job until he went on the road as a musician with the Clark Sisters. In 1996, Island Records signed Moss to a recording contract around the same time they signed his cousin, Karen Clark-Sheard. Although Island was part of a large corporate conglomerate, the black music division was relatively short-staffed. The focus centered on Clark-Sheard and Moss was neglected. However, he won attention as the producer of much of Clark-Sheard's debut CD, *Finally, Karen*, in 1997.

While Moss took a backseat as an artist, PAJAM racked up an impressive list of production credits with gospel and secular artists such as Marvin Sapp, Boyz II Men, Dru Hill, Patti LaBelle, Pam & Dodi, Kelly Price, and Hezekiah Walker. "I'm tired of seeing artists who have warning labels on the cover of their albums but then the last song of their project is a gospel song," he once told GospelFlava.com. "How can God mix and mingle in that? Furthermore, why does radio have to then take a top spot from an up-and-coming gospel artist to give that secular artist play on their format? I think everyone needs to just stay in their own game. You don't see gospel artists doing part-time secular gigs. We don't need part-time gospel artists. We have got to be careful." In spite of his bold statement, Moss has played on non-gospel recording sessions for 'N Sync's *Celebrity* CD and Sisqó's CD *Return of Dragon*, which did feature a parental warning sticker label. His major label debut CD, the high-tech-computerized-urban-gospel *The J Moss Project*, was issued on Gospo Centric Records in fall 2004.

Nicole C. Mullen

ONE OF THE FEW black artists to begin and make their career in the white Christian market, Nicole C. Mullen has become a CCM favorite with her pop-styled hits such as "Redeemer," "When I Call on Jesus," and "On My Knees." Her songs draw on issues of self-esteem, racism, and encouragement, as well as faith. "I sing to a hurting audience because I live in a hurting world," she once said. "So I feel like it's part of my job to present hope." She was born January 11, 1967, in Cincinnati, Ohio. Both of her grandfathers were Pentecostal preachers. Mullen accepted Christ at the age of two and has been singing ever since. Mullen's father, Napoleon Coleman, was a songwriter who once considered a music career. "He could have pursued a music career when he was younger, but instead of leaving us hanging as a family, he worked hard for the telephone company for 38 years and encouraged us to follow our dreams," Mullen told CCM's *U* magazine in 2003.

She began writing songs as a 12 year old, writing from her own emotional issues at the time. A high school counselor tried to gear Mullen toward the more stable career of a lawyer instead of a singer, but singing won out. Mullen won a $6-an-hour job doing background vocals at a friend's recording studio. That gig led to a recording deal with Frontline Records where

Nicole C. Mullen / Word Records promotional photo

she recorded some uneven CCM/dance music in the early 1990s under the name of Nicole Coleman, such as the No. 1 CCM single "Show Me" in 1992. During that period, she met her future husband, musician and performer David Mullen, who enjoyed several major CCM hits in 1990–92. In addition to writing songs together, he helped her get a job as a background singer on Amy Grant's "Baby Baby" tour in 1991. With her lean, athletic build, Mullen also did some choreography work for the Newsboys and Grant.

When Jaci Velasquez had a major hit with Mullen's worship ballad "On My Knees" in 1998, the media attention stirred a new interest in Mullen's recording career. Velasquez's label, Myrrh Records, offered a recording contract. Mullen's self-titled CD featured one of the biggest Christian songs of 2000, "Redeemer." The anthem-like Christian pop ballad won Song of the Year, Songwriter of the Year, and Pop Contemporary Recorded Song of the Year at the Dove awards in 2001. The song was such a major hit in the CCM field that it eventually crossed over to black gospel radio stations. Many gospel music fans thought Mullen was white until she made an appearance at the GMWA convention in 2000. With subsequent albums, Myrrh Records has made greater efforts to get Mullen's music played on black gospel radio stations. "I feel like I've been called to be a bridge, and as a bridge you will sometimes have to get stepped on in order for other people to get across," she told *Urban* magazine. "I've seen God get around the system. I don't make any apologies. I am who I am, and I'm proud of that. I don't feel like I need to try to be something else."

Rich Mullins

ONE OF CHRISTIAN music's most beloved praise and worship artists/composers of the last 20 years, Rich Mullins contributed simple yet classic praise hymns such as "Awesome God" and "Sing Your Praise to the Lord" to the gospel music genre. Born October 21, 1955, in Richmond, Indiana, he mastered many instruments early in life, including the guitar. After college at the Cincinnati Bible College, he joined Zion Ministries and performed his songs at church meetings around the US.

After Amy Grant recorded "Sing Your Praise to the Lord" on her monumental *Age to Age* LP in 1982, Reunion Publishing signed Mullins to a deal. He signed with Reunion Records as an artist in 1986 and released critically acclaimed CDs such as *Winds of Heaven, Stuff of Earth*. Among his Top Ten hits as an artist are "While the Nations Rage," "Awesome God," and "My One Thing," which rested at No. 1 on the CCM hit radio chart for six weeks in 1990. Unfortunately, Mullins was killed in a car accident on September 19, 1997, in Illinois. In spite of the years that have passed, his music continues to be played on Christian radio as if it was just recorded. Moreover, because he was so prolific a writer, artists are constantly recording new versions of his songs. The black gospel audience was largely unaware of "Awesome God" until Helen Baylor, Darwin Hobbs, and Kirk Franklin all made versions that black gospel stations played.

Kristle Murden

ONE OF ANDRAE CROUCH'S featured singers in the 1980s, Kristle Murden possesses a sweet soprano in the Deniece Williams mode, but with less vibrato. One of nine children, Murden was born circa 1956 in the Baltimore-Washington, DC, region. She began singing at the age of three and her parents weaned her on a diet of jazz by Nancy Wilson, Barbra Streisand, and Sarah Vaughn. Her parents separated and her mother couldn't raise the children alone, so they were shuttled off to foster homes. "I grew up feeling unloved and uncared for," Murden once said. Still, she cared enough about her destiny to put herself through Howard University where she met Winona and Harvey Lewis. They recruited her for her brief stint with the Star of Bethlehem Choir. She also did ad libs on Myrna Summer's "Father I Stretch My Hands" on her first Savoy Records LP. During that time, Murden sent a demo tape to Light Records via label executive Gentry McCrary in 1978. "Initially, the people at Light said that I couldn't sing and rejected me," she told *Totally Gospel* magazine in April 1988. McCrary then took the tape to Light's biggest star, Andrae Crouch, who was looking for a unique vocalist for a song he had written. Crouch loved the tape and had Murden fly to California to record the track. The beautiful ballad hit the *Billboard* R&B chart and won a Grammy nomination.

"After doing 'I'll Be Thinking of You,' the record company decided that I could sing and signed me immediately," Murden told *Totally Gospel*. Her debut LP *I Can't Let Go* was produced by Bill Maxwell and Andrae Crouch in 1980. Although it did not chart, it is considered a modern gospel classic. It was reissued on CD in Japan on the Cool Sound label in 1999 because of Japanese demand for the project. Her career was almost derailed after her 1981 marriage. "The situation really threw me, it really hurt me badly," she told the magazine. "I've known since I was a child that I was called by God to do something special. I used to dream of performing onstage with people crying and being moved. I've come to know now that Satan was just trying to block and destroy me."

After she rebounded from her divorce, Murden sang "Jesus, Come Lay Your Head on Me" on Crouch's *No Time to Lose* LP, which also won a Grammy nomination. She can also be heard on his *Mercy* and *The Gift of Christmas* albums in the 1990s. Most recently, she was a background vocalist on Barbra Streisand's "On Holy Ground" (from Streisand's album *Higher Ground)* and *The Ladykillers* film soundtrack. In addition, she was featured vocalist on the tune "Yes" by the Abbot Kinney Lighthouse Choir.

Muyiwa

MUYIWA BURST ON the British music scene in 2002 with the warmly embraced CD *Restoration*, which has brought more attention to England's emerging praise and worship community. He was born Muyiwa Olarewaju on November 26, 1970, in Nigeria. His parents sent him and his sisters to England in 1980 when he was nine so that they could get a "good British education." They were shuttled back and forth between unreliable foster parents. In spite of his unstable home life, he found salvation in Christianity at the All Nations' Centre in South London when he was 13. He drew on that Pentecostal church in Kennington and elements of his Anglican experience in Nigeria to create his own sound. The church made note of his musical development and appointed him as worship leader. Then it was off to University of Westminster for a musical degree. After graduating he had a succession of jobs, including voiceover work for Coca-Cola and the *Daily Telegraph*, and promotions work for Sony Music where he was pushing discs by Mariah Carey, Wyclef Jean, and Aerosmith.

This clean-shaven troubadour then decided to promote his own vision and ministry. He mixed his church influences with elements of soul music and debuted the CD *Restoration* in 2002. The album yielded listener favorites such as "Our God Is Good," "Your Loving Kindness," "Restoration," and "We Want to See You." The album was turned into a live music video in 2003. Since the release of *Restoration*, Muyiwa has been invited to lead worship at events throughout Africa and Europe, including the 25,000-member God Embassy Pentecostal Church in the Ukraine and the "Soul in the City" evangelistic outreach crusade in London. Muyiwa also hosts the *Gospel Tonight* and *Worship Tonight* programs on Premier Christian Radio in London.

Alicia Myers

AN EARLY-'80S soul chanteuse, Alicia Myers was born November 20, 1957, in Detroit. One of nine children, Myers and her brother Jackie used to enter talent contests together. He went on to sing with the Chairmen of the Board, a soul group. Meanwhile, Myers started her professional career with the soul group Al Hudson & the Soul Partners. They later changed their name to One Way and recorded for both ABC and Capitol Records, though a major hit eluded them. Myers made a solo move when she joined MCA Records in 1980 and released the warm LP *Alicia Again*, which opened with the straightforward gospel tune "Keep God in Your Life."

Nothing much happened with that album, but the sophomore project *I Fooled You This Time* made big noise in 1982. The album featured the soft-disco styled gospel love song "I Just Want to Thank You." Myers's sweet swoon of a voice soared over the heavenly lyric.

Although the song stalled at No. 37 on the *Billboard* R&B singles chart, the song has never stopped being played on oldies radio stations. Unlike many crossover gospel songs, the lyrical message was not vague. The opening line was, "I want to thank you, heavenly father, for shining your light on me." The song was the subject of a court battle between its writer Kevin McCord and Mariah Carey in 1994. McCord sued, stating that elements of the song were used in Carey's 1992 hit "Make It Happen." It was later resolved out of court. Myers's 1984 LP *I Appreciate* featured her two biggest R&B hits "You Get the Best from Me" and the title song. The set included another spiritual tune, "Just Praying." After one more LP for MCA, Myers vanished from the musical landscape and has scarcely been heard from since—not even on the oldies concert circuit.

Raymond Myles

THIS FLAMBOYANT gospel singer, a household name in New Orleans, was found dead on a New Orleans street corner on October 11, 1998, at the age of 41. Police said that he died of multiple gunshot wounds and that his vehicle had been carjacked. Myles was known for his high-energy shows. He came up through the gospel ranks and recorded his first single, "Prayer from a 12-Year-Old Boy" as a plea for world peace and an end to the Vietnam War in 1969. Later he founded the RAMS choir (Raymond Anthony Myles Singers), which toured the Bible Belt, reprising songs by Candi Staton, Shirley Caesar, and Al Green. His talent wasn't lost on New Orleans homeboy Harry Connick, Jr., who had Myles open for him a few times, including a huge date at Madison Square Garden in New York. He did all this while holding down a regular job as choir director at the Abramson High School in the Crescent City.

RECOMMENDED RECORDING: *A Taste of Heaven* (Sony/Legacy, 2003) features Myles's Cajun gospel imprint on standards such as "Precious Lord" and Donny Hathaway's "Someday We'll All Be Free."

Johnny Nash

ALTHOUGH HE ENJOYED a handful of Top 40 hits such as "The Teen Commandments," "Hold Me Tight," "Cupid," and "Stir It Up" from 1959 to 1979, Johnny

Nash is most often remembered for his million-seller "I Can See Clearly Now," which topped the *Billboard* pop singles charts for four weeks in 1972. Born August 19, 1940, in Houston, Texas, Nash started off singing in a Baptist church choir. At the age of 13, he began to sing pop cover songs on a local TV show, *Matinee*, which led to his discovery by Arthur Godfrey. Godfrey allowed Nash to perform on his national radio and television programs several times over a seven-year period. Nash signed to ABC-Paramount Records and made his first hit with the song "A Teenager Sings the Blues." Early on, with his honey-sweet tenor and exotic handsomeness, he was considered a pinup rival of crooner Johnny Mathis. He made his film debut in *Take a Giant Step* in 1959. By the mid-'60s Nash had developed a taste for Jamaican music. He scored several hits with reggae-flavored tunes, and his cover of Bob Marley's "Stir It Up" introduced Marley to the American public. After signing with Epic Records in 1972, Nash had Bob Marley & the Wailers back him on a song he wrote called "I Can See Clearly Now." The inspirational pop song allowed Nash to retire comfortably from the music business and live off the royalties. The song has been recorded by more than 30 artists, including Gladys Knight & the Pips, Barbra Streisand, and Ray Charles, as well as the gospel duo the O'Neal Twins.

RECOMMENDED RECORDING: Although it's never been issued on CD, Nash recorded a beautiful gospel LP entitled *The Quiet Hour* for ABC-Paramount. The album featured his easy-listening take on gospel standards such as "I Want Jesus to Walk with Me," "I Believe," and "Nobody Knows the Trouble I've Seen." He also turned in passionate and technically precise performances on "I See God" and "The Eyes of God."

century before. Born January 19, 1932, in Asheville, North Carolina, Rex Nelon enjoyed quartet music as a boy. After his service in the marines, Nelon sang part-time with a handful of gospel groups before he landed a full-time position as the bass singer for the Homeland Harmony Quartet in 1955. By 1957, Nelon had moved on as bass singer and guitarist for the LeFevres. An amiable but ambitious man, Nelon's sharp business mind helped the LeFevres reach new heights (see more in the LeFevres entry). Therefore, it only made sense that the group was sold to Nelon when the original members were ready to call it quits in 1976. Nelon added his teenage children, Kelly and Todd, to the group and they never missed a step. They maintained the LeFevres' audience and drew a new crowd of younger fans who were enticed by the youthful Donny and Marie Osmond appeal of Kelly and Todd. The new lineup produced a string of new Southern gospel hits such as "Come Morning," "I'm Glad I Know Who Jesus Is," and "O for a Thousand Tongues" among a dozen others.

In 1985, the group changed their name from the Rex Nelon Singers to simply the Nelons. They recorded prolifically and maintained a busy concert schedule. After Rex Nelon's first wife died in 1997, Nelon turned the Nelons over to Kelly to manage. He initially thought he was retired until Bill Gaither coaxed him out of his sabbatical to perform on the Gaither Homecoming concerts. Rex and his second wife, Judy, were in London appearing with the Gaither Homecoming Tour when he suffered a fatal heart attack on January 23, 2000. Today, the Nelons are a trio comprised of Kelly Nelon, her eldest daughter, Amber Thompson, and her second husband, Jason Clark, who has sung or been associated with the Nelons since 1994. Clark is studying to become a preacher. In the meantime, he and his family worship at Grace Baptist Church in Powder Springs, Georgia.

Nelons

AFTER THE LEFEVRES sold their name and operation to their bass singer Rex Nelon in 1976 and eventually retired from the stage, Nelon changed their name to the Rex Nelon Singers and continued the legacy of smooth Southern gospel music the LeFevres had begun a half

Bettye Ransom Nelson

ONE OF THE GREATEST sopranos in the COGIC denomination, Bettye Ransom Nelson is the featured vocalist on the COGIC International Mass Choir's biggest sellers *I Can Do All Things* and *Because He Lives*. The Houston-born singer was involved in a severe car accident early in life and lost one lung. Considering her injury, it was a miracle that she was able to continue singing. She tells that testimony on the title track of the *Heritage Travelin Shoes* CD (World Class Gospel, 2000). After COGIC's music department president, Mattie Moss Clark, discovered Nelson's colorful voice, she featured her on several of the denomination's mass choir hit projects in the 1970s. So many of the songs she led were radio and congregational hits that Clark produced her first LP *Jesus Is the Light of My Life* in 1980. She next led "Mustard Seed Faith" from the *A Star Is Born* LP on Gospearl Records in 1982. Nelson went on to record on other COGIC International Mass Choir projects and worked alongside Clark in the national music department, working with the National Children's Choir in particular. In 1994, she was appointed a vice president of the music department after the death of Mattie Moss Clark. She was featured on Bishop T.D. Jakes's *Woman Thou Art Loosed* CD, and her most recent solo project is *Kingdoms of My Heart* (Point of Grace Records, 2001). In July 2004, Donnie McClurkin had Nelson revamp Sara Jordan Powell's classic "When Jesus Comes" for his live concert recording at Virginia Beach, Virginia's Rock Church. Nelson is minister of music and First Lady at the Nelson Memorial Pentecostal (COGIC) in Houston where her husband, Bishop A.C. Nelson, Jr., is the pastor.

Joshua Nelson

THIS JEWISH SPIRITUAL singer is best known in gospel circles for imitating or channeling the voice and style of Mahalia Jackson on a rendition of "How I Got Over" on Bishop Carlton Pearson's *Live at Azusa 3* CD. Nelson was born in Newark, New Jersey, and first discovered Mahalia Jackson's music when he stumbled across one of her old albums at his grandparents' home. Nelson imbibed Jackson's music to the point where he began to sound exactly like her. He honed his musical skills as a student at Newark's Arts High School. After traveling through Israel, Nelson decided to create a new form of music incorporating Jewish liturgical and African-American musical styles. He serves as minister of music at the Hopewell Baptist Church in Newark. He's re-

corded a number of custom CDs that he sells on his personal Web site, www.joshuanelson.com.

Aaron Neville

ONE OF TOP 40 radio's favorite modern-day crooners, Aaron Neville is renowned for pop classics such as "Tell It Like It Is," "Everybody Plays the Fool," and duets with Linda Ronstadt such as "Don't Know Much." Neville was born January 24, 1941, in New Orleans. He grew up idolizing the soft, smooth voices of soul singers Pookie Hudson and Sam Cooke. He recorded for a number of small New Orleans record labels throughout the 1960s and enjoyed a smash hit when the ballad "Tell It Like It Is" spent five weeks at No. 1 on the R&B chart in 1967. However, the Par-Lo label eventually went out of business and Neville wasn't able to capitalize on the song's success. In the next few years, Neville experienced several recording disappointments with other labels, spent time in prison, and was a drug addict.

It was while Neville was high on heroin and burglarizing a clothing shop that he turned his life around. When he and his accomplices were spotted, they all scattered. Neville hid in an old van. "I'm high, so in my head everything is funny to me," he told *Crisis* magazine. "Outside, I hear a voice say, 'Come out of there now,' and 'What are you doing in there anyway?' And I'm just laughing, rolling in the back of the van. And I'm trying to get the door open. But it's stuck. I can't move it. I'm trying everything I could to open that door. And the next thing I know, the parking lot is full of people and the sheriff and all. Then the door opened, and I said, 'Thank you, Jesus.' I was glad it happened. I had been praying for an answer, because I had come there [Los Angeles] to sing, not to rob or nothing. And I had my answer from God. I just sat on that running board, crossed my legs, lit a cigarette, and had a smile on my face." Neville prayed to St. Jude, the patron saint of lost causes, during his court hearing and credits him with the suspended sentence the judge gave him.

He went to work fighting fires, digging ditches, and working on loading docks to support his family before he and his three brothers began recording as the Neville Brothers in 1977. When singer Bette Midler saw them perform, she helped get them a recording deal with A&M Records. They enjoyed a string of Cajun soul albums that found respectable record sales. However, pop star Linda Ronstadt brought Neville back to center stage in 1989. She first met him at the World's Fair in 1984 and was smitten with his heavenly voice. She invited him to sing with her on her *Cry Like a Rainstorm, Howl Like the Wind* CD that year. Their duets on "All My Life," "Don't Know Much," and "When Something's Wrong with My Baby" were all major pop hits. All three songs were further immortalized with music videos that received heavy rotation on VH1 television. The success resulted in Neville's solo career resurgence. Because of his enduring faith, Neville decided to record his first gospel CD, *Devotion*, in 2000 via a partnership with EMI Gospel Records. Propelled by the radio hit "Jesus Is a Friend of Mine," a nice testimonial type of song in which Neville raps about his real-life ups and downs, Devotion reached the Top Ten on the gospel album chart. He has since recorded other gospel music as a soloist and with the late Johnny Adams and Clarence Fountain & the Five Blind Boys.

New Jersey Mass Choir

ONE OF THE MOST popular choirs of the 1980s, the New Jersey Mass Choir's passionate vocals graced such radio hits as "Hold Up the Light," "Look Up and Live," and "I Want to Know What Love Is." Formed October 14, 1981, as an offshoot of the Gospel Music Workshop of America's New Jersey chapter by the chapter president Donnie Harper, their first chart LP was 1984's *Live at the Ritz*. Then fate intervened to take them to the next level. "The label we were signed to at the time and the Foreigner [rock group] team had the same lawyer," Harper told *Totally Gospel* in 1988. "Consequently, the president of our record company asked the Foreigner people how the recording was coming. They said they were about to finish the project, but they had this one song they needed a choir on. Our people submitted some choir albums to them and we were chosen." The song was "I Want to Know What Love Is" and it reached No. 1 on the *Billboard* Hot 100 singles chart. The choir accompanied Foreigner on their media campaign, which in-

cluded a coveted performance on *Saturday Night Live*. The choir then recorded their own gospel version of the song, which reached No. 12 on the *Billboard* dance chart in 1985. The LP of the same name reached No. 7 on the gospel chart. With the momentum behind the group, their subsequent LP *Look Up and Live* soared to No. 1 on the gospel album chart. For a good decade, they continued to make hit after hit, with their last album, *Live*, appearing in 1998 on the Xenon label.

Nicholas

A REPORTER FOR the *Winston-Salem Journal* once wrote: "They offer gospel with a disco beat, a '40s sound, and an easy listening tempo. They have already become a major act in black gospel music circles and they are now crossing over to the inspirational music market at full force." In the 1980s and a good part of the 1990s, Nicholas was one of the top acts in black gospel music. Then they just sort of disappeared.

Philip Nicholas was born February 18, 1954, in Philadelphia. His father was a jazz artist who renounced his past and became a music minister. Under his father's direction, Nicholas performed in church groups all over the City of Brotherly Love. He learned to play the piano and in his junior year of high school in 1971, he formed the Nicholas Chorale Ensemble with his brother Lonnie, their nephew Steve Jackson, and a few other relatives with rotating memberships. He kept the group together through his college years at Drexel University. "I did not have many outside activities because all my time was involved with the group," Nicholas said. "I always had the dream to do this on a professional level."

In 1973, Nicholas's girlfriend, Diane, introduced him to a dorm-mate of hers who was always singing in the shower and waking up everyone on campus. Her name was Brenda Watson (born December 16, 1953, in Salem, New Jersey). Soon after, she joined the Nicholas Chorale, and she and Nicholas became an item. The ensemble toured throughout the northeast before disbanding circa 1976. Nicholas and Watson joined the group Spirit, which was sponsored by the leader of the "I Found It" movement. In October 1977, Motown records producer Frank Wilson offered to help produce an album of the group, but Spirit disbanded within six months.

After getting married on February 18, 1978, the Nicholas couple relocated to Los Angeles and formed a new group simply called Nicholas. They teamed up with another Motown executive, Kent Washburn, who sank $50,000 into Nicholas's first album, but Motown could not manufacture it because it didn't fall within the company's musical demographic. No major company would buy the record, so Philip's brother, Lonnie, sold his own house and loaned the money to Nicholas to manufacture the album themselves. Nicholas formed Message Records in 1981, although Philip continued to work as an accountant with the US Defense Department and Brenda held a secretarial job.

Finally, their first album, *Tell the World*, was released and the group was rounded out with Linda Laury Harold and Steve Jackson. A local DJ who owed them a favor played the record enough for it to create a buzz in the L.A. gospel community. On the strength of the single "God's Woman," the album began to sell. Churches began to call with concert dates. By the time their second album, *Words Can't Express,* was issued in 1983, the group had become a top draw in gospel. That album reached the Top Ten on *Billboard*'s spiritual chart and remained on the chart for 81 weeks.

After arguing with Lonnie over the direction of the company, Philip gave him Message Records and formed Command Records in 1985. They reduced themselves to duo status and secured national distribution via Lexicon/Light Records, one of the largest gospel distributors at the time. In July 1985, the album *Dedicated* was released to great fanfare within the gospel world. The album was voted *Billboard*'s No. 1 spiritual album of 1986 and eventually picked up both Grammy and Dove award nominations. The title song was a soulful love song that recalled the best of R&B duos such as Tammy Terrell and Marvin Gaye. That same year, Command grossed over $750,000. At the time Philip said, "We are not driving Rolls-Royces yet. I don't want to go through that change. But I do drive a nice, new sporty car. And instead of making $300 per performance, we are now getting $3,000 to $4,000." Over the next decade, Nicholas created further hits such as "Tell Somebody," "God's Woman," "Can't Nobody Do Me Like

Nicholas / courtesy of Command Records

Jesus," "A Completed Woman" (to the tune of Carole King's "[You Make Me Feel Like] A Natural Woman"), and "The Closer I Get to You," a gospel remake of the Roberta Flack/Donny Hathaway classic.

Rev. Charles Nicks

ONE OF GOSPEL music's premiere organists, Rev. Nicks was born July 18, 1941 in Lincoln, Nebraska. His father, Charles, Sr., was a Baptist minister and his mother, Alliece, was a pianist and his earliest musical influence. Nicks developed an aggressive organ style that caused spectators to say that he made the instrument talk. When he was 16, Nicks became organist for his father's church, St. James Baptist Church, in Detroit. He eventually became pastor of the church and served as organist with the Harold Smith Majestics. He also produced other artists and enjoyed hits with songs such as "He's So Real," "Something About God's Grace," and "I Really Love the Lord" for the Sound of Gospel label in the 1980s and early 1990s.

Smokie Norful

THIS YOUNG MAN from Arkansas was the saving grace of EMI Gospel Records. The struggling gospel division of the billion-dollar conglomerate never introduced a successful new artist until Norful's debut in 2002. All their previous artists—Londa Larmond, Lamar Campbell, LeJuene Thompson, Sharon Riley, and Darwin Hobbs—have failed miserably. Only established acts such as Donald Lawrence & the Tri-City Singers and Aaron Neville have done well there. However, Norful's gold-selling "I Need You Now" project saved the label from the long-rumored chopping block it was headed for at the time.

Born October 31, 1973, the eldest of three sons born to a Methodist minister and a bank clerk (now a trust officer) in Little Rock, Norful began playing the piano at the age of four. He began singing publicly at the age of six, recorded a custom album at ten, and began playing regularly in his father's church at the age of 12. "I was always involved in music," Norful recalls with a chuckle. "I was in every school play and just did things because I loved music. I listened to everything from jazz to nursery rhymes. You know how people go to libraries and get books? Well, I'd go to the library and check out albums. I liked the music of Daryl Coley, El DeBarge—I sang his song 'Love Me in a Special Way' to many a girl—and Stevie Wonder. But when I turned 13, Vanessa Bell Armstrong became like the premier vocalist in my mind. I studied her riffs and her runs on the *Peace Be Still* album. She was such an inspiration to me vocally."

Since he had already recorded an album, it was no surprise that Norful diligently sought a record deal as a teenager. "My parents scraped and scratched to get me all over town to get in talent shows and to meet this person and to meet that person," he says. "I had many opportunities to get a record deal, but my dad was very protective and very wise. When I was 14, we sat down with some people from Prince's company Paisley Park Records. They flew us to Minneapolis and I did some demos for them. Then, my dad was like, 'You got to get an education first.'" At the time, Norful wasn't happy with his dad's decision. "He simply said, 'I can't live with signing your life away. You'll thank

Smokie Norful / courtesy of EMI *Records*

me one day.' My parents could have sold me out for a dollar, but they didn't do that even though Paisley was talking big money."

Then it was off to the University of Arkansas at Pine Bluff where he majored in political science with a plan to enter law school. Later, Norful switched his major to history and began substitute teaching. He liked teaching so much, he made it his career. He began teaching at his own high school amid his former teachers. "I remember my first time walking into the teacher's lounge," he laughs. "It was eerie. One teacher said 'I know you think you're grown and all, but you ain't that grown to come in here.' I couldn't wait to tell her I was working there now." The kids loved Norful because he was near their age and he could give them insight into their teachers' behavior. By 1998, Norful moved to Chicago to enroll in Garrett Evangelical Theological Seminary's master's degree program. Life began to take a new direction for him when he became a youth and music pastor at a Chicago megachurch. Joanne Brunson of the Thompson Community Choir (the Tommies) had seen him sing in church and asked him to sing on the choir's upcoming project. Norful was flattered, but said he'd rather write a song. He opened for their concert that night and Edwin Oliver, an entertainment attorney for Disney Music, was in the audience. He was awed by Norful's performance and eventually became his manager. Together they financed Norful's solo CD. They had not even begun to shop the CD when Oliver had a chance meeting with an old acquaintance, Ken Pennell, general manager of EMI Gospel. They discussed their respective projects and Pennell asked to hear Norful's CD. When he heard the album, Pennell instantly liked it, but didn't offer him a recording deal until he saw a video tape of Norful performing live. That video sealed the deal.

"When I was 14, I wanted a record deal bad," Norful says. "Now, I'm not about a record deal, it's about furthering my musical ministry. What can I do to make a difference? To make a change? I don't just want to do it here in my local congregation, but how can I reach other folks? A record deal was the vehicle to make that happen." When asked about the potential success of his debut CD, Norful just shakes his head. "I've already been blessed with my wife and our little man Trey. I don't have any expectations but that God is going to do great things. I have great expectations but only in him. I don't even want to fathom what he'll do because I'll under-shoot where I'm supposed to be." The soul-stirring, traditional-styled title track (just Norful singing and playing the piano) became the surprise gospel smash of 2003. After EMI felt the song had run its course, it released other singles. However, radio didn't strongly gravitate to the other singles. Programmers kept playing "I Need You Now" to the point that it eventually crossed over to the R&B singles chart where the song rose to the impressive peak of No. 45. In the summer of 2004, Norful's CD was certified gold and continued to be a Top 40 gospel smash more than two years after its release.

Jessye Norman

ONE OF THE MOST prominent classical sopranos of the last quarter century, Jessye Norman was born September 15, 1945 in Augusta, Georgia, where her father was an insurance man and her mother was a school teacher. She first sang at the Mt. Calvary Baptist Church there when she was four years old. Norman's father insisted on piano lessons for all three of his children. Norman was doing household chores and listening to the radio when she first heard opera music. She began to study the records of operatic greats such as Marian Anderson.

She sang throughout her adolescence but didn't intend on a musical career. She wanted to become a doctor or a nurse, but her high school teachers convinced her to further develop her voice.

At the age of 16, Norman enrolled at Howard University in Washington, DC, where she was a voice major. While in the city, Norman sang in the St. Mary's Episcopal Church Choir and the Lincoln Temple United Church of Christ Choir. She then attended the Peabody Conservatory in Baltimore before earning a master's in music from the University of Michigan in 1968. Later that year, Norman moved to Germany to study at the Institute of International Education and won the Munich Competition which resulted in her professional debut as Elisabeth in Wagner's *Tannhauser* in Berlin. Norman rapidly became the darling of the European opera world with grand performances in *Aida* at La Scala in Milan and in *Les Troyens* at London's Covent Garden. Because of her height, girth, and regal bearing, Norman usually played the roles of commanding figures or queens. By 1975, Norman had brought her wide vocal range (from contralto to soprano) home to America where she made her Carnegie Hall recital debut under the direction of conductor Zubin Mehta. She toured the country in a series of recital concerts until she made her debut as Cassandra in *Les Troyens* at the New York Metropolitan Opera in 1983. In 1997, Norman became the youngest recipient of the Kennedy Center Honors award at the age of 52.

RECOMMENDED RECORDING: *Amazing Grace* (Philips, 1991) features 18 of Norman's greatest spiritual recordings between 1978 and 1987. Among the highlights are the title song, the dramatic "There's a Man Goin' Round," and "Give Me Jesus."

Larry Norman

WHEN LARRY NORMAN surfaced on the Christian music landscape, *Billboard* magazine cited him as the most important songwriter since Paul Simon and *Time* magazine called him the most significant artist in Christian music. The Christian music press labeled him as the father of Christian rock music, and his fans included rock legends such as Bob Dylan, U2, Van Morrison, and John Mellencamp. Born 1947 in San Francisco, Norman was signed by Capitol Records in 1966 when the label was enjoying phenomenal success of the Beatles and the Beach Boys. Over the next four years, Norman recorded faith-oriented songs such as "Riding High" and "We Need a Whole Lot More of Jesus and a Lot Less Rock and Roll" (covered by Linda Ronstadt), "Sweet Song of Salvation," and "I Wish We'd All Been Ready." With the group People behind him, Norman experienced one Top 20 pop hit with "I Love You" in 1968. During the period, Norman's songs were covered by secular artists such as Sammy Davis, Jr., Petula Clark, and Cliff Richard. His stage musical *The Epic* influenced Pete Townshend to write the rock opera *Tommy*.

Since Norman was promoted by a secular record label, many conservative Christians labeled him a heretic simply because of the company he kept. Most Christian bookstores would not carry his LPs such as *Upon This Rock*. During his concerts, Norman rarely smiled and displayed a sardonic wit, but the music was the foundation of what was called the Jesus Movement—born-again Christian hippies during the counterrevolution of the Vietnam era. He later recorded for MGM Records before he opened Solid Rock Records in 1974. However, he spent the rest of the decade battling Christian censors. His albums *In Another Land* and *Something New Under the Sun* were both censored by his distributor, Word Records. They omitted songs from the projects they deemed as controversial.

Norman discovered a number of CCM artists such as Steve Camp, Keith Green, and Randy Stonehill. In 1978, Norman was in a plane accident that caused brain damage and spinal injuries. He had been on the verge of signing to Warner Bros. Records, but the tragedy laid Norman up for the next 12 years. He later started a new label, FIDO (Phydeaux), since he insisted that Christian music was going to the dogs. On the positive side, the plane accident made Norman less judgmental and friendlier. He still refused most interviews (and had a contentious relationship with *CCM* magazine), but, on a personal level, he was more accessible.

Norman suffered a heart attack in the 1990s and has been in unstable health since then. Insurance didn't cover all of his medical needs, so there have been fund-raisers from time to time to help cover those costs. A new generation of artists has discovered Norman's music, which has been covered in recent years by young CCM artists such as Code of Ethics, Tait, Selah, Rebecca St. James, and DC Talk. Norman was inducted into the Gospel Music Hall of Fame in 2001. "I tried to create songs for which there was no anticipated acceptance," Norman once told *CCM* magazine about his musical legacy. "I wanted to display the flexibility of the gospel and that there was no limitation to how God could be presented. I used abrasive humor and sarcasm as much as possible, which was also not a traditional aspect of Christian music. I chose negative imagery to attempt to deliver a positive message, like 'I Don't Believe in Miracles' is actually about faith. 'I Wish We'd All Been Ready' talked about something I had never heard preached from a pulpit as I grew up. 'The Last Supper' and 'Ha Ha World' used very surreal imagery which drug users could assimilate. My songs weren't written for Christians. No, it was not a Christian album for those believers who wanted everything spelled out. It was more like a street fight. I was saying [to Christians], 'I'm going to present the gospel, and I'm not going to say it like you want. This album is not for you.'"

Dorothy Norwood

SHE'S BEEN CALLED Gospel's Greatest Storyteller and it is true that no one tells a story exactly as Dorothy Norwood has on signature tunes such as "Johnny & Jesus" or "The Denied Mother." The third of five children, Norwood was born May 29, 1935, in Atlanta, Georgia. Her father was a full-time minister (at Perrywood Boulevard Baptist Church, which was renamed Norwood Tabernacle after his death in 1986) and her mother was a housewife and occasional singer until she started a clothing shop in later years. Norwood has been singing most of her life. At the age of eight, she toured with her mother's group, the Norwood Gospel Singers (two sisters, her mother, and her brother and his wife). They sang throughout the Southeastern United States until she launched a solo career during her teens. "I wanted to become a nationally known singer," she says. "So I moved to Chicago. I knew I had to leave Georgia in order to be able to accomplish my dream and my goal."

"The first day I went to Chicago," she continues, "Gloria Griffin from the Roberta Martin Singers invited me to go hear Mahalia Jackson sing. I went and heard her and that's when I knew that was my calling." Jackson invited Norwood on the road with her, but it only lasted a few months. "Her health started deteriorating and she stopped traveling so much," Norwood says. She then joined Rev. Clay Evans's Fellowship Choir as a soloist. "That's when Albertina Walker came to the broadcast and heard me sing 'Low Is the Way' and asked me to go on the road with the Caravans." The year was 1956 and the next few years were not lucrative, but they were good training for her career in gospel.

When Norwood's mother fell ill, Norwood returned to Georgia to nurse her. After her mother passed away, "I went back to Chicago and they had already gotten another singer, Shirley Caesar." In the meantime, Norwood wrote songs for the Roberta Martin Singers such as "Ride On, King Jesus" and "Lord, Remember Me." Norwood then joined James Cleveland's group, the Gospel Chimes. In 1964, she organized her own group, the Dorothy Norwood Singers. Her first project, *Johnny & Jesus*, was released on Savoy Records that year and became a gold record. "I had written a couple of stories and I said I was going to pursue that because everybody else was singing and had these big voices," she remembered. "I always wanted to get around the competition. I felt that would not only minister to somebody, even though most of the stories were fiction, that it was a thing whereas somebody had experienced it at some time or another, so that was a good way to start my career and it worked."

In her sandpaper voice, Norwood kept turning out sentimental but hypnotic gospel story songs such as "The Denied Mother," "The Bereaved Child," and "The Bell Didn't Toll." In 1972, Norwood received an unexpected invitation. "I was on tour with my group and the Rolling Stones sent me a telegram," she remembers. "I couldn't believe it. I thought it was a prank asking me to go on the road with them. Right away, I told them I will not compromise, I sing only gospel music. They said they don't want me to sing anything but gospel be-

cause Mick Jagger went into a record store in Los Angeles and asked for a couple of my albums. They gave him *Johnny & Jesus* and another one, and he said he wanted me to go on the road with him."

The 30-city tour kicked off on June 3, 1972, in Vancouver, British Columbia, with Norwood opening. There were also sets by Martha Reeves & the Vandellas and Stevie Wonder. Though Norwood never confirmed it, the tour was wild. Wonder didn't show up for some dates because his drummer was ill and he didn't want to use another drummer. Reeves was booted from some shows. At the Houston concert date, 66 adults and 15 juveniles were arrested for drug possession and one fan overdosed. The critical rock media didn't indulge the Stones' love for Norwood's music. The *Houston Chronicle*'s John Scarborough said, "The crowd politely endured spirituals and hymns."

"The Dorothy Norwood Singers… were not exactly what the crowd had come to see," John Lomax wrote in the Houston weekly newspaper, *Space City*, of the tour's stop at Hofheinz Pavilion. "They played very well—an eight-piece group with organ, bass, drums, guitar, tambourines, and three girl singers—presenting a program of religious numbers like 'I'm So Glad,' 'Just the Two of Us,' and concluding with a rousing version of 'When the Saints Go Marching In.'" When asked about the backstage antics of the tour, Norwood just laughs. "That was a whole other experience," she says. "It just let you know that you could be in the world but not of the world. But I just enjoyed [the Stones'] company. They had the highest respect for me and my group."

From there, Norwood met up with a wealthy entrepreneur, Mike Divies, who opened the Atlanta-based GRC Records label to record artists such as Norwood. After they wrote a song together, Norwood recalls him saying, "'We can make a hit out of this,' so he sent for all the Motown musicians and asked them to come to Atlanta and that's where we recorded." The 1974 inspirational R&B smash "There's Got to Be Rain in Your life (to Appreciate the Sunshine)" reached No. 21 on the *Billboard* R&B chart and No. 88 on the pop singles chart. The song was born from personal experience. She says, "You can't appreciate the good times if you haven't been through the rough times. I had many low points. My mother had passed, I didn't come up with a rich family. We had struggles. I was struggling there in Chicago for a while until I got established."

Norwood enjoyed one more R&B hit with the funky "Let Your Feet Down Easy," which hit the Hot 100 R&B chart in 1975. A song that Atlanta radio announcer Larry Tinsley wrote, "What a Beautiful World This Would Be," also received some crossover radio airplay. "My music stayed right there in the middle," she said. "I didn't try to do hip-hop and I didn't try to do blues. My songs were messages that could reach [from] the stark traditional to the secular." In 1980, Norwood toured Europe where she taped a British television special with Marion Williams, Rev. James Cleveland, and Natalie Cole. The 1980s were a lean period for Norwood musically. She only recorded a few projects, such as *A Mother's Son* for I AM Records. She then recorded for AIR Records without fanfare. In 1990, Norwood joined the Savoy/Malaco Records family and began enjoying hits again. Among her recent hits are "Hattie B's Daughter," "The Lord Is a Wonder," and the 1995 smash "Shake the Devil Off." Of the reggae-styled tune, Norwood says, "Satan is real. I used to think he was a man in a red suit. But I found he can have on a designer suit. It's a spirit that you have to rebuke if you want to move forward."

Over the years, Norwood has produced or presented such recording artists as Cassietta George and Ruby Terry. "The only thing I'm doing now is helping young people," she says. "I'm starting my own school of gospel to help young people and inspire them to keep going. A lot of super-talented people out here won't get a break unless someone gives them a break. Then, some of them need to be taught. They have potential but they need to learn stage presence, how to get a recording deal, and how to get into the media so somebody can hear them. They need to stand on some shoulders and my shoulder is here for them as long as I'm around."

RECOMMENDED RECORDINGS: *Golden Classics* (Collectables, 1994) features all of Norwood's 1970s crossover music. *The World's Greatest Story Teller* (Savoy Records, 2001) features her 1960s story song hits such as "Johnny & Jesus."

Willie Norwood

WILLIE NORWOOD's claim to fame may be his superstar daughter Brandy, but he's been working in the gospel field throughout his life and deserves his own place in the spotlight. Norwood has spent the last 30 years honing his gifts as a musician. After five years as the lead singer and trumpeter for the Los Angeles-based soul band the Composers in the 1970s, Norwood redirected his attentions to church music and assembled a number of choirs over the years that have backed Janet Jackson, Monica, and Quincy Jones, among others.

Norwood was born November 30, 1950, in Lewisville, Mississippi, the oldest of five children. His family later moved to Greenwood, Mississippi, the "cotton capital of the world." The family was poor in material things, but rich in spirit due to their churchgoing. "We lived in Baptist Town," Norwood says. "It was called that because it had one church—a Baptist church. Every time the church door opened, I was there because I loved the Lord."

His faith was born early. He lost a $1 raffle ticket and was worried about replacing it. "If you lost a dollar back then that was a lot of money," he says. "I just looked up to God and asked him to bless me some kind of way because if you lose that ticket you got to pay for it. After I did that, I just happened to look down at the ground beneath me and there was a dollar. After that God became real to me because he answered my prayer. As a young boy you need that sometimes. I think I've kept that childlike faith all of my life. I've always believed that whatever you get into, God can get you out of it—and I have to tell you, as I grew up, I got into some things."

When Norwood was about 14, he picked up music to avoid going to the cotton fields. He played various horns through high school. "I would go to the clubs and play while I was in high school, and I got a scholarship to go to Jackson State University," he says. At Jackson, Norwood became a star student and played horn in the Sonic Boom Band during halftime shows. Before graduating from Jackson in 1970, Norwood joined the Composers, a ten-member dance band, as their lead singer and trumpeter. The Composers were performing at the Elk's Rest club in McComb, Mississippi, when Norwood met his future wife, Sonja Bates. She eventually became the manager for the Composers and got them dates opening for Lou Rawls and Rufus featuring Chaka Khan. Eventually, she pushed them to move to Hollywood. They were never able to catch a recording contract, but they were an in-demand group. "After a while I just got away from church altogether, while my wife began to get more involved in church," Norwood recalls. "She began to pray for me and I was drawn to come and give my life to Christ again. I had gone way astray, but God called me back home."

Norwood had a literal wake-up call. "I was driving through Mount Bayou, Mississippi," he recalls. "I fell asleep at the wheel, cruising down a long country road. I came up to a T in the road where you could just go right or left, and I went straight ahead where there was no more road. I landed in a field just two feet from a telephone pole. I was blessed that nothing happened. There were no cars around. I drove my little yellow Subaru out of that field and went on to my mother's house, but I thought to myself, there must be something left for me to live for."

There was something to live for, but he feared breaking his professional commitments to do so. After Norwood quit the Composers, the Korean owner of the Name of the Game club in Los Angeles had shelled out big money to have Norwood assemble a house band and publicize the new group's debut. "I was new in church," Norwood remembers. "I was working as a Medicare clerk at Blue Cross/Blue Shield and I was getting $750 a night to perform at this club. That was more money than I thought I could ever make. But somehow I couldn't do that…. I couldn't bring myself to do that and do the church thing at the same time." Over the next week, Norwood experienced excruciating headaches while trying to decide which way to turn. "The final thing was that my wife said, 'God wouldn't be pleased with you [being] in the clubs Saturday night and then in church Sunday morning,'… We decided together that I would honor what God was calling me to do."

Then Norwood had to break the news to the notorious club owner, who was known to pack a gun and use it when so provoked. "My name and photo were plastered all over telephone poles and newspapers," Norwood says. "This man had spent a lot of money he was

Willie Norwood (left, with wife Sonja and Marvin Williams) / photo by Bil Carpenter

not going to get back. I was scared about telling him my decision. But I said, 'God, I don't know what you want me to do, but I don't feel good doing this [performing in the club], so make things right when I speak to this man.' One of my friends gave me a scripture that God will make even your enemies to be at peace with you. I held on to that thought and went on and spoke to the club owner. He did not understand. He said to me, 'My wife has been talking to me about going to Korea and this would be a good time to do that.' I thought he was going to shoot me, so I was ready to die. It was like going into the lion's den. I told him my dilemma. I told him I tried to do both and just couldn't. Then he said, 'You know what your problem is?' I said, 'No, what is my problem?' He said, 'Your problem is you think too much.'"

All thinking aside, the Norwoods eventually moved back to Mississippi to re-evaluate their priorities and to start over. In 1979, their daughter Brandy was born and their son, Ray J, came two years later. Meanwhile, Norwood had joined the Church of Christ, which is all a cappella music—no instrumentation in their services. The Southside Church of Christ in Los Angeles heard of Norwood's work in Mississippi and invited him to work with their music department. Back on the West Coast, Norwood did post-graduate study at California State Northridge and spent ten years as music minister at the church. "I would teach music at the Christian school and my kids would go to practice with me all the time," he says. "That's when they began to develop as singers and I'd coach them with the other kids."

Brandy landed a short-lived ABC sitcom, *Thea*, and in 1994 her debut CD for Atlantic Records yielded such smash pop singles as "Baby Baby" and "I Wanna Be Down." Brandy's success continued with her own sitcom, *Moesha*, and further pop hits. Then Ray J made noise with his Elektra Records debut CD in 1997, and he eventually joined the cast of *Moesha* too. Meanwhile, Norwood continued working with his choirs. The Norwood Kids Foundation choir won the McDonald's gospel competition in 1995. They have also backed Monica at the Disney Teacher awards and Brandy and Hezekiah Walker's Love Fellowship Choir on the Essence awards. "Janet Jackson heard about my children's choir and she had us to sing two songs on her *Velvet Rope* album," Norwood beams. "One was a beautiful song that didn't make it on the album. Then Quincy Jones had us on his *Juke Joint* CD."

Because of his association with Brandy, Atlantic Records offered Norwood a recording contract in 2000. He didn't want to record pop music, he wanted to do a gospel album. The label paired him with Victor and Cedric Caldwell, who had produced Take 6 and CeCe Winans, among others. They crafted *'Bout It*, an album that was fresh, but retained the old-school soul flavor that Norwood liked. They gave his renditions of "Put a Little Love in Your Heart" and Stevie Wonder's "Have a Talk with God" a contemporary vibe. Billy Preston was brought in to play organ on the traditional "I'd Trade a Lifetime." Norwood's cousins, the Williams Brothers, produced "No Limit" and "The Search is Over" which both have an urban AC feel. Brandy sang with her dad on the Angie Winans–penned "A Love Shared," which featured a sax solo by Kirk Whalum. Norwood brought his father's deep baritone and his son's tenor together for a trio recording of "Have Thine Own Way." The album closed with a beautiful acoustic pop ballad Norwood wrote called "All That I Need" in which he expresses his thankfulness to God for all of his blessings.

It was a very good CD, but it got caught up in a personnel shift at Atlantic Records when Demetrus Stewart, who executive produced the CD, left Atlantic's Christian division to run CeCe Winans's Wellspring Gospel label. On top of that, Atlantic merged its Christian division with Word Records and stopped promoting gospel projects until they could find a new executive

to run the division. The problem was further compounded when Word was bought by Warner Bros. Records and a new set of suits, who knew nothing about gospel music, began making decisions. At that point, Norwood and his wife had spent their own money to promote the CD since Atlantic had ceased promotional activity. Norwood was able to perform on *The Hour of Power* and TBN's *Praise the Lord*. The television exposure and his own radio campaign led the album to chart at No. 13 on the *Billboard* gospel sales chart in 2002. There was an option to do another album, but Norwood asked to be released from his contract. He now leads music at the Woodland Hills Church of Christ.

A.C. Oliver

THIS ARTIST RECORDED the 45 "You Got to See the Lord for Yourself" with the Gospel Jays in 1976 for Action Records.

O'Neal Twins

THIS SIBLING DUO is best known for the songs "I'd Trade a Lifetime," "I Have Decided to Follow Jesus," and "The Lord Is My Shepherd" during the Nixon administration. Edgar and Edward O'Neal were born August 17, 1937, in East St. Louis, Illinois. Reared in the COGIC denomination, they were greatly influenced by the music of Mattie Moss Clark and Mother Willie Mae Ford Smith. They recorded for Peacock Records in the 1960s with Edgar serving as pianist and song arranger. Edward was the primary vocalist. Their deep, raspy baritones created an earthy, down-home traditional gospel feel on their various recordings. In the 1980s, they recorded for both Savoy and AIR Records. They were profiled in the 1983 documentary film, *Say Amen, Somebody*. Edgar died in 1993.

Sid Ordower

ONE OF THE FEW television outlets for gospel artists, big and small, during the 1960s and 1970s was Sid Ordower's *Jubilee Showcase*. He was an army captain during World War II where he fought in the Battle of Normandy. He received two Purple Hearts and returned home to Chicago where he opened an auto dealership. On January 10, 1963, he began to broadcast *Jubilee Showcase* from his business. It aired on WLS TV and reached 250,000 viewers weekly. The program featured performances by gospel megastars such as the Staple Singers and Thomas Dorsey, as well as lesser-known artists such as Delois Barrett Campbell. "That show literally changed my life," the *Chicago Tribune* quoted Campbell as saying. "No one seemed to realize I could sing before I was on that show, even though I had been singing long before. But when I got on *Jubilee Showcase*, people finally found out that I could get up there and sing out and deliver."

Ordower didn't play favorites either. He presented the full spectrum of black gospel music. "I always used to pride myself on getting the best soloists, the greatest groups, the finest accompanists in gospel," Ordower told the *Tribune* in 1992. "The idea was to get variety.... We didn't want to feature just quartets or just soloists. We wanted everything that was out there, so long as it was the best."

Although he was white, Ordower became colorless to the black fans of the show. He recited the Negro National anthem "Lift Every Voice and Sing" on one episode and always kept his on-air announcements to a minimum. "You see, I wasn't the star of the program, and I didn't pretend to be," he told the *Tribune*. "I wasn't the one who sang and danced. All I did on-screen was introduce the groups, and I had a rule that I made myself and followed religiously: Never talk for more than two and a half minutes." Ordower donated 100 *Jubilee Showcase* episodes to the Harold Washington Library Center. He died January 4, 2002, at Northwestern Memorial Hospital at the age of 82.

Stacie Orrico

FOLLOWING IN THE footsteps of Kim Boyce and Cindy Morgan, who set the standard for Christian dance music almost a half generation ago, Stacie Orrico takes it to another level. Blessed with greater vocal chops and

range than Boyce or Morgan, Orrico has carved out a nice crossover success story for herself while remaining true to her Christian roots. Strongly influenced by the music of Lauryn Hill, Orrico brings an edge to Christian music.

One of five children, Orrico was born March 3, 1986, in Seattle. She began singing early on and first gained recognition in 1998 at the Estes Park Christian Artist Seminar in Denver. That event brought her a record deal with Forefront Records. In 2000, her debut CD *Genuine* was rolled out as a clean alternative to the sensuality of Christina Aguilera and Britney Spears. Her music tackled issues of concern for other teens such as peer pressure, self-esteem, and anorexia. For her self-titled follow-up CD, Forefront and their mainstream label partner, Virgin/EMI, brought out bigger producers. With production work from Dallas Austin, who worked with Pink, and Matt Serletic, who worked with Matchbox Twenty, they positioned Orrico for bigger things. She still held on to her core values, but the music was geared even more toward a non-Christian audience. The single "Stuck" went all the way to the top of the *Billboard* dance singles chart and "More to Life (There's Gotta Be)" made it to No. 2.

With mainstream exposure ranging from *The Tonight Show with Jay Leno* to *American Dreams*, Orrico became a spokesperson for the moral values of her generation. In early 2004, she was in Singapore at the MTV Asia awards when she announced to the press that it worries her to see girls emulating Spears and Aguilera. "The reason that I don't dress trashy is that I'm trying to set an example for little girls," Orrico said at a news conference. "From the time they're seven or eight years old, [girls] are being taught that the only thing that makes them special and beautiful is their sexuality, and I think that's wrong... I don't think that's sexy, I think it's degrading. I think that [being] a truly sexy woman comes from being confident and being classy, respectable, and mature."

Out of Eden

ONE OF THE FEW black gospel acts to launch their career from within the CCM genre, Out of Eden has become a top draw in the Christian music field. Their faces are brown, but many black gospel critics of the pretty sisters say their music is white. Nevertheless, their slick uptown wardrobe and Christian pop hooks have made them stars in the same league with Christian pop royalty such as Rebecca St. James and Rachel Lampa.

Lisa Kimmey Bragg (born 1975) and her two sisters, Andrea Kimmey Baca and Danielle Kimmey, were all born in Richmond, Virginia. They've been singing since childhood when they backed up their mother, DeLice Hall, a classical pianist. The family relocated to Nashville when Hall was offered a teaching position at Fisk University. Hall put her career ambitions aside to groom her daughters' singing ability. In many ways, she mirrors superstar Brandy's mom, Sonja Norwood, who unjustly gained a reputation as an over-zealous, micromanaging stage mother because she was a strong advocate for her daughter. "Our mom is not like a regular mother," Bragg told *CCM* magazine. "She will ask things like, 'How come you girls are not number 1?'" Danielle added that, "She is so straightforward. She is a wonderful woman of God…. She really saw the vision before we did."

Their stepfather made a video of them performing and shopped it to record labels, but there were no takers. It was a friend who took them to a rehearsal of DC Talk at the GMA in 1991 who started their career in earnest. The friend teased them into singing for Toby McKeehan, who liked them and said he'd look out for them if an opportunity ever came up. "The funny thing is we weren't looking for a break," Bragg said in 1995. "We enjoyed singing. We were more focused on doing it behind other people. We had no idea of what would eventually come out of singing in that little rehearsal room. We had no clue what God had in store."

In 1993, McKeehan founded Gotee Records and made Out of Eden his first signing. Their first album, *Lovin' the Day*, sold 100,000 units on the strength of their gospel-dance rendition of Bill Withers's "Lovely Day." The album reached No. 10 on the CCM chart, but never touched the gospel chart. The next album, *More Than You Know*, appeared in 1996 and reached No. 6 on the CCM chart. It sold over 200,000 units. Throughout their career, Bragg has been the group's leading songwriter and she's increased her involve-

ment with each new project. Gotee sought to cross over with 1999's *No Turning Back*, which hit No. 14 on the CCM Chart as they toured with R&B star Monica of "The Boy Is Mine" fame. A fine review in *Vibe* magazine and a guest shot on Brandy's *Moesha* sitcom further helped introduce them beyond the gospel world. The CD was their biggest seller yet with well over 250,000 in sales, but it did not cross over. It did feature a sensual duet track with labelmates the Katinas, entitled "Here's My Heart." About the crossover pitch, Bragg has said, "We have a heart for our peers and a desire to tell our generation that you don't have to lose yourself in today's impressionable society."

In spite of their high profile in the Christian pop world and outright rejection from the black gospel community, the Kimmey sisters don't really feel anyone is embracing their music. "We've had Christian radio promoters look at our CD and say, 'It's not our format,' without ever listening to the music," Bragg told *CCM* magazine in August 1999. "Based on what our album cover looks like, people put us in the black gospel section or the rap section. To me, black gospel is Shirley Caesar. We're pop music. Listen to 'Tomorrow'—that's a pop song. When we first started, we were indignant. We used to say, 'Okay, we're going to get three white girls [to pose for the CD cover], but we're going to sing all the songs and put them out and see how people accept them.'"

For *This Is Your Life* in 2002, the group amended their pop styling to create a more edgy, urban-flavored album meant to finally gain them a black gospel audience. Although it reached No. 11 on the *CCM* chart, the album made no impression on black gospel radio programmers. "They keep playing this one form of music," Bragg complained to *CCM*. "It doesn't make sense. You get tired of just banging down doors. Compared to what is going on in [general market] music with seven of the Top 10 songs being urban, we feel like we shouldn't have to be banging down the doors."

P.I.D. (Preachers In Disguise)

THIS CHRISTIAN RAP DUO was formed by Barry Hogan (born 1969) and Fred Lynch III (born 1967) to present the gospel in a raw language that kids in the street would understand. Between 1989–1992, the group released three Top 40 CCM albums, including *Back to Back* and *Born with the Gift*. They recorded for Benson, Star Song, and Frontline Records. Today, Lynch is a youth evangelist with Josh McDowell Ministries in Dallas, Texas. Hogan is a sound mixer for UCLA's School of the Performing Arts and released a hip-hop–jazz fusion CD, *Thing of Beauty*, on Dome Records in 2004.

Joe Pace

ONE OF THE LEADING black gospel choir conductors of recent years, Joe Pace was born October 20, 1965, in Homestead, Florida. He first gained fame as the leader of the Colorado Mass Choir, which was formed in 1995. Their debut CD *Watch God Move* on Verity Records featured the radio hits "Watch God Move," "Still Have Joy," and "Stir Up the Gift." The choir received a Stellar award for New Artist of the Year in 1997 and several GMWA Excellence award nominations. In 2001, Pace joined Integrity Music as an executive, as well as a performer. His 2004 CD *Sunday Morning Church Service* was another Top Ten gospel hit.

LaShun Pace

ONE OF MODERN gospel's favorite belters, LaShun Pace was born September 6, 1966, in Hapeville, Georgia. She was raised in the COGIC denomination where her mother was a choir conductor. "Before my father got saved, it was very difficult," Pace told *Gospel Industry Today* in April 1999. "I watched her on the floor, listening to the Davis Sisters… She got strength from the church and praying. Literally, we didn't have food—struggling with nine girls and a boy, growing up in a three-bedroom house… Through her, I saw how prayer works, and I saw her live a life. God rewards that. She got ridiculed a lot and so did we." Pace's mother later formed her daughters into a singing group, the Anointed Pace Sisters. After winning Best Gospel Group honors at the annual COGIC convention, the Pace sisters spent the next few years traveling and ministering with Gene Mar

tin, a former evangelist for A.A. Allen's organization before he formed the Action Revival Team. The Anointed Pace Sisters debut album, *U-Know*, appeared on Savoy Records in 1982. In 1987, at one of Edwin Hawkins's Music & Arts Seminars, Pace sang "That Name," which became the title of Hawkins's LP that appeared the following year on Birthright Records. The album reached No. 14 on the gospel chart. Hawkins was so impressed with Pace's vocal power that he personally went to the head of Savoy Records and suggested that they give Pace a solo recording deal apart from her sisters' contract. They did. After marrying Edward Rhodes during this period, Pace changed her name to LaShun Pace-Rhodes. Her debut LP *He Lives* appeared in 1991 and rose to No. 2 on the gospel charts on the awesome strength of her earth-quaking rendition of the old spiritual "I Know I've Been Changed." More good news was in the works as she portrayed the Angel of Mercy in Steve Martin's 1992 film *Leap of Faith*. She has also performed in theatrical productions such as *I Know I've Been Changed* and David E. Talbert's nationally acclaimed *A Fool and His Money*. Her young daughter, Xenia, died suddenly in early 2001 and her marriage unraveled as well. She is currently signed to EMI Gospel Records.

La Wanda Page

COMEDIENNE La Wanda Page gained fame as the fanatical Bible-thumping Aunt Esther on the 1970s TV sitcom *Sanford and Son*. She was born Alberta Peal in Cleveland, Ohio, on Oct. 19, 1920. Page began her career as a dancer and chorus girl on the Negro club circuit where she was billed as "The Bronze Goddess of Fire" because she lit cigarettes with her fingertips and swallowed fire. She befriended fellow humorist Redd Foxx on the Chitlin' Circuit. Page and Foxx both recorded risqué comedy LPs for Laff Records. Uproar Records recently reissued most of Page's catalog, including these titles: *Mutha Is Half a Word* (1970), *Preach On Sister, Preach On* (1973), *Pipe Layin' Dan* (1975), *Watch It Sucker* (1977), and *Sane Advice* (1979). In spite of the X-rated nature of much of the material, which was suggestive more than vulgar, Page often included church humor and even gospel songs.

Page and Foxx both reached the pinnacle of success on television. After landing the role of Fred Sanford on the NBC sitcom *Sanford and Son* in 1972, Foxx called on his old friend Page to play his nemesis and sister-in-law, Esther Anderson. On the show, he always teased her for being ugly while she condemned him for being a heathen. It was a match made in comedy heaven that pushed their respective comedy records to greater success. After *Sanford and Son* and its various spin-off series ended, Page returned to standup comedy and appeared in a gospel musical, *Take It to the Lord... Or Else!* Page died of diabetic complications on September 14, 2002.

RECOMMENDED RECORDING: *Sane Advice* (Uproar, 2001) is a humorous reissue CD that features the reverent recitation "Bible Cake" and the "Mother's Day" monologue. For a discourse on wayward preachers, check out "Pastor's Angels."

Pam & Dodi

MCA RECORDS HAS never had success with gospel music. They launched the Songbird gospel imprint in the 1980s with a Barbara Mandrell release. They got into gospel again in 1991 with a Vickie Winans release. Then in 2000 they jumped back into the fray with an Ametria CD that also went nowhere. With this track record, is it any surprise that the awesomely talented duo of Pam & Dodi hasn't caught fire yet? Pamela Taylor and Audra "Dodi" Alexander hail from Detroit. They were meant to be MCA's answer to Sony's Mary Mary. Just as talented and attractive as the other duo, Pam & Dodi are still waiting on their payday. They first met in the Motor City in 1996. They shared an interest in gospel and R&B and soon were touring as background vocalists with the Clark Sisters, who have a history in both fields.

After being floored by Pam & Dodi at a 1999 talent showcase, an executive from the Diversified Entertainment Group joined forces with the duo and set out to get them a record deal. He landed them at MCA, which had been wanting to get in on the gospel sales boom that Kirk Franklin kicked off with "The Reason Why We Sing" in 1993. The label paired the duo with top R&B

producers, ranging from Randy Jackson (who produced Whitney Houston and Patti LaBelle) to Steve Huff (best known for his work with Avant and Keke Wyatt), but failed to adequately promote the 2002 self-titled CD (featuring the radio singles "Don't Have To" and "What's Wrong?") and it died an unnecessary death.

Papa San

ALTHOUGH HE HAS not received wide fame in the United States as yet, Papa San is a legendary reggae figure in Jamaica. His name is hallowed in the same vintage as Barrington Levy, Jimmy Cliff, and Bob Marley. Sean Paul, who has achieved superstardom in the US, cites Papa San as one of his core musical influences. Nicknamed the Marathon Man for having the fastest tongue in reggae, Papa San left his fortune and fame as a secular DJ and transformed those gifts into a new ministry as a gospel DJ with a dancehall beat.

One of eight children, Papa San was born Tyrone Thompson on July 1, 1967, in Kingston, Jamaica. The ghetto he was raised in was in the Spanish Town, St. Catherine's province. To amuse himself, Papa San began to make up melodies. "We played drums on the wall. We used saucepans to make sounds. We did many things with very little," he once said. His father was a professional drummer, so it's no surprise that Papa San would eventually want to make music his career. While attending the Macauly All Age School as a teenager, Papa San set out to become a rap DJ. He won the Grand Finals in a 1981 Tastee Talent contest. When he decided on his stage moniker, he chose a childhood nickname. "My bother was given the nickname Dirt Man so I was named 'Sand,' which is pronounced San," he once told GospelFlava.com He wanted to be perceived as an authority figure so he called himself Papa San. Soon, he'd laid down his first professional recording, "Touch My Pants, Touch My Shoes." He followed with national hits such as "I Will Survive," "Legal Rights," and the humorous "Round Table," a duet with Lady G (Janice Fyffe).

In the years since, Papa San shared stages with Beenie Man, Doug E. Fresh, Third World, and Sting. "I had lost five family members in a period of three years and with a lot of other things going around me,

Papa San / Gospo Centric Records promotional photo

I got confused and went into a state of depression," Papa San says. "In searching for truth and comfort I had gotten involved with the Rastafarian cult and later found out it was the wrong faith." He then became a born-again Christian and decided to leave secular dancehall music behind him. "I didn't get the opportunity to tell them about the gospel of Jesus Christ and that saddens me at times," he told *Charisma* magazine in 2004. "This is why I have this zeal for the unsaved to know Jesus Christ. My eldest brother who I was very close to was gunned down at the front of his house and I didn't get a chance to tell him about Jesus Christ." Another brother was also gunned down without receiving salvation. However, Papa San takes pride that his parents and many other relatives have accepted Christ as their savior through his proselytizing. Now signed to Gospo Centric Records, Papa San enjoyed a big gospel hit with his reggae-styled single "Step Pon Di Enemy" from his 2003 *God and I* CD.

Kitty Parham

BEST KNOWN AS a member of the Clara Ward Singers, she was born Catherine Parham on November 16, 1924, in Thomasville, Georgia, and raised in Trenton, New Jersey. Before the most famous aggregation of Ward Singers broke up in 1958 over a money dispute, Parham had joined the group. She led their singles of "Every Day Will Be Sunday" and "I Feel the Holy Spirit" on the Savoy Records label. Since they couldn't get a salary raise from the Wards, Marion Williams and Parham left the group and formed the Stars of Faith. The new group starred in the Broadway musical *Black Nativity* in 1962 and Parham sang the lead on "Most Done Traveling" on the Vee-Jay Records soundtrack LP. Later Parham led such Stars of Faith singles as "Let Jesus Lead You," "We Shall Be Changed," and "One Touch from Jesus." She was a member of Philadelphia's Holy Temple COGIC for 55 years and coached the youth choir for most of that period. She also directed the West District Choir and other community ensembles from time to time. She performed at various Ward Singers reunions over the years and was last found on the Bellmark label. She died on June 27, 2003 in Philadelphia.

RECOMMENDED RECORDINGS: Aside from the aforementioned Ward Singers singles on Savoy, Parham can be heard on a 2001 Collectables reissue of *Black Nativity* and on Marion Williams's 1994 Shanachie CD *My Soul Looks Back.*

Winfield Parker & Praise

A TRADITIONAL-STYLED Southern gospel quintet, Winfield Parker & Praise has won small followings in a number of Southern hamlets without attaining national fame. Born in 1942, Parker began his career as a soul music artist. Backed by the Skydells Band, Parker cut his first 45-rpm single "Sweet Little Girl" for Atco Records in 1967 to little fanfare. From there, he moved on to Ru-Jac Records where he recorded more than a dozen sides such as "Go Away Playgirl," "Oh My Love," and "Fallen Star," all in 1968. He still failed to manage a chart hit. Deals with Arctic Records in 1969 and Wand Records in 1970 produced no better results.

Finally, a 1971–72 tenure with Spring Records (where Millie Jackson and Joe Simon were the major label sellers) netted Parker his only R&B singles chart hit with "S.O.S. (Stop Her On Sight)" which peaked at No. 48 in 1971. Further recordings for G.S.F. ("Baby, Don't Get Hooked On Me"), P&L ("I Wanna Be with You"), and "I Want the World to Know" backed by "Momma Bakes Biscuits" for Calla were the death knell for his soul music career. He began singing gospel in 1985. The group Praise is made up of Vanessa Hunter, Emily Watson, Sarah Parker, Stephanie Raleigh, and Edward Lynn. In April 2003, Parker released his first nationally distributed CD, *Sending Up My Timber*, on Jamie/Guyden Records. The project received steady gospel airplay in the mid-Atlantic United States. Parker then reunited with an old friend, Bunny Sigler, who wrote several O'Jays hits in the 1970s such as "You Got Your Hooks in Me." Sigler produced Parker's stellar, traditional-styled 2005 *Miracle* CD that was released on Liaison Records in Baltimore, Maryland.

Janet Paschal

ONE OF THE MOST soulful belters in Christian inspirational music, Paschal was born October 18, 1956, in Reidsville, North Carolina. After graduating from high school, Paschal spent six years with the Neleons, a Southern gospel group, and later sang on Jimmy Swaggart's weekly television show before pursuing a solo career. Debuting in 1988 with an eponymous album on Word Records, her subsequent recordings have included 1994's *Simple Trust* album, which featured the No. 1 inspirational smash "Take These Burdens." The next album, *The Good Road*, featured the soulful "God Will Make a Way," also popular as an accompaniment tape. She later joined the Spring Hill Records roster where she birthed her most successful CD, *Sweet Life* (1998), which featured the pop-styled Top Ten inspirational hit "Shelter" and sold over 50,000 units. She also performs on Southern gospel programs with the likes of Bill and Gloria Gaither. Paschal has taken a performance sabbatical as she battles cancer.

RECOMMENDED RECORDING: *The Good Road* (Chordant, 1997) features the poignant "Another Soldier's Coming Home" about her war veteran grandfather.

Leon Patillo

A HUGE STAR in the white Christian world in the 1980s, Leon Patillo's music lacked the grit and soulfulness to attract a large black gospel audience. However, his Christian pop music had just enough of a soulful edge to attract young white Christians who wanted to get a little funky without offending their parents.

Patillo was born January 1, 1947, in San Francisco. His parents encouraged his music talents early. "My parents really made me practice," he says. "I remember sitting at the piano in the big bay window of my house hating it because all the other kids were outside playing football. But soon they were coming in, listening to me, telling me what a special gift I had." When he was 14, he began to help lead the choir at church and by the time he was 18 and attending San Francisco State College, Patillo had formed a pop group, the VIPs. Eventually, he moved to Los Angeles where he began to do session work for veteran producer Richard Perry. With Perry's guidance, Patillo did background vocal arrangements for the Pointer Sisters, Martha Reeves & the Vandellas, and Funkadelic, among others. A friend was looking for some extra songs for an LP he was working on, so Patillo gave him a tape of five songs he'd written. The friend tried to sell the songs to Carlos Santana. "Santana told him he wasn't interested in the songs but loved the singer," Patillo recalled.

In 1973, Patillo joined Santana, one of the hottest rock bands in the country. He was the featured vocalist on the gold LPs *Borboletta*, *Festival*, and *Moonflower*. One night in 1974, he attended a Bible study with his girlfriend's brother and realized he needed a relationship with God. As Patillo's faith grew stronger, he began to have qualms about the lyrics in some of Santana's songs. He and Santana were having arguments about it, so Patillo left in 1978 and by 1979 he had won a contract with Word Records. Over the next decade, Patillo turned out a dozen solid Christian radio hits, including "Dance Children Dance," "Star of the Morning," and "Cornerstone," which spent an astounding 16 weeks at No. 1 on the CCM hit radio singles chart.

However, the late 1980s would prove to be taxing on Patillo. The tour for his LP *The Sky Is the Limit* featured an all-female band. Many in the conservative Christian music field couldn't get with the idea of a female band. "About 60 percent really liked it," Patillo once said, "and 40 percent hated it." At the close of the tour, he took a sabbatical and dealt with a painful divorce from his wife, Jackie, who is now a record label executive. "For years, ministry came first," Patillo conceded to *CCM*. "I hadn't put my family or my health first."

The Christian music business isn't as kind to veteran artists as the pop world. When artists fall off the charts in the pop world, there's always an oldies-but-goodies revue that can keep them going. The church world doesn't support artists in that manner. In the 1990s, Patillo hosted a late night musical TV program on TBN, but he was absent from Christian radio. He produced some custom CDs but largely fell out of sight. His name resurfaced briefly in 2003 when he was arrested "over a real estate check," according to his current wife, Renee. "It's not ministry related," she told Charisma News Service. "It's from a long time ago. That's all I know." He quietly served time as a federal inmate at the Central Detention Center in San Bernardino, California. By 2005, Patillo was a free man and back on the Christian concert circuit.

RECOMMENDED RECORDINGS: Much of Patillo's biggest hits now sound a bit dated with their '80s synthesizing. There's been no significant compilation of the music as yet. However, on his Web site, www.leon-patilla.org, he has several of his older LPs such as *I'll Never Stop Loving You* available on CD for the first time.

Elder Saint Samuel Patterson

ESTEEMED CHICAGO pastor and musician Elder Saint Samuel Patterson was born in August 1920 in Morgan City, Mississippi. He was the last of 14 children and started singing when he was five years old. He grew up in Memphis where he was active in his church's junior choir and learned to play both the piano and the guitar during his teen years. He was trained in part by the noted guitarist-evangelist Utah Smith, who prayed that Patterson's hands would be "anointed." By the age of 20, Patterson was playing guitar at revivals for a traveling evangelist. When they arrived in Chicago in 1940 for a revival, Patterson attended St. Paul Church of God in Christ, met its leader, the late Bishop Louis Henry Ford, and decided to relocate to the city. In

1941, he became the first organist in the COGIC denomination and directed a choir consisting of some of the church's most gifted songbirds: Ernestine Washington, Goldia Haynes, Emily Bram, and Jessie Mae Renfro. In 1947, Patterson became Mahalia Jackson's guitarist and played on a few of her recordings, such as "Dig a Little Deeper."

In 1956, Patterson founded St. Samuel's Temple COGIC in Chicago and remained the pastor until he retired in 2001. Possessing a full, bluesy voice (amazingly similar to that of blues legend B.B. King), he wrote and recorded a handful of gospel recordings for small labels, such as "Climbing Higher Mountains" and "Two Wings." However, none of them went anywhere. He also did some recording sessions with Evelyn Gay of the Gay Sisters. Through the years, he became beloved or disliked for his fire-and-brimstone preaching style. His daughter once told a local newspaper, "He would always say, 'I'm not hard, the word of God is hard. You have to live up to the word, it is not going to come down to you.' That is what he taught and that is how he lived." He supported his family by working as a maintenance man for the Chicago Housing Authority. A trouper, Patterson performed right up to the end of his life. His last performance was at a September 5, 2004, midnight musical at his church (where his son has assumed the role of pastor). He died of heart failure on September 16, 2004 at the Advocate Christ Medical Center in a Chicago suburb.

RECOMMENDED RECORDING: *The Soul of Chicago* (Shanachie/SpiritFeel, 1993) is an excellent compilation CD that features some of Chicago's obscure gospel artists recording traditional gospel music in the early 1990s. This set shows that many of them were still in phenomenally great voice, particularly Vernon Price Oliver, who could sing rings around anyone in the business. Holding his own, the set features Patterson on two bouncy recordings, "Confidential God" and "This Train." One of the standout cuts is the Golden Harps' a cappella rendering of Patterson's tune "Two Wings." A must-have for fans of heartfelt, old-school gospel music.

Sandi Patti

ASIDE FROM Amy Grant, no other woman has sold more Christian pop records than Sandi Patti. With eight gold or platinum albums, five Grammy awards, and nearly 40 Dove awards, Patti has clearly established herself as one of the most influential women in Christian music history. Born July 12, 1956, in Oklahoma City, Oklahoma, Patti first sang in church at the age of two. She and her brothers formed a singing group, the Ron Patty Family, that sang at church functions throughout their youth. She grew up idolizing pop superstar Barbra Streisand but stuck to pursuing a gospel career. She eventually studied music at San Diego State University before transferring to Anderson College in Indiana, where she sang in the group New Nature and recorded commercial jingles on the side. Around this time, Patti married John Helvering, who became her manager and helped launch her solo career with the custom LP *For My Friends*. A printer's mistake changed her last name from Patty to Patti, and the name stuck.

In 1979, Patti signed to an independent label, Milk & Honey Records, and that year released the LP *Sandi's Song*. She then began a series of musical ministry tours (such as backing the Bill Gaither Trio) and realized she had found her calling. Beginning in 1982, Patti's soaring soprano began to dominate Christian and inspirational religious music radio with such tunes as "How Majestic Is Your Name," "Sing to the Lord," "In the Name of the Lord," "They Say," (with Deniece Williams) and "More Than Wonderful" (with Larnelle Harris) among others. The steady stream of hits earned Patti the distinction of winning more Dove awards than any other woman— Amy Grant comes in second with 21 Doves. All the while, Patti's gold-selling CDs won her mainstream media attention and appearances on television programs such as *Live with Regis & Kathie Lee*, *The Tonight Show with Johnny Carson*, several TV specials, and a primetime broadcast spot at the Republican National Convention in 1988.

Amid the professional high points, Patti projected a wholesome image as a committed wife and a doting mother to four children. Therefore, her evangelical fan base was rocked when news broke in June 1992 that she had filed for divorce—a Biblical taboo. After rumors began to circulate as to why the marriage ended, Patti admitted that she had committed adultery not once but twice. Many conservative Christian radio stations stopped playing Patti's music and several Christian bookstores stopped selling her music. While her previous concert tours could only be contained in arenas, her tours were often reduced to small churches and for a while she took a sabbatical from the stage. Some fans returned to the fold after Patti's life stabilized, she publicly apologized on *ABC News* for letting her fans down by having an affair, and she married singer Don Peslis. However, finding her way back into the hearts of many Christian radio announcers has been slow. For a woman whose albums used to reach No. 1 on the Christian album sales chart and remain on the charts for a year or longer, her recent chart rankings are humbling. Her most recent project, *Hymns of Faith, Songs of Inspiration*, peaked at No. 28 on the Christian album sales chart and fell off the chart after a week. In another career change, Patti has dropped Patti as her last name and taken on her maiden name of Patty again.

RECOMMENDED RECORDING: *The Finest Moments* (Word Records, 1989) features all of Patti's most lasting hits such as "We Shall Behold Him," "In the Name of the Lord," and her epic Larnelle Harris duet "More Than Wonderful."

Carlton Pearson

ALTHOUGH MANY know him as an evangelist who travels in Christian Charismatic circles, Bishop Carlton Pearson was also one of the top-selling traditional gospel artists of the 1990s. With his slicked-back hair, cowboy boots, GQ suits, and well-enunciated Midwestern twang, he cuts a unique picture in the black gospel world. Still, his series of praise and worship albums that have been recorded at his annual all-star Azusa church conferences have made the old-time gospel popular among younger audiences.

Pearson was born the fifth of seven children in San Diego on March 19, 1953. His father was a businessman who at varying times owned convenience stores and several duplex apartment buildings. He was a self-made man. "Nurturing but intimidating" is how Pearson viewed him. There was always food on the table, but few luxuries. "Actually, we missed several Christmases," Pearson recalls. The family was prominent in the Church of God in Christ (COGIC) denomination. Pearson spent hours under the tutelage of his pastor, Bishop J.A. Blake, his mother, and the elders of the church. When he wasn't in church, Pearson was often working in one of his dad's businesses for 35 cents an hour. His future course was set in the eighth grade. He became intrigued by Oral Roberts's World Action Singers when they performed at the First Assembly of God in San Diego. They were recruiting students and Pearson's mother said, "When you go to college, that's where I want you to go."

No one in his family had ever gone to college and Pearson sensed a little jealousy when no one other than his mother encouraged him to go. His parents had no money to pay his tuition. "I said, if my earthly father can't help me, I'll have to depend on my heavenly father." He shut himself in his room for almost a week and only came out to shower. He prayed that God would make a way for him to get to Oral Roberts University in Tulsa, Oklahoma. On the fifth day, Pearson received a call from a family friend who offered to pay his way to the school and give him $100 a month. The doctor Pearson's mother worked for also gave $100. His prayers were answered and he had enough money for his first year of schooling in 1971.

By the time the money stopped, Pearson had become a World Action Singer with a full scholarship. He immediately caught Oral Roberts's eye. The world-renowned evangelist took Pearson under his wing and mentored him. The World Action Singers were celebrities in the Christian arena, performing around the world. Once he was in the group, Pearson became fast friends with Kathie Lee Johnson (now Gifford) and they helped each other get through stressful times on the road. The group taped TV specials at NBC in Burbank during the summers. "We did TV specials with Rodney Allen Rippey, Pearl Bailey, Robert Goulet, Dale Evans and Roy Rogers, Natalie Cole, and others. We did specials in Alaska, Knott's Berry Farm, [and] England. It was very exciting for a black kid out of the ghetto," he recalls.

In 1975, Pearson began a two-year stint as an associate evangelist for the ORU association where he opened concerts for Roberts's son Richard. By 1977, he began traveling on his own as an evangelist. After one home meeting church service with his family and a few friends, Pearson founded the Higher Dimensions Evangelistic Center in August 1981. The first service drew 75 people, mostly ORU students. "The next week that number doubled," Pearson recalls. "In about a month, that number doubled. In about a year, we were running between 800 and 1,000 people." From the beginning, the church was a "stew" of ethnic groups in keeping with Pearson's goal to break down racial barriers. The church now boasts an adoption agency, a home for unwed mothers, a preschool, and a branch that supplies food to over 500 families a month.

Their first official building was a storefront in the Tulsa suburb of Jenks, which at one time had a 6:00 P.M. curfew for blacks. Pearson jokingly remembers debating whether to have a Sunday night service. By the time Pearson pitched his tent there, the law was obsolete, but the mentality was still there. Pearson shrewdly had many of his white associates front for the church so that no one would hold his race against him. "They wouldn't know I was black until the final signing because my color was a hindrance at that time," he says. Just as the ministry was flourishing, the church experienced a setback. Pearson turned the church's financial responsibilities over to a trusted friend. "I was traveling all over the country preaching at revivals to raise the money to pay the bills and buy the sound system and pay the staff," he recalls. "This man squandered $30,000, which broke my heart. I lost that building, we had to sell it, but we didn't make any money. And I moved into another place and leased it until we had to get out of there. We had no collateral; we had no money to put down on this $1.6 million building that we bought. To this day, I can't tell you how that happened because we had no collateral and no money. A man named Mr. Aperton put the money up and acted as our bank."

Since the 1980s, Pearson has been one of the most in-demand Charismatic evangelists in America. In 1988, he held his first Azusa conference, meant to revive the spirit of the 1906 Azusa Street Revival that brought blacks and whites together and gave birth to classical

Pentecostalism. During the 1990s, the convocation welcomed 10,000 registrants a year. Pearson initially was talking to Word Records and Benson Records about recording the musical segments of the choir before striking a deal with Warner Alliance. The Azusa meetings led to the successful series of *Live at Azusa* praise and worship albums Pearson recorded for Warner Alliance Records and then Atlantic Records. The Azusa CD series has included a who's who of gospel talent and featured radio hits such as Pop Winans on "This Train" and Fred Hammond on "Jesus Be a Fence Around Me." In 2003, Pearson began to catch heat when he openly embraced a theology called "The Gospel of Inclusion," which teaches that all people are saved whether they acknowledge it or not. Many churches began to distance themselves from the controversial teaching. However, Pearson seems to be even more adamant that he's taken the right course and refuses to back down.

RECOMMENDED RECORDING: *The Best of Azusa…Yet Holdin' On* (Word, 2003) features all of the traditional radio hits including Pearson's "Mother Sherman Story," Pop Winans's "This Train," and Fred Hammond's "Jesus Be a Fence Around Me."

Pennington Specials

THIS GROUP WAS founded and managed by radio DJ Charles Pennington in the 1960s. Their lead singer Jean Reed's husband sang with the Violinaires and her son sang with the Evereadys.

Dottie Peoples

THE SONGBIRD OF the South, the dynamic Dottie Peoples is known for the songs "He's an On Time God" and "Handwriting on the Wall." The eldest of ten children, Peoples was born August 1947 in Dayton, Ohio. She learned to love music at her grandmother's church in Alabama. She began singing in high school and church choirs during her teens and later sang with her sisters for awhile. Her mother turned down an opportunity for Peoples to tour with Dorothy Norwood in the late 1960s,

Dottie Peoples / photo by DRE P*hotography /* Dr. D. 2004

but the second time Norwood asked, Peoples joined the Norwood Singers when they were touring with the Rolling Stones. Over the remainder of the decade, Peoples sang jazz music in upscale supper clubs.

In 1980, Peoples married and moved to Atlanta with her husband. She began attending Salem Baptist Church where she helped the pastor, Dr. Jasper Williams, Jr., found Church Door Records. She served as general manager for the label and produced several of its releases. In 1991, she signed with AIR Records and released *Live at Salem Baptist Church*. But it was her 1994 CD *On Time God* that put Peoples on top. The title song was a huge radio hit. She followed with further radio hits such as "Show Up and Show Out," "Testify," and "Shut Up and Start Praying" with Candi Staton. With her perfectly coiffed hair and brilliant, eye-catching costumes, Peoples is as well known for her sense of style as she is for her thunderous, traditional singing manner.

"A rock group called Widespread Panic had seen me on a VH1 gospel special and they said that they fell in love with my voice so they called my record label," she once told Kay3music.com. "They said they had a gospel song and asked me to make a special appearance on it and I did. Then, when they came down to Atlanta, I was their special guest. It was sold out. And it was crazy because afterwards I had people coming up to me crying, saying that they were touched that night—I mean, a rock crowd. They were like, 'We are so glad they invited you.' The group said that they got so many e-mails thanking them for having Dottie Peoples at that show. So again, I can't judge people and I am just glad that they at least acknowledge God."

RECOMMENDED RECORDING: Dottie's CDs tend to be uneven in the song selection quality, so the smart money is on *Greatest Hits*, which features "He's an On Time God," "Handwriting on the Wall," and her other radio hits.

Betty Perkins

THIS SINGER RELEASED a delicious traditional gospel LP entitled *Elijah Rock* on Outstanding Records in 1981, featuring Carl Henderson on piano, Shelby Hurns, Jr., on guitar, and John Terry on organ/keyboards. She tackled church standards such as "You Can't Hide" and mixed them with newer songs such as "Why Do You Wait?"

Perri

THIS SMOOTH-JAZZ/SOFT soul female quartet of sisters Carolyn, Darlene, Lori, and Sharon Perry formed their group when they were in high school in 1981. After seeing a Pat Methany concert, they put together a demo tape of themselves singing many of his songs and sent it to him. Methany responded two days later by inviting the group to back him on a recording session. They toured with Methany between 1983–85. They then earned a recording deal with Zebra/MCA Records in 1986. That resulted in their debut LP *Celebrate*, which included faith-oriented songs such as "He Never Sleeps" and the title track. The album reached No. 14 on the smooth jazz chart. One of the members was at a dentist's office when Anita Baker was there for an appointment. Baker asked the group to back her for a week of concerts in Los Angeles and the group ended up singing behind her for a year. They backed Baker on her *Giving You the Best That I Got* CD and her then-producer Michael Powell produced their next album,

The Flight, circa 1989. The lush single "No Place to Go" revolved around the issue of homelessness and reached No. 41 on the R&B singles chart. The album also included the gospel song "Eternal Life." The group made a few other recordings but drifted from public view by the mid-'90s.

Jerry Peters

AN A-LIST R&B music producer/songwriter in the 1970s, Peters has been instrumental in elevating the technical quality of commercial gospel music since the late 1980s. Born in 1946 in New Orleans, Peters's family moved to Los Angeles when he was 14 years old. He learned to play piano by ear and later honed his skills at California State University before pop crooner Eddie Fisher gave him his first big break as his musical director. From there, he went on the road as a musician with Sonny and Cher before earning his first producer credits with the Los Angeles-based, pop-soul quartet the Friends of Distinction. He wrote two of the group's three biggest hits, "Goin' in Circles" and "Love Me or Let Me Be Lonely." He played on innumerable recording sessions for Tina Turner, Marvin Gaye, Earth, Wind & Fire, and a score of other major artists during the period. Toward the end of the 1970s, Peters served as A&R director at Jerry Butler's Memphis Records label and also for Tabu Records.

In 1984, Word Records executive James Bullard approached Peters about handling production on child prodigy DeLeon Richards's *We Need to Hear from You*. The album won a Grammy nomination and Bullard built a strong relationship with Peters. Peters produced sessions for Word and contributed songs such as "He's My Rooftop," a major gospel hit for the Mighty Clouds of Joy. When Bullard left Word Records to launch a black gospel division at the classical recording label Intersound Records in the early 1990s, Bullard followed him there as an A&R executive. There Peters collaborated with Candi Staton, Vickie Winans, and William Becton, among others. In 1997, Bullard and Peters left Intersound Records and formed MCG Records, which has experienced its biggest success with the smooth, Southern quartet group Lee Williams & the Spiritual QC's. Although he occasionally has gone back to his secular roots for certain projects, Peters has largely devoted himself to gospel. "I had once decided that I was going to devote myself completely to doing gospel music, and only gospel music," Peters once said. "But I felt the Lord telling me that he was going to put me wherever he wanted me to be whenever he wanted me to be there, which led me to maintain and nurture my involvement in the pop industry as well, and things have worked out beautifully. Each genre has had a definite impact on the other in my work."

Neville Peter

AN UNCLUTTERED, simple acoustic ambiance permeates the music of Caribbean gospel performer Neville Peter. Born November 17, 1972, in St. Thomas in the US Virgin Islands, the blind vocalist-pianist was diagnosed with advanced glaucoma when he was six months old. He had limited sight for the first 12 years of his life, though his hearing was always good. He had perfect pitch and began to sing in church at the age of five. By the age of 14, he began to study piano with the intention of pursuing a career in pop music. He left St. Thomas when he was 19 years old and entered the University of Miami where he earned a B.A. in jazz music. He began to sing at clubs in the area and won a 1994 *Down Beat* college jazz award. Soon he was on the road touring with Gladys Knight, Natalie Cole, and Cassandra Wilson.

However, all of his efforts to launch a secular career failed and on New Year's Eve 1998 he dedicated his career to Christian music. He wrote two excellent songs, "He Never Will" and "With a Smile," for Gladys Knight's acclaimed gospel CD *Many Different Roads* later that year. He also began to open for gospel artists such as Richard Smallwood, Donnie McClurkin, and the Kurt Carr Singers. In 2003, Peter premiered his debut CD *Messages from the Throne of Grace* on his own recording label. His voice is reminiscent of Stevie Wonder with a slight rasp, while his pop sound recalls early James Taylor. His songs are reflective and have an unplugged, late-night, Quiet Storm quality. The project won three of six Marlin awards (the Caribbean's answer to the Stellar awards).

Pilgrim Jubilees

THEY AREN'T THE best known quartet in gospel, but they are certainly one of the longest standing. They distinguished themselves early on with an engaging mix of delta blues and gritty hard singing during a period when most quartets were noted for tight vocal harmonies and somewhat rural country instrumentation. The history of the Pilgrim Jubilees began with Elgie Graham, who was born November 27, 1919 in Houston, Mississippi. In 1934, he formed a gospel duet with Willie Johnson. They were weekend church singers until they expanded their duo into a group in 1944 with the additions of Graham's brother Theopolis, Monroe Hatchett, and Leonard Brownlee. They sauntered on until about 1950 when Elgie moved to Chicago seeking better employment and left the group to disband. His younger brothers Theopolis, Cleve, and Clay all followed him to Chicago in 1951. In 1952, Clay and Cleve took it upon themselves to relaunch the Pilgrim Jubilees with their two brothers. They more aggressively sought concert dates and soon had a full schedule that was a bit much for their considerably older brothers. Theopolis and Elgie retired under the strain and the remaining brothers brought on baritone Major Roberson, lead singer Percy Clark, bassist Roosevelt English, and guitarist Richard Crume. While operating from their two separate barber shops, Cleve and Clay handled booking and snatched the group's first recording contract with Nashboro Records in 1952 where they recorded tunes such as "Don't Let Jesus Down" and Dorothy Love Coates's "I Got Jesus (and That's Enough)." They didn't produce any major hits there, although the records packed enough steam to keep them working. Roberson and Crume took matters into their own hands in finding a definitive hit record. After some prayer and meditation, they composed "Stretch Out," which they began to perform in their concerts in the late '50s. While singing in Atlanta, Peacock Records radio promoter Dave Clark spotted their act and spoke to his label about signing the group. After signing to the label in 1960, their debut LP *Walk On* finally brought them national gospel prominence in 1961. Buoyed by a new recording of "Stretch Out," which sold over 100,000 copies, after a solid decade of performing they were able to go full-time into singing. Crume left to join the Soul Stirrers, but the core membership of the Graham brothers and Roberson remained.

Later, Ben Chandler, Bobby McDougal, and Michael Atkins would join the group. Their success slowed down in the 1970s, but they continued to record sporadically for Chance and Songbird before joining Savoy Records in 1979. At Savoy they saw a career rebound in the '80s with hits such as "Rich Man, Poor Man" and "Whensoever I Pray." By the end of the decade, Clay's daughter with Josephine Howard of the Caravans, Miki Howard, had become an R&B star with Top Ten hits such as "Baby Be Mine" and "Love Under New Management." She often mentioned her father's career with the Pilgrim Jubilees in interviews, which brought more attention to the group. In 1987, they signed with Malaco Records and released the hit LPs *Gospel Roots* and *Back to Basics*. In the '90s, the Graham brothers' cousin Eddie Graham and Fred Price joined the group. Their 1994 LP *Revival*, a live recording of their better known hits, has proven to be one of their biggest of recent years. The title song of their 1997 CD, *Trouble in the Street*, is a tasty, urban-flavored blues cut featuring Clay Graham's raspy tenor, which eerily resembles that of the late great O.V. Wright. Although they continue to perform, the Jubilees' advancing age has slowed down their performances a bit, and while they are still excellent performers, they lack much of the fiery abandon that was once their trademark.

Pilgrim Travelers

PROBABLY BLACK gospel's first showmen, the Pilgrim Travelers put on the type of entertaining program (rhythmic choreography and stellar vocalizing) in the 1940s that the Temptations would become known for in the 1960s. Formed by Houston-based Joe Johnson and Willie Davis in 1936, the quartet (which included cousins Kylo Turner and Keith Barber) didn't make big strides until they moved to Los Angeles in 1942. Initially, their sound was based on the two major gospel groups of the day, the Soul Stirrers and the Golden Gate

Pilgrim Travelers / courtesy of Specialty/Fantasy Records

Quartet. However, their vocals distinguished them from the pack. Turner was a baritone, but he stretched his voice into a crooning falsetto while Barber sang smoother songs.

J.W. Alexander, a light tenor and former Negro League football player, became the group's manager in 1945 and repackaged the group. Whereas before they would just stand onstage and sing, he pushed them to stretch their voices and to add athletic choreography to their performances to get the church women riled up. It worked. When the guys would jump off the stage and run down the aisles, women would fall out like later generations would at a rock concert. The group signed to Specialty Records in 1947 where the engineer, Bunny Robyn, even miked the floor to catch the sound of their feet moving to the music, thus the phrase "walking in rhythm" that followed them.

Among their greatest hits were the jubilee-styled "Jesus Met the Woman at the Well" and the blues "Mother Bowed." Their doo woppish, a cappella favorite,

"A Wonderful Time Up There," was a No. 4 pop hit in 1958 for Pat Boone. In 1950, Barber's voice was virtually destroyed in a car accident. Although he remained with the group, it wasn't the same. Meanwhile, across the way, Sam Cooke was taking the Soul Stirrers to new heights of fame. Davis had been replaced by Jesse Whitaker, and Turner had been consumed by wine and women. Alexander brought a string of artists through to keep the group alive, including a young Lou Rawls. The gospel audience was rapidly losing interest so Alexander dropped "Pilgrim" from their name and they began to sing secular music that failed to create a new audience. By 1959 the group was disbanded. By the end of the 1960s, Rawls had launched a successful pop career in the style of Nat King Cole, and Turner and Barber were prematurely dead. Whitaker returned to his parents' farm in Missouri. Over the years, Alexander—wealthy from his partnerships with Sam Cooke and his other business ventures—was the spokesperson for the Golden Age of Gospel until his death on July 8, 1996, in Hollywood.

Plus One

BACK IN 1999 when the Backstreet Boys and 'N Sync ruled the pop charts and the hearts of teenage girls (and a few guys too) worldwide, Barry Landis of Atlantic Records Christian music division and Mitchell Solarek put their heads together to create a boy band that their own kids and Christian teenagers in general would embrace. They held auditions and picked five stand-up church boys (three of whom were pastor's kids). The quintet of Nate Cole (born May 19, 1981, in Houston, Texas), Nathan Walters (born March 24, 1978, in Atlanta, Georgia), Jason Perry (born June 1, 1982, in Ft. Thomas, Kentucky), Jeremy Mhire (born May 3, 1980, in Charlotte, North Carolina), and Gabe Combs (born December 11, 1979, in Salem, Oregon) was signed to veteran pop producer David Foster's 143 Records, which was distributed by Atlantic Records. Through Foster's deep industry connections and a big marketing budget, Plus One's debut CD *Promise* rolled out with a huge amount of publicity, including appearances on *Live with Regis & Kathie Lee* and the soap opera *Days of Our Lives*.

Like New Kids on the Block in the 1980s and 'N Sync in the '90s, Plus One's sound was pop with an R&B coating. Songs such as "God Is in this Place," "Here in My Heart," and "When Your Spirit Gets Weak" were all No. 1 Christian radio singles. In spite of coverage in all the major mainstream magazines and oodles of national TV appearances, the CD reached No. 1 on the CCM album chart in 2000, but only No. 76 on the Hot 100 pop album chart. However, the group was never as big as their press projected. Middle-aged Christian music artists have achieved gold status on far less media attention, and for the seven-figure money pumped into Plus One, their project should have generated multi-platinum sales. Their debut was clearly not a successful record. The group's 2002 sophomore CD *Obvious* only reached No. 3 on the CCM chart but reached No. 29 on the Hot 100. Still, it did not achieve gold status.

Those were the least of their troubles, however. The group dissed their own *Christmas* CD as "forgettable" to the press, and both Jeremy Mhire and Jason Perry left the group for other endeavors. Furthermore, there was financial fallout from a disastrous concert tour, and the group was not pleased with their bubblegum pop sound. They tired of being viewed as pinup boys instead of real musicians. "Atlantic wanted us to record another pop album and work with Avril Lavigne's and Nick Carter's producers. Everything they wanted us to do was on another page from what we had in mind, so we left and went to Inpop," Walters told *CCM* magazine.

Their fall 2003 Inpop debut *Exodus* was an alternative rock venture. They wrote and produced most of the music, which didn't appeal to many of their past fans and only netted them a few new ones. "There was one person who waited in line to say, 'Here's your poster back; I don't like you anymore,'" Walters told *CCM*. "We've even had guys who've come to a show ready to make fun of us and ended up saying they looked forward to buying the new record." That particular CD was their worst seller ever. It struggled to reach No. 17 on the CCM album chart and missed the Hot 100 altogether. As of this writing, the group's future is in limbo.

Point of Grace

AFTER THE ROUSING success of their eponymous debut album (five No. 1 Christian radio hits), Point of Grace was hailed by the music media as Christian music's answer to Diana Ross & the Supremes. Heather Floyd Payne (born January 18, 1970, in Abilene, Texas), Denise Jones (born March 22, 1969, in Norman, Oklahoma), and Terry Jones (born May 17, 1970, in Marin County, California) all began singing as the Oauchitones when they were attending Ouachita Baptist University in Arkadelphia, Arkansas. Circa 1991 they added Shelley Phillips Breen (born May 1, 1969, in Belleville, Illinois) to the group and changed their name to Say So. They began touring and won first place at the annual Christian Artists Music Seminar in Colorado, which is where Word Records executives first spotted them. They were signed to the label shortly thereafter. The problem was, there was already a group named Say So, so they started looking for an alternative name. John Mays, who signed them to Word, came up with Point of Grace. "John told us that he read the phrase in a book by C.S. Lewis," Heather once said. "Something like, 'Every day, we as Christians live at the point of God's grace.' That is what it means to me. Always living in his grace."

In the dozen years since their 1993 launch, Point of Grace has become the bestselling female group in the history of Christian music. Just like the Supremes, Point of Grace has continually been ignored by Grammy voters unimpressed with their SoundScans and arena tours. Along the way, they've enjoyed six gold and two platinum albums. Although Point of Grace's sound is upbeat, slick pop, there is a soulful, gospel undercurrent to their music. It shows up well on Terry Jones wrapping her dramatic soprano around "The Wonder of It All" or Heather Payne emoting those high notes on "I'll Be Believing" or "Better Days." Leigh Cappillino (born April 18, 1969, in Belton, South Carolina), who sang with the Christian superchoir TRUTH in the early 1990s, replaced Terry Jones who has retired from the group to devote herself to raising her children.

RECOMMENDED RECORDING: *24* (Word Entertainment, 2003) is the essential Point of Grace collection.

It features all 24 of their staggering No. 1 hit CCM singles and one bonus track on a two-CD set.

Sister Lucille Pope

ONE OF THE MOST popular Southern-styled gospel quartets of the 1970s, Sister Lucille Pope & the Pearly Gates enjoyed hits such as "Somebody's Gone" and "Jesus Was by My Side." She was born Lucille Hall on January 12, 1936, in Concord, Georgia. She was the youngest of the eight children and formed the Pearly Gates with two of her brothers and a brother-in-law. They were regular performers on radio announcer Ed Shane's 15-minute broadcast on WGRI in Griffin, Georgia, in the early '60s. Soul legend Otis Redding was a fan back in those days. Shane had the group record a 45-rpm single of "Almighty God" (Pope on lead) and "Early One Morning" (Larry Bivins on lead) for his small Eddo Records label. After the song began to make some noise, Vee-Jay Records picked it up and

Lucille Pope / courtesy of AIR *Records*

reissued it nationally in 1964. Later that year, Chess Records picked up the group's "Jesus Tore My Heart to Pieces," which was another big hit in early 1965. Sadly, the group didn't record again until the middle 1970s. By that time, Pope's first husband, Willie Pope, had died and her second husband, Louis Alexander, had joined the group as organist. The group signed to Nashboro Records in 1975 and enjoyed an immediate hit with the sad ballad "Somebody's Gone." After Nashboro closed down, the Pearly Gates signed with AIR Records in 1982. They have recorded stunning quartet music such as the 1999 live CD *Real Christians Stand Up*, which showcases Pope's rustic, powerful vocals against the male harmony of the Pearly Gates. Pope has seen her fame and prestige grow abroad due to compilations such as the various Nashboro reissue projects that have been released over the last 15 years. "A lot of people would have sued them whether they got a dime or not," Pope says of the compilation reissues of their Nashboro music. "That stuff was just a dummy track. They put it out and refused to let us fix it. Shannon Williams laid back in his chair and said, 'Sue me.' I said, 'God got it now,' but I'll go to my grave and the world won't know it. He was supposed to let us know before he put that music out. It was Horseman on WLAC just happened to play it and I [nearly] had a heart attack. God wasn't going to let them keep using people like that. They don't believe in God because otherwise they would know God [is] going to get them. Vengeance is his."

Tom and Gwen Pope

THE NO. 1 URBAN NEWS and information radio network in the United States, the Powernomics Radio Network reaches over 1 million listeners daily. Anchored by the daily four-hour call-in program *The Tom Pope Show*, the network has become a tremendous outlet for gospel music. The network begins and ends with the dynamic duo of Tom and Gwen Pope.

Tom was born December 16, 1948, in Sandusky, Ohio. His first industry job was as a copyboy at a radio station. He studied telecommunications at Ohio State University before he became a director at WTVN television in Columbus, Ohio. He later took announcing positions at the Voice of America and WHUR in Washington, DC. Washington, DC, native Gwen Pope (born April 2, 1948) was a school teacher on vacation in South America when she met Tom in 1973. "We met on the beach of Ipanema," she remembers. "Everyone speaks Portuguese there and he walked up and asked me for the time in broken Spanish. Everybody else was in bathing suits and he was standing there in slacks. I said, 'Boy, where are you from?'" They struck up a conversation and exchanged phone numbers. Back in the States, they began courting three months later and married in 1974.

"He was at the top of his game, but there was a void in his life," Gwen says. Tom became a born-again Christian and joined Rev. John Cherry's Full Gospel AME Zion Church. "Tom decided to leave WHUR while he was at the top of his game and go into ministry." When the church leadership noted his dedication to the church, Tom was appointed their director of media between 1987 and 1989. After the church membership mushroomed and expanded, Pope moved on to create new horizons. In 1989, he formed Pope Media Relations, which handled dignitaries such as former DC mayor Marion Barry and the late Dr. Betty Shabazz. In the early 1990s, Pope founded the TPT News radio network and later established the Dudley Broadcasting Network for a black cosmetics firm. However, circa 1997 the Popes took a faith walk and launched their own network, Powernomics Radio Network. The name for the network came from Pope's colleague, Dr. Claud Anderson, who wrote the bestselling book *PowerNomics: The National Plan to Empower Black America*. "I have been on the front line battling for solutions to the socioeconomic challenges facing our society," Pope told the *New Pittsburgh Courier* newspaper in 1999. "I have asked the hard questions, never complaining, rather looking for those solutions within ourselves."

The network's flagship program is *The Tom Pope Show*, which features lively commentary and interviews with headliners. Tom does the interviews and Gwen books the guests, who have included notables such as former First Lady Hilary Rodham Clinton and Bishop T.D. Jakes. Because of their faith, the Popes feature leading gospel artists and religious figures, along with the hard news personalities that their audience has come to expect. "There are only so many opportunities that allow one to touch someone else's life in a real way," Pope told the *Courier*. "My staff and I work to make our show such a vehicle." After a $1 million investment in the network, the ongoing problem has been steady advertising revenue. "For some reason, Madison Avenue and Fortune 200 companies don't value black listeners," Pope told the *Washington Business Journal* in November 1999. "Urban formats have the numbers but don't get the same rate." Further complicating that issue is their determination to keep the network clean. "Through PRN, we have raised a standard in radio broadcasting by not airing beer, liquor, cigarette, or lottery advertisements," Tom told *Purpose* magazine in 2003. "Of course, this means we cannot compromise. We have turned down money from companies with these types of products because of our commitment to the Lord."

"Genial Gene" Potts

IN 1947, FRANCIS FITZGERALD launched Charlotte, North Carolina's WGIV radio station in his two-car garage. He obtained one of the first post–World War II broadcast licenses and named the station WGIV for "We're G.I. Veterans." He had his eye on a potential disc jockey, Gene Potts, whom he thought might be a good fit for his station. Fitzgerald dispatched him out on a test run at the Excelsior Club to host a remote broadcast of the Calypso Four. Fitzgerald liked his work and gave him the job as the morning announcer. To overcome a stammering problem, Potts began to rhyme in an easy rap that became his trademark. One of his famous lines was, "We're setting the pace for others to trace. This is Genial Gene on the air; have you got 15 minutes to spare?" He was one of the Original 13, the first group of full-time black radio announcers in the Southern US.

Sara Jordan Powell

ALTHOUGH SHE'S AN established artist in the gospel world, Sara Jordan Powell's recognition within the

COGIC denomination is iconic. One of gospel's great lyric sopranos, Powell made her name known in the 1970s with a fistful of radio hits such as "Touch Somebody's Life" (1972) and "When Jesus Comes" (1977). She's never achieved superstar status, but she's performed in venues delegated for megastars. She's performed for Presidents Carter and Clinton, as well as Mother Teresa. President Reagan appointed her to the "Year of the Bible" committee during his presidential administration.

The third of 12 children, Powell was born October 6, 1938, in Houston, Texas, and was raised in the COGIC church denomination. Her father was the pastor at Turner Memorial COGIC and her mother was a homemaker. Powell was two years old when she first sang "I Need Thee, O I Need Thee" in front of an audience. Bishop C.H. Mason (who died in 1961) picked her up at the age of two and said a prayer of dedication over Powell's life. "I believe that anointing has followed me all of my life," she says. Her father took his wife and kids on the road as a ministry calling itself the Jordan Family. In order to do this, he bought a long limousine. "We were laughed at," she recalls. "He would pick us up and take us to school, and we were ashamed because the kids would laugh because that long car turns the corner and part was on one street and the rest was on another street." The program for the family group included Powell's father speaking, her mother playing piano, and their children singing.

Later, Powell attended Texas Southern University where she majored in English and minored in history and drama. After graduating, she spent the summer with her sister and brother-in-law, who was a pastor in Chicago. Her sister pushed her to join the board of education there, but her parents really wanted her to come back home. When they realized that Powell wanted to stay, they relented and she took a job at Inglewood High School. While living in the city, Powell sang in various churches. The word spread about the great soprano from Houston. "Sallie Martin called and said, 'I just want to meet you. Can you come over and we'll visit a little bit?'" Powell recalls. Powell was awed to meet the legendary singer. The first time she visited, Martin asked her to sing a song and Martin loved it. "That summer when school was out she asked me if I'd tour with her,"

Powell continued. Kenneth Wood was the pianist and the group was rounded out by Eugene Smith, Cora Martin, and others. They toured the East Coast in a station wagon during the 1964–65 season.

In Chicago, Powell met and married her husband. When her father became ill and passed away, they moved back to Houston to help Powell's mother, who wasn't able to handle the business issues of the church. Powell began to teach in Houston area schools. One of her students saw her sing at a church and asked the school principal if Powell could sing at their graduation ceremony. After she sang at the school, the word spread around Houston and Powell had so many singing engagements that she considering leaving her teaching job.

Powell was performing at a function in Los Angeles where James Cleveland spotted her performance circa 1971. He asked her to meet with him the next morning. He had seen her sing before but never had the opportunity to speak to her. He asked her if she had ever considered recording. She had not. "He said there may be people who never meet you and may never see you in person, but your music may touch their lives because it's anointed," she recalls him saying. He said that he'd be in Dallas within a month for his GMWA con-

Sara Jordan Powell / 1982 LP *cover*

vention and would like to introduce her to his producer and take it from there. Powell said that the new school year would be starting around that time and that she would not be available. Cleveland then asked her to come up to Dallas on a weekend, and she told him that she and her husband would pray about it. He gave her some music to listen to and told her that if she had songs of her own, maybe they could do those as well. A few days later, Cleveland called and asked what they decided. She said they would come. "My husband and I went there on a Thursday," she says. "Went up to his suite and he had a grand piano in there. His producer was there as well. Rev. Cleveland started to play 'Must Jesus Bear the Cross Alone and All the World Go Free.' As I sang that song in his room, his producer said 'Let's go in the studio right now.'"

They went into a studio that afternoon and recorded the whole album within two hours. The debut LP *James Cleveland Presents Sara Jordan Powell* included her first major hit, "Prayer Will Move It." Over the course of her years with Savoy, Powell recorded mostly traditionally styled tunes, usually with contemporary piano accompaniment by Carl Preacher. He had heard her perform and invited her to sing at an event for Houston's Southeastern Choir. Shirley Joiner and Brenda Waters from Preacher's group, known as BCS (for Brenda, Carl, and Shirley), backed Powell on her *I Find No Fault* LP. Preacher then became her accompanist for the next 13 years. "We went to India, Japan, all over Europe," he says. During the last half of the 1970s, Powell was known for her semi-operatic soprano and her ear-piercing vocal gymnastics. Among the other fine recordings she cut included "God Willed It So," "Touch the Hem of His Garment," and "I Must Tell Jesus." However, her biggest hit remains her 1977 remake of the Banks Brothers' 1963 track, "When Jesus Comes."

Powell developed a true fan in soul music icon Ray Charles. Rev. Cleveland had recorded one of Powell's albums at Charles's RPM recording studio and there was a tape left behind. When Ray Charles came in the next morning, he played it—Powell's "I Ain't Got Time to Die." Charles loved it and played it virtually every morning when he came in the studio to start his day. Five years later, Charles was booked to do a Christmas concert in Germany with Aretha Franklin. Franklin had a recording session conflict and bowed out. Charles then sought Roberta Flack, who was also busy in the studio. Charles called Ruth Bowen, Franklin's booking agent in New York, and asked if there was any other way it could work out. Powell's agent at the agency overheard the conversation and asked to speak to Charles. He asked Charles if he would consider taking another artist, a gospel artist. Charles asked who it was and her agent said it was Sara Jordan Powell. "Oh, yes, I'll take her, I listen to her music all the time," Charles said. Powell went to Germany with him and sang Christmas music.

When she returned, Powell's label (New Orleans–based Power House Records) began to suggest that she engage Charles to produce her next LP in 1982. Charles agreed to produce the gospel project on the condition that he have complete control. "When Carl Preacher and I went out to Los Angeles, Ray said that he had my tape and that he listened to it every day," she recalls. "He said, 'That's how I knew who you were, so I agreed to do this. But I must tell you, I will have total control.' [This] allowed me the opportunity to really sit with him and talk with him about my convictions and my commitment to the Lord. He told me that he reads his Bible and that he knows God in a different way. He said, 'I may not go to church every Sunday like other people, but I have a God consciousness. I talk to him and he leads me and guides me.' … I don't feel everyone has to be in church to have a relationship [with God] and I appreciated and respected his opinion about that, so we had a good working relationship. It's just that when it came to the music, it had to be his way."

At their planning session, Charles asked Powell what she wanted to record. She and Preacher played their rendition of "America, the Beautiful." She recalls, "He said, 'Nah, we're not gonna put that on there.' Well, later he used it himself! He got all of the notoriety. I sang that song for him and he loved it. He said that's a beautiful song. I like the way you did it. That was my arrangement and he didn't want me to put that on there and I asked why. He said, 'Just let me handle this,' so I did." The resulting LP, *Affectionately Sara*, was a mix of traditional church numbers and soulful mid-tempo songs. Considering that Powell was a hot commodity on the gospel market and that Charles was a recording legend, it's criminal that the album was not a success. There

were many tracks that could have received radio airplay. The ballad "Thank You Lord (My Prayer)" and the funky chords of "There Is a Way" would have been great candidates. There was no major press highlighting the collaboration and the album failed to find an audience. "I think they got some of their money out of it," Powell says of the label. "But I didn't get anything."

Although the label missed the mark, Powell wasn't totally happy with the project anyway. "I wanted to have more control," she says. "When a person is signed with somebody you are beholden to them. I'm not the kind of person who whines so I worked with them on that. But it was not one of my happiest experiences. After that was done, the company folded. I didn't feel that I did my best. And the problem was that Ray also wanted to control. Everybody wanted the control and I didn't have anything to say. I'd say, 'Ray, can I do that verse this way' and he'd say, 'No no no, you do it the way I told you.' I wasn't free to sing. I was so disappointed."

Following that period, Powell attended Southwest Theological Seminary and earned a Masters degree from the University of St. Thomas. "I'm not a preacher, I'm a reacher," she says of her post-graduate studies. "Over the many years of my life, I have been so disappointed with those who confess but don't possess. I said I'm going to read the Bible all the way through, because I wanted to know for myself that this journey was it…. That it really does pay to serve Jesus. But I wanted to know in a more intimate way. I found the trip is worth the trophy. I wanted to hear the scholars take on issues and I just wanted a deeper understanding. I wanted to communicate to people the love of Jesus." She and her husband moved to Tulsa, Oklahoma, in the 1980s for him to attend law school. Powell became an academic advisor at Oral Roberts University. She also spent a decade as the executive director of the Fine Arts Department for the Church of God in Christ (COGIC). She was inducted into the Oklahoma Jazz Hall of Fame in 2003, joining the ranks of bluesman Taj Mahal, crooner Patti Page, and jazzman Dave Brubeck.

Powell has many other dreams. She and her husband are considering moving West where he'd like to set up a retreat center for ministers and her hope is to open a bed and breakfast in the same complex. "That's one of my hidden talents—cooking," she says. "I do a great seafood gumbo…[The secret is that] you have to know how to do the roux. You put that flour in the skillet and let it almost burn. And when you put that roux in the gumbo everything comes together." However, Powell doesn't want her kitchen cooking to replace the cooking she does onstage. She does want to record again. "Malaco has made some inquiry, but I don't want to go back to that," she says. "I'm not going to play games with the rest of my life. I really can't do hip-hop. I would like to do something with the London Symphony Orchestra or something like that. It has to be meaningful."

RECOMMENDED RECORDING: *The Best of Sara Jordan Powell* (Savoy/Malaco Records, 2004) is an 18-track compilation of every one of Powell's major hits from the 1970s, such as "Touch the Hem of His Garment" and "When Jesus Comes." Powell says, "I don't get a dime from that." Through the persistence of Powell fan and Harrisburg, Pennsylvania, radio announcer Stephen Linen, Malaco issued the project. "They've done all kinds of reissues since the 1970s and I've never gotten anything from them," she says. "I think out of respect they would send me a copy or two, but it was Stephen who sent it to me."

Elvis Presley

HE WAS CROWNED the King of Rock and Roll, though Ike Turner, Chuck Berry, and Little Richard all preceded him and have just as much claim to the throne. When it comes to the more than 100 different albums he sold during his lifetime, it's no doubt that he was the king of rock 'n' roll sales. Born dirt poor on January 8, 1935, in Tupelo, Mississippi, Presley grew up with a love for both gritty black gospel music and smooth Southern gospel music. After he moved to Memphis as a teenager, he became acquainted with even more black culture. He attended concerts by black blues singers such as Rufus Thomas and learned the big R&B hits of the day such as Big Mama Thornton's "Hound Dog" and Arthur Crudup's "That's All Right Mama"—songs that would later become much bigger hits when he recorded them. Producer Sam Philips had success with Rufus Thomas

and other black artists, but the sales always reached a certain ceiling. He was looking for a handsome, young white boy who could make black music palatable to white teenagers. Presley's 1954–55 recordings made some impact in that market, but it wasn't until he left Sun and signed with RCA Records that his career took off at a phenomenal pace with rock 'n' roll standards such as "Hound Dog," "Jailhouse Rock," and "Love Me Tender." That career has been well documented elsewhere, so it won't be rehashed here. In 1960, he recorded his first gospel LP, *His Hand in Mine*, which featured songs associated with black gospel artists such as "Milky White Way" and "I'm Gonna Walk Dem Golden Stairs." Presley's 1967 LP *How Great Thou Art* featured covers of Dorothy Love Coates's "Where Could I Go But to the Lord" and Charles Tindley's "Stand by Me." Presley died of mysterious complications (either heart ailments or drug overdose) on August 16, 1977, in Memphis.

Billy Preston

NICKNAMED THE FIFTH Beatle because of his extensive work with the Beatles in the late 1960s, Billy Preston went on to popularize psychedelic soul instrumentals and organ-peddle romps such as "Nothing from Nothing" in the 1970s before returning to his gospel roots in the early 1980s. Born September 9, 1946, in Houston, Texas, Preston began playing piano at age three. During his youth, he directed special performances of the Houston Symphony Orchestra and the Voices of Victory Baptist Church Choir. By the age of ten, Preston was playing organ for Mahalia Jackson and portrayed W.C. Handy as a child in the 1958 film *St. Louis Blues*. A huge fan of Ray Charles's vocal style, Preston first played secular music on a 1964 European tour with Little Richard. He met Sam Cooke on that tour and recorded the LP *The 16 Year Old Soul* for Cooke's SAR Records label. He then recorded *The Most Exciting Organ Ever* for Vee-Jay Records in 1966 and other albums for a variety of labels. It was while Preston was a member of the house band on the *Shindig* TV series that Ray Charles recruited him for his band. It was when Charles was performing on a BBC television special in London that Beatle George Harrison spotted

Preston and signed him to Apple Records. Aside from releasing his own album *That's the Way God Planned It*, Preston played on Beatles classics such as "Let It Be" and "Get Back." He also played on George Harrison's "My Sweet Lord," and Preston enjoyed a hit with his own version of the song in 1971.

Over the next three years, Preston enjoyed four certified million-sellers with the Top Ten pop and R&B singles "Outa-Space," "Will It Go 'Round in Circles," "Space Race," and "Nothing from Nothing." His songs were recorded by A&M Records labelmates Captain & Tennille ("Song of Joy") and Joe Cocker ("You Are So Beautiful"). After a leap to Motown Records, Preston's hit streak stopped. However, he enjoyed one more Top 5 pop smash with 1980's lush ballad "With You I'm Born Again," which he performed with Syreeta Wright. Preston recorded two average gospel LPs for Myrrh Records, *Behold!* (1978) and *Universal Love* (1980). However, neither project was a bestseller. His 1986 LP *Ministry of Music* reached the gospel Top 40. He has recorded a number of gospel LPs for a variety of small labels in the years since. The best is perhaps *Words & Music: Levitical Worship*, featuring the stirring ballad "Praise God," which demonstrates stellar organ work by Preston and a spoken recitation by Los Angeles radio announcer Edna Tatum. Preston also recorded a very good gospel album with a retro-soul aura with 2001's *Music from My Heart* on MCG Records. In between albums, Preston spent much of the 1990s tangling with the law on numerous occasions. He was charged, at varying times, with sexual harassment, cocaine possession, and insurance fraud. The two-time Grammy winner has also survived a 2001 bout with kidney disease.

Kelly Price

A DYNAMIC SINGER in the mold of Aretha Franklin, Kelly Price was born April 4, 1973, in Queens, New York. She grew up in the COGIC denomination and made her entry into the music business as a background vocalist for Mariah Carey on pop songs such as "Dream Lover" and "I'll Be There." She became an in-demand session singer for rappers and singers alike, and signed to Def Jam/Island Records in 1997. She

then recorded a series of bestselling gold or platinum R&B CDs that produced hit singles such as "Friend of Mine" and "As We Lay." Each of Price's albums included a gospel song, such as "Lord of All," "I Know Who Holds Tomorrow," "Messiah Has Come," and the Clark Sisters' "You Brought the Sunshine." In 2005, Price was a headliner with the sold-out 20-city "Sisters in the Spirit II" concert tour that also featured Yolanda Adams and Prophetess Juanita Bynum.

Prince

PERHAPS THE MOST innovative musical performer of the last 25 years, Prince painted quite a tableau in the 1980s. His bizarre costumes, the scantily clad beauty queen musicians in his bands, his near-pornographic LP cover poses, and simulated sex on concert stages made him a hot topic in entertainment circles. He was born Prince Rogers Nelson on June 7, 1958, in Minneapolis, Minnesota. His parents were both jazz musicians. Prince taught himself to play guitar, drums, and piano by his early teens. He made a demo tape of songs that he got Minneapolis businessman Owen Husney to peddle for him and ended up landing a recording contract with Warner Bros. Records when he was 19 years old. Influenced by funk bands and old-school soul artists, Prince's 1978 debut LP was launched on the provocative single "Soft and Wet." Over the next decade, Prince would thrill audiences and scare censors with his graphic sexual scenarios that spoke of incest, masturbation, oral sex, and lust (as demonstrated on "P Control"). However, his big crossover hits were tamer songs such as "Little Red Corvette," "Kiss," "Purple Rain," and "Wanna Be Your Lover." Regardless of the subject matter, Prince has repeatedly mixed religious metaphors with sexuality in his music, prompting one music critic to say that Prince makes salvation sexy and makes sex our salvation.

Over the years, Prince has battled Warner Bros. over artistic control and royalty accountings. In protest of what Prince considered slavery at the hands of Warner Bros., he changed his name to a symbol and then to The Artist. When his contract with Warner ended on December 31, 1999, Prince reclaimed his stage name of Prince. Through the influence of funk legend Larry Graham of Grand Funk Railroad, Prince converted to the Jehovah's Witness faith in the '90s. He chronicled his conversion on the 2001 CD *The Rainbow Children*, a jazzy soul project filled with religious symbolism and message material. The album was a Top 40 R&B hit and reached No. 4 on the *Billboard* independent album sales chart. During his hugely successful 2004 nationwide concert tour, Prince cut some of his more sensual hits such as "International Lover" from his play list and tweaked the lyrics of some other songs. "I have a responsibility to [young fans] to perform in a manner that I would like my children to be performed in front of," he told *The Early Show* on CBS that summer. "I've changed," he told *Entertainment Weekly* that year. "I'm a different person. I'm about the present and moving forward. New joke, new anecdote, new lesson to be discovered," he says. "You know that old lady in *Sunset Boulevard*, trapped in her mansion and past glories? Getting ready for her close-up? I don't run with that."

Desmond Pringle

DESMOND PRINGLE'S golden tenor can be heard on some of the finest recordings of the last decade. That's him backing up R. Kelly on "I Believe I Can Fly." That's Dez wailing behind Yolanda Adams on her 1996 *Yolanda Live in Washington* album. That's him again on Marvin Sapp's breakthrough single "Not the Time, Not the Place" in 1997. He was also bringing up the rear on the debut CD of Kristy Starling from NBC's *Today Show* talent contest. However, Pringle's fame isn't just in the background. Aside from several hit singles such as "With Arms Wide Open" as a soloist for Tommy Boy Records, Pringle has recently shared duets on new albums by Shirley Caesar and Bishop Paul Morton while creating a new platform for his vast talents as the A&R director for Warner Christian Music's urban music department.

A homegrown church boy, Pringle was born on April 22, 1970, in Charleston, South Carolina. "I was christened in the Reformed Episcopal church," Pringle recalls. "Then my family started attending a Pentecostal church, and when I was 16, I began to play keyboards

Desmond Pringle / courtesy of Desmond Pringle

for a nondenominational church." After high school graduation, Pringle enrolled as a marketing major at Winthrop University in Rockhill, South Carolina. However, he left when he won the role of Clarence in the national touring company of the gospel musical *A Good Man Is Hard to Find* in 1992. The success of the play brought Pringle starring roles in other stage musicals such as *Only the Strong* and *Paint the White House Black*, and his first recording contract with a major record label, A&M Records.

By 1993, Pringle had moved to Chicago, which has a very active and progressive gospel music community. In that creative atmosphere, Pringle began to write songs for Bishop T.D. Jakes, Rev. Clay Evans, and others. When he wasn't writing hit songs, Pringle was singing background vocals on them. During that period, he backed R. Kelly, Twinkie Clark, and Marvin Sapp, among others. In 1999, he didn't wait to be offered a recording contract. He produced and financed his own CD project, *Psalms, Hymns and Spiritual Songs*, which created a foundation for him at gospel radio and opened up an array of opportunities for the psalmist to minister at churches nationwide.

It was not long after when Tommy Boy Gospel offered Pringle a recording contract that would take his calling to the next level. The company pulled out all of the stops as the CD *Loyalty* featured vocal cameos by Tonex and Lexi. Aside from Pringle's production hand, other track producers included Roger Ryan (CeCe Winans), Derek "DOA" Allen (Smokie Norful), Percy Bady (Jennifer Holliday), and superstar artist/producer Fred Hammond.

With such talent behind the project, it's absolutely no surprise that the CD was critically acclaimed. The first single was an urban-flavored rendition of Creed's "With Arms Wide Open." Tommy Boy was facing funding problems and soon would be closed, so the project did not receive the full attention it merited. The single only peaked at 97 on the *Billboard* R&B singles chart but made it all the way to the Top 30 of the Gavin Urban AC singles chart in spite of Tommy Boy's administrative turmoil. In addition, the CD *Loyalty* crossed over to the R&B album sales chart, the Heatseekers chart, the Top Independent sales chart, the Top Contemporary Christian music album sales chart, and reached No. 9 on the *Billboard* gospel album sales chart—no small feat.

After Tommy Boy officially closed in 2002, Pringle was a free agent. A new opportunity was presented to him. Word Entertainment had recently been bought by Warner Bros. Records and wanted to relaunch its legendary black music division. A lover of classic gospel music, Pringle welcomed the chance to become director of urban A&R at the company. One of his first dreams was to dust off a CD Shirley Caesar had recorded with R&B stars. The CD had been shelved during Word's reorganization and forgotten. Pringle located the master tape, which had been lost, and sifted through the red tape and confusing paperwork to get the contracts signed. In spite of grand duets between Caesar and Patti LaBelle, Gladys Knight, and Kirk Franklin, there were only enough songs for half an album. He secured the participation of Oleta Adams, Faith Evans, Kim Burrell, and Dottie Peoples to round out the album, *Shirley Caesar and Friends.*

One of the highlights of Pringle's career has been recording the hymn "Just a Closer Walk with Thee" with Shirley Caesar. Pringle recalls, "One day, Pastor Caesar said, Dez, why don't you sing with me?' I was floored that she would offer me that opportunity alongside all of these legends she has on her project, but that's how it came about. She asked me and I wasn't about to turn her down." The CD was a success, reaching No. 6 on the *Billboard* gospel album chart and winning a Grammy nomination.

A licensed minister, Pringle continues to minister at churches nationwide on the weekends in spite of his position behind a desk during the week. Pringle has appeared on two high-profile projects recently. He wrote and performed the radio smash "High Praise" that propelled Bishop Paul S. Morton's *Let It Rain* CD to No. 1 on the *Billboard* gospel album sales chart. Pringle's tune "Holiness Is Right" graced the Grammy-nominated CD *CeCe Winans Presents the Born Again Church Choir*, which won a Dove award as Traditional Gospel Album of the Year in spring 2004. As for what the future holds, Pringle says simply, "I don't know what's next, but I do know that whatever I do, I'm going to praise God and keep on moving."

Keith Pringle

IN THE 1980S, gospel music had only a handful of male solo stars because choirs were all the rage. However, Keith Pringle was one of the fistful of male artists to make an impact on gospel music during the Reagan administration. Born in Detroit circa 1951, he was raised in the COGIC denomination where he played around with the instruments at church until some adult would run him off. By the age of 16, Pringle was organist for the New Bethel Young People's Choir. After graduating from Smokey Robinson's alma mater, Northwestern High School, Pringle moved to Chicago before settling in Los Angeles where he attended L.A. City College.

While living in Los Angeles, Pringle began to attend Rev. James Cleveland's Cornerstone Institutional Baptist Church. One Sunday morning, Rev. Cleveland asked for a musician to come forward and play during the offering collection. Pringle went up and played. After the service, Cleveland asked Pringle to accompany him to Philadelphia for a concert. Pringle was in the house when Cleveland was doing the live recording of his soon-to-be classic song "No Ways Tired" in

1978. With no warning, Cleveland called on Pringle to sing it. Pringle was nervous since he had never sung before an audience before, but he didn't fail Rev. Cleveland. He turned in a stellar performance that made the song one of Cleveland's signature tunes and a gold record.

In 1979, Pringle formed the Pentecostal Community Choir and Savoy Records gave them a recording deal. Their debut LP *True Victory* featured the smash hit "Call Him Up," which won a Grammy nomination. Pringle also directed the choir on pop star Rod Stewart's *Tonight I'm Yours* LP in 1981. By 1983, Pringle had recorded his first solo LP, *I Feel Like Going On* (produced by D.J. Rogers), which peaked at No. 11 on the gospel album sales chart. Pringle was on a hit streak and churned out further hit LPs such as *Perfect Peace, All to You, Magnify Him,* and the No. 1 *No Greater Love.* Unfortunately, Pringle has vanished from the musical landscape and is now rumored to be an educator. "Keith Pringle was a singer's singer," says Chicago radio announcer Gregory Gay. "His greatest song was 'I Feel Like Going On,' but his finest album was *Perfect Peace* because of Thomas Whitfield's masterful production and the fabulous Whitfield Company Choir."

Rachel & the Joy Gospel Singers

RACHEL DIXSON HAS a sweet, girlish soprano and she's been using it with her Joy Gospel Singers since she founded the group at the Thessalonia Baptist Church in New York City circa 1981 when she was a pre-teen. Now based in the Wilmington, North Carolina, area, the group continues with Dixson's daughters Elisha and Shaneice, and Keva Bradley. Rachel shares lead vocal solos with her mother, Ruby David, who has a folksy, down-to-earth alto. The group's sound is traditional but uptempo with an old-school '70s soul backdrop. Pastor James Uttley of WWIL radio in Wilmington has made them virtual household names in the market. After two decades of concerts, the group released their first CD, *Jesus You've Been Good to Me,* for the Tri Factor Music Group in 2001. Dixson manages the Greentree Inn hotel in Wilmington.

Radio Four

A 1950S GOSPEL QUARTET with a country blues tone, the Radio Four (named for the weekly broadcasts they did on WBDL in Bowling Green, Kentucky) were formed in the 1940s by the Babb brothers: George (born June 11, 1923), Ray (born January 26, 1912), James (born June 6, 1928), Claude, and Morgan. They first recorded for Republic Records when they cut "Blood Done Signed My Name" in 1952. They joined Nashboro Records in 1955 and enjoyed moderate hits such as "How Much I Owe" and "When He Calls." They cut one session that included "If You Miss Me from Praying" and "An Earnest Prayer" before Morgan Babb left the group to become a solo artist. On the latter tune, a January 1956 *Billboard* magazine review said, "Watch this one. The lead singer carries this along at a strong emotional pace, and the supporting singers and instrumentation give it a rolling beat. Will get plays." Robert Priestly replaced Morgan Babb and they performed together until they disbanded in 1965. Morgan Babb recorded several sides for Nashboro and Creed into the 1970s, but never experienced a major hit. Instead, his claim to fame has been his ownership of Nashville's WMDB (which stands for Morgan D. Babb), a low-wattage radio station with an eclectic mix of blues, gospel, and talk programming. The station slogan is "The Big Mouth."

Dottie Rambo

IT WOULD PROBABLY be easier to name the artists who have not recorded one of Dottie Rambo's 2,500 songs than to name those who have recorded them. She was one of mainstream gospel's first female singer-songwriter stars in the 1960s. She brought a unique blend of Southern and black gospel to her pop-gospel platform in the early days of contemporary Christian music. She was born Joyce Reba Rambo on March 2, 1934, in Madison, Kentucky. Raised in a Christian home, Rambo began to write songs at the age of eight, and was in demand to sing at community events as a child. When she was 12 years old, she left home to launch her professional career. Her big break was when the Louisiana governor Jimmie Davis, of "You Are My Sunshine" fame, signed her to a writing contract. She married Buck Rambo at the age of 16 and kept on rolling.

In the late 1960s, Rambo began recording for Heartwarming Records. Her 1968 LP *The Soul of Me* was a major success and won her a Grammy award for Best Soul Gospel Performance. Over the years, Rambo has enjoyed many hit recordings such as "He Looked Beyond My Faults and Saw My Needs" and "You've Never Mentioned Jesus to Me." Vickie Winans's signature song is Rambo's "We Shall Behold Him," and dozens of black choirs and artists have sung "He Looked Beyond My Faults." Whitney Houston and Danniebelle Hall covered "I Go to the Rock." Elvis Presley recorded "If That Isn't Love." In recent years, Rambo has overcome debilitating back ailments and a public divorce from Buck to regain her position as one of gospel's grande dames. A recent recording with Dolly Parton, "Stand by the River" became her first No. 1 song in years on the Southern gospel charts. It also won song of the year from the Christian Country Music Association.

Reba Rambo

THIS WRITER WAS present during a Sunday night concert at the Evangel Temple Church in Washington, DC, in the 1980s when the associate pastor, Wiley Alston, introduced Reba Rambo. Clearly, Rambo was the most soulful of all the top-name white female Christian singers of the 1980s. With songs such as "Because of Whose I Am" and "He Gave Me Music," she made a good name for herself outside of her mother Dottie Rambo's large shadow.

Born in 1951, Rambo began singing with her parents' group, the Singing Rambos, when she was 13. After graduating from high school, she went on the road with Andrae Crouch and the Disciples while maintaining membership in the Singing Rambos. Rambo's 1971 debut LP *Songs My Mama Taught Me* was country with lush, string arrangements, but as the years went on, her subsequent LPs became progres-

sively more mainstream Christian with a healthy dollop of soul.

In 1980, Rambo and her second husband, Dony McGuire, produced the concept album *The Lord's Prayer*, which featured cameos by Andrae Crouch, B.J. Thomas, and the Hawkins Family, among others. The album was one of the bestselling projects of the year and it won a Grammy award for Best Gospel Performance. The highlight was the artists performing a medley from the album on the Grammy awards telecast that year. In 1982, Rambo recorded her solo masterpiece *Lady Live* on Light Records. Recorded at the Anaheim Convention Center in Southern California, it bridged the electricity of the black church experience with the polish of the evangelical church circuit. Her backing band was phenomenal. On bass was Abraham Laboriel, who played with jazz greats such as Nancy Wilson and Stanley Turrentine. Her organist, Harlan Rodgers, played with Gordon Lightfoot. Rambo's drummer, Larrie London, played with country greats Johnny Cash and Chet Atkins. With her dynamic soprano, Rambo had several brilliant moments on the LP, such as the medley "Sacrifice of Praise," which finished with a bluesy rendition of "Somewhere Over the Rainbow." The album featured a number of radio favorites such as "The Land of Ooh's and Ah's," "Because of Whose I Am," and "He Never Turned His Back on Me." Rambo and McGuire created other fine albums through the 1980s, but faded from the music scene in the 1990s. The explanation lay in Rambo's autobiography, *Follow the Yellow Brick Road*, in which she wrote candidly of her turbulent first marriage and her second husband's substance abuse. Rambo and McGuire now pastor The River at Music City, an inner-city church in Nashville.

Ramiyah

A STUDIO-CREATED, urban contemporary gospel quartet, Ramiyah was the result of an open-call audition by producers J. Moss, Paul Allen, and Walter Kearney (who bill themselves as PAJAM) in 2001. Once Detroit natives Stephanie Bonner, Sherise Staten, Tracy Bryant, and DeLaurian Burton were selected, PAJAM convinced

Beyoncé Knowles's manager, Matthew Knowles, to sign the group to his Music World recording label. Their self-titled CD hit stores in 2003. The girls appeared on a round of music shows such as *Showtime at the Apollo* and Candi Staton's *Say Yes*. Six months after the album was initially released, it was reissued with a different CD cover. It reached No. 8 on the gospel chart in February 2004 but did not enjoy a long chart run. Gospel radio didn't pick up on the funky urban tracks, and the album never crossed over to the R&B charts. "Many people that hear us think that we're R&B until they hear the lyrics," says Staten. "Our music is filled with catchy beats and rhythms, but at the same time, we have no problem with breaking out with a hymn or two."

Tarralyn Ramsey

WITH CATWALK BEAUTY, Tarralyn Ramsey appeared on the gospel music landscape with her urban-friendly, self-titled debut CD in 2000. A bishop's daughter, she was born in 1980. She sang in her father's church since her youth and was said to have turned down several offers to record secular music when she decided to sign with Verity Records. The CD *WOW Gospel 2001* produced the radio single "Tell It" and saw the project peak at No. 12 on the *Billboard* gospel sales chart in 2000. However, after a slump in her gospel career, Ramsey was dropped from Verity's roster. She then entered VH1's talent contest, *Born to Diva*, in 2003 and won a pop music contract with Tommy Mottola's Casablanca Records label. That venture proved a major failure too. Her power ballad "Up Against All Odds" and a follow-up of "Baby U Know" with Murphy Lee (and a Minnie Riperton sample) failed to earn the singer bona fide diva credentials. Her CD *Tarralyn Ramsey* reached No. 59 but only spent one week on the R&B chart in June 2004.

Cleo Randle

WITH A BIG VOICE similar to Chi-Town neighbor Mitty Collier's high-voltage range, Randle was a great performer of both gospel and R&B music in the 1960s who never made it big outside of Chicago. Born Cleopatra

Jackson, she recorded for Bob Lee's Sta-Set label (one of many small independents he owned) in the 1960s. "You Got Everything" and the bluesy ballad "Big City Lights" were among her singles. Later in life, she returned to church music. She sang in the COGIC circuit under the leadership of Bishop L.H. Ford and Professor A. Samuel Hawkins. Perhaps best known for the song "Walk with Me, Lord," she passed away in March 2004 in Chicago.

Robert Randolph and the Family Band

ROBERT RANDOLPH WAS born circa 1978 in Irvington, New Jersey. He was raised in the House of God Pentecostal denomination, which emphasizes the use of steel guitars over organs and keyboards in its church music. His mother is a minister and his father is a deacon. When he was 16 years old, Randolph began to play the steel guitar like legendary church gospel steel guitarists Lorenzo Harrison and Ted Beard. However, it was the introduction of Stevie Ray Vaughan's music that showed him how to pick the guitar at a faster rate. He then applied that technique to the steel guitar. When Randolph was playing at a sacred steel guitar convention, he was discovered by Jim Markel who decided to manage him with his buddy Gary Waldman. The duo got Randolph and his band booked in key New York clubs such as the Bowery Ballroom, and the word spread rapidly about this unique steel guitar music that has never been fully introduced to mainstream America.

From there, keyboardist John Medeski (of Medeski, Martin & Wood fame) collaborated with Randolph on a blues-gospel CD, *The Word*. The acclaim for that project led Randolph's band to record their own independent CD, *Live at the Wetlands*, on Dare Records, which defined their bluesy, Southern-rock sound in 2001. That album won them even more fans, spanning from deep blues lovers to college kids who like hard rock music. Warner Bros. picked the album up and reissued it. Randolph has said that he writes his songs around instrumental riffs and inserts lyrics later on. While his music was born in the church, the lyrics are not preachy. "I try to make music as secular as I can make it," Randolph told *USA Today* in August 2003, "but still keep it soulful and give people some kind of message." In 2002, the band won a W.C. Handy award as Best New Blues Artist of the Year. In summer 2003, Randolph's first Warner Bros. CD, *Unclassified*, was released to ecstatic reviews. Although most of the consumers buying the project were outside of the church market, the album peaked at No. 6 on the CCM album chart.

"When people come to see me, they want that uplifting feeling, but sometimes I want to make this a rock and roll night," Randolph told *Glide* magazine in 2003. "But that's always in me, because I come from a gospel background, and I can't help but talk about just good things in life and to just help people. I know what people are going through. Like you said, a lot of white people, when they look at black artists of today, they don't get that kind of good, high, mystical feeling. I get down on some of the new black artists... a lot of these guys grew up in churches and had the same background, but they choose to go the other way, in the wrong direction, instead of the right direction. Years ago, when all these black artists came out, guys like Stevie Wonder, they had something good to sing about all the time. And Aretha and Al Green, they had soul and had a good message. These guys had soul and it wasn't all cheesy and they had money, but it wasn't like they were flaunting it. That's just something about me, I don't think I'll ever get into that." The band is comprised of drummer Marcus Randolph, bassist Danyel Morgan, and organist Jason Crosby.

Lou Rawls

KING OF THE supper-club circuit, Lou Rawls distinguished himself as a soulful crooner dating back to the 1960s with jazzy, R&B songs such as "Natural Man" and "Lady Love." He started his career during the Golden Age of Gospel in the 1950s and has come full circle with recent traditional gospel albums celebrating the faith of his youth. Born Louis Allen Rawls on December 1, 1935, in Chicago, Rawls was mostly raised by his grandmother. His father was a preacher and his mother a beautician. He began singing in church from the age of seven, but came to idolize jazz crooners he saw perform at Chicago's storied Regal Theater. Some of his favorite singers were Nat King Cole and Arthur Prysock. Rawls

and his high school buddy Sam Cooke sang together in a gospel group called the Teenage Kings of Harmony. Later, Rawls joined another gospel group, the Holy Wonders, before replacing Cooke in the Highway QCs in 1951. In 1953, he was recruited for the Chosen Gospel Singers when they traveled through Chicago on tour, but his gig only lasted a few months as he joined the Pilgrim Travelers in 1954. In 1956, he left the group to enlist in the army as a paratrooper. When he was discharged in 1958, he returned to the Pilgrim Travelers. Rawls, Cooke, and others were traveling through the South when the car they were in crashed into a truck. Cooke had minor injuries, but one passenger died on the scene, and Rawls was actually pronounced dead on the way to the hospital. He spent almost six days in a coma, did not fully regain his memory for another three months, and spent the rest of the year recuperating.

After Rawls recovered, he decided to sing pop music and worked his way up from small venues. In 1962, he was discovered at a coffee shop near Capitol Records headquarters by producer Nick Venet. Venet snagged him a deal with Capitol Records where he recorded pop-jazz tunes such as "Stormy Monday" and "Love Is a Hurtin' Thing." In the late 1970s, Rawls had a career resurgence when he signed to Philadelphia International Records and began recording gold-selling albums and smash R&B and pop singles such as "You'll Never Find Another Love Like Mine," "Groovy People," "See You When I Git There," "Let Me Be Good to You," and "Lady Love."

The following year, Rawls kicked off what would become a consuming passion for years to come: the Lou Rawls Parade of Stars Telethon, an annual event that raises millions of dollars for the United Negro College Fund. Through the 1980s and 1990s, Rawls recorded jazzier fare for Epic Records, Verve, and his own recording label. In 2001, he returned to his gospel roots when he recorded an armful of songs for two Malaco Records releases, *I'm Blessed* and *Oh Happy Day*. Years after he had left the gospel circuit, some were still critical of Rawls's decision. Gospel legend Sallie Martin once arrived at a special tribute to gospel music veterans in Los Angeles, right after a reporter had interviewed Rawls about why he left gospel. She recalls, "They interviewed him before I got there and they were asking, 'What did you leave the gospel for, Lou Rawls?' He said, 'I left because I wanted some bread.' I said, 'I wished I'd have been here… I would have told him, I have my bread every morning.' And there must have been something wrong with him because the world is the Lord's…Well, I think it's a mighty poor God who owns the whole world and can't feed you."

Mimi Redd

TRULY ONE OF gospel's one-hit wonders, Mimi Redd came from out of nowhere to have perhaps the biggest gospel recording by a female artist in 1994, and she has returned to that nether-place. Redd was born in April 1955 in Omaha, Nebraska, where her parents, Rev. James and Ruth White, were in full-time ministry. She has been a singer since the age of five and very active in church choirs. She stepped into the limelight in 1994 when she recorded classically trained composer Glenn Burleigh's ballad "Order My Steps." With her piercing high Cs and field-holler wails, Redd gave the song a tour de force performance on the GMWA Women of Worship CD *It's Our Time*. The song catapulted that CD to peak at No. 3 on *Billboard*'s gospel album sales chart. The project remained on the chart for 123 weeks (well over two years)—an astounding feat. The tune was played at school functions, marching band parades, radio stations, and sung during Sunday morning services nationwide. To capitalize on the song's success, Aleho Records rushed out the CD *This Is Mimi* in late 1995, with a new, abbreviated version of "Order My Steps." At the time, label President Al Hobbs said, "Mimi Redd is class, culture, heritage, and yet she is church." However, the production was uneven and the project didn't feature a catchy song that fit Redd's unique gifts. After the album failed to chart, Redd disappeared and was last known to reside in San Antonio, Texas.

Carla Reed

OFTEN TIMES, THE public has no concept of the behind-the-scenes battles that take place to get gospel music on television. One who has fought to keep gospel music visible at Black Entertainment Television (BET) is executive producer Carla Reed, who has worked backstage at BET programs such as *Lift Every Voice*, *Bobby Jones Gospel*, and *Video Gospel* to keep gospel music center stage.

The sixth of seven children, Carla Reed was born in May 1960 in Annapolis, Maryland. Her father was a navy midshipman and her mother was a hairdresser. Her family had a musical history as many of them sang with the legendary local group the Mt. Ebo Gospel Singers. Reed witnessed tragedy early on. One of her sisters was killed in a car accident and her mother died of a blood clot in 1969, but her father kept the family together and raised his children on his own. As a youth, Reed had a reputation around their neighborhood for having a teacher's spirit. "The kids would come from everywhere," she laughs, "and I'd teach them things. Because of that, I always thought I'd be teaching professionally." After graduating from high school, she attended a business school before majoring in communications at both Howard University and the University of the District of Columbia.

In the ensuing years, Reed worked in Howard University's dance department and danced with the WOSE Dance Troupe on the side. She was working as a secretary at *U.S. News & World Report* when she heard of a job opening at Black Entertainment Television. She was hired by BET in July 1989. "It was crazy," Reed says of that chaotic period when the network was expanding rapidly. "None of the shows were developed. They started 24-hour programming that September." She worked as a program coordinator and was soon elevated to a manager. The first program she was given to manage was *This Week in Black Entertainment*, a celebrity news show hosted by Tanya Hart in Los Angeles. One day, Dr. Bobby Jones was in the BET studios for a meeting about his television show. He had been hearing about Reed's great work and said to her, "You're going to work for me."

Reed did come to work with Jones and between the two of them, *Bobby Jones Gospel* became BET's No. 1 rated show for over a decade. The show achieved a wider audience than even the rap and hip-hop videos the network is known to showcase. "He was such a hard worker," Reed recalls. "He would come every week and try to make his show look as good as he could. And whether you could sing or not, he was going to encourage you and give new artists a shot." It saddens Reed that many of today's top gospel artists received their first national exposure on Dr. Jones's show and once they reach a certain level, the producers have to virtually beg them to appear on the show again. Reed was also instrumental in the launch of BET's Sunday morning block of gospel music programming. Aside from shepherding *Video Gospel* (a weekly hour-long gospel video show), she is the executive producer of *Lift Every Voice*, which began as a half-hour interview/video program in 1999 with Brother Gerard Henry as the host. The show has grown in such popularity that BET expanded it to a full hour in fall 2003. An autumn 2003 episode of Vickie Winans's 50th birthday party celebration remains the top-rated program in the show's history with a viewing audience of over 800,000. Reed has her hands in a variety of other BET projects, but the success of *Lift Every Voice* remains close to her heart. "We're always looking for new things to keep it exciting and fresh," she says. Through her work at BET and through her private production company, she has certainly repackaged gospel music for a new generation of believers.

Della Reese

ONE OF AMERICA'S favorite standards singers in the 1960s, Della Reese used her singing career to create an equally successful career as America's first national black female talk show hostess. However, her career began on the gospel circuit and she has returned to that market several times throughout her career. Born Deloreese Patricia Early on July 6, 1931, in Detroit, she began singing at the Olivet Baptist Church when she was six years old. At the age of 13, she went on the road with Mahalia Jackson. While a psychiatry student at Wayne State University, she formed the Meditations Singers gospel group with Earnestine Rundless. Her mother died suddenly and her father took ill, so Reese took whatever jobs she could to help support her family. A beautiful but hardy woman, Reese didn't mind getting her hands dirty. She worked as a truck driver, cab driver, elevator operator, and switchboard operator.

It was on her pastor's advice that Reese began to take secular singing engagements. She performed at the famous Flame Show Bar and notched a gig as a vocalist with the Erskine Hawkins band in 1953. She fluctuated between her secular and church engagements until she won a recording contract from RCA Records. Since her married name—Deloreese Bon Taliaferro—was too long for a theater marquee, Reese divided her first name into Della Reese. In 1957, she signed to Jubilee Records and scored a hit with "And That Reminds Me." In her personal success, she didn't forget the Meditation Singers. She had Jubilee issue an LP entitled *Della Reese Presents the Meditation Singers*. In 1959, Reese garnered a million-seller with her RCA Records debut ballad "Don't You Know," which topped the R&B charts for two weeks and peaked at No. 2 on the pop singles survey. Over the next decade, Reese recorded a number of crisply articulated pop songs such as the stunning "Blues for the Weepers," "A Hundred Years from Today," and "Not One Minute More."

Reese became the first black woman to host a nationally syndicated talk show when she premiered *Della* in 1969. Although she has recorded periodically over the last 30 years, Reese is known to a new generation of fans for her television acting rather than her husky-voiced singing. She's had regular roles in *Chico and the Man* with Jack Albertson and Freddie Prinze, and *The Royal Family* with Redd Foxx among a half dozen other sitcoms. In 1994, Reese became the star of the CBS drama series *Touched by an Angel* which ran for eight seasons and brought God into primetime television. Reese's soundtrack CD *Touched by an Angel: The Album* featured artists such as Faith Hill and Amy Grant. Reese sang the rousing "I'll Walk with You" theme from the series on the project, which sold a million copies in 1998. The CD reached No. 1 on the CCM chart, No. 3 on the country chart, and No. 16 on the pop chart.

In addition to her work as an entertainer, after surviving an aneurism operation in 1980, Reese felt called to the ministry. She then founded the Understanding Principles for Better Living Church in Los Angeles, which she still shepherds today.

RECOMMENDED RECORDINGS: Reese has recorded several fine gospel albums over her career. The most recent is *My Soul Feels Better Right Now* (Homeland, 1998), a ten-track set of church standards done in her robust, bluesy style. Among the standouts is the title song, a Thomas Dorsey tune, and her signature gospel tune "Hush (Somebody's Calling My Name)," which she's recorded a couple of times in the past, the first time in 1959. Also worth seeking out are Reese's 1980s AIR Records LPs *Della Reese* and *Brilliance*, featuring collaborations with Merry Clayton and the late O.C. Smith. Used record shops may have her 1950s gospel LPs *Amen* or *Hush*, which both merit a CD reissue.

Sister Jessie Mae Renfro

BORN OCTOBER 3, 1920, in Witchataxee, Texas, Renfro was raised in the COGIC denomination. She flirted with the idea of becoming a secular singer as a teenager when she sang songs such as Bessie Smith's "Empty Bed Blues" in Dallas-area blues joints, but eventually decided to travel the gospel highway instead. She joined the Sallie Martin Singers in the 1940s and began her gospel career there. She possessed a powerful, bluesy soprano similar to Clara Ward's but with much more punch. She sustained her long, simple notes in much the same manner that Ward did, but expanded them with volcanic eruptions of passion. Her base was in Oklahoma City where her husband pastored a COGIC denomination church. Although she began recording in 1946, her most notable recordings appeared on the Peacock label in the 1950s. In 1951, she recorded her first single for them called "A Wonderful Savior." In 1952, she recorded "I'll Be Satisfied Then" which was backed by a stunning version of "No Room at the Hotel." The following year she recorded the definitive version of "I Must Tell Jesus," with enough gutbucket and verve to appeal to church house and gin house alike. After the Golden Age of Gospel passed, she contented herself with COGIC work and leading denominational revivals.

Reverend Ike

PERHAPS THE MOST notorious African-American televangelist of the 1970s, Rev. Ike preached the Gospel of Green (a get-rich-quick prosperity theology) to the church community long before Creflo Dollar, Robert Tilton, and others took the message to a new level in the 1990s. He was born Frederick Eikerenkoetter on June 1, 1935, in Ridgeland, South Carolina. His father was a preacher and his mother was a school teacher. He began preaching at the age of 14 and later became assistant pastor at the Bible Way Church in Ridgeland for two years. After earning a divinity degree at the American Bible College in Chicago, he served as an air force chaplain for a couple of years. From there, he founded the storefront United Church of Jesus for All People in Boston. Since most people could not properly pronounce his last name, he had the congregation refer to him as Rev. Ike. Almost from the beginning of his ministry in the 1950s—at the height of segregation and when most blacks were working class—Rev. Ike preached a prosperity gospel that drew hundreds to his church and thousands to his crusades around the country. "Money is not the root of all evil," he'd preach. "It's the absence of money that's the root of all evil." In 1966, he moved to New York and founded the Science of Living Institute (Christ United Church), which was housed in the old Lowe's movie house on 175th Street in Harlem. The $600,000 mortgage was paid off in three years. People poured into the complex to hear Rev. Ike's "Cosmic Law of the Mind" prosperity sermons.

Using biblical scriptures that emphasized reciprocal blessings to those who give offerings and freewill offerings, Rev. Ike touched a chord with the downtrodden. Adorned in designer suits, sporting diamond rings, wearing a perfectly styled pompadour and driving around in luxury cars made Rev. Ike the living example of the philosophy he promoted. As he once said, "The Bible says that Jesus rode on a borrowed ass. But I would rather ride in a Rolls-Royce than to ride somebody's ass!" By the 1970s, Rev. Ike was a household name due to his weekly television broadcast and widespread media coverage. His television broadcast was on in 27 markets and his *ACTION* magazine had a mailing list of 1.5 million donors. In the magazine, he spoke of a "money rake" or "how to rake money in." Ike had found his money rake. By 1973, he owned a Rolls-Royce, a Mercedes-Benz, diamonds, custom suits, and estates on both coasts, yet he maintained that he only made $40,000 a year. When he was once asked about race, Ike replied, "I used to be black myself, then I turned green."

Although his name was often used disparagingly in reference to dishonest people or money-driven individuals (it was often invoked on the sitcom *Sanford and Son*, for instance), Rev. Ike never backed from his tenets. Although the media presented Ike as more of a joke than an honorable clergyman, the public still rushed to send him donations in exchange for the anointed prayer cloths and other trinkets the ministry would send to contributors. By the 1980s, Rev. Ike was off of television for a while and kept a lower profile. He still dressed well, but less ostentatiously. In recent years, Rev. Ike has triumphed over accusations of sexual harassment and mail fraud. Today, his Science of Living Ministry still takes in millions of dollars a year via his current cable television and other outreach resources. "I don't care if you are black, white, pink, or yellow," he has said. "As long as your money is green, God will love you."

RECOMMENDED RECORDING: Extremely rare and collectable is Rev. Ike's 45-rpm entitled "Wonderful" backed by "Healing Blessing and Prayer" (Rev. Ike Prays For You Records). On the single, Rev. Ike preaches and Eddie Taylor sings.

DeLeon Richards

THUS FAR, SHE'S NEVER enjoyed a huge hit recording, but DeLeon Richards was a long-time gospel veteran even as a child singer. Her father, Rev. Bob Richards, pastors the Faith Tabernacle COGIC in North Chicago and her mother, Deborah, was a singer who encouraged DeLeon from an early age to honor her gifts. Born September 18, 1976, in Lake Forest, Illinois, Richards began singing publicly at the age of five and later learned to play both organ and piano. In 1982, Chicago mayor Jane Byrne selected Richards to sing at a Chicago Gospel Festival on a bill that included such heavy-

weights as Andrae Crouch, Rev. James Cleveland, and the Mighty Clouds of Joy. The 20,000 people in attendance were ecstatic about her performance and the local TV news covered the little girl with the big voice. Soon, preachers such as Jesse Jackson and Clay Evans were having Richards perform at their convocations. Those experiences led to her recording contract with Myrrh/Word Records. Her debut LP *DeLeon* received a Grammy nomination in 1984 and reached No. 17 on the black gospel album chart.

Richards's music at that point in her career was cute and sugary. With her high voice and sweet arrangements, it was unlikely to appeal to a mass audience, even within the gospel fold. However, her Stacy Lattisaw–like albums were able to sell steadily enough that Myrrh kept her on the roster through her final LP for the label, *New Direction*, in 1992. As she matured, she put down an urban-friendly CD of contemporary gospel called *My Life* for Intersound Records in 1996, but gospel radio wasn't ready for such contemporary vibes and the label didn't have the means to promote the CD on secular radio. Richards was attending college at the same time and graduated from Lake Forest College with a degree in sociology and communication in 1997. At the time, she told *Excellence* magazine about her future plans. "I can see myself in the future being like Oprah Winfrey or Quincy Jones," she said. "More so Quincy because he is involved in literally everything. I see myself being a kind of music mogul, involved in recording, radio, film, television, magazines… the whole spectrum. I definitely see myself where singing is not the entirety of what I do." She briefly put her career on hold to marry Los Angeles Dodgers baseball star Gary Sheffield on February 5, 2000, in St. Petersburg, Florida, with Bishop Noel Jones officiating. Among the singers performing at the nuptials were CeCe Winans, Tonex, and Yolanda Adams. In 2001, Richards was back on track with her career and released a slick contemporary gospel CD for Tommy Boy entitled *Straight from the Heart*, that was lost in the label's subsequent closing. In 2004, DeLeon made national headlines when an extortionist revealed to the media that DeLeon had a sexual relationship with accused child molester/R&B singer R. Kelly when she was a teenager.

Donna Richardson

FITNESS EXPERT Donna Richardson was born November 3, 1962, in Washington, DC. She worked her way through Hollins College by working as a waitress. After a friend challenged her to take an aerobics class, Richardson began to see fitness as her calling. She became the instructor of the very class she was taking and eventually began to teach fitness throughout the Washington, DC, region. In 1986, she and a friend invested $10,000 of their own money into a fitness video. Her big break came in 1992 when the ESPN cable sports network hired Richardson to co-host a show called *Fitness Pros*. She eventually became a fitness correspondent for the *Weekend Today Show* on NBC. With her national platform secured, Richardson began to make a series of bestselling exercise videos. She has made headlines in recent years for marrying legendary syndicated radio announcer Tom Joyner. In 2004, she launched an exercise video aimed at the church market. *Sweating in the Spirit* featured musical performance by gospel artists such as Kirk Franklin and Vickie Winans. In addition to her regular clientele, she now takes her fitness message to religious groups and appeared on the successful Sisters in the Spirit national concert tour with Yolanda Adams and others in 2005.

Rici

IF EVER THERE WAS an example of what bad management, poor distribution, and a small record label could do to extinguish the kindling fire of a bright new star, the story of Rici Bell is a prime example. Her fifteen minutes of fame didn't last three minutes in 1998. As quickly as she rose, Rici fell due to circumstances beyond her control. She was something gospel music has rarely seen: a young, beautiful sex symbol. At the time, the R&B world had Brandy, Monica, and Aaliyah. Gospel had no one to appeal to teenage girls of color. Poised and sophisticated yet down to earth, Rici's music was mellow funk with hip-hop loops. Her record label billed her as gospel's Mary J. Blige, though her style and sound was much closer to that of Aaliyah and her dry alto

more akin to that of Brandy. "My music isn't sexy and it doesn't moan; it praises God and rebukes the devil," Rici once said. "Everybody who knows me knows that I'm a cheerleader and soldier for Jesus Christ. I'm always down with praising his name and sharing his message, especially with my peer group."

Rici Bell was born circa 1981 in Fresno, California. She accepted Christ when she was eight years old and leading the Mt. Mariah Baptist Church Choir. By the age of 11, she sang with the BAAD (Born Again And Delivered) Mass Choir before becoming the 15-year-old opening act for a group called God Quest. Local producer Marcus Davis said in his promotional material on Rici, "She always stood out at the shows. She was the little girl with the big voice." He later said that he felt God nudging him to sign Rici to his startup Devaness Records label. While attending Edison High School and serving on the cheerleading squad, she recorded her first CD, entitled *So Into You*, in 1997.

The album was largely produced without the benefit of live musicians and is technically amateurish. Rici had survived her parents' divorce, losing a friend to cancer, and two other friends slain in drive-by shootings. Her real life gave her credentials to subtly deal with issues of concern to teenagers. Distributed through the trouble-plagued Diamante Music Group, the CD's distribution was spotty and uneven. Davis had no experience running a record label. As of this writing, he has not had the songs individually copyrighted. Although Davis wrote or co-wrote most of the songs, not one of them is registered with ASCAP, BMI, or SESAC so that he and the other co-writers could receive radio airplay royalties. Compounding the problem was that Davis's wife was the radio promoter. Lacking the contacts and political clout to get the music played by many key gospel radio stations, the CD floundered. However, a Diamante executive Marcy Emerick stepped out of her position with the label to give the CD a further push. She convinced Vincent Young at the public relations company Capital Entertainment (which handled gospel heavyweights such as CeCe Winans and T.D. Jakes at the time) to take the project on almost a year after its initial release. Through Young's efforts, Rici made her national television debut on BET's *Teen Summit* singing the infectious single, "Prayin' for You." Young secured national news stories around Rici and saturated the Fresno media with news of her debut.

The excitement over the BET exposure and renewed radio play for "Prayin' for You" by a handful of radio stations such as WPGC in Washington, DC, led to friction between Bell's parents and Davis over the direction of Rici's career. As a result, momentum was lost during the standoff. Meanwhile, Rici tired of the bickering and focused on college. At last notice, she was attending Fresno Pacific University as a child psychology major.

RECOMMENDED RECORDING: *So Into You* (Devaness Records, 1997) is long out of print and, as of this writing, Rici's only recording. Overall, the project's production is weak. However, Rici's vocals are good and controlled. She shines best on "Prayin' for You," a song from a girlfriend to her boyfriend who's going through a tough spot, and "Don't Worry."

Righteous Riders

DON'T LET THE tough-guy image fool you. Although the Righteous Riders know the streets intimately, they have a heart for people. In the past, various members have sold drugs, served time, and had other scrapes with the law. However, they turned that negative into positive and now minister to youth who are where they once were, and try to turn their lives around with the hip-hop music they can relate to and understand.

Members Devon "Knowledge" Golder (born March 11, 1982) and Derek "Logic" Lamont Coleman (born October 23, 1981) first sang with an urban gospel group called Kinnection in the early 1990s with their cousins. The Indianapolis-based kids' group recorded two CDs, *Testimony* (1991) and *Save the Children* (1992), for their uncle Leonard Scott's record label, Tyscot. During their teenage years, the guys got caught up in street life for a period, but eventually came back into the Christian fold. They formed the Righteous Riders with other street ministers named Blue Chip and Specialist (a duo playing under the name Boanerges),

Blood Bought, and Vi Nu. They released their debut CD *The Awakening* in 2001 with a strong rap and hip-hop backdrop. They followed up the next year with the CD *Internal Affairs*, featuring more of the group's singing ability on smooth soul songs such as "Call Him," which showcased Vi Nu's chops. Along the way, various group members had a difference of opinion on the group's direction and quit. Only Golder and Coleman remained until they met a solo singer, Jason Clayborne (born May 30, 1981), on a date in Louisville, Kentucky. They instantly felt a connection with each other. Other people play the dozens, but the Riders started to do freestyle raps on the spot. Everything they gave, Clayborne answered with a quick, clever hook. He eventually joined the group and they continued to perform as a trio. In 2005, the trio disbanded when Golder and Coleman decided to launch an R&B music career. Clayborne refused to sing R&B music and now sings gospel as a soloist.

RiZen

THE DYNAMIC FEMALE quartet RiZen is the opposite of everything up-and-coming female singers are told will sell in today's market. They are full-figured, they downplay sexuality, and they sing a very traditional brand of gospel music. However, in spite of those no-nos, the high heel-wearing group with the slick, Sanctified choreography is one of the biggest female groups to emerge in gospel since Trin-i-tee 5:7 a decade before them.

They all hail from Saginaw, Michigan. Aundrea (born 1977) and Adriann (born 1982) Lewis are daughters of a Galilee Full Gospel Baptist Church pastor. They grew up singing in church and at home they heard the best Golden Age Gospel artists such as Rev. James Cleveland and Albertina Walker. Their parents were more liberal concerning R&B music than many pastors. Although gospel was their foundation, the sisters listened to a healthy dose of R&B growing up as well. In 1996, they took these influences and formed RiZen as an eight-member female singing troupe. Some of the women became impatient that success wasn't coming fast enough and left the ensemble. "We were down to

RiZen / courtesy of Chez Musique

just myself, Aundrea, and Kanika [Trigg]," Adriann once said. "There were times when I really began to doubt if this was really what God was calling me to do, but we were still determined to go on."

In 1999, they held auditions for a soprano and Ashley Jones joined the group. Then they hooked up with veteran producer Sanchez Harley when he founded his own record label, Chez Musique, in 2003. From their explosive debut on BET's *Bobby Jones Gospel* with "View that Holy City" (similar in style to Dorothy Love Coates's "City Built Foursquare"), there was an industry buzz about the girls. Their raw wails, charismatic stage energy, and catchy traditional hooks put them in the spotlight. Their self-titled debut CD reached No. 6 on *Billboard*'s gospel album sales chart, and almost everyone predicts a long career for the young women who are introducing a new generation to an older generation's style of gospel music.

Rev. Lawrence Roberts

INSTRUMENTAL IN THE career of Rev. James Cleveland and the propagation of a new, then-contemporary

choir sound in the 1960s, Rev. Lawrence Roberts was born in Newark, New Jersey, circa 1939. He was a church pianist for the Zion Hill Baptist Church's junior choir and various local gospel groups until he became a staff producer and session player for Savoy Records in 1954. He formed the Gospel Chordettes and saw them record for Savoy. He also recorded for the label as a headliner, but his most commercial successes were supervising recordings by the Davis Sisters and the Gospel Harmonettes, among others. Roberts brought many new recording artists to the label and also helped Rev. James Cleveland and Fred Mendelsohn define Cleveland's trademark sound of creating records that sound like actual church services rather than individual tracks. At the heart of this sound was the trio's use of multi-dimensional vocal parts and contemporary instrumentation. Many of Cleveland's best recordings were recorded with the Angelic Choir at the First Baptist Church of Nutley, New Jersey, where Roberts was pastor. In 1964, Roberts wrote the classic "What Makes a Man Turn His Back on God?" which became one of Rev. Cleveland's biggest hits. "Songs are like people," Roberts once told the *Crossroads Newsletter*. "Some live a long time, and some don't live that long." He stopped touring in 1992 and retired from the pulpit. Roberts and his wife, Bootsy (Delores), now reside in an Atlanta, Georgia, suburb where they attend Mt. Nebo Baptist Church and go fishing from time to time.

Paul Robeson

ONE OF AMERICA'S first black superstars, Paul Robeson gained fame on stage, screen, and record, but he gained notoriety for his political views. Born April 9, 1898, in Princeton, New Jersey, his father was a former slave who became a Methodist minister and his mother died when he was six years old. Only the third African-American to attend Rutgers University, Robeson was lettered in four varsity sports and graduated with honors. He then graduated from Columbia University law school and took a job at a New York law firm. When a white stenographer refused to take dictation from a "nigger," Robeson left law behind and pursued theater at the request of his first wife. In 1922, he landed his first stage role and over the next decade, he appeared in several stage productions. The role of Joe in the musical *Showboat* made him a star. He also starred in *Othello* and performed on stages around the world. The more he traveled, the more his political views changed.

By the 1940s, Robeson returned to America as a communist hell-bent on defeating American racism. When he suggested that Negroes should not fight if America went to war with Russia, the State Department revoked his passport in 1950. Although he still worked in entertainment, much of his work was sidelined when Hollywood blacklisted him for his communistic views. When his autobiography was published in 1958, most of the major media outlets ignored it. Many of his prior friends shunned him and he contemplated suicide twice. In 1958, Robeson's passport was reinstated, so he began to travel and perform in Europe again to wide acclaim. He suffered a massive stroke in late December 1975 and died on January 23, 1976.

RECOMMENDED RECORDING: *The Power and the Glory* (Sony, 1991) is a set of 16 spirituals and sacred songs such as "Balm in Gilead" and "I'll Hear De Trumpet."

Cleophus Robinson

POSSESSING A UNIQUE tenor with a distaff-sounding alto quality, Cleophus Robinson recorded a handful of obscure gospel classics. While never achieving the commercial success of many of his contemporaries, Rev. Robinson remained a prominent figure on the gospel circuit throughout the 1970s. Born March 18, 1932, in Canton, Mississippi, Robinson sang while working in the cotton fields as a child. His mother, Lillie, was a gospel shouter who had great influence on his music. In 1948, he moved to Chicago where he began to sing in a variety of churches. Through the Gay Sisters' Evelyn Gay, he was introduced to Lee Egalnick of Miracle Records. It was there that he recorded his first gospel sides. When those songs flopped, Robinson moved to Memphis where he lived with his uncle, Rev. L.A. Ham-

blin. He hosted a weekly radio program and opened for artists passing through town such as Brother Joe May, who became his mentor. He also formed a relationship with pianist Napoleon Brown, who would accompany him from then on. In 1953, Robinson signed to Peacock Records where he recorded a number of poorly selling songs such as "In the Sweet By and By." In 1956, he finally enjoyed a hit when he and his sister, Josephine, recorded the duet "Pray for Me." They later enjoyed another small hit with "When I Cross Over." Robinson's bluesy recordings emphasized the high-pitched growls of Joe May and the lusty wails of Mahalia Jackson, but his music never found itself at the top of the popularity charts. In the 1960s, he hosted the *Hour of Faith* weekly radio program and in 1964 launched his own television program. Over the course of the decade, he struggled through lackluster record sales on Battle Records, Savoy Records, and finally with Nashboro Records. In 1970, Robinson recorded his signature song, "Wrapped Up, Tied Up, Tangled Up." He later made some sermon albums for Peacock Records such as "Backsliding Heifer." Aside from an appearance at the 1975 Montreux Jazz Festival in Switzerland, Robinson's latter career was downhill from that point on. He died on July 2, 1998.

Eddie Robinson

AN EARLY EXPONENT of the Jesus Movement, Eddie Robinson was one of the first black gospel artists to work in the acoustic, guitar-driven embryonic era of contemporary Christian music in the 1970s. He was born in 1933 in Birmingham, Alabama. Robinson played piano as a child and began to play for Rev. Louis Bodie after his family moved to Chicago. He then became Mahalia Jackson's substitute pianist when Mildred Falls wasn't available. Throughout the 1960s, Robinson accompanied several gospel artists on piano. He recorded the LP *Reflections of the Man Inside* for Myrrh Records in 1974. The single of "I Give My All to Thee" was a moderate radio success. Robinson is now the staff pianist for St. Andrew Temple Choir and a chapel musician for Leak & Sons Funeral Home in Chicago.

Faye Robinson

SHE'S NOT ACHIEVED such mainstream fame as Kathleen Battle or Renée Fleming, but within the opera world, Faye Robinson is an established star. She graduated from Bennett College with a Bachelors degree before setting off on a journey that has seen her perform at virtually every major opera house in the world. Over the years, Robinson has starred in productions of *La Traviata*, a revival of *Don Giovanni*, and *Porgy and Bess*, among others. However, her first solo recording was *Remembering Marian Anderson* on D'Note Records in 1997. In her warm soprano, Robinson covered Anderson's classics such as "Ride On, Jesus," "This Lil' Light of Mine," and "He's Got the Whole World in His Hands." Known as a trouper even under difficult circumstances, Robinson always delivers her best. At a program saluting the music of William Grant Still (the first black classical composer) and Marian Anderson, the *Cincinnati Dispatch* music critic Barbara Zuck was disappointed in the pacing and performance of the Still segment. At one point in her review, she wrote, "The orchestra was just not at its best. It played sloppily and often out of tune." However, she was ecstatic about the Anderson tribute by Robinson. "Robinson was absolutely stunning," she wrote in January 1996. "She sang these songs with such magnificent vocal command and such a commanding emotional presence that she simply transcended whatever problems swirled around her."

Noel Robinson

ONE OF ENGLAND'S best-known and most admired Christian artists, Noel Robinson was born October 11, 1962, in the Willesden area of London. He was raised in church. His father taught him to play the guitar as a child and he picked up other musical education through the church experience he had as a youngster. He later studied classical and jazz studies at Goldsmith College where his instruments of choice were the double bass and the guitar. He continued his studies later at the Royal College of Music. Robinson then formed Jubal Communications, a recording and production

company. Through the company, he has recorded CDs such as *O Taste and See*, *Higher Higher*, and *Worthy in this Place*. Robinson and his backing group, Nu Image, were nominated for seven awards at the British Gospel Oasis awards in 2002 and took four of them home. He also hosts "The Gospel Show" on Choice FM Radio in London.

Roscoe Robinson

THIS DYNAMIC PERFORMER has made his mark in the gospel field with the Blind Boys of Mississippi and in R&B as a solo artist. Robinson was born May 22, 1928, in Dumont, Alabama, and was raised in Arkansas and Indiana. He grew up singing in church and recorded for a series of gospel groups all throughout the West and the Midwest. Among the groups he performed with were the Five Trumpets, the Highway QCs, and the Fairfield Four. Although Robinson was not blind, Archie Brownlee personally recruited him to join the Blind Boys. Robinson was afraid of blind people at the time and refused. However, when Brownlee fell sick and really pushed him to join, Robinson agreed and came to enjoy the group.

While they were on the road in Louisiana in 1960, they heard that Brownlee died. "He didn't take care of himself," Robinson says. Brownlee had suffered with a bleeding ulcer and other problems, and he was in and out of the hospital so much that he contracted pneumonia and died. Robinson continued with the group. When their contract with Peacock Records was up, they tried to get the owner Don Robey to buy them a new car before they re-signed. "The one we had couldn't hardly make it nowhere," Robinson recalls, "and he turned us down." So Robinson called his old friend Leonard Chess at Chess Records, who gave them a contract (and money to buy a new car).

"We recorded an album called *I'll Go*," Robinson says. They had a date in Houston where Robey was based and he called them into his office with a plan. "I hate to tell it, but I got to tell it like it was," Robinson says. "He said Chess has a lot of money and all we have to do is say that the group was still under contract to Peacock. They signed a pre-dated contract that said that we were signed. I didn't sign it because it was wrong and neither did Shorty (Lawrence Abrams), who was the tenor. So that eliminated me from the group… Then it was hard for me to get a job with another gospel group because they made it look like I had left the Blind Boys for the white man. They didn't get it how it should have been that I left because I was trying to do the right thing."

Robinson and Shorty formed a group called the Blind Boys of Ohio. They recorded a song for Vee-Jay Records called "Take Time Out." The lawsuit between Chess and Robey's Peacock label was in full swing and it was still crippling Robinson's career. "People believed it, so promoters didn't want no part of me," he says. Robinson pawned his Cadillac to record four R&B songs. He released them on his own Jerry Records label (named after his second wife). "It was doing good in places," he says. "But Ernie Lena at United Distributors in Chicago said he'd get behind it." Lena gave him spending money, cash to get his car back, and brought him three major label offers. Robinson decided to go with Scepter/Wand Records and told them that he wanted Lena's company to distribute the single of "That's Enough" through the Midwest in 1966. It reached No. 7 on the R&B singles chart and No. 62 on the pop charts in 1967. "They say it's a million-seller, but I ain't never received nothing financially to show me that," he says.

The next few years were rough personally. His second wife (a model for Johnson Publications) was cheating on him when he was on the road and when he confronted her about it, she got *Tan* magazine to run a story that Robinson was a bigamist. His first wife came to his aid and proved that he was not. He later married his third wife, Zanella, and they have a son who is in college now. Robinson's second wife got 40 percent of his earnings in the divorce settlement, so he left recording for a while to work in Nashville with another old friend, John Richbourg, and help launch Joe Simon's R&B career. Later in the 1970s, Robinson rejoined the Five Blind Boys of Alabama and sang with them off and on. His latest CD, *So Called Friends*, is a bluesy, old-school soul project that was released on Sound Mindz Records in 2004.

Smokey Robinson

DURING THE 1960s, Smokey Robinson's unctuous falsetto made teenage hearts swoon and he was considered America's greatest singing poet. He wrote some of the most memorable pop songs of the period, such as the Temptations' "My Girl" and Mary Wells's "My Guy" among a score of others. He was born William Robinson on February 19, 1940, in Detroit. He formed the singing group the Miracles while attending Northern High School in 1957. They teamed up with local songwriter Berry Gordy, who made them the first act on his Tamla/Motown Record label in 1959. The Miracles became the label's first hit group with a string of top-selling R&B/pop singles such as "Shop Around," "You've Really Got a Hold on Me," "I Second That Emotion," and "Tears of a Clown." In 1972, Robinson launched a solo career that featured such hits as "Cruisin'" and "Being with You."

In the late 1980s, Robinson beat a cocaine habit and rebounded from the dissolution of his first marriage, which ended over his infidelities. Through the intervention of his best friend, actor-producer Leon Kennedy, Robinson became a born-again Christian and very active in ministry as an evangelist. In spring 2004, Robinson released his first completely inspirational/gospel project, *Food for the Spirit*, for Liquid 8 Records. Considering Robinson's wealth and musical skills, the production was surprisingly pedestrian and low-budget sounding. However, gospel radio embraced the ballad "I Have Prayed on It," and the album rose to No. 3 on the gospel album chart. "I am certainly not ashamed at all to tell of my relationship with Jesus Christ," Robinson told GospelFlava.com in 2004. "I've known God since I was a child, growing up in the ghetto section of Detroit. My mom was what I call a 'God lady,' she brought me up to know God. She passed away when I was ten, and I was raised by my older sister. So I always knew that Jesus was the Son of God. Then in 1986, I made a personal decision, I decided for myself to accept Christ as my savior."

Woody Rock

A MEMBER OF THE '90s sensual soul vocal group, Dru Hill, Woody Rock stayed in the background during the group's initial success circa 1995. Dru Hill became known for their pillow-talk ballads such as "Tell Me," "In My Bed," "We're Not Making Love No More," "Never Make a Promise," and "How Deep Is Your Love." After the group's charismatic lead vocalist Sisqó appeared to be going solo on the success of his top-selling single "The Thong Song" in 2001, Rock briefly walked away from the group and launched a gospel career. Born James E. Green on September 10, 1978, in Baltimore, Maryland, his mother didn't allow him to listen to any secular music, and Rock grew up on the music of the Winans. During his high school years, Rock and three buddies formed the gospel group Dru Hill, named for the neighborhood they lived in. They sang throughout the Baltimore area. Once they found a manager to shepherd their career, he convinced them to switch from gospel music to R&B. Island Records offered them a record deal after they appeared on *Showtime at the Apollo.* Immediately, they turned out one sensual, soulful hit after another.

Although Rock enjoyed the success and adulation he was receiving, he needed more. He felt a need, especially after the death of his mother to cancer, to return to his gospel music roots. That led to him signing with gospel powerhouse Gospo Centric Records. The label postponed the CD release a couple of times in an effort to make sure the timing and mix of songs was just right. In the end, the 2001 CD *Soul Music* featured vocal collaborations with Mary Mary, B.B. Jay, and the Gospel Gangstaz, among others. In spite of a large press hype and briefly ascending the upper reaches of the *Billboard* gospel, CCM, and R&B album sales charts, the album was not the major success Gospo Centric was anticipating for a singer stepping away from a million-selling soul group. "The only thing I would say is different is the message," Rock said at the time. "Instead of singing about the ladies, I'm singing about the Lord. But the music and the beats are pretty similar." In 2003, Rock was back with Dru Hill, although their fame had dwindled considerably and their sound had been eclipsed by newcomers such as B2K.

D-Boy Rodriguez

A SELF-PROCLAIMED street poet, Christian rapper D-Boy Rodriguez was shot down in the prime of his life in 1990. He was born Daniel Dimitri Rodriguez in November 1967 in the Bronx, New York. His parents, Cookie and Demi, founded the Street Church Academy to help rehabilitate kids in Dallas street gangs. Rodriguez was a counselor there and helped many youth turn their lives around. Rodriguez recorded his first CD, *Plantin' a Seed*, for Frontline Records in 1989. The radio single "Pick Yourself Up" resulted in the only Top Ten CCM single of his career. "D-Boy was very influential on DC Talk," Toby McKeehan told *CCM* magazine. "He had exactly the kind of attitude that we'd like to try and emulate. He encouraged us, telling us he loved us. He wasn't trying to play any kind of games; he was just so humble. Obviously, his ministry was having an impact."

Rodriguez was in the midst of finishing up his sophomore CD and working in his parents' ministry when tragedy struck. He was dropping a friend from the ministry at her home in the Carrollton suburb of Dallas on October 6, 1990, when he was shot in the chest and killed. For a while, media reports suggested that Rodriguez was making trouble. "If you knew him that would crack you up," his sister Genie (gospel rapper MC Ge Gee) said in 1992. "When I went through my stage where I was trying to be bad and trying to cuss, I would get slapped by him. You couldn't say anything like that around him. He never went out. On weekends, he'd hit Blockbuster and rent videos. But he never liked to go out. He never cussed. We called him Disciple Dan… They also tried to insinuate that he was killed by a gang but that was ruled out because of my mom's relationship with the gangs. She hears things before they are going to happen and we would have heard. Someone will brief her or tell her any time of the night. So many of the gang members were upset when this happened that Mom said she hopes that the person who did this gets caught by the police before they get caught in the streets by a gang because that's how bad he'll get it. They all respected Danny."

After his death, rappers from Toby McKeehan to Vanilla Ice spoke of Rodriguez's influence on their lives. Frontline rushed out Rodriguez's last CD, *The*

Lyrical Strength of One Street Poet, which was his first project to chart. It reached No. 35 on the *Billboard* CCM album chart in early 1991. Genie Rodriguez, under the moniker MC Ge Gee, followed with the CD *The Mission Continues* to carry on her brother's ministry. Rodriguez's labelmate Angie Alan dedicated her song "Until We Meet Again" to his memory. MC Ge Gee found Vanilla Ice's thoughts on her brother incredible at the time. She said in 1992, "My brother didn't like him because he was so materialistic. He always wanted women in his car and my brother didn't even really know him. Then, when my brother died, an article comes out where Vanilla Ice says, 'That was my homie'… I thought he was trying to jump on some kind of bandwagon. He doesn't even know what my brother stood for."

D.J. Rogers

IF EVER A MAN walked the fence separating gospel and R&B, it is '70s soul-man D.J. Rogers. Like Curtis Mayfield, Rogers easily mixes biblical metaphors and songs of brotherhood with a mellow contemporary R&B rhythm. However, whereas Mayfield possessed a soft, sweet wisp of a voice, Rogers is the opposite. His voice is full and thunderous with an ear-piercing vibrato that would make the hairs on the similarly gifted Rance Allen's head stand on end.

Born DeWayne Julius Rogers on May 9, 1948, in Los Angeles to a preacher father, Rogers began singing in church at the age of three. He sang with the church's Sunshine Band and later directed the youth choir. As a teenager, Rogers sang with Harrison Johnson's Los Angeles Community Choir over the course of five LPs they recorded for Savoy Records in the 1960s. His lead on the choir's "I Decided to Make Jesus My Choice" was a radio smash in 1969. For a brief spell, Rev. James Cleveland served as Rogers's mentor and gave him the opportunity to record. In spite of his youth, Rogers was a veteran by that point and formed his own group, the Watts Community Choir, which recorded for the Proverb label circa 1969.

Although Rogers's heart was in gospel, many of his church friends such as Billy Preston and Bobby Womack had crossed over to secular music. One day Rogers was in BMI's office switching his songwriting affiliation to ASCAP when he met Don Williams, an executive with rock star Leon Russell's Shelter Records. Rogers handed Williams a tape of songs he had recorded. Williams immediately loved the music and called Russell on the phone to brag about it. Russell instructed Williams to sign Rogers on the spot. In 1973, Rogers's self-titled, message-oriented debut R&B LP appeared but was lost in the shuffle when Shelter changed distributors.

By 1975, Rogers had transferred his recording allegiance to RCA Records where he recorded the late-night masterpiece "Say You Love Me," a moving love ballad. It was not the single from his RCA LP *It's Good to Be Alive*; that single bombed and the label was on the verge of dropping Rogers from the roster until fate intervened. Radio announcer Tony Jones played the "Say You Love Me" track on Thanksgiving morning 1975 and the request lines lit up. Rogers later told writer David Nathan, "The next thing we knew, it was in heavy rotation, and two other L.A. stations—KGFJ and KDAY—were playing it, and the song was No. 1 on all three stations even though it was still just an album cut." After the record began to break across the country (with no help from the label), an RCA executive called Rogers and said the label didn't want to drop him. Rogers wanted to be dropped until the label sweetened the pot with a financial bonus.

Although Rogers sang of romance, even his love songs evoked feelings of church. He didn't leave the church behind. He brought it to his soul music and a majority of his songs revolved around everyday issues and spiritual matters. In 1978, Earth Wind & Fire's Maurice White signed Rogers to his Kalimba production company, which was distributed by Columbia Records. His first single, "Love Brought Me Back," a mid-tempo funk number, was released in July and reached No. 20 on the *Billboard* R&B singles chart. The word "love" was code for God and the song tells the story of a man on the edge who was "sinking fast 'till love brought me back." It was the perfect crossover song because, without spelling it out, it was obvious Rogers was referring to God in the song. Rogers's robust gospel wail further stamped the song as gospel.

Since 1980, Rogers has maintained a low profile, recording sporadically because of label politics and other personal pursuits. However, he kept his church ties intact. He wrote gospel songs such as "I Told Him I Would Sing" for Murphy J. Pace and "My Faith in Jesus" for Keith Pringle. A hero to the current neo-soul music generation, Rogers also has an influence on the young gospel generation. He recorded the duets "I'll Share It" on Darius Brooks's *Simply Darius* CD in 1990, "One More Day" on Keith Pringle's 1982 *I Feel Like Going On* LP, "I'm Determined" with Rance Allen on Chris Byrd's 1996 *Shower Down* CD, and "Constantly" on Melvin William's 2003 *When Mercy Found Me* CD. Rogers's songs continue to be popular cover songs for gospel artists as well. Willie Neal Johnson covered "Trust in Me," Helen Baylor revamped "Love Brought Me Back," and his "(It's Alright Now) Think I'll Make It Anyhow" was the song that made Hezekiah Walker a star in 1989. Although many soul artists such as Natalie Cole and Jennifer Holiday have recorded "Say You Love Me," Rev. James Cleveland transformed it into straight gospel as "Say You Love Him."

In 1997, Rogers had a recurring role on the UPN television sitcom *Good News*, but his name has circulated of late because of the success of his son D.J. Rogers, Jr., on the soul music scene. "I used to be very rebellious," Rogers, Jr., said to *Billboard* magazine. "When I was younger and mentioned my father's name, everyone would look at me like 'The D.J. Rogers?' or people would say, 'Can you sing as good as your dad?' But now I've grown into a greater understanding. The bottom line is, that's my dad. He loves me; I love him."

RECOMMENDED RECORDING: *The Message Man: The Best of D.J. Rogers* (Sony/Legacy, 1998) is a soul hits collection that also features some of Rogers's most delicious gospel sides, such as Walter Hawkins's "Changed" and his own "He'll Be Your All in All." It also includes "Love Brought Me Back" and the breathtaking "You Are My Joy," which is unabashed church wrapped in a love song melody.

Lulu Roman

LULU ROMAN IS best known as a hillbilly comedienne on the long-running *Hee Haw* TV show, but her early life was anything but funny. Born May 6, 1946, in a home for unwed mothers, Roman was later placed in an orphanage. She was born with a thyroid dysfunction that has made her struggle with weight problems all of her life. She's said she felt her weight kept her from being adopted and led to ridicule by other children. Instead of being the butt of jokes, she eventually turned the tables and created a self-deprecating humor as a form of defense. After beginning her career as a comedienne, she landed a spot on the syndicated *Hee Haw* country variety television show that ran from 1969 to 1992. A drug addiction and subsequent arrest for possession got her booted from the show in 1971. After rededicating her life to Christ, she was reinstated on the show and began to sing again.

In 1975, Roman recorded *One Day at a Time*, the first of four LPs for Rainbow Records. Her deep, sultry voice shone on polished Southern gospel tunes with just a wee bit of pop in them. She also enjoyed a happy marriage, motherhood, and great wealth during that period. However, after 13 years of marriage, her husband walked out on her and she lost her money. "The Lord has led me to trust in him," she once said. "I don't have any of the stuff that the world gave me. I have something more precious than silver or gold, or man's applause or worldwide fame. I have Jesus, and that's what makes the difference."

In 1984, Roman joined Word Records' Canaan Southern gospel imprint and recorded the LP *You Were Loving Me*, which won her a Dove award as Best Album by a Secular Artist. The following year's LP, *Take Me There*, was another Southern gospel hit and the title song (penned by Dolly Parton) was a highlight. A duet with Russ Taff, "King of Who I Am," hit No. 1 on the CCM chart that same year. "Two More Hands," a trio recording with Ricky Skaggs and Sharon White, hit No. 1 on the *Gospel Voice* chart in 1988. Over the years, Roman has recorded other fine Southern gospel albums for Homeland, Benson, Wing, and Orchard Records. "I hope my life can make the difference in someone else's life," she says on her Web site. "There's too much grieving in the world to stay down when you could be blessing someone with your ability to make them laugh, even though you sometimes hurt. I have learned that God didn't dump me, he chose me."

Joann Rosario

A PROTÉGÉ OF Fred Hammond, Joann Judith Rosario was born June 3, 1974, in Chicago. Her parents, Nahum and Minerva Rosario, founded Maranatha World Revival Ministries there. Her mother began to teach her how to sing when she was three years old. "My dad, as both my father and pastor, has had a great impact on my life. He raised me with Hispanic values which are very close to biblical values," she once said. Rosario traveled with him to many of the 300 churches he oversees throughout the world. While attending Oral Roberts University in Tulsa, she sang with the ORU Gospel Choir and Bishop Carlton Pearson's Azusa Mass Choir. Later, Rosario sang with rap group ETW at an Azusa television taping. When the program aired, Fred Hammond was snoozing with the television on. He was awakened by Rosario's voice booming through his television set. Hammond loved her voice and made arrangements to meet her. After writing some songs together and singing in his Radicals for Christ Choir, Verity Records released *Fred Hammond Presents Joann Rosario*, her debut CD. Pushed by the percussive, up-tempo song "Serve You Only," the album debuted at No. 11 on the gospel chart in spring 2002. After the single ran its course, the mellow praise and worship ballad "More, More, More" kept the momentum going. Rosario was nominated for a Stellar award as Best New Artist but lost to Smokie Norful. She was also nominated for a Latin Grammy for Best Latin Christian/Gospel Album. Fernando Ortega took that one home.

Diana Ross

SHE'S KNOWN AROUND the world as the First Lady of the Motown Sound that took the music world by storm in the 1960s and '70s. But fashion-plate Diana Ross has also subtly claimed a quiet faith which has resulted in some fine, if overlooked, spiritual music in her vast repertoire of hits. Born March 26, 1944, in Detroit, Ross's parents were educated and raised their six children in a clean, working-class neighborhood. They later moved up to the respectable Brewster Projects which were not the ghetto the Motown PR machine later painted them to be in order to create a rags-to-riches media story. The maternal side of Ross's family hails from Bessemer, Alabama, where her grandfather was a Baptist minister and her mother sang in church as a teenager. Ross attended church in Bessemer and back in Detroit. Her favorite gospel song was "His Eye Is on the Sparrow," which her mother used to sing around the house as her father whistled the melody. "It talks about how God protects all his creatures, even his littlest ones," she said of the song in her memoirs, *Secrets of a Sparrow*. "I think in a sense it was my mother's prayer or her protection for us. She protected us from many things in life, trying to shield us from its harsher realities... I've always looked at the more positive side of things. All the pain I've had in my life, I'll hold on to it for a second and then I'll let it go. I really try to let go of all the negativity and leave the rest up to God." Ross also wrote, "...My childhood gave me the greatest gift available: my profound spiritual faith, a faith that has been simple and unwavering throughout my life. I was still a child when I stood on the church stage for the first time, in front of the congregation, and recited the words to the 23rd Psalm... God gave my life this grace. My faith and truth are so deep, they're my private secret."

In 1961, Barbara Martin, Mary Wilson, and Ross joined Tamla/Motown Records as the Primettes. Their name was later changed to the Supremes and they became the biggest female pop group in history with songs such as "Where Did Our Love Go?" and "Come See About Me." In the '70s Ross went solo and became an all-around superstar entertainer with dozens of hit recordings. She won an Oscar nomination for her portrayal of Billie Holiday in *Lady Sings the Blues* and packed concert halls around the world. Through the years, Ross has occasionally slipped a faith-inspired song on her albums. In 1968, the Supremes recorded

"He" for a gospel album entitled *In Loving Memory* that featured several of Motown's leading stars singing gospel songs in tribute to the life of Martin Luther King, Jr., who was assassinated that year.

Among the other spiritual songs Ross has recorded are Wintley Phipps's "Tell Me Again" from 1986's *Red Hot Rhythm & Blues* CD and 1991's "The Force Behind the Power." The latter was written by Stevie Wonder and featured the Andrae Crouch Singers on background vocals. The 1993 CD *Christmas in Vienna* features Ross singing a beautiful plaintive "Amazing Grace" backed by the Vienna Symphony.

RECOMMENDED RECORDINGS: *Forever Diana: Musical Memoirs* (Motown, 1993). Aside from her big secular hits, this four-CD, 78-song box set includes outright gospels such as "Amazing Grace" and "Ninety Nine and a Half Won't Do." It also includes inspirational songs, such as moving renditions of "What a Wonderful World," "Let's Make Every Day Count," and "Reach Out and Touch (Somebody's Hand)." There's a fine EMI import holiday CD by Ross entitled *A Very Special Season* that features "His Eye Is on the Sparrow," "Amazing Grace," "What the World Needs Now Is Love," and her rendition of Stevie Wonder's "Overjoyed," which a number of gospel artist have adopted as a gospel song.

Nedra Ross

KNOWN AS THE ORIGINAL Bad Girls of Rock 'n' Roll music, the Ronettes were rock music's first tough girls to gain wide acceptance. Nedra Talley (born on January 27, 1946, in New York City), her cousins Estelle and Veronica Bennett, and Ronnie Spector first performed as the Darling Sisters in 1959. As Ronnie's raspy voice took center stage, they became known as Ronnie & the Relatives and finally as the Ronettes. Producer Phil Spector wanted to sign Ronnie as a soloist to his Philles label, but she refused to sign without her group. He signed the group and they scored with the 1963 hits "Baby, I Love You" and the No. 2 pop smash "Be My Baby." They also toured with the Beatles, but tensions within the group forced them to disband. In 1966,

Nedra Ross / Word/New Song promotional photo

while visiting her future husband Scott Ross's family in Maryland, Nedra visited a church and became a Christian. While her husband worked as a radio announcer and founded New York state's Love Inn Christian commune, Nedra Ross was content with domesticity as a wife and mother. In 1978, she resurfaced briefly with a heavily promoted gospel LP, *Full Circle*, on the Word/Myrrh-distributed New Song recording label. The album was easy-listening and contemporary Christian music fare that was somewhat bland, in spite of Nedra's heartfelt dulcet vocals. Legendary guitarist Phil Keaggy wrote and played on the title cut, which reached No. 8 on the CCM singles chart. At the time, Ross said of the project, "…you get what I was, what I was into, and who I am now. I know I've touched a lot of people in spite of my faults… God has used me and my music, and that's exciting." In 2000, the New York Supreme Court granted the Ronettes $2.6 million in their 1988 case against Phil Spector for back royalties. The case revealed that the singers had only been paid a $14,000 advance in 1963 and never received further compensation on their music, which made millions for Spector over the years. The eccentric producer has continued to appeal the case. However, as of 2005, Spector had more pressing court cases, including a murder charge in the death of actress Lana Clarkson, who was found dead at his California home on February 3, 2003.

Royal Sons Quintet

THIS WINSTON-SALEM, North Carolina, group actually consisted of six men, though their group name continued to say they were a quintet. Their music spanned several styles, including gospel. After a period of recording with Apollo, they moved on to King Records in 1954. Around that time, they changed their name to the "5" Royales (the quotation marks were intended to resolve some of the confusion about the six-member group) and enjoyed R&B hits such as "Think," "Tears of Joy" and "Dedicated to the One I Love." They disbanded in 1965, having influenced such artists as Eric Clapton and James Brown.

Rugged Cross Singers

THIS BALTIMORE-BASED male quartet recorded only four sides for Gotham Records circa 1955 in a three-hour session. Only one single was ever issued, "The Time Will Surely Come."

Thermon Ruth &
the Selah Jubilee Singers

BORN MARCH 6, 1914, in Pomaria, South Carolina, Thermon Ruth's parents died when he was quite young. At the age of eight, he moved to New York to live with a grown sister, Beulah. Having grown up in the South, she grounded him in a storefront church in Brooklyn, St. Mark's Holy Church, to build his moral character and protect him from the temptations of the big city. An active church singer all his life, Ruth formed the Selah

Jubilee Singers at the prodigious age of 12. At various times, the group included guitarist Fred "Sonny" Baker, John Ford, Bill Langford, Nathaniel Townsley, baritone Theodore Harris, bass Jimmy Gorham, J.B. Nelson, tenor Junius Parker, baritone Alden "Allen" Bunn (died 1977), Gene Mumford (died 1977), Melvin Coldten, and guitarist Norman "Crip" Harris. A cross between the Southern quartet style of the Fisk Jubilee Singers and the then-modern shouting style of the Soul Stirrers, they developed a local reputation and drew people to the church each week to see them sing during the services. However, the pastor, Mother Lambert, would not allow them to perform elsewhere for fear that her attendance would drop off. Almost a decade later, when they were of age, the group began to perform along the East Coast. They eventually relocated to Raleigh, North Carolina, and had a regular radio program on WPTF where they would sing live each week. Their name grew throughout the South before they ever recorded. Ruth had a strict code for the group: no cursing, no drinking, and no skirt-chasing. The group did often sport flamboyant, colorful suits that set them apart from other groups of the time. They landed a recording contract with Decca Records in 1939. Their earliest recordings such as "I Want Jesus to Walk Around My Bedside" were good but uninspired. As time passed, they became better. They later moved on to Continental Records but never enjoyed a breakout hit record. Among their finer performances were "Royal Telephone," "Stop Playing Numbers and Pray," and "Leak in the Building." During the height of World War II propaganda, they recorded the novelty tunes "Mother, Don't Cry If Your Son Goes to War" and "Wasn't That an Awful Time at Pearl Harbor?" They performed for the troops and were the first gospel group to perform Sunday concerts at the Apollo Theater in Harlem. Ruth kept pushing theater owner Frank Schiffman to give his group a chance. "He told me, 'They'll throw bananas at you,'" Ruth told the *New York Daily News.* "He set it up so I had all the risk. Then we packed the place to the rafters and I made the money." After the group switched from the then-outdated jubilee style to straight gospel, their audience abandoned them. Ruth and Bunn formed a new gospel group with new members and called it the Jubilators. They knew from experience that they would never get royalties on their songs, only advance money. So, in October 1950, they went to Jubilee Records and were paid to record four gospel songs. However, they listed themselves as the Selah Singers instead of the Jubilators. It didn't end there, though. A couple hours later, they had convinced the Braun brothers, who ran Regal Records in Linden, New Jersey, to record them as the Jubilators. They received their money and made their way over to Newark to persuade Savoy's Regency Records imprint to record them. Savoy was game and they recorded four R&B tracks as the Four Barons (although there were six in the group). One song was the risqué "Lemon Squeezer" with the line: "The way I squeeze your lemons is a low-down dirty shame." They were paid and made their way back to Apollo Records and asked for a different executive. They were sent back into the studio as the Southern Harmoneers, but an engineer recognized them from that morning and tipped off label owner Bess Berman. When she confronted them, they admitted that they were broke and had spent the day getting money from labels for singing on the spot. She liked their initiative and loved their music, so she forgave them, though she alerted the other labels to the scam. She got to keep them as her group, but the other labels were allowed to release their material under the names the group signed under. However, Berman didn't really want a gospel group. She wanted an R&B group to compete with the Orioles and the Ravens, so she picked a good bird name, the Larks, and rechristened them an R&B group. They released songs such as "My Reverie" and "I Live True to You." Their only chart hits were "Eyesight to the Blind" and "Little Side Car." Berman spent little on promotion and subscribed to the theory of throwing records in the air and if one stuck, that was the hit. "Every one of the Larks could do a lead," Ruth told the *Daily News*. "We could sing. If Bess had had any money for promotion, the Larks would have been stars." After his failure on the R&B circuit, Ruth returned to the gospel market. He saw nothing wrong with singing both gospel and R&B, but concluded that R&B wasn't for him. Ruth moved back to North Carolina where he became a DJ known as T. Ruth. In his later years, Ruth moved to New York and became active at St. Mark's. He died on September 13, 2002. Within the last decade, both Document

Records and P-Vine Records have compiled CD reissues of the Selah Jubilee Singers' music.

Kim Rutherford

PSALMIST-SONGWRITER Kim Rutherford has written some of Fred Hammond's best-known songs such as "You Are My Daily Bread," "Please Don't Pass Me By," and "That Ain't Nothin.'" She got her break as a member of Fred Hammond's Radicals for Christ choir in the early 1990s. Hammond soon noticed her talents and began to collaborate with her on composing songs. In 1995, Hammond produced Rutherford's debut solo CD *Brand Nu Vision* for Buster Soaries's Sparrow Records imprint, Proclaim Records. Soaries and Sparrow parted company midway through the promotional campaign and the recording died rapidly, although the song "Down Through the Years" received some decent radio airplay.

"She is the real deal," says Cinque Cullar, a singer with the gospel group Fortitude. "She is anointed to lead large numbers of people into the presence of God. I think it is her sole purpose. She is real and has a tremendous connection with the Lord. She's prophetic. She's solid in the Word. She's not like many artists who don't even have a church home. And to hear her speak? She speaks better than she sings and she sings beautifully. But the anointing on her can't be denied. Her writing—if you go back to some of Fred Hammond's best songs, she wrote them!"

The success of Rutherford's collaborations with Hammond led to other artists recording her material. CeCe Winans, Daryl Coley, Marvin Sapp, and many others have recorded her tunes. Perhaps Rutherford's shining achievement is her work on Hammond's *Pages of Life: Chapters I & II* where she contributed greatly to the song repertoire, backing vocals, and did narration on the live concert portions of the project. In addition, she and David Ivey led the ballad "Your Love," which showed off her light soprano. Aside from doing background vocal sessions for a number of recording artists, Rutherford was once the worship leader at Kingsley Fletcher's Life Community Church in Research Triangle Park, North Carolina. She is now based in Los Angeles.

Reggie Saddler Family

FOR YEARS Reggie Saddler sang for his supper in the best hotels in Las Vegas. He opened for such personalities as Patti Page, Bill Cosby, Redd Foxx, Jerry Lee Lewis, and Frankie Valli & the Four Seasons among others.

Born August 26, 1944, in Charlotte, North Carolina, Saddler's parents divorced early in his life and he was raised by his mother. He grew up craving his father's acceptance and attention. Learning guitar chords at the age of 11 helped Saddler take his mind off of his absentee father. As a teenager, he began to play in clubs around Charlotte before he headed out West and began playing on the Vegas strip. Along the way, he secured a recording deal with De-Lite Records in 1973 during the time the label was enjoying success with Kool & the Gang's "Jungle Boogie" and "Hollywood Swinging." He recorded "I Can't Account for My Actions" with Janice & the Jammers, but it failed to become a hit. In the late 1970s, Saddler became a Christian while visiting the late E.V. Hill's Mt. Zion Missionary Baptist Church in Los Angeles. Saddler and his wife, Bridgette, now comprise a Southern gospel quartet with their daughters Shivonne (born October 7, 1981) and Ingra (October 15, 1985).

The group records on their own recording label and has appeared on the television ministries of the conservative Baptist televangelists Jerry Falwell and Charles Stanley. They have also appeared on Bill Gaither's Homecoming concerts. Their biggest hits thus far have been "I've Got a Home," which reached No. 18 and "Anytime, Anyplace, Anywhere," which reached No. 14 on the *Singing News* Southern gospel chart. The family resides in Vale, North Carolina.

Sylvia St. James

SHE'S THE FORCE behind the popular gospel brunch phenomenon that the House of Blues restaurant chain popularized back in the 1990s. Born December 24, 1947, Sylvia St. James first gained fame as a member of the soul music troupe Side Effect. It began as a male trio in 1972 with Gregory Matta, Louis Patton, and their leader, Augie Johnson. In 1974, they decided to add the female purr of Sylvia Nabors, who was replaced by future gospel star Helen Baylor. In 1977, Baylor was replaced by Sylvia St. James, who had begun her career as a background vocalist on LPs by Ronnie Laws and George Duke (*The Aura Will Prevail*) in 1975–76. She remained with Side Effect for two years, singing on songs such as the funky "Goin' Bananas," the jazzy "Cloudburst," and the radio-friendly tune, "Private World." She left in 1978 and was replaced by future R&B balladeer, Miki Howard.

St. James contented herself with session work backing Stanley Clarke & George Duke on "Sweet Baby," Wayne Henderson on "Hot Stuff," and Lenny Williams on "Fancy Dancer," among others. In 1981, Williams helped St. James get her own recording deal with Elektra Records. He produced her debut LP *Magic Minstrel*. She followed up with the album *Echoes & Images*. In the early 1990s, James became national director of the House of Blues restaurant chain's immensely popular Sunday morning gospel brunches. In these brunches, St. James presents both national and talented artists on

Sylvia St. James / Elektra Records promotional photo

the rise. The brunches at the various House of Blues locations have become so popular that all sorts of restaurants have created their own gospel brunches. The outlet has proven to be very beneficial to record labels trying to expose new talent and promote new CDs. It has also helped reignite the careers of various artists. "She has played a very big part in our being successful," Madeline Thompson of the Clara Ward Singers said in 1994. "She keeps us on the news, she keeps us with the politicians. She keeps us with the people we're used to being with back in the old days, and they have really looked out and put us where we're accustomed to working."

RECOMMENDED RECORDINGS: For a taste of the type of music featured at the House of Blues gospel brunch, pick up *Essential Gospel Brunch* (House of Blues Records, 1999). St. James doesn't sing on the project, but there is a 45-second introduction by her on the CD, followed by two dozen gospel classics such as Commissioned's "Ordinary Just Won't Do" and Vickie Winans's "We Shall Behold Him." St. James also served as choir conductor on Harry Connick, Jr.'s *Harry for the Holidays* CD, which reached No. 1 on the *Billboard* jazz chart in 2004.

Samputu

ONE OF RWANDA's best-known vocalists, Jean Paul Samputu was born on March 15, 1962, in Butare Ngoma, Rwanda. Although he grew up on a musical diet of Bob Marley and Stevie Wonder, he put his vocal talents to work with a couple of choirs in his teens. After departing the group he co-founded, Nyampinga, he recorded his first solo album, *Tegeka Isi* (Govern the World), in 1985. After a Rwandan entrepreneur, Valens Kajeguhakwa, began to invest in Samputu's music, his career took off on a higher plane. Following the 1994 Rwandan genocide when millions of people were killed (including Samputu's mother, father, and four siblings), he refocused his music on healing the divisions in his country and finding faith in faithless circumstances. Among the recordings from this period are "Mana Wari Huri He (God, Where Were You?)." Samputu's

music is a blend of African musical traditions (Ugandan, pygmy, rhumba, and soukous). He is the first Rwandan to win a Kora award (a pan-African accolade equivalent to the Grammy).

Marvin Sapp

BEST KNOWN AS A latter-day member of the '80s gospel supergroup Commissioned and for his 1997 breakthrough hit "Not the Time, Not the Place," Marvin Sapp still hasn't developed a neat niche in gospel. Some see him a preacher more than a singer and therefore don't take him seriously as a performer. However, the diminutive vocalist has a velvety boom of a voice that commands attention when it merges with the correct song. His mellow, R&B approach to contemporary gospel (reminiscent of Donny Hathaway) is engaging and has sustained his popularity in spite of uneven recorded material.

Born in Grand Rapids, Michigan, Sapp began to sing in church at the age of four. He always loved music, imbibing a mix of D.J. Rogers and the Winans with Stevie Wonder, Donny Hathaway, and Teddy Pendergrass. He vacillated between a gospel or secular music career until his mother forced him to choose one or the other. He then devoted himself to church music and sang in various gospel groups before becoming an evangelist in 1988. In 1990, he received a surprise phone call from Fred Hammond who was looking for a vocalist to replace Keith Staten in Commissioned. While the group was still successful, their popularity had waned a little and their glory days were behind them. Sapp's first album with the group was *Number 7*. He appeared on two further albums with the group and led on songs such as "Until My Change Comes" and "I Am Here."

After the group disbanded circa 1996, Sapp's self-titled solo debut CD appeared on Word Records and spawned the moderate radio hits "Calling Me" and "In His Presence." However, it was 1997's *Grace and Mercy* CD that created a buzz about Sapp. The CD peaked at No. 11 on the gospel chart and produced the mid-tempo megahit "Not the Time, Not the Place," which remains popular on the radio. His last Word album charted well on the strength of the prior CD, but did not produce any major radio hits. After Word shut down their black music division circa 2000, Sapp moved on to Verity Records where he released the album *I Believe* in 2002. Again, nothing spectacular happened on the radio, but Verity's promotional arm made it Sapp's highest-charting project to date. It reached No. 4 on the gospel chart and No. 62 on the R&B/hip-hop album chart. That same year Commissioned reteamed for a reunion live CD and national tour that were both well-received, though not on the grand scale many of the parties had anticipated. A decade had passed since Commissioned was a significant industry presence, and much of their '80s music (the uptempo numbers in particular) sounded dated, much like '80s R&B group New Edition, which has launched a couple of ill-fated reunion tours in recent years. The tour wasn't embraced by many who were unfamiliar with the group but who came out because they were fans of Fred Hammond's solo material. Sapp now spends much of his time doing community work and preaching through his JOY ministries. "I am not a singer who happens to preach," he's said. "I am a preacher—called of God—who happens to sing."

Rev. Bill Sawyer

SAWYER WAS A striking man with handsomely dark skin and a thick mane of jet black hair that rolled off his shoulders like the Lion's in *The Wizard of Oz*. Born July 25, 1935, in Cleveland, Sawyer was pastor of the city's Christ Tabernacle Church. Tyscot Records founder, Dr. Leonard Scott, once told GospelFlava.com, "Our first 'hit' recording was a project we picked up from Rev. Bill Sawyer from Cleveland, Ohio. He had released the album *Something Old, Something New* that contained the song, 'Near the Cross,' sung by an elderly lady who used to be a nightclub singer years before. He told us he could not keep up with the sales and run his church too. So he asked us to take it over. It became our first recording to move major numbers. It was the first time that radio stations and stores called us for servicing and products." That LP hit No. 18 on the gospel chart in 1984. Sawyer followed with the LPs *Gospel of Yesterday*

and Today and *What a Wonderful Change*. He died April 1, 1990, in Chicago.

Bishop Leonard Scott

ONE OF THE FIRST to bring praise and worship into the black church, Dr. Leonard Scott has never enjoyed a big personal radio hit, but he has enjoyed career longevity as a worship and praise artist. He was born February 28, 1949, in Indianapolis, Indiana, where he became a practicing dentist and active in his church. In 1976, Scott started Tyscot Records with L. Craig Tyson with the intention of promoting his church's choir, the Christ Church Apostolic Radio Choir. The choir's first LP, *Feel Good*, was released in 1977 and the label was on its way. Tyson later sold his share to Scott and left the business. The company made a huge leap when it signed Rev. Bill Sawyer who gave the label their first huge hit with his *Something Old, Something New* LP in 1984. In 1988, Scott's 19-year-old son, Bryant, joined the label as an executive and runs the label today.

Scott continues to record intermittently. One of his most successful albums was 1989's *Holy*, which featured four John P. Kee compositions, including "Come Let Me Tell Ya" and "Worthy to Be Praised." However, 2004's *Hymns for the Nation* may well be his first bona fide hit. With his rapid tenor, Scott delivers that old-time religion on tunes such as "Glad to Be in the Service." The album is sprinkled with Scott's sermonettes and vocal cameos by Albertina Walker, DeAndre Patterson, Nicki Ross-Turnley, and Bishop Clifford Johnson. If Scott's project doesn't take off as it deserves to, it doesn't matter to him because he's just as happy to provide the musical platform for other artists. "Sometimes we get caught up in fame and fortune and forget the main focus: Christ," he says. "Remember where your blessing came from and why you got into this ministry in the first place." It's a theme that he echoed in a *Billboard* magazine interview in 1994. "Some people aren't in the music because they love the music, they're in the music for the business of it—just to make the dollar," he said then. "And I think that anything you're in, you're going to have a greater impact if it's in your heart." Scott is the pastor of the Rock Community Church in Indianapolis, Indiana.

Sensational Jubilettes

THIS GROUP, probably based in Detroit, recorded the wailing "Jordan River" for the Motor City's Message Records label circa 1962.

Sensational Nightingales

OFTEN CALLED The Gentlemen of Song for their dignified yet stirring traditional quartet harmonies, the Nightingales' measured technique and smoothness contrasted nicely with the earth-shattering vocal spontaneity and dynamics of their primary lead vocalist, Julius "June" Cheeks. The group was founded in 1942 by Barney (later Rev. B.L.) Parks, who left the Dixie Hummingbirds to start his own group in Philadelphia. The original members were Howard Carroll (also a renegade Hummingbird), Paul Owens from the Swan Silvertones, Ben Joiner, and William Henry. The Nightingales recorded several sides for Decca Records during the war years and worked sporadic markets, mostly gaining regional fame in certain pockets rather than national stardom.

In 1946, Parks decided that the group was missing something to send them over the top when he discovered Julius Cheeks. The new lead singer brought so much verve to the group that fans started calling them sensational to the point that Parks changed the group's name to the Sensational Nightingales. They joined Peacock Records where their first single was "Will You Welcome Me There?" in 1947. What distinguished the group immediately was Cheeks's preacher's baritone that he used to growl, holler, and reach helium-level falsetto notes. Some of their biggest hits during the 1950s included "New Burying Ground," "Morning Train," "Somewhere to Lay My Head," and "See How They Done My Lord." In 1960, Cheeks left the group, and neither he nor they ever enjoyed the same level of fame without each other.

After Peacock Records was bought by ABC Records, the Nightingales continued to record, with the smoother Charles Johnson taking over Cheeks's former position. However, few of those songs found an audience and in 1979 the group signed to Malaco Records with a lineup consisting of JoJo Wallace, Willie Woodruff, Horace Thompson, and Calvert McNair. Woodruff's signature song with the group was "He Was There All the Time." Over the years, they've done more than a dozen albums that have kept them working the quartet circuit, particularly in the South. Their most recent CD, *Wasted Years* in 2001, featured the group as a duo of Wallace and Thompson with guest accompanists to round out their sound. This new sound has taken on a smoother Southern style without the legendary Cheeks's fiery vocals and persona. The group's influence on the styles of vintage soul singers such as James Brown, Wilson Pickett, Bobby "Blue" Bland, and even B.B. King was due to the Cheeks mystique more than the group's harmonies as a whole. Without Cheeks, the Nightingales were an average-sounding quartet, and it's no surprise that the years without him never returned them to the heights they once reached with him. Still, they will go down in history as one of the most influential quartets during the Golden Age of Gospel.

After his first wife died in 1991, Woodruff moved to Bladensburg, Maryland, where he remarried. He suffered from diabetes and heart ailments, and died July 15, 1995, at a motel in New Castle, Delaware, where he was performing in concert. Woodruff's death left only JoJo Wallace and Horace Thompson as members who date back to the group's glory years in the 1960s. They have since added the far younger singers Larry Moore and Darrell Luster to the group and continue to perform up to 200 dates a year.

7 Sons of Soul

GROUP MEMBER David Lindsey has described the 7 Sons of Soul's sound as the Canton Spirituals meet the Winans. Although there are only six men in this retro-soul gospel group, they say the seventh slot stands for the ultimate son, Jesus Christ. Cliff Jones has extensive experience with artists such as Will Smith and Boys II Men. He first came to public attention as the primary vocalist on William Becton's "Be Encouraged," which was both a major gospel and R&B single in 1995. Jones was then signed to a deal with Atlantic Records. His urban inspirational CD was shelved, though. He later toured in the play *Your Arms Too Short to Box with God* and also produced tracks for Gladys Knight's first gospel CD *Many Different Roads*. In recent years, Jones formed a sextet with a quartet sound when he dreamed up the 7 Sons of Soul. In addition to Lindsay and Jones, the group is rounded out by Nathaniel Fields, Paul Edwards, Sam Kendrick, and Deonte Gray. All of the members were working musicians in the Washington, DC, area before they came together. In 2004, their debut CD *7 Sons of Soul* appeared on Verity Records. Pushed by the mellow, urban adult contemporary–styled inspirational ballad "Run On," the album peaked at No. 24 on the *Billboard* gospel album sales chart and sold 40,000 units.

Rev. Al Sharpton

OVER THE LAST 20 years, Rev. Al Sharpton (born Alfred Charles Sharpton, Jr., on October 3, 1954, in Brooklyn, New York) has served as a lightning rod in US politics— his words at times polarizing the entire country over the issue of racism. He gained national notoriety for his involvement in the Tawana Brawley rape and Howard Beach assault cases in 1987, during which Sharpton launched public protests to draw media attention to the racism he said was prevalent in that part of New York.

Sharpton was baptized at the age of three and delivered his first sermon at the age of four. He was an ordained minister by the age of ten and was billed as the "Wonder Boy Preacher" at the 1964 World's Fair. His family was well-off, as Sharpton's father was what Sharpton Jr. himself called a "slumlord." His mother kicked Sharpton Sr. out of the house for getting her daughter from a previous marriage pregnant. Sharpton Sr. later married the daughter, and Al's mother and the other children were forced to live in a housing project.

Sharpton, who toured as a preacher with the likes of Mahalia Jackson, staged his first protest during high school when he complained about the dress code and cafeteria food. In 1969, he became youth director for Rev. Jesse Jackson's Operation Breadbasket. In 1971, Sharpton formed the National Youth Movement, a grassroots organization that registered young voters and also pressured the entertainment industry to employ inner-city youth. He was later youth coordinator for Shirley Chisholm's 1972 presidential campaign. Sharpton was a student at Brooklyn College when he met the Godfather of Soul, James Brown, in 1973. The two developed a father-son relationship, and Sharpton even adopted Brown's processed pompadour hairstyle. He dropped out of school to become Brown's road manager during that period. On that tour, he fell in love with one of Brown's background singers, Kathy Jordan, and they married a decade later.

Sharpton later worked with boxing promoter Don King and was involved in a number of community programs. Although he was already well-known in the black community for his service, Sharpton wasn't formally introduced to mainstream America until 1986's Howard Beach incident, in which a black man was killed as he was fleeing a white youth mob. However, that incident paled in comparison to what would take place the following year. On November 28, 1987, 15-year-old Tawana Brawley (aka Maryam Muhammad) was found in Duchess County, New York, covered with feces and racial slurs written in charcoal. She claimed to have been abducted and raped by six white men, some of them law enforcement officers. However, a few hours before, a neighbor was looking out her window and witnessed Brawley pack herself into a green trash bag and lay on the muddy ground. The neighbor notified the police, who came out to investigate the suspicious behavior. Brawley gave conflicting stories as to what happened when she was interrogated by the authorities, and forensic tests found no evidence of a sexual assault.

Still, Rev. Al Sharpton and others used the incident to demonstrate what they considered systemic racism within the police and judicial system. The media frenzy over the event brought Sharpton national attention and scorn by many who felt the Brawley case was a trumped-up hoax. The case was eventually thrown out of court in 1988 when a grand jury determined that the story was not credible. Steven Pagones and the other accused were cleared of all charges a decade later (and Pagones later won a $150 million defamation lawsuit against Sharpton and other accusers). In 1991, Sharpton was at the forefront of the Crown Heights riot that pitted blacks and Jews against each other in New York. That same year, Sharpton was stabbed during a Bensonhurst rally. It was while he was recovering that he realized the impact of his often loose, incendiary words.

Sharpton has since worked on reshaping his image to appeal to a more diverse political constituency. He traded his colorful jogging suits for business suits. In 1992, he ran for a Senate seat in New York and then ran a campaign for mayor of New York. Although he didn't win either seat, fans and foes alike applauded Sharpton's new statesmanlike demeanor. He also won high marks for his 2004 campaign for president of the United States. Again, he did not win, but he brought many issues to the campaign and spoke at the Democratic National Convention that year. Since 1991, Sharpton has run the National Action Network, which seeks to educate and empower citizens on a variety of issues, including economics and voting rights.

RECOMMENDED RECORDING: James Brown and Sharpton teamed up to sing and testify on a traditional gospel LP, *God Has Smiled on Me* (Royal King Records, 1981).

Kierra Sheard

THE ONLY DAUGHTER of Karen Clark-Sheard of the legendary Clark Sisters gospel group and Bishop Drew Sheard of Greater Emmanuel Institutional COGIC, Kierra "Kiki" Sheard was born circa 1987 in Detroit. Before Sheard was born, her grandmother, Mattie Moss Clark, predicted that she'd be born to sing the gospel. When she was singing in a children's choir at church, she was given a solo. She floored the church and her mother then knew it was time to groom her for a ministry in gospel music. Sheard made her recording debut on the song "The Will of God" from her mother's 1997 CD *Finally Karen*. It was a traditional duet where the ten year old and her mother swapped trademark Clark Sis-

ters riffs. When they premiered the song at a T.D. Jakes revival at Chicago's UIC Pavilion that year, the 6,000 church folks in attendance went wild after hearing Kierra copy her mother's dynamic runs note-for-note.

As Sheard matured, she began to develop her own sense of faith. "Before my mom recorded *2nd Chance*, she had a minor surgery procedure," she told ChristianityToday.com in 2004. "But she developed complications, and the doctors gave her a two percent chance to live. The family thought she was going to die. I didn't have much faith in God at the time, and I'd decided that if she didn't make it, I was going to live however I wanted to. But with God, all things are possible. He answered my prayers and took the load from my shoulders. My mom recovered.... I've gone through a lot of things that people my age have gone through. I've been through situations that forced me to learn who my true friends are. I've had a broken heart. I've seen friends drift away from God and end up having babies or on drugs. My mom's illness challenged me a lot. That's why I thank God for keeping his hand on my life."

Many of those feelings are spoken of in Sheard's debut single "You Don't Know," arguably the biggest gospel radio hit of the summer of 2004. Produced by R&B producer Rodney Jerkins, the song packed an infectiously fresh urban punch with a strong gospel message. The song spent several weeks at No. 1 on the *Radio & Records* gospel chart and her EMI Gospel debut CD *I Owe You* debuted at No. 1 on the gospel, No. 29 on R&B, and No. 4 on CCM album sales charts—virtually unprecedented for a new artist in gospel and a good barometer for what her future may hold.

Silver Leaf Quartette

A NORFOLK, VIRGINIA–based jubilee-styled quartet in the 1920s, they recorded for a couple of labels, including OKeh Records. Their primary success was the tune "Sleep On, Mother." Various members kept the group's name alive until bass singer Luther Daniels passed in 1979 and the group was permanently retired.

Carole Allen Simmons

ONE OF HOUSTON's great vocal wonders in the 1980s, Carole Allen Simmons perished long before she reached her artistic and commercial peak. She was born on May 20, 1942, in Houston, Texas. Her parents, Bennie and Earline Allen, were prominent leaders in the COGIC denomination. Simmons, her sister, and two brothers sang in the family group, the Allenettes, throughout their youth and teen years. After finishing high school, Simmons recorded with Mattie Moss Clark's UNAC COGIC Choir and with Richard White. In the 1980s, Simmons recorded for a variety of Texas-based recording labels, most notably Lively Records in Dallas. Although her records were not distributed far beyond the borders of Texas, Simmons's dramatic performances earned her a stellar reputation within the COGIC denomination. In 1990, Simmons was performing a concert in Canada when she fell ill. She was unable to keep any food down, so she called her mother and asked her to make some mustard greens for her. "When she got here, she ate those greens and the other things she asked me to prepare and told me how good it all tasted," her mother, Earline Allen, says. "The next day, she called and said that she had been sick ever since she ate the food." Allen suggested she go to the doctor, but Simmons procrastinated for weeks. When she finally went to a doctor, she was told that she had colon cancer that had spread to her liver. The doctor gave her a year and a half to live.

"She was very brave about it," Allen says. "The doctor asked if she cried about it and she said no. So then he asked, 'Are you angry?' She said no. Then he said, 'Well, I am, because a woman with a voice like this and the potential that you have, if you're not angry, then I am." Her mother moved Simmons into her home, took her to her hospital visits and nursed her around the clock. "I did everything I could to save that child's life," Allen says. She even showed Simmons videotapes of her performances to inspire her to become well so that she could sing again. "'That's why I'm sick,' Carole said about her singing for the Lord," Allen says. "[She said] 'The devil don't like it.'" Had she lived, Allen feels Simmons would have become a preacher. "She was

moving further and further into ministry," says Allen. However, Simmons died in August 1992. Her four adult children (Angela Bennett, Yolanda Jones, John Simmons, Jr., and Mark Simmons) all work in the music field. Angela and John are performers. Yolanda gives private voice lessons at her own music school, and Mark is a professional drummer who has played on recordings by such artists as jazz great Al Jarreau.

RECOMMENDED RECORDING: *It's in My Heart* (Lively Records, 1989) is a hard-to-find LP that showcases Simmons's fervent gospel performances. Most of the songs were written and produced by Lively Records owner Willie Stewart, such as "Everything Will Be Alright" and "Real (Jesus Is)." Another Houston singer, Kathy Taylor, wrote "God's Amazing Grace," Simmons's sister Myra Cormier wrote "Oh Lord, I'm in Your Care," and the late Carl Preacher (Sara Jordan Powell's piano accompanist) wrote "Worthy Vessel."

Joe Simon

SINCE LEAVING SECULAR music in the 1980s, Joe Simon has virtually been forgotten by all but his staunchest fans, but for the entire 1970s Joe Simon was a top-draw singer. His music made smooth transitions from '60s bubble-gum pop to Southern soul before closing the decade with funk-disco hits. He is one of the few singers able to sing absolutely any style of music with effortless perfection. No one possesses a voice exactly like Simon's smooth, plaintive drawl, which has been known to croon and squall within the same measure. Born September 2, 1943, in Simmesport, Louisiana, Simon first sang in the choir of the Pilgrim Rest Baptist Church. When Sims was 15, his father moved the family to the Oakland, California, area for better employment prospects. Simon enjoyed the music of Ray Charles and Arthur Prysock, but he later joined the Golden West Gospel Singers. The members were tempted to try secular music so they changed their name to the Golden Tones, the name under which they recorded "Little Island Girl" for Hush Records in 1959. In 1964, label owner Gary Thompson pulled Simon into the studio to record "My Adorable

One." The record made enough money for Vee-Jay Records to buy Simon's contract from Hush. They released "Let's Do It Over" in 1965 and it reached No. 13 on the R&B charts, but the label soon went out of business.

In 1966, Simon was passing through Nashville promoting his latest Vee-Jay single when he encountered the city's 50,000-watt WLAC DJ John Richbourg, an amiable white man who was the most influential R&B radio announcer in the South. Simon expressed his unhappiness with Vee-Jay's handling of his career. "He was the first guy I ever met who could swing that much weight yet be so nice," Simon told the *Tennessean* in 1985. "I had never been to Nashville. I was just passing through. He said, 'Well, man, I've got this label called Sound Stage 7; why don't you give me a chance with your career?' Richbourg became Simon's mentor and producer. Their first single, a sweet doo wop tune called "A Teenager's Prayer," went to No. 11 on the R&B chart that year and was soon followed by Southern soul Top Ten hits such as "The Chokin' Kind" (which won him a Grammy in 1968), "Your Love," and "Farther Down the Road."

Singer Otis Redding was also an aid to Simon's career. They were running partners and were booked to do some joint concert dates before Redding died in a December 1967 plane crash on the way to Cleveland to tape the *Upbeat* TV show. Simon was supposed to be on that plane, but something came up at the last minute. Fellow singers Johnnie Taylor and Joe Tex joined him as pallbearers at Redding's funeral. Macon, Georgia's City Auditorium was packed beyond its 3,000-seat capacity with a who's who of soul music present: James Brown, Wilson Pickett, Sam & Dave, Rufus and Carla Thomas, among others. Over audible sobs, Simon sang Redding's favorite gospel song, "Jesus Keep Me Near the Cross," as Redding's widow, Zelma, broke down. It was a sobering moment Simon has recalled in his rare media interviews.

In 1970, Richbourg moved Simon to the new Polydor-distributed Spring Records which had greater financial resources and inroads to the urban market to take Simon's career to a new level. After initial productions with Richbourg, Simon later collaborated with producers such as Raeford Gerald and Gamble & Huff to create the smash R&B hits "Your Time to Cry," "Drowning in the Sea of Love," "Power of Love," "Trouble in My Home," "Theme from Cleopatra Jones," and

"Get Down, Get Down." After a couple more chart hits in the early '80s and a failed record label venture with Richbourg in 1984, Simon left secular music completely. He then dropped out of public sight, even turning down offers for oldies-but-goodies revues. Thus far, Simon has only recorded one gospel CD, the excellent *I Must Tell the Story*, which peaked at No. 27 on the gospel chart in 1998. The album was done in the smooth, classic Southern soul vein of his early '70s hits. Standout cuts were "Come to Jesus" and "He's Gonna Smile on Me." Simon is now a traveling evangelist with an Illinois home base.

Nina Simone

ONE OF THE MOST indefinable singers of the 20th century, this song stylist recorded blues, standards, gospel, and classical music during her 50-year music career. She's also one of only a few performers who is known more for a body of work than for a signature tune. In spite of that, Simone's work is characterized by a deep-seated anger born from growing up in the segregated South. Those emotions were displayed through black self-pride on songs such as "To Be Young, Gifted and Black" and biting commentary on tunes such as "Mississippi Goddam." She was born Eunice Waymon on February 21, 1933, in Tyron, North Carolina. She grew up in a religious family. Her father, John, was a handyman and her mother, Mary, was a domestic during the week, but they were both Methodist ministers on Sundays. By the age of four, Simone was playing the piano by ear. Later, she was a busy teenager: not only did she play the organ at church, she was president of the student council, sang in the glee club, played on the basketball team, and was the 1950 valedictorian of Allen High School for Girls.

Simone eventually became a piano student at the prestigious Juilliard School of Music in New York. She put herself through school by playing piano in nightclubs. She changed her name from Eunice Waymon to Nina Simone (after the French actress Simone Signoret) when she landed a job at the Midtown Bar in Atlantic City. She changed her name so that her religious parents would not hear that she was singing secular music. Her unique, masculine vocals and trembling vibrato mixed well with her leisurely, jazz style of approaching pop standards. Simone soon became confident enough to seek a recording deal. Her first major hit was 1959's "I Loves You, Porgy" on the Bethlehem label. A switch to Colpix Records included the classic *Forbidden Fruit* LP in 1961. The title track was a hilarious recitation of the biblical Adam and Eve story. Simone enjoyed other hits such as "I Put a Spell on You," "Ne Me Quitte Pas," and "Trouble in Mind." By the end of the 1960s, Simone had evolved from a chanteuse into a black radical. She sang bitterly of the death of civil rights activist Medgar Evars and of four black children in a church bombing in Birmingham in the scathing "Mississippi Goddam." Her music took on an even more "Black Is Beautiful" theme as Simone stopped straightening her hair and began to wear an afro instead. From that period, she recorded sensitive songs such as "Four Women," which examined racism within the black community, and "To Be Young, Gifted and Black" which was a proclamation of self-esteem. By the middle 1970s, Simone's marriage had dissolved, her record sales were down, and at one point, she was broke.

Simone temporarily retired from the business and moved to Liberia with her daughter. In 1978, her manager boyfriend struck a blow to the base of her skull that kept her hospitalized for several weeks. Extremely depressed, she took an overdose of valium, but was found and treated before it could kill her. She eventually rebounded and moved on with her life. Unlike many artists who grew up in church and left it behind to pursue secular careers, Simone never did. Throughout her career, she openly embraced gospel music and inserted whatever she fancied into her vast repertoire.

"The more you listen to the radio—there are about five or six groups I can point out that came straight out of the church," she told *Ebony* magazine in 1969. "I mean the feeling. It's the same! But they just call it soul music. It bridges the gap. You know my people…my parents have a way of looking at it—I always give them a hard time about it because I have never believed in the separation of gospel music and the blues. Gospel music and the blues have always been the same. It's just that Mom and Dad were so religious that they wouldn't allow you to play boogie-woogie in the house, but would allow you to use the same boogie-woogie beat to play a gospel tune."

In her later years, Simone seemed to rarely smile. To many, she was an angry, aging singer. She was known to get into shouting matches with journalists. She was also known to get into verbal spars with hecklers in her audiences. In 1993, Simone left the scene of an accident and was later fined $5,000. In 1995, she was ordered to pay $4,600 to two teenagers she shot at when she claimed they were disturbing the peace while she was gardening. However, the last few years of her life were some of Simon's best financially. She was recognized as the music legend she was and earned upwards of $40,000 a night for the sold-out concerts she gave during that period. She also seemed to smile more often, take things less seriously, and even poked fun at her radical past. Sadly, she knew what the world did not. She had been battling cancer the last few years of her life and the disease claimed her life on April 21, 2003 in Carry-le-Rouet, France.

RECOMMENDED RECORDINGS: Unfortunately, none of the labels Simone recorded for have had the foresight to compile all of her gospel music on a single set. She recorded many gospel songs during her Philips Records years circa 1965–66. During that period, she recorded "Nearer Blessed Lord," "Sinnerman," and "Take Me to the Water" among others. Her 1968 *'Nuff Said!* LP featured a stirring rendition of "Precious Lord, Take My Hand."

Tommy Sims

HE'S THE MAN to call when you want to merge a gospel message with a tight, commercial pop groove. Singer-songwriter Tommy Sims was born in Chicago. Like many children reared in strict Christian homes, gospel music was the only music allowed, though his stepbrother and an uncle introduced him to secular music on the sly. Sims studied music at the University of Michigan for a spell and later toured the US with several bands. In the late 1980s, he moved to Nashville and used it as a base to begin songwriting for various artists. In the 1990s, Sims was mentored by rock icon Bruce Springsteen and was a member of his E Street Band for a while. A song he co-wrote for Eric Clapton and Babyface called "Change the World" was featured in the 1996 John

Travolta film *Phenomenon* and became a No. 1 pop single. It also won a Grammy as song of the year in 1997 and turned a lot of new people onto Sims. He's a top studio session man, having played bass or keyboards on projects by Amy Grant, Michael W. Smith, and Michael McDonald among others. In addition, he's produced McDonald (*Blue Obsession*), CeCe Winans (*Everlasting Love*), Darwin Hobbs (*Vertical*), and an array of gospel artists. In 2000, Sims birthed his first solo CD, *Peace and Love*, on Universal Records.

Sister Cantaloupe

IN THE GUISE of Sister Cantaloupe, Trina Jeffrie tells jokes like this: "Only one thang that really, really, really made me mad," she says. "One man [Louis Farrakhan] could get a million menzzzzzz to march allll the way to Washington, and I can't get one to march down the aisle." Then, when she plays the dozens, she's vicious: "Your mama hair so nappy, Moses couldn't part it!" They call her the First Lady of Gospel Comedy, sort of a Moms Mabley with a Bible in her hand. She's a loud-mouth, gossipy church mother who tells people off and calls them as she sees them, though she really means no harm. Dolled up in a yellow nightcap, grey wig, red Poindexter glasses, a colorful flower-print dress, knee-high stockings, and an oversize pair of house slippers, Trina Jeffrie transforms herself into the Sister Cantaloupe character that has helped put Christian comedy on the map.

Born January 2, 1962, Jeffrie found life anything but funny growing up in Dallas. Her mother suffered from mental illness and spent most of her adult life in a psychiatric institution. After she died, Jeffrie's father remarried and left Jeffrie to be raised by a series of relatives. Living in the projects, Jeffrie joined a street gang and was in such grief from her mother's death that she contemplated suicide. "I felt like I had no purpose," she told the *Arlington Morning News*. "I was waiting for the bus because I didn't have a car. I decided to let the bus hit me instead." But as she was about to step in the path of the bus, Vickie Winans's gospel song "Stay with Me" came over the airwaves of KHVN radio, which was blasting through her Walkman earphones. "God

did have a plan for me," she thought to herself. "I stopped, and the bus just went on by."

Jeffrie began to focus more on acting. She had always lost herself in TV sitcoms and had first noticed she had a talent for comedy at the home of her great-aunt Ruby, who wasn't hip on fashion. "She would dress me in old lady clothes," Jeffrie recalls. "Kids would tease me. To keep them from hurting my feelings, I started to make fun of myself. I'd make them laugh at me and that would take the hurt off of it." Lucille Ball and Carol Burnett were her role models. After graduating from South Oak Cliff High School, Jeffrie worked at a bank and insurance company while pursuing acting on the weekends. While preparing to do a skit at a church banquet, Jeffrie conjured up the Sister Cantaloupe character. She wasn't sure what to call her. It couldn't be offensive but had to be funny. "Right up to the time they called my name I still didn't have one for the character," she says. "As I was passing dinner tables to get to the stage, I saw fruit bowls with cantaloupe in them and I said, 'Sister Cantaloupe,' that will be my name."

A local gospel radio announcer enjoyed the skit and asked Jeffrie to repeat it at a show he was hosting. As expected, the audience was captivated with Sister Cantaloupe, who is based on a slew of characters, including the bag lady performed by Carol Burnett on her 1970s TV variety show. "I put a big old crazy hat on with the Minnie Pearl shopping tag hanging down. I put pads in my bra and in my back-end," she's said. Jeffrie turned the laughter into opportunities. She opened for gospel and R&B recording artists Stephanie Mills, John P. Kee, and Peabo Bryson, among others. BET gospel TV host Bobby Jones booked her as a guest on his weekly TV show where she met Al Hobbs, president of Aleho Records, who signed her to a comedy recording contract. The CD and video *Go Cantaloupe, Go Cantaloupe, Go!* was recorded live at Dallas High School and went on to sell over 30,000 units with little gospel radio airplay. Then her Dallas buddy Kirk Franklin picked her as the opening act for his 1997 "Tour of Life" concert tour (also co-starring Yolanda Adams and Fred Hammond) that put Jeffrie in front of 10,000 new faces every night for over six months. "I'm not just up on stage talking about my family," she says. "I'm talking about my family in church. I'm not just talking about my kids. I'm talking about my kids in church. Everything has to do with church."

In spite of her emphasis on the church, some pastors don't like Jeffrie's brand of humor. She has often been boycotted by churches who feel that Christian comedy is sacrilegious. "But there have been a couple of times when a pastor uninvited me and then saw me perform somewhere else," she recalls. "Then he liked what he saw and invited me again when he realized I wasn't making fun of God." She was once considered for a role on the *Martin* sitcom on Fox TV, but it did not pan out. "They did take some of my ideas and created Shenaynay though," she recalls. Eventually, she hopes to bring her comedy to television, but in the meantime, she's content to be working and knowing that she's inspired a new trend of female gospel comics such as Mother Onion and Small Fry. "All my characters are fictitious because my goal isn't to offend or hurt my audience," Jeffrie explains. "I know how that felt as a kid. I don't talk about Baptists or specific groups. I keep everything focused on Sister Cantaloupe."

RECOMMENDED RECORDINGS: Perhaps Cantaloupe's best project was her second one, *Laffin' Out Loud with the Lord* (Aleho, 1999), which features a lot of black church humor and a little music. For those wanting a sample of a variety of Christian comics, check out *Sister Cantaloupe Presents Some Funny Things Happen in Church* (Aleho, 2003), featuring the comedy of Cantaloupe's peers Small Fry, Ron Baker, Jr., Meeshel, Rod-Z, and Quinn.

65dBA

THE CHAMPIONS OF the British music idiom known as Sanctified Dance (a fusion of techno and jungle rhythms with gospel lyrics), the group was founded by distaff vocalist Shaz Sparks and keyboardist Robbie Bronniman in 1990. The group was rounded out by Phil Ball (drums), Danny Budd (guitar), and Stu Bobson (bass). The Bristol-bred group was initially produced by British Christian pop artist Sheila Walsh's producer, Ray Goudie. He aimed the group at inner-city youth

and they took their name from the decibel level restriction they were given prior to one of their very loud concerts. Their music was first released by Nelson Word Records in England, and later picked up by Integrity Music in the United States. They released two CDs under the deal, *The Great Awakening* and *Shout*. The song "Drowning in the Sea of Love" from the latter peaked at No. 4 on the CCM singles chart in November 1995. However, subsequent recordings failed to match that success. By 1996, Sparks and Bronniman were performing as a duo under the name of DBA after the other members had left the group. The group morphed once again into a group called Hydro and now appears to be on hiatus. The blonde bombshell Sparks, whose voice has a soulful black sound, now records for Detox Records in London as a soloist.

Janet Lynn Skinner

A POPPISH GOSPEL singer who enjoyed a decade of success in the 1980s with hits such as "Just a Prayer Away," Janet Lynn Skinner was born in Cleveland, Ohio, where her white mother was a private duty nurse. Her black father died of spinal meningitis before she was born. Skinner was raised in the Pleasant Grove Baptist Church. When she was four years old she walked to the front of the church and told Pastor Jerry Valentine that she wanted to join the church. He asked why, and she said, "Because I'm ready to serve the Lord." They sat her in the choir stand and she sang with the adult choir from then on.

During high school, Skinner was a member of the Future Nurses club. "During the summers I volunteered at local hospitals," she recalls. "And I was having a hard time with blood. I remember my counselor saying, 'Janet, do you think this is really the career for you?' So I kind of ruled that out." After graduating from Shaw High School in East Cleveland, she attended Cleveland State University as a business major. During her spare time, she joined the Cleveland Church of Christ Choir. "That was Bishop James Haughton's church," she says. "Their choir was well-known in the city. I joined the choir and became one of their featured singers." She

Janet Lynn Skinner / photographer: Michael Mann

came in contact with producer James Bullard when he produced a 45-rpm on the choir called "Yes, He Will" that received radio airplay in the city.

It was during that period that Gentry McCrary, a Light Records executive, sought to have Skinner join the label, with plans for Walter Hawkins to produce the project. "Having no professional experience I was somewhat leery," Skinner says. "I was nervous. My mom was nervous." " So they declined the offer. However, there was a policeman named Dale Edwards who attended the same church as Skinner. He had written and produced an album of music for another singer. As he was shopping the album, the feedback was that the music was good, but the singer was not. He then approached Skinner about rerecording the vocals. Skinner had another idea. She suggested that they write all new songs and open their own record label. "It was unprecedented in those days," she remembers. "We shopped a record where we would own it and just lease it to a record label. We got a lot of opposition to that because our company was unknown. But God was in our midst. We started talking to every major record label. Back in those days it was Light Records, Savoy Records, and a few others."

The dynamic duo could not gain the interest of a label to distribute the LP, *The Beginning*, for their Joy

Records label, so they released it regionally themselves circa 1980. The album received decent airplay and Skinner was performing to promote it. Then Gentry McCrary became an A&R executive for Onyx Records. He caught wind of the project and arranged for it to be released through that label in 1982. "They had Richard Smallwood and Vanessa Bell Armstrong," Skinner says laughingly as she thinks back on the period. "I remember feeling abandoned. She was such a powerful artist. That was eye-opening for me because with Joy Records I was the artist, but when you go somewhere else they have other priorities. But looking back I can't be angry because that may well be her best album ever; she was a phenomenal talent." Onyx was able to get the album sold nationally and the radio single "Just to Be with You" became a modest gospel hit.

"My ministry was growing and we did a lot of things," Skinner says. "If I had applied myself more, maybe things would have happened sooner or on a larger scale." Still, she was apprehensive about dropping her professional career for a gospel career. "If [I had been] at McDonald's flipping burgers, it might have been easy to leave," she reasons. "But I had a middle management job and it was difficult for me to make that change. I met a lot of artists who were well-known in the industry and they were struggling financially." Skinner held on to her position at the Picker X-ray Corporation and her supervisors allowed her to travel for her ministry work when it was necessary. "I had a band and we left here Friday in a van," she explains. "We'd get on the road and we'd go places. Sometimes I'd get back Monday morning about five or six o'clock in the morning, take a shower, and go to work. That was my life for several years and trust me, I did not complain."

By the mid-'80s, Onyx Records had closed. Skinner continued to work off of her one LP until she became reacquainted with James Bullard, who had produced her church choir in the 1970s. He was, at that time, the vice president of black gospel for Word Records. He worked the same sort of distribution deal that Skinner enjoyed with Onyx. "We feel Janet Lynn Skinner is a tremendous new artist who has a great deal of potential," Word Records executive Ken Harding said at the time in a press release. "Her contemporary, pop-oriented style appeals to today's younger gospel audience who is looking for very upbeat, uplifting music." Interestingly enough, her label debut had very little for youth. Skinner's smooth, light soprano shone on *The Beginning*, an album of mostly midtempo pop-gospel styled songs that were more suited for an adult audience. Edwards and Skinner produced all of the material. Skinner laughs thinking back on the recording process. The duo wanted to step up the production and began to do some recording in Hollywood. "We went Los Angeles to lay some tracks; we wanted to hang with the big dogs," she recalls. "John Brinson, who helped coordinate the production, kept saying he was going to have this musician come and he kept calling him Larry. So imagine walking into the studio and there stands Boom-Boom Washington— Lawrence Hilton-Jacobs from *Welcome Back, Kotter*. When he sat down and started playing keyboards it blew my mind because I certainly had no idea he could play that well."

Word Records added Skinner to a promotional concert tour with Shirley Caesar, the Richard Smallwood Singers, the Mighty Clouds of Joy, and Philip Bailey in 1987 and the momentum built for her career. The upbeat, traditional-styled title track "One Prayer Away" propelled the album to peak at No. 25 on the *Billboard* gospel chart in 1987. Being with a big label such as Word opened Skinner's eyes about music politics. Suddenly, music critics were not viewing her music in terms of its ministry. They were appraising it for artistic purposes. Skinner was taken aback. "This guy out of New York ripped my album to shreds," she says. "He said I was neither fish nor fowl, that you couldn't tell if I was a white artist or a black artist and that my music wasn't true to either category." Even more disheartening was that she found a stack of her LPs that were stamped "DO NOT PROMOTE AS BLACK GOSPEL." With her prior album, Skinner had received airplay on both white and black Christian and gospel radio stations.

The things Skinner was seeing bothered her. "There were some business things that didn't work out like we'd hope," she says. "They were doing things and testing the waters, but I'm also not sure the commitment was there. Amy Grant was the queen and they seemed to focus on her a lot." In addition, "I became disenchanted with the industry. I looked on it as a farce. Unfortunately, I had

some bad experiences with some of the companies because of financial things they owed me. A lot of the executives were not interested in salvation and saving souls… it was really a money-making game. After a while, I took notice of that and I really lost interest… I didn't feel God was in it."

At that point, Skinner left the recording aspect of the industry behind her and continued with her position at Picker until Edwards came up with another venture. "Dale was trying to put Cleveland on the map and radio was one of his pet projects," she says. She became a Sunday morning radio announcer on WZAK, an FM urban format station. Their sister company WJMO played oldies. When they changed it to a 24-hour gospel station, Skinner became a co-host for an afternoon drive-time show. On Saturdays she hosted a praise and worship show, and on Sundays, she continued to announce on WZAK. "I loved it," she said of the decade she spent with that hectic schedule. In 2001, Edwards bought WABQ and Skinner began her current weekday drive-time show. In May 2004, Skinner became music minister at the Destiny Church, a small but loving congregation of 300 in Twinsburg, Ohio, where she serves under pastors Calvin Brown, Sr., and Bob Ross. "I like being at a church where the pastor knows who you are and when you're ill, he'll come and see you," she says.

Alvin Slaughter

ONE OF THE LEADING praise and worship artists in the predominantly white Christian music industry and church circuit, Alvin Slaughter was born July 17, 1955, in New York. His parents never attended church, but Alvin was forced to and developed an aversion for it. He met his future wife, Gloria, at a prayer meeting when he was 14 years old. Soon, their relationship became intimate, and they had two children before they finally married when Slaughter was 23. He did not have a well-paying job and became depressed over his failure to provide for his family. They were evicted from two apartments and could barely pay their bills. Finally, "I bailed out," Slaughter told the *Good News Gazette* in June 2003. "I left church. I left my wife. I quit my job. I hated black churches. I hated white churches. I hated everybody, including myself. I remember walking down the streets of Manhattan with balled fists saying to God, 'I hate you. I can't stand you.'"

It was at the urging of his sister that Slaughter attended a service at Brooklyn Tabernacle Church. Under their leadership, Slaughter's defenses softened and he became active in the church. At the same time, his estranged wife had begun attending services at the church and through counseling, their family was reunited. Slaughter joined the church choir and became a featured soloist. His signature song with the choir was "I'm Clean." Around November 1990, Slaughter went into full-time ministry after a series of business ventures failed. After a while, Slaughter was in such demand that Integrity Records offered him a recording contract. From the beginning, Slaughter's music was embraced by the largely white evangelical audience that appreciates praise and worship music. Beginning with the CD *Revive Us Again* in 1995, all of Slaughter's albums have hit the *Billboard* Top 40 Christian albums chart. However, he has never reached the black gospel chart, although his 2003 CD *On the Inside* was produced by gospel producer Kevin Bond and geared toward black gospel radio more so than his previous efforts. For a time, Slaughter also hosted a weekly musical series on the Trinity Broadcasting Network. "God has turned my life completely around," Slaughter told *LA Focus* magazine. "I'm no longer crying to God to bless me, but now I say, 'Lord, make me a blessing.'"

Slim & the Supreme Angels

ONE OF QUARTET music's most enduring acts, Slim & the Supreme Angels have contributed hits such as "Better Make a Change," "People Don't Do," "Where Shall I Be," "Shame on You," and "Death and the Beautiful Lady" to the canon of gospel music. Throughout the years, personnel have come and gone and life has brought change, but the one constant has been Howard "Slim" Hunt.

Hunt was born in 1936. He grew up in Walnut Grove, Mississippi, where his deeply religious family toiled as sharecroppers. "We picked cotton and grew corn for feed. I mean to tell you, I came up on the rough side," he once said. "That was during the war and times

were tough. If we got two pairs of shoes in a year—one pair for work and school—and a Sunday pair too, we thanked God because that meant it had been a good year." Although he sang in church from the age of four, Hunt never dreamed of becoming a singer as an adult. "I remember working in the fields—I must've been eight or nine—and a plane would fly overhead," he says. "I'd get to daydreaming, and tell my mother how one day I'd be traveling, too. She'd fuss at me and say, 'You'd better get back to work, boy. If I get that switch after you, you're gonna do some travelin' right now!'"

When he turned 17, Hunt abandoned the farm life and moved to New Orleans and lived with his sister for six months. He worked on a riverboat steamer for a while and then moved to Milwaukee in 1953 where he stayed with another sister. There he worked briefly for a plumbing company. "That didn't last and I was out of work until I heard about a group that needed a baritone singer," he once said. "So I started on with them, but I still didn't know singing was going to be a career." By 1956, Hunt was playing guitar and singing with a local gospel group called the Soul Seekers while working in a candy factory.

Making a bigger name for themselves in gospel circles was a group called the Paramounts, who had changed their name to the Supreme Angels around that period. They had actually recorded a couple of national singles, "Run to the Rock" and "Jesus Let Me Sleep," that were beginning to make some noise. A few days before a big concert, the Angels' guitarist ran off to Florida, taking the one guitar the group owned. "Our group was rehearsing when one of the Supreme Angels came by and asked me if I would play for them that weekend," Hunt said. "I did, and I guess they liked what they heard, because they asked me to stay on.

"Some of the guys in the group were preachers, and eventually they stopped singing and started pastoring churches. The rest of us decided to try to make a go singing rock 'n' roll and the blues. We were packing out juke joints every night, but the church people begged us not to go that route. Some of the other fellows decided to go out on the road just playing churches. We traveled all over the USA.

"It was pretty rough making a living since we didn't have a record out at that time, and we didn't have good sense either. We'd drive to Philadelphia to sing one night, and then get in the car and drive straight through to California—to make maybe $250. We were young. It never occurred to us, I guess, that we could have just stayed put where we were and done a lot better.... Things were so tight by the late '50s, the group broke up and left me out on the road alone because they couldn't make a living. Three of the guys went into the service. We had recorded 'Lord Bring Me Down,' which was a big record for us and was getting played all over. Promoters had booked the group, but there was no more group! I had to do a few shows solo, but people received me well."

Hunt held on to the group's name, but finding reliable members was hard. He sang solo for most of the 1960s with only occasional backup. In 1969, he found the guys he needed to round out a group: Robert "Sugar" Hightower (vocals, guitar), Quincy King, Larry Young (vocals, keyboards), Michael Richardson (vocals, bass), and Maurice Robinson (vocals, drums). They began to record and finally made a breakthrough with the gold-selling single "Shame on You" in 1974 for Nashboro Records. Other hits followed and they continued to build their audience. In 1986, Hunt felt called to preach and founded the Deliverance Temple in Dillon, South Carolina. However, in spite of his preaching duties, he has always maintained the group. They have continued to hit the gospel Top 40 with albums such as *Death and the Beautiful Ladies* (1989), *Stay Under the Blood* (1995), *Nobody but You* (1996), and *Over Yonder* (1998).

The Angels still maintain the passion that made them leaders in the quartet world. In October 2000, an arts newspaper reporter caught the Supreme Angels' performance at a tribute concert (held at the Emmanuel Evangelistic Temple) for Milwaukee's best-known gospel personality, Andrew Taylor, who was celebrating 32 years on the radio. "Slim, a grim, lanky veteran of 50 years on the gospel highway, was backed with hot-double time vamps and strangely ominous grooves in the less frantic tempos—his fire-and-brimstone fulminating about secret sinners and hypocrites was accompanied by equally incendiary tuneage, including some searing, rocky, bluesy guitar licks," the reporter wrote. "Whether the song dealt with the story of a blind man thought delusional because he told everyone he was already walking on streets of gold, or a rambunctious warning to the audience to start living right, Slim & the Supreme Angels worked their acolytes into a stern and joyous sweat."

Richard Smallwood

HE IS TO BLACK gospel what Frederic Chopin was to classical music: an artisan who composed rich, melodic harmonies for pianists. He is also gospel's finest high-art composer since Thomas Dorsey, who wrote "Precious Lord." Richard Smallwood has built a career and a solid audience by ingeniously fusing the strings and hauteur of classical music with the vocal stylings and piano chords of the traditional black church. As a result, he has created a body of work that is melodic and commercial yet distinguished and intelligent in a musical genre often stereotyped for its emotionally charged earthiness and histrionics. Songs such as "Center of My Joy," "Total Praise," and "In the Shelter" are sung in some church somewhere in America every Sunday of the year.

Born November 30, 1948, in Atlanta, Georgia, Smallwood began to play piano by ear by the age of five. By seven, he was taking formal lessons and by eleven had formed his own gospel group. He graduated cum laude from Howard University with a degree in music. He was a very active student at the college where he

Richard Smallwood / photo courtesy of Richard Smallwood

Left to right: Jacky Ruffin, Dottie Jones, Wesley Boyd, and Richard Smallwood / photo by Peter Nash

developed relationships with fellow classmates such as Donny Hathaway, Debbie Allen, Phylicia Rashad, and Roberta Flack. Smallwood was a member of Howard's first gospel group, the Celestials, who are reputed to be the first gospel group to sing at the Montreux Jazz Festival. Smallwood was also one of the founding members of the Howard Gospel Choir. Following college, Smallwood taught music at the University of Maryland for a while. In 1977, he founded the Richard Smallwood Singers. They were originally a five-to-seven member group that brought a progressive, contemporary sound to gospel music. They performed throughout the Washington, DC, area before they were signed to Onyx Records (the black gospel division of Benson Records) in 1982. Their debut LP *The Richard Smallwood Singers* spent 87 weeks on *Billboard* magazine's Spiritual chart.

With lead vocals fluctuating between the charismatic Dottie Jones, the smoldering Jackie Ruffin, the earth-quaking Darlene Simmons, and Smallwood's dry tenor, they created a distinct sound that caught on with middle-class, mostly black Christian young adults. Whereas most gospel artists of the period appealed to an older crowd, the Smallwood Singers enjoyed a young, savvy following. Their 1984 LP *Psalms* hit No. 1 on the Spiritual chart. They moved over to Word Records' Rejoice black division for the 1987 LP *Textures*, which did

not chart as high (No. 7) as their previous album but produced the biggest hit of the group's career with the ballad "Center of My Joy." Composed by Smallwood with Bill and Gloria Gaither, the song had a soft pop feel that built to a rousing gospel crescendo with a background vocal arrangement alternating between a classical chorale sound and a passionate gospel blow-out. It was the first song to introduce Smallwood to the white Christian community and has since been covered by artists as diverse as Ron Kenoly, Tanya Goodman-Sykes, and the Sensational Nightingales. The group's popularity led to an invitation to perform in the Soviet Union—reportedly the first gospel group to do a concert tour of the country at the time. The group also supplied background vocals for soul/gospel music legend Candi Staton on her 1988 traditional gospel LP *Love Lifted Me* and her 1989 contemporary gospel CD *Stand Up and Be a Witness*. Smallwood shadowed Staton's vocals on the title cut of the latter.

Following another album that charted but didn't sell as well as their prior projects, entitled *Portrait*, the Smallwood Singers moved on to Sparrow Records where they rebounded with the smash radio hit "What He's Done for Me" from the LP *Testimony* in 1992. They did one more LP for the label, a *Live* CD featuring "Stand by Me" and "In the Shelter" the next year before moving on to Jive/Verity Records. "I've been with every major gospel label that there is," Smallwood once said. "I've been able to compare different labels and the way that things are done—the support or lack of. I've been in the position of the new kid on the block, where the importance or focus was put on the names that were known better than I was at the time, and all the energy was put on them…. The label just did not give me the support, and that's a frustrating feeling because you have a lot of ideas and concepts that you'd like to see [happen], and you go to the label and say, 'Hey, I've got this idea about marketing or promotion,' and they say 'Well, we'll see.' They just kind of put [the record] out there, and if it makes it, it makes it on its own, without any serious support from the label. I've been there."

Once he moved to Verity, Smallwood disbanded the Smallwood Singers. He formed a large backing choir named Vision who backed him on his first Verity CD,

Adoration, which featured the smash hits "Angels" and "Total Praise" in 1996. With Vision, Smallwood continued to push out hit after hit CD, such as *Healing, At the Table*, and *Calvary*. Unlike a lot of gospel artists who enjoy a couple of megahits and then fall out of sight, Smallwood has never enjoyed gospel superstardom per se, but he has enjoyed consistent career longevity. Without courting them, Smallwood's music has been embraced by secular artists who have recorded his gems, including Whitney Houston ("I Love the Lord"), Yolanda Adams ("That Name"), and Destiny's Child ("Total Praise"). When asked about the impact of his songs, Smallwood was philosophical in a 1993 *Washington Post* interview. "I don't know that I have all the answers or any of the answers," he said. "But being a minister of music, I need to be open to listen and give a word of encouragement through songs of testimony. Singing is only part of it. The ministry itself is much more than that."

Esther Smith

A GOSPEL BELTER of the Shirley Caesar generation, Esther Smith has paid her dues though she's never enjoyed the recognizable hit records and fame of her peers. Her career has taken her from her teenage years as Little Esther in the Lockhart Singers group in the 1950s, on through her years at Stax Records in the 1970s with the Howard Lemon Singers, to her solo recordings after 1980. Smith has created a body of consistently enjoyable, substantial gospel music that is a proud contribution to the evolution of gospel music in the 20th century.

Born Esther Jones on December 9, 1937, in Guntown, Mississippi, Smith's life has been a wild ride. Her parents separated early. Her father was a womanizer who left the family and moved to Milwaukee. Her mother took a housekeeping job on a wealthy plantation in order to take care of her three children. They lived on the premises and as a child, Smith picked cotton with her family. After her mother was nearly killed by an unwanted suitor, the family fled to relatives in Chicago. There Smith became active in her church and at the age of 13 she escaped her troubled home and was taken in

by a couple named Mom and Dad Lockhart. Smith became the lead singer with the Lockhart Singers, who recorded for Vee-Jay Records. Little Esther led on "Own Me as Your Child," "Walking Up the King's Highway," "Feed Me Till I Want No More," and "I Want to Be a Christian." She was such a great singer that James Cleveland recruited her to go on the road with his Cleveland Singers group. "I was only 15 and the mother of the church told me that it would not be a good idea," Smith once recalled. "She felt the environment was not good for a kid. But I was so honored and almost cried when I had to say no."

At the age of 18, Smith became a missionary and spent the next few years outside of the music business. In 1969 she joined the Detroit-based Howard Lemon Singers who would soon snag a recording deal with Stax Records' Gospel Truth subsidiary. The label was run by veteran R&B promotion man Dave Clark and the music was aimed at inner-city youth. They recorded the LPs *Message for Today* (1972) and *I Am Determined* (1973), but they never scored a major hit. Smith did lead their best-known songs, "Tradewinds" and "Anytime You Need Him." Smith finally departed the group in 1980 and went solo after signing a deal with Detroit's Sound of Gospel Records.

Although her national success was never all she hoped it to be, Smith was beloved in Detroit where she was a mother figure to many aspiring gospel artists, such as Fred Hammond and Vickie Winans. That respect led Detroit's finest artists to collaborate on launching her solo career. Mattie Moss Clark produced her *Trust in Jesus* LP in 1980 and saw the single "Moving in My Heart" take off at traditional gospel radio. The project's success led to her sophomore LP *Soul Winner* in 1982. Marvin Winans produced the title song and provided background vocals for her *Miracles* album, but Smith's biggest album thus far is *Esther Smith...Live in Concert*. It was recorded at her home church, International Gospel Center, in Ecorse, Michigan. Gospel radio made big hits out of the uptempo "Just Call Him" and the worship ballad "More of Thee and Less of Me." Her final LP with SOG was *He Loves Me*, produced by Fred Hammond and Michael Brooks. Most recently Smith has been affiliated with DoRohn Records where her

2000 CD *He Loves Me…Still* produced the funky, up-tempo radio hit "He's Able."

Michael W. Smith

DURING THE LATE 1980s and '90s Michael W. Smith reigned as Christian music's pretty pinup boy and its biggest commodity outside of Amy Grant. His light-weight vocals and pop songs gave him 15 minutes of fame as a crossover artist when his inspirational ballad "Place in this World" reached No. 6 on the *Billboard* Hot 100 singles chart in 1991.

Born October 7, 1958, in Kenova, Washington, Smith became a Christian as a youngster and spent his teens with a group of brethren who strengthened his faith and played music together. However, when he came of age, he strayed into drug and alcohol abuse. After a try at college, Smith began to work on his songwriting skills. In 1978, Smith relocated to Nashville where he played keyboards with bands such as Rose. His drug abuse came to an end in fall 1979 when he had a nervous breakdown that led to him rededicating his life to Christ. He soon joined the CCM group Higher Ground as their keyboard player. In 1981, Smith became a staff songwriter for Meadowgreen Music where he wrote songs for Sandi Patti, Kathy Troccoli, and Amy Grant's breakthrough LP *Age to Age*. He and Grant became fast friends, and Smith went on tour with her as her keyboardist. After "Great Is the Lord" from his debut LP *The Michael W. Smith Project* took off, Smith toured as Grant's opening act.

Smith's success paralleled Grant's and he continued to make his mark through the 1980s with hit Christian radio songs such as "Friends" and "Pray for Me." In order to maintain his youthful audience, in the early 1990s Smith began to turn his music more toward rock and pop with less blatant spiritual messages. When Reunion Records struck a deal with Geffen Records, they were able to cross Smith over to the pop charts with such AC hits as "I'll Lead You Home," "I Will Be Here for You," and "This Is Your Time." However, by the late 1990s and into the millennium, Smith had returned to his musical roots with more church/worship-oriented music such as the platinum albums *Worship* and *Worship Again*.

Rev. Dan J. Smith

ALTHOUGH HE HAD sung gospel blues all of his life, it wasn't until the last quarter of his life that Rev. Dan Smith began to develop an audience and a reputation as a performer. Born February 23, 1911, in Perdue Hill, Alabama, Smith sang in church as a child. "I went to church," he once said. "But I wasn't saved. I just liked singing church songs." He learned to play harmonica at the age of 18 and briefly played the instrument on some of Leadbelly's 1930s recordings. During World War II, he worked in defense contract factories, but he lost his vision in a work accident at a General Motors plant in Tarrytown, New York. Smith didn't begin his career in earnest until the 1960s when he accompanied folk music circuit performers such as Pete Seeger and Rev. Gary Davis. He appeared at the storied Caffè Lena and the Fox Hollow Folk Festival, both in upstate New York. In 1970, Smith heeded a call he heard many years before and became an evangelist in the Fire Baptized Church denomination, though he continued to perform. In spite of his coterie of fans on the folk circuit, Smith's sound had a distinct delta blues feel. In 1992, he released his first CD, *Just Keep Goin' On*, for Glasshouse Records. Smith was in bad health during much of the recording and recorded intermittently as his spirit permitted. Produced by esteemed Americana music producer Buddy Miller, the CD featured guest vocalists Bryan Duncan, Victoria Williams, and Julie Miller. On the CD sleeve, Smith wrote: "My aim is to reach the unreached, lift the unlifted, to strengthen the weak, encourage the discouraged, help the helpless, unburden the burdened, comfort the lonely…. That my joy may be shared with anyone anywhere; that my love may be felt to the deepest depth. To anyone who reads this: look to the foundation from which the living waters flow—Jesus." Smith passed away on November 16, 1994.

Howard Smith

HOWARD SMITH IS one of Detroit's great unknown musical heroes. Depending on the song, he possesses either a sweet tenor or a warm baritone. His gift is in bringing emotional impact to his music without oversinging. He began his career with the a cappella group the Followers of Christ. Smith also did extensive session work as a background vocalist for Stevie Wonder, Dolly Parton, and Smokey Robinson. During this period, Andrae Crouch tagged him as one of his featured singers circa 1984 and featured his lead vocals on projects such as "No Time to Lose." Smith soon became known as Mr. Personality because his voice breathed so much authentic emotion into his songs. He finally had his moment in the spotlight in 1985 when Light Records released his debut LP *Totally Committed*. Filled with top-rate songs written by Marvin Winans, BeBe Winans, Percy Bady, and Debbie Winans, it was a singer's paradise. The standout track "I Will Remember" was an excellent, old-school ballad. The album peaked at No. 20 on the *Billboard* gospel album sales chart. However, Light did not renew Smith's option for a second LP and he resumed his career as a session singer. Then, in 1993, BeBe Winans formed Benjammin Productions, through which he produced Angie & Debbie, the Clark Sisters, and Howard Smith for R&B-friendly albums to be issued via Capitol Records. In 1994, Capitol Records abruptly closed their black music division which ended Winans's production plans for Smith. Over the last decade, Smith has done some background session work for Fred Hammond and others, but he has yet to make a return to the solo spotlight.

Willie Mae Ford Smith

THE HISTORY OF Mother Willie Mae Ford Smith in the gospel field is nearly mythical. Her solos at annual Baptist conventions in the 1930s suggest that she was a spellbinding performer who wrecked church houses coast to coast with her blues-inspired soprano. She was also the inventor of the sermonette. Before her, no artist ever recorded a testimony or spoken dialog within the context of a gospel song. Born June 23, 1904, in Rolling Fork, Mississippi, the seventh in a brood of 14 children, Smith was raised in Memphis before her father, a railroad brakeman, moved his family to St. Louis in 1918. Her mother opened a restaurant there where Smith worked after dropping out of school in the eighth grade. Early on, she sang secular music for her own enjoyment, but

Willie Mae Ford Smith (seated) *in a still from* George T. Nierenberg's film, Say Amen, Somebody

after she formed the Ford Sisters (Emma, Geneva, and Mary) quartet, she decided to solely sing gospel music.

The Fords' debut at the 1922 National Baptist Convention caused a stir with their thrilling rendition of the Negro spiritual "Ezekiel Saw the Wheel." After basking in their fame for a season, the Ford sisters eventually married and departed the group. At that point, Smith became a soloist. Reportedly, Smith toyed with using her high soprano in the classical field before she was inspired by Madame Artelia Hutchins's performance at the 1926 Baptist convention to truly devote herself to church music.

After marrying a man with a struggling business, Smith toured relentlessly to help support the household. A chance meeting with influential gospel songwriter Thomas Dorsey in 1932 led her to co-found the National Convention of Gospel Choirs and Choruses. She later presided over the St. Louis chapter. Smith's fame continued to blossom as the Baptist world embraced her dynamic singing skills. Her reinterpretations of church standards such as "Jesus Loves Me" made her a sought-out musical mentor. Over the years, she counseled Martha Bass, Brother Joe May, Myrtle Scott, and Edna Gallmon Cooke, among others. The late deep soul singer O.V. Wright also cited her as a musical influence. In 1939, Smith joined the Church of God Apostolic where she began to influence the music department in the same manner that she had with the Baptist convention. She did not record herself until the 1950s—more than 20 years after some of her legendary church performances. Her best-known song was "If You Just Keep Still." Smith was unfazed about stardom and instead concentrated on mentoring Brother Joe May, who, ironically, was labeled the male Mahalia Jackson when all of his licks were vintage Smith. She spent the next decades doing evangelistic work while continuing to mentor musicians behind the scenes. In 1982, Smith was featured in the documentary film *Say Amen, Somebody*, which traced the history of gospel music and brought Smith some much-deserved media attention. The accolades won her the Heritage award from the National Endowment for the Arts in 1988. Smith died on February 2, 1994, at the age of 89.

Lois Snead

THIS VETERAN, traditional gospel singer is still waiting for her big break. Born in 1941, Snead had a brief career as a secular artist when she landed on the R&B charts with "This Little Woman," which reached No. 95 on the survey in 1973. In the mid-'70s, Snead teamed up with Dorothy Norwood for a duet LP. She's recorded sporadically over the years. Among her offerings are "He Will Make Everything Alright" (Instinct Records) with the Interdenominational Mass Choir, "Great New Feeling," (Spire, 1977) and "God is Good" (Savoy, 1982). Snead's most recent recording was *Somebody Must Be the Lord: Live in Buffalo*, which was issued on Born Again Records in 1998. "Ms. Norwood was backing her up at the time, so I signed her up," says Born Again's owner Barnett Williams. "But then they got mad at each other and stopped working together." Radio didn't gravitate toward the project and the album failed to

find an audience. In 2000, Snead starred in the play *God Saves My Two Sons*.

Troy Sneed

A YOUNG CHOIR leader in the James Cleveland quasi-contemporary-traditional mold, Troy Sneed has made more noise behind the scenes than center stage. Although he's recorded as a solo artist, he's most identified with the Georgia Mass Choir. Born December 14, 1967, in Perry, Florida, Sneed dreamed of an NFL career when he entered Florida A&M University (FAMU), but a field injury ended his career aspirations. Instead, he joined the university choir and became active in gospel music. The school's gospel choir advisor, Prince J.D. Olds, recognized Sneed's leadership and musical qualities almost immediately and appointed him the minister of music for the choir. During that period, Sneed traveled with the choir as they performed with gospel luminaries such as James Moore, LaShun Pace, Dorothy Norwood, and James Cleveland.

After graduating from FAMU, Sneed taught at Jacksonville's Beach Elementary School until Savoy Records executive Milton Biggham offered him a position as the Georgia Mass Choir's assistant minister of music. Over the course of his decade-long tenure there, Sneed traveled with the choir, arranged music on their CDs, and appeared with them in the Denzel Washington/Whitney Houston motion picture *The Preacher's Wife*. In 1999, Sneed's debut CD *Call Jesus* appeared on Savoy Records. Although he's a young man, the album showed Sneed's love for the older-sounding traditional gospel that most young gospel artists such as Kirk Franklin were distancing themselves from. He joyfully reprised old standbys such as "He's Sweet I Know," "This Old Building," and "Walk Around Heaven." Perhaps the failure of that project to resonate with gospel radio and church consumers led to his decision to make the follow-up CD *Bless that Wonderful Name* more urban contemporary in feel. In spite of the stylistic change, the album still failed to find an audience. Sneed currently serves as minister of music at the Emmanuel Missionary Baptist Church in Jacksonville, Florida, while also directing the Florida Youth Mass

Choir. Perhaps his greatest exposure has been a 2002 cameo on the syndicated court TV show *Texas Justice*, where his group sang as a character witness for his booking agent who had sued a concert promoter.

Soul Stirrers

THE PREMIER GOSPEL group of the post–World War II era, the Soul Stirrers set the gospel standard for the total package—choice of music, showmanship, and vocal dexterity. Under their two great leads, Rebert Harris and later Sam Cooke, the Stirrers raised the bar for gospel music and transformed it from mere church ministry into a profession. Over the years, they have given us such gospel classics as "Bye and Bye," "In That Awful Hour," "Must Jesus Bear the Cross Alone," "Touch the Hem of His Garment," "That's Heaven to Me," and "Nearer to Thee."

The group's history began with baritone Senior Roy Crain, who was born June 7, 1911, in St. Augustine, Texas. As a teenager, he formed a quartet with some other teens from his church in 1927. After one of their performances, a spectator approached Crain and told him how the group "stirred his soul." Crain then named the group the Soul Stirrers. The group disbanded when he moved to Houston in the 1930s and started attending the Pleasant Green Baptist Church. Some of the congregants had heard of Crain's prior group experience and begged him to join their local church group. He agreed on the condition that they change the group's name to the Soul Stirrers. Renowned ethnomusicologist Alan Lomax came across the group in 1936 and had them make a field recording for the Library of Congress. As the group continued to perform, Crain gradually began replacing the Houston members with singers from back in Trinity, Texas, such as baritone T.L. Bruster, bass singer Jesse Farley, and the lead singer Rebert Harris (born March 23, 1916). Harris's father, Rev. James S. Harris, a Methodist pastor, was known in the region for his powerful voice and for teaching others to sing hard gospel. His teaching was not lost on his son. With his new group intact and now based in Chicago, Crain stepped away from group harmonies and traditional songs and began to emphasize two strong lead

voices in their music. The leads would literally out-sing each other until they had the audience in a fever pitch waiting for the song to climax. In Chicago, the group began singing the new songs of Windy City composers such as Kenneth Morris, Thomas Dorsey, and James Medlock. For a period, Medlock sang with the group but was later replaced with Paul Foster (born July 12, 1920, in Shreveport, Louisiana). He sang in various groups in his home town and then in Oakland, California, before joining the Golden Echoes, who recorded for Specialty Records in the late 1940s. After Foster's father died, he left the Echoes and was living in Houston. During this period, Crain asked him to join the Stirrers. In 1950, the Stirrers signed to Art Rupe's Specialty Records label. Their sublime debut single "Bye and Bye Part 1" shows smooth singing and tight harmonies. However, "Bye and Bye Part 2" shows Crain pushing Harris to a more frenetic vocalizing style that audiences would come to expect from the group and Harris in particular. Frustrated singer Reuben L.C. Henry wrote the next singles, "I'm Still Living on Mother's Prayer" and "In That

Soul Stirrers / courtesy of Specialty/Fantasy Records

Awful Hour." All of the records took the group's stature even higher. However, as much as he enjoyed singing for the art and ministry of it, Harris was very uncomfortable. The audiences became frenzied and women would rush the stage. He didn't like that. He was a happily married man and had to run from the stage every night to fight the women off. He was even more angry that many of his group members succumbed to the advances of the women who flocked to their concerts. He thought it was unrighteous and that the focus of the gospel music, a Christian lifestyle, was being lost in the name of mammon.

The gospel public was shocked when Harris abruptly quit the group in 1950. Rupe worried that the group's hit streak would stop and others suggested that Harris's career was over. In many ways, it was. He continued to sing, forming the Christland Singers with ex-Stirrers Taylor, Medlock, and T.L. Bruster. Later he'd also sing with the Gospel Paraders and the Masonic Quintet, but he never enjoyed his prior fame again. The real question of the moment was whether the Stirrers would survive without fan-favorite Robert Harris. Crain had been quietly grooming the Highway QCs' Sam Cooke to replace Harris because everyone knew he was unhappy with his group. When Harris finally left, it was announced that he'd be replaced by Cooke. Many ridiculed the decision and predicted that the relatively inexperienced Cooke would be the downfall of the group. However, when Cooke's sweet, graceful voice premiered on their 1951 78-rpm single "Jesus Gave Me Water," it became the Stirrers' biggest hit yet. Soon, the 20-year-old singer's handsome face, slim build, and fashionable uptown duds all conspired to make him gospel music's first true sex symbol. The concert grind was too much for Bruster, so he retired and was replaced by baritone/guitarist Bob King. In 1954, the raspy-voiced Julius Cheeks briefly joined the Stirrers and recorded with them on "All Right Now." However, prior contract ties forced him out of the group almost as soon as he joined it.

That was okay because Cooke was the group's best meal ticket. He not only attracted throngs of women to their concerts, but he was able to write such hits for the group as "That's Heaven to Me," "Jesus Be a Fence Around Me," and "Touch the Hem of His Garment." Having conquered the gospel world as no man had done before, Cooke decided he wanted to reach beyond the church world with his music. In 1956, he left and scored a year later when "You Send Me" topped the pop and R&B charts. Cooke was replaced by another Highway QCs member, Johnnie Taylor (born May 3, 1934, in Crawfordsville, Arkansas). However, after Cooke's departure, the Stirrers were never quite the same. While attractive, Taylor did not possess the matinee idol looks nor the deft vocal skills that Cooke had. It was akin to Jean Terrell replacing Diana Ross in the Supremes. She sounded like her, but it just wasn't the same. There were many regular personnel changes in the years to come, but the Stirrers basically became something of an oldies-but-goodies act by the 1960s and never regained their glory. Various incarnations of the group continue to perform although none of the personnel are original members. Cooke was murdered on December 10, 1964, under scandalous circumstances. Foster died on August 20, 1995, and Crain died on September 13, 1996, both in Vallejo, California. Taylor reportedly died of a heart attack on May 3, 2000, in Dallas, and Harris died later that year on September 3—largely forgotten. But their music lives on and will never be forgotten.

RECOMMENDED RECORDINGS: For any true fan of Sam Cooke or the Soul Stirrers, put your money on the *Complete Recordings of Sam Cooke with the Soul Stirrers* (Fantasy/Specialty Records, 2002), a three-CD set that boasts 84 tracks such as the evergreen "Touch the Hem of His Garment." The box set also includes detailed liner notes and vintage photos. For a more economical collection, try *Sam Cooke with the Soul Stirrers* (Fantasy/Specialty Records, 1991), which features 25 of the group's best tunes during Cooke's tenure with the group. For purists who dislike the commercial vein of the Sam Cooke period with the Stirrers, there are the recordings led by the more restrained but no less dramatic Robert Harris on *Shine on Me* (Fantasy/Specialty Records, 1994). Among the standout cuts demonstrating Harris's fine vocalizing are "I Have a Right to the Tree of Life" and "I'm Gonna Move in the Room with the Lord."

Souljahz

ONE OF THE MOST unique groups to emerge in the Christian field in recent years, Souljahz is a sibling trio who fuse rap-rock and R&B for a crisp, cutting-edge sound that has found a home on MTV even if much of the gospel industry has yet to embrace the group. Reared in San Diego, Jo'shua (born 1980), Rachael (born 1984), and Je'kob (born 1981) Washington were all athletic teenagers but chose to focus on their mutual love of music instead. Their father sold his business in order to concentrate on making his children's dream of a recording career come true. Eventually, they wound up with Squint Entertainment and spent a summer touring as an opening act for Ashanti, Third Day, and Jars of Clay. Their first radio single, "All Around the World," reached No. 1 on the *Radio & Records* Christian singles chart. Their acclaimed CD *The Fault Is History* followed, produced by singer Tonéx. "The first time I felt like we'd written a good song was when we made one called 'Poor Man,' a song about the way people around the world view people of poverty," Jo'shua once told the *Tennessean* newspaper. "Instead of writing a song about being happy that we're Christian, we wanted to write about a situation, specifically. That song wound up touching people more than if we'd just sung 'I believe in Jesus.' We need to write more songs about things people are going through, not just songs about the happiness of what we have."

Gloria Spencer

SHE NEVER HAD a big hit or a big break, but Gloria Spencer goes down in gospel history because she had a big body. It seems ludicrous that a gospel singer's weight would be their claim to limited fame, but Creed Records used Spencer's size as their primary marketing tool when they debuted her LP *For Once in My Life* back in 1976. In fact, the subtitle of the album was, "The World's Largest Gospel Singer! 615 LBS!"

Born in Pennsylvania, Spencer was singing church solos at the age of three. Eventually, she taught herself to play the piano as well and sang in a number of church groups. She and her two sisters were all born with a thyroid glandular problem that made their weight balloon. The lighter sister weighed 300 pounds, while the heavier one died at 628 pounds and it reputedly took 20 men to carry her coffin. As an adult, the 5'3" Spencer weighed 625 pounds at her heaviest.

After her schooling was finished, Spencer worked during the week as a 115-words/minute typist at the Pennsylvania state capitol in Harrisburg while singing gospel up and down the Atlantic coast on the weekend. She first recorded "I Got It" for the Jay Walking Records label in the early 1970s. Along her travels, she met and married Rev. David Gray, a 135-pound counselor at Kitrell Junior College in Raleigh, North Carolina, who encouraged her career and often traveled with her. She then snagged a record deal with Creed Records where she recorded the *For Once in My Life* LP. In spite of her girth, Spencer's voice was not deep and gravelly as one might expect. She had a sparkling soprano that could easily show a pop feeling or a gritty one. The album featured standards such as "It's in My

Gloria Spencer with her pianist, Rev. Bill Robinson / courtesy of Bil Carpenter

Gloria Spencer / Gospel News Journal, July 1972 / courtesy of Capital Entertainment archives

Heart" and "I'll Fly Away." She and Rev. Isaac Douglas sang a spirited rendition of "Ain't Gonna Study War No More." Throughout the album, Spencer testified about her weight and the miracles of God.

Spencer became a caricature of herself as her handlers would feed the media stories of her weight and she too would regale them with such stories. For instance, she told the *Gospel News Journal* in 1972, "I had a piano bench collapse with me when I started to play, but I just kept right on playing—from the floor." As she performed ten months out of the year, she traveled frequently. On airline trips, Spencer was charged for three seats. At hotels her beds had to be reinforced with blocks. After a while she bought a special van to transport her on her singing trips. In spite of offers to sing secular music, Spencer always refrained. "I'll never sing rock and roll," she once said. "I dedicated my life

to the Lord and I'll never do it." She died April 12, 1976, in Charlottesville, North Carolina. Nadine Rae, who sang at the funeral, says that, "It took 17 men to carry her casket."

Spirit of Memphis

THIS MEMPHIS-BASED quartet was one of gospel's most acclaimed vocal groups during the 1950s. They formed circa 1927 from a group of friends who would get together and sing for the fun of it. In 1930, A.C. Harris, James Darling, Forrest Terrel, and Arthur Wright were backstage waiting to go on next during a concert. The emcee wanted to know how to introduce them because the group had no name. Darling was wiping his face with a handkerchief with the phrase "Spirit of St. Louis" printed on it (a reference to aviator Charles Lindbergh's historic 1927 transatlantic flight). A light clicked on in Darling's head, and the group was anointed as the Spirit of Memphis Quartette. They first recorded for the Hallelujah Spiritual label in 1949 when they cut the regional hits "I'm Happy in the Service of the Lord," "Blessed Are the Dead," and "My Life Is in My Hands." The personnel changed over the years, but the most popular period included Silas Steele's resonant baritone, Jet Bledsoe's smooth croon, and Willie "Little Axe" Broadnax's piercing tenor. Joe Hinton was briefly a member of the group when he led "Lost in Sin" (which was based on Pookie Hudson & the Spaniel's "Peace of Mind"). Hinton later enjoyed some R&B fame with his 1964 hit "Funny How Time Slips Away." The Spirit of Memphis was retired for most of the 1960s, but were poised for a major comeback when they were scheduled to record some tunes with Elvis Presley before he fell ill in 1977. They resurfaced in the 1980s as an eight- or nine-member ensemble and recorded for David Evans's High Water label.

Angela Spivey

A LIVELY, CHARISMATIC traditional gospel show woman, Angela Spivey was born on November 9, 1959, in Chicago. Her father was a pastor at First Corinthians Missionary Baptist Church. In that congregation, Spivey formed a young people's choir when she was 14 years old and eventually became the church's minister of music. After graduating from Lucy Flowers High School, Spivey received her cosmetology license from Debbie's School of Beauty College. She then opened her own beauty shop before veering off into a career in real estate. All the while, she has continued to sing. Spivey released her debut CD, a live recording called *Victorious Praise* on Aleho Records in 1995. Known for her squalling and on-stage clowning gestures, Spivey has enjoyed gospel radio hits with songs such as "Step Out in Faith," "Lift Him Up," and "The Dorothy Love Coates Medley."

Micah Stampley

"MICAH STAMPLEY IS the new talent to watch in contemporary praise music," says longtime ABC radio gospel announcer Andrelle Perry. "Although he's very young, he has the seasoned phrasing and charisma of a Donnie McClurkin." Born September 7, 1971, in Los Angeles, but raised in Baton Rouge, Louisiana, Stampley is one of eight kids born to parents who were ministers in the COGIC denomination. He began singing when he was four years old. By the time he was a high school student, Stampley was playing keyboards and serving as music minister at his father's church. After high school, he sought a career as a model or actor but didn't know how to make it happen. Then, in 1994, he toured the world with an evangelist named Rev. Earl Johnson, who spotted Stampley singing at a church conference in Natchitoches and was so impressed that he hired him as music minister for his ministry. Stampley eventually married and went back to Louisiana to help his father's ministry. In 2001, Stampley moved his wife and kids to Houston when he accepted a music position at St. Agnes Baptist Church. It was there that Stampley entered the Stellar awards Gospel Star Search and won first place. Suddenly, record labels were interested. "For years I couldn't pay a record company to listen to my demos," Stampley told the *Houston Chronicle*. "I would be in the studio sending people CDs and stuff. No one would even call." Bishop T.D. Jakes's Dexterity/ EMI Records label called and offered Stampley a con-

tract in 2004. His debut CD *The Songbook of Micah* premiered at No. 3 on *Billboard*'s gospel album sales chart in April 2005 on the strength of the massive gospel radio hit single "Take My Life (Holiness)."

Lorraine Stancil

ONE OF THE GREAT high-C gospel singers who has never quite found her footing, Lorraine Stancil was born August 1954 in Paterson, New Jersey. She began singing at the age of four. Her mother and siblings formed a family group that performed regularly within the Bibleway denomination churches. After attending Westminster College in Princeton, New Jersey, Stancil first recorded "Touch Somebody" with Rev. Lawrence Roberts and the First Baptist Church of Nutley Voices on their LP *From Us to You*. Through the 1980s and 1990s, Stancil performed in stage shows such as *Your Arms Too Short to Box with God*, *God's Trombones*, and *Let the Music Play Gospel*. However, Stancil is best known as portraying Sister Carrie for four years in Vy Higgensen's *Mama, I Want to Sing*. When Stancil auditioned for Higgensen, she was only 22 seconds into her solo when Higgensen hired her on the spot. The Gospel Music Artists Association of New York voted Stancil the No. 1 gospel artist for 1991 and again in 1992.

Stancil's national reputation grew in 1992 when she was the featured vocalist on the smash single "When We Get Over There" from Hezekiah Walker and the Love Fellowship Crusade's *Live in Toronto* CD, which was No. 1 on *Billboard*'s gospel charts for over a month. Another career highlight came in 1993 when she was asked by former Congressman Walter E. Fauntroy and Coretta Scott King to perform the national anthem at the 30th Anniversary March on Washington before a crowd of 150,000 people.

Stancil was a soloist on Bishop Jeff Bank and the Revival Temple Mass Choir's *He's All Over Me* CD, which reached No. 9 on the gospel chart. Her own 1993 live CD, *More Like You*, received positive reviews from the *Washington Post* and other publications, but it was stymied by Savoy staff and didn't produce a major hit for Stancil. The label halfheartedly pushed the hymn "Come Thou Fount" on gospel radio when the more commercial tracks were the reggae-styled "Holy Holy Holy" and "Every Day with Jesus," which showed off Stancil's melismatics and her higher register. After some artist management versus label disagreements over the promotion of the CD, the label released Stancil from her contract.

Stancil has continued to be an in-demand soloist at church conferences and on various concert bills, but she hasn't connected with a major label yet. When Mimi Redd hit it big with "Order My Steps," many Stancil fans mistakenly went to stores asking for the new Stancil record when it was Redd they were looking for. The two powerhouse singers have remarkably similar voices and vocal ranges. Since then, Stancil has recorded a series of fine, but low-budget custom CDs such as 1999's *You're My Everything*. To see Stancil perform live is to see an artist put their whole body into a song. She shakes, she sweats, she cries, she shouts as she jumps from a baritone to a high C within one measure. "My job—and I take it very seriously—is to put [God] on display and I have to make him look good," she told the *North Jersey Herald & News* in 1994. "At times, I feel there's no one there but me and him. The human side of me gets out of the way, so he can take the stage. I ac-

Lorraine Stancil / photo by Robert Shanklin

tually forget who I am. If he is to be on display, I don't want any distractions, including myself."

Staple Singers

THEY ARE THE ONLY original gospel group to be inducted into the Rock and Roll Hall of Fame and they were indeed the original First Family of gospel music back in the 1950s when their music began to resonate across America. In the 1960s, they were the leaders of a new brand of message-oriented music that was heavy on inspiration and creative in how it weaved in the gospel story. They released message-music classics such as "I'll Take You There," "Respect Yourself," and "If You're Ready (Come Go with Me)" in the next decade and set the stage for future gospel crossover artists such as BeBe and CeCe Winans, Yolanda Adams, and Kirk Franklin.

The group was the brainchild of its patriarch, Roebuck "Pops" Staples. He was born on December 28, 1914, in Winona, Mississippi, where he grew up working in the cotton fields. Although his family was church-centered, Staples picked up the guitar and taught himself to play blues. He embraced the music of Barbecue Bob and Big Bill Broonzy. But after Staples was saved as a teenager, he gave up ambitions of singing the blues and joined a gospel jubilee quartet called the Golden Trumpets in 1931. He soon married his wife, Oceola Ware (born September 10, 1917), and they had two children: Cleotha (born April 11, 1934) and Pervis (born November 18, 1936). The family moved to Chicago in 1936 during the great migration of blacks who moved north in search of better-paying factory jobs. In the Windy City, the family stayed with Pops's brother, Chester Staples, until they were settled into their own place. Eventually, Yvonne (born October 23, 1937), Mavis (born July 10, 1939), and Cynthia Marie (1941–1973) were all born in the city. Pops worked in the stockyards, in a steel mill, and on construction sites. Oceola worked nights at the Morrison Hotel. To entertain his active children, Pops began to teach them gospel songs such as "Will the Circle Be Unbroken." When Pops's sister Katie was staying with them, she heard the kids sing and had them sing at her church one Sunday morning in 1948. When an offering was taken and $7 came in (a good amount for those times), Pops figured they could make extra money singing, so they began to perform throughout the area.

A wise manager, Pops bought time at WTAQ radio and the group began to sing live on the radio on a weekly basis. They developed a strong local following as a result. They made a custom record of "These Are They" under Royal Records circa 1953. Then, family friend Evelyn Gay, of the Gay Sisters, helped the group get a record deal with United Records, where they recorded "Sit Down, Servant." It was not a huge hit, so United owner Leonard Allen pushed them to make secular records or nothing at all. Pops sat on the two-year contract until it expired, at which point Jimmy Bracken signed them to Vee-Jay Records. The first song they recorded was "If I Could Hear My Mother Pray Again." Pops asked Bracken what they needed to sell to make him happy. Bracken said 1,000 copies. Pops felt he could easily sell that. When the record was released, it only sold 300 copies and Pops feared that Vee-Jay would drop the group. However, Bracken believed in the group. They next recorded the traditional hymn "Uncloudy Day" with a dirge-like tempo in 1956. "That thing sold like rhythm and blues," Pops told *Blues & Rhythm* magazine. "Vee-Jay were very pleased. We were doing so well, other record companies began wanting us. Vee-Jay started us off at one cent per record. It went up to three cents, I think. That's all we got from Vee-Jay." The record is reputed to have sold a half million copies. With Pops's delta-influenced guitar tuning, Pervis's falsetto, and Cleotha's high notes contrasting with Mavis's lusty contralto, the Staples created a unique sound that made them instant gospel celebrities. "We called the guitar the devil's music, but you know, the good Lord was with me," Pops told *Blues & Rhythm*. "I was the first person to go into church with a guitar, they wouldn't let nobody else in. I opened it up for all the singers." Other hits followed, including "Will the Circle Be Unbroken," "Help Me, Jesus," and "Swing Down Chariot (Let Me Ride)." At the end of the decade, Yvonne, who was the group's business manager, stepped in as a singer while Pervis served in the military.

By the end of 1962, the Staples had signed to Bill Grauer and Orrin Keepnews's Riverside jazz label.

Through the label's mainstream influence and non-gospel retail accounts, the Staples began to develop a larger, not necessarily church audience. In fact, it is during that period that they began to attract a white college audience as they made songs such as "Wish I Had Answered" and "Hear My Call." After Pervis returned to the group, Cleotha left for a while and Yvonne stepped in again. In 1965, the group signed to Epic Records and began to make inroads to the pop charts with a more message-oriented brand of gospel. "We made the transition to protest songs when we heard about Dr. King and we visited his church," Mavis said in 1992. "Pops called us into his room and said, 'If this man can preach this, we can sing it and put a beat under it.'" During their Epic tenure, the group recorded "Why Am I Treated So Bad" (Pops wrote it in protest of a 1957 Central High School busing incident) and their first crossover hit, "For What It's Worth," which reached the Hot 100 pop singles chart in 1967. They also recorded the stunning LP *What the World Needs Now*, which featured their dramatic versions of hits such as the title song, Curtis Mayfield's "People Get Ready," and Elvis Presley's "Crying in the Chapel." It also featured the startling, earthy "I Wondered Why," a brief but climatic indictment of racism, sung with an immediate gospel fervor.

The group made the transition to Memphis-based Stax Records in 1968, where Otis Redding and Sam & Dave were turning out a string of hits. The group softened their protest posture and began espousing a message of love. Their first releases such as "Long Walk to DC" and "The Weight" were not major hits, although they sold respectably well. In 1969, Pervis left the group for good to concentrate on managing groups such as the Emotions. Working with a variety of producers, the group finally earned a Top Ten R&B single with "Heavy Makes You Happy" in 1971. On that tune, Mavis introduced her famous "shamone" grunt that was later adopted by Michael Jackson on songs such as "Bad." After that point, it was smooth sailing. It seemed that everything the Staples touched turned to gold. Their spring 1972 single "I'll Take You There" spent four weeks at No. 1 on the R&B chart. Mavis wrote the song with Stax Records President Al Bell, but he never gave her writing credit on the song. Although the infectious

Staple Singers / Epic Records
Billboard *magazine advertisement*

song was talking about heaven, many church folks had a problem with it.

"The Staple Singers would like to give the impression that they're still gospel singers, but they're not," Rev. James Cleveland once said in the *Journal of Gospel Music.* "They've decided to do message songs and Mavis has even done a pop album which has no religious things on it at all. I've known the Staples all my life. As little kids we grew up in Chicago together when their father was working in the stockyards…. There was never anybody else around who sang like the Staple Singers. They had a fresh, Mississippi sound. I don't personally feel that in their case it was necessary to change over from gospel to rhythm and blues, except to make more money, because they had climbed to the very top of the gospel ladder. Whenever someone needed gospel talent, they had to think of the Staple Singers." Shirley Caesar also criticized the group in *Jet* magazine during the period.

"DJs started playing our music on the R&B radio stations and people began raising hell, phoning the stations and saying stop playing the Staples, it's a mockery of gospel," Pops told *Gospel Exclusive* magazine in 1995. "Gospel traditionalists were the ones who really kicked up on us, and even today, some of them don't believe in the Staple Singers. But we just kept on singing and praying and we let our music carry the message." Mavis reaffirmed Pops's statement. "They went off on it," she said. "They thought we had gone to the devil. We had to do a lot of interviews explaining ourselves and eventually everybody saw what was happening and we started getting invitations from the churches to come and sing those very songs."

The Staples always had outright gospel songs on their Stax LPs, but it was the inspirational songs such as "Respect Yourself," "If You're Ready (Come Go with Me)," and "Touch a Hand, Make a Friend" that became Top Ten R&B or pop smashes. Before Stax closed in 1975, the Staples had already moved on to Warner Bros. Records where they enjoyed a massive hit with the suggestive "Let's Do It Again" in 1976. Surprisingly, the church community was mute on the subject. "It didn't go that way that time," Mavis said. "[It] was definitely more explicit than anything we'd ever done before. Pops didn't want to sing it at first, but we told Pops, 'Come on, let's do this because we're trying to get a hit record.' The song was so beautiful. I told him, 'It's just a movie score, it's just a song,' so he went on and did it. But he didn't want to do it at first. He just wanted to sing religious stuff or message things." The Warner years didn't produce many big hits, but they did produce many great songs such as the country ballad "God Can," the soulful "Leave It All Up to Love," and the Top 40 R&B hit "Unlock Your Mind."

In the 1980s, the Staples recorded for 20th Century Fox and Priority Records. Their 1984 LP *Turning Point* featured the funky gospel-rock track "Slippery People," which reached No. 22 on the R&B chart in 1984. The rest of the decade was rough for the group. Record sales were down, concert bookings were slow, and the family lost $300,000 in what turned out to be a celebrity investment scam. Cleotha began selling insurance, Yvonne had other business ventures, and Pops' had his publishing royalties. Mavis dipped into her savings and sought to ignite a solo career with various recording projects that never turned out right.

Pops portrayed a voodoo doctor in the 1985 film *True Stories* and played a riveting "Nobody's Fault but Mine" on the Grammy awards that year. In 1987, he recorded a self-titled LP for Chicago's I AM Records. Eventually, Pops signed to Virgin Records' Pointblank subsidiary where he cut the critically acclaimed *Peace to the Neighborhood* (1992) and the Grammy-winning *Father, Father* (1994) CDs. The latter included bluesy renditions of Bob Dylan's "Gotta Serve Somebody," the Consoler's "Waiting for My Child," and the last Staple Singers track, "Hope in a Hopeless World." In between days when fatigue and old age slowed him down, Pops was working on a new CD when he died on December 19, 2000. Mavis plans to eventually release the project.

For her part, Mavis's fortune changed in 1989 when Prince produced her LP *Time Waits for No One*. The album was uneven and not the best presentation for Mavis's skills. However, in 1992, Prince released a masterpiece, *The Voice*, on his Paisley Park Records label. It was a modern soul project that made *People* magazine's Top Ten Albums of the Year listing. None of the singles, including "You Will Be Moved," "House in Order," or "Blood Is Thicker Than Time," received their just airplay. Prince and his label distributor, Warner Bros., were arguing over other issues, and the label stopped promoting the CD. It only sold 60,000 units when it had gold record written all over it. Still, the CD brought Mavis wide media coverage and concert bookings. Besides touring with her family, Mavis performed solo gigs with Prince and others. In 1996, she recorded a Mahalia Jackson tribute CD *Spirituals & Gospel* with pianist Lucky Peterson for Polygram/Verve's subsidiary in France. In 2004, after three years of work and $80,000 of her own money, Mavis released her first CD in almost a decade. The album, *Have a Little Faith*, debuted at No. 5 on the *Billboard* blues chart and received ecstatic praise from music critics for its bluesy gospel tunes such as "I Wanna Thank You" and "God Is Not Sleeping."

Since Pops's death, the Staple Singers are no more. Cleotha has Alzheimer's disease, Pervis works in private industry, and Yvonne is Mavis's business/road manager.

A year before Pops passed, the family was inducted into the Rock and Roll Hall of Fame, which served as an affirmation of just how far the Staple Singers spread the gospel. In August 2004, Mavis reflected on the group's legacy in the *Chicago Tribune*. "They said we were doing the devil's music, but I said the devil doesn't have any music," she said. "All music is God's music. Listen to the lyrics in our songs… These are songs about God being alive for us in the world."

RECOMMENDED RECORDINGS: *Have a Little Faith* (Alligator Records, 2004) is a great place to start for Mavis's solo recordings. *Father, Father* (Pointblank, 1994) is the place to start for Pops's solo recordings, and *The Best of the Staple Singers* (Fantasy/Stax, 1990) features the group's crossover hits from the 1970s such as "I'll Take You There." The compilation *Pray On, My Child* (Liquid 8 Records, 2002) features the group's early hits for Vee-Jay Records such as "Uncloudy Day" and "On My Way to Heaven."

Star of Bethlehem Youth Choir

THIS ENERGETIC YOUTH choir was born from Rev. Harvey Lewis, Sr.,'s Star of Bethlehem Church of God in Christ (COGIC) in Washington, DC, in 1960. They were a bit cutting edge at the time, incorporating elements of jazz and strains of contemporary gospel into their rhythmic sound. The choir was shepherded by the pastor's extraordinary son, Harvey Lewis, Jr. He was born in Red Oak, North Carolina, in 1950 but raised in Washington. His whole family was musical. His mother Gloria is a superb contralto. By the age of nine, Lewis had taught himself to play several instruments, including the piano. He was very active, serving as music minister at his father's church and as a church elder, running the church's daycare center, and serving as Sunday school teacher. He was a founding member and director of the famed Howard University Gospel choir. Lewis was also director of the State Youth Choir under COGIC's Washington, DC, jurisdiction music department where he served under the tutelage of Dr. Theodore King. However, while he held all of these positions, Lewis led the Star of Bethlehem Youth Choir to win first place in the choir division of the International Congress of the Church of God in Christ (aka UNAC Convention) in 1972, 1973, 1974, 1975, and 1977. Lewis performed these feats while carrying on an equally stellar professional career outside of the limelight. A Howard University graduate, he was a psychology instructor at the University of Maryland, a counselor with the DC mental health department, and a researcher at Howard University Hospital.

The Star of Bethlehem Youth Choir recorded a number of independent albums over the years, resulting in radio hits such as "You'll Be Ready When He Comes," "By the Time I Get to Heaven," and "If I Put My Trust in You." However, their first nationally released LP was *He's the Greatest* for Glori Records in 1978. The song was inspired in part by the image of Muhammad Ali. "Harvey was in the middle of a recording session," says traditional gospel sage Gregory Gay. "One of his musicians, Tommy Rodgers, came into the session and said, 'The choir needs a catchy song like the Hawkins Family songs 'Be Grateful' or 'Right on Time.'" They then came up with "He's the Greatest" and the hook was their use of the 1970s ethnic slang phrase, "Right on!" On that tune, Lewis's pregnant sister, Winona Jones, sang from her chair. Her bluesy soprano, rich and full, was the perfect counterpoint to Kenny Spears's smooth tenor on the duet. The album was recorded live at George Washington University's Lisner Auditorium.

The choir's best-known song, "Only Speak the Word," was recorded at a December 1979 session. By that point, Lewis had been diagnosed with cancer and was confined to George Washington Hospital. However, he was determined to see the recording through fruition. He checked himself out of the hospital, went to the session, and directed the choir from his wheelchair. Sadly, the cancer claimed his life on January 9, 1980. In the summer of that year, Savoy Records had created a major hit with the uptempo "Only Speak the Word," which immediately became a favorite with church choirs. Other hit songs from the *Only Speak* LP included, "One of These Mornings," "Let It Be You," and "Oh May My Life (Please You Lord Each Day)."

Under Lewis's heroic leadership and passionate guidance, the choir produced some great vocalists. Its personnel included Tawatha Agee, who went on to fame as one of Luther Vandross's featured background vocalists; Kristle Murden, who gave the choir its jazzy syncopations and later enjoyed a long association with Andrae Crouch; and Donny Crawford, whose vast vocal range brought a wide spectrum of colors to the before-its-time sound of this fiery choir. Lewis also had incredible influence on choir director O'Landa Draper, who was briefly a member during his youth and, like Lewis, died at a painfully young age.

Derrick Starks

"I HAVEN'T HAD ANY tragedies in my life," Derrick Starks says humbly. "But, musically, I didn't have my business straight on my end." Almost a decade ago, Derrick submitted a song to a record label. They used his song and it became a big gospel hit. "I never got paid," he says as he recalls the sad experience. The late Grammy-nominated choir conductor Thomas "Maestro" Whitfield helped Derrick deal with his anger and frustration of being swindled out of the profits of his first composition. "Tommy gave me advice about it," he says. "He told me to take it as a learning experience. I was ready to go to court. I had been reading a book about publishing and that was no help. I thought I had done everything the right way. I filled out my forms and a copy was accidentally sent back to me. Where my name was, someone else's name was typed over it. Now, I have an attorney check over everything."

Today, Derrick has forgiven the culprits, but he was mostly hurt because he thought of them as friends. He has found some true friends, though. Those friends, Brian Spears and Ben Whitfield, run Detroit's Crystal Rose Records and they've done all they can to support Derrick, not exploit him. He wrote or co-wrote nine of the ten songs on his 1999 album *He's on Time*, and he got writing credit for every one of them. Although Derrick was robbed of a song, he's been blessed with favor. When the time came to record the album, he received help from two gospel heavy hitters: Vanessa Bell Armstrong and Rance Allen. Derrick was Armstrong's musical director for several years. "When it was time for me to do my album, she did it for me," he says. "I met Rance at a COGIC convention and at some other events. When I wrote that song 'Choose Ye This Day' I had Rance in mind, so I sent it to him and when he heard it, he said he'd do it." Backed by his choir, Today's Generation, Derrick's unique mix of traditional and contemporary gospel is bridging the gap between young adults and middle-aged gospel lovers.

Born November 27, 1970, in Detroit, Derrick's life was full of faith and music. His father, C.J. Starks, was the pastor of the Prayer Tabernacle Church. His mother, Dorothy, was a housewife and mother of five children. One year Pastor Starks bought the family an organ for Christmas, but Derrick was the only one who took interest in it. He was seven years old when he began to tickle the ivories. At church, Derrick would sit on the stool next to his aunt, the church pianist, and study how she played. Eventually, he began playing at functions around the Motor City. At the age of 17, he played organ on the *Ron Winans Family & Friends Volume I* album. Locally, Derrick's name was being bandied about as the next big talent to rise out of Detroit when he caught the attention of Thomas Whitfield, who became his primary influence. "I was a Tommy fan. I'd go to his concerts and follow him. I hung around him so much that I wanted to do things he had done and he was with Crystal Rose, so I wanted to go there too. So I eventually submitted a tape to Brian Spears."

Whitfield also helped land Derrick his first big job as a staff organist at the Hartford Memorial Church in 1988. The job caused a slight tension between Derrick and his father. Instead of being at his father's church on Sunday morning as he always had been, he was across town playing for another church. "My heart was always at my home church," Derrick says. "I'd finish church, hit the expressway, and rush over to my dad's church to finish his service out. It was a major adjustment at first, but eventually, he supported me. He didn't try to block anything." Opportunities kept coming too. A friend submitted Derrick's name to pianist John Tesh to enlist Today's Generation for the gospel part of his concert at the Fox Theater. The choir has also backed Vickie Winans and others. Today, Starks is the minister of music at the Berean Christian Church in Lithonia, Georgia.

Duawne Starling

ONE OF THE MOST in-demand session singers in gospel music, Duawne Starling was born December 21, 1970. He grew up in the Seventh Day Adventist denomination and attended Oakwood College in Alabama, but earned his degree in recording industry management from Middle State University in 1994. While in college, Starling worked as an *Ebony* magazine Fashion Fair runway model. He got his start as a singer backing Angie & Debbie Winans when they held the opening slot on Whitney Houston's "Bodyguard" concert tour circa 1992. Through Angie & Debbie, he came to work with their sister, CeCe Winans, as one of her featured vocalists for several years. He was background vocalist on CDs such as Michael McDonald's *Motown*, several Donnie McClurkin projects, and albums by various members of the Winans family.

Candi Staton

IN THE 1970S, Donna Summer may have been disco's queen and Gloria Gaynor may have been its first lady, but Candi Staton was its princess. However, in 1982 the third most popular female disco artist of the era surprised her staunchest fans by walking away from the clubs that treated her like royalty in favor of churches that "treated me like dirt," she says. After Staton announced that she had become a born-again Christian, her toughest criticism came from church leaders, who have always been skeptical of secular singers who decide to sing gospel. "Candi has not been fully embraced by the gospel music industry and the reason for the apprehension is that quite a few folks within this industry are judgmental—even subconsciously judgmental. Their 'holier than thou' attitude frowns upon and simply refuses to show love to an artist coming from the secular side," says Percy Williams, a former gospel radio announcer at New York City's WBLS. "But at the same time they will embrace their own even if they know that person is not living the life they sing about. You might call it prejudice or discrimination, but it's alive and well even in the gospel music industry. I see it all the time."

Born March 13, 1943, in Hanceville, Alabama, Staton came from a poor farming family. Her father was an abusive alcoholic and her mother was a strict Christian. Staton and her sister, Maggie, sang in a local gospel group called the Four Echoes before Staton's mother moved the family to Cleveland to escape her husband. It was there that Staton joined the Jewel Gospel Trio circa 1955. They recorded for Nashboro Records and toured with 1950s gospel stars like Mahalia Jackson, the Staple Singers, Sam Cooke and the Soul Stirrers, and Aretha Franklin. The trio was exploited and financially taken advantage of by their founder, Bishop Jewell.

Staton quit the group and returned to Alabama where she finished high school, married, and became a housewife. In the 1960s, Staton raised her children and played keyboards at a strict church before the pastor kicked her out for having a television in her house. "I said forget God and forget everything associated with God," she once recalled. At her brother's urging, Staton began to sing at a Birmingham's 27/28 Club where she opened for blind R&B star Clarence Carter who would take her under his wing, make her his wife, and get her a record deal with Rick Hall's Fame Records label. Over the next five years, Staton churned out

Candi Staton / photo courtesy of
Warner Bros. Records (1976)

a series of country-styled R&B smashes such as the Top Ten hits "I'd Rather Be an Old Man's Sweetheart (Than a Young One's Fool)," "Sweet Feeling," and "As Long as He Takes Care of Home." Her renditions of "Stand by Your Man" and "In the Ghetto" both received Grammy nominations. By 1975, Staton had divorced Carter, signed to Warner Bros. Records, and changed her music from Southern soul to upscale disco. Over the next few years Staton scored with club classics such as "Victim," "Nights on Broadway," "When You Wake Up Tomorrow," and the No. 1 smash "Young Hearts Run Free." However, by 1982 Staton walked away from all of that, saying that God had delivered her from alcoholism and that she would be singing gospel from then on. She and her fourth husband, John Sussewell (a former Ashford & Simpson drummer), produced Staton's first gospel LP *Make Me an Instrument* in 1982. It was the first album where Staton wrote all the songs herself. The album had a contemporary flavor that was still unique to the gospel world. White Christian radio stations played her ballad "Sin Doesn't Live Here Anymore" and black gospel stations played the uptempo "Let Go and Let God." The album reached No. 7 on the gospel chart and received a Grammy nomination. In spite of the album's success, churches were reluctant to book Staton because gospel audiences did not instantly embrace her contemporary music. "The first concert I did in Memphis," she once recalled, "I started singing my songs and one by one the pews started to empty. By the time I finished singing the only people left were on the front row and those were some guys who had just gotten saved who used to come see me sing in the clubs." Staton decided to make her music more traditional in nature and it paid off handsomely with the 1988 hymns LP *Love Lifted Me*, which sold over 75,000 units.

At the same time, R&B radio was still craving a Staton hit. Staton recorded a gospel dance song entitled "You Got the Love" for the 800-pound Ron High's weight loss campaign hit the R&B Hot 100 in 1986 in spite of poor distribution and promotion. The popular refrain "Sometimes I feel like throwing my hands up in the air" was first introduced in the gospel arena by this funky track. A bootleg British remix of the song by John Truelove (Candi's 1986 a capella track on top of underrated Chicago house music master Jamie Principle's

1985 local club smash "Your Love") became such a big underground hit in British clubs that Truelove started a record label to market the song in 1991. Once it was readily available to the public, the song zoomed to No. 4 on the British pop chart and became the biggest dance recording of the year selling over 200,000 copies. After going out of print, the song's notoriety continued to grow to the point that Truelove commissioned a "Now Voyager" remix that shot up to No. 3 on the UK pop chart in 1997. The song finally received a big American audience when it was featured in the final episode of HBO's *Sex and the City* series in February 2004.

The UK success led React Records to offer Staton a recording deal in 1999 to create an entire new CD of inspirational music geared toward the clubs. The resulting CD, *Outside In*, was produced by England's top producer, K-Klass. The pop-dance CD featured club rockers such as Frankie Knuckle's "Whadda Ya Want?" "Love Has Come to Stay," "Reach," and "Outside In," all of which subtly referenced Staton's Savior. There were other song themes such as romance ("The Lightning"), brotherhood ("Wake Up, Everybody" and Boy George's "Love on Love"), and self-affirmation ("Love Yourself" and "Bouncing Back"). The album produced three Top 40 UK pop singles. Because the album was not categorized as a gospel CD in Europe (it was labeled inspirational pop), rumors got back to America that Staton had backslid and gone back to secular music.

"It was terrible," Staton recalls. "K.D. Bowel, a DJ on The Light radio network got on the air and had listeners calling in talking about my salvation. One woman said she knew it was just a matter of time before I went back to R&B which is why she never supported my records in the first place. K.D. never once called me to ask if the rumors were true. The gospel singer Ann McCrary called to see if I was okay. She said she had heard on the radio that I had backslid and gone back to the world. Pastors started canceling my dates. The radio stations playing my music stopped playing my songs. It was devastating for me. There was nothing on that CD that couldn't be sung in a church. It irritates me that people were judging me and yet they had never heard the CD. It wasn't even released in America."

The controversy eventually faded and Staton's gospel career was back on track. She's enjoyed a peren-

nial Mother's Day hit with the country-styled "Mama" (1995). However, her biggest gospel hits have been traditional-styled, bluesy numbers such as "The First Face I Want to See" (1997) with Joe Ligon, "Shut Up and Start Praying" (2000) with Dottie Peoples, and "When There's Nothing Left but God" (2003). Since 1986, Staton has hosted a weekly musical television program on the Trinity Broadcasting Network entitled *Say Yes* (originally *New Direction*). After *Bobby Jones Gospel* on BET, Staton's is the longest-running gospel program on television.

RECOMMENDED RECORDING: *Classic Candi Vols. 1 & 2* (Beracah, 2004) feature all four of Staton's initial 1980s gospel LPs on two separate CDs, including songs such as "Uncloudy Day" and "Sin Doesn't Live Here Anymore."

Maggie Staton-Peebles

THE SISTER OF SOUL star Candi Staton, Margaret "Maggie" Staton-Peebles was born February 12 circa 1940 in Hanceville, Alabama. As preteens, she and Candi formed a group called the Four Echoes with a couple of local girls. The gospel quartet performed throughout the state on the weekends. By the time they were teenagers, the Staton sisters had moved to Nashville to attend the Jewel Academy, a religious boarding school. There they joined Naomi Harrison and became the Jewel Gospel Trio. They first recorded for Aladdin Records in Los Angeles but cut their biggest hits for Nashboro Records beginning in 1953 with "Many Little Angels in the Band." They took turns leading songs, but Maggie led their biggest hit "I Looked Down the Line and I Wondered." Candi led their next biggest hits, "Jesus Is Listening" and "Too Late." The trio was the first gospel group of the era to have their own regular band, which featured a steel guitarist. They toured with the biggest groups of the day such as the Soul Stirrers and the Clara Ward Singers. Their sound and music was traditional with tight vocal harmonies. They sang ballads, but they mostly sang songs that would make the church audiences jump from their seats and shout to the music. Eventually, the group's overseer, Bishop M.L. Jewell, added two other girls and they became the Jewel Gospel Singers. By 1958 they had stopped recording for Nashboro and both Staton girls had left the group angry that they were not being well compensated by Jewel for their recordings and their concerts. Maggie got married and Candi returned to high school.

After graduating from Tennessee State University with B.A. and M.S. degrees, Maggie became a public school teacher in Nashville. After a 20-year tenure, she retired from teaching and reignited her recording career with her then-husband's Winston-Derek Records label in 1988. Her first solo LP, *First Fruits*, was produced by Moses Dillard, who collaborated with Al Green on many of his gospel recordings. It was traditional in tone with sweet arrangements that accentuated her tender yet earthy vocal style. One of the best cuts was her rendition of Sam Cooke's "Touch the Hem of His Garment." She recorded two more LPs, *This Soul of Mine* and *Born Again*. She's now semi-retired from performing. Candi continues to record, and Naomi (who had become a minister) died of colon cancer in 2002.

Silas Steele

FOUNDER OF THE Blue Jays quartet, which was based in Chicago in the 1950s, Steele was born March 29, 1911, in Brighton, Alabama, and formed the group with Clarence Parnell in 1926. They added James Hollingsworth and Charlie Beal. Steele's hard singing would later influence the Soul Stirrers and other groups with what was called the Jefferson County sound. They recorded for Paramount Records songs such as "Standing by the Bedside of a Neighbor" in 1932. They didn't record again until 1947 when they cut "I'm Bound for Canaan" for the Harlem label. Steele eventually left his group and joined the Spirit of Memphis.

Martha Jean Steinberg

THIS FEISTY, SIX-FOOT beauty queen was a pioneer radio announcer in both R&B and gospel music in the 1950s. Born Martha Jean Jones September 9, 1930, in Memphis, Tennessee, she worked as a nurse before marrying a white, Jewish jazz musician (Steinberg herself was black). At some point, Steinberg decided that she wanted to be a DJ so she took a part-time job at WDIA in 1954. Initially management wanted her to stick to women's issues such as sewing or cooking on the *Tan Town Homemaker's Show*, because they didn't think the largely male audience would accept a woman spinning records. However, her high ratings encouraged station executives to take a chance on Steinberg doing a less domestically oriented program. They gave her a weekend shift playing R&B records where she quickly became known as a wild woman for her brassy candidness. Her program ran from 9:30 to 11:00 P.M. and was followed by Rufus Thomas's salacious *Hoot 'N' Holler* program. Steinberg held her own in a male occupation and earned her nickname there. "Every black disc jockey had to have a rhyming, stereotyped name," she later told the *Detroit News*. "One day the staff announcer at WDIA in Memphis introduced me as Martha Jean 'The Queen.' I took that name later when I came to Detroit. It's a trademark now."

In November 1963, Steinberg moved to Detroit where she became a DJ at the Chit Chat Lounge and also took an announcer position at WQBH, a community radio station where she played blues and gospel music. She developed the same warm audience rapport in Detroit that she enjoyed in Memphis. In 1967, she was lured to a wider FM audience at WJLB. During the 1967 Detroit riots, Steinberg helped calm the black citizens by staying on the air for 24 hours straight. "Through it all, she remained regal, righteous, and responsive to the needs of the people," Detroit Congressman John Conyers told the *Detroit News*. "And you can be sure that like most Detroiters, Martha Jean was tough... she was ambitious and extremely tough in difficult circumstances." She also intervened in 1970 when a policeman was slain during a standoff with a group of Black Panthers. She showed up at the crime scene and calmed both sides of a tense situation.

In 1973, Steinberg had a cameo role in the motion picture *Detroit 9000*, and in 1975, she founded the Home of Love, a church community center and low-income housing center on Detroit's West Side. She kept one foot in the church and one foot in the Chit Chat

Lounge nightclub. In 1982, she returned to WHCB as an on-air personality and co-owner. In 1997, she bought the remaining ownership for $3.9 million. Even as her health began to fail, Steinberg continued to host her three-hour, daily talk show. Gospel singer Esther Smith recalls, "She had a program where people would call in and make their complaints or ask questions, especially when it came to dunking on men. She tried to make women stand on their own two feet and was labeled as being a male basher. She had the respect of a large part of Detroit. Every year her Easter program at the Fox Theater was a sellout just from her radio program. She had artists like the Mighty Clouds of Joy and Rance Allen. A few years, she included me, and a few others from time to time, but every year the Clouds and Rance were there." Steinberg was doing the show up to two weeks before her death. She died Saturday, January 29, 2000, in Detroit. She remains so popular that the station (now run by Steinberg's daughter Treniere) still runs Steinberg's commercials and archived radio conversations on politicians, the Lord, and the hazards of dating married men.

Demetrus Alexander Stewart

ONE OF GOSPEL music's most powerful music executives, Stewart was born November 21, 1959 in Nashville, Tennessee. A former professional singer herself (she recorded background vocals on BeBe and CeCe Winans's *First Christmas* and the Clark Sisters' *Miracle* CDs), Stewart began her business career as a receptionist for Nashville-based Warner Alliance Records in 1989. She was soon elevated to promotions director where she flourished by marketing hit Christian albums by Marilyn McCoo, Michael English, and others. There was such a buzz about Stewart's work that New York–based rap/soul music label Jive/Zomba Records hired Stewart to launch their gospel label, Verity Records, in 1993. A year later, Warner Alliance rehired Stewart as a vice president and for a while, she maintained both positions. However, she eventually moved back to Warner Alliance full-time where she signed bestselling artists such as Bishop Carlton Pearson, Jonathan Slocumb, and Beverly Crawford. She courted

Donnie McClurkin for months before he finally joined Warner Alliance and gave the label its first gold CD with his self-titled album that featured the radio hits "Stand" and "Speak to My Heart."

Warner Bros. decided to close Warner Alliance in 1998 and the staff was merged into the Christian division of its sister label, Atlantic Records. However, in 1999, Stewart was recruited by longtime friend CeCe Winans to form the superstar's Wellspring (later renamed Puresprings) gospel recording label. At Puresprings, Stewart has presided over three gold albums by Winans and introduced the label's bestselling new artist, Vicki Yohe, who made a splash in 2003 with her smash hit "Because of Who You Are."

Princess Stewart

OFTEN CALLED THE Grand Lady of Gospel for her regal bearing and bigger-than-life voice, Stewart recorded for Vee-Jay Records in the 1960s. She toured with the Langston Hughes Broadway musical *Black Nativity*, and was best known for the songs "That's God," "Tired, Lord," and "I'm Not Gonna Let Nobody Stop Me." Born as Theodosia Asbury, she died in Februrary 1967.

Freddie Stone

A FOUNDING MEMBER of Sly & the Family Stone, Frederick Stone was born June 5, 1946, in Vallejo, California. He and his three siblings sang as the Stewart Four, a gospel group, during their early teens. Stone spent his teen years singing in a church choir and perfecting his guitar skills. In 1965, he formed a group called Freddie & the Stone Souls. The group played in various San Francisco Bay Area nightclubs for two years. His older brother, Sly, already had producing experience with some national acts. In 1967, they formed Sly & the Family Stone with female trumpeter Cynthia Robinson. In the thick of the counterculture and civil rights movements, the multiracial band created a repertoire of thought-provoking, non-preachy songs touching on issues of the day. After signing to Epic Records, the group enjoyed a run of pop and R&B hits such as "Everyday People," "Dance to the

Music," "Stand!" "I Want to Take You Higher," "Family Affair," "Hot Fun in the Summertime," and "Thank You (Falettinme Be Mice Elf Agin)" among others.

Aside from having one of the best live band shows of the period, the group was a lightning rod for media attention. There was a rumored romance between Sly Stone and America's sweetheart, Doris Day. Sly was also known to miss concert dates and had several run-ins with the law over his drug abuse. By the end of the 1970s, the group had disbanded and Sly was a solo act. In the ensuing years, Freddie Stone, who had a ten-year drug addiction, became a born-again Christian in 1980. In 1988, he became an ordained minister and in 2000 he released his first gospel CD *Everywhere You Are* on his own Geronimo Records label. Stone wrote and arranged the project, which had an old-school soul feeling to it. "My desire is that this CD will uplift and encourage everyone who hears it," Stone said at the time. "I believe old-fashioned principles still work today. You too have everything it takes to make it, and it's amazing what you can do with the Lord on your side." In 1993, Sly & the Family Stone was inducted into the Rock and Roll Hall of Fame. Today, Stone pastors the Evangelist Temple Fellowship Center in Vallejo.

Stovall Sisters

FOR A BRIEF MOMENT in 1971, Warner Bros. Records' Reprise imprint took some time out from promoting Frank Sinatra, Sammy Davis, Jr., and Lola Falana records to spread the gospel via the electrifying music of the Stovall Sisters. Lillian, Netta, and Joyce Stovall were all born in Indianapolis, Indiana. They were the last three of ten children born to Della Stoval. Four older sisters sang as a church group for years until they married and settled into domestic bliss. The three younger girls sang in churches too as the Little Wonders in the 1950s, but by their teens had changed their name to the Valley Wonders. Della managed the group and booked their concerts. She also snagged them a record deal with a small label.

In 1964, the family moved to Oakland, California, where they finished high school, sang in church as the

Stovall Sisters, and took on 9-to-5 jobs. They began to see that there was little money to be made in singing gospel, so they added secular music to their repertoire and started getting nightclub work around the city, lying about their ages because they were still underage. "We were with Ike and Tina Turner for a while," Lillian said in a 1971 press release. "I think we were the 18th set of Ikettes. We did a lot of recording sessions, too, but mostly it was club work. We were [known as] the Sisters Three when we did rock and roll, but we'd still record for the gospel label as the Valley Wonders or the Stovall Family."

Things weren't happening fast enough for their careers, so they took out an ad in the *Oakland Tribune* that read, "Three Black Girls Looking for a Caucasian Band to Sing With." They got a lot of weird calls, but the only decent response from the ad was a keyboardist named William Truckaway. "He came right in and sat on the floor like we'd been knowing him for years," Joyce said back then. Through Truckaway, they did background vocals on "Bluegreens." He also introduced them to his musician buddy Erik Jacobsen, who decided to use them as the background singers on Norman Greenbaum's song "Spirit in the Sky." The song went to No. 3 on the pop charts and became the label's bestselling single up to that time.

Everyone enjoyed the sisters so much that Greenbaum's label, Reprise, decided to record a self-titled LP on them. Reprise issued three singles in 1971 including "Hang On in There," "Spirit in the Sky," and "The World Is in a Change," but none of them took off. The sisters' sound was gutsy gospel wrapped in a rock music package and should have been a huge seller. Of particular interest was "Yes to the Lord," a brilliant gospel reworking of Martha Reeves & the Vandella's "My Baby Loves Me." Also notable were the powerful vocal punches on the ballad "I'm Ready to Serve the Lord" and the sweet "The World is in a Change." Philip Bailey briefly served as their music director before he eventually joined Earth, Wind & Fire. In the meantime, they did background vocals on Greenbaum's follow-up albums *Back Home Again* and *Canned Ham*. They did the same on Tom Fogerty's *Myopia* (1975) and Truckaway's LP *Breakaway* in 1976. There's been no recorded trace of the sisters since then.

Straight Company

THIS CO-ED A CAPPELLA group was every bit as talented as Take 6 and much more adventurous in their musical choices. The original group members were Tierra Watkins, Vette Murrah, Kim Murrah, Jeff Murrah, Jesse "Essej" Murrah (who founded the group with his sister Kim), and Mark Kamp. They were discovered singing in the lobby of the Hilton Hotel at the GMWA convention in 1992 by Benson Records President Jerry Parks. Unlike Take 6, whose arrangements had a sameness quality that leaned toward Negro spirituals, Straight Company brought many elements to their gospel a cappella. They incorporated street corner harmonies, doo wop, calypso, contemporary gospel, and praise and worship styles to their music. Their first album was 1993's *So Excited*, which was all vocals and sold over 50,000 copies. Their second was 1996's *Plugged In*, which was their first to feature instrumentation. In recent years, the group has recorded a number of custom CDs such as *Kentucky Fried Gospel* and their latest, *Courtesy of God*. They are based in Highpoint, NC. Kim died in 1996.

Kim Stratton

ONE OF BLACK GOSPEL'S most prominent yet underrated worship leaders, Chicago-based Kim Stratton was born in 1961. For a time, her family lived in a homeless shelter and worked their way out of that situation. Perhaps because of that, Stratton has spent much of her adult life working in community programs and ministering in churches. She recorded for Integrity Music's black gospel imprint, Glorious Records, in the middle 1990s. During that period, Stratton recorded her best-known songs, including "New Life," "That's How Mercy Saw Me," and "More Than Enough." The latter was later revised by Vickie Winans, who enjoyed a hit with it on her *Live in Detroit* CD in 1997. "I respected her for not allowing her circumstances to dictate her lot in life," says Stacy Merida, who worked with Stratton during her years at Glorious. "She really has a Cinderella story."

Donna Summer

HANDS DOWN, Donna Summer was the most prolific and bestselling female artist of the latter 1970s—worldwide. Summer's record sales topped even those of bona fide pop superstars such as Olivia Newton-John and Linda Ronstadt. Her string of club-oriented hits such as "Bad Girls," "Hot Stuff," and "Love to Love You Baby" earned her the title the Queen of Disco. At the height of her fame in 1980, she became a born-again Christian amid swirling rumors that she'd soon give up pop music and become a church singer. She didn't give up pop music, but she did transform her image from the provocative "Bad Girl" image Casablanca Records cultivated into that of a more sophisticated lady of song. She also turned from the sensual songs that made her famous and began to perform more love songs and message music fueled by her faith.

She was born LaDonna Andrea Gaines on December 31, 1948, in Boston. Summer was raised in the Episcopal church. She loved Mahalia Jackson's music and used to lie on the floor of her parents' bedroom and practice breath control listening to Mahalia. She was eight years old when she first sang in church. "It brought tears to my eyes," her father, Andrew Gaines, once told *People* magazine. "She turned the lights on in the church." As a teenager, she turned the lights on as the lead singer for a rock group called Crow. As her desire to sing professionally increased, her strong-willed father thought she needed to concentrate on a more stable avocation. She ended up running away from home and joining a German stage production of *Hair* in 1968. She lived in Germany and performed in a number of productions before marrying Helmut Sommer. She began hanging around the burgeoning European disco scene where she met her future producers, Girorgio Moroder and Pete Bellotte.

In 1975, the trio was at a party where they heard Serge Gainsbourg and Jane Birkin's song "Je T'aime… Moi Non Plus" on the turntable. Something about the song inspired them to go and write what would become "Love to Love You Baby." The 16-plus minute song with its repeated orgasmic moans eventually became a massive American hit. Its provocative nature caused many radio stations to ban the song. The media attention only made the song bigger. It was the kick-off for a string of pop, disco, and R&B smashes such as "Spring Affair," "Try Me," "I Feel Love," "I Love You," "Bad Girls," and "Hot Stuff." By the end of the decade, Summer was the bestselling female artist of the era with numerous gold and platinum awards to her credit.

Summer became a born-again Christian at an altar call held at her friend and fellow singer Roberta Kelly's wedding circa 1979. Summer, who was never comfortable with her sex-kitten image, began to downplay her sensuality and concentrate on more message-oriented music. In 1980, she signed a reported $25 million contract (the biggest artist deal ever at that point) with David Geffen's newly founded Geffen Records. Over the next few years, Summer recorded message-oriented hits such as "The Wanderer," "She Works Hard for the Money," and "Dinner with Gershwin." Summer also began to include gospel or faith-inspired songs on her projects. The self-penned tune "I Believe in Jesus" appeared on *The Wanderer* LP. Summer's 1983 project *She Works Hard for the Money* was her most overtly inspirational album. The faith-inspired songs such as "He's a Rebel," "Unconditional Love," with the Musical Youth, "Love Has a Mind of Its Own" with CCM star Matthew Ward, and "Woman" received regular airplay at Christian radio formats and scored Summer a cover story in *CCM* magazine that year. Summer won a Grammy for the gospel song "Forgive Me" from 1984's *Cats without Claws* LP and she paid tribute to Mahalia Jackson on the 1987 smash "Dinner with Gershwin." Summer appears to be in semi-retirement, emerging infrequently for short concert tours or sporadic recordings.

Academy of Music, Summer founded the Interdenominational Youth Choir and landed a recording deal with Atlantic Records' subsidiary Cotillion Records . Their first album, *God Gave Me a Song* was issued in April 1970 to wide critical acclaim. A *Billboard* magazine writer wrote, "This debut album by Myrna Summers and the Interdenominational Youth Choir is a robust, full-bodied sing-along to which most lovers of gospel music would automatically gravitate. There is much of the sincerity and enthusiasm of youth in this production. And added to its other enjoyable qualities is some really good gospel singing."

From the start, Summers merged the youthful soul and pop music of the era with the ecstatic enthusiasm of her COGIC foundation. The mid-tempo title tune won Summers a Grammy nomination and brought her much media attention. During her period with Cotillion, Summers recorded other hit LPs such as *Now* and *Tell It Like It Is*. By the end of the decade, Cotillion had stopped recording gospel artists such as Marion Williams, Alex Bradford, and Summers. Summers moved on to Savoy Records where she began a new run of slightly more traditional choir hits such as the 1979 Grammy-nominated "Give Me Something to Hold On To." However, her 1988 project "We're Going to Make It" remains her bestseller. Backed by Timothy Wright and his choir, the album peaked at No. 3 on the gospel chart and won a slew of Stellar award nominations. By the late 1990s, Summers and Savoy had parted company. Her last known CD is *His Love Endureth Forever*, which was released on her own Put God First record label in 2000. Summers is minister of music at the Reid Temple church in Lanham, Maryland.

Myrna Summers

A MAJOR CONTRIBUTOR to the contemporary church choir movement of the 1970s, Myrna Summers was born in the Washington, DC, area March 30, 1949. A church-reared singer, Summers began singing at the age of five. She sang with a number of choirs and groups such as the Girls' Ensemble of the Refreshing Springs COGIC. After formal piano training at the Toutorsky

Swanee Quintet

A COUNTRY QUINTET with a hard backbeat, this Augusta, Georgia–based group was the bread and butter for Nashboro Records in the 1950s. Their early recordings featured Rev. Reuben Willingham (who was called the funkiest lead in gospel at the time), guitarist William "Pee Wee" Crawford, Charlie Barnwell, Rufus Washington, and falsetto James "Big Red" Anderson. In 1956,

Johnny Jones joined the group. By the mid-'60s, both leads had left the group and were replaced by Percy Griffin and Lee Wallace. The Godfather of Soul, James Brown, who was raised in Augusta, grew up on the Swanee Quintet and adopted some of their hard-singing techniques in his own music such as the 1956 church-like workout, "Please Please Please." The group was best known for songs such as "Step by Step," "Sleep On, Mother," and "Sit Down, Servant."

Sweet Chariot Singers

THIS HAND-PICKED group of singers sang at New York's Sweet Chariot Christian nightclub in the early 1960s. During the first wave of crossover gospel music ushered in by the Clara Ward Singers during the early 1960s, this group became known for their somewhat stereotypical portrayal of gospel music. The club featured scantily clad angels (waitresses), served faux cocktails, and conveyed gospel singing with buffoonery. Columbia Records immortalized some of the antics on the 1963 LP *Shoutin' Wailin' Hard Drivin' Pop Gospel Recorded Live at the Sweet Chariot*. At the time, major magazines were predicting that pop-gospel music and religious-themed nightclubs such as the Sweet Chariot would become bigger than the Twist dance craze. They didn't, and in the meantime, established gospel artists were offended by the trend. In an interview with *Down Beat* jazz magazine, Mahalia Jackson was beside herself with disgust over the Sweet Chariot (and the group recorded for her record label, Columbia). "They're making a mockery of the most precious thing in the world—the salvation of God," she said in 1963. "The gospel is good news and good tidings and not meant to entertain. If it [the Sweet Chariot] was helping some lonely soul and doing some good, instead of blaspheming the Holy Ghost, it would be different. I do not see the Catholics doing this; I do not see the Jewish people doing it; I only see my people doing it. For a few measly dollars they will portray our folk-parents' understanding and our religion under the Lord [in this manner]. What is wrong with these Negroes? I have made money in gospel singing, but I have never brought it down to a low level."

Sweet Honey in the Rock

ONE OF THE MOST respected vocal ensembles in the world, the history of this a cappella group begins with Bernice Johnson Reagon (born October 4, 1942, in Albany, Georgia), a child of the civil rights movement. While a student at Albany State College in 1961, Reagon was arrested for participating in a SNCC demonstration. She spent the night singing protest songs with other prisoners and after she was released, she joined the SNCC Freedom Singers to use music as a tool for civil disobedience After earning her B.A. in history from Spelman College in 1970, she founded Sweet Honey in the Rock in 1973. While promoting her group on the weekends, she held down a position as a folklorist for the Smithsonian Institute and earned a Ph.D. in history from Howard University in 1975. The following year, Sweet Honey in the Rock released their self-titled debut LP on the Flying Fish label. From the beginning, the repertoire was gospel ("Jesus Is My Only Friend"), encouraging ("You Make My Day Pretty"), and protest ("Are There Any Rights I'm Entitled To?").

Over the years, the group has remained a critic's favorite as they have preserved African-American music and forged an esoteric form of gospel music that is not commercial by comparison to modern gospel radio station playlists. Still, Sweet Honey in the Rock has recorded over a dozen albums that have been well-received by their upper-crust fan base and by world music aficionados. Since 1993, Johnson has been curator emeritus at the Smithsonian and has served as a professor of history at American University. She developed the Peabody award-winning *Wade in the Water: African American Sacred Music Traditions* for National Public Radio (NPR). Johnson retired from the group in February 2004 and charter members are now managing the aggregation. "With the new ensemble, we're remembering the past and moving on to the future," founding member Carol Maillard told *Billboard* magazine in March 2004. "We're creating new sounds but always being sure that fans of Sweet Honey past, present, and future recognize that there is a continuum from all the formations of the group."

RECOMMENDED RECORDING: *Selections 1976–1988* (Flying Fish, 1997), a double CD, features 34 tracks from the group's first dozen years. Among the many outstanding tracks are "Testimony," "Run, Mourner, Run," and the poignant "More Than a Paycheck." Their vocals are smooth and their multi-part harmonies are complex and spellbinding.

Jubilant Sykes

A CLASSICALLY TRAINED baritone, Sykes began his career in the early 1990s and has performed at the Metropolitan Opera, the Deutsche Oper Berlin, and as guest soloist with the Boston Pops. In 1996, he was named the Vocalist of the Year by *Sacred Music USA*. In spring of 1998, he released his first CD, *Jubilant*, on Sony Classical. His second album, *Wait for Me*, was issued in 2001 and he made the media rounds, including *Good Morning America*. In 1997, his label paired him with trumpeter Terrence Blanchard on the critically acclaimed *Jubilant* CD, which was meant to expand the reach of Sykes's audience. He continues to perform in stately venues worldwide, but his recorded output is far from prodigious.

RECOMMENDED RECORDING: *Wait for Me* (Sony, 2001) is perhaps his most approachable album for non-classical fans. It includes two religious tracks, "John the Revelator" and Sykes's own "Angel's Lullaby," along with folk-rock artist John Hiatt's "Have a Little Faith in Me," which Sykes gives a somewhat secular reading here as a duet. However, for a full picture of his gospel work, try *Jubilant* (Sony, 1998), which features 14 sure-fire, concert hall-styled gospel treats such as "Give Me Jesus" and "How I Got Over."

Russ Taff

A MUSICAL CHAMELEON, Russ Taff started off performing what might be considered Christian Muzak, then shifted into blue-eyed soul before turning country. The fourth of five sons, he was born November 11, 1953, in Farmersville, California. His father was a fire-breathing Pentecostal preacher. He began to sing in his father's church as a child and he formed a local band called Sounds of Joy in 1968. After he opened for the Christian pop group the Imperials, Taff was recruited as their lead singer in 1977 and stayed with them through 1981. In 1983, Taff launched his solo career with Myrrh Records where his debut single "We Will Stand" spent 15 weeks at No. 1 on the CCM singles chart. Over the years, Taff crafted skillfully styled R&B vocals on songs such as the mellow "Silent Love." Other hits included "I Cry," "Farther On," and "Walk Between the Lines." In 1994, Taff briefly replaced Michael English in the Gaither Vocal Band. He then made a couple of forays into country music where the singles "Love Is Not a Thing" and "One and Only Love" made a modest impact in that market. Over the last decade, Taff has vacillated between inspirational country and Christian pop music, amid dates with Bill Gaither's Homecoming concert tours.

Take 6

THIS A CAPPELLA vocal group formed on the campus of Oakwood College in Oakwood, Alabama, circa 1980 as A Special Blend. At the time, the group was comprised of students Claude McKnight, Mark Kibble, Mervyn Warren, Lori Bryan, and Joya Foster. As members graduated, the personnel changed. By 1987, the group was named Take 6 and included Alvin Chea, Cedric Carl Dent, and David Thomas. They signed with Reunion Records in 1988 and released the LP *Doo Be Doo Wop Bop!* They were then signed to Reprise Records where their self-titled 1989 CD featured "Mary, Don't You Weep," "If We Ever Needed the Lord Before (We Sure Do Need Him Now)," "I L-O-V-E U," and "Spread Love." The project received wild praise from mainstream music critics, gold record certification, and reached the Top Ten on the gospel, CCM, and jazz album charts. In 1990, Warren left the group to concentrate on producing and was replaced by Mark's brother, Joel Kibble. The group added instrumentation to their vocals and released the gospelized rendition of Ambrosia's pop hit "Biggest Part of Me" in 1994. The song reached No. 3 on the CCM singles chart and No. 36 on the R&B singles chart. The group, which has always enjoyed an upper-income mainstream audience, is thought of as an artistic group rather than an evangelistic one. They continue to be a top draw at jazz festivals around the world.

RECOMMENDED RECORDING: *Greatest Hits* (Reprise, 1999) features the group's best-known a cappella tunes and their collaborations with CeCe Winans, Stevie Wonder, and Sarah Vaughan.

David E. Talbert

THE MAN RESPONSIBLE for creating the phenomenon known as the gospel stage play in the early 1990s is David E. Talbert (born February 10, 1966). To many, the "E" in his name stands for ego. He bills himself as the People's Playwright and often comes off as arrogant and overly impressed with his own accomplishments. However, one can't argue with his success. No one has produced more hit gospel musicals than Talbert has over the last decade. While attending Morgan State University as a marketing major, Talbert worked as a radio announcer with Baltimore's V-103 and in Washington, DC, at DJ-100. After earning his degree, he was off to Oakland, California. There he was invited to see a production of the show *Beauty Shop*. "I remember sitting there in my seat watching the audience go absolutely wild," he once recalled. "Folks were laughing, and high-fiving each other. It was amazing, the response. That's when the theater bug bit me. That night I went home, pulled out my word processor, and started pecking away on a story of my own." Over the years, he has turned out such hit shows as the spiritually centered *He Say, She Say, But What Does God Say?*, *The Fabric of a Man*, *Mr. Right Now*, and *His Woman, His Wife*.

"For me, it's really about touching lives and making a difference," he once said. "I want to be remembered as someone who made folks laugh, smile, and more importantly, believe. If I can accomplish that, then I know beyond a shadow of a doubt, I'm being who I was created to be."

Ben Tankard

THE LEADING PIANIST in modern gospel, Ben Tankard was born in 1964 in Daytona Beach, Florida. A preacher's kid, Tankard was a college basketball star poised to be drafted into the NBA when he was sidelined by a knee injury. Unable to work and virtually homeless, Tankard began to attend a church to be in a warm building and possibly get a free meal. During a revival service one night, he began to sense a calling in his life. He became a Christian, and the church's pastor anointed his hands with oil and instructed him to sit at the piano and play. Ben had never played piano before, yet he claims he had a miraculous ability to play. In 1989, he released his first LP *All Keyed Up*, but it wasn't until the 1997 CD *Instrumentally Yours* that one of his albums hit the Top 20 gospel chart. His 2004 CD *Piano Prophet* was his first to hit the smooth jazz chart at No. 15.

"When I first started my career in music, I was the freshman who wanted to slam-dunk every time I got in the game," Tankard once said. "I wanted to showcase…to slay demons…raise the dead…make the front page for God! But the more I've gotten to know him and the longer I've walked on this path, he's changed and matured me. The end result is that the ministry has also matured and changed. Every day he gives me more insight into his Word. As my relationship with him grows, so does my faith and the gifts of the Holy Spirit that flow through me and my music."

Ruby Pickens Tartt

ALONGSIDE ALAN LOMAX, Ruby Pickens Tartt was arguably one of the most important folklorists to publish and document African-American folk songs and spirituals in the early half of the 20th century. Born January 13, 1880, in Alabama, she studied art at the Alabama Normal School and the William Chase School of Art, but her real interest was in Negro culture. As a child, she often accompanied her father on his trips to collect rent money from his black tenants. She developed a keen interest in the way blacks talked and what they talked about. She loved to hear them sing songs or tell stories.

She began to collect these tales and send them to the Library of Congress. The Library's archivist, Alan Lomax, was fascinated by what Tartt sent in and went down to Alabama to record various black families. There Lomax discovered singers such as Vera Hall and Dock Reed, who were brought to Washington, DC, where they recorded a variety of songs for the Library of Congress. Among the songs she collected were "Sweet Honey in the Rock," "Another Man Done Gone," and "Last Month of the Year." In 1936, Tartt became the supervisor of the Federal Writers project for Sumter County, Alabama. In 1940 at the age of 60, she took a position as librarian for Sumter County. She died on November 24, 1974. After her death, more than 5,000 of her manuscripts were donated to Livingston University. She was later inducted into the Alabama Women's Hall of Fame along with other luminaries such as educator Helen Keller and actress Tallulah Bankhead.

Spencer Taylor & the Highway QCs

IN THE 1950s, the Highway CQs were not considered a top group. Instead, they were considered stepping stones to better things as both Sam Cooke and Johnny Taylor left the group for higher callings to the Soul Stirrers and then to pop-soul solo music careers. However, they did enjoy two respectable hits with "Jesus Will Fix It" and "Lord, I Just Want to Thank You" for Peacock Records in the 1960s. Spencer "Pretty Boy" Taylor was born March 6, 1928, in Chicago. He grew up in church and first sang with a group called the Holy Wonders (personnel included Lou Rawls, James Walker, and Chris Flowers). He joined the QCs after Johnny Taylor left to replace Sam Cooke in the Soul Stirrers. When Sam Cooke founded the group in 1948, they named themselves after the Highway Baptist Church. The QC in their name may have stood for Qualified Christian. They occasionally filled in for the Soul Stirrers on their WIND radio broadcast when the Stirrers had an out-of-town gig. Although they haven't enjoyed a big radio presence, Taylor has maintained enough enthusiasm for the group to work steadily over the last 40 years. They continue to make the traditional quartet records they made in the early days. Their recent recordings have

appeared on the Marxan Recording label. The 2001 CD *The Legend* features "I Come To Praise Him" and "Prayer Changes Things."

Ted & Sheri

TED WINN AND Sheri Jones-Moffett are two of the most dynamic performers to rise from the gospel music field in the last decade. Their heartfelt vocals and emphasis on real singing have endeared them to many. Joseph "Ted" Winn and Sheri Jones-Moffett were both raised in Memphis, Tennessee, where they had strong church backgrounds. They met when they were members of the Voices of Binghampton Choir in the early 1990s. Ted then formed Ted Winn & Deliverance and Sheri joined him in the group. In spite of performing within a group, they began to receive invitations to sing as a duo. In 1995, Ted disbanded the group, and he and Sheri continued to sing together. While they waited for their career to take off, Ted sang with Richard Smallwood's choir and Sheri sang with Donald Lawrence's choir. In 1999, a door opened and the duo was signed to Neily Dickerson's Church Howze Records label.

On the heels of their dazzling, note-bending reprise of Roberta Flack and Donny Hathaway's "Come Ye Disconsolate," Ted & Sheri were warmly embraced by gospel radio and their 2001 CD debut *The Healing*

Ted & Sheri / photo by Derek Blanks

Starts Right There sold over 30,000 units. They later moved to Word Records where their sophomore project *Celebrate* hit the *Billboard* gospel Top 40, and the festive title song (written by Donald Lawrence) rose to the Top 5 on both the *Radio & Records* and *Billboard* gospel singles charts in 2005.

Ruby Terry

A FRUSTRATED CHOIR conductor once said that good singers are a dime a dozen, and Malaco signed a number of those dime-a-dozen singers in the 1980s. What makes an above-average singer something special is their material. When the music is below average, the singer is often ignored by the industry. Therefore, it's no surprise that since A&R expertise is not a Malaco hallmark, they saddled a good but average singer like Ruby Terry with okay music and they got okay results.

A preacher's kid, Ruby Karen Frances was born in Columbia, Mississippi, in February 1952 and grew up in Lawton, Oklahoma. After high school, she attended Seward County College and Wichita State University. During this time, she married Ivanhoe Terry and they began to raise a family in Lake Charles, Louisiana, where Rev. Terry pastors the Saints Memorial COGIC.

Ruby Terry financed and co-produced her own first recording, entitled "Heeding the Spirit." She mailed a copy of it to Malaco Records executive Frank Williams, who liked what he heard and immediately signed her to the label. Her first LP, *Chapter One*, was released in 1988 and garnered a Stellar award nomination. Terry's most successful album remains *Ruby Terry Live with the Southwest Louisiana Mass Choir*, which was produced by Rev. Timothy Wright in 1992. The album hit No. 11 on the gospel charts and featured Terry's traditional renditions of "Blessed Assurance" and "Old Time Religion."

Terry's 1994 album, *What a Time*, reached No. 39 on the gospel chart but wasn't a strong seller. She did much better with 1996's *God Can Do It*. Produced by gospel legend Dorothy Norwood, the CD was recorded live at the Civic Center in Lake Charles, Louisiana. She was backed once again by the Southwest Louisiana Mass Choir to nice effect. The lead song, "Didn't I Tell You," a tambourine-friendly bounce tune, was written by

Norwood and featured James Moore and Norwood squalling with Terry. It was a high point, although the best tracks were those written by Terry herself, such as the uptempo "My Mind's Made Up" and "The Lord Will See You Through." In 2000, Terry made a guest appearance on Pastor Brandon B. Porter & the GCT Voices Choir's CD *Count Me Lord* where she sang "Hallelujah," a rousing remake of a Mattie Moss Clark classic.

Sister Rosetta Tharpe

SHE WAS PERHAPS the original gospel crossover artist. Having begun her career in the gospel market, Sister Rosetta Tharpe made a few novelty blues records that became major pop hits and expanded her audience in the 1930s as she shocked the church community by performing in secular venues such as Harlem's Cotton Club. Although she left and returned to gospel a number of times over the balance of her career, many of the old fans never forgave Tharpe for singing the "devil's music." However, long before the success of Mahalia Jackson, when most people thought of gospel music, they thought of Sister Tharpe. Her songs such as "This Train," "Up Above My Head" (with Marie Knight), and "Strange Things Happening Every Day" are gospel classics.

She was born on March 20, 1921, in Cotton Plant, Arkansas. Not much is known of Tharpe's father. Her mother was Katie Bell Nubin (1880–1969), a mandolin-playing traveling missionary and gospel shouter who was known as "Mother Bell" throughout the COGIC denomination. Tharpe learned to play guitar by the age of six and was considered a child prodigy. Her mother felt called to preach the word, but women weren't allowed to preach at the time. Therefore, to draw audiences, Nubin hit the tent revival circuit with P.W. McGhee where she preached, sang, and played mandolin alongside her daughter, who was called "Little Rosetta Nubin, the singing and guitar-playing miracle." The miracle was that a child could play so well, and the other oddity of the duo was that it was rare for women to play guitars and mandolins. Blues vocalist Memphis Minnie was the only professional guitarist in the public eye. Little Rosetta thrilled audiences with buoyant, bubbly performances of "Jesus on the Mainline" and other church standards. Mother and daughter accompanied McGhee's revivals through the Southeastern states before they settled in Chicago in the mid-'20s.

At home, Tharpe would play blues, but not in public. Early on in Arkansas, she had soaked up blues and jazz influences while gleaning from blind pianist Arizona Dranes when they were performing together on the McGhee revivals. In 1934, Little Rosetta married ukulele player Wilbur Thorpe (who later changed his name to Tharpe) and formed a trio with him and her mother. Neither the marriage nor the trio lasted long. By the time she moved to New York on the advice of promoters a year later, Wilbur was causing trouble. Since he and Tharpe met in the Sanctified Church, he expected her to adopt the behavior of a Sanctified Church lady. When she debuted her gospel with the Cab Calloway big band at the Cotton Club in Harlem in 1938, she did not wear a hat. At the time, black church women always covered their heads in public. However, Tharpe refused to be restricted by the rules of Wilbur or the Sanctified Church.

Soon, the marriage was over and Tharpe was free to pursue her career without interruption. The performance with Calloway caused a minor stir in the New York music community. Rarely, if ever, had sacred music been performed in a nightclub. While many churchgoers surely went to a nightclub now and again, they believed in separation of church and play. Even more so, Tharpe's religious songs were different from most sacred songs. They were not slow and mournful. She had noticed some time before that secular audiences liked upbeat jump songs. Therefore, she used her sprightly, girlish soprano on uptempo gospel songs and would enhance them with bluesy colors on the guitar. Although Decca Records had never signed a gospel artist before, the buzz about Tharpe was enough to convince them to take her into the studio. In October 1938 she laid down Thomas Dorsey's "Hide Me in Thy Bosom" as "Rock Me," "My Man and I," "Lonesome Road," and "That's All." Lucky Millinder's jazz orchestra backed Tharpe on the recordings. Decca billed her as Sister Rosetta Tharpe and issued "Rock Me" as a 78-rpm single. It became an instant success. Tharpe's winning smile and gregarious personality made her a media darling. In 1939, *Life* magazine profiled her seemingly contradictory career of working nightclubs Saturday night and slipping into church on Sunday morning.

The Sanctified Church was none too pleased. They caused such a fuss over Tharpe's performing with a jazz orchestra that she asked Decca executives if she could record her future songs with only guitar accompaniment. They vetoed that idea, but compromised by giving Tharpe a trio of bass, guitar, and piano. Boogie-woogie pianist Sammie Price became Tharpe's keyboardist and song arranger. Together, Tharpe and Price created a rhythmic, jazzy sound that allowed her to surpass the Golden Gate Quartet as the country's best-selling gospel act. Although Tharpe was able to work in the church market, her records were mostly sold to non-church consumers and she was able to command more money from secular venues than she could at churches. In 1942, Tharpe did her first totally secular recording when "I Want a Tall Skinny Papa" became the B-side to "Shout, Sister, Shout." In 1944, Tharpe's success jumped another notch when the record "Strange Things Happening Every Day" hit *Billboard* magazine's Race Records Top Ten chart. The song was a sly slap at the church hypocrites who sought to besmirch Tharpe's name for performing gospel outside the four walls of the church. She followed up with the smash "This Train," the lyrics of which reinforced that she was a Christian-living woman.

In 1946, Decca kicked the barometer on Tharpe's career up a few more degrees when they paired her with contralto Marie Knight. Tharpe's light, upbeat vocalizing and showmanship contrasted nicely with Knight's reserved vocal style and flat-footed singing. That year, their recording of "Up Above My Head" became another huge crossover hit and the duo hit the road as a team. They became all the rage as they toured football-size arenas around the country, and became close as singers as they recorded other radio hits such as "Precious Memories," "Beams of Heaven," and "Didn't It Rain." In 1949, Tharpe scored again when she and her mother teamed for "Ninety-Nine and a Half Won't Do."

In 1950, Tharpe re-signed with Decca and endured an exhaustive tour with her mother that lasted 115 days and took them to 97 cities. At the height of her fame, Tharpe married former Ink Spots manager Russell Morrison, at a lavish wedding at Griffith Stadium in Washington, DC. More than 25,000 people came out for the spectacle. Over the next few years, Tharpe vacillated between pop and gospel music recordings. After the nuptials, there was a concert with the Sunset Harmonizers, the Harmonizing Four, Vivian Cooper, and the Rosette Gospel Singers. It was these lavish affairs that gave rise to the anniversary concert concept that gospel singers have used ever since. As soon as other performers such as the Ward Singers and the Caravans began to have anniversary concerts, they stole Tharpe's thunder. Tharpe's more secular-oriented presentation didn't hold up against the dynamic church concerts that others delivered. Tharpe rapidly began to lose ground. Besides, many in the church community felt that Tharpe had sold out when she sang pop, and she was never able to win those hearts over again. She recorded sporadically throughout the 1960s but never experienced a major success, though she did not give up trying. Morrison took her through little country hamlets that rarely saw gospel stars and Tharpe still found adoring audiences there. She recorded a couple of LPs for Savoy Records and found herself nominated for a Grammy award in 1969 for a rerecording of "Precious Memories." She lost to newcomer Edwin Hawkins, who won for "Oh Happy Day." In 1970, Tharpe suffered a stroke that confined her to a wheelchair, from which she performed at her last concerts, which were poorly attended. In those last years, she opened up to Anthony Heilbut in his book *The Gospel Sound*. "I'm gonna write the story of my life, the people will cry and cry," she told him. "I've been robbed, cheated, married three times, but God is good." She finally suffered another major stroke and died on October 9, 1973, at Temple University Hospital. She was only 56 years old. In recent years, critics and a new generation of fans of roots music have discovered Tharpe again. The 2003 CD *Shout, Sister, Shout* was an all-star Tharpe tribute project featuring Maria Muldaur and the Holmes Brothers, among others.

RECOMMENDED RECORDING: *Gospel of Blues* (MCA Records, 2003) is a remastered CD collection of 18 of Tharpe's best sides such as "This Train" and "Mansions in the Sky."

Annette Thomas

THE DAUGHTER OF Brother Joe May, Thomas recorded some fine message and gospel singles for Stax Records' gospel division in the early 1970s. She began singing at the age of five and sang as part of the ensemble backing some of her father's Specialty Recordings in the 1950s. In the 1960s, she recorded with Rev. James Cleveland's Southern Community Choir and as a member of his girl group, the Gospel Girls, who recorded for Savoy Records. She and her pianist brother, Charles May, did background vocals for Jerry Lewis and Robert Goulet in the early 1970s. Lewis's musical director, Lou Brown, became Thomas's manager and brought her to the attention of Stax with his business partner Don Gottlieb. She recorded her first song "Nothing Is Everlasting" at Malaco's Studios in Jackson, Mississippi. Gottlieb got the song added to the soundtrack for the film *Class of '74*. Lewis's influence won Thomas a high-profile appearance on *The Tonight Show with Johnny Carson* when Lewis was hosting, but it did little to help increase her radio play. Possessing a handsome, expressive, controlled alto, Thomas did a fine job on her final Stax single. The up-tempo "You Need a Friend Like Mine" was written for Mavis Staples to sing, but the Staple Singers had already left the label for Warner Bros., so it was given to Thomas and she was instructed to sing it as Staples would. The song actually called the name of Jesus and was a well-constructed song with a nice hook. The 45 single was backed with "What Good Is a Friend?" and should have been a much bigger hit. Had the Staples done it, it probably would have been, but Thomas's rendition is flawless. Regardless, Thomas left the stage herself and managed James Cleveland's career the last decade of his life and continues to serve as executor of his estate.

Carla Thomas

THEY CALL HER the Memphis Soul Princess and she was the First Lady of Stax records in the 1960s with a string of solid AM radio R&B hits such as "Gee Whiz (Look at His Eyes)," "Baby," and "Tramp," a duet with Otis Redding. Thomas was born December 21, 1942 in Memphis, Tennessee. Her father, Rufus "Walking the

Carla Thomas / uncredited 1973 publicity shot, courtesy of Capital Entertainment archives

Dog" Thomas, was a popular blues DJ at WDIA radio in the 1950s. She was a member of the Teen-Town Singers at the age of ten and studied both opera and gospel at Hamilton High School. Thomas used to doodle poems and compose songs in her head. One day she thought up a song called "Gee Whiz" and sang it into a reel-to-reel tape recorder. Her father came across it later and, unbeknownst to her, decided to peddle it. Satellite Records (which would eventually be renamed Stax) owner Jim Stewart decided to issue the song in 1960, and it went on to become his label's first million-seller and the first of many more for Thomas. A big fan of Jeanette "Baby" Washington, she'd often sing the songs as she'd imagine Washington might sing them. Even though Washington was a deep, gruff singer, Thomas's music had a sweet quality with a more polished soulfulness.

By the early 1970s, Thomas had begun to record more songs inspired by her faith in God. Because she was with an R&B label, many of these songs took on a message orientation. During this period Thomas's LPs included songs such as "Are You Sure" (which the Sta-

ple Singers did as well), "You're Still Your Daddy's Child," "What Is Love?" and "Love Among People." However, Thomas did a straight-out gospel song that she wrote called "I Have a God Who Loves" (which was recorded to the melody of James Cleveland's "I Had a Talk with My God Last Night"), which she performed at the famous Wattstax Festival at the Los Angeles Memorial Coliseum in 1972. Considering the sweetness and pop-styling of her biggest Stax hits, when one hears Thomas rip through songs such as her duet with Johnnie Taylor, "I Get a Bad Feeling," it makes one think she has a really fine traditional-styled gospel album in her just waiting to come out.

Irma Thomas

THEY CALL HER the Soul Queen of New Orleans because she's the Crescent City's greatest export in the field of soul music. Born February 18, 1941, in Ponchatoula, Louisiana, Thomas became pregnant at the age of 14. Her father forced her to marry the baby's father, but the marriage didn't last. She took a job that paid fifty cents an hour washing dishes at a restaurant and sang in a gospel quartet at Home Mission Baptist Church during what little leisure time she had. By the age of 17, she'd married her second husband and was working at the Copper Kitchen. She was fired for singing on the job because her white boss didn't like the "nigger music" she was singing to keep herself company in the kitchen. Fortunately, she soon snagged a waitressing job at the Pimlico Club where Tommy Ridgely's band played every Wednesday night. One night she asked to sing the Drifters' "There Goes My Baby" with the band and was well-received. Soon word spread about the Singing Waitress, and patrons came in requesting that she sing. Thomas's boss complained that he paid her to wait tables, not to sing. He forbid her to sing again. When she thought he was gone, she went on stage and sang. "He walked in the middle of me doing a couple of songs," she once said, "and he pointed the finger at me and told me I was fired."

Not to worry—Ridgley got her a recording deal with the local Ron Records where she cut the driving

"Don't Mess with My Man" circa 1960. The hit record brought her to the attention of producer and songwriter Allen Toussaint (who would later write Glen Campbell's "Southern Nights" and LaBelle's "Lady Marmalade"). Toussaint signed her to Minit/Imperial Records, where she cut early soul songs such as "It's Raining," "Ruler of My Heart," and "Cry On." However, her first really huge hit was a song she wrote called "Wish Someone Would Care." She once told writer Dawn Eden, "I was really at a low point when I wrote that. I was just looking back at life… At the time, I was breaking up with my husband because he was giving me a hard time about being onstage. It was a song from my heart, that's probably why it sold so well. I really wanted someone to care, to stand beside me and care."

Her next significant track was "Time Is on My Side" which the Rolling Stones recorded and made their first US Top Ten hit. Thomas was bitter that her original version was passed over in favor of the Stones' version. After recording some good, but uncharting tracks for Chess Records, Thomas dropped out of sight. She took a job at Montgomery Wards until Rounder Records coaxed her out of retirement in 1986 to record the album *The New Rules*, a first of a string of respectable sellers for the label. In 1993, Thomas's lifelong dream of recording a gospel album came true when she released *Walk Around Heaven*. The album received widespread praise. "The singer radiates uplifting sincerity throughout," the *Chicago Tribune* noted of the set, which featured traditional arrangements of Bessie Griffin's "Careful Hands" and Cassietta George's "Walk Around Heaven." The *Boston Globe* wrote, "Usually, R&B singers who venture into gospel come out way behind their full-time gospel peers. Thomas is the exception, a stellar vocalist who can hold her own with anyone." Thomas continues to perform at blues and soul music festivals globally.

Shawn Thomas

SHAWN THOMAS hasn't made a big splash in the traditional Christian music industry. However, his poster-boy good looks, pop tenor, and contemporary rhythms have brought him some attention from the gay com-munity. Born in 1968 in Dallas, he was in his mid-twenties before realizing he was gay. His first CDs *Come My Way* and *Typical Male* appeared in the early 1990s, but they were regular love song projects—angry love songs, that is. Since that time, Thomas came to grips with his faith, his sexuality, and overcame an eating disorder. In 1999, he founded Aaron's Rainbow Project, a music production firm. In 2000, he released the CD *Out in this World*, which peaked at No. 1 on the OutVoice.com Web site. "I'm out in the respect that I wouldn't deny it if I were directly asked," Thomas once told *Oasis* magazine about his sexuality. "I have a lot of friends that do know, but I feel it's important to live my life the best way I can and try to live life like I feel God wants me to live." He is based in Huntsville, Alabama.

RECOMMENDED RECORDING: *Best of Shawn Thomas 1993–2003: The First Ten Years* (Aaron's Rainbow Project) features 21 of Thomas's best-known songs touching on love and faith, including the funky "Glorify His Name."

Johnny Thompson Singers

A GROUP WITH a good bridge between traditional black gospel and the showbiz antics that made the Clara Ward Singers international stars, the Johnny Thompson Singers never became big American stars. However, they have had a successful run on stages all over Europe. The group founder, Johnny Thompson, was born August 15, 1942, in Philadelphia. He began to play piano at the age of five and formed his first group, the Blue Robe Boys, in 1955—the same year he wrote his first song, "The Creation." Although the group eventually disbanded, Thompson continued to compose songs. Over the years, he wrote such songs as Shirley Caesar's "Stranger on the Road" and Rev. Douglas Fulton's "If I Perish." In 1965, he formed the Johnny Thompson Singers with charter members Delores Helena Copes (April 2, 1946 to September 21, 1997), Shirley Hunt (born September 1, 1954), Arlene Mills (born March 8, 1934), and George Edmonds (September 1, 1943 to September 15, 1987). A shrewd self-promoter, Thompson was able to get the group booked on gigs that established gospel acts never dreamed of getting. In 1967, they toured France with jazz greats Louis Armstrong and Dave Brubeck. In 1968, they toured eight European countries with Horace Silver and blues idol Muddy Waters. In 1969, the group became the first gospel group to tour the Soviet Union and various Eastern bloc countries. It was just the first of many breakthroughs for the group, such as taking the gospel to the Zurich Opera House and to the Montreux Jazz Festival.

Through the years, the group's personnel has changed frequently and they have recorded 30 albums. Their first recordings for Jersey City's Glori Records in the 1970s were their best. For instance, their 1976 LP *I've Found a Refuge* featured female leads on most of the tracks. Thompson's elastic tenor carried the title song. Thompson's piano counterpoint to the organ swells kept the traditional gospel fervor in the mix, although the percussion gave the music a contemporary sound. In live performances, audiences always swooned over the lanky George Edmonds's voice, which was considered a natural soprano rather than a falsetto. Two of the original members are now deceased, but the group continues to perform with new vocalists all over Europe. Back in the United States, Thompson is the pastor of the First Apostle FBH Church in Coatesville, Pennsylvania.

Big Mama Thornton

TOBACCO-VOICED blues singer Big Mama Thornton is best known for recording the original version of "Hound Dog," which was a million-seller for Elvis Presley in 1956. Although the mainstream culture associates the song with Presley, Thornton's version was no slouch. It held down the No. 1 spot on *Billboard*'s R&B chart for seven weeks in 1953. She was born Willie Mae Thornton on December 11, 1926, in Montgomery, Alabama. Her father was a minister and her mother sang in the choir. After her mother died in 1939, Thornton went to work to help support her family. She eventually found blues music to be a pretty good paycheck and began touring in musical revues. Thornton's mentor and bandleader Johnny Otis nicknamed her "Big Mama" because of her 200-pound frame. In 1951, she was signed to Peacock

Records where she initially hit it big with her sassy rendition of "Hound Dog" in 1953. Thornton, who was only paid $500 to record the song, always claimed that she wrote it over a bottle of Ole Grandad and that the copyrighted authors, Jerry Leiber and Mike Stoller, stole the song from her. Leiber and Stoller claim they wrote the song themselves. Otis claims that they both were wrong and that he wrote the song with Leiber and Stoller. "We had an agreement that if the song needed rewriting in any way that I would help rewrite it and we'd split three ways," he told *Living Blues* magazine in November 1992. "I rewrote 'Hound Dog' with them, they didn't affirm the contract legally and went to court saying they wrote the song. We fell out after they [cheated] me out of my song."

Afterwards, Thornton's career was downhill. She was constantly cheated by managers and a string of record labels. Adding insult to injury, rocker Janis Joplin rose to fame off of Big Mama's "Ball and Chain," a tune that Thornton did write but for which she was never properly compensated. However, she recorded sporadically through the 1970s with commercially respectable sales, even though the albums were panned by music critics. Her one gospel LP, *Saved* (Pentagram Records, 1973), was trashed in a *Rolling Stone* magazine review: "We, her fans, will just have to pass this one up, cross it off and hope that her next album will be one that finally captures her galvanic, profoundly exciting singing in all its sweeping power and emotional directness. It seems we've been waiting for years—but then we know how surpassingly good she can be. I guess we'll keep on hoping and waiting." In spite of the critic's appraisal, it was actually a good project that featured Thornton's bluesy, rock 'n' roll takes on church standards such as "Glory, Glory" and "Oh Happy Day." She continued to perform at small clubs until the end of her life and in spite of rapidly failing health. A heavy drinker, she suffered from cirrhosis of the liver and was emaciated by the time she found herself living in a rundown Los Angeles rooming house. "It was Willie Mae, her sister, and a couple of friends sitting around the table drinking Jack Daniels or something," Johnny Otis recalled. "Willie Mae just put her head down on the table and never came up." It was July 25, 1984, and she had suffered a massive heart attack.

Denise Tichenor

A MUCH-HERALDED rising star in the early 1990s, Denise Tichenor's career was sidetracked by a lack of marketing and a series of personal tragedies. One of eight children, Tichenor was born July 19, 1970, in Indianapolis, Indiana. Her father was a pastor and although everyone in her family sang, she did not. Instead, she excelled in track and field. It wasn't until a high school choir teacher encouraged Tichenor to sing that she began to take her voice seriously. She then passed out flyers around her neighborhood announcing that she was founding a gospel group and recruiting members. The group, the Sounds of Deliverance, became 50 strong and performed throughout the region. Tichenor then attended Lincoln University as a broadcast major. While in college, she won a role in the nationally touring gospel musical, *Mama Don't*. The attention brought her to Tyscot Records, which released her first CD *Refreshingly Neecy* in 1991. The project, a mix of contemporary and traditional numbers, never charted, but she did win a GMWA Excellence award. Her 1992 CD *Lead Me* won a Stellar award nomination. However, Tyscot was never able to identify Tichenor's demographic and the projects never resonated with any particular audience.

Since then, Tichenor has known tragedy. Her brother was slain as he protected his daughter from a street gang. Both of her parents and a sister are now deceased as well. "It helps me to appreciate every day that is given me and keeps me focused on my purpose—why I'm here," she once said. "I don't know what's going to happen to me tomorrow. With your family members passing, you learn to appreciate every minute. I maximize my time to my potential. I live my life with a purpose in mind." When she's not singing lead vocals with the Nashville Super Choir on BET's *Bobby Jones Gospel*, Tichenor is a music minister at both the Higher Calling Community Church and the Emmaus Christian Church in Indianapolis. She runs the Michael Tichenor Foundation for at-risk youth and is working on her first CD in a decade.

Tonéx

ARGUABLY THE MOST hyped man in modern-day gospel, Tonéx's unique approach to the presentation of his ministry has been compared to Prince and Michael Jackson. However, for those who really know music, Tonéx's presentation is much closer to the cutting-edge music of '70s groups like Funkadelic or LaBelle. He was born Anthony Charles Williams, II, on March 13, 1973, in San Diego, California, where his father, A.C. Williams, has been pastor of the Truth Apostolic Community Church since 1992. His father had previously played saxophone with soul bands such as Tank and the Soul. His mother, Betty "E.B." Williams, also sang in a girl group. When he was ten, Tonéx's family recorded an album, *The Hogpen Experience*. By the age of 13, he yearned for a solo career and gave himself the name Toné. Then the soul group Tony Toni Toné surfaced. "I wanted to change the spelling," Tonéx says. "I added the x to represent what I was, but am no longer. We are all x-somethings. I don't pronounce the x because it's no longer alive and functioning in my life. We shouldn't forget where God has brought us from. Anything that is not of God is simply x-ed out."

In 1993, Tonéx recorded a CD that he released regionally via MSS Records, a label he founded at the age of 16. Two years later, Tonéx was selling another custom CD, *Damage*, out of the trunk of his car before signing with Rescue Records. "Nobody would sign me because they said I was too wild or eccentric," he said. The album had poor distribution but was selling for $100 as a bootleg. A buzz began to build in the gospel community after his August 1998 appearance at the GMWA convention in Philadelphia. He lit incense, danced, and put on a show worthy of funkmaster George Clinton in his prime. "Many thought, 'How could a brother dressed in a Dr. Seuss hat and a black and white boa sing with this kind of anointing,'" *Gospel Times* newspaper editor Sheila Belle says. "He was powerful, breathtaking, refreshing, and overwhelming."

By that time, Tonéx was signed by Tommy Boy Records, and the label had hired veteran publicist Phyllis Caddell to build his public profile. Tonéx's penchant for wearing outlandish stage costumes, oversize glasses, clown shoes, and feathered outfits drew immediate and rabid attention in the gospel community. The picture he painted was reminiscent of the outlandish space suits worn by LaBelle and the diapers Parliament/Funkadelic wore in the 1970s. "I want to revolutionize the presentation of the gospel," he once said. "I want the integrity, the Word, to remain the forefront and template for what I do. I want to combine the theatrical arts with the gospel. Young people are more visual than oral. When it's time to go into demonic territory I am like Clark Kent changing into Superman. You can't judge me on how I look. I'm here to educate the body of Christ and be an ambassador…. I believe my birth mission is to change the pop culture for Jesus and introduce him to the mainstream in a way that is new and refreshing. The difference is the anointing and the lifestyle, testimony, and the spirit of God."

"They kept changing the release date [for Tonéx's debut album]," Caddell says of Tommy Boy Records. "So the press was so far in advance of when the CD finally released that some of the momentum had died and

Tonéx / photo by Delphine Fawundu

then it came back." That 2000 CD, *Pronounced Toe-Nay*, was a blend of jazzy and retro soul songs that did not adequately showcase Tonéx's amazing vocal range (from throaty wails to dizzying high notes). Furthermore, the songs lacked the hooks and vamps that usually carry gospel hits. Still, it was quite a good project with a rather mainstream appeal. It just wasn't what gospel radio was accustomed to and most radio programmers didn't give the single "Personal Jesus" a chance to resonate with listeners. It peaked at No. 12 on the gospel sales chart—a far cry from the staggering sales the label and Tonéx's press clippings anticipated. According to SoundScan, the CD sold just over 60,000 units in its first year of release, a major disappointment. As a compromise to get the gospel audience to pay attention to his music and not his wardrobe, Tonéx cut his long hair and started wearing suits. By 2002, Tommy Boy closed and Jive Records released his next CD, O_2, that year. The change in apparel had no major effect on Tonéx's acceptance and the album sales were again lackluster.

Tonéx was as incensed as the candles he liked to light during his personal devotions. In a candid interview with the *Gospel Times* newspaper in August 2003, he told all. He said that Verity Records had forced him to revise the O_2 CD 13 times. He recorded 60 songs before the company found 16 they were happy with. The album was supposed to come out in January 2001 but wasn't released until April 2002. "I truly felt I had been sold into slavery like Joseph [from the Bible] by his brothers," he said. In addition, Tonéx lamented the short setup period to properly market and introduce his projects. While he was recording his double-CD set, *Out of the Box*, he told the newspaper it would be his last for Verity Records. "I feel as though my career has been damaged and hindered and has not reached its full potential due to lack of support, promotion, and proper marketing," he said. "The machine is there but they don't know how to break an artist… I had a following when I got there, but you can't have 22 high-profile acts and only one publicist and [not] think somebody's not going to be happy… Look at Deitrick Haddon on his *Lost and Found* project… He had at least five crossover singles on that project and they let that record fall through the cracks." And as for the GMWA, where many in the gospel industry first discovered him, Tonéx said, "GMWA just doesn't get it. They're stuck in a time warp and apparently aren't ready or willing to evolve."

After several postponements, the star-studded live double CD *Out of the Box* debuted at No. 1 on the gospel chart, peaked at No. 5 on CCM, and No. 15 on the R&B chart in summer 2004. The numbers are impressive until one realizes that a double CD counts as two sales. So, technically, Tonéx's sales did not improve much, further buttressing Tonéx's contention that the label doesn't know how to break artists. In spite of guest appearances by artists such as Kirk Franklin and Yolanda Adams, the album sales dropped significantly after the big first-week sales push. "If I sell 2 million records I still would not be able to recoup the money spent on my first record, because there was a big money exchange for me to come on board with Verity. However, I still have not seen any of that money. I don't get advances," he told the *Gospel Times*.

The CD wasn't the biggest thing on Tonéx's mind that summer. His father, who suffered with diabetes and heart ailments, had a stroke in January 2004. During that period, Tonéx and his mother co-pastored his father's church until Pastor Williams was well enough to resume his position in May 2004. However, he suffered a fatal stroke on July 26, 2004. Since that time, Tonéx has balanced the demands of his recording career with the demands of pastoring his father's church.

Transformation Crusade

ONE OF THE FIRST gospel rap groups in the 1980s, they were comprised of Darryl Fitzgerald, Chris Williamson, Kathy Sims, and Andre Sims. Fred Hammond produced their debut project *Transformation Crusade* (1990) and the follow-up *Makin' It Happen* (1991) on Benson Records. Their motto at the time was that they minister to "the saints in the church pews and the dealer on the streets." Back then, Andre Sims said, "God has ordained us to use the musical language of the streets, which is rap, to relate to the kids the message of salvation, offering them a positive solution to the negative grip Satan has held on their lives. That's what Transformation Crusade is all about." However,

at the time, Christian radio was not open to rap music by black artists (the format did embrace DC Talk's pop-rap blend, though). After the projects failed to make a significant impact, the group was dropped from the roster and faded into the landscape.

Carolyn Traylor

A VIVACIOUS AND charismatic personality, Carolyn Traylor is one of the new breed of young singers keeping traditional gospel music alive. The baby of 12 children, Traylor was born July 30, 1960, in Greenville, Texas. Her mother was a homemaker and her father ran a cemetery service. She sang in church until she sang a bad note one Sunday and a church elder smirked, "I thought that Traylor girl could sing." Her confidence was so wounded that Traylor stopped singing and attending church altogether. After graduating from high school, she enrolled at Texas Southern University as a criminal justice major. A classmate named Cynthia had heard Traylor sing under her breath when R&B music was playing on the radio. She kept prodding Traylor to come to church with her until Traylor finally gave in. "So, I went to a choir rehearsal with her and didn't know that it was a divine setup," she laughs.

The rehearsal took place across the street from the university at the Philadelphia Missionary Baptist Church. There, Traylor met the music minister, Olivia Branch Walker, who was well-known in the Houston gospel community. It turns out that Cynthia had been telling Walker about Traylor's vocal ability. "I was so embarrassed and at that age," she recalls. "The only church song I could remember was 'Trouble in My Way' and I didn't know most of that. But I sat there by the steps while she was at the piano and I sang enough of it for her to say that I had potential. She was a student at Texas Southern in the music department, so everything she learned in class, she came back and taught us in rehearsal. Everything that I know, I learned from her."

Traylor joined the church and Walker became her mentor. Traylor even had her first recording experience under Walker's guidance. She backed Walker on her 1986 LP *New Life* and led the song "Tell It." However, Traylor's music career was cut short. One morning she received two calls from two doctors. "One said that my mother had six months to live," she recalls. "The other said my father had a year to live." She returned home to Greenville and nursed her parents throughout the balance of their lives. Her mother died of a heart attack in December 1987 and her father died of cancer a year later. Traylor was working a 9-to-5 job when Bessie Armstrong staged a big concert with Willie Neal Johnson & the Gospel Keynotes and the Canton Spirituals in 1991. Traylor opened the concert and Johnson took a liking to her.

Traylor spent two years on the road with Johnson and he introduced her to his record label, Malaco. At the same time, she was going through marital problems and eventually divorced. "Thank God for deliverance," she laughs. "It did make me work harder. With a divorce comes a sense of failure. That pushes you to a degree. If nothing else, you want the ministry to work. It also left a lot of free time so I could do ministry."

Although she was signed to Malaco, it was a long time before Traylor's CD would be released. She was extremely discouraged when she ran into Bobby Jones on the road. "I told him all of these things and he didn't say anything," she recalls. "Five months went by and he had his musician Derek Lee invite me to Italy with New Life for their Easter concert. I was saying all these young singers have come up and maybe my time had passed. But what God did was impart some trailblazers like Dr. Jones to encourage me to keep moving on." She came to meet gospel legend Dorothy Norwood when the latter was recording an album in Texas. The singer who was supposed to solo canceled at the last minute. Norwood and Lee tried to think of who could replace her when Lee suggested Traylor. "God has allowed me to get a lot of leftovers," she laughs. "But they are good when you're hungry. But whoever didn't show up, Derek suggested me and Dorothy put me on that." Later, when Malaco finally prepared Traylor for her CD debut, *Don't Wanna Be Left Behind*, they called in Norwood and Lee to produce the album, which was released in 2000 to positive reviews. Traylor is currently working on her sophomore project and is considering rerecording her mentor Olivia Branch Walker's signature song, "New Life."

Trin-i-tee 5:7

IN THE EARLY '90S, distaff soul groups such as En Vogue and TLC were all the rage. So Gospo Centric Records decided to release a project on a female gospel group with a similar vibe. Their name was Trin-i-tee 5:7 and they presented a gospel message with a commercial urban sound on songs such as "Put Your Hands Up" and "Holla."

The New Orleans–reared gospel group was comprised of Chanelle Haynes, Angel Taylor, and Terri Brown when they were high school students. Their manager, Kenneth Grant, brought them to the attention of Gospo Centric Records in 1997. Label owner Vicki Mack Lataillade pictured them crossing over to the urban market as her flagship artist Kirk Franklin had four years before. "A great deal of attention was put into their imaging because there's a fine line you have to walk with female talent with relation to the church and secular audiences as well," Lataillade told *Billboard* magazine in 1998. "Nobody wants to think a female group is not clear about who they are and what they're singing about. They had to be attractive and trendy, but a class act as well."

The label named the group Trin-i-tee 5:7 based on the I John 5:7 biblical scripture that refers to the trinity. R. Kelly and Franklin produced the group's self-titled debut project in 1998. With preorders of 100,000 copies and an aggressive urban marketing campaign, the project debuted at No. 3 on the gospel chart and eventually stepped up to the top slot. It also reached the R&B Top 20 chart and was eventually certified gold. The album created two gospel radio hits in "Mary, Don't You Weep" and "God's Grace." Just as the group was taking off, there was trouble in the ranks. In May 1999, Terri Brown exited the group amid a cloud of scandalous rumors and speculations. She was replaced by the group's hairstylist, Adrian Anderson, and the group issued their second project, *Spiritual Love*, which featured the big hit "Put Your Hands Up" (to the music of L.T.D.'s 1977 R&B hit "Back in Love Again"). "Our videos and our music are really different from most of what's out in the music industry today," says Angel. "We want to convey hope and positiveness, and that's really who we are. The more popular we become, the more attention will be focused on our personal lives. I think that the best thing we can do for God is to show the world what Christianity is all about through the way we live our own lives."

By the time the group's *The Kiss* CD was issued in 2002, they were having issues with Gospo Centric. The sizzling urban radio track "Holla" didn't get the urban radio push they felt the song merited. All their past singles at least made it to the lower reaches of the R&B charts. During that period, Grant left his post as manager, and the group sought to be released from the deal, but the company refused. Pop star Brandy's mother and manager, Sonia Norwood, took over management and brought the group to a higher level of respect by booking them on major nongospel television shows. However, she eventually turned the management over to Beyoncé's father and manager, Matthew Knowles. Now the world awaits what is next for the trio.

Kathy Troccoli

ALTHOUGH SHE'D probably deny it, Kathy Troccoli has been something of a Christian music sex symbol for over 20 years. Her dark locks, natural beauty, and smoky voice have made her a fan favorite of bachelors and a wholesome, but very hip role model for bachelorettes. Her songs (many of which she's written herself) are all Christian music staples, including "Love Has a Name," "Mission of Love," "Go Light Your World," "All the World Should Know," and "You've Got a Way."

Born June 24, 1958, to a big Italian family on Long Island, New York, Troccoli was raised in church but did not commit to Christ until she was 20 years old. However, she always loved to sing and in junior high school, with a teacher's encouragement, she did a three-song mini-concert of Carole King songs during a talent show, which furthered her desire to sing professionally. While attending Berklee College of Music in Boston, she began to sing pop songs in coffeehouses and intimate clubs. In the summer of 1978, a friend led Troccoli to a deeper relationship with God. Soon, she started singing contemporary Christian music instead of pop songs. Members of the a cappella group Glad heard Troccoli sing at a

concert and invited her to open for them on an upcoming date in New York. "The lead singer flew me to Pennsylvania to do a demo of songs," she told *Today's Christian Woman*. "Eight months later, Amy Grant's managers, Mike Blanton and Dan Harrell, heard my tape and came to hear me in concert. They encouraged me to move to Nashville to pursue Christian music." That was in 1982 and with Troccoli's commercial pop voice, cover-girl looks, and strong faith, they felt getting her a record deal would be a no-brainer. Blanton and Harrell, who carried considerable weight in the industry due to Grant's success, were frustrated that label after label turned Troccoli's demo down, so they formed Reunion Records themselves to record her first album.

After the duo secured distribution through Word Records, Troccoli's *Stubborn Love* LP was released in 1982 and it was the fastest-selling debut album by a female Christian artist up to that time. Over the next five years, she'd record two more LPs, featuring the Top 5 CCM singles "I Belong to You," "Talk It Out," and "All the World Should Know." After a while, Troccoli seemed to abruptly leave Christian music. "I had some insecurities, I was hard on myself—especially in the area of weight," she confessed to *TCW* later. "Despite being on the thin side, in college I had become obsessed with food—gorging myself, then abusing laxatives. Although I never threw up, my bulimic tendencies continued for several years. In some strange way, abusing food made me feel like I was in control and comforted me…. I also was immature when it came to relationships. Because I had such a great need to be loved, when the chemistry wore off I'd want to move on. I'm very sorry for the ways I've hurt people…. With the responsibilities of performing, my insecurities grew even stronger, but I didn't have time to work through my pain. I knew things had to change. So in 1986, I packed up and returned to Long Island to deal with my emotional issues and questions about my future in Christian music."

After working through her issues and a stint of doing session work with pop artist Taylor Dayne, Troccoli made a Reunion Records comeback in a big way with the 1991 CD *Pure Attraction*. Christian radio was thrilled to have her back, and five songs from the album all hit the Top Ten on the CCM chart. One of those songs, "Everything Changes," was No. 1 on the CCM chart for four weeks and also crossed over to the pop charts. BMG had bought a stake in Reunion by this point and used all of their mainstream radio contacts to break Troccoli in the field. On the pop charts, the bouncy number jumped to No. 1 on the *Gavin* AC chart, No. 14 on *Billboard*'s Hot 100, and the video was No. 4 on the VH1 *Top Twenty Countdown*. The album featured three other *Gavin* Top Ten AC hits with "You've Got a Way," "If I'm Not in Love," and "Tell Me Where It Hurts."

The success led to Troccoli opening for Jay Leno's Las Vegas act and appearing on *The Tonight Show*. She made all the major media rounds, but in the midst of Troccoli's greatest success, her mother was diagnosed with cancer. She had lost her father to colon cancer when she was 15 and was devastated by the news. In between promoting her album and touring with Michael Bolton, she spent time healing her sometimes combative relationship with her mother. Within a year, Troccoli's mother, grandmother, and grandfather were all dead, and she felt like an orphan, although she was a grown woman.

Troccoli's ever-increasing faith and the outlet of songwriting gradually allowed her to conquer her grief and look to the future. Although she's yet to make it back to the pop charts, the CCM hits have continued to come and Troccoli uses those songs as an outlet for her feelings and emotions. Upon the release of *Corner of Eden* in 1998, she said of the recording, "What shocked me most was that I was really truly able to say 'I've failed God... I've turned my back on God... things that we don't ever really want to say. I want to be abandoned to God more than ever, but I also realize how life is still such a struggle, hanging on is such a struggle. We all want to act like we're in a place we're not." Troccoli continues to record, although her releases are not the huge sellers they once were.

RECOMMENDED RECORDING: *Greatest Hits* (Reunion Records, 2003), a 14-track collection, features Troccoli's pop breakthrough "Everything Changes" and her more Christian-oriented fare such as "Stubborn Love."

Truthettes

A FINE CONTEMPORARY female quartet, they made their name in the 1980s with hits such as "Peanut Butter and Jelly" and "Every Step of the Way." The group started with Velma Morgan. One of four children, she was born in the 1940s in Hollinville, Oklahoma. She grew up in the Friendship Baptist Church and played piano from the age of seven. Her parents were divorced early on and her mother, Dorothy, worked as a domestic to support her family. Morgan sang with a variety of groups including the Gospel Truths, a local gospel group that sang in the surrounding states. In 1974, Morgan took her two daughters Tiffanie and Tammy Jordan and formed a group with the three daughters of a friend who also sang in the Gospel Truths. Their name, the Truthettes, came from the other group as well. They produced their own 45-rpm single called "My Soul" and put "Message to the People" on the flip side. From that one single, they were booked on gospel programs throughout the Southwestern United States.

They were opening for Willie Neal Johnson & the Gospel Keynotes at a concert in Dallas when they got their big break. Johnson loved their music and took them on the road with him for the next three summers. Eventually, he got them a record deal with Malaco Records. They began recording for the label in the late 1970s, but their first major release was the 1984 LP *Take It to the Lord in Prayer*. Fueled by the dramatic story/ballad, "Peanut Butter and Jelly," they enjoyed one of the biggest gospel hits of the year. The album reached No. 11 and spent 81 weeks on the gospel album chart. The girls attended school on the weekdays and hit the road for concerts on the weekend. They weren't the average, sweet-sounding young girl group. They wailed like women with brassy, full alto voices. Many of their albums were produced by the Williams Brothers, who kept that infectious quartet vamp in the music while maintaining a fresh, contemporary sound.

They continued to make hit projects such as the Top Ten *Making a Way* in 1985 and *God Will Make Everything Alright* in 1986. Perhaps their best album is their last project to chart, *Every Step of the Way*, from 1987. The oozy title song is a luscious ballad featuring

Doug Williams of the Williams Brothers. Other stand-out tunes include the catchy "I Need You to Hold My Hand" and the slow drag "Thank You Lord." The project peaked at No. 25 on the gospel chart. Afterwards, Velma Morgan joined the group as other members made their exit. They recorded another two projects for the label. "They didn't renew the contract," Morgan says of Malaco. "[The group] recorded two more albums after that for a company in Los Angeles. But they are still together. They are married now, but they still sing."

Ike & Tina Turner

AT THE HEIGHT of their fame as a married couple and professional singing duo in the early 1970s, Ike & Tina Turner's stage show was the hottest ticket in any town they shook a tail feather in. Drawing on their mutual backgrounds in the Baptist church, their show was the sweatiest, funkiest show on earth. Although they sang raw R&B and blues, their emotion was heavily borrowed from their supercharged church backgrounds.

Ike Turner was born November 15, 1931, in Clarksdale, Mississippi, while Tina Turner was born Anna Mae Bullock on November 28, 1938, in Nutbush, Tennessee. The duo met in 1959 in East St. Louis where Ike's Kings of Rhythm were the hottest act in town. It was a complicated relationship from the start. Tina came from a broken home where she felt unloved by her mother, and Ike, a short man, had a Napoleon complex. After Tina came to see his band perform and he learned that she could sing, they became fast friends.

Initially, the relationship was purely platonic. "Ike walked into the room, and you could feel it…. He had the body then that David Bowie has now—great!" Tina wrote in her autobiography, *I, Tina*. "His suit looked like it was hanging on a hanger…. I thought, 'What an immaculate looking black man.' He wasn't my type, though—not at all. His teeth seemed wrong, and his hairstyle too, a process thing with waves that lay right down on his forehead. It looked like a wig that had been glued on. When he got closer, I thought, 'God, he's ugly.' But I kept listening and looking. I almost went into a trance just watching him."

Tina wanted to be a star and thought Ike could help her, and he looked on her as a little sister. At the time, Tina was pregnant by her boyfriend Raymond Hill and Ike's common-law wife, Lorraine, was pregnant too. The relationship with Tina was so innocent that sometimes Tina slept in the same bed with Ike and Lorraine. After Ike and his wife broke up for a spell, Ike and Tina became an item. Soon Tina was pregnant again, this time with Ike's son. Ike went back to his wife, who was soon pregnant with another child as well. Ike kept Tina around as a confidante and an occasional lover when his wife was acting up.

Ike and Tina had never thought of performing as a duo, however. Ike was recording a demo of "A Fool in Love" for a local singer named Art Lassiter in 1958. Lassiter and Ike had a heated argument and Lassiter stormed out of the studio before he cut the song. Since he already had the studio time, he asked Tina to sing the demo so that he could shop the song and get someone to record it. Tina didn't like the song, but she sang it to help Ike out. A DJ friend of Ike's sent the song out to a bunch of record labels. They all turned it down except Juggy Murray at Sue Records. Murray liked the song because of Tina's raw gospel vocals, so he suggested to Ike that the song be released as Ike & Annie (Tina's name at the time). Ike liked the sexiness of the name "Tina" instead and renamed Annie as Tina Turner even though they were not married. Tina didn't want to become a duo, but after Ike hit her for the first time (with a shoe stretcher), she fell in line. That record took the duo to No. 2 on the R&B charts in the summer of 1960 and created a chain of hits that would follow over the next dozen years. Through the 1960s they would record such R&B hits as "I Idolize You," "It's Gonna Work Out Fine," "Cussin' Cryin' and Carryin' On," "Shake a Tail Feather," and their signature song, "Proud Mary."

They eventually married legally and had one of the funkiest, high-voltage stage shows in music history, highlighted by Tina's slinky outfits (showing off her famous legs), long wigs, and ferocious dance steps with her Ikettes backup trio in tow. Ike's physical abuse of Tina and womanizing eventually led her to divorce him in 1976. In the divorce settlement, Tina

In the beginning there was an idea. Ike & Tina Turner wanted to re-examine their gospel roots in the light of their explosive pop/soul sound.

In the middle there was a recording session. And the results were so uplifting and exciting, Ike & Tina went ahead and recorded all their favorite gospel songs.

In the end there is,

"The Gospel According to Ike & Tina"
A new album from Ike & Tina Turner
on United Artists Records & Tapes
Been to church lately?

Ike & Tina Turner / United Artists and Billboard magazine advertisement

surrendered all of her interest in their property and song royalties to Ike in return for the right to keep the name he gave her: Tina Turner. She used that name to keep working the concert circuit in order to support her mother, her extended family, and the four sons she and Ike raised together. In 1985, Tina transcended the fame of the Ike & Tina Turner Revue when her pop smash "What's Love Got to Do with It?" brought her international fame beyond anything she and Ike ever accomplished together. Her LP Private Dancer went on to sell ten million copies worldwide. Tina continues to record, although she's officially retired from performing. After beating his drug addictions, Ike came back in the 1990s with a new band and was recording blues music again.

One of the last albums the duo recorded before their divorce was The Gospel According to Ike & Tina Turner for United Artists Records in 1974. In the introduction to their biggest hit "Proud Mary," Tina always said, "We never ever do nothing nice and easy… We always do it nice and rough." They approached their gospel the same way. There was not a quiet moment on the LP. Drawing on the style she heard in Sanctified Churches in her youth, Tina brought the same fiery passion to this album of traditional church songs. The instrumentation Ike laid under the project was a swirl of electric guitars and synthesizers that give these gutbucket gospels a rock edge.

One issue this project clearly settles is that Ike needed Tina just as much as she needed him. His vocal solos on "Father Alone," "Take My Hand, Precious Lord," and "Just a Closer Walk with Thee" are an acquired taste. His baritone is enthusiastic though not always attractive. He shines best when he and Tina jointly sing "Amazing Grace" and "When the Saints Go Marching In." However, the authentic star of these sessions is Tina. She turns in tambourine-shaking performances on the rocking, bass-charged renditions of "Glory Glory," "Nearer the Cross," and "What a Friend We Have in Jesus." The ultimate highlights of the album are Tina's bluesy solos on "Walk with Me Jesus" and "The Lord Will Make a Way Somehow." Tina's ad libs and passion makes these evergreens sound showroom new. In 2002, EMI-Capitol Special Markets (Fuel Records) reissued the LP on CD for the first time, allowing Ike & Tina fans to listen to the gospel foundation of the hardest-working duo in show business history.

Tina had grown up singing in the Spring Hill Baptist Church Choir back in Nutbush and was no stranger to the art form. "I wasn't much of one for church…" she recalled in her autobiography. "First you'd have to go to Sunday school, and that was all right, with all the kids there; it was kind of fun. But then, afterwards, you'd have to sit through the service, and it was hot and you'd be sweating—no air conditioning then, you know? And there'd be all these old people singing, wearing all these clothes, and the hats, and you didn't know what the preacher was talking about, and you just had to sit there.… The choir was the only thing I enjoyed. I was the only little girl in it; the rest were teenagers. But I could sing. I wasn't aware that I was singing about God, and how good he was; I just liked the songs. And I would always take the lead on the upbeat ones—you know, the real shouters." After she left Ike, Tina has said that she found comfort in Buddhist chanting. "I had always held on to the Bible and the things I learned as a little girl—the Lord's Prayer, the Ten Commandments," she wrote in *I, Tina*. "And I prayed every night, you can believe that. But now I was really seeking a change, and I knew that it had to come from the inside out—that I had to understand myself, and accept myself, before anything else could be accomplished…. I was looking for the truth of a future that I could feel inside of me." After she'd recite the Lord's Prayer, she'd do a chant. She once told *Jet* magazine that she considers herself a Baptist Buddhist.

Evelyn Turrentine-Agee

IN 2001, a simple traditional-styled gospel boogie called "God Did It" literally took the gospel world by storm and put a veteran, but little-known singer named Evelyn Turrentine-Agee on the musical map in a big way. That song won BMI's Most Played Gospel Song of the Year award, beating out proven stars such as Kirk Franklin, Fred Hammond, and Yolanda Adams for the coveted accolade. After years of struggling to make a name for herself and create good gospel music, Turrentine-Agee had arrived and has since built a solid reputation and following on the back of her song.

The third of 18 children, Turrentine-Agee was born Ruth Evelyn Tyler on February 4, 1946, in St. Louis, Missouri. Her father was a church deacon and the founder of a gospel quartet. When Turrentine-Agee was three years old, her father would hold her in his arms onstage and have her sing. "As I grew, my daddy took me with him when he traveled from church to church and sometimes he would allow me to sing," she recalls. "When my daddy would sing I would cry along with others who were crying and shouting. I didn't understand the feeling I got nor the reason I was crying. Daddy taught me about God and I was saved at the age of nine. Then I discovered what the shouting and crying was about. I could feel the power of God as my father

sang under the anointing of God. He lived the life he sang about. I've always strived to sing under that same anointed power. I grew up listening to all the gospel greats, quartets and otherwise, and taking note of them."

When Turrentine-Agee was 13, her father founded a teen gospel girl group, the Tylerettes, with Turrentine-Agee as the lead singer. They were together for three years before her father dropped four girls from the group and added Turrentine-Agee's three male cousins and they became the Tyler Singers. With Turrentine-Agee still in place as the lead vocalist, they developed a style similar to Gladys Knight & the Pips, though they were still a gospel group and went on to win several awards and acclaim around the St. Louis area.

After graduating from high school at the age of 17, Turrentine-Agee made her first record. The Tyler Singers recorded a 45-rpm called "Precious Lord" that was backed with "He Won't Forsake His Own" on Shippings Records. "Mr. Shippings did everything he could to promote us and take us to national status," she recalls. "However, just as we were beginning to receive calls from across the country for concert appearances, I got married and moved to Detroit. This terminated the Tyler Singers."

After marrying Curtis Turrentine, Turrentine-Agee earned a Bachelors degree in industrial psychology from the University of Detroit. In the Motor City, Turrentine-Agee began singing solos on a Sunday night church radio broadcast. Soon groups began to recruit her. She auditioned and considered joining groups such as the Detroit Harmonettes, the Gideon Singers, the World Travelers, the Wright Specials, the Harlan Gospel Singers, and the Meditation Singers. Ultimately, she briefly became a member of the Masonettes before spending years with the Gospel Echoettes. They recorded for the Billesse label before their manager was tragically killed circa 1972. Around that time, Turrentine-Agee, former Echoettes member Helena Berry, and Darlie Carter formed a new group called the Gospel Warriors. They performed regularly but did not record their first LP until 1981 when they released *War on Sin* for Gospel Express Records in Memphis. That project featured the original version of "God Did It."

The group performed sporadically over the years with no major breakthroughs. In 1990, Turrentine-Agee signed on to the small Chicago-based CGI Records as a solo artist and released the CD *In God's Own Time*, which featured a nice jazzy version of Pete Seeger's folk song "If I Had a Hammer." The project didn't receive much airplay and it didn't pick up any big sales, but it won Turrentine-Agee Stellar, Motor City Music, and Soul Train award nominations as Best Female Gospel Artist. In the meantime, she made guest appearances singing "Hurry Up" on a *Salt of the Earth* CD and "Not for Himself" on the National Baptist Convention's *Let's Go to Church* project. CGI wasn't doing a good job of promoting any of its artists, so they eventually sold out to Platinum Records, a company affiliated with Polygram Records. The company just sat on Turrentine-Agee's second project and would not even allow her to buy the unreleased album back. She was disgusted and disillusioned, so she left the label altogether and questioned whether she was meant to stay in the gospel field.

Eventually, "I decided to get up and do something for myself," she says. She knew many gospel radio announcers who would play her music based on their friendship, so she decided to make a demo and see what happened with it. She founded WOS Records in 1999 and re-recorded her old Warriors song "God Did It." Released in February 2000 with her family pitching in to mail promo packages and call radio stations, "God Did It" slowly but steadily took off in the quartet community. A year later, the song had crossed over to the regular black gospel radio formats and received over 20,000 spins in the first quarter of 2001. By that time, the CD of the same name had spent 40 weeks on the *Billboard* gospel chart and Turrentine-Agee had received airplay on syndicated FM urban radio programs such as *The Tom Joyner Morning Show*, Walt "Baby" Love's *Gospel Traxx*, and *The Russ Parr Show*.

Over the years, Turrentine-Agee has founded the Detroit Gospel Unity awards to honor pioneers in the quartet gospel industry and she hosted the *War on Sin Gospel Radio Hour* for five years. In August 2002, Turrentine-Agee released the well-received *God Did It!* CD via World Wide Gospel Records. Also in 2002, Turrentine-Agee signed a recording agreement with AIR Records and released the modest-selling CD *It's Already Done* in 2003.

12th Tribe

THEY GREW UP on heavy metal and black rap music. They enjoyed the Fat Boys, Whodini, and Kool Moe Dee. When Dave "Rap Galore" Portillo (born 1970) and Eddie Sierra (born circa 1968) began rapping in 1985 as Deity, they sought to make a gospel impact on their mostly Mexican neighborhood, which was plagued by drugs, prostitution, and crime. They eventually changed their name to 12th Tribe after the tribe of Benjamin in the Bible. "They were mighty warriors and skilled archers," Sierra said in 1992. "The Bible says that they were to go out and pierce hearts [with the word of the Lord]. That's where we stand."

Their first rap CD, *Knowledge Is the Tree of Life*, was released on Frontline Records in 1991. "The first album was very evangelical such as exalting Jesus Christ in every single song," Portillo said in 1992. "But in the second album we're talking about issues in the news: AIDS, condoms, sex. Everything you can think of we're bringing out. It's more of a topic album with a concept behind it." However, since there was little church acceptance for hard-hitting rap such as that on their 1992 CD, *Livin' in Babylon*, they received virtually no Christian radio airplay and their sales were even worse. At the time, Portillo, son of a Foursquare Church pastor, recognized this and said, "There should be more openess and more backing from the church. The church we go to backs us up and that keeps us going…. People put us in the hardcore category, but the Lord gave us this ministry. As a Christian artist, I don't believe in censorship... but I think as a parent you have to be on top of it."

They got flak from the church on one side and the cold shoulder from the rap world on the other. "If Ice T or Ice Cube was a Christian and you got them on the album cover looking really hard," Sierra said, "you have some kid in the Midwest wanting it, but the mother isn't going to buy it for him because it's too street. The street rap where we come from is a little harder to sell. The pop rap has it easier [such as DC Talk]. A lot of times in the rap community, Christian rap is always being slammed because your big rappers like Eric B. & Rakim or Poor Righteous Teachers were all Muslims. The Nation of Islam is always exalted in what they do, and… the rap industry supports it totally. But anything to do with Christ, the door is shut immediately because they don't want to hear it. They say it's weak, but it's the realest thing that's out there. It's the real thing. We've tried to get in stores with our albums and it's like, 'They look good, they sound good, their beats are good, but change the message and we'll talk to you.' It's sad, it's really sad." It was sad. After the duo's 1996 CD *Funk Residue* also failed to find an audience, 12th Tribe vanished from the national scene.

Moses Tyson, Jr.

ORGANIST MOSES TYSON is cousin to rock legend Sly Stone and the son of a pastor, Rev. Moses Tyson, Sr., in Vallejo, California. Tyson Jr. was born in 1961 and grew up around music. His mother, a pianist herself, helped Tyson with his first guitar at a young age, but Tyson wanted to play the organ instead because he thought he could attract more girls with it. "I started playing the guitar when I was about eight years old. But I noticed the girls went for the guys who played organ and that motivated me to learn how to play the organ!" He learned to play by ear and received coaching from Sly Stone, playing on one of his records when he was 12 years old. By the 1980s, Tyson had recorded an R&B album that Capitol Records shelved. In between projects, Tyson played behind Billy Preston and Rev. Timothy Wright. By the 1990s, Tyson had become an executive with Al Bell's Bellmark Records. There he produced Rance Allen and Edwin Hawkins. Bell mentored him and Tyson learned what he needed to know to launch his own World Class Records. Tyson sold 30,000 units of his *Music* instrumental CD of gospel hymns before he hooked up with Pioneer Entertainment in 1999. Pioneer had distribution through Atlantic Records, but the company went under a year later and Tyson's catalog of CDs was caught up in the ensuing legal/financial catastrophe. However, after regrouping and going back to his own independent network of distributors, Tyson rebounded with *Music 2*, which has sold over 100,000 units according to SoundScan and includes organ arrangements of the Staple

Singers' classic "I'll Take You There" and Sly Stone's "Thank You (Falettinme Be Mice Elf Agin)."

Ultra Naté

ULTRA NATÉ WYCHE was born in 1968 in Havre de Grace, Maryland. She was a pre-med student when she first became intoxicated by dance music. After she began to frequent house clubs, she met the Basement Boys, a couple of DJs who began to collaborate with her on her music. A track they created, "It's Over Now," won them a contract with Warner Bros.' London office. The song became an international smash but made little noise in America. She made her biggest American impact with the gospel jam "Rejoicing (I'll Never Forget)," which peaked at No. 7 on the *Billboard* hot dance music/club play chart in spring 1992. The following year, she reached No. 2 on the same chart with "Joy." Subsequent Warner albums failed, and she moved on to Strictly Rhythm Records where her 1997 single "Free" topped the pop charts in France and Switzerland in 1998.

Donald Vails

ONE OF THE TRADITIONAL black church's brightest music directors of the '80s, Rev. Donald Vails and his Choraleers made a name for themselves with their 1979 rendition of Margaret Douroux's composition "He Decided to Die." It's been said that the Grammy-nominated album the song hailed from sold 500,000 copies and made the Choraleers one of the most in-demand gospel groups of the early 1980s.

Born December 25, 1948, in Atlanta, Vails was virtually born into church. His family sent him to the Atlanta Gospel Choral Union Day Nursery where he learned to appreciate gospel music early on. His family attended Mt. Zion Baptist Church where Vails really began to show an affinity for music. By the age of 12, he was directing his first choir. As a teenager, Vails left Atlanta to study engineering at the Detroit Institute of Technology. When he didn't have his head in his technology books, Vails was playing piano for gospel groups or singing with choirs. In 1969, he founded the Donald Vails Choraleers and they continued to perform as Vails spread his arms into a variety of musical endeavors. By this point, he'd become an active leader in James Cleveland's Gospel Music Workshop of America (GMWA) and in 1977 assembled the Youth Kaleidoscope, a program that provided intellectual, spiritual, and physical development to more than 3,000 Detroit youth. From this group the Voices of Deliverance choir was birthed. Their debut LP *What a Wonderful Savior I've Found* was on *Billboard*'s Top 40 gospel chart for 104 consecutive weeks. In 1979, the Choraleers' LP *He Decided to Die* earned a Grammy nomination and reportedly sold a half million copies. In 1984, Vails cut a solo project entitled *He Promised a New Life* on Savoy Records, which reached the gospel Top 40.

In 1985, Vails moved to Washington, DC, to earn a graduate degree in music from Howard University. Along with his studies, Vails quickly immersed himself in the church music community. In February of that year, he formed the 80-member interdenominational community choir known as the Salvation Corporation. He also joined the Ebenezer AME Church of Fort Washington, Maryland, where he organized and encouraged their young adult choir's membership to swell from 40 to 175 people in a matter of months.

The year 1987 was one of the most rewarding for Vails. His LP *Until the Rapture* was his highest gospel charter when it rose to No. 11. Furthermore, on June 4th Vails and the Choraleers performed on the PBS special *Night of Music '87*. Taped before a crowd of thousands gathered outside the Lincoln Memorial where Martin Luther King, Jr., gave his "I have a dream" speech, this was a special presentation showcasing classical, country, jazz, and gospel music under the direction of famed conductor Zubin Mehta. The program was broadcast on June 20, 1987 to a global television audience. In spite of his national reputation, Vails was still content to be music director at Ebenezer and create new music as the spirit moved him. Only ill health caused him to step down as music director. He died in 1997 after a long illness, leaving behind a wife and two children.

Tata Vega

ONE OF THE MUSIC industry's most visible behind-the-scenes artists, Tata Vega enjoyed a moderately successful career as an R&B singer with Motown records in the 1970s and most of her albums included one gospel song. However, over the last two decades, she's been a regular featured singer with Andrae Crouch and other gospel singers, along with occasional solo projects of her own.

Born October 7, 1951, in the Panama Canal Zone, Vega went to Los Angeles when she was 16 to join a traveling company of the musical *Hair*. While in the production, Vega met singer Dobie Gray (best known for the song "Drift Away") who got her to join a counterculture band called Pollution from 1971–72. After two LPs with Pollution, Vega joined another band, Earthquire. They recorded for Natural Resources, a Motown records subsidiary. As lead singer, songwriter, and percussionist with the band, Vega was soon signed to Motown's Tamla label as a soloist.

During her tenure at Tamla, Vega recorded four LPs: *Full Speed Ahead*, *Totally Tata*, *Try My Love*, and *Givin' All My Love*. These four albums covered the musical spectrum and they all included one gospel song as a testament to Vega's faith. Vega never moved many units at Motown and she barely dented the R&B charts, but she did respectfully well in the dance market where *Full Speed Ahead* reached No. 18 in 1976. Surprisingly, a 1977 vinyl club single with Vega's gospel tracks "Come in Heaven, Earth Is Calling" "Jesus Will Take You Higher," and "It's Too Late" reached No. 21 on the *Billboard* club chart. Her last club chart entries were a double single of "I Just Keep Thinking About You Baby" and "Get It Up for Love," which hit No. 17 in 1979.

Following the Motown years, Vega began touring internationally with gospel legend Andrae Crouch. At the same time, she stayed active as a session singer, backing artists such as Russ Taff, Randy Stonehill, Leslie Phillips, Stevie Wonder, Madonna, Michael Jackson, Chaka Kahn, Patti LaBelle, and others. Quincy Jones and Crouch tagged her to be the singing voice of Margaret Avery's character Shug in the motion picture *The Color Purple*. She's also performed on the soundtracks for *The Lion King* and *Forrest Gump*, among others.

The queen of cameo appearances, Vega has recorded on literally dozens of albums by other artists. Quincy Jones's Qwest Records released her first gospel CD, *Now I See*, in 1998. The album received a Stellar award nomination but was lost amid Qwest's restructuring and eventual closing. While she's not always center stage on the marquee, Vega's vocals are always front and center even when she's backing artists such as Israel Haughton and Kirk Whalum. In reflecting on her purpose, Vega has said, "I just want to encourage the average Joe because that's who I am. I want to tell people to have faith in God and to have dreams. God has a plan for our lives and that's what's carried me through life. I know that he gave me something to share... and I'll never stop dreaming."

Jaci Velasquez

ONE OF THE BIGGEST stars to rise on the CCM scene in the last decade, Jaci Velasquez has a pleasant, honey-toned delivery that elevates what might otherwise be average songs into Christian anthems. Her signature songs such as "On My Knees" and "God So Loved the World" have made her a superstar in the Christian field. The youngest of five children, Jacquelyn Davette Velasquez was born on October 15, 1979, in Houston. She began singing at the age of ten and won an entertainment pageant in 1990. In 1992, she sang at the White House and began recording independent projects with her parents' worship ministry. In 1995, Velasquez signed with Myrrh Records. Her debut CD *Heavenly Place* was a surprise smash hit. The first single, "If this World," reached No. 4 on the CCM chart. Over the next year, the album would yield five other Top 20 CCM hits such as "Baptize Me," "On My Knees," "Un Lugar Celestial (A Heavenly Place)," "Flower in the Rain," and "We Can Make a Difference." Therefore, it's no surprise that the album has since achieved platinum status and made Velasquez Christian music's first Latin star.

Velasquez's summer 1998 release, *Jaci Velasquez*, swiftly went gold and produced two radio hits, "Look What Love Has Done" and "God So Loved the World."

In summer 1999, Myrrh pushed out *Llegar a Ti*, a platinum CD of her hits re-recorded in Spanish. The hits have kept coming with the gold-selling *Crystal Clear*, another Spanish CD, and a Christmas album. At the height of her career, Velasquez suffered a personal low: her parents' divorce. "The way I started singing was with both of my parents—the three of us started out singing as a group," she says. "When Mom and Dad broke up, it was so, so hard. You have no idea. I felt like my world had been ripped apart. So, now, with this Spanish record [*Mi Corazón*], every song that's on this record is about how I've dealt with my parents' divorce and what happened. I think there were a lot of times where I became really bitter, towards everything and everybody. I think God truly had to do a work in me. My healing process was making *Crystal Clear* and *Mi Corazón*. Sometimes when you make a record, the record label or your management will say stuff like, 'You need to make sure this is a very Christian record.' And I just wasn't concerned with that kind of thing. I said, 'I'm going to make a record that is about me, and I am a Christian.'" While Velasquez remains a significant draw on the Christian concert circuit, her recent CD sales have slid considerably as she has begun to focus more steadily on developing a career as a Hollywood actress.

Jacqui Verdell

A GREAT CONTRALTO, Jacqui Verdell vacillated between a career in gospel and the hope for greater stardom in the secular arena. Born in 1937 in Camden, New Jersey, she began her career singing with the Thelma Davis Specials, eventually becoming second lead. Later, she toured and performed with the Davis Sisters and the Clara Ward Singers. Her hit solos with the Davis Sisters included "We Need Power" and "Lord, Don't Leave Me." However, in the early 1960s she left gospel music to try and make it as a pop singer as the Soul Stirrers' Sam Cooke had done. She launched that phase of her career with a 45-rpm ballad, "I'm Your Girl," that went nowhere. During her tenure there, Decca also released the singles "Are You Ready for This?" "Does She Ever Remind You of Me?" and "Don't Set Me Free." None of them hit for her. She then moved to Peacock Records where she cut "Hush" and "Why Not Give Me a Chance?" Still nothing.

Her singles "He's Mine" and "We're Gonna Have a Good Time" were recorded at GRT Studios in Chicago with guitarist Phil Upchurch. They were initially released on the Gospel Truth label in August 1973, but later reissued on Stax proper in February 1974. Through most of the 1970s, Verdell backed up other performers, joining Judy Clay and Cissy Houston to do background vocals on Van Morrison's LPs *His Band and the Street Choir* and *Moondance*. She also backed up Dee Dee Warwick and Wilson Pickett. She was featured in the *Save the Children* concert film that starred Marvin Gaye and was nominated for a Grammy in 1979 for her contribution to the Jesse Jackson LP *Push for Excellence* that featured her stirring rendition of "Kumbaya" (Andrae Crouch won for *I'll Be Thinking of You*). In 1984, she teamed up with Joe Simon, who produced a Spring Records gospel album on her simply called *Jacqui Verdell,* featuring traditional favorites such as "Lay My Burden Down" and "Can I Get a Witness?" Verdell died of cancer circa 1996.

Shirley Verrett

ONE OF THE BRIGHTEST mezzo-sopranos of the 1960s operatic world, Shirley Verrett was born May 31, 1931, in New Orleans. Her family later moved to Oxnard,

California, where she sang in the choir of the local Seventh Day Adventist Church. She always wanted to sing, but her father insisted she go to college and have an education to fall back on. After graduating from Ventura College, she opened a successful real estate firm, but her heart wasn't in it. She began to take vocal lessons from Anna Fitziu, a former Metropolitan Opera soprano, who secured an appearance for Verrett on Arthur Godfrey's *Talent Scouts* television show. After her performance, a Juilliard School of Music instructor saw the show and recruited her for the school. Composer Richard Rodgers financed Verrett's education there. She made her professional debut in 1958 in Kurt Weill's *Lost in the Stars* with the New York City Opera. Over the next few years, Verrett portrayed such classic operatic heroines as Carmen and Aida. She appeared on *The Ed Sullivan Show* and recorded the excellent LP *How Great Thou Art, Precious Lord* for Kapp in 1964. The 12-song album featured soaring renditions of "The Old Rugged Cross" and "Face to Face." In 2003, Verrett published her candid autobiography, *I Never Walked Alone.*

Vinesong

AN INTERNATIONALLY KNOWN vocal group comprised of itinerant singers from all over the world, the group was formed by a white South African, John Watson, in 1982. His parents were missionaries in Zimbabwe and South

Vinesong / courtesy of John Watson

Africa. For a time, he pastored the church his parents founded in Durban before forming a church in England. Later, Watson moved to Hollywood where he began to collaborate with other songwriters and develop praise and worship songs. Unlike most modern-day recording artists, Vinesong charges no fees to appear at the hundreds of churches they've ministered at around the globe. Their musical style can easily be defined as Christian Muzak, very plain and unvarnished. As Tony Cummings of the British *Cross Rhythms* magazine has written, "Vinesong's music is hugely middle of the road, an anonymous blend of voices whose mix of unison and harmonies with the kind of stilted jolliness once heard on black and white minstrel TV shows of old... And yet, Vinesong, both in performance and in John Watson's material, carry an anointing that many better, and hipper, musical aggregations can only dream about." The longest running group membership included Phil Woolley (from England), Evelina Tonceva (from Bulgaria), Isaac Neuteboom (from the Netherlands), Carol and Hilary Lashley-Bobb (from Guyana), Peter de Fin (born in South Africa), and Donato Seeley (from the United States). Their best-known songs are "Let Your Living Water Flow" and "Peace Like a River," which have been sung in congregations worldwide.

Voices of Binghampton

DISCOVERED BY Wylie Dickerson in 1987, the group performed on recordings of Rev. Lawrence Thompson and Rev. James Moore. In 1989, Kevin Davidson signed on as their choir director and primary songwriter. Like John P. Kee and Hezekiah Walker's respective choirs, this group mixed traditional gospel styles with just enough contemporary rhythms to attract a youthful audience. Their releases have appeared on New Haven records.

Voices of 6th Avenue

A TRIO CONSISTING OF Tyrone Payton, Paul Scott, and Shank Thompson, they recorded a dance-oriented version of Ricky Grundey's upbeat gospel jam "Call Him Up" as a 12-inch single in 1991 on Ace Beat Records.

It boasted a ten-minute extended testimonial mix, an inspirational radio mix, and a jump and shout dub mix. A *Billboard* review read, "Are we on the verge of a club trend that blends house with gospel? Could be. Either way, this powerful track incorporates spiritual choir harmonies with a kickin' beat. Raise your hands to the sky!" The European production team of Brothers in Rhythm remixed it a year later for Stress Records in London. Another *Billboard* appraisal read, "In its new incarnation, the gospel-houser is awash with lush strings and ever-so-delicate techno-colored synths. Of course, the focal point of the track continues to be the rush of rousing choir vocals. Sadly, the act's US deal with Atlantic fell through, and it is currently fielding offers." They recorded one more notable single, "You Gotta Believe," with the Swedish group Intense, featuring Cassondra.

Wades

THIS BRITISH SWING TRIO produced a number of edgy, street-derived gospel numbers during the 1990s. Hailing from a family of seven kids in South East London, the brothers—David, Derek, and Lloyd Wade—formed their group in 1985. Their radical approach to music, from the viewpoint of the Anglican church, which sees sacred music as solemn and orchestral, included fusing traditional American gospel styles with more contemporary flavors. They won the BMA award (a black version of the BRIT awards, which are the equivalent of the American Grammy award) for Best Gospel act in 1994 and won the DMI World Music Gospel award for Best R&B Gospel group in 1995. Their LP *A Touch of Heaven* was the bestselling Christian album in London that year. Among their familiar tunes is the antidrug song "Get Off That Poison," which was a popular track on pirate UK radio stations back in 1993 before it was officially released. Their best-known American project is *A Family Thing* from 2000.

Albertina Walker

EVER SINCE Mahalia Jackson passed to the other side, there has been a debate going as to who her successor is. Is it Shirley Caesar or is it Albertina Walker? Or is it one of the many newcomers who are often called the new Queen of Gospel by some hyperactive PR person who knows nothing about gospel music's history? Granted, Caesar has sold far more records as a solo artist than Walker and has worked like a Trojan to remain on top for almost 40 years. However, a queen is a queen because of her influence and for those she has groomed, as much for her success. On that end, the throne must belong to Walker who has probably supported and groomed more famous gospel singers than anyone else in history. She alone is responsible for giving the first breaks to Rev. James Cleveland, Cassietta George, Inez Andrews, Dorothy Norwood, and even to Shirley Caesar, among many others.

The youngest of nine children, Walker was born on August 29, 1929, in Chicago, where she grew up on the South Side and started singing as a child at Westpoint Baptist Church. Her home church was a magnet for the top gospel stars of the time such as Roberta Martin, Sadie

Albertina Walker (with Benson President Jerry Parks and unidentified man) / courtesy of Benson Records

Dunham, and Professor Thomas Frye. Possessing a deep, lush contralto voice, Walker sang with a number of groups, such as the Pete Williams Singers and the Willie Webb Singers, but it was the Robert Anderson Singers who served as Walker's true musical foundation toward a professional career. Anderson was a generous singer and group leader. Although he possessed a luminous voice himself, he often gave some of the best solos to the other singers in his group. Walker picked up on that philosophy and would become a very altruistic shepherd over the group she founded in 1951, the Caravans.

The original lineup included Ora Lee Hopkins Samson, Elyse Yancey, and Nellie Grace Daniels, all graduates of the Robert Anderson Singers. That early aggregation enjoyed tight, sweet harmonies that featured Walker's dry contralto on most of the recordings such as "All Night, All Day" and "Think of His Goodness to You" for the States label between 1952–1954. When Bessie Griffin, with her volcanic vocal runs, joined the group in 1953, their sound began to change. A natural showstopper, Griffin's dynamic vocal posture forced the other singers to step up their performances. "It was a lot of work and no money," Walker told the *Washington Post* in May 1998. "I wanted to stand up before audiences and deliver the message, win souls for Christ. I wanted to touch dying men and slipping women."

By 1957, they were recording for Savoy Records and all of the original members other than Walker had left the group. The new crop of singers were all powerful soloists in their own right: Inez Andrews, Delores Washington, Dorothy Norwood, and Little Shirley Caesar. James Cleveland was the group's pianist. Walker stood back and let the other singers take center stage. The Caravans quickly eclipsed the popularity of the Clara Ward Singers among black gospel audiences. The Wards had created a corny show aimed at tourists in Las Vegas where they played for more money than they'd ever make on the gospel circuit. This left the field wide open for the Caravans to step up, and they did. The highlight for many was to see Shirley Caesar and Inez Andrews out-sing each other. They had a dozen radio smashes as well. Andrews led "Mary, Don't You Weep," "I'm Not Tired Yet," and "A Friend." Caesar shone on "No Coward Soldier" and "Sweeping through the City." Walker put her stamp on "Show Me Some Sign" and "The Lord Will Make a Way."

There were other hit solos by Josephine Howard, Cassietta George, Eddie Williams, and James Herndon. The group moved to Vee-Jay Records in the 1960s where they enjoyed one more huge hit with Cassietta George's "Walk Around Heaven." But their success was beginning to wane as several other new and exciting groups had risen in the gospel field. By 1966, all of the Caravans stars had left for solo careers. Walker continued on with new members such as future disco star Loleatta Holloway, but the group had seen better days. Further recordings on the Hob and Jewel labels were good but not the ringing hits they had enjoyed before.

In 1975, Walker finally went solo and released the *God Is Love* LP on Polydor Records. There wasn't much fanfare for that project. Gospel's grande dame Sallie Martin remarked, "Well, she ain't done too hot. I shouldn't be saying it." But Walker's heat reignited when she reteamed with James Cleveland on the 1978 LP *Reunion*. They enjoyed a number of bestselling projects together, including the classic "Please Be Patient with Me" from 1979. Through the 1980s, Walker recorded a number of projects with choirs, but did pure solo work when she signed to Word Records. Her debut LP *Spirit* was a contemporary CD geared toward the white Christian market but still managed to reach No. 22 on the gospel album chart. None of her material for Word was particularly memorable. That all changed when she moved on to Benson Records (which morphed into Verity Records) where she went back to her traditional roots with hits such as "Working on a Building" and "I Can Go to God in Prayer." The strategy paid off when she won her first Grammy in 1994 with the CD *Songs of the Church: Live in Memphis*. She's appeared on a number of projects in recent years such as Jeff Majors's *Sacred 2000*, but hasn't recorded an album of her own since 1997's *I'm Still Here*. She has received many tributes and honors of late. Hampered by emphysema from years of smoking early in her career, Walker is often seen at public events with an oxygen tank. It's not a pretty picture, but once she hits the stage, she always rises to the occasion.

RECOMMENDED RECORDINGS: For the Caravans' material, the best set is *The Best of the Caravans* (Savoy Records, 1977), which features the big hits such as "Mary, Don't You Weep" and "No Coward Soldier."

There isn't a compilation to cover Walker's great solo material for Savoy, but *The Best of Albertina Walker* (Verity Records, 2001) covers the hits from her Benson/Verity years such as "I'm Still Here" and "I Can Go to God in Prayer."

Hezekiah Walker

SECOND ONLY IN sales to Kirk Franklin's various choir ensembles, Hezekiah Walker's Love Fellowship Crusade was the second-bestselling gospel choir of the 1990s. Born December 24, 1962, in a crime and drug infested Brooklyn housing project, Walker grew up without a father, and his loving mother died young. Although he had been singing solos in church since the age of eight, Walker didn't give his life to Christ until he was 13 years old. He began the Love Fellowship Crusade Choir in 1985 as a weekend outlet for his musical proclivities. This outlet led to a recording contract with Sweet Rain Records in Bala Cynwyd, Pennsylvania, in 1987. The choir, which started with 12 members and grew to 100, displayed a youthful exuberance with contemporary song arrangements that more than compensated for their lack of vocal technique and finesse. However, most gospel consumers don't buy music for technique, they respond to the emotional connection of the performers to the music and on that account, the Crusade Choir delivered bigtime on their debut LP *I'll Make It* in 1987.

The album was a surprise hit for the struggling gospel label. Beginning with a rousing cover of D.J. Rogers's "I'll Make It" with Walker on lead, the album's other radio hits included "Spirit" and "The Lord Will Make a Way Somehow," which both featured Kervy Brown on lead. The project also featured two tracks written by Stanley Brown, who would go on to be a hit urban producer for Island Records. One of those songs, "Hold On" was led by Aaron Hall, who would have a successful career as an R&B balladeer in the early 1990s. The LP peaked at No. 12 on the gospel chart and was an all-around success for the young choir. After their follow-up LP *Oh Lord We Praise You* reached No. 11 on the gospel chart in 1990, it was obvious that their success was not a fluke.

Benson Records sought the choir out and after the Crusade Choir signed with the label, their debut LP *Focus on Glory* went all the way to No. 5 on the gospel chart. As the group was thrust on the national gospel scene and Walker came in contact with numerous gospel legends, he was initially shocked by the hypocrisy. "I was disappointed to get into the music arena and find out that some of the gospel artists were not really living the life that they were singing about," he told *Gospel Industry Today*'s Teresa Hairston in 2000. "Gospel music was just a job for them. They didn't have the ministry at heart. That bothered me a lot. When I got around them, we all were anointed on stage, but after the concert was over, behind stage, it was a different thing."

It wasn't a different thing for the choir's next CD, *Live in Toronto*, though. Like all their others, this one was a bestseller. On the strength of Lorraine Stancil's uncredited lead on "When We Get Over There" the album soared to the Top Ten on the gospel chart. Arguably, the Crusade Choir's best album is 1995's *Live in New York by Any Means...*, which rose to No. 3 on the gospel chart. The CD features some of the choir's most requested songs, such as "I'll Fly Away," "Second Chance," featuring Walker's wife Monique in a particularly stirring performance, and a remake of Dorothy Love Coates's composition "Ninety-Nine and a Half Won't Do," which was not credited to her on the album and often caused her to criticize the choir for not acknowledging that she wrote the song.

Around this period, Walker founded and began to pastor the Love Fellowship Church in Brooklyn. Within a few short years, the church grew from 500 members to a couple of thousand. Walker's youthful ministry and the real, street nature of his personality attracted many hip-hop artists such as Foxy Brown to the church. "About five years ago, we started attracting a lot of secular artists to the ministry," he told *Gospel Industry Today* in 2000. "We've just been ministering to them. Most of them felt that there was no vehicle back to the church and everybody was shutting them down, but I was able to let them know that we're not going to compromise what we believe, but the church is for all the people. So I extend my hand to them, and I've gained a rapport with them—including Teddy Riley, Puff Daddy, Missy Elliott, Lil' Kim, Dave Hollister."

Along with the mantle of being a pastor to roughnecks from the neighborhood and hip-hoppers, Walker was the center of criticism from church conservatives when he had Sean "Puffy" Combs perform with him on "Let's Dance." "I believe the church ought to trust us enough to know that we're not going to just put anybody on our records," he told *Gospel Industry Today*. "We actually have conversations with them. We find out where they are and what they're doing.... A lot of [secular] artists out there have a heart for the Lord. They [went into secular music] because it was a money thing and nothing more than that. We try to give them an opportunity to come back into the church and to sing about their first love."

The Crusade Choir's most recent CDs, such as *Live in London at Wembley*, *Family Affair*, *Love Is Live*, and *Family Affair II*, have all been Top Ten gospel smashes. When asked his theory on his choir's success, Walker candidly said, "I incorporate the same excitement people find in secular music into gospel music and into what we're doing for the Lord. I believe in positive messages like 'Don't do drugs.' But you also got to tell people where to find the power to stop and how to stay clean, and that's Jesus. I'm not going to sing a song that says, 'Don't cry, baby, it's gonna be al-

Hezekiah Walker / Benson records promotional photo

right.' The truth is that only Jesus is going to dry your tears and make it alright."

Olivia Branch Walker

OLIVIA BRANCH WALKER was a woman who didn't record long enough or live long enough to become the legend she was sure to have become. She was born circa 1954 in Houston, Texas. The pianist/singer studied music at Texas Southern University in the early 1980s. She was also minister of music at the Philadelphia Missionary Baptist Church where her husband, Israel Samuel Walker, was the pastor. In 1986, she recorded the stunning traditional (yet very commercial) LP *New Life* on her own Spirit of Love label, distributed by Wendell Parker's Sure Fine Records in Decatur, Georgia. Prompted by the infectious title song (with its great hook and scintillating piano chords), the album reached No. 31 on the gospel album chart. She appeared on the *Bobby Jones Gospel* TV show and also saw "Poor Pilgrim" receive strong radio airplay. The album did well enough that AOR Records signed her and released her final LP *To Thee* in 1990.

Walker died of a heart attack in 1993. She was only 39 years old. Dr. Caesar A.W. Clark of the Good Street Baptist Church in Dallas gave the eulogy. The funeral was held at Walker's cousin F.M. Williams's church, which was packed to capacity. In 1998, Walker was inducted into the Oklahoma Gospel Music Hall of Fame. Her husband recently had a stroke and now lives in Texas City, Texas. "Her legacy to me is like Mahalia Jackson," singer Carolyn Traylor says. "She imparted [blessings] in everybody's life that she touched. You would think you were her best friend and favorite pupil. But when she died and you went to the funeral, you saw you weren't alone. She touched everyone that way."

Clara Ward Singers

DURING THE 1950s and 1960s, there was no more famous gospel group than the Clara Ward Singers. They conquered Hollywood with the same vengeance that they used to become the bestselling gospel group of the 1950s. In the black church world, they were renowned for their million-sellers, such as "Packing Up, Getting Ready to Go" and "Surely, God Is Able." In the mainstream market, they weren't known for those songs. They were known for Broadway-styled renditions of "Down by the Riverside" and "When the Saints Go Marching In." The group broke many barriers for gospel music. They were the first to perform in Las Vegas hotels, the first to perform in amusement parks such as Disneyland, and they brought a flamboyant elegance to a musical art form that was considered an unglamorous vestige of slavery.

Clara's parents, Gertrude Mae Murphy Ward and George Ward, were raised in abject poverty in South Carolina. They moved to Philadelphia in search of a better life in 1920. George worked for the Link Belt Company and Gertrude worked as a housekeeper. Their first daughter, Willa Ward, was born December 13, 1922, and their second girl, Clara Ward, was born on August 21, 1924. The family worshipped at the Ebenezer Baptist Church, and Gertrude had a vision in 1931 that God wanted her to form a group. So when they came of age, she formed a trio with her two daughters. In 1934, the group made its debut at an anniversary concert that Mother Ward assembled. She brought in gospel stars Thomas Dorsey and Sallie Martin (along with her pianist Dinah Washington), neither of whom had performed in the Northeast before, to make sure people remembered the concert. The concert was a grand success, and the group soon was booked as the Consecrated Gospel Singers. At the same time, Willa began to practice singing pop songs but her parents pressured her to stop. As the girls became young women, they both married against their mother's wishes. In fact, before kicking Willa out of her home, Mother Ward yelled (as recounted by Willa in her autobiography), "Clara wouldn't have done this if you hadn't encouraged it. Damn you! You're only good for having babies; now you want Clara to be the same. I'll break your neck if you don't get the hell out of here now."

In 1943, Gertrude muscled the group onto the National Baptist Convention program in Chicago. After a winning performance there, the delegates went back to their states raving about the Ward Singers, and their fame began to grow. By that time, Clara's marriage had dissolved and Mother Ward kept her from getting involved with another man. The success only pushed Mother Ward to push her girls harder. They worked and worked to the point that when they headlined a concert at Washington, DC's Uline Arena in 1949, over 14,000 fans came to see them. By 1950, the group had added other singers such as Henrietta Waddy, Frances Steadman, Kitty Parham, and Marion Williams. They were called either the Famous Ward Singers or the Clara Ward Singers from then on, and their live program was quite a spectacle. They dressed in the best coordinated stage attire, had their hair stacked into beehive wraps, and sang with divine abandonment. "Marion and I did a spot obbligato in high register and close harmony with Clara ad-libbing," Willa wrote in her book. "We could see listeners twitch in their seats—we knew their reserve was crumbling. By the time we eased into our heavy hitters, the congregation was crying, shouting, and [doing] holy dancing in the aisles."

The group recorded prolifically for Savoy Records for the entire 1950s and scored with staggering radio and retail hits such as "Surely God Is Able," "Packin' Up," and "How I Got Over." The group let everyone's talent shine. Clara and Willa sang most of the alto songs, Waddy and Williams sang the high soprano parts, and Steadman sang bass. Clara wrote and arranged most of the music, and Mother Ward handled all the business and collected the money. They were the top gospel group, and thousands of dollars were coming in the box office as they filled arenas and theaters with the gospel message. However, Mother Ward did not share the wealth. In 1958, Williams quit because she was barely earning enough to live on. Once she quit, Parham, Waddy, Steadman, and Esther Ford left as well. Unmoved by their stand, Mother Ward just hired other singers who were only too happy to join the country's most famous gospel troupe.

The 1960s brought even bigger success for the group as they left much of their early black gospel audience behind and cultivated a new, upper-middle-class white professional audience. They starred on Broadway in *Tambourines to Glory* and performed at the top Las Vegas hotels, which brought them grief from the Amen Corner. "The [Frontier] hotel was dead before we came," Clara told *Down Beat*. "Now we have people standing all around the walls. And when we do ["When the Saints Go Marching In"] and march around the room, a lot of the people get up and march with us." Hollywood's elite came out for the shows, everyone from Dinah Shore to Elvis Presley. Jack Benny took them on the road with him for six weeks. They appeared on all of the major television programs of the day and became so popular that they formed two sets of Clara Ward Singers—one group worked the West and one worked the East. "Miss Ward would pick the costumes," Madelyn Thompson, who was a Ward Singer at the time, said in 1994. "When we were in Mexico, we had Mexican clothes on. When we were in Hawaii, we had their style of dress, and when we were in Japan we wore kimonos. Some things Mother Ward created herself." With Hollywood clout behind them, including the William Morris Agency and Diahann Carroll's husband Monte Kay as their new manager, Clara became extremely well-known outside of the group. She recorded inspirational LPs for Verve and Dot Records with non-gospel fare such as "Born Free" and "What the World Needs Now Is Love."

Meanwhile, Willa and Mother Ward had fallen out over her decision to sing pop music. Willa's female trio, the Willettes, did background vocals for artists such as Chubby Checker, Frankie Avalon, and Patti LaBelle & the Bluebelles. The group, which was also known as the Gay Charmers, recorded pop singles for Savoy, Swan, Moultrie, and Jamie Records. Their 1959 single "Get in and Shut the Door" was becoming a big hit for Swan Records. "My husband wouldn't let us go around to advertise it," Willa sighs. "Jerry Ragavoy was so disgusted because he put out thousands to make it. He and our manager Fred Strauss wanted to make us like the Supremes. They weren't out yet, but we could out-sing them. But my husband wanted all of the control, so they left us alone. I would have been the first colored girl to play a lounge at the Tropicana in Las Vegas, but he wouldn't let me go. My daughter still talks about me to this day. She says, 'Mom, you should have left daddy.'" On the one hand, Willa suffered from her husband's interference in her career, and on the other, her mother was trying to prevent her from becoming a successful secular artist under the Ward name. "She'd tell the people lies about us and people were afraid of her," Willa says. "Bette Midler got her start at the [gay] bath-houses in New York. My mother got a hold of [Herbie Moon from the Queen Booking Agency] who wanted us there and said, 'You better not do that! You can't use the name of Ward,' but that was my name too." Then Sister Rosetta Tharpe invited Willa to tour Europe with her, and her husband wouldn't let her go there either.

"Gospel was not what I wanted to do," Willa says. "My mother made me do it. When I did get away from gospel, my husband didn't want me to do that for his own reasons. He was afraid I was going to leave him. Halle Berry and Vanessa Williams, all of them had these type of husbands, but they were smart, they got rid of them and went on and became famous. But I was in love and did what my husband told me. I thought that's what I was supposed to do." Even after he died, "All of those people who wanted me before didn't want nothing to do with me." Willa was down but not out. Although the big things fell through, Willa continued to work in concert halls, the Ward Singers were working steadily, and Clara Ward was moving closer to a secular career herself. "You're going to hell in a hand basket—just like your sister," Willa quoted Mother Ward's rebuke to Clara. "God is going to fix you."

A divine fixing wasn't necessary. Clara was in poor health. She longed to get married and was rumored to have dated men such as Rev. C.L. Franklin. However, she worked so much that she never had time for a husband and she once said that she'd only had one vacation during her entire adult life. Since she was the star of the show and the accompanying singers could be rotated, Clara's schedule was exhausting. In addition to her concerts and recording schedules, appearances on NBC's *Tonight Show* and *Today Show*, she had roles in the Universal film *Spree* and the MGM movie *A Time to Sing*. Her blood pressure was up and she had splitting headaches, but Mother Ward told her God would take care of her ailments and that she didn't need a doctor. Mother Ward was suspicious of everything as it related to Clara and even listened in on her phone calls.

It all caught up with Clara when she was headlining at the Wreck Bar in the Castaways resort in Miami Beach in 1967. She was watching her warm-up act, comedian Rodney Dangerfield, from the side of the stage. The laughter took her mind off of her throbbing headaches.

Clara Ward / New York Amsterdam newspaper advertisment / courtesy of Capital Entertainment archives

When she was onstage singing "Stand by Me," Clara collapsed. Willa rushed her to the hospital where doctors stabilized Clara. She had a severe aneurysm and had suffered a stroke. C.L. Franklin came down and spent time whispering in her ear and encouraging her to get well. Almost three weeks later, Clara was released from the hospital. "She wasn't supposed to ever sing hard again from the first stroke," says Willa. "They said that if she did, that artery that had burst when she had the first stroke, if that opened up again, she would die."

Mother Ward ignored the doctor's admonitions and pushed Clara to get back on the road. Willa fought her mother on the subject and took Clara to see a cardiologist on a regular basis to keep her strength up. Meanwhile, Mother Ward booked Clara at Caesar's Palace in Las Vegas, then Clara went on the road with Mitzi Gaynor. Mother Ward sincerely believed that God had completely healed Clara and that there was no reason to slow down, so she moved Clara to Los Angeles to get away from Willa's cautionary stance on her health. "My mother had Clara buy her a church, pay for all new furniture, a new organ, a baby grand piano, the pulpit stuff," Willa recalls. "Plus, a new gorgeous house in Baldwin Hills. So, Clara would still sing to help pay for all of that. I had no say in that because she moved her to California. Clara said she didn't want to go, she just wanted an apartment so that when they sang out that way, she'd have a place to stay instead of an expensive hotel. My mother decided she wanted to go out there too."

Things were good for a while. Clara's strength came back, but she was still working like a mule. In late 1972, Clara was negotiating with NBC for her own network television series called *The Sheep and the Lambs*. It was to be a musical program mixing secular and gospel artists with Clara as the host. "She had picked out this $350,000 house across the street from Nancy Sinatra," Willa says. "She was just getting ready to really go out and live and sing different kinds of songs. She was all set, but my mother didn't want that to happen. Why? Because she [would have] had no control." Then Clara had another stroke. "When she had the second stroke, they wanted to close up that artery like Della Reese did and Quincy Jones did [when they had aneurysms]. My mother wouldn't let them do it.... She was sending for prayer cloths from these whack TV preachers.... If [Clara had had the operation], she'd be living today." Clara slipped into a coma and finally passed away on January 16, 1973, at the UCLA Medical Center. There were 7,000 mourners at the Philadelphia funeral, then Clara's body was flown to Los Angeles for a funeral that was covered by the TV networks. She was placed in a crypt at Forest Lawn Cemetery where her neighbors are Nat King Cole and Marilyn Monroe.

Mother Ward made sure that Willa didn't receive the money Clara left her in her will. However, Mother Ward's last years were rough. Without Clara, demand for the Ward Singers fell sharply and she was no longer able to maintain the lavish lifestyle she had become accustomed to. She lost the church and the home Clara had purchased and lived between friends. She didn't want to live in Willa's home after a family friend attempted to sexually assault her there. "I'd send her money whenever she needed it," Willa says. Mother Ward formed a male group of Ward Singers that never

found fame, and she sang as a soloist for free will offerings at churches from time to time. As her health failed, Madelyn Thompson took care of Mother Ward before she died November 27, 1981. After her mother's death, Willa found that much of Clara's wealth had not been spent on material possessions at all. Mother Ward had contributed heavily to television ministries in return for prayer cloths and holy water. Willa found receipts amounting to almost $100,000. Clara's estate then fell into Willa's hands, but she says, "There isn't much. My mother had sold the publishing rights to the songs, so someone else is living off of that."

Willa continued to perform in lounges and nightclubs into the 1990s. She says that she's not rich, but she's happy. She appeared in the 1998 Oprah Winfrey movie *Beloved* and plays piano at a senior citizen's home once a month. Twice-widowed, Willa swims, dances, and keeps a healthy social life with a couple of casual boyfriends. She also tries to keep in touch with the surviving Ward Singers such as Frances Steadman, who—at age 88—married a past sweetheart in 2003 and moved to Baltimore.

RECOMMENDED RECORDING: Shamefully, Savoy Records has not kept the group's stellar music in print. However, if one wants to get a feel for the Ward Singers, *Meetin' Tonight* (Vanguard, 1994), features live recordings from 1961–62 and studio cuts such as "Jacob's Ladder" and "The Storm Is Passing Over," 25 tracks in all.

Dionne Warwick

IN THE 1960S, Dionne Warwick surfaced on the pop scene with a surreal, soft-textured soprano with hues of jazz and gospel to lend it further definition. Backed with the poetic lyrics of Hal David and the complicated rhythms of Burt Bacharach, it was a winning combination that produced 22 Top 40 pop hits. She made sporadic hits in the 1970s before making a larger comeback in the 1980s with more R&B-flavored urban radio hits such as "How Many Times Can We Say Goodbye" and "Whisper in the Dark." What she's become best known for over the last two decades, though, is her valiant battle against the spread of the AIDS epidemic via various charity fundraisers.

Born Marie Dionne Warrick on December 12, 1941, in East Orange, New Jersey, her father, Mancel, was a gospel promoter for Chess Records and her mother, Lee, sang and managed the Drinkard Singers. Warrick first sang at the age of six at the New Hope Baptist Church in Newark and joined the choir thereafter. As a teenager, she formed a singing group called the Gospelaires with her baby sister, Dee Dee, and her young aunt, Cissy Houston.

After graduating from high school in 1959, Warrick attended the Hartt College of Music in Hartford, Connecticut, on scholarship. Meanwhile, the Gospelaires were becoming popular session singers by lending their harmonies to pop songs such as Ben E. King's "Stand by Me" and "Spanish Harlem." Her big break came during a Drifters' session for their song "Mexican Divorce." The song's writer, Burt Bacharach, liked Warrick's voice and asked her to sing some demos of his songs he'd written with Hal David. David pitched one of the songs to Florence Greenberg, who owned Scepter Records—home to R&B stars of the period such as Chuck Jackson and the Shirelles. Greenberg loved Warrick's voice. He signed her to a recording deal and had the David/Bacharach team compose the album. It was a hit out of the box with the single "Don't Make Me Over" becoming a Top 20 pop hit in early 1963. There was just one problem, though. The graphics artist misspelled Warrick's name as Warwick on the *Anyone Who Had a Heart* LP cover. Because the album was a hit, Warwick considered it a good omen, so she kept Warwick as her stage name.

Over the next decade, the trio would record a string of intricate, light pop songs that convincingly displayed Warwick's aching vocals to great dramatic effect on hits such as "Walk on By," "Alfie," and "I'll Never Fall in Love Again." However, amid her fame, Warwick didn't forget her gospel roots. In 1968, she recorded her only gospel LP to date, *Magic of Believing*, which featured the Drinkard Singers backing her. The pop world didn't go for Warwick as a gospel chanteuse, but the black audience took the LP to No. 49 on the R&B album chart. The collection featured

stirring versions of "Somebody Bigger Than You and I," "Blessed Be the Lord," "Jesus Will," and "Steal Away." The following year, Warwick included a very nice cut of the Impressions' pop-gospel track "People Get Ready" on her LP *Soulful*, which peaked at No. 2 on the R&B and No. 11 on the pop album charts.

In the years since, Warwick has enjoyed at least two bona fide career comebacks and earned her Ph.D. in music from Hartt College. In 1998, she recorded *Dionne Sings Dionne* for River North Records. The CD was rumored to have cost over a half million dollars to produce and featured duets with Tyrese and Celia Cruz & the Pete Escovedo Orchestra. Among the featured tracks were Warwick's first gospel recordings in years on Tim Miner's "Humbly I Pray" and "All Kinds of People." Some in the black community were not ready to support any type of new music by Warwick, gospel or secular. Many felt she had betrayed her Christian roots and dignified image when she became a spokesperson for the Psychic Friends Network television infomercials during the 1990s. Warwick acknowledged that she was fascinated with the paranormal, but that the show was not meant to take the place of God. "I am no different from anybody else," she told *Jet* magazine's Clarence Waldron. "And the Psychic Friends Network happens to be a job…. I'm not a psychic. It's something I'm having a good time doing and I don't see anything wrong with it…I feel that there are people who have developed eyes and have an ability that we have to question because we can't do it. My grandfather told me a long time ago that we tend to fear what we don't understand." She went on to stress that "God will always be first. God can't be any place but first. And any of those who doubt that, then they have a problem."

Ella Washington

THIS SOPHISTICATED Southern soul vocalist has never received her just due. A fine, slow-simmer dramatist, Ella Washington recorded a number of stellar R&B songs for a variety of labels such as Octavia Records, which could never adequately promote them. Her most lucrative year as an R&B singer had to have been 1969 when she joined legendary DJ John Richbourg's

Sound Stage 7 Records label. That year Washington released her high-voltage rendition of Harlan Howard's country ballad "He Called Me Baby," which rose to No. 38 and No. 77 on the R&B and pop charts respectively that year. The flip side of the single was James Cleveland's composition, "Stop Giving Your Man Away." The self-titled LP that included these songs was an immediate cut-out bin item, but the moderate success of the single was strong enough to earn Washington a Grammy nomination for Best Rhythm & Blues Vocal Performance. She was competing with Etta James for "Security," Erma Franklin for "Piece of My Heart," and Barbara Acklin for "Love Makes a Woman," but Aretha Franklin won the category for "Chain of Fools."

Washington followed up with the fine 1970 LP *Nobody but Me* but soon wandered off into oblivion, only to resurface in 1983 with the wonderful contemporary soul-styled gospel LP *If You Can Take It, You Can Make It* on the small independent label Solomon Records. In spite of fine ballads such as the title song, "Reach Out and Touch the Man," and "He'll Be Just What You Let Him Be," the album did not resonate with gospel radio programmers who were still not ready for contemporary music, even if they were ballads. In 2001, Orpheus Records released a compilation of Washington's R&B hits called *Starving for Love.*

Madame Ernestine B. Washington

KNOWN ALTERNATELY AS either Madame or Sister Washington, Washington was proclaimed the Songbird of the East by the COGIC music community back in the 1940s when she made her first records. Because Washington was rarely seen or heard outside of COGIC convocations, her obscure career and the tales of those who witnessed her performances have transformed her into a gospel legend of mythic proportions.

Ernestine Beatrice Washington was born in 1914 in Little Rock, Arkansas. Washington grew up with a mother who was a Sanctified Church singer, so she sang from an early age. After high school, she worked as a domestic before meeting her future husband, Rev. Frederick D. Washington, at a COGIC convention where she was singing hosannas to the Lord. They married and

moved to Montclair, New Jersey, where Frederick founded the Trinity Temple COGIC. By the 1940s, they had moved over the bridge to Brooklyn, where he founded the Brooklyn COGIC (later renamed Washington Temple in his honor). Washington sang with her husband's various church choirs from the start, combining the somewhat shrill, nasal, and loud singing style of her Sanctified musical heroine, Arizona Dranes, with the softer eloquence of her Baptist heroine, Roberta Martin. It's an acquired listening taste which nonetheless earned Washington a reputation as a church-wrecker for the pure theatrics of her racy vibrato.

Washington recorded with secular jazz trumpeter Bunk Johnson and his band in the 1940s. Perhaps because she was a respected pastor's wife, Washington received none of the flak that Sister Rosetta Tharpe did for recording with jazz bands. Maybe it was the fact that Washington didn't sing in nightclubs as Tharpe did that kept the critics at bay. Washington's first recording is believed to be "My Record Will Be There," recorded for Manor Records in 1943. The following year she recorded "If I Could Just Make it In" with the Dixie Hummingbirds, "Does Jesus Care?" with Johnson in 1946, and more tracks with the Southern Sons in 1947, but none of those songs were hits. She seemed content to be the First Lady of the church and the official soloist for the COGIC denomination for several years. Because she never had a radio hit, Washington was never in demand for packaged gospel shows, but she did perform on church bills with friends such as Mahalia Jackson, Roberta Martin, and the Selah Jubilee Singers. She remained visible and active with her husband's church until her death on July 5, 1983. Never in wide release, Washington's 1940s recordings were reissued by the Document Records label in the 1990s.

Ethel Waters

IN HER YOUTH, Ethel Waters was a salty blues singer. During the 1940s, she became America's first bona fide black female movie star in films such as *Cabin in the Sky* and *Pinky* and by the end of her life in 1977, she had become a great ambassador for Christianity through her frequent performances during Billy Graham's crusades.

Born October 31, 1896, in Chester, Pennsylvania, Waters grew up near Philadelphia with her eye on a career in the arts. Possessing very clear diction (much like Della Reese), she began that career as a blues singer and recorded for Swan Records, reputedly the first black-owned record label, in 1921. Later, her material became more jazz-oriented, even before that term had been coined. Exploiting her popularity as a singer, Waters became a movie star in the 1930s. She was the artist who introduced songs such as "Dinah," "Am I Blue" (in a 1929 movie), and "Stormy Weather" into the popular consciousness of America. It's been written that her vocal styling influenced jazz greats such as Mildred Bailey.

In the 1930s, Waters toured with her husband, trumpeter Eddie Mallory, and appeared on Broadway in *Mamba's Daughter*. In the 1943 film *Cabin in the Sky*, she introduced the song "Taking a Chance on Love." As she entered later middle age, Waters devoted herself to more devotional projects and signed a recording deal with Word Records. Her first album, *His Eye Is on the Sparrow*, was a polished 13-track collection of Waters's favorite religious songs (mostly Negro spirituals) such as "Just a Closer Walk with Thee" and Charles Tinley's "Stand by Me." Backed by the Paul Mickelson Orchestra and Choir, the album's pop styling made it popular among Word's predominantly white Christian audience. The title song would become Waters's signature song via her many performances of it at various Billy Graham crusades. In 1962, she recorded the LP *Reminisces* for Word Records. The album featured her folksy recordings of "I Am a Pilgrim" and "It Is Well with My Soul." Her great faith and fame made her an obvious guest psalmist for many Billy Graham crusades throughout the 1960s and early 1970s. She died on September 1, 1977. That year Word released the LP *Just a Little Talk with Jesus*.

Kanye West

ONE OF THE HOTTEST rappers to emerge in recent rap music history is Kanye West, who made big noise in 2004 with his hits "All Falls Down" and "Through the Wire." Born June 8, 1977, in Atlanta, Georgia, the Chicago-bred West began rapping in the third grade

and producing tracks when he was 14 years old. In 2002, he signed with Roc-A-Fella Records. In fall 2003, West was involved in a horrendous car accident. He told BET.com, "My whole outlook on life changed—at any given moment, my life could be taken. You just appreciate all the days you get. You take one day at a time and keep God in all your rhymes."

West did just that on his summer 2004 single "Jesus Walks" (from his CD *The College Dropout*), which peaked at No. 11 on the Hot 100 pop singles chart. The song, which openly embraces faith, was edited for Christian radio because the original version had profanity. In it, West raps: "They say you can rap about anything except for Jesus / That means guns, sex, lies, videotapes / But if I talk about God, my record won't get played, huh?" The clean version received airplay on gospel radio stations and on BET's gospel program *Video Gospel*. The song was so embraced that it made the first round of Stellar award nominations for best gospel rap album. People in the gospel community raised a furor because it was the only gospel song on the CD, which was filled with curse words and other song themes they found objectionable. "It just seems that it shouldn't have gotten through," Jadda Gunn of Light Records told the Associated Press. "For this to be the Stellar awards they should have known Kanye West, Roc-A-Fella records, that's not a gospel album." The Stellars have a history of seeking secular artists to participate in their program in order to boost TV ratings. However, they dropped West's nomination when the gospel community started complaining.

Tommye Young-West

BORN IN JANUARY 14, 1949, IN DALLAS, Tommye Young-West's father was Bishop T.L. Young in the COGIC denomination. She first sang at the age of five in her father's church where she and her sister, Lynda, sang as the Young Sisters. In August 1970, she was performing secular songs in a Dallas nightclub when producer Bobby Patterson spotted her raw, innate talent. He signed her to his Shreveport-based Soul Power Records label where she cut the scarce *Do You Still Feel the Same Way?* LP, which went on to become one of the most sought-after soul music albums ever by deep soul record collectors.

Soul Power was short on cash and had a poor distribution network, so it could not keep up with demand for the album when the title song cracked *Billboard*'s Top 30 R&B singles chart in spring 1973. The lack of promotional muscle hurt the second single, "She Doesn't Have to See You (To See Through You)," which only reached No. 68 on the R&B singles chart that summer. Young-West reportedly didn't help matters. Conflicted by the idea of singing secular music, she did few promotional appearances to promote the LP and often returned to her father's church to sing there instead. For a time, Young-West happily worked behind the scenes, offering backing vocals on a Doc Severinsen album and doing commercial jingles for Zales Jewelers. After recording the soundtrack to Cicely Tyson's TV mini-series *A Woman Called Moses*, West abandoned secular music altogether.

Since then, Young-West has been featured on numerous gospel albums by artists such as Mattie Moss Clark and has appeared in half a dozen touring gospel musicals. In 1992, she sang at the Republican convention prior to a speech by former First Lady Barbara Bush. Young-West has recorded gospel projects for a number of poorly distributed, small gospel labels. Her first solo offering was 1987's *The Jordan River*. Her first gospel LP was 1993's *Just Call Me Tommye* on Brenda and Phil Nicholas's Command Records. She's also recorded the solo CDs *Believe* and *Now Is the Time*.

RECOMMENDED RECORDINGS: Possessing a voice not unlike Aretha Franklin's in her prime, Young-West arguably shines best on "He's My All and All" from the Georgia Mass Choir's *I Owe You the Praise* CD in 2002 and "A Path in the Sea" from Bishop T.D. Jakes's 2003 *A Wing and a Prayer* CD.

Rev. Richard "Mr. Clean" White

A CRUSTY-VOICED singer/preacher, Rev. Richard White was born in 1944. He's written more than 300 songs, including "Accept What God Allows," "God Is Not Through Blessing You," and "The Will of God." He was saved in 1957 under Apostle Arturo Skinner. Two years later, he began working in the ministry and was ordained in 1963. In 1978, he founded Corinthian Temple COGIC where he remained until 1984. White then moved to Connecticut for a period before returning to Atlanta in 1987. At that time, he assumed leadership over Greater Hinsley Temple (later Gospel Temple COGIC).

LaBarbara Whitehead

THE VOICE OF THREE of the biggest gospel classics of the 1970s, LaBarbara Whitehead was born September 6, 1938, in Detroit. Her father, James Whitehead, Sr., was the pastor of Mt. Zion COGIC and her mother is an evangelist/missionary. She began taking piano lessons at the age of five and was very active in her church's musical activities. After graduating from high school at the age of 16, she enrolled in the pre-med program at Midwestern Baptist College. Because of the expense of a medical program, she changed majors several times until she decided on a double major in music and theology. "I wanted to be a doctor, but I knew I loved music," she says. She continued to sing throughout her educational studies.

As a teenager, Whitehead was a singer on Mattie Moss Clark's first Southwest Michigan State Choir LP *Lord, Do Something for Me* on Kapp Records in 1959. When the choir began to record for Savoy Records in the early 1960s, Whitehead got her first recorded solo on the beautiful slow tune, "Wonderful, Wonderful." She performed on all of the choir's LPs through 1974. Later, Whitehead's brother met Donald Vails at a church in Atlanta when the former was a student at Morehouse College. He invited Vails to Detroit for a revival and Vails ended up living with the Whiteheads for over a year. Whitehead joined Donald Vails and the Choraleers and sang the song "I Will Serve Thee" on the group's first album. Later Vails featured Whitehead's captivating soprano on the Choraleers' classic hits "He Decided to Die" and "If God is Dead."

While performing with the Choraleers on the weekend, Whitehead played double-duty as music minister at her brother's church in Romulus and her father's church in Ypsilanti. By that time, she was also working full-time as a surgical nurse at Beaumont Hospital. "I was flying every weekend," she says of the choir's heyday. The Choraleers perished when Vails died in 1997. Whitehead has remained active in her church's musical department and has served as the state choir director for COGIC's second jurisdiction for 16 years. She credits the church's annual convocations with keeping the church's music fresh and vibrant. "It's like going to the gas station and getting your oil changed, getting your battery charged," she explains. "You are charged up and ready to go back home. You may not have 50,000 members at your church, but you're ready to go back home, ready to work for the Lord. The fasting, the praying—the convocations are not as long as they were when my mother used to go when I was a little girl because she would stay three weeks. When she'd come home talking about it, you could just see it. There was just something about listening to the preaching and being there with the saints and the worship. Bishop G.E. Patterson has started the fasting again. That's where the growth is. You learn to deny yourself. You may have a small storefront church, but you don't feel that way when you go to Memphis [where the annual convocation takes place every November] because you know you're part of an organization."

RECOMMENDED RECORDING: *He Is Risen* (Malaco Records, 1998) is a compilation CD featuring a dozen songs by choirs such as New York's Restoration Choir and the Florida Mass Choir. The collection includes Whitehead's original take on "He Decided to Die." Sadly, most of the Choraleers' music is out of print, but this one chestnut is worth seeking out.

Thomas Whitfield

IN A LEAGUE OF HIS OWN, Thomas Whitfield is singularly responsible for marrying the uninhibited excitement of the Pentecostal music tradition with the controlled poise of the Baptist music genre. And just to keep things interesting, Whitfield threw in a good measure of European classical music to define his own unique choir blend on songs such as "Let Everything Praise Him," "Hallelujah Anyhow," "He Saved My Soul," "I Shall Wear a Crown," and his arrangement of Aretha Franklin's "Higher Ground," which showcases Franklin singing as Rev. Jasper Williams preaches.

Born on April 30, 1954, in Detroit, he was the eldest of five boys. His great-grandmother inspired him to play the piano and he began taking lessons at the age of five. He began to play the organ at the Nazarene Baptist Church when he was ten and soon was playing all over the Motor City. After graduating from Central High School, he attended the Detroit Conservatory of Music. Upon graduation, he became a music instructor at the city's Finney High School.

Whitfield and his friend T.J. Hemphill founded the Whitfield Company in January 1977. It comprised 40 of the most renowned soloists, music directors, and musicians around Detroit. Whitfield crafted his own unique contemporary gospel style that merged elements of the Baptist, Pentecostal, and classical music genres. Over the years Whitfield produced, composed, or arranged material for gospel luminaries such as Aretha Franklin, Shirley Caesar, Edwin Hawkins, Rev. James Cleveland, Vanessa Bell Armstrong, Yolanda Adams, and Bishop Paul Morton. In 1984, Whitfield received his first of three Grammy nominations, in this case as producer of Armstrong's *Peace Be Still* album.

The Whitfield Company went on to build a name for itself with its albums *Hallelujah Anyhow* and *I'm Encouraged*. The latter was named *Billboard*'s No. 1 gospel album of 1987. That same year Whitfield performed during a papal visit to Detroit and both played and arranged music on Aretha Franklin's bestselling *One Lord, One Faith, One Baptism* gospel album. Toward the end of his life, Whitfield produced Yolanda Adams's debut album, appeared on Quincy Jones's *Handel's Messiah* Christmas project, and was planning songs for future Whitfield Company releases.

June 1992 was a rough time for Whitfield. His mother was diagnosed with cancer, he was unhappy with his recording label (Benson Records), and he turned down a high-profile role in Steve Martin's film *Leap of Faith*. Many of Whitfield's friends had emphasized that they thought he was making a mistake to decline the role of a zany choir conductor in the film. "He weighed the pros and cons," says Donna Harris, Whitfield's hand-picked president for the choir. "He just felt the role was demeaning to church people and he felt it was demeaning to people of color."

Some members of the Whitfield Company wanted to be in the film and on the night of June 20, 1992, their intentions were on Whitfield's mind. He spoke in-depth about the choir's purpose and goals. After a long choir rehearsal, Whitfield, Harris, and others went to Bob's Big Boy for a late night meal. "He talked about record contracts," Harris says. "He talked about people he wanted the choir associated with and ones he didn't want them associated with—things he never talked about. He talked about everything you could think of regarding the business of the choir. It was as if he was preparing to surrender the choir into my care." Before the meal was over, Whitfield clutched his chest and was then rushed to Garden City Hospital where he was pronounced dead. At his funeral, Daryl Coley and Jennifer Holliday sang, Detroit Congressman John Conyers spoke, and hundreds came out to pay their respects.

After Whitfield's death, Harris kept the choir alive. She forged a new recording deal with Crystal Rose Records. They recorded some of the many unpublished songs Whitfield had left behind. In 1998, the Whitfield Company CD *Still...* was released and peaked at No. 29 on the gospel album chart. The album earned the choir the best press of their career and performance slots on NBC's *Today Show* two years in a row. In 2003, Harris, who had reached into her own pockets to fund publicity trips and other opportunities for the choir, stepped down as president in order to concentrate on administering Whitfield's vast song copyrights and to focus on other professional pursuits.

RECOMMENDED RECORDING: *The Best of Thomas Whitfield* (Verity Records, 1999) features 13 of Whitfield's finest moments, such as "Hallelujah Anyhow" and "Nothing but the Blood."

Walt Whitman and the Soul Children

A *CHICAGO TRIBUNE* reporter once described the Soul Children's stage presentation as "heartfelt handclaps, rhythmic foot stomps, flailing arms, choreographed dance steps, and the melodious sounds of gospel music." In terms of mainstream television appearances, they are one of the most popular choirs of recent memory. They performed at the White House during George H.W. Bush's administration, sang on a network television Motown special, and appeared on other TV programs with the likes of Mavis Staples and Patti LaBelle.

The choir's success is directly attributable to their aggressive, strict founder, Walt Whitman (born in 1961), who formed the choir in 1980 when he was a music teacher at St. John De La Salle Elementary School in Chicago. They were called the Gospel Soul Children back then. As the choir grew from two dozen students to over 100 kids from throughout the Chicago area, Whitman changed their name to the Soul Children. It was not an easy choir to join. Of the 250 youth who routinely auditioned each year, there were rarely more than 30 opening spots available. In addition, Whitman enforced a no-compromise policy regarding drug usage, gang membership, pregnancies, use of makeup and jewelry during concerts, and bad grades. Singer Jamie Simond from the gospel-soul group Fortitude was a member of the choir for six years. "We rehearsed twice a week," he says. "Wednesday night and Saturday morning. Because it was a children's choir we only traveled on the weekends. We did a lot of traveling. We'd leave Friday night and get back Sunday evening. Then we'd be back in school Monday morning. He really stressed good grades. If you fell below a B average, he'd get you a tutor." Whitman once told the *Chicago Tribune*, "They must learn not to follow other people's negative standards. Instead, they make their own positive standards and follow those." Another Fortitude member, Cinque Cullar, was also an alumnus of the choir. "Walt Whitman exposed me to a different market than the regular gospel market," he explains. "He was doing Presbyterian churches for their youth conferences, Wesleyan churches. He did a lot of corporate things. Places you'd never think gospel music would go, he takes it there and does it well and with tact."

Allen T.D. Wiggins

SAXOPHONIST Allen T.D. Wiggins (born circa 1967 in Orlando, Florida) made a brief appearance on the gospel scene in the late 1980s. With his handsome looks and polished suits, he was a sophisticated alternative to the sweaty images of gospel performers. His father, R.W. Wiggins, was pastor of the Greater New Hope Missionary Baptist Church. He took vocal and piano lessons as a child, but had focused on the saxophone by the time he reached high school. While studying pharmacy at Florida A&M University, Wiggins produced his own custom LP in 1987. The blend of traditional and contemporary instrumentals sold 1,500 copies throughout the state. Phil and Brenda Nicholas's Command Records label repackaged the project as *One Way* the following year. It peaked at No. 31 on the gospel album sales chart. Wiggins has been out of the spotlight for a decade now, but continues to play sax on most of Allen & Allen's CDs. "Christians should have something to listen to as a form of entertainment," he told *Totally Gospel* in November 1988 of the main purpose for his ministry. "But the Christian entertainer should couple his or her performance with the Word of God in such a way as to act as a magnet in bringing souls to Christ."

Madam Mattie Wiggley

ONE OF THE GRANDE dames of the COGIC denomination, Madam Mattie Wiggley served as vice president in the denomination's National Music Department under the leadership of Mattie Moss Clark. She first met Clark in 1968 and became her right hand in ministry the following year. Although Wiggley regularly sang at denominational events and was a star within that circuit, she recorded very little. In 1959, ethnomusicologist Alan Lomax went through the Southern United States to record rural Negro musicians. He captured on tape a relatively youthful Wiggley on the congregational sing-along "Power." The tune can be found on the four-disc box set *Sounds of the South: A Musical Journey from the Georgia Sea Islands to the Mississippi Delta*, released by Atlantic Records in 1993. In later years, Wiggley adopted Calvin Bridges's composition "I Can Go to God in

Prayer," which was popularized by Albertina Walker as her own signature song. LaBarbara Whitehead says, "When she sang that, she could lift the church." The song was featured on the COGIC International Mass Choir *Leaning on Jesus* CD that was released by Moses Tyson's World Class Gospel label in 1997. "She was a very easy-going person to work with," Whitehead continues. "Sometimes your pastor or your bishop may say something you don't agree with, but she would follow through on whatever they said because she followed leadership. She could help us young people a lot when we got upset or if we were mad with Mattie [Moss Clark]. She'd say, 'All right now,' and calm us down." Wiggley died in 1995 and was believed to be in her late seventies.

Stephen Wiley

CONSIDERED THE godfather of gospel rap, Stephen Lamarr Wiley was born in September 1956. He graduated from the University of Oklahoma in Norman. He began rapping in the 1980s—well beyond the age of most rappers, but since he was a Christian rapper and there was no such field, he was embraced by progressive youth ministers. He was youth minister at Fred Price's 15,000-member Crenshaw Christian Center Church in Los Angeles for years, which helped introduce him to other ministers who would book him for their youth conventions. He produced some brisk-selling custom rap LPs in the late 1980s that brought him to the attention of Star Song Records in 1990. "Rap is the medium that is currently speaking to our youth culture," Star Song Vice President Jeff Moseley said upon signing Wiley to the label. "I can't think of anyone more suited to use the medium than Stephen Wiley. His talents are large, but his heart for kids is even bigger." The two albums Wiley created during his tenure there, *Rhythm and Poetry* and *Rhapsody*, featured poppish hip-hop raps such as "Teenage Mutant Youth Group Member," "Purpose," and "Bible Break." In the long run, Wiley's raps were too tame to be taken seriously by rap aficionados. Harder Christian rappers such as T-Bone and Michael Peace rose to fill the void. Wiley and his wife Pamela currently pastor the Praise Center Family Church in Tulsa.

Barnett Williams

THE FOUNDER OF Born Again Records, which has given the world Christian comic Broderick Rice and the soulful sounds of James Grear and Company, Barnett Williams was born on September 12, 1946, in Bogalusa, Louisiana. He once recorded for Motown Records before he launched his record label in the 1990s.

Beau Williams

A FORMER *STAR SEARCH* contestant, Williams rose to marginal fame in the 1980s for his near-perfect renditions of Sam Cooke songs. Like Cooke, Williams's voice is a soothing, smooth croon. However, when necessary, he can break out into a spine-tingly yelp that will bring the church to its feet. He was born in Houston, Texas, where his father was a preacher and his mother sang the gospel. Early on he auditioned for the Temptations, but was not selected to join because he was only 5'8" and most of the Tempts stood over six feet. He then formed the R&B group Solar Heat. From there, he went on Ed McMahon's *Star Search* talent competition. After breaking future cabaret star Sam Harris's 13-week winning streak on the program, Williams won a recording deal with Capitol Records. He recorded several albums for the label, but none was a major success. His highest charting single was "There's Just Something About You," which barely cracked the R&B Top 40 in 1986.

All along, Williams has said that he was yearning to sing gospel exclusively. "I was uncomfortable with my image in the R&B world," he told *Totally Gospel* in 1989. "I was being marketed like a sex symbol. The songs that I wanted to sing [gospel], no one would pay attention to.... I think we need to be conscious of the messages that we are portraying in the music and the lyrics. I needed to be delivered and now I'm doing gospel and I'm quite happy about that." He could not have been happy with the response from the gospel industry, though. He's recorded for Light Records, Platinum Records, and Insync Music. Although many of his albums charted, he doesn't have a definable signature song within the church community.

RECOMMENDED RECORDING: *The Best of Beau Williams* (Platinum Entertainment, 1995) features three songs associated with Sam Cooke, such as "That's Heaven to Me." He also offers a pleasant version of Stevie Wonder's "Love's in Need of Love Today."

Deniece Williams

THE SONGBIRD, as the music critics called her, was one of soul music's favorite female singers of the late '70s and early '80s. Her multi-octave vocal range and tender love songs such as "Silly," "Free," "It's Gonna Take a Miracle," and her million-selling "Too Much, Too Little, Too Late" duet with Johnny Mathis made her a fan favorite. While still at the top of her game, Williams left secular music for a total immersion into the gospel field. For a few short years, Williams was a top draw in gospel with smashes such as "They Say," "I Surrender All," and "His Eye Is on the Sparrow." After a decade in gospel, the Songbird sought to stage a comeback on the pop scene in the late '90s, but has been out of sight since then.

Born June Deniece Chandler on June 3, 1950, in Gary, Indiana, Williams grew up in a strict Pentecostal church background where her introduction to music was gospel. Her mother, Alma, was a singer and Williams admired her voice as well as those of jazz artists Carmen McCrae and Nancy Wilson. Williams sang in church throughout high school and took an after-school job as a record store clerk. Her boss introduced her to the owner of the local Toddlin' Town Records, where she recorded her first single, "Love Is Tears." Nothing much happened with the song, so the practical-minded singer headed to Morgan State University to study nursing while singing in a nightclub. An early marriage produced two sons before Stevie Wonder caught wind of Williams's Toddlin' Town singles (via her cousin John Harris, Wonder's valet and childhood friend) and asked her to join his backup group, Wonderlove, in 1971. She remained a member for years, contributing backing vocals to Wonder's LPs *Talking Book* and *Songs in the Key of Life*.

Deniece Williams / Word Records promotional photo

By 1975, Williams had decided to pursue a solo career as a songwriter, so she moved to Los Angeles and began collaborating and writing songs with others. In between many background vocal sessions such as Candi Staton's "Young Hearts Run Free" to pay her bills, Williams made a demo of songs she was hoping soul band Earth, Wind & Fire would record. Maurice White, the group's founder, heard the tape and brought her into his stable as a songwriter and singer. He was beginning to produce artists such as the Emotions under his Kalimba Productions Company. His productions were released through Columbia Records, and Williams's first LP, *This Is Niecy*, hit the world in late 1976. The first single, "It's Important to Me," was a moderate R&B hit, but the second single, a moody ballad called "Free," soared to No. 2 on the R&B chart and made Williams an instant star with a gold record to boot. All of Williams's albums for Columbia included one gospel song, and on this album it was the funky "Watching Over."

Williams was initially compared to Minnie Riperton for her rippling vibrato and vein-breaking high notes, but they had two distinctly different styles. Whereas Riperton sang in a higher key and wrote moody, intellectual love songs with Latin and Caribbean flavors, Williams most often sang in her middle range and only used the high notes for dramatic effect at the climax of a song. In addition, Williams's music varied from Riperton's in that it wasn't heady. It was poetically written, but simple. It was emotional with spiritual overtones and connected with the masses more than Riperton's music did. In spite of the massiveness of Riperton's 1975 million-seller "Lovin' You," during her short lifetime she never experienced the consistent commercial success that Williams did with her music in the same time frame.

Over the next few years, Williams was a steady hit maker with R&B smashes such as the No. 1 "It's Gonna Take a Miracle," "Baby, Baby, My Love's All for You," "When Love Comes Calling," "Silly," "I've Got the Next Dance," "Do What You Feel," and a remake of Curtis Mayfield's "I'm So Proud." A 1977 duet with pop legend Johnny Mathis, "Too Much, Too Little, Too Late," took Williams's career to a new high. The ballad of a marriage at its end gave both artists their first No. 1 pop and R&B hits ever. Columbia was so thrilled with the million-selling single that they rushed the duo into the studio to record an entire album of duets. The album, named after one of Williams's compositions, *That's What Friends Are For*, became another gold album. The duo performed on all of the major talk and variety shows of the day, such as *The Tonight Show with Johnny Carson*. In 1984, Williams recorded another No. 1 pop and R&B classic, "Let's Hear It for the Boy" from the soundtrack for the film *Footloose*, which currently stands as her bestselling single yet with multi-platinum sales.

After a short-lived early '80s marriage to an actor-turned-minister, Christopher Joy (who co-starred in the Motown movie *Big Time* with Smokey Robinson), Williams seemed to take a more vocal public stand on her Christian faith by appearing at Christian convocations such as the 1981 "Living Proof" rally at Washington, DC's RFK Stadium. Also in attendance were other saved secular artists such as Pat Boone, McCoo & Davis, and Ray Parker, Jr. In spite of her faith, many of Williams's fans were surprised to learn that she recorded a complete gospel album in 1986 for Sparrow Records. The album, *So Glad I Know*, appeared on the heels of "Let's Hear It for the Boy" and was a huge success on both black and white Christian radio. With her pop approach to soul, Williams's LP produced three Top 15 singles, including the title song, "Wings of an Eagle" and the Sandi Patti duet "They Say," which spent two weeks at No. 1 on the CCM charts. Black gospel played those songs plus Williams's stirring piano-based version of "I Surrender All." The LP went on to sell over 250,000 units (the most Sparrow had ever sold on a black artist at that time) and won Williams the first Grammy awards of her career for "They Say" and "I Surrender All."

Meanwhile, Williams was still at Columbia recording clean pop albums such as *Hot on the Trail*, which appeared in 1986 and produced the vaguely gospel single "Healing" that reached No. 76 on the R&B chart. The following year's LP *Water under the Bridge* resulted in the mild R&B hits "Never Say Never" and "I Confess," but the album won a Grammy award for the gospel song, "I Believe in You." Columbia executives were never excited about Williams recording gospel, but they didn't fight it. However, the label appeared to lose interest in her as Williams's fame grew in the gospel market. Her Columbia singles were not pushed as strongly, but then again, her R&B songs were not as strong as they once were. Columbia was surely none too pleased when Sparrow Records partnered with MCA Records (a direct Columbia Records competitor) to promote Williams's *Special Love* gospel CD to the urban market in 1989. Meanwhile, Columbia was promoting what would become Williams's last new R&B CD for Columbia, *As Good as It Gets*. MCA's urban single "Every Moment" reached No. 55 on the R&B chart while Columbia muscled Williams's catchy R&B single "I Can't Wait" to No. 8 on the R&B chart.

By this point, Williams's third husband, Brad Westering, had taken over management of her career and he was aggressively pushing for her success in the Christian market. Soon, Williams and Columbia parted ways. However, after Sparrow licensed all of Williams's gospel tracks from her Columbia R&B albums—such as 1977's a cappella "God Is Amazing" from the CD *From the Beginning*—they parted company too. Aside from a lullabies CD for Word Records in 1991, Williams disappeared from both the gospel and the pop scene for years. She resurfaced in 1996 with news that she'd divorced Westering and was raising her four sons in Eng-

land where she had a BBC radio show and had performed in the London production of the gospel musical *Mama, I Want to Sing*.

That was the year Williams made a comeback R&B album, *Love Solves It All*. She wrote most of the songs (something she had seriously curtailed during her waning days at Columbia) and they were very good. The catchy, uptempo summertime single "Why You Wanna Do Me?" should have become a major R&B hit, but the small American P.A.R. label and its equally small London counterpart, Upstage Records, lacked the resources to push the album and it failed to ignite. The album closed with a beautiful a cappella rendition of the hymn "Great Is Thy Faithfulness."

A year later, Williams was back living in the US and indirectly recording a gospel album for Sony (which had since bought Columbia Records). The album *This Is My Story* was released on Sony's gospel imprint, Harmony Records. It was an uneven album of contemporary renditions of hymns such as "It Is Well" and "Blessed Assurance." It was not her best work and sold poorly in comparison to her prior gospel releases. Still, it reached No. 14 on the gospel chart and won a Grammy in 1998. Currently, she fluctuates between gospel and secular concert dates. She briefly hosted a radio program on the Los Angeles radio station KKLA in 2003.

Joy Williams

ONE OF THE BRIGHTEST stars to surface on the Christian pop scene in recent years is Joy Williams, who's already racked up an impressive number of Top Ten hits. The pretty young blonde has probably never thought of it, but her sometimes urban and dance-flavored music is helping break down the walls that keep many black artists from succeeding on Christian pop radio. The more CCM radio programmers hear urban sounds and hear that their core audience is more open to it than they are, the more open their ears will be when urban gospel artists approach them for airplay in the future.

Williams was born November 14, 1982, in Mt. Hermon, California. Her father, Roger Williams, was executive director at the Mt. Hermon Christian Conference Center where the younger Williams grew up around esteemed religious leaders. At the age of 14, Williams was offered her first recording contract, but turned it down because she wanted to be a regular kid. When a second contract was offered two years later, she felt she was ready and signed to Reunion Records. With musical influences ranging from Billie Holiday and Nat King Cole to Celine Dion, Williams's self-titled debut CD was considerably mature in tone for a teenager. Released in July 2001, it reached No. 12 on the CCM album sales chart before selling over 100,000 units. While promoting the album on the road, Williams maintained a 4.0 GPA in high school and was also student body president before graduating with honors in spring 2002. The following autumn she released her sophomore CD, *By Surprise*, that peaked at No. 31 on the CCM chart. "I would love for God to use me to impact culture in a way that would direct people toward the Lord," she told *CCM* in 2001. "I would love for people, once they left the building after hearing me sing, to go 'Wow, God is so awesome.'"

Kelli Williams

THEY USED TO call her "the little girl with the big voice" because she could sing explosively dramatic songs even at a young age. After singing around the house and at church for as long as she could remember, Williams made her professional debut in 1988 at the ripe old age of ten when she appeared with Take 6 and Larnelle Harris at the Choice awards. However, it was three consecutive wins on Ed McMahon's *Star Search* in 1993 as a teen champion that really opened doors for Williams. That year, she also performed on *March On*, an all-star Warner/Reprise CD commemorating the 30th anniversary of the historic March on Washington. Word Records signed her soon after and her self-titled debut CD hit stores in 1995.

The CD was produced by the Caldwell Brothers and Sanchez Harley. It's by far her best project to date with a warm mix of urban and pop-styled gospel. A *Billboard* magazine critic wrote, "A long list of singles candidates from a young woman who arrives on the scene a fully developed, mature, and exciting new tal-

ent." For most of 1996, Williams was on the road, opening for CeCe Winans's "Alone in His Presence" tour and even joining Winans on a reprise of the Whitney Houston/CeCe Winans hit "Count on Me."

Of working with Winans, Williams said, "CeCe's example taught me so much. I grew spiritually from being around her, and also learned a lot as a singer. She's such a role model as both a Christian woman and entertainer. And I found out that things don't always go perfectly, even when you're CeCe Winans, and that we all have to lean on the Lord in the very same, humble way." At the same time, Williams aspired for the broad fame of Houston. "Whitney's audience is not just a black audience or a white audience," Williams told *CCM* magazine. "She's singing to people across every racial line. A lot of people thank the Lord for the gift, but I think he deserves something in return, not that I could ever pay him for what he's done. I just want to bless other people, and I want to help them know Christ."

Through several executive-level personnel changes at Word's black music division, Williams was not always given priority treatment. However, R. Kelly collaborator Percy Bady and gospel legend Walter Hawkins were brought in to produce the *I Get Lifted* set, which also featured a nice duet with R&B macho man Dave Hollister on "Love Wouldn't." Williams's final Word CD, *In the Myx*, found her going for an even stronger crossover audience and featured a faithful remake of Tramaine Hawkins's dance classic "Fall Down." In 2002, Word was bought by the Warner Music Group and many of the black artists were released from their contracts, including Williams. Recently, Williams has appeared in some gospel stage plays and has done session work on albums by Helen Baylor and others.

Marion Williams

PERHAPS GOSPEL'S BEST SOPRANO EVER, Marion Williams rose to fame as a member of the Clara Ward Singers, where her famous yodel and thunderous vibrato influenced rock 'n' roll singers such as Little Richard. She later formed the Stars of Faith and then enjoyed a solo career over the balance of her life. She was born August 29, 1927, in Miami. Her father was a West Indian butcher and her mother was a laundry woman. Her father taught her music and her mother taught her religion. As one of her older brothers listened to blues and jazz music, Williams picked out elements of it that she liked and left the lyrics behind. After her father died when she was nine, money became scarce. So, by the age of 14, Williams had quit school and gone to work beside her mother in the laundry. When her mother lost both of her legs to diabetes, Williams was the family's primary source of income. On the weekends, she sang in Sanctified Church programs and even sang on street corners. "I went to work when it was dark and I came home when it was dark," she said in 1994. Then she met Rev. Jerry Pratt. "You don't need to be on nobody's job," she recalled him saying as he gave her a $25 a week ("and that was like millions to me") to sing with his ten-member group, the Melrose Gospel Singers.

Soon Williams became the best-known gospel artist in the Miami area, but her name would be made elsewhere. In 1945, Williams was visiting her sister, Rebecca, in Philadelphia. She and a friend went to a Clara Ward Singers concert. "When I went to the church that night it was jam-packed," she says. "I had never seen singers like that. They were dressed up [white suits with rhinestones] and their hair was styled. They were sharp! The lady I went with [Leola Crosby] was a friend of theirs and she told them I was there from Florida." Williams was called up to sing, and though intimidated, she wailed on "What Could I Do If It Wasn't for the Lord?" to the point that, "it was almost doxology."

The Wards invited Williams to join the group, but since she was only 16, her mother said no. A year later, the Wards still wanted her, and her mother finally consented. Williams met up with the group for a concert at a ballpark in Jacksonville, Florida.

After a few dates, they were off to Oakland, California, circa 1948 to record their first 78-rpm featuring Williams, "Stretch Out in Jesus When Troubles Burden Me Down." Williams says, "My voice was hoarse, but we made it. We sold a gang of records at churches." By the middle 1950s, the Clara Ward Singers were the best-selling group in all of gospel—male or female. Williams led the group on two of their biggest recordings, "Surely, God Is Able" and "Packin' Up." During this period she

became known for her yodel, which Little Richard would eventually come to imitate on the back-end of his infamous phrase "A wop bop a loo bop a lop bam boom" on "Tutti Frutti." The group was as big as any rock 'n' roll act of the day and was filling sports arenas and theaters. However, Williams and the other non-family members of the Ward Singers were not sharing in the wealth. Williams had given birth to a child out of wedlock with a singer from one of the popular quartet groups of the time, and she needed money to take care of her son. She went to Mother Gertrude Ward, who controlled the group finances, and asked for a raise. Ward refused. "They got a little greedy and stingy and they didn't pay us," she said. "I just left on faith that God would see me through." Williams left in 1958 during a particularly busy period where the group was to appear on both NBC's *Tonight Show* and *Today Show*.

After Williams left, Henrietta Waddy, Kitty Parham, Frances Steadman, and Esther Ford all followed her. Media rumors swirled that the Ward Singers would have to disband, but Clara and Mother Ward denied that and said that the walkout was a temporary distraction. They got the Anna Smallwood Singers to fill in until they could recruit new members. Williams wasted no time rearranging her life either. Savoy Records gave her a recording contract and she went into the studio in August 1958 with her Ward Singers cohorts and began to record new songs such as "When He Calls." They even re-recorded "Packing Up." The new group called themselves the Stars of Faith. "We were just sitting around," Williams recalled. "I said, 'The Lord has blessed us to become stars and we have plenty of faith here,' so Miss Waddy said she thought we should call ourselves that." They did not shine instantly. Being in a successful group isn't the same as knowing how to make one successful. Williams lacked Mother's Ward's ability to manage, Clara's competitiveness, and fresh new songs. However, by 1961 their prospects changed.

Williams's manager, Barbara Bryant, booked them to star in Langston Hughes's play *Black Nativity*, which went to Broadway and toured to packed houses coast to coast. They then went to Italy to the Two Worlds Festival. "They had never seen nothing like us," Williams said. "Even movie stars came to see us, like Sophia Loren, Lauren Bacall, Zachary Scott. One of the prettiest theaters you ever saw in your life. We were there a month." From there, they went to London, where even the prime minister attended a performance. "Every night, it was packed," she said. "London was like home to us. When we didn't have other cities to go to [in Europe], we'd stay in London until we did. We went to Paris, then Austria, Copenhagen, Amsterdam, Belgium, all of those places. We even went to Liverpool and the Beatles came to see our show and they were hot at that time. We were playing in Boston the day that President Kennedy died. We did that show for about four years."

After the play finally closed, Williams said that jealousy over her growing media stature caused her to leave the group she founded. "After that, I found out my group didn't appreciate me so I went solo. Well, they always think the group's leader is getting more admiration and really, I was, because I was the star of the show. But you know how some people are." After her mother died circa 1966, she realized that she was all alone in the world and that if she was to succeed, she had to look out for herself. With the help of her longtime fan Anthony Heilbut, she began to sing on white college campuses, such as Yale, which introduced her to a younger audience.

Eventually, Atlantic/Cotillion Records came knocking and offered her a recording deal. The label matched Williams with the best musicians, including Keith Jarrett and Eric Gale. The Dixie Hummingbirds backed her on one project and Roberta Flack produced another. Later, she recorded projects for Columbia and Nashboro Records. In the late 1980s, Williams began recording a series of fine, raw traditional gospel CDs for Heilbut's Spirit Feel Records label. She received another boost of attention when two of her songs were used in the 1992 film *Fried Green Tomatoes*. The same year, her cover of "Up Above My Head" was featured in the movie *Mississippi Masala*. Because of the exposure she received the MacArthur Foundation "genius grant" for $375,000 for outstanding community service in 1993. Later that year, Williams was saluted by Aretha Franklin and Little Richard when she was awarded the Kennedy Center Honors along with Johnny Carson and Stephen Sondheim.

"I can sing sweet, but I sing rough too. Most the time it's rough. A lot of folks say I have a sexy voice,

but I don't know what that's all about," she joked in 1992. "Thank God, I'm still able to sing. There are women my age who aren't able to carry a tune anymore. So far, so good for me. I tell you what. I want to sing until I die. I want to die singing. Let me go away from here singing a song, singing the gospel." In the end, she was too ill to sing before passing away of renal failure on July 2, 1994.

RECOMMENDED RECORDING: All of Williams's Spirit Feel recordings are superlative. However *Remember Me* (Spirit Feel, 2005) covers 24 of Williams's classic performances of songs such as "Strong Again," "O Death," and "The Lord Will Make a Way Somehow."

Mary Lou Williams

ONE OF THE GREATEST stride pianists of the 20th century, Mary Lou Williams was always considered an excellent female musician. However, had she been born a man, she would have most likely been considered a genius on par with Duke Ellington and Art Tatum. She was born Mary Elfrieda Scruggs on May 8, 1910, in Atlanta and taught herself to play piano by ear. She began to work in vaudeville when she was 13 and eventually married saxophonist John Williams. They briefly relocated to Memphis where she made her first records and then on to Kansas City where John joined the Andy Kirk Orchestra. Williams filled in for a pianist on one of Kirk's recordings and played so well that Kirk allowed her to join the ensemble. Her arrangements gave the orchestra a distinctive sound with her stride piano that even caught the attention of Jelly Roll Morton. She wrote songs such as "Roll 'Em," which was a major hit recorded by Benny Goodman, Shirley Scott, and Harry James. Her tune "What's Your Story Morning Glory?" was covered by Jimmie Lunceford and Ella Fitzgerald. She also produced fine arrangements for the Earl Hines and Tommy Dorsey bands. Her second husband played with the Duke Ellington orchestra and that led Williams to write and arrange for Ellington as well. She later played with Benny Goodman and became a proponent of the edgy, bebop movement popularized more famously by Thelonious Monk and Dizzy Gillespie.

During the 1950s, Williams lived in Europe for a while and became a Catholic convert. She retired in 1954 and devoted herself to a lifestyle of prayer and meditation that resulted in jazz hymns such as "Black Christ of the Andes," "Anima Christi," and "Praise the Lord." Her official comeback occurred when Gillespie featured her as a guest soloist at the 1957 Newport Jazz Festival. "The ability to play good jazz is a gift from God," she told *Ebony* in 1966. "This music is based on the spirituals—it's our only original American art form—and should be played everywhere, including church. Those who say it shouldn't be played in church do not understand they are blocking the manifestation of God's will." In her later years, Williams taught at Duke University while continuing to perform and record new music. She died of cancer on May 28, 1981, in Durham, North Carolina.

Lee Williams & the Spiritual QCs

BY THE TIME Lee Williams bounced on the national scene in a big way in the late 1990s with songs such as "I've Learned to Lean," quartet music was considered old hat, but Williams made it look cool. Slim, handsome, and fastidious in a masculine manner, Lee Williams personifies the concept of the gentleman gospel singer. He doesn't strut across the stage, pant, and clown around; he just stands there flat-footed and lets his voice do the talking. His current lineup of QCs includes Al Hollis, Leonard Shumpart, and Roger McKinney.

Lee Williams was born in Tupelo, Mississippi. His uncle sang in a local gospel group, the Gospel Stars. When he was seven years old, Williams and three older brothers formed their own group, the Gospel Star Juniors. Williams's uncle later formed a group called the Spiritual QCs (Qualified Christians). When the group disbanded in 1964, Williams and his brother kept the group going. After a two-year stint in the army, Williams worked as a truck driver during the week and sang with the group on the weekends. Fast-forward three decades. A homemade cassette of the group singing wound up in the hands of a Memphis radio announcer who began playing songs from the cassette on the air. The tape be-

came a local hit and small Memphis label released the group's debut CD *Jesus Is Alive and Well.* When the group was performing in Birmingham in 1996, an executive with MCG Records liked their sound and worked on signing them to the label. Their debut *Love Will Go All the Way* followed and reached No. 15 on the gospel album chart. The album was propelled by the radio smash "I've Learned to Lean" and also included a rousing gospelized take on Wilson Pickett's "In the Midnight Hour."

The group's subsequent CDs have included their hard-driving quartet hits "You Didn't Have To," "You Been Good," and "Right on Time." Williams's tight, controlled yet dynamic vocals reignited the quartet industry, but that came as no surprise to him. "It was gospel quartet music that played a major role in the birth of R&B, soul, and rock 'n' roll," Lee once said. "They all borrowed from us. We've cranked it up considerably since the old days, but the heart of our sound has been consistent for years. If it sounds familiar…if it makes you want to get up and dance, or maybe shed a tear here and there…well, it ought to. This is where it all started."

"In the world of gospel quartet music there are no million selling overnight sensations. There are no Mariah Careys who get handed 28 million bucks whether they sing or not," columnist Ted Holland wrote in the *Good News Gazette* in November 2002. "The world of quartet moves and evolves very slowly. Lee Williams toiled 32 years before 'Love Will Go All the Way.' He sang all over the South on weekends, cutting records for small labels, and driving a truck to feed his family. That is pretty much the blueprint for most of the top-selling groups. Of the entire gospel quartets in existence only about ten are able to make a living singing full-time. The best paid quartets probably make less per night than a backup singer or musician for the Rolling Stones."

For his part, success hasn't changed Williams much. "Every now and then, if the company needs an extra driver, and I've got a couple of days off, I'll take a drive," he says. "That's a real getaway…a mind-relaxer for me, and spending time in the truck stops keeps me in touch with the real world, not to mention giving me good ideas for songs. You're never a stranger in a truck stop."

Michelle Williams

NOT SINCE THE Pointer Sisters in the 1980s and perhaps En Vogue in the early 1990s has a female group impacted the pop charts in the manner that Destiny's Child has in the new millennium. Aside from their slick pop hooks, what they bring to the table is centerfold beauty and a sensual image that is further accentuated with songs such as "Say My Name," "Emotion," and "Bootilicious." The most recent member of the trio, Michelle Williams, created a firestorm of buzz within the black church world when it was announced that she was working on her first gospel project. Just as they had done with Sam Cooke a generation or two before, the gospel community was ready to attack Williams for walking the tightrope separating R&B and gospel. But she rose to the occasion and has developed a base of support among one of the hardest groups of music listeners to please: church folks.

Born Michelle Tenitra Williams on July 23, 1980, in Rockford, Illinois, Williams hails from a religious and musical family. At the age of seven, she sang her first church solo with her rendition of "Blessed Assurance" at the St. Paul Church of God. As a teenager, she sang with the gospel groups United Harmony and Chosen Expression. Singing was a hobby and not a career ambition at that point, so she attended Illinois State University where she majored in criminal justice with her eye on a career in the FBI as an undercover agent. However, she auditioned to become a backup singer for Atlanta-born R&B singer Monica when she was riding high with the pop smash "The Boy Is Mine" in 1999. She snagged that job and the next year, she joined Destiny's Child after a member quit the already superstar-level group. Williams has performed on Destiny Child's No. 1 pop hits such as "Independent Women," "Survivor," and "Bootilicious." As Destiny's Child became the biggest female group in America, the rumors of an eventual breakup surfaced, although all members of their camp denied as much.

Williams has always considered herself a church singer, so she decided to make her solo CD debut a gospel project. To help set up her entry into the gospel world, Williams's handlers paired her with gospel legend Shirley Caesar on the hymn "Steal Away." It was the featured track on Caesar's *Hymns* CD in 2001 and included on William's CD *Heart to Yours* in 2002. Williams has a rather light voice to handle most gospel music, but the mellow urban vibes her producers chose to round her project out covered whatever vocal limitations she may have. She was even able to hold her own with the squalling Caesar on their duet, surely no small feat. The CD debuted at No. 1 on the gospel chart, and peaked at No. 3 on the CCM chart and No. 17 on the R&B charts.

Once Williams's CD was issued, she made herself much more accessible to the press than Destiny's Child had ever been. She walked into the field with a sincere heart and a humility that lesser known gospel singers often never display, and she was immediately attacked for singing songs such as "Bootilicious" while professing to be a Christian. She was attacked because of the glamorous, sexy clothes Destiny's Child often wears. Instead of avoiding the uncomfortable charges of the Christian press, Williams unnerved many by tackling the questions in an unapologetically direct manner.

"I know we sing R&B, but we don't promote premarital sex, drugs and alcohol, or do those things," she told *Gospel Today* magazine. "I'm here to help change the world—not have the world change me…. I can't let anybody tell me that because I'm in Destiny's Child I'm not saved…. When I got in the group my manager knew our style was sort of uncomfortable for me…. I do know that I probably will get some negative feedback from people, but I can't let them discourage me and try to tell me I'm not a Christian and I'm not saved, because they're not God. I know what God has done in my life and I know that God is still with me and he still loves me. I'm here to testify about that." Unbothered, Williams has ignored the critics and watched the CD sell well over 200,000 units—far more than the average gospel CD sells in a lifetime. Her sophomore CD *Do You Know* only reached No. 2 on the *Billboard* gospel sales chart in 2004, but showcased a far better choice of songs and vocal depth than the first project.

Williams Brothers

THEY ARE THE QUARTET that no one thinks of as a quartet. In the 1970s, the Williams Brothers leaped on the music scene with contemporary gospel quartet music even before the Mighty Clouds of Joy created their late '70s hits such as "Mighty High." Over the years, the group has made gospel music that crosses the musical spectrum, from country to traditional quartet to smooth soul. Among their best-known hits are "Jesus Will Fix It," "Cooling Water," and their signature song, "I'm Just a Nobody."

The story of the Williams Brothers began with Leon "Pop" Williams (born November 24, 1908) in Smithdale, Mississippi. He was an old-time believer who sang with the Big Four Gospel singers back in the 1940s. He didn't believe in compromising by singing secular music and he raised his children with the same tenets. His older sons, Frank and Leon, Jr., sang in a group with their cousins, the Southern Sons, in the 1960s. One day, Pop Williams heard his younger children, Marilyn, Leonard, and Melvin out in the yard singing. They sounded very good to him, so he talked to Frank about them and the two of them formed the Williams Brothers in 1960, without Marilyn participating. Instead, another brother, Douglas, joined and "Cousin" Henry Green rounded out the group a year later. Pop had discovered Green singing at Brown's Chapel Primitive Baptist Church in Liberty, Mississippi, where he wowed the congregation with his melodious high notes.

They were initially known as the Little Williams Brothers, but as their name built, they became known as the Sensational Williams Brothers. Pop Williams groomed them meticulously. "He was strict," Doug says. "He really wanted us to be professional in every way from the stage to the way we carried ourselves in public. In those early days, he was mostly spending his own money because we weren't making any money yet." The group fused tight quartet harmonies with both traditional gospel rhythms and a bit of Motown flavor. One of the highlights was Douglas singing the old Hightower Brothers song, "Oh, Lord, I'm Your Child"—his first group solo. As the group toured on the weekends to build their base, they never missed school. "Most Sunday nights we were late getting

home," Doug recalls. "Whether we were in Louisiana or Alabama or wherever singing that weekend, we'd try to get our sleep on the way back home. There have been times where we literally stepped out of my father's car and stepped onto the school bus."

The group's first LP, or half an LP, appeared in 1971. They cut a side of songs on the *He's My Brother* album and the Jackson Southernaires performed the songs on the other side. The Williams Brothers' music was a mix of contemporary and traditional gospel. "We were the first quartet to do any kind of contemporary music," Doug says. "Even though we never got credit for that, it was there. They said it [started with] people like Rance Allen or Edwin Hawkins. But back in the early '70s, we were doing contemporary music mixed with traditional music and we still do it the same way now. That's just the way God was giving us our music. Even before we started recording and were just doing concerts, our arrangements were different from regular quartets. That word 'contemporary' was not even in existence in gospel music at that time."

The first complete Williams Brothers project was 1973's *Holding On* LP on the Songbird Records label. It featured the monster hit "Jesus Will Fix It." Doug says, "That's when things really began to take off. It took off so fast that we weren't ready for the success.... We didn't even know what kind of money to ask for when promoters called." For instance, they were asked to do a concert in Atlanta with Shirley Caesar and James Cleveland. "'Jesus Will Fix It' was the No. 1 song in Atlanta," Doug recalls. The brothers were unsure of how much to charge the promoter for their concert, so they asked their brother Frank, who said they should take no less than $500. "Well, we had never gotten $500 in our lives," Doug laughs. "So we thought that was big, but we probably could have gotten a lot more."

The Williams Brothers continued to turn out hits such as "Jesus Made a Way," "If It Wasn't for the Lord," and "I'll Fly Away." In 1982, their old friend James Bullard brought them to Word/Myrrh Records where they enjoyed three years of hits such as "If I Don't Wake Up," "He'll Understand It Better and Say Well Done," and "A Mother's Love." In 1985, a Word Records executive overlooked the group's biggest hit ever. "We were supposed to do another album," Doug says. "'I'm Just a Nobody' was supposed to be on Word Records. We were in a negotiating period at that time and there were some people at Word that had been put in certain positions who didn't really know and understand black gospel. We already had that album finished basically. We already knew 'I'm Just a Nobody' was going to be a big record. We knew it from the inception of the song. This guy—and I refuse to call his name—he was over that department and he just couldn't hear it. He said we need to go back in the studio and take off most of the songs and redo them. He said 'I'm Just a Nobody' is an okay song and that he didn't see it as being a big hit record and so forth. So we left that meeting that particular day knowing that this is not the place for us to be."

With that said, the brothers met with their brother Frank, who was chief executive of the black gospel division at Malaco Records, the same week. They played the album for Malaco owner Tommy Couch, Sr., and he loved the music. "The deal was done and soon as that record was in the market, it shot straight to the top of the charts," Doug says. The album *Blessed* was such a staggering hit that it rotated the No. 1 and No. 2 slot on the gospel album sales chart with Walter Hawkins's *Love Alive III* LP the entire summer of 1985. The project remained on the sales chart for a total of 89 weeks. "It's still probably the biggest record we've ever had," Doug says. "The people at Word Records were probably scratching their heads like, 'What happened?'"

Over the next five years, the group enjoyed another series of smash hits such as "Sweep Around Your Own Front Door" and "If It Wasn't for the Lord." It was a dream of Pop Williams's for his sons to one day have their own label. "He always said that you should try to own your own because that way you have more control over what happens with your career," Doug says. When their contract with Malaco was up, several labels courted the group. "There were some real lucrative offers on the table," he says. Sparrow Records even upped the ante when the group passed on their offer. "But when we saw that interest, we were unanimous that it was time to start our own label," Doug says as he thinks back on that period. "We didn't even think back or have second thoughts about turning down the money that they were offering us. It was time to move. God had given us the vision and it was time to move forward."

In April 1991, the group launched their record label, Blackberry Records, with distribution through Malaco Records. "It hasn't been easy because it does take a lot of commitment and diligence," Doug says. "You've got to be willing to work those extra hours. They say that most artists are lazy people. They don't like to get up early in the morning and stay late at night to do what they have to do to make things work. That was the one thing we were committed to do once we started the label. We were willing to do whatever it took to make it float and be successful. So if that meant getting up at six A.M. and working until one or two in the morning, that's what we had to do and that's what we did. The early years were rough because it takes a lot of money to run a record company and do it right. At that time, we didn't have the kind of cash flow coming through to make it work the way it needed to work." The company hasn't only been an outlet for the Williams Brothers' projects. Blackberry has released albums on Rev. Clay Evans, the Canton Spirituals, and the Texas Boyz, among others. As for the Williams Brothers, Doug and Melvin have both done separate solo CDs and a duet CD. Leonard no longer sings with the group on a regular basis, but "Cousin" Henry has hung in with the brothers for over 40 years now. Among their recent hits are "Cooling Water," (featuring Lee Williams) "I'm Too Close," (featuring Stevie Wonder) and "I'm Still Here." At times, the solo projects had fans fearing the group was breaking up, but that was never the case. "We don't do anything without all of us being in agreement," Doug says. "We support each other wholeheartedly. The three of us will never leave each other as a group."

RECOMMENDED RECORDING: *The Greatest Hits: Vol. 1* (Blackberry, 1991) features the group's best remembered songs, including "I'm Just a Nobody" and "Mama Prayed for Me."

Williams Sisters

THE WILLIAMS SISTERS enjoyed one of the biggest gospel hits of 1996 when the traditional-styled, toe-tapper "Jesus Will Pick You Up" exploded over gospel airwaves across the country. Then there was seven years of silence until the siblings resurfaced on EMI Records in 2004. Their father, James Williams, was an itinerant evangelist, traveling up and down the East Coast spreading the Good News. His wife, Terry, and their six children (Renee, Janice, Vanessa, Patricia, Juliette on drums, and James, Jr., on bass guitar) formed a group calling itself the Crusaders for Christ to accompany James, Sr., during his religious crusades. They were born in Philadelphia, but spent much of their early childhood in South Carolina until the family relocated to the city of brotherly love in 1978. Once back home, the group changed their name to the Williams Sisters and continued to sing in the tri-state area of Delaware, Pennsylvania, and New Jersey. They recorded their first CD, *Live on the East Coast: Let Every Ear Hear*, for the local First Lite Records in 1996. The snappy song "Jesus Will Pick You Up" became a massive gospel radio hit. Unfortunately, without a big label behind the project, the distribution was uneven and the marketing was virtually nonexistent. Therefore, in spite of the radio hit, there was little consumer identification of the group with the song. People knew the song, but not its creators. Then, for several years, the group was in and out of court, seeking to break an unfavorable management agreement.

Once the court battle was over and settled, the sisters picked up where they left off and continued to wow audiences with their dynamic stage presence. At a performance in Philadelphia where they opened for the Mighty Clouds of Joy, Messiah Records' owner Tony Beck was in the audience. Based on their performance that night, he signed them to his record label where they recorded a couple of live albums. However, his small label was unable to take the projects as far as the group's talent would stretch. In 2001, Beck planned to release an album the sisters recorded live in Switzerland, but he became ill and it was shelved until his health improved. Finally, he released it as *Alive and Kickin'* in 2003, but it was going nowhere with his limited resources. At that point, EMI Records' vice president, Larry Blackwell, contacted Messiah about reissuing the project via EMI. Blackwell had been a fan of the group since their "Jesus Will Pick You Up" days and was thrilled to finally bring the sisters to a national audience. The CD was repackaged as *Power in the House* during the summer of 2004.

Wilmington Chester Mass Choir

IN THE EARLY 1990s, the choir sound was back in vogue and the Wilmington Chester Mass Choir became popular thanks to a series of contemporary gospel songs with strong catchphrases or hooks. Among their best-known songs are "Take It Away," "He's Preparing Me," and "Ride On, King Jesus." The Grammy-nominated group is perhaps best known for backing Patti LaBelle on her Top 5 R&B hit "When You've Been Blessed (Feels Like Heaven)" in 1992. The Pennsylvania-based choir was formed by the late Rev. Ernest Davis in 1978. Aside from making great music in the early '90s, the choir was also known for their readiness to sing at community fundraisers and AIDS benefits. Various members of the choir had been touched by the disease. "I'm looking at the senior citizens," the choir's Tracy Shy told the *Wilmington News Journal* in October 1994. "They are living to be 100, and my peers are falling like flies."

Bryan Wilson

IT'S BEEN SAID that the most soulful music is born from pain. Whether it's heartbreak or hard knocks, nothing seems to beat a kick in the pants for bringing out the best in a vocalist. Singer Bryan Wilson knows this firsthand. Though only in his twenties, he's already lived a lifetime of pain through a broken family and abuse in the music industry. Against this backdrop, it's understandable that when he stood onstage at the age of 12 and belted out one of the most soulful renditions ever of "His Eye Is on the Sparrow" with the Mississippi Children's Choir, the gospel world fell in love with him instantly. Wilson was not just singing a song. He was singing from experience, because like the song says, "His eye is on the sparrow and I know he watches me." Surely, God had been watching over him too.

The singer's story begins in Danville, Illinois, where he was born on November 3, 1981. His mother, Sheila

Bryan Wilson / photo by Robert Shanklin

(who sang with the R&B group WQBC of "We're Thumpin'" fame), and her family sang in a family gospel group called the Davis Singers. Wilson was only about six when he first began singing with them. "My grandfather was the major influence in my life up to that time," Wilson says of his early years. "He was the one who encouraged me to keep singing. He told me to keep on singing and to carry on the family tradition. My grandfather was the leader of the group. The first time I ever sang a solo was at my grandfather's funeral. It was kind of ironic that it was he who started me singing, and that my solo happened to be at his funeral." Aside from his family, Wilson grew up loving the sacred sounds of James Moore, Commissioned, and the Clark Sisters.

Music served as a positive outlet for Wilson. He didn't officially meet his biological father until he was ten. "Before then, he came around every few months or so to speak to my mother, but no one ever said, 'That's your father,'" he recalls. His father was a user, drinker, and womanizer so there was little time for mentoring his son. Wilson's mother worked hard to keep her three sons together and kept them grounded in church life. Growing up in a tough neighborhood, Wilson developed a tough skin and was surrounded by temptations, but he held on to his faith and kept on singing just for fun.

"I used to sing to the grass," Wilson laughs. "I'd be out in the yard playing and pretending that each blade of grass was a member of my audience." His next door neighbor Mrs. Parker often overheard him singing and thought that he was good. She liked his singing so much that she held on to a tape of Wilson singing LaShun Pace's "I Know I've Been Changed" and "His Eye Is on the Sparrow" at a church service. Her daughter, who is married to the nephew of Malaco Records executive director Jerry Mannery, brought Wilson's name up when plans were in action for the Mississippi Children's Choir album. Mrs. Parker sent Wilson's tape down, and everyone at Malaco agreed that Wilson should sing on the project. Recorded live at Callaway High School Auditorium in Jackson, Mississippi, Wilson didn't know what he was going to sing when he showed up for rehearsal. "When they flew me down there, they said just sing a song, and 'His Eye Is on the Sparrow' was one of the

songs that my grandfather had taught me. I began to sing and when I was singing it, the pianist Jerry Smith was saying do this, do that. I am a quick learner, so I just did it. I think that night, he began to structure the song the way he thought that it should go, and it was just like that."

The response was immediate. As Wilson reached and grabbed notes that only a Mariah Carey could snatch, the audience was in hysterics watching this child sing like an adult. Bryan's track became the song that received the most gospel radio airplay and essentially sold the Mississippi Children's Choir album, *A New Creation*. The album reached No. 39 on *Billboard*'s gospel chart and has since sold over 70,000 units. Soon gospel announcers had nicknamed Wilson "Boy Sparrow" because of the beautiful high notes he sang and because the song that brought him fame and acclaim was "His Eye Is on the Sparrow." Wilson's overnight success led Malaco Records to offer him his own recording deal. Among the heavy-hitter producers crafting Wilson's debut were gospel legend Walter Hawkins and John P. Kee. Sticking with a dramatic hymn as the radio single, "Blessed Assurance," took the CD *Bryan's Songs* to No. 21 on *Billboard*'s gospel chart. Instead of capitalizing off the CD's success, Malaco let the momentum for Bryan wane. In the meantime, he suffered through puberty and a voice change that depressed him.

"I can remember times when my voice was changing, I would go places to sing and they would want me to sing 'His Eye Is on the Sparrow,' but I just could not hit the notes," Wilson recalls. "A lot of the times crowds were very displeased because they wanted to hear the little boy with the high voice. I went through a period almost where I couldn't sing, and it was depressing, because I felt like, now God, you blessed me with this voice and you blessed me to do all these things, but now I feel like he was just taking it away from me. Then there came a time when I didn't even want to sing. I was just real hurt, I felt like my career was just coming to an end—like the Michael Jackson story, with the voice change kind of thing. That's the way I felt really. I began to think about Tevin Campbell, who people had always compared me to—I wondered if he went through the same thing…. Eventually, I had my tonsils removed, and now my range is finally going back up and I am just so happy. My voice had changed naturally, and I had to train myself how to sing. Now that I have had my tonsils out, I am in a stage of retraining my voice, learning how to sing all over again."

Wilson showcased his new vocal style on the 1999 CD *Growing Up*, which featured his foray into more urban, youth-flavored contemporary gospel music. It was a good, solid album, but Malaco Records did not promote it aggressively enough. The three-year gap between releases necessitated a reintroduction to gospel radio that Wilson did not get. Unbothered, he moved to Orangeburg, South Carolina, to stay with his surrogate father, Shane Wall, and to attend Claflin University as a theology and music major. He graduated in May 2004. After earning a scholarship to Princeton University, Wilson enrolled in their graduate school with his sights set on earning both Masters and Doctoral degrees.

Nancy Wilson

AMERICA'S PREMIER female jazz vocalist and one of the last vestiges of the golden age of the field, Nancy Wilson is noted for her collaborations with Cannonball Adderly, Ramsey Lewis, and George Shearing. In 1964, Wilson had four LPs on the charts, her record sales at Capitol Records were second only to the Beatles, and she won her only Grammy award to date. That same year *Time* magazine called Wilson the "Greatest Pre-

tender" to Ella Fitzgerald's position as the First Lady of Jazz. Though no one is Ella, no one is Nancy Wilson either. She sings ballads and blues, pop, and even gospel. She sings them all low, high, hot, cool, sweet, and blue. As Duke Ellington might have put it, Wilson is indisputably a "Sophisticated Lady."

Born February 20, 1937, in Chillicothe, Ohio, Wilson's father was a factory worker who later moved his family to Columbus. Wilson sang in the Methodist church as a child and quickly became known as a child prodigy. Her biggest musical influence was the androgynous singer Little Jimmy Scott whose vocal dynamics are unparalleled in the field of jazz. She developed her own style as early as the age of 12 and used that style to win a talent contest at the age of 15. The prize was her own local television show, *Skyline Melodies*. Her show ran almost four years and continued as she entered Central State College in Wilberforce, Ohio. After a year of matriculating, Wilson left college and joined saxophonist Rusty Bryant's Carolyn Club Band with whom she made her first record. However, because she was so known in Columbus, she sat in with sax legend Cannonball Adderly during a date in the city. His manager, John Levy, was there and saw a star in the making. Within six months, he'd placed her with Capitol Records where she recorded her first LP, *Like in Love*, in 1959.

Wilson, through Adderly's introduction, was meeting all the right people and by the early 1960s was commanding $5,000 a night to perform. Her chic show took her to upscale venues such as the Waldorf Astoria in Manhattan, Mr. Kelly's in Chicago, and the Coconut Grove in Hollywood. Although she was branded a jazz singer, Wilson sang everything from show tunes to the most urban of R&B songs such as Stevie Wonder's "Uptight (Everything Is Alright)." Her records sold far in excess of what most jazz artists sold because she appealed across the board to pop and R&B audiences. Songs such as her live version of "Guess Who I Saw Today," "Face It, Girl, It's Over," and "You Don't Know How Glad I Am" were all major radio hits, and her LPs routinely reached the Top Ten pop and R&B charts.

By the early '70s, Wilson's glamorous life offstage was as written about as her music. After her divorce from drummer Kenny Dennis in 1969, the tabloids romantically linked Wilson to Congressman John Conyers, actor

Robert Hooks, Gary, Indiana, mayor Richard Hatcher, and Venezuelan TV producer Julio César Cova Ruiz. But she surprised the press by marrying Rev. Wiley Burton in 1974. At the time, she also hosted her own weekly Los Angeles television show for which she won two Emmy awards. Wilson branched off into things other than performing. She managed a group called the Checkmates for a time, invested in a Wyoming cattle ranch, and restored antique cars. Over the years, Wilson has held a handful of acting roles. She portrayed a heroin addict in an episode of *Hawaii Five-O* and appeared in Fred Williamson's *The Big Score* feature film.

After leaving Capitol Records circa 1980, Wilson spent almost 20 years at Columbia Records, where she recorded more urban AC material than jazz material. It's also during that period that Wilson recorded a handful of deliciously elegant gospel songs. The first gospel outing was her stunning, smooth jazz tune "Puttin' My Trust" with its bluesy modulations. This dramatic tune can be found on her 1987 LP *Forbidden Lover*. The following year the LP *Nancy Now!* featured the somewhat mediocre "Power & the Glory," an uptempo gospel song without a strong hook. The overall album was not up to Wilson's usual high standards.

However, Wilson was back on her old game on 1989's *Lady with a Song* LP, which featured two spiritual songs. The first was the romantic "The Other Side of the Storm," a love ballad citing divine intervention for the triumph of love through rough times. The album closed with a rousing gospel song by young writer Lorrin "Smokey" Bates entitled, "Heaven's Hands." The all-star group backing Wilson was a who's who of R&B music, with Natalie Cole, Philip Bailey, the Emotions, Teena Marie, Freda Payne, and others conducted by Andrae Crouch. After a couple of albums with no gospel, 1994's *Love, Nancy* CD reached No. 6 on the contemporary jazz album chart. The album was driven by the radio success of the singles "Love Won't Let Me Wait" and "I Can't Make You Love Me." However, a high point of the project was the closing song, "Your Arms of Love," written by gospel artist BeBe Winans. Sung with just ace session man Jerry Peters at the piano and a boisterous background vocal group, Wilson turns the simple song into a beautiful plea for God's love. In recent years, Wilson has deeply curtailed her performance schedule and

only records sporadically. She has nurtured relationships with gospel artists such as Yolanda Adams, BeBe Winans, and Bobby Jones. Wilson has appeared on Jones's weekly BET gospel TV show several times.

Natalie Wilson

ONE OF CONTEMPORARY gospel's first female choir directors, Natalie Wilson was born September 23, 1975, in Newark, New Jersey. Her father, Bishop Nathaniel Simmons, pastored the St. Paul Church in the city. She was always active in music at the church, but was planning a cosmetology career when tragedy struck in 1992. Her brother, Glenn, who was the director of St. Paul's S.O.P. (Sounds of Praise) Chorale, died, and her father asked her to take over the choir. "I never dreamed of this," she once said. "I only did it to keep the choir going in the church until a real director was found. I didn't know how to direct. The only skill I knowingly brought to the job was how to teach three-part harmony. God filled in the blanks, which gave me confirmation that it was meant to be. From the first day, the anointing was there, as if my brother's mantle had just fallen on me. Everyone was amazed, no one more so than me! The Holy Spirit just gave it to me, and still is."

After the distributor for Wilson's 1998 debut custom CD abruptly closed shop and floundered, Wilson found a record deal with Gospo Centric Records. Her street urban sound was featured on the hit CD *Girl Director*, which reached No. 8 on the gospel sales chart in 2000. Gospel radio enthusiastically embraced the singles "Act Like You Know" and "Calvary." She followed up in 2003 with the *Good Life* CD, which peaked at No. 12 on the sales chart. Along with her brother's death, Wilson has since lost her mother and father. She has also survived a painful divorce, but still she keeps the faith. "I know the Lord has done far more than simply orchestrate my pain," she once said. "These trials have all been monumental events in my life. They've been the final tests before promotion from God. No matter where my life goes from here, I would hope that people would always be able to say that I had been encouraging and uplifting to everyone I met and encountered, and that they felt the genuineness and sincerity of my spirit and heart."

Winans

PERPHAPS THE MOST popular male gospel group of the 1990s, the Winans defined the art of contemporary gospel music for the 1980s decade. With songs such as "Bring Back the Days of Yea and Nay," "It's Time," "Ain't No Need to Worry," and "Tomorrow" among others, the group was the paradigm for contemporary gospel during the period. The Detroit-based group of brothers was comprised of Marvin and Carvin (born March 5, 1958), Michael (born June 5, 1959), and Ronald (born June 30, 1956). They grew up singing in their great-grandfather's Mack Avenue (COGIC) Church and later, the Shalom Temple. Their parents, David and Delores, knew they loved to sing and were supportive of their music as the Testimonial Singers (founded in 1975). They sponsored their local concert programs and "Just hoped and prayed that someone would show up," Delores Winans laughs. A friend introduced the group to a godfather of gospel, Andrae Crouch. Crouch was so moved by their music that he got them signed to Light Records and took them on the road to perform in his concerts in the early 1980s. Their debut LP *Introducing the Winans* appeared in 1981 and produced the radio hits "The Question Is" and "Restoration." The 1983 follow-up, *Long Time Comin' (Holdin' On)* found a hit in the title song. However, the 1984 release *Tomorrow* established the group as gospel superstars. The album reached No. 3 on the gospel charts, pushed there by Carvin's sweet tenor on the title song ballad. Other hit songs from the project included the uptempo "Uphold Me" and dramatic downtempo tune, "Bring Back the Days of Yea and Nea," which featured Marvin's urgent vocals.

With the aggressive management of Barry Hankerson (who later discovered both R. Kelly and Aaliyah), the Winans reached new and rare heights for gospel artists. It's a credit to Hankerson's tenacity that he negotiated a contract for the group with Quincy Jones's Qwest Records label, which had never had a gospel artist on its roster before the Winans. With the legendary producer's R&B/pop clout and Hankerson's push, the first three albums were all solid crossover smashes. The first, *Let My People Go*, was released in 1985 and became their first No. 1 gospel album. The title song reached No. 42 on the R&B singles chart and "Choose Ye This Day," a scintillating urban soul duet with Vanessa Bell Armstrong, was a massive gospel hit. The hits kept coming as their 1987 LP *Decisions* featured the Top 20 "Ain't No Need to Worry" mellow tune with Anita Baker (and extra vocals by Melvin and Doug Williams). Other hits included "Millions" and "Love Has No Color" with Michael McDonald. It was No. 1 on the gospel chart and also hit the pop and R&B sales chart. One distraction was that the first lot of albums was recalled from retail stores after Elton John objected to the group's changing the words to his song, "Don't Let the Sun Go Down on Me." The song was dropped from subsequent shipments and the consumers with the first-run LP have a collector's item.

In 1989, the group recorded a stellar album, *Live at Carnegie Hall*, which was also a bestseller. That fan-favorite is owned by Hankerson and the Winans's Selah record label and has never been reissued. In 1990, the group recorded what remains their bestselling album ever, the gold-selling *Return*. The album made the Hot 100 pop album chart, No. 12 on the R&B album chart, No. 4 on the CCM chart, and No. 1 on the gospel album chart. The album featured production by R. Kelly and Teddy "Newjack Swing" Riley and was the group's most successful attempt at bridging gospel and urban music. The funky track "It's Time" reached No. 5 on the R&B singles chart and even graced the *Billboard* dance chart before spending 8 weeks at No. 1 on the CCM radio chart. The ballad "A Friend" reached No. 11 on the R&B chart. Two more songs, "Don't Leave Me" and "When You Cry" also hit the R&B Top 40 singles chart. The track "Every Day the Same" also spent two weeks at No. 1 on the CCM singles chart. During that period, the group was ubiquitous. They starred in their own top-rated *The Real Meaning of Christmas* TV special and they had a cross-country Winans family tour in 1992. The tour featured BeBe & CeCe Winans, Angie & Debbie Winans, Mom and Pop Winans, and Vickie Winans. The tour was a sold-out, gospel-soul extravaganza. They reprised the tour a decade later and videotaped it for home video, but it has yet to be released.

In the 1990s the Winans begin to gradually fade away from the musical scene. Before Qwest closed, the Winans enjoyed other radio hits such as "Payday" and "Heart and Soul." Marvin Winans devoted more time to his flourishing church. He is the pastor at Detroit's Perfecting Church and has been in great demand as an evangelist. In addition, Marvin has made vocal cameos on numerous CDs by Helen Baylor, Tim Bowman, and even CeCe Winans with whom he re-recorded "Bring Back the Days of Yea and Nay" in 2001. Michael and Carvin have both done touring plays. Carvin was head of the black music department at Word Records in the late 1990s and managed Winans Phase 2 for a while. Michael and his wife Regina have recorded music for MCG Records and perform as a couple.

As for Ronald, he experienced heart failure in 1997. His heart stopped beating on the operating table and his family says that he was miraculously healed. "I had no idea any of that happened, I was feeling like I was having a cold," he said. "I had no idea of the gravity of it. The family had to tell me what happened because I was out of it." Even at the height of the Winans fame, Ronald had a side project. He had always dreamed of recording a choir album. So, in 1989, he released his first Family & Friends Choir album, which reached No. 22 on the gospel album sales chart and featured Debbie Winans and Donnie McClurkin among others. The next three projects *Family & Friends II* (1990), *Family & Friends III* (1992), and *Family & Friends IV* (1996) all reached the Top Ten on *Billboard*'s gospel sales chart.

In May 2004, Ronald recorded the fifth installment of *Family & Friends* at Detroit's Greater Grace Temple. It features soul-stirring performances by Ruben Studdard, Gladys Knight, Rance Allen, Justin Campbell, and Marvin and BeBe Winans. "A whole bunch of people," he said. "I wanted to keep it fresh. Each one of the albums has its own personality and revolved around different things happening in our lives at the time. This one celebrates my healing. That's why we call it *Family & Friends: A Celebration*." Ronald was also writing a book about his recovery and other important points in his life when he suffered a relapse and died of heart complications on June 17, 2005, in Detroit's Harper Hospital. Meanwhile, fans wait and hope that one day the Winans will reunite and give them at least one new album.

RECOMMENDED RECORDING: For the Winans's music, check out *The Very Best of the Winans* (Rhino, 2002),

which features their greatest hits from both their Light and Qwest recordings. For Ronald Winans's material, *The Best of Ron Winans Family & Friends* (EMI, 2003) features guest shots by Karen Clark-Sheard, CeCe Winans, and Donnie McClurkin, among others.

Angie Winans

BEST KNOWN AS half of the Angie & Debbie urban gospel duo, Angie Winans has now carved out a solo career as a smooth jazz gospel singer. She was born Angelique Winans on March 4, 1968. Growing up, she studied orchestral etudes and gospel piano. As she grew older, Angie fell in love with the music of jazz pianists such as Joe Sample, David Foster, and David Benoit. Her favorite jazz vocalist is Michael Franks. "I love Michael Franks's music so much! He's been such an influence on me that I would die if he ever did a riff," Angie laughs of the smooth, laid-back singer. She sang at home and at church as a child. Her older brothers' group, the Winans, burst on the gospel scene in the early '80s with a string of gospel and crossover hits such as "Tomorrow" and "Ain't No Need to Worry." Their siblings, BeBe and CeCe, followed with several soul-gospel million-sellers such as "I'll Take You There" and "Addictive Love" at the end of the decade.

At 15, she joined her sister Debbie and friend Sherry Reynolds Kibble for a ten-year stretch as background vocalists for BeBe & CeCe. It was while on the road with BeBe & CeCe that Angie met her future husband, Cedric Caldwell, the renowned record producer, who was the duo's keyboard player at the time. However, after BeBe & CeCe stopped touring in 1993 and began to pursue solo projects, Angie & Debbie began to sing together as a duo and released their first eponymous album on Capitol Records in the summer of 1993. The critically acclaimed album received major write-ups in *USA Today*, *Entertainment Weekly*, and other publications. The album was nominated for Grammy and Soul Train Music awards and was supported with an opening slot on Whitney Houston's national tour that year. The album sold over 100,000 copies. Eventually, Capitol Records closed their black music division, and Angie & Debbie pursued other opportunities.

Left to right: Debbie Winans, Toni Braxton, Monie Love, Angie Winans, and CeCe Winans, 1993 / Capitol Records photo

Angie concentrated on writing and producing other artists. She co-wrote and produced the urban-styled "Never Alone" for *Star Search* winner Kelli Williams's debut album. She composed the overture, sang, and arranged most of the background vocals on CeCe Winans's gold album, *Alone In His Presence*. She also wrote "I Love You" for BeBe & CeCe's hit Christmas album and recently wrote a song for pop star Brandy.

Together, Angie & Debbie have done background vocals and vocal arrangements on the albums of various members of their family. They also backed Donnie McClurkin on his smash hit, "Speak to My Heart." The duo wrote four songs for football star Reggie White's autobiographical film *Reggie's Prayer*. They also joined their sister CeCe for the trio record "Always Sisters" which rose to No. 24 on the CCM charts in 1996. Angie & Debbie reteamed for the smash hit CD *Bold* in 1997. In the future, Angie plans to write more instrumental music and compose film scores. Her smooth jazz-styled solo debut CD *Melodies of My Heart* debuted in spring 2001 and was nominated for a Grammy award. She sings and plays the keyboards on the Top 40–styled CD that also features guest appearances by saxman Kirk Whalum and Take 6.

BeBe Winans

IN ANOTHER WORLD or perhaps another life, BeBe Winans would have been a soulful crooner in the style of a Luther Vandross or perhaps even a Lionel Richie. However, because he grew up in a gospel household, he seems to have been caught between upholding the family honor of only singing gospel and his own ambitions to become a pop superstar. His smooth vocal style and soothing soul rhythms are a perfect match for Quiet Storm R&B radio formats. That intimate sound BeBe created took him (with his sister CeCe) to the top of the R&B and gospel charts with crossover songs such as "I.O.U. Me," "Lost Without You," and "Addictive Love." He continued that style as a solo artist with further hits such as "In Harm's Way" and the trio recording of "Coming Back Home" with Brian McKnight and Joe.

The seventh of ten children, BeBe was born Benjamin Winans on September 17, 1962, in Detroit. His major musical influences were Andrae Crouch, Danniebelle Hall, Stevie Wonder, and the Hawkins Family. After graduating from Mumford High School, BeBe and CeCe were singing in church one day circa 1983 when a family friend and fellow singer, Howard McCrary, suggested they audition for the PTL Singers at Jim and Tammy Faye Bakker's *PTL* religious television broadcast in Charlotte, North Carolina. They both auditioned but only CeCe passed the test. "I went along with her because dad didn't want her to go alone," BeBe once said. "After three days there, they asked me to join the cast of regulars." It was a quick learning experience. They were in awe of the *PTL* surroundings and the opportunity to meet the gospel artists they admired and looked up to, such as Rosey Grier and Candi Staton. Their first month away from home, they ran up a $2,000 phone bill.

BeBe and CeCe were not a duo per se, but they were the only two black members of the PTL Singers, so they stood out from the other singers. One day Tammy Faye Bakker was in a record store and heard Joe Cocker and Jennifer Warnes's love song "Up Where We Belong" and thought it would be a good song for BeBe and CeCe to record. After she presented the idea to them, BeBe met with Larnelle Harris and began to change the lyrics to fit the Christian perspective. Then BeBe and CeCe recorded it that same week. The subsequent LP, *Lord, Lift Us Up*, sold over a million copies to the *PTL* donors. Along with the *PTL* work, BeBe also did background vocals on Keith Green's *Jesus Commands Us to Go* LP for Sparrow Records.

After Sparrow Records and Capitol Records created a unique partnership where they would jointly promote BeBe & CeCe, the duo was on their way. Sparrow would promote them in the Christian market and Capitol would promote them in the urban/mainstream market. They were a hit out of the box with their self-titled 1987 debut LP. The first single "I.O.U. Me" reached the Hot 100 R&B singles chart. The album produced further hit singles "Change Your Nature" and "Love Said Not So" that made the CCM singles chart. The mainstream press made much ado about the duo, who were bringing gospel into the new age with slick R&B grooves and inspirational messages. Later in 1987, BeBe co-starred with Chip Fields, Glynn Turman, and Vanessa Bell Armstrong in the touring musical *Don't Get God Started*, composed by his brother Marvin.

The next BeBe & CeCe project would prove that their success was no fluke. The *Heaven* LP produced three Top 40 R&B hits with the title song, "Celebrate New Life," and "Lost Without You," which reached all the way to No. 8 on the R&B singles chart. The album also featured an uptempo collaboration with Whitney Houston on "Hold Up the Light." However, the next project would really put the group on top. The platinum-selling *Different Lifestyles* CD in 1991 featured two No. 1 R&B singles with "Addictive Love" and a remake of the Staple Singers' "I'll Take You There" featuring a cameo by Mavis Staples. Other songs from the project that hit the R&B singles chart included "It's O.K.," "Depend on You," and "The Blood" with MC Hammer.

As the duo's urban profile increased, they toured as the opening act with Al Green one year and then toured as the headliner with the Sounds of Blackness. BeBe & CeCe recorded one more CD, *Relationships*, before they decided to take a hiatus in late 1994. At that point, CeCe launched a solo career with 1995's *Alone in His Presence* CD. In 1997, BeBe Winans opened his solo career with the *BeBe Winans* CD, pushed by the mellow Top 20 R&B single "In Harm's Way" and the club hit "Thank You." He's recorded subsequent music on Motown and Hidden Beach Records, including the dragging ballad "I'm Coming Home" with Brian McKnight and Joe. With all of Motown's muscle, the best the song could do was No. 50 on the R&B singles chart. "Do You Love Him?" (a sluggish gospel remake of the Chi-Lites R&B classic "Have You Seen Her?") didn't chart on the R&B singles chart at all, though it made some strides on the urban adult contemporary singles chart.

BeBe hasn't restricted himself to gospel. He's performed on pop albums by Brandy, Gladys Knight, Anastacia, Dave Koz, Kelly Price, and Gerald Albright. He's written songs for Nancy Wilson, Stephanie Mills, and Bobby Brown. He's also produced tracks on Trey Lorenz, Chanté Moore, and the flipside to Whitney Houston's "I Will Always Love You" single, which sold four million copies in 1993. Through his erstwhile Benjammin' production company he produced Angie & Debbie's debut CD in 1992, the Clark Sisters' 1994 *Miracle* CD, and Eternal's 1994 *Always & Forever* CD. Angie & Debbie and Eternal's projects were run through Capitol/EMI Records. However, by the time the Clark Sisters' project was ready, Capitol had effectively shut down its black music division. BeBe took the project to Sparrow Records instead. The latest news is that BeBe is planning to launch his own record label with distribution via

BeBe & CeCe Winans / *courtesy of Capital Entertainment archives.* July 1987 Totally Gospel *magazine*

Hidden Beach which has had success with R&B starlet Jill Scott.

RECOMMENDED RECORDING: *BeBe Winans* (Atlantic, 1997) is by far Winans's best solo project. An album with Luther Vandross, Deborah Cox, and Fonzi Thornton singing backup, Billy Preston playing organ, Paul Jackson, Jr., on guitar, and Louie Vega and Arif Mardin producing can't be that bad. In fact, it's great late-night listening music with subtle religious references. Aside from the smooth title song, standout cuts include the ballad "Did You Know" with baby sister Debra Winans and the uptempo pop track "I Wanna Be the Only One" with the female group Eternal.

CeCe Winans

NO WOMAN OTHER than Mahalia Jackson has accomplished as much as CeCe Winans has in gospel music in recent years. In fact, she's often been cited as the Mahalia of her generation. Over her two decades in the music business, Winans has stepped out from the long shadow of BeBe & Cece, who dominated both gospel and R&B radio playlists in the 1987–92 period with a string of Top Ten smashes such as "Addictive Love," "Celebrate New Life," and "I'll Take You There." As a soloist, Winans has solidified her standing with commercial endorsements, several gold records, and high-profile television appearances just as Mahalia did 50 years previously.

Born October 8, 1964, in Detroit, CeCe was the eighth of David and Delores Winans's ten children. She once told *People* magazine that "Our parents raised us with Christian values, and you don't always understand that as a kid—I didn't wear make-up until I was 18. And my first movie was *Tootsie* when I was good and grown. But it saved me from a whole lot of trouble." The family was rooted in the church and Winans sang her first church solo at the age of eight. However, she was selling chilidogs at Detroit's Coney Island while working toward her beautician's license when she decided to become a singer with Jim and Tammy Faye Bakker's PTL Ministries in Charlotte, North Carolina, in 1982. Her brother BeBe went along as her chaperon and they ended up becoming a duo there where they recorded their first million-seller *Lord, Lift Us Up* in 1984 for PTL Records. By 1987, they had won an unprecedented gospel recording contract with Sparrow Records that allowed Capitol Records to promote BeBe & CeCe's music in the urban market. The unique blend of R&B grooves with a spiritual foundation made BeBe & CeCe the most successful sibling duo of the '80s. They churned out a dozen R&B chart smashes, including "Addictive Love," "Lost Without You," "Heaven," "It's Okay," and "I'll Take You There."

In October 1995, Winans released her first solo album, *Alone in His Presence*, a praise and worship collection. The album spent more than a year in the Top 10 of *Billboard*'s gospel charts, won CeCe her first solo Grammy award, and achieved gold certification. In addition, CeCe made history when the album won her the Dove award as Female Vocalist of the Year. It was quite a feat considering that no African-American woman had ever won the award in the history of the Dove awards. In support of the album, CeCe launched her first solo concert tour, which won her critical praise. A *Los Angeles Times* reviewer wrote that "CeCe reveled in the spotlight…quickly developing an intimate rapport with the audience. It may as well have been Sunday at church…. Her soaring vocals were well suited to her inspirational message."

Winans's solo stature was further buttressed by numerous high-profile media appearances. She sang at President Clinton's inaugural prayer service and was the first gospel artist to perform on *The Rosie O'Donnell Show*. During this period, she also served as spokeswoman for Crest toothpaste and Bell South. She also tackled Broadway, starring in a sold-out run of *Born to Sing* with Shirley Caesar at Madison Square Garden in 1996. Winans joined longtime friend Whitney Houston to tape a special performance of "Bridge over Trouble Water" for a VH-1 Honors special. It was such a success that they reteamed to record "Count on Me," a duet from the multi-platinum *Waiting to Exhale* soundtrack. The song sold two million copies and hit the Top Ten on pop, R&B, and adult contemporary charts. In March 1998, Winans released her second solo album, *Everlasting Love*, an urban adult contemporary set that included the Top 50 R&B single "Well, Alright" and the apocalyptic "On that Day," produced by superstar rap-maven Lauryn Hill. Following this triumph, Winans cut her first solo Christmas album, *His Gift*. Over the next year, she hosted *CeCe's Place* on the Odyssey/Hallmark Channel; completed a sold-out, 80-city arena tour with Kirk Franklin; released her inspirational autobiography, *On a Positive Note*; and recorded a Hallmark Entertainment album of Christmas duets, *Listen! It's Christmas*, with Johnny Mathis that sold two million units.

Over the summer of 1999, Winans formed her own record label, CW Wellspring, in Nashville. Their first effort was the gold-selling *Alabaster Box* praise and worship CD. CeCe shared the stage with Pope John Paul II at the Vatican's 15th annual World Youth Day, which drew 1.5 million youth from around the world to Rome. The next CD, simply entitled *CeCe Winans* and released in 2001, was an album that sought to em-

brace listeners of popular music. "I just knew this album would be totally different than *Alabaster Box*," Winans said at the time. "With this album, we wanted to reach the world. I want people to feel encouragement and passion from this record." The first single "More Than What I Wanted" reached the Top 10 of the urban adult contemporary charts.

In recent years, Winans has become interested in acting. She's landed meaty parts in Fox Television's *Living Single* and PAX's *Doc*, among others. She later changed the name of her record label to PureSprings Gospel and signed acts such as Vicki Yohe, the Born Again Church Choir, and her mother, Delores Winans. Under the guidance of label President Demetrus Stewart and general manager Stacy Merida, all three projects charted and the Yohe project was one of the bestselling gospel albums of 2004. In terms of Winans's recordings, she signed a unique deal for Sony Music to distribute her personal PureSprings Gospel recordings. The first, September 2003's *Throne Room*, a 16-track praise and worship album, debuted at No. 1 on the gospel chart and racked up the best first-week sales of Winans's career: 27,000 copies. Within a year, the album was certified gold, also Winans's fastest RIAA gold certification. "At first I shied away from the limelight, I didn't want to be out front," CeCe once said in looking back at her career. "Every time I sang, I had to be pushed to do it, and every year I cried when the time came for me to sing 'Fill My

Left to right: Soledad O'Brien, CeCe Winans, and David Bloom, Today Show *at Rockefeller Plaza, August 2000 / photo by Bil Carpenter*

Cup, Lord.' Now I'm glad family and friends pushed me. I'm glad they pushed me into my purpose…. Every year 'Fill My Cup, Lord' became more and more real to me until slowly, gradually, God healed me of my fears. He used music to do it."

RECOMMENDED RECORDING: For a taste of Winans in her urban pop groove, check out the astonishing *Everlasting Love* CD (Pioneer, 1998). It features the definitive fusions of R&B and gospel on songs such as the Caribbean-styled "On That Day," the hypnotic Quiet Storm vibe of "Slippin'," and Winans's self-penned power ballad, "Just Come." For Winans's worship music, one can't go wrong with *Throne Room* (PureSprings/Sony, 2003), featuring standout tracks such as "Hallelujah Praise," "Thirst for You," and "Mercy Said No." Her 2005 *Purified* CD featured the urban radio smash "Pray" that was produced by her nephew, Mario Winans.

Daniel Winans

CONSIDERED THE country member of the Winans dynasty, Daniel actually isn't a country artist. He's eclectic and has taken more musical chances than the rest of the family to create his own unique body of work. He was born July 22, 1961, in Detroit. In spite of growing up in a household of faith, Winans didn't become saved himself until his high school years. After school, he went to work at a soft drink factory before he made some demos and sent them around to recording labels. "I was called the country singer of the family," Winans told GospelCity.com in 2002. "They thought I sounded like a white country singer, but that's okay; one of my best friends is now Vince Gill."

Winans's first recordings were issued through Myrrh Records in the late 1980s. In a time when most major labels were cutting back on 45-rpm single manufacturing and most religious labels didn't make any singles, Myrrh felt compelled to release two singles, "Runnin' with the Vision" (featuring Pop Winans) and "Tonight" from his debut LP *Daniel Winans and the Second Half* in 1987. The music was promoted at both CCM and black gospel radio. Neither of those singles made much radio impact and the album never charted,

though it was a very good album with no traces of Winans's country bent. In fact, it was very much a pop album with a soulful edge. On songs such as "Oh, I Know" and "When I Think of You," Winans came off closer in style to adult contemporary radio staples Stephen Bishop or Christopher Cross rather than a member of the Winans clan. There was even a '50s-styled doo wop song, "The American Way," that showcased a Sam Cooke–like yodel.

The second LP, *Let Brotherly Love Continue*, barely reached the CCM album sales chart in 1989 but did win a Grammy nomination. Winans then moved to Integrity/Glorious Records where he finally hit the black gospel sales chart with the CD *Not in My House*, which peaked at No. 33 in 1995. The album featured cameos by Andrae Crouch and Mark Kibble from Take 6. Along with original songs, it included Winans's unique arrangements of "Drift Away" and "Love Lifted Me." The album received a Grammy nomination, but was beat out by his sister CeCe's *Alone in His Presence* album that year. Although Winans has recorded other albums in the ensuing years, he's recently appeared in gospel music plays.

Debbie Winans

BEST KNOWN FOR her work with Angie & Debbie, the deep-voiced singer is now a solo artist with a children's ministry. Debbie Winans was born September 3, 1972, in Detroit. She started singing at the age of 12 when her siblings BeBe and CeCe were launching their music ministry and needed background vocalists (Debbie, her sister Angie, and their friend Sherry Reynolds Kibble formed the backup trio). Debbie was on the road so often that finishing at Motor City's Mumford High School was a chore. This was complicated by the fact that at the age of 16 Debbie joined the touring production of the gospel musical *Don't Get God Started*, which starred the Winans, Vanessa Bell Armstrong, and Chip Fields. She began as an orchestra pit singer, but eventually graduated to a featured role. She was with the show for a year and took a tutor while the musical was on Broadway.

"At first I was surprised my mother let me go," Debbie recalls. "I said, 'But I'm only 16!' But Mama said,

'If you don't know Jesus by now, you ain't gonna know him.' She told my brothers to keep me in line and watch over me." Her brother Ronald wanted Debbie to attend Manhattan's prestigious High School of the Performing Arts, but she wasn't interested. After the play closed, Debbie remained in the city to finish her tutoring. She stayed in Trenton, New Jersey, with friends of the family and drew closer to God. "I was all alone. I was so worried about becoming a huge sinner that the first thing I did was go to a Bible bookstore and bought a big Dake's Bible that broke it all down in ghetto terms," she laughs. "My mom wasn't there and my brothers were never around, so I was afraid that without their supervision I was going to be drinking and getting into all kinds of trouble. But that's when I really began to develop a strong spiritual life."

Debbie later rejoined BeBe & CeCe on the road. Surprisingly, a vocal career was never on Debbie's mind. She studied cosmetology at the Michigan Barber School and has a license to style hair. However, as BeBe & CeCe's backup group, she and her sister Angie became as much of an attraction as BeBe & CeCe. BeBe pushed Angie & Debbie to form a duo and family friend Whitney Houston provided background vocals on their first single, "Light of Love." Later, Whitney managed them and had them open for her on her *Bodyguard* concert tour. After the tour, Capitol Records' black music division had fizzled and the duo went back to private life. Debbie then returned to cosmetology intermittently doing hair for Capitol Records photo shoots while concentrating on her songwriting skills. She's written album cuts for Ben Tankard, Vickie Winans, BeBe & CeCe Winans, Ann McCrary, and the Clark Sisters. She also wrote Helen Baylor's hits "Worthy Is the Lamb" and "Stand My Child." Angie & Debbie made a huge comeback in 1997 with their smash CD *Bold*, which featured the hits "I Believe" and "Not Natural." The latter song was labeled an antigay song because of one line about comedienne Ellen DeGeneres outing herself on her ABC sitcom during that period. For a year, Angie & Debbie were the subject of national news stories, and it was their record that set the stage for football player Reggie White and others in the Christian right to take up homosexuality as a political platform. The album debuted at No. 3 on *Billboard*'s gospel charts and remained on the charts

a full year. Later Debbie joined big brother BeBe for two duets on his album *In Harm's Way* and has acted on stage in the touring musical *What's Love Got to Do with It?* Recently, Winans has devoted herself to a children's project entitled, *Debbie Winans Presents Fruity Fruits*.

Mom & Pop Winans

"DETROIT IS THE singingest city," Pop Winans says. "Smokey Robinson was around the corner, Eddie Kendricks was there too. The Four Tops. Marvin Gaye was over on Armor Drive. The Clark Sisters were over there on Cerranto [a Detroit street]. Vanessa Bell Armstrong went to McKenzie High School. Detroit was just blessed." However, no one family of singers seemed to be as blessed as the Winans family. It's no exaggeration to say the Winans are the most successful family of singers from the Motor City. First, the four brothers billed themselves as the Winans and were discovered by gospel legend Andrae Crouch. They became the best-selling gospel group of the 1980s with hits like "Tomorrow" and "My Time." BeBe & CeCe took things higher with "Addictive Love" and a remake of "I'll Take You There." Daniel Winans's group appeared on the scene as Marvin's wife Vickie made her name on "We Shall Behold Him." Lastly, came their babies Angie & Debbie Winans, who scored hits such as "Light of Love" and "Not Natural."

Born David Glenn on April 20, 1932, in Detroit, Pop's parents never married, and his father denied his paternity. Pop's mother, Laura Glenn, sang with the Zion Congregational COGIC, but her mother saw to it that Pop attended Mack Avenue COGIC, where his father's father, Isaiah Winans, was the pastor and recognized Pop as his grandson. When Pop was a grown man, his grandfather asked him to take the family name he was entitled to and at that point he became David Winans. Mom Winans was born Delores Ransom on September 22, 1934, in Detroit. Her dad was a baker and her mother was a homemaker. Though presiding over such a large dynasty, Mom and Pop come from small families themselves. Pop was an only child and Mom had a sister. They were both raised in the church. As a teenager, Mom had spent ten years as a singer/

pianist with the Lemon Gospel Chorus choir. Pop, who had previously sung in a quartet called the Nobelaires, joined the group in 1950. "My mother made me go," he says. "I couldn't stay at home on a Sunday by myself. She knew I would've gotten into something. She pushed me into the choir. Every Sunday I'd sit and look at my watch. Next thing I knew I made up my mind to join the choir. They had a lot of girls in the choir and a young man's going to be impressed." He was soon impressed by the tranquil nature of Delores Ransom, but it wasn't love at first sight. "He wasn't my type," Mom laughs. ("Oh, you don't have to tell it all," he cautions.) It took him three years to win her over. On November 21, 1953, they married and moved into his mother's home temporarily. By the time their first child arrived, they moved into a flat and he worked for Chrysler. Over the years, he also drove a taxi and was a barber. Mom was a typist. "I've always had a couple of jobs," Pop recalls, "but through it all it was nice. If I had it to do all over again, I would. We never had problems regarding food or anything. My grandmother was a great inspiration in our marriage.… She would always tell me the darkest part of day is just before dawn. Don't worry, things will change, and it has. She didn't live to see it, but it changed greatly." The ten Winans children were raised in the church and only listened to gospel music. Pop says, "I found out music has a spirit. When you get into the gospel as parents, kids can see we're their ex-

ample. I was the example to the boys and Mom was the girls' example. I'm not going to tell [the kids] something that I'm not going to do [myself]. Gospel was my life! That's what I believe in…. By me being the parent and the leader of the home, that's what you're going to believe in… The Bible says, be ye doers, not just sayers. They might have heard [secular music] outside, but they didn't bring it inside."

In 1968, Pop started a youth organization to keep kids off the street. He had 300 kids, ten Little League baseball teams, a track team, and arts and crafts. He was a surrogate father to the community but never failed to be hands-on with his own children. Pop also taught the kids a strong work ethic. BeBe & CeCe worked at the Coney Island chilidog stand. They helped him clean a local McDonald's and a Social Security office. It was through these jobs that Mom and Pop were able to raise enough money to finance the Winans's early showcases and their first album. After the entire family had become famous and sang on the Grammy awards circa 1989, a Sparrow Records executive asked Mom and Pop if they'd record an album for the label. Their CD debut, titled *Mom & Pop Winans*, was a mix of traditional-styled tunes and synthesized contemporary gospel tracks. It received a Grammy nomination and peaked at No. 31 on the gospel album chart in 1990. The album was distinguished by Mom's solo on the laid-back jazz number, "He's the One," which showed off her smooth and colorful vocal textures. Their final Sparrow Records project, *For the Rest of My Life*, featured a slightly edgier sound. It failed to chart but included two pulsating performances on the rocking rendition of "Go Tell It on the Mountain" and the sweaty aerobic workout, "Golden Crown."

Aside from touring with their children periodically and singing at church convocations, Mom & Pop were out of the public eye until June 1999 when they returned with solo CDs on Against the Flow Records (owned by Angie & Debbie and Victor and Cedric Caldwell). Angie personally wrote and produced material for Mom's album, *An Affair to Remember*, which was a hymn-like album backed by the London Symphony Orchestra. Pop's album, *Uncensored*, was the polar opposite. It was a funky, bluesy quartet collection that featured Winans Phase 2 on background vocals. His rough, raspy vocals

Left to right: Former National Council of Negro Women executive director Jane E. Smith, Delores "Mom" Winans, Yolanda Adams, and David "Pop" Winans at the Lincoln Memorial in Washington, DC, September 1999 / photo by Bil Carpenter

and boundless energy recalled the great Sam Cooke recordings of the 1950s. He wrote the beautiful jazz ballad "Is There Any Hope?" and the Delta blues "I'll Always Remember." However, it was the rambling rendition of Sister Rosetta Tharpe's "This Train" that received radio airplay and helped earn the project both Dove and Grammy award nominations. In 2004, Mom Winans returned to the studio to record the hymn CD *Hymns from My Heart* on daughter CeCe's PureSprings Gospel label.

Vickie Winans

VICKIE WINANS HAS had more lives than a cat. She's constantly reinvented herself to remain relevant and in demand as a gospel artist. After years of paying dues , she's now rightfully hailed as the Hardest Working Woman in gospel music. Sometimes, she'll do three concerts within the same day in three different cities while conducting cell phone media interviews between trips. Over the years, she has vacillated between the allure of contemporary gospel crossover success and the pull of traditional gospel fans. Just when she was categorized as a traditional church singer with songs such as "As Long as I Got King Jesus," "Been to the Water," and "We Shall Behold Him," she shocks everyone and releases the biggest single of her career, the funky urban jam "Shake Yourself Loose."

She was born Viviane Bowman, the seventh of ten children, on October 18, 1953, in Detroit. Her mother was a housewife and her father sometimes worked as many as four jobs as a laborer, contractor, carpenter, and mason. Winans's entire family was a musical one and deeply religious as well. She first sang in the bathtub with her sisters. One day they were harmonizing when Vickie's voice rose above the others. "One of my sisters jumped out of the tub and ran and told my mother, 'Mama, Vickie can sing for real, for real,'" she once told the *Detroit Free Press*. She was eight years old when she first began singing outside of the tub at the International Gospel Center. After high school, Vickie had an early marriage to Bishop Ronald Brown of Faith Tabernacle Deliverance Temple in Orangeburg, South Carolina, a union that produced a son, Mario "Skeeter" Winans (he later took on the last name of Vickie's second husband).

She grew up loving to hear Tramaine Hawkins sing, but never thought of herself as a lead vocalist. However, after marrying Marvin Winans in June 1978, his siblings encouraged her to join Winans Part II, a Detroit gospel group comprised of BeBe & CeCe Winans, Daniel Winans, and neighborhood friend Marvie Wright. After BeBe & CeCe left to join Jim and Tammy Faye Bakker's *PTL Club* in the early 1980s, the group broke up and Vickie reluctantly began to sing solo.

Vickie was a gifted fashion designer and made beautiful stage costumes, but Marvin felt she needed to be recording. He eventually secured a recording deal for her with Light Records where his group, the Winans, was the biggest money-maker the label had seen since Andrae Crouch in the 1970s. Winans and Marvin produced her debut LP *Be Encouraged*, an urban contemporary album in the style of the Winans signature sound, which reached No. 3 on the *Billboard* gospel chart in 1987. Several songs received gospel airplay, such as a remake of Gladys Knight & the Pips' "Midnight Train to Georgia" as "First Trumpet Sound," a Marvin-penned ballad "Sweeter Than the Honeycomb," and his upbeat "Give It One More Try." However, the smash hit of the album was the full-throttle cover of Dottie Rambo's "We Shall Behold Him." Vickie's young, pure voice soared and reached melismatic ecstasy on the rousing orchestral piece. It was such a show-stopping, tour de force performance that listeners' memories of it kept Winans's concert dates coming in even when she didn't have a new hit record. Good thing too. Winans's follow-up LP, *Total Victory*, was a total flop. It reached No. 7 on the gospel chart off the success of the prior LP, but it was not a long-term seller and produced no signature hits. By this point Light was in financial trouble, and the Winans had already left to join Quincy Jones's Qwest Records label, so Vickie walked too.

Circa 1990, Vickie signed with Geffen Records where she was going to create a gospel sound that would cross over to urban radio. However, through the company's acquisition by Universal Records, Winans's contract was shifted to sister label MCA Records. Suddenly, she was dealing with executives who never signed her, such as Ernie Singleton and Louis Silas, Jr. They subtly pushed Winans to tone down the Christian message in her music. "They don't tell you, but you get the vibe," she told *Gospel Today* in 1999. "I don't ever, ever, ever want to be in that predicament again. It's one thing when you just sing a song where you don't use the actual name of Jesus, but it's a whole 'nother thing when you *try* not to use the name. For me, the name of Jesus will never be distasteful in my mouth. He'll always be the answer."

In spite of the name of Jesus being largely absent from *The Lady*, it was a very good album. The measly nine-song project opened with the dance number "Don't Throw Your Life Away," which Winans wrote with her son Mario (who would eventually hook up with Puff Daddy's camp and make a career in R&B). A positive, inspirational dance song with a fine hook and nice vocals from Vickie, it failed to take off on R&B radio, the music video was not put into regular mainstream rotation, and gospel radio turned its collective nose up at the obvious attempt for a crossover hit. There were other fine message songs, such as *West Side Story*'s "Somewhere," which Barbra Streisand had popularized during that period (and she hit every note Streisand hit) and the bouncy "Hooked," which Vickie wrote with Marvin, Kenneth Hickson, and Clark Sisters sideman Antun Foster. The saddest thing about Winans's tenure with MCA is that Quiet Storm radio never had the opportunity to fall in love with soulful ballads such as "The

Vickie Winans / courtesy of Vickie Winans

Way You Love Me," a song about healing a broken marriage entitled "The Right Place," and an awesome spiritual duet between Vickie and Marvin called "Just When." On the tail end of "Just When," Vickie lets out a spine-tingling note one wishes would never stop.

When *The Lady* appeared, MCA sent Winans to perform on the Stellar awards TV broadcast with dancers. Many in the church community found it sacrilegious to mix gospel music with what they considered worldly dancing. There was a huge and immediate outcry. Some radio announcers stopped playing Winans's music and TV viewers sent the Stellar awards office letters criticizing the performance. "I was contemporary when I went down, but they slapped me so hard, when I got up I was traditional," she told *Gospel Today* years later. Days after the taping, Winans went into a recording booth and recorded a heartfelt apology to anyone who was offended and promised to never make such a spectacle of the gospel again. She then sent the tape out to 1,500 radio stations at her own expense. Some people forgave her and it would take a while before others did. It didn't matter to MCA executives, who found the tiff silly and unfounded. Since the gospel community didn't support the album and they could not break the record on R&B radio, MCA dropped Winans and it was three years before she'd find another recording home.

Former Word Records executive James Bullard, who always had a soft spot in his heart for underdog artists, lured Winans over to Atlanta-based Intersound Records, a classical recording label where he was launching a black gospel music division. He matched Winans with legendary R&B producer/songwriter Jerry Peters, who had become a Christian. They produced her label debut, *Vickie Winans*, which rose to No. 10 on the gospel chart in 1994. The album was more geared toward the church market, but it did not have a standout hit. Winans had nodes on her vocal chords by this point and didn't hit all the notes on a new version of "We Shall Behold Him." Intersound was ill-equipped to promote the dance track "Work It Out" (which she wrote with Antun Foster) on urban radio. Winans reportedly spent $50,000 of her own money to create a music video of the song to help push the sales of the album beyond the church market. BET and a few other gospel video outlets aired the video and it helped push sales among younger audiences. However, the older audiences still found the music too contemporary, yet her traditional numbers such as "Precious Lord" sparked little excitement among gospel programmers. Sadly, the best songs on the project were the urban/smooth jazz cuts "Only One" and "Mary, Did You Know?" which had the potential to make her a star in that field.

Not long after, the bottom dropped out of Winans's world. Her marriage was falling apart. She was so stressed that she had ulcers on her esophagus and she developed diabetes. She began to eat excessively to soothe the pain, and she and Marvin finally divorced circa 1995. "It was a very hurting experience," she later told the *Detroit Free Press.* "Both of us took it for granted that everything was okay. But, you know, after a while, it doesn't even matter whose fault it was. We are still friends and I still love him." During that depressing period in her life when Winans packed on weight and mourned the loss of her fairy-tale marriage, she was preparing songs for her first live album. She picked songs that helped her deal with the emotions she was feeling at the time. "Until you've experienced something, you don't have anything to talk about," she told the *Detroit Free Press.* "A child can't sing about being hurt. He just got in this world the day before yesterday." Winans was sure that once the marriage was over that her career would be too. "I knew I was going to have to be a secretary at a bank or something," she told *Gospel Today.* Instead, out of the blue, Bishop T.D. Jakes invited her to perform at one of his convocations and new doors opened for her as if she were a brand new artist. Winans had managers in the past and never felt she was handled correctly, so she began to manage herself and book her own concerts. She reasoned that, at the end of the day, she'd have no one to blame but herself if she was not successful. Pastors loved the fact that she called them herself, and they felt a stronger connection to her and eagerly booked her at their churches over and over again. There have been times where she booked herself in three cities within the same day and would then go out in the church lobby and sell her product herself, thus truly earning the title of the Hardest Working Woman in gospel.

It was not long after that *Live in Detroit* was released. Recorded live at Bishop Andrew Merritt's Straight Gate Church, Winans went all the way traditional to give the gospel programmers exactly what they said they wanted from her. She gave them faithful, simple arrangements of "Great Is Thy Faithfulness," Bill Gaither's "Because He Lives," and Candi Staton's "The Blood Rushes." However, the megahits were Rev. James Cleveland's "No Cross, No Crown" and "Long as I Got King Jesus," which both featured the Straight Gate Mass Choir. The album did so well so quickly that CGI (the Polygram-owned company that bought Intersound circa 1996) invested in a music video of "Long as I Got King Jesus," which certainly helped keep sales steady. The album eventually peaked at No. 6 on the gospel chart and sold well over 200,000 units—a staggering success for a project with no crossover single. Winans hustled the record at her many concerts and in numerous radio interviews she set up herself. "I did all that," she said with no arrogance. "The label didn't get on the record until after I made it hot. Then they came in and caught on to the vision."

CGI was so pleased with Winans that they gave her a $75,000 check on her birthday and announced an ambitious trilogy project for 1999. They planned to release three albums within the year beginning with a May release of *Live in Detroit II*, followed by the *Share the Laughter* comedy album in July, and capping the year with an October release called *Woman to Woman: Songs of Survival.* CGI rolled out the big guns. They launched their most expensive marketing campaign ever to promote the project. They bought full-page color ads in magazines, shot a concept video for the song "Already Been to the Water," and hired Capital Entertainment (which handled CeCe Winans and Bishop T.D. Jakes at the time) to handle Winans's press coverage. They were able to book her on *Queen Latifah,* various BET shows, and *Jenny Jones,* among other television programs and got her the most press coverage she'd had since she toured with the Winans Family Tour in 1992.

The first installment of the trilogy, *Live in Detroit II,* crested to No. 3 on the gospel chart and was only stopped from hitting No. 1 by Kirk Franklin projects that were receiving mainstream radio play. Still, the album sold over 250,000 units—a bona fide success.

The second installment, *Share the Laughter*, was a compilation of Winans's comedic comments to the audience between songs at the *Live in Detroit* taping. The gregarious singer has a gift of gab and a naturally humorous personality, so she delivered the jokes well. Considering that many church folks don't seem to find gospel comedy very funny, it's a credit to Winans's popularity that the album reached No. 20 on the gospel chart. However, the third installment of the project was never released. "Now, that was the album that was going to outsell all of my earlier albums," Winans once said. Winans paid for that part of the series herself and owned the masters to it. She refused to allow CGI to release it because they began to have financial problems and would not stand by everything in their contract with Winans. Rather than allow CGI to profit on the album without fulfilling their end of the contract to her, Winans withdrew the project.

After being courted by Vicki Mack Lataillade at Gospo Centric Records and other companies, Winans briefly flirted with opening her own label before old singing pal Marvie Wright signed her to Tommy Boy Gospel in 2001. Before Winans released a new project, the label closed down the gospel division and she was without a recording home again. In 2002, Winans was signed to Verity Records and released *Bringing It All Together*, which turned out to be the biggest hit of her career thus far. The album spent over seven weeks at No. 1 on the *Billboard* gospel chart and was her first No. 1 project. The song "Shake Yourself Loose" was such a massive radio hit that it kept the CD on the gospel chart for over 75 weeks. Other hits from the album included "Shook" and "We Need a Word from the Lord."

By the end of the year, Winans married businessman Joe McLemore and had turned down an offer to star in a Broadway production of *The Color Purple*. In spring 2004, she launched a musical play that she wrote and starred in called *Torn Between Two Loves*. The play had a successful run and Winans then decided to open her own online record label, Destiny Joy Records. In the future, the comedic and charismatic singer hopes to branch off into film and television work. "I love what I do," she told the *Detroit Free Press* in 2003, as she reflected on her career and its many trials. "I love, first of all, the fact that I've been in church all of my life. All I know how to do is to sing about Jesus. I love to let people feel what I feel. The Lord has blessed me to make it so that it's safe to laugh and sing gospel in the same setting."

RECOMMENDED RECORDINGS: Absolutely essential is Winans's debut CD *Be Encouraged* (Light Records, 1985), which featured contemporary hit after hit such as "You Turn Me," "Last Trumpet Sound," and "We Shall Behold Him." The next project to get is *Bringing It All Together* (Verity Records, 2004), which is packed with solid contemporary grooves that are every bit as classic as Winans's debut project.

Winans Phase 2

THE THIRD GENERATION of the Winans clan came together because their aunt Debbie (of Angie & Debbie fame) had a dream about her nephews singing as a group. After she told them about the dream, her brother, Carvin, Sr., began to coach his sons, Carvin, III, and Juan, and his nephews, Michael and Marvin, Jr., on how to make their group work. "I didn't even know they could sing," their grandmother, Delores "Mom" Winans, once said. "They had never shown any interest before Debbie had that dream." The dream became reality as Carvin, Sr., gave them vocal, choreography, and finishing school lessons. In the 1980s, the Winans (brothers Marvin, Sr., Carvin, Sr., Ronald, and Michael, Sr.) had created a string of gospel favorites such as "Tomorrow," "The Question Is," and "Bring Back the Days of Yea and Nay." The younger group was named Winans Phase 2 to signify a new generation of singers to carry on the Winans legacy. After bringing in secular producers such as Narada Michael Walden, who produced Aretha Franklin's *Freeway of Love*, and Rodney Jerkins, who had done several songs for Brandy, the CD *We Got Next* appeared in summer 1999 on Word/Myrrh Records. In spite of a very good, smooth R&B-styled gospel project that should have crossed over to the R&B world, Word records was ill-equipped to make such a feat happen. The project was marred by a series of bad executive decisions from the label. Phase 2 recorded a fine duet with Amy

Grant on her classic "El Shaddai." It received major airplay on CCM radio and was intended to introduce the group to that largely white demographic. Yet, it was foolishly not included on the *We Got Next* CD. Babyface contributed the awesome song "Just for the Day" which didn't take off on urban or CCM radio, as it should have. The funky "Send Me" received the most radio airplay but never caught on beyond the gospel audience. Still, in spite of several personnel changes at Word, the CD sold 300,000 copies—an impressive debut for any gospel artist, let alone a new act. After touring on the Winans Family "Together We Stand" tour in 2002, the group disbanded. Marvin "Coconut" Winans has been producing other artists, including his mother, Vickie Winans, on her Grammy-winning *Bringing It All Together* CD.

Witness

COMMISSIONED'S KEYBOARDIST Michael Brooks handpicked the ladies rounding out his group, Witness. Initially, the ensemble was comprised of his sister Tina, Marvie Wright (sister of Commissioned guitarist Michael Wright), Yolanda Harris, Diane Campbell, and Lisa Page, whose late father, Warren Harris, was a member of the Motown group the Motions. "Michael Brooks…was working with his sister who wanted to do a solo thing," Page told manhunt.com in 2004. "So Pastor Brooks suggested we get together and it took off from there. When we got together we were considered the female Commissioned."

From the beginning, the group's sound was built on traditional, thick harmonies and the mellow contemporary gospel style that the Winans and Commissioned had popularized. The Detroit quintet's debut LP *Keep Looking Up* appeared on Tyscot in 1987 and featured the moderate radio hit "Oh, How He Loves Me." They moved on to Fixit Records. Page's husky alto soon became the drawing card. She was featured on radio hits such as "Song in the Night," "You'll Never Walk Alone," "Resting in Him," and "Standard." The group's 1991 CD *We Can Make a Difference* won them a Grammy nomination and they walked away with a 1991 GMWA Excellence award for Best Group.

However, there was trouble in the camp. In April 1992, *Billboard* magazine reported that Fixit Records released an incendiary press release stating that, "Certain differences have arisen that have made it necessary to terminate the agreement. No further radio promotion, marketing, or publicity will be undertaken by Fixit for the Witness project." Shortly thereafter, Fixit signed a former Witness singer, Liz Lee, to a recording deal, but her career never took off since the label eventually closed. "We had several group changes and it seemed like as we got used to one set of members then we had to adjust again and it was trying at the time," Page told manhunt.com. "We had several changes including the record company falling through, which kind of took the cake."

By 1997, Lisa Page had married Michael Brooks and embarked on a solo career. Her CD *More than You'll Ever Know* on CGI Records peaked at No. 32 on the gospel sales chart. Page-Brooks won a 1997 Dove award nomination and took home the Stellar award as Best New Artist. The original members of Witness disbanded and Page-Brooks enjoyed a temporary industry buzz that eventually dissipated. In 2003, Michael Brooks decided to resurrect the group with Leah Page-Jones, Lou Stewart, Lisa Page-Brooks, and their daughter, Natasha Page. The comeback CD *Appointed Time* on Axiom Records featured the catchy "Clap Your Hands." Michael Brooks is pastor of the Restoration Fellowship Church in Detroit.

Bobby Womack

BACK IN THE 1970S, Bobby Womack was alternately hailed as the Preacher or the Poet of Soul Music. He wrote and recorded soul music with a preacher's cadence but also sang those love songs with the sensitivity of a poet. Born on March 4, 1944 in Cleveland, Ohio, his guitarist father, Friendly Womack (born April 5, 1919), created a strict, religious home environment. He organized his sons Cecil (born September 25, 1947), Harry (born June 25, 1945), Curtis, and Friendly, Jr. (born 1941) into a gospel quintet called the Womack Brothers. One of their earliest gigs was opening for the Soul Stirrers in 1953. Friendly, Sr., heard the group was coming through

Cleveland, so he showed up at the venue and leaned on the Stirrers' manger, S.R. Crain, to let his sons sing. Crain gave in, the boys performed and received thunderous applause from the audience. Ever the salesman, Friendly got on the horn and let several concert promoters know that the Womack Brothers had opened for the Soul Stirrers—then the biggest male group in gospel. With that spot on their résumé, the group was soon working steadily.

Years later, after Cooke had left gospel for pop stardom and launched his own SAR Records label, Roscoe Robinson of the Five Blind Boys brought the Womack Brothers up to him as a group he should sign. Cooke agreed and added the boys, who were then teenagers, to his roster. Bobby Womack and Cooke became fast friends. Friendly, Sr., assumed that Cooke would keep his sons in church music. However, after they cut Robinson's tune "Somewhere There's a God," Cooke started to have other ideas. Using the same instrumental track, he stepped into the recording booth and recorded the same song as "Somewhere There's a Girl." It was a subtle hint to the Womack Brothers that there was a world beyond the church market. Their first gospel record was a flop and didn't earn them any money or any greater notoriety. When they returned to SAR for another session, Cooke showed them his big house with the shiny new cars in the driveway. He told them to think about those things the next time they recorded and "That'll make you sing real hard," according to his biographer Daniel Wolff.

When the brothers returned home to Cleveland, they told their father they were leaving gospel to sing secular music. Friendly, Sr., broke down and cried at the thought of his sons leaving God for the devil, as he called secular music. "That was the first time I saw my father cry," Bobby says. When Friendly finished crying, he kicked all of his sons out of the house. Cooke wired them enough money to buy a car and drive out to Los Angeles. Once there, Cooke renamed them the Valentinos and they began taking gospel songs and transforming them into love songs. Aside from "Somewhere There's a Girl," they took "Couldn't Hear Nobody Pray" and made that into "Lookin' for a Love," which became a No. 8 R&B chart hit. They followed up with "I'll Make

It Alright" and "It's All Over Now." The group toured with James Brown and Cooke pulled Bobby out to be his guitarist. After the Rolling Stones covered "It's All Over Now" (which Bobby wrote) in 1964 and saw it top the British pop charts, the singer was suddenly rich. However, after Cooke's tragic murder in December 1964, Womack fell into a depression and the Valentinos disbanded. Womack had become one of Cooke's closest friends and idolized him as a mentor and big brother. From Womack's perspective, he felt he was helping take care of Cooke's family as Cooke would have wanted him to—and at the same time being closer to his idol—when he married Cooke's widow, Barbara Campbell, three months later. The R&B community was outraged that a man who Cooke had treated as a brother would marry Cooke's wife so soon after his death. Some felt he was cashing in on Cooke's legacy and estate. "I was getting static from all around the world," Womack told writer Leo Sacks of that period after he released his first singles on Chess Records. "It was devastating. Radio people were throwing my records in the garbage. I started wearing shades just to hide my pain. I didn't want you to look into my eyes, that's how hurt I was. But I wanted everybody to know how I felt. That I loved Barbara. That Sam was my partner. That I was in living hell. Then someone said, '[Wilson] Pickett's your ticket. Channel your energies through him.' So I wrote 'I'm in Love.' When I played him the demo, he ran around the room screaming, 'Womack! You're crazy! All this hurt comin' out of you! I'm gonna tell this story!' he sang it with the feeling I wanted, of someone who was crying out, because he knew my situation." The songs he wrote for Pickett, such as "I'm in Love" and "I'm a Midnight Mover," became Top Ten R&B hits.

By 1970, Womack's past was forgotten and he was a rising star. Over the next few years, he recorded R&B smashes such as "Sweet Caroline," "That's the Way I Feel About 'Cha," and "Woman's Gotta Have It." Although Womack had left the church behind and was running with a fast crowd, he still sprinkled his albums with gospel songs. The 1971 LP *Communication* had the gospel standard "Yield Not to Temptation" and the inspirational "Everything Is Beautiful." The 1972 LP *Facts of Life* featured a deliciously raspy take on Sam Cooke's "That's

Heaven to Me," and the 1975 LP *What's This World Coming To?* featured a couple of gospel-inspired chant interludes. In spite of the fact that Womack had adopted a hard, partying lifestyle (perhaps confirming his father's worst fear about his sons going into secular music), he kept his faith with him and closed the album with a refreshing, bluesy rendition of "Yes, Jesus Loves Me." In the late 1970s, Womack's career waned considerably. He also recorded great soul songs with his running buddies Candi Staton and David Ruffin. He had divorced Barbara in 1970, and by the end of the decade, he had married Regina Banks (Rev. James Cleveland officiated) in spite of his depressive emotional state. Tragedy followed when their baby son died suddenly and, in a separate incident, their house burned down. Womack moved on to Arista Records where he still couldn't find his groove. Finally, the small, independent Beverly Glen label was the entity to turn Womack's career around. His 1981 LP *The Poet* featured the ballad "If You Think You're Lonely Now," which reached No. 3 on the R&B chart and put him back on easy street. He followed over the next few years with hit songs such as a duet with Patti LaBelle, "Love Has Finally Come at Last," and "I Wish He Didn't Trust Me So Much." In the intervening years, Womack has cleaned up his life and continues to perform. When the *Detroit News* asked Womack how drugs killed his friend David Ruffin but passed him by, Womack said, "It could have been me. But watching them fall by the wayside gave me a determination, a resolve to say, 'I'll tell the story; I'll finish it.' They say God only knows how much you can bear. I can take a lot."

In 1999, Womack fulfilled a promise he made to his father that he would one day record a gospel album. The album *Back to My Roots* was released through EMI's The Right Stuff imprint with a direct order television campaign. When the campaign was over, the CD was sold in stores where it reached No. 27 on the gospel chart and sold upwards of 50,000 units.

RECOMMENDED RECORDING: *Back to My Roots* (The Right Stuff, 1999) is a fine piece of traditional gospel music for anyone wanting a taste of earthy, Southern-style gospel. Its 17 bluesy tracks with Womack's crusty vocals bring the knowing quality that comes with hard-earned survival to church standards such as "What a Friend We Have in Jesus" and "Oh Happy Day."

Stevie Wonder

THE MOST PROLIFIC and acclaimed male singer-songwriter of the 1970s, Stevie Wonder was an icon before the age of 30. His prestige has only deepened with the passing years. Wonder's music was a fusion of social commentary, spirituality, and simple good times. Gems such as "You Are the Sunshine of My Life," "Living for the City," and "I Wish" have more profound meanings than their commercial success would dictate. At the same time, like Aretha Franklin, Wonder is one of very few secular artists who has always been as welcome in the gospel world as he is in the mainstream. Therefore, he's collaborated with scores of gospel artists over the years, from the Williams Brothers to BeBe Winans.

Born Steveland Hardaway Judkins on May 13, 1950, in Saginaw, Michigan, Wonder was born prematurely. As he lay in an oxygen tank until his condition stabilized, he was given too much oxygen, which caused his blindness. In 1954, his family moved to Detroit, where Wonder sang in his church's choir. He was playing piano, drums, and harmonica by the age of nine. Seeing Wonder perform for some of his friends circa 1961, Ronnie White (who sang with the Miracles) decided to arrange an audition for Wonder with Berry Gordy at Motown Records. Gordy signed him immediately and paired him with producer Clarence Paul. Because they found his talent so "wonderful," label executives decided to rename the 11-year-old singer Little Stevie Wonder. His first LPs were cover albums and didn't sell well. It was his third LP, *The 12 Year Old Genius*, featuring "Fingertips," which put him on the charts and into the hearts of America.

Wonder's voice was changing, so he took some time off and studied classical piano at the Michigan School for the Blind. In 1964, his voice had changed to the tone that it now has, he dropped "Little" from his stage name, and came back strong with the infectious dance tune "Uptight (Everything's Alright)," the first hit that he wrote himself. The signs of Wonder's future social activism via music were displayed in 1966 when he decided that he wanted to cover Bob Dylan's lyrical protest song "Blowin' in the Wind" and the follow-up hit "A Place in the Sun." Although Motown executives wanted him to stay in the non-political world of puppy love songs, Wonder refused to pander. As he took the reins of his career, his love songs were mature in spite of his youth, including the Top Ten R&B hits "Hey Love," "I Was Made to Love Her," "My Cherie Amour," "Signed, Sealed, Delivered," and "For Once in My Life." By the time the 1970s opened, Wonder started slipping stronger social and faith-oriented messages into his albums. The LP *Signed, Sealed, Delivered* featured the inspirational tunes "Heaven Help Us All" and "Joy (Takes Over Me)." The former reached No. 2 on the R&B chart in 1970. The 1973 LP *Innervisions* became a hit off of the caustic radio singles "Higher Ground" and "Living for the City," which were both indictments on American society and politics in particular. However, the project also included "Jesus Children of America," another stunning critique that has been covered by gospel artists since, including Shirley Caesar on her 1978 *First Lady* album. Wonder joined BeBe and Marvin Winans for another rocking version on BeBe's *Love and Freedom* CD.

Wonder's masterpiece, *Songs in the Key of Life*, came in fall 1976. *Billboard* magazine called it "phenomenal… a gorgeous communication from a genius soul at peace with itself." One of the ten best albums of the rock era, by anyone's account, it was loaded with music that gospel artists have made full use of in the years since. The mid-tempo "Have a Talk with God" has been covered by Willie Norwood, the Dixie Hummingbirds, Nysa Shenay, and Jon Gibson. The ballad "Love's in Need of Love Today" has been reworked by Take 6, Beau Williams, Donald Lawrence's former group Company, and Rev. John P. Kee. Clarence Fountain and the Five Blind Boys have done "Higher Ground." Nichole Nordeman has recorded "As." All of these classics come from this one landmark album.

Wonder's involvement in other artists' projects doesn't stop there though. He co-wrote the gospel jam "Try Jah Love" for the reggae band Third World in 1982. Ben Tankard, the Steele Family, and Mary Mary have all put their stamp on Wonder's 1987 Quiet Storm ballad, "You Will Know." He wrote Diana Ross's 1991 hit "Force

Behind the Power" that featured thunderous background vocals by the Andrae Crouch Choir. Wonder co-wrote "Why I Feel This Way" with Mark Kibble for Take 6's 1994 *Join the Band* CD. He surfaced on the track and the video of "I'm Too Close to Heaven" on the Williams Brothers' *Still Standing* CD in 1997.

Rev. Maceo Woods

CONSIDERED BY MANY to be gospel's finest organist (since pop music can claim sometime gospel artist Billy Preston as their best), Maceo Woods was born April 23, 1932, in Chicago. He first recorded for Apollo Records in 1952 but is best known for his Vee-Jay recordings. His stirring 1954 organ instrumental of "Amazing Grace" easily sold 200,000 copies that year alone and has continued to sell over the years. It is arguably the bestselling instrumental in gospel music history. Rev. Woods formed the Christian Tabernacle Concert Choir in 1960 and began touring the 32-member ensemble. After Woods signed to Stax Records' Volt subsidiary in the 1960s, they enjoyed a huge R&B smash with the muddy, down-tempo ballad "Hello Sunshine." Co-written by sax great Curtis King and Ronald Miller (who wrote the Rolling Stones hit "Mercy Mercy"), the song first appeared on Aretha Franklin's *Aretha Now* LP in 1968. The following year, Woods released his bluesy, organ-driven version with George Jordan and the late Pearl McComb deliberately singing out of sync. It was one of gospel's finest moments. The single eventually peaked at No. 28 on the R&B singles chart and the LP rose to No. 45 on the R&B album chart in 1969.

Woods has only recorded sporadically in the intervening years but continues to bring his traditional style of gospel to the concert stage. "Even though I am traditional, I don't dislike contemporary music," he told the *Milwaukee Journal* newspaper in June 2004. "But let me tell you this: when you take the *con* out of contemporary, you have temporary. I am not temporary. I am permanent. And that is how I approach my ministry." He also continues to serve as pastor at the Christ Tabernacle Church on Prairie Avenue in Chicago that he founded over 40 years ago.

World Wide Message Tribe

FORMED CIRCA 1991 in Manchester, England, this band was a bridge between the church and the dance floor. The original lineup included Elaine Hanley, fashion designer Andy Hawthorne, and David Mark Pennells, Jr. Hanley had a gospel squall equal to that of American dance mavens such as Robin S or Loleatta Holloway. In 1996, they experienced two US releases when Warner Bros. issued the *We Don't Get What We Deserve* and *Jumping in the House of God* CDs. An integrated group of British and South African musicians/singers, the current lineup includes Lindey West, George Mhondera (from Zimbabwe), Quintin Delport (from South Africa), and Tim Owen and his wife Emma. The group now performs simply as the Tribe.

Betty Wright

"TO ME, BETTY'S like a preacher in everything she sings," British soul siren Joss Stone told the *Philadelphia Inquirer*'s Tom Moon in 2004. With her 1971 million-selling anthem "The Clean Up Woman" and other tell-it-like-it-is tunes such as "The Babysitter" and "Tonight's the Night," Betty Wright developed a reputation as a preaching soul practitioner in the 1970s. In spite of her soul pedigree, Wright has been a behind-the-scenes player in gospel music circles for two decades while maintaining her soul music career.

Born Bessie Regina Norris on December 21, 1953, in Miami, Florida, Wright first sang as a child with her siblings Jeanette, Philip, and Milton in the gospel group the Echoes of Joy. In 1966, the 13 year old recorded her first single for Deep City Records and even hosted a local Miami TV show. In 1968, she was signed to Alston Records where she scored her first Top 20 R&B hit with "Girls Can't Do What the Guys Do." An impressive string of R&B smashes followed, such as "The Secretary," the Grammy-winning "Where Is the Love?" and the sassy "The Clean Up Woman," which spent eight weeks in the No. 2 slot on *Billboard*'s R&B singles chart.

After stints with Epic and other recording labels, Wright formed Ms. B Records and produced further soul music hits in the 1990s such as "No Pain, No Gain."

While many veteran singers fall from sight when they hit 40—and new, younger faces emerge—Wright has worked steadily over the years doing session work, songwriting, or vocal coaching with artists such as Johnny Mathis, Gloria Estefan, Erykah Badu, Jennifer Lopez, and P. Diddy. That's Wright and Michael Jackson doing the background vocals on Stevie Wonder's tribute to Martin Luther King, Jr., "Happy Birthday to Ya." An ordained minister, Wright wrote Dorothy Norwood's "Ole Rickety Bridge" hit, songs for Regina's *It Ain't Over* CD, and handled vocal arrangements on Jaci Velasquez's *Crystal Clear* and *Milagro* projects.

One of Wright's recent recordings, "U-R-A-Ho (And You Don't Know)" from her 2001 CD *Fit for a King* raised a few eyebrows with its racy title. However, she has said the song is based on Ezekiel 23, where the scripture discusses the whoredoms that grew up between the cities of Jerusalem and Samaria. "I've been preaching on my records all my life," Wright has said of that particular song and her back catalog of songs. "You can't get this studying theology, you can't get this in the seminary. What God ordains for you to do, you do—I don't care how many years you go to school. God gave this to me. Every song I sing, I would get those melodies in my head. I'm glad people think I'm so deep, but I'm not doing this, it's God. It's his gift."

Timothy Wright

TIMOTHY WRIGHT WAS born June 17, 1947, in Brooklyn, New York, where his family attended St. John's Fire Baptized Holiness COGIC. It was there that he began playing piano at the age of 12 and also began to compose music for the church's choir. By 1969, he had moved on to Bishop F.D. Washington's Washington Temple COGIC, where he presided over the music department—a high-profile position within the COGIC denomination. Soon, Mattie Moss Clark, Rev. Isaac Douglas, and Benny Cummings were seeking him out for songs. He wrote all but one track on Rev. Douglas's landmark debut LP *Let's Go Higher*, in 1971. In 1976, Wright formed the Timothy Wright Concert Choir. They soon released the well-received albums *Who's on the Lord's Side?* and *Do You Know the Light?* He teamed with Myrna Summers on her smash project *We're Gonna Make It*. Wright is the pastor and founder of the Grace Tabernacle Christian Center in Brooklyn.

Marvin Yancey

ALTHOUGH HE'S BETTER known as Natalie Cole's first husband, Rev. Marvin Yancey was a pillar of the Chicago gospel scene in the 1970s and recorded several hit albums. Born May 31, 1950, his mother was an active gospel singer. He studied at the Chicago Baptist Institute and the Mooney Baptist Institute of Theology. As a teenager, the keyboardist accompanied gospel greats such as Rev. James Cleveland when they came through Chicago. Yancey was backing an incarnation of the Caravans at an Operation Breadbasket Expo in the early 1970s when Expo-founder Jesse Jackson's brother, Chuck, approached Yancey about co-writing some songs to pitch for an Aretha Franklin LP. It would be Yancey's entrée into secular music. The pair started collaborating and attended R&B crooner Jerry Butler's Songwriters Workshop, financed by Chappell Music. The workshop leaders loved the music Jackson and Yancey composed and offered them paid positions as Unichappell Music songwriters, an unusually quick leap into the big time.

Some of their first songs were placed with an R&B group called the Independents. Later, their manager, Bob Schwaid, was visiting fellow manager Kevin Hunter, who was looking for songs for Nat King Cole's daughter, Natalie, who'd just graduated from college and was looking to start a singing career. Cole went to visit the duo in Chicago and they went into Curtis Mayfield's Curtom studios and laid down some tracks, including some of the songs they intended for Aretha Franklin such as "This Will Be." Once their demo was complete in late 1974, they approached every record label, and every label executive turned them down except Larkin Arnold at Capitol Records, the recording home of Cole's father. "This Will Be" and the second single "Inseparable" zoomed to the top of the R&B charts. Eventually, Cole and Yancey married. Over the next five years, they wrote all of Cole's biggest hits such as "Sophisticated

Lady (She's a Different Lady)," "I've Got Love on My Mind," and "Our Love." The couple had a bicoastal marriage, some weekends on the West Coast and others in Chicago where Yancey assumed the role of pastor at his late father's church, Fountain of Life, on the South Side. While churning out hits for his wife, Yancey was making hits of his own on the gospel circuit. Yancey and Cole had a tumultuous marriage in part due to Cole's drug abuse and hectic schedule. They later divorced, but were on the verge of a reconciliation when his biggest gospel LP *Heavy Load* reached No. 4 on the gospel charts in 1985. Just as his life seemed to be the best it had been in years, Yancey died suddenly of a heart attack at the age of 34.

Vicki Yohe

SHE IS ONE OF THE first white gospel artists to reach the Top Ten on the black gospel chart with her soulful praise and worship songs such as "Because of Who You Are" and "The Mercy Seat." Vicki Yohe was born July 13, 1965, in Normal, Illinois, to a minister and his homemaker wife. When she was four, her family moved to Rapid City, South Dakota, for ten years before resettling in Loranger, Louisiana. The Yohe home jumped with music and worship. In this atmosphere, she wrote and sang her first song at the age of five. Her earliest musical influences were Tramaine Hawkins and Aretha Franklin. She and her sister, Terri, formed a singing duo that performed at church convocations for years. By the age of 17, Yohe had left home and enrolled at Jackson College of Ministry. After two years there, she became a music director at a church in Baton Rouge, where she led an 80-member choir that taught her every good and bad lesson about working in ministry. "I learned from that experience," she says, "and I grew in my walk with the Lord." Unbeknownst to Yohe, her family decided it was time for her to record an album and raised the money for her to record her eponymous debut CD in 1992. When she decided to do it, she called upon her Minneapolis-based cousin Nate Sabin (who has collaborated with the Sounds of Blackness among others) to produce it.

While not a great commercial success, the album opened up national ministry opportunities for Yohe and led to a recording contract with Giant Records. Her freshman CD, *Everlasting Love*, yielded the Christian inspirational chart hits "The Mercy Seat" and the title track. The former had been pitched to Yohe by longtime friend Mark Caruthers who had co-written it with Steve Richardson and Jeff Harpole. He recited the words and Yohe agreed to record it without even having to hear the melody. "It was such a powerful message I had to record it," she says. "The Mercy Seat" was an integral part of the four-year spiritual phenomenon known as the Brownsville Revival in Pensacola, Florida. The song was sung every night during the altar call over the course of the four-year revival, which was covered by CNN and led over four million people to dedicate their lives to the Lord. Yohe only sang the song at Brownsville a handful of times herself, but the soundtrack for the song has sold over 60,000 units nationally—making it one of the Top Ten bestselling Christian accompaniment tapes of all time.

Yohe released the *I Give You Me* CD in 1995 and *He Knows My Heart* in 1997. The latter featured the tune "Comforter," later covered by CeCe Winans. Yohe had never heard of the Trinity Broadcasting Network (TBN) when Alvin Slaughter first invited her to appear on his TBN television program. "We never did watch TV in my household because we thought if we watched TV our eyeballs would fall out," she deadpans. That appearance with Slaughter was seen by TBN co-founder Jan Crouch who instantly fell in love with Yohe's ministry and started booking her for the network's primetime TV shows such as *Praise the Lord*. The television exposure took Yohe's ministry to a new plateau. She and her husband were reading *Charisma* magazine when they spotted an ad there for a conference where Bishop T.D. Jakes was speaking. They wondered out loud why she had never sung at one of the Charisma church conferences. As quickly as they raised the subject, the next day a church called to cancel Yohe's scheduled meeting for a Friday night service. Two hours later Charisma called out of the blue to ask Yohe to sing prior to Jakes's sermon at the conference she had seen in the magazine ad. Jakes stood at the edge of the stage during her whole set

and watched her minister. At the end of the evening, he approached her and asked her to sing at a "Woman, Thou Art Loosed" conference. Later, Juanita Bynum had her sing "The Mercy Seat" at the Ice Palace in Tampa before an audience of 35,000.

Yohe has had great success in predominately black churches although she has never marketed or promoted to them. Because her musical style is praise and worship, she can easily fit all Christian and gospel radio formats. "I just feel like I should be on gospel radio even though I'm a white girl," she says teasingly.

On the recording side of things, life began to turn around when CeCe Winans and Yohe were booked to appear on *Praise the Lord* on the same night. "I was in my car and I was thinking it would be so neat to go to CeCe's dressing room and talk to her because I'm such a fan," she recalls. "I wasn't going to push myself, but if it happened, it would be nice, I just wanted to say hi. So I get to TBN and these two ladies tell me CeCe wants me to come to her dressing room. As I was going, I told myself to be calm and cool, don't act crazy. When I walked in, CeCe yelled, 'Vicki!' And I yelled, 'CeCe!' Everything I was going to do went out of the window. She said she enjoyed my singing and that she saw me on TBN all the time."

Vicki Yohe / photo by Michael Gomez

To make a long story short, Demetrus Stewart, president of Winans's PureSprings label, signed Yohe and the rest is history. Yohe's debut CD for PureSprings, *I Just Want You*, hit the marketplace in September 2003 and has been a bestseller ever since. The album has been propelled by radio's support of the soaring praise ballad "Because of Who You Are," which earned a Dove award nomination for Best Contemporary Gospel Recorded Song of the Year in spring 2004. The CD peaked at No. 7 on the *Billboard* gospel chart and reached the Top 40 on the *Billboard* CCM chart.

In spite of her success, "I'm an open book," says Yohe. "I'm a worshipper, but I tell jokes about funny experiences that have happened to me. When I first started touring, I would sing, but I didn't have anything to say [between songs]. I really started praying, 'God, I can sing these songs and I'm hitting every note, but it's petrifying.' Finally, God says, 'Vicki, just act like they are in your living room. Just be real, be open, be honest and that will take all the pressure off.' That has really helped me because now I go out there and I'm totally relaxed." Yohe and her husband, Troy Hodges, live in Nashville where they attend Christ Church.

Zion Travelers

THIS LOS ANGELES–BASED group signed to Dootsie Williams's Dootone Records in 1956. The lead singers were L.C. Cohen (from Greenville, Mississippi) and Bartha L. Watkins (from Little Rock, Arkansas). Their sound was on the sweet side, similar to the Orioles in the R&B field. They performed up to the 1990s. A couple of their best-known songs were "Two Little Fishes" and "Soldier of the Cross."

Darlene Zschech

AN AUSTRALIAN PRAISE and worship vocalist, Darlene Zschech enjoyed the biggest praise song of the entire 1990s with her signature tune, "Shout to the Lord." According to *Charisma* magazine, that one song is sung in churches, worldwide, by over 25 million people every Sunday morning. Zschech was born September 8, 1965, in Brisbane, Australia. She began singing professionally at the age of ten when she was a regular on the *Happy Go Round* children's TV program. When her parents divorced when she was 13, Zschech blamed herself for their breakup. She felt renewed when she became a Christian at the age of 15. Through her teen years, she fronted several local bands and became an in-demand session singer. She recorded commercial jingles for McDonald's, Diet Coke, Special K, and Kentucky Fried Chicken. She also organized choirs for the Australian concert tours of pop stars such as Barry Manilow and Michael Bolton.

Then, circa 1986, Zschech left the pop music field behind her and became vocal director and then worship leader at the Hillsong Church in Sydney, Australia. As the Hillsong Church began to record its choir, Zschech was very instrumental in the praise and worship recordings that were eventually released internationally through Integrity Music. Although she was the face of the projects, they were ensemble projects. The first to take off was the title song of 1996's *Shout to the Lord*, which became an instant radio success and was quickly adopted by local church choirs the world over. Zschech is now worship pastor at Hillsong Church, as well as associate director of the Hillsong Conference, an annual music and leadership gathering that draws more than 15,000 attendees.

Glossary of Terms

A&R (Artist & Repertoire)   An individual who scouts for talent to sign to a recording label. This person signs the artist to a contract, develops them as an artist, and picks songs and producers to bring the artist's music to life.

BET   Black Entertainment Television, a leading cable television network specializing in African-American–oriented programming.

COGIC   The Church of God in Christ is the largest African-American religious denomination based in the United States. Based in Memphis, Tennessee, the church has created some of the biggest gospel artists of all time.

diamond award   In 1999, the Recording Industry Association of America (RIAA) established the "diamond award" certification to mark album sales of 10,000,000 (ten million) or more copies.

GMWA   The Gospel Music Workshop of America, an annual music convention founded by Rev. James Cleveland.

gold record   In 1958, the Recording Industry Association of America (RIAA) established the "gold album" certification to mark album sales of 500,000 or more copies. It now represents album (CD, cassette, or LP) shipments (as opposed to sales) of 500,000 or more copies to retail outlets. The first gold album was Gordon McCrae's cast album for *Oklahoma*. The standard for sales of cassette singles, CD singles, and 45-rpms is 1,000,000 units shipped. Perry Como's "Catch a Falling Star" was the first gold single. That same year, 13-year-old boy soprano Laurie London enjoyed the first certified gold gospel single with his rendition of "He's Got the Whole World in His Hands."

gospco   Term coined by former '70s disco star Candi Staton to describe disco music with gospel lyrics, such as her songs "You Got the Love" and "Change in My Life." Songs by other artists falling into this category include Tramaine Hawkins's "Fall Down (Spirit of Love)" and the Mighty Clouds of Joy's "Mighty High."

label   A company that creates, manufactures, or distributes music is called a recording label. Well-known gospel labels include Benson, Word, and Verity Records.

LP   Long-playing record album that plays at 33 and a third revolutions per minute. Before the advent of the CD in the late 1980s, it was the primary music configuration.

multi-platinum record   In 1984, the Recording Industry Association of America (RIAA) established the "multi-platinum album" certification to mark album sales of 2,000,000 or more copies. It now represents album (CD, cassette, or LP) shipments (as opposed to sales) of 2,000,000 or more copies to retail outlets. Michael Jackson's *Thriller* was one of the first multi-platinum album certifications.

platinum record   In 1976, the Recording Industry Association of America (RIAA) established the "platinum album" certification to mark album sales of 1,000,000 or more copies. It now represents album (CD, cassette, or LP) shipments (as opposed to sales) of 1,000,000 or more copies to retail outlets. The Eagles' *Greatest Hits 1971–1975* was the first platinum album. The standard for sales of cassette singles, CD singles, and 45-rpms is 2,000,000 units shipped. Johnnie Taylor's "Disco Lady" was the first certified platinum single.

producer   The individual in charge of making sure a recording is completed. The producer often picks the songs, the musicians, background vocalists, and even the studio where the project will be recorded. For independent projects, the producer is also often the person who raises the capital to pay for the project to be completed. In return for his investment and labor, the producer often receives points and royalties on the sales of the recordings.

TBN   Trinity Broadcasting Network, the largest religious cable television network.

Gospel Trivia

Once you've read this book, you'll be able to answer these questions, which are all answered at some point in the book.

1. What gospel star was once Mahalia Jackson's newspaper boy?
2. What group did Albertina Walker leave to found the Caravans?
3. What gospel star had a post office named after him?
4. Where did Aretha Franklin meet the Staple Singers for the first time?
5. The song "What Is This?" was popularized by the Hawkins Family in the 1970s, but who recorded it first?
6. What gospel singer once weighed 615 pounds?
7. Who replaced Sam Cooke in the Soul Stirrers?
8. Where was Aretha Franklin born?
9. What singer started with the Robert Anderson Singers and became a star on her own?
10. Who was the first praise and worship artist to receive a gold record?
11. Which one of the Gay Sisters played piano for Mahalia Jackson?
12. What gospel artist lived on a plantation as a child in the early 1940s?
13. Who was the first gospel artist to grace the cover of *Black Enterprise* magazine?
14. What gospel song was associated with Dick Gregory's Bahamian diet in the 1980s?
15. What gospel song was built around the hook of funk band Brick's 1977 Top Ten R&B smash "Ain't Gonna Hurt Nobody"?
16. What black gospel group sang with Amy Grant on a remake of her tune "El Shaddai"?
17. Who was the first gospel singer to perform at the White House during the Kennedy administration?
18. What four female gospel artists were on US postage stamps in 1998?
19. What Red Sovine song became a gospel hit for a gospel group in 1979?
20. What recording artist co-coordinated the "Jesus at the Roxy" stage production in 1981?
21. What recording artist adopted Marion Williams's yodel as their signature vocal trick?
22. What gospel group toured with the Commodores in 1981 and joined the group to sing "Jesus Is Love" as the finale in their concerts?
23. Who was the first gospel artist to win a Grammy award?
24. What three gospel artists have stars on the Hollywood Walk of Fame?
25. What gospel artist featured Lawrence Hilton-Jacobs (aka Freddie "Boom-Boom" Washington from the ABC sitcom *Welcome Back, Kotter*) playing keyboard on one of their LPs?

Answers

1. Rev. James Cleveland
2. The Robert Anderson Singers
3. Milton Brunson
4. A gas station
5. Rev. Willie Morganfield
6. Gloria Spencer
7. Johnnie Taylor
8. Memphis
9. Albertina Walker
10. Ron Kenoly for "Lift Him Up"
11. Evelyn Gay
12. Esther Smith
13. CeCe Winans
14. "You Got the Love" by the Source featuring Candi Staton
15. "No Stoppin' the USA" by MC Hammer
16. Winans Phase 2
17. Mahalia Jackson
18. Roberta Martin, Mahalia Jackson, Clara Ward, and Sister Rosetta Tharpe
19. "Teddy Bear" by the Williams Brothers
20. Philip Bailey
21. Little Richard
22. East St. Louis Gospelettes
23. Mahalia Jackson
24. Rev. James Cleveland, Mahalia Jackson, and Andrae Crouch
25. Janet Lynn Skinner

Bestselling Gospel Singles of All Time

In the gospel world, the market has always emphasized album sales over single sales. However, there are a handful of singles that have managed to sell very well over the years.

Edwin Hawkins Singers – "Oh Happy Day" (1969)	7 million***
Whitney Houston – "Jesus Loves Me/I'll Always Love You" (1992)	4 million
Candi Staton – "You Got the Love" (1991)	2.4 million**
Mahalia Jackson – "Move on Up a Little Higher" (1948)	2 million*
Staple Singers – "I'll Take You There" (1972)	2 million*
Marian Anderson – "Ave Maria" (1937)	1 million*
Louis Armstrong – "When the Saints Go Marching In" (1938)	1 million
Carter Family – "Will the Circle Be Unbroken?" (1935)	1 million
Chuck Wagon Gang – "I'll Fly Away" (1948)	1 million
Clara Ward Singers – "Packing Up" (1957)	1 million*
Clara Ward Singers – "Surely, God Is Able" (1955)	1 million*
Thomas Dorsey/Marion Williams – "Precious Lord" (1973)	1 million*
Fairfield Four – "Don't Let Nobody Turn You Around" (1947)	1 million*
Fisk Jubilee Singers – "Swing Low, Sweet Chariot" (1909)	1 million*
Whitney Houston – "My Love Is Your Love" (1999)	1 million
Impressions – "People Get Ready" (1965)	1 million
Staple Singers – "Uncloudy Day" (1957)	1 million
Sister Rosetta Tharpe – "Strange Things Happening" (1945)	1 million
Mahalia Jackson – "Dig a Little Deeper" (1949)	500,000*
MC Hammer – "Pray" (1990)	500,000
Staple Singers – "Respect Yourself" (1972)	500,000
Staple Singers – "If You're Ready, Come Go with Me" (1973)	500,000

All songs are based on RIAA figures, except where noted.

* Most independent record labels did not allow the Recording Industry Association of America (RIAA) to audit their sales figures before the 1970s because they didn't want the artists or the Internal Revenue Service (IRS) to know exactly how many records they sold. Therefore, many records that are universally accepted as having sold half a million or more copies have never been officially certified. These songs with one asterisk fall into that category.

** Documented by Warner Chappell Music in London.

*** Various renditions of the Edwin Hawkins adaptation of the song have accounted for an accumulated sales total of over 18 million copies.

Bestselling Gospel Albums/CDs of All Time

God's Property – *God's Property* (1997)	3 million*
Barbra Streisand – *Higher Ground* (1997)	3 million
Rev. James Cleveland – *Peace Be Still* (1962)	2 million
DC Talk – *Jesus Freak* (1992)	2 million
Aretha Franklin– *Amazing Grace* (1972)	2 million
Kirk Franklin – *The Nu Nation Project* (1999)	2 million
Whitney Houston – *The Preacher's Wife* (1996)	2 million
Elvis Presley – *Amazing Grace* (1999)	2 million
Yolanda Adams – *Mountain High, Valley Low* (1999)	1 million
Commodores – *Heroes* (1982)	1 million
Kirk Franklin – *Kirk Franklin & the Family* (1993)	1 million
Kirk Franklin – *The Rebirth of Kirk Franklin* (2002)	1 million
Kirk Franklin – *Whatcha Lookin' 4* (2001)	1 million
Amy Grant – *Age to Age* (1982)	1 million
Fred Hammond – *Pages of Life: Chapters 1 & 2* (1998)	1 million
Walter Hawkins – *Love Alive III* (1990)	1 million
Ron Kenoly – *Lift Him Up* (1993)	1 million
Donnie McClurkin – *Live in London* (2001)	1 million
Della Reese – *Touched by an Angel* (1998)	1 million
Take 6 – *Take 6* (1988)	1 million
BeBe & CeCe Winans – *Different Lifestyles* (1991)	1 million
CeCe Winans – *Alabaster Box* (1999)	1 million
CeCe Winans –*Alone in His Presence* (1995)	1 million
Yolanda Adams – *Believe* (2001)	500,000
Barnes & Brown – *Rough Side of the Mountain* (1983)	500,000
Kurt Carr – *Awesome Wonder* (2003)	500,000
Kirk Franklin & the Family – *Christmas* (1995)	500,000
Fred Hammond – *Purpose by Design* (2001)	500,000
Fred Hammond – *Spirit of David* (2002)	500,000
John P. Kee – *Not Guilty* (2001)	500,000
Mary Mary – *Incredible* (2003)	500,000
Mary Mary – *Thankful* (2000)	500,000

Donnie McClurkin – *Donnie McClurkin* (1996)	500,000
New Life Community Choir – *Show Up* (1997)	500,000
Smokie Norful – *I Need You Now* (2001)	500,000
Sandi Patti – *Let There Be Praise* (1989)	500,000
Run D.M.C. – *Down with the King* (1993)	500,000
Sounds of Blackness – *Africa to America* (1994)	500,000
Sounds of Blackness – *Evolution of Gospel* (1991)	500,000
Trin-i-tee 5:7 – *Spiritual Love* (2000)	500,000
Trin-i-tee 5:7 – *Trin-i-tee 5:7* (1998)	500,000
Take 6 – *Join the Band* (1994)	500,000
Winans – *Return* (1989)	500,000
BeBe & CeCe Winans – *Heaven* (1988)	500,000
BeBe & CeCe Winans – *Lord, Lift Us Up* (1984)	500,000
BeBe & CeCe Winans – *Relationships* (1994)	500,000
CeCe Winans – *CeCe Winans* (2001)	500,000
CeCe Winans – *Everlasting Love* (1998)	500,000
CeCe Winans – *Throne Room* (2003)	500,000
Darlene Zschech – *Shout to the Lord* (1996)	500,000
Various Artists – *Fighting Temptations*	500,000

* Amy Grant's *Heart in Motion* is the bestselling CD by a gospel artist, at 5 million units. However, since it's a pop album, it's not listed here.

Gold Videos

Brooklyn Tabernacle Choir – "He's Been Faithful" (1996)

Shirley Caesar – "Live in Memphis" (1995)

DC Talk – "Narrow Is the Way" (1994)

Ron Kenoly – "God Is Able" (1996)

Ron Kenoly – "Lift Him Up" (1995)

Ron Kenoly – "Sing Out" (2000)

Donnie McClurkin – "Live in London" (2002)

Gospel Songs on the R&B Charts

The following are gospel songs or inspirational songs by gospel artists that have appeared on the *Billboard* Top 125 R&B singles airplay charts since 1942, when the magazine began to document activity on black music radio formats.

Song Title – Artist	Chart Peak	Year of Release
"Crying in the Chapel" – The Orioles	No. 1	1953
"Be Thankful" – William DeVaughn	No. 1	1974
"Stomp" – God's Property	No. 1	1997
"I'll Take You There" – Staple Singers	No. 1	1972
"If You're Ready, Come Go with Me" – Staple Singers	No. 1	1973
"I'll Take You There" – BeBe & CeCe Winans	No. 1	1991
"Addictive Love" – BeBe & CeCe Winans	No. 1	1991
"Oh Happy Day" – Edwin Hawkins Singers	No. 2	1969
"My Love Is Your Love" – Whitney Houston	No. 2	1999
"Strange Things Happening" – Sister Rosetta Tharpe	No. 2	1945
"Jesus Walks" – Kanye West	No. 2	2004
"People Get Ready" – Curtis Mayfield/Impressions	No. 3	1965
"Pray" – MC Hammer	No. 4	1990
"Somebody Bigger Than You and I" – Whitney Houston	No. 4	1996
"City in the Sky" – Staple Singers	No. 4	1974
"Knockin' on Heaven's Door" – Randy Crawford	No. 4	1989
"Ya Mo Be There" – James Ingram and Michael McDonald	No. 5	1983
"It's Time" – Winans	No. 5	1990
"Up Above My Head" – Rosetta Tharpe and Marie Knight	No. 6	1948
"It's Okay" – BeBe & CeCe Winans	No. 6	1992
"Fall Down (Spirit of Love)" – Tramaine Hawkins	No. 7	1985
"Count on Me" – CeCe Winans and Whitney Houston	No. 7	1996
"Praise the Lord and Pass the Ammunition" – Southern Sons	No. 7	1942
"Open Up My Heart" – Yolanda Adams	No. 8	2000
"Milky White Way" – Trumpeteers	No. 8	1948
"Lost Without You" – BeBe & CeCeWinans	No. 8	1989
"A Change Is Gonna Come" – Sam Cooke	No. 9	1965
"Gospel Train" – Marie Knight	No. 9	1949

Song Title – Artist	Chart Peak	Year of Release
"Lift Every Voice" – Melba Moore and Various Artists	No. 9	1990
"Down with the King" – Run D.M.C.	No. 9	1993
"Belle" – Al Green	No. 9	1977
"Our Father" – Original Five Blind Boys of Mississippi	No. 10	1950
"Praise the Lord and Pass the Ammunition" – Royal Harmony	No. 10	1942
"Jesus Walks" – Kanye West	No. 11	2004
"A Friend" – Winans	No. 11	1990
"Testify" – Sounds of Blackness	No. 12	1992
"Heaven" – BeBe & CeCe Winans	No. 12	1988
"Touch Me, Lord Jesus" – Angelic Gospel Singers	No. 13	1949
"Little Boy" – Rev. Samuel Kelsey	No. 13	1948
"Precious Memories" – Marie Knight	No. 13	1948
"Do Not Pass Me By" – Hammer	No. 15	1991
"I Believe" – Sounds of Blackness	No. 15	1994
"Ain't No Need to Worry – Winans and Anita Baker	No. 15	1987
"You Brought the Sunshine" – Clark Sisters	No. 16	1983
"Amen" – Curtis Mayfield/Impressions	No. 17	1965
"My Main Man" – Staple Singers	No. 18	1974
"Shackles (Praise You)" – Mary Mary	No. 19	2000
"I L-O-V-E U" – Take 6	No. 19	1990
"Love Brought Me Back" – D.J. Rogers	No. 20	1978
"There's Got to Be Rain" – Dorothy Norwood	No. 21	1973
"Everything's Gonna Be Alright" – Al Green	No. 22	1987
"Jesus to a Child/One More Try" – George Michael	No. 22	1996
"Mighty High" – Mighty Clouds of Joy	No. 22	1976
"Hold On, Change Is Comin'" – Sounds of Blackness	No. 22	1997
"Slippery People" – Staple Singers	No. 22	1984
"You Are the Only One" – God's Property	No. 23	1997
"My Sweet Lord" – Billy Preston	No. 23	1971
"I Belong to You" – Rance Allen Group	No. 24	1979
"Depend on You" – BeBe & CeCe Winans	No. 24	1992
"Celebrate New Life" – BeBe & CeCe Winans	No. 25	1989
"Lean on Me" – Kirk Franklin and Various Artists	No. 26	1999
"In the Morning Time" – Tramaine Hawkins	No. 26	1986

Song Title – Artist	Chart Peak	Year of Release
"Why We Sing" – Kirk Franklin & the Family	No. 28	1994
"Miracle Worker" – Rance Allen Group	No. 32	1991
"Time" – Mighty Clouds of Joy	No. 32	1974
"God's Grace" – Trin-i-tee 5:7	No. 32	1998
"Be Encouraged" – William Becton Featuring Cliff Jones	No. 32	1995
"I'll Make It Alright" – Beautiful Zion Baptist Church	No. 33	1973
"Jesus Is Love" – Commodores	No. 34	1980
"Midnight Hour Pt. 1" – Mighty Clouds of Joy	No. 34	1984
"Don't Leave Me" – Winans	No. 34	1991
"Love of My Life" – BeBe & CeCe Winans	No. 35	1995
"Biggest Part of Me" – Take 6	No. 36	1994
"I Want to Thank You" – Alicia Myers	No. 37	1982
"I Want to Know What Love Is" – New Jersey Mass Choir	No. 37	1985
"It's in God's Hands Now" – Anointed	No. 40	1999
"No Charge" – Shirley Caesar	No. 40	1975
"We Fall Down" – Donnie McClurkin	No. 40	2001
"When You Cry" – Winans	No. 40	1990
"Let My People Go" – Winans	No. 42	1985
"Border Song (Holy Moses)" – Dorothy Morrison	No. 43	1970
"I Need You Now" – Smokie Norful	No. 45	2003
"Mighty Cloud of Joy" – Mighty Clouds of Joy	No. 47	1975
"Light of Love" – Angie & Debbie Winans	No. 47	1993
"Lord, Don't Move the Mountain" – Inez Andrews	No. 48	1973
"Wholy Holy" – Aretha Franklin	No. 49	1972
"Jesus Is the Reason for the Season" – Kirk Franklin	No. 50	1995
"Hey, Did You Give Some Love?" – Street Christians	No. 50	1972
"In the Morning" – Mary Mary	No. 52	2002
"If Anything Ever Happened to You" – BeBe & CeCe Winans	No. 52	1994
"There's Love/God Is Not Dead" – Mighty Clouds of Joy	No. 53	1977
"Thank You" – BeBe Winans	No. 53	1998
"Workin' Out" – William Becton	No. 54	1997
"Say Amen" – Howard Hewett	No. 54	1987
"Every Moment" – Deniece Williams	No. 55	1989
"The Rock" – Tramaine Hawkins	No. 56	1987

Song Title – Artist	Chart Peak	Year of Release
"More Than What I Wanted" – CeCe Winans	No. 57	2001
"The Lady, Her Lover and Lord" – T.D. Jakes	No. 58	1998
"Revolution" – Kirk Franklin	No. 59	1999
"Beautiful Black People" – James Grear & Company	No. 59	1998
"I Sings" – Mary Mary	No. 59	2000
"Ain't No Need of Crying" – Rance Allen Group	No. 61	1975
"Fear No Evil" – The Mission	No. 61	1974
"Stay with Me" – BeBe & CeCe Winans	No. 62	1995
"Glow Love" – Mighty Clouds of Joy	No. 63	1982
"The Lord Is Real" – Blackstreet	No. 64	1996
"I'll Be Thinking of You" – Andrae Crouch	No. 69	1980
"Feels Like Heaven" – BeBe & CeCe Winans	No. 69	1996
"I'm Gonna Be Ready" – Yolanda Adams	No. 71	2002
"In the Middle of the Night" – Little Richard	No. 71	1973
"Loves Me Like a Rock" – Dixie Hummingbirds	No. 72	1973
"Never Give Up" – Yolanda Adams	No. 73	2002
"Lean on Me" – Thelma Houston & the Winans	No. 73	1989
"The Battle Is the Lord's" – Yolanda Adams	No. 74	2003
"Payday" – Winans	No. 74	1993
"Lighthouse" – New Direction	No. 75	1999
"Healing" – Deniece Williams	No. 75	1986
"I.O.U. Me" – BeBe & CeCe Winans	No. 77	1987
"Let My Life Shine" – D.J. Rogers	No. 78	1976
"The Blood" – BeBe & CeCe Winans with Hammer	No. 78	1992
"Need to Know" – Dawkins & Dawkins	No. 79	1998
"You Bring Out the Best in Me" – Vanessa Bell Armstrong	No. 80	1987
"Intervention" – Lavine Hudson	No. 85	1988
"Let's Ride" – Beautiful Zion Baptist Church Choir	No. 87	1973
"You Got the Love" – Candi Staton	No. 88	1986
"Don't Give Up" – James Grear & Company	No. 89	1998
"If at First You Don't Succeed" – Edwin Hawkins	No. 89	1990
"Heart & Soul" – Winans	No. 89	1995
"Something on the Inside" – Vanessa Bell Armstrong	No. 94	1993
"Let Your Feet Down Easy" – Dorothy Norwood	No. 96	1975

Song Title – Artist	Chart Peak	Year of Release
"Gotta Have Love" – Yolanda Adams	No. 97	1996
"With Arms Wide Open" – Desmond Pringle	No. 97	2001
"The Battle Is the Lord's" – Yolanda Adams	No. 101	2002
"A Brighter Day" – Kirk Franklin	No. 102	2002
"Put Your Hands Up" – Trin-i-tee 5:7	No. 103	1999
"Let's Dance" – Hezekiah Walker	No. 103	2000
"Thank You" – Kirk Franklin & Mary Mary	No. 105	2001
"911" – Kirk Franklin & Bishop T.D. Jakes	No. 106	2002
"Anybody Wanna Pray?" – CeCe Winans	No. 109	2001
"Mary, Don't You Weep" – Trin-i-tee 5:7	No. 111	1998
"Yeah" – Yolanda Adams	No. 113	1999
"You Can Always Call His Name" – Trin-i-tee 5:7	No. 113	1999
"My Body" – Trin-i-tee 5:7	No. 116	2000
"O Holy Night" – Smokie Norful	No. 121	2004
"The Prayer" – Donnie McClurkin & Yolanda Adams	No. 121	2003
"Tonight Tonight" – BeBe & CeCe Winans	No. 121	2001
"Won't Be Afraid" – Damita	No. 122	2001
"Celebrate (He Lives)" – Fred Hammond	No. 123	2004
"Now Behold the Lamb" – Kirk Franklin & the Family	No. 124	1996
"Fragile Heart" – Yolanda Adams	No. 125	2000

Gospel Grammy Winners

In 1957, a group of recording industry executives came together to form an organization to recognize artistic achievement by recording artists, songwriters, and behind-the-scenes people who help create the music. They named the organization the National Association of Recording Artists and Sciences (NARAS) and the trophy they handed out each year was nicknamed the Grammy, after the gramophone-shaped trophy. NARAS created the first Grammy gospel category in 1961 specifically so that they could honor Mahalia Jackson for the incredible mainstream success that she had enjoyed up to that point.

Over the years, in order to recognize the burgeoning diversity of gospel music styles, NARAS has created several other gospel music categories. If the following categories seem erratic or incomplete, it is because NARAS has changed the name of various categories over the years. They have also dropped certain categories and added others. For instance, in 1986, the category of Best Inspirational Song was dropped, and in 2005 the new category of Best Gospel Performance was added—the category existed briefly in the late 1970s. The latter allows artists who have recorded one song (as opposed to a whole album) to be nominated for an award. For the purposes of this book, I've also identified established gospel artists who have won Grammys in non-traditional Grammy categories, such as Pops Staples's gospel CD *Father Father* winning the Best Contemporary Blues album Grammy in 1994. Since this book primarily deals with the black gospel idiom, I've also identified gospel artists such as CeCe Winans who have won Grammys in Grammy categories that fall outside of the realm of black gospel music.

Best Contemporary Blues Album

Pops Staples – *Father Father* (1994)

Best Contemporary Soul Gospel Album

Smokie Norful – *Nothing Without You* (2004)

Donnie McClurkin – *Again* (2003)

Eartha – *Sidebars* (2002)

Yolanda Adams – *The Experience* (2001)

Mary Mary – *Thankful* (2000)

Yolanda Adams – *Mountain High, Valley Low* (1999)

Kirk Franklin – *The Nu Nation Project* (1998)

Take 6 – *Brothers* (1997)

Kirk Franklin & the Family – *Whatcha Lookin' 4* (1996)

CeCe Winans – *Alone in His Presence* (1995)

Take 6 – *Join the Band* (1994)

Winans – *All Out* (1993)

Various Artists – *Handel's Messiah: A Soulful Celebration* (1992)

BeBe & CeCe Winans – *Different Lifestyles* (1991)

Take 6 – *So Much 2 Say* (1990)

Best Gospel Choir or Chorus Album

Brooklyn Tabernacle Choir – *Live…This Is Your House* (2004)

Bishop T.D. Jakes & the Potter's House Mass Choir – *A Wing and a Prayer* (2003)

Brooklyn Tabernacle Choir – *Be Glad* (2002)

Hezekiah Walker & LFT Church Choir – *Love Is Live!*
(2001)

Brooklyn Tabernacle Choir – *Live: God Is Working*
(2000)

Brooklyn Tabernacle Choir – *High and Lifted Up*
(1999)

O'Landa Draper & the Associates – *Reflections* (1998)

God's Property – *God's Property* (1997)

Shirley Caesar's Outreach Convention Choir
– *Just a Word* (1996)

Brooklyn Tabernacle Choir – *Praise Him!* (1994)

Love Fellowship Crusade Choir – *Live in Atlanta*
(1994)

Thompson Community Singers – *Through God's
Eyes* (1994)

Brooklyn Tabernacle Choir – *Live: We Come
Rejoicing* (1993)

Music & Arts Seminar Choir (Edwin Hawkins)
– *Live in Los Angeles* (1992)

Sounds of Blackness – *The Evolution of Gospel* (1991)

Southern California Community Choir – *Having
Church* (1990)

Best Gospel or Other Religious Recording

Mahalia Jackson – *Great Songs of Love and Faith*
(1962)

Mahalia Jackson – *Everytime I Feel the Spirit* (1961)

Best Gospel Performance, Contemporary or Inspirational

Ray Charles and Gladys Knight – *Heaven Help Us All*
(2004)

Various Artists (Reba Rambo, Walter Hawkins, etc.)
– "The Lord's Prayer" (1980)

Best Gospel Performance, Female

Amy Grant – *Lead Me On* (1988)

Deniece Williams – "I Believe in You" (1987)

Sandi Patti – *A Morning Like This* (1986)

Amy Grant – *Unguarded* (1985)

Best Gospel Performance, Male

Larnelle Harris – *Christmas* (1988)

Larnelle Harris – *The Father Hath Provided* (1987)

Philip Bailey – *Triumph* (1986)

Larnelle Harris – "How Excellent Is Thy Name"
(1985)

Best Gospel Vocal Performance by Duo, Group or Choir

Take 6 – "The Savior Is Waiting" (1989)

Sandi Patti and Deniece Williams – "They Say"
(1986)

Sandi Patti and Larnelle Harris – "I've Just Seen
Jesus" (1985)

Sandi Patti and Larnelle Harris – "More than
Wonderful" (1983)

Best Gospel Vocal Performance, Female

CeCe Winans – "Don't Cry" (1989)

Best Gospel Vocal Performance, Male

BeBe Winans – "Meantime" (1989)

Best Inspirational Performance

Jennifer Holliday – "Come Sunday" (1985)

Donna Summer – "Forgive Me" (1984)

Donna Summer – "He's a Rebel" (1983)

Barbara Mandrell – *He Set My Life to Music* (1982)

B.J. Thomas – *Amazing Grace* (1981)

B.J. Thomas – *You Gave Me Love When Nobody Gave Me a Prayer* (1979)

B.J. Thomas – *Happy Man* (1978)

B.J. Thomas – *Home Where I Belong* (1977)

Bill Gaither Trio – *Jesus, We Just Want to Thank you* (1975)

Elvis Presley – *How Great Thou Art* (1974)

Bill Gaither Trio – *Let's Just Praise the Lord* (1973)

Elvis Presley – *He Touched Me* (1972)

Best Pop/Contemporary Album

CeCe Winans – *CeCe Winans* (2001)

Deniece Williams – *This Is My Song* (1998)

Various Artists – *Tribute: The Songs of Andrae Crouch* (1996)

Andrae Crouch – *Mercy* (1994)

Best R&B Performance by a Duo or Group with Vocal

Take 6 and Stevie Wonder – "Love's in Need of Love Today" (2002)

Michael McDonald and James Ingram – "Ya Mo Be There" (1984)

Best Soul Gospel Performance

Mahalia Jackson – *How I Got Over* (1976)

Andrae Crouch & the Disciples – *Take Me Back* (1975)

James Cleveland & the Southern California Community Choir – *In the Ghetto* (1974)

Dixie Hummingbirds – *Loves Me Like a Rock* (1973)

Aretha Franklin – *Amazing Grace* (1972)

Shirley Caesar – *Put Your Hand in the Hand* (1971)

Edwin Hawkins Singers – *Every Man Wants to Be Free* (1970)

Edwin Hawkins Singers – *Oh Happy Day* (1969)

Dottie Rambo – *The Soul of Me* (1968)

Best Soul Gospel Performance, Contemporary

Al Green – *Higher Plane* (1982)

Andrae Crouch – *Don't Give Up* (1981)

Shirley Caesar – *Rejoice* (1980)

Andrae Crouch – *I'll Be Thinking of You* (1979)

Andrae Crouch & the Disciples – *Live in London* (1978)

Edwin Hawkins Singers – *Wonderful!* (1977)

Best Soul Gospel Performance, Female

Aretha Franklin – *One Lord, One Faith, One Baptism* (1988)

CeCe Winans – "For Always" (1987)

Deniece Williams – "I Surrender All" (1986)

Shirley Caesar – "Martin" (1985)

Shirley Caesar – *Sailin'* (1984)

Sandra Crouch – *We Sing Praises* (1983)

Best Soul Gospel Performance, Male

BeBe Winans – "Abundant Life" (1988)

Al Green – "Everything's Gonna Be Alright" (1987)

Al Green – "Going Away" (1986)

Marvin Winans – "Bring Back the Days of Yea and Nay" (1985)

Andrae Crouch – "Always Remember" (1984)

Al Green – *I'll Rise Again* (1983)

Best Soul Gospel Performance, Traditional

Al Green – *Precious Lord* (1982)

Al Green – *The Lord Will Make a Way* (1981)

James Cleveland & the Charles Fold Singers – *Lord, Let Me Be an Instrument* (1980)

Mighty Clouds of Joy – *Changing Times* (1979)

Mighty Clouds of Joy – *Live and Direct* (1978)

James Cleveland – *Live at Carnegie Hall* (1977)

Best Soul Gospel Vocal Performance, Male or Female

Al Green – "As Long as We're Together" (1989)

Best Soul Gospel Vocal Performance Duo, Group or Choir

Daniel Winans – *Let Brotherly Love Continue* (1989)

Winans – *Live at Carnegie Hall* (1988)

Take 6 – *Take 6* (1988)

Winans and Anita Baker – "Ain't No Need to Worry" (1987)

Winans – *Let My People Go* (1986)

Winans – "Tomorrow" (1985)

Shirley Caesar and Al Green – "Sailin' on the Sea of Your Love" (1984)

Bobby Jones and Barbara Mandrell – "I'm So Glad I'm Standing Here Today" (1983)

Best Rap Song

Kanye West – "Jesus Walks" (2004)

Best Traditional Soul Gospel Album

Ben Harper & the Blind Boys of Alabama – *There Will Be a Light* (2004)

Blind Boys of Alabama – *Go Tell It on the Mountain* (2003)

Blind Boys of Alabama – *Higher Ground* (2002)

Blind Boys of Alabama – *Spirit of the Century* (2001)

Shirley Caesar – *You Can Make It* (2000)

Shirley Caesar – *Christmas with Shirley Caesar* (1999)

Cissy Houston – *He Leadeth Me* (1998)

Fairfield Four – *I Couldn't Hear Nobody Pray* (1997)

Cissy Houston – *Face to Face* (1996)

Shirley Caesar – *Live: He Will Come* (1995)

Albertina Walker – *Songs of the Church: Live in Memphis* (1994)

Shirley Caesar – *Stand Still* (1993)

Shirley Caesar – *He's Working It Out for You* (1992)

Mighty Clouds of Joy – *Pray for Me* (1991)

Tramaine Hawkins – *Tramaine Hawkins Live* (1990)

Grammy Hall of Fame Award

This award was created in 1973 to honor individual recordings (at least 25 years old at the time of the award) that are of lasting qualitative or historical significance.

"Amazing Grace," the Dixie Hummingbirds, Apollo Records single, 1946 (awarded in 2000)

Amazing Grace, Aretha Franklin, Atlantic Records album, 1972 (1999)

"I'll Take You There," the Staple Singers, Stax Records single, 1972 (1999)

"Move on Up a Little Higher," Mahalia Jackson, Apollo Records single, 1948 (1998)

"Oh Happy Day," Edwin Hawkins Singers, Buddah Records single, 1969 (1999)

Peace Be Still, Rev. James Cleveland, Savoy Records album, 1962 (1999)

"People Get Ready," the Impressions, ABC Records single, 1965 (1998)

"Respect Yourself," the Staple Singers, Stax Records single, 1971 (2002)

"Schubert: Ave Maria," Marian Anderson, RCA Victor single, 1936 (1999)

Songs in the Key of Life, Stevie Wonder, Tamla album, 1976 (2002)

"Uncloudy Day," the Staple Singers, Vee-Jay Records single, 1958 (1999)

Lifetime Achievement Award

This Special Merit award is awarded to performers who made a significant contribution to the field of recording. Listed here are only artists who have some affiliation with the gospel music genre.

The Staple Singers (2005)

Al Green (2002)

Sam Cooke (1999)

Paul Robeson (1998)

Stevie Wonder (1996)

Curtis Mayfield (1995)

Aretha Franklin (1994)

Little Richard (1993)

Marian Anderson (1991)

Mahalia Jackson (1972)

Trustees Award

This Special Merit award is given to individuals who have made a significant contribution to the field of music, outside of being a performing artist.

Thomas A. Dorsey (1992)

Dove Awards

The Gospel Music Association (GMA) founded the Dove awards in 1964 to expose, promote, and celebrate the gospel through music.

Contemporary Gospel Album of the Year

(Formerly Contemporary Black Gospel Album of the Year)

Israel & New Breed – *Live from Another Level* (2005)

Smokie Norful – *Limited Edition* (2004)

Kirk Franklin – *The Rebirth of Kirk Franklin* (2003)

CeCe Winans – *CeCe Winans* (2002)

Fred Hammond & Radical for Christ – *Purpose by Design* (2001)

Anointed – *Anointed* (2000)

Kirk Franklin – *The Nu Nation Project* (1999)

Andrae Crouch – *Pray* (1998)

Kirk Franklin – *Whatcha Lookin' 4* (1997)

Anointed – *The Call* (1996)

Take 6 – *Join the Band* (1995)

Helen Baylor – *Start All Over* (1994)

Various Artists – *Handel's Messiah: A Soulful Celebration* (1993)

Take 6 – *He Is Christmas* (1992)

Take 6 – *So Much 2 Say* (1991)

Commissioned – *Will You Be Ready?* (1990)

Take 6 – *Take 6* (1989)

Winans – *Decisions* (1988)

Clark Sisters – *Heart & Soul* (1987)

Winans – *Let My People Go* (1986)

Andrae Crouch – *No Time To Lose* (1985)

Bobby Jones & New Life – *Come Together* (1984)

Leon Patillo – *I'll Never Stop Loving You* (1983)

Walter Hawkins Family – *Live* (1982)

Larnelle Harris – *Give Me More Love in My Heart* (1981)

Contemporary Gospel Recorded Song of the Year

(Formerly Contemporary Black Gospel Recorded Song of the Year)

"Again I Say Rejoice" – Israel & New Breed (2005)

"Hallelujah Praise" – CeCe Winans (2004)

"In the Morning" – Mary Mary (2003)

"Anybody Wanna Pray?" – CeCe Winans (2002)

"Alabaster Box" – CeCe Winans (2001)

"Power" (from *The Prince of Egypt* soundtrack) – Various Artists (2000)

"Let the Praise Begin" – Fred Hammond & Radical for Christ (1999)

"Up Where We Belong" – BeBe & CeCe Winans (1998)

"Take Me Back" (from *Tribute: The Songs of Andrae Crouch*) – CeCe Winans (1997)

"The Call" – Anointed (1996)

"God Knows" – Angelo & Veronica (1995)

"Sold Out" – Helen Baylor (1994)

"Real" – Daryl Coley (1993)

"Addictive Love" – BeBe & CeCe Winans (1992)

"I L-O-V-E U" – Take 6 (1991)

"With My Whole Heart" – BeBe & CeCe Winans (1990)

"If We Ever Needed the Lord Before (We Sure Do Need Him Now)" – Take 6 (1989)

Traditional Gospel Album of the Year

(Formerly Traditional Black
Gospel Album of the Year)

Lynda Randle – *A Tribute to Mahalia Jackson* (2005)

Born Again Church Choir – *CeCe Winans Presents the Born Again Church Choir* (2004)

Blind Boys of Alabama – *Higher Ground* (2003)

Shirley Caesar – *Hymns* (2002)

Shirley Caesar – *You Can Make It* (2001)

Richard Smallwood & Vision – *Healing: Live in Detroit* (2000)

Shirley Caesar – *Christmas with Shirley Caesar* (1999)

Shirley Caesar – *A Miracle in Harlem* (1998)

Shirley Caesar's Outreach Convention Choir – *Just a Word* (1997)

Shirley Caesar – *He Will Come* (1996)

Various Artists – *Live at GMWA* (1995)

Kirk Franklin – *Kirk Franklin & the Family* (1994)

Sandra Crouch & Friends – *With All of My Heart* (1993)

Yolanda Adams – *Through the Storm* (1992)

Tramaine Hawkins – *Tramaine Hawkins* (1991)

West Angeles COGIC Mass Choir – *Saints in Praise* (1990)

Shirley Caesar – *Live in Chicago* (1989)

Aretha Franklin – *One Lord, One Faith, One Baptism* (1988)

Shirley Caesar – *Christmasing* (1987)

Shirley Caesar – *Celebration* (1986)

Shirley Caesar – *Sailin'* (1985)

Sandra Crouch – *We Sing Praises* (1984)

Al Green – *Precious Lord* (1983)

Shirley Caesar – *Go* (1982)

Teddy Huffman & the Gems – *Incredible* (1981)

Traditional Gospel Recorded Song of the Year

(Formerly Traditional Black
Gospel Recorded Song of the Year)

"Through the Fire" – The Crabb Family featuring Donnie McClurkin (2005)

"Poor Man Lazarus" – Fisk Jubilee Singers (2004)

"Holding On" – Mississippi Mass Choir (2003)

"Hold On" – Selah (2002)

"We Fall Down" – Donnie McClurkin (2001)

"God Can" – Dottie Peoples (2000)

"Is Your All on the Altar?" – Yolanda Adams (1999)

"I Go to the Rock" (from *The Preacher's Wife* soundtrack) – Whitney Houston (1998)

"Stop by the Church" – Babbie Mason (1997)

"Great Is Thy Faithfulness" – CeCe and Delores "Mom" Winans (1996)

"He's Working It Out for You" – Shirley Caesar (1995)

"The Reason Why We Sing" – Kirk Franklin (1994)

"'Twill Be Sweet" – Richard Smallwood Singers (1993)

"Through the Storm" – Yolanda Adams (1992)

"The Potter's House" – Tramaine Hawkins (1991)

"Wonderful" – Beau Williams (1990)

"Hold My Mule" – Shirley Caesar (1989)

Stellar Awards

Inaugurated in 1985 by Chicago businessman Don Jackson, the Stellar awards were launched as an alternative to the Grammy and Dove awards, which often gave little attention to black gospel artists. The Stellars were created to celebrate current and past black gospel music artists and personalities. Some of the award categories have been introduced or omitted after the initial launch of the award in 1985, therefore some categories are incomplete or inconsistent.

Artist of the Year

Tonéx & the Peculiar People (2005)

Vickie Winans (2004)

Kirk Franklin (2003)

Donnie McClurkin (2002)

Yolanda Adams (2001)

Kirk Franklin (2000)

Fred Hammond & Radical for Christ (1999)

God's Property from Kirk Franklin's Nu Nation (1998)

Kirk Franklin (1997)

Kirk Franklin (1996)

Song of the Year

"Make Me Over" – Tonéx (2005)

"The Presence of the Lord Is Here" – Byron Cage (2004)

"Hosanna" – Kirk Franklin (2003)

"We Fall Down" – Donnie McClurkin (2002)

"Never Seen the Righteous" – Donald Lawrence & Tri-City Singers (2001)

"Lean on Me" – Kirk Franklin & Friends (2000)

"Let the Praise Begin" – Fred Hammond (1999)

"Stomp" – Kirk Franklin (1998)

"Melodies from Heaven" – Kirk Franklin (1997)

"Be Encouraged" – William Becton (1996)

"The Battle Is the Lord's" – Yolanda Adams (1995)

"On Time God" – Dottie Peoples (1994)

"The Reason Why We Sing" – Kirk Franklin & the Family (1993)

"My Mind Is Made Up" – Rev. Milton Brunson & Thompson Community Choir Featuring Darius Brooks (1992)

"He's Preparing Me" – Rev. E. Davis, Jr. (1991)

"Wait on Him" – John P. Kee (1990)

"Heaven" – BeBe & CeCe Winans (1989)

"Center of My Joy" – Richard Smallwood (1988)

"I Surrender All" – Deniece Williams (1987)

"Completely Yes" – Sandra Crouch (1986)

New Artist of the Year

Martha Munizzi (2005)

RiZen (2004)

Smokie Norful (2003)

Excelsior (2002)

Mary Mary (2001)

Maurette Brown Clark (2000)

Love Fellowship Tabernacle Choir (1999)

God's Property from Kirk Franklin's Nu Nation (1998)

Colorado Mass Choir (1997)

William Becton (1996)

Anointed (1995)

Kirk Franklin & the Family (1994)

War on Sin (1993)

Mississippi Mass Choir (1992)

War on Sin (1991)

Shun Pace (1990)

Cathedral of Faith (1989)

Mississippi Mass Choir (1988)

Take 6 (1986)

BeBe & CeCe Winans (1987)

Calvin Bridges (1986)

CD of the Year

Another Level – Israel & New Breed (2005)

Prince of Peace – Byron Cage (2004)

The Rebirth of Kirk Franklin – Kirk Franklin (2003)

Mountain High, Valley Low – Yolanda Adams (2002)

Live in London – Donnie McClurkin (2001)

The Nu Nation Project – Kirk Franklin (2000)

Pages of Life: Chapters 1 & 2 – Fred Hammond &
    Radical for Christ (1999)

God's Property from Kirk Franklin's Nu Nation (1998)

The Nu Nation Project – Kirk Franklin (1997)

I've Got a Testimony – Rev. Clay Evans & AARC (1996)

American Quartet Awards

Founded in 1997 by George W. Stewart, a former Tuscaloosa, Alabama, disc jockey, the American Quartet Convention was formed to preserve and promote the traditional sound of quartet gospel music.

Hall of Fame Inductees

The Caravans (2006)

The Soul Stirrers (2005)

Williams Brothers (2004)

Dixie Hummingbirds (2003)

Swanee Quintet (2002)

Rev. Howard "Slim" Hunt (2002)

Pilgrim Jubilees (2001)

Five Blind Boys of Alabama (2000)

Five Blind Boys of Mississippi (2000)

Willie Neal Johnson (1999)

Rev. Thomas J. Spann (1999)

Jackson Southernaires (1998)

Robert Blair (1997)

Joe Ligon (1997)

Highway QCs (1996)

Angelic Gospel Singers (1995)

Rev. Claude Jeter (1994)

Dr. R.H. Harris (1993)

Willie Banks (1992)

Frank Williams (1992)

BMI Christian Music Awards (Contemporary/Traditional Gospel)

In 2001 Broadcast Music International (BMI), one of the three leading performance rights organizations in the U.S., began honoring the most played Christian/gospel songs of the year.

2005

"Celebrate (He Lives)" – Fred Hammond

"Let Go and Let God" – Keith "Wonderboy" Johnson

"One Thing" – Marvin Sapp

"The Presence of the Lord Is Here" – Byron Cage

"Suddenly" – Bishop Eddie Long

2004

"I'm Coming Out" – Dorinda Clark Cole

"I'm Walking" – Donnie McClurkin

"Oh How Wonderous" – John P. Kee

"Praise Is What I Do" – William Murphy III

"Shake Yourself Loose" – Vickie Winans

"The Prayer" – Yolanda Adams

2003

"Closet Religion" – Dottie Peoples

"God's Got a Blessing" – Norman Hutchins

"He Reigns" – Kirk Franklin

"Holla" – Trin-i-tee 5:7

"Hosanna" – Kirk Franklin

"I Believe" – Marvin Sapp

"Thank You" – Yolanda Adams

2002

"God Did It" – Evelyn Turrentine-Agee

"In the Sanctuary" – Kurt Carr

"Say a Prayer" – CeCe Winans

"Show Up and Show Out" – Dottie Peoples

"Thank You" – Kirk Franklin & Mary Mary

2001

"I Know It Was the Blood" – Fred Hammond

"Jesus Be a Fence" – Fred Hammond

"Lean on Me" – Kirk Franklin

"Open My Heart" – Yolanda Adams

"That's What I Believe" – Donnie McClurkin

Soul Train Music Awards – Best Gospel Album

Former Chicago WVON news announcer Don Cornelius' weekly syndicated musical television series *Soul Train* has been running non-stop since October 2, 1971. After graduating from broadcasting school, Cornelius and his classmates were advised that they'd probably never get a real broadcasting job. So Cornelius had the idea for a black dance show. He pitched the idea to WCIU in Chicago and financed the pilot at his own expense. The show was a runaway success in the local market. Johnson Products (Afro Sheen, etc.) founder George Johnson approached Cornelius about having his company sponsor the show if it went national. The rest is history. It's now the longest-running musical weekly program in television history. For years, *Soul Train* was the only national television outlet for R&B artists whose music did not cross over to the pop charts. R&B artists with pop hits such as Bobby Womack, Gladys Knight & the Pips, Candi Staton, and the Commodores had the added television outlets of Burt Sugarman's *Midnight Special*, Don Kirshner's *Rock Concert* and Dick Clark's *American Bandstand* to shine their lights before the non-black masses in the 1970s. The black megastars such as Natalie Cole, Diana Ross, Aretha Franklin, and Stevie Wonder had the ultimate reward of sitting on the couch on Johnny Carson's *Tonight Show* or chewing the fat on the Dinah Shore, Merv Griffin, or Mike Douglas shows. However, *Soul Train* featured a wide spectrum of performers ranging from one-hit wonders to legends such as Ike & Tina Turner. Along the way, the show has also featured the most popular gospel artists of the day such as the Staple Singers (the first gospel artists to appear on the show), the Mighty Clouds of Joy, Rev. James Cleveland, Anointed, and Smokie Norful, among many others. In 1987 Cornelius created the Soul Train Music Awards to honor black recording artists in a manner that many felt the American Music and Grammy awards never have. The show has become one of Hollywood's biggest nights and features the leading artists of today and yesterday. In the first two years of the awards broadcast, a gospel award was given for both best gospel album by a solo artist and best gospel album by a group. However, in order to add more R&B categories while keeping the show on a tight schedule, the two categories were reduced to one that could result in a solo or group winner.

2005   *Another Level* – Israel & New Breed

2004   *The Prince of Praise* – Byron Cage

2003   *The Rebirth of Kirk Franklin* – Kirk Franklin

2002   *Live in London* – Donnie McClurkin

2001   *Thankful* – Mary Mary

2000   *God Can & God Will* – Dottie Peoples

1999   *The Nu Nation Project* – Kirk Franklin

1998   *God's Property* – God's Property from Kirk Franklin's Nu Nation

1997   *Whatcha Lookin 4* – Kirk Franklin & the Family

1996   *Show Up* – The New Life Community

1995   *Africa to America* – The Sounds of Blackness

1994   *It Remains to Be Seen* – Mississippi Mass Choir

1993   *He's Working It Out for You* – Shirley Caesar

1992   *Different Lifestyles* – BeBe & CeCe Winans

1991   *Return* – The Winans

1990   *Heaven* – BeBe & CeCe Winans

1989   *Take 6* – Take 6

1988   *Following Jesus* – Vanessa Bell Armstrong (solo album)

1988   *Decisions* – The Winans (group album)

1987   *He Is the Light* – Al Green (solo album)

1987   *Let My People Go* – The Winans (group album)

Soul Train Lady of Soul Awards – Best Gospel Album

2004   Ceremony not held

2003   *Dorinda Clark Cole* – Dorinda Clark Cole

2002   *Believe* – Yolanda Adams

2001   *Thankful* – Mary Mary

2000   *Mountain High…Valley Low* – Yolanda Adams

1999   *His Gift* – CeCe Winans

1998   *Finally Karen* – Karen Clark-Sheard

1997   *A Wealthy Place* – Lashun Pace

1996   *More Than a Melody* – Yolanda Adams

1995   *The Live Experience* – Helen Baylor

Gospel Poll Results

In spring 2004, a poll of ten questions was sent to more than 200 gospel radio announcers, gospel industry personnel, and everyday gospel fans. This is the result of that poll.

The Best Gospel Group of All Time

The Winans	29.16%
The Hawkins Family	19.44%
The Clark Sisters	17.01%
Commissioned	14.58%
The Caravans	12.15%
The Soul Stirrers	4.86%
All others	2.43%

Best Female Gospel Artist of All Time

Shirley Caesar	21.87%
Mahalia Jackson	19.44%
CeCe Winans	19.44%
Tramaine Hawkins	17.7%
Vanessa Bell Armstrong	7.29%
Vickie Winans	4.86%
Candi Staton	4.86%
Karen Clark-Sheard	2.29%
Kim Burrell	1.14%
All others	1.14%

Best Male Gospel Artist of All Time

Donnie McClurkin	24.3%
Daryl Coley	17.1%
Andrae Crouch	12.15%
James Cleveland	9.72%
Sam Cooke	9.72%
Tonéx	7.29%
Marvin Winans	7.29%
Fred Hammond	4.86%
Rev. Claude Jeter	2.43%
Brother Joe May	2.43%
Rev. Al Green	1.21%
All others	1.21%

Best Gospel Song of All Time

"Oh Happy Day" (1969) – Edwin Hawkins Singers	18.18%
"Touch the Hem of His Garment" (1956) – Sam Cooke	12.12%
"Total Praise" (1999) – Richard Smallwood	12.12%
"What Is This?" (1981) – The Hawkins Family	12.12%
"Center of My Joy" (1986) – Richard Smallwood	6.06%
"The Reason Why We Sing" (1993) – Kirk Franklin	9.09%
"Stomp" (1997) – God's Property	9.09%
"Praise Is What I Do" (2001) – William Murphy	6.06%
"Jesus Can Work It Out" (1980) – Cosmopolitan Church of Prayer Choir	3.03%
All others	6.06%

Best Gospel Album of All Time

Love Alive I (1975) – The Hawkins Family	20%
Amazing Grace (1972) – Aretha Franklin	16%
Heaven (1988) –BeBe & CeCe Winans	12%
Take Me Back (1975) – Andrae Crouch	8%
Alone in His Presence (1995) – CeCe Winans	8%
Thankful (2000) – Mary Mary	8%
Kirk Franklin & the Family (1993) – Kirk Franklin	8%
Mercy (1993) – Andrae Crouch	6%
Give Us Peace (1985) – Edwin Hawkins	4%
All others	4%

Most Overrated Gospel Artist of All Time

Kirk Franklin	23.52%
Rev. James Cleveland	11.76%
Dr. Bobby Jones	11.76%
Yolanda Adams	8.82%
Shirley Caesar	8.82%
Albertina Walker	5.88%
Dottie Peoples	5.88%
Hezekiah Walker	5.88%
Byron Cage	5.88%
Smokie Norful	5.88%
Eartha	2.94%
All others	2.94%

Most Overrated Gospel Song of All Time

"Rough Side of the Mountain" (1983) – F.C. Barnes and Janice Brown	28.7%
"Open My Heart" (2000) – Yolanda Adams	12.3%
"Oh, Happy Day" (1969) – Edwin Hawkins Singers	12.3%
"We Fall Down" (2001) – Donnie McClurkin	8.2%
"What if God Is Unhappy" (1997) – Christopher Brinson	8.2%
"The Reason Why We Sing" (1993) – Kirk Franklin & the Family	8.2%
"The Presence of the Lord" (2003) – Byron Cage	8.2%
"One Day at a Time" (1973) – Various Artists	4.1%
"The Gospel Slide" (2001) – Dana Divine	4.1%
All others	4.1%

Best Dressed Gospel Singer of All Time

Vickie Winans	33.30%
Dottie Peoples	26.64%
Yolanda Adams	13.32%
Shirley Caesar	9.99%
Bobby Jones	6.66%
CeCe Winans	6.66%
All others	3.33%

Most Underrated Gospel Group of All Time

The Clark Sisters	25.00%
Witness	18.75%
Brent Jones & T.P. Mobb	12.50%
The Christianaires	12.50%
Commissioned	12.50%
The Williams Brothers	12.50%
All others	6.75%

Most Underrated Gospel Performer of All Time

Vanessa Bell Armstrong	29.6%
Lynette Hawkins-Stephens	22.2%
Tarralynn Ramsey	11.1%
Andrae Crouch	11.1%
Richard Smallwood	7.4%
Tonéx	7.4%
LaShun Pace	7.4%
All others	3.7%

Gospel Poll Participants

A cross section of gospel radio announcers, gospel music critics, and gospel music consumers participated in this poll. A few of the participants did not want their names printed. Here is a list of those who participated on the record.

Alexander, Donte – Consumer (Houston, TX)

Bell, Jerome – Maryland Family Christian Center (Upper Marlboro, MD)

Byrne, John – *Stage* newspaper (London, England)

Creer, Donna –KIPR (Little Rock, AR)

Dr. D – WHCR (Brooklyn, NY)

Daniels, B.J. – WPGC (Washington, DC)

Ellis, Patrick – WHUR (Washington, DC)

Ely, Gordon – *Billboard* magazine (Richmond, VA)

Fitzpatrick, Janelle – WDAS (Philadelphia, PA)

Frazer, Jason – WKRC (New York, NY)

Gales-Webb, Jacquie – WHUR (Washington, DC)

Gay, Gregory – WKKC (Chicago, IL)

Gray, Johnathan – KFXZ (Lafayette, LA)

Gregg, Stacy – WUSC (Columbia, SC)

Hamby, DeWayne – *Christian Retailing* magazine (Cleveland, TN)

Harris, Alexander – The Management Group (Brighton, MA)

Hartley, Richard – WTHE (New York, NY)

Hildebrand, Lee – *San Francisco Chronicle* (San Francisco, CA)

Hill, Denise – WKYS (Lanham, MD)

James, Lenita – Consumer (Long Beach, CA)

Kennedy III, Robert – Kay3Music.com (Lancaster, MA)

Love, Sherry – Consumer (Pensacola, FL)

McGarvey, Seamus – *Juke Blues* (London, England)

McIntyre, Donald – Gospel EUR (Houston, TX)

Matthews, Miko – Sirius Satellite Radio (New York, NY)

Merida, Stacy – Gospel executive (Nashville, TN)

Moseley, Ken – Potter's House (Dallas, TX)

Parker, Bobby – WAUG (Raleigh, NC)

Paula – Hot 105 FM (Miami, FL)

Petit, Loretta – WYLD (New Orleans, LA)

Pollard, Deborah – WJLB (Detroit, MI)

Powell, Stephen – *Inspirational Vybes* (Brooklyn, NY)

Smith, Beverly – WTCL (Chattahoochee, FL)

Smith, Edwin – WURC (Jackson, MS)

Smith, Esther – Recording artist (Detroit, MI)

Smith, G. Aundrei – WTCL (Chattahoochee, FL)

Terrell, Calvin – *Sister 2 Sister* magazine (Philadelphia, PA)

Terry, Shavone – Consumer (Greenbelt, MD)

Wall, Shane – Pastor (Orangeburg, SC)

Waller, Wayne – WPGC (Washington, DC)

Williams, Andrea – Tehillah Enterprises (Washington, DC)

Williams, Percy – WBLS (New York, NY)

Winans, Sabrina – Consumer (Jacksonville, FL)

Woods, Lin – *Urban Network* magazine (St. Louis, MO)

Personal Interviews

Aikens, Margaret. 2004.
Allen, Earline. Summer 2004.
Allison, Margaret. March 24, 1992.
Angelo & Veronica. November 1993.
Armstrong, Vanessa Bell. 1989.
Bailey, Philip. 2003.
Barge, Gene. Spring 2004.
Barnes, Luther. 2003.
Berry, Rev. Delores. 2004.
Bowman, Tim. 2004.
Boyd, Leomia. Spring 1988.
Brown, Ruth. 1994 and 1998.
Burke, Solomon. 1992.
Burks, Mosie. January 2003.
Caesar, Shirley. February 29, 1992.
Caldwell, Victor & Cedric. 2000.
Campbell, Lamar. 2001.
Clark, Jacky. 1994 and 2004.
Coley, Daryl. December 1993.
Crouch, Andrae. February 28, 1994.
D.C. Talk. 1992.
Darrett, Montrel. 1998.
Dillard, Ricky. 2002.
Divine, Dana. 2004.
Dixon, Jessy. 2004.
Dixon, Marcia. 2005.
Dorsey, Willa. 2004.
Falana, Lola. 1994.
Fortitude. 2004.
Gay, Donald. 2004.
Gay, Gregory. 2004.
Glenn-Durrah, Vanessa. 1995.
Haddon, Damita. 2002.
Hairston, Teresa. 2005.
Hardeman, Gabriel. 2002.
Harris, Donna. 1998.
Hartley, Richard. 2004.
Hawkins, Edwin. 1999.
Hearn, Billy Ray. 2004.
Henry, Gerard. 2004.
Hewett, Howard. January 2003.
Hill, Fairest. 2000.

Holliday, Jennifer. April 19, 1993.
Huff, George. 2004.
Hutchins, Norman. July 19, 1993.
Jackson, Millie. 1992.
Jasper, Chris. 2001.
John, Mable. 1992.
Jones, Brent. 2004.
Jones, Dottie. 2003.
Keeble, Stanley. August 2004.
Kelly, Roberta. 2004.
Kenoly, Bingo. 1999.
Kenoly, Ron. 1996.
Kenoly, Sam. 1999.
Lawrence, Donald. 1995.
Lee, Derrick. 2004.
Love, Patrick. 1998.
Lowe, J. 2004.
Lubinsky, Herman. 2005.
McFadden, Gladys. 2005.
McClary, Thomas. 2004.
McClurkin, Donnie. 2002.
McComb, Liz. 2002.
McCrae, Gwen. 1998.
McCrary, Ann. 1999.
Majors, Jeff. January 2003.
Melson, Bertha.
Merida, Stacy. 2004.
Mitchell, Vernessa. 1990s.
Moffet-Jones, Sheri. 2004.
Montgomery, Ed. January 2003.
Moore, Dorothy. 2004.
Morgan, Velma. 2004.
Morganfield, Rev. Willie. October 2004.
Norful, Smokie. 2002.
Norwood, Dorothy. 2004.
Norwood, Willie. 2001.
Omartian, Michael. March 11, 1992.
Parks, Barney. 2004.
Pearson, Bishop Carlton. 2000.
Pope, Sister Lucille. 2003.
Powell, Sara Jordan. July 2004.
Pringle, Desmond. 2004.

Pugh, Bryant. 2004.
Pugh, Sullivan. 2004.
Rae, Nadine. 2004.
Reed, Carla. 2004.
Richards, Emma. 2004.
Rodriguez, MC Ge Gee. June 22, 1992.
Robinson, Roscoe. 2004.
Skinner, Janet Lynn. 2004.
Smallwood, Richard. October 31,
     1991 and spring 2004.
Smith, Esther. 2003.
Staples, Mavis. 1992.
Starks, Derrick. 2001.
Staton, Candi. Fall 2002.
Thompson, Madelyne. 1994.
Tratlor, Carolyn.
Turrentine-Agee, Evelyn. 2002.
Tyson, Moses. 1999.
Wall, Shane. 2003.
Ward, Willa. 2004.
Warwick, Dionne. 1992.
Whitehead, LaBarbara. 2005.
Williams, Doug. 2004.
Williams, Marion. April 10, 1992.
Wilson, Bryan, Fall 2002.
Winans, Angie. 1997.
Winans, Carvin. 1992.
Winans, CeCe. Fall 1999.
Winans, David. 1999.
Winans, Debbie. 1997.
Winans, Delores. 1999.
Winans, Ronald. August 2004.
Winans, Vickie. Spring 1998.
Winn, Ted. 2004.
Womack, Bobby. 1994.
Yohe, Vicki. 2003.

Radio Programs

*The Georgia Peach Radio Show with
Imagene Stewart.* WOL Radio, January
12, 2003.

Selected Bibliography

Boyer, Horace Clarence. *How Sweet the Sound: The Golden Age of Gospel.* Washington, DC: Elliott & Clark Publishing, 1995.

Branch, Taylor. *Parting the Waters: America in the King Years 1954–1963.* New York: Simon & Schuster, 1988.

Brothers, Jeffrey L. *Hot Hits Christian Radio: 20 Years of Charts, Artist Bios and More.* CCM Books, 1999.

Burnham, Kenneth E. *God Comes to America: Father Divine and the Peace Mission Movement.* Boston: Lambeth Press, 1979.

Clifford, Mike, editor. *The Illustrated Encyclopedia of Black Music.* New York: Harmony Books, 1982.

Darden, Robert. *People Get Ready: A New History of Black Gospel Music.* New York: Continuum Publishing, 2004.

Franklin, Aretha, and David Ritz. *From These Roots.* New York: Villard, 1999.

Goldberg, Marv. "The Larks," Marv Goldberg's online "R&B Notebooks," 2000.

Goodman, Vestal, with Ken Abraham. *Vestal! "Lord, I Wouldn't Take Nothin' for My Journey Now."* Colorado Springs, CO: Waterbrook Press, 1998.

Graham, Rhonda. "And the Choir Sings On: AIDS has cast a pall of silence over the black gospel community," *Sunday News Journal,* Wilmington, DE, October 23, 1994.

Guralnick, Peter. *Sweet Soul Music: Rhythm and Blues and the Southern Dream of Freedom.* New York: Harper & Row, 1986.

Harris, Sara. *Father Divine.* New York: Collier Books, 1971.

Heilbut, Anthony. *The Gospel Sound.* New York: Limelight Editions, 1997.

Hoshor, John. *God in a Rolls-Royce: The Rise of Father Divine: Madman, Menace, or Messiah.* New York: Hillman-Curl, 1936.

Howell, Ann Chandler. *African-Americans in Gospel Children's Activity Book* (Kmart Share the Word/ Celebrating Black History). Chicago: Chandler/White Publishing Company, 2001.

Jones, Bobby, with Lesley Sussman. *Make a Joyful Noise.* New York: St. Martin's Press, 2000.

King, B.B., with David Ritz. *Blues All Around Me: The Autobiography of B.B. King.* New York: Avon Books, 1996.

LaBelle, Patti, with Laura Randolph. *Don't Block the Blessings: Revelations of a Lifetime.* New York: Riverhead Books, 1996.

LaZell, Barry, editor. *Rock Movers and Shakers: An A–Z of People Who Made Rock Happen.* New York: Billboard Publications, 1989.

Lydon, Michael. *Ray Charles: Man and Music.* New York: Riverhead Books, 1998.

McCoy, Eugene B. *Climbing Up the Mountain.* Nashville: Sparrow Press, 1994.

Mother Divine. *The Peace Mission Movement.* Philadelphia: The Imperial Press, 1982.

Nathan, David. *The Soulful Divas.* New York: Billboard Books, 1999.

Pruter, Robert. *Chicago Soul.* Urbana, IL: University of Illinois Press, 1991.

Reagon, Bernice Johnson, editor. *We'll Understand It Better By and By.* Washington, DC: Smithsonian Institution Press, 1992.

Salvatore, Nick. *Singing in a Strange Land.* New York: Litle, Brown & Co., 2005.

Smith, Esther. *Programmed for Failure… But God.* Detroit: Affirmation Publishing, 1998.

Smith, Wes. *The Pied Pipers of Rock 'N' Roll: Radio Deejays of the 50s and 60s.* Marietta, GA: Longstreet Press, 1989.

Stambler, Irwin. *The Encyclopedia of Pop, Rock and Soul.* New York: St. Martin's Press, 1989.

Staton, Candi. *This Is My Story.* Lanham, MD: Pneuma Life Publishing, 1994.

Turner, Tina, with Kurt Loder. *I, Tina.* New York: Avon Books, 1986.

Ward-Royster, Willa, and Toni Rose. *How I Got Over: Clara Ward and the World Famous Ward Singers.* Philadelphia: Temple University Press, 1997.

Warren, Gwendolyn Sims. *Ev'ry Time I Feel the Spirit.* New York: Henry Holt/Owl Books, 1999.

Watts, Jill. *God, Harlem USA.: The Father Divine Story.* Berkeley: University of California Press, 1992.

Weisbrot, Robert. *Father Divine and the Struggle for Racial Equality.* Urbana, IL: University of Illinois Press, 1983.

Williams, Jr. Nolan & Delores Carpenter. *African-American Heritage Hymnal.* Washington, DC: GIA Publications, 2001.

Winans, CeCe. *On a Positive Note.* New York: Pocket Books, 1999.

Winans, David and Delores, with Lisa T. Grosswiler. *Stories from Home.* Newport Beach, CA: FMG Distribution, 1992.

Wolff, Daniel, with S.R. Crain, Clifton White, and G. David Tenenbaum. *You Send Me: The Life and Times of Sam Cooke.* New York: William Morrow and Company, 1995.

Young, Alan. *Pilgrim Jubilees.* Jackson, MS: University Press of Mississippi, 2002.

Young, Alan. *Woke Me Up This Morning: Black Gospel Singers and the Gospel Life.* Jackson, MS: University Press of Mississippi, 1997.

In gathering information for the book, I read feature stories, record reviews, concert critiques, and obituaries from literally dozens of newspapers and periodicals. Some of the publications I consulted most frequently were *Totally Gospel* magazine, *CCM* magazine, the *Gospel Voice*, the *Gospel Times*, *Charisma* magazine, *Ebony* magazine, *Jet* magazine, *Right On!* magazine, *Sepia* magazine, and *Black Stars*. Daily newspapers such as the *Washington Post*, *Atlanta Journal-Constitution*, the *Chicago Tribune*, the *Chicago Sun-Times*, the *Los Angeles Times*, the *New York Times*, and the *Baltimore Sun* were also of tremendous value. Also, these gospel music Web sites have been a tremendous aid in information on current gospel artists: www.GospelFlava.com, www.GospelCity.com, www.ccmcom.com, and www.manhunt.com.

Photo Credits

Adams, Yolanda / courtesy of Elektra Records
Allen, Earline / courtesy of Earline Allen
Allen, Rance / Bellmark Records publicity photo
Angelic Gospel Singers / courtesy of Margaret Allison
Barnes, F.C. & Sister Janice Brown / courtesy of AIR Records
Blind Boys of Alabama / courtesy of Specialty/Fantasy Records
BL& S Singers / Savoy Records publicity photo
Bowman, Tim / courtesy of Tim Bowman
Bradford, Alex / courtesy of Specialty/Fantasy Records
Brunson, Milton / photo by Mike Borum for Rejoice Records
Caesar, Shirley / Hob Records LP cover
Caldwell Brothers / photo by Erick Anderson for Father's Image
CBS Trumpeteers / uncredited publicity photo, courtesy of Capital Entertainment archives
Chosen Gospel Singers / courtesy of Specialty/Fantasy Records.
Clark Sisters / photo by Arnold Turner, courtesy of BET Celebration of Gospel
Cleveland, Rev. James / Savoy Records promotional photo
Coley, Daryl / courtesy of Sparrow Records, 1996
Cooke, Sam / ourtesy of Specialty/Fantasy Records
Crawford , Beverly / photo by Bill Carpenter
Dillard, Ricky / courtesy of Crystal Rose Records
Dorsey, Willa / 1973 Word Records LP cover
The Emotions / courtesy of Stax/Fantasy Records
Falana, Lola / photo by Robert Shanklin
Gay Sisters / courtesy of Gregory Gay, Gay Family Estate
Green, Al / courtesy of A&M Records
Griffin, Bessie / Savoy Records photo
Hairston, Teresa / courtesy of *Gospel Today* magazine
Hammond, Fred / courtesy of Verity Records
Harris, Larnelle / courtesy of Benson Records
Hawkins, Edwin / courtesy of Capital Entertainment archives
Hawkins, Edwin / courtesy of Edwin Hawkins
Hawkins, Tramaine / A&M Records publicity photo
Houghton, Israel / photo by DRE Photography / Dr. D. 2004
Huff, George / photo by Robert Shanklin, 2004
Jackson, Mahalia / sheet music courtesy of Margaret Aikens
Jackson, Mahalia & Duke Ellington / Columbia Records publicity photo
John, Mable / courtesy of Stax/Fantasy Records
Jones, Bobby / courtesy of Word Records
Kee, John P. / photo by Robert Shanklin
Kelly, Roberta / photo by Ron Slenzak, 1978. Casablanca Records publicity photo
Kenoly, Ron / Integrity Records pomotional photo
King, Curtis / courtesy of the Black Academy of Arts & Letters
LaBelle, Patti / photo by Robert Shanklin
Ladies of Song / courtesy of Margaret Aikens Jenkins
Lawrence, Donald / courtesy of Crystal Rose Records
Lee, Laura / Hot Wax Records LP cover

Ligon, Joe / photo by Aaron Rapoport
Lil iROCC / courtesy of Authority Music
Little Richard / courtesy of Specialty/Fantasy Records
Majors, Jeff / courtesy of Music One
M.C. Hammer / Capitol Records promotional photo
McClendon, Debbie / photo by Harry Langdon, courtesy of Star Song Records
McClurkin, Donnie / courtesy of Verity Records
Miller, Douglas / courtesy of Joe Williams, Matador Management
Mullen, Nicole C. / Word Records promotional photo
Nicholas / courtesy of Command Records
Norful, Smokie / courtesy of EMI Records
Norwood, Willie / photo by Bill Carpenter
Peoples, Dottie / photo by DRE Photography / Dr. D. 2004
Pilgrim Travelers / courtesy of Specialty/Fantasy Records
Pope, Lucille / courtesy of AIR Records
Powell, Sara Jordan / 1982 LP cover
Rizen / Chez Musique publicity photo
Ross, Nedra / Word/New Song promotional photo
St. James, Sylvia / Elektra Records promotional photo
San, Papa / Gospcentric Records promtional photo
Skinner, Janet Lynn / photo by Michael Mann
Smallwood, Richard / courtesy of Richard Smallwood
Willie Mae Ford Smith / from film *Say Amen, Somebody*
Soul Stirrers / courtesy of Specialty/Fantasy Records
Spencer, Gloria (1) / courtesy of Capital Entertainment archives
Spencer, Gloria (2) / courtesy of Bill Carpenter
Stancil, Lorriane / photo by Robert Shanklin
Staple Singers / Epic Records *Billboard* magazine advertisement
Staton, Candi / courtesy of Warner Bros. Records
Ted & Sheri / photo by Derek Blanks
Thomas, Carla / courtesy of Capital Entertainment archives
Tonéx / photo by Delphine Fawundu
Turner, Ike & Tina / United Artists *Billboard* magazine advertisement
Vinesong / courtesy of John Watson
Walker, Albertina / courtesy of Benson Records
Walker, Hezekiah / Benson records promotional photo
Ward, Clara / courtesy of Capital Entertainment archives
Williams , Deniece / Word Records promotional photo
Wilson, Bryan / photo by Robert Shanklin
Winans, Angie / photo by Michael Gomez for ATF Records
Winans, Angie & Debbie / Capitol Records photo
Winans, BeBe & CeCe Winans / courtesy of Capital Entertainment archives
Winans, CeCe / photo by Bill Carpenter
Winans, Mom & Pop Winans / photo by Bill Carpenter
Winans, Vickie / courtesy of Vickie Winans
Yohe, Vicki / photo by Michael Gomez

About the Author

An avid record collector and history buff, Bill Carpenter holds a B.A. in history from the American University in Washington, D.C. Over the last decade, he has worked both as a music journalist and a record label publicist. He was a contributing editor to the first edition of the *All Music Guide* and has written hundreds of articles for publications such as *People*, *The Washington Post*, and *Living Blues*. He has also written liner-note essays for various CD compilations for Sony Legacy, Warner Bros., and EMI Records. In addition, he has handled publicity campaigns for such diverse subjects as Aaliyah, various members of the Winans gospel dynasty, and Coretta Scott King's 30th anniversary march on Washington. Carpenter's songs have been recorded by Grammy nominees David "Pop" Winans and Candi Staton, among others. He lives in Washington, D.C., where he runs Capital Entertainment, a public relations company.

Index